TRANS-HIMALAYA

1. LORD MINTO, VICEROY OF INDIA. *Frontispiece*

TRANS-HIMALAYA

DISCOVERIES AND ADVENTURES IN TIBET

BY

SVEN HEDIN

WITH 388 ILLUSTRATIONS FROM PHOTOGRAPHS, WATER-COLOUR SKETCHES, AND DRAWINGS BY THE AUTHOR AND 10 MAPS

IN TWO VOLUMES

VOL. I

MACMILLAN AND CO., LIMITED
ST. MARTIN'S STREET, LONDON
1909

ISBN : 978-81-212-0341-8

Published, 2018

Published by

Gyan Publishing House
5, Ansari Road
Daryaganj, New Delhi-110002
Phone: 011-47034999, 9811692060
www.gyanbooks.com
E-mail: books@gyanbooks.com

Printed at: G. Print Process, Delhi.

TO

HIS EXCELLENCY

THE EARL OF MINTO

VICEROY OF INDIA

WITH GRATITUDE AND ADMIRATION

FROM THE AUTHOR

PREFACE

In the first place I desire to pay homage to the memory of my patron, King Oskar of Sweden, by a few words of gratitude. The late King showed as warm and intelligent an interest in my plan for a new expedition as he had on former occasions, and assisted in the fulfilment of my project with much increased liberality.

I estimated the cost of the journey at 80,000 kronor (about £4400), and this sum was subscribed within a week by my old friend Emmanuel Nobel, and my patrons, Frederik Löwenadler, Oscar Ekman, Robert Dickson, William Olsson, and Henry Ruffer, banker in London. I cannot adequately express my thanks to these gentlemen. In consequence of the political difficulties I encountered in India, which forced me to make wide detours, the expenses were increased by about 50,000 kronor (£2800), but this sum I was able to draw from my own resources.

As on former occasions, I have this time also to thank Dr. Nils Ekholm for his great kindness in working out the absolute heights. The three lithographic maps have been compiled from my original sheets with painstaking care by Lieutenant C. J. Otto Kjellström, who devoted all his furlough to this troublesome work. The astronomical points, nearly one hundred, have been calculated by the Assistant Roth of the Stockholm Observatory; a few points, which appeared doubtful, were omitted in drawing the route on the map, which is based on points previously determined. The map illustrating my narrative in the *Geographical Journal*, April 1909, I drew roughly from memory without consulting the original sheets, for I had no time to spare; the errors which naturally crept in have been corrected on the new maps, but I wish to state here the cause of the discrepancy. The final maps, which I hope to publish in a voluminous scientific work, will be distinguished by still greater accuracy and detail.

I claim not the slightest artistic merit for my drawings, and my water-colours are extremely defective both in drawing and colouring. One of the pictures, the lama opening the door of the mausoleum, I left unfinished in my haste; it has been thrown in with the others, with the wall-paintings and shading incomplete. To criticize these slight attempts as works of art would be like wasting gunpowder on dead crows. For the sake of variety several illustrations have been drawn by the British artists De Haenen and T. Macfarlane, but it must not be assumed that these are fanciful productions. Every one of them is based on outline drawings by myself, a number of photographs, and a full description of the scene. De Haenen's illustrations appeared in the London *Graphic*, and were ordered when I was still in India. Macfarlane's drawings were executed this summer, and I was able to inspect his designs and approve of them before they were worked up.

As to the text, I have endeavoured to depict the events of the journey as far as the limited space permitted, but I have also imprudently allowed myself to touch on subjects with which I am not at all familiar — I allude in particular to Lamaism. It has been unfortunate that I had to write the whole book in 107 days, during which many hours were taken up with work connected with the maps and illustrations and by an extensive correspondence with foreign publishers, especially Albert Brockhaus of Leipzig, who never wearied in giving me excellent advice. The whole work has been hurried, and the book from beginning to end is like a vessel which ventures out into the ocean of the world's tumult and of criticism with many leaks and cracks.

My thanks are also due to my father, who made a clean copy from my illegible manuscript; and to my mother, who has saved me from many mistakes. Dr. Carl Forstrand has revised both the manuscript and the proof-sheets, and has compiled the Swedish index.

The seven and thirty Asiatics who followed me faithfully through Tibet, and contributed in no small degree to the successful issue and results of the expedition, have had the honour of receiving from His Majesty the King of Sweden gold and silver medals bearing the portrait of the King, a crown, and an inscription. I humbly beg His Majesty to accept my warmest and most sincere thanks for his great generosity.

The book is dedicated to Lord Minto, as a slight testimony of my gratitude for all his kindness and hospitality. It had been Lord Minto's intention to further my plans as Lord Curzon would have done if he had still been Viceroy of India, but political considerations prevented him. When, however, I was actually in Tibet, the Viceroy was free to use his influence with the Tashi Lama, and the consequence was that many doors in the forbidden land, formerly tightly closed, were opened to me.

Dear reminiscences of India hovered about my lonesome years in dreary Tibet like the pleasant rustling of palm leaves. It will suffice to mention men like Lord Kitchener, in whose house I spent a week never to be forgotten; Colonel Dunlop Smith, who took charge of my notes and maps and sent them home, and also forwarded a whole caravan of necessaries to Gartok; Younghusband, Patterson, Ryder, Rawling, and many others. And, lastly, Colonel Longe, Surveyor-General, and Colonel Burrard, of the Survey of India, who, with the greatest kindness, had my 900 map-sheets of Tibet photographed, and stored the negatives among their records in case the originals should be lost, and who, after I had placed my 200 map-sheets of Persia at the disposal of the Indian Government, had them worked up in the North-Western Frontier Drawing Office and combined into a fine map of eleven printed sheets — a map which is to be treated as "confidential" until my scientific works have appeared.

It is with the greatest pleasure that I avail myself of this opportunity of expressing my sincere gratitude for all the innumerable tokens of sympathy and appreciation which I received in all parts of the United Kingdom, and for all the honours conferred on me by Societies, and the warm welcome I met with from the audiences I had the pleasure of addressing. I shall always cherish a proud and happy remembrance of the two months which it was my good-fortune to spend in the British Isles; and the kindness then showered upon me was the more delightful because it was extended also to two of my sisters, who accompanied me.

Were I to mention all the ladies and gentlemen to whom I am especially indebted, I could fill several pages. But I cannot let this book go forth through the English-speaking world without expressing my sincere gratitude to Lord Curzon for the great and encouraging interest he has always taken in myself and my journeys; to Lord Morley for the brilliant speech he delivered after my first lecture — the most graceful compliment ever paid me, as well as for many other marks of kindness and sympathy shown to me by the Secretary of State for India; to the Swedish

Minister in London, Count Herman Wrangel, for all the valuable services he rendered me during and after my journey; to Major Leonard Darwin and the Council and Members of the Royal Geographical Society, to whom I was delighted to return, not as a strange guest, but as an old friend; to the famous and illustrious Universities of Oxford and Cambridge, where I was overwhelmed with exceptional honours and boundless hospitality; to the Royal Scottish Geographical Society, where twice before I had received a warm reception. Well, when I think of those charming days in England and Scotland I am inclined to dwell too long upon them, and I must hasten to a conclusion. But there is one more name, which I have left to the last, because it has been very dear to me for many years, that of Dr. J. Scott Keltie. The general public will never know what it means to be the Secretary and mainspring of the Royal Geographical Society, to work year after year in that important office in Savile Row, to receive explorers from all corners of the world and satisfy all their demands, without ever losing patience or ever hearing a word of thanks. I can conceive from my own experience how much trouble I have caused Dr. Keltie, but yet he has always met me with the same amiability and has always been a constant friend, whether I have been at home or away for years on long journeys.

Dr. M. A. Stein started and returned from his splendid journey in Central Asia at the same times as myself. We crossed different parts of the old continent, but we have several interests in common, and I am glad to congratulate Dr. Stein most heartily on his important discoveries and the brilliant results he has brought back.

It is my intention to collect in a third volume all the material for which there is no room in *Trans-Himalaya*. For instance, I have been obliged to omit a description of the march northwards from the source of the Indus and of the journey over the Trans-Himalaya to Gartok, as well as of the road from Gartok to Ladak, and the very interesting route from the Nganglaring-tso to Simla. I have also had to postpone the description of several monasteries to a later opportunity. In this future book I will also record my recollections of beautiful, charming Japan, where I gained so many friends, and of Korea, Manchuria, and Port Arthur. The manuscript of this later volume is already finished, and I long for the opportunity of publicly thanking the Japanese, as well as our representative in Japan and China, the Minister Extraordinary, Wallenberg, for all the delightful hospitality and all the honours showered down on me in the Land of the Rising Sun.

Lastly, the appetite of young people for adventures will be satisfied in an especial work.

I am glad to be able to announce at the eleventh hour that the Madrassi Manuel, who in Chapter IX. was reported lost, has at length been found again.

In conclusion, I must say a few words of thanks to my publishers, and first of all to Herre K. O. Bonnier of Stockholm, for his valuable co-operation and the elegant form in which he has produced my book, and then to the firm of F. A. Brockhaus, Leipzig; the "Elsevier" Uitgevers Maatschappij, Amsterdam; Hachette & Cie., Paris; "Kansa," Suomalainen Kustannus-O-Y, Helsingfors; the Robert Lampel Buchhandlung (F. Wodianer & Söhne) Act.-Ges., Budapest; Macmillan & Co., Ltd., London and New York; J. Otto, Prague; Fratelli Treves, Milan.

SVEN HEDIN.

STOCKHOLM, *September*, 1909.

CONTENTS

CHAPTER VIII

CHAPTER IX

CHAPTER X

CHAPTER XI

CHAPTER XII

CHAPTER XIII

CHAPTER XIV

CHAPTER XV

CHAPTER XVI

ILLUSTRATIONS

MAPS

CHAPTER I

SIMLA

In the spring of the year 1905 my mind was much occupied with thoughts of a new journey to Tibet. Three years had passed since my return to my own country; my study began to be too small for me; at eventide, when all around was quiet, I seemed to hear in the sough of the wind a voice admonishing me to "come back again to the silence of the wilderness"; and when I awoke in the morning I involuntarily listened for caravan bells outside. So the time passed till my plans were ripened and my fate was soon decided; I must return to the freedom of the desert and hie away to the broad plains between the snow-clad mountains of Tibet. Not to listen to this secret voice when it speaks strongly and clearly means deterioration and ruin; one must resign oneself to the guidance of this invisible hand, have faith in its divine origin and in oneself, and submit to the gnawing pain which another departure from home, for so long a time and with the future uncertain, brings with it.

In the concluding lines of my scientific work on the results of my former journey (*Scientific Results*) I spoke of the impossibility of giving a complete description of the internal structure of Tibet, its mountains and valleys, its rivers and lakes, while so large a part of the country was still quite unknown. "Under these circumstances," I said (vol. iv. p. 608), "I prefer to postpone the completion of such a monograph till my return from the journey on which I am about to start." Instead of losing myself in conjectures or arriving at confused results owing to lack of material, I would rather see with my own eyes the unknown districts in the midst of northern Tibet, and, above all, visit the extensive areas of entirely unexplored country which stretches to the north of the upper Brahmaputra and has not been traversed by Europeans or Indian pundits. Thus much was *à priori* certain, that this region presented the grandest problems which remained still unsolved in the physical geography of Asia. There must exist one or more mountain systems running parallel with the Himalayas and the Karakorum range; there must be found peaks and ridges on which the eye of the explorer had never lighted; turquoise-blue salt lakes in valleys and hollows reflect the restless passage of the monsoon clouds north-eastwards, and from their southern margins voluminous rivers must flow down, sometimes turbulent, sometimes smooth. There, no doubt, were nomad tribes, who left their winter pastures in spring, and during the summer wandered about on the higher plains when the new grass had sprung up from the poor soil. But whether a settled population dwelt there, whether there were monasteries, where a lama, punctual as the sun, gave the daily summons to prayer from the roof by blowing through a shell,—that no one knew. Tibetan literature, old and recent, was searched in vain for information; nothing could be found but fanciful conjectures about the existence of a mighty chain, which were of no value as they did not accord with the reality and were not based on any actual facts. On the other hand, a few travellers had skirted the unknown country on the north and south, east and west, myself among the number. Looking at a map, which shows the routes of travellers in Tibet, one might almost suppose that we had purposely avoided the great white patch bearing on the recently published English map only the word "Unexplored." Hence it might be concluded that it would be no easy feat to cross this tract, or otherwise some one would ere now have strayed into it. In my book *Central Asia and Tibet* I have fully described the desperate attempts I made in the autumn and winter of

1901 to advance southwards from my route between the Zilling-tso and the Pangong-tso. One of my aims was to find an opportunity of visiting one or more of the great lakes in Central Tibet which the Indian pundit, Nain Sing, discovered in 1874, and which since then had never been seen except by the natives. During my former journey I had dreamt of discovering the source of the Indus, but it was not then my good fortune to reach it. This mysterious spot had never been inserted in its proper place on the map of Asia — but it must exist somewhere. Since the day when the great Macedonian Alexander (in the year 326 B.C.) crossed the mighty stream with his victorious host, the question of the situation of this spot has always stood in the order of the day of geographical exploration.

It was both impossible and unnecessary to draw up beforehand a complete plan of a journey of which the course and conclusion were more than usually uncertain, and depended on circumstances quite beyond my control. I did, indeed, draw on a map of Tibet the probable route of my journey, that my parents and sisters might know roughly whereabouts I should be. If this map be compared with my actual route it will be seen that in both cases the districts visited are the same, but the course and details are totally different.

In the meantime I wrote to Lord Curzon, then Viceroy of India, informed him of my plan, and begged for all the assistance that seemed to me necessary for a successful journey in disturbed Tibet, so lately in a state of war.

Soon after I received the following letter, which I reproduce here with the consent of the writer:

VICEREGAL LODGE, SIMLA,
July 6, 1905.

MY DEAR DR. HEDIN — I am very glad that you propose to act upon my advice, and to make one more big Central Asian journey before you desist from your wonderful travels.

I shall be proud to render you what assistance lies in my power while I still remain in India, and only regret that long before your great expedition is over I shall have left these shores. For it is my intention to depart in April 1906.

Now as regards your plan. I gather that you will not be in India before next spring, when perhaps I may still see you. I will arrange to have a good native surveyor ready to accompany you, and I will further have a man instructed in astronomical observations and in meteorological recording — so as to be available for you at the same time.

I cannot say what the attitude of the Tibetan Government will be at the time that you reach India. But if they continue friendly, we will of course endeavour to secure for you the requisite permits and protections.

Assuring you that it will give me the greatest pleasure in any way to further your plans, — I am yours sincerely,

CURZON.

It may easily be conceived how important this active protection and help on the part of the Viceroy was to me. I was especially pleased that I was allowed to take with me native topographers experienced in survey work, for with their co-operation the maps to be compiled would be far more valuable, while, released from this complicated work which takes up so much time, I could devote myself entirely to researches in physical geography.

With this kind letter at starting I commenced my fifth journey to Asia. Lord Curzon had, indeed, when I reached India, already left his post, and a new Government was shortly to take the helm in England with Sir Henry Campbell-Bannerman as premier. But Lord Curzon's promises were the words of a Cæsar, and I had not the slightest doubt that a Liberal Government would respect them.

On October 16, 1905, the same day on which I had started twelve years before on my journey through Asia, I again left my dear old home in Stockholm. This time it seemed far more uncertain whether I should see all my dear ones again; sometime or other the chain that binds us must be broken. Would it be granted me to find once more my home unchanged?

I travelled viâ Constantinople and the Black Sea, through Turkish Armenia, across Persia to Seistan, and through the deserts of Baluchistan to Nushki, where I reached the most western offshoot of the Indian railway system. After the dust and heat of Baluchistan, Quetta seemed to me a fine fresh oasis. I left this town on May 20, 1906, descended in four hours from a height of 5500 feet to a country lying only 300 feet above sea-level, and found in Sibi a temperature of 100° F. in the evening. Next day I passed along the Indus and Sutlej through Samasata and Batinda to Ambala, and I was now, in the hottest part of the year, the only European in the train. The temperature rose to 107°, the height I had shortly before recorded in Baluchistan, but it was much more endurable in the shady carriage, which was protected by a roof and hanging screens from the direct heat of the sun; it was well, however, to avoid touching the outside of the carriage, for it was burning hot. Two window openings are covered with a tissue of root-fibres which are automatically kept moist, and a wind-catcher sends a draught into the carriage through the wet matting. At a window like this the temperature even at noon was only 81½°, and therefore I had nothing to complain of. At some stations there are excellent restaurants, and natives travelling on the train sell on the way lemonade and ice as clear as glass.

Nevertheless in India's sultry dried-up plains one longs for the mountains with their pure cool air. From Kalka a small narrow-gauge railway carries one in 6½ hours to a height of 7080 feet, and one finds oneself in Simla, the summer residence of the Viceroy and the headquarters of the Indian Army. The road is one of the most charming and magnificent in the world. The little railway climbs up the steep flanks in the boldest curves, descends the slopes into deep and narrow ravines, passes along steep mountain spurs, where the train seems as though it would plunge into space from the extreme point; then the train crosses bridges which groan and tremble under its weight, enters pitch-dark tunnels, and again emerges into the blinding sunshine. Now we run along a valley, catching a glimpse of the bottom far below us, then mount upwards to a ridge affording an extensive view on both sides, then again traverse a steep slope where several sections of the marvellously winding line can be seen below. The scene changes every other minute, new contours and landscapes present themselves, new points of view and lights and shades follow one another, and keep the attention of the traveller on the stretch. There are 102 tunnels on the route, most of them quite short, but the longest has a length of three-quarters of a mile.

We pass through one zone of vegetation after another. The flora of the plain is left far behind; now the eye notices new forms in new zones — forms characteristic of the various heights of the southern slopes of the Himalayas — and at last appear the dark deodar forests, the royal Himalayan cedars, with their luxuriant green foliage, amidst which are embedded the houses of Simla like swallows' nests. How fascinating is this sight, but how much more imposing as a symbol of the power of the British Empire! Here the eagle has its eyry, and from its point of vantage casts its keen eyes over the plains of India. Here converge innumerable telegraph wires from all the corners and extremities of the British Empire, and from this centre numerous orders and instructions are daily despatched "On His Majesty's Service only"; here the administration is carried on and the army controlled, and a host of maharajas are entangled in the meshes like the prey in the nest of a spider.

I approached Simla with some anxiety. Since Lord Curzon's letter I had heard nothing more from the authorities in India. The singular town on its crescent-shaped ridge appears larger and larger, details become clearer and clearer, there remain only a couple of curves to pass, and then the train rolls into the station at Simla. Two servants from the Foreign Office, in scarlet liveries, took possession of my luggage, and I was welcomed in the Grand Hotel by my old friend Colonel Sir Francis Younghusband — we kept Christmas together in Kashgar in 1890, and he was just as friendly and pleasant as then. I was his guest at dinner in the United Service Club. During half the night we revelled in old reminiscences of the heart of Asia, spoke of the powerful Russian Consul-General, Petrovski, in Kashgar, of the English expedition to Lhasa, which was led by Younghusband, of life in Simla and the coming festivities in the summer season — but of my prospects my friend did not utter a word! And I did not ask him; I could believe that if everything had been plain and straightforward he would have told me at once. But he was silent as the grave, and I would not question him, though I was burning with impatience to learn something or other.

When I went out on to my balcony on the morning of May 23, I felt like a prisoner awaiting his sentence. Below me the roofs of Simla glittered in the sunshine, and I stood on a level with the tops of the cedars; how delightful it was here far above the heavy sultry air of the plain. To the north, through a gap in the luxuriant woods, appeared a scene of incomparable beauty. There gleamed the nearest ranges of the Himalayas covered with eternal snow. The crest shone white against the turquoise-blue sky. The air was so clear that the distance seemed insignificant; only a few days' journey separated me from these mountains, and behind them lay mysterious Tibet, the forbidden land, the land of my dreams. Later on, towards midday, the air became hazy and the glorious view vanished, nor was it again visible during the few weeks I spent in Simla. It seemed as though a curtain had fallen between me and Tibet, and as though it had been vouchsafed to me to see only once from a distance the mountains over which the road led into the land of promise.

It was a sad day; at twelve o'clock I was to hear my sentence. Younghusband came for me and we went together to the Foreign Secretary's Office. Sir Louis Dane received me with great amiability, and we talked of Persia and the trade route between India and Seistan. Suddenly he became silent, and then said after a pause:

"It is better you should know at once; the Government in London refuses you permission to pass into Tibet across the Indian frontier."

"Sad news! But why is this?"

"That I do not know; probably because the present Government wishes to avoid everything which may give rise to friction on the frontier; the granting of your request throws responsibility on us should anything happen to you. Yes, it is a pity. What do you think of doing now?"

"If I had had any suspicion of this in Teheran, I would have taken my way through Russian Asia, for I have never met with any difficulties from the Russians."

"Well, we have done out here all we could to forward your plans. The three native surveyors Lord Curzon promised you have been trained for six months, and hold themselves in readiness at Dehra Dun. But probably this too will be countermanded from London. Still, we have not yet given up all hope, and we expect the final answer on June 3."

To have to wait eleven days for the final decision was unbearable. Perhaps a personal application might have a favourable effect. I therefore sent the following telegram to the English Prime Minister:

> The friendly words, in which your Excellence referred two years ago in Parliament to my journey and my book, encourage me to apply direct to you, and to beg you in the interests of geographical science to grant me the permission of your Government to pass into Tibet by way of Simla and Gartok. I propose to explore the region, mostly uninhabited, to the north of the Tsangpo, and the lakes lying in it, and then to return to India. I am thoroughly acquainted with the present political relations between India and Tibet, and as I have held peaceful intercourse with Asiatics since my twenty-first year, I shall also this time behave with circumspection, follow the instructions I am given, and consider it a point of honour to avoid all disputes on the frontier.

And now we waited again; the days passed, my three native assistants held themselves ready in Dehra Dun for the journey, the Commander-in-chief, Lord Kitchener, assured me that he should be pleased to place at my disposal twenty armed Gurkhas — only the permission sought from the Secretary of State for India, Mr. John Morley, must first arrive; for it was he who held the keys of the frontier, and on him everything depended. Lord Minto, the new Viceroy of India (Frontispiece), did everything in his power. He wrote long complete statements of affairs and sent one telegram after another. A refusal could not discourage him; he always sent off another despatch beginning with the words: "I beg His Majesty's Ministry to take once more into consideration that," etc. When the assurance was given from London that the refusal was not intended for me personally, but that the same answer had been communicated to several British officers, Lord Minto in his last telegram begged that I might be permitted to accompany the British officer who was to travel to Gartok in summer to inspect the market there. But the Secretary of State kept immovably to his resolution, and I received the following reply to my telegram in a despatch of June 1, 1906, from the Secretary to the Viceroy:

> The Prime Minister desires that the following message be communicated to Sven Hedin: "I sincerely regret that I cannot, for reasons which have doubtless been explained to you by the Indian Government, grant you the desired assistance for your journey to and in Tibet. This assistance has also been refused to the Royal Geographical Society in London, and likewise to British officers in the service of the Indian Government."

The contents of the last London telegram intimated, then, that nothing was conceded to me. The Indian Government and the Viceroy could, of course, do nothing but obey, as usual, the orders from London. They were willing to do everything, and displayed the warmest interest in my plans, but they durst not help me. They durst not procure me a permit or passport from Lhasa, they durst not provide me with an escort, indispensable in the insecure country of Tibet, and I lost the privilege of taking with me three efficient topographers and assistants in my scientific observations, from which both sides would have derived advantage. But this was not all. Should I fall in with circumstances and cross the frontier with a party of natives on my own responsibility, the Indian Government had orders to stop me. Thus Tibet was barred to me from the side of India, and the English, that is, Mr. John Morley, closed the country as hermetically as ever the Tibetans had done. I soon perceived that the greatest difficulties I had to overcome on this journey proceeded not from Tibet, its rude climate, its rarefied air, its huge mountains and its wild inhabitants, but — from England! Could I circumvent Mr. John Morley, I should soon settle with Tibet.

Hope is the last thing one resigns, and so I still hoped that all would turn out well in the end. Failure spurred my ambition and stretched my powers to the uttermost tension. Try to hinder me if you can, I thought; I will show you that I am more at home in Asia than you. Try to close this immense Tibet, try to bar all the valleys which lead from the frontier to the high plateaus, and you will find that it is quite impossible. I felt quite relieved when the last peremptory and somewhat curt refusal came and put an end to all further negotiations. I had a feeling as though I was suddenly left in solitude and the future depended on myself alone. My life and my honour for the next two years were at stake — of course I never thought of giving in. I had commenced this fifth journey with a heavy heart, not with trumpets and flourishes as on the former expeditions. But now it was all at once become my pet child. Though I should perish, this journey should be the grandest event of my life. It was the object of all my dreams and hopes, it was the subject of my prayers, and I longed with all my soul for the hour when the first caravan should be ready — and then every day would be a full chord in a song of victory.

I do not venture to pass an opinion on the policy which then piled up in my way obstacles apparently insurmountable. It was at any rate prudent. For the future it will be necessary. If I had gone under British protection and accompanied by British subjects and then been killed, probably a costly punitive expedition must have been sent out to make an example; whether I were a Swede or an Englishman would have made no difference in this case. The view the English Secretary of State took of the matter is shown in his answer to Lord Percy's question a month after I had received my answer: "Sven Hedin has been refused permission to penetrate into Tibet for political

2. COLONEL SIR FRANCIS YOUNGHUSBAND,
Commander of the English Expedition to Tibet,
Resident in Kashmir.

3. COLONEL J. R. DUNLOP SMITH,
Private Secretary to the Viceroy.

reasons, in accordance with which even British subjects are not allowed to visit that country. The Indian Government favours the expeditions of experienced explorers, but the Imperial Government has decided otherwise, and considers it advisable to continue the isolation of Tibet which the late Government so carefully maintained."

During this time I received many proofs of sympathy and friendship. I had true friends in India, and they felt it hard that they could not help me. They would have done it so gladly. I durst not ask them for anything lest I should place them in an awkward, troublesome position. Sir Louis Dane had informed me that if my petition were granted I should have to sign a bond, but what this would have contained I have never found out. Perhaps it dealt with some kind of responsibility for the men who accompanied me, or a promise not to visit certain districts, and a pledge to place the results of my journey at the disposal of the Indian Government — I know not. But now I was absolved from all obligations; freedom is after all the best, and he is the strongest who stands alone. Still, it would be exaggeration to say that I had then any great affection for the name of Mr. John Morley. How could I foresee that I should one day reckon him among my best friends, and think of him with warm respect and admiration?

After my first visit to the Foreign Office, Younghusband (Illustration 2) conducted me to the Viceregal Palace, to enter my name in the visiting list of Lord and Lady Minto. Younghusband is a gallant man, a type of the noblest that a people can produce. He was more annoyed than myself at the refusal of the Government; but he had in this connection a far more bitter experience — his expedition to Lhasa, which ought to have thrown open Tibet to scientific exploration, had been in vain. He took me on the way to Lord Minto's private secretary, Colonel J. R. Dunlop Smith (Illustration 3), in whom I found a friend for life. He is one of the finest, noblest, most generous, and learned men that I have ever met. He is well educated in many subjects, and has a thorough knowledge of India, for he has lived there four-and-twenty years. When we see such men in the most responsible posts, we can well conceive that the ruling race will weather many a violent storm, should they arise, among the three hundred millions of India.

My life at this time abounded in contrasts. How little did my sojourn at Simla resemble the years of solitude and silence that awaited me beyond the mountains veiled in dark masses of cloud! I cannot resist recalling some reminiscences of these extraordinarily delightful days.

Go with me to the first State dinner on May 24, 1906. Along the walls of the great drawing-room in the Viceregal Palace are assembled some hundred guests — all in full dress, in grand uniforms of various colours, and glittering with orders. One of them is taller than the rest by a whole head; he holds himself very upright, and seems cool-headed, energetic, and calm; he speaks to no one, but examines those about him with penetrating, bright bluish-grey eyes. His features are heavy, but interesting, serious, impassive, and tanned; one sees that he has had much experience and is a soldier who has stood fire. His uniform is scarlet, and a whole fortune in diamonds sparkles on his left breast. He bears a world-renowned, an imperishable name: Lord Kitchener of Khartum, the conqueror of Africa and Commander-in-chief of the Indian Army.

A gentleman comes up to me and asks if I remember our having sat together at a banquet of Lord Curzon's. The Lieutenant-Governor of the Punjab is also one of my old acquaintances, and Sir Louis Dane introduces me right and left. A herald enters the room and announces the approach of the Viceroy, and Lord Minto, accompanied by his staff, makes the round of the room, greeting each one of his guests, myself only with the words, "Welcome to Simla." The melancholy tone of the words did not escape me; he knew well that I did not feel as welcome as he and I should have wished. To the sound of music we move to the dining-room, are regaled with choice French dishes, eat off silver plate, and then rise again to take part in the levée, at which five hundred gentlemen are presented to the Viceroy, who stands at the steps of the throne.

4. VICEREGAL LODGE IN SIMLA.

Their names are called out one by one as they pass rapidly in front of the throne. Each one halts and turns to the Viceroy, who returns his deep reverence: he bowed this evening nine hundred times! When Indian princes or Afghan ambassadors pass before him, he does not bow, but lays his hand on the hilt of his guest's sword as a sign of friendship and peace.

Next day I was invited to transfer my quarters to the palace (Illustration 4), and henceforth I was the guest of Lord and Lady Minto. The time I spent with them I shall never forget, and these weeks seem to me now like a dream or a fairy tale. Lord Minto is an ideal British gentleman, an aristocrat of the noblest race, and yet simple and modest. In India he soon became popular owing to his affability and kindness, and he does not think he occupies so high a position that he cannot speak a friendly word to any man out of the numerous tribes of the immense Empire committed to his rule. Lord Minto formerly served in India, and took part in the campaign against Afghanistan; after various experiences in three continents he was appointed Governor-General of Canada. In 1904 he returned to his estate of Minto in Scotland, intending to spend the remainder of his life there; then the King of England and Emperor of India invested him with the office of Viceroy and Governor-General of India. He is not the first Earl of Minto who has held this post, for his great-grandfather was Governor-General of the British possessions in the Indian peninsula a hundred years ago. Then one had to sail round the Cape of Good Hope in order to reach the country of the Hindus, a long, troublesome voyage. Therefore the first Lord Minto left his family at home. The letters exchanged between himself and his wife are still extant, and display an affection and faithfulness quite ideal. When his period of service in India had at length expired, he embarked on a vessel which carried him over the long way to his native land, and he hurried with the first coach straight to Minto. There his wife expected him; she looked along the road with longing eyes; the appointed time had long passed, and no carriage could be seen. At length a rider appeared in a cloud of dust, and brought the news that Lord Minto had died only one post stage from his house. A small label on the packet of letters bears the words "Poor fools." They were written by the first Lady Minto.

But now a new Minto family has blossomed into life. Comfort, simplicity, and happiness prevail in this charming home, where every member contributes to the beauty of the whole. A viceroy is always overwhelmed with work for the welfare of India, but Lord Minto preserved an unalterable composure, and devoted several hours daily to his family. We met at meals; some guests were usually invited to lunch, but at dinner we were frequently alone, and then the time passed most agreeably. Then Lady Minto told of her sojourn in Canada, where she travelled 116,000 miles by rail and steamer, accompanied her husband on his official tours and on sporting expeditions, shot foaming rapids in a canoe, and took part in dangerous excursions in Klondike. We looked over her diaries of that time; they consisted of thick volumes full of photographs, maps, cuttings, and autographs, and were interspersed with views and descriptions of singular interest. And yet the diary that Lady Minto had kept since her arrival in India was still more remarkable and attractive, for it was set in Oriental splendour and the pomp and gorgeousness of Eastern lands, was filled with maharajas bedecked with jewels, receptions in various states, processions and parades, elephants in red and gold, and all the grandeur and brilliancy inseparable from the court of an Indian viceroy. Three charming young daughters — the Ladies Eileen, Ruby, and Violet — fill this home with sunshine and cheerfulness, and, with their mother, are the queens of the balls and brilliant fêtes. Like their father, they are fond of sport, and ride like Valkyries.

Is it to be wondered at that a stranger feels happy in this house, where he is surrounded daily with kindness and hospitality? My room was over the private apartments of the Viceroy. On the ground-floor are State rooms, the large and elegant drawing-rooms, the dining-room, and the great ball-room decorated in white and gold.

5. LADY MINTO AND THE AUTHOR ON THE TERRACE OF THE VICEREGAL LODGE.

The various rooms and saloons are reached from a large ante-chamber adorned with arms and heavy hangings; here there is a very lively scene during entertainments. An open gallery, a stone verandah, runs round most of the ground-floor, where visitors, couriers, *chaprassis*, and *jamadars*, wearing red viceregal uniforms and white turbans, move to and fro. Behind is the courtyard where carriages, rickshaws, and riders come and go, while well-kept paths lead to quiet terraces laid out from Lady Minto's designs. Behind these terraces begins the forest with promenades in the shadow of the trees (Illustration 5).

From the great hall in the middle of the house a staircase leads to the first storey, where the family of the Viceroy occupy rooms which surpass all the rest in the tastefulness of their decoration. Two flights up are the guest-rooms. From an inner gallery you can look down into the great hall, where the scarlet footmen glide noiselessly up and down the stairs. Outside my window was a balcony, where every morning I looked in vain for a glimpse of the mountains on the borders of Tibet. The highest official of Peshawar, Sir Harold Deane, with his wife, and the Maharaja of Idar, were guests in the palace of the Viceroy for a couple of days. Sir Harold was a man one never forgets after once meeting him; strong, tall, manly, and amiable. The half-savage tribes and princes on the frontier of Afghanistan fear and admire him, and he is said to manage them with masterly tact. This meeting was very important to me, for Sir Harold gave me letters of introduction to the Maharaja of Kashmir and his private secretary, Daya Kishen Kaul. At my return to India, Sir Harold was, alas! dead. In him India has lost one of its best guardians.

The Maharaja of Idar was a striking type of an Indian Prince: he had a very dark complexion, handsome features, and an energetic bearing; he dressed for entertainments in silk, gold, and jewels, and altogether made an appearance which threw all Europeans quite into the shade. Yet he was exceedingly popular with them, and always a welcome guest. He is a great sportsman, a first-rate rider, and an exceedingly cool-headed hunter. He owes his great popularity to the following incident: Once when an English officer died in the hot season near his palace, there was difficulty in finding a man to bury the corpse. As every one else refused, the Maharaja undertook the odious task himself. Scarcely had he returned to his palace when the steps were stormed by raving Brahmins, who cried out to him, with threats, that he had forfeited his rank, must be ejected from his caste, and was unworthy to have rule over the state. But he went calmly up to them and said that he knew only of one caste, that of warriors; then he ordered them to go away, and they obeyed.

I met many men in Simla whom I shall always count among my best friends — Generals Sir Beauchamp Duff and Hawkes, with their amiable consorts, and Colonel Adam and his wife, who spoke Russian; he was Lord Minto's military secretary, and died during my absence; also Colonel M'Swiney and his wife. I was their guest at Bolaram, near Haidarabad, in 1902, and I had met the Colonel in the Pamirs in 1895; he, too, has been called away by death, only a month before he would have received his expected promotion to the command of the Ambala brigade. He was an exceptionally excellent and amiable man. I also made acquaintance with many members of Younghusband's Lhasa expedition, one of whom, Captain Cecil Rawling, ardently wished he could get back to Tibet. We often met and concocted grand plans for a journey together to Gartok — hopes which all ended in smoke. The German Consul-General, Count Quadt, and his charming wife were also especial friends of mine. Her mother belonged to the Swedish family of Wirsén, and we conversed in Swedish. I shall never forget a dinner at their house. Dunlop Smith and I rode each in a rickshaw along the long road to Simla, through the town and as far again on the other side, to Count Quadt's house, which was the Viceregal residence before Lord Dufferin built the new palace, the "Viceregal Lodge," in the years 1884–1888. The road was dark, but we had lamps on the shafts; our runners strained at the carriage like straps, and their naked soles pattered like wood on the hard earth. We were late; Lord Kitchener was there already, and every one was waiting.

After dinner the guests were invited to go out into the compound forming the summit of the hill on which the old palace is built. The light of the full moon quivered through the mild intoxicating air, the hills around were veiled in mist and haze, and from the depths of the valleys rose the shrill penetrating rattle of grasshoppers. But this hill, where lively laughter resounded and conversation was stimulated by the effects of the dinner, seemed to be far above the rest of the world. Here and there dark firs or deodars peeped out of the mist with long outstretched arms like threatening ghosts. The night was quiet, everything but ourselves and the grasshoppers seemed to have gone to rest. Such an impression is never effaced. Etiquette forbade that any one should leave before Lord Kitchener—he had to give the signal for breaking up the party; but he found himself very comfortable here, and we talked in French with the wife of Colonel Townsend, drawing comparisons between the matrimonial state and the advantages of uncontrolled freedom. It was after midnight when the dictator of the feast rose, and then ladies and their cavaliers could make for their rickshaws. Silence reigned on the moonlit hill; only the shrill song of the grasshoppers still rose to heaven.

A couple of State balls also took place during my stay in the Viceregal Lodge. Then an endless succession of rickshaws streams up to the courtyard, winding like a file of glow-worms up Observatory Hill. One is almost astonished that there are so many of these small two-wheeled vehicles in Simla, but only the Viceroy, the Commander-in-chief, and the Governor of the Punjab are allowed to use horse carriages, because of the narrowness of the roads. Then elegant ladies rustle in low dresses of silk, with agrafes of diamonds in their hair, and pass through the entrance and hall escorted by cavaliers in full-dress uniforms. One is frightfully crushed in this flood of people who have spent hours in adorning themselves so brilliantly, but the scene is grand and imposing, a *non plus ultra* of gala toilets, a kaleidoscope of many colours, of gold and silver; the red uniforms of the officers stand out sharply against the light silk dresses of the ladies in white, pink, or blue. Here and there the jewelled turban of a maharaja hovers over a sea of European coiffures. Then there is a sudden silence, a passage is opened through the crowd; the herald has announced the advent of the Viceroy and his party, and the band plays "God save the King." The Viceroy and his lady walk slowly through the ranks, saluting on both sides, and take their seats on the thrones in the great ball-room; then the first waltz is played. The illustrious hosts summon first one and then another of their guests to converse with them; there is a rustling of silk, a humming and buzzing, shoe-soles glide with a scraping noise over the floor, and the dance-music hurries on its victims with irresistible force. The guests flock in small parties or large groups into the adjoining dining-room, and there sup at small tables. At length the ranks grow thin, the hosts retire, the wheels of the last rickshaw rattle over the sand of the courtyard, the electric lights are extinguished, and the palace is quiet again.

Lord Kitchener's residence stands at the end of the town of Simla, and is called Snowdon. The visitor enters first a large ante-room, which, with its tasteful arrangement and decoration, makes rather the impression of a reception room or a hall of honour bedecked with trophies. A fine portrait of Gordon Pasha is placed on an easel; opposite stand busts of Alexander and Cæsar. In the wainscot of the staircase is inserted the arm of the presidential chair which Uncle Kruger used in Pretoria, and on the tables, shelves, and friezes are valuable Chinese vases of the Kang-hi (1662–1722) and Kien-lung (1736–1795) periods; for Lord Kitchener is an enthusiastic collector of old Chinese porcelain, but only the very finest finds favour in his eyes. But what strikes the stranger most in this unique hall, and above all attracts his attention, are the trophies and flags from Lord Kitchener's victories in the Sudan and South Africa. They hang down from their staves from an upper gallery, among them the standards of the Mahdi and the dervishes of Omdurman and Om Debraket, besides several Boer flags from the Transvaal and the Orange Free State. In the inner drawing-room we find the same luxurious decoration with Chinese porcelain vases and rare

6. Herbert, Viscount Kitchener of Khartum,
Late Commander-in-Chief of the Indian Army.

ethnographical objects, among which certain Tibetan temple friezes carved in wood are of great value; they were brought by Younghusband's Lhasa expedition. On the tables lie albums of photographs of Lord Kitchener's numerous tours of inspection in India, and of his journey through the cold Pamir. At receptions the table is adorned with costly services in solid gold, gifts of the English nation to the victor of Africa (Illustration 6).

My time in Simla came to an end; it was useless to stay any longer after I had received the last decisive answer from London. On June 9 I took leave of the Viceroy and his youngest daughter, who were going to ride to Mashroba and pass the Sunday there. I cannot describe the leave-taking; it was so warm and hearty. Lord Minto wished that I might still carry out my intentions, and he hoped sincerely that we should again meet in India. I could not on the point of departure express all the gratitude I felt. He had done all that was in his power to help me, and had exposed himself to unpleasantnesses on my account. He had played an important part in my life's course, and I knew that I had gained in him a lasting friend. It was a trial to have to say good-bye to him. He was more grieved than myself that our plans had miscarried, and for my part I felt that my honour now demanded that I should do my best.

On Sunday morning Lady Minto and her two eldest daughters also drove off to Mashroba. I bade them a last farewell, and thanked them for the boundless hospitality I had enjoyed in the Viceregal Lodge. The moment of parting was fortunately short; bitter it certainly was. Two fine carriages drove up with outriders, and escorted by native cavalry soldiers in red and gold, carrying lances in their hands. The ladies, in light bright summer toilets and hats trimmed with flowers, took their seats — the group of ladies of bluest blood, which through centuries and generations had been ennobled and refined, seemed to me like a bouquet of flowers themselves. I remained on the lowest step as long as I could catch a glimpse of the waving sunshades, but soon the red uniforms of the soldiers disappeared among the leafy trees of the avenue which leads down to the main guard, and the romance was at an end.

When I again entered my room the royal palace seemed lifeless and desolate, and I had no heart to remain any longer. I packed my things, hurried into the town and paid a couple of short farewell calls, made arrangements for my heavy luggage, and was soon ready to start. On the 13th I went off. The number thirteen plays a rôle of some importance in this journey: on November 13 I left Trebizond on the Black Sea; on December 13 I reached Teheran, the capital of Persia; and on June 13 I left Simla; but I was not superstitious. Younghusband was the first to welcome me and the last to say good-bye; I was soon to see him again in Srinagar. Then the train sped downwards through the 102 tunnels. From a bend in the road I caught sight of the Viceregal Lodge with its proud towers and lofty walls, the scene of so many joyful reminiscences and disappointed hopes.

CHAPTER II

DEPARTURE FROM SRINAGAR

MANUEL was a singular fellow. He was a Hindu from Madras, small, thin, and black, spoke good English, and with his parents had joined the Roman Catholic Church. He had presented himself at the last moment with a huge packet of testimonials and declared confidently: "If the gentleman thinks of making a long journey, the gentleman will want a cook, and I can cook." I took him into my service without looking at his testimonials (Illustration 15). He behaved well, was honest, and gave me more satisfaction than annoyance. The worst he did was to get lost in Ladak in some mysterious way, and to this hour I have heard nothing more about him.

In my compartment we sat as close as herrings in a barrel. The air became hotter and hotter; from the pleasant coolness of the heights we came again into the oppressive heat of the Indian plains. Passing Kalka, Ambala, and Lahore I came to Rawalpindi, where I put up at a passable hotel. But the room was hot and stuffy, and the punkah, the great fan hanging down from the ceiling, was in motion all through the night, but did not prevent the gnats from paying me importunate visits.

On June 15 a *tonga* and three *ekkas* stood before the hotel; I took my seat in the former, and the baggage was securely packed on the latter — and Manuel. The road runs between fine avenues of trees straight to the foot of the mountains. The traffic is lively: carts, caravans, riders, tramps, and beggars. Before us lie slopes of no great height, and beyond the higher mountains of the

Himalayas. Are they walls erected across my path by hostile spirits, or do they await my coming?

Beyond Malepur the *tonga*, drawn by two spirited horses, passes through the first hills with dark and light tints of luxuriant green. The road winds up among them, and I am glad to leave the fiery glow of the plains behind; certainly the sun is still burning, for the air is clear and the first forerunners of the cloud masses of the south-west monsoon have not yet appeared. Thus we pass one stage after another. We have often to drive slowly, for we meet long trains of native soldiers in khaki uniforms with forage and munition waggons, each drawn by two mules — how glad I should have been to possess a couple of dozen of these fine animals! Cool winds blow in our faces and conifers begin to appear among the foliage trees. We leave the summer station Murree behind us, and now the snow-clad mountains at Gulmarg are visible. After crossing a pass near Murree we ascend again. Beyond Bandi we reach the right bank of the Jhelam, but the river lies far below us; the scenery is beautiful, and its grandeur and magnificence defy description. Lower and lower we go, drive close along the river's bank, and pass the night in the *dak bungalow* of Kohala.

Next day we cross a bridge and slowly mount the slopes of the left bank. The morning is beautifully fine, and the not over-abundant vegetation of the hills exhales an agreeable summer perfume. On our left rushes the stream, often white with foam, but its roar strikes our ears only when we make a halt; at other times it is drowned by the rattle of the *tonga*. I follow with the closest attention the changes of scenery in this wonderful country. The road is carried through some of the mountain spurs in broad vaulted tunnels. The last of these is the longest, and opens its gaping jaws before us like a black cavern. Within it is delightfully cool; the short warning blasts of the signal horn reverberate melodiously in the entrails of the mountain.

In Gurie we breakfast, and rest a quarter of an hour on a comfortable couch in the verandah. Here, four years previously, I spent a memorable hour with Sir Robert and

7. THE MAHARAJA OF JAMMU AND KASHMIR.

Lady Harvey. The wind whistles through the same poplars, elms, and willows to-day; I feel extraordinarily forlorn and melancholy. Then I had come from a great journey, now the future seems to me hopelessly dark. Before me rise the softly rounded but steep slopes of the wooded mountains on the right side of the valley; down yonder the village of Gurie lies on both sides of the river. The air is mild. I dream of eternal spring and forget my cares. Beyond Chinawari tall conifers are again seen on the cliffs. My driver, who speaks Persian, points to a huge block of stone embedded in the margin of the road; ten days ago it fell and killed a man and two horses. At dangerous spots, where landslips may be expected, small white flags are stuck up. The mountain landscape becomes wilder, and its sharp outlines become more distinct in the shades of evening. We come to Urie and Rampur and often drive through dense forest. When we arrive at Baramula we have covered 106 miles in fourteen hours.

On June 17 it rained in torrents, but we determined in spite of it to travel the last six stages to Srinagar. We canter along the straight road between endless rows of poplars. The mud splashes up, the rain beats on the roof of the *tonga*, heavy clouds involve us in semi-darkness, and there is not a trace of the mountains to be seen. The weather suits the mood in which I arrive at Srinagar, the capital of Kashmir on the bank of the Jhelam. Here I had to make several preparations for my journey — to Turkestan, it was stated officially; there was no more talk of Tibet. The persons whom I called upon on the first day of my sojourn in the capital of the Maharaja were away, but at last I found the superintendent of the Mission Hospital in Srinagar, Dr. Arthur Neve. In 1902 he had treated my sick cossack, Shagdur, and rendered me many other services, for which I owe him an eternal debt of gratitude. One of my best friends in India had advised me to try to persuade Dr. Arthur's brother, Dr. Ernest Neve, to accompany me, but now I learned that he too had applied for permission to visit western Tibet, chiefly in connection with missionary work round about Rudok, and had likewise met with a refusal; he was now on his way back from the

Tibetan frontier above Leh. Dr. Arthur Neve is one of the men I most admire. He has devoted his life to the Christian Mission in Kashmir, and his hospital is one of the best and most completely equipped in India. There he works indefatigably day and night, and his only reward is the satisfaction of relieving the sufferings of others.

This day everything seemed to go wrong, and out of spirits I returned to Nedou's Hotel just as the gong announced eight o'clock. I sat down at the long table among some thirty ladies and gentlemen, all as strange to me as I to them. But in some of the parties the conversation turned on me.

"Have you heard that Hedin is in Srinagar?"

"No, really? When did he come?"

"To-day. Of course he wants to go to Tibet."

"Yes, but he has been forbidden, and the Government has orders to prevent him crossing the frontier."

"Well, then, he can pass round Tibet and enter it from the north."

"Yes, he has done it before, and can of course find the way again."

It was exceedingly unpleasant to have to listen to this conversation, and I almost drowned myself in my soup-plate. I could scarcely understand how I could be thus spoken of. It seemed as though the dreams and illusions of my soul were sorted out, named, and ticketed, while my corporeal part sat at the *table d'hôte* and swallowed soup. When we had happily arrived at the coffee I quietly withdrew, and thereafter always ate in my own room. My position was such that I had to avoid all contact with Englishmen; they could do me no service, and I would on no account reveal my real designs. What a difference from any former journeys, which I had always commenced from Russian soil, where every one, from the Czar to the lowest *chinovnik*, had done everything to facilitate my progress!

Next day I called on the private secretary of the Maharaja, the Pundit Daya Kishen Kaul, a stately, distinguished man who speaks and writes English perfectly. He carefully read through my letter of introduction, and kindly promised to get everything ready for me as quickly as possible. During the conversation he took notes. His agents were to receive his orders on that same day, mules would be procured, four soldiers be told off to accompany me during my whole journey, provisions, tents, and pack-saddles be bought, and he would find a pleasure in fulfilling all my wishes. No one would have an inkling that all this was done for me; every outlay would be lost among the heavy items entered under the heading "Maintenance of the Maharaja's Court." And Daya Kishen Kaul kept his word and became my friend. The business proceeded slowly, but still it did go forward. Not a word was spoken of Tibet. I was ostensibly getting ready for a journey to Eastern Turkestan, but his meaning smile told me that he divined my intention.

Even at a base of operation where one has full liberty it is not quite easy to get a caravan ready for the march; how much more difficult here where I was in the midst of intrigues and political vexations. But my self-respect and energy were stimulated, and I felt certain of succeeding in the end. The whole affair reminded me of a drama with an interminable list of rôles; the complications were great and I longed only for action. One act of the play was performed at Srinagar, and I cannot pass it over, as it had a sequel later on. When everything else had been denied me from London the road to Eastern Turkestan still lay open.

On June 22 I received from the Resident, Colonel Pears, the following letter:

> The Indian Government has ordered me by telegraph not to permit you to cross the frontier between Kashmir and Tibet. They have no objections to your travelling to Chinese Turkestan, taking it for granted that you have a Chinese passport. But as you have lately informed me that you do not possess such a document, I have telegraphed to the Indian Government for further instructions.

Now I telegraphed to the Swedish Minister in London, Count Wrangel, and begged him to procure me a passport for Eastern Turkestan, a country I never thought of visiting, and then informed the Government in Simla of this step and of the satisfactory reply. Nineteen days later I received the following letter from Sir Francis

Younghusband, who meanwhile had arrived in Kashmir as the new Resident:

> I have received a telegram from the Government informing me that you may set out before the arrival of the Chinese passport, but on the condition that you do not travel beyond Leh. As soon, however, as the Chinese Government, or the Swedish Minister (in London), telegraphs that your passport is drawn out, you may cross the Chinese frontier at your own risk; your passport will then be sent after you.

Then I telegraphed to Count Wrangel again, asking him to assure the Indian Government that the passport had really been granted me and was already on the way. It was already awaiting me in Leh when I arrived there. It was a pure formality, for I did not need it, and it would have to be decided first where the boundary lay between Eastern Turkestan and Tibet. The representative of China in London subsequently expressed his astonishment to Count Wrangel that I was travelling about in Tibet with a passport made out for Eastern Turkestan, but Count Wrangel replied very justly that he could not possibly control me and the roads I followed in Asia. The English Government had done its best to prevent my travelling through Tibet, and so there was no resource left but to outwit my opponents. How I succeeded will appear in the pages of this book.

On one of the first days, accompanied by Daya Kishen Kaul, I called on the Maharaja of Jammu and Kashmir, Sir Pratab Sing, whose brother, Emir Sing, was also present. His Highness is a little middle-aged man of dreamy, melancholy aspect (Illustration 7). He received me with great friendliness, and promised to meet my wishes in every respect. He had heard of my journey through the desert in 1895, and when I had narrated its incidents I had won him over to my side; he would be pleased, he assured me, to see my new expedition start from his territory.

On June 29 I was invited to a great fête at the Maharaja's palace in honour of the Emperor's birthday. The birthday of the King of England falls on November 9, but the Emperor of India was born on June 29. How that happens I do not know. At the appointed time I went to

8. PALACE OF H.H. THE MAHARAJA OF KASHMIR IN SRINAGAR.

Younghusband, and at the quay of the Residence we were taken on board a *shikara* of the Maharaja — a long, elegantly decorated boat, with soft cushions and an awning with hanging fringes and tassels, and manned by about twenty rowers in bright red clothing. We glide swiftly and noiselessly down the Jhelam, see palaces, houses, and thick groves reflected picturesquely in the swirling ripples, sweep past numerous house-boats and canoes, and come to a halt a little below the bridge at the staircase to the palace, where Emir Sing received us on the lowest step in the red uniform of a major-general. On the platform above the steps the Maharaja awaited us. And then we mingled with the varied crowd of Englishmen and natives, all decked out in their best. Then a court was held; all the guests filed past in slow single-file, and His Highness distributed friendly shakes of the hand and nods. Then in the same order all sat down in rows of chairs, just as in a theatre. But we did not rest long, for soon dinner was announced, and we made free with what kitchen and cellar provided. After the feast was over, the Maharaja, his brother, and his little nephew, the heir to the throne, entered the hall and took their places at the middle of the table at which we sat. The Maharaja called for a cheer for the King-Emperor, another toasted Younghusband, who returned thanks in a neat and partly humorous speech. Then the guests were invited to go out into an open gallery with thick pillars, where they witnessed a display of fireworks. Between suns and Bengal fires, rockets and serpents flew into the air from boats lying on the river, and on the further bank "God save the King-Emperor" was spelled out in red lamps. Taste and elegance had been less studied than noise; there were detonations and sprays of fire in every nook and corner, and the whole gave an impression of unswerving loyalty. When we went down to our boat again all around was veiled in darkness; brilliant light streamed only through the colonnade of the palace façade. We rowed upstream and enjoyed a more beautiful and quieter illumination; the moon threw sinuous lines of gold across the ripples of the river, and flashes of blue lightning darted over the mountains on the horizon.

The Pundit Daya Kishen Kaul Divan Sahib was unwearied in his kind efforts. He procured me forty mules, which he bought from the Raja of Poonch. I rejected four; the rest were in good condition, but they were of a less sturdy breed than the Tibetan, and all foundered in Tibet. He also furnished me with an escort of four soldiers who had been in the service of the Maharaja. Two of them, Ganpat Sing and Bikom Sing, were Rajputs, and spoke Hindustani; they had certificates of good conduct, and the former wore a service medal. Like the cook Manuel, they declared themselves prepared to sacrifice their lives for me, but I calmed them with the assurance that our campaign would not be so bloody. Fortunately both belonged to the same caste, so that they could mess together; but, of course, they could not eat with other mortals. In camp I always saw them seated at their own fire a good distance from the others. The two others were Pathans, Bas Ghul from Cabul, and Khairulla Khan from Peshawar. Daya Kishen Kaul provided all with guns and ammunition at my expense, and their pay was fixed. They also received money for their outfit, and I prepared them to expect cold. My amiable benefactor looked after tents for me, saddles, pack-saddles, and a number of other necessary articles. Meanwhile I made purchases myself in the bazaars. I got about twenty *yakdans*, small leather-covered wooden boxes such as are used in Turkestan; kitchen utensils and saucepans; furs, ordinary blankets and frieze blankets; a tent-bed with mattress and a gutta-percha undersheet; warm material and *bashliks*; caps, Kashmir boots, cigars, cigarettes and tobacco for a year; tea, and several hundred boxes of preserved meat; also woven stuffs, knives, daggers, etc., for presents, and no end of other things (Illustrations 10, 14).

In all my purchases and transport arrangements I received invaluable help from Cockburn's Agency. It provided me with stores of rice, maize, meal and barley; for it was impossible to get together sufficient quantities in Leh. It also looked after the transport of this heavy baggage, and I had every reason to be satisfied with its arrangements. I had myself brought a boat with oars, rudder, mast, sails, life-buoys and centre-board, in the

9. THE JHELAM IN SRINAGAR.

large chests I had sent out to India. Then I had the same scientific instruments as before: an alt-azimuth, two chronometers, meteorological instruments, compasses, photographic apparatus and plates, writing-blocks, sketch- and note-books, writing materials, field-glasses, hunting-rifles, revolvers, etc.

Burroughs and Wellcome of London had been so kind as to present me with an unusually complete medicine-chest, which was in itself a tasteful and elegant work of art, and contained drugs specially selected for a high, cold, and dry climate. All the remedies were in tabloids, well and orderly packed, and could easily be found with the aid of a printed catalogue. The whole was carefully stowed in a pretty aluminium chest which shone like silver. The medicine-chest was from the first exceedingly popular in the caravan; every one had a blind confidence in it. I had a suspicion that many ailments were feigned just to get another look at the chest. At any rate it contained the best portable medical outfit I have ever seen.

I had some difficulty in finding an assistant for meteorological observations. There was none at the Central Institute in Simla, and therefore I applied to the Meteorological Station in Srinagar. The chief recommended a youngster to me who had been assistant at the station and had been baptized under the name of Rufus, but he was a fat Bengali, who always walked about with an umbrella even when it did not rain. I was not troubled about his corpulence; he would soon be cured of that on the mountains; but, what was worse, he had certainly never seen an aneroid barometer, and I could not, try as I would, teach him to read it. I therefore dismissed him, for at the worst I could read the instruments, though I had a superabundance of other things to do.

Then just at the right moment a Eurasian, three-and-twenty years old, presented himself, named Alexander Robert. In his first letter to me he gave himself no other title than the very correct one of a "stranger in Srinagar"; this indicated modesty. He came to my hotel, showed me his testimonials, which were all excellent, and he struck me as a pleasant, strong, and healthy man. Among other employments he had worked on the railway at Peshawar and had been an assistant in Dr. Neve's hospital. Dr. Neve recommended him most warmly, and as, besides, he acquired a good knowledge of the instruments after a single lesson and needed only a few days' practice in Srinagar in handling and reading them, I was very glad to engage him. He left his mother and young wife at home, but they were in no straits, and a part of his wages was paid to him in advance. I did not regret taking him, for he had a knowledge of many things, was capable, cheerful, and ready for work of any kind. When I knew him better I entrusted all my cash to his care, and could do it without hesitation, for his honesty was beyond suspicion. He was a companion to me during the long winter evenings, was a favourite in the caravan and among the Tibetans, and carefully watched that every one did his duty. Robert was only once a cause of grief to me, when he left me in December 1907, in consequence of sad news he received of his family through Gartok (Illustration 13).

After Robert joined me matters went on more easily. He superintended the packing of the baggage and the weighing of it out into equal loads, and helped me in stowing and distributing the heavy money-bags which held 22,000 silver and 9000 gold rupees. Thus the days passed, and at last the hour of release struck. I had longed for it as for a wedding feast, and counted the intervening hours. I took leave of my old friend Younghusband, who at the last moment recommended to me a caravan leader, Muhamed Isa of Leh, and bade farewell to the Maharaja, Emir Sing, and Daya Kishen Kaul; and Mrs. Annie Besant, who on several occasions had shown me great kindness, expressed the best and most sincere wishes for the success of my journey.

My people were ordered to be ready on the morning of July 16, 1906, in the courtyard of the hotel (Illustration 16). The start should be delayed not a day longer; I had now waited long enough. It was evident that some hours would be required to get all in marching order for the first time. At eight o'clock the men from Poonch came with their mules, but only to tell me that they

10. The Start from Ganderbal.

11. My Escort.

must have 5 rupees each for new clothes. The purchase of these articles of clothing took up four more hours, and in the afternoon the preparations had progressed so far that there was only the loading-up to see after. Some hours elapsed before the pack-saddles and loads had been adjusted. The mules were very excited, danced round in circles, and kicked so that the boxes flew about, and at last each animal had to be led by a man (Illustration 17). The hired horses were more sensible. Manuel on his steed presented rather a comical appearance: he had never mounted a horse in his life, and he looked frightened; his black face shone in the sun like polished iron. The whole company was taken by at least half-a-dozen amateur photographers (Illustration 18). At length we moved off in detachments, exactly twelve hours behind time; but the long train was at any rate on the way to Gandarbal and Tibet—and that was the main thing. What did it matter what time it was? Feeling as though my prison doors were opened, I watched my men pass along the road (Illustration 10), and the whole world lay open before me.

Of all these men none knew of the glow of delight within me; they knew me not, and I did not know them; they came from Madras, Lahore, Cabul, Rajputana, Poonch, and Kashmir, a whole Oriental congress, whom chance had thrown together. They might as well be robbers and bandits as anything else, and they might think that I was an ordinary *shikari sahib* whose brain was filled with no other ideal but a record in Ovis Ammon's horns. I watched the start almost pitifully, and asked myself whether it would be vouchsafed to them all to return home to wife and child. But none was obliged to follow me, and I had prepared them all for a trying campaign of eighteen months. What would it have profited me to have made them anxious by anticipating troubles? Trying days would come soon enough.

I was most sorry for the animals, for I knew that famine awaited them. As long as there were opportunities they should satiate themselves with maize and barley that they might subsist as long as possible afterwards on their own fat.

At length I stood alone in the yard, and then I drove

to Dal-dervaseh, where a long, narrow, five-oared boat awaited me at the stone steps, and placed myself at the tiller, when the boat put off and I was at last on the way to the forbidden land. All the long journey through Persia and Baluchistan had been only a prologue, which had really no result except to land me in the spider's nest in which I found myself caught in India. Now, however, I was free, out of the reach of all that is called Government; now I could rule, myself.

The canal, on the bright mirror of which we now glided along, was varied by water plants, ducks, and boats, almost sinking under their loads of country produce. On the banks washerwomen crouched, and here and there a group of merry children were bathing; they scrambled up projecting points and mooring places, let themselves tumble into the canal, splashed and threw up the water like small whales. The canal becomes narrower, only a few yards broad, our boat takes the ground, and the oarsmen get out and draw it over the shallows. The waterway is very winding, but runs on the whole to the north; the water is shallow, but the current is with us. On either side stand picturesque houses of wood and stone as in a street of Venice. At every corner the eye encounters a new charming subject for the brush, which gains additional effect from the motley figures, the vegetation, and the light lancet-shaped boats. The lighting up of the picture is also fine now that the sun is setting, bathing everything in its warm glowing beams, and causing the outlines to stand out clearly against the deep shadows. Between the houses the water is as black as ink. We draw near to a small projecting height, behind which the road runs to Kangan and Leh. Side branches debouch into the canal, but we make for a lake called Anchar; its water is greyish blue, and comes from the Sind, or Send as they here pronounce the name of the river.

After a while eddies and sandbanks show that we are in the river. The sun has set; the summer evening is quiet and peaceful, only the gnats buzz over the water.

Though the rowers work steadily, putting forth all their strength, we make slow progress, for the current is strong

12. My Three Puppies.
13. Robert, the Eurasian.
14. Ganpat Sing, the Rajput.
15. Manuel, the Cook.

PROMINENT MEMBERS OF THE FIRST EXPEDITION.

against us. I have therefore opportunity to peep into the domestic affairs of a whole series of English families in the house-boats. It is just upon nine o'clock and the inmates are gathered round the table in dress coats and elegant toilets. At one table sat three young ladies; I thought that they had spent too much trouble over their toilet, for there was nowhere any sign of a cavalier to be charmed with their appearance. Through the open windows the glaring lamplight fell on the water; they saw us pass, and perhaps puzzled their heads over the reason of so late a visit. Now the century-old planes of Gandarbal appear, we row into a creek of stagnant water and go on shore.

This was my first day's journey, but the day was far from being over. Scouts were sent out, but not a soul was to be found at the appointed halting-place. We settled down between mighty tree-trunks and lighted a blazing signal fire. After a time Bas Ghul comes like a highway pad into the light of the flames; he leads a couple of mules, and at ten o'clock Robert and Manuel also lie beside our fire. But the tents and provisions are not yet here. At eleven scouts are sent out again, and we do not see or hear of them again before midnight; they report that all is well with the caravan and that it will soon be here. But when one o'clock came another scout vanished in the darkness and it was not till a quarter to three that my people arrived, after I had waited quite five hours for them. But I was not at all angry, only happy to be *en route*. New fires and resinous torches were lighted, and illuminated brightly the lower branches of the plane trees, while through the crowns the stars twinkled above our first bivouac on the way to Tibet.

What noise and confusion in this throng of men and baggage animals! The place was like a fair where all scold and scream and no one listens. The escort tried in vain to get a hearing, the Rajputs were quieter, but the Pathans abused the disobedient Kashmiris and the saucy men from Poonch as robbers and murderers. The animals were tethered with long cords to the foot of the trees, and on a small open space my tent pegs were for the first time driven into the ground. The tent was a present from my friend Daya Kishen Kaul, and was my home for a long time. The baggage was piled up in walls of provision sacks and boxes, and Manuel got hold at length of his kitchen utensils and unpacked his enamelled ware. The animals neighed and stamped and occasionally gave their neighbours a friendly kick, but when the barley nose-bags were carried round and hung on their necks only a whinnying was heard, which signified impatience and a good appetite. And then these children of the East, this gathering of dark-skinned men who strode about in the red firelight with tall white turbans — what a fine striking picture on the background of a pitch-dark night! I smiled to myself as I saw them hurrying hither and thither about their numerous affairs.

But now dinner is ready in the lighted tent, and a box lid serves as a table. A carpet, a bed, two boxes for daily use, and the young dogs are the only furniture. There are three of the last, of which two are bitches. They are pariahs; they were enticed away from the street in Srinagar and have no trace of religion (Illustration 12). Robert and I, who always speak English, call the white and the yellow ones simply "Puppy"; the third soon received the name of "Manuel's Friend," for Manuel and he always kept together.

And all this company which the sport of fortune had collected around me was to be scattered again, one after the other, like chaff before the wind. I was the only one who, six-and-twenty months later, reached Simla again, and the last of all the men and animals who now lay in deep sleep under the planes of Gandarbal.

But I was not the last to lay myself down to rest on this first night, for when I put out my light at three o'clock the firelight still played on the side of the tent, and I seemed to feel the brisk life out in Asia like a cooling breath of pine forests and mountains, snowfields and glaciers, and of broad open plains where my plans would be realized. Should I be tired of it? Nay, should I ever have enough of it?

16

18

17

16. In Front of Nedou's Hotel in Srinagar.
17. Some of our Mules.
18. An Amateur Photographer Photographed.

CHAPTER III

THE ROAD TO LEH

THE day ended late. Next morning I was awaked late, and the sun stood high in the heavens before we were ready to start. It took four hours to get the whole camp under weigh, to pack up and load the animals; but the work would be done more expeditiously when all knew their parts.

The long train begins to move, troop after troop disappears among the trees. On both sides of the road country houses and villages peep out between willows, walnut and apricot trees, and small channels of water murmur through the rice-fields, where men are hoeing, moving in regular order, and singing a rhythmical encouraging song; the singing lightens the work, for the weeds are torn up in time with the air, and no one likes to be behind another.

A bridge crosses the Sind, which rolls its greyish blue water, rushing and roaring, through several large arms. Now the road ascends the valley of the river, then we turn eastwards, and soon the broad valley of Kashmir with its level country disappears behind us. The rise is already noticeable, and we are glad of it, for the day is warm. Trees become fewer, and we ride for greater and greater stretches in the blazing sun; but all around us is green and abundantly watered, the mild air is full of life and productive energy, and the whole valley resounds with the roar of the river and the echo it calls forth. I have passed this way twice before, but on both occasions the Sind valley was covered with snow; now summer reigns in the deep hollows and on the heights.

At Kangan we pitched our tents in a thick copse. This time the camp was marked out and the tents set up fairly expeditiously. The *Numberdar* of the village procured us everything we wanted — we did not wish to touch our own stores until it became impossible to obtain local supplies. The four coolies who had carried the boat were here relieved by four others, who were to carry it up to Gunt.

So we had accomplished another day's journey. We all delighted in the free, active life. But the day was declining, the shadows grew longer, the sun disappeared an hour sooner than usual, for it was concealed by the mountains, and after we had listened for a while to the plaintive bark of the jackals we also went early to rest. In the stillness of the night the roar of the stream sounded still louder; its water came from the heights which were the goal of our hopes; but with still greater longing would my eyes one day watch these eddies on their way to the sea.

When I came out of my tent in the cool of the morning the rest of the caravan had already set out, and the camp looked empty and deserted. The new day was not promising, for it rained hard, and thunder growled among the mountains; but the summer morning gave forth an odour of forest and fresh green vegetation, and after a good breakfast my detachment, to which Robert and Manuel belonged, started on its march.

The sun soon came out, and with the warmth great swarms of flies, which tortured our animals and made them restive. The road ran down to the river and through the trees on its right bank. On the crest of the left flank of the valley some patches of snow still defied the summer sun, and the wood opposite was much thicker than on our side. Here and there a conifer raised its dark crown above the lighter foliage. At the village Mamer, where a mill-wheel swished through the waterfall, and an open booth invited the traveller to refresh himself, Khairullah remained awhile behind in company with a smoking narghilé. At Ganjevan we crossed the river by three shaking bridges. In the background of the narrowing valley rose a mountain covered with snow. The scenery was fine, and we enjoyed a ride really elevating in a double sense. Our caravan had to halt several times when a mule threw off its load; but the animals were already quieter, and I looked forward with anxiety to the time when they would become meek as lambs, and when no objurgations would induce them to move on.

The camp at Gunt was already in order when we arrived. My first thought is always for the puppies; in the morning, during the first hours of the march, they whine, finding the movement of the mule very uncomfortable, but the rocking soon sends them to sleep. But as soon as they are taken out of the basket they fall foul of one another, and then they wander all the evening among the tents, gnawing and tearing at everything.

Even with a temperature of 52.2° F. I felt so cold in the night, after the heat of the plains, that I woke and covered myself with a fur rug. The river in the morning marked only 46.2°. Upstream the view became ever finer. Sometimes we rode through narrow defiles, sometimes up steep dangerous slopes, sometimes over broad expansions of the valley with cultivated fields. Then the precipitous rocks drew together again, and cool dense shadows lay among willows and alders. The roar of the stream drowned all other sounds. The river had now become smaller, so many tributaries having been left behind us, but its wild impetuosity and its huge volumes of dashing water were the more imposing; the water, greenish blue and white, foaming and tossing, boiled and splashed among huge blocks of dark green schist. In a gully, close to the bank, a conical avalanche still lay thawing, and up above small waterfalls appeared on the slopes like streaks of bright white paint. When we came nearer we could perceive the movement, and the cascades that resolved themselves into the finest spray.

Then the valley spread out again, and conifers alone clothed its flanks. We bivouacked at Sonamarg, where I set out some years before from the *dak bungalow* on a winter's night, with lanterns and torches, for a venturesome excursion over the avalanches of the Zoji-la Pass.

The Governor of Kashmir had sent a *chaprassi* with me, and at a word from him all the local authorities were at our service. But it was not easy to keep some of the members of the caravan in order. Bas Ghul and Khairullah proved to be great brawlers, who began to quarrel with the others on every possible occasion. Bas Ghul evidently considered it his chief duty to appropriate a coolie for his own service, and Khairullah thought himself much too important to help in unloading. The others complained daily of annoyance from the Afghans, and I soon saw that this escort would give us more trouble than help. Among the rest, also, the Kashmiris and the men from Poonch, there were petty pilferers, and the Rajputs were ordered to watch that none of our belongings went astray. In Baltal there was a great commotion, for people from Sonamarg appeared and declared that my servants had stolen a saucepan as they passed through. And it was actually found among the Poonch men. The complainants received their pan back again as well as compensation for their trouble (Illustration 19).

The state of the road from Baltal over the Zoji-la Pass was very different now from what it was in the year 1902. Then the whole country was covered with snow, and we slided almost the whole way down over glaciated slopes. Now some five hundred workmen were engaged in mending the road up to the pass. Their industry was indicated by thundering blasts, and now and then great blocks of stone fell down uncomfortably near to us.

Now our heavily-laden caravan had to cross the pass. Slowly and carefully we march up over hard and dirty but smooth avalanche cones, in which a small winding path has been worn out by the traffic. Water trickles and drops in the porous mass, and here and there small rivulets issue from openings in the snow. After a stretch of good road comes a steep slope along a wall of rock — a regular staircase, with steps of timber laid across the way. It was a hard task for laden animals to struggle up. Now and then one of them slipped, and a mule narrowly escaped falling over — a fall from the steep acclivity into the deep trough of the roaring Sind would have been almost certain destruction, not a trace of the unfortunate beast would have been found again. From our lofty station the river looked like a thread. After some sacks of maize had fallen overboard, each of the animals was led by two men.

19. The Road to Baltal.

The train advanced slowly up. Piercing cries were constantly heard when one of the animals was almost lost. But at last we got over the difficulties, and travelled over firm snow and level ground. The thawed water from a huge cone of snow on the south side flowed partly to the Sind, partly to the Dras. The latter increased with astonishing quickness to a considerable river, and our small and slippery path followed its bank. A treacherous bridge crossed a wild tributary, with agitated waters of a muddy grey colour. One of the mules broke through it, and it was only at the last moment that his load could be saved. Then the bridge was mended with flat stones for the benefit of future passengers.

The Dras is an imposing river; its waters pour over numerous blocks that have fallen into its bed, and produce a dull grinding sound. And this mighty river is but one of the thousand tributaries of the Indus.

We reached Matayun in drizzling rain, and had scarcely set up our camp when the caravan-men came to loggerheads. We here overtook a hired contingent of 30 horses with forage. Their drivers had received orders to travel as quickly as possible to Leh; but now it appeared that they had remained stationary for several days, and wanted to be paid extra in consequence. The authorities in Srinagar had done their best to make my journey to Leh easy, but there is no order in Kashmir. In Robert I had an excellent assistant; he did everything to appease the refractory men. I now saw myself that stringent measures must be resorted to, and I waited impatiently for a suitable occasion for interference. About three-fourths of the Poonch men reported themselves ill; they wished to ride, and that was the whole cause of their illness. The mules, when not wanted, were to go unloaded, in order to economize their strength, and on that account we had hired horses in Srinagar. Some men had been kicked by our hot-tempered mules, and now came for treatment.

Then we go on to Dras and Karbu. On the heights above the Dras we pass the famous stone figures of Buddha, and then we descend a narrow picturesque valley to Karbu. The river constantly increases in volume, and presents a grand spectacle; small affluents fall between the rocks like silver ribands, and spread out over the dejection fans. The pink blossoms of the hawthorn wave gracefully in the wind, which cools us during the hot hours of the day. Fine dark juniper bushes, tall as cypresses, adorn the right bank.

In front of the station-house in Karbu an elderly man in a white turban came up to me. "Good day, Abdullah," I said to him, for I immediately recognized the honest fellow who had helped me up over the snowfields of the Zoji-la on the former occasion.

"Salaam, Sahib," he answered, sobbing, fell on his knees and embraced my foot in the stirrup, after the Oriental custom.

"Will you go on a long journey with me?" I asked.

"Yes, I will follow you to the end of the world, if the Commissioner Sahib in Leh will allow me."

"We will soon settle that. But, tell me, how have you got on since we last saw one another?"

"Oh, I am the *Tekkedar* of Karbu, and provide passing caravans with all they want."

"Well, then, think over the matter till to-morrow, and if you wish to accompany me, I have a post free for you among my people."

"There is no need of consideration; I will go with you, though I only get a rupee a month."

But Abdullah was too old and infirm for Tibet, and the conditions which he afterwards put before Robert were much more substantial than he had represented them in the first joy of meeting me again: 60 rupees monthly, everything found, his own horse, and exemption from all heavy work were now his demands. Consequently next morning we bade each other an eternal farewell.

Now a traveller turned up from the preceding station, and complained that the Poonch men had stolen a sheep from him. As they denied it, I made the plaintiff accompany us to Kargil, where the case could be tried before the magistrate.

We approached the striking spot, where two valleys converge and the Dras joins the Wakkha, passed the sharp

20. KARGIL.

21. CHHORTEN IN LAMAYURU.
Sketches by the Author.

rocky angle, and rode up close by the bank of the Wakkha. The valley has a very great fall, and the powerful stream rushes down in wild commotion, swells up and leaps over the blocks in its way, or breaks into foaming, tumultuous surge. Several old acquaintances and the Vezir Vezarat himself came to meet us, and before we reached Kargil we were accompanied by a whole cavalcade. We bivouacked in a cool grove of poplars and willows, and intended to rest the following day (Illustration 20).

This day brought some picturesque scenes. Surrounded by the authorities of Kargil with the pundit Lashman Das and the Vezir Vezarat at their head, I held judgment over the heterogeneous rabble which had caused so much embarrassment in the first week of my journey. Firstly, all the Kashmiris, with their leader Aziza, were dismissed. Then came the turn of their fellow-countrymen, who had transported hither on hired horses the maize and barley for our animals, and lastly we came to the Poonch men. As regards the sheep-stealing the following procedure was adopted. The suspected men were tied to a couple of trees, and though there was a cool shade, they grew weary, and after waiting three hours for a rescuing angel, confessed all, and were thereupon sentenced to pay double the value of the sheep. Then Khairullah stepped forward and interceded for his friend Aziza; as his request was not granted he was annoyed, and positively refused to undertake the night watch. So he, too, was dismissed, and was allowed to take with him the other Afghan, Bas Ghul, who suffered from periodical fits of insanity, and was moreover a rogue. It was quite a relief to me to get rid of these esquires of our bodyguard. Of the original "Congress of Orientalists" in Srinagar only four men now remained, namely, Robert, Manuel, Ganpat Sing, and Bikom Sing.

When we left Kargil on July 26 we took with us 77 hired horses with their leaders, and the forage of the animals formed 161 small heaps. A native veterinary surgeon was to accompany us to see that the mules were well tended. After we had bought all the barley we could get hold of, our caravan had much increased, and the weeding-out effected in Kargil made the succeeding days of our journey to Leh much more agreeable than the previous.

At Shargul we passed the first lama temple on this route; beyond Mullbe they gradually became more numerous. At every step one finds evidence that one is in the country of the lamas; the small white temples in Tibetan style crown the rocky points and projections like storks' nests, and dominate the valleys and villages below them. But a monk in his red toga is seldom seen; the temples seem silent and abandoned among the picturesque *chhorten* monuments and *manis*. The whole relief of the country is now much more prominent than in winter, when the universal snow-mantle makes all alike and obliterates all the forms. The fantastic contours of the mountains stand out sharply with their wild pinnacles of rock and embattled crests, which above Bod-Karbu mingle with the old walls and towers, of which only ruins are now left.

On July 28 we crossed the river by a tolerably firm bridge, and continued to ascend the valley which leads to the Potu-la. Just beyond the pass the authorities of Lamayuru came to meet us with flowers and fruits, and each one, according to the custom of the country, offered a rupee, which, however, we needed only to touch with the hand. A little further the first *chhorten* appeared, followed by a long row of others; the stone heaps pointed towards the famous monastery of Lamayuru. Passing round a projecting corner a little farther on, we had a clear view of a small valley between lofty mountains, and here rose a precipitous terrace of detritus, on which the monastery is built. Some white buildings up there stood out sharply against a grey background, and in the depths of the valley cultivated fields spread out among a few groups of trees (Illustration 21).

As soon as our party was visible from the valley, music was heard, and long brass drums boomed from the temple roofs with a deep, solemn, organ tone, which was joyously echoed among the mountains. Would the lama monasteries of Tibet give us such a friendly welcome? As we entered the village, there stood there about thirty

23

24

22

22. Church Music in Lamayuru.

23. Portrait of a Lama. 24. Portrait of a Lama.

Sketches by the Author.

women in their best clothes, in fur-trimmed coloured mantles, with blinkers firmly plaited into the hair, and with turquoises on the top. All the inhabitants had turned out, and formed a picturesque group round the band, which started a deafening tune with its flutes and drums (Illustration 22).

In the afternoon we went up to the monastery, where the prior and the monks received us at the main entrance. They led us into the open court of the monastery, surrounded by old buildings, *chhorten*, and flagstaffs. From here one has a grand view of the valley which slopes down to the Indus. Under dark masses of cloud, and in fine rain, seven monks executed an incantation dance; they had tied on masks of wild animals, evil spirits, and monsters with laughing mouths, tusks for teeth, and uncanny staring eyes. Their motley coats stood out like bells as they danced, and all the time weird music was played. How the monks must be wearied in their voluntary imprisonment! Evidently their only relaxation is to display their religious fanaticism before the inquisitive eyes of passing strangers.

Immediately beyond the village we descend a dangerously steep road in the small, narrow, and wild ravine which leads to the Indus. The deep trough of the Dras is crossed by small, neat wooden bridges, and after a couple of hours' journey one rides as through a portal into the great, bright valley of the Indus, and has the famous river before one. It is a grand sight, and I halt for some time on a swinging wooden bridge to gaze at the vast volume of water which, with its great load and its rapid current, must excavate its channel ever deeper and deeper. The station-house, Nurla, stands just above the river, which tosses and roars under its windows.

The day had been broiling hot; the rocks and soil of this grey, unfruitful valley seem to radiate out a double quantity of heat, and even in the night the thermometer marked 61°. Even the river water had a temperature of 54° in the daytime, but still, though dirty-grey like porridge, it was a delicious drink in the heat.

As far as Saspul we rode along the right bank close to the river. Here the road is often dangerous, for it is cut like a shelf in the steep wall of rock, and one feels at ease only when the valuable baggage has passed safely. The danger is that a pack-horse on the mountain-side may thrust itself past another, and force this one over the edge of the rock, so that one may in a moment lose one's instruments, photographic apparatus, or sacks of rupees.

At Jera a small emerald-green foaming torrent dashes headlong into the Indus, and is lost in its bosom — the clear green water is swallowed up instantaneously by the muddy water of the Indus. One is delighted by the constantly changing bold scenery and the surprises encountered at every turn of the road. The eyes follow the spiral of a constantly moving vortex, or the hissing spray which the wind whips off the crests of the waves. One almost envies the turbid eddies of this water which comes from the forbidden land, from Gartok, from the regions north of the Kailas mountain, from the unknown source of the Indus itself, whither no traveller has yet penetrated, and which has never been marked down on a map.

The bridge of Alchi, with its crooked, yielding beams, seemed just as dangerous as on my last visit, but its swaying arch boldly spans the interval between the banks, and during a pleasant rest in the shade the bridge was reproduced in my sketch-book. The waves dashed melodiously against the stone embankment of the road, and I missed the sound when the route left the bank and ascended to Saspul, where we were received with the usual music and dancing-women (Illustration 26).

Basgho-gompa has a fine situation in a side valley of the Indus. The monastery is built on the left side of the valley, the white walls of three storeys, with balconies, effective cornices and pennants, standing on a long cliff. A quantity of *chhortens* and *manis* surround Basgho. The sacred formula "Om mani padme hum" is carved on a slab of green slate, and lizards, as green as the stone, dart about over the words of eternal truth.

The first of August was the last day of our journey to Leh. A bright, peaceful morning; the rays of the sun crept warm and agreeably through the foliage of the apricot trees, and threw green reflexions into the station-room.

29 28 25 26 27

25. The Sumto Valley. 26. Bridge of Alchi. 27. Girl in Niemo. 28 & 29. Palace of the Kings of Ladak in Leh.
Sketches by the Author.

We rode near the Indus as far as where the monastery, Spittol, stands on its hill, beyond which the road turns aside from the river and runs straight up to Leh, which is visible from a distance, surrounded by verdant gardens. Mohanlal, a merchant of Leh, who had undertaken a large part of the final equipment of the expedition, came to meet us, and, as we rode past an enclosed field of fine clover, told me that he had bought it for my mules.

We dismounted at the gate of a large garden, and went in. In the midst of the garden stands a stone house among poplars and willows. It is usually the residence of the Vezir Vezarat, the representative of Kashmir in Ladak, but now it was to be my headquarters for twelve days. Here I had a roof over my head for the last time for two long years, and I found myself very comfortable in my study up one flight of stairs. Robert occupied another room, and an open, shady balcony was fitted up as a meteorological observatory Manuel and the two Rajputs had the control of the ground-floor; in the courtyard purveyors and new servants were continually coming and going, and adjoining the garden was our stable, where the newly obtained horses were posted in the open air.

Leh is the last place of any importance on the way to Tibet. Here our equipment must be finally completed. Nothing could be omitted; if we forgot anything we could not obtain it afterwards. Here the silver stream of rupees flowed away without intermission, but I consoled myself with the thought that we should soon be in a country where, with the best will in the world, we could not spend a farthing. A large caravan sucks up money, as a vampire blood, as long as it remains in inhabited cultivated lands; but when all contact with human civilization is cut off, it must live on its own resources; consequently, it gradually dwindles and approaches its dissolution. As long as it is at all possible we let the animals eat all they can; the best clover to be had must be procured, and both horses and mules must be so well tended that they can afterwards live on their own fat and endure the hardships that await them.

CHAPTER IV

THE LAST PREPARATIONS

CAPTAIN PATTERSON was now Joint-Commissioner of the province of Ladak. He received me from the first with the greatest hospitality and kindness, and was one of the finest men I have ever come in contact with. Having a thorough knowledge of India, Ladak, and Tibet, he was able to give me valuable hints and advice, and was untiring in assisting to equip the great caravan, the object of which was still, officially, Eastern Turkestan, without overstepping his instructions by a hair's breadth. I found in him a true friend, and after dinner, which I always took at eight o'clock in the evening, we often sat together till long after midnight, talking of the future of Asia and the doings of the world.

Sir Francis Younghusband had recommended to me a well-known caravan leader, Muhamed Isa. I had seen him in Kashgar and Srinagar, and knew that he had been present at the murder of the French explorer, Dutreuil de Rhins, on June 5, 1894. During about thirty years he had travelled in most parts of Central Asia, and was also acquainted with many parts of Tibet. Besides a number of shorter journeys which he had accomplished in the service of various sahibs, he had also been Carey's and Dalgleish's caravan leader on their great march through Central Asia, and had served a couple of years under Dutreuil de Rhins. He accompanied Younghusband on his famous march over the Mustagh Pass (1887), and had been his caravan leader in the campaign to Lhasa (1903–1904). On Ryder's and Rawling's journey in the valley of the upper Brahmaputra he had had the management

30. Muhamed Isa.

of the baggage caravan. During all these journeys he had acquired experience which might be very useful to me, and I gratefully accepted Younghusband's proposal, especially as Captain Patterson, in whose service Muhamed Isa then was, did not hesitate to place him at my disposal. Besides, Muhamed Isa spoke fluently Turki, Tibetan, and Hindustani, and wished for nothing better than to accompany me. Without knowing that he had been warmly recommended, he had earnestly begged his master to allow him to enter my service (Illustration 30).

His father was a man of Yarkand, his mother a Lamaist of Leh. The mixed race of such unions is called Argon, and is generally distinguished by physical power and extraordinarily well-developed muscular structure. Muhamed Isa also was a fine man, tall and strong as a bear, with great power of endurance, reliable and honest, and after a few days' journey with him I found that my caravan could not have been entrusted to better hands. That the first crossing of Tibet was so successful was due in great measure to his services. He kept splendid discipline among the men, and if he were sometimes strict, it was for the good of the caravan, and he permitted no neglect of duty.

He entertained Robert and myself, and even the caravan men, for hours together with tales of his fortunes and his adventures in the service of other Europeans, criticising some of his former masters without much reserve. The remembrance of Dutreuil de Rhins especially seemed to affect him; he frequently returned to his account of the attack made on the unfortunate Frenchman. He was also a good boaster, and declared that once in midwinter he had carried a letter in ten days from Yarkand to Leh, with all his provisions on his back — a journey that an ordinary mortal takes a month to accomplish. But there was no harm in his exaggerations; he was always witty and amusing, always cheerful and ready for a joke, and kept up the spirits of the rest in depressing circumstances. Poor Muhamed Isa! How little we suspected, when he and I set out together, that he would never return to his wife and home!

I had scarcely taken possession of my new dwelling in Leh when Muhamed Isa appeared with a pleasant, kindly "Salaam, Sahib."

"Peace be with you," I answered; "you have not changed much in all the years since we met in Kashgar. Are you disposed to accompany me on a journey of two years through the high mountains?"

"I wish nothing better, and the Commissioner Sahib has allowed me to report myself to you for service. But I should like to know whither we are to travel."

"We are going northwards to Eastern Turkestan; you will hear about our further movements when we have left the last villages behind."

"But I must know the details of your plan because of the preparations."

"You must take provisions for horses and men for three months, for it may happen that we shall be so long without coming into contact with human beings."

"Then, surely, we must be making for Tibet — that is a country I know as well as my house in Leh."

"What are your terms?"

"Forty rupees a month, and an advance of two hundred rupees to leave with my wife at starting."

"All right! I take you into my service, and my first order is: buy about sixty strong horses, complete our store of provisions so that it may last three months, and get together the necessary equipment for the caravan."

"I know very well what we want, and will have the caravan ready to march in ten days. But let me suggest that I be allowed to choose the servants, for I know the men here in Leh, and can tell which are fit for a long trying journey."

"How many do you want to manage the caravan?"

"Five-and-twenty men."

"Very well, engage them; but you must be responsible that only useful, honest men enter my service."

"You may depend on me," said Muhamed Isa, and added, that he knew it to be to his own interest to serve me well.

During the following days Muhamed Isa was always on

his feet, looking out for horses. It was not advisable for many reasons to buy them all at once — for one thing, because the prices would then rise; so we bought only five or six each day. As, however, the peasants from the first asked exorbitantly high prices, a commission of three prominent Ladakis was appointed, who determined the real value of the horses offered for sale. If the seller were satisfied with the assessment, he was paid at once, and the horse was led to his stall in our open stable. Otherwise, the seller went away, but usually returned next day.

Altogether 58 horses were bought, and Robert made a list of them: 33 came from various villages in Ladak, 17 from Eastern Turkestan, 4 from Kashmir, and 4 from Sanskar. The Sanskar horses are considered the best, but are difficult to get. The Ladak horses, too, are good, for, being bred in the mountains, they are accustomed to rarefied air and poor pasture; they are small and tough. The Turkestan horses have, as a rule, less power of endurance, but we had to take them for want of better, and all ours had crossed the Karakorum Pass (18,540 feet) once or oftener.

As the horses were bought they were numbered in the list, and this number on a strip of leather was fastened to the mane of the horse. Afterwards I compiled a list of the dead, as they foundered, in order to ascertain their relative power of resistance. The first that died was a Sanskar, but that was pure chance — he died some days after we marched out of Leh, of acute disease. Later on the losses were greatest among the Yarkand horses. The prices varied considerably, from 37 to 96 rupees, and the average price was 63 rupees. A horse at 95 rupees fell after three weeks; another, that cost exactly half, carried me a year-and-a-half. The commission was very critical in its selection, and Muhamed Isa inspected every four-legged candidate before it was accepted. As a rule we did not hesitate to take horses ten or twelve years old; the tried horses were more reliable than the younger ones, though these often appeared much more powerful. But not one of them all was to return from Tibet; the lofty mountains let none of their prey escape. "Morituri te salutant," said

Captain Patterson forebodingly, as the first caravan passed out of Leh.

The caravan, then, consisted of 36 mules and 58 horses. It is always hard at the last to make up one's mind to start; after a few days we should find ourselves in country where we could procure nothing but what grows of itself on the ground. Certainly we were in the very best season; the summer grass was now in the greatest luxuriance, but it would soon become more scanty, and in about ten days we should reach a height where there was no pasturage. Therefore it was necessary to take as much maize and barley as possible with us, and here a difficulty came in: we durst not overburden the animals with too heavy loads, for then the strength of the caravan would be broken in the first month, while, in the second month, it would come to grief if we should find ourselves, as was most probable, in a barren country. And as the days pass, the stores diminish and come to an end just when they are most wanted. In the first weeks we had the ascent to the border region of the Tibetan plateau before us, and had consequently to expect the most troublesome country to traverse just at the commencement of the journey. Therefore our first marches were short, and all the shorter because the loads were heavier. This is a pretty complicated problem for an army commissariat.

After consultation with Muhamed Isa I resolved to hire an auxiliary caravan of 30 horses from Tankse to accompany us for the first month and then return. Hence arose a financial problem. The men of Tankse asked 35 rupees a month for each horse, or 1050 rupees in all; of course they ran great risk, and I must therefore undertake to pay 30 rupees for every horse that fell on the outward journey, and 10 rupees for one that fell on the return home. In the worst case, then, the cost would amount to 1950 rupees. On the other hand, if I bought these horses at 60 rupees a head, the total expenditure would be 1800 rupees, and the horses would belong to me. Then the old problem was repeated: I should have to take fodder for these thirty horses, and engage ten men to attend to them, and for these men provisions must be obtained.

After many pros and cons we at length decided to hire the horses only, for then their owners would accompany them at their own risk and supply themselves with rations carried by seven yaks. The provisions for the first month were to be taken from our own animals, to lighten their loads and economize their strength; for a horse or mule always gets tired at the beginning of the journey, and must be spared. But if one of the hired horses became exhausted, its owner was at liberty to send it home before the expiration of the month.

As forage and grazing was dear in Leh, we sent off as early as August 10, 35 mules and 15 horses with their loads, and 15 men and a *chaprassi*, to Muglib, which lies beyond Tankse and has good pastures. Sonam Tsering, whom Captain Rawling had strongly recommended, was chosen as leader of this caravan. He received 100 rupees for the expenses of the caravan. Muhamed Isa accompanied it part of the way to see that everything went on smoothly.

A few days after his engagement Muhamed Isa presented to me 25 men, who, he proposed, should enter my service. There was no difficulty in finding men willing to come; all Leh would have followed me if wanted. The difficulty was to make a proper choice, and appoint only serviceable men who could fill their posts and understood their duties.

It was a solemn moment when the main body of the caravan assembled in my garden, but the spectacle had its humorous side when Muhamed Isa, proud as a world-conqueror, stepped forward and mustered his legions. At my request Captain Patterson was present to have a look at the fellows; he now delivered a short address, and impressed on them how important it was for their own sakes to serve me honestly. Their pay was fixed at 15 rupees a month, and half a year's pay was advanced to them. The Rev. Mr. Peter was so kind as to undertake to distribute the money to their families. Lastly, I promised each a present of 50 rupees for good behaviour, and bound myself to guarantee their journey home to Leh, with expenses, from whatever place we might separate.

In the course of my narrative I shall have abundant

opportunities of introducing these men individually to my readers. Besides Sonam Tsering, already mentioned, who had served under Deasy and Rawling, I will here name old Guffaru, a grey-headed man with a long white beard, who thirty-three years ago accompanied Forsyth's embassy to Jakub Bek of Kashgar. He had seen the great Bedaulet ("the fortunate one") in all his pomp and state, and had many tales of his experiences on Forsyth's famous journey. I at first hesitated to take with me a man of sixty-two, but he begged so earnestly; he was, he said, Muhamed Isa's friend, and he was so poor that he could not live if I did not employ him. He had the forethought to pack up a shroud that he might be buried decently if he died on the way. That everything should be properly managed in such case, and that his outstanding pay might be transmitted to his family, he took his son, Kurban, with him. But Guffaru did not perish, but was in excellent condition all the time he was with me (Illustration 31).

Another, on whom I look back with great sympathy and friendly feeling, was Shukkur Ali. I had known him in 1890 in Kashgar, where he was in Younghusband's service, and he, too, remembered that I had once drawn him in his master's tent. He was so unconsciously comical that one almost died of laughter as soon as he opened his mouth, and he was my oldest acquaintance among this group of more or less experienced Asiatics. He had taken part in Wellby's journey, and gave us the most ghastly descriptions of the sufferings the captain, who afterwards fell in the Boer War, and his caravan had to endure in North Tibet, when all the provisions were consumed and all the animals had perished. A year later he shared in my boating trips on the holy lake, Manasarowar, and was as useful as he was amusing. Shukkur Ali was an honest soul, and a stout fellow, who did his work without being told, quarrelled with no one, and was ready and willing for any kind of service. He was always in the highest spirits, even during a violent storm in the middle of the lake, and I saw him weep like a child on two occasions only — at the grave of Muhamed Isa, and when we said the last good-bye.

31. Guffaru.

These three were Mohammedans, as their names show. The caravan contained eight sons of Islam in all; the leader, Muhamed Isa, was the ninth. The other seventeen were Lamaists. Then came two Hindus, a Catholic, Manuel, and two Protestants, Robert and myself. I will not vouch for the religious convictions of the Lamaists. As regards some among them, I found that they sometimes changed their religion. For instance, Rabsang, when he travelled to Yarkand, was a Mohammedan and shaved his head, but on the way to Tibet he was just as zealous a believer in Lamaism.

The oldest of my companions was Guffaru, sixty-two, and the youngest Adul, twenty-two, and the average age of the whole company was thirty-three years. Eleven of these men came from Leh, the others from different villages of Ladak. Only one was a foreigner, the Gurkha Rub Das from the frontier of Nepal. He was quiet and faithful, and one of my very best men. It was a pity he had no nose; in a hot scuffle in Lhasa an opponent had bitten off that important and ornamental organ.

I may pass quickly over the equipment; it is always the same. For the men rice, flour, *talkan*, or roasted meal, which is eaten mixed with water, and brick tea in bulk were taken. For myself several hundred tins of preserved meat, tea, sugar, tobacco, etc., all provided by the merchant Mohanlal, whose bill came to 1700 rupees. New pack-saddles, ropes, frieze rugs, horseshoes, spades, axes and crowbars, bellows, cooking-pots, copper cans, and the cooking utensils of the men with other articles cost nearly a thousand rupees. The pack-saddles we had bought in Srinagar were so bad that we had to have new ones made, and Muhamed Isa enlisted some twenty saddlers, who sewed all day under the trees of the garden. But everything was ready in time and was of first-rate quality. Captain Patterson declared that a better-found caravan had never left Leh. How stupid I had been to linger so long in Srinagar and associate with the lazy gentlemen of the Maharaja. Everything that came from there was either exorbitantly dear or useless. Only the mules were good. Yet I always remember my sojourn in Srinagar with feelings of great thankfulness and pleasure.

The Moravian missionaries in Leh rendered me invaluable service. They received me with the same hospitality and kindness as before, and I passed many a memorable hour in their pleasant domestic circle. Pastor Peter had endless worries over my affairs; he managed both now and afterwards all the business with the new retainers. Dr. Shawe, the physician of the Mission, was an old friend I had known on my former journey, when he treated my sick cossack, Shagdur, in the excellent Mission Hospital. Now, too, he helped me both by word and deed. He died in Leh a year later, after a life devoted to suffering humanity.

Many of my dearest recollections of the long years I have spent in Asia are connected with the Mission stations, and the more I get to know about the missionaries the more I admire their quiet, unceasing, and often thankless labours. All the Moravians I met in the western Himalayas are educated to a very high standard, and come out exceptionally well prepared for the work before them. Therefore it is always very stimulating and highly instructive to tarry among them, and there is none among the Europeans now living who can vie with these missionaries in their knowledge of the Ladak people and their history. I need only mention Dr. Karl Marx and Pastor A. H. Francke as two men who are thoroughly at home in strictly scientific archæological investigation.

Some young coxcombs, to whom nothing is sacred, and whose upper storeys are not nearly so well furnished as those of the missionaries, think it good form to treat the latter with contemptuous superiority, to find fault with them, to sit in judgment on them, and pass sentence on their work in the service of Christianity. Whatever may be the result of their thankless toil, an unselfish struggle for the sake of an honest conviction is always worthy of admiration, and in a time which abounds in opposing factors it seems a relief to meet occasionally men who are contending for the victory of light over the world. In Leh the missionaries have a community which they treat with great gentleness and piety, for they know well that the religion inherited from their fathers has sunk deep into the bone and marrow of the natives, and can only be overcome by cautious, patient labour. Even the Ladakis who never visit the Mission stations always speak well of the missionaries, and have a blind confidence in them, for apart from their Mission work they exercise an effect by their good example. The Hospital is made great use of, and medical science is a sure way of access to the hearts of the natives.

During the last days of my stay in Leh I saw my old friends again, Mr. and Mrs. Ribbach, in whose hospitable house I had spent many pleasant winter evenings four years ago.

One day Captain Patterson proposed that I should go with him to call on the wealthy merchant Hajji Nazer Shah. In a large room on the first floor, with a large window looking over the Indus valley, the old man sat by the wall, on soft cushions, with his sons and grandsons around him. All about stood chests full of silver and gold-dust, turquoise and coral, materials and goods which would be sold in Tibet. There is something impressively patriarchal about Hajji Nazer Shah's commercial house, which is managed entirely by himself and his large family. This consists of about a hundred members, and the various branches of the house in Lhasa, Shigatse, Gartok, Yarkand, and Srinagar are all under the control of his sons, or their sons. Three hundred years ago the family migrated from Kashmir to Ladak. Hajji Nazer Shah is the youngest of three brothers; the other two were Hajji Haidar Shah and Omar Shah, who died some years ago leaving numerous sons behind them.

The real source of their wealth is the so-called Lopchak mission, of which they possess a monopoly. In accordance with a treaty nearly 200 years old the kings of Ladak sent every third year a special mission to the Dalai Lama, to convey presents which were a token of subjection to the supremacy of Tibet, at any rate in spiritual matters. However, after Soravar Sing, Gulab Sing's general, conquered Ladak in 1841 and annexed the greater part of this country to Kashmir, the Maharaja of Kashmir took over the duty of carrying out the Lopchak mission, and always entrusted it to one of the noblest, most prominent families of Ladak. For some fifty years this confidential post has been in the family of Nazer Shah, and has been a source of great profit to them, especially as several hundred baggage animals are provided for the mission gratis, for the journey from Leh to Lhasa. A commercial agent is also sent yearly from Lhasa to Leh, and he enjoys the same transport privileges.

The mission had left eight months before under the charge of one of the Hajji's sons. Another son, Gulam Razul, was to repair in September to Gartok, where he is the most important man in the fair. I asked him jokingly if I might travel with him, but Hajji Nazer Shah replied that he would lose the monopoly if he smuggled Europeans into Tibet. Gulam Razul, however, offered me his services in case I should be in the neighbourhood of Gartok, and I afterwards found that this was not a mere polite speech. He will play a most important part in this narrative. After my return to India I had an opportunity of drawing attention in high quarters to the importance to English interests of his commercial relations in Tibet, and I warmly recommended him as a suitable candidate for the much-coveted title of Khan Bahadur, which he, indeed, received, thanks to the kind advocacy of Colonel Dunlop Smith.

Now, too, he rendered me many valuable services; perhaps the greatest was to take a considerable sum in Indian paper in exchange for cash, part of which consisted of a couple of bags of Tibetan *tengas*, which proved very useful four months later.

The old Hajji was a fine Mohammedan of the noblest type. He obeyed faithfully the commands of the Koran, and five times daily tottered into the mosque to perform his devotions. He had more than enough of the good things of this world, for his extensive business connections brought him in yearly a net profit of 25,000 rupees, and his name was known and respected throughout the interior of Asia. Before my return he had left the stage and taken possession of his place, with his face turned towards Mecca, in the Mohammedan graveyard outside the gate of Leh.

34

35 32

33

32. The Raja of Stok. 33. Portal of the Palace in Leh. 34. View over the Indus Valley from the Roof of the Palace in Leh. 35. Lama of High Rank in Leh.

Sketches by the Author.

The small town itself is full of the most attractive and fascinating examples of Tibetan architecture. On all sides are seen quiet nooks with motley figures, temple portals, mosques, houses rising one above another, and open shops, whither customers flock; and the traffic became brisker every day after the summer caravans from Yarkand over the Kardang Pass began to arrive at Leh. Round the town stands a crescent of bare, lumpy, sun-lighted hills; to the south and south-east the dry gravelly plain slopes down to the Indus, where a series of villages among green fields and woods impart some life to the picture. On the farther side is seen the Stokpa, a lofty summit, below which the village Stokpa peeps out of a valley mouth. Here resides an ex-king of the third generation, the Raja of Stok, whose grandfather ruled as king of Ladak but was deprived by Soravar Sing of his dignity and State.

The Raja of Stok, or, to give him his full name and title, Yigmet Kungak Singhei Lundup Thinlis Zangbo Sodnam Nampar Gelvela, Yagirdar of the state of Stok, awakes one's sympathy in his somewhat sad position; he is evidently painfully sensitive of the loss of the honour and power which fate has denied him. He was on a visit to Leh, for he owns an unpretending but pretty house in the main street. The Tibetans still look upon him as the true and rightful king, while the ruler of the country, the Maharaja of Kashmir, is only a usurper in their eyes. We therefore concluded that a letter of recommendation from this Raja of Stok might be very useful some day or other. He was evidently flattered by my request and quite ready to grant it. In his open letter he ordered "all men in Tibet of whatever rank, from Rudok, Gartok, and Rundor to Shigatse and Gyantse, to allow Sahib Hedin to pass freely and unmolested, and to render him all necessary assistance." This highly important document, with the date and the red square seal of the Raja affixed, was afterwards read by many Tibetan chieftains, on whom it made not the slightest impression. They quietly answered: "We have only to obey the orders of the Devashung in Lhasa." (Illustration 32.)

The old palace of Leh stands on its rock like a gigantic

monument of vanished greatness. From its roof one has a grand view of the town, the Indus valley, and the great mountains beyond the river. In the foreground stretch fields of wheat and barley, still staringly green amidst the general grey, small groups of garden trees, groves of poplar, farm-houses, and small knobly ridges, while the dreary Mohammedan graveyard stands out sharply and obtrusively in the evening sunshine. Immediately below us lies a chaos of quadrangular houses of stone or mud, with wooden balconies and verandahs, interrupted only by the main street and the lanes branching out of it. On the point of a rock to the east is seen a monastery, for which a lama gave the name of Semo-gungma. Semo-yogma stands in the palace itself. The temple hall here is called Diva, and the two principal images Guru and Sakya-tubpa, that is, Buddha. The portal of the palace with its pillars has a very picturesque effect. Through this portal you enter a long, dark, paved entrance and then pass up a stone staircase and through gloomy passages and corridors, with small offshoots running up to balcony windows; in the interior, however, you roam about through halls all equally dark. No one dwells now in this phantom castle, which fancy might easily make the scene of the most extravagant ghost stories. Only pigeons, which remain for ever young among the old time-worn monuments, coo out their contentment and cheerfulness (Illustrations 28, 29, 33, 34).

Still the palace, in spite of its decay, looks down with royal pride on the town far below, with its industry and commercial activity, and on this central point on the road between Turkestan and India. The wind sweeps freely over its roof, its flat terraces, and breastwork with prayer strips flapping and beating against their sticks. A labyrinth of steep lanes lead up to it. Wherever one turns, the eye falls on some picturesque bit: whole rows of *chhortens*, one of which is vaulted over the road, small temples and Lama houses, huts and walls.

On the hill behind Captain Patterson's bungalow lies a burial-ground with the graves of five Europeans: the names Stolicza and Dalgleish especially attract our attention. Over Stolicza's grave a grand monument has been erected.

36. MONUMENTS TO STOLICZKA AND DALGLEISH, LEH.

The inscription on a tablet in front informs us that he was born in June 1838 and died in June 1874 at Murgoo, near the Karakorum Pass. The Indian Government erected the memorial in 1876 as a mark of respect and gratitude for the service which Stolicza had rendered during the journey of Forsyth's embassy. The same inscription is repeated on the other side in Latin. Dalgleish's tombstone is simpler, but is also adorned with a tablet of cast-iron. He was born in 1853 and was murdered on the Karakorum Pass in 1888. Both terminated their life pilgrimage in the same country high above the rest of the world, and both sleep their last sleep under the same poplars and willows. Now the evening sun gilded the mountain crests, reddish-yellow light fell on the graves and the trunks of the poplars, a gentle wind murmured softly through the tree-tops, and spoke in a melancholy whisper of the vanity of all things; and a short time later, when the lamps in the Government buildings had been lighted, champagne corks popped at the farewell dinner given by Captain Patterson to another pilgrim who had not yet ended his lonely wanderings through the wide wastes of Asia (Illustration 36).

CHAPTER V

THE START FOR TIBET

THE time at Leh passed quickly, as we were working at high pressure, and the result of our efforts was a splendid caravan in excellent order for the march. Robert and Muhamed Isa seemed to be infected by my eagerness to start, for they worked from morning to night and saw that every one did his duty. I took leave of Captain Patterson, who had helped us in so many ways, and on August 13 the loads of the second great caravan stood in pairs in the outer yard, and had only to be lifted on to the pack-saddles of the horses.

Muhamed Isa started at four o'clock next morning, and I followed a few hours later with Robert and Manuel, four riding horses, and nine horses for our baggage. Hajji Nazer Shah and his sons, our numerous purveyors, the officials and pundits of the town, and many others, had assembled to see us off, and sent us on our way with kind wishes and endless "Salaams" and "Joles."

A crowd of beggars escorted us along the main street, the merchant Mohanlal bowed to us from the steps of his house, and we passed through the gate of the town into the lanes of the suburbs. At the first turn the horse which carried my boxes of articles for daily use became tired of his burden and got rid of it at once. They were put on another horse, which seemed quieter and carried them as far as the Mohammedan burial-ground, when he, too, had

37. Religious Objects from Sanskar.

38. Images of Gods. A Miniature Chhorten on the Right. Holy Books, Temple Vessels. On Either Side of the Small Altar-Table Wooden Blocks with which the Holy Books are Printed.

enough of them, shied, broke loose, disappeared among some *chhortens*, and flung the boxes so violently to the ground that it was a marvel that they did not fly to pieces among the pebbles and blocks of stone. The jade got clear of all the ropes in a second, and galloped, with the pack-saddle dragging and dancing behind him, among the tombs in which the Mohammedans sleep. That the boxes might not be quite destroyed we hired a quiet horse for the day. This is always the way at first, before the animals have got used to their loads and pack-saddles. Here a couple of buckets rattle on the top of a load, there the handle of a *yakdan*, or, again, a pair of tent-poles jolt up and down and knock together at every step. The rest in the stable had made the horses nervous, the fragrant trusses of juicy clover had made them sleek and fat, strong, lively, and ready to dance along the road. Every horse had now to be led by a man, and at length we came to the open country, and our companions left us one after another, the last to say farewell being the excellent, noble-hearted Mr. Peter.

Then we went down from Leh past innumerable *mani ringmos* and through narrow gullies between small rocky ridges, and so drew near to the Indus again. A rocky promontory was passed, then another close to a branch of the river, and then Shey came in sight with its small monastery on a point of rock. The road runs through the village, over canals by miniature stone bridges, over grassy meads and ripening corn-fields; here and there lies a swamp formed by overflowing irrigation water. To our left rise granitic rocks, their spurs and projections ground down and polished by wind and water.

After we had lost sight of the river and ridden through the village, where the people almost frightened our horses to death with their drums and pipes, we found ourselves in front of the monastery Tikze on a commanding rock, with the village Tikze and its fields and gardens at the foot. The tents were already pitched in a clump of willows. The highway and its canal ran past it, and here stood our mules and horses tethered in a long row before bundles of fresh grass. The puppies were released immediately; their basket was already too small for them; they grew visibly, could bite hard, and began already to guard my tent — barking furiously when they smelled anything suspicious.

Barely half an hour after the camp is set in order comes Manuel with my tea and cakes. He is rather sore after his day's ride, and looks dreadfully solemn, dark-brown and shiny; he is darker than usual when he is cross. Robert is delighted with his horse, and I have every reason to be content with mine — a tall, strong, dapple-grey animal from Yarkand, which held out for four months and died on Christmas Eve. At Tikze we are much lower than at Leh, and then we begin to mount up again. The day had been very hot, and even at nine o'clock the thermometer stood at 70° F. Muhamed Isa is responsible for my twenty boxes; he has stacked them up in a round pile and covered them with a large tent, and here he has fixed his quarters with a few other chief Ladakis. Robert and Manuel have a tent in common; the kitchen, with its constantly smoking fire, is in the open air; and the rest of the men sleep outside (Illustration 39).

Now the new journey had begun in real earnest — we were on the way to the forbidden land! I had had to fight my way through a long succession of difficulties and hindrances before reaching this day. Batum was in open insurrection; in Asia Minor Sultan Abdul Hamid had provided me with a guard of six mounted men to protect me from robbers; in Teheran revolutionary tendencies were even then apparent; in Seistan the plague was raging fearfully; and in India I encountered the worst obstacle of all — an absolute prohibition to proceed into Tibet from that side. Then followed all the unnecessary complications in Srinagar and on the way to Leh, and the stupid affair of the Chinese passport which I did not need, but had so much trouble to obtain. Does not this remind one of the tale of the knight who had to overcome a lot of hideous monsters and hindrances before he reached the princess on the summit of the crystal mountain? But now at last I had left behind me all bureaucrats, politicians, and disturbers of the peace; now every day would take us farther and farther from the last telegraph station, Leh, and then we could enjoy complete freedom.

39. Tikze-gompa, Monastery in Ladak.
Sketch by the Author.

On August 15 exactly twenty-one years had elapsed since I started on my first journey in Asia. What would the next year bring? the culminating point of my career or a retrogression? Would opposition still continue, or would the Tibetans prove more friendly than Europeans? I knew not: the future lay before me as indistinct as the Indus valley, where dark masses of cloud swept over the mountains and the rain beat on the tent canvas. We let it rain, and rejoiced to think that, if the precipitation extended far over Tibet, the pasturage would be richer and the springs would flow more freely.

After a short march we come to the village Rambirpur, reconstructed thirty years ago, and to the right of the road the small monastery Stagna-gompa stands on a pinnacle of rock. On the left bank is seen the village Changa, and a little higher up the well-hidden, small, and narrow valley where the famous temple of Hemis lies concealed. Thunder rumbles over its mountains as though the gods stormed angrily on their altar platform.

At a corner where a small, shaky, wooden bridge spans the Indus, stand some more long *mani ringmos*; they are covered with well-cut stone flags, on which the letters are already overgrown by a weathered crust, and stand out dark against the lighter chiselled intervals. Former kings of Ladak caused them to be constructed as a salve to their consciences, and to gain credit in a future life. They are a substitute for the work of the Lamas; every one is at liberty to propitiate the divine powers by this means. Thus the monks acquire a revenue, and every one, travellers and caravans included, rejoices at the pious act, while the stone slabs speak in their silent language of bad consciences and manifold sins, in rain and sunshine, by day and night, in cold and heat.

Now we leave the Indus for good and all. "Farewell, thou proud stream, rich in historical memories. Though it costs me my life I will find some day thy source over yonder in the forbidden land," I thought, as, accompanied by *jamadars* and *chaprassis* of the Kashmir state and some of my men, I turned the rocky corner into the side valley through which the road runs up past the monasteries Karu and Chimre to the Chang-la Pass. The road now becomes worse; every day's journey it deteriorates, sometimes changing into an almost imperceptible footpath, and at last it disappears altogether. The great road to Lhasa along the Indus and to Gartok was closed to us.

Our company makes a grand show; a sheep is killed every evening, and the pots boil over the fires in the centre of the various groups which have combined into messes. I make no attempt to learn the names of my new servants; coolies and villagers are always moving about among them, coming and going, and I scarcely know which are my own men. It must be so in the meantime; the time will soon come for me to know them better, when all outside elements are removed. A melancholy air is heard in the darkness; it is the night watchmen who sing to keep themselves awake.

At Chimre we are at a height of 11,978 feet, and we ascend all the day's journey to Singrul, where we find ourselves 16,070 feet above sea-level. The road keeps for the most part to the stony barren slopes on the left side of the valley, while the brook flows nearer to the right side, where bright green fields appropriate so much of its water that little is left to flow out of the valley. A path to Nubra follows a side valley on the right. In Sakti we wander in a labyrinth of narrow passages and alleys between huts and *chhortens*, boulders and walls, *mani ringmos* and terraces which support cultivated patches laid out in horizontal steps. Above us is seen the Chang-la, and we are quite giddy at the sight of the road that ascends to it with a tremendously steep gradient (Illustration 42).

Tagar is the last village before the pass; here I had halted twice before. Its wheat-fields extend a little distance further up the valley and then contract to a wedge-shaped point, continued by a narrow winding strip of grass along the central channel of the valley bottom. The sections of the caravan climb higher and higher, some are already at the goal, and we have overtaken the hindermost. The path runs up steeply between huge blocks of grey granite, so that our Ladakis have to take care that the boxes do not get banged.

40. MASKED LAMAS IN THE COURT OF CEREMONIES IN HEMIS-GOMPA (LADAK).

41. GROUP OF MASKED LAMAS IN HEMIS-GOMPA.
(Taken by a photographer in Srinagar.)

After four-and-a-half hours we are up on the small terrace-shaped halting-place, Singrul, and the bluish-grey smoke of the fires of yak dung floats over the soil, scantily carpeted with grass and traversed by a rivulet of crystal clear water. An alpine, cold, barren landscape surrounds us. Muhamed Isa sits enthroned like a pasha in his fortress of boxes and provender sacks, the usual sheep is killed and cut up, and is then thrown into the general cauldron, stomach, entrails, and everything. The head and feet are broiled before the fire on stones. Some of the men take possession of the skin, and spend the evening in rubbing it and making it soft — probably it is for use as bed furniture.

The two Rajputs sit a little apart from the rest by their own small cooking-pot, and, I perceive, make a very light meal of spinach, bread, and rice. The rarefied air seems to be of no consequence to them, nor the cold; the puppies, on the other hand, were very downhearted when the thermometer in the evening marked only 45°; they howled piteously, and, crawling under my tent bed, rolled themselves up together. The four coolies, who carried the boat, went beyond Singrul to a cave, where, they said, they would be more protected from the cold in the night. Towards evening the brook rose, and one of its arms made straight for my tent, which had to be protected by a temporary dam. The Ladakis sat till late and sipped their red tea mixed with butter, and at many points reddish-yellow fires illumined the night.

The temperature fell to 21°, and it was really very uncomfortable in this high, raw region where the wind had free play and the sun had not yet got the better of the snow; rather large snowdrifts still lay on the ground, and clear streamlets trickled down from their edges, juicy moss and grass sprouting up beside them and forming a fine grass lawn. Accustomed to the heat of India, we feel the cold particularly severe on rising, when the snow particles beat like grains of sugar against the tent. A bluish-black raven sits on a stone, sometimes flying down to examine what we have left, snaps his beak loudly, and seems contented with his morning's catch.

Slowly and heavily the horses and mules zigzag up through the grey granitic detritus and round the boulders on the way. Our troop is considerably strengthened, for the animals need help on the acclivities and the loads easily get out of place. To climb up these heights with loads on their backs, as our coolies do, they must have especially constructed lungs, good chests, and strong hearts. We mount higher and higher to the pass in the mighty range which separates the Indus from its great affluent, the Shyok. We still see the green fields down below at the bottom of the valley, the bird's-eye view becomes more and more like a map, and the landscape behind us grows more distinct and extensive. Sharply marked orographical lines indicate the direction of the Indus valley, and the great range on its farther side rises darkly before us and covered with snow. Fifty mules from Rudok laden with salt threaten to block our way, but are driven to one side by our men. From time to time we call a halt to allow our animals to recover their wind. Then we go on a little farther; the rests become more frequent; the horses puff and pant and distend their nostrils. And then on again to the next halt.

At last we were at the top, 17,585 feet above sea-level. Certainly the thermometer marked 41.4°, but the wind was in the north, thick clouds obscured the sky, sweeping over the crest of the mountains, and soon hail came down, slashing us like a whip. On the summit of the Chang-la Pass stands a stone heap with sacrificial poles, which are decked with ragged streamers torn by the wind. All these streamers bear in Tibetan characters the prayer of the six sacred letters; coloured or faded, they flap and rustle in the wind as if they would drive the prayers up higher and higher by unknown paths to the ears of the gods. Horns and skulls adorn this elevated altar. Here all our Ladakis in turn come to a halt, raise a cheer, dance, swing their caps, and rejoice at having reached this critical point without mishap.

The descent, however, on the eastern side of the pass, is still worse: nothing but detritus, boulders of all sizes, sharp-edged pieces of granite, and between a muddy paste

42. From Singrul, looking towards the Pass, Chang-la. Sketch by the Author.

43. View from Sultak, August 17, 1906. Sketch by the Author.

44. Drugub. Sketch by the Author.

in which our horses flop and splash at every step. Sometimes the path is more like a rough staircase, where you might fall headlong, but our horses are sure-footed and accustomed to bad ground. It is cold, dreary, raw, and grey — how different from the warm, sunny country we have so lately left!

At the foot of the descent from the actual pass old Hiraman, a friend of mine on former journeys, was waiting. The old man was just the same, perhaps a little more wrinkled than before (Illustration 45).

After a night with 12.8 degrees of frost we rode on from Sultak by a small lake dammed up by moraines, and down a valley full of detritus. Now the puppies had to run alone, and they did the short day's march without complaining, but they were heartily sorry for their exhibition of strength when we got to Drugub, and were so tired out that they omitted to ferret about as usual (Illustrations 43, 44).

Drugub lies at a height of 12,795 feet, and on the short way to Tankse we ascended only 299 feet; from there, however, the route again ascends slowly until at length one reaches the great open plateau, where the differences of elevation show little alteration in a month of marching. Beyond Tankse a massive, finely sculptured mountain rises in the background; deep valleys open on either side; through the southern runs a road to Gartok, which I was to follow later; through the northern, the road to Muglib, which I had travelled by before; this I was to take now, and for two days keep to roads I was well acquainted with.

The Tankse river has a fair volume of water; we crossed it at a broad, shallow place, where the fall is very slight. The water is almost quite clear, of a bluish-green tinge, and glides noiselessly as oil over its gravelly bed. The whole village was on foot, and watched the pitching of my tent in a small clump of willows, which had resolutely struggled against the elevated situation and severe climate. These, however, were the last trees, worthy the name, that we saw for half a year.

We rested a day in Tankse, and settled with the men who were waiting with their thirty hired horses. On the early marches one gains all kinds of experience, and now we had to make one or two alterations. Muhamed Isa set up for the caravan men a large Tibetan tent with a broad opening in the roof to let out the smoke. The sacks of provender were to form round the inside a protection against the wind, and at the same time be themselves sheltered from rain. Furthermore, roasted meal, spices, and tobacco were purchased for the men, and all the barley that could be procured in the neighbourhood. The headmen of Tankse and Pobrang offered to accompany us for some days on a pleasure trip, and to see that everything went on smoothly.

Late in the evening a bright fire in Muhamed Isa's camp lighted up the surroundings, and the noisy music sounded more merrily than ever. The caravan men held a jollification on taking leave of civilization, and had invited the notables of the village and the dancing-girls to tea and music. It was a very jovial party; the barley beer, *chang*, Ladak's national drink, raised the spirits of guests and hosts, and as I went to sleep I heard female voices and the notes of flutes and bagpipes echoed back from the mountain flanks.

On August 21 we were again on the move; at our departure all Tankse turned out, besides the natives who had come in from the surrounding villages, and all sent us off with friendly cries of "Jole" and "A good journey."

Here I commenced to draw my first map-sheet, being the first stroke of a work that for more than two years kept my attention riveted on every mile of the route and on every object that could be seen from it. At the same time the collections of rock specimens was begun. Specimen No. 1 was of crystalline schists *in situ*, while the bottom of the valley was still covered with large and small blocks of granite.

We left the Tankse monastery on its rocky spur to our left, and henceforth kept to the right side of the Muglib brook, now at the foot of the mountain and past its cones of detritus, now over easily recognizable denudation terraces, and again along the bank of the brook, where here and there we came across a miniature meadow. Down in the valley

45. My old Friend Hiraman from Ladak.

46. Chiefs of Tankse and Pobrang; Muhamed Isa, the Caravan Leader, in the Background.

at Muglib there is good rich pasture; close by the brook the meadows are swampy and treacherous, but higher up the soil is sandy, and even thistles crop up among the grass.

Here our 130 animals grazed and were hurriedly inspected. Sonam Tsering had to give a report of his stewardship, which he had managed admirably, and our mules looked fat and plump after grazing for five days on the open pastures of Muglib. Our camp was now for the first time fully mustered, and with its four tents and its various groups of men seated round, the camp-fires had a very imposing appearance. Horses neigh and mules bray on all sides, the men remove the pack-saddles to see that the under side is smooth and cannot rub and cause sores, the animals are groomed and fed, their hoofs are examined and re-shod, if the old shoes are worn out on the stony ground.

The village of Muglib consists of three wretched huts, and its twelve inhabitants cultivate barley and peas. The barley harvest was expected in ten days, but the peas were still in full blossom, and would not be ripe before the frosts set in. They are then used as horse fodder while they are still soft and green. I asked some Muglib men what they did in winter. "Sleep and freeze," they answered.

Next morning the sun had not risen when a shouting and jingling, loud voices, and the stamping and neighing of horses woke me out of sleep — the heavy cavalry was marching off under the command of Muhamed Isa. Then the puppies discovered that my bed was a grand playground, and left me no more peace. Manuel's fire in the kitchen began to crackle, and a fragrant steam gave notice that there were mutton cutlets for breakfast. I was accustomed to camp life, but I had never been so comfortable before and had never had so large and perfect a caravan.

Beyond the village we crossed the brook six times; it is quite small, and seems always to contain the same amount of water, for it comes from a small lake, where I had encamped on the eastern shore in December 1901. Now we followed the northern shore over many very difficult mountain spurs of black schist and quartzite; the ground is covered with gravel, sometimes with small patches of coarse grass, and then again is very sandy. Sometimes torrents of clear water gush down from the mountains, where huge fan-shaped cones of dejection descend from the mouths of ravines to the valley.

A heap of stones bedecked with flags and a *mani* mark the point of hydrographical importance, which is the watershed between the Panggong-tso and the Indian Ocean; here the height is 14,196 feet. From this point the valley descends slowly to the lake, and we ride in the channel through which at one time it discharged itself into the Shyok and Indus.

Now, the Panggong-tso is cut off from the Indus and consequently contains salt water. Behind a spur on the right side of the valley which hides the view, the western extremity of the lake peeped out, and a few minutes later a grand panorama unfolded itself before us; the great bluish-green lake between its colossal cliffs. Five years before I had skirted its northern shore with my camels, my old sturdy veterans, which caused so much excitement in Ladak that there I was still called the Camel Lord.

Just where the Pobrang river enters, forming a flat delta full of lagoons, we halted for a while to control our determination of heights by a boiling-point observation, and then rode along the river, which in 1901 was choked up with drifted sand, but was now full of water. When the drainage water fails in winter, the bed is at once filled up with sand, but the dunes are swept away again as soon as the spring flood sets in.

Lukkong is a small village with a couple of stone huts, a field of barley, a *chhorten*, a meadow, and a stunted mountain poplar. From this place the road runs north and north-east through the broad pebble-strewn valley, where we have a foretaste of the flatter conformation of the Tibetan plateau. We are in a region which has no drainage to the sea; we have already crossed three important thresholds, the Zoji-la, the Chang-la, and, to-day, the small Panggong Pass, but we have still two great passes in front of us before we finally enter the wide expanses of the tableland. Beyond the first we must again descend to the basin of the Indus, behind the second lies an enclosed hydrographical area which we must traverse in order to reach the country draining to the ocean through the upper valleys of the Brahmaputra.

From a small pass with a few stone cairns we had a surprising view over a valley which ran parallel to the one we had just travelled through, and was full of green meadows. Many tents and camp-fires were seen above and below the village Pobrang, and the meadow land was dotted over with dark caravan animals, for mine was not the only party that was paying Pobrang a flying visit: an English *shikari*, too, was there, a Mr. Lucas Tooth, who had been hunting in the mountains and was very well pleased with his collection of antelope horns. We talked in my tent till midnight, and he was the last European I saw for a space of more than two years.

CHAPTER VI

TO THE EDGE OF THE TIBETAN TABLELAND

We had another day's rest in Pobrang; there we found the last good pasture land on the way to Tibet; it was, moreover, important that men and horses should gradually become accustomed to the increasing elevation. I had also received my letters from Sweden and India, and was a long time occupied with my letters and answers; the post-carrier was to return to Leh on the next day. But it was arranged that a mail-runner should be sent after us from there. From Pobrang he was to have a companion, for the country is infested with wolves. After the road came to an end the track of the caravan could easily be traced, and it was agreed that we should pile up small heaps of stones at doubtful points for the guidance of the letter-carriers. However, we never heard anything of them, and I do not know how they prospered. Pobrang, then, was the last point where I was in contact with the outer world.

Here we bought thirty sheep for fresh meat; we thought we should not want more, as the chase would yield us some supply, and some of my men were clever sportsmen.

At Muhamed Isa's suggestion Sonam Tsering's pay was raised to 20 rupees, and he was appointed caravan-bashi of the mules. Old Guffaru was leader of the horse caravan, and Tsering, the short name we gave to Muhamed Isa's brother, had the management of the small caravan which transported my daily necessaries, Robert's tent, and the cooking outfit.

The *jamadar*, Rahman Khan, who had been my leader in 1902, and had come with us from Lamayuru, was discharged and well paid, and also the two *chaprassis*, Razul and Ishe. Old Hiraman insisted on keeping us company for another day's journey, while the *Numberdar* of Pobrang and the *Kotidar* of Tankse were to remain with us, as already mentioned, up to the plateau. Thus our party was gradually lessened; last of all the hired horses and their ten attendants would leave us.

I consulted every evening with Muhamed Isa; Robert, too, was generally present, for he was the first of all my servants, conducted the business of the caravan, and kept accounts of the expenditure. We now resolved that some of the hired yaks should carry the boat, and that the last of the coolies should turn back. Then we took stock of our provisions: the maize and barley must last for 68 days; the meal for our thirty men would hold out for 80 days, and with economy for three months; the rice would not be all consumed for four or five months. But, however carefully calculations and estimates may be made, it is a risky, adventurous undertaking to cross the whole of Tibet, and the calculations seldom turn out correct. One may be sure of losing animals wholesale; matters may, too, come to a crisis, when the loads become too heavy for the surviving animals, and part of the baggage must be sacrificed. It may also happen that the provender diminishes more quickly than the animals, and then the latter must put up with smaller feeds, and at last find what nourishment they can on the ground.

My chief anxiety now was to maintain the caravan until we might meet the first nomads to the north of Bogtsang-tsangpo; had we good fortune so far, we should manage to get on by some means or other. I now drew up a provisional plan of campaign, the chief point being that it was based, not on time and distances, but on pasturage and water. The length of a day's march was, then, fixed by the occurrence of these indispensable resources, and even a march of one hour in the day was enough when it led to tolerable pasture. Where, however, the land was quite barren we might travel any distance we liked. No one had any suspicion of my actual plans; I meant to reveal all only when the last men and their horses had left us. If I let anything transpire now, my plan would be made known in Ladak, and would reach the ears of my opponents. Then, as so often before, a merciless "Thus far and no farther" would have sounded in my ears even at Bogtsang-tsangpo.

On August 24 we left Pobrang, the last village, and rode up the valley. Fine tame yaks were sunning themselves on small grassy patches. To the left stretches out the Ldata valley, with good pasture lands in its lower part. Seen from a flat hilly rise with a couple of stone cairns, the country to the east assumes more of a Tibetan character, with low, rounded forms, and small, slightly marked open valleys and dried-up river beds. Everything seems dreary and barren; small hard *yapkak* plants are alone visible. The ascent is extremely slow, but the path is still easily perceptible in the tiring gravel or sand. Not a drop of water is to be seen. The weather is quite Tibetan: burning hot when the atmosphere is calm and clear; raw and cold when the sun is overcast, and the wind envelops horse and rider in sand.

At Lunkar we encamped near some deserted stone huts. A couple of hundred yards from us were grazing a pair of *kulans* or *kiangs*, as the wild asses are called in Tibet and Ladak. Nine fires lighted up the darkness, and snow hissed among the firebrands, continuing to fall, so the night watchman reported, till early morning.

Consequently in the morning was heard the crunching sound caused by footfalls on frozen snow; my tent bulged inwards under the burden, while all the landscape disappeared under a white wintry mantle, and dense clouds hung over all the crests. Manuel and Ganpat Sing had never seen snow falling before; they appeared extremely astonished and curious, and looked very cold in their *pustins* or Yarkand fur coats. The puppies were highly displeased at this new occurrence, and barked at the snow in their disgust till they found that it was no use. They also disapproved of our impudence in adding two large dogs from Pobrang to the caravan. Another reinforcement consisted of ten goats to supply me with milk, which were obtained in Lunkar.

We were all of a sudden transferred from the summer

that reigned in Tankse to midwinter on the heights, and received a foretaste of the cold of the neighbouring Tibet. We saw little more of the summer this year — Pamzel might allow us to take a last farewell of the warm season.

The main caravan was still there when I left my tent, and we started all together. Old Hiraman took leave of us, and rode back down to his hut. The sun came out, and all around became dazzling white; even the Ladakis were forced to protect their eyes with a tuft of wool, which they fixed in front under their caps, and they looked very comical with this by no means becoming frontal decoration.

The long train now wound up to the pass like a huge black snake. The forty sheep and goats with their drivers led the way, but were soon overtaken by the mules, which now marched all day at the front. Next came Muhamed Isa with the horse caravan, and at his heels the hired horses with their leaders, and the yaks belonging to them. In their tracks followed our seven hired yaks, which carried the heaviest boxes and the boat; they did their work very well, and were first-rate animals — great black beasts; they did not seem to be affected by the high elevation of the pass, nor to feel the weight of the boxes; and kept up with the rear of the caravan all day long. Behind the yaks I rode, with Robert, the *Kotidar* of Tankse, and a runner who held my horse when I dismounted to search for rock specimens, take bearings, or make sketches. Last of all came Tsering and Manuel with my small caravan (Illustration 47).

We had not ridden far when we came up with the horse entered as number 52 on the list; it came from Sanskar, and cost 90 rupees. It had eaten nothing the day before, and was evidently on its last legs, for its leader could only make it stumble on a step at a time. It bled from the nostrils, its belly was swollen, and its muzzle was cold — all bad symptoms. It seemed to suffer from giddiness, and at last fell down and could not be induced to get up again. After a time, however, it raised itself up with a last effort, but rolled over again on the other side. We saw it from the pass still lying motionless, its attendant beside it; the latter overtook us later and reported that there was nothing to be done with the horse. So it was numbered 1 in the list of the lost, and we decided that the *Kotidar* might keep it, should it unexpectedly recover.

This pass, the Marsimik-la, had looked quite easy from our camping-ground at Lunkar, but now we found that it would be a very serious matter to cross it. The horses had to stop and recover their wind every five minutes at first, then every minute and a half, and at last they could not go more than a minute at a time, and then must stand still for as long. The snow now lay a foot deep, and the caravan marked out a coal-black winding line through the white expanse. Curious yellowish-grey and violet clouds rose above the mighty snowy range to the south and west. When the sun was visible our faces and hands were scorched; but when it was hidden behind clouds the day was pleasant, and the glitter of the sunshine on the snow, so trying to the eyes, was extinguished by the shadows of the clouds.

The caravan in front of us seems hardly to move, so slow is the progress in this highly rarefied air. Still it does move onwards, as we can tell by the constant shouts of the drivers. Some of the Ladakis sing together to lighten the toil of themselves and the animals. They are as cheerful and contented as though they were going to a harvest festival. From time to time Muhamed Isa's voice growls forth like rolls of thunder, shouting out *Khavass* and *Khabardar*. We see him standing up above at the last turn up to the pass, and hear him distributing his orders from the centre of the semicircle now formed by the caravan. His sharp, practised eye takes in every horse; if a load threatens to slip down he calls up the nearest man; if there is any crowding, or a gap in the ranks, he notices it immediately. With his hands in his pockets and his pipe in his mouth he goes up quietly on foot over the Marsimik-la.

Now the first column of mules reaches the ridge of the pass. A joyous shout goes out over the mountains; it is heard clearly and distinctly, but is indescribably thin, cold, and toneless, and at once dies away without awaking the feeblest echo; the air is too rare for that. Every detachment as it comes to the pass raises the same shout of

47. THE WAY TO THE MARSIMIK-LA.

48. SPANGLUNG.

triumph. With a feeling of relief I watch the last horse disappear below the white outline of the pass summit.

At the highest point I made, as usual, a fairly long halt to take observations, while Tsering's detachment filed past me, and the yaks tramped, grunting, over the Marsimik-la. The absolute height was 18,343 feet, the sky was partly clear, and it was as warm as in an oven, though the temperature had risen only to 34.7°. Before we began to move again the tail of the procession had vanished behind the point of rock which marks the entrance to the valley that leads downwards. The fallen horse lay lonely and forlorn, a dark spot in the snow. It was the offering the gods of the pass had exacted as toll.

Eastwards the high range appears more uniform, as though planed down, and no prominent summit rises above the crest. The descent from the pass is bestrewn with pebbles and small blocks, which may be said to swim in mud. The snow thaws, and a continual trickling murmuring sound is heard. The route of the caravan is marked by an endless succession of small deep ditches filled with water, and meandering in dark lines through the white surface. Numerous trickles of water collect into a rivulet, which rushes down among the stones. Where the ground is level a swamp is formed, dome-shaped clumps of moss render it uneven, and between these stand pools, often of deceptive depth. For a long distance we follow a perfectly bare slope, and we are almost impatient at descending so slowly to the layers of denser air.

At length we go down steeply into the valley over a disagreeable slope of detritus crossed by a number of small water channels. On the left opens a large trough-shaped valley, where we can perceive in the upper part three snow-covered glacier tongues with fissures in the ice-front standing out clearly. From these a large brook issues, which unites with the brook from the pass into a greenish-grey foaming river. From their confluence we see the whole length of the valley which we must traverse to reach our camping-ground. It is deeply and boldly eroded; the foaming river occupies the whole of its bottom. We must therefore keep to the steep banks on the right side, 300 to 600 feet above the river. Here the ground is detestable — coarse, sharp pebbles forming the edge of a terrace — and as we have to ride along the outer edge we should roll down the slope and break our necks if the horses made a false step.

Here one of the Pobrang dogs came towards us; he made a wide detour to avoid us, and did not once look at us when we tried to coax him. Probably he suspected that we were on the way to inhospitable regions, and thought he could lead a more peaceful life at the miserable huts of Pobrang. At length we came down over swampy moss-grown rubbish mounds to the camp, which was situated just where our valley ran at an angle into the Spanglung valley, in the midst of lofty mountains where nothing could be heard but the monotonous roar of the two streams. Wearied out, we threw ourselves into our tents and enjoyed the pleasant heat of the brazier. Bikom Sing went up the mountains and shot at an antelope, but missed. Muhamed Isa said jestingly that hitherto the Rajputs had done no more than the puppies. He did not include them at all in our muster roll; in his opinion they did nothing but consume our stores of meal and rice; but he was unjust in condemning them before they had had an opportunity of distinguishing themselves (Illustrations 48, 49).

The moon shone, a cold pale sickle, over the mountains, and we were glad to get to rest; after such a day the night comes as a friend and deliverer.

Our route to Pamzal continued downwards along the Spanglung valley, sometimes about 150 feet above the bottom, where some snowdrifts resisted the warmth of the short summer, sometimes on sharply defined terraces forming several steps. The road was bad, for the whole country was full of detritus. On the right opened the Lungnak valley with small snowy peaks in the background, and before us towered the great dark range lying on the north side of the Chang-chenmo valley. The Manlung valley runs up from the south-west, and its stream contributes a large addition of muddy water to our valley.

As we advanced farther, other grand snowy mountains and jagged peaks came into view — these are the heights

49. SPANGLUNG.

50. CAMP NEAR PAMZAL.

51. THE CHANG-CHENMO AND THE WAY TO GOGRA.

that enclose the Chang-chenmo valley. At last the path turned into this valley, and we bivouacked on the small strip of vegetation on the left bank of the river (Illustration 50).

Towards evening the river rose considerably; when we measured its volume next morning we found the discharge to be 494 cubic feet a second, and large strips of the stony bed were still wet from the highwater in the night. In summer one cannot ride through the river at this place; then it rolls enormous floods down to the Indus. Its name is Kograng-sanspo, while Chang-chenmo denotes rather the whole country around. The Ladakis said that the summer would here last twenty days longer; after that the nights would become cold but the days remain fairly warm; then, however, winter would come with ever-increasing rigour.

Eastwards five days' march brings one to the pass Lanak-la, which belongs to the colossal ridge of the Karakorum mountains running right through Tibet. Some English travellers have crossed this pass. To me the road was closed. I had promised Lord Minto not to act against the wishes of the English Government, but I should like to know who could have prevented me now.

On August 28 we left this pleasant, quiet spot, and now it would be long before we came again to so low a level. We were constantly increasing the distance from roads and human dwellings; for some time yet we were to remain in known country, and then the vast unknown land in the east awaited us. The day was fair and warm when I set out with my usual companions, Robert, Rehim Ali, one of our Mohammedans, and the two drivers from Tankse and Pobrang.

The terrace on the left bank, on which we ride, is washed by a branch of the stream which is very muddy, forms small rapids, and usually divides into several arms. The whole of the valley bottom is grey with rubbish; the river water has much the same colour, and therefore is not conspicuous in the landscape. There is no living thing anywhere around, neither tame yaks nor wild animals, and not a sign of men. But a faintly beaten footpath shows that mountaineers occasionally wander here. It guides us down to the river again, at a point opposite the narrow, deep, and boldly sculptured transverse valley Kadsung with the usual terraces, from which emerges a brook of clear, blue, beautifully fresh water and mingles with, and is lost in, the dirty grey water of the main stream. Here the path again turns upwards and affords a short cut over a small pass to our camp for the night. We could see at a distance that in the middle of the steep slope where the path runs there had been a landslip, and a deep fissure formed which we could hardly cross until some alterations had been effected. A troop of men were sent in advance with spades and pick-axes, and meanwhile the various sections of the caravan collected together on the bank.

Some men examined the ford on foot, for here we had to cross the main stream. The water certainly foamed up to the houghs of the horses as they were led over in long files, but the depth was nowhere more than 2½ feet, and all came safely to the other bank. The yaks evidently liked the bath; they waded through the water as slowly as possible, and my boat was poised over its own element without touching it. The most difficult task was to get the sheep and goats over. The whole flock was driven to the water's edge, and some were seized by the horns and thrown into the river, though they struggled frantically. But the rest found the situation too disagreeable, turned tail and made a wild dash up the nearest terrace. Again they were all driven to the bank, and were there shut in by a line of men and pushed into the water, and as the first had now made up their minds to wade, the others followed and bravely struggled against the current (Illustrations 51, 52).

Immediately after, the caravan was seen labouring up the steep slope; it was a pretty sight, but not without danger. The sheep did not keep to the path, but climbed about in search of food.

A couple of minutes after the little pass Mankogh-la is left behind there is a bird's-eye view of the valley of the Kograng-sanspol, at any rate of the upper part, which we had followed from Pamzal; it makes here a sharp turn, and we came over hills and spurs down again to the river-bank. The camping-ground, which has fairly good pasturage, is

52. Muhamed Isa in the River Chang-chenmo near Pamzal.

called Gogra. From here two valleys run up to the main crest of the Karakorum range, the Chang-lung-barma and the Chang-lung-yogma or "the middle and the lower north valleys." Both valleys would take us to a nasty pass; we chose the second. We must get over somehow or other, and at dangerous places the most valuable baggage could, if necessary, be carried by men. With his cap on the side of his head, his fur coat thrown negligently over his shoulders, and the inevitable pipe in his mouth, Muhamed Isa stalked like a field-marshal through the smoke of the camp-fires and issued his orders for the next day's march. None of our men, indeed, knew the road, but from their uncertain reports we could gather that we had a nasty bit of work before us.

We did not reach a much greater height during our march, but we had to go up and down over so many hills and steep declivities that the day's journey was as trying as though we had surmounted a number of passes. The river was now considerably smaller, as many of its tributaries had been left behind. Nevertheless, it was more troublesome to ford than before, for the whole volume of water was confined to one channel, and the fall was greater. It seemed hopeless to drive the sheep into the cold water where the current would carry them away. The shepherds were at a loss what to do when I lost sight of them, and I do not know how the passage was accomplished; but they came across somehow, for they reached the camp all safe and sound. The dark-green schists in this neighbourhood are partly much weathered, partly hard and untouched. A large cairn stands on a hill, and one of the men asserted that an old road to Yarkand ran past here, while Guffaru affirmed that some, at least, of Forsyth's companions travelled through this country.

The headwaters of the river flow from a large valley to the north-west, its background formed by snow mountains, while we follow the heights above a side valley, which, seen from above, has a grand and almost awesome aspect. A small, clear brook murmurs melodiously along the bottom. Then again we descend over soft red dust and rubbish. Small cairns mark the route, and guide us down to the bottom of the valley, here very narrow, and confined between steep, dark schistose rocks. A little higher up the rocky walls are perpendicular, and the river finds its way through a dark gorge. We therefore have to climb up the right side to avoid the difficult spots, and the ascent is very steep. Here the caravan came to a standstill; Muhamed Isa's gigantic form was seen at the worst point of the ascent. Every horse had to be assisted up by five men. One tugged at the bridle, two supported the load at either side to prevent it slipping off, and two pushed behind; as soon as somewhat easier ground was reached the baggage was put to rights and the cords tightened, and then the horse had to get along the track without help.

In the Chuta district, where we again find ourselves at the valley bottom, warm springs of sulphurous water rise out of the earth. One of them has built up a pyramid 10 feet high, somewhat like a toad-stool; the water bubbles up from the centre of the crown, and drops down the sides, forming a circle of stalactites around. The water as it leaves the orifice has a temperature of 124° F. Another spring, which sends a jet of water right into the river, has a heat of only 108°. At many places on the bank and in the river-bed the water bubbles up with a simmering noise.

After more rugged slopes of rubbish and loose yellow dust we arrived at last in the Chang-lung-yogma valley, where the pasturage was very scanty. In the evening it snowed hard, and the valley was veiled in a mystic light, which was perhaps a faint reflexion of the moon. A couple of fires flashed out of the mist and lighted up the large tent of the Ladakis. Only the murmur of the brook broke the silence. Suddenly, however, repeated shouts resounded through the stillness of the night — perhaps some horses had taken into their heads to stampede to more hospitable regions.

We needed a day's rest in this camp, for before us was the high pass which forms a watershed between the Indus and the isolated drainage of the plateau. Muhamed Isa and Sonam Tsering rode up the valley to reconnoitre, and, meanwhile, Robert and I repacked my boxes amidst

53. Rabsang, Adul, Tsering, and Muhamed Isa.

54. Our Horses at the Karakorum.

alternations of sunshine and snowfalls; winter clothing and furs were taken out, and the tent bed was put aside; henceforth my bed was to be made on the ground, on a foundation consisting of a waterproof sheet and a frieze rug; by this method it is much easier to get warm.

On the last day of August the ascent was continued. The country was white with snow, but before noon the ground was clear again. I now rode a small, white, active Ladak pony; it was sure-footed, and we were soon good friends. A small stone wall at a bend of the route shows that men have been here; but many years have probably elapsed since their visit, for there is no sign of a path or other indications of their presence. All is barren, yet it is evident that wild yaks have been here not long ago. Muhamed Isa set up three cairns at the mouth of a very small insignificant side-valley for the guidance of the expected post-runners. Here we turned aside from the main valley. The contours of the mountains now become more rounded, the relative heights diminish, and the valleys are not so deeply excavated as on yesterday's ride. The rivulet, which we follow up to its source in the main ridge, is the last connected with the system of the Indus, but still it is a child of the Indus, and carries to the sea news of this elevated region. Winter will soon chain up its waters, soon it will fall asleep in the cold and frost, until the sun calls it to life again in spring (Illustration 55).

An old yak skull was set up on a rocky projection and grinned at us — another of Muhamed Isa's waymarks. There were several *yapkak* plants, hard as wood, in a small hollow, but even this meagre forage was no longer to be despised. We therefore pitched our camp here at a height of 16,962 feet, or about 1300 feet higher than Mont Blanc. This camp was distinguished as No. 1, for we were now in a country beyond the range of topographical names. A huge stone pyramid was erected among the tents, for the men had nothing else to do while the animals were gnawing at the *yapkak* stalks close by.

CHAPTER VII

OVER THE CREST OF THE KARAKORUM

We had a hard day on September 1. The ground was white, and the sky had a threatening aspect, but a small blue strip to the south gave hopes of fine weather. We started early, and as I jumped into the saddle I saw the whole narrow valley filled with the various sections of the caravan. When I consigned my tent to its fate, that is, Tsering and the Hindus, our deserted camp-fires were still smoking, and the new cairn stood out black against the snow. We left camp No. 1 with some excitement, for now we were approaching wild lands in real earnest, and were to cross a pass of the first rank, which none of my people was acquainted with, and of which we knew only that it was called Chang-lung-yogma; it lies a little east of the pass marked on the large English map of north-east Ladak, and, as far as I know, no European has yet made use of it.

The terraces along the river bank gradually come to an end, and, where they do occur, they are only a couple of yards high, and disturbed by frequent landslips. Our route runs to the north-east. In front of us appears a pure white saddle, now flooded with sunshine; we take it for the pass; but no, the mules, as shown by their tracks in the snow, have turned in another direction.

The flanks on both sides consist of loose, extremely fine material, wet and crossed by clefts a foot deep. At the edge of some spurs these clefts run like the curved fissures of a glacier tongue. The ground is unstable; the slopes slip down and are displaced by their own weight, for they are soaked through, and there are no roots to hold the fine material; they are in a state of motion, and the gently rounded forms prevailing in the landscape are the result of this phenomenon.

The silence of the desert reigns in this country where the feet of man have never wandered; only now and then are heard the warning shouts of the caravan men. Not one of the animals is left behind, all goes on satisfactorily. May all this hard day's march pass fortunately! The valley becomes quite narrow, the water trickles out of the gravelly soil in quantities barely sufficient to form a brook. But even on this gravel the animals sink in the mud.

At the foot of a trough leading up to a side-pass, which had led us astray, the caravan came to a halt, and an accessible passage was searched for.

I rode forwards up innumerable zigzags, and stopped at every corner to take breath. Muhamed Isa reported that the true pass had been found, but I rode with Robert up to a height rising above all the land around, to reconnoitre.

The view from this point was far too striking to be sought merely for the purpose of orientation. Above and behind the mountains in the foreground, some of them coal-black, appeared a white horizon and a jagged line of mighty Himalayan peaks. A really magnificent landscape! The sky was almost clear; only here and there floated a few white clouds. Down below us lay the small valley through which we had struggled so laboriously; here it looked ridiculously small, an insignificant drain in a world of gigantic mountains. Some detachments of the caravan were still toiling up the narrow way, and the shouts and whistles of the men mounted up to us. The horizon was quite clear, not enveloped in haze, as it frequently was; its outlines were exceedingly sharply drawn; silver-white, sun-lighted summits towered up above and behind one another; generally the fields of eternal snow gleam in blue tints of varying intensity, now dull and now dark according to the angle of the slope in relation to the sun's altitude; now shade and light pass gradually and insensibly into each other, now they are sharply defined. Here physical laws work out their perfect complicated scheme, exacting absolute obedience. On a shelf below us a part of the caravan halts and puffs; the animals appear like black spots on the snow. Up here the south-west wind enwraps us in swiftly passing clouds of whirling snowflakes.

All this agitated sea of the highest mountains in the world seems singularly uniform as the eye passes unhindered over its crests. You conceive that no summit rises above a certain maximum height, for before its head lifts itself above the crowd, wind and weather, denudation, have worn it down. In this the mountains are like ocean waves; when these, too, rise in foaming wrath, their undulations, seen from the ship's deck, are of equal height, and the horizon is a straight line; and it is just the same with the small ridges between the furrows thrown up by the plough, which are all of uniform height; so that the field seems in the distance quite level.

The horizon seemed to be very far off; nearer heights broke the sky-line only to the north and north-east, hiding those behind, and in this direction thick clouds were hanging, white above and dark and bluish underneath, and lay like soft cushions on the earth. There was, then, no suggestion of a plateau, but far in the north a mountain range seemed to rise right up to heaven. In the north-west a main crest was plainly visible, starting from our point of observation, that is, the height on which we stood. This is the Karakorum range. The whole ridge here took the form of a rounded back, without solid rock, and intersected by numerous small valleys, all starting from the crest, and cutting gradually deeper and deeper into its flanks. The main ridge winds like a snake over the highlands, and the erosion valleys diverge on all sides like the boughs of a tree. Here horizontal lines predominate in the landscape, but lower down, in the peripheral region, vertical lines catch the eye, as in the Chang-chenmo lateral valleys. Down there the scenery is more imposing and picturesque, up here the surface of the earth appears rather flat; here is the abode of storms, and their boundless playground in the long dark winter nights.

Chilled through to the bones we walked down to the pass gap, where the whole caravan was assembled; here the height was 18,963 feet, and the temperature 2° above

55. In the Snow, N.E. of Chang-lung-yogma.

56. My Tent.

57. Lake Lighten.

freezing-point. The men were too tired to sing, but we had good reason to be satisfied, for all the animals had got up safely with their burdens. We slowly descended along a small valley running northwards. The ground consisted entirely of mud, in which the animals sank at every step, and in the footprints they left behind muddy grey water collected immediately. Round about us lay a chaos of comparatively low, flat hills, furrowed everywhere by clefts which indicate landslips. A tiny rivulet winds silently down the middle of the valley without forming rapids. For the rest, all the country was flooded, and so we had no immediate fear of scarcity of water.

Where we encamped not a blade of grass could be seen; there was, therefore, no object in letting the horses run about loose, so they were tied together in couples, and had to stand waiting till the sun went down. Then Guffaru sat down on a rug, had a sack of maize placed before him, filled a wooden bowl with the grain, and emptied it into a nose-bag, which a Ladaki hung on the muzzle of a horse. And so the men ran about till all the animals had received their rations, and the dry, hard maize corns cracked under the teeth of the hungry beasts. The Ladak horses positively refused to eat maize, and were given barley instead; they whinnied with delight when the bags were brought, but the pleasure did not last long; the chewing gradually ceased, and with lowered heads and blinking eyes they wearily waited for the long night.

Some spare horses were laden with dry *yapkak* plants; at camp No. 2 there was not a particle of fuel. We were now at a height of 18,215 feet.

In the morning we took leave of Chenmo, the *Kotidar* of Tankse, and Zambul, the *Numberdar* of Pobrang, who turned back here. They would be able to enjoy warm winds and bright sunny days again. Besides a liberal reward for their valuable services they each received a testimonial in flattering terms. They took my letters with them, and were to give the messengers instructions about the route, should they fall in with them. Our party was thereby diminished by six men, three horses, and seven yaks (Illustration 46).

There were now only three men in my detachment, namely, myself, Robert on horseback, and Rehim Ali on foot. We turned with the brook to the north, and had hilly elevations on both sides. The country was, as it were, dead — not a blade of grass, not a track of a strayed antelope; all organic life seemed to be banished from the neighbourhood. But when we had advanced a little further we found signs of the visits of man. A faint light streak on the ground seemed to be a path which had not been used for a long time, and beside it stood a cylindrical cairn surmounted by a slab of stone. At one spot, too, lay several skulls of horses and yaks; yet hunters, they say, never wander hither. Perhaps it was a memento of the cartographical work of the Survey of India, or was connected with the European pioneers who many years ago travelled backwards and forwards between Eastern Turkestan and India.

The weather was quite Tibetan. One shower of hail after another chilled us through, and drove a cold douche into our faces, but the sun was always shining somewhere within sight. Long sheets of hail fell from the clouds, which seemed of very insignificant volume, but they could not whiten the ground. It seemed dry as tinder, in contrast to the wet slopes on either side of the Karakorum Pass. Dust even rose now and then behind the horses. Far in front of us we saw two dark points on the yellowish-grey land — they were a horse and its guide which had lingered behind the others.

The long procession of the caravan moved extremely slowly along the descent. It made a halt, so pasturage had been found! Ah, no — the soil was just as barren here as along the other 12 miles we had travelled this day. So, as yesterday, the horses had to stand tied together, and the nose-bags of barley and maize were strapped round their necks.

In the twilight I summoned Muhamed Isa to a council of war.

"How long can the animals hold out, if we find no pasture?"

"Two months, sir; but we shall find grass before then."

"If the marches are no longer than to-day's we shall take ten days to reach Lake Lighten, which Sahib Wellby discovered twenty years ago, and the route lies through Ling-shi-tang and Aksai-chin, which are some of the most desolate regions in all Tibet."

"Then we will try to make forced marches, to get through the bad country as quickly as possible; in the neighbourhood of Yeshil-kul the grazing is good, according to Sonam Tsering, who has been there."

"How goes it with the animals?"

"They are in good condition — only a horse and a mule are tired out, but we will let them travel awhile without loads. As for the rest, their loads are a little heavier now that we no longer have the seven yaks. But that will soon right itself."

"How are the hired horses?"

"They are all right except two, which are on their last legs, and which we shall soon lose."

"See that the animals are spared as much as possible and are well cared for."

"You may depend on me, nothing will be neglected. In camps like this they get more maize and barley than usual, but where there is pasturage we will be more sparing of our supplies."

On September 3 the level plateau was hidden in snowdrift and mist, and it was hard to decide in which direction to proceed: we agreed, however, that none of us should lose sight of the brook, for apparently no other water was to be found. We had not gone far when snow began to fall, a sharp south-west wind arose, and the whirling snowflakes hid even the nearest hills. It now snowed so thickly that we were afraid of missing the track of the caravan, which was far in front of us. According to the English map we could not be far from a small salt lake, but in this weather we were unable to obtain any notion of the lie of the land, and it was no use to climb a hill in order to look round. We sat in the saddle pelted with snow, but the snow soon thawed on our clothes, leaving an unpleasant smell of dampness behind.

But this weather did not last long; the heavy dark blue

and purple clouds parted asunder like curtains, and continued their rapid course to the east; the view was clear again. Some scouts, who had gone in advance, discovered some fine *yapkak* plants on the left bank of the river, and our hungry animals were glad to put up with these. Three antelope tracks we crossed were regarded as a good sign; there must be pasturage somewhere about, but where?

The next day's march led us over an apparently level plain, begirt by a ring of mountains, and our direction was on the whole north-east. We started simultaneously. I rode all along the caravan, which made a fine show. The animals did not march in file but in scattered troops, and their footprints combined to form a broad highway. The mules keep up bravely, and are always in the van. Several of the horses are suffering, and lie down from time to time, only to be roused up immediately by the Ladakis. Muhamed Isa leads the way on foot; he is the lodestone which draws after it the whole company.

Now we tried to cross the broad swampy bed of the stream. Muhamed Isa mounted his horse, but his steed sank in up to the belly; we had to give up the attempt and follow the bank instead. At times we had to cross side channels with the same treacherous ground. When the pilot had shown the way, some laden mules followed; then the other animals came all together. They sank up to the knee in the squelching ooze, and the ground behind them looked like an indiarubber sponge.

At ten o'clock the daily storm set in. In the north-west its outer margin was marked with great sharpness. It rolled, huge, black, and heavy, over the plateau. Now the storm is over our heads and its first black fringes swallow up the blue expanses of the sky. Two ravens, which have faithfully followed us for some days, croak hoarsely; a few small birds skim twittering over the ground. The hail lashes us with terrible violence; it comes from the side, and the animals turn their tails to the storm, and thus leave the trail, and have to be driven again into the right direction. We do not know where we are going. I halt with Muhamed Isa for a moment's rest on a hill.

60

58 b 59 58 a

58 a, 58 b. PANTHOLOPS ANTELOPE. 59, 60. OVIS AMMON.
Sketches by the Author.

"It would be better if we filled some goatskin sacks with water, in case we lose sight of the stream," he suggests to me.

"No, let us go on; it will soon clear up, and then we can consider the matter."

And the train moves on in spite of the drifting snow and the wintry darkness. It grows light, and the eyes survey unhindered the dreary, hilly, snow-covered land; westwards extend the plains of Ling-shi-tang; to the south-east stretches the immense Karakorum range with peaks covered with eternal snow, where thunder rolls among blue-black leaden clouds. Soon this storm also reaches us, and we are enveloped in dense, fine, dry snowflakes, while the darkness of night reigns around us. I am riding at the tail of the train. The caravan is divided into four columns. We travel in the wake of the last, which looks almost black through the mist; the one in front of it appears as a dirty grey patch; the next is hardly perceptible, and the foremost is almost quite invisible. Muhamed Isa has vanished. The snow now changes into large feathery flakes, which sweep almost horizontally over the ground. All is silent in our company; no one speaks: the men walk with their bodies bent forward and their fur caps drawn over their ears. The whole party looks now like snow men, and the snow makes the loads heavier for the animals than they need be.

At last our old friend, the brook, peeped out again from the duskiness, and we pitched our camp on the bank. Tsering discovered abundance of *yapkak* plants close at hand — some green, to which the animals were led, others dry, and very acceptable as fuel. In the evening there were $5\frac{1}{2}$ degrees of frost. The moonlight fell in sheaves of rays through an atmosphere full of fine snow crystals. Absolute silence! One can hear the puppies' hearts beat, the ticking of the chronometer, the cold of night descending and penetrating into the earth.

The country we marched through on September 5 was good and level, especially near a small lake, which now showed its blue surface in the south-east. Like all other salt lakes in Tibet it seems to be drying up, for we travelled for some distance over its dry muddy bed, and saw, higher up, plainly marked old terraced banks. Muhamed Isa reported that an exhausted mule would probably not be able to cross a pass in a small ridge which barred our way. It managed, however, to get over, and came into camp in the evening, but was thin and exhausted. Two Pantholops antelopes, easily distinguishable by their long, lyre-shaped horns, sped away southwards, and we came across a wolf's spoor. In some spots the pasture was so good that we halted a few minutes to let the animals feed. We were sometimes tempted to pitch our camp, but yet we passed on. At last we bivouacked in an expansion of the valley with a stagnant creek, *yapkak*, and thin grass. We had scarcely hoped to find these three things so necessary to us — pasturage, fuel, and water, so soon and so close to the Karakorum. In this camp, No. 6, we decided to give the animals a day's rest after all their exertions (Illustrations 58 a, 58 b).

On September 7, at daybreak, six miserable jades were picked out from the hired horses, and, as their loads were already consumed, were allowed to return home with their two guides. The sick mule lay dead. The sky was perfectly cloudless and the day became burning hot. In another respect we entered on new conditions, for, though we had covered 19 miles, we had not seen a drop of water before we reached the place where our camp was pitched. It seemed not unlikely that the monsoon clouds would come no more over the Karakorum, and then scarcity of water might render our situation very critical.

The direction of the march was determined for us by open country lying between low, round, reddish hills. The ground would have been excellent if field-mice had not undermined it, so that the horses continually stepped into the holes and almost fell on their noses. The mice certainly did not show themselves, but it was too early in the year for their winter sleep. The broad valley opened into a colossal cauldron, skirted on all sides by grand mountains, a regular *Meidan*, as the men of Turkestan call such a valley. To the north the mountains between the Karakash and Yurungkash lift up their lofty peaks, and in the south the Karakorum diverges farther and farther from our course.

Antelopes career over the plain in light flying leaps; they stand motionless, watching us, but as soon as we come near dart off as though on steel springs, and soon vanish in the distance.

A mountain spur in front of us seemed a suitable point to make for, where water would surely be found. But hours passed and it seemed no nearer. A dying horse detained me; he was relieved of his load, but he was quite done for. I was very sorry for him, and regretted that he could not come with us any farther. I stayed awhile to keep him company, but the day was passing, and the two men who were with him were ordered to cut his throat if he could not get on. My Ladakis thought it dreadful to desert a horse as long as it lived; its death-struggle might last for hours, and its last moments would be horrible if wolves got wind of it. It was a tall, black Yarkand horse; in the evening its number was entered in the list of the dead.

The caravan was moving in a black line to a ravine between the hills, where a faint greenish tinge seemed to indicate grass. A short time after, however, it came down again and marched out of sight; probably there was no water there. Another fairly long space of time went by before we distinguished on the plain westwards small black spots and lines, whether wild asses or our own mules we could not determine. The field-glass would not reach so far. At the foot of a mountain in the west shone a silvery brook, but it was a long way off, and all distances were so great that the atmospheric effect misled us, and what we took for a caravan might be only a shadow on an erosion terrace.

But Robert's sharp eyes detected the smoke of a signal fire at the foot of the mountain. The caravan had, then, reached it and set the camp in order, and after a ride of an hour straight across the plain we joined it. Here the height was 16,250 feet.

We were now in a country belonging to the unannexed region Aksai-chin, in north-west Tibet. Or tell me to what Power this land belongs? Does the Maharaja of Kashmir lay claim to it, or the Dalai-Lama, or is it a part of Chinese Turkestan? No boundaries are marked on the map, and one looks in vain for boundary stones. The wild asses, the yaks, and the swift-footed antelopes are subject to no master, and the winds of heaven do not trouble themselves about earthly boundary marks. From here, therefore, I could move eastwards without acting in direct opposition to the wishes of the English Government, and the Chinese would certainly forgive me for not using their passport.

The distant mountains in the north, which had but now stood out in rosy colours like rows of houses in a great city, now grew pale in the grey twilight, and the grand contours were obliterated as another night spread its dark wings over the earth. A flute sounded softly and sweetly among the tents, and its tones lulled our weary wanderers to rest.

The following morning the camp looked unusually small, for the hired horses and mules had remained behind on the plain, where their guides had found water by digging. They were thus spared a considerable detour. As a precaution we took a couple of goatskin vessels full of water, and filled all the bottles and cans. Just before starting we saw our Ladakis lying full length by the overflow of the spring thoroughly quenching their thirst, and the horses were allowed as much water as they liked.

This day's route was excellent, firm and level; the great trunk road in India could not be better, and hardly a highway in Sweden. Masses of clouds appeared from the east round to the south-west; a storm was probably raging in the Karakorum, but its outskirts never reached us. Here the ground was dry, and the exceedingly fine dust stirred up by the caravan hung like steam over the earth. The other columns, like ourselves, made for a goal previously agreed upon, a mountain spur in the north-east. As we approached it, we speculated whether we should see beyond it Aksai-chin, the lake Crosby passed in 1903.

North of the spur a large flat plain extends, and here the mirage was marvellously perplexing. The mountains seemed to be reflected in a perfectly calm lake, but the

61. A Gully at Camp 8 (Aksai-chin).

surface did not look like water — it was bright, light and airy; it was as transitory as a play of colours in the clouds, and seemed as though it had a foundation of transparent glass. The mule caravan, now in front of us, was also the sport of the mirage: we saw it double as if it also were passing beside a lake.

At last we reached the spur and rested there awhile. Robert climbed up the side to look for the expected lake; as he came down the detritus began to move, our horses were frightened and wildly stampeded towards the east. Fortunately, they followed the track of the caravan, which was in the act of pitching the camp. The grazing at camp No. 8 was the best we had seen since Pobrang, and water was obtained by digging at a depth of 22 inches. Kulans had supplied the fuel, for their dung was plentiful. The place was so comfortable that we remained here the following day, and made an excursion to an elevation of sandstone and conglomerate almost in the form of an upturned dish, which stands on the south of the plain and turns its sharply clipped margin to the north. On the top Muhamed Isa erected a cairn — he had a mania for cairns. Little did I dream then that I should see these landmarks again a year and a half later (Illustration 61).

At dawn next day we made another advance into the forbidden land. The air was not quite clear, and we saw it quivering over the ground; but above it was clearer, for the crests of the mountains were more sharply defined than their feet. We marched eastwards; on our right was blood-red conglomerate, which lay upon green schists. On the left the lake was now visible, its deep blue surface contrasting vividly with the dull tones which prevailed elsewhere. The sight of a lake was refreshing; it gave the crowning touch to the scene. The country was open eastwards to the horizon; only in the far distance one snowy mountain appeared in this direction, but probably our longitudinal valley extended along the north or south side of this elevation. In short, the land was as favourable as it was possible to be, and remained so for several days; and I suspected that Lake Lighten, the Yeshil-kul, and the Pul-tso, known from Wellby's, Deasy's, and Rawling's travels, lay in this valley, which in every respect was characteristic of the Tibetan highlands.

The ground was like a worm-eaten board; the holes of the field-mice lay so close together that all attempts to avoid them were vain. Even on the intervals between them one was not safe. Frequently the roof of a subterranean passage, consisting of dry loose soil mixed with gravel, broke in. Robert once made a somersault with his horse. These troublesome rodents, which live on the roots of the *yapkak* plants and grass, are very irritating.

The caravan had camped close to the shore, beside splendid water, which a brook poured down in great abundance into the salt lake. Late in the evening we saw a fire burning in the far distance. Was it another traveller, or had hunters wandered thus far? No, it was some of our own people, who were watching the animals and had kindled a fire to keep themselves warm. There were no men in this desolate country but ourselves.

CHAPTER VIII

TO LAKE LIGHTEN

We left camp No. 9 (16,171 feet) with a feeling of satisfaction, for the country, as far as the eye could reach, was quite level; its elevation above the lake shore was so insignificant that it could not be detected without instruments. The atmosphere was hazy; the pure blue of the lake, a reflexion of the sky, had quite disappeared, and now the water looked dull and grey. One of the hired horses was left behind at the camp; its owner hoped to save it, but he was disappointed, and he also betrayed the horse, for he took another way home and mercilessly abandoned the poor animal to solitude and the wolves.

We rode a long distance on the old lake bottom and perfectly level stretches of clayey mud. Afterwards the soil was of fine gravel, and as hard as though it had been compressed by the weight of a steam-roller. Only in an isolated drainage basin can such level expanses occur among huge mountains. Weathering, precipitation, flowing water, storm and wind work together in levelling the land. All heights and ridges are thereby reduced, all hollows are filled up with mud, sand, and rubbish. Far in the east the country is quite open. Here giants riding on Indian elephants would have room enough to play a game of polo in grand style, and the swift-footed Jambas dromedaries might run till they were tired, for even the restless west wind finds no obstacle in its path. Antelopes and kulans appeared in timid herds. Of human beings not a sign. Yesterday some of the men saw three stones placed together to form a hearth; perhaps they had to do with Crosby's expedition (1903), for he, too, passed eastwards from the Aksai-chin lake to Lake Lighten.

In the north, on the left side of our route, we could descry three stages or crests; nearest to us a row of small dark-green hills; farther off a continuous chain without snow on it, and quite in the background a main range with a number of snowy peaks. On the south our longitudinal valley was bordered by mountains gradually increasing in height towards the east. At camp No. 10 we found all we wanted, though the water was a little salt. Good luck followed us, and we had reached, quite fortuitously, a much more kindly country than we had ventured to expect.

Near the camp we crossed a stagnant creek and we passed several others on September 12. It soon turned out that a large river-bed, containing, however, little water, ran to the lake, and all day long we fell in with indications of its proximity. The landscape was monotonous, and showed little variety during the day's march. But the ground was all that could be desired, and if it so continued, it would help us to make good progress into the heart of the forbidden land. Grass now cropped up in larger quantities than we had hitherto met with. It thrived best where the soil was sandy. It grew in small tufts, green and succulent only in the middle, for the rest was yellow and hard from the frosts at night. The west wind, which swept all day over Tibet, rustled pleasantly through the grass. Who would have looked for a true prairie up here in North Tibet? The ground was of a deep straw-yellow, but the vault of heaven above us was clear and blue in spite of the wind; it seemed to me as though an immense flag of the colours of my native country enveloped heaven and earth. North and south rose dark purple, greyish-yellow, red, and white-capped mountains.

The land was so level that the caravan, though it was an hour's march ahead, was visible as a short, narrow black line against the horizon, not the slightest rise ever hiding it from sight. In consequence of the mirage it seemed to hover a little above the surface, and the animals looked like fantastic long-legged camels.

At a spot where the grass was unusually good the

62. The Hired Ladakis and the Provision Sacks in North-West Chang-tang.

63. Namgyal with a Sack of Yak-Dung.

hired detachment had made a halt; it had lost another horse, and wished to try and save two other death candidates. The packs were strewed about the ground, the animals were grazing eagerly, and the men sat at the fire with their backs to the wind and smoked in turns from a common pipe.

Salt made the soil in some places white as chalk, in others a thin layer of coarse quartz sand occurred with a tendency to form dunes. The caravan had encamped, and small scattered black points showed us that the animals were grazing. A couple of spots, which were far removed from the others, were riders in search of water. It was not easy to pitch the tents; all the men must hold on with all their strength, lest the canvas should be blown away or torn into shreds, and at the same time coarse sand blew into their faces. We were glad to get under cover at last, but even then the wind roared and whistled through all the holes and chinks, and the puppies were very uneasy. But such a westerly storm has one advantage: it makes the march easier, pushing on behind. One needs only to turn and try riding against the storm to learn the difference.

The 13th began badly, for nine horses had made off in the night, and Muhamed Isa with some Ladakis had gone in search of them. Meanwhile we waited in a regular snowstorm. Manuel was engaged in a very lively dispute with Ganpat Sing; it was about a pair of stockings which the latter had bought from our cook in Leh. But now Manuel found that he could use them himself, and talked over Ganpat Sing to retract the bargain. Manuel often amused Robert and myself with his broken English. If it snowed, he said "The dew falls"; if it stormed, "There seems to be a breeze in the air to-day"; and when we left the lake he asked when we should come to the next "pond." He thought the Aksai-chin lake a wretched puddle compared with the boundless ocean at Madras.

After five of the lost horses had been caught I started on the track of the mules. The land rose as slowly as before, nothing was seen of the mountains through the drifting snow; we might as well have been on the plains of Mongolia or the Kirghiz steppe. The camp this day was pitched by a source at the foot of the mountains on the northern side of the valley, where there was good pasture. In the absence of a tent we were housed in Sonam Tsering's round fortification of provision sacks, where a fire burned in the middle and we were sheltered from the wind. Towards evening Muhamed Isa sent word that another horse had been recovered, but that it was impossible to look for the others in the driving snow, and he asked for furs and provisions from the main camp. The man, however, whose unenviable duty it was to return with these things to camp No. 11 through the darkness and snow, could not find the caravan-bashi and his companions, who had therefore to spend the night in the open, exposed to the frost and without food and drink. They were much exhausted when they rejoined us next day with all the missing horses. I gave my night watchmen a scolding, and insisted strongly that this must not occur again, for the animals were tired by these wanderings and exposed to the attacks of wolves, and the march was delayed. It was, however, really wonderful that we had so far lost only a mule and two horses (Illustration 64).

And now we went on eastwards, still in the same great longitudinal valley. The river contained more water the higher we mounted, for below the water was lost by evaporation and percolation into the ground.

The red conglomerate continued on our right, on the left were green schists. In the midst of the sterile valley we passed a small round oasis of grass, like a coral island in the ocean. The day's storm brought us rain and muggy weather; about mid-day it poured down and the thermometer marked 39°. All was uncomfortably wet and dirty when we formed our camp, and the damp fuel would not catch fire. Then it began to snow, and late in the evening the country was again clothed in wintry white. We had hoped in vain to reach the saddle whence Lake Lighten might be seen. According to Wellby's map it might be still a couple of days' march off, but under favourable circumstances it must be visible from a long distance.

Icy east wind blew next day. It was cold and raw

64. Shelter of Provision Sacks.

65. Camp in a Narrow Valley (Camp 41).

66. Robert, Muhamed Isa, and Two Servants by a Fire.

as it passed over the snowfields, and the vile weather was not only uncomfortable physically, but it had a depressing effect on the spirits, so that we sat listlessly in the saddle, were sleepy and indifferent, and longed for the brazier in the evening. The antelopes were bolder than usual; at this season they are fat and strong. We rode past a horse which had fallen and died on the track; nothing could have been done for him. He lay with wide-opened eyes as though looking for a land in the east, and he was still quite warm. The pack-saddle had proved useful, for Muhamed Isa had thoughtfully had all the saddles stuffed with hay for future use. So the animals could little by little consume their own pack-saddles. In camp two sheep were slaughtered, for they showed signs that they would not hold out much longer.

In the morning a dying horse lay among the tents. A wolf crouched in a side valley, watching our departure and looking forward to a grand meal; but he would not have the pleasure of killing the horse, for we put an end to its life with a knife. We had now entered on a critical period, for scarcely a day passed without our losing one or more of our animals.

We still mounted slowly eastwards, and, trusting to Wellby's map, I had promised my people that they should this day get sight of a lake. We ascended a rise in the ground, but from the summit only another was visible, which quite blocked up the view, and when we had surmounted this there was a third in front of us. Now, however, our expectations were no longer to be disappointed. Part of the blue lake appeared in the east-south-east, encased in hills. On its southern shore, where Wellby had travelled in 1896, rose singular irregular points and groups, the continuation of the red snowy range which we had seen for several days past, and now, in fine weather, stood out in all its wild beauty. We had mounted for six days towards the expected pass, and found it just above the lake. Its height was 17,300 feet.

Now the horses were so exhausted that we must find good pasture at any cost, and let the animals rest a few days. Camp No. 15 was pitched on the strand, and afforded a view over all the lake. To the south rose the singular range in shades of yellowish-red and scarlet, pink, and light brown, and fantastic precipitous rocks stood out between soft snowfields of a glistening bluish tinge.

Camp No. 15 was to be a notable station in our bold raid into the forbidden land (Illustration 57). We had scarcely got things in order when the last eight of the hired Tankse men, attended by Muhamed Isa, appeared before my tent, fell on their knees after the Ladak custom, touched the ground with their foreheads, and then sat motionless as images while their leader and foreman spoke as follows:

"Sahib, we have nineteen horses left; eight of them are still strong, but the rest will not last much longer. Oh, Sahib, let us return home before winter comes and our animals perish."

"It was agreed that you should accompany us as far as the Yeshil-kul; do you mean to break your word?"

"Sahib, we know that we are in your hands, and are dependent on your favour; our provisions will not last more than ten days; if we go as far as Yeshil-kul we shall all die on the return journey. Oh, Sahib, have pity on us, and let us go home."

"Very well. If I let you go, which road will you take?"

"Sahib, we will travel over the mountains here in the south, and pass by Arport-tso to the Lanak-la, which one can reach in ten days."

"Can you find your way, and are you sure that your supplies will last out?"

"Yes, sir."

"Then make ready to start." Turning to Muhamed Isa I continued: "Manuel and the two Rajputs cannot bear this climate, and it is best to let them go also before the cold winter comes."

Muhamed Isa was a diplomatist, and tried to conceal his satisfaction as he answered: "Yes, if we take them with us farther into the country in winter they will freeze to death. Already they crawl together like marmots to the fire, and yet their teeth chatter and they tremble from cold in their furs."

"We can easily do without them."

"Hitherto they have done no more work than the puppies, or, rather, less, for they are either too lazy or too grand to collect fuel for their own fire; two of our Ladakis have to attend on them and their horses. It would be a great gain if we were quit of them."

"Let them go, and then we shall have the use of their horses, for I can hire some of the Tankse horses to be at their disposal on the journey to Ladak."

"Yes, sir, they have three saddle-horses, besides two others for their baggage. We are now losing the Tankse horses, some of which, indeed, have only carried fuel, but, by their departure, the baggage to be carried by our own horses will be increased by fifteen other packages. Therefore the black men's horses are a very necessary reinforcement."

Next day the plates and rock specimens, to be forwarded to Srinagar, were packed up, and I wrote letters home and to friends in India. I begged Colonel Dunlop Smith to send after me, in October, to the neighbourhood of Dangra-yum-tso, with the permission of the Viceroy, all letters that had come for me up to that time. They must be sent through Gyangtse and Shigatse, and the Tashi Lama, who had recently been so well received in India, would certainly be very pleased to see that the post-bag was transmitted to me. I thought that, even if I were forbidden to travel further in the interior of Tibet, my letters would not be held back — at the worst I could make the forwarding of the mail a condition of the acceptance of the demands of the Tibetans. I accordingly requested that a post-runner should receive orders to reach Dangra-yum-tso at the end of November, there to await my arrival.

On the morning of September 17 three of our own horses lay dead among the tents. The following night the great spotted Yarkand horse, which had carried our boat, died (Illustration 67). When the sun rose on the 19th two more victims had followed the others, and lay, with neck and legs outstretched, frozen hard after a night frost of a degree below zero. I summoned Muhamed Isa.

"How many more animals have we?"

"We have 83: 48 horses and 35 mules; 10 horses and a mule have died."

"It will be bad if this dying goes on at the same rate as in the last three days."

"I do not think it will, Sahib; the weakest have succumbed, the strongest remain."

"But six horses are gone, and that means six more loads for the survivors, besides the fifteen of the Tankse horses."

"The six fallen horses have carried nothing during the last few days."

"But at any rate the loads will now be heavier."

"Since we have been camping here I have given the animals double measures of maize and barley, partly to strengthen them, partly to lighten the loads. On the first days, when we start from here, we must make short marches, and rather let the horses eat their fill than throw away a single sack of barley."

"Good. We have 510 English miles before us to the Dangra-yum-tso, and that makes 51 days' marches at the rate of 10 miles a day. If 15 days of rest be added, we should arrive at the lake on November 25, that is, in two months and six days. The mules seem hardier than the horses; we must try to keep a stock of strong mules; later on we shall contrive something when we have met the first nomads."

"Oh, yes, if it comes to the worst the Ladakis can carry what is absolutely necessary, and we can all go on foot."

"Yes, Muhamed, remember that I shall certainly not turn back unless I am compelled by superior force."

"No, I know that; all will be well."

Four horse-loads of maize and barley were consumed in this camp; and henceforth a horse-load would be used daily, not including the men's rations. But probably we should also lose a horse a day, often, perhaps, two or more. Still, there always remained a chance of finding better pasturage, where the horses might recover their strength, when we turned off to the south-east. We had at present no ground for complaint. The hired horses had done us very great service. We were able to leave the western shore of Lake Lighten with 83 laden animals. Two horses were required for our boat and all its appurtenances, but I intended to

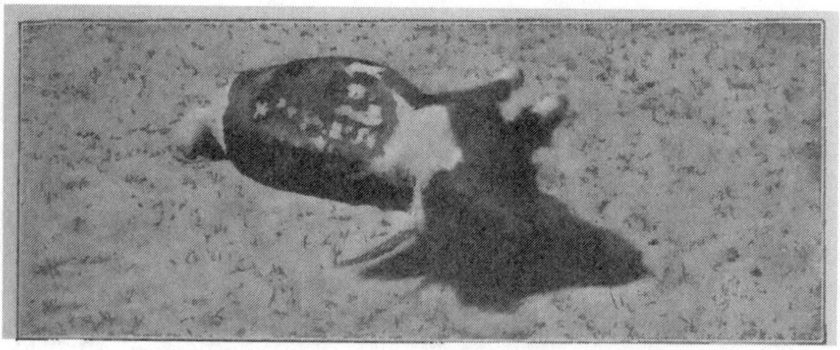

67. THE LARGE PIEBALD YARKAND HORSE.

68

69

68, 69. THE SLAIN YAKS: TUNDUP SONAM, THE HUNTER, ON THE LEFT IN 68.

spare them a couple of days, and let the boat be taken over the lake.

So far we had succeeded in keeping our stages well in advance, and that was good. Wellby, Deasy, Rawling, and Zugmayer, who were all in this region, and brought back such excellent, meritorious results, had here and at Yeshil-kul caravans in a far less efficient condition than mine. Leh and Tankse were my starting-points. But the last connections with them were severed at Lake Lighten, and here commenced a bold march towards an unknown destiny.

CHAPTER IX

ON THE LAKE IN A STORM

On September 19 we took leave of the Hindus and the natives of Tankse. I was sorry for the former; it was not their fault that they could not bear the climate, and they had had no opportunity of showing what they were worth. On the last evening Bikom Sing had sung his swan-song in our party, the same monotonous, melancholy Sanskrit hymn which had so frequently reminded himself and his fellow-countrymen of a warm country with pleasant huts in the shade of palms and mango trees, of laden ox-carts on dusty roads, and of the warning growl of the royal tiger in the jungle by the river bank, when the full moon shines from heaven on mild spring nights. I thanked them for their good, faithful, and honest services, paid them well, provided for their return journey, and handed them good testimonials. They received supplies of meal, sugar, tea, and rice, and a sheep for butcher's meat. Manuel was allowed to take with him one of the puppies which he was fond of. Muhamed Isa had sewed together a tent of empty corn sacks, to protect them from the frosts at night.

They intended to travel on the first day only to the foot of the red mountain chain, and the day was already far advanced when they shook hands and mounted their horses. We remained standing awhile, watching the little party grow smaller under the sun in the south-west, and soon disappearing behind the nearest hills.

I have never heard anything more of them. Eighteen months later Manuel's father wrote to inquire where his son was, but I did not know. So much I ascertained, that he had arrived safely at Leh, but I could not track him any farther. However, I hope that he will turn up all right at home after his wanderings. We missed them sorely, but we consoled ourselves with the boat, which was unpacked and put together on the bank.

A bright clear day after 30 degrees of frost. The rivulet at our camp was frozen into a shiny riband, meandering to the strand, and along the bank a belt of ice two yards broad flapped up and down under the beat of the ripples. The water of the lake may be drunk in case of necessity; probably its affluents reduce the salinity along our shore, where the river descending from the pass and numerous springs pour into it. The sand on the bottom of the lake is finely and sharply rippled by the oscillating movement of the waves, and the water is crystal clear.

Now our horses, which had lost another comrade in camp No. 15, were laden with heavy packs. The caravan had orders to skirt the northern shore of the lake, and to encamp at some suitable spot near it. Robert was to draw a rough sketch of the shore-line; Tsering, Muhamed Isa's brother, accompanied me at his own request. And so we left at the same time this dreary place, where we had parted with our companions and had lost seven horses. Amid the silence of the desert it lay rocked to sleep, as it were, by the murmur of the waves against the shore — a burial-ground forgotten by gods and men.

Tsering soon got used to the oars, and afterwards the west wind came to our assistance. We made across to the north-western corner of the lake, and had a much less distance to cover than the caravan, which had to make a wide detour. The sail was only a trial trip, but I was delighted from the first moment with the English boat, which was solid and comfortable, and easy to steer. The greatest depth we measured was 159 feet. After rounding a promontory we caught sight of the bluish-grey smoke of our camp a little distance from the shore, drew the boat on to the beach, and rejoined our people.

The camp was arranged as follows: Muhamed Isa, Tsering, two other men, and the kitchen were accommodated in a large tent, quadrangular below and pyramidal above. The principal Ladakis lived in the Tibetan tent, while the rest found shelter within the ramparts of the provision sacks. Robert had Manuel's tent to himself, and he had piled up so many boxes of all kinds round his bed that it looked like a Parsee tomb. Outside, on the right wing, stood my tent, a little apart from the others. The black Pobrang dog was missing; probably he was enjoying a feast on the seven dead horses; and so it was in fact: when Muhamed Isa sent a man back to camp 15 there was the dog fat and bloated, like a tightly stuffed bag, and so lazy and stupid that he could hardly move. He had thoroughly overeaten himself, and would not look at his food for a whole day after.

September 21 was a memorable day in our chronicles. The boat lay on the shore ready to sail, and I resolved to spare the horses its weight once more. Eastwards the lake seemed quite small, and it could not be far to its eastern bank, near which the caravan could encamp wherever there was passable grazing. If it became too dark before they heard anything of me, they could light a beacon fire on the shore. But, of course, we should turn up in good time. We looked upon the trip as a mere trifle, and did not think of providing ourselves with food, drinking-water, fuel, and warm clothing for the night. I was dressed as usual, wore my leathern vest, and took my ulster with me, and a fur coat was spread over the back bench only to make a soft seat.

Yes, we were too thoughtless on this occasion. In the forenoon I inspected the animals, as usual, and then gave Rehim Ali a lesson in rowing, for he was to come with me this time, and he did so well that he was solemnly appointed *Kemibashi*, or admiral of the fleet. Just at starting I decided to row across the lake, to sound its depth and ascertain its breadth. The distances, or, more correctly, the course, I measured with a log by Lyth of Stockholm, and the depths were to be sounded every quarter of an hour. We should certainly reach the rendezvous before dark. At eleven o'clock the temperature of the water was 43° F., and it rose afterwards a few degrees higher. The

70. REHIM ALI, ONE OF MY LADAKIS ON THE FIRST CROSSING OF TIBET.

day was bright and quite calm; at one o'clock we noted 53° F. I took the dark opening of a bank terrace as the point to steer for. We could do without drinking-water, for the hydrometer marked 1000 in the lake; it therefore floated as low as in fresh water (Illustration 70).

The lagoons on our shore were covered with ice fully half an inch thick. Six wild yaks were seen at the foot of the mountain to the north. The lake lay deceptively quiet and smooth; only a slow gentle swell, the last reminder of the effect of the expiring night wind, could be felt. Not a wisp of cloud, not the slightest breeze — weather all the more enjoyable after the storms of the past days. The lake shone against the light turquoise-blue vault of heaven, when we looked southwards, with as bright a green as the tender foliage of birches in the spring.

For a few minutes we heard the bells of the mules as they tramped off, but the black line of the caravan soon vanished in the hilly lands along the shore. Rehim Ali rowed like a practised boatman. At the second sounding-station the depth was 115 feet, and at the third 161. When my oarsman shipped his oars the next time the sounding-line, 213 feet long, did not reach the bottom; unfortunately we had no reserve lines, for I had never found before such great depths in a Tibetan lake.

"This lake has no bottom at all," groaned Rehim Ali.

"Of course it has a bottom, but we have no more line."

"Does not the Sahib think it dangerous to go further when the lake is bottomless?"

"There is no danger on that account; we can row to the shore, which is not far, and then we have only a short distance to the camp."

"Inshallah, but it may be farther than it looks. Bismillah," he cried, and he set to work again.

About two o'clock the lake was as smooth as a sheet of glass, and showed curious confused reflexions of the mountains. We became quite dizzy in the head; the lake had now assumed the same colour as the sky, and we might have been soaring in a space of bright blue ether within a magical spherical planet. Behind us, to the north, the panorama of a mighty crest unrolled itself, with flattish lofty domes covered with eternal snow. The sun was scorching hot, Rehim Ali wiped his brow, the smoke of my cigarette hung motionless in the air, there was not a ripple except those produced by the boat and the oars — it was a pity to spoil the surface. All was quiet and peaceful as a day in late summer which had lingered among the mountains.

"God protect us from the darkness," said Rehim Ali; "it is dangerous to be on the water after the sun has set."

"Do not be afraid."

Now the sounding-line touched the bottom at 95 feet, and next time at 34 feet. A quarter of an hour later we jumped ashore.

I drew a panorama of the northern mountains, while Rehim Ali munched a piece of bread which he had providently brought with him.

It was a quarter to four when we put off again. In two hours it would be dark, but then we should see the camp-fire on the shore. The east end of the lake seemed quite close, but we were easily deceived by the mirage. We rowed for a while east-north-eastwards along the shore. It would be extraordinary if the west wind did not get up on this day. I asked Rehim Ali repeatedly, for he had the western horizon in front of him, if the view was clear in that direction, or if the westerly storm was making its appearance.

"No, there is no storm," he answered quietly.

"Yes, now it is coming," he said, after a short interval; "and it will be a bad one."

I turn round and see in the west, above the pass we had crossed some days before, high, light-yellow vortices of sand and dust, which soon tower up to 30° above the horizon; they rise rapidly, condense into a dark cloud, and hide the view of the western heights. Yes, that is a westerly storm coming on.

But the danger to us is not great; we can land wherever we like; we have matches to light a fire, and sufficient *yapkak* can be found, so we shall not freeze even with 29 degrees of frost; and we can do without food for once.

But we will not land; perhaps the camp is close to.

71. Starting on a Voyage.

"Row on, Rehim Ali — no, wait a moment, set up the mast and loose the sail before the storm breaks, and then we shall get help for a part of the way. If the storm becomes too violent we will go ashore."

It is still deadly quiet. But now comes the first forerunner — a ripple skims over the surface, the wind catches the sail, puffs it out like a ball, smoothing out all its folds, the boat darts forwards, and a whirling, boiling track is formed in our wake. We keep to the southern shore; there lie a series of lagoons and spits of sand and pebbles. A pair of black geese sit on one of these spits; they gaze in astonishment as we pass; they perhaps take us for a huge water-bird which cannot fly, because it has only one wing. The lake is getting rougher; we fly towards a spit to the north-east; oh, heavens! the water is only 3 feet deep under our keel. If we run aground the boat will be dashed to pieces; its oiled sailcloth is as taut as a drumskin. I put the helm over as far as possible, and graze the spit amidst the raging surf; the manœuvre succeeds, and the next minute we are in deep open water where the waves are more moderate.

Now a spit shows itself to the east-north-east projecting far into the lake, but it is a long distance off, and we are out on the agitated lake, where the white horses are getting higher and higher and their roar becomes louder and louder; the whole lake is in the wildest commotion; if we can only reach that landspit safe and sound we can get under its lee and land safely. Yes, we must land by hook or crook, for the storm is upon us; it becomes more violent every moment and the mast cracks; I dare not sail any longer with the sheet made fast. We have a grand sailing wind, the water roars and rages under the stem and boils and bubbles behind us. We have to look out, for if the mast breaks, which already bends like a whip, the boat will tip over, will fill in a moment, and will be sunk by the weight of the centre-board, which is not in use but is carried as cargo. We have two life-buoys as a last resource.

Rehim Ali sits in the bow. He clings to the mast, keeps a look-out forwards, and reports that the lake beyond the landspit is as extensive as in the west. We have been the victims of an illusion, and cannot reach the eastern shore before complete darkness overtakes us. Would it not be better to land and wait for the day? Yes, let us land and get into the lee of the landspit. The sun sinks, the storm grows in strength, we can hear it howling through the chasms to the south; fine spindrift flies like a comet's tail over the crests of the waves; it is a most critical and trying moment. The dust clouds have disappeared, and the western horizon is dimly perceptible. The sun sinks to its rest, a ball of liquid gold, and a weird, mysterious gleam spreads over the whole country. Everything is coloured red except the dark-blue white-edged lake. The night rises out of the east, dark purple shades lengthen out behind the mountains, but the most easterly pinnacles and the summit T, rising above all the others with its glittering snowfields, stands out fiery red against the dark background, like volcanic cones of glass lighted within by glowing streams of lava; a couple of riven clouds rush eastwards, their crimson colour vying in beauty with the snowfields and glaciers below them. All shades of rose-colour play on the sail, and a purple foam quivers on the crests of the waves as though we were being driven over a sea of blood.

The sun sinks; now the sail and spray turn white, and soon only the last tint of the evening red lights up the highest snowfields. The night spreads further westwards, and the last glow, the final glimmer of day, dies out on the summits in the south-east.

Rehim Ali crouches at the bottom of the boat while we shoot towards the landspit, tossing, rolling, and pitching. All outlines are still sharp and clear. I steer the boat out of the surf round the landspit, but then pause a moment; it would be easy to get into lee-water; but no, all is well now—the moon shines brightly, and before it goes down we may perhaps reach another point.

Through driving spume and hissing foam we fly past the point, and in a second it is too late to get under its lee, however much we might wish to do so, for the roar of the surge dies away behind us, and open water again yawns before us black as night, bounded in the distance by a

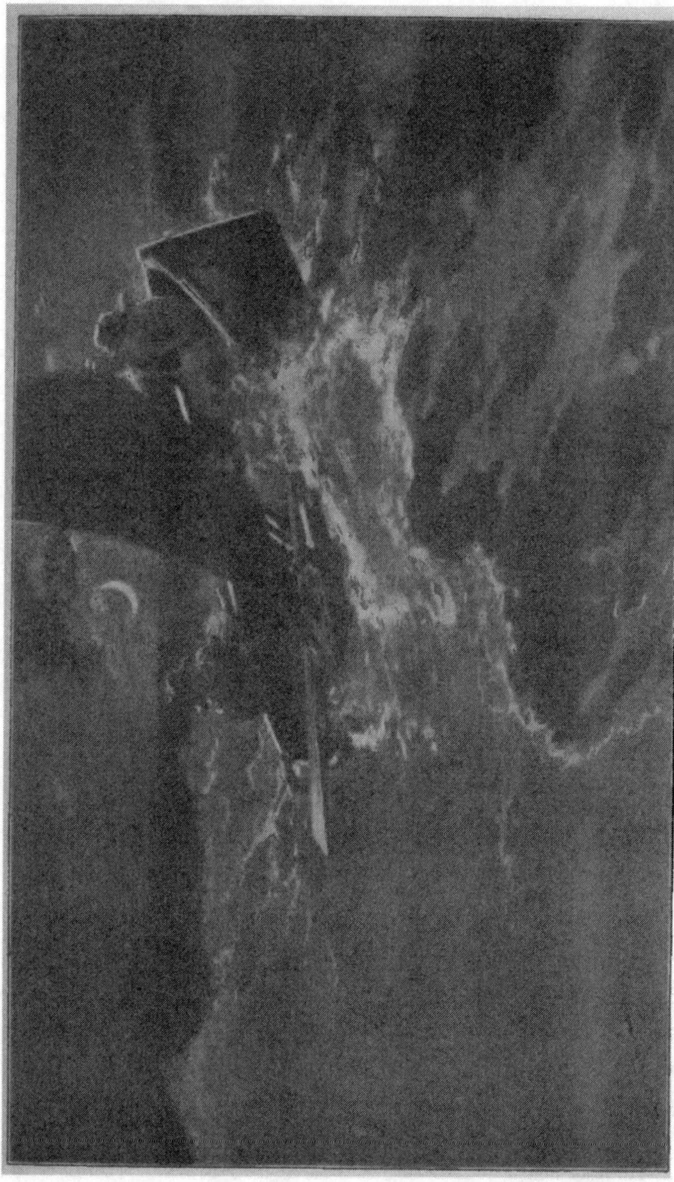

72. In Peril on Lake Lighten.

scarcely perceptible strip of land, another spit of the gravel so abundant on the southern shore.

So we speed over the disturbed lake. We start with a fright, for we hear the huge waves rolling over behind us. The dull droning comes nearer, and I turn round — we must inevitably be buried under the heavy, rolling crests. A faint gleam of the dying day still lingers in the west. The spray, driven by the storm, gives us a cool bath. Then the waves reach us, but they lift up the boat gently, and then roll on towards the eastern shore, which Rehim Ali does not expect to reach.

Now the sail is white in the moonshine, and my shadow passes up and down it with the movement of the boat. Rehim Ali is almost dead of fright; he has rolled himself up like a hedgehog on the bottom of the boat and buried his face in my ulster, so as not to see the agitated water. He says not a word, he is quite resigned and is awaiting his last moments. The distance to the eastern shore cannot be estimated, and it is certainly impossible to effect a landing there without shipwreck. If there are cliffs and reefs on the shore we shall be mangled and crushed amid the breakers, and if the strand slopes down gently we shall capsize, and be thrown ashore by the great rolling billows like a piece of cork (Illustration 72).

In the midst of the dark, indistinct chaos the surf at the point of the landspit flashes out; it is more furious than at the other point, for the waves have become larger as we have left a wider expanse of lake behind us. I try to get into the lee, but the storm drives us out again, and we are away from the land before we are aware. It now becomes colder, but I do not feel it, the excitement is too great, and our lives are at stake. I look in vain for the beacon of my servants; have they not obeyed my orders, or are they so far from the shore that the fire is invisible? I succeed in removing the back bench and sit on the bottom, where I am somewhat protected from the cutting wind. Behind us, the broken streak of moonlight on the water makes the waves look more weird than before; they have become gigantic, and the nearest hides all behind it.

The hours pass one after another; the moon sets.

Now all is pitch darkness; only the stars flicker like torches over our heads, otherwise the deepest blackness surrounds us. My right hand is gone to sleep, cramped with grasping the rudder; the boat seems to dart eastwards, but the waves roll past us — they are still quicker than we. Now and then I ask Rehim Ali whether his cat's eyes can see the breakers on the eastern shore. He casts a hurried glance over the gunwale, answers that they are still very far off, and buries his face again in the ulster. The tension becomes more acute; whatever happens we are certainly approaching the moment when the boat will be cast helpless on the strand. I hope that the lake is so broad that we may continue our wild career till daybreak. But no, that is incredible, for there are no lakes so large in Tibet. We have the whole night before us, and in this flying course we can cover immense distances.

There is something uncanny and awe-inspiring in such a sail, when the crests are visible in the darkness only when they lift the boat, to roll onward the next moment. We hear nothing but their swish, the howling of the wind, and the hissing of the foam under the stem.

"Look out, Rehim Ali," I call out; "when you feel that the boat has grounded, jump out and pull it with all your strength to the beach." But he makes no reply; he is quite paralyzed with fear. I pack up my drawings and sketch-books in a small bag.

But what is that? I hear a thundering roar that drowns the growling of the storm, and in the pitch-black darkness I see something like a bright streak close to us. That must be the surf on the shore. "Loose the sail!" I cry, so loudly that my throat nearly cracks, but Rehim Ali is helpless and does not move an inch. I undo the rope and let the sail flap and beat just as the boat grinds against the bottom and suddenly sticks fast.

"Jump into the water and draw the boat up," I shout, but he does not obey; I poke him in the back, but he takes no notice. Then I seize him by the collar and throw him overboard just as the next roller dashes up the beach, fills the boat, turns it over, and soaks me to the skin. Now I may as well jump out myself, but Rehim Ali at last realizes the situation and helps me to draw the boat beyond the reach of the waves (Illustration 73). The fur coat and ulster are as wet as myself, and only after a long search do we recover all the things that have been scattered in our shipwreck.

We were half-dead with weariness and excitement; one almost loses one's breath altogether with such exertions in this rare atmosphere. We mounted a sandy hillock and sat down, but the cutting icy wind drove us away. Could the boat provide us with shelter? We must draw out the bolts which held the two halves together, and at last we succeeded with the help of the centre-board. Uniting our forces we heaved up one half of the boat, propped it up with a plank, and crept under its shelter. We were quite numbed; no wonder, for the water froze in our clothes so that they crackled when touched. The water on the bottom of the boat turned to ice; my fur coat was as hard as a board, and was absolutely useless. Hands and feet were stiff and had lost all feeling; we must get up again or we should be quite frozen. There was only one thing to do. In the shelter of the boat I took off my Kashmir boots and my stockings, and Rehim Ali shampooed my feet, but I felt no life in them till he had opened his *chapkan* and warmed them for a long time against his naked body.

There was no sign of life anywhere about. Amid the roaring of the surf we had to shout to make ourselves heard. How were we to pass the night with 29 degrees of frost, and wet clothes already stiffened into cuirasses of ice? Could we keep alive till the sun rose? Rehim Ali disappears into the darkness to search for fuel, but he comes back empty-handed. To my joy I discover that my cigarette-case and matches are still available; I had stood in the water only up to my breast, even when the last breaker had done its best to wet me through. So I light a cigarette and give one to Rehim Ali to cheer him up.

"Is there nothing here, then, that we can burn? Yes, wait, we have the wooden roller of the sounding-line and the frame in which it is fixed. Fetch them at once."

We ruthlessly break up this masterpiece of Muhamed

Isa's skill in carpentry, and hack in pieces the frame with our knives; we lay aside the wet shavings, and use the dry, inner sticks as firewood. They make a very tiny heap. Only a couple are sacrificed at once, and I get them to burn with some blank leaves from my note-book. Our fire is small and insignificant, but it warms us famously, and our hands thaw again. We sit close over the fire, and keep it up with the greatest economy, putting on one splinter at a time. I take off my clothes to wring them as dry as I can; Rehim Ali dries my ulster, on which I depend for the night; the fur coat is left to its fate. How long is it to the dawn? Ah, several hours yet. The roller and the handle are still in reserve, but this small stock of wood cannot last long, and I look forward with trepidation to the moment when the cold will compel us to sacrifice the mast and the benches. The time passes so slowly; we say little to one another, we long for the sun. As soon as our clothing is a little dry we can boil water in the baler, so as to get something warm into our bodies.

However, we had good reason to rejoice that we had got off so well. I shall never forget Lake Lighten, Wellby's and Deasy's lake. It had kept us company for several days, we had lost seven horses on its banks, and our friends had left us with the last letters. We had seen this lake strikingly beautiful in bright light hues, but also pitchy black, like a tomb, in the arms of night; it had lain smooth and shining in the burning sunshine, but it had also shown us its teeth, white shining teeth of foam and spindrift. Not long ago we were almost roasted in the heat of the sun on its unknown depths of crystal-clear, vernal-green water; now we were on its bank nearly frozen in the bitter, wintry cold; then it lay so still that we hardly ventured to speak lest we should disturb its peaceful repose; now it raved in unbridled fury. Its shores had yielded us grass, spring-water, and fuel, but to the voyagers in the night it had seemed almost boundless: the eastern bank had retired before us all day long; we had seen the sun rise, sink and set in a sea of purple and flames, and even the moon accomplish its short journey before we reached our goal where the surf thundered and

73. The Author and Rehim Ali pull the Boat out of the Waves up on to the Shore.

folded us in a wet and cold embrace. We had made a notable voyage in the small boat, full of variety and excitement; thrice our lives had hung by a hair as we almost ran aground on the landspits, for had we capsized there we could hardly have reached land before our hands were paralyzed on the life-buoys in the icy-cold water. Wonderful lake! Only yaks, wild asses, and antelopes find freedom on thy shores; only glaciers, firn-fields, and the everlasting stars are reflected on thy surface; and thy silence is only interrupted by the music of thine own waves and the victorious war-song that the western tempest plays on thy strings of emerald-green water.

At any rate we were still alive and on land without any broken limbs. We longed for the grey of dawn, and kept a tight hand on the fire, feeding it only now and then with a fresh chip to prevent its going out altogether. Sleep was out of the question, for we should be frozen. Sometimes we nodded a moment while we sat cowering over the flickering flames, and Rehim Ali occasionally hummed an air to make the time pass.

I am just thinking how I should enjoy a cup of hot tea, when Rehim Ali gives a start, and cries out:

"A fire in the distance."

"Where?" I ask, somewhat incredulous.

"Yonder, northwards, on the shore," he replies, pointing to a feebly luminous point.

"That is a star," I say, after searching through the darkness with a field-glass.

"No, it is on this side of the mountains."

"Why, then, have we not seen the fire before? They would not light a beacon fire in the middle of the night."

"It is not a fire, it is a lantern; I see it moving about."

"Yes, indeed, it is a light which changes its position."

"Now it is gone."

"And it does not appear again; perhaps it was only an optical illusion."

"No, there it is again."

"And now it is gone again."

And it remained so long invisible that we lost hope, and cowered over the embers of the last chips of the roller.

"Does not the Sahib hear something?"

"Yes, it sounds like the tramp of horses."

"Yes, and like men's voices."

The next moment the shadowy outlines of five large horses and three men appear against the sky. The riders dismount and approach us with joyful, friendly greeting. They are Muhamed Isa, Rabsang, and Adul. They sit down by us and inform us that camp No. 18 lies an hour's journey to the north, a little distance from the shore. As soon as the camp was pitched they had sent out men to look out for us, but had given up the search, as these men had found no signs of us and had seen no fire. Late at night, however, Robert, feeling uneasy because of the storm, had climbed a hill, and had seen our small fire. He at once sent the three men after us. They said that they had kept up a large beacon fire all the evening, but apparently the inequalities of the ground had concealed it; certainly we could not see it from the lake.

I borrowed two sashes from the men to wind round my feet. Then we mounted, and with the lantern in front the little cavalcade moved off northwards to the camp, while the billows continued their ceaseless race towards the shore.

74. Camp at the Yeshil-kul.

75. The Pul-tso, looking East.

76. Horses and Mules in Open Country.

CHAPTER X

DEATH IN THE JAWS OF WOLVES — OR SHIPWRECK

WHEN we marched on September 22 over the old terraces of the lake and up to the threshold of the pass separating its basin from that of Yeshil-kul, the view of Lake Lighten opened up more the higher we rose, and at length the whole of the great blue lake in all its beauty lay before us at the foot of the snowy mountains. The pasturage was excellent everywhere, and the Pantholops antelopes in their surprise and perplexity often did not know in which direction to make their escape, and prompted by curiosity came thoughtlessly to meet us. The pass has a height of 17,392 feet. We had proceeded only a few paces on the other side when a complete change of scenery presented itself, as though a leaf of a large book had been turned over. The forms which had hitherto riveted our attention vanished forever, and new mountains lay before us, a new basin, and a new turquoise-blue lake — the Yeshil-kul. To the south and south-west of the lake extend great flats of pure white salt; concentric rings and isolated pools indicate that Yeshil-kul also is contracting (Illustration 75).

During the following days we encamped in a country where the grazing was good but the water slightly salt. On the wide, flat plains on the west side of the lake stand long rows of cairns, heaps of earth or skulls, piled up at a distance of two or three yards apart. They look like boundary marks, but, in fact, have been erected by antelope hunters of the Changpa tribe, Tibetan nomads, who are the "Northmen," or natives of the northern plateau, Chang-tang, and who in this way drive the game into their nooses laid in a hole. It should be explained that antelopes have a decided objection to leaping over such lines, and will rather run along them till they come to the end. But before they reach it one of them has had the misfortune of putting his foot in a ditch with a noose in it. Only a son of the wilderness, who passes his life in the open like the wild animals, could devise such a mode of capture. My Ladakis informed me that the Changpas no longer hunt here, for fear of the people of Eastern Turkestan, who have often shown themselves hostile.

The 24th of September was another memorable day — my sails on Tibetan lakes, curiously enough, almost always ended in adventures. Of my Ladakis five had been in the service of Deasy and Rawling, and two of them affirmed that a shiny spot east-south-east was the spring where Captain Deasy had encamped for ten days in July 1896, and which he names in his narrative "Fever Camp." Their indication agreed with Deasy's map; so Muhamed Isa was ordered to lead the caravan thither, light a large beacon fire on the nearest point of the shore as soon as darkness set in, and keep two horses in readiness.

Our plan was to sail in an east-north-easterly direction for the northern shore, and thence southwards again to the signal fire. Rehim Ali was on this occasion assisted by Robert, who subsequently developed into an excellent boatman. The lake was nearly quite calm; its water, owing to its small depth, is greener, but quite as clear as that of its western neighbour. It is so salt that everything that touches it, hands, boat, oars, etc., glitters with crystals of salt. The shore and bottom of the lake consist chiefly of clay cemented together by crystallized salt into slabs and blocks as hard as stone, so that great care must be exercised when the boat is pushed into the water, for these slabs have edges and corners as sharp as knives. The lake is a salt basin of approximately elliptical outline with very low banks; nowhere do mountains descend to the strand. The three-foot line runs about 100 yards from the shore; but even 650 yards out the depth is only 15 feet. We executed our first line of soundings across the lake in the most delightful calm, and I steered the boat towards the point I had fixed by observations. At one o'clock the temperature was 49° F. in the water, and 50½° in the air. The depth increased very regularly, the maximum of 52.8 feet occurring not far from the northern shore. Robert was much delighted with the sail, and begged that I would always take him with me in future, which I the more readily granted that he was always cheerful and lively, and that he gave me valuable help in all observations. A little bay on the north shore served us as a landing-place. We surveyed the neighbourhood, and then hurriedly ate our breakfast, consisting of bread, marmalade, *pâté de foie*, and water. My companions had brought sugar, a tea-pot and enamelled bowls, but left the tea behind; but this forgetfulness only raised our spirits.

Then we put off again to make for the spring to the south-east. A row of stone blocks and lumps of salt ran out from the landing-place east-south-eastwards, and the water here was so shallow that we had to propel our boat with great care. Just as we had passed the last rock, of which I took a specimen, the west wind got up, the surface of the lake became agitated, and a couple of minutes later white horses appeared on the salt waves.

"Up with the sail and down with the lee-boards."

The lake before us is tinted with shades of reddish purple, a reflexion from the clayey bottom; there it must be very shallow, but we shall soon pass it.

"Do you see the small white swirls in the south-west? Those are the forerunners of the storm, which stirs up the salt particles," I said.

"If the storm is bad, the boat will be broken on the sharp ledges of the bottom before we can reach land," remarked Robert.

"That is not clouds of salt," said Rehim Ali; "that is the smoke of fires."

"But Muhamed Isa should be camping at Sahib Deasy's source; that lies towards the south-west."

"There is no smoke there," replied Robert, who had the field-glass; "perhaps they have not been able to cross the salt flats on the south of the lake."

"Then it is their beacon fires which we see; but we cannot cross over in this boat in a storm."

"Master," suggested Robert, who always addressed me thus, "would it not be more prudent to land again before the storm reaches its height? We should be safe behind the stones, and we can gather a quantity of fuel before sunset."

"Yes, that will perhaps be best; this lake is much more dangerous in a storm than Lake Lighten. We have, indeed, no furs, but we shall manage. Take in the sail and row behind the boulders. What are you gazing at?"

"Master, I see two large wolves, and we have no guns."

He was right; two light, almost white, Isegrims were pacing the shore. They were so placed that they must be able to scent us in the boat; the odour of fresh live meat tickled their noses. When we stopped they stopped too, and when we began to move they went on close to the margin of the water. "Sooner or later you must come on shore, and then it will be our turn," perhaps they thought. Rehim Ali opined that they were scouts of a whole troop, and said it was dangerous to expose ourselves to an attack in the night. He had only a clasp-knife with him, and Robert and I only pen-knives in our pockets; we had, therefore, little chance of defending ourselves successfully. Robert, for his part, preferred the lake in a storm to the wolves. I had so often slept out of doors unarmed, that I no longer troubled myself about them. But in the midst of our consultation we were suddenly compelled to think of something else. The storm came whistling over the lake.

Fortunately, the sail was still standing and the centre-boards were down; the wind caught the canvas, the water began to rush under the stern, and we shot smoothly southwards with a side wind. Robert gave vent to a sigh of relief. "Anything but wolves," he said. I made Robert and Rehim Ali row to save time, and soon the two beasts were out of sight. "They will certainly gallop round the lake, they know quite well that we must land somewhere," said Robert. He was quite right, the situation was

77. DEATH IN THE JAWS OF WOLVES — OR SHIPWRECK.

exceedingly unpleasant; we had only a choice between the storm and the wolves. We could not depend on our people; they were evidently cut off from us by salt morasses, which it was dangerous to venture into. We would therefore try to reach a suitable point on the south shore before dark (Illustration 77).

The hours fled past, and the sun sank in glowing yellow behind the mountains. For two hours we held on our course towards Deasy's camp, but when the beacon fires became more distinct in the gathering twilight we changed our direction and steered southwards to reach our people. The distance, however, was hopelessly long, and just from that direction the storm blew, and in the broken, freakish light of the moon the waves looked as weird as playing dolphins. Sometimes I was able to take some rapid soundings; they gave depths of 32 and 36 feet. Our fate was just as uncertain as on the former occasion on Lake Lighten; we steered for the shore, but did not know how far off it was. Rehim Ali judged from the length of the path of moonlight on the water that it was a long distance. Two more hours passed. I gave my orders to the oarsmen in English and Turki. We had now the waves on our quarter, and if we did not parry their rolling, foaming crests they would fill the boat and sink it; so we had to sail straight against them.

The situation was not a little exciting, but good luck attended us. The boat cut the waves cleanly, and we got only small splashes now and then. The spray trickled down our necks, was pleasantly cool, and had a saline taste. I again took soundings, and Robert read the line: 33 feet, then 25, and lastly 20.

"Now the southern shore cannot be very far," I said; but my companions remained still and listened. "What is it?" I asked.

"A heavy storm from the west," answered Rehim Ali, letting his oar fall.

A regular humming noise was heard in the distance, which came nearer and nearer. It was the storm, which swept over the lake with redoubled violence and lashed up foam from the waves.

"We shall not reach the shore before it overtakes us. It will be here in a minute. Master, we shall capsize if the waves become twice as high as they are now."

The waves swelled with incredible rapidity, the curves in the streak of moonlight became greater and greater, we rocked as in a huge hammock. The sounding-line had just marked 20 feet. How long would it be before the boat would ground on the hard, salt bottom, if it found itself in a trough between two waves? The lee-boards beat against the sides, the boat pitches and rolls, and any one who does not sit firmly and stiffen himself with his feet must go overboard. A terrible wave, like an all-devouring monster, comes down upon us, but the boat glides smoothly over it, and the next moment we are down in a trough so deep that all the horizon is concealed by the succeeding crest. We were not quick enough in negotiating this new wave; it ran along the gunwale and gave us a good foot-bath (Illustration 78).

"Master, it looks dangerous."

"Yes, it is not exactly pleasant, but keep quiet. We cannot land in such a sea. We must turn and make for the open lake. About midnight the storm may abate, and then we can land."

"If we can only keep on rowing so long."

"We will help ourselves with the sail."

"I am not tired yet."

To land on the southern shore would be certain shipwreck; we should all be drenched to the skin, and that is dangerous on this night when we cannot reckon on the slightest help from the caravan. We shall be frozen before the dawn. To look for fuel before the sun sets is not to be thought of, for the saline plains in the south are absolutely barren. No, we will turn.

At the same moment we felt a violent blow, which made the boat tremble. The larboard oar, which Rehim Ali worked, had struck against the ground and started loose from the screw which fastened it to the gunwale. Rehim Ali managed to catch hold of it just in time, while he shouted, "It is only a stone's throw to the land."

"Why, how is this?—here the lake is quite smooth."

"A promontory juts out into the lake. Master, here we shall find shelter."

"All right, then we are saved; row slowly till the boat takes ground." That soon happened, the sail was furled, the mast unshipped. We took off our boots and stockings, stepped into the water, and drew the boat on to dry land. My feet were so numbed in the briny water, cooled down to 41°, that I could not stand, and had to sit down and wrap my feet in my ulster. We found a patch of lumps of salt, thoroughly moist, indeed, though drier than elsewhere, and the best spot to be had; for water lay all around us, and the bank was extremely low. How far it was to really dry ground we could not ascertain; the moon threw a faintly shining strip of light for a considerable distance farther towards the land.

While I endeavoured to restore life to my feet by friction, the others carried our belongings to our wretched salt island. Then the boat was taken to pieces, and the two halves were set up as shelters. At nine o'clock we noted 31° on the thermometer, and at midnight 17½°; yet it was warmer now than on the previous days, for the water of the lake retains some of the heat of the summer air. Muhamed Isa had made a new roller for the sounding-line, with frame and handle, out of an empty box; it was of course immediately utilized as fuel.

The provision bags and the water-cans were brought out again, and we drank one cup of hot sugar-and-water after another, and tried to imagine it was tea. As long as the fire lasted we should not freeze — but then, what a night! Towards ten o'clock the wind abated — now came the night frost. We lay down on the life-buoys to avoid direct contact with the briny soil; Robert had the fur coat, I the ulster, and Rehim Ali wrapped himself in the sail. He slept huddled up together, with his forehead on the ground, as is the Mohammedan custom, and he did really sleep. Robert and I rolled ourselves together in a bunch, but of what use was it? One cannot sleep just before freezing. My feet were, indeed, past feeling, but this consolation was a sorry one. I stood up and stamped on the salt patch, and tried to walk without moving, for the space was very limited. I sang and whistled, I hummed a song, and imitated the howl of the wolves to see if they would reply. But the silence was unbroken. I told anecdotes to Robert, but he was not amused by them. I related adventures I had had before with wolves and storms, but they had little encouraging effect in our present position. We looked in vain for a fire; there was nothing to be seen in any direction. The moon slowly approached the horizon. The wind had sunk entirely. Little by little the salt waves, splashing melodiously against the shore, also sank to rest — an awful silence reigned around. We were too cold to think much of the wolves. Twice we raised a wild scream, but the sound of our voices died away suddenly without awaking the slightest echo; how could it reach the camping-ground?

"Now it is midnight, Robert; in four hours it will be day."

"Master, I have never been so starved in my life. If I get back to India alive, I shall never forget this dreadful night on Yeshil-kul and the hungry wolves on the shore, though I live to a hundred."

"Oh, nonsense. You will think of it with longing, and be glad that you were here."

"It is all very fine to look back on, but at present I should be delighted to have my warm bed in the tent and a fire."

"Life in Tibet is too monotonous without adventures; one day's journey is like another, and we want a little change occasionally to wake us up. But we will take tea and firewood with us next time."

"Shall you have more of such lake voyages, Master?"

"Certainly, if there is an opportunity; but I fear that the winter cold will soon make them impossible."

"Will it, then, be still colder than now?"

"Yes, this is nothing to what the cold will be in two months."

"What time is it, Master?"

"Two o'clock; we shall soon have been lying six hours on the morass."

We nodded a little once more, but did not really sleep for

78. A Dangerous Situation on the Yeshil-kul. In Moonshine.

a minute; from time to time Robert told me how badly his feet were frozen. At three o'clock he exclaimed, after a long silence: "Now I have no more feeling in any of my toes."

"The sun will soon come." At a quarter past four begins a faint glimmer of dawn. We are so chilled through that we can hardly stand up. But at length we pull ourselves up and stamp on the ground. Then we cower again over the cold ashes of our fire. We constantly look to the east and watch the new day, which slowly peeps over the mountains as though it would look about before it ventures out. At five o'clock the highest peaks receive a purple tinge, and we cast a faint shadow on the bottom of the boat, and then the sun rises, cold and bright-yellow, over the crest to the east. Now the springs of life revive. Rehim Ali has disappeared for an hour, and now we see him tramping through the swamp with a large bundle of wood, and soon we have kindled a sparkling, crackling fire. We undress to get rid of our wet and cold clothes, and warm our bodies at the flames, and soon our limbs are supple again.

Then Muhamed Isa's tall figure appears on horseback in the distance. He ties a cord to the foreleg of his horse and leaves it at the edge of the swamp, while he proceeds on foot. When I was suffering most severely from cold I had composed a sharp curtain-lecture for him as soon as we met. But now when I caught sight of my excellent caravan leader I forgot it all, for I had to admit the validity of his reasons for delay. The caravan was long detained in dangerous, unstable ground, and the men had to carry everything. We went together to Deasy's camp, which the caravan reached also. When the sun attained its highest altitude at mid-day, it found me still in the arms of Morpheus. I take it for granted that my two companions also requited themselves for the loss of their night's rest.

On the morning of September 26 two horses were nearing their end; they could not get on their feet and had to be killed; one had died in the previous camp, and one fell on the march. We had lost 15 horses out of 58, and only 1 mule out of 36; these figures are distinctly in favour of the mules.

We now rode along the great longitudinal valley, where favourable ground made our progress easy, and passed a salt basin, with a pool in the middle surrounded by concentric rings of desiccation as regular as the benches of an amphitheatre. Before us in the distance was seen the caravan in two detachments, appearing like two small black spots in the boundless open landscape. I was deeply impressed by my own insignificance compared to the distances on the earth's surface, and when I remembered that we travelled at most 13 miles a day, I was overwhelmed at the thought of the length of way we must traverse before we had crossed Tibet. Wolves were seen at the foot of a hill; perhaps they were our acquaintances of yesterday. We had to leave them, much against our will, an abundant banquet at the last camp, where six ravens had swooped down on our fallen horses.

One of the uppermost "benches," which stood some 160 feet above the surface of the pool, afforded a capital road. Round about the soil was chalky white with salt. To the right of us was a low, brownish-purple ridge. Soon, with my usual companions, Robert and Rehim Ali, I came up with a worn-out horse. He did not look at all emaciated, but he had been relieved from duty for several days in hopes of saving his life. His guide came into camp in the evening, and reported that he had collapsed on the road and expired. The country is somewhat hilly, but solid rock seldom crops out, and then it is limestone and light-green clay-slate.

The camping-ground on this day, No. 22, had an interest of its own. Captain H. H. P. Deasy, on his remarkable expedition through West Tibet and Eastern Turkestan during the years 1896–1899, had great difficulties to contend with, and lost so many animals that, in order to save the expedition and its results, he had to leave behind a large part of his baggage and provisions, in short, everything that could be spared at all. In the year 1903 Captain Cecil Rawling made an equally meritorious journey of exploration through the same parts of Tibet, and as he found himself in a very critical situation through want of provisions, he decided to search for Deasy's depôt, which, according to the map, must be somewhere in the neighbourhood. Two of Rawling's men, Ram Sing and Sonam Tsering, had also accompanied Deasy, and Sonam Tsering was able to point out the place where the baggage and provisions had been buried. Thanks to the stores of rice, meal, and barley, found there in the wilderness, Rawling was able to save his horses, which would otherwise have been lost, and a small bag of horse-shoes and nails came in very usefully for their hoofs.

Sonam Tsering now accompanied me on my expedition. I had ordered him in the morning to halt at Deasy's and Rawling's camp, and therefore he marched on this day in the front with the mules. It was, of course, of great importance for my route survey to visit a spot so accurately fixed.

There was not the slightest difficulty in finding the spot, and when we reached the camp, which lay on a small flat space between gently rounded hills, Muhamed Isa had already digged out seven boxes. One of them contained flour, which had gone quite bad in the long interval, and probably was already spoiled when Rawling was here three years before. Only one box was of Tibetan workmanship, for Rawling, as Sonam Tsering informed me, had exchanged some of his worn-out Kashmir boxes for Deasy's Turkestan chests, which were much better. But even Rawling's boxes were better than the easily damaged wooden boxes from Leh, in which we kept candles and tinned meats. We therefore appropriated some of them and used our own as firewood. After all, Rawling had so thoroughly ransacked the depôt that there was very little left for me; but I was not in such urgent need of the goods. Some boxes of American beef were very welcome to the dogs, but the men despised them as long as we had fresh mutton. Cubical tins, which had contained Indian meal, lay all about the place. One of the boxes held a quantity of empty cartridge-cases; they had not been used, and Sonam Tsering believed that the Changpas had been here a couple of years after Rawling, and had picked out the powder; he pointed out to me one or two fireplaces, which seemed much more recent. In another box we found a shipping almanac and some map-sheets of Upper Burma — Deasy had planned to pass into that country, but had been prevented by sickness and death in his caravan. A packet of blotting-paper came in very handy, for Robert had started a herbarium for me; and Muhamed Isa discovered some ropes in good condition. Besides these things, we took only a couple of novels and Bowers' description of his journey in Tibet in 1891, a welcome addition to my very scanty library (Illustration 79).

We were now in a country which several travellers had visited before me. Wellby and Malcolm, who discovered Lake Lighten, a lake already touched by Crosby, I have already mentioned. Dutreuil de Rhins, Wellby and Malcolm, Deasy, Rawling, and the Austrian naturalist, Zugmayer (1906), had been at Yeshil-kul. I crossed the route of the last a couple of months after his journey; he, like the Frenchman and the English explorer, has written a valuable book on his observations. At the time I knew nothing of his journey, but now I find that I crossed his route only at one point. Wellby's and Dutreuil de Rhins' paths I crossed only once, but Deasy's at two points. In the following days it was harder to avoid the districts where Wellby and Rawling had been, and where the latter especially, with the help of native surveyors, had compiled such an accurate and reliable map that I had no prospect of improving it.

Consequently, I longed for country which had never been touched by other travellers. My camp 22 was identical with Rawling's No. 27, and his expedition had skirted the lake Pul-tso, which lay a day's march in front of us, both on the northern and southern side. Therefore, to avoid his route, I made for the middle of this lake, which stretches north and south, an unusual orientation.

When the great caravan is loaded up, and starts at sunrise, the camp is usually full of noise and commotion. In consequence of our daily loss of baggage horses the loads have always to be re-arranged; when, however, the crowd has moved off, all is quiet again, the iron brazier and the hot bath-water are brought, and in my tent, with its opening turned to the east, because the prevailing wind blows from the west, it is soon as hot as in a vapour bath. This heat often tempts one to put on lighter clothing, but one soon regrets it, for it is always cold outside. Then we go on through the desolate country where three expeditions have converged to the same point.

The soil is brick-red, the pasturage good everywhere. To the south lie low hills with arched tops, to the north stretches the immense mountain system of the Kuen-lun with several imposing mountain masses covered with eternal snow, and just in front of us rises the colossal dome-shaped, snow-covered massive, which Rawling named the "Deasy Group." We had seen this gigantic elevation from Yeshil-kul, and it would serve us for a landmark for several days to come.

The caravan encamped on the bank of the Pul-tso (16,654 feet) near a small rock of limestone. Tundup Sonam, the "Grand Court Huntsman" of the caravan, begged to be allowed to go out shooting, and was given four cartridges. After a few hours he returned with three cartridges, and showed a yak's tail as a proof that he had killed a huge beast, which he had found grazing peacefully by itself behind the hills to the south. Now the caravan had fresh meat to last ten days; "and when it is consumed, Tundup will shoot us another yak," said Muhamed Isa, who was always much pleased when men he had picked out made a good job of their work. I had marrow from the yak's bones for dinner—a dish that would not have disgraced the table of Lucullus (Illustrations 68, 69).

CHAPTER XI

GREAT LOSSES

We had scarcely pitched our camp on the west shore of the Pul-tso when Muhamed Isa came to ask for a day's rest. The grazing, he said, was good, fuel abundant, and the animals needed a little time to recover. I fell in with his wishes the more readily that they fitted in with my own plans — another lake voyage. I intended to go with Robert and Rehim Ali early in the morning across the lake in the direction of a precipitous mountain which lay 56° east of north; then we would sail over to the south bank and pass the night at a mountain 62° east of south. The following morning we expected to reach the north-east corner of the lake, where the caravan would wait for us on the yellowish-green pastureland. We should thus take two days on the lake to cover a distance which the caravan would traverse in one day. We would take with us food, warm clothing and bedding, and a quantity of fuel, that we might not be in such straits as last time. Water was not wanted; the lake water was potable, though it had a rather queer taste.

The lake looked very inviting and picturesque at even, its perfectly smooth mirror lying dark, dreamy, and silent between the mountains capped with eternal snow. Great, reeking fires of dung burned cheerfully among the tents, the men prepared their supper, or mended the pack-saddles, chatting merrily the while; all was quiet and peaceful, and the moon floated, silvery white and cold, among rose-coloured clouds.

Then I hear far in the east a droning sound, which

79. At Deasy's Camp.

80. Afternoon Tea in the Open Air.

81. Melting Snow for Drinking-Water.

swells up rapidly, comes nearer, and changes into deafening thunder, and in a moment a very violent storm sweeps over the shore. I call men to close the opening of my tent. I hear Robert raise a whoop as his airy dwelling flaps about and threatens to split up into shreds. But a dozen men set it to rights again. Then my tent is strengthened with sand heaps and boxes; I am shut in with my brazier, but a small spy-hole is left in the tent opening. The moonshine glistens on the surf of the billows rolling against the shore — a grand spectacle — wild, weird, almost theatrical in its beauty. A storm of unsurpassed violence rushes ruthlessly along. It sounds like express trains rolling through covered stations; it lashes, roars, and howls, and dashes the surf thundering against the beach. The fires, but now flickering so cheerfully, are put out; the spray is spurted out like rockets; I hear Muhamed Isa's tent flapping about; then the sound of men's voices is heard no more, only the howling of the storm and the thunder of the waves disturb the silence of the wilderness. If I do but look out of my spy-hole I am almost suffocated by the pressure of the condensed air. Only the yaks delight in such weather; they grunt and snort with pleasure when the long black fringes of hair on their flanks flutter in the gusts.

September 28, however, was clear, the storm had sped off on its course to the west, and the dull splashing of the swell on the beach was all that was left of its fury. Before we were half way along the first line of soundings, the lake was again as smooth as a mirror; it was only flecked with small flakes of foam left behind by the storm. The water had been too thoroughly stirred up to be clear. We took little more than an hour to reach the rocky promontory, sounding on our way a maximum depth of nearly 56 feet. We left on the north a considerable bay which the caravan would have to go round.

After a short rest we continued our voyage to the south-east, and were well helped on our way by a gentle northerly breeze. This time we reached the shore without any adventures and before sunset. We landed with all our belongings. Rehim Ali collected heaps of dry dung,

Robert set the camp in order, and I cruised about in the evening breeze till twilight came, and cold and darkness surrounded our bivouac. We sat down by the fire, talked, and cooked. The mince of fried sheep's brains and kidneys tasted delicious in the open-air. To the west we could see the fires at camp No. 23. Later in the evening a strong east wind rose up again, and the waves dashed against the shore barely two yards from us. We rolled ourselves in our furs and gazed into the fire; the head is never so full of projects and aspirations as when the eyes follow the play of the blue flickering flames and the fiery forms that arise in the glow.

But the storm increased in violence, we could hardly keep the fire alive, and soon we crept under the boat, which we used as a shelter without taking it to pieces. We all three lay in this improvised tent, and strengthened it with the sail and two tarpaulin cases, which covered the halves of the boat on the march, and which we had brought with us to protect our night wraps and beds in bad weather. Above us hung a lantern which we extinguished when we were ready; now the moon shone on the sail, the tempest howled and moaned round the boat, and the surf soon lulled us to sleep.

The minimum thermometer marked 14°; it is always warmer near lakes. We were early on our feet, a good fire put new life into us, and we breakfasted beside it, the sun looking on. Our berth for the night was restored to its element, the baggage was packed in, we stepped on board and steered eastwards to the entrance of a passage which divides the Pul-tso into two basins. Its breadth is about 65 yards; in the southern basin the water was often almost red with small crustaceæ. We crossed it south-westwards, and found depths of barely 46 feet. Then a strong breeze came up from the north-west, and the waves splashed and lapped against the boat. If we only got a south-west wind we could easily sail to the appointed rendezvous. We would wait a little by the shore. It curves gracefully, and has four terraces, each about two yards high.

On the sail back a new line was sounded, the maximum

depth being about 60 feet. Now we had a favourable wind on the quarter, let down the weather-board, hoisted the sail, and danced along to the strait. As we came up to its eastern point, a rider with spare horses and several men on foot came in sight. It was Muhamed Isa coming to meet us. Now Rabsang relieved Rehim Ali, but he was so awkward with the oars, that we preferred to take back our old oarsman. We said good-bye to the rescue party, and steered northwards over the northern basin of the lake, where the depths were 10 feet at most. Unfortunately the wind veered to the north, so that we were thoroughly chilled through during the two hours' sail to the north shore.

Muhamed Isa had brought us sad news: two more horses and a mule had died at camp No. 23; in the evening another horse died. Otherwise the caravan at camp No. 25 was sound and lively. Therefore we were the more astonished to see a large fire at the abandoned camping-ground in the west. The caravan had started towards eight o'clock in the morning, and now it was four o'clock in the afternoon. Not a soul had remained behind in camp No. 23, and yet there was the fire; we saw flames and smoke, which hung like a great veil over the shore. Rehim Ali thought that the post from Ladak had caught us up at last.

"No, that is impossible; a post-runner cannot travel so far and carry his rations with him."

"But the camp-fire must have gone out immediately after the departure of the caravan. A fire does not burn so brightly with no one to attend to it."

"The smoke of camp No. 25 can be plainly seen from camp No. 23. If the post had reached camp No. 23 it would not have stayed there a minute, but would have hurried on to join us before night."

"Yes, Sahib, but perhaps the messenger is so exhausted that he is signalling for help."

"May it not be Changpas?" remarked Robert.

"Yes, certainly, it may be Tibetans, sent from the south to order us to stop, or at least to watch us, and report to the nearest headman."

"Master, perhaps we shall have to stop sooner than we think. What is to happen then?"

"I do not think that the Tibetans can interfere with us so far to the north; they cannot force us to turn back. At the worst we shall have to pass eastwards through Central Tibet to China or Burma, as Bower did."

"Look, now, how it smokes; this great fire must mean something."

"Yes, it is a regular will-o'-the-wisp, a Saint Elmo fire. The gods of the lake have lighted it to lead us astray."

"I believe it is the post, but the fire looks uncanny," said Rehim Ali, and rowed with all his might.

"Do not disturb yourself. If it is the post we shall hear of the messenger before evening; I believe that the camp-fire has not gone out, but has smouldered on in a sheltered spot all day long; when the wind changed, some reserve heap of dung caught fire, and, fanned by the north wind, it has burst into flames."

At six o'clock we were home again. After I had taken a much-needed meal I summoned Muhamed Isa and Sonam Tsering to a consultation.

"How many horses have we left?" — "Forty."

"How many mules?" — "Thirty-four."

"Are they in fairly good condition?" — "No, Sahib, not all; four of my horses and six of Sonam's are at the point of death, and five mules."

"We shall, then, have more losses soon?" "Yes, alas! But to save all we can, the strongest animals must now have maize and barley; the sickly ones must forage for themselves till their hour comes. They are certainly doomed."

"That is barbarous; give them at least something. Perhaps some may be saved." — "We must be very sparing with the forage, Sahib."

The management of the caravan-bashi was prudent, but cruel.

At seven o'clock the storm came. It was the third evening we had had violent east winds, a direction exceedingly infrequent in Tibet. It came like a stroke, and put an end to all our peacefulness, stopped all conversation, interfered with all kinds of work, extinguished the camp-fires, blew sand and dust into my tent, and prevented the tired animals from grazing; for they will not feed in a storm. They place themselves with their tails to the wind, keep all four legs as close together as possible, and hang their heads. So they remain standing, and wait till it is quiet again. They had to wait all night long, and perhaps, sleepy and heavy-headed, dreamed of the heart-lessness of men and the peaceful, sunny slopes at Tankse and Leh. In the evening Muhamed Isa and I inspected them. The moon shone brightly, but its cold, bluish light made the piercing wind seem more icy than usual. The animals stood, like ghosts, so motionless in the night, that one would think that they were already turned into ice. Not the cold, but the wind, kills our horses; all my people say so. Winter was coming down upon our mountains in all its severity. The rarefaction of the air and the scanty pasturage were the worst troubles.

The wind whistled mournfully round the corners as I went to sleep, and the same sound fell on my ear in the morning as Tsering, muffled up in a thick fur coat, brought the brazier in. A dreary morning! Everything in the tent was buried under a thick layer of dust and drift sand, and I was thoroughly frozen before I had dressed. The horses and mules had gone forward eastwards, but I did not start till nine o'clock — in a furious storm. Just outside the camp the last horse that had perished lay cold and hard as ice. Tsering told me that he was scarcely a stone's throw from the body when the wolves had already crept up to feast on it.

The ground is good, sand, dust, and fine gravel. Afterwards the soil becomes brick-red. One cannot see far, the air is hazy and the sky overcast, but as far as the sight can carry, only low mountains are visible. One or two brooks, almost frozen up, run out of side valleys on the north. We slowly ascend to a pass, whence the country eastwards seems just as level and favourable as hitherto. Here I am following Rawling's route; his map corresponds to the actual conditions in the smallest details.

It is quite a different thing to ride against the storm

over rising ground, and to have the wind on one's back going downhill. We work our way through the wind, which penetrates our furs, and in ten minutes are quite numbed. I can scarcely use my hands for mapping work; now and then I thrust them into the sleeves of my coat, lean far forwards, and let the horse find its own way. Two more horses die before the evening; a third was led nearly to the camp; he looked fat and sleek, but he tumbled down.

When I rode into camp I had had more than enough of this terrible day. A bright fire was burning in the fort of provision boxes, by which we chatted awhile, waiting for Tsering. The camp fort shrank up day by day at an alarming rate, but the animals died so quickly that the loads were, nevertheless, too heavy. But it was Muhamed Isa's opinion that enough mules would be left till we got to the Dangra-yum-tso, and that no baggage need be left behind. In case of necessity the boat and a couple of tents might be sacrificed. Empty provision chests were consumed at once as firewood. Undoubtedly we should reach the distant lake in a state of utter helplessness. Without assistance we could proceed no further. Then the Tibetans could easily stop us. We were therefore a prey to great anxiety, which increased every day.

"If the animals founder at the same rate as at present, we shall not reach the nearest nomads."

"Sahib, the strongest are still alive."

"Yes, that is always your consolation; but in a few days some of the strongest will be dying."

"The wind kills them. If we had only a few days of calm weather!"

"There is no prospect of that at this season of the year. This storm has now lasted 27 hours. Then come the winter storms from the south-west."

On October 1 I wrote in my diary: "What will be our experiences in this new month? At eight o'clock the tempest still raged, and the ride to-day was worse than before."

Flat, open country. Only one or two hills of red sandstone and conglomerate with green schist — otherwise no hard rock. The Deasy Group, towering to the south, seems nearer and nearer. The horse, No. 27, lies in a pool of frozen blood, cold and bare, for the pack-saddle has been removed for the sake of the hay. During the night three horses had stampeded, and were searched for by Muhamed Isa and three Ladakis. Stupid animals, to tire themselves out for nothing! Some unaccountable restlessness seemed to have driven them from the spot where they were unloaded. The poor things perhaps thought they could find better grass than our hard-heartedness allowed them.

We approached a very small freshwater lake, by which both Wellby and Deasy had rested. A fourth of its surface was frozen over, and on its west bank the storm had reared up a wall of ice fragments a foot high. An icy brook descended from the Deasy Group into the lake. The water of the lake was cooled down below freezing-point; a few more hours of perfect calm and the whole lake would be frozen over. On the bank Sonam Tsering found three old tent-poles with the iron rings still on them. He could not remember that Rawling had left them here: probably they were a memento of Wellby's visit.

Tundup Sonam had killed an antelope, and for my dinner I was served with fragrant *shislik* roasted on a spit. Tsering knew his work; he had been cook to Beach and Lennart, whom I met in Kashgar in 1890, and was more skilful than "the black fellow," as Muhamed Isa contemptuously styled the late Manuel.

The Lamaists among my Ladakis told me in confidence that they prayed every evening to their gods for a lucky journey. They were just as eager as myself to reach Shigatse and the holy monastery Tashi-lunpo, where the Tashi Lama resides. For then they would receive a title of honour, just as a Mohammedan becomes "Hajji" when he has been in Mecca. They would willingly pay their Peter's pence, seven rupees for butter for the altar lamps, nay, would give up a whole month's pay as a present to His Holiness, the Tashi Lama. Their aim was to bring a pilgrimage to a successful termination; mine to fill up as many blanks as possible in the map of Tibet. We must succeed! Heaven befriend us!

No one minded that we had not a single man as escort. Yet with every day we were getting nearer to inhabited country, and were advancing into a land which had recently (1904) been at feud with its powerful neighbour on the south. The Tibetans were ever hostile to Europeans, and after the slaughter at Guru and Tuna they would probably be still more bitter against them. We had neither passport nor permission to enter the forbidden land. How should we prosper? Our excitement was always increasing. Should we be received as open enemies, and after all wish ourselves back with the wolves on the banks of Yeshil-kul?

October 2. Thirty-six degrees of frost in the night — and we hear nothing of Rabsang! Has anything happened to him? Shukkur Ali is sent back along the caravan track with meat, tea, and bread. A mule, which can no longer keep on its feet, is killed in the camp. When the wind falls occasionally, it is singularly quiet. The landscape is still monotonous — a boundless, gently rising plain. North and south the two mountain ranges with their snow-peaks still run on. Grass and *yapkak* grow on all sides. Hour after hour we ride east-north-east without any change of scenery. I look forward to the moment when we shall turn towards the south-east, but that is far off, for I must first pass round all the region that Rawling explored. The animals will then have still harder work, for we shall have to cross several passes. The ranges run from east to west; meanwhile we are marching between two of them, later on we shall have to go over them. I examine the animals daily with great anxiety, and fix my hopes on the strongest, the select troop which will hold out to the last. How depressed I feel when one of them slips its collar.

At camp No. 28, beside a salt pool, the animals are mustered as usual. They understand the summons when the corn-bags are ready. Then they are turned out to graze. Empty provision sacks and pack-saddles serve as cloths to protect the animals from the cold at night. For the mules small triangular pieces are cut to bind over their foreheads, where they are supposed to be most susceptible to cold. Outside the Ladakis' enclosure stand our twenty goats and sheep, tied head to head into a compact group, so that they may keep one another warm.

This day the moon rose blood-red over the mountains in the east. It became quickly paler the higher it rose, and the snowy mountains shone as white as the steam of an engine. The evening was calm, and the tent was easily heated in camp No. 28. Yet the temperature sank to $-8°$ — and Rabsang was still missing. Had the wolves torn him in pieces?

Next morning, however, he turned up in Shukkur Ali's company, but without the horse. He had followed the trail of the wandering animal for a long distance, and in the sand on the shore of the small lake had been able to read the story of a tragic incident with almost dramatic vividness. The tracks showed that the horse had galloped madly about, pursued by a troop of wolves on either side. They had chased their victim on to a narrow strip of mud ending in a point. There he had found only one track of the horse, which disappeared in the slowly deepening bed of the lake. But the wolves had left a double track — they had come back. They thought to fall upon the horse on the landspit, where he could not run further, but they had made a mistake. Rabsang maintained that their confusion was reflected in their backward trail. The helpless horse, driven to desperation by the wild and hungry jaws opened wide to devour him, plunged into the water, preferring to drown rather than fall into the clutches of his persecutors. Not a drop of blood could be seen. If he had attempted to swim across the lake, he must have died of cramp; if he had turned back to the shore, the wolves would have waited for him and not have retired into the mountains. He was a hero, and now I felt his loss doubly; he was one of the best in the caravan, a Sanskari, and had long carried the heaviest boxes of silver. The picture of his bold spring into the water, and of his desperation bordering on frenzy, long haunted my imagination, when I lay awake at night, and I thought of the horse on which Marcus Curtius plunged into the abyss.

The day's march took us further along the same even plain, where at length every trace of vegetation ceased.

At camp No. 29 there was, alas! no pasturage, and so we had to lead the horses to the foot of the mountains where grass grew sparingly.

October 4. We continue our journey to the east-north-east, and there is not the slightest change in the country. Like a squirrel in a revolving cage, we go on and on and yet find ourselves always in the same country; north and south the same summits appear, and their profiles change but slowly. Deasy named this great open longitudinal valley "Antelope Plain." Rawling traversed its south-western portion in two directions, and my route runs between them on the left bank of its very broad, but now waterless, drainage channel. We suppose that the salt lake, which Wellby skirted on the south, must lie to the east-north-east, but it is not yet visible. Yellow grass again appears on both sides, and the camp is pitched beside a small basin of splendid spring-water. As soon as the animals are relieved of their loads and let loose, we notice that a third begin to graze at once, another third stand resting with drooping heads, and the remaining third lie down immediately. The first are the best and strongest horses, the last those that are most exhausted. Among these is horse No. 10, which has to be killed next morning; he is entered in the list of dead as No. 25.

Muhamed Isa does not now set out before half-past eight in the morning. He has noticed that the animals feed with a better appetite in the early hours after sunrise. The broad, hard river-bed is an excellent road, quite a highway, descending with an extremely slight gradient. During the last days the needles of the aneroids have remained almost stationary at the same figure. To the north we have still the Kuen-lun, sometimes as masses of dark rock, sometimes with snow-capped, rounded summits.

At one o'clock I always make a short halt with Robert and Rehim Ali to read the meteorological instruments. The journal is kept by Robert with the greatest care. I draw a panorama and take bearings, while our horses stray about grazing. We take no food at that time, for we eat only twice a day — at eight o'clock in the morning and six in the evening. Yet the short mid-day rest is very welcome.

We are by that time thoroughly frozen; we can more easily keep ourselves warm on the ground than in the saddle, where we are fully exposed to the wind.

We have not seen a drop of water all day long, and the caravan is evidently looking for a spring, for we see scouts making off from time to time to the right and left. At length they discover a large pond, and there the tents are set up. We have marched lately about nine miles a day—we cannot do more.

We had scarcely set out on the morning of October 6 when the camping-ground was inspected by wolves on the look-out for another horse. They follow us as faithfully as the ravens, and perhaps receive reinforcements from time to time. Strict orders are issued that the night watch must be responsible for the animals, and will be punished if we suffer any loss from the wolves. The six ravens also still stick to us. They settle when we encamp, they set out with us, and follow us all day long with their hoarse croaking.

We pass over the river-bed, now containing water and ice, but still the low hills hide the expected lake. Otherwise the ground is level, so level that only the languid movement of the stream shows in which direction the land dips. Yellow sand-whirls in the north-west indicate the approach of a storm, which comes upon us out of a clear sky. Within half an hour it passes into an easterly storm, a typical cyclone. Worn out with the cold we arrive at camp No. 32.

The puppies are now quite big, and up to all kinds of mischief. It is recorded against the white puppy that she has torn up one of my map-sheets. Fortunately, none of the fragments is wanting. Tsering also found a toothbrush in front of my tent, which the silly dog must have considered superfluous. The brown puppy bit in two a hydrometer, which was lying about in its leathern case. Their education is very defective, but they are foundlings from the streets of Srinagar, and we cannot therefore expect much of them. They have not the slightest notion of discipline, and they do not obey when they are called. But when Tsering brings the dinner they come to heel at once, put on a show of amiability, and force themselves to the front by some means or other. They are not of much use; they keep my feet warm at night, for then they lie rolled up together on my bed.

Forty-five degrees of frost in the night! That was perhaps why I had such a horrid dream: a whole host of dark Tibetans came to meet us, and drove us back to the north. The water in the basin and the ink are lumps of ice.

Now we have left Rawling far behind us, and Wellby and Malcolm's is the last route which has been traversed in this region. We are still following the same valley as that expedition.

Our store of yak meat was just at an end when Tundup Sonam killed an antelope. A second, unfortunately, he only wounded, and it escaped on three legs. One of our wolves was pacing about on a hill. He had closely watched the chase, and the wounded animal would probably become his prey.

Muhamed Isa, in his thick grey winter suit and with his pipe in his mouth, moves about, and is guiding the caravan up between the hills when we overtake him. We ascend to the summit of a hill. A white line appears, and below it a bluish-green stripe which gradually increases in dimensions. After a few minutes we have the salt lake we have been looking for immediately below us, for the hills slope steeply to the southern shore. Now the Ladakis commence one of their finest march songs in soft, melting tones; they are glad to have reached this lake which I have spoken of constantly, and, like myself, remind themselves that we have reached another stage on the long journey to Dangra-yum-tso. To the north-west the scenery is grand, with the great mountains, their snow-capped peaks and great glaciers. Continuing the direction of the sea westwards is flat land white with salt, and there white eddies dance, whirling along the dismal shore.

East-north-east the longitudinal valley is as open as before; there Wellby travelled. We can now, if we wish, turn aside to the south-east without again coming in contact with Rawling's route. There new country awaits us, the great triangle between Wellby's, Bower's, and Dutreuil de Rhins' routes. It had been one of my most cherished hopes to cross, at least once, the great white patch which bears on the English map of Tibet nothing but the one word "Unexplored."

CHAPTER XII

IN UNKNOWN COUNTRY

In the middle of the night I was awaked by seven mules, which stood close to my tent stamping about on its ropes. I went out to drive them away, but when I saw how piteously cold they were, and how closely they crowded together, I let them alone. One of them lay dead in the morning beside my tent, with its belly swollen all out of shape.

Green schists form small ledges and strips on the otherwise soft ground, so that at a distance the land seems striped with black. Here and there veins of quartz crop out. Reddish-purple hills appear on the western horizon, and the country becomes more uneven. After a while we pass the sheep driven by the men in the wake of the caravan. They travel very slowly, grazing as they go; we have still 18 left. To-day the water is a difficulty. Some is found by digging at a depth of a foot, but it is briny. The day's march is therefore longer than usual, 12 miles, but then we come to a spring.

On the eve of a day of rest we feel as though it were Saturday evening and there were no school next day. We intended to spend October 9 in camp No. 34; I had not given a day's rest for 17 days. All were delighted, and the Ladakis, in anticipation of the day of rest, arranged an *al fresco* feast round a great camp-fire. The refreshments were the same as usual: tea in wooden bowls, parched meal, and roasted antelope meat — spirituous liquors of any kind were prohibited in our caravan. But, nevertheless, the men were in a right jovial mood; they danced round the fire, and sang a lively song with a chorus culminating in barbaric, shrill-sounding laughter. They rejoiced that they had proceeded so far and still possessed sufficient power of resistance to undergo severe hardships. We have travelled 331 miles from the Karakorum, and there are 400 more to the Dangra-yum-tso. But we are nearer the lake than we are to Leh, and so have really more than half the journey behind us.

After 41 degrees of frost in the night, October 10 dawned with brilliant weather, sunny and calm. Horse No. 3 was the twenty-sixth martyr of the caravan; he lay dead on the field. We passed another which was reduced to a skeleton and never reached the camp. We travelled east-south-east, and had now to leave the longitudinal valley through which Wellby had traversed the whole of north Tibet. A small hollow in the ground was crossed, and the camp was pitched among the hills on its south side. The brown puppy had behaved so disgracefully that she had to lie outside as a punishment. She howled and whined piteously, but slept after she had been covered with a frieze rug. Next day she had to travel with the mules to her shame. In the night another horse died.

Red and yellowish-grey hills begirt the way, which led up in three hours to a small flat saddle, whence the view eastwards seemed boundless. Had it been our intention to proceed farther in this direction we should have encountered no difficulties in the nature of the ground for many days to come, but my unalterable goal was the Dangra-yum-tso, and therefore we must direct our course south-eastwards. There a dark chain with an irregular, toothed crest soon came into view. Between its summits were seen deeply-cut saddle-formed gaps; but, to our chagrin, they were more difficult to surmount than they appeared, and the slightest rise in the ground was felt by our caravan in its prostrate condition.

The ground was all honeycombed with the holes of the abominable field-mice, but the holes were not so treacherous now, for the soil was frozen, and held firm when we rode over the subterranean catacombs connected by a network of passages.

Again we mounted a small swell in the ground (17,234 feet). We saw before us a dark point in the track of the caravan; it was a dead mule, which slept his last sleep with wide-open eyes beside his pack-saddle. Behind a hill we surprised a large, handsome fox, which made off in a great hurry as we drew near. But he could not refrain from frequently turning round and staring at us; he had probably never seen a human being before.

At camp No. 36 there was not a drop of water, but we were not able to travel further. We had with us two goat's leather bottles filled with ice which sufficed for our tea; but the animals had to go without water. However, we could not complain; it was the first time since Leh that we had had no water.

An unusual sight greeted us on the morning of October 12; the whole country was covered with snow. But scarcely had the sun mounted up, when the snow melted and the ground was dry. The caravan set out early for the sake of the thirsty animals. Now we kept on a south-easterly course, leaving out of the range of our vision the lake discovered by Rawling, and named "Lake Markham" after the former distinguished President of the Royal Geographical Society in London.

Again we pass a horse with its throat cut; it is reddish-brown, and contrasts strongly with the grey, sandy soil. The eyes have already been picked out by the six ravens which sit like black ghouls round the fallen beast and hold a wake. A little farther something suspicious again appears in the track of the caravan — it is the sixth mule. He has collapsed on the march and has not to be killed; he is still soft and warm, and his eyes have not lost their brightness, but the ravens will soon be here, for they follow the caravan like dolphins in the wake of a vessel. For every animal that falls there is a horse-cloth to spare for his comrades. They will need it when the severe cold of winter comes. The two victims to-day have long been released from duty, but they had to follow on till they died, for there was always a hope that they would recover — a vain one, indeed.

The trail leads us to the mouth of a valley, where we

soon come up with the caravan—all the animals have their heads in a brook, they have had to thirst so long. The valley must come down from a pass, so we march up it. It becomes narrower and narrower, till at length there is a passage only five yards broad between walls of schists tilted up vertically. By the brook lay the bleached skull of an Ammon sheep with fine horns (Illustrations 59, 60). We found shelter from the cutting wind at the foot of a precipitous wall of rock on the left side of the valley, and there set up our tent poles. Muhamed Isa climbed a height opposite, taking the field-glass. "A labyrinth of small mountains," was his unsatisfactory report. By this time we had lost 29 horses and 6 mules, and had only 29 horses and 30 mules. "The strongest animals are still living," was Muhamed Isa's consolation.

October 13. The night with 39 degrees of frost deprived us of another horse and a mule. Their bones are bleaching in camp No. 37, and are tokens of our visit. A heavy march over very undulating ground. We had to cross over three small, trying passes. A good deal of snow still lay on the ground. To our right extended a red mountain crest, and in a gorge a waterfall was congealed into a mass of ice. Muhamed Isa had erected three cairns to show us the way where the track of the caravan became indistinct on pebbly ground. On the first pass the prospect was dreary, nothing but pink, purple, and yellow mountains. On the north the Turkestan mountains still dominated the landscape with their majestic peaks, a row of imperial crowns far above the rest. Fifty degrees east of north we fancied we perceived a large lake, but it might equally well be a plain transfigured by the mirage. Many of the hills and spurs consist of creeping soil from above, which in consequence of its slow motion is frozen into concentric rings and other patterns. The third pass rises in perfectly barren land. Here Tsering gave himself enormous trouble in setting up a cairn, which was quite unnecessary, for no one would come after us; but it was an act of homage to the gods of the mountains, an earnest prayer that they would let us pass safely.

At last we came down into open country, a main valley

running eastwards, where there was a glimpse of yellow grass in the distance. Tundup Sonam shot two Ammon sheep, and their flesh prolonged the lives of our 18 sheep. In this cold, windy weather we are never properly warm. When I sit, sketching the panorama of the mountains or taking a solar observation, I must have the brazier beside me to warm my numbed hands a little, so that I can use them. Only Muhamed Isa, Tsering, Sonam Tsering, and Guffaru are exempt from night duty; all the rest are obliged to turn out into the cold, dark, wintry night. When darkness falls I fill up the drawings I have sketched in the day, study maps, or read light literature, or Supan's *Physische Erdkunde*, and a couple of books on Buddhism and Lamaism. At nine o'clock Robert takes meteorological readings, and sets up the hypsometer, which I read off in my tent. Then we talk awhile and go to sleep. My bed is laid on an India-rubber sheet and two folded Turkestan frieze blankets. On these is laid a great square of goatskins sewed together. I lay myself down on one half of the square and cover myself with the other, and then Tsering tucks in the edges under the felt blankets, so that the whole is converted into a sack. Lastly, he spreads two more felt blankets, my ulster, and my fur coat over me. I have my fur cap on my head and a *bashlik*; otherwise I undress as usual. In stormy weather the morning bath is not exactly pleasant; my clothes have become icy cold during the night. The Ladakis have no notion of cleanliness, and consequently carry about with them small colonies of vermin, for which I have not the least use. But those who make my bed, clear up, and wait on me in my tent, cannot help giving me a most liberal share of their surplus, and therefore my underclothing has to be frequently washed in boiling water. My sensitiveness in this respect is a wonderful source of amusement to the Ladakis; I hear them laughing heartily at my horror of all kinds of blood-sucking creatures. But I tell them that I feel comfortable only when I am quite alone in my clothes.

The winter evenings grew longer and longer, and our life passed in monotonous solitude. The worst was that my light reading was put a stop to. To occupy the leisure hours I made the Ladakis relate to me traditions and legends of their own country, and noted some of them down. I also made each of my servants narrate his own experiences; but the notes I made of them were not very remarkable, for the men had not much to tell, and thought it all quite natural and unimportant. You must question and draw them out, and even then the result is unsatisfactory. They very seldom know the name of a European whom they have served for months, and they cannot state their own age. But they know exactly how many horses there were in a caravan they accompanied years ago, and the colour of each horse. One Ladaki, who has traversed the inhabited parts of western Tibet, can tell me the name of every camping-ground, describe it accurately, and tell me whether the pasture there was good or bad. They have also a marvellous memory for the character of the ground.

Having regard to the compass of this narrative, I cannot allow myself to wander into diffuse biographical notices, but I must very briefly introduce my little party to the reader. We will begin, then, with Rabsang, who went in search of the horse that was baited by the wolves. He is a Bod, or Buddhist, strictly speaking a Lamaist; his father is named Pale, his mother Rdugmo, from the village Chushut-yogma in Ladak. By occupation he is a *zemindar* or farmer, grows barley, wheat, and peas, owns two horses and two yaks, but no sheep, pays 23 rupees (about 31 shillings) in taxes to the Maharaja, but no contributions to the lamas. Once a year he travels in the service of Afghan merchants to Yarkand, and receives 50 rupees for the whole journey. The merchants carry clothing materials, coral, tea, indigo, etc., to Yarkand, where they put up in the *serai* of the Hindus, and stay twenty days to sell their goods and purchase silk, felt rugs, ordinary rugs, etc., which they get rid of in Peshawar. Rabsang had served chiefly the Hajji Eidar Khan, a rich merchant of Cabul. Six years ago he had an adventure on the Suget-davan, where twelve Badakshan men, who owed the Hajji money, met the caravan. The twelve men had led a wild life in Yarkand, and could not pay their debts

The Afghans, who numbered five, fell upon them and a violent scuffle ensued, ending in bloodshed. That was Rabsang's worst adventure. He had served Captain Deasy five months and another Englishman as long. When he was away himself, his wife and a brother tilled his land and looked after his affairs.

"Can you depend on your wife's faithfulness for so long a time?"

"No," he answered, "but we do not think much of that in Ladak."

"What happens if she misconducts herself with another man?"

"Then he must give me a sheep as compensation."

After this not a word more could be extracted from Rabsang.

In our caravan he is under Tsering's immediate command, and leads the four horses which carry my tent, my bed, the four boxes of articles for daily use, and the kitchen utensils. He is assistant to the head cook, and has to keep me supplied all the evening with fuel. He brings Tsering fuel and water for cooking, and is an exceedingly sturdy, useful fellow. A year later he had a prominent part to play.

I have already spoken of the Mohammedan Rehim Ali. He is my right-hand man on the march. Guffaru is the oldest of the company, and guide of the horse caravan; consequently the more horses die, the less he has to do. The Hajji Gulam Razul has been twice in Mecca; he is Muhamed Isa's cook. Shukkur Ali has made many remarkable journeys, which would fill a whole chapter themselves; with us he is leader of a section of the horse caravan, but has now only two charges. Gaffar is a young Mohammedan, who follows the horses, gathers fuel, and fetches water. Young Tsering has the same occupations, and Ishe, Tundup, and Adul belong also to this party; the last, a hard-working, sturdy man, has entered my service in order to buy himself a house in Leh and to enable him to marry. Islam Ahun is horse watchman. Bolu belongs to my caravan, and is one of Tsering's assistants. Galsan, who has travelled much in western

82. Preparations for Dinner at Camp 41.

Tibet, serves as a mule-driver. Ishe Tundup is responsible for the sheep. Lobsang Rigdal, nicknamed the Lama, has to attend to my horses. He is come with me to earn money to give to his father and elder brother, because they have always taken good care of him. He is the jester of the caravan, and has a very comical appearance. Tashi, who accompanies the horses, is one of our best men. Tundup Sonam keeps up the sporting reputation of the caravan and provides us all with fresh meat. He scarcely ever misses, and is as quiet and composed as a pan of clotted milk. He had served under me before, in the winter of 1902, when I travelled from Leh to Yarkand. Gartyung belongs to the mule caravan, and entered my service to restore order in his financial affairs. A small, short, black-bearded fellow, fifty years of age, answers to the name of Tashi Tsering; formerly he was called Islam Ahun, he says, so he has changed his religion, though it seldom happens that a Mohammedan goes over to Lamaism. He also leads a troop of horses. Rub Das is a Gurkha from Sitang, and does all sorts of work; he is silent and works like a slave, without needing the slightest reminder. Tundup Geltsan is the reciter of tales, whose voice is heard when all the day's work is over; he is also chief cook in the black tent of the Ladakis. Namgyal is a mule-driver, and one of our best; Sonam Tsering is overseer of the mules, Kurban nothing but Guffaru's son, and Tsering is my head cook.

Herewith the list closes. Each of these men had his duty to perform; all were willing and good tempered, and quarrels and disputes were never heard. But Robert and Muhamed Isa knew excellently well how to maintain discipline. Every man had a warm sheepskin, and they made themselves bedding of the skins of the slaughtered sheep or the wild animals that were shot; as the winter cold abated they used empty provision sacks as blankets. As they all travelled on foot they soon wore out their soft Ladak boots, and they had to re-sole them repeatedly; for that purpose they utilized pieces of skin with the wool turned inwards.

On October 14 we passed a series of large river-beds

which intersect the ridge to the south along flattish valleys. Kulans and antelopes were grazing in large numbers. At the camp, situated between reddish hills, the grass was good. Our direction was east-south-east. In the night a horse died. The country preserves henceforth the same character: it consists of a number of small ridges extending from east to west, and much time is lost in crossing them; between them lie longitudinal valleys. Not infrequently we can count southwards three or four such ridges, and we have to pass over them all. We have lost ourselves in a sea of rigid undulations; we are like a ship that has lost its rudder and is on the point of sinking: no islands of refuge, no ships coming to meet us, boundless sea on all sides. We should like to pour oil on this rough sea; we long for calm waterways, but as long as a plank remains we will cling fast to it. At camp No. 40 there was good grazing, and water we could obtain from ice.

The men have sewed up a felt coat for the brown puppy, which they put on her when it is cold at night. She looks very ridiculous in her new night-dress when she runs about, steps on a corner, and then rolls over. The white puppy sits at first quite disconcerted and gazes at her, but then finds the sight so alluring that she cannot refrain from making fun of her comrade, dancing about her and biting her cloak. The brown one, on the other hand, sits resolutely quiet and lets the white one sport about her.

We penetrate further into the forbidden land. On October 16, the anniversary of my departure from Stockholm, we had still 380 miles to travel to Dangra-yum-tso, but now were seldom able to march more than 7½ miles a day. In Camp No. 41 (Illustration 65) some articles that we could spare were left behind, to lighten the loads, among them several books that I had read and Bower's narrative, which had now served their turn in my travelling library. The tents were set up in a sheltered valley at the foot of a rock. Tundup Sonam had gone in advance, and had surprised a four-year-old yak which was lying on a slope in the sun. Taking advantage of inequalities in the ground, the sportsman had crept up quite close to it. The first ball had entered the pelvis. The yak, thus unpleasantly aroused from his meditation, sprang up and received a second bullet in his hough. Then he rushed down the slope, turned a somersault on to the bottom of the valley, and lay dead as a mouse; and here, therefore, the tents were pitched. He was already skinned and cut up when we arrived, and the dark-red flesh with a purplish tint at the legs lay in the sun. The stomach was immense, and full of grass, lichen, and moss — no wonder that the animal needed rest after such gourmandizing. The head was set up as a decoration at the foot of a mountain spur, and the hunter was photographed beside this trophy. The Ladakis were ordered to eat their fill of the meat, for we could not burden ourselves with any extra weight. All the fat, however, was taken with us, and the marrow was reserved for me. When we left the place, there was not much left of the yak, and I have my suspicion that the Ladakis carried some fine pieces with them in their private bags.

The ravens, in company with an eagle, sat feasting round the bloody skeleton. Now there are eleven of them, and their wings shine in the sun like blue steel. They feel, alas! quite at home in the caravan and are half tame. The dogs take no notice of them, and are treated by the ravens with sarcastic contempt.

October 17 was a trying day; there was a strong wind from the west, and the temperature did not rise above 23° at noon. We were approaching a pass, but we encamped before reaching the summit. At nine o'clock the thermometer marked 9.3°, and I could make it rise in the tent only to 24.5°, for the little warmth radiating from the brazier was at once driven out by the wind. The minimum thermometer stood at −18.8°, the lowest temperature that we had hitherto recorded. A white mule, which had carried no load for the past ten days, was frozen to death. Now I had 27 mules, 27 horses, and 27 servants in the caravan. We had not seen a man for 57 days. Should we all remain together till we fell in with the first nomads?

Antelopes and yaks were grazing on the slopes of the pass, the height of which is 17,575 feet. A labyrinth of mountains spreads itself out in the direction of our march, and therefore we turn aside to the north-east and encamp in the mouth of a valley. The white puppy, which faithfully follows Robert and myself, is always soundly thrashed by her brown sister when we arrive in camp. She has no hope of defending herself, so she lies quietly on her back as if she were made of papier maché, and does not dare to utter a sound. Now they are both bloated from over-indulgence in yak flesh; but however bad the brown puppy may feel, her little sister must get her licking as soon as she appears.

In the night of October 19 two more of our horses were frozen to death, and a sheep. Of the latter we had now only 16; puffed up with gas the three dead animals lay on the slope and stared at us with dark bloodstained eye-cavities; the ravens had already been at them. The ground was very difficult, constantly sloping upwards and then down again. We saw the caravan struggle up to a pass, but beyond appeared another still higher, with patches of snow. The crests of the mountains in this country run in general to the east-north-east. In the south lies a lake at a distance of about 20 miles, but it is far to the right of our route.

When we reached camp No. 44, at a height of 17,539 feet, in the midst of terrible mountains, it was announced that Muhamed Isa was ill. He had suffered for some days with severe headache, and had been well dosed with quinine. As he could not reconnoitre as usual, Robert asked permission to climb the high pass which barred the way to the east, and to look around. He did not come back till dark, and then informed us that we should soon emerge from these troublesome mountains if we turned to the south-east. Muhamed Isa therefore received instructions for the following day in accordance with this information.

What a difference from the previous evening when the stars twinkled down from a blue-black sky and the fires blazed bright and red! Now heavy masses of cloud lie over mountain and valley, so low that they seem almost within reach of the hand. It snows unusually thickly; the ground is white, and the inequalities and tufts of moss throw long shadows about the fires. A pale light rises out of the provision fortress, now reduced to small dimensions, and casts a feeble glow on the black tent of the Ladakis. Tsering sits with his men round the kitchen fire, wrapped in furs, and delivers a lecture more than two hours long, without pausing a second. His tongue is like a windmill in a breeze. They have all known one another for years. What on earth can he have to tell them that they have not heard already twenty times over? But Rabsang, Rehim Ali, and a couple of other men listen attentively, and express their satisfaction from time to time. I join them for a while. They rise to greet me, and lay a fresh armful of dry dung cakes on the fire. The flickering flames throw a glaring light over the snow, which crunches under the feet of the men. But the brightness does not extend far, and, beyond, the darkness of night yawns on all sides. The grazing animals can neither be seen nor heard, but the snow hisses as it falls continuously into the blaze of the yak-dung fire.

CHAPTER XIII

UNFORTUNATE DAYS

OCTOBER 20, 1906, was a bad day. The snow lay three inches deep, and all around was dazzling white in the sunshine; only to the west blue shadows spread over the slopes. We were to cross the pass. In the universal whiteness the distance seemed short, but after the caravan had advanced half way, the pass still appeared as a small, black, fixed point. The field-mice were awake and scurried about between their holes in the snow, which became deeper as the way became steeper. It was soon a foot deep, and we had to keep carefully in the track of the caravan, lest we should roll over into the snowy abyss. Spots of blood were seen; one of the animals had hurt its foot against the sharp-edged detritus. Step by step we mount upwards, blue-black clouds gather threateningly together behind us, and in an instant we are enveloped in the wildest driving snow: the dry particles, fine as flour, whirl round us, like comet tails, with a rushing sound. They collect into drifts, the track of the caravan is hidden, and we can no longer see how far it is still to this deadly pass.

A dead horse lies on the way, without its eyes — the wicked ravens must always have the eyes while they are still warm and soft. The wind had driven the snow over his back and neck, as though to make him a nice and comfortable couch. He lay as on a bed of state, exposed to all the winds of heaven, with clean white pall, and the black ravens as a guard of honour — the only thanks he got for his services.

On the pass we make the usual halt for observations; the height is 18,409 feet; it blows and snows, with 18 degrees of cold. We perceive, however, some sign of the saddle to the south-east which Robert reconnoitred yesterday, and which is supposed to lead down into level country. But Muhamed Isa has taken his own way down a valley running north-east, and that is serious for us. Far in front as he is, we must, though much against our will, follow his track, lest we should lose one another. It is now difficult to see whither the caravan had marched. If we lose one another in such country, and the snow continues to fall, we are done for.

So we follow him down the valley. The pass behind us looks weird — a white saddle against a background of blue-black clouds, which resemble whirling, suffocating smoke. Tsering reaches the pass with his two men and four horses, and salutes it with a loud salaam. Treacherous frozen rivulets are crossed, as hard as glass and as smooth as cooling grease; our riding horses stumble and slide. It is very seldom that a small hill of dark schist peeps out above the snow.

As the valley runs too much to the north, the caravan perceives its mistake, turns aside to the east, and buries itself in a labyrinth of hills where not a blade of grass grows. We ride past the shepherd with the 16 sheep and the goats; the white puppy teases them as usual, till a bold wether puts her to flight. The goats are remarkably hardy and get on splendidly, and yield me a cup of milk every morning and evening.

We found the caravan behind a second saddle. The camp was formed, but in a most unfavourable spot; there was neither grass nor *yapkak*, neither dung nor water — absolutely nothing. The animals stood in a dark group, standing out sharply against the white snow. Thus they had to stand, quietly and patiently, all night long, and doubtless felt how slowly the time passed, how hunger and thirst increased, and the cold again diminished. They had to wait standing for the morning red, which might perhaps fail to appear, for dark masses of cloud still covered the sky.

Robert and I took refuge in the tent of the Ladakis, where a fire burned, which was fed with fragments of a box and antelope dung. We could at any rate obtain water by melting snow; my dinner consisted of parched meal, bread, and coffee, for nothing else could be cooked. In the twilight Rabsang appeared and asked me to come outside. Two large wild yaks stood on a neighbouring hill and gazed at our camp with astonishment. But we left them in peace, for we did not want their flesh, and would not add to our loads. They trotted slowly away when they were convinced that we were not of their species. The night was pitch dark, so that I had to inspect our weary beasts with a lantern.

We set out early from this unlucky camp, where a mule had fallen at his post. The footprints between the tents, made in the snow the evening before, were filled up with fresh snow, and a new set of paths had been formed. Scarcely two minutes' walk from the camp a horse lay dead, which had carried his load only the day before, and the black corpse-watch was beside it. A dead wild-duck also lay in the snow. Is there a lake in the neighbourhood? No; the ducks come long distances, and this one had probably lost its way.

Now the sun burns, now a snowstorm envelops us in its fine dust, now we are roasted, now chilled through—regular Tibetan weather, unreliable and changeable. Another dead horse! The men had cut its throat to shorten its sufferings; swiftly whirling snow covers the stream of blood that congeals in the cold. We make our way up to a pass, and then follow a ridge, but the ground is frightful. At length we ride down a flat valley which gradually winds round to the north; on the south rises a formidable crest. Muhamed Isa had orders to take, if possible, a south-easterly direction, but as he was not sure of the way, he had encamped at the bend of the road. He had gone forwards with two men to reconnoitre. Towards four o'clock he returned, and reported that we should reach open country within three hours. My first thought was to set out at once, for in camp No. 46 there was no grass, and the animals were so hungry that they bit one another's tails and the pack-saddles. One horse had actually not a hair left on his tail, but that one had been eaten up the night before. The old, experienced hands, however, gave their opinion that it would be better to start in the early morning.

I therefore gave orders to reserve as much rice as we should require for forty days, and to give the rest, mixed with barley and maize, to the animals. While, however, they were eating from their nose-bags, the men changed their minds, and Muhamed Isa asked if they might make a start.

"I am quite willing, but it will be pitch dark in an hour."

"I will find the way. You have only to follow the trail in the snow."

Then began the tumult of breaking up camp, and the sound of tramping in the snow; but there was no singing. There were 27 degrees of frost with a boisterous wind from the west. Everything was taken except my things and Robert's and the cooking utensils. A mule, which refused to move, remained with us. No fires lighted up the dark procession led by the horses and closed by the sheep. It moved off slowly, and the shouts of the men reached us more and more feebly till at length the caravan disappeared in the pale moonlight. I entered my tent stiff with cold. A quarter of an hour later a man came back with another mule which could not get on any further. So we had two dying animals with us.

And then came the night. The air was clear and calm, the stars twinkled like diamonds in the brightness of electric light, and the cold settled keenly round our tent. Outside, Tsering, Rabsang, Rehim Ali, and Bolu had rolled themselves together into a heap under all their belongings. As long as I was awake I heard the irrepressible Tsering telling his tales in the depth of his cave of furs, and the others occasionally giving vent to a subterranean giggle. Curious fellows, these Ladakis! No amount of cold seems to affect them, while I, in my tent, can only sleep a minute at a time.

An awful, terrible night in the lonely mountains of

Tibet. The temperature sank to $-17°$, and that was too much for the two mules which had been left behind. One expired about midnight; he was the animal which Sonam Tsering had wished on the first day to send back to Leh as useless. We tried then to exchange him for a horse, but as no one would have him, he had to come with us after all. He was accustomed to travel with horses, and later on always went with them. To the astonishment of all he became strong and led the van — a good example for the horses. Now he lay cold and hard as iron, with his legs stretched out; if he had been lifted on to his feet he would have remained standing. Sonam Tsering wept when he heard that the animal was gone.

The other mule was heard moving about in the night and nibbling at the yak grass, which is too short for other animals except the yak; the tongue of the yak is provided with horny barbs which pluck up the fine velvety grass. Early in the morning I heard the mule squeal, and was glad that one at least still survived. But when the sun rose his strength too was spent, and when Tsering woke me he said that the animal was dying. He looked healthy and well nourished, but we tried in vain to raise him up and feed him with maize, and he was sacrificed to the gods of this valley of death. He did not move a limb or twitch an eyelid as the blood spurted out on to the snow; he seemed only to experience a welcome sense of peace and resignation, while his eyes were turned full on the sun.

As we were on the point of leaving this horrible camp, there came fresh tidings of misfortune. Tundup Sonam appeared to show us the way, and reported that the horse caravan had wandered off too far to the left, while the mules under Muhamed Isa had taken the opposite direction. Muhamed Isa, as soon as he found out his mistake, had descended into the first valley he could find, to wait there for the dawn. As for the flock of sheep, Tundup Sonam could only say that it had at first followed the track of the horses, but had afterwards turned away. The greatest confusion reigned everywhere, but the worst news Tundup Sonam kept to the last: four more mules had died during the night.

Our situation was desperate. We could not go on much longer; we were coming to a crisis. The ground, the weather, and the cold were all against us, the horses died wholesale, and it might be a hopeless distance to the nearest nomads. What did it matter whether the Tibetans would be friendly or hostile? Now the only question was: should we be able to drag ourselves along to inhabited districts? For, if these losses continued a few days longer, we should soon be compelled to abandon all the baggage and continue our journey on foot. But could we carry ourselves enough provisions to last us through this uninhabited country? Should we perish one after another in these icy deserts of the Tibetan Alps? And if at length, in a wretched, half-dead condition, we met with Tibetans, they could do what they liked with us. At any rate we could not force our way through to Shigatse and the unknown country to the north of the Tsangpo, the goal of all my most cherished dreams.

A journey straight across Tibet looks pleasant and easy on the map. In reality it is a serious and difficult undertaking, costing suffering, excitement, and tears. The meandering line is drawn in red on the map, for it is really marked with blood. We set out under the guidance of Tundup Sonam, and it soon became evident that we should never have found the way without him. Up and down, over hills and through valleys we threaded this intricate maze, where the deep snow smoothed down the inequalities and quite misled us in estimating the heights of the steep declivities. We left the track of the horses on our left; there a load of maize was left, but Tundup Sonam assured me it would be fetched. To the right appeared the high ground where the mules had wandered in the night trying their strength uselessly. An icy south-west wind blew over the bitterly cold snowfields. From time to time Tundup Sonam reared up a slab of schist to show the way to Tsering, who was coming behind without a guide.

Now we cross the trail of the mules and see the valley where they have passed the night. "Yonder, on the slope, lies a mule," says Tundup Sonam, "and two behind the hill, and a little farther on a fourth." We could not see them from where we were, but the ravens resting here, sleepy and satiated, confirmed his words.

At last we reached the pass, whence we caught sight of the plain and a small lake to the south-east. The height was 18,048 feet. At one o'clock there were 18 degrees of frost, the wind was high, and it snowed so thickly that the view disappeared again. We did not stay a minute longer than was necessary for observations, and then rode down a steep descent. We rested at the first grass we came to; the horses were almost mad with delight when they saw it — their stomachs were so empty.

Now we saw five men on a height. They were Muhamed Isa and four companions, who had come out to look for the missing men and animals — 14 horses, 8 men, 16 sheep, and 2 dogs. We were able to inform them that their track ran north-eastwards, and after they had given directions how to find the camping-ground of the mules they vanished again in the snow. After searching in vain for the track and looking out for the smoke of the camp-fire, we came to a halt on a smooth plateau, where the grazing was good, and collected dung for a fire — it was high time, for Robert and I were half dead with cold.

We were in a terribly sad plight. We did not know where the mules were encamping, and had not the slightest notion where the horses had gone. The sheep, in this country swarming with wolves, were probably lost. Tsering had remained behind, and might easily miss our track in the snowstorm. We could do nothing but thaw our clothes. After we had been sitting an hour, and had somewhat recovered in the heat of the fire, the "Lama" came over the plain bringing with him Sonam Tsering, who had been camping with the mules behind some hills. The good fellow wept bitterly at our losses; Muhamed Isa had proved a bad pilot this time, he complained. Nine mules had perished within a few hours in these frightful mountains, which were probably the western prolongation of the system called by the Mongols, dwelling farther to the east, Buka-magna, or the "Head of the Wild Yak." Twenty mules still remained, but two of them had received their death-warrant. Of the twenty-three surviving horses one was left behind with his pack-saddle in a hollow, and was probably dead by this time. At a late hour of the night only one of the missing ones, namely, Tsering, had put in an appearance.

Under these circumstances it was a matter of course that we should have a day's rest in camp No. 47. When day broke, I was awakened by the bleating of sheep. The shepherd had at first followed the track of the horses, but soon abandoned it when he noticed that the mules were not there, and he began to look for the track of the latter. In the darkness he got completely lost, and in a pass one of the sheep had refused to go any farther. He had carried it awhile, but as he soon felt that it had become cold and stiff he threw it away as dead. Frightened of the darkness and the wolves, he had taken refuge in a gorge, tied together the sheep and goats in a circle, and set himself in the middle to keep himself warm and look out for the wolves. However, they had not ventured to attack him. In the morning twilight he had found one of the many tracks leading to camp No. 47.

Two of the missing men turned up in the forenoon, carrying boxes. A horse had been left behind. Islam Ahun, who had led the horse caravan, had cleverly conducted them down by the shortest way to the lake, and had encamped there beside good pasture. Muhamed Isa and his companions had lost themselves in the night, and had slept beside a fire, with nothing to eat or drink but snow. But they, too, found their way to us again, and so the remnants of the caravan were gathered together to one place.

Here everything was sorted out that could be spared: sacks, bags, ropes, horse-shoes, tools, and cooking utensils. Boxes were burned after their contents had been transferred to others; no one was allowed to burden the caravan with unnecessary articles. The rejected goods formed a large heap, and we thus got rid of two horse loads. Then we took stock, and found that we had still 32 loads including the boat. We had 20 mules, of which 2 were on their last legs, and 21 horses also, including 2 ready to drop, or 37 serviceable animals in all. Only Robert and I were allowed to ride, so that we had 3 spare horses; but in the evening the loads were so distributed that all the animals carried something, except the sickly ones. Four animals were to be laden with maize and barley, the rice made seven loads more, the meal five, the bread one, and the butter, which the Ladakis took in their tea, only half a load. We estimated that the meal would last a month longer; five loads of rice were to be given up to the animals, and I directed all the men to take the greatest care of the veterans. Tundup Sonam shot three antelopes just when our meat was finished. Some of the Ladakis had to cut them up, and at even when they returned with the spoil they intoned the antiphonal song they sing when they carry a *dandy*, or an ordinary load, at home in Ladak. One of the antelopes, however, was all devoured by the wolves before they found it.

We decided to rest a couple of days at the next camp, and Tundup Sonam undertook to conduct us to a small lake lying to the east, where the grass was particularly good.

In the night of October 24 a horse and two mules died, so we had 38 animals. "The strongest are still living," said Muhamed Isa as usual.

To the north rose the lofty mountain system which had caused us so much suffering, and its crests were seen stretching to the east. We advanced over even ground, and after a short march reached a small round lake firmly frozen over, and surrounded by yellow grassland. Water was supplied by a spring which filled a small frozen basin; the animals drank as much as they would from a hole cut through the ice; they had had no water for three days. The sandy soil was frozen so hard that the iron tent-pegs bent when they were driven into the ground. The sky was overcast, and there was a strong wind, but the ground to the east-south-east seemed favourable. The four tents stood in a row, mine to windward, that I might not be annoyed by the smoke of the other fires.

At ten o'clock at night a flock of wild geese passed over our camp in the brilliant, silvery-white moonshine.

They flew very low, and quacked the whole time. Probably they intended to settle at the spring, but went on when they found the place occupied. "There is plenty of light, and in a short time we shall be at the next spring." Such, we may suppose, was the gist of the conversation between the leading goose and the others. No doubt it had given its orders at sunset, remarking: "To-night we will stay at the spring on the shore of the small lake, where we rested last spring." All were agreed, and the flock, flying in a wedge, had gradually dipped lower towards the ground. But when they had passed over the hills which concealed the spot from view, and saw the frozen lake glancing like a mirror in the moonshine, the leading goose called out, "Men! we cannot stay so near to tents and fires. Up again, and onwards." And all the flock answered: "We can rest at the next spring in the valley behind the hills to the south." That was the conversation I heard above my tent when all was quiet in the camp. Perhaps the lively chatter was about something else, but I think that I interpreted the wild geese correctly. For it is quite certain that they hold consultations on their long journeys, and discuss their plans. And why should they not be endowed with intelligence? Why should they speed away at random like soulless flying-machines? They are just as dependent as ourselves on the earth and winds. If they can cover 120 miles on a clear, calm day, they must take a longer time over the same distance when storm and contrary winds prevail. Therefore they cannot every year pass the nights at the same springs, but must adapt their arrangements to circumstances. But the wild geese know every spring along the course they follow twice a year, and when they are tired they settle at the first they come to. On my travels in various parts of Tibet I have come to the conclusion that the same parties or tribes of wild geese, which have for generations bred at the same watercourses, follow always the same routes through Tibet. The geese which we saw on this occasion came, let us say, from one of the lakes along the Tarim river below Shah-yar, and intended to spend the winter in the neighbourhood of Khatmandu, the capital of Nepal. In spring they return to the Tarim lakes, and follow exactly the same course as in autumn, and so on from year to year. The young ones, which are born on the Tarim, make the journey over the mountains for the first time in autumn, but they remember the way in the following autumn, and afterwards the time comes when they in turn teach their young ones the position of the sources. Thus the knowledge of the route is never lost in the family, and the leading geese would never dream of trying any other course. We had already on several occasions seen wild geese flying southwards, but they had certainly taken other roads, come from other breeding-places, and had other destinations. They belonged to other tribes. If it were possible to draw on a map of Tibet all the tracks of the various tribes of geese, they would form a whole system of lines running more or less in a meridional direction. Perhaps many of these lines would in parts merge into one another like the fine ripples on the surface of a sand-dune. Perhaps now and then a line runs in sharp zigzags. It may then be taken for granted that it was thus drawn in the most remote antiquity when the patriarchs of each tribe first sought out the way from one spring to another. Each tribe is divided into a number of communities, and each of these into families. Probably all the geese of one community are closely related to one another. Each community remains together on the journey, but how do they choose a leader? It may be supposed that the oldest goose flies at the head of the flock, for it must be the most experienced, and if it dies the next oldest is its natural successor. I am fond of the wild geese, and admire their intelligence and their wonderful bump of locality; we shall hereafter come into closer contact with them.

In camp 48 we remained fully three days inactive, and the south wind howled continuously: "Patience! Patience!" To us the days seemed very long, but the animals must have rest. On the first morning horse No. 39 lay dead on the ground, and was entered with the same number in the list of the dead.

The wolves were impudent, and howled just outside

our camp, but they were more polite after Tundup had shot a brute, which ran off on to the ice, and lay down to die in the middle of the lake. The scoundrel soon had as companion a raven, which had taken into his head to peck the manes of the living horses and disturb them while grazing. At nine o'clock in the evening the thermometer indicated $-6°$, and in the night $-18\frac{1}{2}°$.

In the morning Muhamed Isa reported that the dung-gatherers had discovered something which they described as ruins of stone houses. Robert and I went at once to look at them. We found that there actually were three quadrangular walls constructed of slabs of schist, probably of very ancient date. They rose but just above the ground, and on digging we discovered that they went down fully 3 feet. Probably they had been constructed only as foundations and wind screens for permanent tents, for such walls were afterwards met with on several occasions. There was no trace of a hearth. The Ladakis, who had travelled much in west Tibet, thought that the place had once been the permanent abode of some Changpas who had wished to avoid paying taxes to the Devashung, or the Government in Lhasa.

At any rate this discovery had a very encouraging effect on us. We had not seen men for 65 days, and now we found the first sign indicating their proximity. We felt invigorated, and the tale-teller in Muhamed Isa's tent in the evening was longer winded than ever. He sang a song, all joining in the chorus. Now we must keep a sharp look-out in the country before us, for this first sign of man must surely be succeeded by others.

The caravan moved on towards the east-south-east on October 28 in a very violent south-west storm. A mule had died in the night, and so we had 36 baggage animals, but since the last inspection the provisions had diminished by nearly three loads. In this camp, also, superfluous articles were left behind. I threw away *Sonja*, by Blicher-Clausen. Robert and I sat at the morning fire, while the men saddled the horses, and I amused myself by tearing out one leaf of the book after another and throwing the whole collection into the air, where the wind swept the flying leaves with tremendous velocity to the north-east. The ten ravens puzzled their heads as to what new species of flying creatures they could be, but made little effort to get out of their way, and the dogs soon gave up the attempt to pursue the leaves; but one of Tsering's pack-horses was so alarmed that it shied, broke loose, and rushed up the hills, and was not caught again for a good half hour. Meanwhile Sonja swept on, fluttering over mountain and valley, much to my satisfaction, for I had felt annoyed the evening before because she left her good-hearted husband. When and where would these leaves come to rest after flying over endless stretches of unknown country? Certainly a book has seldom had so wide a distribution.

We follow the track of the caravan in an open, flat valley between low mountains. After riding some hours we were so perished that we had to make a halt in a hollow way and light a fire. My small white Ladak horse was in excellent condition; he treated the cold and other disagreeable incidents with philosophical calmness. The tall dapple-grey which I had ridden from Leh was usually off duty, for he showed symptoms of exhaustion. At this day's camp there was no water, only snow in a cleft of the mountain. Yet we were in very high spirits, for the men had seen fireplaces built of three stones laid crossways, which were intended to hold a kettle. It must have been a long time, however, since they were used, for neither ash nor soot was seen among them. An iron ladle, too, was found, such as the Tibetans use to melt lead for bullets. So either robbers or hunters must have halted here sometime or other.

83. THE AUTHOR, ROBERT, AND REHIM ALI ATTACKED BY A WOUNDED YAK.

CHAPTER XIV

IN THE LAND OF THE WILD YAK

WE broke up our camp on the morning of October 29, after a night of 49 degrees of frost, at an early hour, so as to find water for our thirsty animals as soon as possible. A small lake and two springs we passed were frozen as hard as rock; beside one lay the skull of a yak, which had evidently had its throat cut with a knife; we also saw two fireplaces on the way, and at camp No. 50 a path, which, however, might have been worn by wild yaks. We therefore were no doubt coming near to other men, and we were always on the look-out for tents.

Next day the storm increased in strength, and it was only with the greatest effort of will that I could use my hands for map-sketching. We seemed paralyzed and could no longer think clearly. We were like the field-mice, which run from one hole to another seeking to find shelter from the wind and cold.

On arriving at a spring I slipped down wearily from my horse, and thought I should be frozen before the fire was kindled. Muhamed Isa, also, and four other men, were ill, and could not assist in setting up the tents. When my tent was ready, I crept into bed in my clothes, boots and all. While Robert and Tsering were covering me up with warm wraps I was seized with violent ague, my teeth chattered, and my head ached terribly. Robert, who had been trained in nursing in Dr. Arthur Neve's school, now proved an excellent doctor, and took every care of me. As soon as we were under cover he plunged into the study of Burroughs and Wellcome's medical instructions.

The Tabloid Brand Medicine Chest stood open, as frequently happened, in my tent. Stanley, Emin Pasha, Jackson, Scott, and many other travellers have prized this ideal travelling dispensary as highly as myself. My case, a present from the English firm, had been filled with especial regard to the climate of Tibet.

At ten o'clock at night Robert and Tsering undressed me. There were 47.9 degrees of frost in the night, and the storm howled dreadfully. Robert took my temperature every two hours, and it rose to 106½°, high-fever mark. As he told me after, he pondered whatever he was to do if I remained for good at camp No. 51. I could not sleep, and Robert and Tsering watched beside my bed in turn; glowing lumps of fuel were brought in all through the night, and a burning candle was placed behind a box, where it was protected from wind and draught. I was constantly delirious and the men were much concerned, for they had never seen me ill before.

Next day the fever had slightly abated, when Muhamed Isa slipped gently into my tent to inquire how the Sahib was. He informed us that the wounded yak was dead, and that, in cutting it up, two Tibetan bullets had been found; also at three places hearths had been seen, which could not be more than two months old, for ashes still lay among the stones. So hunters had been here in autumn, and he was quite convinced that we should soon meet with the first nomads.

It was still as the grave, only the storm howled and moaned. All the men in the camp were afraid of disturbing me, but I gave orders in the evening that they should sing as usual. I could not lift an arm without help, and I lay hour after hour watching the curious lights in the tent. Within, the stearin candle emitted a dull light, and the yellowish-red blaze of the fire and the bluish moonlight penetrated from without. The singing sounded melancholy and wistful, and was accompanied by the howling of the storm.

On November 2 the storm still raged, having now continued to the sixth day. I had slept a few hours, though the cold sank to 52° below freezing-point. I was getting a little better, but I was still extremely weak. Robert, who was troubled because his horse had died in the night, read to me one of the novels we had stolen from Deasy's depôt. Tsering and Rehim Ali massaged me in the Asiatic manner to restore my strength. And so we arrived at the fourth evening. I had been confined to my bed for four-and-eighty hours, the soil of Tibet seemed determined to keep me, and perhaps I should be allowed only to dream of the forbidden land at a distance.

Surely on November 3 the god of the winds must have said to the westerly storm, "Six days shalt thou labour — on the seventh thou shalt become a hurricane." Dust and sand penetrated the thin canvas and covered everything in the tent. The men, who had led the animals to water, had rings of dust round their eyes, and their faces were ashy grey. For my part I felt like one of our poor worn-out brutes, which does not know whether he will reach the next camp. Then I decided to remain here with some of the men and some provisions, while Robert and Muhamed Isa went in search of natives, whom they might send to fetch me. But no; I would try to hold myself in the saddle, for I did not wish to remain in this miserable fever-camp. I wore a whole wardrobe of winter clothes: several trousers, my leather jersey, the ulster, fur coat, cap, and *bashlik*; it was a heavy weight for my weak, tottering legs as I walked to my horse and was lifted into the saddle.

We followed the shore of the small lake near our camp. But I soon perceived, after nearly falling again and again, that the exertion was too much for me, so we halted and lighted a fire. After a short rest we rode on, and were delighted when at length we saw the smoke of our caravan rising behind a hill, where it had camped by a source and had found fireplaces erected last summer, with skulls and horns of tame sheep around them. Yak dung was very plentiful; the source was, therefore, a watering-place of wild yaks. A third of the men were really ill, most of them suffered from headache, and all were more or less indisposed. Robert alone was in good health, and he nursed us.

On November 5 the tracks of men became more frequent. A yak's skeleton lay beside a hearth, and the ashes piled up among the stones could not have been cold longer than the day before. We climbed up troublesome hills and then descended into a gully leading down to a large valley begirt with fiery red heights. A number of excavations, each with a heap of sand beside it, attracted our attention. The sand contained gold, so not ordinary nomads but gold-seekers had been here, probably every summer, to dig for gold.

In the lower part of the valley warm springs burst forth with a temperature of 57°, so that the water seems quite hot. A few yards farther, however, it forms a large sheet of ice.

In the next valley, a hollow between precipitous terraced slopes, a huge wild yak lay dead on the ground with twelve of our men standing round it. Tundup Sonam had surprised a whole herd which had come down into the valley to drink. The other animals had torn up the valley in headlong flight, but this one, struck by a bullet, had made for the hunter, and Tundup clambered up the edge of a terrace only just in time. The yak remained at the foot, uncertain what to do, and received a second shot in the heart.

I photographed him from several points of view before he was skinned. It was not easy to raise him into a suitable posture; the twelve men had to put forth all their strength. The raven-black coat of the beast formed a strong contrast to the red soil; his long side fringes serve him as a mattress when he lies down (Illustrations 68, 69).

On November 7 we skirted a lake; to the right we had steep mountains with disagreeable cones of sharp-edged débris. Two troops of fine Ammon sheep, numbering nine and five respectively, skipped with bold leaps over the smooth abrupt rocks. Large numbers of hares were seen, and frequently the holes of marmots where the inmates were still hibernating. Two Tibetan cairns proved to us that we were on the right way, that is, the one the gold-diggers use.

Now we leave this part of the mountains on the right, and proceed along the southern, open and extensive plain

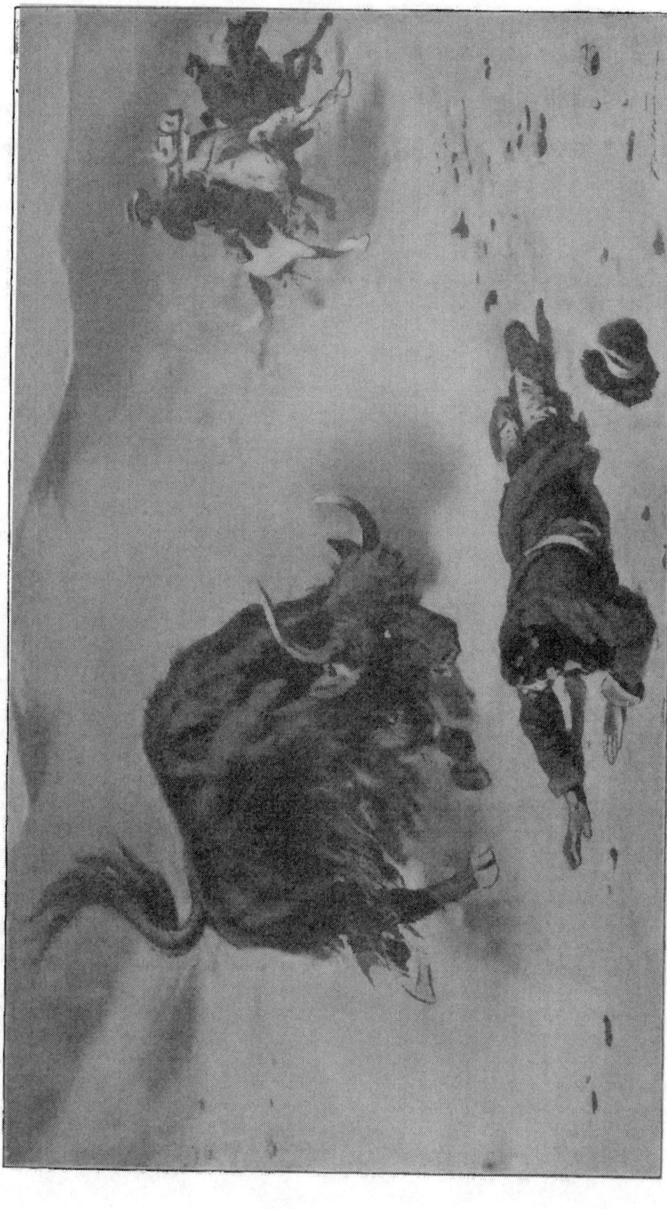

84. Rehim Ali falls to the Ground and thus rescues us from the Furious Yak.

by the lake shore. There grazed a herd of perhaps fifty yaks. Twenty antelopes, probably frightened by the caravan, scampered away with elastic springs like the shadow of clouds moving over the earth. Soon the tents and all the details of camp No. 56 could be clearly distinguished, and we had only a few minutes' march more, when even this short distance would have been too far for one of us, if fate had so willed.

For close beside the tents, near our animals, a large black yak appeared. Rehim Ali drew our attention to it, but we took no farther notice of it. I took my last bearing of the tent, and was in the act of laying down the ground on my map-sheet, when a shot cracked from Muhamed Isa's tent, and the yak, evidently hit, rushed madly northwards. We followed him with our eyes, expecting to see him fall. But no; he turned and came running wildly towards us. Rehim Ali's face was contorted with frantic fright, and he raised his hands to heaven, crying out, "Allah, Allah, we are lost!" The brute drew near in a cloud of dust, his fringes waved and flew about, and he lowered his horns for a rush. I did not move, for I thought that he had not seen us and would turn back again, but he held on his way and grew larger to the sight. Rehim Ali ran screaming to the tents, but suddenly turned round, and as our horses took fright and galloped off, he caught hold of the tail of Robert's steed, hoping to follow us at a run. The wild chase swept quicker and quicker over the plain, and the yak changed his course and made a circuit towards us in a mad rage. His breath rose like clouds of steam from his nostrils, his muzzle almost grazed the ground—he was ready to catch his victim on his horns, toss him into the air, and stamp him to a jelly under his forefeet. Nearer and nearer I heard him, panting and gasping like a steam saw. Turning in my saddle I saw him about twenty yards off, his small, fierce eyes blazing with fury and madness and rolling so as to show the blood-stained whites. It was a question of a second. I rode straight to the right; my horse and I would be the first to be caught on the horns of the yak. Now the horses stretched their legs like bow-strings. I tore off my red *bashlik* and waved it behind me to attract the yak and stop him, but he did not look at it. Then I tore my belt off in order to take off my fur coat and throw it over the yak's eyes and blind him, just when he was on the point of thrusting his horns into the belly of the horse and stiffening the muscles of his neck for the toss. A second more and the yak would hoist the horse, break my back, and trample on my chest — I seemed to hear the cracking and breaking of my ribs, and I well deserved it, for it was my fault alone that all the animals left behind us had to suffer so much. Then was heard a heart-rending cry of despair. As I turned quickly round, I saw Rehim Ali with uplifted arms fall senseless to the ground, and the yak turn and rush at him. He remained prostrate, a lifeless mass, and I saw the yak, with lowered horns, and his purple tongue hanging far out of his mouth, dash down upon him in a cloud of dust. Now all the horses made off, and I had some difficulty to keep my seat on my grey Ladaki. When I looked round again, a second later, the yak was running up the valley with his dust cloud about him.

"Turn back and see if there is still a spark of life in Rehim Ali, and if he can still be saved," I called out.

"Master, it is too dangerous, the yak is still near, and may come back. Muhamed Isa and all the rest are running out of the camp to look after Rehim Ali."

But I had already turned, and I rode to the fallen man. He lay dead on his face with arms outstretched — both Robert and I thought, at any rate, that he was dead. But when we had dismounted beside him he slowly turned his head, and with a look of horror waved his hand, as much as to say: "Do not trouble about me, I am dead as a mouse." We could not repress a smile when, turning him over like a joint at the fire, we examined his bones and joints, and found that the fellow was still sound, though severely bruised. The yak had trodden upon the inner side of the left shank, where a bloody stripe showed the mark of his hoof.

Two strong men bore the fallen hero to Muhamed Isa's tent, where he was well tended by Robert. He seemed stupefied for several days, and we feared that his adventure had affected his brain. He did not eat or speak, and had to travel on horseback, and one of his fellow-countrymen was told off to attend on him After some time, when his head was clear again, he was able to tell us his impressions. When he saw the yak preparing to attack my horse, he turned round and threw himself flat on the ground. Perhaps irritated by the red and violet *chapkan* floating about in the air, the yak left me, made an unexpected change of front, and rushed with lowered horns on the fallen man. He had half unconsciously made a quick movement to one side, and the horns had struck the ground instead of entering his body, and so close beside his head that Rehim Ali felt the panting breath of the brute in his face. Then he lost consciousness, and did not revive till we came up, and then he thought that the yak was on him again. He had intended to save himself by this manœuvre, and thereby had become our deliverer. After the adventures he had taken part in lately he had an immense horror of Tibetan lakes and wild yaks (Illustrations 83, 84).

Temperature — 16½° on the night of November 28. One would expect that the temperature would fall with the advance of winter, but it remains constant, owing in great measure to our progress southwards. Beyond a small pass we came to a new longitudinal valley, where the country was open towards the south-east. Game was abundant, spoors crossed one another in all directions, and two bold yaks awakened in us greater respect than before. At six places we saw large herds of wild asses, and antelopes grazed on the plains. We lost a mule here, and had now 16 animals of both kinds.

Another day's journey across flat country. We were traversing the large white patch of unknown land, and were approaching Bower's route at an acute angle, though we were still rather far east of it. A wild yak ran across our path, and we wondered if it were our enemy of the previous day. Where we pitched our camp, No. 58, we found some hearths which could not be more than a couple of days old. Our excitement and eagerness increased day by day; now the uttermost margin of inhabited Tibet could not be far distant. As I let my eyes rove over these red or black, snow-capped or bare crests, I could fancy I could perceive a whole host of dancing notes of interrogation, some in fantastic draperies, mocking us because we had ventured without an escort into the forbidden land, others motioning us onwards, but all doubtful and speculative. Step by step, day by day, with failing strength, we approached the solution of all these questions. Any moment a troop of mounted men might appear on the horizon, bringing orders from the Devashung that we must immediately evacuate the country and retire northwards.

I was still convalescent, went to bed at seven o'clock, and was not much the better for it, for I always felt terribly languid. Tsering was very despondent because I did so little honour to his cooking. "How can the Sahib regain his strength if he eats so little?" he used to remind me. He was a comical fellow, Tsering, as he marched day after day with his stick in his hand at the head of his detachment, self-conscious and pompous as a chanticleer.

Late at night we heard the dismal, long-drawn howling of wolves close at hand. We could tell from the wild complaining tone that hunger had made the brutes bolder and that the odour of fresh meat excited them. They were on the other side of the source, and Tundup Sonam stole off to scare them away by firing into the troop, though there was small chance of hitting one in the darkness. The brutes retired, but in the night chased our animals, which scampered off to the north as though there were a fire behind them. But the men followed their trail, and found them at dawn a good day's journey from the camp.

On November 10 we had good ground again, and saw to the east-south-east a lake which looked like a bright white ring, the middle being deep blue. Near this day's camp, No. 59, were clear traces of a man who had driven five tame yaks to the lake. The footprints were at most three days old, and excited a great stir in the caravan. We were undoubtedly close to human dwellings, and I thought with regret of the interval of nearly three months during which we had no cause to dread hostile tribes. We held a council of war: should we as long as possible avoid contact with men, and keep out of the way of their tents, so that we need not turn back until further progress became quite impossible? Or should we seek out the nearest nomads at once, and beg them for assistance? At this moment Tundup Sonam ran up out of breath. He had been scouting to the west and had descried a black tent. I immediately sent him to it with two other men, and gave them a handful of rupees. But the news they brought from this first meeting with human beings was not particularly interesting.

The tent was inhabited by a woman and her three children. She had come from the district of Gertse in the south-west, and had covered the distance in twenty-five short days' marches. She had arrived seventeen days before with her two husbands, but both had returned a few days ago to Gertse, after they had filled the tent for her with wild-ass meat. She was daily expecting her parents, who were to keep her company for three months, during which time they would live on game — yaks, kiangs, and antelopes. She owned a few yaks and a small flock of sheep, which she and the oldest child tended and milked. The inside of the tent was very wretched, but a warm fire burned in the centre. She knew that four more tents were standing in a neighbouring valley. When Tundup Sonam told her that we were a party of Ladakis on a pilgrimage to the holy places, she replied that we had chosen a very bad route, and would have done better to take a more southern road where there were men. Her geographical knowledge was limited. The country in which we were now she called Gomo-selung. The gold placers we had passed lay in the La-shung country, and the lake at camp No. 55 she called La-shung-tso. My servants, who had already been in Tibet, held that this information was reliable, for they had heard the names before.

Now, then, the ice was broken. After seventy-nine days of complete isolation from the outer world, some of our men, at least, had seen human beings. But other connections would soon follow this lonely woman, this daughter of the wilderness, this real lady of the mountains, and again we discussed the line of policy we must adopt. The woman dwelt alone, and no news of our approach could be conveyed through her instrumentality to the south. We could, then, take the matter for the present quite coolly as heretofore, and when we were surrounded on all sides by nomads, among whom reports are rapidly dispersed, we must then think of hastening our movements.

We granted the animals a day's rest, for the pasturage was good, and it was pleasant to spend this day under canvas. The storm whistled and howled through the grass and round the stones. Everything that was light and loose was blown away, and the ground was swept clean. The sky was cloudless and the air clear, the wild commotion was only in the layer of air close to the ground, and the important part played by the wind in the deformation of the surface was evident; in such a storm huge masses of material must be removed from their original position.

In the night the storm ceased all of a sudden, and it became so still all at once that I awoke. It was as though we had encamped by a waterfall which in an instant ceased to roar. One starts up and wonders what has happened, but one soon becomes accustomed to the stillness, and finds the absence of the noise and the draught a relief.

85, 86. The First Tibetans.

CHAPTER XV

THE FIRST NOMADS

SAD news again on the morning of November 12: two of our best horses were dead, and a third, which had carried two boxes, made in Stockholm, all the way from Leh, was at the point of death. All three had been sound on the preceding evening, and they died with exactly the same symptoms. They became giddy, lost control of their legs, fell down, and were unable to get up again. I hoped to rescue the remnants of my caravan, and was already thinking of the time when I could lead the poor beasts to mangers in Shigatse full of sweet-smelling clover, and now those that we had reckoned the strongest had broken down. Now only 13 horses were left, and the loads would soon be too heavy for the survivors.

But it had not come to that yet, for this day, which commenced so sadly, brought us joy before the sun went down. Following the track of the caravan we rode among hills, and saw below us camp No. 60 in a deep valley. I had just entered my tent when Muhamed Isa announced that Tundup Sonam was coming from the upper valley in the company of two Tibetans, one mounted, the other on foot. Timorous, and doubtful whether Tundup Sonam had allured them to a robber band, the Tibetans laid their long clumsy guns on the ground and came forward cautiously. Tundup had needed all the fascinations of his eloquence to induce them to come with him. He had told them that we were pilgrims accompanying an eminent lama from Ladak to the holy places. Then they had answered that they would come and show their reverence for His Holiness, and bring with them a sheep's stomach full of butter, and another with goat's milk, as a testimony of their deep respect. Muhamed Isa, who was accustomed to deal with Tibetans, allayed their fears, taking them into his tent and talking and joking with them. Then they were brought to me, and they laid their presents on the ground, fell on their knees, put out their tongues, and made a low obeisance. Instead of a holy man they found a European, but seemed by no means displeased with the change. Muhamed Isa acted as interpreter. They must first give us information on the geography of the country and the character of the land through which our route lay. The information received from the lady of the mountains was confirmed in every respect, and they told us that we should meet with no men for several days, but after that should pass black tents daily.

Our guests might be fifty and forty years old respectively. The elder was quite a typical specimen, more like an ape than a man; the younger looked as though he had already met with many adventures, and he would have passed very well for a robber chief (Illustrations 85, 86).

The conversation now commenced may have little intrinsic interest, but to us in our condition it was as exciting as a tale — our salvation was involved.

"How long is it by the nearest way to Shigatse?"

"Four long, or five short, days' march."

"Will you guide us?"

"Yes, if we are paid to do so."

"How much do you want?"

"That the Bombo Chimbo (great chief) shall decide himself."

"Have you any horses you can sell us?"

"We have two, but we will not sell them."

"Have you any yaks for sale?"

"Yes, we will sell five, if we get 20 rupees for each."

"Will you give us some of your sheep?"

"You may have six, if you will pay 4 rupees a head."

"Good. Bring all the animals you are ready to sell, and if we are satisfied with them you shall be well paid."

"The Bombo Chimbo must remain here till to-morrow if we are to do this."

It was then agreed that we should remain. But I knew the Tibetans, and was aware that they promise much and perform little. We therefore kept the fellows with us for the night, and they slept in Muhamed Isa's tent. In the evening they were enraptured by the tones of our flutes, and felt so much at home that their tongues were loosened, and rattled like praying-mills. I heard their cackling until I went to sleep.

And this night I slept well. After eighty days of complete solitude we again had men as guests in our tents; we had obtained fine, rich goat's milk, and next day we should feast on well-fed mutton; we had received information about the country and the marches before us on the way to our far-off destination. And what was best of all, our veterans, our caravan animals, would get help. And this help was a boon from heaven; for this day, after we had lost three more horses at once, and when Rehim Ali must unfortunately be reckoned among the baggage, the loads had become too heavy for the animals. The future seemed more promising. Certainly the ridge of the Samoma-sakcho mountains did not exhibit a more purple colour in the evening light than the mountains which we had seen glowing in a grand display of colours on many a lonesome night; the blue smoke of the camp-fires danced a fairy dance on the steppe grass just as before, and the night came down just as dark and cold over the mountains to the east, but all around us to-day inspired us with cheerfulness and hope.

The new day had hardly broken when our two Changpas set out homewards with some of the Ladakis, to make preparations for the great business transaction. Two hours later we were the fortunate owners of five fine yaks, which, the Tibetans affirmed, could easily carry four boxes each, whereas our horses and mules had carried only two. One of the yaks was to take over the boat, and the horse which had carried it from Lake Lighten was relieved of the work. I breathed freely again when I saw the faithful animal without anything to carry. Then we bought four sheep at 4 rupees each, and exchanged our last three sheep for two fresh ones, paying 2 rupees in addition. At the Gomo lake our last eight goats obtained their well-earned rest, being exchanged for as many Tibetan and a money payment of 1 rupee a head. In the evening I had three times as much milk as usual, and richer and better than our exhausted goats had supplied. Both parties were thoroughly satisfied with the bargain (Illustration 88).

Good old Changpas! The wandering cavaliers of the wilderness came to us, looking picturesquely savage with their black coarse hair hanging down over their shoulders and back, and making their furs greasy, with long, dark matchlocks on their shoulders, clumsy sabres and knives in their belts, and mounted on small, tough, long-haired horses. Though wild and dirty, they were yet kindly, friendly and good-tempered, and were certainly not cold in their old dingy fur coats. The elder wore a small round fur cap, the younger a *bashlik* of fur, which covered his whole head except the face. They had their provisions and all kinds of other articles they wanted on their journey stuffed into their fur coats in front, and from the belts which held their fur coats together, hung knives, awl, flint and steel, pipe and tobacco pouch, which swung and knocked together at every step. They wore felt boots, originally white, but now black and worn-out, but had no trousers — it must be far too cool to sit trouserless in the saddle with 36 degrees of frost.

As they came from Gertse, the country to the south-west, they had hardly any knowledge of the region through which we were to travel, but they thought that we should require at least fifty days for the journey to Shigatse. They pass the winter in the Gomo district, living on the game there. They could easily serve a little breakfast with which the most exacting gourmand might be satisfied. Is not the following menu tempting?

A bowl of goat's milk with rich yellow cream.
Yak kidneys, fried a golden yellow in fat.
Marrow from yak bones, toasted over the fire.
Small, delicate pieces of tender, juicy meat from the vertebræ of the antelope, laid before the fire and slowly browned.

Antelope head, held in the flames with the hide and hair on till it is blackened with soot.

Their taste is in general very different from ours. When they have killed a wild ass, they cut it up and keep the pieces in the tent, piled up around it as far as possible from the fire. The longer it has lain there, the better it is supposed to taste. The Changpas prefer to eat their meat raw, hard, dry, and old. They take out from the recesses of their fur coats a yak's rib, which looks more like a piece of blackened wood than anything edible. Then the knife is brought out, and the hard meat is removed in strips or lumps from the bone. Chinese brick-tea is their greatest luxury, and the thicker and dirtier it is, the better they like it. They stir it up with a piece of butter.

Like the wild geese, they have learned by traditional experience where the best camping-grounds are. One may be sure that their tent is always pitched at places where there is little or no wind; that there is good pasture at hand for their tame yaks, sheep, goats, and horses, if they have any; that good hunting-grounds are to be found not far from the tent, and that water is always to be had. At the Gomo lake they have excellent table-salt cost free. When their domestic animals have eaten up the grass around, and the game has been frightened away, they transfer their camp to another district. The tents are set up at the same spots where their forefathers have pitched them for innumerable generations, and where frequently old votive cairns have been erected of loose stones to propitiate the spirits that rule over mountain and dale.

To the Changpas, or "inhabitants of the north," who spend the winter in the north, the chase is the chief resource, and cattle-breeding is of secondary importance. The Tibetans in Gertse and Senkor, on the Bogtsang-tsangpo, or in Naktsang, who own large herds, do not move northwards in winter, for with them hunting is an occasional occupation. The hunting tribes pursue the yak, the kiang, and the antelope. In hilly country they stalk them against the wind. Constant life in the open air has wonderfully sharpened their intelligence. They know the peculiarities and habits of the yak as well as he does himself, and know how far they may go without overstepping the limits of his acuteness. They know that his senses of sight and hearing are not particularly well developed, but that he soon scents the huntsman, so that the attack must be made from the lee side. Though he goes on the chase in his thick fur coat, the huntsman creeps as noiselessly and as lithe as a panther till he approaches within range of his prey. Then he lays his gun on the rest, strikes fire from the flint with his steel, catches it in tinder, sets light to the end of the match, and sees that the hammer brings the fire at the right moment into the touch-hole. All is done so quietly, so deliberately and carefully, that the hunter has every prospect of bringing down the game.

Another time he watches for hours together behind a wall which he or his forefathers, perhaps his great-great-grandfather, has built beside a spring, and waits with angelic patience for a troop of wild asses, which come at sunset to quench their thirst. But the antelopes, wild sheep, and gazelles are too wide-awake to be caught by the most skilful hunter. Yet the antelopes do not always succeed in escaping his cunning toils. He lays nooses for them on the old established antelope paths; among the hunting nomads in the interior of Tibet, the quantities of antelope meat garnishing the sides of the tents are astonishing.

While the men are away, the women look after the yaks and sheep, and when the hunter returns at sunset he sees the former chewing the cud in front of the tent, while the latter are shut up in a pen-fold of stone. The yaks remain at night near the tents, and hence the dung, the only fuel of the nomads, has not to be carried far. When it is dark, all gather round the fire on which the tea-kettle boils. Then they talk of the monotonous incidents of their life, of the day's bag, the condition of their herds, and the work of next day. One mends his soles with sinew and an awl, another dresses a yak hide with his hands, and a third cuts straps from the skin of a wild ass. Their life seems void and uneventful, but they have no wants — they know nothing better. They have a severe

87. SMOKING CAMP-FIRES IN THE HEART OF CHANG-TANG.

88. OUR YAKS, BOUGHT FROM THE FIRST TIBETANS.

struggle for life in this unproductive corner of the world, which is called the Chang-tang, or the north plain, where it has been their fate to be born. Amidst poverty and danger they live victorious in God's free Nature; the awful storms are their brothers, the lordship of the valleys they share with the wild beasts of the desert, and at night the everlasting stars twinkle over their black tents. If they were given comfortable huts down south in the shade of walnut trees, they would always be longing for the grand solitude of the mountains, for the icy cold, the drifting snow, and the moonlight of the peaceful winter nights in Tibet.

Then Death comes one day and looks in through the tent door; in vain is the constant prayer "Om mani padme hum" repeated; vain are all attempts to conjure or propitiate the evil powers that are inimical to the children of men. Bent, wrinkled, and grey the old hunter finishes his course, and is borne on strong shoulders to some shallow cleft near the mountain crest, and there abandoned to the wolves and birds of prey. When his grandchildren are grown up, they do not know whither he has been taken; in life he had no abiding dwelling-place, and after death he has no grave. And no one asks where the bones of the dead are bleaching, for the place is haunted by evil spirits.

November 14. Calm! In the night there were again 49 degrees of frost, but it was fairly warm riding southwards towards the sun. The two horses of the Tibetans had stampeded. But if this were a trick contrived to give them an excuse for making off themselves, it did not succeed this time; for I sent off one of them with two of my men to look for the horses, while the other had to accompany me and tell me the names of the places we passed. We did not know our men yet, and therefore did not dare to let them out of our sight, or they might have despatched mounted messengers to give information to the authorities in Gertse. Then we should have been ordered to halt sooner than it suited us. Now we could feel easy, at least till we came to the next tent. But the horses were recovered, and the old man stumped after us leading them by the bridle. Then we rode together between the hills and over small passes. Here, too, gold occurred in two places. Men come every summer, dig up the sand, throw it into the air, and collect the grains of gold on a cloth spread out on the ground. If the output is abundant, the number of gold-diggers is doubled the following summer.

In camp No. 61, also, the Tibetans showed no desire to desert us; they were friendly and attentive, helped us in unloading and setting up the tents, collected fuel, and undertook to be answerable for the horses. They seemed not to have the slightest suspicion that the country was forbidden to us, and not an echo of any especial orders had reached them from the south. I could not learn how matters stood. The plan of my journey had been alluded to in the Indian press, and there was nothing to prevent tidings being carried to Lhasa through Darjiling or Pekin; and I knew also from experience how soon an order against a European is handed on among the nomads. I had counted on hurrying on, like a thief in the night, as soon as possible after the English mission to Lhasa, and appearing on the scene before the Tibetans had quite made up their mind about the political state of affairs. But perhaps I was wrong, perhaps stricter regulations than ever had been passed.

The western shadows move over the plain; only in the east are the hills deep crimson, in the west they show a pitch-black outline. Another night spreads out its dark-blue pinions, and rises up to the zenith, driving before it an expiring reflexion of the setting sun. When the stars begin to shine we are out of doors examining the animals, which rejoice at being more lightly loaded on the march. At seven o'clock I am massaged and go to bed. At nine o'clock Robert comes with the hypsometer, and we talk for an hour. Then the light is allowed to burn till it flickers out. I lie a long time awake, watching the shadows come and go, as the wind shakes the canvas. I gaze at them till they turn into monsters and wild yaks, dancing mockingly round my prison. Now it is striking midnight in the towns of Siberia and India which lie on our meridian, and at length comes the deliverer sleep and drives away the shadow-pictures: they melt away and vanish on the horizon, which recedes more and more into the distance, no longer bounded by the thin web of the tent. Now a low murmur seems to call to mind forests, meadows, and small rocky islands. I dream that a strong hand leads me to a parting in the ways. It points to a road, and a voice tells me that this will lead me to a land of peace, hospitality, and summer, while the other leads to dangers and privations among dark lofty mountains. When Tsering brought the brazier in the morning, I was glad that I had in my dream chosen the latter road without hesitation.

We penetrated further and further into this mysterious Tibet. During the next day's march we passed a succession of deserted fireplaces, and in some places saw rows of stone cairns to entice the antelopes into snares. Then we ascended a valley, in which a small strip of ice gradually expanded into a cake, filling all the space between the firm slabs of greenstone. The Seoyinna came in sight — a dark mountain to the south, which would remain visible for a couple of days longer.

Our Tibetans are already as intimate with us all as though we had been friends from childhood, and say that they have never met with such decent people. The elder is called Puntsuk, the younger Tsering Dava. We sit for hours together at Muhamed Isa's fire and talk pleasantly, and I take notes as they describe to me in detail all the routes in Tibet they are acquainted with. Tsering Dava has accomplished the pilgrimage to Tso-rinpoche, or the holy lake Manasarowar, which I long to reach, and which has been the subject of my dreams for many a day. The two men were to accompany us only three days more; they had left their yaks and sheep to the care of their wives and children, and wolves were extraordinarily numerous; otherwise they would have travelled any distance with us. They had arrived from Gertse nineteen days before, and intended to stay six months; forty or fifty parties come every year from Gertse to this country.

They told us that the Tokpas, or gold-diggers, when they go up to the goldfields for two or three months, take as provisions meal and meat, which are carried by their sheep and yaks. When the provisions are consumed they return home, passing the salt lakes, where they load their animals with salt, which they barter in inhabited districts for barley. Thus they make a twofold profit on their journey, and can live the rest of the year on their gains.

In the evening a dead horse, emaciated and wretched, lay on the ice in our valley. I had procured him for 70 rupees from a dealer in Leh, who in December 1901 had bought my last nine camels. Next morning a mule died just as unexpectedly. He looked brisk and sound, and allowed himself to be loaded as usual, but had not gone a hundred paces when he fell dead. The two small Tibetan horses, which travel with us, take a great interest in their fellows; but they do not seem quite sure that the animals, so thin and wretched, are really horses. At this day's camp, No. 63, we saw them run up to their masters for two large pieces of frozen antelope flesh, which they eagerly ate out of their hands like bread. They are just as fond of yak or sheep's flesh, and the Tibetans say that this diet makes them tough and hardy. We cannot help liking these small shaggy ponies, which live to no small extent on the offal of game, are at home in the mountains, and bear rarefied air with the greatest ease; their lungs are as well adapted to it as those of the wild asses. The cold does not trouble them in the least: they remain out all through the night without a covering of any sort, and even a temperature of $-22.7°$, which we had on the night of November 17, does not affect them. Though they are not shod, they run deftly and securely up and down the slopes, and the men on their backs look bigger than their horses. We notice with great amusement how heartily they greet each other at every camp. Puntsuk, who shows Muhamed Isa the way, rides a small bay pony, which is already grazing when we appear. As soon as the pony catches sight of his grey comrade with Tsering Dava he neighs with delight, cocks his ears, and runs up to him; and the grey one exhibits just as much satisfaction. This is very different from the conduct of our dogs, which fight wildly as soon as they see each other.

Now we passed the Seoyinna mountain; one flank was

dotted over by numerous wild yaks engaged in feeding, and Tundup Sonam shot two. My men took the best joints with them, the rest of the meat our guides would fetch on their way home. They were evidently much impressed by Tundup Sonam's skill, but Dava Tsering declared that he had shot more than three hundred yaks in his lifetime, which was probably no exaggeration, seeing that these men live on the products of the chase.

Now we ascend rapidly to the Chak-chom-la pass. Tsering Dava rides in front. His little pony trots up the ascent. When we have still a good distance to cover, we see the profile of the man and his horse on the summit, sharply defined against the sky. There stands a cairn of granite blocks, and many trails of gold-diggers run at a height of 17,825 feet. Sitting beside a fire, rendered necessary by the cold and the wind, we gaze southwards over a vast extent of country, a chaos of yellow, reddish, and black crests. No plains appear between them, and we suspect that we have troublesome ground before us. Near at hand, towards the south-south-east, a flat basin with a small lake occupies a large expanse. We ride down a very steep path to the camp where the Tibetans proposed a day's rest on behalf of the yaks we had purchased.

In the course of the day we settled accounts with our guides, who had been so friendly and helpful, and who now wished to return to their bare cold mountains where the winds and wolves howl in rivalry. They received each 3 rupees a day as recompense, and a sheath-knife from Kashmir, and a whole heap of empty tin cigarette-boxes, which seemed to please them more than the money. And then they vanished, swiftly and lightly as the wind, behind the nearest hills, and we were alone again.

With 36 degrees of frost our nine Mohammedans celebrated their "Aid" after Ramazan with flute, dance, and song, and with a freshly slaughtered sheep. In the night the thermometer fell to $-23°$. The ink was always freezing in my pen, even when I sat bending over the brazier; after a few minutes my washing-basin contained only a mass of ice.

After a few hours' march we descried from a pass 22 grazing horses, 300 sheep, and some evidently tame yaks, and these were near a tent. Farther to the west 500 sheep and a number of yaks were feeding. Five more tents were pitched in a sheltered place in a deep valley, and a troop of snarling dogs ran out to meet us. Men, women, and children turned out to see what was the matter. The caravan encamped near, on the western shore of the lake Dungtsa-tso, and presently received a visit from four Tibetans. These, too, came from Gertse, had arrived ten days previously, and intended to stay three months. The six tents contained 40 inmates, who possessed together 1000 sheep, 60 yaks, and 40 horses. The oldest of our new friends was a lame man of fifty-three years of age, and was named Lobsang Tsering. He presented to me a dish of sour milk and a bundle of joss-sticks, such as are used in temples. He was willing to sell us three large yaks for 23 rupees, and we took them without a moment's hesitation.

When the caravan had set out next morning two other Tibetans presented themselves, very eager to sell us two more yaks. When I told them that our money was on in front, they asked permission to go with us to the next camp, where the purchase might be completed. That evening, then, we were the fortunate owners of ten excellent yaks, and Tundup Sonam was appointed to be their chief and leader. Our remaining mules and horses now carried only very light loads, and I was rejoicing that I could keep them all alive. But at this very spot another mule was frozen to death; true, there were 59.2 degrees of frost.

Our day's march ran round the lake and into a broad valley extending in a south-easterly direction. Some 150 kulans were peacefully grazing among the tame yaks of the nomads. A youth acted as guide to the caravan, and old Lobsang Tsering rode like a herald before me, mounted on a fine yellowish horse, which he would not sell at any price. As he rode he muttered prayers at an incredible pace — it sounded like the buzzing of a swarm of midges about a lime tree on a summer evening. I myself rode my dapple-grey from Yarkand again, in order that my small white Ladaki might have a couple of days' rest.

The camp was pitched beside a pool of fresh water, where the most wonderful sounds were emitted from the firm ice all night long. It cracked and clappered, gurgled and snorted like camels and yaks, and one might fancy that a bevy of water-nymphs were dancing under the icy roof. The dogs barked furiously at the ice till they at last perceived that this noise must be put up with like everything else.

At the evening fire Lobsang Tsering asked Muhamed Isa whether we had met with Changpas at the Gomo. But Muhamed Isa had promised Puntsuk and Tsering Dava not to betray them. Then Lobsang winked an eye and said that Islam Ahun had already told him that we had not only seen nomads, but had bought yaks from them and had taken them as guides for several days. Muhamed Isa tried to turn the affair into a joke, and answered laughing that Islam Ahun had concocted the story himself. But the old man was sharp; he smiled cunningly, and seemed to regard the first version as the more probable. It was a great advantage to us that we had first come into contact with Gertse nomads, who were themselves strangers in the country we passed through. They had received no orders from Lhasa concerning us, and were beyond all comparison better disposed and more friendly than the eastern Tibetans, who on my former journey had sent off messengers at once to the south. But we now found that the Gertse nomads were afraid of one another; the first had begged us to tell no one that they had helped us, and had turned back at the right moment in order not to be seen by their fellow-tribesmen from Gertse.

Lobsang Tsering did not seem to be of a timid disposition; he led us to other tents, gave us instructions about the way to Bogtsang-tsangpo, and was able to give us much interesting information. He told us, for instance, that nearly four thousand sheep and several hundred yaks are yearly employed in transporting salt from the lakes we had lately passed, and that the salt was carried to Shigatse and Lhasa. From these towns came most of the gold-diggers, and in the north were many other gold-placers which we had not seen.

We soon perceived that Lobsang was a man of importance, for all showed him the greatest respect, and we could see from his camp that he was rich. He spoke with dignity, and with an educated, refined accent. In his appearance he reminded me of a decayed actor, without a trace of beard, and with an animated expression in his dirty, copper-coloured face. Unlike the rest, who wore sheepskin caps, he sported a red turban, and his fur coat was trimmed with red woollen stuff. In the front of his coat all sorts of things were stuffed, among them a vile pocket-handkerchief — a thick, coloured, square rag, constantly in use, but never washed. There also he kept his snuff-horn, which he could handle even in a wind with a certain dexterity. The fine yellow snuff was scooped up on the tip of the forefinger under the protection of the thumb-nail, and conveyed to its destination somewhat noisily.

Every evening Muhamed Isa made his report. This time he presented himself with the following statement: "Sahib, Rehim Ali is still bad, and he begs permission to offer a sheep to Allah."

"Very well, if he will be any the better for it."

"Oh yes, certainly, Sahib."

"I think it is all humbug, but it will do him no harm and the Mohammedans will get an extra meal. I will give the sheep then."

"No, Sahib, that will not do; then the sacrifice would have no effect."

"Indeed. Can I have the kidneys for dinner to-morrow?"

"No, Sahib, only Mohammedans may eat of a sheep offered in sacrifice."

"Just so; of course in your opinion I am a *kaper*" (heathen).

He laughingly protested, but changed the subject. "Now we have 13 mules and 11 horses, or 27 animals altogether, of the original caravan."

"Thirteen and eleven make only twenty-four," I replied.

"Oh! then I must count them again," said my conscientious caravan leader, and he gave himself much unnecessary trouble to make the figures agree. At last it proved that we had still twenty-five animals beside the yaks.

CHAPTER XVI

OUR FORTUNES ON THE WAY TO THE BOGTSANG-TSANGPO

DURING the preceding five days we had covered forty-two miles in a direction 33 degrees east of south, and on November 22 travelled a little farther on the same course. We are now on a great, easily recognizable road, consisting of about fifty paths running parallel to one another, which have been worn by the sheep of the salt caravans and the yaks of the gold-diggers. In the country Kebechungu, where nomads were encamped, our new friends turned back. In this part of Tibet the sharply-defined configuration of the mountains occurring farther east, where longitudinal valleys alternate with lateral ranges, does not prevail. Here one travels day after day among crowded hills of gentle outline, and small, level expanses are much less common. No lofty commanding mountain masses rise above this maze, and the eye searches in vain for the isolated, glaciated summits seen in East Tibet.

The weather had been quite calm during the season of severe cold, but when the storms returned at night, the temperature fell only to $-4.7°$. Next day it was hard riding. We marched to the south-south-east in a strong south-west storm, and were almost suffocated in the gusts of dust-laden air which swept along the ground. We suffer greatly and cannot use our hands, the map-sheet is torn in pieces, and we wonder if we shall live to reach the next camp. Our faces are distorted and assume quite a different expression, for we involuntarily draw the facial muscles together in the wind, to protect the eyes, producing a quantity of fresh wrinkles which are filled with white dust.

The eyes are bloodshot and water, tears run down the cheeks, catch the dust, and freeze. The lips swell and burst, and the skin round the nails cracks so that the finger-tips bleed.

At last, more dead than alive, we reach the camp, where the men have, with great exertion, set up Muhamed Isa's tent, and after many attempts have induced the fire to burn, which, now that it has caught, blazes with flickering tongues of flame and scatters sparks all round into the gyrations of the whirlwind. We hasten to restore our circulation, but that takes time. By degrees our facial muscles recover their elasticity and return to their proper position, and we regain our former aspect; there is no longer a twitch at the corners of our mouths when we laugh, though, indeed, we have precious little cause for laughter. Half-a-dozen of our remaining mules come up, attracted by the warmth. Sonam Tsering wishes to drive them away, but I let the poor frozen creatures stay. The fewer they become, the more carefully we look after the survivors, and are always hoping to reach more hospitable country. There is, indeed, little hope of it; the barley and maize are almost consumed, and there is only one sack of rice left.

In such nights one longs for a warm bed. The noise outside is as though artillery waggons were racing over a pavement of undressed stones. The wind comes in gusts as though driven by pulsations. A gust is heard whistling through the grass and dying away in the distance, only to be followed by another which rushes down the mountains like a waterfall, and seems determined to carry away the tent with it in its headlong flight. One does not look back with regret on the day now drawing to a close, but longs to get away — away from the Chang-tang.

November 24. In a month it will be Christmas Eve. Shall we remain together so long? At the former camp the animals had no water, and at to-day's camping-place also we found nothing but hard ice at the mouth of a very narrow gorge, and consequently two mules passed away in the night, and a third followed them in the morning. My dapple-grey was suffering; I now rode a tall, yellowish horse which had carried the boat, and afterwards the box of cooking utensils. The latter was transferred to a mule, but he died before the next camp and a horse had to fetch the box.

Four mules in one day! We had now only eight. The yaks, the splendid yaks, carried all the baggage. When we left the bodies a troop of wolves sneaked out of the ravines. Islam Ahun, who had travelled with Robert and myself since Rehim Ali's adventure, tried to frighten them away, but in vain. Four great vultures had already mutilated one of the corpses; they must have begun early, for they were already satiated, and staggered slowly away as we rode past. The ravens waited at some distance for their turn to come.

Of 58 horses and 36 mules, 12 and 8 respectively now remained. The ratio between the survivors was therefore nearly the same as between the original numbers. It would, however, be hasty to infer that mules are as efficient as horses in the highlands of Tibet. Had we had small, tough Sanskar horses in the place of the Yarkand horses, the result would certainly have been in favour of the horses. On the other hand, our mules came from Poonch. Had we had Tibetan mules, they would probably have held out better than the horses. But Tibetan mules are seldom to be found in Ladak.

Lower down the valley we came to a *mani-ringmo*, a stone cist covered with *mani* slabs, and our men became quite lively at the sight, for it reminded them of their home. We rode up a height with an extensive view. To the south-east appeared rather a large lake, begirt with white fields of gypsum and terraces. Crossing three rocky ridges running out to its western shore, we reached the southern bank, where we encamped. This must be the Rinak-chutsen ("The hot spring of the Black Mountain"), for every detail agreed with the description given us by Lobsang Tsering.

The date is November 25, the day I had fixed on, when with Colonel Dunlop Smith, as the most likely date of our arrival at the Dangra-yum-tso. The post must therefore be at the lake long before us. The post? We did not know whether we should find on the shore a hospitable tent or an impenetrable wall of soldiers and horses and a fence of matchlocks.

This is the lake which Dutreuil de Rhins discovered in 1893 and named "Lac Ammoniac." We did not cross his route, for he skirted the lake on the east, we on the west side. But just to the south of the lake we crossed Bower's route of the year 1891. We shall again remain for some days in unknown country until we intersect Littledale's track of the year 1895, mine of 1901, and Nain Sing's of 1873.

In the night the temperature sank to $-27.8°$, the greatest cold we had hitherto experienced. We were, however, advancing southwards to lower regions. Though the winter still continued, it could scarcely bring us lower temperatures. For four days we travelled towards the noonday sun, slowly marching over passes and through winding valleys, over small plains, where kiangs enjoyed their free delightful life, over a hard-frozen river, and by springs, round which emerald-green ice glittered in the sun, past a flock of sheep and four tents, and finally we emerged on to an open plain, enclosed by mountains, which sloped towards the south and contained in the middle a lake nearly dried up, where the crystallized salt and gypsum emitted a brilliancy like that of fresh-fallen snow.

The country was called Mogbo-dimrop; at the foot of the red mountains we descried six black tents surrounded by stone walls. Namgyal and Tundup Sonam found only eight inhabitants, children, boys, and old men, for the strong men and women had gone out with the cattle. These nomads belonged to the province of Naktsang, and were under the rule of the Devashung, the Government in Lhasa, and therefore could give us no information about the country near the Dangra-yum-tso, where the nomads are under the administration of Tashi-lunpo. They would be very glad to sell us yaks and sheep if we would be so good as to wait here till the next day.

Then Muhamed Isa went off to the tents, and came back full of gloomy forebodings. An elderly man from a neighbouring group of tents had come to warn the others. He had declared in sharp commanding tones: "We know that you have a European with you, and to such our land is closed. We cannot stop you at present, but we shall take care not to sell you yaks or sheep, and we cannot give you any information. It would be better for you to make haste back again, or you will get into trouble."

"We are on the way to the Tashi Lama, who is expecting us."

"Here we have nothing to do with the Tashi Lama; we are under the direct rule of the Government in Lhasa."

Tundup Sonam, who had also gone to the tents, noticed that two youths were absent, and was convinced that they had been despatched as express messengers to the nearest *Bombo* or chief, in the south. We must therefore make all haste to reach a district which was under the control of Tashi-lunpo.

Later on a wanderer came to our camp. He was ragged and miserable, and said that he was one of a party of 35 pilgrims from Nakchu, who with 600 sheep and 100 yaks had visited the holy lake and mountain in Ngari-korsum, and were now on their way home to Nakchu, where they would arrive in three months. The pilgrimage takes two years or more to accomplish, for the people remain for days, and often weeks, together where there is good pasturage. They followed the north side of the Chargut-tso along an old established pilgrim route.

We broke up our camp early on December 1, with a temperature of $-24.2°$, which cost us the loss of another mule. He was at once devoured by the wolves, which were so bold that they did not go away when we rode past. When we had accomplished about half our march we came to a tent of which two snappy light yellow dogs seemed to be the only masters. But no doubt the inmates were afraid to show themselves, and examined us only through their spy-holes. Near this day's camp there were more tents, and my usual dealers obtained two yaks, three sheep, and a can of dirty milk. Before the Tibetans would deal, they first inquired whether there was not a *Peling* (a European) in our party, and declared that they would visit our camp to convince themselves that such was not the case. The answer given them was that the principal personage in our company

89. "WHERE ARE YOU GOING?" THEY ASKED ME.

was a *Kalun*, or high official, from Ladak, and that we had several dangerous dogs. On that they gave up their visit. But when we started off two of them were present, one of whom Muhamed Isa took as a guide. The other remained standing by us and looked at me, trying to find out whether I was a *Peling* or a *Kalun*. He was certainly doubtful, for he looked exceedingly disturbed as we rode off.

This day Robert and I lost our way. We had taken the Hajji as guide, but he lost the trail, and stupidly wandered about aimlessly. As he had to seek for the track again, we settled down on an open space beside a fire, while the storm roared above our heads and dark threatening snow-clouds swept over the mountains to the north. At last Muhamed Isa became uneasy and sent out scouts, who at length found us out.

Camp No. 77 was situated in the higher part of a lateral valley, where a spring was frozen into huge clumps of ice. At the fire we encountered two strangers in red turbans, round which their locks were twisted, with ivory rings, silver image cases, and fur coats trimmed with red and green ribands; they were armed with sabres encased in silver-mounted scabbards, richly encrusted with inferior coral and turquoise; they wore new coloured felt boots, and had their black muskets hanging from their shoulders. They belonged to the troop of pilgrims from Nakchu. Our Ladakis, however, were convinced that they were come to spy upon us. If we seemed too strong for them, they would only ask — as, in fact, happened — if we had anything to sell; otherwise they would steal our horses. Meanwhile they behaved very civilly, were exceedingly friendly, and promised to return next morning with some yaks and sheep, which we might buy.

"We will remain near you till it is dark and will return before daybreak, for if any one saw us trading with a *Peling*, we should pay dearly for it."

"You need not be afraid, we shall not betray you," I said.

"Even if you did betray us, Bombo Chimbo, we should not be easily caught. There are many pilgrims on the way to the holy mountain Kang-rinpoche (Kailas)."

"You may be quite at ease. Come with your animals, and you shall be well paid."

"Good. But tell me, are you not the *Peling* who came five years ago with two companions to Nakchu, and was compelled by the Governor to turn back?"

"Yes, that was I."

"We did not see you ourselves, but all the province was talking about you, and you had Shereb Lama as a guide. You had also a large caravan with camels and several Russians in your service."

"How can you remember all that?"

"Oh, it was repeatedly said that it would be a marvel if you escaped the robbers."

I clearly perceived from this not very flattering popularity that, if the common people were so well informed of my doings, the authorities would find it easy to follow my track. Now the Tibetans knew that it was I, and no one else, who was penetrating to the heart of the forbidden land. How speedily this fact would be transmitted to the south! How quickly would the Devashung bring us to a halt! Where would our grand progress come to a standstill, checked by a peremptory "Thus far and no farther," backed up by muzzle-loaders and sabres? Ah, where would my dreams again be shattered and my aspirations cease to pulsate?

In the morning, when the pilgrims had returned, I was waked early and went out to view the market that had been created in the wilderness as by an enchanter's wand. The sun had not yet risen above the mountains, the camp lay in icy-cold shadow, and the air was dull and raw. The smoke circled round the fires in suffocating density, and through it I saw six splendid yaks with wooden saddles. The Tibetans in their picturesque costume, with sabres jingling at their sides, knives and amulets, gesticulated vehemently, and in a torrent of well-chosen words extolled the exceptional qualities of the grunting oxen. The result of the affair was that all six yaks passed into our possession, and we also bought two packets of brick-tea, a bag of Bhotan tobacco, and a couple of bladders of butter. Robert piled up the shining silver coins in rows at the door of my tent, and the eyes of the Tibetans shone with delight at the sight of so much money, and at hearing the ring of the silver. An empty tin and a tin cigarette box found their way, as usual, into the front of their fur coats.

"Do you know the way to the south?" I asked.

"Yes, we know it well."

"If you are disposed to accompany us, you shall receive three rupees a day."

"We should like to, but we dare not."

"What are you afraid of?"

"We have heard that to the south of this pass the country has been roused and that soldiers are being collected to render your further journey impossible. We must go quickly northwards. Our people are already ahead."

"Where do you think that the soldiers are waiting for us?"

"That no one knows, but it is certain that they are gathering together."

"What, in your opinion, do they mean to do with us?"

"They will prevent you going farther southwards, but will do you no harm."

"How do you know that?"

"Because the Bombo Chimbo was friendly last time, and did not refuse to march westwards when he was required to do so."

"Which way will they ask us to take this time?"

"Probably the same as before, to Ladak."

The silver money rattled in the tin boxes as they mounted and disappeared down the valley, while we, now owners of eighteen fine yaks, struggled laboriously up the small steep pass overlooking camp No. 77. We had a wide view southwards over side ranges separated from one another by broad valleys. But it was not long before heavy snow drove us away. Numbed with cold, we rode down to the level country.

From the plain the Hajji pointed back to the pass, where three riders showed black against the snow; they rode down at a smart trot and soon overtook us. Their black, snorting horses steamed, they carried guns at their shoulder-belts, and sabres in their girdles. Their reddish-purple mantles were rolled up on the saddle behind them, and they rode in sheep-skins, black and greasy from the soot of camp-fires, and the blood and fat of slaughtered game, which in the course of years had hardened into a smooth crust intersected with cracks. As we were the object of their ride, they followed at our heels, slackened their pace, and rode up to my side. A coarse fellow asked shortly and boldly (Illustration 89):

"What are you?"

"Pilgrims."

"Where do you come from?"

"From Ladak."

"Whither are you travelling?"

"To the Dangra-yum-tso."

"People from Ladak never come from the north."

"That is quite possible, but we come from the north. Where have you been yourself?"

"With relatives who are camping to the east. We have two more days' journey before we reach home."

Then they spurred their horses and rode after the caravan, which was encamped at the foot of a rock. Here they let their horses graze, behaved as though they were at home, and subjected Muhamed Isa to the same cross-examination. Shortly before sunset they rode off westwards. We had an uncomfortable feeling that something ominous, something decisive, was brewing, and that our fate might perhaps be settled next day. For it was clear as day that the men must have been spies. They were a patrol of the numerous express messengers sent into all the valleys by orders from Lhasa to beat up the men fit for military service. Soon these incorruptible riders would crop up like mushrooms from the ground.

The camp No. 78 and the weather were in harmony with our mood as we awaited our fate. There was no pasturage, only ice, and the fuel was scanty. Opaque clouds obscured the sky, snow was falling on the mountains, the north-west storm moaned round the corners, and whirled the ashes and scraps of dung about so that they found their way into my tent, where the dogs lay rolled in a corner to keep themselves warm.

Again, on December 4, we left a mule behind. The land was covered with snow, and the ride was fearfully cold, icicles hung from my moustache, and my right foot lost all feeling. Hundreds of antelopes and kiangs were grazing to the left of our road; the dogs dashed at them, but soon came back again, for the animals would not move an inch. No men appeared, and we thought that the real opposition would be encountered at the Bogtsang-tsangpo, that is, where I had last time been forced to turn westwards.

The next day's march took us over rather tiring hills where small points of weathered porphyry cropped up here and there out of the ground. Spoors of wild animals ran in all directions, and cattle and sheep tracks were equally numerous.

But not even at the Bogtsang-tsangpo did anything suspicious appear. We calmed down again and rested here on the 6th. Our store of rice and flour was consumed; there was only a little for me, so that I had my freshly-baked bread every morning and evening. The others had to live exclusively on mutton, so that every day one sheep at least was needed. Just as Tundup Sonam and two other men returned from a foray, bringing with them six fat sheep, we saw six men on foot coming to our camp. Our grand vizier, Muhamed Isa, received them before they were brought before me. The principal among them thus introduced himself:

"I am the *Gova* (District Chief) of this country, and have received tidings from the north that you are on the way southwards. You passed through here five years ago with twenty-five camels. I am now come to inquire your name, how many servants and pack-animals you have, and whither you intend to go."

"Why do you put these questions?"

"Because I must forward information to the Governor of Naktsang; if I do not, he will cut my head off."

He was given the particulars he wanted, and then he asked:

"Will the Bombo Chimbo be so kind as to wait here until the answer comes back?"

"Where is the Governor of Naktsang?"

"In Shansa-dzong on the Kyaring-tso."

"How long will it take a messenger to reach him?"

"Ten days."

"Then the answer will be here in twenty days. No, thank you, we have no time to wait so long."

"But you must wait three days, until I have sent for a man who can write."

"No, we are off to-morrow."

So far all had passed off well. Instead of encountering an armed force, we found the country open for twenty days longer. But after that things would be different; the Governor of Naktsang would not let me take another step farther southwards; I knew him in the year 1901 and found him inflexible. The least we could expect was that he would detain us till the answer of the Government was received. Like Dutreuil de Rhins and Grenard, I should have to wait one, perhaps even two, months.

Our chief, however, pursued a little private policy of his own, and said that the relations of the Devashung and India were now friendly, and therefore he would treat us as friends. He dared not sell us baggage animals or provide us with guides without the consent of the Governor, but he would gladly impart to us all the information we desired. He mentioned some names according with those given by Nain Sing, and showing how conscientiously the celebrated Pundit had performed his task. The conical height to the north of our camp he named Tugu-lhamo; the Gobrang is a ridge to the north-east of it, and a side valley is called Ragok. Nain Sing gives the names Dubu Lhamo, Gobrang, and Ragu. He reckons the distance to the Dagtse-tso, the salt lake by which I encamped in 1901 at the mouth of the Bogtsang-tsangpo, at nine days' journey. It is easily explained how Nain Sing fell into an error here, and also represented the river as flowing into the Chargut-tso, for he was not there himself and trusted too much to the frequently unreliable information of the chiefs.

In the course of the evening the chief became still more friendly, and proposed to travel with us for three days under the pretence of keeping an eye on us. He would, however, keep some distance from us, and, like a night-owl, join us only when it had become quite dark. In the night he pitched his chieftain's tent, green above and white below, beside ours.

We passed quickly eastwards along the Bogtsang-tsangpo in only five and a half short marches, partly close beside the river, partly along parallel valleys which skirt its southern bank. On December 7 we lost sight of it, but in the district Pati-bo it again emerged from a narrow transverse valley. Eastwards the fall is extremely slight, and the river winds in most capricious curves, so that the path touches the bank only at the southern bends. A quantity of hearthstones and fenced-in sheepfolds show that many nomads spend the summer on the Bogtsang-tsangpo. The volume of water is very insignificant, for the river is principally fed by sources which are called into existence only by the autumn rains, and fail in winter. Thick ice lies over it all, and is deeply hollowed by the constant fall of the river. The ranges on both sides run in an east and west direction, and frequently three such crests are seen at the same time towards the south. One is often astonished at the whim of the stream in turning sharply to cut through a rocky crest, whereas it would seem much easier to flow on along the open longitudinal valley. But, like most mountainous countries, Tibet presents many such puzzling problems, difficult of solution. At a place where comparatively warm rivulets flow in on our side there is a short, wide reach of the river where Robert caught fish, a very welcome variation in our monotonous diet.

In the night we had 54 degrees of frost, and on December 12 the thermometer sank to $-24.7°$. The caravan now consisted of 11 horses and 4 mules, besides the 18 yaks. The yaks are not accustomed to long day's marches, so we proceeded very slowly eastwards. We could not hurry our marches, much as we should have liked to do so. There were several men sickly, and the medicine chest was in great demand. Muhamed Isa especially suffered from headache, and many a time as we passed by he was lying on his back on the ground. He was dosed with antipyrine and quinine, and I advised him to walk as little as possible.

The chief became more and more at home with us, and no longer observed his former caution. He sometimes called on nomads on the way, but his tent was always set up among ours. Every day he brought to me one or two nomads, who gave me information about the country and sold us milk and sheep. Several were from Ombo, a village and district on the north shore of the Dangra-yum-tso, where a couple of stone huts stand and barley is cultivated. The pasturage round the lake is said to be so poor that the inhabitants of its shores have to migrate northwards with their flocks in winter. Unfortunately they had not heard of a post messenger from Shigatse, but they were equally ignorant of any order directed against us.

On December 12 we left the Bogtsang-tsangpo and directed our steps towards the south-east. At night a violent storm arose, but the minimum temperature was only 13.5°; the night before there were 56.7 degrees of frost.

Another mule died in the night, and the surviving animals had to be carefully guarded from the wolves, which were unusually daring. We started on December 13 to the pass La-ghyanyak (16,932 feet high), where a pyramidal cairn marks the divide between the Bogtsang-tsangpo and the Dangra-yum-tso. The former can be seen meandering along its valley to its termination in the lake Dagtse-tso; the latter is not yet visible, but we can guess where its basin lies among the huge mountain massives. Yonder lay the holy lake Dangra-yum-tso, which had long been our aim, and whither I had requested Colonel Dunlop Smith to send my letters. To the south-west arose two dominating snowy peaks above a sea of mountainous undulations, and in the same direction lay a small round lake, the Tang-yung-tsaka, already seen by Nain Sing, and named by him Tang-yung-tso (Illustration 90). The country seemed desolate and uninhabited, and no riders spurred through the valleys to block our way. Farther down we passed two tents, where the inmates told us we were on the wrong way if we wished to go to the Dangra-yum-tso, for it could be reached in a direction due south in four short marches. All Naktsang knew, they said, that a *Peling* was coming, a report that, however, had probably spread from the north, not from the south. If the mail-runner had actually reached the lake, he would hear that we were not far off, and would look out for us.

Now the thermometer sank to -24° again, and we let the animals rest a day. Meanwhile I, with Robert and Shukkur Ali, made an excursion on foot through a singularly wild romantic valley, which was little over a yard broad in some places, and was cut out between vertical walls. Often the bottom is filled with fallen blocks, which obstruct the way, but elsewhere it is occupied by a brook, now frozen up. The rapids and waterfalls of this brook are also congealed into glassy ice, and shine with a bluish-green tinge in the depth of the valley, where the summer flood has excavated curious caves. Here the wind is confined as in a pair of bellows, and roars and whistles round the cliffs. In an expansion of the valley we kindle a fire and take a rest. Along the precipice above us six proud eagles soar with motionless wings.

According to previous arrangement Rabsang came to meet us with some of our yaks, so that we could ride back. He brought us disturbing news. At the tents we had seen farther up the valley on the day before, twelve armed men had collected to waylay us. An express messenger had, it seems, brought word from Shigatse that we must be driven back to the north. I did not question him further, and we rode home in silence. It was a bitter experience now, when we had looked down from La-ghanyak on the great unknown country crossed only by Nain Sing's route of the year 1874, which we had intended to intersect at one point only, to see all the grand discoveries, of which I had dreamt so long, blown away like mist. And it was especially irritating to think that others might come here later and rob me of these conquests. Reminiscences of the past autumn and early winter came into my head; we had successfully executed an immense traverse over the Chang-tang, and at the critical moment the nomads had come to our assistance. It had been a splendid bold journey hitherto, but I had always considered it only as a prologue to the grand plans which kept me awake at night and had occupied my thoughts during the long weary ride. And now they would receive their death-blow. Now my dreams of victory would be resolved into blue haze, like the smoke of the camp-fire which marked the southernmost point of our advance into the forbidden land.

CHAPTER XVII

CHRISTMAS IN THE WILDS

MUCH depressed but outwardly composed, I dismounted from the yak and entered my tent just as Tsering brought in the brazier. The tent seemed more dismal than usual, the brazier made me feel weary, and at this moment I seemed to realize how lonely and dull my life had been all through the winter; but Tsering was as tranquil as usual, and raked the fire with the tongs to remove some still smoking dung.

"Now you see that I was right; how often have I told you that we should be ordered to halt at the Bogtsang-tsangpo?" I said.

"Ordered to halt?" exclaimed Tsering in astonishment.

"Yes, now we are stuck fast, but I will not move a step from the spot until the Tibetans have provided me with a new caravan, though I have to wait all the winter. Then we will go north-eastwards, look for the Mongolian pilgrim road, and hasten to Pekin. I will force the Mandarins to allow me to see the parts of Tibet where no European has yet been."

"I do not understand what the Sahib means; hitherto no one has hindered us, and the country southwards lies open before us."

"What are you talking about? Have they not come this very day to stop our further progress?"

"No, on the contrary, three Tibetans are sitting with Muhamed Isa, and they are most civil and friendly."

"Has, then, Rabsang played a trick on me and the Babu Sahib?"

"Ah," replied Tsering, laughing, "now I understand the matter. Rabsang was up at the tents this morning, and allowed himself to be frightened by a Tibetan, who told him that we should be forced to remain where we are, for we had no right to travel southwards to Naktsang. But that was only the Tibetan's own notion, and Rabsang, who had to go immediately after to the valley with the yaks, had not heard how matters really stood with us."

"Bravo, Tsering, slay the fattest sheep we have got, and invite every one to a feast. I will have the kidneys fried in their own fat."

Now the storm-beaten tent seemed more comfortable and the brazier sent out a pleasant kindly heat. I sat buried in thought, wondering whether this were a good omen, when Muhamed Isa announced a visit of the three Tibetans. I invited them to take a seat at the fire. Turning to the chief man, who wore a blood-red fur coat and a brick-red fox-skin cap, I asked him who he was.

"I am Karma Tamding from Tang-yung," he answered; and I was astonished that he gave his name at once, for the Tibetans are generally shy of doing so, lest they should bring upon themselves retaliation on the part of their superiors when their names are known.

"We are, then, in the province of Tang-yung?"

"Yes, Bombo Chimbo, the pass you crossed yesterday is its northern boundary; to the west Tang-yung extends for three days' journey, and as far to the east, and southwards to the Dangra-yum-tso."

"Why have you come to my tent, Karma Tamding? Has one of your superiors sent you?"

"No, but idle rumours have been current here for some time. First it was an old woman, who would have it that two hundred men were coming down from the north. Large bands of robbers from Nakchu have plundered the nomads in the north, and we felt sure that they were robbers who were coming into our country. The day before yesterday we heard that it was only a peaceful European, who took, indeed, yaks, sheep, butter, and milk from our people, but always paid well for them. I am now come to see our guests with my own eyes, and I am very glad to find you instead of a robber band."

"You have not heard, then, that any messenger from Shigatse has been inquiring about us?"

"No, not a word. But this very day I have heard that an express has been sent from the Bogtsang-tsangpo to Shansa-dzong, and that messengers will travel thence to Lhasa."

"Will you be so good as to sell us yaks, Karma Tamding?"

"Yes, willingly. I saw you five years ago at the Bogtsang-tsangpo. Then you were conducted over the frontier by a large escort and two officers, but now Europeans seem to be privileged to pass through the country."

"Will you procure us guides?"

"Certainly; but which way do you think of taking? If you wish to go to the Dangra-yum-tso, you must cross the Kam-la, which lies a little farther up this valley. But if you prefer the route to the Ngangtse-tso, you must travel on eastwards. It is all the same to us which way you take, but I must know for certain. I will ride back to my tent and fetch parched meal, which you can buy when I overtake you in a few days. The yaks I will send to-morrow morning."

Karma Tamding seemed so trustworthy that I handed him half the purchase money in advance, and the next day we bought 3 yaks at 20 rupees a head, and received a guide, who conducted us over two difficult passes, eastwards to the Rara country, and on December 16 over the Pike-la, a gap in a longitudinal valley running parallel to the Bogtsang-tsangpo.

We were compelled to camp early by one of our three mules, which could not travel any farther. He came up to the fire with trembling legs and laid himself down. "The news of his death will be the first I shall hear in the morning," I thought, but I had not to wait so long, for before the stars had begun to twinkle he lay stiff and cold in the smoke of the camp-fire. Only two of the Poonch mules were left.

Then Karma Tamding rode up with twelve other Tibetans, two of them women. They sat down by the fire and looked at me; and I looked at them. The older woman had a fine sheepskin, and on the forehead an ornament of pendent coral and silver coins from Lhasa. The younger was similarly dressed, and had a huge lambskin cap. Little could be seen of her, but the little that was visible was dirty beyond belief. The men were strongly built and well proportioned — one could perceive that, when they drew off the right sleeve and exposed their breasts to the heat of the fire.

When we had gazed at one another long enough, and I had learned that the small lake near by was called the Tar-matse-tso, the whole party crawled into Muhamed Isa's tent to offer their edibles for sale. And there parched meal and barley was bought to the value of 68 rupees; it was quite a pleasure to see with what an appetite our last twelve animals emptied their bags of barley; they had so long had to put up with the execrable grass of the desert.

Next day we took leave of honest Karma Tamding. "On the boundary of Naktsang you will meet with an elderly man, named Chabga Namgyal, who is just as nice as I am," were his last words. We continued our long winter journey through Tibet eastwards along the same convenient longitudinal valley, and bivouacked in the district Neka, an ominous name (it means in Swedish to refuse), which might perhaps have brought us bad luck had the supreme chief of Tang-yung, whose headquarters are here, been at home at the time. Fortunately he had a short time before set out with his wife and children to Tashi-lunpo for the New Year festival, and had consigned his large herd of yaks and flock of sheep to the care of his servants and his herdsmen. They sold us milk and butter, but disapproved of my disturbing the gentle fish in a neighbouring pool. Within an hour I had twenty-five on dry land, which were a great treat at dinner. Robert had been unwell for some days, and now developed high fever, which confined him to his bed. Sonam Tsering suffered from a curious mountain sickness, in consequence of which all his body swelled up and assumed a livid hue. Two others were unwell, and the medicine chest stood open again. Sonam Tsering's tent was like an hospital, where all the sick found shelter as soon as they were incapacitated. Only old Guffaru was still healthy, did the work of two, and had at present no use for the shroud he brought from Leh. His large white beard had turned yellow in the smoke of the fires, and his hands, frost-bitten in winter, were dark and hard as iron. We stayed two days in camp No. 90, to give the invalids a rest. My dapple-grey from Yarkand was nearly drowned in a spring; fortunately he was seen from the camp, and ten strong men pulled him out of the mud. Then he was dried at the fire, rubbed well down, and covered with cloths. But his days were numbered.

On December 20 we ride on along the longitudinal valley parallel to the Bogtsang-tsangpo, and encamp at the mouth of a transverse valley, which belongs to the southern mountains, and is called Kung-lung. Frozen springs are seen on all sides; the farther we advance southwards the more the country is fertilized by the monsoon rains. The ground is honeycombed by millions of mouse holes; they are so close together that there is no room for more. The field-mouse here does the work of loosening and ploughing up the ground that the worm does in our soil. But the herbage derives no benefit from it, for the mice subsist on the roots and destroy the grass.

When we had passed the boundary between Tang-yung and Naktsang, and had just pitched our camp at the source of the brook draining the Kung-lung valley, three riders with guns suddenly appeared, who were making for the same spot, and behind them came a dark group, perhaps soldiers. Probably they were about to arrest us here, at the first camp in Naktsang. No; another false alarm. They were simply peasants from the Bogtsang-tsangpo, who had been to Naktsang to barter salt for *tsamba* (parched meal) and barley, and were now on their homeward journey. The troop consisted of members of several tent villages, among which the goods would be distributed. The *tsamba* and the barley were carried by yaks, horses, and sheep, and seemed sufficient to last many households all the winter.

Here I heard for the first time of the lake Shuru-tso, but I little thought that I should bivouac on its shore next spring. The range on the north, in which the Keva is the highest summit, is the water-parting between the Dagtse-tso and the Kung-tso, a lake visible to the east. On the south we had the range which we had first seen at the Dangra-yum-tso, and which afterwards skirts the south side of the Tang-yung-tso.

In the night the continued westerly storm increased to a hurricane, which blew down my tent. It was fastened up again, but at dawn I was awakened by a report like a gunshot, for one of the strained tent ropes broke, and another tore itself out of its iron cap, which fell with a sharp clatter against the tent. A shower of stones and coarse sand beat about my airy dwelling, so that it required a certain amount of resolution to issue forth in weather worse than we had experienced in Chang-tang.

"How much longer will the storm last?" I asked our guide, as he joyfully and thankfully pocketed his 18 rupees after he had handed us over to another guide of the Nakt-sang tribe.

"Six months," he replied.

We marched eastwards, gradually diverging to the south, and thus passed round the chain which had hitherto lain on our right. On the way we found Adul in a hollow, and asked him how he was.

"I am dying," he answered, without moving a muscle. I sent one of his comrades and a horse from the camp to bring in his corpse, but next morning he was as lively as a cricket. Such weather is certainly not enjoyable, but it is no use to complain of wind and weather. My horse staggers about as if he had drunk too much. At the opening of every lateral valley we may be sure of a buffet that will make us reel in our saddles. We bend sideways against the wind to help the horse in maintaining his equilibrium, and we draw ourselves together so as to present a smaller surface to the wind — indeed, we are like a sail that must always be set according to the direction of the wind, and

90. Near the Dangra-yum-tso. In the Valley below is seen the Little Lake Tang-yung-tso.
Sketch by the Author.

we have to trim ourselves just as one would handle a sailing-boat in a high sea. We rested awhile in the shelter of a rock, to recover our breath, and when at length we reached the camp in Nadsum we had suffered as much as we were able to bear. To the north-east, beyond the mountains, lies the Dagtse-tso, which Bower, Dutreuil de Rhins, Littledale, and I have visited; on the way thither a lake is passed, called the Goang-tso.

On the 22nd we took our way to the south, where a range of considerable height bars the road to the Ngangtse-tso. We followed the river Sertsang-chu upwards; a little water still bubbled and trickled down under its thick covering of ice. In the evening we received a visit from eight Tibetans, two of whom had lost all their yaks by a kind of cattle-plague. We ascended the same valley for another day's journey, and found five tents in an expansion of the valley which was called Torno-shapko; at several spots we saw large flocks of sheep guarded by dogs as snappy and impudent as the nomads themselves. Some of these fellows came into our camp and used very rude language, daring even to say that we must not remain here but must pack off with all speed. To buy milk and butter was out of the question. Muhamed Isa drove them away and threatened to report their conduct to the Governor of Naktsang. Our guide, a boy of fifteen, was frightened, but was persuaded to accompany us a day longer.

December 24. When I woke an old mendicant lama sat singing before my tent. He had a little withered woman with him, and their small light tent was pitched quite close to us. In his hand he held a staff bedecked with coloured strips and with brass plates, coral, shells, tassels, and other ornaments, which he made to spin round as he sang. The old man had in his lifetime wandered far and wide, begging his way from tent to tent, but when I asked him to accompany us and to bring in the Christmas festival with song at our camp at night he declared he was too tired.

The road led us higher up the same valley, soon leaving the sources behind. We passed two *manis* with prayers inscribed on the slabs, one of which was 23 feet long. Two tents stood at a spot where two large valleys converged. The unfriendly men we had met yesterday had gone on before us and had warned the people not to sell us anything if we asked them. Two of our men tried to trade, but met with a refusal, whereupon Muhamed Isa laid his riding-whip smartly across the backs of the mischief-makers. Then the whole company fell on their knees, became remarkably civil, and brought out at once all the butter and milk they had on hand.

Our valley now runs eastwards, and at last rises in a south-easterly direction to a pass. Evidently no great road runs over it, for there is no cairn on the summit. It turned out later that the youth had led us astray, omitting to turn aside through a southern valley to the pass Gurtse-la. However, it was of no consequence, for the view from our pass was grand, and below us lay a lake not marked on Nain Sing's map. The valley descending from the pass is so deeply eroded that we had to keep for some distance to the heights on the right side. Islam Ahun led my tall dapple-grey, which was weak and sickly; he took only a few steps at a time, but he could still graze. We had made a long march, and the camp could not be far distant, so he would perhaps reach it. I therefore only stroked him as I passed, while he held his nose to the ground and plucked up the grass. But when I left him to his fate and rode on, he raised his head, sighed heavily, and gazed after me. I was deeply grieved afterwards that I did not remain with him. He had carried me faithfully on the long dreary journey from our departure from Leh until his back became one great sore; then he was not worked till his back was healed. Afterwards he was degraded to a pack-horse, but when our caravan was reinforced with yaks, he was exempted from work of any kind. Latterly we had had abundance of barley for the animals, but he had shown no signs of recovery. This day, however, he had managed to climb the pass, and would surely be able to get over the short remaining distance. But Islam Ahun came into camp alone. The horse had stumbled on a very steep descent, rolled over several times in the débris, and then remained lying. Islam, who had received strict orders to be careful of the dapple-grey, stood and waited, but the horse did not move again, and died where he was. Why did I not understand him when he so plainly said a last good-bye? I was much grieved at it, and for a long time could not forget the troubled expression of his eyes as he saw me ride away. The remembrance haunted me when it grew dark at night and the winter storm howled in cold dreary Tibet.

Down below in the valley basin lay the Dumbok-tso asleep under its ice mantle, out of which rose a small rocky ridge, the Tso-ri or "Lake Mountain." Up above the heights were still bathed in sunshine. The Dumbok-tso was the most important discovery of the day. The watch-fires burned in front of the tents and threw a yellow light on the surroundings.

Then the day's notes were filled in, and Robert, as usual, labelled the rock specimens we had collected. "Dinner is ready," says Tsering, as he brings in fresh fuel, and the *shislik* and sour milk are served and placed on the ground before my bed. Then I am left alone with a thousand memories of Swedish Christmas feasts, and the words: "Christmas is now under every roof," and "Frozen is the limpid lake, it waits for the winds of spring," from the poet Topelius' Christmas song, rings in my ears. The Christian community in our camp consisted only of Robert and myself, but we determined to celebrate the Christmas festival so that the heathen also might have their share in the enjoyment. For some time we had kept all the candle ends, and now had forty-one pieces of various lengths. We set up a box in the middle of my tent, and arranged the candles on it so that the largest stood in the middle, and the others became smaller and smaller towards the corners. That was our Christmas-tree. When all the candles were lighted we threw back the flaps of the front of the tent, and the Ladakis, who meanwhile had assembled outside, gave vent to a murmur of astonishment. They sang softly in rising and falling tones. I forgot for a time the solemnity of the moment, and gazing into the flickering flames of the candles let the minutes of the holy night glide slowly by. The sentimental air was now and then interrupted by a thundering *khavash* and *khabbaleh* in which all joined, howling like jackals. The flutes performed the accompaniment, and a saucepan served as a drum. Lamaist hymns at a Christmas festival under the constellation of Orion! Dimly illuminated from the tent, and flooded by the silvery light of the moon, my men presented a weird appearance as they turned themselves round in their native dance, keeping time to the noise of the saucepan. The Tibetans of the neighbouring tents perhaps thought that we had all gone mad, or perhaps that we were executing an incantation dance, and had lighted sacrificial lamps to propitiate our gods. What the wild asses, grazing on the lake shore, thought of it, no one can tell.

Our young guide, who had been placed in the middle of the tent door, caused us much amusement. He stared, now at the lights, now at me, without uttering a sound, sat like a cat on the watch with its fore-paws on the ground, and did nothing but gaze. He would have wonderful stories to tell his fellow-tribesmen, which would certainly lose none of their effect by the embellishments added by himself and amplified in the course of repetition. Perhaps the memory of our visit still survives in the country, in a legend of singular fire-worshippers who danced and bellowed round an altar adorned with forty-one burning candles. When the youth was asked how he liked the illumination, he made no answer. We laughed till our sides ached, but that did not disturb him; he continued to glare with eyes full of astonishment. When he had somewhat recovered his senses next morning, he told Tundup Sonam in confidence that he had had many experiences, but that he had never met with anything so extraordinary as the evening's entertainment. He would not sleep with us that night, but went off to the tents of his people, and on the first holiday he begged permission to return home.

The lower the candles burned down, the brighter the stars of Orion shone into the opening of the tent. The corner lights had long gone out, and only a couple in the middle continued to flicker. Then I distributed a small sum of money among the men, beginning with Robert and Muhamed Isa. That was the only Christmas present.

After this the men retired to their fires, which had in the meantime gone out. Two had to stay behind to explain to me one of the songs in which the word Tashi-lunpo had repeatedly occurred. It was more difficult than I expected to translate the song. In the first place, the men did not know it well themselves, and, secondly, they did not know the meaning of some of the words it contained. Other words they understood well enough, but they could not translate them into Turki or Hindustani. First we wrote out the hymn in Tibetan, then Robert translated it into Hindustani, and I into Turki, and finally from the two translations we concocted an English version which had no sense or meaning. But by repeatedly taking the song to pieces and analyzing it, we at last made out what the subject was — it was a glorification of the monastery Tashi-lunpo, which was the goal of our hopes. The learned who happen to be acquainted with ancient Tibetan hymns will be very much amused if they take the trouble to read the following translation. It certainly has the merit of forming a record in poetic license.

Now rises the sun shining in the east,
From the eastern lands over the heights of the east.
It is now the third month that the sun mounts up,
Pouring forth floods of heat.
First fall the beams on the temple,
The house of the high gods, and caress
The golden battlements of Tashi-lunpo,
The roof of the venerable cloister temple,
And with threefold brilliance glitter the pinnacles in the sun.
On the highest meadows of the temple vale
Shy antelopes graze in thousands.
Hard is its crumbly soil, but still
Rich is the vale and green and lovely,
And grass thrives on its poor land,
And brooks ripple down with cool water.
The highest, ice-covered mountains glitter
Like transparent glass. The nearer summits
Rise like a row of lofty *chhortens,*
And close at their feet beat the blue waves
Of the Yum-tso, playing on the holy strand.
Take water from the lake and fill

The sacrificial bowls of the holy idols,
Moulded of brass. Then decorate with silk cloths
Of every kind and colour, which from Pekin come,
And adorn also with veils the tall golden images of the gods,
And fill the temple halls with hanging standards.
Take *kadakh* cloths, holy and dear,
Of best silk from the town of Lhasa,
And lay them on the forehead of Buddha's image.

So ended our Christmas Eve in the wilderness, and while the glow of the Christmas fire sank down in the ashes I read the old Bible passages relating to this day, put out my light, and dreamed of Christmas festivals in the north, and of Tashi-lunpo down in the south behind the mountains, the goal towards which we had been struggling amid suffering and privation all through the cold winter, and which was still far off and perhaps even beyond our reach.

CHAPTER XVIII

TEN DAYS ON THE ICE OF NGANGTSE-TSO

FROM the Christmas camp we travelled southwards over two passes, of which the second, called Laen-la, forms a watershed between the Dubok-tso and the Ngangtse-tso. The great lake itself we do not see yet, but a distant bluish background of mountain chain which rises from the southern shore of the lake. A yak was lost; he was not exhausted, but his fore-hoof had split so that he had become lame. When once he had laid himself down no power on earth could induce him to get up again; tugging at the rope, which was passed through his nasal cartilage, availed nothing. We therefore left him behind, and gave him to the natives nearest to our camp. Several yaks and the surviving veterans from Leh were in need of a thorough rest, so we decided to remain a fortnight at the great lake. It was certainly risky to linger so long at one place in Naktsang, where I had met with such determined opposition in the year 1901, for we should give the authorities time to make their preparations. But we must rest; we had no choice.

After a night temperature of $-24.2°$ we marched down the longitudinal valley to a point immediately above the place where the valley emerges into the lake-plain, and bivouacked near a group of tents containing six households. The whole country is corroded with mouse holes, and sometimes they lie in stages one above another. If one reckoned in the central parts of Tibet only one field-mouse to the square yard, the resulting total would be marvellous. At camp No. 97, for instance, it was impossible to lay down my bed without covering several holes, and I was awaked in the morning by the mice, which were making a noise and squeaking beneath my bed, and wondering why they could not get out of their house door.

The nomads of the district were friendly disposed, and sold us sheep, butter, and milk. They said that the high road to Shigatse skirted the east side of the lake; another to the west of the Ngangtse-tso was much longer and more difficult. The highway to Lhasa runs eastwards through Shanza-dzong. Thus far it had been followed by Nain Sing, whose route we crossed here; for from the Marku-tso, a small lagoon on the north shore, the road he took passes to the west-north-west. Many nomad communities winter on the extensive plains of the lake shore, especially on the south side. The nomads never travel over the lake, the most direct and quickest way, for they mistrust the ice, and our last guide would on no account accompany us over the lake, but warned us of the thin ice. His statements seemed to me more probable when he said that the lake was salt, that the water was not fit for drinking, and that there were neither fish nor plants in it.

The long period of rest must be utilized somehow. It had, moreover, been one of the aims proposed in the original scheme of my journey, to investigate the country round the central lakes discovered in 1874 by Nain Sing, and to execute soundings in several of them. If the ice held firm we could go over the lake, and sound through holes. Two men were therefore sent out to examine the ice: 100 paces from the bank the ice was 11 inches thick, at 200 paces $10\frac{1}{4}$ inches, and even at 300 paces 10 inches; so I determined to commence at the nearest point to our headquarters.

Robert and Muhamed Isa were to remain behind to watch over our animals and attend to them. It might, indeed, be risky to split up our caravan just at this time, but I could not remain idle for a whole fortnight. There was everything we needed at the headquarters — nomads, pasturage, water, and fuel; the place seemed to be of some importance, for a round *mani* stood in the valley, and Robert found on a ridge a *samkang*, a hermit's cave, with a small stone wall in front of it. There the lama Togldan was wont to dwell in summer, earning his bread from the neighbouring nomads by murmuring formulæ to conjure evil spirits, and offering up prayers for the prosperity of their flocks. We had an hour and a half's journey to the northern shore, and there innumerable camping-places indicate summer visits of nomads. There the tents are situated among excellent pasture lands, exposed to the noonday sun, with the great lake, often agitated by boisterous storms, in front of them.

We got ready provisions for ten days for myself and half a dozen Ladakis. Two live sheep were taken. The men were to take Robert's small tent, but I intended to sleep under a half of the boat, which was to be pushed over the ice as a sledge, laden with all the baggage, bed, furs, and instruments. The boat would also be a source of safety should we at any time venture on to too thin ice. The white puppy was to go with us to keep me company. During my absence Robert occupied my tent, where the barograph and the thermograph ticked on my boxes.

On the afternoon of December 29 I rode down to the Ngangtse-tso, where camp No. 98 was pitched on a lagoon under the shelter of a shore embankment. Towards the east-south-east the country is open as far as the sight can carry; the eastern shore of the lake is scarcely perceptible, the western not at all; in the south-west snow mountains rise up, which, I said to myself, must be Nain Sing's "Targot Lha Snowy Peaks." Rabsang was my valet, Bulu my cook; they arranged my improvised hut, and the building material consisted of half of the boat, the stand of my photographic camera, and a frieze rug. For dinner I was given leg of mutton, sour milk, bread, orange marmalade, and tea; and then I smoked an Indian cheroot and gazed at the lake, which was to be thoroughly investigated during the succeeding days.

The 30th of December, a Sunday, began brightly with 45.2 degrees of frost. Puppy had kept my feet warm. It was rather tight work washing and dressing in my den, but when at last I was ready, I could enjoy the fire, the sight of the sun and of the great lake. The baggage was quickly packed, and the boat was dragged on to the ice and kept in equilibrium by two runners, while six men pushed it forward. But the ice gave us much trouble. The salt separated out on freezing had collected on the surface like dry potato flour, sometimes forming continuous sheets, sometimes swept up into banks, ridges, and drifts, in which the runners and keel stuck fast. However, in spite of it, we worked our way on in a direction 9° east of south, where I had selected a small dark cliff on the south shore as a landmark. The first hole was cut out; the ice was 8½ inches thick, and the depth of the lake, reckoned from the edge of the ice, only 13 feet.

After we had wandered on for some time we held a council; I saw that we could not go on as we were. We took off the runners and put together three simple sledges, on each of which a third of the baggage was tied. And in this way we struggled on a short distance farther, while I went on foot. At the next hole the depth was 18.7 feet; probably we were on one of those extraordinarily shallow salt lakes, such as I had often met with in north-eastern Tibet. Again we held a consultation; our sledges made such slow progress that we should never get over the lake at all, far less traverse it several times. When two of the baggage sledges, which had lingered far behind, came up, I sent a message to Robert to send me more men and all the pieces of old boxes that were in the caravan.

Meanwhile we took off the two zinc runners, which were screwed into the gunwale and into which the mast thwart was fitted. They were then fastened as sledge cheeks to two benches bound together; to the sides of this singular vehicle two long poles were attached, meeting at an angle, through which the towing-rope was slung. A Caucasian *burkha*, which I had bought at Trebizond, was laid in several folds on the benches. For the sounding apparatus, the field-glass and other articles, we stretched a hammock between the poles. When the structure was complete it astonished us; for we had only to give this newly devised sledge a push and off it ran a good way by itself. Now the boat was contemptuously discarded, and

91, 92, 93. ON THE NGANGTSE-TSO.

when Rabsang with the towing-rope over his shoulder hurried off southwards over the ice unaided, the boat soon diminished to a black speck and disappeared. The others had orders to follow the track of the runners at their leisure; they would soon get help when the other men came (Illustrations 91, 92, 93).

Wrapped in my large sheepskin I sat cross-legged on the sledge, which glided merrily over the ice by the hour together, while Rabsang had no need to over-exert himself. The sledge cut through the salt ridges as though they were nothing, and bumped with a pleasant rumbling noise over the places where the ice was lumpy; it jumped over cracks and fissures, where the edges of the ice shone green, and clear as glass, and on smooth patches shot noiselessly forward, so that its point reached Rabsang's heels if he did not jump on one side just when the line became slack.

It was really not dangerous on the ice, which was nowhere less than 7 inches thick. So the Tibetans' dread of drowning was exaggerated. But they have always the greatest respect for the spirits inhabiting the lakes, and would rather go all round a lake than cross it, mistrusting the winter repose of the raging storm-beaten waves.

Many singular effects of congelation may be observed, which change their forms in various parts. Sometimes they are innumerable vertical figures in perfectly clear dark ice; seen from the side they have the form of oak leaves, but looked at from above they resemble stars with four arms thin as paper. At other places you find blocks of white porous ice embedded in clear ice, the result of a storm which has broken up the first ice-sheet of early winter, whereafter the blocks are enclosed in new ice on the final freezing over. Water is squeezed out through long narrow cracks, and is congealed into screens sometimes a yard in height, forming fantastic sheets and domes, and edges and points often as sharp as a knife. Rabsang has only to give them a kick to clear a passage for the sledge, but these thin ice-fences are very misleading, and render it difficult to estimate distances.

We sounded in eight holes, and the greatest depth was only 32 feet. The bottom consists of dark clay mud. It took a good quarter of an hour to cut out a hole in the ice with axes and crowbars. As soon as the last blow drove through the bottom of the ice, clear, cold, dark green water welled up and filled the cavity, and then the sounding weight was let down by its rope.

The first line of soundings had occupied far too long a time, chiefly owing to the interruptions and repeated re-arrangement of the baggage at starting, and we were still far from the nearest shore when the sun set in clouds of red and gold. But the full moon shone in the heavens, the rocky promontory was sharp and clearly perceptible, and we made all haste we could. The ice was uncomfortably lumpy, so that I had to traverse long stretches on foot. Cold, white, and desolate the ice mantle of the lake extended on all sides; all was silent and quiet, only the crunching sound of our own footsteps could be heard. If nomads had pitched their tents on the shore we were approaching they would be much perplexed by the black specks moving out on the lake. But no fire illumined the night and no wolves howled. In the darkness we could, of course, gain no notion of how much further we had to go. At the last hole the promontory had not appeared much larger. And so we marched onwards until Rabsang suddenly came to a halt with the information that we were only a few hundred paces from dry land.

There we left the sledge and advanced to the outlying mountains, where several fallen blocks of stone lay at the foot. Under one of them we sat down to wait. Then Rabsang collected as much fuel as he could in the dark. We must light a signal fire to guide the others. At length they tramped up, Tashi, Ishe, Bulu, and Islam Ahun, all heavily laden, for they had preferred to leave the sledges behind and carry the baggage. Two hours later some dark points were noticed out on the ice; it was the reinforcement, and now I had ten men with me. They had seen from the lake fires at four places; we were therefore surrounded by nomads on all sides, but we had no need of them, so we did not trouble ourselves about them.

Profiting by experience, we made the most practical arrangements possible for our next day's wanderings. Islam Ahun was to return to headquarters, collecting all the things we had dropped on our way, and was to see that the boat was fetched. Rabsang and Tashi drew my sledge, the others carried the baggage. At first they followed a road along the shore before taking to the ice and making for the goal for the day, in the north-west. We keep them in sight all day. They march in Indian file, trotting, swaying, and singing, and sometimes sitting down for a rest. Then they use the firmly tied bundles as back-rests. But they cannot get up again without help; it is very easy for six of them, but the seventh, that is, the one who has to get up first, finds it more difficult. He rolls over on to his stomach, wriggles up with the help of a stick, and when he has at length accomplished the feat, he helps the others to get on their feet.

The ice was excellent, far better than on the first traverse. Also the salt was less abundant, owing to the westerly storms which sweep it eastwards. For long distances the ice lay pure and smooth in front of us, and had a dark green colour. I did not know what to make of it when we tramped over the dark patches. Were there warm springs at the bottom which prevented the lake from freezing over in parts? But we soon became accustomed to the sight, the ice was firm and at least 6½ inches thick, while the greatest depth amounted to 31¾ feet. I sat like a statue of Buddha cross-legged on my toy sledge, smoked, took observations, made notes, and rejoiced that I could keep New Year's Eve on the ice of Ngangtse-tso. About mid-day a south-westerly wind arose, and I had to ride backwards so as not to get frozen. A lead running north and south puzzled us greatly. It was 5 feet broad, and ran in either direction as far as the eye could reach; open water lapped between the margins of ice. Probably it had come into existence during a storm, when the whole ice-sheet was slightly disturbed towards the east, and had left behind it a yawning channel. After a long search we found a place where fresh ice was being formed below. Using the sledge as a bridge we crossed over dry-footed.

How the others got over the difficulty I do not know, but they were not afraid of wetting their feet.

We went ashore rather early, at a place where 19 horses were grazing on the wide plain and a youth was watching 500 sheep. He scampered off in a hurry when he saw us coming, and I was not surprised that he was afraid when he saw ten great fellows stealing like ghosts over a lake that had never been trodden by human foot. The Ladakis sat round a large fire, sang, and blew their flutes, and the moonlight poured down a cold, peaceful flood of light over the unknown strand where a party of wandering strangers were passing a single night of their lives. It was the last night of the year 1906, and the camp was our hundredth.

A splendid New Year's morning in 1907! With joyful hopes for the new year and its work I began the third line of soundings in a direction south, 19° E., towards a dark spur lying between two valleys where ice-clumps glistened in the sun. The spur seemed to fall steeply to the lake and the distance seemed tremendous, but it was an illusion: the low plain extending from the foot of the mountains to the lake could not be seen from the ice. We had to cross the fissure of the day before, but it had frozen over in the night. But water stood in many other fissures and spurted up as we passed over. This day our porters kept up with us, and their songs resounded far and wide over the ice-fields. At every new hole they settled down and awaited the result of the sounding with genuine interest. Singular men, always cheerful and contented, never down-hearted and complaining, taking everything as it comes, and calm and composed in all kinds of wind and weather.

Puppy has had enough of running over the ice, suffers from cold feet, jumps on the sledge as soon as it comes to a halt, but has a decided objection to riding.

A conical summit to the south of camp No. 99 dominates the whole lake like a lighthouse. Nain Sing, who touched the north shore of the Ngangtse-tso, has drawn the outline of the lake on the whole correctly, but has made the south-western part too broad. There also the sheet of water narrows down to a point, and the whole has the form of a half-moon. The mountains, which the Pundit has inserted in his map on the south side of the lake, are very erroneously portrayed, and no wonder — for he saw them only from a great distance, and could not possibly, in these circumstances, obtain any proper notion of their configuration. It is just as hard to form an idea of a lake by viewing it from the shore; this is possible only from a pass or a crest.

We wondered whether we could reach the southern shore before twilight, for the distance seemed still enormous. About noon the wind began to blow strongly, whirled up white clouds of dry salt, swept them along the ice, and obscured our view. Sitting on the sledge I was exposed to its full onslaught, and had to be careful not to open my mouth. Here and there the ice rose in undulations, as though it had been formed in a high sea; the ice-waves also have a steep slope towards east-north-east, the way of the wind. In the troughs between them the salt-dust driven by the wind collects, and lends to the ice-field a curious appearance like watered silk. All the eastern half of the lake is concealed by the rocky promontories near which our camp, No. 99, is pitched. We penetrate more deeply into the southern bay. Yaks graze on the slopes, and towards evening are driven down by a man. To the south also we catch sight of tents, yaks, and groups of kiangs. From our low point of view they seem to be moving in the midst of the lake; the acuteness of the angle of elevation deceives us. At the last sounding-hole the axe and crow-bar bored deeper and deeper into the ice without breaking through. Not till a depth of 17¼ inches was reached did the water burst violently up, full of the usual small red crustaceæ — the salinity of the lake cannot therefore be very great. Somewhat further the ice was found to lie directly on the clayey bottom without a layer of water beneath it. Then we came to the sterile shore, and were glad that we were this day independent of vegetation. We found fuel and obtained water by melting lumps of ice. The greatest depth on this line was 30.8 feet, or a little less than on the others.

We had another boisterous storm towards evening. The lake ice, only a couple of yards distant, vanished completely from sight, and the dung-gatherers suddenly emerged from the mist when they were only a few steps from the fire. I could not understand how they found their way in such a thick atmosphere. They erected a shelter from the wind with the sledge and three sacks of fuel, and sat behind it by their fire, the flickering flames almost singeing their faces. The group was exceedingly picturesque in the dark night and the struggling moonbeams. And how it blew! I could scarcely keep my feet when I read the thermometer, and my cap flew in all directions. In the night the men slept huddled up together in the shelter of the tent.

The temperature on January 2 was − 8°. To-day the fourth line had to be executed; it was short, it is true—barely five hours, but trying. We had to march southwestwards, straight in the teeth of the wind. Moreover, the ice proved rough and heavy, doubtless in consequence of the slight depth of the lake. The maximum depth was 10.6 feet. In my diary, this day is described as one of the worst, if not absolutely the worst, day of the whole journey. But we always think that what is present is the worst, forgetting the horrors of the past. The storm drove the salt before it in thick clouds, which scoured the ice with a swishing sound and dashed into my face. When I ordered my two "towing horses" to keep the direction, a quantity of salt flew into my mouth, and I had the greater dfficulty in getting rid of the disagreeable taste that the powder also made its way into my nose. My eyes became red, watered, and ached. My hands, from constant contact with the sounding-line for several days, were encrusted with salt, and the skin cracked so deeply that the blood ran. Sometimes my hands turned blue, were stiff, and lost all feeling, so that it was only with the greatest difficulty that I managed, holding the pen in the fist like a chisel, to jot down the results of the soundings, the times, and distances; other notes were not to be thought of. Rabsang and Tashi at all events kept themselves warm, for they had to put forth all their strength to drag the sledge against the storm. Where the ice was smooth they could not get firm foothold, slipped and fell; once Tashi was thrown into my lap, capsized by the gale. Often the wind was so strong that sledge and team were driven backwards, and the men could only stop themselves by sitting down and planting their feet against a ridge of salt. I became so benumbed and helpless that I could not rise, and had to remain sitting while the holes were hacked out. But at one hole, which was broken in a field of ice as smooth as a mirror, the wind seized the sledge and myself and carried us in a dizzy race over the lake like an ice-yacht. I tried to put on the drag with my feet, but I had no power in them, and my boots of soft felt glided lightly and jauntily over the ice mirror without reducing the speed in the least. The runners were too short, and the sledge revolved in a circle, but still it moved onwards, and if the ice had been all smooth, the storm would have blown me back in a few minutes all across the lake to camp No. 98. Then my vehicle fortunately tilted over in a fissure, I was thrown out, shot a little way farther over the ice, and landed on a salt ridge. Rabsang hurried sliding after me, picked up me and the sledge, and drew me back to the hole unharmed (Illustration 94).

Our appearance was enough to frighten one another. We looked like swollen disinterred corpses, dried in the sun and daubed with white oil paint. Faces, hands, and clothes were white with salt. I could not wear my sheepskin again; it was stiff, had given way at the seams, and had to be thrown away with other clothes.

We had not yet covered half the distance. The men exerted themselves as though they had to struggle through water 3 feet deep. Oftentimes I could not see through the clouds of salt, and nothing was visible of the ice beneath the sledge; it seemed as though we stood still while a foaming white flood poured down on us ready to swallow us up. I wondered whether we should ever reach the shore alive. There was very little life in me when we at length landed. The sledge was anchored to prevent the storm carrying it away, and then we climbed five terrace banks, one after another, to seek shelter behind the wall of a sheepfold erected on the sixth. Fortunately we found dry yak dung there in great abundance, and soon had a roaring fire, at which I had to sit a good hour before my limbs became at all supple again.

From camp No. 102 to the southern extremity of the lake the distance measured 3260 paces. There large herds were feeding, and six tents were set up at the mouth of the valley. About five o'clock the storm ceased as suddenly as it had sprung up, and it became strangely calm. When I took the meteorological observations at nine o'clock all my men were lying in a row, with their heads against the wall, their foreheads on the ground, and their legs drawn up, and as close to one another as sardines in a tin. They slept well; that I could tell from the tunes their nasal organs emitted.

There were shells of freshwater molluscs on the strand, and a quantity of goose feathers in a bank formed of decaying algæ. At present the water of the lake is not fit to drink, but the Ngangtse-tso was a freshwater lake formerly, that is, when it still discharged into one of its neighbours.

Wearied by our exertions on the previous day we slept till late, and then started off in a north-easterly direction towards the red porphyry mountains which jut out into the lake to the west of camp No. 99. We had no storm, but a brisk wind, and when it blew at our backs we glided like oil over the ice. I had a pole to steer with.

Beyond the promontory we encamped in a deep hollow to obtain shelter from the wind. A shepherd was feeding his sheep on a slope and tried to make his escape, but Rabsang overtook him. He thought we were robbers. He had nothing to sell, for he was in the service of another man. But Rabsang requested him to bring his master to us. Meanwhile the others had arrived, except Ishe, who had fallen ill, and was left lying in the middle of the lake. Two of his comrades fetched him in the evening. All were tired out, and begged that they might make a short march on January 4, and that suited us well, for the shepherd's master came and sold us a sheep, butter, sour milk, and a bag of tobacco. It was high time, for the provisions were almost consumed. The tobacco was quite a

94. In a Snowstorm on the Ice of the Ngangtse-tso.

godsend to the men, for latterly they had been reduced to smoking yak dung! The old man gave much interesting information about the Ngangtse-tso, and told us that there were then fifty to sixty tents pitched in the valleys of the southern shore. So far all was well, but the day was not yet ended.

CHAPTER XIX

DRIVEN BACK

A DISMAL, inauspicious day was January 4, 1907. Towards noon Islam Ahun appeared, half dead with weariness. He had left headquarters on the morning of the 2nd, and searched up and down the lake for us; had been on the west and on the south shore; and at last, following the most recent track of the sledge, had found us in our dell. He brought me a letter from Robert:

> Yesterday, on January 1st, six armed men came to the camp, made a few inquiries, and went off again. To-day, the 2nd, they returned with some other men, and said the Governor of Naktsang had ordered them not to allow us to proceed further, because we had no passport from the Devashung, and that we must remain where we are. They wanted an answer from Master, in order to report to the Governor, who would communicate immediately with Lhasa. They are waiting impatiently for a reply, so I am sending off this letter.

After Islam Ahun had rested and eaten, he had to take back a letter to Robert at camp No. 97. Robert was to inform the ambassadors that I would not give an answer until I had seen them in person; if they were so anxious to hear it, they might come on the afternoon of the 5th to the northern shore at a distance of three miles from camp No. 98. If they did not, they must be answerable for the consequences. Muhamed Isa must come with them as interpreter.

Now matters were coming to a head. This time it was not a false alarm. Tidings of our journey had been sent to Lhasa, and we were in the hands of the Governor of

Naktsang. I had put off the decisive moment in order to get time for at least one more line of soundings. If I could advance no farther in Naktsang, at any rate I would complete my investigation of the Ngangtse-tso. Afterwards the great retreat might commence. The intense excitement in which we had lived during the past months had now reached its culmination, and the Ngangtse-tso was to be the turning-point of our journey. I heard distinctly the creaking and grinding of the hinges as the great gates of the land of holy books, the forbidden land in the south, were slammed in my face.

At length we set off to camp No. 104, which was situated on the southern shore to the east of camp No. 99.

January 5. Every blade and stalk was covered with rime in the early morning when we marched over the ice in a direction north, 19° E. The day was fine and calm, the air pleasant, almost warm. Was the spring coming? Did spring set in so early in these more southern regions? It had seemed so far off that we had not thought of looking forward to its mild air while the long winter of Chang-tang still lingered in our limbs. We needed more warmth to thaw properly. The ice cracked and groaned wildly in the night, but it was not on that account that I slept badly.

Here the ice-fields form long waves; banks of water pressed up and then frozen, brittle as glass, came in sight every minute. The greatest depth, 32.9 feet, occurred when we were 6.6 miles from the shore, and was the deepest we sounded in the Ngangtse-tso. The lake is, then, deeper in the east; the west wind silts up its western half with sand and dust.

Half way across we saw a small dark speck on the ice in the direction of the Laen valley. It was the Hajji with a letter. The envoys had received fresh orders from the Governor of Naktsang. In four days he would appear in his own exalted person, and meanwhile his representatives were to watch us closely. Consequently they remained with the caravan, but they had allowed Robert and Muhamed Isa to transfer our headquarters to a place south-east of camp No. 97, where the pasturage was better.

We had therefore freedom for a couple of days longer. The Governor of Naktsang! It was he who in 1901 had made me halt at the south side of the Zilling-tso. I could expect no mercy from him. On the contrary, I had on the former occasion given him so much trouble and annoyance that he would be furious at my return to his province.

On January 6 Ishe was so ill that the Hajji was obliged to take him home. Now we crossed the lake again in a direction north, 49° E. We had just arrived at our second sounding-hole when three men, who had followed our track, came in sight behind us. They made signs that we should stop, so fresh news must have arrived. We were able to cut out our hole and take a sounding before they came running up to us. They were Muhamed Isa with two other of my men, perspiring and breathless, and I invited them to make themselves comfortable on our lawn.

"What is the news?" I asked.

"Sahib, twenty-five Tibetans have pitched their tents round about ours. We wished this morning to move our headquarters to the shore, in order to be nearer to you. All the animals were laden, and we were about to set out, when the men came out of their tents and forced us to unload the animals again, and ordered us to stay where we were."

"Have you heard anything more of the Governor?"

"He is to be here in three days. Mounted messengers are coming and going daily, often several in one day, and they seem to ride fast. They are in constant communication with the Governor and send him reports."

"What do they say to my remaining away so long?"

"They are exceedingly astonished at it, and repeatedly ask us what the Sahib is doing out on the ice. They have had spies on the shore, and believe that the Sahib is dredging up gold through the holes from the lake bed."

"Are they civil to you?"

"Yes, but determined and immovable. They say that the Governor himself will decide our fate. Their number has been greatly increased during the latter days, they have provisions brought to them, and they expect further reinforcements."

"What is their intention, do you think, Muhamed Isa?"

"Ah, the outlook is not bright. They certainly intend to render our further progress impossible, and to force us to go northwards."

"We have to thank for this that ill-omened fellow on the Bogtsang-tsangpo, who has despatched an express messenger to Naktsang. If we come to a deadlock here, they must provide us with a new caravan, and we will travel to Pekin. There I will procure permission from the Chinese Government to travel through Tibet. How is the caravan?"

"All's well. A mule died the day before yesterday, and my black saddle-horse yesterday. Eight horses and a mule are left. The yaks are in splendid condition."

"We shall have plenty of time to rest at this lake, for if we have to negotiate with Lhasa, it will be a couple of months before the question is settled. Now, go back and remember me to the others."

We went on with our sounding and found a maximum depth of 27.4 feet. On the shore old banks were plainly perceptible; they have here been exposed to the breakers of the western storms. The highest might be about 50 feet high. There paced a solitary wolf, farther back 25 kiangs were grazing; they looked at us inquisitively for a long time, and then darted away as lightly and swiftly as the wind. We saw no sign of our porters, and on the shore, where we walked along the highest bank, we did not find a track. Why did they not signal by lighting a fire? At last we caught sight of them far off in a northerly direction. They were tired and lay down to sleep as soon as they reached land. I did not scold them, but Rabsang seized the first he could get hold of by the hair, and then gave them all a thrashing in turn, which, however, did not prevent them singing as merrily as usual in the evening.

Now my work on the Ngangtse-tso was finished, after marches over the ice aggregating 66 miles.

On January 7 the porters with all our belongings, except my tent, set off for headquarters. I waited for my riding horse, did not allow my mind to be disturbed, and was in no hurry to give myself up to the Tibetan militia — those horrid black riders who had so often interfered with my plans. No news came from Shigatse, no post from India. I had ordered it to arrive at the Dangra-yum-tso on the 25th of November, and now it was January 7. Had Ganpat Sing lost the letters, or had they never reached Leh? Was it, perhaps, impossible, for political reasons, to send me my letters from India?

I had to wait a long time. It was not till one o'clock that a man appeared with my horse, and at the same time a caravan of 50 yaks appeared on the inner terrace embankment, driven by Tibetans. We supposed that it was the Governor's baggage train, but the Tibetans said that they were natives of Laen, and had been attending the market in Naktsang.

We were three hours from the camp. Seven wild asses trotted in front of us for an hour; the wind was strong against us. Clouds of sand and dust swept along the bank, the icy surface became invisible, and the wild asses disappeared like ghosts in the mist. The light was curious and confusing, the ascent became steeper, and fresh hills continually appeared out of the dense air, which was like muddy water. Often a small troop of Goa gazelles sprang lightly past. We did not see camp No. 107 until we were close upon it.

A deep erosion channel running towards the lake. On its right flank are our four tents, looking eastwards. Muhamed Isa stands at his fire, his hands in his pockets, his pipe in his mouth (Illustration 66). All the others come out. The Tibetans peer out of their tents like field-mice out of their holes. Robert reports: "All quiet on the Shipka pass." The day before our horses, chased by wolves, had stampeded and had taken the Tibetan horses with them, but they were all found again in scattered groups along the shore.

I entered Muhamed Isa's tent; when I was seated the principal Tibetans were summoned. They presented themselves immediately, bowed low, and thrust out their tongues as far as possible; this time this original mode of salutation seemed to me a mockery. A man with a red turban, dark-blue fur coat, and a sabre in his belt, had been in 1901 in Hlaje Tsering's camp on the eastern shore of the Chargut-tso, when we encamped together, and he reminded me of that time.

"Is Hlaje Tsering still ruler of Naktsang?" I asked.

"Yes, it is he who is coming the day after to-morrow."

"Is he bringing with him as large a following as last time?"

"No; he perceived then that the troops of mounted men did not frighten you, and he trusts that you will be amenable to his wishes."

January 8 was spent in repacking the baggage, and on the 9th the Tibetans set up another tent, intended, they said, for the Governor's kitchen. At dusk two riders arrived, who announced that the Governor begged to be excused for not arriving at the stated time. He was an old man, had had the storm against him on the way, and could only travel slowly, but he would certainly be here on the evening of the 12th.

Then I sent for the chiefs of the Tibetans, and told them that they would not be admitted to my presence again if they did not speak the truth this time.

"Bombo Chimbo," they replied, "if the Governor is not here in three days you may cut off our heads."

"That is not necessary; it will suffice if you bind yourselves in writing to pay me a fine of ten horses if the Governor is not here in three days."

"We will give you twenty horses."

"No, ten are enough." And now the contract was drawn up and signed.

"Have you any fresh information?"

"Yes; the Governor has brought only his own twelve servants. He knows that the Bombo Chimbo is come back, for he received a letter from the Bogtsang-tsangpo, saying that the same traveller who had been there five years ago with a camel caravan was there again. Then he sent an express to Lhasa, and waited ten days for an answer, but at length decided to come himself."

Our patience was put to the trial again, as though we

had not had already occasion enough to exercise it. At last, on the 11th, a small group of cavaliers appeared against the hills, and soon after a blue-and-white tent stood in the camp of the Tibetans — they had now seven in all. Then followed a party of mounted men, one of whom sat very much bent, wore a red *bashlik*, and was carefully wrapped in furs. "That is Hlaje Tsering," we were told. His followers carried guns decked with red pennants. They seemed very starved, quickly withdrew into their tents, and we heard nothing more of them.

January 12. All too soon a messenger came to ask if I would go to the Governor's tent, or whether he should first pay me a visit. I sent an answer that I would let him know when I could receive him. My poor storm-beaten tent was made as fine as circumstances allowed; there was no room for more than two guests, but frieze rugs and cushions were laid down for them, and between these seats and my bed a large brazier was placed, so that the old man might get a good warm. My messenger was just gone, when two horses were led up to the blue-and-white tent, and the old man mounted one, a young lama the other; the horses were led by the bridle, the other Tibetans fell in on foot, and the procession moved off slowly to our tents.

Hlaje Tsering, for it was really my old friend, came in a parade costume of Chinese cut, with a Chinese cap, decorated with two foxes' tails and a white glass button, and in boots trimmed with velvet and with thick white soles. On his silken robe with wide hanging sleeves he wore a short collar of otter skin, and in the lobe of the left ear a large earring of pure gold studded with round turquoises. When he appeared I went to meet and salute him. We at once recognized each other, exchanged warm greetings, nay, almost embraced, and remarked how singular it was that we should meet here again in the midst of the wilderness after five long years. Holding his hand in mine, I conducted him to the modest seat of honour, and invited the lama, his secretary, a son of the Yunduk Tsering of 1901, to take a seat. I sat cross-legged on my bed beside him, Robert and Muhamed Isa in the

95. Hlaje Tsering and his Travelling Companion, a Lama, at my Tent on the Ngangtse-tso.

tent door, while the rest of the space framed by the opening was filled with a mosaic of Tibetan heads. Muhamed Isa, the interpreter, wore a robe of ceremony presented to him by Younghusband in Lhasa: it was made of thick, cerise-coloured Tibetan woollen material, and was confined round the waist by a coloured girdle; on his head he wore a tall gold-embroidered turban from Peshawar. He put us all in the shade with his finery (Illustrations 30, 95.)

After I had taken out a box of Egyptian cigarettes, and Hlaje Tsering had for a time examined everything in the tent, he said with a solemn, troubled manner:

"In my capacity as Governor of Naktsang I cannot allow you to proceed further, to Shigatse or in any other direction within the boundaries of Naktsang. Soon after the English expedition to Lhasa I received orders from the Devashung to allow no European in future, as formerly, to travel about in Naktsang. My instructions are that if any European forces his way into Naktsang it is the duty of my office to stop him and force him to turn back."

I replied: "It is impossible that the conditions remain the same as five years ago, when you held up my caravan with your militia of 500 men. Since then the Indian Government has concluded a treaty with the Devashung in Lhasa, and now the two Governments are on most friendly terms."

"Hedin Sahib, you will remember what took place last time. You were then so kind as to turn back at my request, but you do not know what befell me. All the expenses of the levy raised against you I had to pay, and the Devashung demanded from me 2000 rupees in addition. I was ruined, while my colleague, Yunduk Tsering, enriched himself by exploiting the people, and now lives, a wealthy man, in Lhasa. We are old friends, but I cannot expose myself to new vexations on your account."

"It is true, Hlaje Tsering, that we are old friends, but you cannot expect me to undergo another journey through Chang-tang on your behalf. I owned 130 animals when I left Ladak five months ago. Now, as you can see yourself, I have only 9. I will not be persuaded to return by the same way, and by the treaty of Lhasa you have no means of compelling a stranger by force."

"The treaty of Lhasa was concluded with England. You are not an Englishman but a Swede-*Peling*."

"You have the more reason to show me hospitality. England forced a war on you against your wishes; my country has not done so."

"You are right; your people has never injured us. But in my instructions no distinction is made between different nations. I shall certainly not force you to retrace your steps to Ladak by the long troublesome route by which you came; I know that this is impossible without a large strong caravan. It is of no consequence to me whether you succeed in reaching Shigatse or not, but you must not travel thither through my province. In Naktsang there is only one road open to you, namely, the one by which you came. I do not mind what road you take afterwards, and if you can force your way to Shigatse from the northern and western shores of the Dangra-yum-tso, that is not my affair."

"You know that the Tashi Lama was in India a year ago, and how well he was received there. He expects me in his capital, and no one else has the right to hinder me on my journey to him."

"Naktsang is under the Devashung, not under the Tashi Lama."

"The Dalai Lama took to flight when the English troops drew near to Lhasa. The Tashi Lama is now, therefore, Tibet's foremost Grand Lama."

"Quite right; we do not understand the action of the Dalai Lama, and do not approve of it. He should have been the first to protect his country from its enemies. But that has nothing to do with the question. I receive my instructions solely and only from the Devashung."

"And I shall not leave Naktsang until the Tashi Lama has confirmed your statement that the way is closed. I will, then, forward a letter to the representative of the Indian Government in Gyangtse, Major O'Connor, and if he replies that the political situation forbids my travelling further, I will leave Tibet. I will await his answer here, at the Ngangtse-tso. And I have another reason for this resolution. I am expecting letters from India, which are to be forwarded through Major O'Connor. You will understand that I am not disposed to leave Naktsang before the arrival of my letters, which will doubtless be sent on by order of the Tashi Lama."

"That is all very fine, but have you any proof that the Tashi Lama will assume the responsibility of forwarding your letters? You have no passport from the Devashung. Have you one from the Tashi Lama? It is not my duty to serve your pleasure. If I send your letter to Gyangtse on my own responsibility I shall lose my head."

"I will send two of my own Ladakis with the letter."

"No; the land is closed to them as much as to you. And, besides, how long do you expect to have to wait here for the answer? Several months?"

"Oh no; it is 165 English miles to Gyangtse, and the journey will not take more than twenty days, even with short marches."

"I shall not leave this place till you have started northwards and passed the frontier of Naktsang."

"And I will not start till I have received an answer to my letter from Gyangtse."

"You cannot possibly remain here long. You cannot feed your men; there are no nomads here, and those who dwell in the neighbourhood are poor as rats."

"I saw many tents on the southern shore and large flocks. At the worst we can live by hunting; there is plenty of game here. As I ask nothing but that you will allow me to wait here for an answer, you might oblige me so far."

"There you make a mistake. In my position neither Shigatse nor Gyangtse has anything to do with me. When the English had evacuated Tibet the Devashung sent a proclamation round to every *dzong* (governor's residential town) in Tibet that we had certainly been beaten, but that we had lost none of our territory and were still masters over it, so that the old regulations with regard to European travellers were still in force. I will try to meet you as far as I can, and will now withdraw to my tent to take counsel with my people."

At the same time I held a council of war with Robert and Muhamed Isa. It was perfectly evident that we could not continue our journey southwards. On the other hand, it seemed possible that, making a detour to the Dangra-yum-tso, we might penetrate into the country on its west side, which was governed, Hlaje Tsering said, from Saka-dzong. Were we driven from there, we would direct our course to Pekin. Why? I am certainly very optimistic, but I had a conviction that I could befool the Chinese Emperor as Marco Polo did, and obtain his permission to travel about freely in Tibet, with some kind of special mission as a pretext. Muhamed Isa thought it was an enormous distance to Pekin, but Robert was enthusiastic about the journey. We would only take our best men; for the others I could procure permission to return to Ladak through Gartok. We should have a hard journey at first, but through Southern Mongolia we should fly on Bactrian camels like wild deer over the steppe. I would on no account return home vanquished. I tried to infect the two others with my enthusiasm, and depicted our camel ride as a fairy tale and a romance.

Now two of Hlaje Tsering's men presented themselves, bringing a dish of rice and a lump of butter as a present from their master. The secretary lama sent an apron full of rice. In return I sent Muhamed Isa with a whole piece of *pashmina* cloth and a knife from Srinagar for the Governor, and a similar knife and a turban bandage for the secretary.

I returned the visit about three o'clock, accompanied by Robert and Muhamed Isa. Hlaje Tsering's tent was large and handsomely fitted up, and all his secretaries and servants were sitting round the fire, which blazed up towards the upper opening. At the sides lay sacks of rice and *tsamba*, and several whole slaughtered sheep; everything showed that the old man was prepared for a long stay. Guns with rests and pennants, sabres and lances, harness, bridles, saddles and saddle-cloths, lent a picturesque and warlike aspect to this chieftain's tent. Along the shorter side, opposite the entrance, thick cushions were piled up, and covered with small Lhasa rugs, and round cushions laid upon them served as supports for the back. I was invited to take my seat there beside Hlaje Tsering; a small red lacquered table was placed in front of us. On our right stood an altar shrine with gilded images of gods and *gaos*, small silver cases with figures of Buddha, which on a journey are suspended by a red strap from the shoulder. And before them flickered a wick, fed with butter, in a bright brass bowl.

A servant brought cups of Chinese porcelain on copper saucers and with silver covers. Another poured out of a picturesque tea-pot the thick tea mixed with butter which the Tibetans are so fond of, and which I now drank apparently with pleasure, though to me it tasted horrible — but Hlaje Tsering had lately praised my English tea.

The conversation was carried on calmly and agreeably as in my tent. But the negotiations made no progress, but rather the contrary, for Hlaje Tsering now said:

"I can on no account let you go to the Dangra-yum-tso; the lake is holy, and, besides, watchmen have already been posted there."

"The road to the east is also barred?"

"Yes, the country is entirely closed to you on the south, west, and east, and I cannot, as I now perceive, send you back to the north."

"Am I, then, to travel through the air, or sink down to the lower regions?"

"No, but you must wait here."

"And you will send my letter to Gyangtse?"

"No, I will not do that, but I will not prevent you from sending two of your men on your own responsibility."

"Will you sell me some horses for them?"

"No; then it would be said that we were in the same boat, and that I had allowed myself to be bribed."

"You are a fine governor, Hlaje Tsering; you cannot even sell me a couple of horses. I shall consequently have to send my men on foot, and they will take twice as long."

"Well, I will sleep on it, and let you know my decision in the morning."

Rub Das and Tundup Galzan received their instructions in the evening. They were to take a letter to Major O'Connor in Gyangtse, and a sum of money was given them, which was sewed up in their girdles for safe keeping. They were to start on their adventurous journey the following evening as soon as it became dark.

CHAPTER XX

ONWARDS THROUGH THE FORBIDDEN LAND

JANUARY 13. Again this ominous number, which is regarded by so many people as unlucky, and is surrounded by a cloud of superstition! Would the 13th be unfortunate for us also?

The sun had scarcely risen when Hlaje Tsering sent to announce a visit. Accompanied by his private secretary, the lama Lobsang Shunten, and all the rest of his retinue, His Excellence the Governor of Naktsang came to my tent on foot. They took their seats on the cushions, and Hlaje Tsering opened the conversation with the following remarkable declaration:

"Hedin Sahib, we have, neither of us, time to stay here for weeks and months, waiting for an answer from Gyangtse. I cannot help you in your correspondence with Gyangtse. I have thoroughly considered the situation, and have discussed it with my secretaries, who, like myself, are responsible to the Devashung. We are of the opinion that all you can do is to pass southwards into the territory of the Labrang (Tashi-lunpo). I beg you to set out the day after to-morrow."

What did this most unexpected change of front mean? Yesterday I was not to be allowed to take a single step southwards, and to-day I was requested to start as soon as possible to the forbidden land. Had Hlaje Tsering received secret orders from Lhasa? Had he been informed that the Tashi Lama was really expecting me? He said nothing on the subject, and I cautiously refrained from asking him. Or were we the victims of a ruse, and when we had been induced to travel with all speed to Gyangtse, should we be compelled to return thence to India through Darjiling? For there the Devashung could appeal to the terms of the treaty, in which it is emphatically stipulated that only those who are in possession of a passport from Lhasa have a right to travel about the country, and so my journey would be speedily ended.

Might it not be better to make for the unknown country west of the Dangra-yum-tso, which after all was the main object of my journey? Hlaje Tsering's change of front was so absolutely at variance with my former experiences in Tibet, that I had some misgivings, and wondered whether I was about to fall into the jaws of the English, Chinese, and Tibetan authorities, and should shortly be delivered unconditionally into their hands.

But this opportunity must on no account be lost. Between the Ngangtse-tso and Shigatse stretches the eastern part of the great white patch north of the Tsangpo, which no European, no pundit, has trod, the land of which not even hazy and uncertain reports at second-hand have ever found their way into geographical text-books. Even if I had an opportunity of making only a single traverse over it, my labour would not be in vain. Nain Sing has two rivers on his map, which flow east and north-east to the Kyaring-tso, and their upper courses he places in the country south of the Ngangtse-tso. At present I knew nothing of them, but I should learn everything if I accepted Hlaje Tsering's proposal. But I had already perceived that the mountains on the south side of the lake were quite fanciful and arbitrary as inserted in Nain Sing's map. At any rate, I must not now betray my satisfaction, so I answered very calmly and thoughtfully:

"Well, I will march southwards the day after to-morrow if you will provide me with horses by then."

"I have sent men into all the valleys in the neighbourhood with orders that all the available horses are to be brought here. Two roads lead from here to Shigatse. If you travel by the west side of the lake you will be in four days in the territory of the Labrang, but by the east side you will reach it in two days. You may choose yourself which way you will take, but I shall be better pleased if you decide on the eastern, for with me the main thing is that you should clear out of my province as quickly as possible."

"No, I will fix on the western road, that I may be able to make an excursion to the Dangra-yum-tso; for I wish to see the lake, and also I must go there because I have given it as my postal address, and the messenger of the Tashi Lama is awaiting me there."

This was a very undiplomatic utterance. I ought to have avoided disclosing my plans. Hlaje Tsering bristled up at once and exclaimed: "To the Dangra-yum-tso? Never! The lake is holy; the mountain Targo-gangri on its southern shore is holy, and there lies the great monastery Sershik-gompa, in which influential intriguing monks dwell. Your visit to the lake would lead to complications. No, if such is your intention, I will leave only one road open to you, namely, that along the eastern side of the Ngangtse-tso. I cannot and will not compel you, but I implore you to give me your word of honour that you will not go to the Dangra-yum-tso."

Thus I lost the holy lake a second time; but I gave my word of honour, that I might not lose the important route still open to me. My premature candour vexed me at the time, but I was soon to have reason to be thankful for it. Had I gained an opportunity of visiting the holy lake at this time, I should certainly have been arrested on its shore; but that is another story which will be related in a later chapter.

"Tell me, Hlaje Tsering, do you think that I shall be stopped in the territory of the Labrang?"

"As you have not been arrested here, in Naktsang, probably you will not be there. I do not know how I shall get on, but I have been Governor for seven years, and my term of office expires in five months, so it is of no consequence if I lose my post. The Devashung has plundered me so thoroughly that I have few cattle and little other property left. Now, for instance, I am travelling in my province at the expense of the people; the nomads have to provide me with baggage animals and provisions for the whole time."

"The Devashung must be a nice institution. How glad you must be that your time of service will soon expire."

"Yes, but I must settle down in some place where I can live cheaply."

"Does the Devashung know that I am here?"

"I have not heard anything from it up to the present, but I despatched another report on your affairs yesterday by express messenger. How they will treat you I do not know; I have gone as far as I could for old friendship's sake."

After that we again paid him a return visit. Some of Hlaje Tsering's men had seen us engaged in rearranging our baggage, and this caused him to ask me if he could have an empty chest. Four of the best were given him, and also all kinds of other superfluous articles.

January 13 was a memorable day in our chronicles, and the 14th was to bring with it still more wonderful incidents. Our life during the past months had passed rather monotonously, but now the facts of our daily experience were stranger than fiction. The alt-azimuth had been placed on its tripod near my tent, and I had the chronometer, an aneroid, and a thermometer close at hand. There I stood for fully three hours, observing the phases of the eclipse of the sun. About nine-tenths of the sun's disc were obscured. Shortly before the maximum the temperature of the air was 16.7°, and soon after the maximum 11.5°. The violet line of the thermograph fell sharply, and a slight breeze swept along the earth's surface. Some Tibetans had betaken themselves to Muhamed Isa's tent to sell us horses, but when the singular darkness fell, they shook their heads and returned to their tents. The Ladakis are outside, sitting at their fire and murmuring prayers. The ravens are quiet and do not move. An eagle circles with heavy pinions close above the ground. Our sheep come in of their own accord from the pastures, just as they are wont to do in the evening, and yet the vanishing sun stands at its mid-day altitude. The puppies break off their play, creep timidly into the tent, and lie down on my bed. Only the horses graze on and display no surprise that the day is so short. All is strangely still and quiet.

96. Servants of Hlaje Tsering.

97. Messenger with Letters from Home, and his Travelling Companion.

98. Hlaje Tsering setting out.

But then the small sickle of the sun, which has not been extinguished in interstellar space, increases again. It becomes lighter, and the shadows that have just before shown a double outline, become sharp again. The sheep stand a moment irresolute and then go slowly back to the pasture. The dogs return to their play, and the Tibetans, one after another, peep out of their tent doors. The ravens shake themselves and fly off croaking to a hill. The prayers of the Ladakis are heard no more, and the eagle is borne aloft by swishing beats of his wings to the sun, which again shines out in all its splendour.

Then old Karpun came to visit us, and was given some tea, tobacco, and a piece of cloth.

"Does the Bombo Chimbo remember that I tried to detain him five and a half years ago with a large levy?"

"Yes, on the north shore of the Selling-tso (Zilling-tso). I gave you a great deal of trouble then, and you could not induce me to stay."

"The trouble is all forgotten, and I am very glad to see you again in good health and brisk."

"We did not expect then that we should meet again. You, too, are looking well. But tell me why you are come just now."

"I have brought a message to the Governor from Shansa-dzong. The officials remaining there have ordered me to call out the people. Now all the militia must stand under arms to ——"

"You surely do not intend to detain me again?"

"By no means. But news is come from the black tents on the middle course of the Bogtsang-tsangpo that a large band of robbers has pillaged ten tents and driven off all the owners' cattle and all the flocks of sheep."

"When?"

"A few days ago."

"Then we may thank our stars that we did not fall into their hands, for we passed along the middle course of the Bogtsang-tsangpo for five days, and we have a large quantity of silver money in our boxes."

"The Bombo Chimbo is a friend of the gods. No harm can befall you."

"In which direction have the robbers retired with their booty?"

"They are still in the territory of Naktsang. We shall pursue them, catch them, and cut off their heads."

Then I visited Hlaje Tsering with the corner pillars of my caravan. He sat at his lacquered table drinking tea, and had his long Chinese pipe in his mouth.

"Why is it that it has just been so dark?" I asked him. "The gods of the Dangra-yum-tso are angry because you will not allow me to visit their lake."

"No, certainly not. A big dog roams about the sky and often conceals the sun. But I and the lama Lobsang have prayed all the time before the altar, and have burned joss-sticks before the images of the gods. You have nothing to fear; the dog has passed on."

"Very fine," I cried, and made a desperate attempt to explain the phenomenon. Robert held up his saucer to represent the sun, and I took two rupees to represent the earth and moon crossing each other's orbit. Hlaje Tsering listened attentively to Muhamed Isa's translation of my demonstration, nodded approvingly, and finally expressed his opinion that all this might do very well for us, but that it did not suit Tibet.

At this moment the flap of the tent was thrown back, and Rabsang entered panting and calling out to me:

"The post is here!"

Muhamed Isa and Robert jumped up as though there were fire under their feet, and exclaimed, "We must be off." I sat quite still, and thrust my feet against the ground so as not to show that I was trembling with excitement. Was it possible? Letters from home, from India, from Gyangtse, and perhaps from the Tashi Lama!

"Who has brought the mail?" I asked, as if nothing had happened.

"A man from Shigatse, accompanied by two others," answered Rabsang.

"Where is he? Let him bring the mail-bag."

"We have already told him to come, but he replies that he has strict orders to hand over the letters to the

Sahib himself in his own tent. He refuses to do so in the tent of the Governor."

"What is the matter?" asked Hlaje Tsering, astonished at the general commotion.

"I have news from the Tashi Lama," I returned very coolly. It was now Hlaje Tsering's turn to look disconcerted. The news made a very deep impression on him. He quickly gave an order, two men hurried out and returned with a confirmation of my statement. Then he gave me a friendly clap on the shoulder and said, smiling:

"Hedin Sahib, this news is of much greater importance to me than to you. It is of no consequence what kind of tidings you receive, but the arrival of the post from the Tashi Lama is, in itself, a proof that His Holiness is actually expecting you, that Labrang is open to you, and that I acted rightly when I told you that you might continue your journey. If I had not already granted you permission yesterday, I should do so now."

"I have always said that I should receive my letters from the Tashi Lama."

"That is true; but now I have for the first time tangible proof, now I am perfectly satisfied, and do not intend even to wait for your departure. I shall travel back to Shansadzong the day after to-morrow."

Now I could no longer curb my impatience. I took leave and hurried to my tent, whither the post-messenger was summoned. He was a young powerful Tibetan, a servant of Kung Gushuk, one of the highest officials in Shigatse, and younger brother of the Tashi Lama. Lieutenant Bailey, who had taken the place of Major O'Connor, absent on furlough, had, according to orders from India, sent the carefully packed post-box to the Tashi Lama with a request that he would forward it to me. The forbidden Dangra-yum-tso appeared in the Tibetan address also. By command of the Tashi Lama the man was furnished with an open passport from the Labrang, the Vatican of Tashi-lunpo, which empowered him to demand horses and provisions along the route. The men with him were the nomads who had last supplied him with horses at the Dangra-yum-tso, and now that they were sure of tips would not leave him. He had taken eighteen days to travel to the holy lake, and had looked for us there for three days, when he heard by chance that we were encamped on the Ngangtse-tso. Then he had hastened to us in order to execute his commission. But why was he so late? I had arranged for November 25. Yes, but Kung Gushuk had let the box lie for forty days, and Kung Gushuk is a blockhead. But this was a piece of good luck. Had Kung Gushuk done his duty, the post would have arrived at the right time, while I only reached the place agreed upon at the end of December. A higher providence had overruled the whole affair, and everything turned out well (Illustration 98).

Now the box was broken open. What excitement! It contained packets of letters from my home, from the Government House in Calcutta, from Colonel Dunlop Smith, and many other friends. I first ascertained from the last letter that all were well at home, and then read all the letters in chronological order with the most eager interest. The letters were the more welcome that they contained nothing but good news. I received a quantity of Swedish newspapers; they were old as the hills, but I should now have no lack of reading on my way to Shigatse.

The caravan did not see much of me that evening. I lay on my bed engaged in reading, and made my men heat the tent well. The Ladakis, too, were merry, kindled a large fire, danced and sang. I was invited to go and look on at their merry-making for a moment, and availed myself of the opportunity to make a short speech, in which I told them that they had all served me well and faithfully, and that hitherto we had met with good fortune. Now the road to Tashi-lunpo was open to us, and they would attain their wish of making a pilgrimage to the holy town. There they would rest after their exertions. Then I returned to my letters, and read on till the day dawned in the east, till long after the brazier had grown cold, and there were 45 degrees of frost in my tent. But I was well wrapped up in furs and did not feel the cold. Near my tent a troop of wolves made such a noise that Tsering had to go out and silence them with a few shots.

On the 15th I still lay down and read. On the 16th Hlaje Tsering paid me his farewell visit. We talked very pleasantly together, joked, and wondered whether fate would ever bring us together again. Then I attended him to his horse, which was snowy white, had a crimson saddle-cloth, and was bedecked with ornaments of shining brass and a chest-cloth with jingling bells. He mounted into the saddle, gave me both his hands at parting, and disappeared with his small retinue behind the hills. Then I again went back to my letters, but I felt a dull void now that the amiable Governor of Naktsang was gone (Illustration 97).

January 17. What did it matter if the day were gloomy, if freshly fallen snow veiled the surrounding mountains, and heavy greyish-blue clouds rolled over the lake as though to hide it from our sight at the moment of our departure? To us everything seemed bright, cheerful, and smiling. A powerful governor had come to prevent us from travelling further, and yet the route to the south was as free to us as the uninhabited Chang-tang had lately been. But now we were much better off. We should pass black tents daily, be able to buy all we wanted, and have no cause for alarm because we had provisions for only five days longer. We enjoyed unlimited freedom, and had not a single man with us as escort or watchman. Before us lay a country which might be said to be the most interesting in the world from a geographical point of view, and in which every day's journey might lead to discoveries of the highest importance. What did we care if the air was raw and cold? Spring must come sometime. We could count on warmer weather for three reasons: we were advancing to more southern climes, we should soon reach districts at a lower level, and the spring was daily approaching. And for three reasons the Ngangtse-tso would ever be memorable in the diary of my reminiscences: there freedom of movement had been unexpectedly accorded to us, there connection with the outer world had been again established, and there I had an opportunity of determining the depth of the lake by a complete series of soundings, and of drawing its contours in a map.

We had obtained three new horses fairly cheaply, on which Robert, Muhamed Isa, and Tsering rode, while I kept to my small Ladak white. Accompanied by the post-messenger and his two comrades, we rode in a south-easterly direction down to the lake, and along the eastern shore to the southern part, where we bivouacked near two black tents. Kiangs and wolves were frequently seen. A kiang had been torn in pieces by the wolves, and the white puppy and the Pobrang dog remained by the body to enjoy a good feast. We were terribly starved during the long march of 13.2 miles, and in the night the thermometer marked 61.9 degrees of frost, the worst cold of the whole winter.

The next day's march took us up a transverse valley of the mountains which rise on the south shore of the Ngangtse-tso. It was rather narrow, and a small source murmured under its covering of ice. We followed a plainly marked path, leaving a couple of tents behind us, and passed sheepfolds, grassy plots, and dark spots where tame yaks had lain and worn off the grass; everything was black, the tents, the Tibetans, the half-naked children, and the dogs. At length the gully turned westwards; just at the bend was a waterfall congealed into milky white ice. Far up the valley we encamped on a plateau, where we had a very interesting view to the north-east. We could see almost the whole of the lake which Nain Sing left at some distance to the south of his route, and which he called Daru-tso. I cannot dispute its correctness, but none of the Tibetans whom I questioned had ever heard this name for the lake; they called it Marchar-tso, and it now figures in my map under this name. It often happens that a lake has different names among different nomad tribes. In camp No. 109 it lay just below us as on a map; its form is not so simple as on Nain Sing's map, but abounds in peninsulas and bays, and it is extremely narrow in the middle. The isthmus between the Ngangtse-tso and the Marchar-tso is only a few miles broad; at the highest point the old shore terraces of the two lakes touch one another. At the time when the water stood higher the two lakes were therefore connected. The Marchar-tso is said to be as salt as its neighbour, but its ice was smooth and blue, and we saw no fields of free salt on its surface.

We had seen nothing of the white puppy and the Pobrang dog after we had left them behind, so I sent the Hajji back to the lake. But he came back without having found any sign of them. We never saw them again, and I sorely missed the white puppy, who had been a faithful friend in the tent and on the march. Either they had had a fight with wolves and got the worst of it, or they had lost our track and had been adopted by nomads. The former was the more probable, for the Hajji when he came to the lake saw a troop of wolves careering over the ice.

On the 19th we surmounted the neighbouring pass, the Chapka-la (17,474 feet), on which a stone pyramid is erected in honour of the gods. As a watershed it is only of secondary importance, for the water from both sides flows to the Ngangtse-tso. The valley leading down makes a curve to the south; in the Lamblung valley we had eleven tents as neighbours, and were able to provide ourselves with all we needed for several days. The country was still in the Naktsang territory, but the nomads were subjects of the Labrang, and paid their taxes to Tashi-lunpo.

We remained here two days, which we ought not to have done, and we would not if I had properly considered the matter. It was not the furious snowstorm which caused us to waste forty-eight hours, but Ngurbu Tundup, the postman. I had intended to keep him with us as long as possible, for it would evidently be an advantage to us, and would increase our dignity, to have with us a servant of one of the highest officials of Shigatse. He was our living passport; if he were not with us, we might perhaps again be regarded as freebooters, and be ordered to stop by some despotic chief. But Ngurbu Tundup was deaf to our entreaties, and declared that he had strict orders to return immediately his task was accomplished, and give in his report. He had already disobeyed his orders and had lost several days, but he consented to remain with us if we would rest in the Lamblung valley. I had great need of the time to get all my huge correspondence ready. On January 20

I wrote for sixteen hours, and by noon of the 21st the mail was ready and packed up. Ngurbu received a present of 82 rupees for his excellent service, and if he handed over the packet of letters to the British commercial agent in Gyangtse he was to receive further especial reward, when we met again at Shigatse. But he was to make all speed, changing his horse several times a day. If he loitered and covered only 18 miles a day, that is, reaching Gyangtse in ten days, he was to expect only 10 rupees. If he completed the journey in nine days, he was to receive 20, and if he accomplished his task in eight days, I would give him 30 rupees, and so on, at the rate of 10 rupees for every day saved. He actually arrived in eight days. I really committed a blunder in making this arrangement, for I gave notice of our approach to the south, and it might have happened that the Tibetans might have conceived evil designs against us. Nay, had the Chinese received news of our march, we should most certainly have been very soon stopped.

When Ngurbu had ridden off over the hills, we were again cut off from contact with the outer world, and were left to ourselves.

The following morning we ascended eastwards along the valley in which we had encamped, and where some *mani* cists stand, the longest of which measures 33 feet, and is covered with slabs of sandstone bearing the holy formula in incised letters. Continual snowstorms and huge masses of cloud with or without snow — that was the characteristic weather in January.

The Pongchen-la (17,621 feet) is a low threshold, like the preceding of secondary importance. On its summit stands a votive stone heap, with a bundle of rods, on which pennants, cloth rags, and ribands flutter. Smaller cairns radiate out from it. Here we had a last glimpse of our dear old Ngangtse-tso, and to the north-east a valley ran down to the Marchar-tso. To the south-east rose a dark range with several snowy peaks, which is called Pabla. The valley we traversed is broad and open, and is enclosed in low mountains. We saw no tents all the day, but numerous traces of summer encampments. Namgyal, however, who is a quick intelligent man, spied out two tents in the neighbourhood of our camp No. 111, which was pitched in a district called Namachang, and there bought some sheep, parched meal, barley, milk, and sour milk. He also brought a young Tibetan with him, who was good-looking, honest, and gentle, and did all we asked him willingly and pleasantly. His accent was so soft and refined that it was a pleasure to hear him speak. He gave me a quantity of credible information and promised to accompany us a day's journey.

It snowed so thickly all night and the following day that I frequently could not see Rabsang, who marched with the Tibetan guide just in front of my horse. The snow enveloped us, whirled about us, and piled itself into small drifts on the sheltered side of every stone, grassy hillock, and hollow. The valley slopes gently to the south-east, and its frozen river is called Buser-tsangpo, and is a tributary of the Tagrak-tsangpo, which debouches into the south-western corner of the Ngangtse-tso. We are therefore still in the basin, of which the lake occupies the lowest part, and of which the border on the north-west and east lies close to the lake, but on the south is removed many days' journey from it. The camping-ground this day is called Kapchor; eastwards extends an open longitudinal valley, through which runs the road to Shansa-dzong; on the north side also of the Ngangtse-tso and Marchar-tso a road runs thither, and by this Hlaje Tsering had reached our camp in twelve days. This road is known from Nain Sing's journey in 1873–74.

On the morning of the 24th we were nearly blinded on going out of our tents, so brilliant was the reflexion from the thousands of small facets of the snow crystals which had spread their white cloak over hill and valley in a thick continuous sheet. The sky was clear, and blue as the purest turquoise from Nishapur, but the wind swept bitterly cold over the snowfields a night old. Our route ran southeastwards to the exit of the narrow valley where the Tagrak-tsangpo, now frozen to the bottom, rested mute and motionless in the arms of winter. We followed the river, the largest watercourse that we had seen since the

Chang-chenmo, upwards. At some places small nomad communities had their winter pastures, and there large herds of yaks and flocks of sheep roamed over the slopes. The name of the valley is Kayi-rung, of the spot where camp 113 was pitched Kayi-pangbuk, and of the district Tova-tova. Nain Sing's Dobo Dobá Cho, from which he brings the river Para-tsangpo to the Kyaring-tso, was not known to the inhabitants. The Pundit makes the water drain eastwards, but as a matter of fact it runs westwards and north-westwards to the Ngangtse-tso. This is due to his not having been here himself, for the statements of the natives are usually very unreliable.

Immediately beyond the camp we crossed on the 25th a small saddle, where we obtained an instructive insight into the lie of the land. The eyes swept unhindered over all the wide plain, with the three streams forming the Tagrak-tsangpo meandering over the level ground in capricious curves and bends like silver ribands in the brown and grey country. Close to us on the south-east is the Kesar-tsangpo, which receives the Naong-tsangpo at the foot of our gap, and then cutting through our mountain begins its course in the Kayi-rung valley. Farther off to the north-east the Naong-tsangpo has already absorbed the waters of the Kung-tsangpo, and with them makes its way to the Kayi-rung valley and the Ngangtse-tso. The great plain is enclosed by moderately high, rounded mountains and hills.

After crossing the Kesar-tsangpo we follow the right bank, upwards as far as Toa-nadsum, where we bivouac. A quadrangular wall of earth marks the spot where the *bombo*, or chief of the district, usually erects his tent; now he is in Tashi-lunpo to pay his tax. In the adjoining valleys there are at the present time twenty-two tents, but only four near our camp, and in these beggars are wintering in great poverty. The country is said to be noted for its cold, raw climate even in summer. It rains in June and July, but the fall varies very much from year to year. If it rains hard for a long time, all the rivers swell, draining water from a thousand valleys, and the Tagrak-tsangpo is then sometimes unfordable.

When we started on the following day in a twilight caused by heavy clouds, the poor natives came up holding out their hands for *tsamba* or money, and each received a coin. Our way ran to the east-south-east, to the Naong-rung valley, traversed by the Naong-tsangpo, now frozen to the bottom. We now ascended gradually, and at camp No. 115 found ourselves at a height of 16,844 feet.

Two large black nomad dogs fell in love with the brown puppy, and followed us as though they belonged to the family. One limped, having at some time hurt his leg; he was old and shaggy, and was received with stones and abuse. Yet he clung to us faithfully, and put up with hard words from the men and the offal from slaughtered sheep. He was at last admitted a member of our travelling company, and hobbled, with drooping head and tongue hanging out, over lofty passes and through deep valleys, and answered to the name of "Cripple." As he was old he often lagged behind, but in spite of his slow pace he always turned up and took his place before Muhamed Isa's tent. He was the grand dog of our tent court, and was much concerned about us when danger threatened. Naturally he became a friend of us all, was allowed to eat as much as he liked, and acquired a position in the caravan. Then we would gladly have forgotten we had had the heart to beat him, and to greet him with stones and whips — he, our Cripple, who had come to us of his own accord to defend us and guard our tents, only asking free board in exchange; for free lodging of course he had under the everlasting stars in great desolate winterly cold Tibet.

CHAPTER XXI

OVER THE TRANS-HIMALAYA

JANUARY 27. Storm as usual. We march in a south-easterly direction, guided by the river system of the Tagrak-tsangpo, which branches off into smaller and smaller ramifications, and no one interferes with us or takes the slightest notice of our advance. From a small pass we look down on the two tributaries of the Naong-tsangpo, the Pupchung-tsangpo, and the Kelung-tsangpo, and follow the latter. It conducts us to a second saddle with a stone cairn and prayer streamers; from a pole in the middle strings radiate out to the four cardinal points, bearing rags and ribands, and fastened to the ground by small stones. From a third watershed of secondary rank the guide points out a pass of the first order in the Pabla mountains which we shall cross to-morrow. We now find ourselves in a high alpine region without herbage; only moss grows among the pebbles. Camp No. 116 is pitched in the valley of the Pupchung-tsangpo. The brook descends from the Pupchung-ri, a part of the main crest. To the south-east we see the two mountains Tormakaru and Sangra covered with snow. Here nomads never encamp, for the elevation is too great. Only when officials from Tashi-lunpo travel here on duty are the nomads living nearest obliged to set up tents for them.

The wind sank in the evening, and the sound of the flutes echoed clearly and sweetly in the valley. The moon rose high, and poured down its light over the peaceful wondrous land. The night advanced cold and silent, and

99. Three Tibetans saluting.

the thermometer fell to $-29°$. At such a temperature there is no need of draughts through the chinks to cool the sleeping-tent. The cold wakes me up, and I have to wrap myself more closely in my blankets.

January 28 was a great day in our records. We knew that we had a trying way before us, and therefore we made an early start. The horse that bore the number 22 on the label attached to his mane lay before my tent frozen hard, with his legs stretched out; he had served us faithfully for nearly half a year. Seven horses and a mule were left. They carried nothing but the cloths that protected them from cold in the night. The new Tibetan horses were in splendid condition: they were fat and sleek compared to our old horses, which had passed through the winter on the Chang-tang.

Even at ten o'clock the wind is icy cold, and not the smallest cloud floats over the earth. Dull weather is much better if the air be still. Now the sun looks down sneeringly on our sufferings and makes no attempt to lighten them. We march towards the east-south-east, over an endless, slightly undulating plain, where the ground consists of troublesome moss-grown stones and sharp débris. On our right is the Sangra peak and other parts of the Pabla crest, whence short transverse valleys descend, and are continued over the plain in insignificant furrows of erosion. To the left the land is undulating, where the affluents of the Naong-tsangpo wind among softly rounded hills. Higher hills and ridges, lying to the north of the right bank of the Naong-tsangpo, intercept the view in this direction.

So we mount slowly up till a deeply eroded valley suddenly and unexpectedly appears on the right side of our route. It is not included in the Ngangtse-tso basin. I am about to leave the isolated hydrographic region, and puzzle my head about the surprises that await me. The valley is called Sangra-palhe, runs south-eastwards, and receives the southern transverse valleys of the Pabla, which are just as deeply excavated. To the south-east we see the dark extremity of a spur of the Pabla, round which the great main valley and its stream bend towards the south and pass on — but whither? On this point the guide could give us no information; we were to find out later. Farther on we reach a valley running in a northerly direction, and therefore connected with the Naong-tsangpo. Northwards the country slopes gently, but steeply, to the south, and we ascend to the low pass forming the watershed. Immediately beyond the hill Sereding we march up a steep ascent towards the conical mountain Serpo-tsunge, which we afterwards leave close on the right of our road. From its western and eastern sides, and also from the gap where we now stand, a number of deep erosion valleys run down to the Sangra-palhe. To the left of our route a valley, which still belongs to the system of the Naong-tsangpo, slopes to the north-west. We are therefore on the water-parting ridge. The Serpo-tsunge is a geographical boundary pillar, and marks where the domain of the Ngangtse-tso ends. The whole configuration is singularly complicated.

Here we left one of our yaks, which could not be induced by coaxing or scolding to move a step farther, but lowered his horns and rushed at those who attempted to drive him on. He was abandoned, the second animal of his kind. He had here abundance of yak-moss, snow, and fresh air, and would probably fall into the hands of the nomads some time or other.

A little higher and we stood on the very summit of the pass, marked by a pole with streamers, which flap and flutter in the wind. It was quite time that we made a small fire, for we were half dead with cold. It was not easy to make the hypsometer boil. Robert sat on the ground and improvised a tent round the instrument with furs and a rug, while I lay on my stomach on the lee side and read the thermometer through a small opening. The temperature was 15°, with a west-south-west wind No. 8, that is, half a gale. The valley leading down, the Sele-nang, lay now, at mid-day, in dark shadow. Through its opening appeared a vast sea of rigid mountainous undulations, steep cliffs, and deep valleys, no level stretches, no vegetation, only a labyrinth of mountains, a much bolder, more marked, and wilder relief than we had seen in Chang-tang. The nearer parts of the Pabla ridge intercepted the view to the west.

The pass, where we now were, is called the Sela-la, and attains the great height of 18,064 feet above sea-level. I perceived clearly that it must be situated in the main chain, which, farther east, bears the well-known peak Nien-chang-tang-la on the south shore of the Nam-tso or Tengri-nor, and has been crossed by a few Europeans and pundits. It is one of the greatest and grandest watersheds of the world, for from its northern flank the water flows down to the undrained lakes of the plateau, and from its southern flank to the Indian Ocean. The course of this watershed and the configuration of the mountain system crossed by our route between the Ngangtse-tso and Ye-shung on the Tsangpo was till this January of 1907 as unknown to geographers of European race as the side of the moon turned away from the earth. On the other hand, the seas and mountains seen in the full moon have been known from ancient times much better than the region of the earth's surface whither it is my good fortune to be able to conduct my readers. I venture to describe this geographical problem that I have succeeded in solving as one of the finest, perhaps the most striking, of all problems connected with the surface of our earth that awaited solution.

But on the Sela-la we crossed the immense watershed only at a single point. I will not anticipate events. We must first muster our acquisitions in order, and then we will draw our conclusions from the material collected. And now we will continue our arduous passage through the unknown world of mountains which still separates us from the great river.

After I had hastily sketched the panorama with hands turned blue with cold, inserting the names the guide was able to give me, we hurried down the slopes of detritus, partially covered with snow, on the south side of the pass. In the valley bottom, with its patches of ice, we mounted our horses again, and met three mounted Tibetans driving before them eight loose horses. As soon as they caught sight of us they turned aside and made a great detour to avoid us. We supposed that they belonged to a band of robbers, who wished to escape with their booty by untrodden paths.

It was delightful this evening to sit at length in the warmth of the camp-fire. In silent meditation my eyes swept from the rocky crests, brightly lighted by the moon, down to the dark shadowy depths of the valley, where there were only wolves crouching in their holes. It seemed as though all belonged to me; as though I had marched into this land a conqueror at the head of victorious legions, and had crushed all opposition. Oh, what splendid legions! Five-and-twenty ragged fellows from Ladak, ten lean jades, and about twenty worn-out yaks. And yet I had succeeded! Marius could not have been prouder of the triumphs he achieved in the war against Jugurtha than I was when I had won my first victory over the "Trans-Himalaya" at the Sela-la, that Sela-la which, now bathed in moonlight, seemed to us the extreme outpost on the limits of boundless space.

Our march on January 29 was pleasant. We were sheltered from the wind in the deep valley, travelled towards the sun, and felt the first touch of the approaching spring. We rode at first towards the east-south-east, but gradually made a curve round to the south. Just at the bend the valley Tumsang runs in, and in the background we again caught a glimpse of a part of the great range we crossed at the Sela-la. Innumerable valleys such as ours must descend from the crest more or less parallel to it. The valley becomes broader, and the ice strip of the Sele-nang winds along the middle. We see no tents, but places where they are pitched in summer, and some *manis* are erected for the edification of travellers. Camp No. 118 is pitched in an expansion of the valley called Selin-do.

During the past days we had often remarked how desirable it would be if we could hire some yaks from the nomads. Our own were exhausted and kept us back, and in the high country with its abundant detritus, where we were now travelling, their hoofs became sorer every day. As long as the land lay open before us we must make all haste we could. Delay might be dangerous, but the yaks marched as though they had a log at their heels. We saw no tents in Selin-do, but Namgyal came in the evening with two Tibetans he had met in a side valley.

They were willing to provide us with 25 yaks, if they were paid a *tenga* (about 5½ d.) for every day's march, and they reckoned eight days' march for the journey to Ye-shung on the Tsangpo. They would accompany us themselves only for one day, and insisted that other men should take their place when they turned back. We could not do any better; we should spare our own animals, make longer marches, and obtain good guides as well.

In the evening we received a visit from seven well-armed riders in search of a band of robbers who had stolen several horses from them. We informed them of the party we had met the day before and they rode off, thanking us warmly, up the valley.

January 30. In the morning our new friends turned up with the yaks; when all was in order we found that we possessed only eighteen loads of the heavy baggage with which we set out from Leh. Our last two guides were paid, and immediately set out for the Sela-la.

Immediately below camp No. 118 the Selin-do valley unites with the Porung valley, along which we again ascended to the south-east. I was surprised that our guides tramped up to higher ground again, but they followed a plainly marked path, while the valley that we left on the right seemed to slope down to the west-south-west and south-west. They said that it debouched into the valley of the My-tsangpo, a northern tributary of the Yere-tsangpo (the upper Brahmaputra). I had afterwards an opportunity of ascertaining that their statements were correct. But now, on first crossing the country, the arrangement of the mountain ranges and watercourses was ill-defined and confusing to me. At every camp I interrogated Tibetans who seemed reliable, and made them draw small maps with their fingers in the sand, which I copied into my diary. But the map changed every day, even if the chief lines remained the same.

From the point where we began to ascend again a desolate chaos of mountains is visible towards the south-west. On the right bank of the Porung several warm springs well up from the pebble bed, containing sulphurous water at a temperature of 127.9° and filling basins in which the hot steaming water simmers and bubbles. The place is called simply Tsaka-chusen, or "The Hot Salt Water." The terraces of the valley indicate powerful erosive action. Side valleys run in on both sides; sometimes we cross the frozen stream, sometimes pass over steep mountain spurs. At a bend in the way we meet a party of armed riders who are on the way to Chokchu, a country west of the Dangra-yum-tso.

We come to an expansion in the valley, a very important spot, for here several valleys converge to a gigantic focus of erosion in this sea of wild mountains. The largest is the Terkung-rung, which, joined by a whole series of side valleys, descends from the main crest of the Pabla in the north-east. The track through the valley passes several large summer pastures. I made a long halt on a broad rocky projection with a *mani* to get my bearings in this extremely interesting country. Here, too, we met a mounted party, which was in pursuit of a freebooter who had eloped with another man's wife — just as with us. The injured husband was in the party and looked very furious. Then we met a caravan of 55 yaks laden with great bales of Chinese brick tea from Lhasa, which they were carrying to the Chokchu province. A dozen dark bare-footed men followed the animals, singing and whistling, spinning woollen thread with the help of vertical rotating spools, or engaged with their prayer mills. They hired their yaks, and were to exchange them for fresh animals at Selin-do. They had also 50 sheep with them, carrying small loads of barley. The farther we advanced the more lively became the traffic.

Small footpaths from the side valleys join our road, which is now broad and shows signs of considerable traffic. All our guides tell us that this is the great highway to Shigatse, and is also a section of the main road connecting Chokchu with the capital of the country. The road is a collection of parallel footpaths, and where it crosses slopes and steep declivities appears like stripes on the ground.

We continue our ascent in a south-south-easterly direction, and find ourselves about 100 feet above the valley bottom, which is occupied by a huge ice-belt of uniform breadth resembling a great river; we could fancy ourselves transplanted to the Indus valley in its winter dress as seen from Saspul. But the resemblance is only apparent, for after we have passed some rather large side valleys we reach the abundant springs of Mense-tsaka with warm freshwater at a temperature of 118°, which farther down forms pools where small fishes dart about among slimy weeds. The water gradually cools down and forms ice, and runs down over it farther and farther until, as now in the end of January, it has filled the whole valley bottom from the foot of one flank to the other.

From the great meeting-place of the valleys we have passed four *manis*, in general not more than 10 feet long, but covered with unusually well-dressed slabs of red, white, or green sandstone and slate. On the former, the letters in the weathered crust stand out bright red against the chiselled intervals with their white surface. We are tempted to take away some specimens, but we shall probably have later opportunities of committing sacrilege.

In front of us stands the trough up to the pass; surrounded by the concave crest, where the caravan is seen on the top, the pass seems unpleasantly steep. Above the valleys Shib-la-yilung and Chugge-lung the ascent is difficult, and the horses often pause on the slopes of detritus. At last, however, we are up at the votive cairn with its streamer pole amongst smaller pyramids of stones. This is the Shib-la, which has a height of 17,549 feet. The view is magnificent and is free on almost all sides, for no summits in the foreground obstruct it. Down in the valleys we were sheltered from the wind, but up on the summit it sweeps unhindered over the agitated sea of crests.

The guide points south-westwards to the next pass we have to cross. Between it and the Shib-la stretches a deep boldly eroded ravine, sloping to the west-south-west. Its river, or rather its ice-belt, unites with all the watercourses we have crossed this day — with all, indeed, that we have met with since the Sela-la. We have therefore crossed a number of tributaries, but the main stream, which receives them all, lies to the west of our route and is not visible from any point. It is the river called My-chu, My-tsangpo, or My-chu-tsangpo.

We had still a fairly long march to the camp. It grew dusk. We descended the steep slope on foot, stumbling over the rubbish and the mouse-holes. Darkness came on, but a white streak was seen in the valley, the ice of the river. The light of the camp-fire looked tempting in the cold and darkness. But nothing is so deceptive as a blaze of light in the darkness; you go on and on, but the fire seems no larger. At last, however, tired and starved, we arrived at the camp and sat as close as possible to the glowing *argol*, and the conversation with Muhamed Isa began — cheerful and animated, as usual.

Four of our spare yaks were thoroughly exhausted and must have a day's rest. Had I known what was coming behind in our track, I would have left them and hurried off next morning. But we knew nothing, and spent the last day of January quietly in camp No. 119. The thermometer fell to $-29.9°$: the third time we had recorded the same reading.

I spent the leisure day in studying the maps I had drawn, and endeavouring to form a clear conception of the mountains and valleys among which we had been wandering. This much was evident, that the great watershed between the isolated lake basins of the Chang-tang and the Indian Ocean ran along the main Pabla range, and that this was the immediate western prolongation of the mighty chain Nien-chen-tang-la. We had crossed the Pabla mountains at the Sela-la, and were now in the wide-stretching intricate river system of the My-chu. Nearly parallel to the My-chu flows farther east the Shang-chu, and along its valley the Pundit Krishna (A. K.) travelled in the year 1872 and Count de Lesdain in 1905. Between the My-chu and the Shang-chu there must therefore be a secondary watershed and a considerable mountain elevation, which is really nothing else than an offshoot from the main range of the Pabla. All the watercourses we had crossed from the Sela-la onwards flow westwards, and the secondary watershed, where they take their rise, lies to the east of our route. It is, however, possible that between the My-chu and the Shang-chu another, or perhaps several valleys lie, equal in importance to the valleys of these rivers.

The Pabla is only a part of the main chain of the "Trans-Himalaya," and the Trans-Himalaya is not only a watershed of the first rank, but is also a geographical boundary of exceptional importance. I have now and then wandered through mountain regions of awful grandeur, but have never seen anything to equal the country to the south of the Trans-Himalaya. In Chang-tang the predominating lines of the landscape are slightly undulating and horizontal; now we had reached the peripheral regions, having a drainage to the sea, and immediately vertical lines came into prominence. On the south side of the Trans-Himalaya the valleys are much more boldly excavated in the rock masses than in any part of the plateau country. And why? Because the precipitation from the monsoon clouds is incomparably more abundant on the south side of the Trans-Himalaya than on the northern flank. It is the same in the Himalayas, where the south side, facing the west monsoon, catches the lion's share of the precipitation, and is irrigated by much more abundant and more continuous rains than the northern. Now we found springs, brooks, and rivers in every valley, while not very long before we were always in danger of finding no water. In climatic relations, then, the Trans-Himalaya is a boundary line equalled in magnitude and importance by few on the earth's surface.

My excitement and expectation were constantly increasing; every day I saw plainer indications of the proximity of a religious metropolis — votive cairns, *manis*, travellers, caravans were all signs of it. My Ladakis were inspired by the same feeling of exultation which the pilgrims of Islam experience when they approach the Arafat mountain, and remember that from that elevation they will behold for the first time the holy Mecca.

Early in the forenoon fresh men with fresh yaks presented themselves to take over our loads on February 1. I could not understand why the nomads were ready to serve us without the slightest suggestion. Certainly the highway is divided into stages, and fresh yaks are kept in readiness for the transport of baggage and goods, but these advantages are intended only for Tibetans, not for a European caravan, which had not even a passport. At any rate Ngurbu Tundup had done us no harm; on the contrary, it was known everywhere that I was coming, and that he was a messenger sent to me by the Tashi Lama. At every halting-place we were told how many days ago he had passed through the place. The readiness of the nomads to provide us with yaks was due in no small degree to the good pay and kind treatment they received. Now our own yaks travelled without loads, and also the seven Ladak horses and the last surviving mule. But we were prepared for any emergency. We had agreed that if we could not at any time find transport animals, I, with Muhamed Isa and Namgyal, would ride on our three Tibetan horses in forced marches to Shigatse, while the caravan would follow slowly under Robert's command.

We had 58½ degrees of frost in the night, and the morning was horribly cold, dull, and stormy. We ascended to the next pass along a new valley. We had not gone far before we were half dead with cold; Robert wept, he was so frozen. When it was warmest, there were still 27½ degrees of frost, and a biting wind blew in our faces. Our faces, and especially our noses, would have been frost-bitten if we had not constantly put them in the openings of our long fur sleeves, where, however, the breath turned so quickly to ice that the sleeve froze on to the moustache. It is not easy to do map work under such circumstances. Before I have taken my observation and looked at the watch my left hand is dead; and, however much I hurry, I have not recorded the result before my right hand has lost all feeling. It is impossible to march on foot in face of the storm up a steep ascent and in the rarefied air if one has the least respect for one's heart. We crept into a cave and crouched down on the sheltered side; we thrust our hands between the horse and the saddle-girth to thaw them; we stamped our feet, and looked intensely miserable when the muscles of our faces were so benumbed that we could hardly speak. "Let us ride on; we will light a fire

100. PASS OF LA-ROCK. *MANI* HEAP WITH FLUTTERING PRAYER-STREAMERS.

101. ON THE BANK OF THE TSANGPO (BRAHMAPUTRA).

up above." And so we struggled painfully up through sharp-edged detritus and among stones.

At last we are up on the flat arch of the Chesang-la at an absolute height of 17,599 feet. This pass is therefore a little higher than the Sela-la, but nevertheless it is only a pass of the second rank, for it separates two of the affluents of the My-chu. When we came up, there were three large grey wolves on the pass, but they quickly took to flight. Here the storm raged in uncontrolled freedom, and we could scarcely keep on our feet. Robert and I crouched on the ground on the sheltered side of the large cairn, while Rabsang and our Tibetan guide collected dry yak-dung. We set it alight with the help of flint and steel, and then we all four cowered over the fire. We opened our fur coats to let a little heat penetrate our clothes and took off our boots to warm our feet, but we sat an hour and a half before we felt anything like human beings again. Then we hastened down in a south-south-westerly direction and encamped in the Sham valley near some wretched stone huts.

CHAPTER XXII

TO THE BANK OF THE BRAHMAPUTRA

THE Sham valley narrows like a pear, and at the entrance of this funnel huts stand at three different spots, and large herds graze on the mountain slopes. A *mani*, 148 feet long by 5 feet high, was covered with clods to protect the upright stones sculptured with prayers. At length the Sham valley enters a large valley coming from the east, which occupies a prominent place in this river system. It is traversed by the Bup-chu-tsangpo, the largest river we have yet seen. Immediately below the place where the two valleys unite is the confluence of a third river, which is called Dangbe-chu and flows from the south-east. Thus three considerable streams meet in this small expansion of the valley. The explanations of my guide made this complicated river system of the My-chu-tsangpo clear to me. The sources of the Bup-chu-tsangpo lie two long days' march to the east, and are of course to be found in the great offshoot of the Pabla which forms on the east the watershed of the My-chu-tsangpo. From the confluence where we now stood the Bup-chu-tsangpo continues its course for two short days' journey south-westwards, and then at the monastery Linga-gompa enters the My-chu-tsangpo, which has its source in the main range of the Pabla.

The Bup-chu-tsangpo was at this season converted into a huge sheet of ice, but had an open water channel. We crossed dry-footed at a place where the ice formed a bridge all across the bed of the stream, and then marched in a south-easterly direction through the narrow Dangbe valley.

At camp No. 121, on February 3, we left Tundup Sonam and Tashi behind with our own yaks, which were so exhausted that they could be driven only very slowly. The men were given money for their keep, and were ordered to move on towards Shigatse at a very slow pace. The rest of the caravan set out early, in good weather and at a minimum temperature of only 11.3°.

Our course is south-south-east and afterwards east. All the valleys are full of ice, which we strew with sand as the caravan passes. The pass to-day is the Dangbe-la, decorated, as usual, with a cairn and streamers; its height is 17,224 feet, or much less than that of the preceding pass. It is interesting, as lying on the watershed between the Bup-chu (My-chu) and the Rung-chu. The latter river does not unite with the My-chu, but takes its own course direct to the upper Brahmaputra. When I asked why we could not descend the Rung valley to avoid the two passes in front of us, I was told that the valley is very narrow, is confined by precipitous mountains, and is filled with ice. There is, however, a path used in summer which runs sometimes along the slopes, sometimes over the valley bottom, but is hard to follow after rain, for then large volumes of water pour down the valley, thundering over falls and rapids.

We bivouacked in a locality called Ngartang in the Rung valley, where twelve tents remain standing all through the year. The valley is considered cold, whereas the Sham is reputed warm. Indeed, we had found there some juniper bushes, and were so delighted at seeing them that we had adorned the inside of our tents with branches. It never snows in summer in the Sham valley, but it does in the Rung valley. In many years there is much rain in both valleys.

As though to prove the truth of the Tibetans' assertions, the thermometer again fell in the night to −19.1°. We were prepared for a long day's journey and a difficult pass, and therefore it was still dark when I heard the yaks being driven into the camp. After we have left the Ma-lung river behind us we ride up hills consisting of firm soil overgrown with moss, and an inextricable entanglement of mountains is displayed to our view. We ride steeply upwards along the valley coming down from the pass, passing over detritus and among boulders, with votive cairns here and there. A stretch of almost level ground follows, and then at last the path rises steeply to the pass, which is strewn with innumerable blocks of grey granite. This is the Ta-la or "Horse Pass," and its absolute height is 17,835 feet.

If the ascent among the boulders is troublesome, and both horse and rider have to twist their bodies in all kinds of acrobatic feats, the pilgrim is richly rewarded when he stands at the top of the Ta-la beside the streamer-decked cairn; for anything grander and more overpowering I have never yet seen, unless it were on the top of the Chang-lung-yogma. The panorama to the south-east and east-south-east is so fascinating that we almost forget to dismount. We command a somewhat limited portion of the horizon, for two peaks of the Ta-la crest, like the portal of a great temple, close in the landscape in front of us. Below is a zone of reddish-brown, dome-shaped hills, behind them a nearly black spur, intersected by numerous short transverse valleys, and farther in the background a dark grey ramification. All seem to run westwards and from the watershed, which we have supposed to lie to the east of our route since we crossed the Sela-la. Such scenery as this we had gazed upon time after time. But high above the dark-grey ridge rises a world of mountains which seems to belong to the heavens rather than the earth, so lightly and airily is it poised above the rest of the earth under a canopy of white clouds. It is so far from us that the individual contours are indistinguishable, and it rises like a wall of a universal light blue hue, which, however, is a little deeper than the colour of the sky. The boundary between the two expanses of blue is sharply marked by an irregular bright white line; for what we see before us is the snow-covered crest of the Himalayas, and behind it lies India with its eternal summer. These are the most northern chains of the Himalayas, on the frontier between Tibet and Bhotan. Between them and the dark grey crest, comparatively near to us, yawns an abyss, a huge fissure on the earth's crust, the valley of the Brahmaputra or Tsangpo. The river itself is not visible, but we feel that we are now not far from our destination. Ah, you fearful ranges and passes which we have surmounted in the Chang-tang, where dead horses mark the miles and show in which direction we travelled, at last we have you behind us, and only a single mountain system, the Himalayan, separates us from India! This view strikes us dumb, and it seems wonderful to me that I have succeeded in forcing my way so far.

Tsering and Bolu now reach the pass with the small caravan. They fall on their knees before the heap of stones and recite their prayers, and Tsering tears a strip off his ragged coat to tie as an offering on to one of the strings. We all feel as though we were on a pilgrimage. The Tibetans who let their yaks on hire see after the loading and unloading, gather fuel, and relieve the Ladakis of many of their duties. The older men of our own people are allowed to ride. They have easier work in every way, but still they are pilgrims on the way to one of the greatest centres of Lamaism. Old Tsering holds his cap in his hand as he goes over the pass, and cannot turn his eyes aside from the dreamy light-blue mountains which gleam in the distance among the clouds. He reminds himself that they rise far beyond Tashi-lunpo and that we have not to cross them to reach our longed-for destination.

But we must leave this grand pass, the never-to-be-forgotten Ta-la. Down we go on a break-neck descent among boulders, between steep cliffs, over landslips and spurs, and the Himalayas gradually vanish from sight. Now we see only the line of the crest tipped with eternal snow; after we have descended a couple of slopes, it also is concealed by the dark grey ridge, and our horizon is bounded by its sharp outline. Kabbalo is a village of two tiny stone cabins in the Permanakbo-tang valley where we encamp. Several Tibetans are out of doors and stare at us; for dinner I have butter and radishes, and see no more of the perpetual mutton.

On February 5 we made a short march down the same valley, which is called Dokang, where we set up our camp

No. 124. Forty Tibetans stood at the camp-fire. When I rode up they all thrust out their tongues as far as they would go, and their bright red colour formed a strong contrast to the dirty faces. Those who wore caps took them off with the left hand and scratched their heads with the right — another form of salutation. When we spoke with them they repeatedly shot out their tongues, but only from politeness and friendliness; they could not do enough to show their goodwill. Near the camp are the ruins of a *dzong*, or fort, which is called Dokang-pe, and a deserted village called Arung-kampa testifies that the valley was formerly more densely populated than now.

The march on the 6th is one I shall never forget; for now we rode down the gigantic staircase, the edge of the Chang-tang, into the Ginunga gap which we had seen from the Ta-la, and in the depths of which flows the upper Brahmaputra. From the camp we marched towards the south-south-east, leaving our river on the right, which, cutting through the mountains in a deep ravine, flows to the Rung-chu. At the entrance of the narrow valley stands a small temple, the Chega-gompa. A pack of wolves howled dismally in a gorge. The ascent to the pass La-rock (14,567 feet) is short and easy, and before we were aware we were up at a great cairn amid smaller heaps of stones, where the *tarpoche* (votive pole) stands grey and cracked, and much worn by wind and weather (Illustration 100). Several blocks of stone lying in heaps on the east side of the pass were white-washed on their upright sides. We had to cross over two more smaller ridges before we had a free and uninterrupted view. The scene is grand, and reminds one of the landscape seen from the palace at Leh. The northern ranges of the Himalayas were distinctly visible, but heavy clouds rested like a canopy on their peaks. Mount Everest, therefore, the highest mountain of the world, could not be seen. The Tsangpo appeared as a very small bright riband, still at a considerable distance. Below us flowed the Rung-chu, which we could see from the place where it emerges from the mountains. Most imposing are the colossal offshoots and ramifications of the mountains lying to the east and west of our position, which fall suddenly to the valley of the Brahmaputra like an endless row of tiger's claws.

The plain stretched out before us is a very large expansion of the Brahmaputra valley, and is named Ye, or Ye-shung, while the river is here called the Yere-tsangpo. It is densely peopled; the great number of dark specks are all villages. To the right, at the foot of a mountain spur, stands the large monastery Tashi-gembe, which with its numerous white-washed houses has the appearance of an Italian coast town. Thence a road runs to the famous monastery Sekya. A fine line meandering towards the south-east is the great highway to Shigatse, Tashi-lunpo, and Lhasa.

From the last platform the path plunges down headlong, so we descend on foot these steep slopes of grey granite rounded by wind and weather. Where loose material fills up the interstices the path is sunk in to the depth of a yard. Many pilgrims, horses, and yaks have passed here before the path became so small. Sometimes we have abysses beside us, sometimes we slide down over the sheets of granite, sometimes we step down as on a staircase, but down we go, ever downwards, and we rejoice to think that every step brings us nearer to warmer, denser air, where we can breathe more easily. Here and there tower up great round granite blocks on a pedestal of loose rubbish, like glacier tables; rain and wind have sculptured out these singular forms.

At last we are down on the great plain into which all the valleys open. We ride past barley-fields, poplar groves, farms and villages with white houses, where blue and red pennants and flags decorate the roofs. We leave the monastery Tugden on our left; a little farther, at the foot of a mountain spur, Muhamed Isa had made a halt. About a hundred Tibetans of all ages and both sexes, exceedingly black and dirty, but very friendly, surrounded the tents. They sold us sheep, fowls, milk, radishes, and malt beer (*chang*), and our tired animals were supplied with plenty of hay and barley. Women with a round arch on their necks by way of ornament, carried wicker baskets of dung to the fires, and were never tired of sitting with us, astonished at us and our wonderful occupations. Here Ngurbu Tundup presented himself and gave me the welcome information that his master, Kung Gushuk, would forward my correspondence. He received only a part of his reward at present, and the remainder would be paid him as soon as I had news that the letters had actually reached Gyangtse. He handed me a *kadakh*, or cloth of welcome, from his master, and said that he was ordered to accompany us and assist us on the way to Shigatse. This was most important news. It signified that we should meet with no obstructions.

Here the absolute height was 12,956 feet, and the air was warm and pleasant. At nine o'clock we had only 5½ degrees of frost, and therefore the tent flap was left open. I held a long consultation with Robert and Muhamed Isa. Should we spend ten days instead of only one in this delightful locality, where there was all we wanted and where the animals could recover their strength, while I visited the curious monasteries perched like storks' nests on rocky promontories, or glittering white at the mouths of valleys? No; we knew nothing definite about the reception that awaited us; it was only eleven days' journey to Lhasa, and we could reach our destination, Shigatse, in three days. We had heard nothing from the Government, but we were expected in Shigatse. Any moment might bring a change unfavourable to us. We would not therefore lose a single precious day, but would start early in the morning, and hurry on as long as the road was open to us.

Our excitement was becoming acute. After all the severe trials and adventures we had experienced should we succeed in reaching our goal? At night the Ladakis sang their Tashi-lunpo hymn more softly and earnestly than ever. At midnight they were singing still, and I listened attentively, though I had so frequently heard the song on the Chang-tang.

Then the fires went out in our first camp in the valley of the Brahmaputra. The crowd collected before the tents on the morning of the 7th was a very mixed one. Horses, mules, and cows were to carry the luggage, for there were no yaks here. A south-west storm blew when I started

102. The Tsangpo with Floating Ice.

103. The Valley of the Tsangpo above Shigatse.

fully an hour later, and the whole population of the neighbourhood collected to witness our departure. Just as I was mounting into the saddle three emissaries appeared from a certain Cheppa Deva, a friend of Kung Gushuk. They brought me a present from him consisting of a whole slaughtered sheep, a thick sweet cake, with figures in relief and preserved fruits on the top, three large lumps of butter, and thirty eggs. I could not send any present in return, for the caravan was already gone on, but I gave them 15 bright rupees and begged them to convey my hearty greeting to the unknown Cheppa Deva. Then the chief of the three said: "We must hand over this money to our master, and therefore it would be well if the Bombo Chimbo would give us an extra tip." This was a cute, sensible speech; they received an additional sum of money and went away contented.

A number of other people accompanied us, giggling and chattering, as far as the highroad to Shigatse. The attractive monasteries on the right and left of the road passed out of sight, and we rode through part of the village Dzundi, inhabited by smiths, and past a warm medicinal spring, over which a bath-house is erected — unfortunately it was just then occupied by a patient, and we could not enter; white clouds of steam issued through the roof, windows, and doors. And further proceeds our picturesque party, through more villages and barley-fields, past fresh monasteries, rocky cliffs and valley openings, till the road winds over a barren plain more and more to the south, towards the Brahmaputra, just as one approaches the Indus from Leh, and, as there, loose stones have been removed from the road and lie along the sides.

Where the valley contracts we have the large monastery Tarting-gompa on its rock to the left, and on the right or southern bank of the river the village Rokdso with its ferry; and now we reach the first granitic spur, which extends to the neighbourhood of the river. Beyond the village Karu with its cornfields and small gardens we ride through a hollow way 13 feet deep, a corridor in the yellow löss; here and there the banks are broken through by rain gutters, and through the gaps, as from the windows of a gallery, we have a glimpse of the great side valley So, which drains from the south into the Tsangpo. The rain has modelled the loam into pyramids, sometimes as much as a yard high, like a forest of gigantic mushrooms. We meet dark bare-headed peasants, driving before them laden horses and mules, and women and children with baskets on their backs, containing fuel or roots. An old woman sat astride on her mule and rose in her saddle with the step of the animal; a man of higher position, on horseback, accompanied his wife; some country people whistled as they followed their cows laden with hay; a party of men and women in picturesque costumes of blue, red, and yellow were making a pilgrimage to the New Year's festivities in Tashi-lunpo, which my Ladakis had long hoped to attend. All the traffic was making eastwards, and we met only men who were going on business from one village to another.

The road now runs over low land which is flooded in summer, so that those who pass this way are then obliged to travel along the flanks of the mountains. Even now the Tsangpo is an imposing stream, and we rest for a while on its bank, which our road touches for the first time. For the first time in my life I drink of the holy water of the Brahmaputra. Bluish-green and almost perfectly transparent, it flows slowly and noiselessly in a single bed to the east, while here and there fishes are seen rising. Only a very thin crust of ice confines the water at the margin, but a bright clump of ice, like a mountain crystal, frequently sweeps past us. A raft laden with barley floats down on the way to the great market in Shigatse, and soon vanishes round the next corner, where the steersmen with their long poles must keep a good look-out — a sight reminding me vividly of my voyage on the Tarim in the year 1899.

To the east of this point the soil is sandy and rises into barren dunes 6 feet high. One can tell at the first glance how they are formed, especially on a day like this, when the westerly storm sweeps the drift-sand before it in clouds, often hiding completely the steep rocky walls on the right bank of the river. During high-water the river deposits quantities of mud and sand on the shallows, which are exposed and dry up in winter. The west wind carries away the silted material to pile up dunes farther east; where these lie low enough, the next high-water clears them away, and when it has fallen the process is repeated. Thus in the valley of the Tsangpo a continuous displacement of solid matter from west to east is going on. It is not alone that the river excavates the bed with its own weight, and loads its water with masses of mud; but also the material deposited at the banks is borne away by the wind which comes to the help of the water. Wind and flowing water work together in harmony to the same end, washing out this gigantic drainage channel deeper and deeper. They have laboured at the work for untold thousands of years, and the result is the Tsangpo valley as we see it to-day.

After a ride of eight hours we came to a small village composed of thirty houses, called Rungma (Illustration 104), where the tents were set up in a garden among poplars and willows. How pleasant it seemed to us, who had passed a whole half-year on the desolate Chang-tang plateau, to hear the wind soughing again through the leafless branches of the trees! Now the fires were no longer fed with dried dung; dry faggots crackled between the tents and threw a bright light on the trees and the Tibetans.

On February 8 we had another long ride. Ngurbu Tundup complained that his mule had run away, so that he must stay behind, and begged me to pay him the remainder of the reward I had promised. But this trick was too transparent.

We suspected that the letters had not reached Gyangtse after all. However, we were not far from the village when Ngurbu came riding after us on a borrowed horse with jingling bells. When we had pitched our camp, Ngurbu was immediately sent off as a punishment to Shigatse, to inform Kung Gushuk that we should arrive the next day, and that I wished to have a good house prepared for me. That was a thoughtless step, for if Kung Gushuk had told what he knew to a Chinaman, we should have been stopped at the last moment before reaching the town.

The winding highway runs further and further eastwards along the northern bank of the Tsangpo, past fields laid out in terraces and watered by the river. It is astonishing to find in Tibet so much cultivable land, and such a number of inhabited villages with solid stone houses and gardens.

At Lamo-tang the river washes the mountainous foot of the left bank, and here a narrow break-neck path runs in zigzags up the slopes. But it need not be used except when the water is high. Now we travel along the embankment beside the river. The river has quite a different appearance to-day: its surface is half covered with porous ice-blocks, but then at night there were 33.8 degrees of frost. Leaping and clattering they drive downstream and graze the fringe of ice attached to the bank, piling up on it small white walls of ice. They keep in the line of the strongest current, and often remain stranded on sandbanks which show a reddish-brown tinge amid the clear green water. A grand landscape under a blue sky and among ponderous fissured mountain masses! In the afternoon the drift-ice had decreased in quantity, and in the evening, before our camp, had disappeared altogether (Illustration 101).

Upwards over the extreme point of a rocky projection by a stony staircase where we prefer to go on foot. Then we descend again to the level valley-bottom, past more villages and monasteries, always surrounded by *chhortens* and *manis*, and often, like the Tikze-gompa in Ladak, perched on rocks. Tanak-puchu is a great valley coming down from the north, and its river irrigates the fields in Tanak. I could not obtain a clear description of this valley: all I heard was that it came from a pass to the north; so I do not know whether it comes from the Trans-Himalaya, like the My-chu and Shang-chu valleys. If such is the case, however, then the eastern watershed of the My-chu is a hydrographic boundary between it and the Tanak-puchu, not the Shang-chu. The question can only be solved by future investigations on the spot.

In the Tanak ("The Black Horse") valley we encamped in a pretty garden (Illustration 105), where a small house with a gaily painted verandah is occupied by the Tashi Lama, when the prelate pays his annual visit to the temple

104. House in the Village of Rungma.

105. Garden of the Tashi Lama in the Village of Tanak.

Tashi-gembe. The garden is situated on a terrace of detritus, which descends sheer down to the river and affords a magnificent view of the Tsangpo. The river is here called Sangchen, or sometimes Tsangpo-Chimbo, that is, the great river. The Tsangpo is the river of Tibet *par excellence.* According to Waddell this name is sometimes so written that it is a strict translation of the name Brahmaputra, which means "Son of Brahmạ." We have already mentioned the name Yere-tsangpo, and farther westwards we shall meet with other names. In the lower part of its passage through the Himalayas it is called Dihong, and it assumes the name of Brahmaputra only when it emerges from the mountains to water the plains of Assam.

CHAPTER XXIII

DOWN THE TSANGPO BY BOAT — ENTRY INTO SHIGATSE

THE 9th of February dawned, the great day on which our caravan of yearning pilgrims would reach the goal of their dreams. The day before had been stormy, and in the evening a strange reddish-yellow light spread over the valley in consequence of the dust that floated about in the air; the mountains were indistinct, and the horizon to the east was quite invisible. But the morning was beautiful and the day was calm. Early in the morning Sonam Tsering and some Ladakis went on board two boats with part of the baggage, while Muhamed Isa and Tsering kept along the road with the caravan. That was a stratagem we had devised. If any one appeared at the last moment ordering us to halt, the prohibition would only affect Muhamed Isa and the caravan, while I should slip into Shigatse by water unnoticed.

All the others were on the way when Robert, Rabsang, and I made our way from the terrace down a steep gully, and stepped on board the excellent boat that was to bear us down the holy stream. These Tsangpo boats are both simple and practical. A skeleton, or rather framework, of thin tough boughs and laths is tied fast together, and is covered with four yak hides sewed together, which are attached to a rim of wood forming the gunwale — and the boat is ready. It is very dumpy, of a long rectangular shape, but somewhat smaller in front than behind. It is not heavy, being only an ordinary load for a man. All the boats now descending the river with pilgrims going to the New Year festival, and the boats which convey country produce or fuel to Shigatse and Tashi-lunpo, will be carried back by the owners along the river-bank. A large proportion of the inhabitants of Hlindug-ling, the part of Tanak where we had encamped, gain their living by such transport. These boats are very buoyant; there were four men in mine, and it could have borne a much heavier load.

The rower sits on a thin board and rows continuously, but faces forwards, for he must be able to see the waterway downstream. The blades of the oars are divided like a fork, and a piece of leather is sewed between the prongs like the web of a duck's foot. Our boatman is a self-confident fellow, and receives my advice with a smile of superiority when I venture to air my experience in river navigation. The current does most of the work, but the oars are in constant use to keep the boat under control.

At first we glided along slowly till we came to the village Segre, with white, clean, and neat houses standing picturesquely on the left bank, and a short distance beyond, to where the river washes the foot of a steep mountain spur. But then the velocity of the boat increased, amounting on an average to 4 feet a second. I was able to look down the river, note the intervals of time, take my bearings, measure the velocity, and draw a map of the river's course, just as I had before done on the Tarim. We passed no cataracts, but the water formed small rapids in narrow contracted reaches, and seethed round the bends. It was a splendid voyage, the most delightful that I have experienced. The last day's journey could not have passed more pleasantly. In Tibet, where hitherto Nature had only placed obstacles in our way, we were now borne along by one of Nature's forces. During half a year we had worked our way through Chang-tang with constant losses, and now the gates stood wide open and I glided as smoothly as on oil to my destination. One of the greatest erosion valleys of the world displayed its wonderful panorama, the air was so still that not the slightest ripple ruffled the surface of the Tsangpo. Undisturbed by the winds of heaven, the emerald-green water gives itself up to the sport of silent eddies, which, coming into existence at cliffs and projecting points, dance rapidly downstream in ever wider circles, and finally vanish altogether. They are born and die, come and go, and the same tongue of land calls forth new ones to life, but every new vortex whirls its spirals in other water of the holy river, which has for thousands of years pursued its course to the mysterious narrows of the Dihong.

What an intoxicating pleasure to be borne along eastwards by the Tsangpo! Is the river one of the forbidden paths of Tibet? If they come now and stop me I shall return: "I am not in Tibet; I am on the holy river of the Hindus; let me alone." The view changes with quite perplexing frequency: we have a dark wall of rock in front of us; at the next turn it has disappeared, and another comes into sight on the opposite side of the stream. We often wonder what above and below mean here; we seem to remain motionless while the panorama revolves round us. Robert is plunged in thought, looks over the gunwale, and, misled by the water and ice-blocks about us, exclaims with astonishment: "Why, Master, surely we are not moving." "Look at the sandbank yonder on the left," I reply, and he is puzzled at seeing it move upstream. And where the river is shallow and the bottom can be seen, it seems as though the gravel, rounded stones, and sandbanks were all passing upwards underneath the boat.

We fall into reverie on this fairy-like voyage. A thought occurs to me: shall we travel on to the mouth of the Ki-chu and thence go up to Lhasa on foot? We can travel by night, and hide ourselves during the day; and Tibetan is Rabsang's mother-tongue. But it passes away as quickly as the eddies beside the boat. In Lhasa I could add nothing to the knowledge acquired by Younghusband's expedition two years before; my hopes were fixed on the friendship of the Tashi Lama. On the Sela-la I had conceived a great fancy for the Trans-Himalaya, and no geographical problem on earth had greater attractions for me. All my future enterprises should have the object of making as thorough a scientific investigation of the Trans-Himalaya as could possibly be accomplished by one man in a single journey. Yes, this

106. Ferry-Boats.

107. Pilgrims on the Way to Tashi-lunpo.

task was so tremendous that my former longing for Lhasa died away like the red of even in the Tsangpo valley, this gigantic colonnade of granite, this royal highway of Buddha, which, breaking through the mountains and becoming hazy in the far east, leads direct to the mouth of the Lhasa valley, while we now glide along on its floor of liquid emerald to the holiest town of Lamaism. Fascinating and attractive as fairy dances the current carried my thoughts eastwards, but it also prompted new plans of campaign in districts which had hitherto lain outside my sphere of interest. In the valleys which pour their water to the My-chu, I had heard more than once of Nain Sing's Raga-tsangpo, which some Tibetans had described as quite as important as the Tsangpo, itself. Was, perhaps, the Raga-tsangpo the main stream? Had it, perchance, tributaries deriving their water from the heart of the mysterious country to the north? Not an evening had passed during the whole winter when I had not studied attentively Ryder's and Nain Sing's maps. Was it certain where the source of the Brahmaputra lay? Had I not here a task before me much more profitable than following in the steps of Tommy Atkins to Lhasa? The sun-lighted waters bearing our boat brought me intelligible messages from distant ravines, from the melting margins of perpetual fields of firn, from bluish glaciers and green ice grottoes in the heaven-kissing crest of the Himalayas, nay, a sonorous echo from the valley where the source of the Brahmaputra bursts out from the rock.

But we must not forget the demands of the present amid dreams of the future. The golden gods of Tashi-lunpo expect us at their festival. Sometimes the river contracts and deepens, and the bottom ceases to be visible, sometimes it spreads out and the velocity decreases. Below the village Pani, where a valley opens out, the river makes a bend to the south-east, but quickly turns eastwards again, where it traverses the great bed which in summer lays almost the whole breadth of the valley bottom under water. We seldom pass a high, clearly defined bank covered with grass, which is not flooded at high-water. From time to time the river sends out a side channel, which, however, soon rejoins the main bed. Wild-geese stand on the bank and scream as we pass by; black and white ducks, herons and other waterfowl, are fearless and trustful, as though they well knew that it is strictly forbidden in Tashi-lunpo to quench the light of life in any living thing.

Just as we were leaving Tanak a dozen boats passed the village; some were tied together in couples so that they could not capsize. The passengers were pilgrims from farther up the river on their way to the New Year festival. There women sat in their most elegant holiday attire, with necklets of coloured glass beads from which little silver boxes containing images and relics or silver coins were suspended, and with high arched frames at the back of the neck covered with red woollen material and adorned with turquoise and coral. There sat greybeards, men, and boys, and a couple of lamas in their red togas had joined the party of laymen. Most of the boats carried small prayer streamers on rods tied to the gunwale, and small reliquaries hung over it to bring a blessing on the boat journey. In some boats sand was laid on the bottom and slabs of stone, where a fire could be kindled and tea infused. They took little notice of us, but talked and gossiped continually and seemed very merry. Evidently the passengers of some boats were well known to one another, and were travelling together from the same village. All the boats on the river were engaged on a day like this, and a continuous succession of pilgrims streamed down the water highway to the holy monastery. Where the banks were low these small black points could be seen both up and down stream (Illustrations 106, 107).

We float past a sandbank, where some blocks of ice are stranded, warning us of danger. The boat only twice grazes the bottom, for our boatman is watchful and steers well. He knows the way, too, and here it is not so easy as it looks to find the course; for the river splits into arms, and only a boatman acquainted with them all can choose the best and shortest. Sometimes he guides us into a narrow channel where the water rushes swiftly.

Now the river turns towards the right, southern side of

the valley, where a mountain falls sheer to the water, leaving only sufficient room on the bank for a road buttressed up with stone blocks. There a dozen boatmen are carrying their skin boats on their backs, and, seen from behind, resemble a row of gigantic beetles. And in the other direction caravans of mules laden with firewood are being driven to Shigatse. Here begins a succession of views of inconceivable grandeur, picturesqueness, and wildness. One cliff after another falls steeply to the river, and is washed by the water murmuring at its foot. Often a block of ice is tilted up in a whirlpool, rises above the surface, brightly glistening in the sun, and then falls back again.

We waited for an opportunity of landing, but the current was too strong. At length the boatman succeeded in getting us into a backwater, and I got out on to a promontory just as a party of pilgrims were passing by, and was in time to take them with my camera. They could not make out what I was doing, and they ceased talking; they seemed relieved, and breathed freely again, when they found that they had got off with a whole skin, and that my camera was not a firearm. Wherever I turned my eyes new subjects presented themselves and invited me to stay sketching all day long. But there was no time; it was my last day, and I had ventured on too great a game to let everything depend on a single card. "It is still far," the skipper said, pointing at starting to a point behind which lay the Shigatse valley, a considerable distance off (Illustration 103).

When we come again into the middle of the valley the river becomes as broad as a lake, is smooth as a mirror, grand and majestic, flows slowly as oil, and reflects the forms of the mountains and the boat. The spurs and cliffs of the mountains on the northern bank have a rosy hue, the water, usually green, shines blue from the reflexion of the sky, and all is solemnly quiet and peaceful. Robert and Rabsang sleep in a corner, but I grudge to lose a minute of this pilgrim voyage. Here and there stands a cairn with a streamer-decked rod — these are the places where routes cross the river. At one ferry a large caravan of yaks were halting, and their loads of sheep's wool were piled up in a wall on the bank. The black men stood out sharply against a background of yellow sand dunes. Farther down Tsering was engaged in getting his detachment into a boat, while his horses were being driven on to another by coaxing and scolding. Here the great road from Tanak crosses the river, and Tsering shouted to us as we shot rapidly past that Muhamed Isa was far ahead. Fishermen in two boats were at work with their net in a bay of the river, trying to drive the fish into the net by throwing stones; they had a poor catch, but promised to bring us fish for sale in the morning to Shigatse. We again make a bend to the south-east and approach the mountains of the southern side, at the foot of which we pass the villages Chang-dang, Tashi-gang, and Tang-gang, prettily situated among gardens. The river now flows slowly in a single channel, as though it must be careful in passing the mouth of a valley leading to a monastery.

There is much life and movement at the foot of the next promontory; many boats laden with barley, straw, firewood, and dung are on the point of putting in, and from others the cargo is being cleared amid shouts and singing. Rows of boats are drawn ashore, and lie turned upside down like large hairy toads. The boatman who has conveyed us to the mouth of the Nyang valley receives four times the usual pay, and can scarcely believe his eyes. He will be able to give himself a day's rest to-morrow.

At this singular landing-stage Guffaru is waiting with our horses. I mount my small white Ladak horse and Robert his Tibetan bay, and while the sun is setting we ride up the Nyang valley with Rabsang as outrider. We soon plunge into a labyrinth of hollow ways and fissures in yellow loam. But we do not need a guide, for several travellers and mule-drivers are on their way, and give us instructions, and none is uncivil. A little to the left of our road flows the Nyang-chu, the river of Gyangtse, one of the largest southern tributaries of the Tsangpo, with several villages on its banks. Twilight falls; I feel my heart beating; shall we succeed? It becomes dark; a large white *chhorten* stands like a ghost close on the right of our way. Rabsang asks a belated wanderer how far it is, and receives the answer: "Follow the road and you will come soon to a lane." On the right rises a hill, and on its summit the outlines of the Shigatse-dzong, the Council House, are faintly seen against the sky. Now we are between white houses and follow a narrow lane, in which it is still darker. In an open place some Chinese stand and stare at us. Snappy dogs come out of the houses and bark at us. Otherwise the town is asleep, and no popular assembly witnesses our entry. But where are our men? We do not know where they are quartered. Ah! there stands Namgyal, waiting to show us the way, and he leads us to a gate in the wall behind which Kung Gushuk's garden lies.

Here Muhamed Isa and all the other men meet and greet us, as though they would offer me their congratulations on a great triumph. We dismount, and cross the court to the house which Kung Gushuk has placed at my disposal. But it is cold and cheerless, and I prefer my tent set up under the poplars of the garden. While we are waiting for Tsering we sit by a large fire of brushwood, whither also several Tibetans gradually gather. I pay no heed to them; I am too much engaged with my own thoughts. I had been fortunate, and after a six months' journey through Tibet had reached my first goal. It was late at night when my dinner was ready; it was very welcome, for we had had no provisions on the boat. Then I had two hours' good work at the notes I had made during the day. But I was disturbed by a gentleman who belonged to the secular staff of the Tashi Lama. He said that he was not acting upon orders, but that he had been told that an unusual visitor had arrived, and he begged me to furnish him with particulars. Then he wrote down the names and nationality of us all, and the size of the caravan, and inquired by which way we had come, whither we intended to travel, and what was the object of my visit to Shigatse. He was exceedingly polite, and hoped that we had not suffered too severely in the cold of Chang-tang. He was, he said, an official of too low a rank to venture to address the Tashi Lama, but he would communicate the information he had obtained to his superiors. I never heard anything more of him. Seldom have I slept so well as on this night — yes, perhaps, when I had fortunately completed my college course.

When the next day passed without any one, lay or spiritual, giving himself the least trouble about us, I sent Muhamed Isa up to Tashi-lunpo. Its golden roofs shone fierily in the rays of the evening sun on a slope in the west close to our garden, which was situated in the southern suburb of Shigatse. My excellent caravan leader sought out a lama of high position, who answered that he would send some one next day to inquire particularly about my intentions and he would then communicate with me further. At the same moment a Chinaman of high rank named Ma paid me a visit. He introduced himself as the commander of the *lansa*, or detachment of 140 Chinese soldiers, which, it seems, garrisons Shigatse. Ma, who was a Dungan and a follower of Islam, became my particular friend from the first moment, and smirked with good temper and cheerfulness. He had arrived from Lhasa five days previously, and was to stay until the Amban, the Governor-General, Lien Darin, recalled him.

"It is inconceivable," said Ma, "how you have contrived to get through to Shigatse without being stopped."

"Yes, to speak frankly, I had expected all kinds of annoyances, if not sooner, at any rate a couple of days' journey from here."

"I did not hear a word of your coming; if I had known that you were approaching the town, it would have been my duty to stop you."

"Then it is fortunate for me that you are strange here."

"Yes, but the worst is, that I shall come off badly as soon as the Amban hears that you are living here, in Shigatse. But now it is too late; I cannot help it now."

"Tell me, Ma Daloi, do you think that the Tashi Lama will receive me?"

"I doubt it. Immediately on my arrival I begged for an audience with the Grand Lama, but he has not even condescended to give me an answer. And yet I am a Chinese officer."

108. Court of Religious Ceremonies in Tashi-lunpo.

109. Religious Decorations on the Roofs of Tashi-lunpo to exorcise Evil Spirits.

This was little encouraging to me, a stranger, who had come from the north without permission, and of whom no one knew what spirit he was. And then next day was the New Year festival, which I could not attend without some understanding, especially as the Tashi Lama himself would be present. But he must know something about me, or how could Ngurbu Tundup's arrival at Ngangtse-tso with the letters be explained?

Meanwhile we awaited the course of events, and went out with a paper lantern to inspect one of the horses which had died in his stall and must be removed. Why could he not remain alive now, when the mangers were so full of barley, straw, and chaff, and the animals stood against a wall which sheltered them from cold and wind, and had an idle ti: e before them? Five of the veterans and the last mule from Poonch were still living, the last six of the splendid caravan which had set out from Leh six months before. All the rest lay in Chang-tang and the storms roared above them. These six should be cherished as the apple of my eye and be well cared for. Their sore backs should be washed and rubbed, their flanks groomed, at night they should sleep in cloths, and of barley and chaff they should have abundance. The ground beneath them should be strewn with straw, and they should be led to water at regular times. I stroked my small grey, but he bit and kicked as usual. He, of all the veterans, was in the best condition, and Guffaru declared that he could cross the Chang-tang again if necessary.

We were very comfortable in the garden. To right and left of my tent stood Robert's and Muhamed Isa's, and that of the Ladakis a little farther off, and huge fires burned as usual before the latter two. A man and woman of Kung Gushuk's household lived in a wretched hut in the entrance gate, and procured for us anything we wanted. The woman was old and infirm, and her face was bedaubed with black, but she was exceedingly friendly. She was always coming to my tent, bowing, giggling and grinning out of pure good-will.

On February 11 I was awaked at half-past six with the news that two men wished to speak to me at once. The brazier and warm water were brought, I dressed in great haste, the tent was swept and put in order, and then I sent to invite my guests to enter. The one was a tall lama of high rank, named Lobsang Tsering, and he was a secretary of the Tashi Lama; the other, Duan Suen, was a Chinaman, with handsome and refined features. Both were extremely polite and had polished manners. We talked for two hours on all kinds of subjects. Singularly enough, my arrival in Shigatse seemed to be a complete surprise to both gentlemen. They inquired my name, the route by which I had come, and my intentions, and, of course, had never heard of poor little Sweden; but they wrote down the Swedish, English, and Chinese names of my country.

"I intend to be present to-day at the New Year festival," I said. "I cannot leave Shigatse without witnessing one of the greatest church feasts."

"A European has never attended our festivals, which are intended only for Tibetans and pilgrims of our faith, and permission will never be granted to witness them."

"The Panchen Rinpoche (the Holy Teacher, the Tashi Lama) must have been informed of my coming some months ago. His Holiness also knew from which direction I should come, or he could not have sent my mails to the Dangra-yum-tso."

"The Panchen Rinpoche never meddles with worldly matters; these are looked after by his brother, the Duke (Kung Gushuk)."

"Still, I must see His Holiness, for I know that he expects me."

"It is vouchsafed only to a small number of mortals to appear before the face of the Holy One."

Now the letter of the Raja of Stok and the Chinese passport came into my mind. The letter made no impression on them; but the young Chinaman, when the passport with its blue border and red stamp was unfolded before him, became very interested, and opened his eyes wider the farther he read. He read it once through, and then translated it slowly to Lobsang Tsering.

"Why," they then both asked, "did you not show us

this paper at once? It would have saved us all discussion."

"Because the passport is made out for Eastern Turkestan and not for Tibet," I answered truthfully.

"That does not matter, now that you are here. You have an excellent Chinese passport, and therefore are under Chinese protection."

The young Chinaman took the passport and went off with it, while Mr. Lobsang Tsering put further questions to me and examined our weapons and other articles. At last I asked him whether he would like to see our garden, and I hurriedly ate my breakfast during his absence. Then the Chinaman came back and declared shortly that I might attend the festival, that especial seats were reserved for myself and a couple of my people, and that a chamberlain of the Tashi Lama's court would call for us at the proper time. Now I blessed the Chinese passport which had caused me so much vexation at the time, and I blessed the Indian Government which had forced me to procure it; I blessed Count Wrangel, who had obtained it so quickly, and I blessed the Chinese ambassador in London, who had written out the passport with permission of his Government. But I had never dreamed that it would be of the slightest use to me, being issued for another country than Tibet.

This was our entry into Shigatse, and these were our first experiences there. Not a finger had been raised to stop us, no inquisitive people had jostled us in the streets to gaze at us. But now, when we had already set up house in the town, our presence in the place excited as general astonishment as if we had dropped down straight from heaven. That this stroke had succeeded, and through no action of mine, was due to certain peculiar circumstances. Hlaje Tsering had himself for some unexplained reason reopened the bag in which he had caught us, and the chieftains dwelling south of the Ngangtse-tso probably thought: "If the Governor of Naktsang lets them pass, we cannot stop them." It was also lucky for us that some of these chiefs had betaken themselves to the New Year festival at Tashi-lunpo, and that we ourselves were lost in the crowd of other pilgrims when we came to the great highway; for during the days of the New Year the Tibetans are like capercailzies at breeding time: they neither see nor hear. And, lastly, I, the only European of the caravan, had ridden into the town when night had already spread a veil of darkness over the earth.

110. THE UPPER BALCONY OF THE COURT OF CEREMONIES IN TASHI-LUNPO

CHAPTER XXIV

THE NEW YEAR FESTIVAL

THE Lamaist Church has, in addition to the monthly festivals, four great annual ceremonies, and the greatest is the New Year feast, the Losar, which is celebrated in remembrance of the Sakya-muni, Buddha's victory over the six heresies, the victory of the true religion over infidelity. It is always held at the beginning of February, and is therefore a festival of spring and light, in which the children of Buddha welcome the victory of the lengthening days over the darkness of winter, the passing away of the cold weather, the awakening of life and of the sprouting seeds after the winter sleep, and the approach of spring, when mild breezes, heralds of a warmer, brighter season, play with the streamers on all the temple roofs. The Losar is therefore an extraordinarily popular feast, which for quite fifteen days draws the labourer from his work, the herdsman from his yaks, and the merchant from his counter; a season of joy and pleasure, of feasting and dancing; a time for paying and receiving visits, and of giving and receiving presents; when the houses and temples are swept and garnished, and the best clothes and ornaments are taken out of the trunks; when friends gather to drink together in their apartments, and then in humble meditation squash their noses against the floor before the images in the dark temple halls; when broad anecdotes and strange stories of robbers are related to visitors from a distance, frequently interrupted by the hum of the prayer mills and the eternal truth "Om mani padme hum."

All are admitted to the great temple festivals: no

distinction is made between clergy and laity, monks and nomads, rich and poor, men and women, greybeards and children. A begging woman clothed in rags is seen beside a duchess loaded with precious stones. The Losar is a feast of the whole people, a carnival of Lamaism, like the Lupercalia and Saturnalia in ancient Rome.

It was my good fortune to arrive just in time for the greatest annual festival of Lamaism, and to be present at its celebration in the monastery town of Tashi-lunpo. At half-past ten appeared Tsaktserkan, a young chamberlain from the vatican, in a very elegant yellow robe of silk and a hat like an upturned dish, with a hanging tassel, and announced that he had come from His Holiness to fetch me to the festival, and that he was commissioned by the lama Lobsang Tsering to attend on me during my sojourn in Shigatse. He requested me to put on the finest clothes I had with me, for I should sit where I could be seen during the whole time from the seat of the Grand Lama. At the bottom of my box I had an old dress coat, several dress shirts, and patent leather shoes, which I had brought especially for the benefit of the Tashi Lama, and when Robert had rummaged out my shaving implements from another box, I assumed the appearance of a European gentleman among the bare mountains of Tibet. But I could not compare in gorgeousness with my interpreter Muhamed Isa, for his gold-embroidered turban surpassed everything. Of the rest only Robert, Tsering, Rabsang, and Namgyal were allowed to accompany me.

We mount the new horses from the Ngangtse-tso and ride to the monastery, a distance of twelve minutes. We leave on the right the Shigatse-dzong, which stands picturesquely on its hill in the sunshine, and reminds me of the palace at Leh. Our way passes across an open place, by detached houses and courtyards, fields, pools, and ditches; the crowd increases, the road becomes narrower; people stream in dense masses to the monastery — townsmen and nomads, pilgrims from distant lands and dirty ragged beggars; and old women sit at every corner offering with loud voice sweetmeats and cakes for sale. Boys, dogs, and Chinamen are all mingled together as in a huge ant-heap.

But Tsaktserkan and his marshals open a way for us and we ride up the lane, beside which rows of great upright prayer mills are enclosed in white-washed masonry. A little higher the way becomes a proper street with tall white houses containing the cells of the monks, and we dismount at one of the chief entrances, a large gateway. High above us rises a brick-red temple building, the Tsogla-kang, and above all shines the white façade of the Labrang with a black frieze on the top and with awnings before its windows. We admire the imposing singular architecture, visible in all its lines and details and making an impression of uniformity and solidity. It is, perhaps, owing to my affection for Tibet that everything in this wonderful land is bewitching and magnificent in my eyes.

Now we mount up to the holy dwellings; the steep, corridor-like passages between the mysterious walls are paved with flagstones, varying in form and dimensions, but all smooth and bright as metal, though very uneven and worn, for they have been trodden for centuries by the feet of innumerable pilgrims and the soles of hurrying monks. Sometimes the crowding in this tightly packed stream of pilgrims is very uncomfortable, and in the lanes there is a musty odour of human beings. We mount higher and higher, go along winding passages, turn frequently at right angles left or right, pass through a gateway roofed over and with a massive threshold, and follow passages and corridors, dimly lighted, dark or pitch-dark, crowded with lamas in red togas, who have one or both arms bare, closely cropped hair, and no covering on their heads. They welcome us with kindly good-tempered smiles, and then move aside to let us pass. Where treacherous steps lurk in the darkness, I feel a strong arm ready to support me in case I stumble; it is some attentive lama at my elbow.

Now it becomes lighter in the monastery walks, and the profiles of the monks stand out black against the light. We enter a gallery with massive wooden pillars, and we take our places in a balcony shut off from the gallery by curtains of yak's wool with horizontal white stripes at the bottom. An arm-chair of European form was placed for me, and I needed it; for this day's spectacle, the grandest of the whole New Year festival, lasted three hours. Here we sat as on the second tier of an open-air theatre, and had an excellent view of the scene of action, like a rectangular market-place, and surrounded by open platforms or terraces supported by colonnades of wooden pillars. The whole reminded me of a vast roofless auditorium. In the centre of the paved court rose a tall mast which had suffered severely from the wind, and had been fissured by many summers and the frosts of the succeeding winters, and from its top long flags hung down to the ground. Immediately below our balcony ran the uppermost terrace, and beyond its edge we looked down over the whole courtyard where the religious ceremony was to take place, and over the galleries opposite and at the sides, one storey above the court below (Illustration 108).

Everywhere, on all the balconies and roofs, on all the projections and terraces, even right up under the gilded roofs curved in the Chinese style of the mortuary chapels, where departed Grand Lamas sleep, the people swarmed. From our elevated point of vantage we looked down on a sea of heads, a conglomeration of human beings, a mosaic of vivid glaring colours, an exhibition of national costumes, among which the Tibetan dress was certainly the most conspicuous, but where the eye lighted on figures hailing from Bhotan and Sikkim, Nepal and Ladak, while Chinese merchants, or soldiers and pilgrims from the grassy steppes of Mongolia, were easily distinguishable. An old lama of high rank, who had shown us to our places, informed us that there were more than 6000 spectators present, and this estimate was below rather than in excess of the truth. Right in front of the highest platform opposite us sits the Consul of Nepal, a young lieutenant in a round black cap with a gold band but no peak. He blows rings from his cigarette, and is the only one guilty of such a desecration of the holy place. Behind him sit a number of other Nepalese and representatives of other Himalayan countries attracted hither by business affairs or religious zeal. To the left of them are long rows of men in dresses entirely of red or of yellow, long kaftans with coloured girdles and sashes round

111, 112. THE *PROFANUM VULGUS* AT THE NEW YEAR FESTIVAL IN SHIGATSE.

the waist, and mushroom-shaped hats, also red or yellow, which have the circumference of a parasol and are fastened with a string under the chin; they are officials of different ranks, are either the city fathers, or are attached to the civil court of the Lama, or to the administrative bodies of the province Chang. On the gallery below them sit their wives and other ladies of rank, quite buried under the most varied and extraordinary adornments: their dresses are red, green, and yellow; they wear necklaces and silver pendants, silver cases inlaid with turquoise, and at the back of the neck tall white aureoles, thickly set with jewels and other ornaments. Their coiffures are of various forms: some have a parting in the middle, and hair, like polished ebony, puffed up at the sides; others have the hair plaited in a number of thin switches, which are fixed up and decorated with beads, etc. There are seated women from Pari and Kamba-dzong, from Ngari-khorsum in the west and Kham in the east, and from the black tents on the shores of Tengri-nor. They remind me of Leksand, Mora, and Vingåker, for there is life and colour in these female groups. Beauty, according to European ideas, will be sought in vain, but many seem agreeable and merry; they are healthy, strongly and symmetrically built, and evidently are much pleased with their pretty dresses. But if their relationship to the Venus de Milo is very remote, they are at any rate women; they talk and chatter, nibble dried peaches and sweets, blow their noses with their fingers, and throw glances at their neighbours which betray their firm conviction that they have outstripped their sisters in the elegance of their attire. How very different these ladies are to the women we have seen in Chang-tang! They do not, indeed, wash themselves every day, but to-day they have washed their faces for the festival, and one is astonished to see so many fair complexions — quite as fair as with us, with scarcely a tinge of yellow, and often with a colour on the cheeks as fresh as an apple.

On the platform under our balcony there are no dignitaries: there the people sit sociably together, there the *profanum vulgus* has its place; there sit country mothers hushing their crying children, and there stand ragged beggars leaning on their sticks, or sit on the ground with their backs against the wall, while they hum their usual begging songs, which are lost in the confusion of voices. Many have brought small cushions, or folded clothes to make a comfortable seat. In some groups tea is drunk out of wooden cups, in others acquaintances meet and lay their heads alternately in one another's laps. Fresh spectators are constantly coming on to the platforms, and the crush becomes dreadful. The railing is low, so as not to hide the view of the scene below. The last-comers have to look for a place against the house wall, and stand that they may see over the heads of those seated before them. Some places right up under the roofs seem rather dangerous, but the people behave well and with great self-control; there is no jostling, no fighting for places, no one falls over the low balustrades, but the greatest harmony and the most perfect order prevail everywhere (Illustrations 111, 112).

The weather was all that could be desired for an *al fresco* festival. What an unpleasant odour must rise from the crowds of human beings when it rains during a festival in late summer! Towards the end a slight wind arose, causing the flags which hung down from the galleries to unfold and blow out. To-day every one was in a holiday mood, and little attention was paid to us, though we sat in the full sunlight in a position where we could be seen from all sides. Occasionally some one turned towards us and made a remark which caused merriment among the others.

As in the two preceding years the New Year festival of 1907 was of a more solemn character than usual, and had attracted larger bands of pilgrims, for the Dalai Lama had taken flight when the English advanced to Lhasa, and this cowardly pope dwelt, misunderstood and despised, in Urga in Mongolia, after abandoning his country, where all was in confusion, to the mercy of the invaders. Many a pilgrim, who would otherwise have gone to Lhasa, now resorted to Tashi-lunpo in preference, where the Panchen Rinpoche, the Pope of Chang, had stuck to his post when the country was in danger. The Chinese had posted up a long proclamation at all the street-corners in Lhasa, in which they

113. LAMA WITH SHELL-TRUMPET.

114. LAMA WITH FLUTE USED IN RELIGIOUS SERVICES.
Sketches by the Author.

declared that the Dalai Lama was deposed because he had exposed his people to danger instead of defending them, and appointed the Tashi Lama in his place as the highest administrator of the home affairs of Tibet. True, the mob had torn down this proclamation and trampled it in the dust, and the Tashi Lama had refused his acquiescence, but nevertheless it was still apparent, two and a half years later, that the Tashi Lama enjoyed a far higher reputation than the Dalai Lama. For though the Dalai Lama was supposed to be omnipotent, all-seeing, and omniscient, his troops had been defeated by infidel strangers; although he had promised his warriors invulnerability, they had been shot down like pheasants by the English machine guns; although he had solemnly sworn that no harm could befall Lhasa, the abode of the gods, the enemy had occupied the town, while the invincible one, the almighty, the incarnation of the deity, had taken to headlong flight like the most cowardly of marauders, more cowardly and meaner than the worst mercenary from Kham. The Tibetans may be forgiven for beginning to doubt the infallibility of the Dalai Lama after the butchery at Guru and Tuna, though the priests were ready with plausible explanations of these events.

The Tashi Lama, on the other hand, had stuck to his post, and was the object of the reverence and respect traditionally paid to the chief priests in Tashi-lunpo. He was the highest prelate in Tibet, while the Pope of Lhasa was wandering a homeless fugitive about Mongolia. At the New Year festival of 1907 it was easy to perceive what great prestige and what boundless confidence were attached to the person of the Tashi Lama. The crowds in festive robes who thronged the platforms and balconies were soon to behold with their own eyes the holiest of the holy in Tibet. And the nearer the time approached, the greater became the excitement and expectation. They had been sitting here for hours, for weeks and months they had toiled through desolate mountains, and now ——

Suddenly from the uppermost platforms on the roofs ring out deep, long-drawn-out blasts of horns over the country; a couple of monks show themselves against the sky; they blow on singular sea-shells, producing a penetrating sound, which is echoed back in shrill and yet heavy tones from the fissured rocks behind the convent; they summon the *Gelugpa*, the brotherhood of yellow monks, to the festival. The venerable lamas whose duty it is to attend on me, explain everything to me, but I do not find it easy to follow them, especially as their words are translated to me by a Mohammedan. They say that this first blast gives notice that the monks are drinking tea together. Then a shout of joy bursts forth from the lips of all the assembled multitude, for now the ceremonies begin.

On the right hand, on the other side of the court, a gallery is placed obliquely resting on five pillars, and from it a stone staircase of eleven steps leads down to the court. The gallery is now concealed by heavy black curtains characteristic of all lama monasteries. Invisible choristers, among whom we seem to distinguish voices of men and youths, now intone a mystic chant. It is subdued, deep, and slow; it quavers in religious enthusiasm beneath the dark vaults of the gallery, and seems to proclaim with full conviction:

"In every land the whole world round
This song of praise shall soon resound."

The murmuring voices are silent and the chant swells up crescendo and then falls again, and seems to die out in some distant under-world, as though the singers had reached the portals of Nirvana. Enthralling, mystical, full of yearning and hope is this wonderful Losar hymn in Tashi-lunpo. Nothing of the kind I have heard, neither the chanting in the Isaac Cathedral in St. Petersburg, nor in the Uspenski Sobor, the cathedral of Moscow, has made a deeper impression on me; for this chant is grand and powerful, and yet at the same time soothing as a cradle song, intoxicating as wine, and sedative as morphia. I listen to it with a solemn feeling, and miss it when the murmur of voices begins again, drowning the final notes.

Above this gallery is a second, which is open to the Dojas-chimbo, as the court is called. Only the middle

115

116

117

115, 116, 117. LAMAS IN DANCING MASKS.
Sketches by the Author.

is covered with a curtain of yellow silk with red stripes, and with heavy gold fringes and tassels at the bottom. Behind this curtain the pope takes his place; he is so holy that his whole person may not be exposed to the gaze of the multitude, but a small rectangular opening is made in the curtain that he may be able to watch the proceedings. After an interval long copper trumpets give forth a new signal; the holy one has left the Labrang, and is on his way to the performance. A procession of high lamas enters the gallery, each bearing some of the robes and pontifical insignia of the Tashi Lama. A low, reverential, and subdued murmur is heard, the multitude rises, on the tip-toe of expectation, all is still as the grave, and all eyes are turned towards the door of the gallery through which the procession enters. He comes, he comes! Then there is a murmur more reverential than before among the crowd, who all rise and remain standing, with their bodies bent and their hands on their knees, inspired with deep devotion at the approach of the Panchen Rinpoche. He walks slowly to his place, sits down with crossed legs on a couple of cushions, and then only his face can be seen through the opening in the silken curtain. Apparently he is rather a young man; on his head he wears a large yellow mitre, which, however, resembles a Roman helmet or a French infantry helmet; his pontifical robe is of yellow silk, and in his hand he holds a rosary. At his right hand sits his younger brother, Kung Gushuk, the Duke, our host, in a dress of red and yellow, and at the right hand of the latter we see three other secular lords in yellow. To the left of the Tashi Lama sits the minister of state, Lobsang Tsundo Gyamtso, a little fat cardinal with a head like a billiard ball, and beside him the tutor of the Tashi Lama, Yonsin Rinpoche, and his deaf and dumb mother Tashi Lamo, a little woman with a shaven head and a red and yellow dress embroidered with gold — I should have taken her for a man if I had not been told who she was. In the semi-darkness behind them is a row of high lamas, all in yellow garments — their ordinary dress is red. It is truly an imposing scene. We seem to have before us the whole conclave of venerable cardinals of Buddhistic catholicism. And this impression is not weakened by the way in which they move and speak. One can imagine how softly they speak to one another in the presence of His Holiness; their movements are dignified and formal, slowly and gracefully they assume the sitting posture of Buddha; their gestures are noble; when they converse, bending slowly towards one another, an air of genuine striking nobility pervades the whole picture without the slightest touch of anything that can be called vulgar.

The crowd has seated itself again, but frequently pilgrims from far-distant lands stand up embued with religious awe, bow, fall on their knees, press their foreheads against the ground, and pay homage to the Grand Lama as to a god. My eyes frequently meet his; apparently he is extremely interested in his guests. Before the commencement of the spectacle he had sent a lama to my garden to present me with a large *kadakh*, a long narrow piece of fine white silk, as a greeting of welcome and a polite token of esteem. Now several monks came gently behind my chair; a table, or more correctly a stool, was set down, and a whole collection of brass bowls were placed on it, filled to overflowing with the finest mandarin oranges from Sikkim, dried fruits from Nepal, raisins from India, figs from Si-ning-fu, sweetmeats from Bhotan, dried peaches from Baltistan, and Tibetan cakes. And tea-cups of Chinese porcelain were filled again and again with thick buttered tea. They said: "The Panchen Rinpoche begs you to partake of these." I immediately caught his eye, rose and bowed, and he nodded to me with a friendly smile. All the refreshments left over — and the quantity was not small — were given to my companions.

Now the religious ceremonies begin. The Tashi Lama takes off his mitre and hands it to an acolyte. All the secular lords on the open platforms also take off their mushroom-shaped hats. Two dancers with gruesome masks, in coloured silken dresses with wide open sleeves, come forth from the lower gallery, the curtain being drawn aside, and revolve in a slow dance over the quadrangle. Then the Grand Lama is saluted by the eleven principal standards in Tashi-lunpo; every idol has its standard, and every

118. View of Tashi-lunpo.
Sketch by the Author.

standard therefore represents a god of the copious Lamaistic mythology, but only the standards of the eleven chief deities are brought out. The flag is square, but strips or ribands of a different colour protrude at right angles from the three free edges; there are white flags with blue strips, blue flags with red ribands, red with blue, yellow with red strips, etc. The flag is affixed in the usual way to a long painted staff, round which it is wrapped when a lama brings it out. He marches solemnly up, halts before the box of the Tashi Lama, holds out the staff horizontally with the assistance of a second lama, and unrolls the flag, and then the emblem of the god is raised with a forked stick to salute the Grand Lama. It is then lowered again, the flag is rolled up, and the staff is carried sloped on the shoulder of the bearer out through a gate beneath our balcony. The same ceremony is observed with all the standards, and as each is unfolded a subdued murmur of devotion rises from the assembly.

After a short pause the trumpets sound again, and now appear some lamas with white masks and white robes, heralding a procession of monks, each of whom carries some article used in the ritual of Buddhism, holy temple vessels, golden bowls and chalices, censers of gold swinging in their chains and emitting clouds of sweet-smelling incense. Some of these monks appear in harness and accoutrements; three masked lamas almost collapse under the weight of their exceedingly costly vestments of red, blue, and yellow gold-embroidered silk. Behind them six copper trumpets, 10 feet long and bound with brass, are carried, and are so heavy that their sound-bells must be supported on the shoulders of young novices. They are followed by a group of flutists, and then come forty men in fanciful motley costly dresses, who bear drums held up vertically on carved poles, and beat them with drumsticks resembling a swan's neck. Now come the cymbals clashing loudly and in regular time in the hands of monks clothed in red silk. Nakchen, "The Great Black Man," is the name of a dressed-up monk who bears a hand-bell. Below, at the stone steps, the court is spread with a square of carpets. There the orchestra seats itself, the forty drums are held up parallel to one another, and likewise the trumpets, which are now allowed to slope down to the pavement. All the musicians wear yellow mitres somewhat like the mitre of the Grand Lama. Three monks of high rank come out on the gallery, which is situated on the short side of the quadrangle immediately above the arena. They wear yellow vestments and yellow mitres, and ring from time to time brazen bells which they hold in their hands. Each of them, I am told, is the superior of a thousand monks; only three are present, for the fourth is ill. Tashi-lunpo has 3800 monks at the present time.

The curtain at the top of the stone staircase is opened and a masked figure, named Argham, comes out with a bowl full of goat's blood in his hand. He holds it horizontally with outstretched arms while he executes a mystic dance; suddenly he pours the blood over the steps. With both arms extended, holding the bowl upside down, he continues his dance, while some serving brothers hurry up to wipe up the blood. Undoubtedly this ceremony is a relic of the time when the original Bon religion prevailed in Tibet, before the Indian monk Padma Sambhava in the eighth century A.D. laid the foundation stone of Lamaism by introducing Buddhism into Tibet; for Lamaism is only a corrupt form of pure Buddhism, and under an outward varnish of Buddhistic symbolism has incorporated a number of Sivaistic elements, and has also retained the superstitions which in pre-Buddhistic times found expression in wild fanatical devil dances, rites, and sacrifices. The object of these ceremonies was to exorcise, banish or propitiate the powerful demons which reign everywhere, in the air, on the earth, and in water, and whose only function is to plague, torture, and persecute the children of men. At that time the god of war and the demons were appeased by human sacrifices, and the ceremony I have just described is certainly a relic of these offerings. Of course Buddhism had a better prospect of becoming popular in Tibet if as much as possible of the old religion were incorporated in the new. But the first command of the fundamental law of Buddhism forbids to "quench the vital spark," to kill. This does not, however, prevent the monks from eating

119. STREET IN TASHI-LUNPO, WITH LAMAS.

meat or making use of goat's blood in certain religious rites — the sheep and goats are killed by ordinary butchers, while the lamas themselves do not transgress the commandments of the law.

Bagcham is the name of a dancer in a frightful devil's mask; as he circles over the quadrangle, pieces of coloured cloth flutter about on all sides. He is followed by eleven masked lamas who execute the same movements. They are joined by a troop of new performers in coloured garments with necklaces, beads, and ornaments. They wear a square collar with a round hole in the middle, which is passed over the head, so that the collar rests on the shoulders and stands out horizontally when they dance. A great number of strips tied about the body swing out like the skirts of a ballet-dancer when the dancers spin round. They hold in their hands various religious objects and long light strips, ribands, and streamers.

Again the curtain parts asunder, and preceded by two flutists Chöjal Yum appears at the top of the steps, the impersonation of a female spirit, and with a trident in his hand performs a dance on the topmost step. Lastly, lamas dance in hideous masks with large evil eyes and Mephistophelian eyebrows, distorted features, and huge tusks; others represent mythical wild beasts, all equally terrible (Illustrations 115, 116, 117). At every new number the three high priests ring their bells, and the music continues without interruption, the discordant noise awakening a thundering echo from the stone façades of the narrow court. The drummers beat their instruments slowly and in strict time, accompanied by the clash of the cymbals, the weird, prolonged blasts of the trumpets, and the more agreeable notes of the flutes. But now and then the time is accelerated, the beats of the drum follow one another more and more closely, and the claps of the clashing basins pass into one continuous resonance. The musicians seem to stimulate one another, and there is a great crescendo; there is more than enough noise to deafen one, so it is useless to attempt to speak to one's neighbour. The dancing becomes more furious, and undoubtedly the fanatical spectacle makes a deep impression on the spectators. Now and then a fanatic is overpowered by it, jumps up, and, turning towards the Tashi Lama, grabs at his head with his hands, falls forward with his hands and forehead on the ground, and repeats this obeisance thrice — he has a deified man before him. A greybeard from Chang-tang, sitting in his fur coat just below our balcony, is unwearied in these observances, and is constantly jumping up to make his reverence to the Grand Lama; but once he slips on a piece of mandarin peel and makes a frightful contortion, to the great amusement of his neighbours. Other pilgrims take from their girdles a small bag of rice or barley, and throw a pinch or two into the court. This is an offering to the temple, and is appropriated by the pigeons and sparrows.

Only the northern third of the quadrangle is required for the religious diabolical masquerade; the other two-thirds are left free for the poor of Shigatse and its environs. There the crush is terrible, but now and then lictors, as they may be called, armed with whips and rods, clear a space. They strike right and left, and all the people bend their backs under the blows, but their interference seems only to increase the disorder. Among the pilgrims on the platforms tea is distributed gratis by monks of low rank; they carry large brass-bound copper cans on the right shoulder, from which they fill the wooden cups held out by their guests. *Panem et circenses!* The monks know how to treat their lambs. What does it matter to them if they give a few yak-loads of brick tea once or twice a year, when they live exclusively at the expense of the people and from the Peter's pence which flow continuously from the bags of pilgrims into the temple treasury?

At length the lictors clear a space in the crowd below us, where a fire is lighted. Two monks step forward and hold a large sheet of paper horizontally over the fire at as great a height as possible; on this paper is written down all the evil from which protection is desired during the year now commencing, and all the affairs in which a triumph is hoped for over the designs and influence of wicked demons. The paper also represents the past year with all its sufferings and all its sins. A lama walks up to the fire with a

120. STREET IN TASHI-LUNPO.

wand in one hand and a bowl in the other. He recites some formulæ of incantation, performs all kinds of mystical hocus pocus with his arms, and throws the contents of the bowl, some inflammable stuff, into the flames, which blaze up brightly and consume in a moment the paper, the passing year with its sins, and all the power of the demons. All the spectators rise and break out into prolonged shouts of rejoicing, for now evil is crushed and every one may rest in peace. The last number of the day's programme was a general dance of all the lamas in the courtyard.

Now the Tashi Lama rises and slowly retires from the scene of the festival, followed by his retinue. After his departure the pilgrims withdraw in perfect order, quietly and without crushing, and take their way down to Shigatse in a black stream of humanity. When the last have disappeared, we look for our horses, accompanied by our new friends.

The jugglery we had witnessed was in every respect brilliant, gorgeous, and splendid, and it is easy to imagine the feelings of humility such a performance must inspire in the mind of the simple pilgrim from the desolate mountains or the peaceful valleys. While the original signification of these dramatic masquerades and these mystic plays is the exorcising and expelling of inimical demons, they are in the hands of the clergy a means of retaining the credulous masses in the net of the Church, and this is a condition of the existence both of the Church and of the priests. Nothing imposes on ignorance so thoroughly as fearful scenes from the demon world, and therefore devils and monsters play a prominent part in the public masquerades of the monasteries. With their help and by representations of the King of Death, Yama, and of restless wandering souls vainly seeking new forms of existence in the sequence of transmigrations, the monks terrify the multitude and render them meek and subservient, and show many a poor sinner what obstacles and what trials await him on the rough road to Nirvana through the valley of the shadow of death.

On our way back we returned the visit of my friend Ma. His *yamen* was built in the usual Chinese style and was surrounded by a wall. I was invited to take my place on the seat of honour beside a small table, on which attentive servants placed tea, sweetmeats, and cigarettes. The whole room was full of Chinamen, but Ma was as amiable as before.

Lobsang Tsering and Tsaktserkan were waiting in my garden. They had brought a whole caravan of mules laden with *tsamba*, rice, meal, dried fruit, and barley for our horses — supplies sufficient for our whole party for a full month. They also handed me 46 silver *tengas* (barely 20 shillings) wrapped in paper, with which, they believed, we should buy meat, for the Tashi Lama must have no hand in anything which involved the extinction of the vital spark. The envoys also said that His Holiness expected me at nine o'clock the following morning, and that they would come to fetch me. But I was not to tell Ma or any one else that the Tashi Lama was going to receive me. For the rest, I had only to say a word and all my wishes would be fulfilled. Later in the evening a subordinate official presented himself with the information that no one would fetch me; I was to be at the great portal at nine o'clock — for the Chinese might become suspicious. At night I took out of Burroughs and Wellcome's large medicine chest all the drugs which I thought we might want, and we packed them in labelled bags. The chest itself, of aluminium, and all its elegant tabloid boxes, bottles, cases, bandages, and instruments were rubbed and polished up till they shone like silver, and then wrapped in a large piece of yellow silk which Muhamed Isa had picked up in the bazaar, for it was next day to be my friendship's offering to the Panchen Rinpoche.

121. THE LABRANG, THE PALACE OF THE TASHI LAMA, TO THE RIGHT.
In the foreground, a part of the Court of Ceremonies.

CHAPTER XXV

THE TASHI LAMA

THE 12th of February came, the day on which I was to be received by the holiest man in Tibet. I therefore made myself as spruce as I had ever done for a ball in a British Government House, and then, accompanied by the same men as to the performance, rode up to the main entrance to Tashi-lunpo, where Tsaktserkan, Lobsang Tsering, and some monks awaited us. In their company we ascended to the higher regions, through a labyrinth of gloomy lanes and dark narrow cloisters, to the Labrang, where the Tashi Lama lives — the Vatican, with its white façade, its large quaint windows, and its solid balconies standing high above this town of temple buildings (Illustration 121). Our conductor leads us into cold dark rooms, up unusually steep staircases. The steps, in which the soles of the monks have worn deep hollows, are edged with iron, and the round bars of the balustrade are polished by innumerable hands. The steps are dark, and our friends warn us to mount slowly and cautiously. Then there is light, and we are taken out on to a gallery, a roof, but only to plunge again into a maze of dark passages and flights of steps. I am asked to wait in a room with red cushions on the floor. Before long we are informed that the man next in rank to the Tashi Lama, the honourable fat little lama, who holds the post of a minister of state, is ready to receive us. His audience chamber, or rather his private cell, is quite a small room, but from its single window he enjoys a beautiful view over the sacred town of Shigatse and the rocky mountains of the neighbourhood. The room is fitted up with solid, unpretentious, and genuine Lamaist luxury. Red carpets lie on the floor, and the ceiling and walls are also red, that is, all that can be seen of them, for most of the walls are hidden by artistically carvéd cabinets with red lacquer, and decorated in colours and inlaid metal work. On these stand large silver *gaos* containing images of the gods, and before them smaller ones of solid gold, between bowls with offerings or wicks burning with a dull flame in butter. Other objects may be seen which the monks use in their services: bells, cymbals, holy water vessels, and a *dorche*, the thunderbolt, emblem of power, which resembles a sceptre. To the left, in a window niche, hangs a flag-like picture (*tanka*) of the first Tashi Lama, and to the right a similar portrait of the ecclesiastical prince Sakya Pandita.

The venerable prelate sat cross-legged on a bench fixed against the wall and covered with red cushions, and before him stood a small, yellow, carved table with silken material inserted in the top. He beamed with fat, inward complacence and goodwill, like any other cardinal; his features were finely cut, and his eyes indicated great intelligence. When I entered he rose with a polite smile and invited me to be seated on a chair by the table, whereupon the inevitable tea was served. Just as indispensable is it to exchange *kadakhs* and presents. I gave him an engraved dagger from Kashmir, and he presented to me a gilt idol — there is the difference between secular and ecclesiastical presents. We talked about an hour over one thing or another, and His Eminence begged me to excuse the delay, but the Panchen Rinpoche was absorbed in meditation and occupied with his daily prayers, and might not be disturbed till he himself gave a sign.

This moment came at length: a lama whispered to the cardinal that I was expected. We go still higher up smooth steep staircases to open landings, up more steps, higher and higher to the holiest of holies in the monastery of Tashi-lunpo. The conversation is carried on in lower, more subdued tones, one dares no longer speak loud; small groups of lamas stand in the corridors and passages, silent as statues, and look at me as I pass by. Lobsang Tsering tells me in a whisper that we are now in the last antechamber, where I can make myself ready and put on the black shoes. Here my servants are ordered to remain, except Robert and Muhamed Isa. If I could have dispensed with interpreters His Holiness would have seen me quite alone.

We enter, not without feeling solemn. I make a deep bow at the door, and two more before I stand before him. The Tashi Lama is sitting on a bench in a window recess and has in front of him a small table with a tea-cup, a telescope, and some printed sheets. He is dressed as simply as an ordinary monk, wears a cerise costume of the usual style, coat, waistcoat, vest, and the long scarf which is thrown over the shoulder and wound round the body like a toga; between its folds peeps out a yellow under-vest with gold embroidery; both arms are bare and the head is uncovered.

His complexion is fair, slightly inclining to yellow; he is somewhat below the middle height, is well proportioned, looks healthy, and at his twenty-fifth year, lately completed, has every prospect of attaining a good old age. In his small, soft, delicate hands he holds a rosary of red beads. His short-cropped hair is black, and there is scarcely any down on his upper lip; his lips are not thick and full like those of other Tibetans, but thin and gracefully formed, and his eyes are of a chestnut-brown colour.

Nodding kindly, he gives me both his hands and invites me to sit in an arm-chair beside him. The apartment, in which he spends the greater part of the day, is astonishingly plain, quite a contrast to that of the cardinal in the lower regions. It is small and consists of two parts: the outer is a kind of roofless ante-room, exposed to all the winds of heaven, to the snow in winter and the pouring rain in autumn; the inner is raised a step, and is again separated by a division ending in a grille, behind which his bedroom is situated. There is not a single idol, no wall painting or other mural decoration, no furniture except what has been already mentioned, not a thread of carpet, only the bare stone floor — and through the window his melancholy and dreamy, but clear and open, glances wander over the golden temple roofs, over the town below them with its dirt and sinfulness, over the dreary mountains which bound his earthly horizon, and away through the azure-blue sky to a Nirvana invisible to us, where his spirit will one day find rest. Now he descended from his heaven and became a man for a moment. But all the time he preserved a wonderful calmness, a refined, amiable politeness and dignity, and spoke in a charmingly soft and subdued voice, modest, almost shy; he spoke quickly and in short sentences, but in a very low tone.

What did we talk about? Why, about all kinds of things in heaven and earth, beginning from his own religion, in the Pantheon of which he himself takes the highest rank among living prelates, down to the yaks that roam wild over Chang-tang. He displayed an alertness, an interest in everything, and an intelligence that surprised me in a Tibetan. I have never been interviewed so thoroughly and with so much tact. Firstly, he inquired if I had suffered much from the cold and hardships in Chang-tang, and whether we had had great losses. Then he hoped I would excuse the sorry entertainment I had met with; it was all owing to my having arrived quietly and unnoticed, and no one knew whether I was the man who was expected and of whose probable arrival information had been received from India. But now everything possible should be done for my welfare and convenience, and he wished and hoped that I should carry back with me a pleasant remembrance of his country.

Then followed inquiries about my name, my age, my caravan, the routes by which I had come; my country, its size and population, its position with regard to Russia and England; whether Sweden was dependent on a neighbouring country or had a king of its own; the best way to travel to Sweden, how long it took to travel there, and what season was the most suitable — just as if he intended to return my visit. Then he asked about the various European countries and their rulers, their relative power and extent; about the war between Russia and Japan, about the great naval battles and the armoured vessels which had sunk; the effect the result of the war would have on Eastern Asia; about the Emperor of Japan and the

Emperor of China — apparently he had the greatest respect for the latter. He asked what countries I had visited, and whether I had seen much of India, where he had been so well received a year ago. He spoke with pleasure of his impressions of India, of the large cities with their fine buildings, of the Indian army, the railways, the splendour and wealth everywhere apparent, and the hospitality shown him by the Lord Sahib (the Viceroy). "Promise me to greet the Lord Sahib from me when you write, and tell him that I still think of his kindness, and greet Lord Kitchener;" and then he showed me a photograph with the autograph of the great General. He was particularly pleased at having been able to visit the holy places he knew so well from descriptions and pictures, which were connected with the great founder of his religion, Buddha, especially Buddh Gaya in Magadha, where Prince Sarvarthasidda, the son of Buddha, had passed six years in solitude and meditation, overcome Mâra, the tempter, the ruler of the world of lust, and had attained to perfect wisdom.

To the Tashi Lama, then, the journey to India had been of the nature of a pilgrimage, though from the English point of view the invitation had been rather connected with political considerations. It was, of course, important to the English in India to have a neighbour on their northern frontier on whose faith and friendship they could rely in unsettled times. As long ago as the year 1774 the great Warren Hastings had sent Bogle as ambassador to the third Tashi Lama, to obtain information about the country, and, if possible, to establish commercial relations. And in 1783 he had sent Turner to the fourth Tashi Lama. Now, 120 years later, the sixth Tashi Lama had been invited to visit India himself, that he might observe with his own eyes the wealth, might, and prestige of the English. No efforts were spared to make a lasting impression on the influential ecclesiastical prince. Later events have proved that this project has failed. The journey of the Tashi Lama to India met with great opposition in Tibet, and gave rise to much suspicion. And great was the joy when he returned in safety; for the Church could not afford to lose, perhaps, the Tashi Lama also, when the Dalai Lama had disappeared from the country. What would become of the re-incarnation when no one knew where the two popes were dwelling?

Then he turned the conversation to the European Powers, and thought that Europe was a singular mosaic of states. He brought out a picture showing all the more powerful supreme rulers of the earth. Under each portrait the name and country were written in Tibetan characters. He put many questions about each monarch, and showed the liveliest interest in their fortunes — he who is more powerful than all the kings of the world, for he rules over the faith and the souls of men from the Kalmucks on the Volga to the Buryats on Lake Baikal, from the shores of the Arctic Ocean to the burning sun of India.

I am not the first European whom Tubden Chöki Nima Geleg Namgyal, the sixth Tashi Lama, has received in the Labrang at Tashi-lunpo. After Younghusband's expedition, Major W. F. O'Connor was admitted to an audience in the autumn of 1904 as representative of the Indian Government, and on this occasion he was accompanied by four officers of the Gartok Mission, Major Ryder, Captains Rawling and Wood, and Lieutenant Bailey. O'Connor, who knows the Tibetan language, was Younghusband's interpreter in Lhasa and the Tashi Lama's in India, and in his capacity as British Trade Agent in Gyangtse had frequently occasion to negotiate with the pope in Tashi-lunpo. Also, immediately after his return home in 1906, the Tashi Lama received Captain Fitzgerald, Lord Kitchener's aide-de-camp, and Mr. David Fraser.

Of the two supreme pontiffs of the yellow-caps Köppen says: "Of these the Panchen Rinpoche at Tashi-lunpo is usually supposed to be an incarnation of the Dhyani Buddha of the present age of the world, Amitabha, but also an incarnation of the Bodhisattvas, Manjusri and Vajrapani, and lastly almost as a re-birth of the reformer Tsong Kapa, the founder of the yellow-caps; the Dalai Lama, on the other hand, is always held to be a reincarnation of the Bodhisattva Avalokiteshvara (Padmapani). . . ." In the same work the functions of teacher and

122. INTERIOR OF THE PALACE OF THE TASHI LAMA.
The little corner near the two windows is the place where Tashi Lama passes his free time.

king are divided between the two Lamaist popes, the former being especially assigned to the Panchen, the latter to the Dalai Lama. And this is also signified by the titles of the two potentates, for the former is called Panchen Rinpoche, "the Great Precious Teacher," and the latter Gyalpo Rinpoche, "the Precious King." In consequence of this idea the Dalai Lama has at length become the temporal ruler of the greater part of Tibet, though he owes his position more to the situation and historical connections of his capital than to this scholastic theory of sanctity, just as the Vicar of Christ on the seven hills owes his supremacy to the importance of the city of Rome. The great teacher (the Tashi Lama) has therefore for the present to content himself with a comparatively small territory, combined with a reputation for sanctity and omniscience, and the privilege of acting as tutor and guardian to an infant Dalai Lama.

And Waddell says of the respective spheres of the two popes: "The Tashi-lunpo Grand Lamas are considered to be, if possible, holier even than those of Lhasa, as they are less contaminated with temporal government and worldly politics and more famous for their learning."

I shall show later that this relation between the two Lamaist popes underwent great modifications in favour of the Tashi Lama during the period of my last journey. The expectations of the English, that they would gain an influence in Tibet through the friendship of the Tashi Lama, were to a certain extent justified; but they had not taken into consideration that the temporal power lost by the Dalai Lama by no means passed over to the Tashi Lama, whose temporal authority was confined within the boundaries of the province Chang, and even there was limited by the universal supremacy of China. The Dalai Lama accordingly had much to lose, the Tashi Lama little or nothing. The Dalai Lama was an ambitious intriguer, who by his incautious policy provoked the offensive measures of Lord Curzon so disastrous for Tibet, and thereby lost almost everything. And if the Tashi Lama had already enjoyed a greater reputation for holiness and learning than his colleague in Lhasa, his renown and his spiritual influence were much enhanced when the result of the war proved that the fine promises of the Dalai Lama were all lies and humbug, and only tended to secure more firmly the heavy yoke of the Chinese on the necks of the Tibetans. Shortly before my visit the Tashi Lama had had an opportunity of reminding the Lamaist hierarchy of his illustrious existence. When he reached the age of twenty-five he sent presents of money to all the monasteries of Tibet, inviting all the monks to a great banquet in their own convents at his expense; a special embassy of monks was despatched to Ladak, and others to Lhasa, Sekiya, Tashi-gembe, and other places. The twenty-fifth anniversary of his birth was celebrated throughout the Lamaist world.

But we will return to the audience. Lamas, walking on their toes and silent as phantoms, handed us tea and fruits continually. The Tashi Lama drank a sip from his plain cup with me, as though to show that he did not consider himself too holy to sit at table with an unbeliever. Some Lamas who stood in the room at a distance were now and then dismissed by a wave of the hand when he wished to put some question he did not want them to hear. This was particularly the case when he requested me not to let the Chinese know that he had entertained me, though it could hardly escape their penetration.

I seized the opportunity to beg for certain favours. I asked permission to photograph him. Oh, certainly, I might come again with my camera, if I liked. I asked to be allowed to see the whole of Tashi-lunpo, and to draw and photograph in the cloister town at my pleasure. "Yes, by all means; I have already ordered the lamas to show you everything." And, finally, I begged for a passport for future journeys in his country, for an official of the Labrang, and some reliable men as escort. This, too, was granted me, and all was to be in order when I had fixed the day of my departure. All these promises were fulfilled to the smallest detail, and if China had not just at this time seized Tibet more tightly than ever in its dragon's claws, the Tashi Lama would certainly have been powerful enough to throw every door open to me. But at any rate his friendship and favour were an excellent recommendation in all my subsequent journeys, and extricated me from many a

123. View of a Part of Tashi-lunpo, with the Façade of a Mausoleum of a Grand Lama.

difficult situation. Pilgrims from all parts of Tibet had seen with their own eyes how well I was received. They had boundless respect for the Tashi Lama, reposed in him the most sincere confidence, and reasoned as follows: "Whoever this stranger may be, he must be an eminent lama in his own country, or the Panchen Rinpoche would never have treated him as his equal." And then these pilgrims returned to their black tents in distant provinces and related to others what they had seen, and when we arrived with our small caravan all knew who we were. Eighteen months later it came about that chiefs and monks said: "Bombo Chimbo, we know that you are a friend of the Tashi Lama, and we are at your service."

When we had conversed for two hours, I made a move to leave him, but the Tashi Lama pushed me back on to the chair and said: "No, stay a little longer." And this was repeated till quite three hours had passed. How many millions of believers would have given years of their lives for such a privilege! The pilgrims who had travelled hundreds of miles to get a sight of him must be content with a nod of the head and a blessing from a distance.

Now was the time to present my offering. The elegant English medicine chest was taken out of its silk cloth, opened and exhibited, and excited his great admiration and lively interest — everything must be explained to him. The hypodermic syringe in its tasteful aluminium case with all its belongings especially delighted him. Two monks of the medical faculty were sent for several days running to our camp to write down in Tibetan the contents of the various tabloid boxes and the use of the medicines. But I warned them, as well as the Tashi Lama, against making a trial of their effect before consulting Major O'Connor's physician in Gyangtse. There was not much danger, however, for the lamas believe that their medical knowledge is much superior to that of Europeans.

Wonderful, never-to-be-forgotten Tashi Lama! Never has any man made so deep and ineffaceable impression on me. Not as a divinity in human form, but as a man, who in goodness of heart, innocence, and purity approaches as near as possible to perfection. I shall never forget his expression: it displayed unbounded kindness, humility, and philanthropy; and I have never seen such a smile, a mouth so delicately formed, so noble a countenance. His smile never left him: he smiled like a sleeper dreaming of something beautiful and desirable, and whenever our eyes met, his smile grew broader, and he nodded kindly and amiably, as much as to say: "Trust in my friendship implicitly, for my intentions are good towards all men."

The incarnation of Amitabha! The earthly shell in which the soul of Amitabha lives on through time! Therefore a deity full of supernatural wisdom and omniscience. The Tibetans believe that he knows not only what is and has been, but also all that is to come. Can he be Amitabha himself? This much is certain, that he is a very extraordinary man, a singular, unique, and incomparable man. I told him that I thought myself fortunate to have seen him, and that I should never forget the hours I had spent in his company; and he replied that he should be very pleased if I came back again.

After I had thanked him once more for his generous hospitality and kindness, he called some lamas and ordered them to show me the temples. Then he gave me both his hands, and followed me with his wonderful smile as I bowed myself out. His friendly eyes did not leave me till I had passed through the door leading into the antechamber. At the foot of the first staircase several lamas were waiting; they smiled in silence, and with wide-opened eyes, no doubt thinking that so long an audience was an unusual favour. Henceforth they all treated me with greater respect, and it was evident that very evening that the whole bazaar and all the town of Shigatse knew that I had spent three hours with the holy one. For my part I could hardly think of anything else but the Tashi Lama and the powerful impression he had made on me. I left the Labrang, his cloister palace, intoxicated and bewitched by his personality. This one day was worth many days in Tibet, and I felt that I had now beheld what was most remarkable in the country, scarcely surpassed by the massive mountains with their snow-capped summits, which from remote periods have looked down on the births and

124. FAÇADE OF THE MAUSOLEUM OF THE FIRST TASHI LAMA. THE COURT OF CEREMONIES IN THE FOREGROUND.

deaths of generations in the valleys which wind about their feet.

During our sojourn in Shigatse we made many friends among the monks of Tashi-lunpo, who gave us right willingly all the elucidations we asked for. One told us that a Tashi Lama, when he feels the approach of death, must in accordance with the directions of the holy law remain in a sitting position, with his legs tucked under him and his hands palms upwards in his lap, for he must die in the same attitude as the meditating Buddha. His last moments are soothed by a number of monks who surround him on all sides, fill the air with the murmur of their prayers, and continually prostrate themselves with their hands and foreheads on the ground, paying divine honours to him and his departing spirit. When he has lost consciousness, has no longer any control over his body, and becomes limp, he is held up, and when life has flown he is so placed that he grows rigid in the orthodox position. The corpse is clothed in priestly vestments, all new and never worn before, and then the tall mitre is placed on his head. Prayers for the dead are recited, mystic rites are performed, and the corpse is placed as quickly as possible, still in a sitting posture, in a metal vessel which is filled with salt and hermetically sealed. Then his mortuary chapel must be prepared, and as this must be erected in a massive stone building, and be decorated within with great art and expense, it may be a long time before his dust is finally laid to rest. The cost is borne by the pilgrims and devotees of the country, and in consequence of his death the Peter's pence flow in more plentifully than ever, for it is a good deed to contribute to the interment of a Tashi Lama. Such liberality secures privileges to the donor in his soul's wanderings.

After the decease, Amitabha clothes himself in the body of a newly born boy, and the difficulty is to discover where this boy is. Therefore letters are sent to all parts of Tibet and to all the adjoining Lamaist countries, in which inquiries are made whether a child of the male sex, endowed with extraordinary spiritual gifts, has appeared. Numerous replies come in. After one after another has been rejected, the boy must certainly be among the remainder, and the right one has to be found out. The names of the boys are written on strips of paper, which are rolled up and deposited in a covered bowl, and this is placed before the image of one of the chief gods, probably before Amitabha or Tsong Kapa, whereupon high cardinals offer up prayers before the bowl, recite appropriate texts from the holy scriptures, present gifts to the gods, burn incense and perform other ceremonies, and then the cover is removed, and the first ticket taken out gives the name of the new Panchen Rinpoche. The decision of this lottery must, however, be ratified by the Dalai Lama before it can have legal force, and from him the new pontiff, an innocent child, receives his consecration. If the Dalai Lama is absent, or is himself a minor, this is conferred by a conclave of the higher priests.

125

126

125, 126. INTERIORS OF TWO MAUSOLEUMS OF GRAND LAMAS IN TASHI LUNPO.
Sketches by the Author.

CHAPTER XXVI

THE GRAVES OF THE PONTIFFS

VOLUMES would be required in which to describe a monastery such as Tashi-lunpo in all its details, its intricate conglomeration of stone buildings connected with one another by passages, corridors, staircases, and terraces, or separated by narrow deep lanes or small open squares; its many temple halls with an innumerable host of images; its monks' cells, lecture halls, mortuary chapels, kitchens, factories, warehouses for provisions and materials; its complicated organization in spiritual and temporal affairs, its festivals and ceremonies. Such a description could only be compiled by an intimate acquaintance with the Lamaist hierarchy and Church, and this knowledge could only be attained by the ardent study of a whole lifetime; for those who would penetrate deeply into the mysteries of Lamaism must gain a thorough knowledge of Buddhism and its relations to Brahminism and Hinduism, and understand the influence which Sivaism has exerted on the religion of the Tibetans, and must be familiar with the elements of the ancient Bon religion and its fetichism and Shamanism, which have crept in and corrupted the Lamaistic form of Buddhism. Such a task lies beyond the scope of this work for many reasons, not least because I have only a dim conception of the essentials of Lamaism.[1] I shall therefore content myself with depicting the system from its

[1] I would especially recommend the following works to those who desire to make a thorough study of Lamaism: Köppen's *Die Lamaistische Hierarchie und Kirche*; Waddell's *The Buddhism of Tibet*; and Grünwedel's *Mythologie des Buddhismus in Tibet und in der Mongolei*. I have borrowed much of the historical and ritualistic information in the following pages from these works.

picturesque side, and describing the outward ordinances I had an opportunity of observing personally. I shall write the names phonetically, without all the silent consonants which render a conscientious translation unintelligible to those who have not devoted much time to the study of the Tibetan language.

Tashi-lunpo must not be conceived as a single vast block of buildings, but as a cloister town within an enclosing wall, a town of at least a hundred separate houses, very irregularly built and grouped, joined together in rows divided by narrow lanes (Illustration 118). On the south side of the Tsangpo a rocky spur projects from the mountains eastwards into the valley of the Nyang-chu; below and to the east of this cliff lies Shigatse in the broad valley on the northern, left bank of the river, while the monastery is built on the lower part of the southern slope of the ridge, and therefore faces south. Looking from the plain to the south of the monastery at this conglomeration of white houses, one notices at once some striking features which facilitate the orientation. On the extreme right is a high thick wall without windows, from the top of which large pictures are exposed to view during certain summer festivals. A little to the left of it, the grand white façade of the Labrang, with its solid, simple, and tasteful architecture, rises above all the cloister town, and in front of and below the Labrang five buildings, quite alike in appearance, catch the eye — massive towers with golden roofs in the Chinese style. They form a line running from west to east, and are the mausoleums of the five earlier Tashi Lamas. The remaining space within the wall around and below them is occupied by all the other houses, and wherever you stand on their flat roofs the first and the last objects you see are these mausoleums; for Tashi-lunpo has also a system of aerial streets and places, as they may be called, that is, the roofs protected by low parapets. In the deep lanes one is quite unable to find the way unless one is very familiar with them, for only the nearest high walls can be seen, consisting either of an unbroken smooth surface or interrupted by large long windows in black frames. The walls all slope a little inwards,

127. THE KANJUR-LHAKANG IN TASHI-LUNPO.
Sketch by the Author.

so that all the lanes between the houses are narrowest at the bottom. The pavement is irregular, worn, and smooth; some lanes and open squares are not paved at all. All these constructions are solidly and firmly built, and planned so as to defy time as well as the rude climate of Tibet.

Tashi-lunpo was founded in the year A.D. 1445 by Ge-dun-dup, the nephew of Tsong Kapa, who in the year 1439 was installed as Grand Lama of the Gelugpa sect, though he did not yet bear the title of Dalai Lama. The present Grand Lama of Lhasa, Ngavang Lobsang Tubden Gyamtso, who has now held the office for thirty-four years, is the thirteenth in succession. This number is not to be compared with the long list of Roman Popes. The first Panchen Rinpoche of Tashi-lunpo was named Panchen Lobsang Chöki Gyaltsan, and held the dignity of pope from 1569 to 1662, or ninety-three years — certainly a world record. His mortuary chapel, Chukang-sher, or the East Tomb, is the one to which we shall first direct our steps.

Its façade faces the rectangular court where the ceremonies are performed, its portal stands at a level with the uppermost platform for spectators, and above the door hang large white awnings beneath a symbolic decoration — a wheel between two gilded stags. The roof is made of gilded copper sheeting, and is divided into two sections by a platform with a parapet (Illustration 124).

The interior of the mausoleum is a cubical room, illuminated only by the daylight, which enters through the portal and mingles effectively with the pale gleam of the butter-fed wicks in a row of silver saucers and brazen bowls. The middle bowl is larger than the others, is like a caldron, and has a cover with a round hole through which a sacrificial flame rises from the melting butter. Before this cordon of butter lamps, on a rather higher super-altar, stand a row of pyramidal figures of baked paste, painted in front with various colours and representing different Lamaistic symbols. Behind them is a row of bowls and chalices of solid gold and silver, donations of wealthy pilgrims. They contain pure water, meal, barley, rice, and other edible offerings.

The tomb itself, in the interior, is a *chhorten* in the form of a pyramid with steps, ledges, and cornices, and may be 20 to 23 feet high. All the front is decorated with gold and silver in arabesques and other designs, and is studded with precious stones. At the very top stands a *gao*, a yard high, somewhat like a sentry-box, with a front of lotus leaves, and in it sits a statue of the deceased wearing the usual mitre, with which Tsong Kapa is always represented, and of which we saw so many specimens during the festival. A number of long silken *kadakhs* have been placed in the uplifted hands of the statue, and hang down over the monument in long festoons and streamers. This is also draped with a multitude of *tankas*, temple banners which are painted in Lhasa and Tashi-lunpo, and represent scenes from the life of the founder of the religion and of the Church fathers. Among and behind them also hang standards and pennants of coloured cloth narrowing to a point at the bottom, and all are old, dusty, and dingy (Illustrations 125, 126).

This *chhorten* with its richly decorated front and its motley surroundings stands alone in the cubical chapel, and a narrow, pitch-dark passage runs round it; at the back, by the light of a paper lantern, the solid foundation of masonry, on which the monument rests, may be seen. The pilgrims circle round it, the more times the better, and the orthodox "Gelugpa," members of the "sect of virtue," always walk in the direction of the hands of a watch, that is, they turn on entering to the left. The monks, who act as guides, insist that we also shall conform to this regulation.

Now we cross again the court of ceremonies, and are conducted slowly through narrow corridors to a somewhat lighter gallery, where we can look down into a *dukang*, a hall where the high office is performed five times a day. Red mattresses, much the worse for wear, lie in rows on the smooth stone floor, on which the monks sit cross-legged during the mass. In the middle of the shorter side stands a papal throne, with back and arms, and covered with yellow silk — it is the seat of the Grand Lama, who on certain occasions teaches and preaches here.

Then we are led to the Yalloa-champa, a holy apart-

128. PORTAL OF THE MAUSOLEUM OF THE THIRD TASHI LAMA IN TASHI-LUNPO.
Sketch by the Author.

ment with a curtain formed of a network of iron rings, through which we catch a glimpse of some dark idols and a quantity of Chinese porcelain bowls. Illuminated by butter lamps and draped with long silken cloths, here stands a figure of Dolma, one of the two wives of Srong Tsan Ganpo, the first Tibetan king, both very popular in Tibet, and immortalized in most Lama temples. It is said of the statue here that it once exchanged words of wisdom with a monk. In another compartment we find Tsong Kapa's statue veiled in silken draperies, and also a figure of the second Tashi Lama, the Panchen Lobsang Yishe.

The library is called Kanjur-lhakang, and here the bible of the Tibetans in 100 to 108 folios, the Kanjur, is kept, studied, and explained. It contains a collection of canonical works which were translated from the Sanscrit originals in the ninth century. The hall is as dark as a subterranean crypt, its red-painted wooden pillars are hung with unframed pictures, *tankas*, painted with minute artistic detail, and on the walls also a host of gods are depicted in colours. At the upper, shorter side is a row of altars, with images of gods in niches, and figures of Tashi Lamas and other great priests. Before these, too, butter lamps are burning, and smooth bright brazen bowls are filled to the brim with offerings. The illumination is scanty and mystical as everywhere in Tashi-lunpo; it seems as though the monks needed darkness to strengthen their faith in the incredible and supernatural literature that they read and study here (Illustration 127).

Proceeding westwards along the lane which runs in front of the mausoleums, we look into the monument of the second supreme pontiff and then into that of the third. They were named Panchen Lobsang Yishe (1663–1737) and Panchen Lobsang Palden Yishe (1737–1779). The mausoleums are built after the pattern of the one already described, but between the entrance pillars of the third hangs a shield bearing the name of the Emperor Kien Lung in raised characters. Köppen gives in his book some interesting information about the relations of the great Manchu Emperor with this Tashi Lama. Kien

Lung (1736–1795) sent many letters to the Grand Lama from the year 1777 inviting him to come to Pekin, but the latter suspected treachery and made all kinds of excuses. But the Emperor was so persistent that at length in July of the year 1779 the prelate had to set out. After a journey of three months he reached the monastery Kum-bum. Wherever the holy caravan passed crowds of pilgrims collected to worship the Grand Lama and offer him presents. He passed the winter at Kum-bum, and made daily several thousand impressions of his hand on paper, which were well paid for as relics. One rich chief alone is said to have presented him with 300 horses, 70 mules, 100 camels, 1000 pieces of brocade, and 150,000 shillings in silver. Escorted by princes, governors, officials, and soldiers, and also by the chief court lama of the Emperor, Chancha Khutukhtu, he reached, after a further journey of two months, Kien Lung's summer residence, where he was received with magnificent pomp and state and brilliant fêtes. The Son of Heaven was pleased to allow himself to be instructed by the holy man in the truths of religion. While the Emperor was visiting the tombs of his ancestors in Mukden, the Tashi Lama made his triumphal entry into Pekin, where all, from the imperial princes to the mob in the streets, wished to see him and receive his blessing. Even the imperial favourites insisted obstinately on seeing His Holiness, on which occasion he sat dumb and motionless behind a transparent curtain, casting down his eyes so as not to be polluted by the sight of beautiful women.

But all this worldly glory came to a sudden and deplorable end. The Tashi Lama fell ill and died, and it was affirmed that the powerful Emperor had caused him to be poisoned, because he suspected him of a design to free himself from the supremacy of China with the help of the Governor-General of India; for it was to this third Tashi Lama that Warren Hastings had sent Bogle as ambassador six years previously. If our friend, the present Tashi Lama, had thought of this circumstance he would perhaps have preferred to omit his visit to India. The Emperor pretended to be inconsolable, had the body

The Namgyal-lhakang with the figure of Tsong Kapa,
in Tashi-lunpo.
Water-colour Sketch by the Author.

embalmed, and masses said for three months over the golden sarcophagus, and then the body was carried on men's shoulders all the way to Tashi-lunpo, the journey lasting seven months, and was there deposited in the splendid mausoleum to which we paid a flying visit (Illustration 128).

Our next visit is to the so-called Namgyal-lhakang, the temple of Tsong Kapa, a large pillared hall with a huge statue of the reformer; before it and its companion images stand the usual battery of lamps, sacred vessels, and Lamaistic emblems. The temple watchman, housed in a small recess in the entrance hall, is a jovial septuagenarian who has lived sixteen years in Mongolia, and always comes out to inquire after my health when I pass the temple of Tsong Kapa on my way from or to the western buildings of Tashi-lunpo (Illustrations 129, 163).

Tsong Kapa's name is as famous and as highly revered in the Lamaistic Church as that of Buddha himself: I cannot recall to mind that his statue is absent in one of the many temples I have visited in Tibet. He was born in Amdo in the year 1355, and of course his birth was attended by all kinds of supernatural circumstances. At the age of three years he decided to retire from the world, and therefore his mother cut off his hair, which became the roots of the famous miraculous tree in Kum-bum (the temple of the "hundred thousand statues"), on the leaves of which Father Huc read with his own eyes holy inscriptions. Unfortunately my own visit to Kum-bum was in the winter of 1896 when the holy tree was leafless. After a thorough course of study Tsong Kapa formed the resolution of reforming the dissolute and corrupted Lamaism, and in several public conferences he silenced, like Luther, all his opponents. The number of his followers rapidly increased, and in the year 1407 he founded the monastery Galdan, near Lhasa, becoming its first abbot, and subsequently the equally large and famous monasteries Brebung and Sera. Tsong Kapa introduced celibacy among the monks of his sect, which he called "Gelugpa," the sect of virtue, and whose badge was the yellow cap; for yellow was the sacred colour of the old Buddhist monks. Among other precepts he enunciated was the regulation that the virtuous monks should retreat into solitude at certain times, to give themselves up to meditation and study, and prepare themselves for disputations. At the present day the yellow-caps are much more numerous in Tibet than the red-caps. Tsong Kapa died in the year 1417, and lies buried in Galdan, where his sarcophagus or *chhorten* stands in the open air. He is regarded as an incarnation of Amitabha, and at the same time of Manjusri and Vajrapani, and he still lives on, therefore, in the person of our friend the present Tashi Lama, after living in the other five Tashi Lamas in succession, whose graves we have just visited. No wonder, then, that he is in exceptionally high repute in Tashi-lunpo.

As we were sitting before the statue, contemplating Tsong Kapa's kind smiling features under the usual pointed mitre, young lamas appeared with fruits, sweetmeats, and tea, and with greetings from the Tashi Lama, who hoped I would not overtire myself. Some monks sat by the wall in the semi-darkness reading aloud from their holy scriptures, which lay before them on small stools; they held in the hand a *dorche*, the symbol of power, and a bell which they rang from time to time (Illustration 130). When we again went out into the sunshine the Indian elephant of the Tashi Lama was taking exercise in the lane; he is the only one of his species in the whole country, and is said to be a present from a wealthy merchant, who brought him from Siliguri.

The fourth Tashi Lama, Panchen Tenbe Nima (1781–1854) has also a mausoleum, similar to those of his predecessors. At either side of the entrance are seen on the walls of the ante-chamber painted portraits, double life size, of the "four great kings," Namböse, Yukorshung, Pagyepo, and Chenmigsang, whose duty it is to ward off the demons and prevent them from disturbing the peace of the temple. They are painted in staring colours and have a hideous appearance, are armed with sword, bow, and spear, and surrounded by a confusion of clouds, waves and tongues of flame, tigers, dragons, and other wild beasts. These four figures are hardly ever absent from the entrance to a temple in Tibet, and one of these four guardian kings is represented in relief on each of the four sides of the five mausoleums.

130. READING LAMA WITH DORCHE (THUNDERBOLT) AND DRILBU (PRAYER-BELL).

131. LAMA WITH PRAYER-DRUM.

Sketches by the Author.

Our guides told us that this mausoleum was erected the same year in which the fourth Tashi Lama died. On either side of the chapel proper is a smaller shrine, to the left the Yamiyang-lhakang, with several images, and an altar front decorated with gilded sphinxes having red wings on the back, nape of the neck, and paws. On the right stands the Galdan-lhakang, with an image of Tsong Kapa projecting from the petals of a lotus flower, which indicates his heavenly origin.

Lastly, we turn our steps to the chapel in which the fifth Tashi Lama, Panchen Tenbe Vangchuk (1854–1882) sleeps his last sleep. As this mausoleum is only about twenty years old, it looks fresher and cleaner than the others, and is particularly richly and gorgeously decorated without and within. The front of the *chhorten* glitters with gold, turquoise, and coral. A glass candelabrum from India looks out of place amid the pure Lamaist convent style, as also some common balls of blue glass and looking-glass — cheap wares, such as are seen in country gardens and in front of village inns. They hang from a ledge in front of the sarcophagus receptacle. On the altar stand the usual votive vessels, many of them strikingly elegant and tasteful. A large bowl on a tall foot is of gold, and contains a burning wick. On the right, on nails, hang simple gifts of poor pilgrims — cheap *kadakhs* like gauze bandages, bangles, necklaces, amulet cases, rosaries — all of the cheapest kind, and all presents from pilgrims who, carried away by their enthusiasm, offered up the insignificant ornaments they happened to be wearing. Here we see the impression of a child's foot on a tablet of stone in a red and yellow frame; a full description in raised letters informs us that it is the print of the foot of the present Grand Lama when he was a child six months old. To this tomb gifts flow more profusely than to the others, for there are still many people living who remember the deceased.

The first four tombs were secured by many solid complicated locks, were opened to admit us, and were closed again when we left. But the chapel of the fifth Grand Lama stood open to the public, and a string of

pilgrims passed to and from it. The monks accompanying us wished to drive them away, but I would not suffer them to be disturbed; it was, moreover, interesting to observe their worship for a while. Murmuring "Om mani padme hum," they stand with bent head before the sepulchral monument, fall on their knees, let their hands slide forward over the stone floor until they lie full-length, touching the ground with their foreheads; then they get up and repeat this gymnastic feat again and again. Afterwards they bow before the idols, lay a handful of rice or meal in the offerings bowls, and go round the dark passage about the monument.

In each of these monuments the Grand Lama is interred at the top, in the pyramid behind his own image. From the street in front of the mausoleums you ascend some stone steps to a portal which gives access to a paved forecourt surrounded by a gallery resting on wooden pillars. Within the pillars the walls are adorned with frescoes representing smiling gods and dancing goddesses like nymphs and odalisks, historical and legendary personages, wild animals, allegorical figures, and the circular disc which betokens the universe with the worlds of the gods, men, and devils. The walls in the forecourt of the fifth tomb were remarkable for the fresh bright colours of their bold effective decoration, while those in the others had suffered from the action of time, and in parts were so much obliterated that they were almost past restoration. When age has set its mark equally on the whole painted surface the picture gains in beauty, for its colours are more subdued and less crude, but the worst is, that frequently the whole decoration has fallen off. A large bronze bell hangs in front of each mausoleum.

The outer courts are so small that the elegant portals cannot exhibit their full beauty; they are too near, and they are seen much foreshortened. From the outer court of the fifth tomb a wooden staircase leads up to the entrance hall; the staircase consists of three divisions, and has therefore four banisters, the two in the middle being closed at the top and bottom by ropes. The middle steps may only be used by the Tashi Lama himself, while those

Entrance to the Tomb of the Fifth Tashi-Lama in Tashi-lunpo.
Water-colour Sketch by the Author.

at either side are free to Tom, Dick, and Harry, and therefore are much worn—almost hollowed out. When the visitor reaches the top of the staircase, he has the door of the mausoleum in front of him, and to the right and left the short sides of the entrance hall, each with a figure of one of the four spiritual kings, while the two others are painted on the wall at either side of the massive door-posts. The entrance hall opens on the forecourt, and its richly carved lintel and beams are supported by two red polygonal wooden pillars with carved and painted elongated capitals. Before the door hangs heavy drapery of a coarse pattern. The very massive heavy panels of the door are lacquered dark brick-red, shine like metal, and are ornamented with mountings, shield-shaped plaques, and rings of yellow brass partly blackened with age. A pair of tassels hang from the rings of the shields. When the two doors are opened the mysterious gloom of the sepulchral chamber and the flickering lamps are exposed to view (Illustrations 132, 133).

Our first inspection of Tashi-lunpo was now ended, and, satiated with strange impressions, we betook ourselves in the twilight to our tents in Kung Gushuk's garden. Darkness fell sooner than usual, for a storm was gathering in the west, and it came down on us before we reached our camp.

CHAPTER XXVII

POPULAR AMUSEMENTS OF THE TIBETANS

The credulous people at whose expense the monks live in laziness — and live well — are not satisfied with religious spectacles alone, which minister only to their spiritual needs; they must also be amused with profane exhibitions, which are more congenial to their lower instincts, and are more adapted to stimulate the senses. On February 15 an exhibition of this kind was to take place on the plain outside the town of Shigatse, and I and my people were invited. We mounted our horses in good time and rode northwards through the small town, which has not more than 300 houses — towns in Tibet are few and insignificant. The houses are white, with a black or red band at the top; with few exceptions they are only one storey high; the roof is almost always flat and guarded by a parapet; the windows and doors are in the same style as those of the monastery. From the street you enter into a yard where generally a large savage dog is chained. The roofs are adorned with a forest of bundles of twigs and rods hung with prayer streamers in all the colours of the rainbow; their object is to drive away devils. Between the irregular lines of houses run narrow lanes and roads, where black swine wallow among the discarded refuse, dead dogs lie about, and stinking puddles stagnate; and we also pass open squares, sometimes with ponds.

There is something uniformly dull about the whole town, in vivid, humiliating contrast to the dzong (Illustration 134), the castle proudly enthroned on its rock, and the golden temple roofs of Tashi-lunpo at the foot of the mountain.

133. Staircase to the Mausoleum of the Fifth Tashi Lama in Tashi-lunpo.
Sketch by the Author.

The ground is yellow dust, and here and there we pass abrupt terraces of löss; dust whirled up by the wind lies on all the houses and roads.

A black, continuous procession of pleasure-seekers streams out to the great plain on the north-east of the dzong; the farther we go the thicker it grows; most are on foot — men with prayer mills and tobacco pipes, women with round red aureoles at the neck and crying children in their arms, boys, beggars, monks, and all the pilgrims from neighbouring countries. Here and there rides a fine gentleman with one or more attendants, while hawkers transport dried fruit and sweetmeats on mules to sell among the people.

Arrived at the show-ground, we leave our horses in charge of Rabsang, and watch with keen interest the curious festive scene presented to our sight. It is a sea of human beings, thousands and thousands of Tibetans and travelling strangers in varied costumes, any one of whom is a subject worthy of an artist's brush. Before us, to the east, we have the gardens of the villages at the foot of the mountains in the Nyang-chu valley, and behind us stretches a whole town of blue-and-white tents with spectators of more or less importance, and in the best position stands a blue-and-white tent open towards the show-ground — there sit, cross-legged, on soft rugs, the officials of the dzong in yellow raiment, solemn as statues of Buddha, and take refreshments now and again. All these tents rise like islands above the sea of heads.

Right through the crowd from north to south runs a race-course, only 6 or 7 feet broad, and flanked on both sides by ridges of earth a foot high. The ground slopes down from the canvas town to the course, and the spectators collected here, ourselves among the number, have seated themselves in groups; but on the east side, where the ground is level, they remain standing. And here the crowd is separated into three divisions by two broad clear lanes. At the end, close to the race-course, two targets are erected, consisting of round discs suspended from poles with a white and a black ring, and a red spot in the middle. The lanes are kept clear lest any one should be hurt during the shooting. Policemen in red-and-white coats with yellow hats, and pigtails both in front and behind, keep the people in order; the pigtail swings backwards and forwards, while a rope's end is in constant use to drive too inquisitive spectators off the course. Two of these policemen are attached to me, to keep me a clear view, but they cause me more annoyance than satisfaction, for I have constantly to restrain them when they would strike half-naked youngsters who are not at all in the way.

Now the show commences! All eyes are turned to a troop of seventy cavaliers in extraordinary motley costumes, who ride slowly in single file northwards along the race-course, so slowly that there is plenty of time to examine the various dresses. All wear red flat mushroom-hats with waving, drooping plumes, white thin vests with a waistcoat over them, and white trousers with patches on the knees. But in some details there is a great variety. One rider, for instance, is dressed in a white silk waistcoat bound with black, over a yellow silken jacket with wide rucked sleeves; while another wears a bright blue jacket on a yellow vest, and has also blue knee-caps on his yellow pantaloons. In general the knee patches are red. The quiver, covered with red material, hangs from a shoulder-belt, and is decorated with shining metal plates, shields, and buttons, and contains a bundle of long arrows tipped with single feathers or tufts. The saddle with its clumsy high wooden frame rests on a saddle-cloth worked in colours. The tail of the horse is wrapped round with red, yellow, and blue ribands terminating in a tassel, which is stretched out by a ring of wire so as to be more effective. A similar rosette also adorns the root of the tail, and from it ribands and cross strips running along the flanks of the horse are attached to the saddle, and flutter in the wind. Between the ears the horse carries a towering plume of peacock's feathers stuck in a bunch of down; on the forehead is a bundle of strips of material of various lengths and colours; the bridle is thickly studded with plates of metal, and across the chest is a broad belt with bells, which ring at the slightest movement.

The party is therefore decked out fantastically in rich

134. Shigatse-dzong (the Fortress).
Sketch by the Author.

colours, and now it turns and rides along the course in the reverse direction, but this time in full career. They ride as fast as the horses can gallop, fling their legs and elbows up and down, the plumes wave, the quivers rattle, and all the tassels, streamers, and ribands fly and flutter in all directions during this wild career. The horses snort, the bridles are covered with flakes of froth, and each rider leaves a cloud of dust for the one behind him. This evolution is repeated twice, and then at the third lap the riders shoot with their long bows at the two targets. The distance between the two is about 60 yards, and an arrow is aimed at each target. The first shot is easy, but then the shooter must be very smart in his movements to catch hold of the quiver, swinging and jumping on his back, take out the arrow, place it against the string and discharge it before he is past the second target. Many marksmen hit both targets, others sent the first arrow into the target, but the second into the ground. Sometimes the arrow glanced against the wooden frame of the target, while some of the riders got over the difficulty by turning round and discharging the arrows backwards, to the great danger of the spectators (Illustrations 137, 138).

The horses are small and active, some of them half-wild and fiery; they have long hair, are badly groomed and shaggy. During the shooting their legs are at full stretch, and the reins hang loose on their necks.

At the fourth career the riders shot with loose powder, and at the fifth with the gun at the first target, and with the bow at the second. They use long, heavy, clumsy muskets, and have not even taken off the inconvenient crutch. A ball of crushed-up paper is inserted in the mouth of the barrel, which is scattered around when the shot is fired — to make a show. The start is made at a considerable distance, and the rider is at full gallop when he comes up to the first target. He holds the gun in the left hand, raises it slowly and gracefully to the right shoulder, grasps the butt with his right hand, holds the muzzle in front of him in the direction of the course, and at the moment he is flying past the target turns the barrel towards it and fires, the match having been lighted at starting. Many produced a red cloud from the target, all a white, of paper, if the gun went off; for it failed when the tinder was not held at the right moment to the touch-hole. Some marksmen discharged their guns a little too late, when they were past the target, and then the spectators most exposed to danger began to rush away in all directions, for they had good reason to fear that their eyebrows would be singed. Immediately the shot is fired the gun-sling is quickly thrown over the shoulder, and now there are two seconds in which to catch hold of the quiver, take out an arrow, and discharge it at the second target. The interval was so short that most of the riders missed; when one made a hit, the crowds gave vent to prolonged applause, and a miss caused still more delight. It must be very hot and trying work to ride in this gorgeous costume with gun, bow, and quiver in full sunshine, every now and then buried in a cloud of dust. Some horses were so restive that their riders could not shoot, and that caused great amusement to the people. One of the marksmen loses his hat, and the next horse shies at it when he is opposite the target, and, leaving the marked course, springs into the crowd of sightseers. Another handles his gun well and raises a red cloud from the target, and also hits the second, but in his hurry has discharged two arrows. One shatters the target and another breaks his gun, and rides on with only the butt in his raised hand, all to the great amusement of the people. Attendants collect the arrows, repair the targets, and fill in the bull's eyes with fresh powder (Illustration 138).

This is a Tibetan popular diversion, fresh, rich in colouring, and picturesque. The spectators have evidently their favourites among the competitors, as may be gathered from the increased buzz of voices when certain cavaliers draw near. Others are not expected to win laurels, for they are received with bursts of laughter. The people are all eyes and ears as they stand or sit for hours together, eating nuts and sweet stuff. In the crowd we see many old acquaintances from the monastery, and also lamas from Ladak, who are studying in the theological seminaries of Tashi-lunpo; merchants from Nepal and Bhotan, Mongolian pilgrims in fur caps with large ear-flaps of fox-skin, and

135. Shigatse, Capital of the Province of Chang, 11,880 Feet.

about a score of merchants from Ladak and Kashmir, in tall white turbans and black kaftans with waist-belts. The Chinese, who play the same part in Tibet as the English in India, sit in small groups, smoking their pipes; they seem to take no interest in the prize-shooting. They wear blue dresses, black vests, and black skull-caps with a coral button on the top.

Two horses, which probably had never before taken part in such sports, took fright, rushed among the crowd on our side, knocking down some and jumping over others, and were caught at length when they had fallen down entangled in human bodies and clothing. Last of all, a ragged fellow jolted along the course on a wretched brute, causing great merriment. This was the signal that the sports were ended, and now the riders dismounted and passed in a long procession before the dzong tent, where each bowed his head before the "Chairman of the Town Council," and a *kadakh* was laid over his neck. This inexpensive mark of favour was also bestowed on them by their friends and acquaintances, and some favourites went about with as many as sixty white neck-cloths. I treated the whole party to tea, and gave them a present of money for the amusement they had afforded myself and my retinue. When we at last rode into Shigatse, we were escorted by quite a host of black Tibetans.

On February 21 Ma Daloi invited me to witness some performances in the inner court of his *yamen* in commemoration of the Chinese New Year. The performers were to be soldiers of the garrison, but the spectacle was put on the stage by the four Chinese temples in Shigatse. It was late at night and pitch dark, and the whole effect depended on the illumination. Two chairs with a table between them were placed in the verandah, and while Ma regaled me with genuine Chinese tea, cakes, and cigarettes, twenty men entered, each carrying two large lanterns of white material in the form of a clover leaf, and painted with flowers and dragons. In the centre a wick is so fixed, that the lanterns do not catch fire when they are swung round. The men dance, and swing their lanterns in an advancing line of uniform undulations; they then place themselves so that the lanterns form various patterns, constantly changing; they whirl themselves round with lightning speed, and the bright lanterns resemble great fireballs hovering about in the darkness. All the time squibs and crackers are thrown about, and fizz and explode among the legs of the spectators, for the court is full of Tibetans who come in quite at their ease. Lastly, the lanterns are left standing and a gigantic bird with a long movable tail and a long curved neck stalks solemnly across the court. The next item is performed by Nepalese. Each of them carries two lanterns like beehives; the top of the one in front consists of a horse's head, with a full flowing mane of paper, and at the point of the hinder hangs a paper tail. Therefore they seem to be riding on horses illuminated from within, as they execute a very lively dance round the court. They sing all the while a melancholy song in slow time. And now a green and yellow dragon comes writhing on to the scene. His head is of wood and paper, and is borne by a man from whose back a painted cloth, the body of the dragon, hangs down and envelops a second crouching man. The dragon dances, twists itself about, opens its jaws, and makes as though it would swallow all present. During the play, weird noisy music drones from drums, cymbals, and flutes, which produce notes like those of a bagpipe. These buffoons present themselves in the courts of all people of rank during the New Year season, to make a little money. They threatened us one evening, but I begged them to come in the daytime, that I might immortalize them on a photographic plate (Illustration 136).

136. Chinese New Year Festival in my Garden.

137. Some of the Members in the Shooting Competition at the New Year Festival.

CHAPTER XXVIII

MONKS AND PILGRIMS

DURING the period of forty-seven days which the force of circumstances compelled me to spend in Shigatse, I had an opportunity of making numerous visits to the monastery, of drawing and photographing interesting details, of making myself familiar with the daily life and habits of the monks, being present at their studies and recitations, and ever increasing my knowledge of the hierarchical metropolis. I used to ride up to Tashi-lunpo with one or two attendants, and pass the whole day in its dark sepulchral chapels and temples. At twilight some of my men came for me with horses. I will recall a few of the impressions I received on these visits, before we start again on our travels.

On February 14 I sat on the uppermost of the western galleries and drew a sketch of the façade of the eastern tomb (Illustration 124), but the pilgrims who were assembling this day for a religious spectacle proved so inquisitive that I had to stop my work and postpone it till a more favourable occasion. I then ascended to a roof platform in front of the Labrang, protected with a balustrade, and posted sentinels at the foot of the steps to prevent the people from following me. Up there the eye falls on a number of cylindrical frames, a couple of yards high, some covered with black and white materials, others enveloped in folded draperies of different colours and length, very like petticoats (Illustration 109). Between them gilded tridents, flagstaffs, and other holy symbols protrude, which protect the temples from demons. While I was sketching a view of the façades of the middle three mausoleums, the head steward of Tashi-lunpo appeared, who supervises the provisioning, cleaning and lighting, etc., caused rugs and cushions to be laid down, and set out the usual refreshments. He is an old lama who has already served thirty years in Tashi-lunpo, after preparatory studies in the monastery Tösang-ling.

From our point of view we can see several smaller gilded copper roofs in Chinese style, standing in front of the façades of the mausoleums and rising directly from flat roofs without any intervening course. Under each roof is ensconced an idol of importance in a temple hall.

We moved about on the roof and enjoyed the wonderful view over the cloister town and its forest of roof ornaments, and came to a place where groups of clerical tailors were sewing together pieces of coloured materials with a zeal and despatch as if their lives depended on it. Had it not been for the religious environment and the waving emblems, one might have thought that they were busy with dresses for a ballet or masquerade. Oh, no, the idols were to have new silken dresses, and were to be hung round with new draperies and standards in honour of the twenty-fifth anniversary of the birth of the Tashi Lama. The clerical knights of the needle sat in the full sunshine, sewed, chattered together, and seemed quite happy. They boldly asked me for money to buy tea, and I gave them a handful of rupees.

Below the place where we had first seen the Tashi Lama at the performance, lies an open gallery, a colonnade looking on the court; the pillars are of wood, and are wound round with red stuff at the top and white below. This gallery is very picturesque, especially the part where the statues of the four spirit kings are placed. The pillars stand out dark against the light background of the open court, and among them move figures which are far from marring the picture, namely, monks in red garments and pilgrims in motley attire (Illustration 142).

Now, too, a religious ceremony was being held in the court. A kind of throne was erected on the northern, shorter, side, and on both sides of it sat monks in yellow kaftans.

138. POPULAR DIVERSION IN SHIGATSE.

Two lamas, also clothed in yellow, advanced bare-headed to the throne and remained there motionless with their bodies bent. Then three lamas in red togas and yellow skull-caps walked slowly over the quadrangle with shrill cries and singular gestures, took off their caps and put them on again with mystical movements. This ceremony was continued so long that we followed the example of most of the pilgrims and left the clergy to their own devices.

Next day another ceremony took place, of which, unfortunately, I could obtain no trustworthy explanation. The Tashi Lama took his seat on the throne of yellow silk, on the short side of the court, in full pontificals, and two monks in red dresses came before him in tall red helmet-shaped head-coverings. After His Holiness had greeted them, one advanced to the eleven steps of the stone staircase and stationed himself on the lowest, whereupon a very curious conversation began. The lama on the step calls out something, probably a quotation from the holy scriptures, or, perhaps, puts a question, claps his hands so that the court rings with the sound, and makes a movement with the right hand as though he were throwing something straight at the head of the other monk. This one replies in the same loud tone and also claps his hands. Occasionally the Tashi Lama puts in a word himself. Lobsang Tsering, who is with me, says that this ceremony is a kind of disputation, and that the two disputing monks will attain a higher degree in the scale of the priesthood if they pass the examination satisfactorily.

Below, to our left, six monks in yellow garments sit on a carpet. Between the pillars the gallery is packed with lamas of lower rank in red dresses, and before them sit superior monks in red kaftans richly worked in gold. Beside the Tashi Lama, on his right, is the seat of Lobsang Tsundo Gyamtso. The dark-red and straw-yellow robes are very effective against the dirty-grey colour of the court.

Now a number of serving brothers come on the scene and set long rows of small tables on the open space in front of the Tashi Lama, which are immediately covered with bowls of dried fruits, confectionery, and mandarin oranges. And now begins a feast in honour of the graduation.

When the tables and bowls are emptied, they are removed as quickly as they were brought, and then comes a solemn procession of monks with tea-pots, and a kind of tea ceremony begins, less complicated but quite as imposing as in Japan. Two priests of high rank place themselves in front of the Tashi Lama and remain there, bending a little forwards, and quite as motionless as the priests praying at the altar in our own churches. It is their duty to serve tea to His Holiness. The first monk in the procession bears a pot of solid gold, which one of the monks before the throne takes from him to fill the cup of the Tashi Lama. The other monks in the procession carry silver pots, each of which is valued at £45, and from these tea is poured out for all the other monks who are not re-incarnations. Every monk carries his own wooden cup in the folds of his toga, and holds it out when the monk who pours out the tea comes round with his pot (Illustration 143).

All through the ceremony the two candidates continue to dispute and clap their hands without intermission. After sitting cross-legged for three hours, as motionless as a statue of Buddha, His Holiness leaves the throne, and, supported by two monks, slowly descends the staircase, on which a narrow strip of coloured carpet is laid; for the Tashi Lama may not touch the unclean earth with his holy feet. Behind him walks a monk, holding above his head a huge sunshade of yellow silk with hanging fringes. One can hardly help feeling that the little man in papal robes and the yellow mitre, who disappears in the darkness among the pillars of the gallery, while the deepest silence prevails, is really a saint, and one of the most powerful in the world. He is now going up to his apartments in the Labrang, where he can pass his time in peace till some new ceremony calls him forth to discharge his ecclesiastical duties (Illustration 145).

Restraint seemed to be lifted from the quadrangle after he had withdrawn. The monks, who had but just been so quiet, began to talk and laugh, the younger ones played and wrestled together, and dirty bare-armed novices drove away with sticks two mangy dogs which had found their way into the holy place.

139. Nepalese performing Symbolical Dances at the New Year Festival.

It was, however, not only the absence of the Tashi Lama that relieved the gloom of the quadrangle: clouds of yellow dust were being swept by a westerly storm over Tashi-lunpo. All the streamers, window curtains and awnings, and the long white flags, began to flutter and clap, and the strokes of the thousand temple bells were blended into one clang, which filled the air and seemed to rise like a hymn to the dwellings of the gods; for at all corners, projections, and cornices are hung brazen bells with clappers attached to a spring, so that a very slight breeze is sufficient to produce a sound. It is very pleasant to listen to this great carillon played by the wind as one wanders through the maze of Tashi-lunpo.

A lama from Ladak, who had been studying for five years in Tashi-lunpo, informed me that there are four different grades of learned priests. If there are several sons in one family, one must always be devoted to the monastic life. In order to be received into a monastery he must first take the oath, binding him to live in chastity and abstinence, not to drink, to steal, to kill, etc. He is then admitted as a novice into the fraternity of the yellow monks. After preliminary studies he attains to the first order in the priesthood, which is called the *Getsul*, and it is his duty to study certain holy writings and listen to the instruction imparted by a Kanpo-Lama. He is also bound to perform certain services, present tea to the superior monks, carry wood and water, see after the cleaning of the temples, fill the votive bowls, snuff the butter lamps, etc. The next order, the *Gelong*, has three subdivisions: *Ringding*, *Rikchen*, and *Kachen*, of which the last qualifies a member to act as teacher. Then comes the rank of *Kanpo-Lama*, or abbot, and lastly the *Yungchen*, who stands next to the Panchen Rinpoche.

The Getsul-Lama has to pay a fee of 20 rupees in order to be promoted to the rank of a Ringding-Lama; it is only a question of money, and the rank may be conferred on a monk a month after he enters the convent, but may be postponed for years if he is penniless. A Ringding-Lama must study a great number of scriptures and pay 50 or 60 rupees before he can become a Rikchen-Lama, and other

300 to become a Kachen. According to another informant the Ringding and the Rikchen are attached to the Getsul order, and only the Kachen belongs to the Gelong order. In these orders, however, it is easier to collect the necessary fees, for the monk has now an opportunity of exercising his sacerdotal office among the people. No payment is demanded on promotion to the rank of Kanpo-Lama, but this appointment is in the hands of the Tashi Lama; it is comparatively seldom conferred, and great learning is a necessary condition. On his appointment the lama receives a certificate bearing the seal of the Tashi Lama. A thorough knowledge of the holy books is required for the rank of Yungchen, and a conclave of high priests present recommendations for the conferment of the dignity.

At the present time there are 3800 monks in Tashi-lunpo, but during festivals the number rises to 5000, for then many come in from the neighbouring convents. Of the 3800 there are, it is said, 2600 of the Getsul and 1200 of the Gelong order. The Gelong Lamas are not obliged to meddle with worldly matters, but have only to superintend the temple services and take part in the rites. There are four only of the Kanpo order now in Tashi-lunpo and two of the Yungchen: one from the Chang province, and the other from Kanum in Beshar, the convent where the Hungarian Alexander Csoma Körösi lived as a monk eighty years ago in order to study the records of Lamaism. This Yungchen-Lama, who is named Lotsaba, is abbot of the monastery Kanum and of three others near the Sutlej. He came as a nine-year-old boy to Tashi-lunpo, and has lived here twenty-nine years. He longs to return to his home, but the Tashi Lama will not let him go thither until the Dalai Lama has returned to Lhasa.

Of the 3800 monks, 400 in all come from Ladak and other lands in the western Himalayas; a few are Mongolians and the rest Tibetans; 240 monks provide the church music, and dancing is performed by 60. They dance only twice a year. In the intervals their valuable costumes are deposited in sealed chests in a store-room called Ngakang. As they are little worn they last for centuries.

140. Dancing Nepalese at the New Year Festival, Tashi-lunpo.

The disputation just described is connected with promotion to the Kachen order, the graduation taking place only during the New Year festival, when eighteen lamas are annually promoted from the rank of Getsul to that of Gelong. The ceremony lasts three days: on the first day two graduate in the morning and two in the afternoon; on the second day six, and on the third day eight.

On February 16 I again rode up to the monastery to sketch gateways and photograph the Tashi Lama, who had sent me word in the morning that this day would suit him if I had time to spare. The weather was all that could be wished, calm and clear. There was a dense crowd on the uppermost platform, in a broad open space before the eastern mausoleum. It was particularly interesting to see an interminable procession of nuns, who had come in from the neighbouring temples to seek the blessing of the Tashi Lama for the new year. All ages were represented, from wrinkled old women to quite young girls. They were fearfully ugly and dirty, and in the whole collection I could find only two who were fairly good-looking. They had short hair and were dressed like the monks: some I should have taken for men, if I had not known that they were women. But, unlike the monks, they wore small yellow caps with turned-up brims, red on the underside.

Lamas and pilgrims swarmed on the courts, platforms, roofs, and staircases — all come to receive the sacred blessing; the devout and patient assembly, here forming queues, made a deep impression on the spectators. To us they intimated a long wait, and therefore we went to the tomb of the Grand Lama, and I drew the handsome portal. I had scarcely finished when Tsaktserkan appeared to inform me that His Holiness was waiting for me, so we hurried up the staircases, past the usual groups of monks, who were loitering all about and appeared to have little to do. On the great quadrangle preparations were being made for the disputation ceremonies.

This time Muhamed Isa accompanied me, and the Tashi Lama received me in the same half-open roof chamber as on the former occasion. He was as charming as ever, and again turned the conversation to distant

countries far remote from this carefully isolated Tibet. This time he spoke chiefly of Agra, Benares, Peshawar, Afghanistan, and the road from Herat to the Khyber Pass.

"What lies to the west of Yarkand?" he asked.

"The Pamir and Turkestan."

"And west of that?"

"The Caspian Sea, which is navigated by large steamers."

"And west of the Caspian Sea?"

"The Caucasus."

"And where do you come to when you continue to travel westwards?"

"To the Black Sea, Turkey, Russia, Austria, Germany, France, and then to England, which lies out in the ocean."

"And what is there to the west of this ocean?"

"America, and beyond another ocean, and then Japan, China, and Tibet again."

"The world is immensely large," he said thoughtfully, and nodded to me with a friendly smile.

I asked him to come to Sweden, where I would be his guide. Then he smiled again: he would like to travel to Sweden and London, but high sacred duties kept him constantly fettered to the convent walls of Tashi-lunpo.

After tea and refreshments he walked about his room like an ordinary man, and asked me to get my camera ready. A yellow carpet was laid in the sunny part of the room, and a chair was placed on it. He did not, alas! wear his refined, charming smile when the three plates were exposed, but had a solemn look — perhaps he was considering whether it might not be dangerous to allow an unbeliever to take his portrait in the midst of his own cloister town (Illustration 146). A tall young lama with a pleasant countenance knew how to take photographs, and took a couple of portraits of me for the Tashi Lama. He had a dark room, where we could develop our plates — Lamaist temples are excellently adapted for dark rooms.

Then we resumed our seats, and the Tashi Lama inquired how I had liked the show of riders on the preceding day. I answered that I had never experienced such amusement. He had never attended these worldly

141. THE KITCHEN IN TASHI-LUNPO.

142. COLONNADE IN TASHI-LUNPO.
Sketches by the Author.

spectacles, for he was always engaged in his religious duties on that day. Then he made a sign, and some monks brought in a gift of honour for me: two bundles of cerise-coloured woollen material, woven in Gyangtse; some pieces of gold-embroidered stuff from China; two copper bowls with silver edges, and a gilded saucer for a porcelain cup, with a cover to match. With his own hands he gave me a gilded image clothed in red and yellow silk, and a large light-yellow *kadakh*. The image he gave me, a seated Buddha with blue hair, a crown, and a bowl in the hands, from which a plant sprouts, he called Tsepagmed. This, according to Grünwedel, is the form of the Amitabha Buddha, called Amitayus, or "he who has an immeasurably long life." It is significant that the Tashi Lama selected this particular image to give me, for he is himself an incarnation of Amitabha, and he is almighty. The figure of the Tsepagmed was therefore intended as a pledge that a long life was before me. This I did not understand at the time; it was only when I looked through Professor Grünwedel's *Mythologie* that I grasped the significance of the present.

This time the audience lasted two and a half hours, and it was the last time I saw the Tashi Lama face to face; for afterwards all sorts of political complications arose which might have been dangerous to him — not to me — and I considered myself bound not to expose him to any annoyance through my visits, which might excite the suspicion of the Chinese. But it grieved me to stay near him for weeks, knowing that he saw every day my tent from his small cloister window, and yet not be able to visit and converse with him; for he was one of those rare, refined, and noble personalities who make other people feel that their lives are fuller and more precious. Yes, the memory of the Tashi Lama will cleave to me as long as I live. His friendship is sincere, his shield is spotless and bright, he seeks for the truth honestly and humbly, and knows that by a virtuous and conscientious life he renders himself a worthy temple for the soul of the mighty Amitabha.

The Tashi Lama was six years old when destiny called

him to be the Pope of Tashi-lunpo, a dignity he has held nineteen years. He is said to have been born in Tagbo, in the Gongbo country. He, like the Pope, is a prisoner in the Tibetan Vatican in spite of his great religious influence, and leads a life prescribed by religious regulations, every day of the year having its particular ecclesiastical functions and occupations. For instance, on February 20, he must bow the knee before the graves of all his predecessors, accompanied by all the superior clergy. When I asked where he himself would be interred when it pleased Amitabha to be re-incarnated in a new Tashi Lama, I was told that a sepulchre would be erected for him as handsome as the others, and that a conclave of the higher priests would select the site. Either the sixth mausoleum will be erected on the west side of the others in a line with them, or a new row will be commenced in front of the former.

One day all my Lamaist followers were admitted to the presence of His Holiness. It was agreed beforehand that they should not pay more as temple offerings than three rupees per man. Of course I paid for them, and they afterwards assured me that the sacred blessing would benefit them during the rest of their lives.

I did not succeed in getting information as to the number of pilgrims who flock annually to Tashi-lunpo. When I made inquiries on the subject I was answered with a laugh, and the statement that they were so numerous it was quite impossible to count them. Pilgrims of rank and fortune make large contributions; others only a small silver coin, or a bag of *tsamba* or rice; and others again come in companies in the train of some well-to-do chief who pays for them all. If the concourse is too large, the blessing is imparted by the higher monks through laying on of hands; when the numbers are smaller, they receive the blessing from the Tashi Lama himself, not with the hand, but with a staff bound with yellow silk. He only blesses people of position and monks with his hand.

We saw laymen as well as clergy among the pilgrims. We have already seen the nuns forming a queue and waiting for the blessing. Four hundred nuns had come in from the neighbouring convents. During their stay they receive free lodging in the Chini-chikang, a building in Tashi-lunpo, free board, and a small present of money at their departure. They do not appear every year, but this year they arrived on the second day of the festival and departed on February 18.

We also saw novices from other monasteries, who are regaled with tea at stated times; but they must be content to sit on the ground in front of the kitchen, where they fill the narrow lane, so that it is difficult to get past.

There are also wandering lamas among the pilgrims. One day I made a sketch of one who had roamed far and wide. He wore a rosary round his neck, a necklace of shells, and a *gao* with an idol, which had been given him by the Tashi Lama. Not long before he had performed a prostration pilgrimage round all the monasteries of Lhasa, and had just completed this feat, so acceptable to the gods, round Tashi-lunpo. He moves in the direction of the hands of a watch, and measures the distance round the monastery with the length of his body. He folds his hands over his forehead, sinks on his knees, lays himself full length on the ground, stretches both arms forward, scratches a mark in the soil, stands up, steps up to the mark and falls again on his knees, and repeats this process till he has gone all round the monastery. Such a circuit of Tashi-lunpo demands a whole day, but if he also goes into the lanes and round all the mausoleums and temples, this religious gymnastic feat requires three days. We saw daily whole rows both of clerical and lay pilgrims encompassing Tashi-lunpo and all its gods in this fashion. I asked several of them how many times they prostrated themselves on the ground during a circuit, but they did not know; for, they said, "We pray all the time, Om mani padme hum; there are twenty manis to each prostration, and we cannot therefore count the prostrations as well." Many of them encircle the wall several times.

This wandering lama was one of a brotherhood of nine monks, who often visited us in our garden, sat down in front of the tents, turned their prayer mills, and sang. They had free lodging in a building in Tashi-lunpo, called

Hamdung. Another member was the seventeen-year-old Tensin from Amdo, who had taken four months to travel thence to Tashi-lunpo. They had come for the festival, and intended to return home through Lhasa and Nakchu (Illustration 216).

The contributions of the pilgrims are one of Tashi-lunpo's chief sources of revenue. But the monastery also possesses extensive estates and herds, and certain monks, who superintend the agricultural affairs and have the disposal of the produce, also carry on trade with the neighbourhood and with Nepal. The produce of the whole of Chang is devoted to the use of Tashi-lunpo, which is therefore wealthy. Each of the 3800 monks, irrespective of rank, receives 15 rupees annually, and, of course, lives gratis in the convent.

Another large source of income is the sale of amulets, talismans and relics, idols of metal or terra cotta, sacred paintings (*tankas*), joss-sticks, etc. The priests also get very good prices for small, insignificant, almost worthless clay idols, and paper strips with symbolical figures, which the pilgrims carry round the neck as talismans, when these things have been duly blessed by the Tashi Lama.

On February 21 I spent nearly the whole day in parts of the monastery I had not previously seen. We wandered through narrow winding corridors, and lanes in deep shadow, between tall white-washed stone houses, in which the monks have their cells. One of the houses was inhabited by student monks from the environs of Leh, Spittok, and Tikze, and we went into the small dark cubicles, hardly larger than my tent. Along one of the longer sides stood the bed, a red-covered mattress, a pillow, and a frieze blanket. The other furniture consisted of some boxes of books, clothing, and religious articles. Holy writings lay opened. A couple of bags contained *tsamba* and salt, a small altar with idols, votive vessels, and burning butter lamps, and that is all. Here it is dark, cool, damp, and musty — anything but agreeable; very like a prison. But here the man who has consecrated his life to the Church, and stands on a higher level than other men, spends his days. Monks of lower rank live two or three in one cell.

Gelongs have cells to themselves, and the chief prelates have much more elegant and spacious apartments.

Each monk receives daily three bowls of *tsamba*, and takes his meals in his own cell, where tea also is brought to him three times a day. But tea is also handed round during the services in the temple halls, in the lecture-rooms, and in the great quadrangle. No religious rite seems to be too holy to be interrupted at a convenient time by a cup of tea.

One day from the red colonnade (Kabung) I looked down on the court full of lamas, who were sitting in small groups, leaving only narrow passages free, along which novices passed to and fro with hot silver and copper pots, and offered the soup-like beverage stirred up with butter. It had all the appearance of a social "Five o'clock tea" after some service. But the meeting had a certain touch of religion, for occasionally a solemn, monotonous hymn was sung, which sounded wonderfully beautiful and affecting as it reverberated through the enclosed court. On March 4 the quadrangle and other places within the walls of Tashi-lunpo swarmed with women — it was the last day on which the precincts of the monastery were open to them; they would not be admitted again till the next Losar festival (Illustration 150).

The young monk who, when accompanying the Tashi Lama in India, had had an opportunity of learning about photography, had his dark room beside his large elegant cell. I, too, was able to develop my plates there. He asked me to come frequently and give him instructions. He had solid tables, comfortable divans, and heavy handsome hangings in his room, which was lighted with oil lamps at night. There we sat and talked for hours. All of a sudden he took it into his head to learn English. We began with the numerals, which he wrote down in Tibetan characters; after he had learned these by heart he asked for other of the more common words. However, he certainly made no striking progress during the few lessons I gave him.

Care is necessary in walking through the streets of the cloister town, for the flags, which have been trod by thousands of monks for hundreds of years, are worn smooth and are treacherous. Usually there is a good deal of traffic, especially on feast days. Monks come and go, stand talking in groups at the street-corners and in the doorways, pass to and from the services, or are on their way to visit their brethren in their cells; others carry newly-made banners and curtains from the tailor's shop into the mystical twilight of the gods; while others bear water-cans to fill the bowls on the altars, or sacks of meal and rice for the same purpose. Small trains of mules come to fill the warehouse of the convent, where a brisk business is going on, for a family of 3800 has to be provided for. And then, again, there are pilgrims, who loiter about here only to look in on the gods, swing their prayer mills, and murmur their endless "Om mani padme hum." Here and there along the walls beggars are sitting, holding out their wooden bowls for the passer-by to place something in, if it is only a pinch of *tsamba*. The same emaciated, ragged beggars are to be found daily at the same street-corners, where they implore the pity of the passengers in the same whining, beseeching tone. In the narrow lanes, where large prayer mills are built in rows into the wall, and are turned by the passers-by, many poor people are seated, a living reproof of the folly of believing that the turning of a prayer mill alone is a sufficiently meritorious action on the way to the realms of the blessed. In one particularly small room stand two colossal cylindrical prayer mills before which a crowd is always collected — monks, pilgrims, merchants, workmen, tramps and beggars. Such a praying machine contains miles of thin paper strips with prayers printed on them, and wound round and round the axis of the cylinder. There is a handle attached, by which the axle can be turned. A single revolution, and millions of prayers ascend together to the ears of the gods.

CHAPTER XXIX

WALKS IN TASHI-LUNPO — THE DISPOSAL OF THE DEAD

IMMEDIATELY below the red colonnade stands the Sokchin-rungkang-chimbo, the kitchen, with its walled-up stove of colossal dimensions and six huge caldrons embedded in masonry. The first supplies all the 3800 monks with tea at one boiling. On the part of the caldron which rises above the masonry are inscriptions and cast ornaments (Illustration 141). Each caldron has a wooden cover which is put on when the caldron is not in use. Tea was being prepared in two of these gigantic pots; probably allowance was made for any chance guests. Glowing, blazing fire-places yawn below the caldrons, and faggots of branches and sticks are thrust in with long iron forks. There is an opening in the roof for the smoke, which rises up in grey rings and produces a picturesque illumination in the holy kitchen. A continuous succession of young lamas and workmen ascend the steps leading up from the street, carrying on their backs water-tubs of different capacity according to the strength of the bearer; for there are quite small boys among them, who have recently been consigned by their relations to the care of the monks. One after another tips his tub over the edge of the caldron, while the stoker thrusts fresh faggots of wood into the stove. Other serving brothers bring in a quantity of cubes of brick tea which they throw into the boiling water, whence clouds of steam ascend and mingle with the smoke. At the side of the caldron stand two cooks, who stir with huge staves larger than oars, and disappear in the rising steam, becoming visible again, like shadow figures lighted from above, when a slight draught from the door clears the air. They sing a slow rhythmical song over their work.

When the tea is ready, it is poured into large bright copper pots with shining yellow brass mountings, handles, and all kinds of ornamentation. Novices carry the vessels on their shoulders to all the various halls and cells. A loud signal is given on a sea-shell from a temple roof that the monks may not miss their tea, but may be on the look-out. I frequently looked into the kitchen, the scene was so picturesque, and the cooks were ready for a joke and were not averse to being sketched (Illustration 148).

Two large and several small *chhortens* are erected on an open square in front of the mausoleums, of exactly the same design as those so frequently seen in Ladak. There are also stone niches filled with idols and other objects. A crowd of people was collected on the terrace when I was sketching, and it was not easy to get a clear view. It was a striking picture, with all the red and many-coloured garments against the background of the white-washed walls of the memorial towers (Illustration 151).

One day when I had sat a long time talking in the cell of the photographing lama, it was dark when I went home. We passed, as we often had before, the entrance gate to the forecourt of the Namgyal-lhakang, the temple in which the Tashi Lama had once provided us with refreshments. There the evening service was in full swing, and of course we entered to look on. The illumination was more dimly religious than usual, but we could at any rate make out our surroundings after coming straight out of the outer darkness. The monks sat on long red divans, and their black profiles were thrown up by the row of forty flames burning in bowls before the altar. The gilded lotus blossoms of the pedestal were brightly lighted, and the yellow silken scarves in the hands of Tsong Kapa's statue and the garlands draped over the images stood out conspicuously. But the upper parts of the figures under the roof were plunged in darkness, and Tsong Kapa's countenance, with plump rosy cheeks and broad nose, was so curiously lighted up from below that his smile was not perceptible. The four coloured pillars in the middle of the hall appeared

144. PART OF SHIGATSE.

145. THE TASHI LAMA RETURNING TO THE LABRANG AFTER A CEREMONY.

black against the altar lamps. The monks wore yellow robes, sat bare-headed, and chanted their melancholy litanies, now and then interrupted by ringing of bells and the roll of drums. At first the leather head of the drumstick falls slowly and regularly on the tight skin, then the beats become more and more frequent, and at last the drum becomes silent in an instant. A monk recites "Om mani padme hum" in rising and falling tones with the rapidity of an expert, and the others join in, making some kind of responses. The recitation passes into a continuous hum, in which often only the words "Om mani" are heard aloud, and the word "Lama" uttered more slowly. The whole ritual has a singularly soporific effect; only Tsong Kapa listens attentively, sitting dreamily with wide staring eyes, and ears hanging down to the shoulders. Here, too, the indispensable tea is handed round; a monk with an oil lamp attends the server that he may be able to see the cups. The monks were now quite accustomed to my visits and took no particular notice of me, but they always greeted me politely and asked what I had been sketching during the day.

A lama gave me information about a remarkable custom. Certain monks consent of their own free will to be walled up in dark grottoes or caves for the space of three, six, or at most twelve years. Near a small monastery, Shalu-gompa, a day's journey from Tashi-lunpo, there is a monk who has already spent five years in his grotto, and is to remain there seven more. In the wall of the grotto is an opening a span in diameter. When the twelve years are over, and the hermit may return to the light of day, he crawls out through this opening. I insinuated that this was a physical impossibility, but the lama replied that the miracle does take place, and, besides, the enclosed monk has become so emaciated in the twelve years that he can easily slip through the opening. One of the monks of the monastery goes daily to the grotto with tea, water, and *tsamba*, and pushes these provisions through the opening, but he may not speak to the prisoner or the charm would be broken. Only sufficient light penetrates through the opening to allow the anchorite to distinguish between day and night. To read the holy scriptures, which he has taken with him into the cave, he must use an oil lamp, and a fresh supply of oil is placed from time to time in the opening. He says his prayers all day long, and divides the night into three watches, of which two are spent in sleep and one in reading. During the twelve years he may not once leave his grotto, never look at the sun, and never kindle a fire. His clothing is not the usual monk's dress, but a thin cotton shirt, and a girdle round the body; he wears no trousers, head-covering, or shoes.

Among other abstruse subjects, this penitent must study a composition on some kind of magic, which renders him insensible to cold and almost independent of the laws of gravity. He becomes light, and when the hour of release arrives, travels on winged feet: whereas he used to take ten days to journey from Tashi-lunpo to Gyangtse, he can now cover the distance in less than a day. Immediately the twelve years of trial are ended, he must repair to Tashi-lunpo to blow a blast of a horn on the roof, and then he returns to Shalu-gompa. He is considered a saint as long as he lives, and has the rank of a Kanpo-Lama. No sooner has he left his grotto than another is ready to enter the darkness and undergo the same test. This lama was the only one in this neighbourhood then confined in a grotto, but there are hermits in abundance, living in open caves or small stone huts, and maintained by the nomads living near them. We were later on to hear of fanatical lamas who renounce the world in a much stricter fashion.

In Tashi-lunpo the cloister rule seems to be strictly enforced: there are especial inspectors, policemen and lictors who control the lives of the monks in their cells and take care that no one commits a breach of his vows. Recently a monk had broken the vow of chastity; he was ejected for ever from the Gelugpa confraternity and banished from the territory of Tashi-lunpo. He has, then, no prospect of finding an asylum in another monastery, but must embrace some secular profession.

One day we visited the Dena-lhakang, a temple like a half-dark corridor, for it is lighted only by two quite inadequate windows. In the middle of the corridor there is a niche which has doors into the hall, for the walls are very thick. Thus between the doors and the window is formed a small room in which the lama on duty sits as in a hut. He belongs to the Gelong order, is named Tung Shedar, came from Tanak, and is now seventy years old, has short white hair, and a skin as dry as an old yellow crumpled parchment.

On entering, one sees on the right a bookcase with deep square pigeon-holes, in which holy books are placed. On the outer, longer wall, banners painted with figures hang between the two windows, in the deepest shadow, most of which are of venerable age, and are dusty and faded — a Lamaist picture gallery. Pillars are ranged along the longer wall, of red lacquered wood, and between them is suspended trellis-work of short iron rods, forming geometrical figures. They are intended to preserve the valuables from theft. In such a niche we see hundreds of small idols set round in rows, four to eight inches high, in silken mantles. Before them are taller statues of gods, and Chinese vases of old valuable porcelain. Especial reverence is shown to a cabinet with an open door, within which is preserved a tablet, draped with *kadakhs*, and inscribed with Chinese characters, in memory of the great Emperor Kien-Lung who was admitted by the third Tashi Lama into the confraternity of the yellow monks. Above, covering the capitals of the pillars, is hung strange, shabbily-fine drapery, of pieces of variously coloured cloth and paper strips. For the rest, the hall abounds in the usual vessels, brazen elephants with joss-sticks, large chalices and bowls, small and large flags, and other things.

Another time I had been drawing in a sepulchral chapel and taken the opportunity of making a sketch of some female pilgrims who were praying there. When the work was finished, we crossed a paved court fully 20 yards broad by 90 long, which was situated just under the façade of the Labrang. It was full of people waiting to see the Tashi Lama, who was to pass by on his way to some ceremony. He came in a red monk's frock and the yellow mitre; above his head was held the yellow sunshade, and he was accompanied by a train of monks. He walked with his body slightly bent and an air of humility. Many fell down before him full-length and worshipped him, while others threw grains of rice over him. He did not see me, but his smile was just as kind and mild as when we last met. So he is evidently affable to all alike.

I made daily visits to the monastery and so gained a thorough knowledge of the solitary life of the monks. Gompa signifies "the abode of solitude," or monastery; the monks in the convent certainly live isolated from the outer world, its vanities and temptations. Once, in the Kanjur-lhakang, I purposed to draw the images with the lamps burning before them on the innermost, darkest wall, but just as I was about to begin monks filled the hall. Their places on the long divans were made ready for them, and before each seat a huge volume of the holy scriptures, the Kanjur, lay on a long continuous desk. The large yellow robes which are put on at service time, but may not be worn in the open-air, were laid ready. The young, brown-skinned, short-haired monks entered in red togas, threw the yellow vestments over their shoulders, and sat down cross-legged before the books. An older lama, a Kanpo, mounted the pulpit on the shorter wall and intoned the sacred text in a harsh, solemn, bass voice. The pupils joined in a monotonous rhythm. Some read from the pages in front of them, while others seemed to know the words of the chant by heart — at any rate they looked all about. Exemplary order is not observed. Some young fellows, who certainly were much more at home in the world than in the Church, talked during the chant, giggled, and buried their faces in their robes to stifle their laughter. But no one took any notice of them; they caused no disturbance. Others never raised their eyes from the book. The hall was as dark as a crypt, being lighted only by a narrow skylight, and through two small doors (Illustration 154).

After they had sung awhile there was an interval, and lama boys passed along the gangways between the rows of benches and poured tea, with wonderful adroitness and without spilling a drop, into the wooden cups held out to them. But almost before the pupils have begun to drink,

146. THE PANCHEN RINPOCHE, OR TASHI LAMA.

the deep bass of the leader drones out in the gloom above, and the proceedings recommence. Meanwhile pilgrims pass along the gangways to the altar and place small heaps of *tsamba* or meal in the bowls standing before the images, from the bags and bundles they bring with them.

A tall lama stands erect at the entrance door. A pilgrim says to him: "I will pay 3 *tengas* for a blessing." The lama sings out aloud the contribution and the purpose for which it is given, and then a strophe is sung especially on behalf of the pilgrim, after which all the monks clap their hands. This is repeated whenever fresh pilgrims come up. I myself paid 5 rupees for a blessing, and received it together with a noisy clapping. For ten minutes the lamas stand up, run along the passages outside the lecture-hall, or take stock of me while I am sketching the schoolroom and the pupils. Often a handful of rice rains down upon the youths — some pilgrim is passing by the window opening. At these readings and at the high mass the monks who have been longest in the monastery occupy the front seats, and the last-comers the back seats. When the lecture is over the Kanpo-Lama counts the receipts that have flowed in from the pockets of the pilgrims, wraps the coins in paper, which is sealed up and conveyed to the treasury, and enters the amount in a large account book.

The images on the altar table of the Kanjur-lhakang are small, and composed of gilded metal, and most of the other idols in Tashi-lunpo are of the same kind. Some are of carved wood, and a few, like the great statue of Tsong Kapa, are composed of powdered spices cemented together by a gum extracted from roots of plants. The statue of Tsong Kapa is said to have been constructed seventy-two years ago, and to have cost as much as one of gold. The Tashi Lama has 1500 small gods cast for the New Year festival, each costing 7 rupees; they are manufactured in Tashi-lunpo, and are given away or sold. The manufacture of these images is regarded as a peculiarly blessed work, and the lamas engaged in it may count with certainty on a long life. Especially is this the case with those who make images of the Tsepagmed. The oftener they utter his name and produce his likeness from the rough metal, the longer it will be before their poor souls have to set out on their travels again. No idol, however, possesses any miraculous power or the slightest shadow of divine influence unless it is properly consecrated and blessed by an incarnated lama.

I must by this time have tried the patience of my readers with my personal recollections of the monastery of Tashi-lunpo. I have unintentionally tarried too long with the fraternity of the yellow-caps, and quite forgotten events awaiting our attention elsewhere. I might have remembered that temples and monks' cells may not have the same interest for others as they have for myself, but the remembrance of this period is particularly dear to me, for I was treated with greater friendliness and hospitality in Tashi-lunpo than in any town of Central Asia. We came from the wastes of Tibet to the greatest festival of the year, from solitude into the religious metropolis swarming with thousands of pilgrims, from poverty and want to abundance of everything we wanted, and the howling of wolves and storms gave place to hymns and fanfares from temple roofs glittering with gold. The balls in Simla and the desolate mountains of Tibet were strange contrasts, but still greater the solitude of the mountain wilderness and the holy town, which we entered in the garb of far-travelled pilgrims, and where we were hospitably invited to look about us and take part in all that was going on.

It is now time to say farewell to Tashi-lunpo, its mystic gloom and its far-sounding trumpet blasts. I do so with the feeling that I have given a very imperfect and fragmentary description of it. It was not part of my plan to thoroughly investigate the cloister town, but on the contrary it was my desire to return as early as possible to the parts of Tibet where I might expect to make great geographical discoveries. Circumstances, however, which I shall hereafter refer to in a few words, compelled us to postpone our departure from day to day. As we were always looking forward to making a start, our visits to the monastery were curtailed. Moreover, I wished, if possible, to avoid exciting suspicion. Tashi-lunpo had on two occasions, more than 100 years ago indeed, been pillaged by Gurkhas from Nepal. The English had quite recently made a military expedition to Lhasa. Many monks disapproved of my daily visits, and regarded it as unseemly that a European, of whose exact intentions nothing was known, should go about freely, sketch the gods, see all the treasures of gold and precious stones, and make an inventory. And it was known that the dominant race in Tibet, the Chinese, were displeased at my coming hither, and that I had really no right to sojourn in the forbidden land. If, then, I wished to accomplish more, I must exercise the greatest caution in all my proceedings.

A few words on funeral customs before we take leave of Tashi-lunpo.

South-west of Tashi-lunpo lies a small village, Gompa-sarpa or the New Monastery, where, according to tradition, a temple formerly stood which was plundered by the Dzungarians. Here is now the cemetery of Shigatse and of the monastery, the Golgotha where the bodies of monks and laymen are abandoned to corruption in the same fashion.

When the soul of a lama grows weary of the earthly frame in which it has spent its human life, and the lama himself, after living perhaps fifty years in his dark cloister cell, perceives that the lamp of life is going out for want of oil, some brethren gather round his sick-bed, recite prayers, or intercede with the gods set up in his cell, whose prototypes in Nirvana or in the kingdom of the dead have something to do with death and the transmigration of souls. As soon as life is extinct, special prayers for the dead are recited to facilitate the severance of the soul from the body, and console it during its first steps on the dark road beyond the bounds of this life. The corpse of a lama lies in his cell for three days, that of a layman as long as five days, that there may be sufficient time for all the funeral rites and services. Rich people retain the corpse longer in the house, which is certainly more expensive, but allows more time for prayers which will benefit the deceased. Monks fix the date of interment and the moment when the soul is actually freed from its earthly fetters and soars up in search of a new habitation.

The dead lama in a new costume of the ordinary cut and style is wrapped in a piece of cloth and is carried away by one or two of his colleagues; a layman is borne on a bier by the corpse-bearers. These are called *Lagbas*, and form a despised caste of fifty persons, who live apart in fifteen small miserable cabins in the village Gompa-sarpa. They are allowed to marry only within the guild of corpse-bearers, and their children may not engage in any other occupation but that of their fathers, so that the calling is hereditary. They are obliged to live in wretched huts without doors or windows; the ventilators and doorways are open to all the winds of heaven and all kinds of weather. Even if they do their work well they are not allowed to build more comfortable houses. It is their duty also to remove dead dogs and carcasses from Tashi-lunpo, but they may not enter within the wall round the convent. If they have any uneasiness about their souls' welfare, they pay a lama to pray for them. When they die, their souls pass into the bodies of animals or wicked men. But in consequence of the afflictions they have endured they are spared too hard a lot in the endless succession of transmigrations.

The Lagbas have only to hack in pieces lamas, their own relations, and the bodies of the homeless poor. Well-to-do laymen have this operation performed for their own people without calling in professional aid.

When the monks come with a dead brother to the place of dissection they strip him completely, divide his clothes among them, and have no compunction in wearing them the very next day. The Lagbas receive 2 to 5 *tengas* (11d. to 2s. 3d.) for each body and a part of the old clothing of a lama; in the case of a layman the Lagba receives all the raiment of the deceased, and the ear-rings and other simpler ornaments of a woman. The monks who have brought the body hurry off again with all speed, partly because the smell is very bad and partly that they may not witness the cutting up of the corpse, at which only the Lagbas need be present; even when the body is that of a layman, it is divided only in the presence of Lagbas.

147. Portrait of the Tashi Lama.
(before retouching).

A cord fastened to a post driven into the ground is passed round the neck of the corpse, and the legs are pulled as straight as possible—a feat requiring great exertion in the case of a lama, who has died and become rigid in a sitting posture. Then the body is skinned, so that all the flesh is exposed; the Lagbas utter a call, and vultures which roost around come sailing up in heavy flight, pounce down on the prey, and tear and pluck at it till the ribs are laid bare. There are no dogs here as in Lhasa, and even if there were, they would get no share in the feast, for the vultures do their work quickly and thoroughly. We afterwards visited convents where sacred dogs were fed with the flesh of priests. The Lagba sits by while the vultures feed, and these are so tame that they hop unconcernedly over the man's legs.

The head is usually cut off as soon as the body is skinned. The skeleton is crushed to powder between stones, and is kneaded with the brains into a paste, which is thrown to the birds in small lumps. They will not touch the bone-dust unless it is mixed with brains. The guild of corpse-cutters pursue their task with the greatest composure: they take out the brains with their hands, knead it into powder, and pause in the midst of their gruesome employment to drink tea and eat *tsamba*. I am exceedingly doubtful if they ever wash themselves. An old Lagba, whom I summoned to my tent to supplement the information I had received from the monks, had on that very morning cut up the body of an old lama. Muhamed Isa held his cap before his face all through the conversation, and had at last to go out, for he began to feel ill. The man had an unpleasant rough aspect, wore a small grey soft cap, and was dressed in rags of the coarsest sacking. He had his own theories of post-mortem examination and anatomy. He told me that when an effusion of blood was found in the brain it was a sign that the man had been insane, and that when the substance of the brain was yellow the man had been an habitual snuff-taker.

In some cases, so a monk assured me, the corpse is not skinned, but the head is cut off, the trunk is divided in two along the spine with a sharp knife, and each half is cut into small pieces, and the vultures are not called till this has been done. Small children and grown-up men are cut up in the same manner. There is not the least respect shown for the nakedness of dead women. The whole aim of this method of disposing of the body is that the deceased may have the merit of giving his body to the birds, which would otherwise be famished. Thus even after his death he performs a pious deed which will promote the peace of his soul. The vultures here act the same part as in the Towers of Silence among the Parsees of Bombay and Persia.

As soon as the demands of religion are fulfilled, the relatives take leave of the deceased. He is then gone away, and his body is quite worthless; when the soul has recommenced its wanderings, the body may be consigned to the brutal treatment of the Lagbas without the least hesitation. No one follows the corpse to the home of the vultures when it is carried out of the house at night to be cut up before the sun rises. There is no legal regulation, and when the bodies are numerous, the sun has generally risen before the work is finished. After that, one, or at most two, of the corpses are left till evening and are taken in hand after sunset. This is also because the vultures are satiated with their morning's feed and must have a rest before supper. It is seldom that more than two deaths are reported in Gompo-sarpa in one day. About twelve years ago when an epidemic of smallpox raged in Shigatse, forty to fifty bodies were removed daily. Then, after the vultures had gorged themselves, the rest of the bodies were wrapped in thin shrouds and buried.

One would suppose that the dying man would shudder at the thought that, at the very moment when the gates of death were opened for him, his body, with which he was so closely connected during his life, which he had cared for so anxiously, endeavouring to shield it from danger and sickness, nay, from the slightest pain, would be consigned to such barbarous treatment. But probably he thinks more of his soul in his last moments, and counts up the good deeds he has performed and the millions of *manis* he has recited.

There is, then, not the slightest touch of sentiment in the funeral customs of the Tibetans and their attitude towards the dead. The children of Islam visit the graves of their loved ones and weep out their sorrow under the cypresses, but the Tibetans have no graves and no green-covered mounds where they may devote an hour to the remembrance of a lost happiness. They weep not, for they mourn not, and they mourn not, because they have loved not. How can they love a wife whom they possess in common with others, so that there is no room for the idea of faithfulness in marriage? The family ties are too loose and uncertain, and the brother does not follow his brother, the man his wife, and much less his child, to the grave, for he does not even know if the child is really his own. And, besides, the corpse in itself is a worthless husk, and even a mother who has tenderly loved her child feels not a shadow of reverence for its dead body, and has no more horror of the knife of the corpse executioner than we have of the doctor.

CHAPTER XXX

OUR LIFE IN SHIGATSE

THE time that was not taken up by visits to Tashi-lunpo I occupied in many ways. We had friends to visit us, and I frequently spent many hours in transferring types of the people to my sketch-book, and I found good material among the citizens and vagrants of the town and the monks of the convent.

On one of the first days the Consul of Nepal paid me a visit. He was a lieutenant, twenty-four years old, was named Nara Bahadur Chetteri, and bore between his eyes the yellow marks of his caste. He was dressed in a black close-fitting uniform with bright metal buttons, and a round forage cap on his head without a shade, but with a gold tassel, and in front the sun of Nepal surrounded by a halo of rays. He had been four months in Lhasa and two here. He and his young wife had taken two months to travel from Khatmandu; they had ridden the first week, but had then sent their horses back, and had tramped through very dangerous, pathless, mountainous regions for fifteen days; the rest of the journey they had accomplished on hired Tibetan horses. Here he had to protect the interests of the 150 Nepalese merchants and assist the pilgrims of his country when they were in difficulties. The merchants have their own *serai*, called Pere-pala, for which they pay an annual rent of 500 *tengas*; they buy wool from the nomads in the north, and pay for it with corn and flour, which therefore is scarce and dear in Shigatse, especially during the festival time when so many pilgrims flock in. The Consul received 200 *tengas* a month, or rather less than £60 a year, and

148

149

149

148

148. LAMAS WITH COPPER TEA-POTS. 149. FEMALE PILGRIM FROM NAM-TSO AND MENDICANT LAMA.

Sketches by the Author.

considered that the Maharaja paid him very badly. Bhotan has no consul in Shigatse, though many pilgrims come from that country.

On February 14 I received a very unexpected visit, a lama and an official from Lhasa. When the Devashung, the Government, had received the letter of Hlaje Tsering announcing my arrival at the Ngangtse-tso, the Chinese Ambassador and the Government, after consulting together, had despatched these two gentlemen in forced marches to the lake, where, however, they arrived several days after my departure. Singularly enough they had been given quite erroneous information about the route we had taken, perhaps because our wanderings over the ice across the lake in all directions had confused the nomads. Therefore they had sought for us for twenty-two days on the shores of the Ngangtse-tso and the Dangra-yum-tso, until they had at length discovered that we had gone off southwards a long time before. Then they had followed our track and had made further inquiries among the nomads, all of whom said that they had been kindly treated, and well paid for all they sold us. The gentlemen rode on, and heard in Ye-shung that we had passed through a couple of days before; our camp-fires were scarcely cold. They changed horses, and spurred them on at a faster pace, for they had been ordered to force us at any cost to return northwards by the same way we had come. But I had got the better of them, for they did not reach Shigatse till thirty-six hours after us, and another party sent from Lhasa to intercept us by a more direct road had quite lost our trail in the labyrinth of valleys and mountains into which we had plunged.

"We have carried out our mission as well as we have been able," they said, "and it only remains for us to ask for your name and all particulars of your journey and companions."

"I have already communicated everything to Ma Daloi and Duan Suen, who have seen my passport, but if you want a second edition, you are welcome to it."

"Yes, it is our duty to send a report to the Devashung. In virtue of the treaty of Lhasa only the market-towns of Yatung, Gyangtse, and Gartok are free to the Sahibs under certain conditions, but no other routes. You have come by forbidden roads and must turn back again."

"Why did you not close the way to me? It is your own fault. You can inform the Devashung that I shall never be content till I have seen the whole of Tibet. Besides, the Devashung will not find it worth their while to place obstacles in my way, for I am on good terms with your gods, and you have seen yourself how friendly the Tashi Lama has been to me."

"We know it, and it seems as though you bore the sign of the favour of the gods on your forehead like caste-markings."

"How is Hlaje Tsering getting on?"

"He is suspected of receiving a bribe from you; he has been dismissed, and has lost his rank and all his property."

"It is very mean of the Devashung to persecute him. But the Government is composed of the most despicable rogues in all Tibet. You ought to be glad that you are at length properly under Chinese protection."

At first they exchanged meaning looks, but gradually they came round to my opinion and admitted that their Government was a disagreeable association. The reason they had not shown themselves immediately after their arrival was that they wished first to spy out our occupations and our associates; for, if they found out that we had friends, these would of course be denounced. Otherwise they were decent men, and readily partook of tea and cigarettes. Unfortunately Tsaktserkan was just then with me, and he must have thought the affair serious, for he made himself scarce as soon as they entered my tent, but afterwards asked me to tell him what they had said.

It impressed them most of all that, in spite of all the ambushes and traps in the form of scouting patrols, who were on the look-out for us, we had after all succeeded in advancing to Shigatse. Now they would wait for orders from Lhasa. No heed was paid to the Dalai Lama, who was as good as dead and buried.

They came frequently during the following days to greet us, and then expressed their opinions of their

150. The Great Red Gallery of Tashi-lunpo.
Sketch by the Author.

superiors more and more frankly. Their remaining on the scene proved, however, that both the Chinese and the Government had their eyes on me. I wondered how the affair would terminate.

When I returned from the equestrian performance on the 15th, I found a large packet of letters from Major O'Connor, and greedily seized letters from home and from friends in India, Lady Minto, Colonel Dunlop Smith, Younghusband, and O'Connor himself, who welcomed me most heartily, and expressed a hope that we should soon meet. He had also kindly given me a great surprise with two boxes containing preserved meats, cakes, biscuits, whisky, and four bottles of champagne. Fancy my drinking champagne alone in my tent in Tibet! I drank a glass at dinner every day to the health of Major O'Connor as long as the supply lasted.

In the chapter on Leh I mentioned the Hajji Nazer Shah and his son Gulam Razul. The old Hajji had another son in Shigatse, named Gulam Kadir, who had been ten years in Tibet and now managed the branch in Shigatse. He sold chiefly gold-embroidered stuffs from China and Benares, which the lamas bought for state robes, and he told me that he made a yearly profit of 6000 rupees. A bale of such material as he showed me was worth 10,000 rupees. Gulam Kadir rendered me many services at this time, and supplied us with anything we wanted.

There is a fine view from the roof of his house of the Dzong, or fort, the stately front of which seems to grow out of the rock. The windows, balconies, roof decorations and streamers have a harmonious and picturesque effect. In the middle of the structure is a red building; all the rest is white, or rather an undecided greyish-yellow colour, which the plaster has assumed in the course of time.

At the southern foot of the Dzong hill lies the open market-place, where trade was carried on two hours a day. There are no tables and stands, but the dealer sits on the dusty ground and spreads out his wares on cloths or keeps them beside him in baskets. In one row sit the dealers in implements and utensils, in others boards and planks are sold, ironware, woven goods, coral, glass beads, shells, sewing thread, needles, dyes, cheap oleographs, spices and sugar from India, porcelain, pipes, figs and tea from China, mandarins from Sikkim, dried fruits and turquoise from Ladak, yak hides and tails from the Chang-tang, pots, metal dishes, covers and saucers manufactured in the town, religious books and other articles for the use of pilgrims, etc. Straw and chaff, rice, grain, *tsamba* and salt are sold by many traders. Walnuts, raisins, sweets, and radishes are other wares in which there is a large trade. Horses, cows, asses, pigs, and sheep are also on sale; for the last, 7 rupees a head are asked. In Chang-tang we had paid at most 4 rupees, and a sheep can be got for 2 rupees. Every kind of ware has its particular place, but the traders, so far as I could see, were all Tibetans; for the merchants of Ladak, China, and Nepal have shops in their own houses.

Most of the traders are women, and they sell even hay, firewood, and meat. They wear huge coils of hair with inferior turquoise, glass beads, and all kinds of pendants, which contrast strongly with their faces smeared with black salve. If they would dispense with this finery and give themselves a good washing instead, some of them would perhaps look quite human. What was the original colour of their clothes is hard to guess, for they are now caked with dust, soot, and dirt. But these hucksters are always polite and obliging; they sit in rows parallel to the north wall of the Chinese town, which is little more than a ruin. Now and then a mule caravan passes along the pathway between the rows, bringing new goods to market. Frequently gentlemen partly dressed in Chinese fashion ride past from the Dzong; and among the swarms of customers are seen all kinds of people — clergy and pilgrims, children of the country and strangers, white turbans from Ladak and Kashmir, and black skull-caps from China. In the market all the gossip of Shigatse is hatched; all sorts of reports more or less probable reach us from there. As soon as any one comes from Lhasa he is driven almost frantic with questions, for all take a deep interest in the new Chinese régime. It was current in the bazaar that lamas in Lhasa were organizing a bloody insurrection against the

151. CHHORTEN IN TASHI-LUNPO.
Sketch by the Author.

Chinese, because the latter had demanded that half the lamas should serve in the army. It was further reported that I and my companions would soon be compelled to leave the country, and that before very long the English commercial agency in Gyangtse would be closed. Every one who has heard anything fresh carries it at once to the market, where the visitors who come to hear news are as numerous as those who make purchases. In a word the market is Shigatse's only newspaper.

Gulam Kadir told me that the two gentlemen from Lhasa employed spies, who reported daily all that they could find out about us. These men used to come as hawkers into our tents and sit there by the hour. Ma also encompassed us with spies. With the help of Gulam Kadir I set two Ladakis as spies to spy upon the spies of the Lhasa spies. We could now be on our guard, for we knew what was going on around us.

My own Ladakis enjoyed in Shigatse a very necessary period of rest. I gave them money for new clothes, which they made up themselves; in a few days they appeared in all the glory of a new outfit from head to foot. Nor could I refuse them a jug of *chang* daily; they very seldom drank too much, after one of them one day under the influence of beer painted his face black, and in this guise made ridiculous pirouettes about the court. Muhamed Isa happened to come home from the market just at the moment, and, catching hold of the dancer, gave him such a thorough drubbing that he never thought of painting himself again. Both Chinamen and Tibetans said that the conduct of my men was exemplary and gave no cause for quarrels. But to hear Tsering's singing in the evening! It was like the creaking of a badly oiled wicket-gate to a shed in my own country, and therefore I listened with pleasure to his rude song. When he had sung for three hours on end, it became a little too much, but I put up with it — it is so pleasant to have cheerful, contented men about one.

Under February 19 the following entry stands in my diary: "In spite of the windy, dusty weather I have all day long been sketching various types, chiefly women, who sat for me as models in front of my tent." The first were from Nam-tso (Tengri-nor) (Illustration 155), wore head-dresses decorated with shells, china beads, and silver spangles, and in their sheepskins trimmed with red and blue ribands looked like girls from Dalecarlia. They had large bones, were strongly built, looked fresh and healthy, and their broad faces were remarkably clean. The women of Shigatse, on the other hand, had smeared their faces with a brown salve mixed with soot which looked like tar. This mask makes them hideous, and it is impossible to tell whether they are pretty or not; the black colour interferes with the lights and shadows, and confuses the portrait painter. One had painted only her nose and rubbed it bright as metal. This singular custom is said to date from a time when the morality of the Lhasa monks was at a low level, and a Dalai Lama issued orders that no female should show herself out of doors unless painted black, so that the charms of the women might be less seductive to the men. Since then the black paint has remained in fashion, but seems now to be going out.

The clothes are always black with age, dirt, and soot. The women pay most attention to their head decoration, and the higher they are in the social scale the more profusely they deck their coiffures with bows, pendants, and jewelry. The hair is frequently so closely entwined with all this finery that it can scarcely be let down every night, but only when it becomes so entangled that it must be put straight. Those who are rich wear large heavy ear-rings of solid gold and a few turquoises, but others simpler and smaller rings. On the neck are worn chains of various coloured beads and *gaos*, small silver cases studded with coral and turquoise and containing amulets. Poor women have to be contented with copper *gaos* of the clumsy kind so common among the Tsaidam Mongols.

A woman of forty belonging to Shigatse was named Tashi-Buti; she looked sixty, for women age very soon here. Above her ordinary clothing she wore a coarse shawl over the shoulders, fastened in front with brass clasps, plates, and rings.

A nomad woman from Kamba had the right arm and

152. PORTAL IN TASHI-LUNPO.

153. GROUP OF LAMAS IN TASHI-LUNPO.

shoulder bare, and was as powerfully and muscularly built as a man, but was so horribly dirty that it was impossible to perceive her complexion. She had no head-dress; but the dark hair was plaited into innumerable thin rat's tails hanging over the shoulders, and tied together on the forehead into a mane of cords. She would have been good-looking if her features had not been so masculine; she sat still and solemn as a statue of Buddha. A fifteen-year-old girl had a parting in the middle, and her hair frizzed in two pads down to the ears, which were combed, oiled, and shiny like those of a Japanese, and she wore a diadem studded with coral. She was dainty and clean and had rosy cheeks (Illustrations 157, 158, 159).

Burtso was a little Shigatse lady of seventeen summers, and bore the dirt of those seventeen summers on her face. Like most of the others her features had the sharply marked characteristics of the Mongolian race — oblique narrow eyes contracting to a point at the sides, and the lower part of the eyelid telescoped into the upper so that a slightly curved line is formed and the short lashes are almost covered; the iris is dark chestnut brown, and appears black within the frame of the eyelids; the eyebrows are usually only slightly marked, are thin and irregular, and never form the finely curved Persian and Caucasian arch like a crescent. The cheek-bones are rather prominent, but not so high as with the Mongolians; the lips are rather large and thick, but the nose is not so flat as among the Mongols. Faces with handsome features are seen among the male Tibetans. But the differences between individual Tibetans are often as great as between Tibetans on the one hand and Mongols, Chinamen, and Gurkhas on the other. The nomads of the Chang-tang are apparently a tribe of themselves, and seldom, if ever, intermarry with the others. Otherwise the Tibetan people is undoubtedly much mixed with neighbouring elements. Chinamen living in Lhasa and Shigatse marry Tibetan women. In the Himalayas, south of the Tibetan frontier, live the Bothias, a mixed people, sprung partly from Indian, partly from Tibetan elements. The people of Ladak have mingled to a large extent with their Aryan and Turkish neighbours, because they have been in closer and more active contact with them. The Tibetan people present remarkable and peculiar problems in anthropological, ethnographical, and linguistic science, which must be solved by future investigation.

I drew on and on, and one type after another found its way into my sketch-book. The expression of my models is listless and devoid of animation; they seem absent-minded and passionless. They take little interest in the proceedings; all they care about is to pocket the rupees after the sitting. They sit motionless, without laughing or complaining. They are rather too solemn, and not a smile plays round the corners of their mouths when their eyes meet mine. I passed the greater part of the day in this silent, apathetic female society.

Now and then comes a party of inquisitive people to watch me, Tibetans, Chinamen, or pilgrims who want to have something to tell when they get home again to their black tents. They stand round me, wondering whether it is dangerous to be drawn by a European and what is the object of it. Of course there are many spies among them. There is an endless variety of types and costumes, and as I ride through the streets and see the inhabitants at their various occupations, I feel oppressed by the thought that I have not time to draw them all. Here stands a man splitting wood, there come two young fellows driving before them asses laden with twigs and branches. There go a couple of women with large water-jugs on their backs, while small girls collect cattle dung from the street. Here a group of officials approaches in yellow garments on fine horses, while some lamas stroll slowly towards the monastery. All is so picturesque, so charming for the pencil; one is constantly delighted with attractive subjects, genre pictures of unusual character, strikingly grouped parties of salesmen and customers; one could spend months here, drawing again and again. I am grieved at the prospect of an early departure.

In the afternoon a company of dancers, male and female, frequently appears in the court and gives no despicable performances, reminding me strongly of the

154. LECTURE IN TASHI-LUNPO.
Sketch by the Author.

dances in Leh. They are always introduced by our little old mother Mamu, who has the management of the garden, and hops about smiling and friendly as a sparrow. She speaks Urdu, so Robert employs her as interpreter. Then come caravans, bringing hay, firewood, chaff, and barley for our remaining animals, or provisions for ourselves, and people are constantly coming to sell all kinds of goods — chickens, eggs, butter, or fish from the Tsangpo; milkmen run with their clattering metal cans, and stringed instruments and flutes make music in our groves. A beggar comes up like a troubadour to my tent with a lute, and sings a melodious air. When I look at him he stops singing and puts out his tongue. Barefooted boys, who could be no blacker if they were drawn twice up a chimney, run about laughing loudly, and peep out from among the trees. Three of them perform on a tight rope, dance like professional rope-dancers, and beat drums, while they turn summersaults all mixed up together (Illustration 164).

Pious visitors also frequent my courtyard: two nuns, for instance, with a large *tanka* representing a series of complicated episodes from the holy scriptures. While one chants the explanation, the other points with a stick to the corresponding picture (Illustration 165). She sings so sweetly and with so much feeling that it is a pleasure to listen to her. Or a mendicant lama comes with his praying mill in his hand and two hand-grooves hung by a strap round his neck. In these he pushes his hands as in a curry-comb, when he prostrates himself on the ground in making a circuit of the temple. They are much worn, and this moves the hearts of the people to generosity, so that his alms bowl is filled daily.

These pious men are the parasites of Tibet, living at the expense of the working population. And yet they are endured and treated by every one with the greatest consideration and respect. To give them a mite brings a blessing on the giver. The people are kept by the lamas in spiritual slavery, and the lamas themselves are docile slaves to those tomes of narrow-minded dogmas which have been stereotyped for centuries, which may not be interfered with or criticised, for they are canonical, proclaim the absolute truth, and stand in the way of all free and independent thought. The clergy form a very considerable percentage of the scanty population of this poor country. Without the Peter's pence Tibet could not make both ends meet. Tashi-lunpo is, then, a huge savings-box, in which the rich man places his pile of gold, the poor man his mite. And with what object? To propitiate the monks, for they are the mediators between the gods and the people. Scarcely any other land is so completely under the thumb of the priests as Tibet. And while the people toil, the monks gather round their tea-pots and bowls of *tsamba* at the summons of the conch.

On three evenings in succession large numbers of wild-geese have flown low over our garden from north-west to south-east. The ravens and as bold as usual; of other birds only sparrows roost in our trees. Our camp within the wall is quiet, but we have posted a night-watch outside, for in a town like Shigatse, full of all sorts of vagabonds, there are many scoundrels. Two monks, who were with me one evening to answer my inquiries, durst not return to Tashi-lunpo in the dark, unless I sent some of my men armed with guns to take them home. Recently a lama was attacked at night between the town and the monastery and stripped to the skin.

On February 20, after only 17.6 degrees of frost, it snowed all day long, the wind howled dismally through the poplars, and the snow fell on my tent. Nothing was to be seen of the golden temple roofs, and the ground and the mountains were white; there was no one in the bazaar, and no inquisitive visitors pestered us. It was just as in the Chang-tang.

On March 4 Gulam Kadir paid me a farewell visit, for he was going next day to Lhasa, which, according to his reckoning, was nine days' journey distant. As he would pass through Gyangtse, he took a large letter-bag to Major O'Connor. On the day before, he had sent off a caravan of 201 yaks laden with brick tea to Ladak. A yak carries 24 bricks, and a brick costs in Shigatse 6 rupees, but in Ladak 9 to 11. It is only the refuse of the tea, which is despised in China, but is good enough for Tibetans and

155. Female Pilgrims from the Nam-tso.

156. Tibetans in Shigatse.
Sketches by the Author.

Ladakis. Gulam Kadir hires the yaks at a cost of 5 rupees a head to Gartok — uncommonly cheap, but they follow the mountain paths and their keep costs nothing. They are five months on the way, for the caravan makes short marches and stays at places where grass grows luxuriantly. From Gartok, where the Hajji Nazer Shah has a large warehouse, managed by Gulam Razul, the tea is transported on other yaks. By a single caravan of this kind the commercial house of the Hajji makes a very large profit. Musk, coral, Chinese textiles, and other valuable goods are forwarded on mules along the great highway which runs along the Tsangpo and the upper Indus.

I had on several occasions met Kung Gushuk, the Duke, in the monastery, and had thanked him for his kindness in sending my letters to the lakes, but it was not till March 7 that I paid him a visit in his house. The walls in the entrance hall are painted with tigers and leopards. In the court, round which the stables and servants' quarters are situated, a large black watch-dog, with red eyes and a red swollen ring round his neck, is chained up, and is so savage that he has to be held while we pass. After mounting two ladder-like staircases we come to the reception-room, which is very elegant, and has square red pillars with carved capitals in green and blue. Along the walls stands a row of shrines of gilded wood with burning butter-lamps in front of them, and over them hang photographs of the Tashi Lama which were taken in Calcutta. The rest of the walls are draped with holy banners (Illustration 167).

The trellised window pasted over with paper, which occupies nearly the whole length of the wall towards the courtyard, and is draped with white curtains on the outside, is placed rather high above the floor. Immediately below the window runs a long divan mattress, on which a square cushion covered with panther skin marks the seat of honour. Before this cushion stand two small stool-like lacquered tables on golden feet. Seated here one has on the left hand, against the shorter wall, a cubical throne with steps leading up to it, and here the Tashi Lama takes his seat when he visits his younger brother, now twenty-one years of age.

Kung Gushuk is, then, quite young. He is very shy, and is evidently relieved when his guest talks and he is not obliged to strain his own small, poorly furnished brain. His recollections of India, whither he had accompanied his illustrious brother, were very hazy: he did know that Calcutta is a large town, and that the weather was excessively hot there, but for the rest the journey seemed to be to him only an unintelligible dream. He did not venture to give an opinion on the journey before me, but said openly that the lamas did not like to see me so often in Tashi-lunpo. His wife had sent to ask me if I would take her portrait, and I now begged to be told what time would suit her. "Any time." When I went away, Her Highness was standing with her black court ladies at the other end of the open gallery surrounding a court (Illust. 168). I saluted her politely, and certainly fascinated the lady as I passed; there was no danger, as she was quite *passée*, for she had belonged in common to Kung Gushuk and an elder brother, who died in Sikkim on the return from India. It is said that she rules the house and keeps the finances in order, and with good reason, for Kung Gushuk leads a fast life, is over head and ears in debt, and plays hazard. This is bad form in a brother of the Tashi Lama.

On March 22 the portrait-drawing came off; it was executed in the large saloon and in pencil. The Duchess is big and bloated, and asserted that she was thirty-three years old—I should put her down at forty-five. Her complexion is fair and muddy, the white of her eyes is dull. She had put on for this occasion all the finery she could find room for; a pearl pendant which hung on the left side of her façade had cost 1200 rupees. In her hair were thick strings of pearls, bunches of coral and turquoises. She was friendly and amiable, and said that she did not mind how long she sat, if only the result were good. Her small carpet-knight of a husband sat by and looked on, and round us stood the other inmates of the house, including a small brother of Kung Gushuk and the Tashi Lama.

157

158

159

157, 158, 159. TIBETAN GIRL AND WOMEN IN SHIGATSE.
Sketches by the Author.

They drank butter tea, but did not offer me any, \
made the visit all the pleasanter (Illustration 170).

Then we were shown the other apartments, which on sunny days are dark as dungeons, for the windows small, the paper thick, and the white curtains outside l to increase the gloom. A small oratory with red pil was so dark that the images of the gods could scarcely distinguished. In the study of the Duke a low divan sto at the window, with paper, inkstand, pens, and a religio book on a table in front of it. The bedroom was adorne with *tankas*, statues, and cups. Here and there butte lamps struggled with the darkness, while braziers of bras on stands of dark carved wood were used to counteract th chilliness of the air. The whole house is like a temple, which is quite as it should be when the owner is brother of the Grand Lama.

Two passages connecting parts of the upper storey are not covered in, so are exposed to all the winds of heaven. A third staircase leads to the top of the roof, which is surrounded by a parapet a yard high, and is white-washed. A thicket of roof decorations and bundles of rods with streamers frightens away evil spirits. There was a violent wind, and dust and bits from the streets of Shigatse flew up in the air, so that our eyes received their share. With the portrait-drawing the visit lasted four good hours, and at the end I had become as intimate with the family as if I had known them from childhood.

CHAPTER XXXI

POLITICAL COMPLICATIONS

In the first chapters of this book I described very briefly the difficulties placed in my way by the English, and told how the Liberal Government in London had not only refused the favours I had asked for, but had even tried to suppress my expedition altogether. In consequence I had been compelled to make a wide detour all through the Chang-tang, where more than once our lives hung by a thread, and we had suffered great losses. Then we met with a weak resistance on the part of the Tibetans, but, nevertheless, came to Shigatse; it was pure good luck that the patrols sent out to intercept us had not fallen in with us. On February 14 the representatives of the Tibetan Government had intimated to me that I had no right to make a prolonged sojourn in Tibet, and that I must leave the country. As though I had not enough to do with the English, Indian, and Tibetan Governments, the Chinese Government also appeared on the scene on February 18. I was now opposed to a fourfold combination of Governments, and wished all politics and diplomatists at Jericho.

On this day the young Chinaman Duan Suen appeared on behalf of Gaw Daloi, the Chinese political agent in Gyangtse. He brought me a letter from him with the following curt contents:

Agreement between Great Britain and China, signed in Pekin in the year 1906, § 2: The Government of Great Britain binds itself not to annex any Tibetan territory, and not to interfere in the

162

161

160

163

160. A CHINAMAN IN SHIGATSE. 161. A TIBETAN IN SHIGATSE.
162. A LAMA IN TASHI-LUNPO. 163. DOOR-KEEPER IN TSONG KAPA'S TEMPLE.

Sketches by the Author.

administration of Tibet. Convention concluded on September 7, 1904, § 9b: No representative or agent of any foreign Power shall receive permission to visit Tibet.

Duan Suen also conveyed to me by word of mouth Gaw Daloi's message that I must on no account travel to Gyangtse, as I had forced my way to Shigatse without a passport or permit, and that only one route was open to me, that through the Chang-tang, by which I had come. I answered as curtly that Gaw Daloi should apply to Major O'Connor, the British representative in Gyangtse, if he wished to learn anything about me, instead of sending me impertinent letters.

It had been my plan and desire to visit O'Connor. I knew him very well by repute; he had loaded me with kindnesses, and I knew that he was one of the very few who had a thorough knowledge of Tibet.

We had been in constant correspondence with one another since my arrival. I had explained to him my ideas about the western continuation of the great mountain system, and O'Connor had replied that he had always longed to explore the extensive unknown parts in the interior of Tibet, and had long suspected the existence of a mighty mountain system to the north of the Tsangpo. I had still an imperfect knowledge of this system, and therefore I proposed to O'Connor that we should in future call the mountains Nien-chen-tang-la after the lofty peak on the south shore of the Tengri-nor. It would have been of the greatest advantage to me to meet a man like Major O'Connor just at this time (Illustration 171).

Meanwhile I soon began to regard the affair in a different light, for I perceived that in Gyangtse I should find myself in a worse position than in Shigatse. As long as I remained in Shigatse, the Chinese did not know what to do with me, but in Gyangtse the provisions of the treaty would at once become applicable to my case, and I might be obliged to retire southwards to India. Gaw Daloi's prohibition with regard to Gyangtse irritated me a little, but I suspected him of using it as a stratagem, and all the more because the authorities of Shigatse offered at the same time to let me baggage animals on hire for my journey thither. Tsaktserkan, as well as Ma, knew that I had received a letter from Gaw, and Ma had long negotiations with the gentlemen from Lhasa. Evidently a political intrigue was going on, and all depended on my playing my cards well.

As early as February 20 I had noticed that the lamas were afraid of the Chinese because of my frequent visits to the monastery, and were becoming more reserved daily. I, however, quietly continued to place myself under their noses, and even to draw the Sakya-tubpa (Buddha). The Chinese pretended to fear that the English would reproach them with a breach of the treaty if they suffered me to sojourn on forbidden ground. My English friends, on the contrary, rejoiced at my success and hoped that I should continue to hold out. Meantime a change might come any day, and therefore I lived in the greatest agitation.

In my answer to Gaw Daloi I begged him to have no anxiety lest I, a Swede, should have any intention of annexing Tibetan territory, and as to § 9, he had not quoted it fully, for it ran as follows: "The Government of Tibet undertakes not to allow a representative or agent of any foreign Power to visit Tibet without the previous consent of the Government of Great Britain." This paragraph did not apply to my case, for I was already in Tibet, and it did not concern me what agreements the two Governments had made together. My case must be treated from quite a different standpoint.

Ma had at first consented to send my letters to Gyangtse, but now he refused, with the excuse that he might seem too ready to oblige me. Therefore Muhamed Isa had to ride off on February 24 for Gyangtse, to carry my letter and passport to Gaw Daloi, and also to take 3000 rupees in sovereigns, which Major O'Connor had promised to exchange for silver coins.

I also sent a long telegram to the English Prime Minister, asking for the "consent of the Government of Great Britain," as the Government of Tibet had hitherto placed no practical obstacles in my way. To this telegram I received no reply.

164. DANCING BOYS WITH DRUMS.
Sketch by the Author.

On February 27 Gaw's answer arrived — not by Muhamed Isa, but by a special messenger; this was diplomatic but imprudent. Gaw wrote that he could not believe I would break a treaty between two great nations for the sake of scientific exploration, that my Chinese passport was not valid here, and that if I were allowed to travel about in Tibet, Russians and Englishmen might claim the same privileges. He concluded with the words: "I have received orders from my Government to arrest you at once, should you come to Gyangtse, and send you with a guard of soldiers across the Indian frontier." I afterwards learned that he had not a single soldier, and that if he had had the whole Chinese army at his command, he could not have used it against me, if I were staying in Gyangtse as a guest in the British Agency. I replied, however, that I was quite willing to set out, in a north-westerly direction, if Gaw could provide me with a sufficiently large caravan.

On March 1 Ma visited me. He was quite beside himself. The Amban Lien in Lhasa had sharply reprimanded him because, with 1000 native and 150 Chinese soldiers under his command, he had not been intelligent and watchful enough to prevent my coming to Shigatse. He had now to inform me that I must leave the town at once, and asked me to tell him on what day I proposed to start. "Not for a good while yet," I replied. "The caravan which is to take me back across the Chang-tang must be ready first." The monks also had been advised from Lhasa to have as little to do with me as possible.

My sojourn in Shigatse had, then, given rise to an exchange of notes and telegrams between Lhasa, Gyangtse, Shigatse, Pekin, Calcutta, and London, and quite against my will I had become a small apple of discord among politicians. My position was so uncertain that I left no stone unturned. The Swedish Minister, Herr G. O. Wallenberg, did all he could in Pekin to obtain for me the permission of the Chinese Government and a passport; he spoke with all the high mandarins, but they with the greatest affability appealed to the treaties in force. The Japanese Embassy in Pekin also made representations, at the request of Count Otani (Kioto), but received the astonishing answer that, if I were in Tibet at all, which was very doubtful, I must be at once expelled from the country. So I met with refusals on all sides. But I was strong in one respect: I stood alone, while my opponents were hampered by having to pay respect to one another's susceptibilities.

Meanwhile I was initiated little by little into the mysteries of Tibetan politics. Tsaktserkan, sent by the Tashi Lama, used to visit me at dusk. He asked me how it came about that, after the English had been victorious against Tibet, China reaped all the advantages of the victory, and China's power increased in the country while England's prestige declined. The Tashi Lama was much disturbed by the continued absence of the Dalai Lama. Immediately after his return from India he had sent presents to the Dalai Lama, and written several letters to him, but had never received a reply. The Dalai Lama had been his tutor, and he was grieved that he could not help him in his difficult situation. The authorities at Lhasa were incensed against Tashi-lunpo, and asserted that the Tashi Lama had been bribed by the English not to take part in the war. The Tashi Lama sent to ask me if I thought that the Emperor of China was angry with him because of his journey to India, to which I answered that in my opinion the Emperor would be pleased if the Tashi Lama maintained peace with his powerful neighbour to the south, and if there was a good understanding between Tibet and India.

Then on March 5 I received a remarkable letter from Gaw Daloi. He advised me "in strict confidence" to write to Chang Yin Tang (Tang Darin, or the Imperial Chinese Chief Commissioner in Tibet), and to the Amban Lien Yü in Lhasa, requesting Their Excellencies to grant me permission as a particular favour to travel through Gyangtse to Sikkim; he had no doubt that they would agree to the proposal. First, he had written to me that his Government had ordered him to arrest me if I came to Gyangtse, and now he advised me to go there. But by acting contrary to the orders of his Government, he gave me a dangerous hold over him: I had him now in my power, and regarded him as out of the running. I then learned in a roundabout way that his letter had been written in accordance with orders from Lhasa, where it was feared that I might not be easily got rid of if I were permitted to penetrate further into Tibet on my return journey. Ma informed me that he had orders to keep couriers in readiness for me, and that a letter would reach Lhasa in five days.

I now wrote to the Tang Darin, telling him that I would on no account act against the wishes of the Chinese Government by travelling through Gyangtse, but intended to return towards the north-west, if His Excellence would command that yaks should be placed at my disposal. As a Swede, I belonged to a country which had from ancient times been on friendly terms with China, and had no political interests in Tibet.

At the same time I wrote also to Lien Darin, and represented that neither the Chinese nor the Tibetan Government had any reason to complain of my journey to Shigatse; if my coming were displeasing to them, they should have prevented me in good time. On the contrary, they ought to be grateful to me for calling attention to the possibility of traversing their country, and I advised them to be more watchful in future if they wished to exclude Europeans. I should not think of travelling to India, for my people were mountaineers and would drop down in the heat like flies; they were, moreover, British subjects, and I was answerable for their safe return to Leh. It was impossible to travel through the Chang-tang, but I would willingly follow a route on the north side of the Tsangpo, where there were nomads. If they wished to get rid of me, they should not render my return more difficult, but rather facilitate it in every way.

When, therefore, the Lhasa gentlemen and the deputies from the Shigatse Dzong urged me that same day to start without delay, I was able to reply that it could not possibly be done till ten days later, for it would take so long to receive an answer from Lhasa.

Our position was still like an imprisonment, though everything was done to get rid of us. On March 4 I was in Tashi-lunpo for the last time. Now I was excluded from the monastery, for I had been expressly requested to cease my visits for fear of the suspicion of the Chinese. I promised, but on condition that I should first be permitted to see the Ngakang, where the vestments and masks are stored. When this was declared impossible, we at last came to an agreement that some vestments, masks, and instruments should be brought to my garden, where I should have an opportunity of sketching them. The objects were brought at night, and while I drew them in the daytime, a watch was kept round the house so that the lamas need not fear being caught. So we came to March 10, when Tashi arrived with my last 13 yaks, which were so worn out that they were handed over to a dealer at a nominal price.

Under March 12 the following entry appears in my diary: "In this holy land the spring is heralded in by kettle-drums and trumpets shriller than any that are sounded at dawn from the temple roofs, and summon the lamas to their first tea. Storms, dark masses of cloud, and dust whirling along the ground, and hiding all the environs except the Dzong fort, which peeps through dust-mist like a dismal phantom ship. The temperature rises, and in the day is several degrees above freezing-point, but there is no other sign of spring. It will come sometime or other, if it is now turning in bed and trying to rub the winter sleep out of its frozen eyes. To-day raged one of the most violent storms we have experienced. The bells of the monastery rang like storm bells, but their sound did not reach us amid the howling of the tempest. The kitchen has been removed into the house, no one is seen on the courtyard, and there is a cracking and whistling among the poplars. Now and then are heard the bells of a courier's horse which canters by the outer wall, and perhaps brings new instructions regarding me. Ma makes no sign, Lobsang Tsering has disappeared, and Tsaktserkan comes only when I send to ask him. We are more and more isolated, no one dares associate with us. Our position is exciting and even interesting. It is evident that we must leave Shigatse, but by which route? I have already told them that I will not go through Gyangtse or Khatmandu (capital

165. Wandering Nun with a Tanka depicting a Religious Legend and Singing the Explanation. (In our Garden in Shigatse.)

166. Gandän-chö-ding-gompa, a Nunnery in Ye.

of Nepal), as Ma proposed to me, and to equip here a caravan for the Chang-tang is out of the question. I have only one goal, the north of the Tsangpo, where most important discoveries await me. At the moment we are on the point of leaving Shigatse we find ourselves for the first time actually prisoners; as long as we remain here we have at any rate freedom within our own walls. And as long as I am in Tibet, I am *tabu* to the English, but as soon as I cross the British frontier I am done for. I cannot go to Eastern Turkestan, for the Chinese Government has, as I hear from Gaw, cancelled my passport, because it has been used for another country. To travel direct to China with Ladakis will also not do. But if I am compelled to make for Sikkim, I must dismiss the Ladakis and travel alone to Pekin to explain the affair to the mandarins."

On March 15 the two gentlemen from Lhasa came to me again. They had been to Gyangtse, and had received orders from Gaw to watch all my movements carefully. Again they wished to know the day of my departure, and I replied that I could come to no decision until I knew by what road I should travel. If it were to the Chang-tang, they might count on a long delay, and might meanwhile buy a house and marry at their leisure. They now complained themselves of the increased power of the Chinese in Tibet, and gave their opinion that only the unrest arising from the new strict régime in Lhasa had rendered it possible for me to travel across Tibet unnoticed.

In this they were probably quite right. The blunder of the Dalai Lama and the unexpected change of front on the part of the English had given the Chinese an opportunity of establishing their supremacy over Tibet more securely than they had been able to do since the days of Kang Hi and Kien Lung in the seventeenth and eighteenth centuries. Of the prestige of England I could not perceive a shadow, and I heard that the Tashi Lama regretted his journey to India. Perhaps it was prudent of the Liberal Government in London to give up Chumbi, and by barring the frontier to exclude all possibility of boundary disputes and friction on the Indian side; for in our times the old

Asia is beginning to waken out of its deep sleep, and the Great Powers of Europe which have interests there should rather seek to retain what they already possess than endeavour to make fresh acquisitions. At any rate the Chinese statesmen exhibited on this occasion admirable prudence and vigilance, and gathered in all that the English gave up. If ever the Dalai Lama returns safely to Lhasa, he must content himself with the reverence accorded to him in the Potala as an incarnation, and he will not be allowed to have anything further to do with political affairs. The country of Tibet will doubtless in the future be closed as strictly as hitherto; for the supremacy over Tibet is a political question of the first importance to China, not only because Tibet is, as it were, a huge fortress with ramparts, walls, and ditches protecting China, but also on account of the great spiritual influence which the two popes exercise over all Mongolians. As long as China has the Dalai Lama in its power, it can keep the Mongols in check, while in other circumstances the Dalai Lama could stir them up to insurrection against China. And Mongolia is also the buffer state between China and Russia.

On March 19 our prospects grew bright at last. Ma had had a meeting with the two Lhasa gentlemen and the authorities of the Shigatse Dzong. The last came to me and begged me to inform them whither I meant to travel. I answered: "Along the Raga-tsangpo to its source."

The gentlemen who had held the meeting, had meanwhile apparently come to the decision of taking the responsibility on themselves of the consequences of my journey to the west. But they firmly insisted that I must take exactly the same route back to Yeshung by which I had come, that is, through Tanak and Rungma, or they would get into trouble.

When it was thus settled that we were not to go to Gyangtse, I sent Muhamed Isa to Major O'Connor with all the maps, drawings, and the results hitherto acquired; the whole despatch afterwards reached Colonel Dunlop Smith in Calcutta in good condition. We had 3000 rupees more in gold exchanged for silver money, and I wrote a letter of farewell to my good friend O'Connor, and likewise to my numerous friends in India. I also wrote home, as usual, in the form of a complete journal.

On the 20th Ma came through our gate, triumphantly waving a letter with a large red seal, and called out from a distance: "From the Tang Darin." The letter was dated on March 15 at Lhasa, and I reproduce it here as a specimen of Chinese diplomatic correspondence:

DEAR DR. SVEN HEDIN — I was much pleased to receive your letter of the 5th instant, and to hear that you are come to Shigatse in order to investigate the geography of the unknown parts of this country. I know that you are one of the famous geographers of Europe, that you move about here without meddling in the affairs of Tibet, political or otherwise, and carry out only geographical work.

I have a great respect for you as a man of science, who seriously advances the progress of earth knowledge. I always value such men most highly and show them the greatest reverence.

But, to my great regret, I must inform you that the last treaty between China and Great Britain contains a paragraph declaring that no stranger, whether he be an Englishman or Russian, an American or European, has any right to visit Tibet, the three market-towns, Gyangtse, Yatung, and Gartok, excepted. You are, then, not the only one to whom the country is closed.

I shall be glad, then, if you will return the same way you came, and you will thereby put me under a very great obligation.

China and Sweden are really friendly Powers, and both peoples are true brothers.

I hope you will not judge me harshly, for I am bound by the treaty not to suffer you to travel further.

I have issued orders to the Chinese and native authorities along your route to afford you all the facilities in their power.

Wishing you a successful journey, I am, yours truly,

CHANG YIN TANG.

The letter leaves nothing to be desired as far as obliging amiability is concerned, but its contents are diplomatically obscure. Chinese and native authorities in the Chang-tang, where we had not seen a living soul for eighty-one consecutive days! Like Gaw, he falls back on the treaty signed by Great Britain to close the most interesting country in the world to exploration.

Ma knew the contents of the letter, and asked if it were still my determination to follow the Raga-tsangpo upwards. If so, the route was open to me. I answered in the affirmative, without showing any sign of my satisfaction, for this road was not sanctioned by Tang's letter. Now some of the gentlemen of the Dzong had to look after the procuring of provisions — all by Tang's orders.

All of a sudden the authorities of Shigatse became very polite, and showered down visits on me, after they found that I was in the good books of the most powerful man in Tibet in temporal affairs. Six sacks of *tsamba*, a sack of rice, and twelve cubes of brick tea were brought to my courtyard, and exact information was asked for as to the points I intended to touch on beyond the mouth of the Raga-tsangpo. However, I did not satisfy them, but said that not a single name up there was known to me. I thought to myself that it was most prudent not to excite suspicion by too many details; the farther we got away from the central authorities the greater prospect we had of being left alone. They inquired how many horses we wanted, and I at once said 65, so as to be well provided; they went away very quietly, as though they thought that this was a very large number.

On March 24 Muhamed Isa came back with the silver money, more letters, and all kinds of articles which Major O'Connor, with his usual kindness, had procured for me. In the afternoon a great council was held: Ma, the two Lhasa gentlemen, the whole Shigatse Dzong, and Tsaktserkan — in all, nearly 20 officials, about 100 servants, Chinese soldiers, and newsmongers; so that the whole court was filled. The new passport was solemnly read to me. Therein the places were mentioned through which I might pass: the Raga-tsangpo, then Saka-dzong, Tradum, Tuksum, Gartok, Demchok, and the Ladak frontier. I must not stop at any point, must make long day's marches, and travel straight along the valleys of the Brahmaputra and the Indus. I considered it useless to make any objections to the regulations; not a word was said of the country north of the Tsangpo, where I suspected the existence of the great mountain system. But I thought that we might contrive ourselves in some way or other an excursion thither, and resolved to give them plenty of trouble before

167. DUKE KUNG GUSHUK, BROTHER OF THE TASHI LAMA.

they got rid of me. Two Chinamen, an official of the Labrang and one from the Shigatse Dzong, were to accompany me for the first part of the journey, and then be relieved by four others. The escort was introduced to me. The gentlemen insisted that we should start next day, but I declared that we required two days more to complete our preparations. All the provisions they had hurriedly collected were weighed in their presence, and paid for by me.

The brown puppy arranged for the morning of the 25th an interlude which certainly was not unexpected. Inspired by uncivilized ideas about the sanctity of my tent, the bitch had not ventured in for a long time, but now, just as I sat writing my last letter, she came and scratched a hole with her forepaws in a corner of my tent, whined uneasily, laid her head on my knee, and looked very unhappy, as though she wished me to understand how helpless she felt. Before I was aware two very small puppies lay squeaking at my feet. While the young mother was licking her first-born with great tenderness, Muhamed Isa made a soft lair for the family. Puppy had scarcely taken her place on it when two more puppies made their entrance into this queer world. Then she probably thought that this was enough, for after a good meal of meat and a bowl of milk she rolled herself up with her well-tended young ones and went to sleep. The new puppies were black as coal and small as rats. I bought a basket for them to travel in until they could follow on foot the caravan in which they were born, and become good caravan dogs. We had tried here, too, in vain to get some good dogs, for our vagabonds from the Ngangtse-tso were good watch-dogs but unpleasant companions. Now we had suddenly a whole pack, and it would be an amusement to us to watch their development. Whatever might be our future fate, we could not reach Ladak in less than half a year, and by that time the puppies would have grown big and comical. Henceforth Puppy was allowed to live in my tent, and we became the best friends in the world, for I was as anxious and careful about the young ones as she. But she would not allow any one to approach who had no business here; scarcely half an hour after the catastrophe she dashed at two boys who were loitering about the court. There was a dreadful whining in the corner of the tent, but both the mother and young ones were as well as could be expected under the circumstances, as it is expressed in society bulletins.

In the meantime there was a very busy commotion in our courtyard. The heavy baggage was packed; rice and *tsamba* for the men, and barley for the horses, sewed up in bags accurately weighed; Chinese macaroni, cabbages, onions, fine wheaten flour, spices, potatoes, and as many eggs as we could get, were brought in from the market. The books, which I had received from O'Connor, filled a box to themselves, and would be thrown away, one after another, as soon as they had been read. When all had been packed up, my tent looked very bare.

On March 26, our last day in Shigatse, the packing was finished and Ma Chi Fu, a young official in Chumbi, came from Lhasa, bringing me greetings from Their Excellencies. He was a Dungan (Mohammedan), spoke gently and politely, and was one of the noblest, most refined, and sympathetic Chinamen whom I have known. He was also exceptionally handsome, had large bright eyes, which had scarcely any characteristics of his race, and pure Aryan features, and wore a valuable silken cloak. He regretted that he had had no opportunity of showing me hospitality, and begged me to believe that the escort would be only a guard; it was only to watch over our safety, and had orders to serve us to the best of its ability. Ma Chi Fu brought a kind letter from Lien Darin, the Amban of Lhasa, in which he wrote:

> I knew that you were a learned geographer from Sweden. I am sorry that in consequence of the treaty I am not now able to make better arrangements for you in Tibet, but you are a wise man, and will therefore understand the difficulty in which I find myself much against my will.

In all my personal contact and correspondence with the Chinese they always showed me the greatest kindness and consideration. They were the masters of the country, and I had no right to travel about in Tibet, yet they never made use of hard words, much less of the means of actual compulsion that were at their command, but carried their hospitality as far as was consistent with loyalty to their own country. Therefore I retain the most agreeable memories of this and all my former travels.

In the evening I bade farewell to good old Ma, gave him three useless horses, which would, however, recover with good treatment, and thanked him for all his kindness to me. He expressed a hope that we might meet once more in this life. All who had been of service to us received considerable presents of money, and Kung Gushuk demanded 45 rupees as rent for his garden. I would have gladly given him several times the sum for the memorable days I had spent under the slender poplars, when the soughing of the spring winds roused me out of sleep.

CHAPTER XXXII

TARTING-GOMPA AND TASHI-GEMBE

I WAS awaked early on March 27. I mounted my horse, accompanied by Robert, Muhamed Isa, and three men of the escort, while the fourth had gone on with the caravan. Muhamed Isa conveyed my hearty greetings to the Tashi Lama, and my wishes that the course of his life might run as smoothly and happily as heretofore. Meanwhile, I paid a short return visit to Ma Chi Fu, and had not yet left him when my excellent caravan leader returned with the kindest greetings from the Tashi Lama and a large silken *kadakh*, which I keep as a souvenir with the image he presented to me. Then we rode in close order through the forbidden streets for the last time, and the golden temple roofs disappeared behind us. So, farewell for ever, grand, lovable, divine Tashi Lama!

When we left the side valley of the Nyang-chu and came out into the Tsangpo valley, we were exposed to the storm coming from the west and covering all the country with a thick cloud of dust. The long white foaming waves of the river rose so high that the farther bank was invisible. The horses were restless and would not go into the skin boat, but at last we brought them all safely over. I now rode a rather large brown horse which I had bought in Shigatse. My small white Ladaki was still in good condition, but he was exempt from work. Only three veterans from Leh remained, two horses and a mule. Robert rode one of the horses from the Ngangtse-tso, and Muhamed Isa a large white horse from Shigatse, where we had also bought two mules; the baggage was transported on hired horses

168. THE LITTLE BROTHER OF THE TASHI LAMA, THE WIFE OF KUNG GUSHUK, AND HER FIVE SERVANTS.

the *lhakang* (God's House) of Tarting-gompa, and behind stands the house of the Grand Lama, picturesque and unique, built in the usual cubical style, with white steps and flat roof. Above it Tarting-gompa is throned on its hill like Chimre or Tikze in Ladak (Illustrations 173, 174, 178).

We enter the court of the *lhakang* with its red walls; on two sides a roof is supported by posts, a shed for the riding horses, pack-mules, men and women who carry fire-wood and goods — a cloister and a caravanserai at the same time, where labour finds harbourage under the protection of religion — and over it waves a long flag from a *tarchen*, a mast standing in the midst of the court. The convent dog is chained up. The gate has an unusually high threshold; on the side walls of the entrance a tiger is painted in fresh colours. We now enter the *lhakang*, and I must confess that I started with surprise in the portal, for we had seen many halls of the gods in Tashi-lunpo, but never yet one so large, ancient and so wonderfully fascinating in its mysterious light.

What rich and subdued colouring! The Sego-chummo-lhakang, as it is called, is like a crypt, a fairy grotto, recalling to mind the rock temples of Elephanta; but here all is of red-painted wood, and 48 pillars support the roof. The capitals are green and gold, carved in intricate and tasteful designs, and carved lions, arabesques, and tendrils adorn the projecting beams of the ceiling. The floor consists of stone flags, their cracks filled up with the dust of centuries, so that it is smooth and even as asphalt. The daylight falls into the hall through a square impluvium, spanned by a network of chains. There stands the throne of the Tashi Lama, who visited the convent two years ago, and is expected again in two years, and opposite is a pyramidal stand, which is hung with lamps at certain festivals. A lama sits all day long at a tall prayer-cylinder (*korlo* or *mankor*) about 6 feet high, with a pile of loose leaves a foot high in front of him, which he turns over rapidly, and gabbles their contents so quickly that one wonders how his tongue can move so fast. Frequently he beats a drum, then he clashes cymbals, or turns the prayer-cylinder in the heterodox direction (Illustrations 179, 254).

In another saloon, beside this, repose Grand Lamas of the Pembo sect, high priests of Tarting-gompa. We find here the same four-sided passage as round the sepulchres of Tashi-lunpo. But as I was going, as usual, from right to left, lamas hurried up to stop me. The monuments are like *chhorten*, and are covered with gold plaques and precious stones. Twelve statues of deceased high priests have behind them huge gilded halos, richly carved with carefully executed detail. Beside Shen Nime Kudun's monument lie two black smoothly-polished round blocks, apparently of porphyry or diabase. On one of them is seen the impression of the foot of the above-named Grand Lama. On the edge of the other are four impressions, his four fingers, just as though the flat hand with the fingers a little expanded had been pressed against a piece of hard butter. One can try it with one's own hand; the fingers fit in exactly, and the hollows are about $\frac{3}{4}$ inch deep. It is well and naturally executed — *pia fraus!*

"When was the monastery founded?" I asked.

"That was so long ago that no one now living knows."

"Who founded it, then?"

"Gunchen Ishe Loto, long before Tsong Kapa's time."

The lamas spend all their lives in the convents, but have no idea how old these are.

Then we ascend to the top of the hill, where several convent buildings stand, and are received by a whole pack of vicious dogs. The chief temple hall, Dokang-chummo, is built on the same plan as the one below, and has numerous images, some of which are covered with strips and silver cases. We are led from one sanctuary to another, and are astonished at the extremely finely-executed frescoes that cover the walls. A temple in an elevated situation is surrounded by an uncovered passage with balustrades and prayer mills. A grand panorama of wild fissured mountains extends all round.

We had heard that the evening before our arrival an octogenarian lama had died, and I begged to be allowed to see his cell. But the excuse was made that some monks were reciting the prayers for the dead, and must not be disturbed. However, the house of the deceased was

170. THE AUTHOR DRAWING THE DUCHESS KUNG GUSHUK.

pointed out to us, and we went and knocked at the door of the courtyard. After a long wait a man came and opened it. Half of the small court was occupied by a black tent, where two men and a woman were cutting chips of wood 2 feet long, on which prayers and holy texts would be written, and then they would be used to kindle the funeral pyre of the deceased. One was drawing religious symbols and circles on a large paper, which would also be burned. We mounted a short staircase and came to a narrow open verandah before a store-shed with leathern chests containing the clothing of the deceased, and a compartment where his servant lived, who was now engaged in printing prayers in red, on white paper, with a wooden stamp; 700 such strips of paper are burned with the body, and the prayers follow the soul through the unknown realms of space.

From here we reach his cell, which is little more than double the size of my tent. There sit two old monks, with their backs against the trellised window. Books containing the prayers for the dead lie on a table before them. Two others sit on the floor in the middle of the room. All four must pray thrice twenty-four hours, day and night, for the soul of the deceased. The cell has a pillar, and is full of idols, holy vessels, banners, and books — a small museum. I asked if I might buy any of the things, but was told that they must all be handed over to the monastery.

The divan bed, partly draped with red hangings, stood against the shorter wall, the head to the window. Here sat the body, bent very much forward and with the legs crossed, and the back to the light. It was dressed in coloured garments with shoes on the feet, a thin *kadakh* over the face, and a head-covering of red and blue stuff somewhat like a crown. Before it on the bed stood a stool with images, bowls, and two burning candles.

The body is not consumed in this dress. A white frock is put on, and a square cloth is spread over the knees, on which a large circle and other symbols are drawn. A crown (*vangsha*) of paper is set on the head, a square brimless hat, on which a button is fixed within eight broad teeth; it resembles an imperial crown. Thus attired the body, in a sitting position, is burned in the hollow of the valley below the temple. A lama carries the ashes to Kang-rinpoche (Kailas), where they are deposited in a holy *chhorten*.

At the age of five years this Yundung Sulting was consigned by his parents in the year 1832 to the care of the confraternity of Tarting-gompa, and his convent name was thenceforth Namgang Rinpoche. He, too, was an incarnation, and stood in high repute for his holiness, wisdom, and learning. On account of these merits he was burned, while the other monks in Tarting are cut in pieces. His sister and only relation, an old wrinkled woman, was present. The watchers of the dead were just in the act of eating their dinner, which was placed on a stool — cold dried meat, *tsamba*, and *chang* (beer). They were shy and astonished, had never seen a European, and did not know whether they should answer my questions as I sat by them on the floor and took notes. I noticed, however, that they were less concerned for themselves than for the deceased. Twenty-four hours out of the prescribed seventy-two had passed when I came to interrupt the masses for the dead, and to disturb the soul which was nearly set free. But Namgang Rinpoche sat still, meditating over the endless enigmatical perspective that the formula "Om mati moyi sale do" opened out to him; and as long as I remained in his cell, no awful wonders and signs were seen.

For my part, I thought of the singular fate of the man whose life had come to an end the day before. As a novice he had left for ever in childhood the free existence among the black tents and grazing herds, said farewell to the world and its vanities, and was received into a community of monks, of whom none now remained alive. He saw his elders die one after another, the young ones grow up to manhood, and new recruits come in. They wandered for a season through the temple halls, lighted the candles, and filled the water-bowls before the statues of the gods, and then passed on to other scenes on the endless road to Nirvana. Seventy-five years he had been an inmate of the monastery, and had lived in the cell in which his body now lay. How

171. Major W. F. O'Connor, British Trade Agent in Gyangtse, now Consul in Seistan.

172. Captain C. G. Rawling.

many soles must he have worn out on the same stone floor! For seventy-five years he had searched the holy scriptures and had pondered over an easier existence beyond the funeral pyre; for seventy-five years he had seen the westerly storms driving the sand along the Brahmaputra valley. Only yesterday, at the point of expiring, he had listened to the sound of the temple bells, which, with their clappers bound with large falcon's feathers, had rung in his passage to the world beyond. And then with tottering steps he had followed the uncertain track of the brethren who had passed away before him.

Such a life seems hopelessly sad and gloomy. And yet a man who will venture to shut himself day and night within the walls of a dim convent must possess faith, conviction, and patience, for it is a prison which he in the tumult of his mind has chosen of his own free will. He has renounced the world when he allows himself to be walled in alive in the dark courts of Tarting; and when the smoke of his pyre ascends, it must, if equal justice be meted out to all, be a pleasant savour before the eternal throne.

But evening was coming on, and we must set out again. Below in a field a woman was ploughing with two oxen. She was singing loudly and cheerily to lighten her work. We rode on between low mountains, leaving Tanka-gompa on our left. When we came down to the plain the darkness was impenetrable, being made denser by thick clouds. A violent north wind arose, bringing cold air from the Chang-tang. At length we caught sight of comet tails of shooting sparks — our camp-fire in the Ye, where we had halted for a night's rest two months before.

We remained two days in the Ye or Yeshung, and here took some liberties which were not in accordance with the terms of our passport, but the escort made no protest. On the first day we rode to Tugden-gompa, a row of cubical, two-storeyed houses painted dark greyish-blue with vertical white and red stripes. The monastery is said to be of the same colour as the famous Sekiya, south-west of Tashi-lunpo, and also belongs to the sect which allows lamas to marry under certain conditions. The convent has thirty monks, and is directly under the Labrang (Tashi-lunpo).

I will not enter into a full description, but will only say that the *tsokang*, the assembly saloon and reading-room of the lamas, had four red pillars, divans in the nave, and handsome banners on the walls of the side aisles, which were painted on Chinese silk, some with dragons on the lower border, some without. The statues for the most part represent monks of high rank (Lama-kunchuk, *i.e.* divine lamas or incarnations). Before the portal stands a huge bundle of rods with streamers in all the colours of the rainbow, which are already torn by the wind. In an upper hall is enthroned a figure of Hlobun-Lama, a regular bishop, with mitre, cassock, and crozier. Some of these statues are very comical — fat, jolly old boys with a divinely gentle smile on their rosy lips, wide-opened eyes, and chubby cheeks, sometimes with moustaches and imperials. The likeness is probably more than doubtful, but at any rate they are very unlike one another. Most of them are wrapped in silken mantles. The Labrang here was closed, for the head lama of Tugden was gone to the tent of a dying nomad to the north. We visited a monk's cell instead. It had a yard, a stall for the monk's horse, a small dark closet for a kitchen, where a cat kept company with two pots, and a large lumber-room crammed with clothes, rags, images of Buddha, books, and tools, in which a novice, the pupil of the monk, lodged.

Immediately to the south-east of Tugden a small poor nunnery, Ganden-chöding, lies buried among hills. The *dukang*, a dark crypt with red pillars and neatly carved capitals, is reached through an unpretending portal in the middle of the façade. Beggarly offerings, scraps of iron and other rubbish, are hung on nails driven into the pillars. The *serku-lhakang*, the holy of holies, receives its light from the larger hall, and as this is dark, it must be pitch dark in the inner shrine. The statues of Chenresi (Avalokiteswara) and of the Tsepagmed (Amitayus) can only be seen with a lamp.

The sixteen nuns of the convent are under the control of Tashi-lunpo, and the Tashi Lama provides them with tea once a day; the rest of their food they must beg in the houses and tents, so that some of them are always on the

173

174

175

176

177

173, 174. TARTING-GOMPA. 175. LINGA-GOMPA. 176. LUNG-GANDEN-GOMPA NEAR TONG. 177. INSCRIPTION AND FIGURE OF BUDDHA CARVED IN GRANITE NEAR THE VILLAGE OF LINGÖ.

Sketches by the Author.

road. Now there were only five sisters at home, all dirty, with short hair, and poorly clad. Two were young and shy, the others were old wrinkled women with silvery-grey bristles, and in clothes which had been red once, but were now black with dirt, partly soot from the kitchen — a miserable hole, where they spend most of the day. I asked them whether they had attended the festival in Tashi-lunpo, but they replied that their means would not allow them except when a charitable person gave them travelling money. I always left a few rupees in the convents I visited, and the inmates were never too holy to take the valuable metal from the hands of an unbeliever.

The whole broad valley at Ye is begirt by a circle of monasteries. Our Chinamen had given notice of my visit on April 2 to Tashi-gembe, a large convent of 200 monks, who belong to the same colour as the monks of Tashi-lunpo. We had an hour's ride to this town of white sanctuaries, which are erected at the foot of a mountain spur. About 100 brethren gave me a civil greeting at the entrance, and led me to the paved court of ceremonies, which has the same appearance as the one in Tashi-lunpo, is surrounded by pillared galleries, has numerous pictures of Buddha painted in fresco on the walls, and a throne for the Tashi Lama, who celebrates a mass here once a year. By a staircase of wood and stone, between two pillars of the entrance hall, where the four spiritual kings keep watch on the walls, we enter into a *dukang*, with the usual pillars and divans. On two of these pillars hang complete suits of armour with shirts of mail, casques and tasses of iron scales fastened together with iron rings, maces, spears, tridents, and lances; on one of these lances hangs a white pennant with a brown border; on the pennant are written characters, and on the point of the lance a skull is placed. Among the harness *tankas* are suspended, which, surrounded by silken cloths, look like escutcheons. Amid this harness and weapons, which are worn by divine powers when contending with devils, one may fancy oneself suddenly transplanted into an ancient Asiatic castle.

A gallery runs round three sides, and standards and banners hang down from it, all in fresh colours, tasteful and handsome. In the middle of the altar rank is enthroned Sakya-tubpa, the Buddha, and before the statues stands a row of polished brass bowls with lights which, mingling with the daylight, cast a magic gleam over the dusky hall. Some are filled with crystal-clear water, the nectar of the gods.

On one of the longer sides the folios of the Kanjur, the collection of canonical books contained in 108 volumes, as many as the beads in a rosary, are arranged in pigeonholes. The Tanjur, the other collection, consists of 235 folios — a caravan of about 150 horses would be necessary to carry the two bibles of the Tibetans. Only rich monasteries are able to keep both. The thought that no one but themselves has waded through these endless scriptures must inspire a feeling of security in the monks. A layman is unable to confound a monk; he has never had an opportunity of dipping deeply into these everlasting truths.

Above the idols and the altar runs a frieze of small Buddha images forming, perhaps unintentionally, a highly decorative element of the internal architecture of the hall.

Beside it lies the Kasang-lhakang, a temple with sixteen pillars and a statue of the Sakya-tubpa. The hall is well lighted with skylights, and abounds in gold and valuables, climbing flowers, sacred trees, and lacquered shrines inlaid with gold. Here, too, are holy writings with unusually elegant margins; an embroidered silk cover is laid over each volume. A copper gong is sounded whenever fresh water is poured into the votive bowls.

The Tsokang is a more elevated hall, which is draped with black hangings striped white at the bottom.

Monks were sitting in a small open space with a quantity of small articles before them; it was an auction, at which the worldly goods of a departed brother were being sold. I acquired some wooden blocks with which the holy scriptures are printed by hand.

In the Ganden-lhakang we see two *chhortens* of gold and precious stones. In one of them are preserved relics of a Grand Lama, some of his blood, his bones, and his intestines. In a room situated beside this hall we saw with surprise six curious figures of cast iron, representing

178. TARTING-GOMPA.

179. SEGO-CHUMMO LHAKANG IN TARTING-GOMPA.
Sketch by the Author.

Europeans in the dress of the thirties of the nineteenth century, with tall chimney-pot hats, stiff folded neckcloths, upstanding collars, and dress coats with high collars, whiskers, and moustaches. They had come from Pekin, and were quite out of place here before the tasteful group of Buddhas, which was set up in a red lacquered niche, where climbing plants, dragons, and small figures like Cupids or angels were beautifully carved.

The Mankang-lhakang has figures of the higher gods on the walls, and in the middle a prayer cylinder rises from the floor up to the ceiling, 11½ feet high, and of such circumference that I laid my outstretched arms four times round it, measuring from finger-tips to finger-tips. Its red surface is covered with gigantic golden characters, and round the middle of the cylinder dances a string of goddesses. A smaller hall of the same kind is called Mankang-chang. On the upper edge of its prayer cylinder is a peg which, as the cylinder revolves, strikes against the clapper of a bell. An old lama sat before it and kept the cylinder in constant motion by means of a string attached to a crank on the iron axle. It is the duty of himself and another monk to keep this monstrosity humming all the day and half the night, or from sunrise to midnight. As he sat turning, he said his prayers, but he did not murmur them in the usual way. No, he bellowed, he howled out inarticulate sounds, so that he foamed at the mouth, perspired, and groaned, throwing himself violently back at each revolution, and then bending forward again. He was, so I was told, in a religious ecstasy, and did not hear, however loudly one shouted to him. I should prefer the oar of a galley slave to this monster, which cripples any capacity of thinking freely in the darkness of the crypt, where only musty dumb gods can be witnesses of its rotations. I looked at my watch; the bell sounded nine times in a minute, so that the machine makes 10,000 revolutions before the midnight hour comes to release the weary monk.

We passed the whole day in the wonderful monastery Tashi-gembe, which, after Tashi-lunpo, is the richest and finest I have seen in Tibet. As to cleanliness and good taste, it surpasses all. The temple halls were well lighted by numerous windows, the midday sun shone in between the pillars and produced a bewitching play of light and shade, and revealed a charming arrangement of colours between red and gold. Some monks sat on a divan and conversed with our companions; they made a clear and effective picture in the sunlight, red on a red background. Others leaned against the pillars, solemn as Roman senators in their togas, in a flood of sunshine, while a dense group of their brethren was dimly seen under the shadows of the gallery. And where the sunbeams played on the gold of Buddha's robe and broke on the leaves of the golden lotus-flower, out of which he rises, reflexions were scattered through the fairy hall, and the pillars shone like transparent rubies. We were dazzled by these effects of light, and might have been transplanted to the halls of the gnomes.

In contrast to all this wealth, an old blind man of eighty sat at a street-corner with a staff in each hand, and sang a beggar's ditty. Beside him lay a half-starved dog, his only friend in this world. The pitying love of Sakya-muni did not extend so far as to release this old man from the bonds of age and suffering. He also found a place in the picture gallery of my sketch-book, which on this memorable day received considerable additions. As ever, I felt myself to be only a passing pilgrim, a wanderer who had crossed the threshold of Tashi-gembe for a few hours, and a stranger and guest in the dreary valleys of Tibet and its mysterious enchanting temples.

The sun had set when we rode home, but the crests of the eastern mountains still glowed as in a rain of transparent gold. In the gently rippling water-channels the wild-geese gathered, screaming, for their spring migration, and the shadows of evening fell over the wide fields of Yeshung.

180. Bridge to the Monastery Pinzoling (on the right).

CHAPTER XXXIII

THE RAGA-TSANGPO AND THE MY-CHU

ON April 3 we journeyed steadily along the way to the west by smiling villages and small convents, and again we approached the bank of the Tsangpo, at a place where a swaying rope-bridge is stretched between two loose blocks on the banks. Here the river forms rapids, and above this point it is only 50 yards broad, often still less, and the valley above the Yeshung expansion is narrow and confined. From the village Pusum, where we encamp, is seen the mountain Nayala, one of the fixed points in Ryder's triangulation. His and Rawling's expedition travelled to the south of the Tsangpo, and it would be two months more before I should first come in contact with their route. The river will rise a month longer in consequence of the melting of ice in the higher parts of its course in the distant west.

The village Pusum lies on a steep terrace above the river. Cones of detritus descend to the bank, and steep mountains rise on the southern side. The valley is narrow and quite straight, so that Pinsoling, the end of the next day's march, can be seen from Pusum; it is perched on its rocky promontory like a castle on the Rhine. The path passes over steep disagreeable slopes of pebbles. Only grey and red granite, with black schist, is seen both in the solid rock and in the débris.

Almost immediately south of Chagha, a village of a couple of stone houses in a grove of old willows, the monastery and dzong of Pinzoling appear on the right bank. The river is narrow, and the bank full of round granite boulders a yard in diameter, so the necessary material for a bridge is at hand. Two huge pyramids of stone are erected on the banks, and two smaller ones behind them. Two thick chains are stretched between them, which pass on to the smaller pyramids, and are made fast again to them. Between the chains a network of ropes is stretched like a hammock, and on this narrow planks are laid; on these passengers walk, using the chains as hand-rails. The Pinzoling bridge has not been used for three years; any one who wants to cross to Pinzoling from Chagha must go upstream to Ladse-dzong and make use of the ferry there. I inquired how old the bridge was. "As old as the monastery," was the answer. "And how old is the monastery?" A villager answered at random, "A thousand years." Another said that this was an exaggeration, for the monastery had been founded two hundred and fifty years ago by a lama named Yitsyn Tara Nara. Two hundred monks belong to the monastery of Pinzoling, but half of them had gone on their travels. An official of the dzong, with the title of Dsabo, lived in Chagha, and examined our passport (Illustration 180).

The river was at its lowest level, but during high-water it is said to come up to the chains of the bridge, which seems to me improbable, for they hang fully 6 feet above the surface of the water at their lowest part. A channel remains open in the middle of the river even in cold winters. Boats reach the side valley in which Shigatse lies in four to five days, but during the summer in two or three days, for then the river flows down with tremendous velocity. It is considered less dangerous to travel in a high flood, for then the boats glide smoothly over boulders and sand-banks, and it is said that a man is very seldom drowned, or a boat's cargo lost.

Black and dark-purple mountains rise around the village, their surface only visible in some places in strips between belts of driftsand; they are like tiger skins. Near a ridge to the south-west lies a large dune as though it were attached to it.

The order of the day for April 5 was that Muhamed Isa with the hired animals and the baggage should encamp at the point where the Raga-tsangpo flows into the upper Brahmaputra. The rest of us rode up to a small pass, Tsukchung-chang, on a spur of the mountains which extends to the bank of the main river. From the summit there is a grand view over the main valley and its stream, which meanders over gravel and sand in two arms. Below we caught sight of mule caravans, mere specks, but their bells filled the valley with their noise. The way runs headlong down to the valley bottom so that we had to engage extra men to carry the baggage, with which the horses could not clamber down the precipitous slopes. Large dark fish swam in a stopped-up arm of the river, and here sat Shukkur Ali with his rod. Sand-dunes ten feet high are a common occurrence, and on the steep side, turned from the wind, that is, the east side, pools are often formed.

To the south-west opens a large portal with shelving mountains in the background and short side valleys, the whole forming a beautiful scene. Through this portal the Brahmaputra comes down towards the Raga-tsangpo, but this river is known here in its lowest course by the name Dok-chu, while the main river is known as the Dam-chu (= Tamchok). At the confluence no tents were to be seen, and Muhamed Isa told me afterwards that he could not stay there as the country was quite barren. We therefore rode up the Dok-chu valley to the village Tangna, consisting of ten stone houses. The inhabitants cultivate peas, wheat, and barley, but cannot count with certainty on a harvest.

I would on no account miss seeing the confluence of the two rivers, and therefore ordered my men to descend the Dok-chu valley next day to this point. But the escort would not hear of it. It was clearly stipulated in the passport that we must not go backwards and forwards as we liked, but must march straight to Ladak. At last they yielded under the condition that the excursion should not last more than one day.

In the morning Muhamed Isa took the boat and the oars down to the river, while ropes, stakes, axes, poles, and provisions were carried by Ladakis down to the confluence by the way we had come the day before. On arriving at the bank I found the boat already put together, and took my seat in it with a Tibetan who was familiar with the river and handled the oars as skilfully as though he had done nothing else all his life, but he was accustomed to steer his own boat between the banks at Tangna, and knew the channel downstream.

Our voyage through the rapids is exciting and adventurous. The fall of the river is by no means uniform, but changes from place to place, roaring rapids alternating with deep quiet basins. Large and small boulders have fallen into the river from the mountain flanks and sometimes it seems impossible to get through them. But the oarsman knows how to steer the boat. We hear the roar of the next rapid from a distance, and keep a sharp lookout in front. Some of our Ladakis run along the path on the bank and warn us of serious dangers.

The boat rushes flying downstream. The boatman sits silent with his teeth clenched and his feet firmly planted against the bottom, and grasps the oars so tightly in his horny hands that the knuckles become white. We had passed successfully several rapids and were gliding pleasantly over a reach of smooth water, when we heard the warning roar of the next rapids, this time louder than ever, and two Ladakis stood shouting and gesticulating. I got up in the boat and saw that the Dok-chu split into two arms, and that the water dashed foaming among dark sharp-edged boulders. The place looked impassable, the intervals between the boulders seemed much too narrow for the boat, which might any moment have its bottom torn by treacherously hidden stones; over some of these the water poured in bright-green hillocks, and then was scattered into foaming spray. "I shall be glad if all goes well," I thought, but I left the boatman to his own devices. We were soon in the sucking current, which endures no resistance, and flew quicker and quicker towards the two rapids. With powerful strokes the oarsman forced the boat to enter the left branch. The Ladakis stood speechless on the bank, and waited till we were wrecked to wade into the rapids and rescue us. Now we dashed towards

181. Group of Tibetans in the Village of Tong.

182. Inhabitants of the Village of Govo.

the first block, but the boatman guided his boat into the deepest water and let it slip down a small waterfall, after which we received a thrust from the other side. Now the channel became broader but also shallower, and we grazed the bottom, fortunately only with the keel and without springing a leak. The current was strong enough to carry us away over stones and rubbish.

After a while the two arms re-unite and the river becomes smooth and deep. The boatman has never changed countenance, and now he helps on with the oars. We are on the north side of the valley, and just at the bend where the river turns southwards the water rages and boils more furiously than ever, and here the undaunted boatman declares that we can go no farther. I hold my breath at the sight of the white foaming water which breaks over the threshold of the fall; the boat will be carried away in a second by the suction of the water and will be infallibly capsized. But just at the right moment the boatman steers our nutshell aside into a bay with a back current, and we are able to land. The Ladakis hurry up, draw the boat ashore, and set it afloat again below the waterfall.

Now we float pleasantly past the steep rocky walls of the southern bank, where the depth is sometimes 5 feet, and sometimes less than a foot. I have a pole and help to hold off the boat from the bank. Again we are carried to the northern side of the valley and dance and rock through a series of small lively rapids, usually quite deep enough. Now and then we graze the bottom, but the wooden keel resists the thumps. Below a gigantic boulder lying in the middle of the stream is a sucking whirlpool, into which we nearly stumble, but we get past safely, and at last arrive at the point where the Dok-chu pours its snow-fed waters into the flood of the Brahmaputra.

The tributary here forms a delta with two branches between gravelly banks 5 feet high. A post was driven in on the left bank of the main arm, to which we fastened one end of a rope, with the other end I rowed over to the right bank, where the rope was fastened to another post. The breadth was 59 yards. Then I measured the depth at eleven points at equal distances apart, and found that it did not exceed 3⅓ feet. The velocity was measured on the surface, half-way down, and at the bottom, with Lyth's current meter. Taking the breadth and the average velocity we arrive at the discharge, which in the two arms of the Dok-chu amounted to 1165 cubic feet per second.

Where the two streams unite the Dok-chu is rapid and tumultuous, the Brahmaputra slow, deep, and quiet. Its breadth was 50 yards and its maximum depth 15.3 feet; the bed is therefore narrow and very deeply excavated. The discharge amounted to 2966 feet in the second, or two and a half times that of its tributary the Dok-chu.

When I had finished this work, our friends Tso Ting Pang and Lava Tashi accompanied me on a short excursion down the main stream, and then we landed on a promontory where our men lighted a fire and served up the best provisions we had, namely, hard-boiled eggs, slices of cold chicken, and milk. A cordial and mixed party, a Swede among Tibetans, Chinamen and Ladakis, we partook of our late dinner amidst the grandest, and most boldly sculptured landscape conceivable. While the others smoked their pipes and sipped their greasy tea, I drew a sketch of the mighty gate of solid granite through which the Brahmaputra rolls its volumes of water on its way to the east, to the valley of the Dihong and the plains of Assam. We should have liked to stay here longer, watching how moment after moment the insatiable stream gathers in its abundant tribute from the Dok-chu, but it was growing dark and we had a long way to go back, so we packed up our boat and stowed it on hired horses with the other baggage, mounted into the saddle, and rode up the valley. As had often happened before, we were to-day overtaken by the darkness. Rabsang went in front with a Tibetan on either side, and all three bellowed as loud as they could. All were in excellent spirits, it was so fresh and pleasant under the twinkling stars, and the merry singers, accompanied by the jingle of the bells on the Chinese horses, awoke a shrill echo in the recesses of the mountains. At a dangerous place near a village, where the road runs above the river over a ledge built up of stones, men came to meet us with paper lanterns, and soon after we sat resting in our tents after a hard but very instructive day's work. Next day we marched gently up the Dok-chu valley in a north-westerly direction, a charmingly beautiful road, where one would like to dismount repeatedly to enjoy conveniently the wild mountain scenery.

But now I cannot loiter; one page after another of my journal must be turned over if I am ever to come to an end of my description of this journey on which so many hard experiences and disagreeable adventures awaited us.

We ride through rubbish and coarse sand, the weathering products of the grey granite, and pass a succession of transverse valleys and several picturesque villages. One of these, Machung, is finely situated at the foot of steep rocks on the northern side of the valley, from which an oval block has fallen down and stands like a gigantic egg in the sand, a pedestal waiting for an equestrian statue. On its eastern side, smoothly polished by wind and weather, a regular tricolour is painted, white in the middle, red on the left and blue on the right, but neither Bonvalot nor Dutreuil de Rhins has left this memorial behind, for no traveller has ever been in the neighbourhood. It is the inhabitants of the village who have made this flag, and beside the tricolour is another symbolical painting, a white cross on a black field. Near the village some gnarled trees are reflected in a pool. The villagers stand staring at the corners and in the house-doors, and a man offers my servants a drink of *chang* from a wooden bowl. The rocks are sculptured into singular forms; the granite is in vertical dykes and stands in perpendicular crags in the valley. We often pass by *mani* cists, for we are in a country where monasteries are numerous and the whole road is adorned with religious tokens. At every cist the road divides, for no one, except adherents of the Pembo sect, omits to pass it on the left, the direction in which the prayer mills revolve. On the tops of many of the rocks are seen ruins of walls and towers, a proof that the valley in bygone times was more densely peopled. At two places sheltered clefts in the rock harbour some stunted juniper trees. On the northern side of the valley the river has at some time polished the base of the granite wall, and on the smooth surface two rock drawings have been executed. They consist of outlines of Buddha pictures, and are very artistically drawn. The western has two others beside it, now scarcely traceable, and below them all kinds of ornamentation, tendrils, and designs are hewn in the granite. We encamped just above this spot in a very picturesque and interesting expansion of the valley at the village Lingö.

Part of the inhabitants of Lingö migrate in summer with their herds, six or seven days' journey northwards, for the soil round Lingö is very poor and the harvest cannot be depended on. The Dok-chu cannot be crossed here in summer except by boat; in the winter it freezes over, but seldom so firmly that the ice will bear. The interesting point about this expansion is that the Dok-chu, or Raga-tsangpo, coming from the west, here unites with our old friend the My-chu, which discharges 534 cubic feet a second. I had the day before calculated 1165 feet as the discharge of the Dok-chu, so the difference of 631 cubic feet is the volume of water brought down by the Raga-tsangpo, and consequently the My-chu is only a tributary. On the other hand the Dok-chu pours through several delta arms with rapids into the My-chu which lies lower and flows more gently, and by this test the My-chu should be the main river; it is all a question of choice.

We had another fine day on April 8, 52.5° in the shade at one o'clock. We were to make a closer acquaintance with the My-chu, a river we had hitherto known only from hearsay, but we had more knowledge of its eastern tributaries which we had crossed on our journey south. As usual we change our baggage horses in almost every village at which we encamp, and Robert pays the hire to the villagers, that the escort may not have an opportunity of putting it into their own purses, at any rate not in our presence. Generally the caravan marches a little in advance, while two villagers come with me and give me information about the country.

Immediately beyond Lingö we turn into the My-chu valley, riding northwards, and now leave behind the

183. LAMA IN TONG.

184. OLD TIBETAN.

Sketches by the Author.

westerly valley of the Raga-tsangpo. Right at the turn we come to a colossal cone of round blocks of granite, among which the path winds up and down in zigzags, sometimes transformed to a staircase, which laden animals cannot possibly pass. We therefore take with us some peasants from the village to help in carrying the baggage. We have the river on our left, deep and sluggish. The fallen boulders of grey granite contrast strongly with the dark-green water in which whole shoals of black-backed fishes swim and rise. On a surface of granite is a Buddhist rock-drawing half obliterated by time. Then follows one *mani* after another. A smith is housed in a cave with a vaulted roof blackened with soot, and sheltered by a small screen of stones, and offers his services to travellers. High up on a rocky terrace stands Gunda-tammo, a small nunnery, and below a chain bridge between two stunted pyramids spans the river. It is only for foot passengers. The river bed is deeply excavated between its bank terraces, and two strips of clear green ice yet remain. The bed is as regular as a canal. On a rocky wall at the entrance of a side valley a face 6 feet in diameter is painted in black, with eyes, nose, and mouth in red.

The farther we go up the more frequently we are reminded that we are on a hallowed road leading from one temple to another, a sacred way of the monks, a pilgrim route on which "Om mani padme hum" is murmured more repeatedly than on ordinary roads. Sometimes boulders and cliffs are painted red, sometimes cairns are heaped beside the way, now we see chimney-like monuments with bundles of rods decked with streamers, then again long *mani* mounds, one of them nearly 400 feet long. Two blocks lying on the road are covered all over with raised characters — a formidable piece of work. We are also in a great commercial artery, more frequented than the bank of the Tsangpo. We constantly meet caravans of yaks and mules, mounted men and foot-passengers, monks, peasants, and beggars. They salute me politely, scratching their heads with their right hands, while they hold their caps in their left, and putting their tongues far out of their mouths, and they call out to me: "A good journey, Bombo!"

Clear rivulets trickle across the road, the valley contracts and its contours become bolder and more pronounced; the granite ceases and is replaced by fine-grained crystalline schist. In the district of Tong, where several villages stand high above the river, we encamp below the monastery Lun-ganden-gompa (Illustration 176), in which 21 monks of the Gelugpa sect live, and, as usual, a prior of Kanpo rank dwells in the Labrang. We paid them a visit, but preferred the lovely view over the valley to the images of the gods in the darkness. The brethren are maintained partly by the Tashi Lama, and obtain the rest of their food from the produce of their fields, for the convent has large glebe lands. A blind man, who was not of the fraternity, sat like a machine at the prayer mill, turning it for the monks, and complained of his hard lot. The Gova, the district chief, of Tong rules over several villages in the neighbourhood, and lives like a prince in his solid house.

On April 10 we continued along the course of the My-chu, past villages and convents hitherto unknown. The villages stand just below the mouths of side valleys where the water can be most effectively applied to irrigation. A caravan of about 100 yaks, driven by men and women and some carrying riders, had been at Tok-jalung and had sold there *tsamba* from Tong; they had spent three months on their return from those gold-diggings in western Tibet. They follow a route through the mountains where there is suitable pasture for yaks. Thus the produce of the soil in the more favoured parts of the country reaches the nomads, who give in exchange for it wool, hides, and salt. After a short march we bivouacked in Ghe, which has nineteen houses. An *angdi* (musician) scraped and plucked a two-stringed instrument (Illustration 185), while his wife danced before us.

Here our escort from Shigatse turned back, after handing our passport to four other men, the chief of whom was the Gova of Tong. They had done us excellent service, so I gave them good testimonials and presents. They were satisfied and would pray for my prosperity till

185. Strolling Musicians.

their lives' end. I felt particular sympathy for one of the Tibetans who had lost his two sons in the battle at Guru; the one was twenty-three years old, and the other twenty-five, and the father could not understand why they had fallen, for they had done nothing wrong.

Next day the escort, jingling like a sledge party, accompanies us up the My-chu, which retains the same character. Granite and schists alternate. The river tosses about, though it has occasionally quiet reaches. In the background of the side valleys are often seen great mountains lightly covered with snow, and at their entrances villages with stone houses and fields where only barley and peas are grown, seldom wheat. The black tents we see occasionally belong to merchants who are on their way from or to western Tibet. Bridges cross the affluents, flat slabs of stone on a pair of beams between rather high slightly overhanging piers of stone. The religious stone heaps are still numerous; one has caused a sand-dune to be formed. Wild ducks, wood pigeons, and partridges occur here, and the latter, sorely against their will, make acquaintance with Tsering's kitchen. In the village Sir-chung the population is large, for here several routes and side valleys converge. Among the crowds of spectators was a young woman so extraordinarily pretty that I took two photographs of her. She was twenty years old and was named Putön (Illustration 186).

The day following we visited the adjacent monastery Lehlung-gompa, where the twenty-six monks belong to some heterodox sect, for they recognize neither Tsong Kapa nor the Tashi Lama; the prior had shut himself up in his dwelling sunk in deep speculations. A lama and three inhabitants of the neighbouring village Nesar had died the day before, so our Tibetan escort warned us not to go up to the monastery lest we should catch the infection, and when we nevertheless went, they begged to be allowed to stay behind. This dreary dilapidated monastery stood proudly on its point of rock, pretty far up a side valley which descends from the left to the My-chu. From its flat roof we had a splendid view and could make out the topography of the My-chu valley.

A novelty to us was a row of stuffed yaks, hard as wood and dry as bone, with their horns, hoofs, and hides, hung up on the ceiling of a verandah. None of the monks could remember when they had been hung up. They looked very old, and apparently were for the same purpose as the four ghostly kings and the painted wild animals, that is, to scare away evil spirits.

Below the monastery twenty-four *manis* stand close together in a row like a parish boundary on a topographical map. All the way up these sacred structures are so numerous that they even outnumber those near Leh. The country assumes a more alpine character, and the valley becomes wilder and more desolate; but some trees form a small thicket at Lehlung-gompa. At length we ride over a pebble terrace, perhaps 130 feet above the stream, which now pours over small falls and murmurs pleasantly among boulders. The caravan has pitched its tents in the narrow valley on the bank of the My-chu and not far from the side valley Kathing. Most of the luggage has been carried by Tibetans, for no pack animals were to be had, and now some hundred black-headed fellows sit in groups by their fires among the large boulders.

Here we were at a height of 13,875 feet, and therefore had only mounted up 1175 feet from Shigatse (12,700 feet). But the air was cooler; the night before we had noted 23 degrees of frost.

186. The Handsome Woman, Putön.

CHAPTER XXXIV

TO LINGA-GOMPA

THE day's march on April 13 takes us along the valley of the My-chu like a hollow way excavated in the solid rock of fine-grained granite, porphyry and crystalline schist, and the landscape is one of the grandest I have ever seen. We follow the western bank, from which rise wild precipitous rocks like the ruins of old walls and embattled forts. A footpath runs along the left bank also, and looks extremely dangerous, passing up above abrupt walls of rock. Here and there valleys open out on the west side, affording views of part of a snow-covered crest in the background. This is, however, a subsidiary range, for it branches off from the Trans-Himalaya southwards and borders the basin of the My-chu on the west. It in turn sends out ramifications eastwards, between which flow the western tributaries of the My-chu. And these again give out branches of the fourth and fifth order; the whole appears in a plan like a tree with its branches and boughs.

The road runs on steep pebble terraces high above the river, which here rages among the boulders in its deeply eroded bed and forms whirlpools. On our left rocky precipices tower above our heads, and avalanches of detritus have slipped down from them and fallen across the road. Many are quite fresh; in other places there has been time to set up the blocks in protecting walls on the inner side and in a breastwork at the outer. And often we pass places where a new landslip may take place at any moment, and where huge blocks are poised in the air and seem ready to roll down the declivity. Flourishing hawthorns in large numbers grow on the stony banks, and high up above rock pigeons have built their nests. Still higher eagles soar with outspread pinions along the mountain flanks. We are 150 feet above the river, where here and there on the bank is room for small tilled fields; a juniper bush has in some places struck root in a fissure of the rock.

The valley is like a trough, and I obtain fine views of constantly changing scenes. We might fancy we were passing through a Gothic cathedral with a colonnade of huge shafts attached to the walls and spanned by a roof of grey and white canvas, the clouds to wit, between which small patches of light blue cloth appear.

The guide, accompanying us on this day, is a half silly old fellow, who laughs and chatters continuously, and frequently begins to dance on the road, flinging his legs about, stamping on the ground and turning round so quickly that his long pigtail flies round him. He tells us in confidence that his wife is a wicked hideous old dragon, whom he has long wished to carry off to the home of the vultures, for there will be no peace in his house till he has done so. When I halt to sketch, he takes his breakfast out of his coat, lays it out on the sand, fetches water from the river in a small bag, shakes *tsamba* from another into a wooden dish, pours water over it, stirs it with his forefinger and then swallows bowl after bowl of this delicious mixture. He hopes to receive so much pay, that for once he can afford himself a plentiful meal while his old woman cannot see him eat. As often as one looks at him, out shoots his tongue and hangs like a fiery red flag in the middle of his black face. When he has finished he licks his plate clean and rubs it with sand to dry it. Then he wraps his things up in a bundle and hides it under the stones. When Robert tells him that people are about who have seen him hiding it, he quickly takes his bundle out again, thinks over the matter for a while, rummages about and at last finds another hiding-place. Then he sits down beside me, puts out his tongue as far as it will go, winks at me with his little pig's eyes and takes a large pinch of snuff. When he walks in front of my horse, he turns round every hundred paces and puts his tongue out at me — a token of pure goodwill and deep respect.

Beyond the nunnery Döle-gompa the valley of the My-chu unites with the large side valley Lenjo running in from the west, in which, farther up, three villages are situated. From this valley the My-chu receives a very considerable tributary, which is crossed by a solid bridge of three arches resting on four stone piers; thick belts of ice still lie along the banks. Here we find two fine *manis* with turrets at both ends, where six-pointed stars are cut into the flat stones. These perpetual *manis* often stand in long rows so near together that they look like a long luggage train, and one expects to see them move and start off for the abodes of the blessed. Everything here denotes a great highway, a mighty commercial artery connecting the sedentary people of the lower-lying lands with the nomads of the plateaus. The road itself is the largest and best kept that I have seen in all Tibet. Bridges span all the affluents which might interrupt the traffic in summer and autumn, and wherever a landslip has occurred, the road is repaired at once. Sacred cairns, walls, and streamers indicate to the traveller at every step that a monastery is near, where the monks expect a visit and a present of money. We are always meeting caravans, riders, peasants, and beggars who extort money from merchants returning home after a good stroke of business. Many of these beggars turn into robbers and pillage undefended huts, but when they meet us they begin to hobble, gasp, and whine. After the harvest the traffic will be still more active than now.

The valley now contracts to a corridor, and the broad shallow stream occupies all its bottom. On the right side, which we follow, the cliffs of schist fall perpendicularly to the river, and the dangerous, narrow road runs like a sill along the wall of rock. Here nature has opposed endless insurmountable obstacles to the engineering skill of the Tibetans. The baggage has to be carried past these dangerous places, and it is astonishing that the horses can get past. Flat slabs of schist, branches, and roots have been inserted into cracks and fissures of the precipice 120 feet above the river, and on these planks, poles, and stones are laid forming a gutter a foot broad, without a scrap of railing, where one must even keep one's tongue in one's mouth lest one should lose one's balance. Of course we traverse this stretch of road, called Tigu-tang, on foot, leaning inwards and supporting ourselves by the rock. We breathe freely again when we are safely over, and the great basin lies before us where, at Linga, two important valleys converge.

Here is the confluence of the My-chu with a river flowing from the east, the Sha-chu, which farther up is called Bup-chu, and which we crossed two and a half months before on its thick coating of ice. On April 15 the Bup-chu brought down 215 cubic feet of water and the My-chu 222, so the rivers were nearly equal, but the ratio may of course vary considerably according to the distribution of the precipitation.

In a short valley in the western mountains the monastery Linga-gompa is placed on the uppermost ledge of a steep flight of terraces, and is as fantastic, fascinating, and attractive as a fairy castle. Its white houses are perched like storks' nests on mountain pinnacles; a row of *manis* points out the way up to where the pious, blameless saints dwell in deep silence, far above the riot and tumult of the villages and the roaring and tossing of the stream. Below the monastery stands the village Linga-kok, where our camp is pitched not far from a bridge of ten arches on eleven piers which crosses the My-chu. A crowd of Tibetans, black as Moors, dirty, ragged, capless and trouserless, watch our arrival in silent amazement (Illustration 188).

Not a single tree is seen in the neighbourhood; only up at the monastery there are two. This consolation, then, is no more, and only in our memory do we hear the thick foliage of tree-tops rustling in the wind. Again we may expect the moaning of the storm on the passes of bare alpine ranges. Moreover, the spring has not set in in

187. On the My-chu near Linga.

188. Village and Monastery of Linga.

earnest, for in the night there were still 30 degrees of frost.

I spent all Sunday till twilight in the monastery, with Rabsang and Tundup Sonam. We mounted the acclivity past rows of well-kept *manis*, which had the appearance of broken-down walls, with red-painted inscriptions chiselled out of the blocks of schist and framed in red. Then we passed through a gate in the convent wall, and mounted higher and higher between forty old and more recent white houses clinging to the rock. The situation is like that of the Hemis monastery in Ladak, but there the houses are not so scattered. Several of them are unoccupied, for the custom prevails here that, when a lama dies, his relations claim possession of his house, lock the door and take away the key. His movable property reverts to the convent. If a newly-come lama takes a fancy to an empty house, he can buy it from the heirs of the former owner; a good house is worth 100 rupees (Illustration 175).

Linga has thirty monks, some of whom accompanied us on our rounds and were always pleasant and friendly, and never bold like the monks in Kum-bum, which I visited in the year 1896. The monastery is subordinate to Sekiya, and the Sekiya-Lama is its highest spiritual superior and contributes towards its maintenance. Linga-gompa also possesses lands, which, however, have not yielded much of late, for the crops have failed several years in succession. The monks are not dependent on the Tashi Lama, and have not a single statue of Tsong Kapa, whence it may be concluded that their sect is older than the reformed church. But it was, as usual, impossible to get any information about the age of the monastery. It seems to be in the interest of the monks to date back its origin to the remotest antiquity, of which no human records are extant. I was told, however, that the abbot, Yimba Tashi, knew its age, which was recorded in an old chronicle of the monastery. Unfortunately, he was not at home, having gone northwards to a district called Kumna, there to track out a band of robbers who had plundered him the year before and carried off all his caravan animals.

Down below the convent is a gorge with a black slope of schist on its side, on which the six holy characters are exhibited in fragments of white quartz, and call out to heaven the eternal truth, "Om mani padme hum," in all kinds of wind and weather.

A staircase of flags of schist leads up to the Dopcha, an open platform paved with flagstones where the religious spectacles take place on feast days. The usual flagmast stands in the centre, but there is no breastwork of any kind, so that one dares not go there after dark, for bottomless abysses yawn round the open sides. Here the monks had laid carpets and cushions and invited me to tea. I enjoyed for a while the fine view over the valley, the confluence of the two streams, the scattered villages, and the fields like chessboards. Far to the east, behind the Bup-chu valley, the lofty mountains are seen over which we travelled on the way from the Ngangtse-tso.

On the south side of the square is the entrance to the chief temple (*dukang*), which in all monasteries is in a red-painted stone building. We enter, look round, and are carried away by the singular mysteriousness, though we have often seen it before with trifling variations. I sink on a divan and fancy myself in a museum crammed full of modern trophies and flags of victory, where impenetrable darkness lurks among the pillars, and rows of drums, gongs, prayer cylinders, and trombones are set up. The hall is darker than usual, but bright light falls through a skylight on to the images of the gods. They seem to be soaring from their pedestals in the darkness into the glorious light of the upper regions. The monks glide inaudibly like ghosts and shadows among them, busied with the votive bowls. A wonderfully weird scene! We have wandered into a cavern where gnomes and hobgoblins creep about.

This grotto resounds the whole time with the chant of the monks on the divans, which rises and falls in rhythmical waves, like the roar of the billows and the lapping of ripples on a strand. They sing in unison, keeping faultless time and without exerting themselves, though with astonishing rapidity. Among them are greyheaded men with cracked voices, men in the prime of life, and youths and boys with fresh young voices. The sound is like horses trotting quickly over an endless wooden bridge; all the monks clap their hands and then the horses seem to trot over a paved street, but the next moment they are on the bridge again and the consonants roll like peas out the monks' lips. Now and then a bass voice rises above the din calling out "*Laso, Laso*" (an exclamation of thanksgiving). During a short pause there is tea. Then the chant goes on again. There is no excitement, no hurrying of the tempo, all goes on in the same even quick trot. The monks have no books before them; they know their liturgy by heart. But the charm of the rhythm seems to render them oblivious of time and space; they do not suffer themselves to be disturbed, but trot on over the bridge that leads to the home of the gods and to Nirvana. As we go out again we hear the chant die away like the humming in a bee-hive.

We visited some other halls, where I noted down the names of the images. At length there remained only two convent buildings on a sharp ridge of rock. The first was named Chörigungkang, and had a sort of shed in which swords, guns, drums, masks, tiger-skins, and other lumber were stored. In the very front, on the point of the rock, is a cubical house called Pesu. It is surrounded on three sides by a gallery without balustrades, and here the abyss is deeper than elsewhere. Here I stayed to sketch the panorama, but the weather was anything but pleasant, and snowstorms veiled the mountains from time to time. Nevertheless it was hard to leave this terrace. The flat roofs down below look no larger than postage-stamps. Bright as silver, or dark, according as they are lighted, the two rivers hasten to meet each other. Then I could not help thinking how singular it was that the loftiest and grandest alpine country in the world, which must surely impress the human mind more than any other, had not been able to instil into the Tibetans a higher, nobler form of religion than this narrow, limited, dogmatic Lamaism. I grant that it was imported from India more than a thousand years ago and was first modified into the so-called northern Buddhism, but after all it flourishes vigorously in Tibet. One would think that the ancient Bon religion with its copious demonology, its widespread superstition, and its spirits haunting all the mountains and lakes, would be more suitable here. But we have indeed, discovered that Lamaism has absorbed many of its elements. At any rate the Linga monks have a splendid view of an artistically sculptured corner of the world. From their loopholes of windows and their flat roofs they can see winter spreading its white carpet over the mountains and putting the rivers in fetters, and then the spring shedding its gold over the valleys, the summer conjuring out new fresh grass, and lastly the rain torrents of early autumn washing the slopes and swelling the rivers.

We now ascended, as if the mountain itself were not high enough, two steep pitch-dark flights of steps, where it is easy to break one's neck, into the entrance hall of the Pesu temple. In a smaller room the flame of a butter-lamp struggled vainly with the darkness, casting its dull light on some idols. Pesu is the hall of the gods *par excellence*, with innumerable statuettes of metal, very old, artistically worked and certainly very valuable. Some figures were of medium size. I stood in front of the altar rank and inspected the gods. *Tankas* and long narrow scarves in many colours hung from the ceiling. On the right was the small, dark room, and on the left was a shutter creaking as it banged to and open in the wind. Before the gods stood a row of bowls with barley, wheat, maize cobs, and water. I asked a monk who had come up with me how long it took the gods to eat it all. He smiled, and answered evasively that the bowls must always be full; but on entering I had caught sight of some mice which quickly scuttled away in the darkness. What cruel irony, what a picture of self-satisfied vanity and religious humbug! The serving brother has been in the Pesu, has filled the bowls and said his daily prayers, has descended the steps and locked the door behind him. When all is quiet the mice come out of their holes. They climb upon the altar table, stand on their hind-legs, curl their tails round the votive bowls, and consume the nectar and ambrosia of the gods.

Could I not buy some of these charming figures? No, it could not be. The monk showed me a label which is attached with wire to each image. Every object belonging to the furniture of the convent has its number, and this number is entered in the general inventory. The prior is usually elected for a fixed term of years, and when he resigns his office he hands the list to his successor to be checked. If any object is missing, he is responsible and must pay the value.

A monk came up to bring tea for Rabsang and Tundup, who had seated themselves in the outer hall. I remained alone and gazed at the gods, mesmerized by their smiling gilded faces, their portly double chins, and their arched eyebrows. Then something wonderful happened. Their features changed and all turned their heads and looked at me. A curious feeling of awe took possession of me; had I insulted them through some want of delicacy? No, next moment they turned their heads away again and stared straight at the opposite wall. It was only a banner which in the draught from the window had moved so as to alter the shadow on the faces and give them an appearance of motion.

Linga is a ghostly castle, but Pesu was the most ghostly part of it all. There large drums and grinning masks shimmered like ghosts in the gloom, and the wind whistled mournfully through all the loopholes and openings. A man of strong nerves would get the horrors if he were compelled to spend a stormy autumn night alone in this hall of the gods, with the light of the moon falling through the loopholes on the images. He would listen with bated breath for every sound and crack. If the door below banged against its frame, he would hear some one entering the ante-chamber, and when the streamers on the roof fluttered in the wind, he would imagine the unknown person was approaching the hall with light steps and would in a second be bending over him; and the mice running over the floor, and the shutters swinging in the wind on creaking hinges, and the wind moaning in the window recesses and among the rafters, all would strain his imagination to the utmost and make him count the minutes till the dawn. After the gods had turned their heads towards me I felt that I should not like to be in such a position, but would rather go down again to my tent in the valley and sleep.

END OF VOL. I

1. The Latest Map of Tibet.

From the *Geographical Journal*, 1906. Note the blank space north of the Upper Brahmaputra with the word "Unexplored."

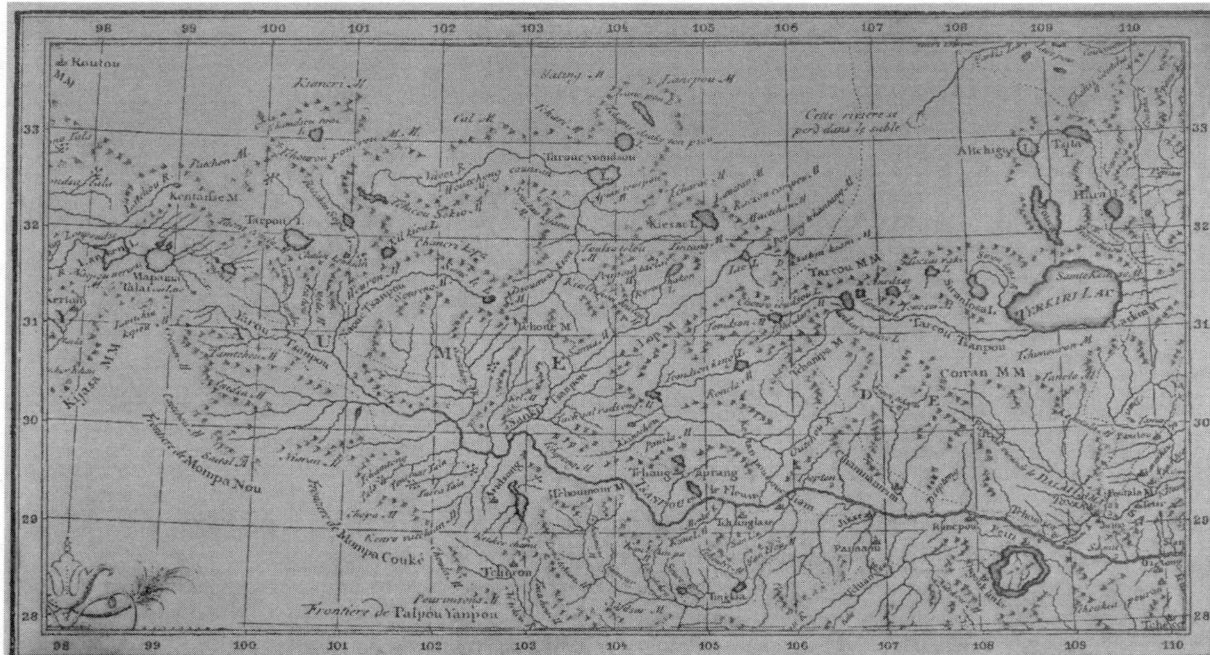

2. Carte Générale du Thibet ou Bout-tan.
(Avril 1733.) D'Anville, *Nouvel Atlas de la Chine, etc.* Paris 1737.

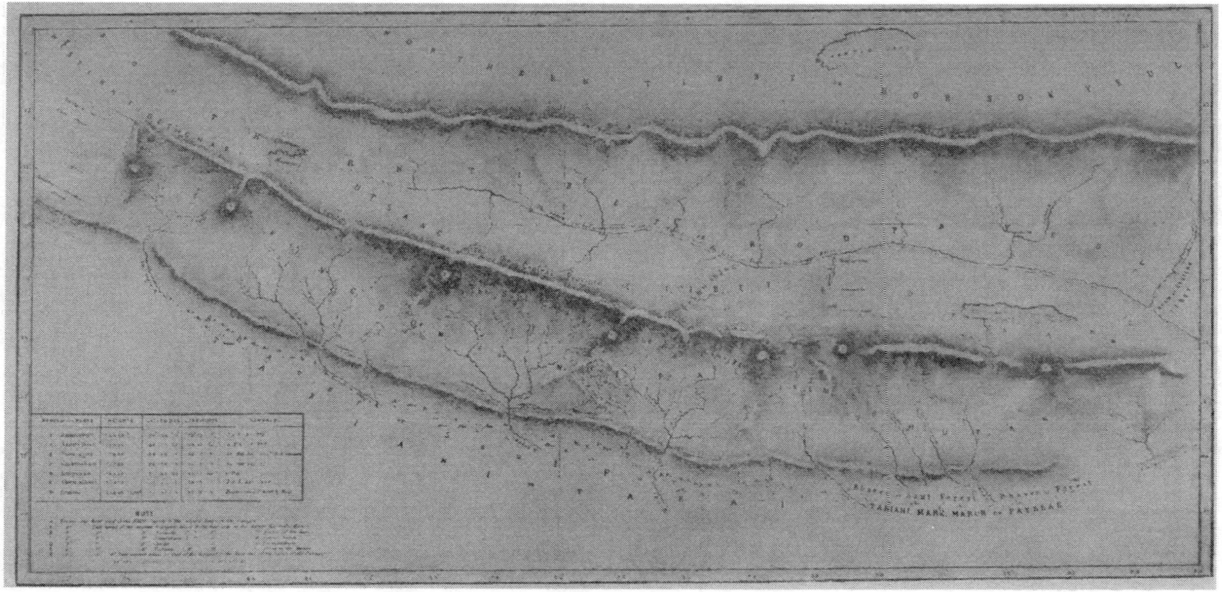

3. Map of Southern Tibet.

From *Selections from the Records of The Government of Bengal.* No. XXVII. Papers relative to the Colonization, Commerce, Physical Geography, etc. etc. of the Himalaya Mountains and Nepal. By Brian Houghton Hodgson, Esq., M.R.A.S. Calcutta, John Gray, *Calcutta Gazette* Office, 1857. Hodgson's "The Nyenchhen Thangla Chain, separating southern from northern Tibet" is only hypothetical, and does not represent the actual configuration.

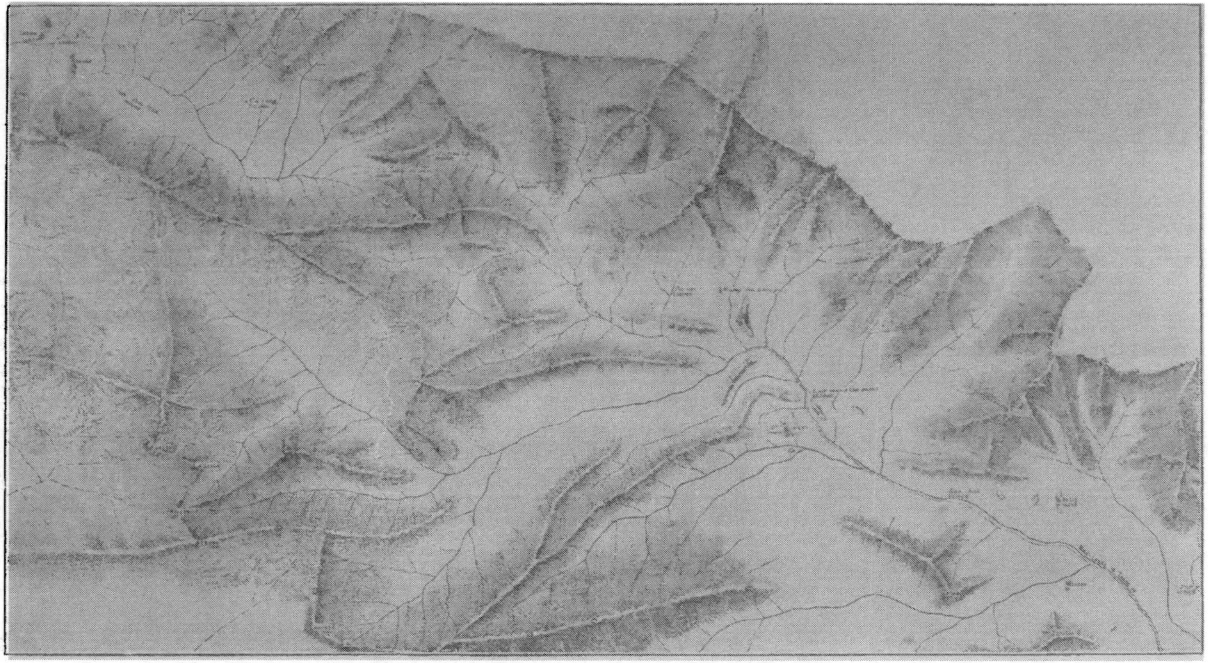

4. The Source-Region of the Brahmaputra.

After Major Ryder, 1904. The Chema-yundung is drawn as the main river, while the Kubi-tsangpo is shown as an affluent. In reality the Kubi-tsangpo is the source-stream, and the Chema-yundung, which receives the Marium-chu, only a tributary.

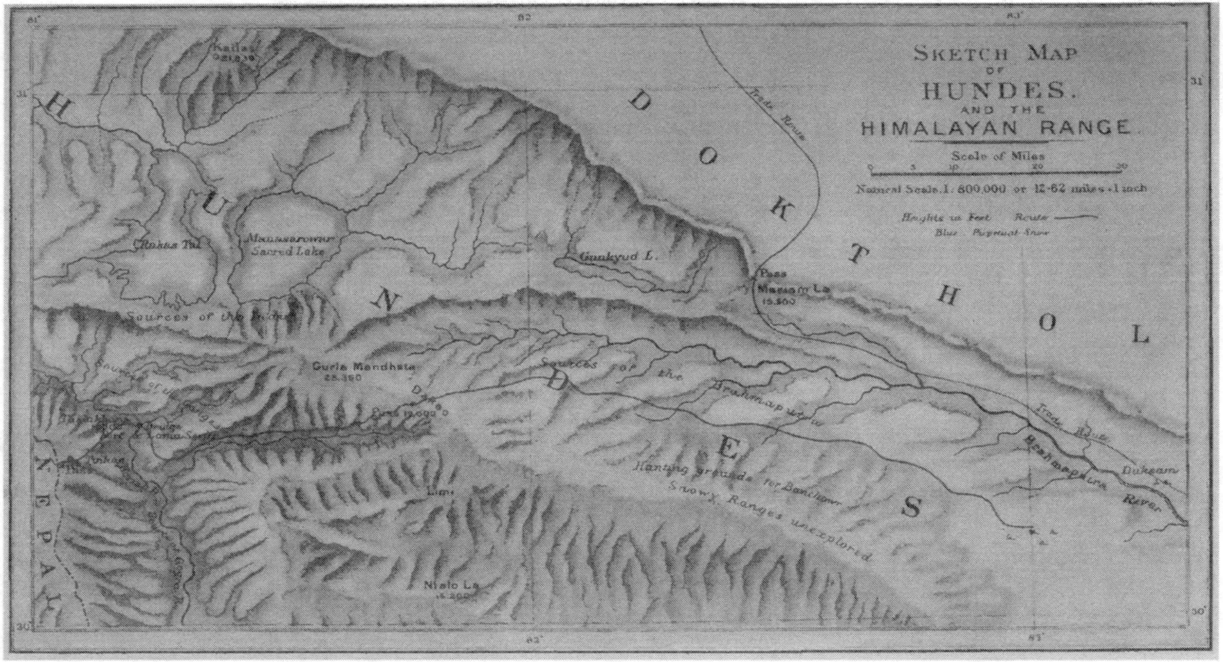

5. SKETCH-MAP OF WEBBER'S ROUTE IN 1866.

The Forests of Upper India. By Thomas W. Webber. London, Edward Arnold, 1902.

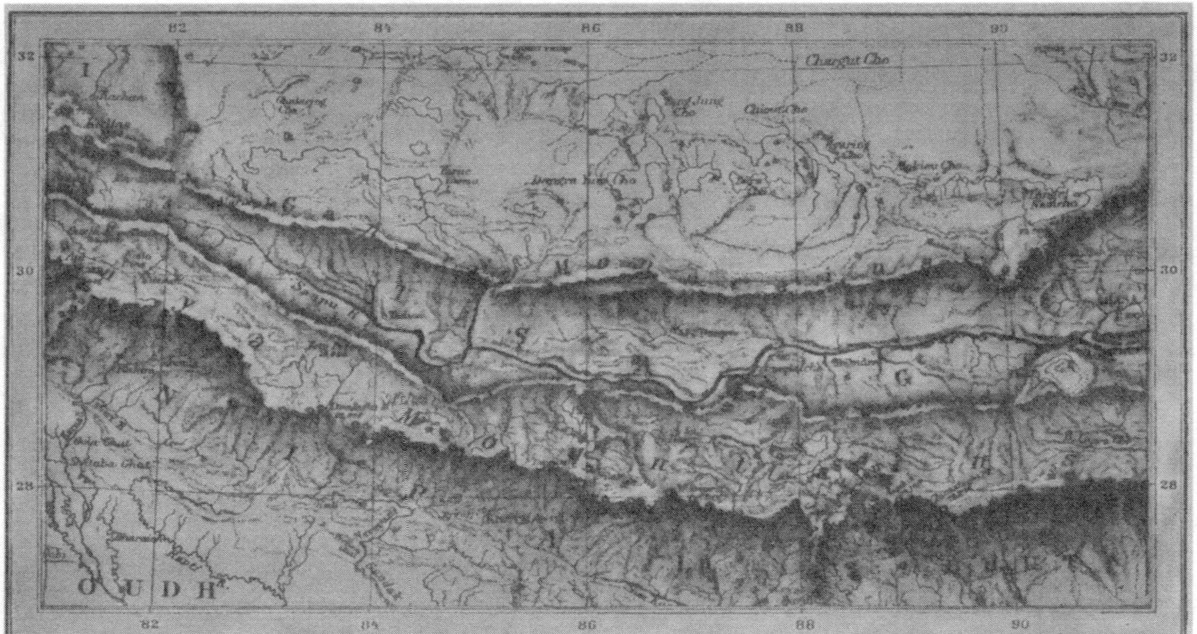

6. Saunders' Map of South Tibet.

From *Narratives of the Mission of George Bogle to Tibet and of the Journey of Thomas Manning to Lhasa.* By Clements Markham. London, Trübner and Co., 1879. Hypothetical form of the Trans-Himalaya ("Gangri Mountains") from 81° to 88½° E. long. Quite incorrect.

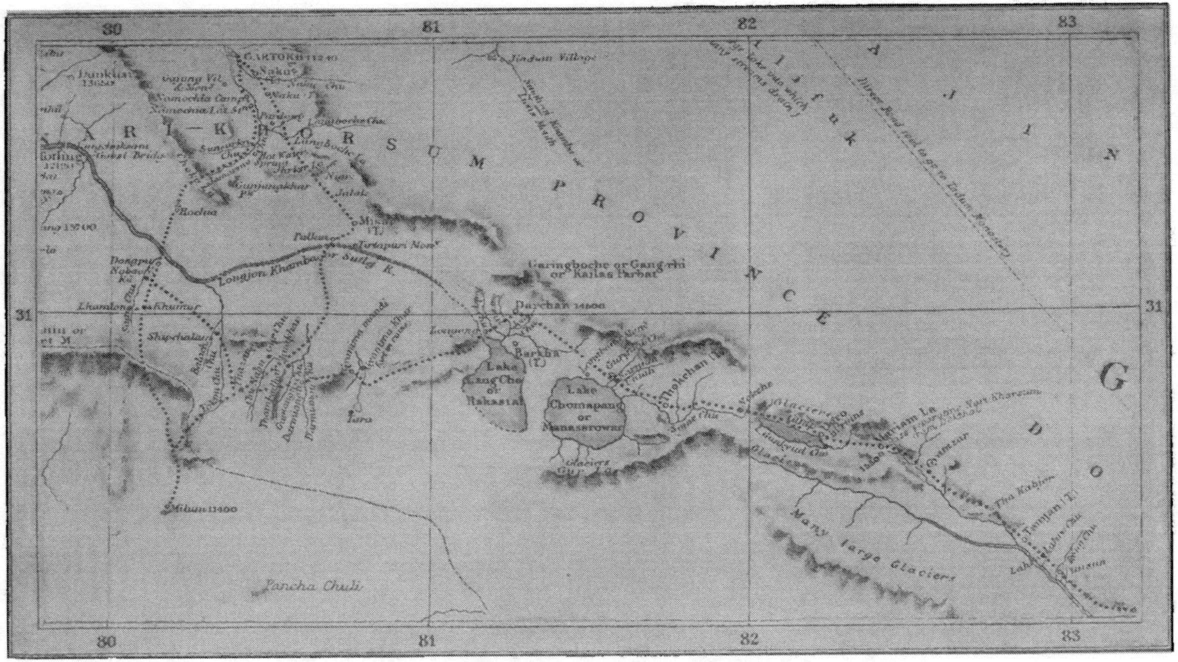

7. THE SOURCE-REGION OF THE BRAHMAPUTRA.
After Nain Sing, 1865. His route is shown by a dotted line.

WILLIAM E. CARSON'S
Mexico, the Wonderland of the South

Illustrated, cloth, 12mo, $2.25 net

Mr. Carson knows Mexico thoroughly, and he has drawn an accurate and fascinating pen picture of the country and of the people, of their everyday life and the everyday sights and scenes. It would be hard to discover anything worth seeing that he has not seen. He has wandered around the Mexican capital and other old cities; he has explored the gold and silver mines and visited some of the quaint health resorts; he has gone mountain climbing and tarpon fishing — and he tells of these many experiences in a most engaging manner. Many pictures of curious and out-of-the-way places add greatly to its beauty and to the value of the book for travellers and general readers.

DR. WILFRED T. GRENFELL'S
Labrador: The Country and the People

Illustrated, cloth, 8vo, $2.25 net

In this volume Dr. Grenfell supplies the only full and adequate account of Labrador — the country, its natural resources, the climatic conditions, and its people. In addition to the main body of the book, with its chapters on Physiography, the People of the Coast, the Missions, the Dogs, the various Fisheries, there are short chapters on the Flora, the Fauna, the Geology, etc., each by a scientific author of standing. The volume, profusely illustrated from photographs in the author's own collection, reveals an unknown land to the vast majority of readers.

ELLA HIGGINSON'S
Alaska: The Great Country

Illustrated, cloth, 12mo, $2.25 net

"No other book gives so clear an impression of the beauty and grandeur and vastness of our northernmost territory, nor so inspires one to explore its vastnesses. She has mingled enough of history and statistics to make it authoritative, and has embellished the tale with stories and anecdotes to prevent its being dull, and has succeeded in writing what might well be called a great book on a great subject." — *The Boston Evening Transcript.*

JAMES OUTRAM'S
In the Heart of the Canadian Rockies

Illustrated, cloth, 8vo, $2.50 net

"It is so inspired with the glories of the mountains, their sublime solitudes and silences, and their fascinating perils that it might well be called the epic of American mountaineering." — *World To-day.*

PUBLISHED BY

THE MACMILLAN COMPANY

64-66 Fifth Avenue, New York

CLIFTON JOHNSON'S BOOKS

Among English Hedgerows

With an introduction by HAMILTON W. MABIE, and over 100 illustrations

Cloth, 8vo, $2.25 net

"This book deserves to succeed, not only in America but in the country which it so lovingly depicts." — *The Spectator*, London.

Along French Byways

Fully illustrated, cloth, 8vo, $2.25 net

"Gives a singularly faithful and complete and well-balanced idea of the French peasantry and French rural life, manners, and customs." — *Boston Herald.*

The Isle of the Shamrock

Fully illustrated, cloth, 8vo, $2.00 net

"A most interesting book, full of lively sketches and anecdotes." — *London Daily News.*

The Land of Heather

Fully illustrated, cloth, 8vo, $2.00 net

"Not only Scotchmen, but every student of human nature will be pleased with this entertaining book. It describes typical people and scenes with much sympathy and appreciation." — *Brooklyn Standard Union.*

AMERICAN HIGHWAYS AND BYWAYS SERIES

Highways and Byways of the Mississippi Valley

Illustrated, cloth, 8vo, $2.00 net

Highways and Byways of the South

Illustrated, cloth, 8vo, $2.00 net

Highways and Byways of the Pacific Coast

Illustrated, cloth, 12mo, $2.00 net

New England and Its Neighbors

Illustrated, cloth, 8vo, $2.00 net

The Picturesque Hudson

Illustrated, cloth, 12mo, $1.25 net

---

and asses. The caravan had encamped in the village of Sadung on the north bank of the Tsangpo. Ishe had carried the four puppies in his dress on his breast, and had led Puppy with a string, that the young ones might be suckled on the way.

Next morning we awoke in beautiful weather. Eastwards were seen a series of brown mountain ridges with shading growing lighter and lighter as they dipped to the river, which stood out in still brighter colouring. The dwellers on the bank here called the Brahmaputra Tamchok-kamba, and said that it would fall for two months more, and would then rise till it attained its maximum at the end of July. Then it floods most of the valley bottom, and rolls majestically down, while all around assumes a fresher hue in the calm air of summer. At the end of September the level of the water becomes lower, and the river freezes only in cold winters.

We again retire from the holy districts, and ride through villages standing at the mouths of side valleys, past granitic promontories of the northern mountains, over fields and dunes, and camp, as before, in the garden of the Tashi Lama in Tanak. The four gentlemen that accompany us have brought their servants with them, and provide their own shelter, horses, and food. They have received on setting out a certain sum for this purpose, but for all that live at the expense of the villagers, eat and lodge free of cost, and order fresh horses for every day's march without paying any hire. They keep their travelling money intact in their pockets, and are therefore well pleased with their commission.

Both on the 28th and on the 29th, when we bivouacked in Rungma, we had violent storms from noon onwards, which blew in our faces. Nothing could be seen of the surroundings, and frequently I could not perceive the man just in front of me. We were pestered with sand, which grated under our teeth, irritated our backs, and made our eyes smart. Where the valley was contracted, the compressed wind blew with double strength, and the sand-clouds rolled in a greyish-yellow mass along the Brahmaputra valley.

We went on the 30th on to Karu in brilliant weather, still along the Tsangpo, which, green and free from ice, gently lapped against the southern foot of the mountains. Occasionally a boat glided downstream. The wild ducks on the shore are very tame, for no one is allowed to kill them, and, indeed, no one wishes to do so. Only a slight local traffic is noticeable. We miss the pilgrims we saw on the journey down; they are now at home again. We leave on the right the small convent Chuding with its nine nuns. On the steep mountain flanks are rocky paths used during high water, for the road we follow is quite covered in summer when the river is 5 feet higher.

In Karu wheat, barley, peas, and radishes are cultivated. We had made a short march, and I had ample time to interrogate the wise men of the village about the geography of the country, the means of communication, the climate, the habits of the river, and the directions of the wind; but I have no room for such particulars in this book. I would rather, instead, introduce our escort to the reader. Vang Yi Tyn is a Dungan, born in Shigatse; Tso Tin Pang has a Chinese father and a Tibetan mother, has his home in Shigatse, holds the Lamaistic faith, and murmurs prayers on the way; Lava Tashi and Shidar Pintso are pure Tibetans. All four are friendly and ready to help, and tell me in confidence that they mean to do their very best, that I may be pleased with them and give them good testimonials.

The last day of the month of March is marked in my journal with an asterisk. While the caravan marched straight towards Ye, the rest of us rode up a side valley, at the mouth of which lies the village Tarting-choro, surrounded by fields and willow trees. A small well-kept *mani-ringmo* is covered with stones polished by the river, in which the usual formula is not incised, but another in red and blue characters, namely, "Om mati moyi sale do." The figure 卍 is many times repeated, and indicates a connection with the Pembo sect, while the figure 卐 is a mark of the orthodox yellow-caps.

Farther up lies another village, having a *chhorten* with a gilded turret in a copse of old trees. A red house is

169. The Little Brother of his Holiness with a Servant.

TRANS-HIMALAYA

Aron Jonason Photogr

189. SVEN HEDIN. *Frontispiece*

TRANS-HIMALAYA

DISCOVERIES AND ADVENTURES IN TIBET

BY

SVEN HEDIN

WITH 388 ILLUSTRATIONS FROM PHOTOGRAPHS, WATER-COLOUR SKETCHES, AND DRAWINGS BY THE AUTHOR AND 10 MAPS

IN TWO VOLUMES

VOL. II

MACMILLAN AND CO., LIMITED
ST. MARTIN'S STREET, LONDON
1910

ISBN : 978-81-212-0342-5

Published, 2018

Published by

Gyan Publishing House
5, Ansari Road
Daryaganj, New Delhi-110002
Phone: 011-47034999, 9811692060
www.gyanbooks.com
E-mail: books@gyanbooks.com

Printed at: G. Print Process, Delhi.

CONTENTS

CHAPTER XLII

CHAPTER XLIII

CHAPTER XLIV

CHAPTER XLV

CHAPTER XLVI

CHAPTER XLVII

CHAPTER XLVIII

CHAPTER XLIX

CHAPTER L

CHAPTER LI

CHAPTER LII

CHAPTER LIII

CHAPTER LIV

CHAPTER LV

CHAPTER LVI

CHAPTER LVII

CHAPTER LVIII

CHAPTER LIX

CHAPTER LXIX

CHAPTER LXX

CHAPTER LXXI

CHAPTER LXXII

CHAPTER LXXIII

CHAPTER LXXIV

ILLUSTRATIONS

MAPS

CHAPTER XXXV

IMMURED MONKS

WE had heard of a lama who had lived for the last three years in a cave in the valley above the monastery of Linga, and though I knew that I should not be allowed to see either the monk or the interior of his ghastly dwelling, I would not miss the opportunity of at least gaining some slight notion of how he was housed.

On April 16, 1907, eighteen months to a day after I had left Stockholm, dreary windy weather prevailed, with thickly falling snow and dense clouds. We rode up to Linga, past rows of fine *chhortens*, left the last dormitories behind us, saw an old tree-trunk painted white and red, passed a small pool with crystal-clear spring water thinly frozen over, and heaps of *mani* stones with streamer poles, and then arrived at the small convent Samde-puk, built on the very point of a spur between two side valleys. It is affiliated to the Linga monastery, and has only four brethren, who all came to greet me heartily at the entrance.

It is a miniature copy, outwardly and inwardly, of those we have seen before. The *dukang* has only three pillars and one divan for the four monks, who read the mass together, nine prayer-cylinders of medium size which are set in motion by leathern straps, a drum and a gong, two masks with diadems of skulls, and a row of idols, among which may be recognized several copies of Chenresi and Sekiya Kōngma, the chief abbot of Sekiya.

A few steps to the south-west we passed over a sheet of schist with two stone huts at its foot containing brushwood and twigs for burning. In Samde-pu-pe were two small temples with altars of mud. In one of them were idols of medium size and sea shells, and before them incense smouldered, not in the usual form of sticks, but in powder. It was strewn in a zigzag line, was lighted at one end, and allowed to smoulder away to the other. Within was a statue of Lovun with two lights before it, and a shelf with writings called Chöna. Rain water had percolated in and formed white vertical channels in the plaster, and under the ceiling *kadakhs* and draperies fluttered in the draught. Here the mice were less disturbed than in the ghostly castle Pesu.

Close at hand at the foot of the mountain is the hermitage, *dupkang*, in which a hermit spends his days and years. It is built over a spring which bubbles up in the centre of the single room, a square apartment with each side five paces long. The walls are very thick, and are in one solid mass, unbroken by windows. The doorway is very low, and the wooden door is shut and locked; but that is not enough, so a wall of large blocks and smaller stones has been built before the door, and even the smallest interstices between them have been carefully filled up with pebbles. Not an inch of the door can be seen. But beside the entrance is a tiny tunnel through which the hermit's food can be pushed in. The amount of daylight which can penetrate through the long narrow loophole must be very small; and it does not shine in direct, for the front of the hut is shut in by a wall, forming a small court, which only the monk who brings the anchorite his daily ration may enter. A small chimney rises from the flat roof, for the hermit may make himself tea every sixth day, and for this purpose some sticks of firewood are pushed through the loophole twice in the month. Through the chimney, too, a feeble light may fall, and by means of these two vents the air is renewed in the cell.

"What is the name of the lama who is now walled up in this cell?" I asked.

"He has no name, and even if we knew it we durst not utter it. We call him merely the Lama Rinpoche" (according to Köppen, lama means *quo nemo est superior*, one who has no one over him; and Rinpoche means gem, jewel, holiness).

"Where has he come from?"

"He was born in Ngor in Naktsang."

"Has he relations?"

"That we do not know; and if he has any, they do not know that he is here."

"How long has he lived in the darkness?"

"It is now three years since he went in."

"And how long will he remain there?"

"Until he dies."

"May he never come out again into the daylight before his death?"

"No; he has taken the strictest of all oaths, namely, the sacred vow only to leave the cell as a corpse."

"How old is he?"

"We do not know his age, but he looked about forty."

"But what happens if he is ill? Cannot he get help?"

"No; he may never speak to another human being. If he falls ill he must wait patiently till he is better again or dies."

"You never know, then, how he is?"

"Not before his death. A bowl of *tsamba* is pushed every day into the opening, and a piece of tea and a piece of butter every sixth day; this he takes at night, and puts back the empty bowl to be filled for the next meal. When we find the bowl untouched in the opening we know that the immured man is unwell. If he has not touched the *tsamba* the next day our fears increase; and if six days pass and the food is not taken, we conclude he is dead and break open the entrance."

"Has that ever happened?"

"Yes; three years ago a lama died, who had spent twelve years in there, and fifteen years ago one died who had lived forty years in solitude and entered the darkness at the age of twenty. No doubt the Bombo has heard in Tong of the lama who lived in the hermitage of the monastery Lung-ganden-gompa for sixty-nine years, completely shut off from the world and the light of day."

"But is it not possible that the prisoner may speak to

the monk who pushes the *tsamba* dish into the loophole? There is no witness present to see that all is correct."

"That could never happen and is not allowed," answered my informant with a smile; "for the monk outside would be eternally damned were he to set his mouth to the loophole and try to talk to the recluse, and the latter would break the charm if he spoke from within. If the man in there were to speak now, the three years he has passed there already would not be put down to his credit, and he would not like that. If, however, a lama in Linga or Samde-puk falls ill, he may write his complaint and a request for the anchorite's intercession on a piece of paper, which is placed in the *tsamba* bowl and pushed into the opening. Then the recluse prays for the sick man, and if the latter has faith in the power of prayer, and holds no unseemly conversation in the meantime, the intercession of the Lama Rinpoche takes effect after two days and the patient gets well again. On the other hand, the recluse never makes any communication in writing."

"We are now only a couple of paces from him. Does he not hear what we are saying, or, at least, that some one is talking outside his den?"

"No, the sound of our voices cannot reach him, the walls are too thick; and even if it were the case, he would not notice it, for he is buried in contemplation. He no longer belongs to this world; he probably crouches day and night in a corner, repeating prayers he knows by heart, or reading in the holy books he has with him."

"Then he must have enough light to read by?"

"Yes, a small butter lamp stands on a shelf before two images, and its light suffices him. When the lamp goes out it is pitch-dark inside."

Filled with strange thoughts, I took leave of the monk and went slowly down the path which the recluse had only passed along once in his life. Before us was the splendid view which might never delight his eyes. When I had descended to the camp I could not look up the monastery valley without thinking of the unfortunate man sitting up there in his dark hole.

Poor, nameless, unknown to any one, he came to Linga,

where, he had heard, a cave-dwelling stood vacant, and informed the monks that he had taken the vow to enter for ever into darkness. When his last day in this world of vanity dawned, all the monks of Linga followed him in deep silence, with the solemnity of a funeral, to his grave in the cave, and the door was closed on him for the rest of his life. I could picture to myself the remarkable procession, the monks in their red frocks, silent and grave, bending their bodies forward and turning their eyes to the ground, and walking slowly step by step as though they would let the victim enjoy the sun and light as long as possible. Were they inspired with admiration of his tremendous fortitude, compared with which everything I can conceive, even dangers infallibly leading to death, seems to me insignificant? For, as far as I can judge, less fortitude is required when a hero, like Hirosé, blockades the entrance of Port Arthur, knowing that the batteries above will annihilate him, than to allow oneself to be buried alive in the darkness for forty or sixty years. In the former case the suffering is short, the glory eternal; in the latter the victim is as unknown after death as in his lifetime, and the torture is endless, and can only be borne by a patience of which we can have no conception.

No doubt the monks escorted him with the same tenderness and the same sympathy as the priest feels when he attends a criminal to execution. But what can have been his own feelings during this last progress in the world. We all have to pass along this road, but we do not know when. But he knew, and he knew that the sun would never again shine warmly on his shoulders and would never produce lights and shadows on the heaven-kissing mountains around the grave that awaited him.

Now they have reached their destination and the door of the tomb stands open. They enter in, spread a mat of interlaced strips of cloth in a corner, set up the images of the gods, and lay the holy books in their place; in one corner they place a wooden frame like those go-carts in which infants learn to walk, and which he will not use till death comes upon him. They take their seats and recite prayers, not the usual prayers for the dead, but others which deal with the glorified light and life of Nirvana. They rise, bid him farewell, go out and close the door. Now he is alone and will never hear the sound of a human voice except his own, and when he says his prayers no one will be there to hear him.

What were his thoughts when the others had gone, and the short hollow echo had died away of the noise he heard when the door was shut for the last time, only to be opened again when he was a corpse? Perhaps something like what Fröding has expressed in his verse:

> Here breaks the soul from every bond
> That fetters to this life its pinion;
> Here starts the way to the dark beyond,
> The land of eternal oblivion.

He hears the brethren rolling the heavy stones to the door with levers, piling them up one on another in several layers, and filling up all chinks with smaller stones and fragments. It is not yet quite dark, for there are crevices in the door, and daylight is still visible at the upper edge. But the wall rises. At length there is only a tiny opening through which the last beam falls into the interior of his tomb. Does he become desperate; does he jump up, thrust his hands against the door and try to catch one more glimpse of the sun, which in another moment will vanish from his sight for ever? No one knows and no one will ever know; not even the monks who were present and helped to block up the entrance can answer this question. But he is but a man and he saw how a flagstone was fitted over the hole through which a last ray of daylight fell; and now he has darkness before him, and wherever he turns there is impenetrable darkness.

He assumes that the other monks have gone down again to Samde-puk and Linga. How shall he pass the evening. He need not begin at once to read his holy books; there is plenty of time for that, perhaps forty years. He sits on the mat and leans his head against the wall. Now all his reminiscences come with great distinctness into his mind. He remembers the gigantic characters in the quartzite, "Om mani padme hum," and he murmurs half dreaming the holy syllables, "Oh! thou jewel in the lotus. Amen!" But only a feeble echo answers him. He waits and listens, and then hearkens to the voices of his memory. He wonders whether the first night is falling, but it cannot be darker than it is already in his prison, his grave. Overcome by the travail of his soul, he sleeps, tired and weary, in his corner.

When he awakes, he feels hungry, crawls to the opening and finds the bowl of *tsamba* in the tunnel. With water from the spring he prepares his meal, eats it, and, when he has finished, puts the bowl in the loophole again. Then he sits cross-legged, his rosary in his hands, and prays. One day he finds tea and butter in the bowl and some sticks beside it. He feels about with his hands and finds the flint, and steel, and the tinder, and kindles a small fire under the tea-can. By the light of the flame he sees the interior of his den again, lights the lamp before the images, and begins to read his books; but the fire goes out and six days must pass before he gets tea again.

The days pass and now comes autumn with its heavy rains; he hears them not, but the walls of his den seem to be moister than usual. It seems to him a long time since he saw the sun and the daylight for the last time. And years slip by and his memory grows weak and hazy. He has read the books he brought with him again and again, and he cares no more for them; he crouches in his corner and murmurs their contents, which he has long known by heart. He lets the beads of his rosary slip through his fingers mechanically, and stretches out his hand for the *tsamba* bowl unconsciously. He crawls along the walls feeling the cold stones with his hands, if haply he may find a chink through which a ray of light can pass. No, he hardly knows now what it is like outside on sunny paths. How slowly time passes! Only in sleep does he forget his existence and escape from the hopelessness of the present. And he thinks: "What is a short earthly life in darkness compared to the glorious light of eternity?" The sojourn in darkness is only a preparation. Through days and nights and long years of solitude the pondering monk seeks the answer to the riddle of life and the riddle of death, and clings to the belief that he will live again in a glorified form of existence when his period of trial is over. It is faith alone which can explain his inconceivable fortitude of mind.

It is difficult to picture to oneself the changes through which the lama passes during successive decades in the darkness of his cell. His sight must become weak, perhaps be extinguished altogether. His muscles shrink, his senses become more and more clouded. Longing for the light cannot pursue him as a fixed idea, for it is in his power to write down his decision to curtail his time of trial, and return to the light, on one of the leaves of his books with a splinter dipped in soot. He has only to place such a paper in the empty *tsamba* bowl. But the monks had never known a case of the kind. They only knew that the lama who had been walled in for sixty-nine years had wished to see the sun again before he died. I had heard from monks who were in Tong at the time that he had written down his wish to be let out. He was all bent up together and as small as a child, and his body was nothing but a light-grey parchment-like skin and bones. His eyes had lost their colour, were quite bright and blind. His hair hung round his head in uncombed matted locks and was pure white. His body was covered only by a rag, for time had eaten away his clothing and he had received no new garments. He had a thin unkempt beard, and had never washed himself all the time or cut his nails. Of the monks who sixty-nine years before had conducted him to his cell, not one survived. He was then quite young himself, but all his contemporaries had been removed by death, and new generations of monks had passed through the cloisters; he was a complete stranger to them all. And he had scarcely been carried out into the sunlight when he too gave up the ghost.

In analysing the state of such a soul, fancy has free play, for we know nothing about it. Waddell and Landon, who took part in Younghusband's expedition to Lhasa, and visited the hermits' caves at Nyang-tö-ki-pu, say that the monks who have there retired into perpetual darkness first underwent shorter experiences of isolation, the first lasting six months, and the second three years and ninety-three days, and that those who had passed through the second period of trial showed signs that they were intellectually inferior to other monks. The cases which the two Englishmen have described seem not to have been so severe a trial as the one I saw and heard about in Linga, for in the Nyang-tö-ki-pu caves the lama who waited on the recluse tapped on a stone slab which closed the small opening, and at this signal the immured lama put his hand out of this door for his food; he immediately drew the stone shutter to again, but in this way he would at least see the light of the sun for a moment every day. In the cases described by Waddell and Landon the immured monks had passed some twenty years in confinement. Waddell, who has a thorough knowledge of Lamaism, believes that the custom of seclusion for life is only an imitation of the practice of pure Indian Buddhism, which enjoins periodical retreats from the world for the purpose of self-examination and of acquiring greater clearness in abstruse questions. In his opinion the Tibetans have made an end of the means.

Undoubtedly this opinion is correct, but it is not exhaustive. It may be that the future hermit has in religious delusion come to the decision to allow himself to be buried alive. But does he clearly conceive what this means? If he became dull and insensible like an animal in his cell, all his energy and his power of will would be deadened, and what seemed to him, when he entered, to be worth striving for, would gradually become more and more indifferent to him. But this is not the case, for he adheres firmly to his decision, and therefore his energy must remain unimpaired. He must possess a steadfast faith, an immovable conviction, which is exposed to a harder trial because he is alone and death alone can visit him in his cave. Possibly he becomes by degrees a victim of self-delusion, so that his longing for the last hour in the long night of his den gives place to the feeling that he is always at the moment when the hour-glass of time has run down. He must have lost all idea of time, and the darkness of the grave appears to him only as a second in eternity. For the means he formerly had of marking the flight of time and impressing it on his memory no longer exist. The changes from winter to summer, from day to night, are only made known to him by the rise or fall of the temperature in his den. He remembers that several rainy seasons have passed by, and perhaps they seem to him to follow closely on one another while his brain is clouded by monotony. It is inconceivable that he does not become insane, that he does not call out for the light, that he does not jump up and run his head against the wall in the agony of despair, or beat it against the sharp edges of the stones till he bleeds to death and frees himself by committing suicide.

But he waits patiently for death, and death may delay its coming for ten or twenty years. His remembrance of the world and life outside his cell becomes fainter and fainter; he has long forgotten the dawn in the east and the golden clouds of sunset; and when he looks up his dimmed eyes perceive no stars twinkling in the night, only the black ceiling of his cave. At last, however, after long years have passed in the darkness, suddenly a great brilliancy flashes out—that is, when Death comes, takes him by the hand, and leads him out. And Death has not to wait, entreat, and coax, for the lama has waited and longed for his welcome and only guest and deliverer. If he has had his mind still clear, he has taken the little wooden stand under his arms so that he may die in the same sacred position in which Buddha is represented in all the thousands of statues and pictures which have come under our notice in our wanderings through the cloister temples of Tibet.

When the *tsamba* bowl, which has been filled daily for so many long years, remains at last untouched and the six days have expired, the cave is opened and the abbot of the monastery sits down beside the deceased and prays for him, while all the other monks pray in the *dukang* hall for five or six days together. Then the body is wrapped in a white garment, a covering called *ringa* is placed on his head, and he is burned on a pyre. The ashes are collected, kneaded together with clay, and moulded into a small pyramid, which is deposited in a *chhorten*.

The Linga monks said that an ordinary lama, when he dies, is cut in pieces and abandoned to the birds. This process is performed here by five lamas, who, though they belong to the monastery, attend the service in the *dukang*, and drink tea with the other monks, are still considered unclean, and may not eat with the other brethren. Also when nomads die in the neighbourhood, their services are required, but then the relatives are bound to provide them with horses and to undertake that the property of the deceased shall pass into the possession of the monastery.

For days and weeks I could not drive away the picture I had formed in my mind of the Lama Rinpoche, before whose cell we had stood and talked. And still less could I could forget his predecessor, who had lived there forty years. I fancied I could hear the conch which summoned the monks to the funeral mass of the departed. I pictured to myself the scene in the cave where the lama, crouching in rags on the floor, stretches out his withered hands to Death, who, kindly smiling like the skull masks in the temples, gives him one hand while he holds a brightly burning lamp in the other. The features of the monk are transfigured in a reflexion of Nirvana, and forgetting the "Om mani padme hum" that for tens of years has reverberated from the walls of his den, he raises, as the trumpet blasts sound out from the temple roof, a song of victory, which calls to mind the following strophe from the myths of another people (*Frithiof's Saga*, Blackley's translation):

> Hail, ye deities bright!
> Ye Valhalla sons!
> Earth fadeth away; to the heavenly feast
> Glad trumpets invite
> Me, and blessedness crowns,
> As fair, as with gold helm, your hastening guest.

CHAPTER XXXVI

OVER THE CHANG-LA-POD-LA

WE had stayed three days near the monastery Linga, when we went on north-westwards on April 17 up the narrow My-chu valley, in which the volume of water was now considerably diminished. Space does not permit me to describe in detail this wonderful road and its wild beauty. From the expansion of the valley at Linga routes run eastwards and westwards into the mountains, with branches to numerous villages, of which I noted down the names and approximate positions. The traffic is now much less, but still numerous *manis* and other religious symbols stand beside the solitary path.

We ride along the steep slopes of the right bank; below us the river forms rapids, and the way is dangerous, especially with a horse that is not sure on its feet. Robert's small bay filly stumbled and fell, so that the rider was thrown headlong to the ground. Had he rolled down the slope he would have been lost; but fortunately he fell towards the mountain.

We encamped in the village Langmar, consisting of a few scattered houses, at the entrance of the small side valley Langmar-pu.

We still have hired horses, and now yaks also, and the caravan is divided into the same detachments as before. Sonam Tsering and Guffaru command their sections. Tsering's party sets out last and is the last to come to rest, and Muhamed Isa supervises the whole. In the evening he is massaged by two men selected for the purpose, of whom Rehim Ali is one. There is still *chang*,

190. Hermit's Grotto near the Chang-la-Pod-la.

the harmless, but still intoxicating, beer. Among the singers at the camp-fires, Tsering, as usual, deserves the first prize. He gives me no end of amusement; he sings like a cow, or at best like a burst temple drum. His voice cracks continually, and he loses the time and the melody without being the least put out. But he considers his singing very fine, and the others take pleasure in it; one can tell from a distance that the tears are coming into his eyes. Sometimes he pauses to explain the subject of the ballad and take a drink, and then he goes on again. When all the others are asleep, and all is so quiet in the camp that the rushing of the stream is audible and from time to time the bark of a dog, Tsering's rough voice trilling harshly still resounds among the mountains.

Next day we draw near to the main crest of the Trans-Himalaya, for to my great surprise and delight we have been conducted in this direction. Granite still predominates, and in it erosion has excavated the wild forms of the valleys; the way is tolerably good, but very stony; small strips of ice lie along both banks of the stream, within which the bright green water fills the valley with the roar of its impetuosity. The dark green of a kind of juniper called *pama* is a relief to the eyes, which otherwise perceive nothing but grey slopes of detritus.

The river here is named Langmar-tsangpo, but it is really only the upper course of the My-chu. It is formed by the Ke-tsangpo coming from the north and the Govo-tsangpo from the west. The former, called in its upper course Ogorung-tsangpo, descends from the main watershed of the Trans-Himalaya, and must therefore be considered the main stream. I was told that its source may be reached in a day and a half from the junction of the valleys. On the left bank of the Govo a thicket of *pama* shrubs grows, and a safe bridge of three arches spans the river. Over this bridge runs the important trade route to Tok-jalung which I have mentioned above. Herds of yaks and flocks of sheep graze on the slopes, and circular penfolds remind us of our life in the Chang-tang. A little farther up we cross the Govo, which is half frozen over; springs and brooks from the side valleys adorn the scene with cascades of ice. The river is said to be here so swollen in summer that it cannot be crossed at any point. To the north and south snowy mountains are visible.

In the village of Govo, consisting of seven stone houses, barley is cultivated and yields a moderate crop; but the inhabitants are not dependent on the harvest, for they also possess sheep, goats, and yaks, with which they migrate northwards in summer. Govo is the last village where agriculture is pursued, so we here find ourselves on the boundary between tillage and grazing, and also between stone houses and black tents (Illust. 182).

We have, then, still time to look into an ordinary Tibetan stone hut belonging to a family in comfortable circumstances. The walls are built of untrimmed bare stones, but the crevices are stopped with earth to keep out the wind. Through a labyrinth of walls and over round stones where the tripping foot seldom touches the ground we come to two yards where goats and calves are kept. In a third is a loom, at which a half-naked coppery-brown woman is working, and in a fourth sits an old man engaged in cutting up *pama* shrubs.

From this yard we entered a half-dark room, with a floor of mud, and two openings in the roof, through which the smoke escapes and the daylight enters. The roof consists of beams overlaid with a thatch of brushwood, which is covered all over with soil and flat stones—it must be nice and dry when it rains. There sat an elderly woman telling off her *manis* on a rosary of porcelain beads.

The next room is the kitchen, the general living-room and the principal apartment of the house. At a projecting wall stands the stone cooking-range with round black-edged holes for saucepans and teapots of baked clay. A large earthen pot, standing on the fire, contains barley, which is eaten parched; a stick with a stiff piece of leather at the end is twirled round in the barley between the palms so that it may be roasted equally. It tastes delicious.

I went about, turned over all the household utensils and made an inventory, and not in Swedish only, but also in Tibetan. There were many different vessels of iron, clay, and wood for all kinds of purposes, a large wooden ladle, a tea sieve of sheet-iron, an iron spoon, an ash shovel, iron fire-tongs, and a thing called a *thagma*, an iron blade fitted into a piece of wood, something like a closed pocket-knife, and used to dress newly woven material. A large clay jug was filled with *chang*. A small cubical vessel divided into four by small cross pieces of wood is used to measure corn. Brick-tea is pulverized with a stone shaped like a cucumber in a deep wooden cup. A knife-blade with a haft at either end is used in preparing and tawing hides. Under one of the smoke vents stood a small hearth for an open fire with an iron tripod. A large leathern sack was filled with *tsamba*, and two sheep's stomachs held fat and butter. On a rack a quantity of sheep's trotters, dusty and dirty, were arranged; when they are several months old they are used to make soup, which is thickened with *tsamba*. Tea, salt, and tobacco are kept in large and small bags.

We saw likewise all kinds of religious objects, votive bowls, joss-sticks, and small image cases; also bales of home-woven textiles, coloured ribands for sewing on skin coats and boots, knives, hatchets, sabres and spears, which, we were told, are for fighting thieves and robbers; a pair of bellows, two sacks of dry dung for fuel, baskets, hand-mills for grinding barley, consisting of two round flat stones with a handle on the upper one; lastly, an oil-lamp and an oil-can, and a cylindrical tub with iron hoops full of water. In a corner lay heaps of skins and garments, and against the wall were two sleeping-places still in disorder.

In another store-room there were provisions in sacks, barley, green fodder, peas, and great joints of meat. Here three young women and a troop of children had taken refuge; we left them room to escape, and they ran away screaming loudly as if all the knives in the house were at their throats. In the room were balances for weighing, consisting of a rounded staff with a stone weight at one end and a dried yak hide at the other. Behind a partition straw was kept. There are high inconvenient thresholds between the rooms, and the usual bundles of rods on the roof to protect the house from evil spirits.

After this expedition we inspected the tents of our escort, where a fire was burning in a broken clay pot, and a skillet stood over it on a tripod. The smoke escapes through the long slit between the two halves of which the tent is composed. The owners of the tent were writing their report to the authorities in Shigatse, informing them that we were on the right road. At the same time they were eating their dinner of mutton, a year old, dry and hard; it must not come near the fire. One of them cut it into strips and distributed it among his comrades. He had been for twenty years a lama in the monastery Lung-ganden in Tong, but a few years before had been ejected from the confraternity because he had fallen in love with a woman. He spoke of it himself, so it was doubtless true.

Robert's bay horse was reported dead on the morning of April 20. His late tumble now seemed to us like an omen; though fat and sleek, he died suddenly about midnight. We now ride on again towards higher regions over uncomfortable blocks of stone, but the valley becomes more open and the relative heights diminish. Though the little that is left of the stream still swirls and foams, the ice becomes thicker, and at last covers almost all the bed, and the water is heard rushing and murmuring under it. Juicy moss skirts the banks, the view becomes more extensive, and the whole character of the landscape becomes alpine. We saw ten men with guns in a sheep-fold, carrying gun-rests with yellow and red pennants on one of the prongs; perhaps they were highway robbers. Dark clouds sweep over the ridges, and in a minute we are in the midst of icy-cold drifting snow, but it does not last long.

The last bit of road was awful, nothing but boulders and débris, which we could sometimes avoid by riding over the ice of the river. The camping-ground was called Chomo-sumdo, a valley fork in a desolate region, but the escort had seen that some straw and barley were brought up on yaks for our horses.

From here we had to ride on the ice, smooth and firm after 27° degrees of frost in the night. The neighbourhood is not, however, uninhabited, for yaks and sheep were seen grazing in many places, belonging to nomads migrating northwards or merchants coming from Tok-jalung. At two black tents the people were packing up for the day's march; they had goats, with strips of red cloth bound round the ears.

A little farther up is a precipitous rock on the right side of the valley, and two caves open their black mouths in the wall. The lower one (Illust. 190) is the entrance to a passage leading to the upper, where a famous hermit has fixed his solitary abode. The upper opening has a partly natural balcony decorated with streamer-poles and ribands. Below the lower stand *mani* cairns, long garlands of string with coloured prayer-strips, a prayer-mast, and a metal idol in a niche of the rock.

We tethered our horses at the edge of the ice and went up to the lower grotto. Here two young nuns from Kirong (on the border of Nepal) met us, and two mendicant monks from Nepal, one of whom spoke Hindustani, so that Robert could converse with him. The nuns were pretty, well-grown, sun-burnt, and somewhat like gypsies; their large black eyes had the shimmer of velvet, and their black hair was parted on the forehead and fell in luxuriant waves over their shoulders; they were clothed in red rags and wore Tibetan boots adorned with red ribands. They spoke cheerfully and pleasantly in strikingly soft, extremely sympathetic voices, and were not in the least timid. Their simple dwelling, which we saw, was in the great entrance of the grotto, under a smoke-blackened vault, surrounded by a small wall and a palisade of *pama* branches, and partly hung with cloth. A sleeping-place was made of rugs of interwoven strips of cloth, and a tea-kettle was boiling on the fire. One of the men had a thick pigtail and a red lama frock; the other wore a sheepskin, and had not had his hair cut in the present, twentieth, century. The dwelling proper was situated in a higher part of the cavern.

All four had come in autumn, and were waiting for the warmer season to proceed to Lhasa, and return thence home again. In the meantime they voluntarily waited on the two holy hermits sojourning in this mountain, and thereby earned their living and gained merit, according to the ideas of their order. When they go off again on their wanderings, other serving brethren and sisters will be found ready to take their place.

A winding staircase on the left, partly natural and partly constructed of flagstones, leads to the upper regions of the cavern. At first it is dark, but becomes lighter as we approach a loophole in the rock. Here and there are streamer-poles, and the holy syllables are incised. From the loophole the staircase turns steeply to the right; if we slipped on the smooth stone we should tumble down right into the nuns' kitchen, which from here looks like the bottom of a well. The passage ends at a point where a small stone staircase goes up to a trap-door covered with a slab. Pushing aside the slab, one reaches the larger grotto chamber of which we had seen the opening from the valley. But the serving brothers and sisters would not take us so high.

In this upper grotto, Choma-taka, the 100-years-old hermit, Gunsang Ngurbu, of high repute in all the country for his holiness, has dwelt for seven years. Gunsang means hermit, and Ngurbu is a very common name signifying precious stone. Every seventh day his attendants place *tsamba*, water, tea, and fuel on the steps under the trap-door, and these things are taken in by the old man, who may not speak with men, but only with the gods. Through a hole under the slab I caught sight of a *chhorten* constructed of stones and mud, and some painted pictures of gods on the wall of the grotto. Behind the *chhorten*, and unfortunately out of sight, the old man sat in a niche in the wall, crouching down and saying his prayers; now and then he blows a shell horn.

I wished to push aside the shutter and mount into the upper grotto, but the consciences of my companions would

191. Robert and Rabsang by the Ice on the Way to the Chang-la-Pod-la.

192. A Lhadse decked with Mani-Stones and Prayer-Streamers.
(N.W. of the Kore-la.)

not permit such a thing for all the money in the world. It would disturb the old man in his meditations, and interrupt the period of his seclusion, and, moreover, the old man would throw stones at us. The life of the hermit Ngurbu must be idyllic compared to that of the immured Linga monks, for he sees the valley, the sun, the whirling snow, and the stars sparkling in the sky; but he must suffer from ennui. In another grotto, side by side with Ngurbu's, lives another hermit, but the two have never met and know nothing of one another. They may eat no meat, only *tsamba* and tea, and they receive these from the neighbouring nomads and the travellers passing along the road.

After this digression we cross the ice of the river again and pass up over the ever-present detritus. Before us is the flattish saddle of the Chang-la-Pod-la. We accomplish the ascent with great effort, the icy wind blowing right in our faces. I cannot commence my observations at the cairn till I have warmed my hands over a dung fire. The view is limited, flat, and of little use for orientation. However, towards the way we have come, we can see the deeply eroded valleys, and we seem to be higher than the ridges enclosing them. The height is 18,284 feet. Chang signifies north, north country; Pod or Pö, Tibet, *i.e.* Tibet proper, chiefly inhabited by a settled population. Chang-la-Pod-la is, then, the pass between the northern tableland of the nomads and the country to the south having drainage to the sea. It is this property of a boundary between these two regions which renders the Trans-Himalaya of such prime importance, and therefore there are many passes called Chang-la-Pod-la. Often and often I was told that a pass, whatever might be its especial name, was a Chang-la-Pod-la when it lay on the watershed between the inland drainage of the north and the river basin of the Tsangpo in the south. I had then crossed the Trans-Himalaya a second time by a pass lying 44 miles to the west of the Sela-la, and had been able to ascertain that the huge range of the Nien-chen-tang-la extends thus far. It was still more my earnest desire to follow it step by step to the west.

After we had encamped on the pass, where the thermometer fell at night to $-9\frac{1}{2}°$, we rode on April 22 slowly down the valley of the Shak-chu river, which gradually becomes broader, and is begirt by flat rounded mountains, in which rock *in situ* seldom occurs. We have passed from the maze of mountains intersected by the affluents of the My-chu, abundantly fed by the rains, on to the wide plains of the plateau country, and notice again that the Trans-Himalaya is also an extraordinarily important climatological boundary.

The Lapsen-Tari is a heap of clods with a sheaf of rods stuck in the middle, from which streamer strings are carried to other rods. From this point there is a fine view over the plateau and its wreath of mountains. To the north, 55° west, we see the Targo-gangri again, but more majestic, more isolated, and more dominant than from the Ngangtse-tso, where, shrouded in clouds and surrounded by other mountains, it was less conspicuous.

Just at the mound we passed the last corner which obscured the view, and suddenly the whole grand mountain appeared in its dazzling whiteness, shining like a lighthouse over the sea of the plateau, in a mantle of firn fields and blue glistening ice, and rising bold and sharply against the sky of purest azure blue. The mound is therefore placed where the traveller coming from Shigatse first comes in sight of the holy mountain. Our guides bared their heads and murmured prayers. Two pilgrims, whom we had seen at the grotto of the hermits, lighted a fire and threw into it a scented powder, an offering of incense to the gods of Targo-gangri. South and south-west runs a lofty range, of uniform height, with patches of snow glittering in the sun on its brownish-purple summit—another part of the Trans-Himalaya.

As we sat here a trading caravan came along the road to Penla-buk, which lies on the west side of the Dangra-yum-tso, and is a rendezvous for gold-prospectors and wool-dealers. Our tents formed a little village on the Kyangdam plain, where wild asses abound, and some sixty nomads of the neighbourhood encamped around it.

In the evening the escort from Ghe presented themselves to inform me that as we were now in the Largep district, subject to the Labrang, they would return home and consign us to a new guard. The latter consisted of five men far advanced in life. Their leader was a small grey-headed man with trembling hands and very indistinct enunciation. When the Ghe men, who longed to return to their warmer villages, had gone off next morning in spite of a violent storm, I had a serious talk with the new men. They intended to lead us over the pass Sha-la (Trans-Himalaya) in the south-west, where the Targo-tsangpo rises, on the banks of which we had passed the day. According to Nain Sing's map this river flows round the east side of Targo-gangri, and then enters the Dangra-tso, as the holy lake is called here. But Nain Sing was never there, and I wished to gain an insight into the geography of the country. So we came to an agreement that we should travel north-westwards; and I pointed out to the men that Raga-tasam was put down in our passport as the next place; that two roads led thither, one over the Sha-la, the other deviating northwards to the Targo-gangri, and that I had chosen the latter. The passport prohibited us from visiting Lhasa, Gyangtse, and the monastery Sekiya-gompa, but contained not a single word about the road to the Dangra-yum-tso. They ought then to comply with my wishes. The old man hesitated, pondered awhile, and summoned his followers to a council. His tent was soon full of black, bare-headed men in grey sheepskins. Then the consultation was adjourned to Muhamed Isa's tent. After some consideration they agreed to my proposals, on the condition that I should pay them a whole *tenga* per day for each yak instead of half a *tenga*. I rejoiced at the hope of seeing the holy mountain coming closer and closer, and its finer details becoming more conspicuous, of beholding it in cloud and sunshine, disappearing behind the hills and peeping out again like a man-of-war in a rough sea with high white waves round the bow, or, more correctly, like a ship under full sail on the sea of the plateau. Of course I exposed myself to annoyances by ignoring the passport, but geographical discoveries were concerned and all considerations must be set aside.

On Vega day, April 24, we had a strong wind in our faces, it was cold, and Targo-gangri partly disappeared behind the clouds. Escorted by the old gentleman and four horsemen who were as much alike as if they had been cast in the same mould, and who had all matchlocks on their backs, I rode along the bank of the Targo-tsangpo in the contracting valley which slopes with an extremely gentle gradient, imperceptible to the eye, to the lake. At last the valley becomes so narrow that the ice fills all its bottom. The road therefore leaves the river on the left, and passes over flat hills, among which we cross a succession of small affluents. Black tents, tame yaks grazing, stone folds for sheep, wild asses, and millions of field mice recall to mind the Chang-tang. The wild yak, however, does not occur in this country. The feathered kingdom is represented by ravens, wild ducks, and occasionally a small bird. When we came to the Bumnak-chu, a right-hand tributary of the Targo-tsangpo, a large number of men came to meet us, saluting with the tongue, and gazing at us cheerfully and good-temperedly with their long black unkempt hair, their small grey skins, and their torn boots.

On April 25 we rode over the Ting-la pass; at its foot is a *mani* in good preservation, with a yak skull as ornament, a form of prayer being incised in the frontal bone between the horns. From the top of the pass Targo-gangri is seen expanded into a row of peaks covered with snow. The whole region is like a sea with a strong swell on, and the Targo-gangri is as white foaming surf on the coast. A little later the summits of the mass stood clearly out white on a background of bluish-black clouds; the highest two, twin peaks, had the form of a Tibetan tent on two poles.

Our camp in the Kokbo valley contained not fewer than eleven tents, for now we had about forty companions of all ages, and at least a hundred yaks. The loads were transferred to other yaks on the march to spare the animals. When the caravan moves over the rounded hills it is like a nomad tribe on the march. Most of our Tibetans ride yaks or horses.

We had made a short march, and plenty of time was left for me to go about, make a visit to each tent, and see how the men were getting on. They were all drinking tea and eating *tsamba*, their greatest pleasure in life. The dung fire burns in the middle, and the form of the tent certainly is the cause of the draught which prevents smoke from collecting inside. Round about stand kettles, tea-pots, and wooden cups. A huge quantity of provisions lies at the sides. Saddles and harness are deposited in a row before the tent. When I enter, all rise, but I beg them to sit down again and go on eating, while I take a seat on a barley sack at the door of the tent. All have the right arm bare, and many both arms; when they let their sheepskins fall down their backs the whole body is naked down to the waist. They are copper-brown and covered with a layer of dirt, but well-grown, powerful, manly, and in good proportion. The cook of the tent community pours out tea for all, and then each one brings out his own bag and takes out a pinch of *tsamba* to sprinkle into his tea. They eat meat either raw or boiled in a pot. They are all quiet and orderly, no angry words are heard, no quarrelling and shouting, they are all the best of friends, and make themselves comfortable after their day's march, talking and laughing together. Their wigs are dust-traps and make them look like Indians. Most of them wear a pigtail, consisting mostly of plaited threads with white bone rings and small silver image boxes which have a couple of turquoises inlaid in the lid. Some have the pigtail wound round the head, forming a singular crown, the diadem of the wilderness.

In another tent the dinner was finished and the "covers" were empty. There a man sat with an awl, cobbling a torn boot; another sewed the girths of his saddle on firmly; and a third lay on his back, with legs crossed and an arm supporting his head, and took his after-dinner nap. Seen from above he makes a very absurd figure with his huge nostrils, into which mice might easily walk in mistake for their holes. A smirking youth is smoking his pipe, while his neighbour busily and carefully searches for suspected lodgers in his sheepskin.

I drew several of them without exciting the least uneasiness; on the contrary, they made a joke of the sitting, and laughed heartily when they saw their counterfeits, which they embellished with prints of their buttery fingers on the margin. They asked me why I drew them, and for what purpose I wished to know their names and ages. They were all sympathetic, polite, and friendly, and I enjoyed their society (Illusts. 193, 194).

A begging lama, too, looked in; he was on the way to Kailas, and was quickly sketched, to the intense amusement of the other men. He bore a lance with a black tassel and red strips, a timbrel, an antelope horn to protect himself against snappy dogs, and a trombone of human bone, which he set in a corner of his mouth when he blew it. It caused him much amusement to be the object of universal attention, and he took advantage of it to make acquaintance with the nomads with a view to an appeal to their liberality (Illust. 195).

193   194

195   196

193, 194. Nomads South of Targo-gangri. 195. Mendicant Lama blowing on a Human Bone. 196. Tibetan Boy.

Sketches by the Author.

CHAPTER XXXVII

TARGO-GANGRI AND THE SHURU-TSO

HITHERTO we had experienced no difficulties, but at Kokbo the state of affairs seemed disquieting. Our old man informed me that he had sent a message to the nomads at the Targo-gangri mountain, asking them to hold yaks in readiness. They had answered that they could not think of serving a European without express orders, and that they would resort to force if our present guards led us to the lake. The old man, however, was not put out, but believed that he could soon bring them to their senses.

On April 26 we march north-westwards in a sharp wind over the pass Tarbung-la. The sacred mountain exhibits all the beauty of its sixteen peaks, and north, 33° west, is seen the gap where we expect to find the Dangra-yum-tso. The view is of immense extent. The valley widens out and passes into that of the Targo-tsangpo. Four antelopes spring lightly over the slopes; black tents are not to be seen.

When we again reach more open ground, one of the most magnificent views I have seen in this part of Tibet opens out to the west-south-west, a gigantic range of uniform height, with snow-covered pinnacles and short glaciers between, which is scarcely inferior to Targo-gangri in imposing beauty and massiveness. The chain is bluish black below the snowy points; at its foot lies a lake unknown to us, the Shuru-tso. The journey to the Ngangtse-tso north-north-east by the way of the Shang-buk-la pass is reckoned as only three days' march. On the eastern flank of Targo-gangri five glaciers are deeply embedded, while to the east of the mountain the flat open valley of the Targo-tsangpo comes into sight, which we gradually approach, passing over five clearly defined terraces, relics of a time when the Dangra-yum-tso was much larger than now. Two wolves make off in front of us, and the old man gallops after them, but turns back when they stop as if to wait for him. "If I had had a knife or a gun," he says, "I would have killed them both."

At length we descend to the valley of the Targo-tsangpo down a bold terrace with two ledges, and here the river is divided into several arms, and wild ducks and geese swarm. Brushwood grows on the banks. On the right bank lies our camp, No. 150, not far from the foot of the majestic Targo-gangri (Illust. 198).

Thus far we were to come, but no farther. Here a troop of twenty horsemen armed to the teeth awaited us, who had been sent by the Governor of Naktsang from Shansa-dzong, with orders to stop us "in case we should attempt to advance to the holy lake." This time they had kept a sharper watch, and had anticipated that I would take all kinds of liberties. They had left Shansa-dzong fifteen days before, and had been camping here three days, awaiting our arrival. If we had hurried we should have been before them again. One of the two leaders was the same Lundup Tsering who, as he told me himself, had stopped Dutreuil de Rhins and Grenard, and had been in January with Hlaje Tsering at the Ngangste-tso. He informed me that Hlaje Tsering was still in office, but had had much trouble because of us, and had been obliged to pay a fine of sixty *yambaus* (about £675) to the Devashung. When I remarked that Hlaje Tsering had told me himself that he was so poor that he had nothing left to lose, Lundup answered that he had extorted the money from his subordinates. All, too, who had sold us yaks and served us as guides had been heavily fined. The next European who attempted to get through without a passport would have no end of difficulties to contend with (Illust. 200).

Lundup pointed to a red granite promontory, 200 yards north of our camp, and said: "There is the boundary between the Labrang (Tashi-lunpo) and Naktsang (Lhasa).

So far we can let you go, but not a step farther; if you attempt it, we have orders to fire on you."

They read the passport from Shigatse, and affirmed that the words therein, "on the direct way to Ladak," did not mean that we had permission to make all sorts of detours, and, above all, we might not go to the Dangra-yum-tso, which is holy and is in the territory of Lhasa. Gaw Daloi had given orders that he should be informed daily which way we were travelling. If they did not obey this order they would lose their heads. It was evident, then, that I should have to give up the Dangra-yum-tso for the third time, and just when I was only two short days' march from it.

The outline of the mountain stood out sharp and white in the moonshine against the blue-black starry sky. The next day there was a storm, and not even the foot of Targo-gangri was visible, much less the icy-cold heights where the winds sing their heavenly choruses among the firn fields. In the evening, however, when the weather had cleared, the whole mass stood clearly out, covered with freshly fallen snow.

Again we held a long palaver with the horsemen from Naktsang. I told them that I would not leave this camp till I had at least seen the lake from a distance. To my delight they replied that though they were obliged, much against their inclination, to cause me the disappointment of not visiting the lake, they would not prevent me from seeing it from a distance, but that they would keep a good watch lest I should ride off behind yonder red mountain to the north.

They had scarcely gone when our old Kyangdam guide came to complain that the horsemen from Naktsang had threatened his life because he had brought me here. I sent for the Naktsang men again and impressed on them strongly that they had no cause of complaint against my escort, for it was entirely my fault that we were here. They promised that they would not again treat the Kyang-dam men harshly, as they had most fortunately caught me just at the right moment. The Kyangdam men could not thank me enough for restoring peace, and their joy was still greater when I presented the whole party with money to supplement their scanty store of provisions. They gave vent to their delight by performing games, dances, and wrestling bouts in front of my tent, and their happy laughter and shouts were echoed till late in the night from the mountains.

Then came twelve more soldiers from Naktsang with fresh orders that we were under no circumstances to be allowed to proceed farther northwards. But all were friendly and polite; we joked and laughed together, and were the best of friends. It is singular that they never lose their patience, though I am always causing them worry, perplexity, and troublesome journeys.

The chief of Largep was more unyielding than our old friends the Naktsang gentlemen. He would not let me climb the red mountain, but insisted that we should leave the district next day and travel straight to Raga-tasam. However, I snubbed him, demanding how he, a small chieftain in the mountains, could dare to speak so peremptorily. Even the Chinese in Lhasa, I said, had treated us pleasantly and had left us the fullest freedom. I would not leave the spot until I had seen the lake. I threatened to tear the Shigatse passport in pieces, and send off at once a courier to Tang Darin and Lien Darin, and wait for their answer at the foot of Targo-gangri. Then the chief became embarrassed, got up in silence, and went away with the others. But they were with me again in the evening, and with a humble smile they said that I might ride up the red mountain if I would promise not to go to the shore of the lake.

A thin veil of mist lay over the country all day long. But when the sun set, the western sky glowed with purple flames, and the cold glaciers and snowfields were thrown up by a background of fire.

At last, on April 29, we take to the road and ride up the affluent Chuma, flowing down from the right and called in its upper course Nagma-tsangpo. We climb higher and higher up regularly curved lake terraces; the view widens out the nearer we approach the summit, where the Ladakis are waiting for us with a fire. The southern basin of the

200. Lundup's Squadron. To the Left a Part of Targo-gangri. Camp 150.

Dangra-yum-tso was clearly visible as a bluish sabre-blade, and the valley of the Targo-tsangpo widens out like a trumpet to the broad plain beside the shore. It was the easier to trace the course of the river to the neighbourhood of the lake because it was marked all along by white glistening ice flakes and dark spots where bushes grow. At the end of July the river is said to rise so high that it cannot be crossed. So when letters have to be delivered to nomads on the eastern foot of the mountain they are weighted with a stone and thrown across a narrow part of the stream.

The water of the lake is said to be as salt as that of the Ngangtse-tso, and is not fit for drinking; but nevertheless pilgrims drink it, because it is holy. At this time the winter ice was breaking up, and long sheets of ice lay only at the shore. In contrast to most other lakes of Tibet, the Dangra-yum-tso runs north and south, and it narrows in the middle, just as Nain Sing has drawn it on his map; but he has made the lake a little too large, and has especially exaggerated the dimensions of the southern basin. A horseman can travel round the lake in five ordinary or seven short days' journey; the pilgrim road closely follows the lake shore. The pilgrims always make the circuit of the lake in the direction of the hands of a watch, if they are orthodox; but if they belong to the Pembo sect, like the monks of the Sershik-gompa, they begin their march in the opposite direction. Most of them come in late summer or autumn. I was told that the pilgrimage round the lake, which of course must be made on foot, was in honour of Padma Sambhava, the saint who came to Tibet in the year 747, became the founder of Lamaism, and enjoys almost as great a reputation as Buddha himself. He is called in Tibet Lopön Rinpoche, and his image is generally found in the temples.

Sershik-gompa, of which we had frequently heard, and which Nain Sing names Sasik Gombas on his map, stands on an even slope at the eastern foot of the mountain. The monastery is under the Devashung, and has twenty Pembo brethren and an abbot named Tibha. Some of the monks are said to be well off, but on the whole the convent is not rich; it is supported by nomads in Naktsang, Largep, and Sershik. The monastery is constructed chiefly of stone, but it also contains timber transported hither from the Shang valley. There is a *dukang* and a number of small images of gods. The Targo-gangri massive can also be travelled round, and only one pass has to be crossed, namely the Barong-la (or Parung), which lies between Targo-gangri and the mighty range on the west of the Shuru-tso.

The short, lofty, meridional range which is called Targo-gangri, and is rather to be considered an isolated massive, ends in the north not far from the lake, the flanks of the last peak descending gently to its flat plain. Nain Sing calls the massive Targot-la Snowy Peaks, and the district to the south of the mountain Társgot Lhágeb (Largep). The river is marked Targot Sangpo on his map. His Siru Cho to the east of the lake is known to no one here, and his Mun Cho Lakes marked to the south of it actually lie to the west of the lake. His representation of the mountains to the south of the lake is confused and fanciful. Some nomads named the holy mountain Chang-targo-ri.

On the way back I took levels, assisted by Robert, and found that the highest recognizable terrace lay 292 feet above the level of the river. The Targo-tsangpo is here certainly not more than 6½ feet higher than the surface of the lake. As the Dangra-yum-tso is surrounded, particularly on the south, by rather low, flat land, the lake must formerly have been of very large extent. At that time the Targo-gangri skirted the western shore as a peninsula.

In the night there was a noise like an avalanche falling; it became feebler and died away. The horses and yaks of the Tibetans, frightened by something or other, had stormed the detritus slope of the terrace. Half an hour later I heard whistling and shouting; the men were coming back with the runaways.

Before we took leave of our troublesome friends they were photographed on horseback (Illust. 201). They all wore roomy, dark cerise-coloured mantles, and, unlike

201. LUNDUP (on horseback to the left) AND HIS RETINUE PREVENT ME FROM PROCEEDING TO THE DANGRA-YUM-TSO.
Targo-gangri and the river Targo-tsangpo in the background.

the bareheaded Largep men, a bandage round the head, in many cases drawn through silver rings like bangles. One had a tall white hat like a truncated cone, with a flat brim, a head-covering I remembered seeing in Nakchu. Their guns, with the military pennants on the forks, they had slung over their shoulders, and their sabres stuck out horizontally from their girdles in silver-bound scabbards decorated with three pieces of imitation coral. Over the left shoulder some carried a whole bandolier of *gao* cases with glass fronts, through which were visible the little innocent gods which bring their wearers good fortune on their journey. Their fat little horses stamped and snorted, longing for their old well-known pastures on the shores of the Kyaring-tso. They also were decked with needlessly heavy but dainty ornaments. The white horses with red riders on their backs made a particularly striking picture. It was a varied scene in the blazing sunshine, with the snowy summits of Targo-gangri as a background and Nain Sing's lake to the north. I begged them to greet Hlaje Tsering heartily from me, and tell him that I hoped to see him again.

And then they struck their heels into their horses, drew together into close order, and trotted gaily up to the level surfaces of the river terraces. Captivated by the appearance of the departing troop I ran after it, and watched the dark column grow smaller at the red spur, where the old shore lines seemed to run together. Singular people! They rise like goblins from the depths of their valleys, they come one knows not whence, they, like us, visit for a few short days the foot of the snowy mountain, and then they vanish again like a whirlwind in the dust of the horses' hoofs and beyond the mysterious horizon.

We, too, set out, and I left the Dangra-yum-tso to its fate, the dark-blue waters to the blustering storm and the song of the rising waves, and the eternal snowfields to the whisper of the winds. May the changing colours of the seasons, the beauty of atmospheric effects of light and shade, gold, purple, and grey, pass over Padma Sambhava's lake amidst rain and sunshine, as already for untold thousands of years, and the steps of believing, yearning pilgrims draw a chain around its shores.

Accompanied by Robert and our aged guide, I rode across the river, which carries about 140 cubic feet of water, and up to a spur of Targo-gangri in order to procure a rock specimen. One glacier tongue after another of the long series on the east side of the mountain passes out of sight, and now the gap disappears through which we had seen a corner of the lake, and far away to the north on its other side the outlines of light-blue mountains.

Six hundred sheep were grazing on a slope without shepherds. Now and then a hare was started in the thick tufts of steppe grass. From the screes on our right was heard the pleasant chirp of partridges. When we were far away two shepherds came up out of a gorge and drove the sheep down to the river. At the lower end of the moraine of a glacier stood a solitary tent. I asked our old man what the spot was called, but he swore by three different gods that he had no notion. The most southern outskirt of Targo-gangri hid the rest of the range, but before we reached camp No. 151 it appeared again foreshortened. This camp stood on the left bank of the river.

May 1. Spring is come; we have, indeed, had as much as 29 degrees of frost during the preceding nights, but the days are fine and clear, and it is never as trying as in the Chang-tang, even riding against the wind. At camp No. 150 we had been at a height of 15,446 feet; now we go slowly down, following the river at first, but leaving it on the left when we see it emerge from the mountains as through a gate. Over a singularly uniform and continuous plain without fissures or undulations we now approach in a south-westerly direction the threshold which separates the Shuru-tso from the Dangra-yum-tso. On the south-west side of Tangro-gangri appear six glaciers, much smaller than those on the north and east, and rather to be regarded as spurs and corners of the ice mantle which covers the higher regions of the massive. The Shuru-tso is seen as a fine blue line. We approach its shore and find that the lake is completely frozen over.

203 

 204

202, 203, 204. Targo-gangri from the South.

We make a halt to photograph and to draw a panorama. Our old man smokes a pipe, and Robert and Tashi try which can snore loudest. When I am ready we sneak off quietly from the two sleepers. Tashi is the first to awake, understands the joke, and also sneaks off. At last Robert awakes and finds himself alone, but he soon overtakes us on his mule.

Now we have the lake close on our right. To the south rise grand mountains, one of the loftiest chains of the Trans-Himalaya, raven black beneath the sun, but the firn-fields glitter with a metallic lustre. Considerable terraces skirt the bank, and the valleys running down from the east to the lake cut through them, forming hollow ways in which a solitary tent stands here and there guarded by a savage dog. We encamp on the terrace above the Parva valley, our eight black tents contrasting strongly with the yellow soil (15,594 feet). Our old Tibetans from Kyangdam now bid us farewell and receive double payment as a present. In front of us are the congealed waters of the Shuru-tso, longing to be released by the warm spring winds; to the south rises the Do-tsengkan, a mighty elevation clothed in eternal snow; in the south-west the sun sinks behind the huge crest of the mountains and the shadows pass silently across the ice. Soon the evening red lingers only on the peaks of Targo-gangri and Do-tsengkan, and then another night falls over the earth. It is a pity that the Tibetans do not understand the relations of the sun and the planets, for they might regard the solar system as a unique immeasurable prayer-mill revolving in space to the glory of the gods. In the darkness the lofty mountains to the north-west are misty and indistinct, but when the moon rises they and the lake are illuminated alike and seem to be connected. From our terrace we seem to have a bottomless abyss below us.

On May 2 we ride southwards along the shore (Illust. 205). Like the Dangra-yum-tso, the Shuru-tso runs almost north and south, lying in a longitudinal valley which has this direction, so unusual in Tibet. There is open water along the bank, and the waves splash against the edge of the porous ice, on which wild ducks sit, often in long rows.

Owing to the swell the water on the bank is black with decayed algæ and rotting water-weeds, in which wild geese cackle and scream. As we come to the regularly curved southern shore of the lake, with its bank of sand, we see the well-known signs of a storm on the plain before us, white dust swirls, stirred up in spirals from the ground by the wind, like the smoke of a shot. After a time we find ourselves in the path of the storm—it will not need many such storms to break up the whole lake and drive its loosened ice-sheets to the eastern bank. We ride across the river Kyangdam-tsangpo, which comes from the Trans-Himalaya, and bivouac on its western terrace (15,548 feet). Here we have the whole lake in front of us to the north, and behind it Targo-gangri, now smaller again.

Here our attendants were changed. The Largep chief, who had been so overbearing at first, was as meek as a lamb at the moment of parting, and gave me a *kadakh*, a sheep, and four skins of butter. Every morning when the caravan sets out Ishe comes to my tent to fetch my two puppies; Muhamed Isa has the third, which he means to train up to be a wonderful animal, and the fourth has been consigned to Sonam Tsering. They have grown a deal already, and howl and bite each other on the march, when they ride in a basket on the back of a mule. They are graceful and playful, and give me great amusement with their tricks.

From the little pass Dunka-la we had a grand and instructive view over the great Shuru-tso, which is of a somewhat elongated form and is convex to the west. Next day we crossed the pass Ben-la in a south-westerly storm. It raged and blew day and night, but the air remained quite clear. On the 6th we rode up a steep path to the Angden-la. In the rather deep snow and the tiring rubbish the horses can get on only a step at a time, and have often to stop and rest. Tsering rides past us with his yak caravan, and four Ladakis have stayed behind in the valley suffering from acute headache. At the top of the pass (18,514 feet) stands a huge cairn with strings and streamers, their prayers rising to the dwellings of the gods on the wings of the wind (Illusts. 207, 209, 210).

205. The Shuru-tso, with Targo-gangri in the Background.

No words can describe the panorama around us. We stand above a sea of mountains with here and there a predominant peak. To the south we see the Himalayas clearer and sharper than before, and can perceive where the valley of the Brahmaputra runs on this side of the white ridge. To the north the Shuru-tso is much foreshortened, and the Dangra-yum-tso is hidden by Targo-gangri, which is sharply defined, though we are six days' journey from it. Nay, even the contours of the mighty mountains on the north-east shore of the lake, which we saw in winter from the north, are distinguishable, and they lie fully ten days' journey from here. I sit at the fire, drawing and making observations, as on all the passes. I am again on the Trans-Himalaya, 53 miles from the Chang-la-Pod-la, and now cross it for the third time. Northwards the water drains to the Shuru-tso, southwards to the Raga-tsangpo. My feet stand on the oceanic watershed, my eyes roam over this huge system, which I love as my own possession. For the part where I now stand was unknown and waited millions of years for my coming, lashed by innumerable storms, washed by autumn rains, and wrapped in snow in winter. With every new pass on the watershed of the gigantic rivers of India which I have the good fortune to cross, my desire and hope become ever greater to follow its winding line westwards to regions already known, and to fill up on the map the great white blank north of the Tsangpo. I know very well that generations of explorers will be necessary to examine this mighty intricate mountain land, but my ambition will be satisfied if I succeed in making the first reconnaissance.

We leave the cairn and the fire, its smoke covering the summit of the pass as with a torn veil, and follow the brook, of which the water will some day reach the warm sea after a thousand experiences. I turn a page and begin a new chapter in my life as an explorer; the desolate Chang-tang remains behind me, and Targo-gangri sinks below the horizon—shall I ever see its majestic peaks again?

We descend rapidly with the wind in our faces. Large

blocks of ice fill the valley bottom between walls of black schists and porphyry. Several large side valleys open into ours, and deserted hearths are signs of the visits of nomads in summer. Our valley unites with the large Kyam-chu valley, which is 6 miles broad and descends from the Sha-la, the pass of the Trans-Himalaya over which our Tibetans had wished to guide us. The land round the nomad tents of Kyam is flat and open.

On May 7 we march on in a terrible wind with the blue mirror of the Amchok-tso on the south. The ground is flat and hard. A hare runs like the wind, as if his life were in danger, over this flat, where he cannot find the slightest cover. Eight sprightly antelopes show us their graceful profiles as they spring lightly along, rising from the horizon against a background of sky. Robert has drawn his fur over his head, and sits in the saddle like a lady, with both his legs dangling on the sheltered side, while Tashi leads his mule. But as the wind still blows through him, he lays himself on his stomach across the saddle. My horse sways when the wind catches the broad breast of its rider. The wind howls and moans in my ears, it whines and whistles as it used to do in the Chang-tang, a whole host of indignant spirits of the air seem to complain of all the misery they have seen in the world.

The plain is called Amchok-tang, and we march over it, following the main stream. Amchok-yung is a village of five tents, where are some fine *manis* bedecked with yak skulls, antelope horns, and slabs of sandstone, one of them, of a regular rectangular form, measuring 40 inches. The inhabitants of the village disappeared as if by magic; only an old man gave us his company as we inspected two of the tents. But when we had ridden on, the people crept out again from behind dung heaps, hillocks, and grass tufts, where they had hidden themselves.

The wind bores thick yellow sand out of the ground into a spout, which is so dense that it looks black on the shady side. It winds up in cyclonic spirals like the smoke of a tremendous explosion and, like a strange ghost, dances across the plain, and does not fall to pieces till it reaches the foot of the eastern mountains.

206. On the Upper Raga-tsangpo.

207. Angden-la.

208. Chomo-uchong from the East.

In our camp of this day, situated on the north-west shore of the Amchok-tso, we heard Chinese and Tibetan officials spoken of who were shortly to ride through the country in all directions, counting the tents, people, and herds. It was thought that this inspection was connected with the new taxation which the Chinese intend to introduce.

My boat lay ready on the strand, for May 8 was to be devoted to an excursion on the Amchok-tso.

CHAPTER XXXVIII

TO THE OUTLET OF THE CHAKTAK-TSANGPO IN THE BRAHMAPUTRA

THE lake was free from ice, and only on the northern shore some blocks rocked on the surf. A south-west wind swept constantly over the country, and there was no prospect of good weather. A dozen Tibetans followed me at a respectful distance. I begged them to come nearer and see us start. The boat was brought down to the water, Rehim Ali and Shukkur took their places, and Lama carried me to the boat through the slowly deepening water. A promontory to the south, 34° E., was fixed as our goal, and the oarsmen began their struggle with the waves. For the first hour the lake was so shallow that the oars struck the bottom and stirred up inky-black mud. Shukkur cries out in time with the oars, "Shubasa, ya aferin, bismillah, ya barkadiallah"—to cite only a few words of his inexhaustible repertoire. Rehim Ali's oar gives me a splash as it dips in, but I am soon dry again in the wind. The swell stirs up the mud from the bottom, and the water is so shallow that the waves show a tendency to break even out in the middle of the lake.

Now the sandspouts begin their threatening dance on the western shore, and in that direction the water gleams white. The storm sweeps over the Amchok-tso, and the two Mohammedans must put forth all their strength to force the boat forward against wind and water. The swell grows heavier, the depth is 7.9 feet, and the water assumes a greener hue. Shukkur Ali, our old fisherman, puts out his line, but nothing but floating algæ will bite.

209, 210. Angden-la, a Pass on the Trans-Himalaya.

In several places are seen wild ducks, gulls, and wild geese. Nomads have just arrived and are putting up their tents in a gorge on the eastern shore. At length we reach the promontory, having sounded a maximum depth of only 12 feet.

After observations have been taken, a panorama sketched, and dinner eaten, we again set off in a northerly direction, and the boat dances before the brisk wind lightly as a wild duck over the waves. We sail past three more tents, sound 10.2 feet, and approach the northern shore, where the water is only 20 inches deep, and is a muddy soup. We run aground at a distance of 100 yards from the bank. Rabsang comes up running, leading my horse by the bridle, and some other Ladakis follow him. They help us to land, and light a much needed fire at the foot of the sand terrace which here rises from the bank.

The river Kyam-chu enters the Amchok-tso on the north side, and only $1\frac{1}{4}$ miles to the west of its muddy delta the Dongmo-chu flows out of the lake towards its confluence with the Raga-tsangpo in the east. Properly speaking, the Dongmo is only the continuation of the Kyam-chu, with the lake hanging like a bag on its right bank.

After the boat has been folded up, Muhamed Isa has to show us the way on horseback over the grass-grown sandhills. He guides me across the twenty shallow and treacherously swampy delta arms of the Kyam-chu. It is dark, but a beacon fire has been lighted in the camp, and the cakes of dung are heated to whiteness in the strong wind, and shine like electric light.

Next day I was up before the sun, in order to take an observation. The thermometer had sunk in the night to 0.3°, and the wind blew regularly as a trade-wind. It is pleasant to see the day dawn in the east, and life begin anew among the tents. The hired yaks have lain tethered during the night, and now they are allowed to wander freely over the pasture. Sleepy yawns are heard in the tents, and men come out and make up the fires; the jug bubbles in which the morning tea is stirred up with butter, and kettles are set on three stones over the fire. The puppies play in the open, and are glad that they have not to roll about to-day in a basket.

The days and months fly by to a chorus of storms, and spring still delays its coming. In the evening songs of the Ladakis I fancy I hear an undertone of home-sickness, and they rejoice at every day's march which brings us a little further westwards. When we woke next morning, it blew as fresh as ever, and Robert had made himself a mask with Tibetan spectacles sewed into the eye-holes; he looked very comical in this contrivance, which was very appropriate in this land of religious masquerades.

The road, ascending the broad valley of the Pu-chu, led over open, slightly undulating ground to Serme-lartsa. Here old Guffaru was reported sick; he suffered from colic, and was well nursed. But late at night Robert came breathless to my tent to tell me the old man was dying. When I came to the tent the son, whose duty it was to keep the shroud ready, sat weeping beside his father, while the other men warmed their caps over the fire and applied them to the body of the patient. I ordered him a cold compress, but he asked me, to the intense amusement of others, just to go back to my tent again. Muhamed Isa laughed till he rolled over. Guffaru sat upright on his bed, moaned and groaned, and begged me to go away. I gave him a strong dose of opium, and next morning he was so brisk that he walked all the way, though a horse was at his disposal. The remains of Burroughs and Wellcome's medicine chest had saved his life; he was thankful and pleased that his shroud was not required this time.

On May 11 we mounted to the pass Lungring (17,697 feet) in a bitterly cold snowstorm, and descended the valley of the same name to the bank of the upper Raga-tsangpo. On the 12th we marched upstream; the valley is broad, and is bounded on the north by great mountains. The thermometer had sunk to $-0.8°$, and the storm was dead against us. Occasionally it abated so much that we could hear the footfalls of the horses on the detritus, but we were benumbed when we came to the camp. Thick snow

211. Manis on the Way to the Angden-la.

fell all the afternoon. My puppies sat together in the tent door and growled at the falling flakes, but when they saw it was no use, they snapped at the flakes as though they were flies and pawed at them. Then they went back into the tent, lay on the frieze blanket in the corner, and let it snow on.

On the next day's march we passed Kamba-sumdo, where the two head sources of the Raga-tsangpo unite; the one, coming from the west, is named Chang-shung, the other, from the south-west, Lo-shung, *i.e.* "Northern" and "Southern Valley." The Chang-shung is the larger. The Lo-shung we had to cross twice, and found the bed full of stones connected by slippery ice. In the west a large snow-covered ridge appeared, the Chomo-uchong, or "High Nun," which was discovered by Nain Sing. Ryder measured it and produced an exact map of it. Belts of snow descend from the white summits down the dark flanks. Other Tibetans called it Chōōr-jong (Illust. 212).

Still marching south-westwards we approached at an acute angle the great main road between Lhasa and Ladak, the so-called *tasam.* As though to show its importance a caravan was just at the time travelling westwards in three columns. It moved so slowly through the landscape that we had to watch the mountain spur behind to convince ourselves that the small black lines were moving at all. Soon afterwards we pitched our tents in Raga-tasam (16,234 feet), a station on the great high-road, where we came in contact with the route of the English expedition under Ryder and Rawling for the first time since leaving Shigatse. Whatever the immediate future had in store for me, it was above all things my desire to avoid this route as much as possible. For the map which Ryder and Wood had executed is the best that has been surveyed of any part of Tibet; I could add nothing new to it with my modest equipment. But if I passed to the north or south of their line of march, I could supplement their map with my own explorations. In this I actually so far succeeded that out of eighty-three days' marches to Tokchen on the Manasarowar only two-and-a-half days' march ran along their route.

As I now perceived that we should have to travel on the road which Nain Sing in the year 1865, and Ryder and Rawling and their comrades in 1904, had passed along, I wrote, after consultation with Robert and Muhamed Isa, to Tang Darin and Lien Darin in Lhasa. I represented in an urgent appeal to the former, the High Commissioner, that it could not clash with any treaty if I, being already in Tibet, travelled to Ladak by one road or another, provided that I actually did go thither, and that I therefore begged permission to take the following route: I wished to take my homeward way past the lake Tedenam-tso, of which Nain Sing had heard, then to visit the Dangra-yum-tso, and thence to proceed to Tradum and to the Ghalaring-tso, the holy mountain Kailas, the Manasarowar lake, the sources of the Indus and the Brahmaputra, and lastly Gartok. To the other, the Amban of Lhasa, I also wrote about the way I desired to take, and promised to send him a report about it from Gartok. I told both that I wished for a speedy answer, and would wait for it in Raga-tasam.

As soon as I had come to a decision, I called Tundup Sonam and Tashi, and told them to get their sleep over by midnight. Then I wrote the above-mentioned letters and letters to my parents and to Major O'Connor. When my correspondence was ready, it was past midnight. The camp had lain several hours in sleep when I made the night watchman waken the two messengers and Muhamed Isa. Their orders were such as they had never received before. They were to travel day and night along the 220 miles to Shigatse and hand over my letters to Ma. They need not wait for an answer, for I had asked the Mandarins to send me special couriers. Provisions they need not take, for they would be able to get everything on the great high-road, and I gave them money to hire the horses they required. They would be able to reach their journey's end in ten days, and in a month we ought to have an answer. If they did not find us in Raga-tasam on their return, they were to follow in our track.

Tundup Sonam and Tashi were in good spirits and full of hope when Muhamed Isa and I accompanied them outside the camp, and watched them disappear into the dark night. They made a detour to avoid the twelve black tents standing here, lest the numerous dogs of the village should bark. It was not far to the great high-road, and at the next *tasam*, as the stations are called, they could hire horses at daybreak. Muhamed Isa and I sat a while in my tent in lively conversation about our prospects. Not till I had crept into bed after a tiring day did it occur to me that it was perhaps cruel to let the two men ride alone day and night through Tibet. But it was too late, they must now fulfil their mission.

There was no hurry now. We stayed here seven days. Westwards the way was open, but not the way I wished to take, and therefore we were prisoners in our own tents. "Patience," whispered the ceaseless winds. The unknown land lay to the north; I could not give it up till all my efforts had proved fruitless. We had cold unpleasant weather, with frequently more than 36 degrees of frost, and on the night of May 15 as much as 46.4 degrees. The Tibetans said that this neighbourhood is always cold, even when spring reigns all around.

I lay on my bed and read *David Copperfield*, *Dombey and Son*, and *The Newcomes*, for I had now a whole library to read through, the gift of the obliging Major O'Connor. Robert gave me lessons in Hindustani, and I drew types of the people. A puppy of the same age as our own warily came up to my tent and got a breakfast. Mamma Puppy was by no means pleased with this wayside guest, who looked comical, as shy and quiet as a mouse; he sat by the hour together at the fire and looked at me, at length falling asleep and turning on his side. When he appeared again at dinner, he was thoroughly worried by Puppy, but nevertheless went calmly to the family mat and laid himself down. Puppy was furious, but so dumbfoundered at this unexpected impudence that she laid herself down on the ground beside the mat.

Tibetans came every day to my tent and implored us to make a start. When this proved useless, they declared at length, that they could no longer supply us with provisions, for no more were to be had in the neighbourhood.

I asked them, as an experiment, whether they would forward two letters to the Mandarins in Lhasa, but they replied that they had no authority to do this. They were much astonished when they heard that I had sent off letters five days previously. For two days I lay in bed, for I was quite at an end of my strength, and made Robert read to me.

On Whitsunday, May 19, we had another long palaver. The Tibetans read to me the instructions they had received from Lhasa, which were dated "on the tenth day of the second month in the year of the fiery sheep." I was there called Hedin Sahib, and the orders contained the following clauses: "Send him out of the country. Let him not turn aside from the *tasam*, and guide him neither to the right nor to the left. Supply him with horses, yaks, servants, fuel, grass, and everything he wants. The prices he must pay are the usual prices fixed by the Government. Give him at once anything he asks for and refuse him nothing. But if he will not conform to the directions on his passport, but says he will take other routes independently, give him no provisions, but keep firm hold of him and send off messengers at once to the Devashung. Do not venture to think for yourselves, but obey. Any one in the provinces who does not obey will be beaten; so run the regulations you have to conform to. If he gives no trouble, see that the nomads serve him well and do him no harm on the way to Gartok. Then it will be the business of the Garpuns (the two Viceroys) to take him under their protection."

And yet I was not satisfied. I told them that I could not think of conforming to my passport, which was contrary to my religion, and that I must go northwards from the Chomo-uchong to Saka-dzong. They were quite at liberty to send messengers to the Devashung. We would wait. Then they held a council, and at length agreed to let us take the northern route, but we must set out on May 21.

I lay on my bed and dreamed of the tramp of horses coming both from the east and the west, of the roads open to me to the mysterious mountain system in the

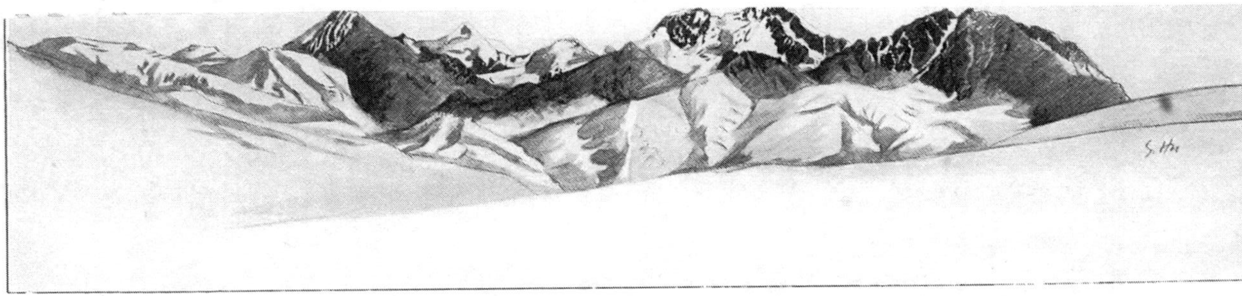

212. CHOMO-UCHONG FROM LAMLUNG-LA.

213. PANORAMA FROM THE TA-LA. (The Brahmaputra Valley and the Himalayas in the background.)
Sketches by the Author.

north, round which my plans and my dreams circled continually like young eagles.

So we set out on May 21, north-westwards, and saw the summits of the Chomo-uchong disappear behind its outskirts. From the camp we could see several valleys in the north-west drained by the source streams of the Raga-tsangpo. Just beyond Raga-tasam we again left the route of the English expedition, and on the 22nd climbed up to the pass Ravak-la, which lies on a low ridge between two of the source streams of the Raga-tsangpo. On the 23rd we crossed four passes. The Kichung-la is the watershed between the Raga-loshung and the Chungsang, a river which takes an independent course to the Tsangpo. The ascent to the fourth pass, the Kanglung-la, was very tiresome, the ground consisting of wet alluvium, wherein the horses sank so deep that we preferred to go on foot and splash through the mud. We were now on the heights whence the water flows down to three of the northern tributaries of the Brahmaputra; the third flows to the Chaktak-tsangpo, which runs to the west of Saka-dzong. Here and there the snow, owing to wind, melting and freezing again, has assumed the form of upright blades, two feet high and sharp as a knife. Far to the south appear parts of the Himalayas, and we are here in a grand landscape of wild and fantastic relief. Now and then the view is obscured by dense showers of hail.

On the morning of the 24th all the country was hidden by thickly falling snow, and the weather at the end of May was more winterly than on the Chang-tang in December. We ride between steep cliffs down a deeply eroded valley, and side valleys run in with narrow deep openings. In one of them is a frozen waterfall. We often cross the clear water of the river which rushes along on its way to Saka-dzong and the Chaktak-tsangpo. Violent gusts of snow sweep through the valley from time to time, and then we can hardly see our hands, and the ground and the mountains become white. In the beautiful junction of valleys called Pangsetak our tents and those of the Tibetans were heavily weighted with snow.

On the 25th we go down further. Nomad tents are as rare as on the preceding days, for people come here only in summer. The path runs frequently up along the left terrace, high above the valley bottom, where the river has formed two large basins of dark-green water. We amused ourselves with rolling stones down the steep slope; they knocked against other boulders, dashed with a thundering noise into the valley, tearing up sand and dust, bounced up from the ground, and finally plunged into the basin, raising a cloud of spray. It was childish but very diverting. The valley passes into a plain, in the southern part of which runs the great high-road between Raga-tasam and Saka-dzong. The river we had followed down is the Kanglung-bupchu, but in Saka it is called Sachu-tsangpo. We pitched our camp in the mouth of the valley Basang on the north side of the plain.

From here to Saka-dzong is a short day's journey. But, instead of travelling along this road, which Ryder has already laid down on his map, I wished to see the place where the Chaktak-tsangpo unites with the upper Brahmaputra. That would involve a long detour of four days' journey, and to this our friends from Raga would not consent without the permission of the Governor of Saka. We therefore stayed a day in the Basang valley, while a messenger was sent to him. When the answer came it was, to our surprise, in the affirmative, but under the condition that the main part of the caravan should proceed straight to Saka-dzong. I even received a local passport for the excursion.

Among other natives who at this time sat for me as models was a youth of twenty years, named Ugyu, who had lived some years before with his mother and sisters in a valley to the north, where their tent was attacked and pillaged by robbers. They had defended themselves bravely with sabres and knives, but the robber band had had firearms, and Ugyu had been struck by a bullet, which had passed through his shoulder-blade and lung, and had come out at his breast. Large scars showed the course of the bullet. When one remembers that the leaden bullets of the Tibetans are as large as hazel-nuts, one is astonished that the boy did not die of internal hæmorrhage. He appeared, on the contrary, extraordinarily healthy and blooming, and had an amiable, sympathetic disposition.

I sat on a barley sack before Muhamed Isa's tent and sketched. Meanwhile, the baggage and provisions were made ready for the excursion. My excellent caravan leader stood, tall and straight as a pole, watching the others filling the sacks we were to take with us. He had the boat also and everything we wanted for river measurements packed up. In the evening he arranged a farewell ball for Tsering, Shukkur Ali, Rabsang, Islam Ahun, and Ishe, who were to accompany Robert and me to the Tsangpo. He had bought in Shigatse a large fine guitar, on which he played himself in his tent. This evening the dancing and singing went off more gaily and merrily than ever. We expected good news from Lhasa, and were glad that the people in Saka had granted the permission I had asked for.

On the morning of May 27 the weather was really fine after a minimum of only 23°; had the spring come at last? The main caravan had already gone off westwards to Saka, and my party was ready when Muhamed Isa came to say farewell. He was ordered to remain in Saka till I returned, and to try by all means to gain the confidence of the officials by friendliness and prudent conduct. My small caravan was on the road to the south, and we stood alone on the deserted camping-ground. After he had received his instructions we mounted into our saddles at the same time and I rode after my men. I turned once more in the saddle and saw Muhamed Isa's stately form upright on his grey horse, his pipe in his mouth, his green velvet cap on his head, and the black sheepskin loose on his shoulder, trotting quickly in the track of the caravan. It was the last time I saw him thus.

Soon we cross the great high-road, the *tasam*, and ride slowly up to the pass Gyebuk-la (15,846 feet), marked by four *manis*, which are covered with green flags of schist with incised Buddha images. The well-worn path, and three caravans of yaks which are just coming over the pass on the way to Saka-dzong, show us that this is an important trade-route. Two of the caravans came from the great town Tsongka-dzong, which lies five days' journey southwards, not far from the frontier of Nepal. From Saka the caravans go over the Gyebuk-la, cross the Brahmaputra, ascend the Samderling valley, and by the Sukpu-la and Negu-la passes reach Tsongka-dzong, which supplies the nomads living in the north with barley. From Gyebuk-la there is a grand view over the sharp peaks and the glacier tongues of the Chomo-uchong. On the southern slopes of the pass there are *pama* bushes almost everywhere, and it is pleasant to see their fresh green needles again.

The road runs down the Kyerkye valley. On a smooth wall of rock "Om mani padme hum" is hewn in characters a yard high. At camp No. 167 the Tibetans of the neighbourhood came kindly to meet me and bid me welcome, and two of them led my horse by the bridle to my tent, as is the custom in this country.

Next day we march down the valley with fresh guides, and see several ruins telling of happier times now gone by. Terraced structures for irrigating the fields indicate that barley is grown in the district. In front of us is now the broad valley of the Brahmaputra, and we come to an arm of the river where a ferry is established to transport caravans and goods on the way between Tsongka-dzong and Saka-dzong from one side of the river to the other.

Camp No. 168 was pitched at the extremity of the tongue of gravel between the two rivers. The Chaktak-tsangpo had here a breadth of 92.2 feet, a maximum depth of 2.4 feet, an average velocity of 4.56 feet, and a discharge of 664 cubic feet per second. Its water was almost quite clear, and in consequence of its greater velocity forced its way far into the muddy water of the Brahmaputra. The latter had at mid-day a temperature of 48.9°, while the water of the tributary was a little warmer, namely, 49.8°. Our companions told us that all who come to the great river drink of the water, because it comes from the holy mountain Kailas, or Kang-rinpoche, in the far west.

Shukkur Ali sat with his ground line at a deep bay

with slow eddies and pulled out of the water ten fine fish, a species of sheat with four soft barbs. He had raw meat as bait on his five hooks; at one end of the line a stone was tied, so that it could be thrown far out into deep water, and the other end was made fast to a peg driven in to the bank, and a stone was laid on the line so lightly in the fork of the peg that it fell when a fish bit. The fisherman can then occupy himself meanwhile with some manual work, such as mending shoes. He puts his fish in a small enclosed basin. The fish had white flesh, and were delicate.

On May 29 we measured the main river at a place where a low island divides it into two channels 175.5 and 180.4 feet broad respectively, with a maximum depth of 3.8 feet. Here the Brahmaputra carries 2532 cubic feet of water, and 3196 after receiving the Chaktak-tsangpo. At the confluence of the Dok-chu we had found only 2966 cubic feet, but the measurement was made a month and a half earlier. The ratio of the Brahmaputra to the Dok-chu was 5 : 2, and of the Brahmaputra to the Chaktak-tsangpo 7 : 2. The Dok-chu is therefore considerably larger than the Chaktak-tsangpo.

On May 30 we followed the broad valley of the Chaktak-tsangpo towards the north-west and west-north-west till we came to a district named Takbur, whence we intended to ride next day over the Takbur-la to Saka-dzong. But it did not come off; for before I was awakened, came a chief with five attendants and made a horrible disturbance with my men and our Tibetans from Kyerkye. The latter he beat with the flat of his sword, and he took away from the former the milk and butter they had bought the evening before, saying that no one had permission to sell us provisions. He told Robert that he had orders not to let us pass through to Saka-dzong, and that he would make us stay here three months. We might not hire yaks also—which was very inconvenient, as we had only a horse and a mule after all the hired animals had gone. We might not buy provisions; but this was not of much consequence, for Robert had shot four wild-geese and found a large quantity of eggs, and the river was full of fish.

I accordingly sent Islam Ahun and Ishe to Saka with a message that Muhamed Isa should send us five horses immediately. Then I summoned the supercilious chief to my tent, where he confirmed the accounts of my men. He declared that I had no right to deviate a single step from the great high-road, and that the district in which we were was under him, not under Saka-dzong, and therefore the local passport was worthless. He intended to carry out the orders he had received, as he valued his head. When I told him that I should report his uncivil behaviour to the Mandarins in Lhasa, he jumped up and drew his sword threateningly, but when he saw that my composure could not be shaken he quieted down. In the evening he came to tell us that we might cross the Takbur-la, and brought us both yaks and provisions. Who he was we could never discover, for in Saka no one would acknowledge that he knew him. Perhaps it was only a childish attempt to cure me of further deviations from the main road. However, it was a pity that we had lost a day here. When the morning of June 1 dawned, Islam Ahun and Ishe came with our horses, which we did not now need, and brought me greetings from Muhamed Isa, who sent word that all was well with the caravan; they were on friendly terms with the authorities, and were permitted to buy all they required.

We set off again northwards and marched through the Takbur valley, where there was abundance of game—hares, pheasants, and partridges—some of which Tsering shot, and foxes, marmots, and field-mice. In the distance we saw a grey prowling animal which we took for a lynx. There were also kiangs, which seemed very unconcerned. North-west, north, and north-east huge snowy mountains were seen from the Takbur-la (16,621 feet), of which Ryder and Wood had taken bearings. Like those Englishmen, I considered it certain that these peaks lay on the watershed of the Tsangpo, and belonged to the crest of the Trans-Himalaya. I had afterwards an opportunity of proving that this was a mistake. From the pass a river runs down to join the Sachu-tsangpo. Here we saw a number of yaks in the luxuriant grass, and a nearly tame kulan kept them company.

214

215

216

214. Beggar at Tashi-gembe. 215. Young Tibetan at the Mouth of the Chaktak-tsangpo. 216. Wandering Lama with a Wooden Glove in his Hand, such as is used to protect the Hands in the Prostration Pilgrimage round the Holy Mountain Kailas.

Sketches by the Author.

Where the river emerges into the Saka plain, we passed on its left side over a last small spur of the mountain on which the pass is situated, and here I rested for an hour with Robert, to draw a panorama of the interesting country. Tsering marched on with his men, and disappeared as a speck on the great plain. To the east-north-east the white houses of Saka-dzong could be seen in the distance, and with the glass we could make out the camp, two black tents and a white, the latter Muhamed Isa's.

Then we too passed across the plain. On the left stood four tents, where the sheep were being driven into the fold for the night. At one place the road divides; travellers who have nothing to do in Saka-dzong take the southern road. We cross the Sa-chu river and the over-flow of a spring; there is a strong wind from the west, and we long for the tents and the warmth of the camp-fires. At last we are there. Guffaru comes to greet us, and all the others call out to us "Salaam!" and "Ju!" I look in vain for Muhamed Isa's stalwart figure, and inquire for him. "He is lying in bed and has been ill all day," they answer. I suppose that he has his usual headache again, go to the brazier in my tent, and let Robert, as usual, unpack the things I require for my evening work. We were tired and chilled through and longed for our supper.

CHAPTER XXXIX

MUHAMED ISA'S DEATH

We had not been sitting long when Rabsang came to say that Muhamed Isa had lost consciousness, and did not answer when he was spoken to. I now perceived that he had had an apoplectic fit, and hurried off with Robert to his tent, which stood close beside mine. An oil-lamp was burning beside the head of his bed, where his brother Tsering sat weeping. The sick man lay on his back, tall, strong, and straight. The mouth was a little drawn on the left side, and the pupil of the left eye seemed very small, while that of the right eye was normal. The pulse was regular and strong, beating 72. I at once ordered hot bottles to be laid at his feet, and a bag of ice on his head. His clothes were loosened; he breathed deeply and regularly. The eyes were half open, but were lustreless. I called his name loudly, but he gave little sign; he tried to turn his head and move his right arm, uttered a low groan, and then remained still again. Robert was shocked when I told him that Muhamed Isa would not see the sun rise again.

While we were sitting beside his bed I inquired the circumstances from Rehim Ali and Guffaru, who had been with him all day long. During the four days they had waited for us here, he had been quite well, and had never complained of headache. He had tried, in accordance with the last instructions I had given him at the camp in the Basang valley, to win the friendship and confidence of the authorities. The day before he had been still in excellent spirits, had drunk tea with his most intimate friends in the caravan, and had sung to the accompaniment of the guitar.

On this day, June 1, he had got up with the sun, drunk tea, and had had a stormy interview with two Tibetans from the dzong. They had refused to supply the caravan with provisions, and then insisted that the caravan should leave the place at once. He had answered that the Sahib would soon be back, and that it would go badly with them if they did not obey him. They had gone away in anger, and then Muhamed Isa had breakfasted about ten o'clock, and had slept an hour. When he rose, he had complained of headache.

When the sun had reached its noonday height he had gone to look out for us, and had then had a violent attack of sickness, fallen on his left side and lain senseless. The other men hurried up, carried him to his tent, and massaged his body. He was restored thereby to consciousness, and spoke much but indistinctly, and chiefly with the god of Islam:

"I was a Lamaist but went over to Islam; help me now, O Allah, out of this severe illness; let me recover; forgive me my sins and all the wrong I have done to others; let me live, O Allah, and I will always keep thy commandments and will never omit my prayers."

Then he had admonished the others to do their duty as heretofore, and thanked them that they had so patiently assisted him in his misfortune. Now and then he had asked for cold water. He had felt his left arm with his right hand, and asked whose arm it was, and had also said that he did not feel the shoe on his left foot. The whole left side was quite paralysed. Sitting upright, and supported by cushions, he had made the following request to Guffaru: "Thou, who art old, and keepest the commandments of religion, wilt not pollute thy hands if thou takest a knife and cuttest my neck; cut deep down to the spine, for that will relieve my infernal headache." In his fearful suffering he struck his right hand against a box. About an hour later another stroke deprived him of speech, and after that he had only made a sign with his right hand, as though in despair at the approach of death. Towards four o'clock Tsering had come and thrown himself over him, weeping loudly. Muhamed Isa had also wept, and pointed to his lips to intimate that he could not speak. When we entered his tent about five o'clock his consciousness was almost gone. He remained in the same condition for an hour and a half, breathing quietly, with his mouth closed. I went therefore to my dinner, which Adul had prepared for me.

Robert and I studied Burroughs and Wellcome's medical handbook, to see that nothing had been omitted. About eight o'clock we returned to the sick-bed. Muhamed Isa was now breathing with his mouth open—a bad sign, showing that the muscles of the jaws were relaxed; the pulse beat 108, and was very weak. The despair of old Tsering when I told him all hope was gone, was heart-rending. Half an hour later the breathing became slower and weaker, and about nine o'clock the death-rattle commenced, and the struggle of the muscles of the chest to supply the lungs with sufficient air. About every fortieth respiration was deep, and then there was a pause before the next came. They were followed by moans. His feet grew cold in spite of the hot bottles, which were frequently changed. At a quarter-past nine the breathing became still slower and the intervals longer. A death spasm shook his body and slightly raised his shoulders; it was followed by another.

The Mohammedans whispered to Tsering that he should leave his place at the head, for a Mohammedan must hold the lower jaw and close the mouth after the last breath. But the sorrowing brother could only be brought to leave his place by force. A third and last spasm shook the dying man, produced by the cold of death. After a deep respiration he lay still for 20 seconds. We thought that life had flown, but he breathed again, and after another minute came the last feeble breath, and then old Guffaru bound a cloth under the chin and covered the face with a white kerchief. Then all was still, and, deeply moved, I bared my head before the awful majesty of Death.

Horrified and dismayed, the Mohammedans poured into the tent, and the Lamaists after them, and I heard

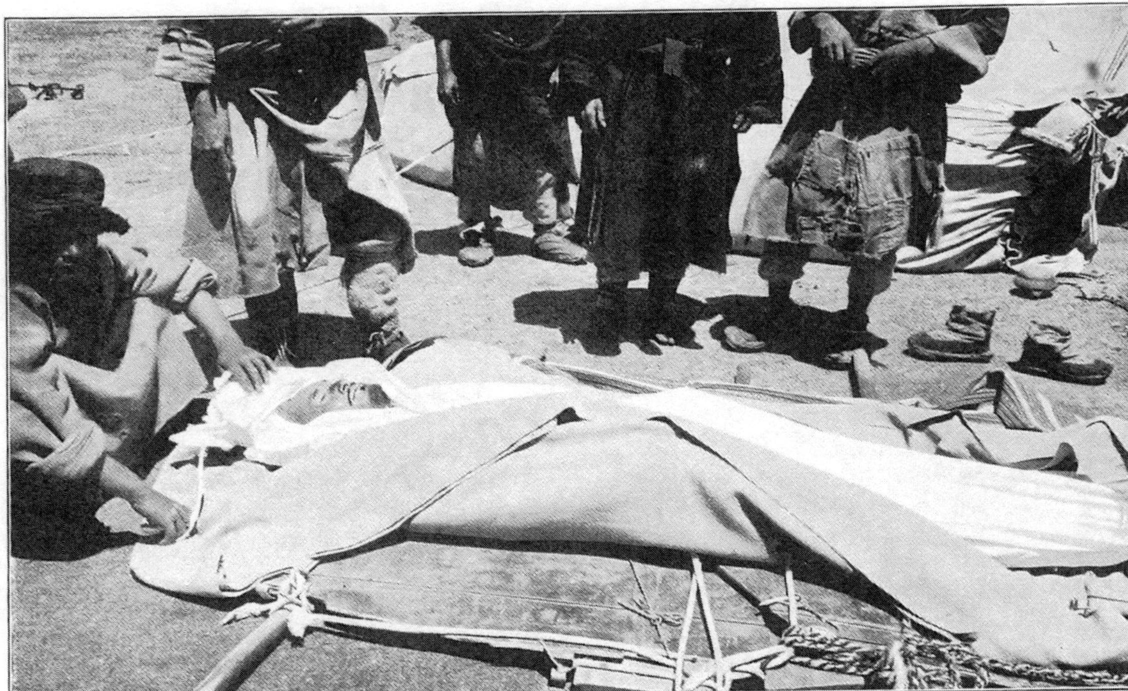

217. The Corpse of Muhamed Isa.

them from time to time call out in low tones, "La illaha il Allah!" Tsering was beside himself: he knelt by the dead, beat his forehead with his hands, wept aloud, nay, howled and bellowed, while large tears rolled down his furrowed sunburnt face. I patted him on the shoulder, and begged him to try and compose himself, go into his tent, drink tea, and lie down and rest. But he neither heard nor saw, and the others had to carry him to his tent, and I heard him wailing in the night as long as I lay awake. Yes, Death is an awful guest. We could hardly realize that he had so suddenly entered our peaceful camp.

I had a long conversation with Robert in my tent, and old Guffaru was sent for to receive my orders for the funeral. The Mohammedans were to watch in turn beside the body through the night. Early next morning the permission of the authorities would be obtained for the choice of a burying-place, and then the interment would take place.

At midnight I paid a last visit to my excellent, faithful caravan leader, who had fallen at his post in the prime of life. He lay long and straight, swathed in a shroud and a frieze rug, in the middle of his tent. At his head burned his oil-lamp, slightly flickering in the draught. The dead watch of five men sat mute and motionless, but rose when I entered. We uncovered his face; it was calm and dignified, and a slight smile played round the lips; the colour was pale, but slightly bronzed from the effect of wind and sun (Illust. 217). Arched over him was the half-dark bell of the tent—the tent which had fluttered in all the winds of heaven on the way through the Chang-tang, and from which Muhamed Isa's merry jests had so often been heard in quiet cold Tibetan nights amidst the sound of flutes and guitars. Now depressing silence reigned around; only the stars sparkled with electric brilliancy.

How empty and dreary everything seemed when I woke on Sunday, June 2, the day of Muhamed Isa's funeral! I went out and looked at the grave; it lay about 300 yards to the south-west of the camp. The Mohammedans had been early in the village to borrow a door, and had washed the body on it. Then they had wrapped it in Guffaru's shroud, which was of thin linen, but quite white and clean. Muhamed Isa and I had often laughed together over the old man's singular fancy of taking this death garment on the journey. Over the shroud (*kafan*) they had wrapped a grey frieze rug. The body lay now in the bright sunshine before the tent, on a bier consisting of the bottom of the two halves of the boat fastened together, and provided with four cross-poles for the bearers.

When all was ready the eight Mohammedans raised the bier on to their shoulders, and carried their chieftain and leader, royally tall, straight and cold, to his last resting-place. I walked immediately behind the bier, and then came Robert and some Lamaists; the rest were occupied at the grave, and only two remained in the camp, which could not be left unguarded. From Tsering's tent a despairing wailing could still be heard. He had been persuaded not to come to the grave. He was heart and soul a Lamaist, and now he was troubled at the thought that he would never see his brother again, who had looked forward to the paradise of the Mohammedans. Some Tibetans stood at a distance. Slowly, solemnly, and mournfully the procession set itself in motion (Illust. 218). No ringing of bells, no strewn fir-branches, no chants spoke of an awakening beyond the valley of the shadow of death. But above us the turquoise-blue sky stretched its vault, and around us the lofty, desolate mountains held watch. In deep mournful voice the bearers sang, "La illaha il Allah," in time with their heavy steps. They staggered under their burden, and had to change it frequently to the other shoulder, for Muhamed Isa was big, corpulent, and heavy.

At length we ascended a gravel terrace between two source streams. The bier was placed at the edge of the grave, which was not quite ready (Illusts. 219, 220, 221). It was deep, lay north and south, and had a cutting or niche on the left side, under which the body was to be laid, so that the earth might not press on it when the grave was filled in. Four men stood in the grave and

218. MUHAMED ISA'S FUNERAL PROCESSION.

received the body, and placed it, wrapped only in the white shroud, under the arch, arranging it so that the face was turned towards Mecca, where the hopes of all true believing pilgrims are centred.

Scarcely was all set in order when a painful incident occurred, an evil omen: the overhanging vault of loose, dry gravel fell in, burying the corpse completely, and partly covering the four men. There was silence, and the men looked at one another irresolute. Shukkur Ali broke the oppressive silence, jumped into the grave, out of which the others clambered, dug out the body again, and removed the gravel from the shroud as well as he could. A wall was then erected of sods cut from the bank of the brook so as to protect the body, the outer space was filled in with sand and stones, and finally a mound a yard high was thrown up over the grave, two stone slabs being placed at the head and foot.

When all was done the Lamaists went home, but the Mohammedans remained at the grave to pray for the deceased, sometimes kneeling, sometimes standing up with their palms before their face. Shukkur Ali, who had been Muhamed Isa's old friend and comrade on many of his journeys in Asia, broke out into violent weeping and wailing, but the others mourned more quietly. Finally, I said a few words in Turki. During all my journeys I had never had a more efficient, experienced, and faithful caravan leader; he had maintained discipline in the caravan, been a father to the men, and taken the best care of the animals; he had been an excellent interpreter, and had treated the natives with prudence and tact. By his happy, humorous disposition he had kept all the others in good temper. In difficult situations he had always found the right way out. In unknown country he had climbed passes and summits to look for the best route—he had always gone himself and not sent others. His memory would always be cherished and honoured among us, and he had also earned a great name in the exploration of Asia, for during thirty years he had served many other Sahibs as faithfully and honestly as myself.

We went silently home after our day's work.

In the lectionary of this Sunday occurred the Bible text, "Thou fool, this night thy soul shall be required of thee."

Muhamed Isa had travelled far, and was highly respected in Asia. He had been in Saka-dzong before, in the year 1904, as Rawling and Ryder's caravan leader. He little thought then that he would return once more, and here set up his tent for the last time after his long wanderings. In the *Geographical Journal* of April 1909, p. 422, Rawling refers to him as follows:—

> Having mentioned Saka Dzong, let me break off one moment to pay a token of respect to the memory of that faithful servant of Sven Hedin who died here. Mohamed Isa was one of the finest characters it has been my fortune to be thrown with. Trustworthy and indomitable in his work, his knowledge of Asia was unequalled by any native, for he had accompanied Younghusband in his famous journey from China, he was with Carey, with Dalgleish who was afterwards murdered, and with Dutreuil de Rhins, when he was a helpless witness of his master's violent death at the hands of the Tibetans. He acted as my caravan bashi in the Gartok expedition, accompanied Sven Hedin during his recent journey, and died, after thirty years of faithful service, at this desolate spot.

From letters I subsequently received from Younghusband, O'Connor, and Ryder, I learned that they also deeply mourned his loss.

The grave terrace rose close to the great high-road between Ladak and Lhasa on its northern side. The mound was next day covered with cut sods arranged in steps, and a small flagstone was set in the ground at the head of the grave, whereon passing Mohammedans could spread out a carpet and pray for the repose of the deceased. On a slab of slate, smoothed down with a chisel, I scratched the following inscription in English and in Roman letters:

MUHAMED ISA
CARAVAN LEADER UNDER
CAREY, DALGLEISH, DE RHINS, YOUNGHUSBAND
RAWLING, RYDER AND OTHERS
DIED
IN THE SERVICE OF SVEN HEDIN
AT SAKA-DZONG, ON JUNE 1, 1907
AT THE AGE OF 53 YEARS.

219, 220, 221. THE INTERMENT OF MUHAMED ISA.

The writing was then cut in the stone by Islam Ahun. The name was also engraved in Arabic, and at the top the formula, "Om mani padme hum," in Tibetan characters, that the people of the country might respect the grave. Future travellers will find the stone in its place—if the Tibetans have not taken it away.

In the afternoon of June 3 I sent for Tsering to my tent. He was now calm and resigned. He was to be my cook and body-servant as before, but his pay would be raised to 20 rupees a month, and this rise was to date back to our departure from Leh. He was allowed to keep the watch I had given to his brother. Guffaru, the oldest of the men, was Muhamed Isa's successor as caravan bashi, received the same increase of pay as Tsering, and was allowed to use Muhamed Isa's grey horse and saddle. In future he would live with two other men in the tent of the deceased.

As I foresaw that the discipline would not be what it was in Muhamed Isa's time, I spoke seriously to the men, telling them that they must obey Guffaru as blindly as they had his predecessor, that they ought to hold together as before and continue to serve me faithfully If any one began to quarrel and was disobedient, he would at once be handed the pay due to him and be sent off to go where he liked. Now that we travelled with hired yaks I could very well spare half the men, and therefore it was their interest to conduct themselves so that they might be retained. Rabsang and Namgyal answered in the name of all, that they would hold together, serve me faithfully, and follow me anywhere.

Then Robert was commissioned to look through the property of the deceased in the presence of Tsering, Guffaru, Shukkur Ali, Rehim Ali, and the Hajji, and after he had made an inventory, to pack it in separate boxes, which were ultimately to be delivered to his wife in Leh together with his outstanding pay. Among his things were some articles of value which he had bought in Shigatse—carpets, tea-cups with metal saucers and covers, ornaments, and woven materials. He had left behind only 10 rupees in ready money, a proof that he had been thoroughly honest in his management of the business of the caravan.

After all relating to the interment had been carried out, the Mohammedans came to ask for a few rupees to enable them to hold a memorial feast in the evening in honour of the deceased. They would make a pudding, called *halva*, of flour, butter, and sugar, drink tea, and kill a sheep. The heathen also, as the Mohammedans called their Lamaist comrades, were to be present. They sang, ate, and drank, and probably hardly thought of the departed.

Two gentlemen from the dzong had been with me on June 2. The Governor himself was absent, travelling in his province to number the tents under his administration and to draw up a list of all the inhabited valleys—all by order of the Chinese. Pemba Tsering, the second in command, was very agreeable and polite, but regretted that he could not supply us with provisions any longer, as he must be prepared to furnish necessaries to the men who were constantly passing to and fro between Gartok and Lhasa. To confirm his words he called up the five Govas or district inspectors of the country, who declared that the poor country could not supply all the *tsamba* and barley we required. I intimated to them that we should still remain a few days awaiting the answer from Lhasa; then they rose, protesting that I might stay here as long as I liked, but that they would not provide me with provisions.

On the same day a large white-and-blue tent was set up by our camp, but it was not till June 4 that the occupants, the Govas of Tradum and Nyuku, paid me a visit. They had heard of our long stay, and wished to find out the state of affairs for themselves. The Nyuku Gova began the conversation:

"Saka and Tradum are put down on your passport, but not Nyuku. Should you, nevertheless, go thither, I will allow you to stay one night, but not longer, for it is stated in the passport that you must travel straight to Tradum."

"My dear friend," I replied, "when once I am in your place we shall become such good friends that you will ask me to stay a whole month to consolidate our friendship. Should you afterwards visit me in India, your visit will be the more agreeable the longer it lasts."

He nodded with a roguish smile, and no doubt considered me a wag, but added that he must obey the orders he had received from the Devashung.

"When I am in correspondence with the Mandarins in Lhasa, and am waiting for their answer, the Devashung has no right to interfere."

"Very well, then it will be best for you to remain here and not come to Tradum or Nyuku; provisions are still scarcer there."

Afterwards Pemba Tsering came again, bringing two sacks of barley and a sheep. He had become much more compliant since he had talked with the other officials, and promised he would try to procure what we needed. We had still two poor horses and a mule from Shigatse, and he was to have one of the animals as a reward. After some consideration he chose the mule. The two horses we sold for a mere trifle to a stranger.

Now we longed to get away from this miserable Saka-dzong and its sad associations. Out in God's open, glorious Nature the winds blow away sorrow. We daily calculated, Robert and I, how long it would be before Tundup Sonam and Tashi returned. If the answer were sent by the so-called Chinese flying post, it might arrive any moment. But the days passed and there was no news. One day some horsemen rode past our camp on the way to the west, and reported that they had seen my two messengers in Kung Gushuk's garden in Shigatse, but they knew nothing of their further intentions. "Patience," whispered the west wind again. In the maze of difficulties in which we became ever more involved, my hopes rested on the answer of the Chinamen. I had told the officials here that I would set off at once if they would allow us to take a more northern route to Nyuku, but, as they would not hear of it, we remained where we were.

When I looked out of my tent my eyes were attracted to the dark grave on its hill. It seemed as if the grave held us fast, though we longed to get away from it. All was dreary and dismal; we missed Muhamed Isa, and his absence caused a great blank. But life goes on as usual. When the sun rises, the women of the village stroll about collecting dung into baskets, while the men drive the yaks and horse to pasture. They sing and whistle, children scream and dogs bark. Blue smoke rises from the chimneys of the village or from the black tents standing within walls among the houses. From the roof of the Saka-gompa with a statue of Padma Sambhava the single lama of the monastery blows his conch. Ravens and bluish-grey pigeons pick up all kinds of morsels among the tents, and the wolves which have come down in the night retire again to the mountains. Riders and caravans pass eastwards to a better land, where poplars, willows, and fruit trees are clothed in their finest summer dress. But we are prisoners in this desolate country, with Muhamed Isa's grave as a focus.

I soon perceived what a depressing effect the loss of the big powerful caravan leader had on my men: they became home-sick. They talked of the warmth of their own firesides, and they took to crocheting and knotting shoes for their children and acquaintances. They gathered round the evening fire and talked of the pleasant life in the villages of Ladak. Robert remarked how dreary and disagreeable Tibet was, and how warm and delightful it was in India; he was pining for his mother and his young wife. I should like to know whether any one was more eager to be off than myself, who had so much before me which must be accomplished. Yes, I saw only too plainly that I could not achieve all I was striving for with my present caravan; it was worn out and used up, which was really not to be wondered at after all it had gone through. My fate was driving me back to Ladak. But I must endeavour to make the most of my chances on the way. And then? All was dark to me. But I knew that I would never give in, and would not leave Tibet till I had done all that lay in my power to conquer the unknown land on the north of the upper Brahmaputra.

On the morning of the 5th came our old friend the

Gova of Raga-tasam. He had heard that we were in difficulties, and offered to speak a good word on our behalf to Pemba Tsering. Afterwards the two came to my tent and informed me that I might take the northern route to Nyuku. The Gova received one of our best horses for his trouble. Now we had six left of our own horses, among them three veterans from Leh, two other horses and a mule. Next evening Guffaru came for the first time to receive instructions, and on June 7 we set out early.

I stopped a moment at the grave. It was striking and imposing in all its simplicity. In its dark chamber the weary one slumbers till the end of time. He listens to the howling of the western storms and the wolves, he freezes in the cold of winter, but he does not see the summer sun, and with longing for the well-remembered past he hears the horses stamping on the hard pebbles. I thought of the Lama Rinpoche in his dark den at Linga.

Farewell, and grateful thanks!

CHAPTER XL

ALONG BYWAYS TO TRADUM

THE day was brilliant ; it was not spring, it was summer. Flies, wasps, and gadflies buzzed in the air, and worms of all kinds crept out of the ground to enjoy the warm season, all too short here. It was hot, 70.2° at one o'clock. The sun seemed to be as scorching as in India. The Sa-chu valley widens out westwards; wild-geese, herons, and ducks sit on the banks of the river, and choughs croak on the mountain which we skirt on the right side of the valley. The fresh grass has sprouted out of the earth in its green summer garb, but it will not really thrive till after the warm rains. We meet a caravan of 200 yaks in five sections, each with two whistling drivers.

" Whence have you come ? " I ask.

" From Tabie-tsaka, where we have been to fetch salt."

" Where does the lake lie ? "

"To the north, in Bongba, thirty days' journey from here."

" Does the road cross over high passes ? "

" Yes, there is a high pass twelve days to the north."

And then they passed on with their light-stepping yaks towards Saka-dzong. It was the first time I had heard this important lake mentioned, and I envied the men of the salt caravan who had traversed this way through the Trans-Himalaya quite unknown to Europeans.

We left the *tasam* on our left ; we turned aside north-westwards straight to the Targyaling-gompa standing with its red *lhakang*, its small white buildings, and its large *chhorten* on a terrace immediately above the spot

222. Woman at the Mouth of the Chaktak-tsangpo in the Tsangpo.

223. Tibetan of Saka.

224. Lama in Saka-dzong.

Sketches by the Author.

where Guffaru has pitched the camp. Twenty lamas came down to find out whether we were thieves and robbers who intended to attack the convent. "Certainly not," Guffaru answered, "we are peaceful travellers passing the night here." "We will not allow it," they replied; "you must remain on the high-road." I now sent Rabsang up, and he was surrounded at the gate by thirty monks. He was told the same; a European had never been here, and none should ever enter the monastery. If the gentlemen of the *dzong* attempted to get us in, they should pay the penalty with their lives. Charming ecclesiastics! Even Rabsang, who was a Lamaist and wore several *gaos* on his neck, was not allowed in. He was in the service of a European. So inimically disposed were these monks that they stopped up the channel we drew our water from. The Devashung, they said, had nothing to do with them. We had heard in Saka-dzong that these monks were bellicose and independent; there they had said that the free-booter who had stopped us on May 31 must have been a disguised monk. But we could do without them and their monastery, which seemed small and unimportant.

Here our four puppies fell ill of a peculiar complaint: they ran about restlessly, snuffed and sneezed, had matter in their eyes, and no appetite. At night I heard one of my tent companions whine and howl, and next morning he lay dead on his rug.

Leaving Rawling's and Ryder's route to the left, we proceeded to the bank of the Chaktak-tsangpo and then northwards along the river. It has a swift current, but does not form rapids; to the south is seen the portal through which it emerges from the mountains. At the village Pasa-guk, which is larger than Saka-dzong, we bivouacked on the right bank. The river here was 141 feet broad, 2 ft. 7 in. deep at most, and carried 629 cubic feet of water. On May 28 it carried 664 cubic feet, but it receives the Sa-chu and other tributaries below the village Pasa-guk.

In the middle of the village is a *serai* with a large store of salt in bags. Here a market is held from time to time, salt being the medium of exchange. I tried to obtain further information about the country in the north, but when I compared the different data together, the result was a hopeless muddle. For instance, I asked travellers who came from Tabie-tsaka, how far they marched each day, and where they passed lakes, rivers, and passes; and when I added the distances together and laid down the direction on the map, the line reached to Kashgar, all through Tibet and Eastern Turkestan! It was impossible to obtain useful data about the country to the north. I must see it with my own eyes. But how would that be possible?

The Hajji came to me, angry and excited, to complain that Guffaru had struck him. I sat in judgment and heard evidence. The Hajji had refused to watch the horses when his turn came, and the caravan bashi had therefore thrashed him. The sentence was, that the Hajji should receive his discharge in Nyuku.

Robert and I sat on the velvety grass on the bank and gazed with longing eyes at the half-clear water dancing merrily on to its destination at the coast. An old man and a youth joined us, and entertained us with dance and song. The old man danced and stamped on the ground in a three-cornered mask of goat leather with red strips and bells, and the youth sang this unintelligible song:

Hail, O God, god of the pass!
Many stars sparkle in the night.
To-day is a fine day.
Would that rain might come!
Give me a bit of tea or a small coin.
O, Cook, give me a pinch of meal and a radish.
Such is the mask that is worn in the Chang-tang.
At the right ear a curl, neither large nor small,
At the left a pin, neither large nor small;
Neither shade nor sun.
There is a father's pin and a mother's pin.
Everywhere we have pins with branches,
For they guard us from all dangers.
The horse holds his head high,
And the rider holds his head high.
The gods are high, the earth is low.
You have gold and silver galore.
May your cattle multiply, your flocks and your property increase!
May your family increase!
The King of Ladak sits between a golden and a silver king.
Now is the song ended.

On June the 10th I left the Chaktak-tsangpo to the right, unfortunately without having learnt whence it comes. We ascended a side valley named Rock, in a north-westerly direction. We had previously passed two towers which had formerly been the fort of a rebellious lama. He was at feud with Saka-dzong, but was defeated. In the camp at the pool Churu the evening seemed to me fearfully long. Home-sickness had become infectious. The Ladakis sang no more, but made shoes for their children, and thereby turned their thoughts more intently to their home. I too found no rest after the day's work. If we only knew what answer the Mandarins would send, but our messenger did not return. We seemed to have stumbled into a morass and to be stamping in it without moving on. Oh, thou dreary, awful Tibet, thou black, poor superstitious folk! In the stillness of the night the step of the camp watchman was pleasant company.

After a night temperature of 14.4° we rode on westwards over a very flat pass, a watershed between the Chaktak-tsangpo and Nyuku, along a road which had once been a *tasam*; numerous ruins and *manis* were memorials of that time. The district was thickly peopled by nomads, and black tents were often seen where sheep bleated and dogs barked; women and boys guarded the flocks, and yaks grazed on the slopes. The country calls to mind the summer pastures on the Pamir. A second puppy died in the night, and was almost eaten up by ravens before morning.

On June 12 we came again to the *tasam* at Nyuku where we set up our camp. The Gova of Nyuku, whose friendship I had gained at Saka-dzong, was very obliging, and said that I was quite at liberty to make another detour to the north, as I seemed to dislike the high-road. It would take me up to a pass, where almost all the mountains of the world could be seen, especially Lumbo-gangri immediately to the north. Here we should come in contact with people of the province of Bongba, who perhaps would sell us all necessaries. In Nyuku the third puppy died. The Tibetans said that it suffered from a throat complaint called *gakpa*, which is very common in the country. Mamma Puppy gave herself no trouble about her little ones when they were ill, but seemed rather to avoid them. We washed them with warm water, and tended them to the best of our power, and did everything we could think of to save the last. The Tibetans could not understand how we could make such a fuss about a dog.

Bluish-white flashes quivered over the mountains all the evening, and their outlines stood out sharp and dark in the lightning. That is a sign of the setting in of the monsoon rains on the southern flank of the Himalayas, and all look forward to them. When rain falls up here, the grass grows up in a couple of days, the cattle become fat and sleek, the milk is thick and yellow; at the present time it is thin and white, and produces little butter. The existence of the nomads, and indeed the prosperity of the whole country, depends on the monsoon. It is the summer pasture which helps the herds to endure the scarcity of the rest of the year. If the rains fail, the stock languish and die.

The night is silent. Only occasionally is heard the hearty laugh of a girl or the bark of a dog. The camp watchman hums an air to keep himself awake.

The 13th was a lazy day; we had to wait for Tundup Sonam and Tashi. I always shave myself on rest days—it is pleasant to feel clean, even when there is no one to smarten oneself up for. Robert shot three wild-geese, and caught two yellow goslings which walked into his tent and made hay there. We put them in the crystal-clear Menchu river, hoping that some kindly goose-mamma would take to them.

From here it is said to be only four days' journey to a district in Nepal, where there are fir-woods. Just fancy: fir-wood as in Sweden and in Simla! But we must remain in this dreary land.

Just as we were starting on the following day the Hajji, Islam Ahun, and Gaffar came to me, and demanded exemption from night duty and separate rations if they were to stay with me. I called all the other men together, and asked if any one else would join them now that they were to be dismissed. But no one wished to. Our Hajji, the only one of the Mohammedans who had been in Mecca —had indeed been twice there—was the only rascal in the caravan. He had instigated the others. In my experience Mecca pilgrims are always scoundrels. The Hajji declared that he preferred robbers and tramps on the road to Guffaru and the other Ladakis. The three men vanished from sight as we marched north-westwards up the valley of the Men-chu.

In camp No. 177, on June 15, I held a grand reception, for some chiefs from the direction of Bongba came to visit me, and our old friend, the Gova of Tradum, arrived. They decided that I might ride a short distance to the north, but only on condition that I came back the same day. So on the 16th we rode on fresh hired horses up to the Kilung-la, where the view was instructive and showed the lie of the land. Before us was the dark Lumbo-gangri with its deep wild valleys and steep cliffs, its small glacier tongues and caps of eternal snow. The men of the district said that the mountain was holy, and was a kind of portal or forecourt to the Kang-rinpoche, the celebrated pilgrimage mountain near the sources of the Indus. Behind Lumbo-gangri are the valley and river of the Rukyok-tsangpo, which flows to the Chaktak-tsangpo. It was now clear to me that these summits, of which bearings were taken by Ryder and Wood, could not lie on the watershed of the rivers flowing to the ocean. But no one knew the true aspect of the country farther north, and the Bongba men had been ordered to stop us if we tried to force our way in that direction. I could not by entreaties or threats obtain more than the view from the Kilung-la. The further we proceeded westwards the more of the blank space on the map was left behind us. That was exceedingly annoying, but my hopes were still fixed on the Chinese letters from Lhasa.

On the morning of the 17th all the mountains were covered with snow, but the day was warm and fine as we rode up to the Serchung-la, and saw to the south-west the northernmost crest of the Himalayas and the broad valley of the Brahmaputra. The valley descending from the pass is full of brushwood and drifting sand, which is piled up in dunes to a height of nearly 20 feet.

After an interesting and successful march we came to the valley junction Dambak-rong. But the day was not yet over. We heard that Nazer Shah's son had arrived the day before at Tradum on his way to Ladak with twenty-two mules. A messenger was therefore despatched to ask him to wait for us, and give us tidings of Tundup Sonam and Tashi. The Gova of Tradum also rode home to get all in order against our arrival. A short time passed by, and then a horseman came up at a smart trot from the Serchung valley. He had evidently followed our track; he rode straight to my tent, dismounted, and handed me a letter with a large seal, bearing the words, "Imperial Chinese Mission, Tibet," and the same in Chinese characters.

Now our fate would be settled. The Ladakis crowded round my tent. I perceived that they hoped we should be obliged to return by the direct road to Ladak. They longed for home, and were not inspired by the same interests as myself. The tension was extreme as I opened the letter. It was dated at Lhasa on June 3, and had been fourteen days on the way. It was written in faultless English by Ho Tsao Hsing, first secretary to H.E. Chang (Tang Darin), and ran as follows:

DEAR DR. HEDIN—Your letter to His Excellency Chang dated the 14th May was duly received. Knowing that you have arrived at Raka-tatsang, that Devashung hindered you to proceed foreward. His Excellency is very sorry to hear such occurrence; and he instructed me to write you the following:—

That in His Excellency's last letter to you he wrote you to return by the way you came; and now he does not understand why you are taking another road contrary to what he wrote you, consequently, you have met with such inconveniences, to which His Excellency regrets very much indeed. His Excellency has, now, again ordered Devashung and officials along the way to give you all possible protection and comfort, but he sincerely wishing you *not* to change your direction to the N.W., where both the country and people are wild [I wonder how he could know that], and that accidents might happen, which His Excellency can hardly bear any responsibility.

Therefore, His Excellency wishes you only to return by the way as you came, not to venture in other directions.

226

228

225, 226, 227, 228. TIBETAN BOYS AND GIRLS OF SAKA AND TRADUM.
Sketches by the Author.

His Excellency gives his best regards to you and wishing you a happy and safe return.—I am yours very truly,

Ho Tsao Hsing.

That was all I got by the stratagem which had cost us so much loss of time. A positive prohibition to proceed north-westwards to the land of my dreams. Now the Devashung would issue fresh orders, and we should be watched more closely than ever. Now the iron gates would be closed again from the south, and the way to the forbidden land barred. Tang Darin was as immovable as the State Secretary for India, Lord Morley. But he stimulated my ambition, and for that I have to thank him. To begin with, we seized the copy of our passport, which was to be transferred from Gova to Gova all along the road.

But not yet had this fateful day come to a close. At sunset came Tundup Sonam and Tashi, dusty and ragged, with their bundles on their backs. "Welcome and well done, 20 rupees each and new suits of clothes is your reward. What news?" No letters, but only a note from Ma that he had forwarded my letters to Lhasa, and sent a letter from Gulam Kadir to Muhamed Isa. They had reached Shigatse in eleven days, and had rested there three days. Then they had set out from Tashi-lunpo directly westwards. They made a fast and long march on the first day, and climbed up to the pass Ta-la at sunset, where nine highwaymen, two with guns and the others with swords, fell upon them and threw them to the ground. The two guns were set on their rests and the barrels pointed to the men's heads, the seven swords were drawn, and one of the robbers said:

"If you value your lives, hand out everything of value you have."

Frightened out of their wits, the two Ladakis begged them to take all they wanted if they would only spare their lives. The nine robbers then opened their bundles and thoroughly plundered them, taking even their little *gaos* and images, as well as their cooking utensils and 18 rupees in silver. They were allowed to keep the clothes they had on their backs. By pure chance the robbers had overlooked a small packet of 30 *tengas*, which Tundup Sonam had put at the back of his girdle. The robbers cleared them out in a minute, and then disappeared into the mountains. Our two defeated heroes remained weeping on the battle-field till dark, and then they went off very slowly at first, turning round frequently and fancying they saw a robber in every shadow, but afterwards they quickened their pace almost to a run. Deadly tired, they crept under two boulders by the wayside, and next morning came to three black tents, where they got food, and were told that a lama had been robbed and stripped naked on the Ta-la two days before. But now they were safe, and it was touching to see how delighted they were to be with us again. They had seen Muhamed Isa's grave, and the conversation about it reminded Tsering of his sorrow.

On June 18 we travel across open country to Tradum, our route following the northern side of the valley while the *tasam* runs along the southern. The ground was sandy. Small irritating horseflies buzz in the nostrils of the horses and drive them frantic. They walk with their noses on the ground like the wild asses to escape the flies. To the right is the Tuto-pukpa, a mountain to which corpses are carried on yaks from Tradum to be cut up. We ride between pools where wild-geese are plentiful with their pretty yellow goslings. At a projecting rock, cairns and streamer poles are set up; the wall of rock is black, but all the side facing the road is painted red—"Ah, this is blood on Balder's sacrificial stone." Here the village of Tradum can be seen, its temple and its *chhorten* on a hill. To the south-west the dark snow-crowned rampart of the Himalayas appears, wild, grand, and precipitous. To the south-east lies the *tasam*, a light winding riband, and our path runs into it; it is 40 feet broad between grass-grown terraces of sand; it is the great trunk-road of Tibet.

We had scarcely set up our camp when the discharged Hajji and his two companions came up and salaamed. But I was angry, and drove them away. I afterwards heard that they wept, and I was heartily sorry that I had been so unkind. But it was too late, for they were seen tramping out wearily into the steppe when the shades of evening fell.

The monastery Tradum-gompa is subject to Tashi-lunpo, and its five monks live on the produce of their sheep and yaks, and carry on trade with Nepal. Round the temple are eight *chhortens*, and in the *lhakang*, the hall of the gods, the immortal son of Sakya is enthroned between the eleven-headed, six-armed Avalokitesvara and other deities. On a small hill of schist above the convent is a hermit's dwelling, where there is a splendid view over the Brahmaputra valley and the Tsa-chu-tsangpo as it emerges from the mountains.

Here died our fourth puppy, which I had hoped to keep as a remembrance of Shigatse. Mamma Puppy had now her mat to herself, and outside the tents lay the two black dogs from Ngangtse-tso.

The Gova of Tradum was an excellent, genial rogue, and had a thorough contempt for the Devashung. He would not let me follow up the Tsa-chu valley, but made no objection to an excursion to the Kore-la pass, two days' journey off to the south-west, and belonging to the Himalayan range which is the watershed between the Ganges and the Brahmaputra. He also let us hire six horses, and gave us two guides for the journey, which was to be commenced on the morning of June 20.

The first night we were to encamp at the spot where the Tsa-chu-tsangpo enters the upper Brahmaputra. I rode south-south-west with my usual retinue over grassy steppe and sand-dunes. In front of us were three wanderers with bundles on their backs and staves in their hands. When we overtook them they stopped, came forward, and laid their foreheads on the ground at my feet. It was the Hajji and the two other men. I was glad of the opportunity of taking them into favour again. For the future they were to follow our yaks.

The camp was pitched on the right bank of the river, at the foot of the hill crowned by the ruins of the old Liktse monastery. Here an important trade-road crosses the river and a ferry maintains communication between the banks. The Tsa-chu river had here a breadth of 35½ yards, and a depth of barely 40 inches, while the Brahmaputra was 120 yards broad by 5¾ feet deep, and was much more imposing than farther down. The absolute height was 14,977 feet. It was not easy to carry the rope across the stream, for a strong south-west gale was blowing and the waves were high. Robert rowed out from the right bank with the rope, and from the left some Ladakis waded out as far as they could in the shallow, slowly deepening, water to catch the end thrown to them and secure it on shore. When at last we had stretched the rope across, it broke with the pressure of the wind and the waves, and the work had to be done again. We noted a temperature of 53.6° in the air and of 59.7° in the water, but the men were so chilled by the wind that they had to make a good fire. It also rained heavily—the first rain we had had since we left Ladak—and thunder rolled among the mountains.

For the first time the minimum temperature in the night, 37.8°, was above freezing-point, and the morning was beautiful after the storm: the sky was only half covered with bright summer clouds, not a breath of air stirred, and the surface of the river was smooth as a mirror, only slightly broken by slowly moving whirlpools. The ferry was already plying across with passengers and goods. The ferryman is paid a *tenga* for each passage, and he crosses over twice in the hour. Our horses and yaks were made to swim over the river after they had grazed at night on the steppes on the left bank.

We rode 21½ miles on the 21st, but first paid a visit to the little Liktse-gompa monastery, which stands on the inner side of the hill, and therefore has not the fine view obtained from the old ruined monastery on the summit. From its window-openings the monks could watch the oscillating life of the river during the various seasons of the year: its slow fall in spring; its rise during summer, when volumes of turbid water come down from melting snow-fields and glaciers; its decline in autumn, and the freezing of the river in the cold of winter. And they could see the breaking-up of the ice in spring, and the

229   230

231   232

229. WOMAN OF NYUKU. 230 TWO TIBETANS. 231. THE GOVA OF TUKSUM.
232. GIRL AT PASA-GUK.

Sketches by the Author.

great clattering slabs dancing down the current. But now the prospect before the eyes of the ten monks is only a wretched loamy valley between barren hills, for their convent lies apart from all roads. Liktse-gompa is a dependency of Sera, but receives no support from it, and possesses no herds. The profits from the ferry are the only revenue of the monks. The abbot, Punjun Dung, with a red turban and a grey beard, showed me the gods in the *lhakang*, Buddha, Padma Sambhava, etc. Among the usual sacred objects on the altar were two human skulls converted into drinking vessels, one of them lined with silver. In the courtyard the holy dog was chained up.

Then we mounted and rode off quickly. We perceived at once that this road is much frequented. On the steppe and in open soft valley bottoms it is less clearly marked, for there every one marches where he likes; but over passes and on spurs with hard stone the tracks converge from all sides, and there the road has been trodden down and worn in the course of centuries. On the small pass Tsasa-la we met a large caravan laden with barley.

"Where have you come from?" I ask.

"From Mundang in the country of Lo Gapu."

Mundang is marked on the English maps of Nepal, but who was Lo Gapu, "the King of the Southern Land"? It sounded so grand.

The next pass is called Dorab-la, and from the top we see the Chockar-shung-chu, a broad valley with a brook draining partly from the Kore-la, and flowing to the Brahmaputra.

While we are resting, Guffaru passes with his black baggage-train in close order, a troop of laden yaks, whistling and singing Tibetans, and some Ladakis with our own horses as a rearguard. They soon disappear in the dust of the road, two of our men resting a while in a cleft to take a puff or two from their weather-worn narghilés. From this point they march westwards to the rendezvous, while we continue southwards.

In the valley leading up to the Ngurkung-la a large salt caravan on the way to Nepal was encamped. The twelve leaders had piled up a fine shelter of sacks of salt against the violent wind. We then came to the very broad valley which ascends to the saddle of the pass visible in the south. We rode up for hours, though the ascent was not noticeable, but the wind was dead against us. To the right is the water-parting chain of the Himalayas which we had seen from Tradum. A curious, sharply outlined cloud, like a white torpedo, covered it, and from the northern extremity small fleecy flakes parted from time to time and floated away. We camped near some black tents in a side valley close to the extraordinarily flat pass.

CHAPTER XLI

A PEEP INTO NEPAL

It was on June 22 that I stood on the platform of the Kore-la pass and gave a stolen glance into Nepal, and tried to get a glimpse of Dhaulagiri peak, 26,670 feet high. But the morning was dull, heavy clouds lay like pillows on the earth, and nothing could be seen of the surrounding mountains. "We must wait till it clears," was the only order I could give. But just then a milk-girl came from a camp of 20 tents which was near at hand. The people were Nepalese subjects, but were camping on the Tibetan side. The girl said that it was only a short day's journey to the nearest permanent dwellings and gardens, and two days' journey to Lo Gapu's summer residence.

Then we thought: "We may as well ride down the southern side of the pass as stay up here in the wind." No sooner said than done! The tents are folded up, the animals laden, we mount and ride along the eastern side of the valley up to the Kore-la, which from the Tibetan side little resembles a pass, for to the eye the grass-grown or unfruitful loose ground seems quite level. Of the snowy mountains on the western side of the valley only the dark base is visible; layers of clouds lie close above the earth; one feels as though one could push one's head against the roof. A ruined house, where perhaps a frontier guard once dwelt, a couple of long *manis*, and loose blocks of conglomerate stand on the top. A caravan comes up from Nebuk in the bottom of the valley.

We look round in vain for the actual watershed, and

find it only by noticing rivulets running together and flowing southwards. Here we light a fire and take observations. The view is marvellous, at any rate a relief such as we have not seen for a long time. The mighty snowy mountains to the south, which yesterday broke through the clouds, are, indeed, obscured, but our valleys fall steeply and unite into a large valley, in the depths of which grassy plots and fields shine in deep spring verdure amid the everlasting grey, yellow, and red landscape. Down below the sun is shining, and behind us the sky is clear above the Brahmaputra valley, while here and round all the snowy mountains float opaque clouds. From the saddle lying west of our point of vantage innumerable valleys radiate out; the surface of the ridges between them is nearly level, or dips gently to the south-east, while the valleys are deeply cut in like cañons, and the promontories at the meeting of the valleys are broken short off. Perhaps some of the nearest peaks of the Himalayas rise like islands above the sea of clouds, for here and there a reflexion from sun-lighted firn-fields seems to be trying to break through the veil of clouds (Illust. 233).

We stand on the frontier between Tibet and Nepal. Behind us to the north we have the flat, level land on the southern bank of the Tsangpo. We have mounted only 315 feet from the river to the Kore-la, where the height is 15,292 feet. And from the pass there is a headlong descent to the Kali Gandak, an affluent of the Ganges. By means of a canal cut through the Kore-la the Brahmaputra might be turned into the Ganges. Northern India needs water for irrigation, but the gain would perhaps be small, for the Brahmaputra in Assam would be as much diminished as the Ganges was increased. Tibet would lose by the change, and a number of villages on the Kali Gandak would be swept away. A new road would be opened for the invasion of India from the north, and therefore on the whole it is perhaps best for all parties concerned to leave things as they are. But the changes here indicated will some time come to pass without artificial aid, for the tentacles of the Kali Gandak are eating back northwards into the mountains much more quickly than the

233. View from the Kore-la towards the South-West.

Tsangpo is eroding its valley. Some time or other, perhaps in a hundred thousand years, the Ganges system will have extended its tentacles to the bank of the Tsangpo, and then will be formed a bifurcation which, in the course of time, will bring about a total revolution in the proportions of the two rivers and their drainage areas.

Now we are in Nepal and go on foot down the declivities. Here little has been done to improve the road. Occasionally an awkward block of granite has been rolled away, leaving a gap in the breastwork; in other respects the caravan traffic has done most for the road, wearing it down. It is easy and pleasant to go down southwards towards denser air; it becomes warmer, and we breathe more easily; the verdure increases, and flowers of different colours make the grass gay. We try to forget that we must toil up all these slopes again; let us go down, down, to enjoy a summer life, if only for twenty-four hours, and forget dreary Tibet. An hour ago the wind blew icy cold on the pass, and now we feel the soft zephyrs gently caressing the heights. Robert takes in deep draughts of the tepid air and fancies he hears a whispered welcome to India; Tsering and Rabsang become lively and contented, and I muse over a visit to the King of the Southland.

Three horsemen rode slowly up the ascent. Two of them were turning their prayer-mills. They looked astonished. We asked whence they came and whither they were going. They were going to the tent village on the plateau. When they were told who we were, in answer to their question, they dismounted and begged pardon for not greeting us at first. I readily forgave them, for I looked like a ragged tramp. They advised us to pass the night in one of the houses of Lo Gapu, and invited us to visit them in their tent village on our way back.

The gradient becomes less steep, and we come to an expansion where three valleys meet, the Kungchuk-kong, which we have followed, in the middle, the Pama on the east, and the Damm on the west. From the Damm valley only comes a small gushing brook. We pass along the right side of the united valley. On the same side a very large valley opens, the Yamchuk-pu, with an irrigation channel running down from its brook to the villages and fields below. In the village Yamchuk we come to the first houses and trees. On the left side of the valley lies a large monastery with avenues of trees and long rows of *manis*; it is called Gubuk-gompa. Fields, grassy patches, and bushes become more numerous. Then comes a succession of villages on the left side of the valley, which is barely 2½ furlongs broad.

Below the side valley Gurkang-pu, on the left, pebble beds stand in perpendicular walls with numerous caves and grottos. These are apparently used as dwellings, for they are connected with the houses and walls in front of them. Lower down we come to the village Nebuk, among gardens. The architecture is of the usual Tibetan style, white and red masonry, flat roofs, and decorations of streamer poles. The vegetation becomes more luxuriant and the fields larger. We frequently pass ruined walls and towers, perhaps relics of the time when Nepal was at feud with Tibet. Now the densely peopled and well-tilled valley has a peaceful aspect, and no frontier guards hinder our advance.

The usual *manis* lie along the road, and a large red *chhorten* or *stupa* has a touch of the Indian style. Below three villages lying close together the valley contracts slightly. Near a lonely house we encamped in a lovely garden, with fine green trees, among waving cornfields. A woman told us that this place, called Nama-shu, belonged to Lo Gapu, and that no one might stay in the garden without his permission. However, we established ourselves there, and inhaled with delight the mild dense air, and heard the wind rustling through the tree-tops.

Soon two men appeared, who were in the service of Lo Gapu, asking for information about us. They said that we were in the district Tso, and that the river was called Tso-kharki-tsangpo. A village we can see just below our camp was named Nyanyo, and from there Mentang, the residence of Lo Gapu, could be reached by crossing only two spurs of the mountains, He, they said, was a frontier chief, who paid no tribute to the Maharaja of Nepal, but was obliged to pay a visit to His Highness every fifth year. He had 500 subjects. The people for three days farther south were Lamaists and spoke a Tibetan dialect, in which, however, many Indian and Persian words were incorporated.

When one of the men had obtained all the information he desired, he rode down the valley to make his report to the frontier chief. Meanwhile we held a consultation. I had only Robert, Tsering, Rabsang, and two Tibetans with me, and our funds consisted of only 24 rupees. The temptation was great to wander a few days more southwards through the wild deep valleys of the Himalayas. Here, in the Nama-shu camp, we were at a height of 12,487 feet, and therefore 2805 feet lower than the Kore-la. Every day's journey southwards would bring us into a denser atmosphere, and even now we were not far from shady coniferous woods. But would it be prudent to advance further into Nepal? We were much puzzled, and considered the matter from all sides. Our money would not last more than two days. Our horses belonged to the Gova of Tradum, and we had agreed with him that we would only take a look into Nepal from the Kore-la, and now we had crossed the boundary and descended into a land where our position was less secure than in Tibet. We might fall into a trap before we were aware of it. Lo Gapu might arrest us and ask for orders from Khatmandu. The greatest danger, however, was that the Tibetans might close the frontier and render our return impossible, and then say that now we had left their country we might not enter again. And then we should be cut off from the main caravan, and all the results of my journey would be endangered. I therefore decided to turn back early next morning before Lo Gapu's men had time to come up and arrest us.

The evening was fine and long, and we enjoyed it thoroughly under the rustling of the thickly foliaged trees. I felt perfectly comfortable and breathed freely: the heart had not to labour so heavily as on the Chang-tang; it worked for hours together without an effort; our feet were warm, and we slept as we had seldom done. For in the

Chang-tang if one sleeps even eight hours one does not feel rested and refreshed on rising; one does not derive the proper benefit from sleep. Here we experienced a thoroughly comfortable feeling after our night's rest, and our only disappointment came from the clouds, which concealed the summits of the Himalayas to the south and south-south-west. Only now and then the peaks looked forth for a minute.

On June 23 we mounted our horses again. We had heard no word of Lo Gapu. When the messenger had left us he was convinced that we should continue our way down the valley, and the little potentate was perhaps now expecting our arrival. He might wait! We rode slowly up to the Kore-la, left our old road to the right, and camped at Kung-muga.

I was sitting at my drawing when a horseman came clanking up. He held in his hand a green flag, a messenger's badge among the Chinese and Tibetans. I felt sure that he had some connection with strict measures against us, but found that he was only the bearer of a proclamation from Lhasa to all the stations as far as Gartok, that horses and baggage animals should be supplied to two Chinamen who had been despatched to find me out and talk with me, and convey to me a letter from His Excellency, Lien Darin. They might be expected any moment.

Midsummer Day was as dull as possible. The whole country was buried in impenetrable fog, and even the adjoining tents were invisible. And when it had cleared a little, the mountains were still concealed. We rode north-westwards on an excellent road, and were astonished at the numerous *manis* with their close, fine, raised inscriptions on purple and dark-green schist; other prayer stones had characters 1.2 or 1.6 inches high, while the largest characters were nearly 8 inches high, so that there was only room for one character on each slab. Then six slabs were placed in a row to spell out the sacred formula, "Om mani padme hum." On some votive stones the characters were red, cut out in round pieces of granite with a white underlayer. The largest *mani* was 262 feet long.

234. Gulam Razul's Tents in Gartok.

235. Landscape in Upper Nepal.

View looking South from Camp 182, Nepal.

We passed encampments with large herds; wild asses grazed along with tame yaks. All the men we met halted and saluted us. The Gova of Tradum came to meet us; he pulled a very solemn face, and wondered whether Lo Gapu would be angry at our visit to Nepal. We reached Bando, near the small lake Tsotot-karpo, over the small saddle Tasang-la, and found Guffaru waiting for us with the caravan.

On the 25th we made a short march up to Chikum, whence the Tsotot-karpo is still visible. We had only provisions for one day, but the Gova of Tradum offered to procure more if we would pay well for the horses we had to hire. He had no fear, he said, of the Chinese who were coming; if they scolded him for allowing us to travel on the south bank of the Tsangpo, he would reply that it was easier to supply us with provisions there than on the north side. He had formerly been a lama in Tashi-gembe, but had lost his heart to a lady. To hush up the affair he had started on a pilgrimage to Kang-rinpoche, but was caught and forbidden to return. Then he had gradually worked his way up, and was now chief of Tradum, and was just as great a rascal in secular life as he had been in the religious life. However, he rendered us good service.

The view from our elevated camp was magnificent. When the full moon had risen up in the sky the small lake shone like a silver blade. The sun had left only an after-glow on the western horizon, but the whole plain of the Brahmaputra and the mountains of Chang-tang in the north were clearly defined in dull clear shades, which left all the finer details indistinguishable. A cloud with bright, silvery, white margins floated before the moon. A little to the right another cloud caught a reflexion of the sun, and showed golden margins. They were the angels of night and day fighting for supremacy. Soon night had won the victory, and now the moon cast a bright path over the lake, while all around was involved in a general mist.

When day had resumed its sway we rode in the morning air through swarms of flies, stinging gnats, and horseflies up over the Tagu-la and down the Tambak valley. To the west the most northerly chain of the Himalayas made a magnificent display, and to the north-west lay the broad open valley of the Brahmaputra, the river winding along the middle like a blue riband. This evening, too, the return of night called forth a brilliant play of colours and tone-effects. Light, restless, motionless to the eye, but riven by the upper winds like old prayer-streamers on a pass, the clouds sailed at sunset in the vault of heaven. The moon, the friend of all nocturnal wanderers and sleepers in the open air, illumines the surroundings of our tents, among which the blue smoke of the camp-fires lies like a veil over the ground. The yaks stand still as shadows, and now and then their teeth are heard grinding against the cartilaginous process of the upper jaw. The Tradum Gova and his servants hum their evening prayer and rattle their prayer-mills.

In the morning comes a quickly passing shower and another before noon. We notice all the signs of the sky, and wish for rain as much as the Tibetans, not on our own account, but for the light-footed antelopes, the wild asses, and the mountain sheep. The clouds are blue-black over the mountains to the south, and from them hang down elegantly curved fringes and draperies heavy with rain. One can hear in imagination the drops splashing on the stones, and new-born torrents rushing down the valleys. The trifling rain that has fallen in our neighbourhood can only moisten the ground for a short time. The drops made a pleasant sound as they pelted on the Tradum Gova's umbrella and on my Curzon hat. Thunder rolled heavily and solemnly round about in the mountains, like an echo of the trumpet of the last judgment.

Then we cross the Nerung-tsangpo, come out into the great valley plain of the Brahmaputra, and encamp in a country inhabited by numbers of nomads. The Gova of Nagor was a tall, agreeable man, who procured us *tsamba*, *chang*, and goose eggs—a pleasant change from our perpetual diet of mutton. Robert and Shukkur Ali caught fish. The Gova told me that his parents, who belonged to Kham, had made a pilgrimage to the Kang-rinpoche and

236. A CHHORTEN IN NEPAL.

237. GROUP OF TIBETAN WOMEN.

had left their little son behind, either by mistake or on purpose. The youngster had grown up in the tents of the wild nomads, and now, though a stranger, had become the chief of the district.

On the morning of the 28th we rode up to Namla-gompa, on a rocky prominence, where the view was extensive and instructive. At the eastern foot of the projecting mountain lies the village Namla, a few poor stone cabins, and here the river Pung-chu, flowing out of the lake Ujam-tso, enters the plain. The monastery contains some images of gilded bronze, and seven monks, of whom one, a man of sixty-six, has lived fifty years within its walls. They are poor and have to beg, but they receive freewill offerings from the nomads living in the neighbourhood.

Across a plain of cracked loamy soil, which is flooded at high water, we gain our camp on the bank of the Tsangpo; the river looks like a lake, and that this is also the case in late autumn is shown in Ryder's remarkably conscientiously drawn and accurate map. The breadth here is 973 yards broad, and the maximum depth only 2.4 feet. It may, therefore, be easily waded, and the yak caravan marches quietly through the water. How different it is farther east, where the river, hemmed in between steep mountains, is deep and tumultuous! In late summer it cannot be waded here, and even a boat dare not venture over because of the treacherous, shifting sand-banks. During our measurements the Ladakis went across the river, measuring the breadth with poles and ropes, and held the boat still while I investigated the velocity of the current. When the work was finished, Rehim Ali began to carry Robert to the bank, but he slipped on the smooth, clayey bottom, and both took an involuntary bath, causing all the rest of us to laugh heartily.

Next day the fragile baggage was conveyed across in a boat, and the rest on hired yaks, which tramped through the turbid dirty-grey water. On the northern bank we ride through peculiar country. Here are lakes and swamps, caused by arms of the river, and lying amid a collection of sandhills as much as 26 feet high. We try all directions to avoid sandhills and deep creeks, and frequently ride straight through basins with yielding ground; in some there is a slight current, while others are stagnant. Here and there islets of sand rise out of the water, some barren, others with grass and stalks. It is a thoroughly disintegrated country, but full of pleasing variety. Gnats pursue us in regular clouds. Some men go in front to pilot us. We often get into deep water and have to turn back. The high water washes away the greater part of the driftsand, and deposits it on the banks of the Brahmaputra lower down. But when the river falls, fresh sand accumulates and forms new dunes. The driftsand therefore finds a resting-place here on its way to the east. We encamped by the last lagoon, and heard the fishes splashing in the water. The whole country reminds me of Lob, the swampy region in Eastern Turkestan, and the continual struggle there between driftsand and flowing water. The district is named Dongbo, and here the Gova of Tuksum and other chiefs awaited us. The first-named had heard that the Chinamen, of whose coming we had been informed, had left Saka-dzong and were on their way hither. He expected that they would arrive before evening.

On June 30 we made most of our march along the *tasam*, on which Nain Sing and the English expedition had travelled; for I durst not pass round Tuksum, which was mentioned on my passport. The greater part of the way runs among fine, regular, crescent-shaped dunes, which move eastwards over the plain before the prevailing wind. They are ephemeral phenomena: they live and die, but are always replaced by others. The horns of the crescent protrude far in the direction of the wind, and the slope is very steep on the windward side, as much as 17 degrees, while on the sheltered side it is as steep as the falling sand will allow.

Ganju-gompa stands on an isolated hill to the west of the Ganju-la. It is subordinate to the Brebung monastery, and has a *lhakang* with twelve pillars and four rows of divans, as well as four large drums. The statues of the gods look down with gentle smiles on the homage paid to them by nomads and travellers. Only five monks and as many dogs live in Ganju.

The whole population of Tuksum came out to meet us before their village. It was agreed with the Gova that Guffaru and the main caravan should proceed to Shamsang, while I with a couple of attendants travelled by forbidden roads on the south side of the river. In the evening a deputation of Ladakis came to wait on me with the request that they should be allowed to give a feast in honour of Muhamed Isa, to be paid for out of his outstanding pay. But I thought this a little too cool, seeing that the money belonged to the widow of the deceased. They might have a feast, however, at my own expense, but there would be nothing but mutton, *chang*, and tea.

On the morning of July 1 I had another application, this time from five young beggar girls, ragged and black, with bundles in frames of wood on their backs, and large pilgrims' staves in their hands. They had been, like so many others, at the Kang-rinpoche, and reckoned it a year's journey to their home in Kham. They beg their way from tent to tent. It must be a serious burden to the nomads to maintain the numerous pilgrims that pass along this road.

We said good-bye to Guffaru and his followers on July 2, and riding in a south-westerly direction over the plain, set up our camp 191 on the left bank of the Brahmaputra, which here carried down 1978 cubic feet of water. Next morning the baggage was taken over, and we had also the honour of helping over the river a high lama, whose acquaintance I had made in Tashi-lunpo. He wore a yellow robe with a red mantle, and had a small yellow wooden hat as bright as metal. His servants were armed with guns and swords, and took all their baggage over the river on yaks. But, unfortunately, the yaks got into deep water and began to swim, so that, of course, all their baggage was thoroughly soaked. We also helped a shepherd with some lambs over to the other side, and if we had waited longer we might have done a ferryman's work all day with our boat (Illusts. 240, 241).

Then we crossed over two other arms, and the total

discharge of the Brahmaputra at this place proved to be 3249 cubic feet. The figures, however, obtained on gauging the river so near its source, are of inferior value, especially when the melting of the snow has quite set in, partly because the source streams rise towards evening, carrying the water from the day's thaw down to the main valley, partly because the volume of water depends to a great extent on the weather. At the first downpour of rain the rivers are little affected, for the water is absorbed by the dry soil; but when this is soaked through, the water runs off, and the rivers swell enormously after a single rainy day. When the sky is overcast without rain they fall, but in quite clear weather the sun thaws the snow and causes the rivers to rise again.

It was a long day's journey, for in many of the tents the people refused to give us the help we wanted, and therefore we passed on to the great tributary Gyang-chu, which comes from the south and receives many streams from the northernmost range of the Himalayas.

I have no time to give an account of the geography of this region on the south side of the Brahmaputra. I will only say that during the following days we were cut off from the main river by low mountains, and that we did not encamp again on its bank till July 6, when we came to the Cherok district. We had left several tributaries behind us, and the main stream carried only 1554 cubic feet of water.

After another short day's march we rejoined Guffaru's party in Shamsang (15,410 feet) on the great high-road, where twenty-one tents were now standing. The chiefs of the neighbourhood were very attentive, and did not say a word against my proposal to go up to Kubi-gangri, which shows its snowy peaks to the south-west, and in which the sources of the Brahmaputra were said to lie. They procured us provisions for twelve days, and we had not had so free a hand for some time. Here nothing had been heard of Chinese or Tibetan pursuers from Lhasa.

238. Women in the Village of Namla.

239. Inhabitants of the Village of Namla.

CHAPTER XLII

IN SEARCH OF THE SOURCE OF THE BRAHMAPUTRA

Now we were already far to the west ; the force of circumstances had forced us to leave behind us step by step ever larger areas of unknown country to the north. I was vexed, but I would, at any rate, endeavour to do all that was possible in my hampered condition. At Shamsang, Ryder's Lahtsang, we were at the place where the actual source streams of the Brahmaputra converged from various directions. I had long determined to push on to the unknown source, unless the Tibetans placed unsurmountable obstacles in my way.

The learned and clear-sighted Colonel Montgomerie had sent Nain Sing in the year 1865 up the valley of the upper Brahmaputra (Illust. 380). From our Shamsang the Pundit crossed the Marium-la, and said in his report that the sources of the river were certainly in the huge chain seen in the south, and were fed by its glaciers. He did not, however, go to look for the actual sources, but continued his journey westwards.

The next year, 1866, Thomas Webber made an excursion into Tibetan territory, and his route lay a little to the south of Nain Sing's. On his sketch-map it may be seen that he crossed some of the source streams of the Tsangpo, but of the tract in which the sources are situated he gives no further indication than "Snowy ranges unexplored." And when he says in his text that here are the sources of the great Brahmaputra, which have their origin in the Gurla glaciers, the confusion is hopeless; for the sources of the river lie 60 miles from Gurla, a mountain which has nothing whatever to do with the Brahmaputra.

The political expedition which, under the command of Rawling in the close of the year 1904, had Gartok for its destination, and the chief result of which was the admirable map of the upper Brahmaputra valley surveyed by Ryder and his assistants (Map 7), travelled from Shamsang over the Marium-la and north of the Gunchu-tso to Manasarowar. It was therefore of the greatest importance to me to travel to the south of their route through country they had not touched on. They travelled by the same road as Nain Sing, and left the source of the river at a distance of 40 miles to the south. From Ryder's report it might be supposed that he considered the Marium-la to be the cradle of the Brahmaputra; but in a letter I have recently received from him, he states that such is not the case, but that he always recognized that the actual source must lie among the mountains in the south-west, which he has set down on his map from bearings taken of their peaks. Ryder also remarks in his report that the principal headwaters come from there.

Instead of entering into a diffuse discussion of the problem, I introduce in this book small sketches of the maps of my three predecessors, Nain Sing, Webber, and Ryder. No other traveller had ever been in this region, and I would on no account miss the opportunity of penetrating to the actual source of the Brahmaputra and fixing its position definitely.

How was this to be done? At Shamsang the source streams meet, and below this point the united river bears the name Martsang-tsangpo. First of all, I must, of course, gauge the quantities of water in the source streams, and, if they were nearly equal, we must be content to say that the Brahmaputra has several sources.

With ten men, the boat, and the necessary measuring apparatus, I betook myself first, on July 8, to the point on the southern side of the valley where two streams run together, the Kubi-tsangpo from the south-west and the Chema-yundung from the west. A short day's march farther west the Chema-yundung receives the Marium-chu, which comes from the Marium-la. First the united stream was gauged, and found to discharge 1554 cubic feet of water per second, and immediately after the Chema-yundung, which discharged almost 353 cubic feet. Subtracting this from the volume of the united river, we get 1201 cubic feet as the discharge of the Kubi-tsangpo. This river is then three and a half times as large as the Chema, and it should be remembered that the Chema also receives the water of the Marium-chu, so that its 353 cubic feet represent the united volumes of two tributaries.

When we encamped in the evening with the main caravan in the Umbo district (15,427 feet), where the Chema-yundung and the Marium-chu unite, the rivers were very considerably swollen, and the water, which had been clear in the morning, had become turbid. Therefore only the two measurements taken at the same time were directly comparable, and I will pass over all the subsequent measurements. To arrive at the source we had only to know that the Kubi-tsangpo is far larger than the two others, so we had to follow its course up into the mountains, which none of my predecessors had done. The Tibetans also said that the Kubi was the upper course of the Martsang-tsangpo.

On July 9 we parted from Guffaru and the main caravan, which was to keep to the great highroad and cross the Marium-la to Tokchen, while Robert and I with three Ladakis and three armed Tibetans followed the Kubi-tsangpo up to its source. Our way ran west-south-west. Where we crossed the Chema-yundung, a good distance above the last delta arms of the Marium-chu, the river carried little more than 140 cubic feet of water, and therefore the Kubi-tsangpo, flowing to the south-east of it, is here fully eight times as large. At the ford our Tibetans drove a peg with a white rag into the edge of the bank, and when I asked why, they answered: "That the river may not become tired of carrying its water down the valleys."

At Tok-jonsung, where we bivouacked among some black tents, the Chema looked very large, but its water ran very slowly. The nomads of the district go up to the Chang-tang in winter. Here also we heard, as on many former occasions, that smallpox was raging frightfully in Purang, and that all the roads leading thither were closed. No country lies so high that the angel of death cannot reach it.

In the night the thermometer fell to 15.4°, but we were at a height of 15,991 feet. The snowy mountains in front of us to the south-west became more distinct. The Chema river meandered with a slow fall, and we left it on the right before we came to our camp in Sheryak.

We ride on July 11 on to the south-west in a strong wind, passing already porous, melting snowdrifts. Solid rock is not to be seen, but all the detritus consists of granite and green schist. We follow a clearly marked nomad path, leading up to the small pass Tso-niti-kargang on the ridge which forms a watershed between the Chema-yundung and the Kubi-tsangpo. The large valley of the latter is below us to the south. The water of the Kubi-tsangpo is very muddy, but on the right bank is a perfectly clear moraine lake. From the south-east the affluent Lung-yung flows out of its deeply cut valley. The view is grand on all sides. From north-west to north-east extends a confused sea of mountains, the crests and ramifications of the Trans-Himalaya, intersected by the northern tributaries of the upper Tsangpo. To the south we have a panorama magnificent and overpowering in its fascinating wildness and whiteness, an irregular chain of huge peaks, sharp, black, and fissured, sometimes pointed like pyramids, sometimes broad and rounded, and behind them we see firn-fields from which the snow slides down to form glaciers among the dark rocks. Prominent in the south is the elevation Ngomo-dingding, and from its glaciers the Kubi-tsangpo derives a considerable part of its water. To the west-south-west lies the Dongdong, another mass with glaciers equally extensive, and to the right of it are heights called Chema-yundung-pu, from which the river of the same name takes its rise, and flows down circuitously to the confluence at Shamsang. To the south-east the position of the Nangsa-la is pointed out to

240. LAMA IN MY BOAT.

241. LOADING THE BOAT WITH BOXES ON CROSSING THE BRAHMAPUTRA.

me beyond the nearest mountains, where the river Gyang-chu, which we came across a few days before, has its source.

We go down among moraines, granite detritus, and boulders. Here three small clear moraine pools, called Tso-niti, lie at different heights. The ground becomes more level, and we pass a *mani*, a rivulet trickling among the rubbish, and a small pond, before we reach camp 200 in Lhayak, on the bank of the Kubi-tsangpo, where the pasturage is excellent and we find numerous traces of nomad camps. In several places we come across large sheets of fine thin birch bark, which have been detached by storms and carried by the wind over the mountains from the south.

Our three musketeers told us that all the nomads now sojourning in the Shamsang district would come up here in a few weeks to stay a month and a half, till the snow drove them away again. In winter the snow lies 5 feet deep, and many men and animals perish in the snowdrifts, when the herds go too high up the mountains and are surprised by early heavy falls of snow. The autumn before, I was told, 23 yaks were grazing up at the foot of Ngomo-dingding when it began to snow furiously. Several herdsmen hurried up to drive the animals down to lower ground, but the snow was heaped up in such large quantities that they had to turn back lest they should perish themselves. In the spring they went up, and found the skeletons and hides of the unfortunate animals. The Shamsang Gova had lately lost some horses in the same way. Even the wild asses cannot escape from the spring snow. They cannot run when the snow is deep, and after trying in vain to reach bare ground, they die of starvation and are frozen in the snowdrifts. Our three guides, who themselves pass the summer up here, assured me that the wild asses are frozen in an upright position, and often stand on all fours when the summer sun has thawed the snow. They had seen dead wild asses standing in herds as though they were alive.

The snow, which falls in winter on the source region

of the Brahmaputra, melts in spring, and together with the river ice produces a flood of far larger volume, it is said, than the summer flood produced by rain. This is probably true of the uppermost course of the Tsangpo, but lower down the rain-flood is certainly the greater. In general, the variations in the water-level are more marked in the higher lands, and the further the water flows downstream the more the fluctuations tend to disappear.

"Is not our country hard and terrible to live in? Is not the Bombo Chimbo's country (India) better?" asked my Tibetans.

"I cannot say that; in India there are tigers, snakes, poisonous insects, heat, fever, and plague to contend with, which are not met with up here in the fresh air."

"Yes, but that is better than the continual wind, the sharp cold, and the fruitless waiting for rain. This year we have only had a couple of light showers, and we shall lose our herds if more rain does not come."

"Well, the summer in Tibet is very pleasant when it rains, while in India it is suffocating; on the other hand, the winter in Tibet is severe and cruel, but comfortable in India."

"Tell us, Bombo Chimbo, is it you, with your glass and measuring instruments, that is keeping back the rain this year? At this season it usually rains heavily, but you perhaps prefer clear weather, to be able to see the country and that the roads may not be soft."

"No, I long for rain as much as you, for my animals are getting thin, and cannot eat their fill of this poor grass, which has stood here since last summer. Only the gods can control the weather, and the sons of men must take the rain and sunshine as they are sent to them from above."

They looked at one another doubtfully. It was not the first time that they had ascribed to me powers as great as those of their own gods, and it would have been difficult to have convinced them of their error.

At midnight the men heard a one-year-old child crying and calling for help on the bank of the Kubi-tsangpo.

They woke one another in astonishment, and Rabsang and two Tibetans went off with a gun, thinking that it was a ghost. When they came near they heard the child weeping quite distinctly, and our heroes were so frightened that they thought it safest to make all haste back again. When I asked them how they knew that it was a year-old child, they answered, that from the sound it could not have been younger or older. When I suggested that it might have been a wolf cub, as there were no human beings in the neighbourhood, they declared that it must have been an uneasy spirit wandering about the bank.

There must have been something supernatural about, for I dreamed in the night that all the fragments of birch bark which we had seen on our day's ride were letters of invitation from the Maharaja of Nepal, that I had accepted the invitation, and was lying half asleep on a soft carpet of grass and listening to the rustle of the warm wind among the cedars of the Himalayas. The dream was so vivid that I could not think all day long of anything else but the warm beautiful land behind the mountains.

Even in camp No. 200 I perceived fairly clearly how the land lay, but we were not yet at the actual source, and therefore we continued our march south-westwards on July 12. The foot of the snowy mountains seemed quite near. The river is broad, and divided by islands of mud into several arms. On the left side of the valley, where we march, are a couple of walls of green and black schist, but elsewhere old moraines extend on all sides. We cross a stream flowing from the country below Dongdong to join the Kubi-tsangpo. The Tsechung-tso is a small moraine lake. The valley bottom rises slowly, and consists of loose material sparsely covered with grass. Occasionally a small erratic block of grey granite is seen. Rags, dung, and fragments of bone lie on the summer camping-grounds. At length the river becomes as broad as a small lake, enclosed in morainic rubbish and driftsand.

We camped at the stone wall of Shapka, one of the headquarters of the nomads. Here, on the right bank of the Kubi-tsangpo, stands a dark purple ridge of medium height with patches of snow, which melt in the course of the summer. The land at the foot of this colossal mountain is remarkably flat, and instead of a cone of detritus there is a stream expanded into a lake. The water from the melting snow has washed away all solid matter.

As we came to camp No. 201, at a height of 15,883 feet, the peaks disappeared in clouds, but just before sunset the sky cleared and the last clouds floated away like light white steam over the glaciers of Ngomo-dingding, which clearly displayed their grand structure, with high lateral moraines and concentric rings of grey lumpy terminal moraines. The surface, except where here and there blue crevasses yawned in the ice, was white with snow and the porous melting crust.

When the sun had set, nine peaks in a line from south-east to south-west stood out with remarkable sharpness. Raven-black pinnacles, cliffs and ridges rise out of the white snowfields, and the glaciers emerge from colossal portals. A whole village of tents rising to heaven! The source of the Brahmaputra could not be embellished with a grander and more magnificent background. Holy and thrice holy are these mountains, which from their cold lap give birth and sustenance to the river celebrated from time immemorial in legend and song, the river of Tibet and Assam, the river *par excellence*, the son of Brahma. One generation after another of black Tibetans has in the course of thousands of years listened to its roar between the two loftiest mountain systems of the world, the Himalaya and the Trans-Himalaya, and one generation after another of the various tribes of Assam has watered its fields with its life-giving floods and drunk of its blessed water. But where the source lay no one knew. Three expeditions had determined its position approximately, but none had been there. No geography had been able to tell us anything of the country round the source of the Brahmaputra. Only a small number of nomads repair thither yearly to spend a couple of short summer months. Here it is, here in the front of three glacier tongues, that the river so revered by the Hindu tribes begins its course of some 1800 miles through the grandest elevations of the world, from which its turbid volumes of water roll first to the east, then southwards, cutting a wild valley through the Himalayas, and finally flowing south-westwards over the plains of Assam. The upper Brahmaputra, the Tsangpo, is truly the chief artery of Tibet, for within its drainage basin is concentrated the great mass of its population, while its lower course is surrounded by the most fruitful and populous provinces of Assam. The Brahmaputra is therefore one of the noblest rivers of the world, and few waterways have a more illustrious descent and a more varied and more glorious career, for nations have grown up on its banks and have lived there, and their history and culture have been intimately connected with it since the earliest times of human records.

Busied with such thoughts, I went out again in the evening to gaze at the cliffs of the nine peaks which showed like dim misty shadows, while the ice and snow-fields below, of the same colour as the sky, were not perceptible in the night. Then a flash of lightning blazed up behind Kubi-gangri, as the whole massive is called, and the crest crowned with eternal snow stood suddenly out in sharp pitch-black contours. Singular, entrancing land, where spirit voices are heard in the night and the sky blazes up in bluish light. I listened for a long time to the brook Shapka-chu, gently trickling down its stony bed to the bank of the Kubi-tsangpo.

We had still some way to go before we came to the actual source, and I could not conscientiously leave Kubi-gangri without determining the absolute height of the source by the boiling-point thermometer. Our Tibetans were exceedingly friendly, and seemed to take an interest in showing us this point, of which I had spoken so often during the past days and about which I had put so many questions. I was really thankful for, and overjoyed at, this unexpected favourable opportunity of fixing the position of the source, though I knew that my excursion to Kubi-gangri could only be a very cursory and defective reconnaissance. A thorough exploration of this neighbourhood would require several years, for the summer up here is short and the time for work is over in two months. But though I succeeded in learning only the chief outlines of the physical geography, I can count this excursion as one of the most important events of my last journey in Tibet. Accordingly, we decided to ride up to the source next day, July 13. Only Rabsang, Robert, and a Tibetan were to accompany me. The rest were to wait for our return under the command of Tsering.

CHAPTER XLIII

THE SOURCE OF THE SACRED RIVER—A DEPARTURE

We started off in beautiful weather, not a cloud hanging over the summits of Kubi-gangri. We followed the left bank of the Kubi-tsangpo, and rode along the foot of the huge moraines, which here rise fully 470 feet above the valley bottom, and which were formerly thrown up on the left or western side of the gigantic glacier, whence proceeded all the glacier tongues now remaining only in short lengths. The morainic character is plainly recognizable, sometimes in curved ridges and walls falling steeply on both sides, sometimes in rounded hillocks rising one above another. The surface is often covered with fine pebbles, grass, and lovely alpine flowers trying to make the most of the short summer. Here and there a landslip has taken place, and then it can be seen that the rock shows no trace of stratification. Occasionally we pass granite boulders, but they are small, the largest not more than 280 cubic feet. On the valley bottom are swamps with rank grass, and wild-geese are enjoying the summer in the ponds. We twice met with fresh spoor of small herds of wild yaks which had moved off to the right bank of the Kubi-tsangpo. The horses' hoofs splashed in the swampy ground, seldom varied by small patches of boulder clay.

Numerous rivulets descend from the moraines. They are fed by the melting snowfields, and therefore, in contrast to the glacier brooks, are crystal clear. They have eroded deep valleys in the moraines, and one of them has deposited a great dejection cone at the mouth, over which the brook falls in ten channels, carrying 106 cubic feet of water. A very considerable proportion of the upper Brahmaputra's water is derived from melted snow. Rivulets rushed and spurted all about in the rubbish, and all came from the snowfields, which struggled in vain against the heat of the spring sun.

Now we have right in front of us the immense glacier which descends from an extensive firn basin on the western foot of the Mukchung-simo massive. Between its terminal moraines and the older moraines we have skirted, a rather voluminous stream has eroded its valley. Its water is tolerably clear and green, so that it proceeds from snowfields. A little below the terminal moraine it unites with the numerous arms of the muddy glacier stream, of which the largest is the one which flows nearest to the foot of the Mukchung massive. Even 200 yards below the confluence the green water can be clearly distinguished from the brown, but afterwards the cold currents intermingle. Where the river, still divided into a number of meandering arms, turns past camp 201 to the north-east, it receives considerable additions from the glaciers lying further east, and thus the Kubi-tsangpo is formed.

Then we ride up, zigzagging among boulders and pebble beds, over ridges, banks, and erosion furrows, over brooks and treacherous bog, over grass and clumps of brushwood, to a commanding point of viewon the top of the old moraine (16,453 feet). Before us is a chaos of huge, precipitous, fissured, black, bare rocks, summits, pyramids, columns, domes, and ridges, moraines, tongues of ice, snow and firn fields—a scene hard to beat for wild grandeur.

Here we made a halt, and I drew the panorama while the horses grazed on the slopes. The largest glacier, which comes from the Kubi-gangri proper, is entirely below us, and we have a bird's-eye view of it. It is fed by three different firn-fields, and has two distinct medial moraines, which here and there rise into ridges where the ice has been thrust aside. The right lateral moraine is well defined, and is still partially covered with snow. The left is broad in its upper part but narrow below, where the green stream washes its base. Up above, a glacier from the west runs into the main glacier, and where the two join the side glacier is thrown up into a mighty wall, which merges into the left lateral moraine of the other. All the bottom of the glacier front is buried in rubbish, and the ice peeps out only here and there. Here are several small sheets of water, some of an intensely blue colour, others brown, with finely pulverized matter, showing that they are connected with the water of the ground moraine. Two of these small pools have vertical sides of blue ice like entrances to marvellous fairy grottos. A series of marginal crevasses are still partly covered with snow. The terminal moraine is a chaos of mounds, pebbles, and boulders, with patches of snow on the shady side. In a hollow between these hillocks flows the middle glacier stream, after passing two pools. The terminal moraine does not increase in size, for its material is slowly disintegrated and washed away by the stream, which winds in several arms over the even bed of the valley bottom just below in the most capricious curves.

An excursion over the surface of the glacier would not be difficult when one was once up on it. There are many dangerous crevasses concealed under the snow which may be avoided by keeping to the rubbish heaps of the medial moraines. The mass of the Kubi-gangri, which from our point of view lies farthest to the right, to the west-north-west, is called Gave-ting; from it descends the great side glacier.

The front of the main glacier, where the largest of all the glacier streams of the Kubi-gangri rises, is the actual source of the Brahmaputra. The other streams which enter it south-east of camp 201 are smaller and shorter. We could not get to them, for the horses sank too deep in the sand and mud of the main stream.

On our return we made a halt at the place where the principal branch of the Kubi-tsangpo comes out from under the ice, and I found that the source of the Brahmaputra lies at an altitude of 15,958 feet above sea-level. I must leave details for the scientific report of this journey, which will be published in due time.

On July 14 it seemed very hot in my tent, for even at

seven o'clock in the morning the temperature was 45.1°; in the night there had been nearly 14½ degrees of frost. The sky was perfectly clear, and therefore I could not refrain from seeking another point of view to investigate the beautiful glaciers of the Kubi-gangri.

After arranging with Tsering that he should meet us in the valley of the Dongdong river we rode up the banks and ridges of the old moraine, through its hollows and over its terraces of barren soil, which was now soft and treacherous from the melting of the snow, past pools of clear, green water, and to the highest point of its ridge, where there was nothing to hide the view.

I first took nine photographs, forming a consecutive series. Then a cloak was thrown over the stand to make a shelter against the strong wind, and in this sentry-box I sat for nearly four hours drawing a panorama which embraced the whole horizon. Meanwhile my companions lay down and snored, and I was glad to sit alone face to face with these royal mountain giants. The whole architecture is fantastically wild, and the only law which is strictly observed is that each glacier is confined between two huge black crests of rock.

In order to give the reader a notion of the scene I here reproduce a part of the panorama embracing the Kubi-gangri (Illust. 242). To the south, 27° E., is a tetrahedral peak, which our guide called Ngoma-dingding. To the south, 11° E., rises another summit, of almost precisely the same form, which is called Absi. On the east of it lies the Ngoma-dingding glacier, and on the west the Absi glacier. West of this stands the lumpy Mukchung-simo group, with its culminating point lying south, 24° W. The northern side resembles a stable with straight short stalls, each containing a small hanging glacier. To the south-west rise two sharp pinnacles, and in the south, 57° W., a couple of dome-shaped summits consisting only of ice and snow; they belong to the Langta-chen massive, and their firns feed to a great extent the glacier in the front of which the Brahmaputra takes its rise. So the glacier may be called the Langta-chen. To the south, 70° W., 88° W., and north, 83° W., rise the summits

112. Panorama of Kubi-gangri and the Langta-chen Glacier, with the Source of the Brahmaputra, from a Height of 16,433 feet, July 13, 1907.

Sketch by the Author.

of the Gave-ting group. To the north, 55° W., three peaks of the Dongdong appear, from which one of the sources of the Brahmaputra takes its rise, quite insignificant compared to the Kubi-tsangpo.

Towards the north-east the sharply defined valley of the Kubi-tsangpo runs downwards, and in the distance are seen the mountains of Chang-tang, pyramidal peaks of singular uniformity, and crowded together in great numbers, which form a finely jagged horizon, and in consequence of the great distance merge into the pink tint of the insignificant snowfields. The Trans-Himalaya seems on this side to widen out and become flatter than in the east.

It was late when we rode down the steep path to the camp on the Dongdong. And now we had to hurry westwards and make as many discoveries and collect as much information as possible on forbidden paths, in spite of the Mandarins and the Devashung.

On July 15 we left our former route to the right and directed our steps northwards over intricate moraines, seeing the snowy peaks of Dongdong and Chema-yundung still more clearly from the pass Kargan-la. On the 16th the sky was overcast, a couple of hail showers fell, and the hills around us changed to white. We rode north-westwards past two small lakes, and again fell in with solid rock—green and black schist. From the Tugri-la we had a fine view over a world of mountains, the names of which I have no time to record. We crossed another saddle, Sen-kamba-la, to reach the broad open valley of the Chema-yundung river, which descends from a very extensive glacier in the south belonging to the Chema-yundung-pu massive. Here were several nomad tents, and seven tents inhabited by pilgrims from Bongba stood on a rise. They were on their way with kith and kin to Kang-rinpoche to make the pilgrimage round the holy mountain. Most of the pilgrims from the far east take this southern route and return over the Marium-la.

July 17. It was very hot in the saddle with a temperature of 50° and quite calm air. The brown puppy was very tired of travelling, and drops fell from her hanging tongue, but she could not leave the antelopes and hares in peace. She darted after them full speed, but never caught them, and came back to me disappointed, but began again the useless pursuit. The Ronggak-chu is an affluent of the Chema, and comes from the north-west. We left the little double lake Kuru-chok in the south. To the west-south-west is the place where the Chema-yundung receives the Angsi-chu, the most westerly of all the headwaters of the Brahmaputra.

In the valley of the Tynchung we encamped beside some accommodating nomads, who quickly procured me fresh yaks, for the three musketeers turned back here to Shamsang, after doing their work well. The whole excursion to the sources of the Brahmaputra had cost 110 rupees, and it was well worth more. The natives said that ten robbers had recently made the neighbourhood unsafe, but immediately it was reported that a European caravan was approaching Tynchung, they had entirely disappeared, and therefore we were regarded as deliverers, and the people could not do too much for us A Hindu merchant from Almora was camping here, buying sheep's wool and salt from the nomads, and selling them frieze rugs and textiles from Agra and Amritsar.

Next day we crossed the Marnyak-la (17,395 feet) and had the Angsi-chu immediately below us, and on the 19th we left the river behind and followed its small tributary, the Loang-gonga, up to its source at the very low pass Tamlung or Tag-la, which is nothing more than a rise in an open longitudinal valley. But this pass is exceedingly important, for it is the watershed between the Brahmaputra and Manasarowar. Its height is 17,382 feet. To the south is spread out a succession of snowy peaks, and to the west-south-west is seen Gurla Mandatta or Memo-nani, a majestic and imposing group which belongs to the same Himalayan range as Kubi-gangri. The pass is situated among old moraines, where is the little insignificant lake Tamlung-tso, from which the Loang-gonga flows out. At some distance to the south is seen the low watershed between the Angsi-chu and the Ganglung, a stream that comes from a massive of the same name, and, as the Tage-tsangpo, falls into Manasarowar. The very latest maps of western Tibet give a very incorrect representation of this country, which has never been visited by a European before. Instead of a clearly marked meridional range we found an open, hilly, longitudinal valley with the watershed running among its moraines. Here we took leave of the Brahmaputra, after passing half a year in its basin since crossing the Sela-la. We encamped at a place where the Gang-lung river breaks through a rampart of moraines, forming foaming cascades.

During the following day's journey it flows through granitic moraines, drift sand, and morasses, and becomes a considerable stream, receiving numerous affluents from the south. A caravan of 50 yaks, and eight men from Purang, armed with guns, and clad in blue with fur-lined cloaks, were on the way to the fair in Gyanima. In the district Tagramoche, where we bivouacked, were many nomads and beggars with staves and bundles on the way to the holy mountain. We also met six merchants from Ladak, who were carrying dried peaches for sale on 45 asses. They had left home a month and a half previously.

On July 21 we rode down the Tage-bup valley among savage cliffs. On its bottom flows the Tage-tsangpo, changing its colour from light green over sandy ground to bluish-purple over dark detritus. Langchen-kamba is a small side-valley on the right, from which robbers are wont to sally forth against defenceless travellers. Just below the valley a spring bubbles forth with crystal-clear water at a temperature of 38°. It is considered holy, and is marked by a pole bedecked with rags and streamers like a scare-crow. This spring is also called Langchen-kamba.

A little farther down the spring Chakko stands on a steep slope on the right bank, and its water (40.3°) is collected in a round pit 3 feet deep. A wall is erected about it, covered with flat stones, on which figures of Buddha and holy texts are carved. Leaves from the holy scriptures are thrust between the stones of the wall, and streamers and rags fly from a pole. Through the water, clear as a mirror, could be seen blue and red beads, two inferior turquoises, some shells, and other trash, thrown in as offerings by pious pilgrims. The water is supposed to have miraculous powers. Murmuring prayers, our guide filled a wooden bowl with water and poured it over the head and mane of his horse to protect it from wolves. With the same object he tied a rag from the pole on to his horse's forelock. He drank himself a good draught to render him invulnerable to the bullets of robbers. If a sheep or other animal is ill it is only necessary to sprinkle it with the holy water to make it well again. When a traveller or pilgrim stands at the well and pours water with both hands over his head, it guards him against falling into the hands of footpads, and from other misfortunes. And if he sits and meditates, drinks, and washes his head, hands, and legs, and has sufficient faith, then he finds gold coins and precious stones at the bottom of the well. The sick man who bathes his whole body in the miraculous water becomes strong again. It is a Lourdes in miniature. While my men were engaged in their ablutions I sat at the edge of the well and listened to the mystical music of the fluttering prayer-streamers, and found this fascinating Tibet more enigmatical at every step.

Then we rode over the Tage-tsangpo, where its valley opens into the flat basin of Manasarowar—a new chapter in the chronicles of our journey. Again Gurla Mandatta showed itself in all its glory, and in the north-west Kang-rinpoche or Kailas, the holy mountain, like a great *chhorten* on a lama's grave, rose above the jagged ridge which forms the horizon in that direction. On seeing it all our men suddenly jumped out of their saddles and threw themselves down with their foreheads on the ground. Only Rabsang, a confirmed heathen, remained seated on his horse, and was afterwards well scolded by Tsering.

We are now out on open hilly ground, and see a glimpse of the holy lake Tso-mavang or Manasarowar. We encamp by a small lake called Tso-nyak, whither come Islam Ahun and Shukkur Ali, sent by Guffaru, who is become uneasy at our long absence. We send them back again to Tokchen with orders to Guffaru to proceed to the

243, 244, 245. THE MOUNTAINS AT THE SOURCE OF THE BRAHMAPUTRA.

monastery Serolung-gompa on the holy lake, where we will meet him.

On July 22 we rode over the Tage-tsangpo, which here carried 291 cubic feet of water, where Rabsang got a thorough wetting in consequence of his horse coming a cropper among the boulders in the bed. Tsering said that he deserved a dip because he had not saluted Kang-rinpoche. Camp 210 was set up in the broad valley Namarding, where a clear brook flows to the Tage-tsangpo. The wind blew strongly, and the Tibetans said that the waves on Tso-mavang were as high and dark as nomad tents. Should we venture in our little canvas boat on the lake, exposed to all the winds? It must be very rough before I consented to give up the trip, for the lake had long been the subject of my dreams.

Next morning Tundup Sonam appeared with the news that the Gova of Tokchen would not let his yaks on hire for the journey to Serolung. I had therefore to ride to Tokchen by a road over the pass Karbu-la, and down the river Samo-tsangpo; it is full of fish, but we were asked not to disturb them, for they came up from the holy lake. We were all together again in Tokchen, and I found the Gova a decent fellow, who welcomed me with a large *kadakh* and a bowl of *tsamba*.

Now an hour of parting was come, for I sent from Tokchen thirteen of my men home to Ladak. I had several reasons for this. I did not need so many men in western Tibet; twelve were enough, and a small, light caravan accomplishes more and does not excite so much notice. The men were to travel along the great highway to Gartok under the experienced leadership of Guffaru, and there deposit all the baggage I could spare with the British agent, Thakur Jai Chand. I also sent to him a letter packet of three hundred pages to my parents, beside other correspondence. Of particular importance was a letter to Colonel Dunlop Smith, in which I asked for 6000 rupees, provisions, books, revolvers and ammunition, and things suitable for presents, such as gold and silver watches, as well as all the letters which must have accumulated at the Viceregal Lodge.

On the first evening, when I called together all the twenty-five men and told them my decision to send away thirteen, and asked which of them wished to go home, no one answered. They declared that they would follow me until I was tired of Tibet. Then I picked out thirteen and retained the best twelve men. Among these was Tashi, who with Tundup Sonam had accomplished the adventurous journey to Shigatse. But when he saw that I was in earnest about the dividing of the caravan, he begged me to let him go home, so he was exchanged for another man.

We stayed here two days to put everything in order. After the baggage was re-arranged I had only four boxes left, and the rest were to be carried away by Guffaru. Robert sat in my tent like a money-changer and piled up sovereigns and rupees in small heaps, the pay, gratuities, and travelling expenses of the men who were going home. Our treasury was relieved of 2118 rupees all at once. The important correspondence was enclosed in a case, which Guffaru carried in his belt. The men with him were allowed to keep two of our five guns. Late in the evening Guffaru came to my tent to receive his last instructions. Honest old Guffaru, he had in the autumn of his life performed wonders in the winter in Chang-tang, always composed and contented, always doing his duty in the smallest particular. Now he sat, with the tears falling on to his white beard, and thanked me for all I had done for him during the past year. I bade him weep no more, but rejoice that the hard time was over for him, and that he could return safe and sound to his people with 400 rupees in his purse. When we left Leh he was as poor as a church mouse, and now he was a rich man for his position, and he had not needed his shroud. I told him that I should miss him very much, but that I could not entrust the valuable baggage and important letters to any other hands but his.

When I came out of my tent early on the morning of the 26th the 13 yaks were laden and the thirteen men were ready to march off with their Tibetan guides. I thanked them for their faithfulness and patience during the time when they were exposed to so many dangers in my service, begged them to remember that they were responsible for the caravan on the way home, and told them that they must obey Guffaru, and that their character would suffer if they did not bear with one another on the way. If they were as conscientious on this journey as in my service, it would be well for them in the future, and perhaps our paths might cross again.

Then old Guffaru came forward, and fell on his knees before me, weeping loudly, and all the others in turn followed his example amid sobs and tears; I clapped them all on the shoulder and hoped that this bitter hour would soon be over. Then they took leave of their comrades, who, deeply moved, sent greetings to their parents, wives, and children in Ladak, and they marched off on foot, as they had travelled so many hundred miles, silent, drooping, and downcast, and soon disappeared behind the hills.

CHAPTER XLIV

A NIGHT ON MANASAROWAR

AFTER Guffaru had set out with his men, the small caravan was organized which was to accompany me. It was led by Tsering, and the other men left were Bulu, Tundup Sonam, Rabsang, Rehim Ali, Shukkur Ali, Namgyal, Adul, Ishe, Lama, Galsang, and Rub Das. The Gova of Tokchen was given a Kashmir shawl, a turban, and some rupees for the services he had rendered us, and all the other Tibetans who had been friendly and helpful received presents. The dividing of the caravan had also the advantage that the Tibetans supposed that we were all making for the same destination by different routes, and that I should join Guffaru in Gartok and continue my journey to Ladak, as directed on the passport.

With Robert, Rabsang, and two Tibetans I now ride down the Tokchen valley and up over the hills to the south-west. To the right of our route the turquoise-blue surface of the holy lake is displayed; how beautiful, how fascinating is the scene! One seems to breathe more freely and easily, one feels a pleasure in life, one longs to voyage over the blue depths and the sacred waves. For Manasarowar is the holiest and most famous of all the lakes of the world, the goal of the pilgrimage of innumerable pious Hindus, a lake celebrated in the most ancient religious hymns and songs, and in its clear waters the ashes of Hindus find a grave as desirable and honoured as in the turbid waters of the Ganges. During my stay in India I received letters from Hindus in which they asked me to explore the revered lake and the holy moun-

246. Tibetans on the Bank of the Soma-tsangpo.

247. Group of Natives of Langmar.

tain Kailas, which lifts its summit in the north under a cupola of eternal snow, where Siva, one of the Indian Trinity, dwells in her paradise among a host of other deities; and they told me that if I could give them an exact description of the lake and river, they would remember me in their prayers and their gods would bless me. But that was not why I longed to be there. The lake had never been sounded—I would sink my lead to the bottom and make a map of its bed; I would follow its periphery and calculate how much water pours into its bosom on a summer day; I would investigate its hydrographic relation to the adjacent lake on the west, the Rakas-tal, a problem which various travellers in this region, from Moorcroft and Strachey to Ryder and Rawling, have explained differently; I would learn something of the monasteries and the life of Hindu and Tibetan pilgrims, for the lake is sacred in the eyes of Lamaists also, who call it Tso-mavang or Tso-rinpoche, the "Holy Lake." How can Manasarowar and Kailas be the objects of divine honours from two religions so different as Hinduism and Lamaism unless it is that their overpowering beauty has appealed to and deeply impressed the human mind, and that they seemed to belong rather to heaven than to earth? Even the first view from the hills on the shore caused us to burst into tears of joy at the wonderful, magnificent landscape and its surpassing beauty. The oval lake, somewhat narrower in the south than the north, and with a diameter of about 15½ miles, lies like an enormous turquoise embedded between two of the finest and most famous mountain giants of the world, the Kailas in the north and Gurla Mandatta in the south, and between huge ranges, above which the two mountains uplift their crowns of bright white eternal snow. Yes, already I felt the strong fascination which held me fettered to the banks of Manasarowar, and I knew that I would not willingly leave the lake before I had listened, until I was weary, to the song of its waves.

We sat an hour and enjoyed the incomparable beauty of the scene. A slight ripple ruffled the surface of the water, but in the middle the lake was as smooth as if oil had been poured on it. The Tibetans said that it was always smooth in the middle except when a storm raged. To the south-south-west and south-west are seen the two summits of Gurla Mandatta, the western very flat, and reminding me of the Mustag-ata in the eastern Pamir. The Tibetans called the mountain sometimes Namo, sometimes Memo-nani. South, 60° W., a row of snowy heights rise behind the Purang valley. To the west-north-west is seen the small pyramidal hill where Chiu-gompa stands on the bank of the water channel which once ran into Rakas-tal. To the north-west a couple of lagoons lie on the shore of Manasarowar, and behind them rise chains and ramifications belonging to the Trans-Himalaya, and among them Kailas or Kang-rinpoche, the "Holy Mountain," called also Gangri or the "Ice Mountain," dominates the horizon unless its summit is veiled in clouds. And lastly, to the north, 20° W., we see the double-peaked Pundi, not far from the shore, and in the north the two valleys Pachen and Pachung, with roads which lead over the watershed of the Trans-Himalaya to Chang-tang.

When I asked our guides what they thought of a boat trip across the lake, they answered unhesitatingly that it was impossible; mortals who ventured on the lake, which was the home of the gods, must perish. Also in the middle Tso-mavang was not level as on the shore, but formed a transparent dome, and up its round arch no boat could mount; and even if we succeeded in getting the boat up, it would shoot down the other side with such velocity that it must capsize, and we should perish in the waves because we had excited the wrath of the god of the lake.

We mounted again and rode south-south-west over the hills to Serolung, the golden valley, where the monastery Serolung-gompa is hidden in the hollow. There I stayed four hours, making sketches and notes. Serolung, which contains thirty monks, most of whom were away wandering among the villages, is one of the eight convents which are set like precious stones in the chain which the pilgrims stretch round the lake, in the hope of acquiring merit in a future form of existence, of being freed from the burden of sin and the tortures of purgatorial fires, nay, perhaps, of sitting at the feet of the gods and eating *tsamba* out of golden bowls.

Our camp No. 212 was pitched immediately south of the mouth of the Serolung valley at the water's edge. The strip of ground on the bank is quite narrow, and on the hills rising to the east of it are visible six horizontal strand lines, the highest lying 162 feet above the present level of the lake, which is 15,098 feet above the sea.

On July 27 I had a good sleep, and spent the rest of the day in making preparations for the first line of soundings, which was to cross the lake in a direction south, 59° W., where a gap appeared in the hills framing the lake. We waited for good weather, but the wind blew violently and the surf beat and foamed against the shore. I therefore resolved to wait till night, for of late the nights had been calmer than the days. On a trial trip we had found a depth of 130 feet not far from the shore, so we made ready a sounding line 490 feet long. Perhaps even this would not be long enough, for a lake lying among such high mountains is sure to be deep. Shukkur Ali was to go with me, and he accepted his fate with his usual composure, but Rehim Ali, the other victim, was frightened; it was all very well in the day, he said, but in the dark gloomy night on such a great lake! We should certainly have the same trouble as on Lake Lighten, he thought.

When the sun set the wind increased in strength, and heavy clouds spread up from the south-west. At seven o'clock it was pitch dark all round, not a star shone out, not a trace was visible of the outline of the shore and of the snowy mountains, and the sea was buried in the shades of night. But an hour later the wind fell, the air became quite calm, but the waves beat in a monotonous rhythm on the bank. The smoke of the camp fires rose straight up into the air.

Then I gave orders to set out. The baggage was stowed and the mast stepped to be ready if we had a favourable wind. Provisions for two days were put in the boat. I wore a leathern vest, Kashmir boots, and an Indian helmet, and sat on a cushion and a folded fur coat on the lee side of the rudder, on the other side of which the sounding-line with its knots lay ready on the gunwale. The log, Lyth's current meter, was attached to the boat to register the whole length of the course, and compass, watch, note-book, and map sheets all lay close beside me, lighted by a Chinese paper lantern, which could be covered with a towel when we did not want the light. I used the towel after every sounding to dry my hands. Rehim Ali took his seat forward, Shukkur Ali in the stern half of the boat, where we were cramped for room and had to take care that we did not get entangled in the sounding-line.

Tsering took a sceptical view of the whole adventure. He said that the lake was full of wonders, and at the best we should be driven back by mysterious powers when we had rowed a little way out. And a Tibetan agreed with him, saying that we should never reach the western shore though we rowed with all our might, for the lake god would hold our boat fast, and while we thought that it was advancing it would really remain on the same spot, and finally the angry god would draw it down to the bottom.

Robert had orders to wait at camp No. 212 for our return, and when we put off from the bank at nine o'clock all bade us farewell in as warm and gentle a tone as though they thought that they had seen the last of us. Their spirits were not raised by the lightning which flashed in the south and might portend a storm. The darkness, however, was not so intense, for the moon was coming up, though it was still covered by the hills rising behind our camp. But its light threw a weird gleam over the lake, and in the south Gurla Mandatta rose like a ghost enveloped in a sheet of moonshine, snowfields, and glaciers.

At my command, the boatmen took a firm grip of the oars and the boat glided out from the beach, where our men stood in a silent thoughtful group. Our fires were seen for a while, but soon disappeared, for they were burning almost on a level with the water. Robert told me afterwards that the little boat sailing out into the darkness was a curious sight; owing to the lantern and the reflexion of the light on the mast the boat was visible at first, but when it reached the moon-lighted part of the lake it appeared only as a small black spot, which soon vanished.

The great lake was dark and mysterious in the night, and unknown depths lurked beneath us. The contours of the hills on the shore were still visible behind us, but we had not gone far before they were swallowed up by higher mountains farther off, which gradually came into view. After twenty minutes' rowing we stopped and let down the line, sounding 135 feet. The roar of the surf on the beach was the only sound in the silence of night, except the splash of the oars and the voices of the oarsmen singing in time with their strokes. At the next sounding the depth was 141 feet. If the bottom did not fall more rapidly our line would be long enough. Every hour I recorded the temperatures of the air and the water. Now the god of sleep paid us a visit; Shukkur Ali yawned at every ninth stroke, and every yawn was so long that it lasted three strokes.

The air is quite still. A long, smooth swell causes the boat to rock slightly. All is quiet, and I ask myself involuntarily if other beings are listening to the splash of the oars as well as ourselves. It is warm, with a temperature of 46.9° at eleven o'clock. The next two depths are 143 and 164 feet. My oarsmen follow the soundings with deep interest, and look forward to the point where the depth will begin to decrease. They think it awful and uncanny to glide over such great depths in the dark night. Again blue lightning flashes behind Gurla Mandatta, which stands forth in a pitch black outline, after appearing just before in a white robe of moon-lighted snowfields. A little later all the southern sky flames up like a sea of fire; the flashes quickly follow one after the other, and shoot up to the zenith, seeming to stay a moment behind the mountains, and it becomes light as day, but when the glow dies out the darkness is more intense, and the sublime, poetic solemnity of the night is enhanced. By the light of the flashes I can see the faces of the two men, who are startled and uneasy, and do not dare to disturb the awful stillness by their singing.

When I let down the line at the fifth point, the two men asked permission to light their water-pipes. The depth was 181 feet. A slight south-westerly breeze rippled the surface. The cry of a water-bird broke shrilly on the silence of the night, and made us feel less lonely. A slight hiss of the surf breaking on the south-eastern shore was audible. In the south the clouds gathered round the summit of Gurla Mandatta, the breeze fell. We glided slowly over the inky black water, and between the wave crests the path of moonlight wound in bright sinuosities; the depth increased slowly 183.4 feet, 189.3, 192 and 212.6. The temperature was still 45.9°, and I did not want my fur coat.

The queen of night, with diamonds in her dark hair, looks down upon the holy lake. The midnight hour is passed, and the early morning hours creep slowly on. We sound 203, 200, 184, 184, 180, and 190 feet, and it seems therefore as if we had passed the deepest depression. Leaning on the gunwale I enjoy the voyage to the full, for nothing I remember in my long wanderings in Asia can compare with the overpowering beauty of this nocturnal sail. I seem to hear the gentle but powerful beat of the great heart of Nature, its pulsation growing weaker in the arms of night, and gaining fresh vigour in the glow of the morning red. The scene, gradually changing as the hours go by, seems to belong not to earth but to the outermost boundary of unattainable space, as though it lay much nearer heaven, the misty fairyland of dreams and imagination, of hope and yearning, than to the earth with its mortals, its cares, its sins, and its vanity. The moon describes its arch in the sky, its restless reflexion quivering on the water, and broken by the wake of the boat.

The queen of night and her robe become paler. The dark sky passes into light blue, and the morn draws nigh from the east. There is a faint dawn over the eastern mountains, and soon their outlines stand out sharply, as though cut out on black paper. The clouds, but now floating white over the lake, assume a faint rosy hue, which gradually grows stronger, and is reflected on the smooth water, calling forth a garden of fresh roses. We row among floating rose-beds, there is an odour of morning and pure water in the air, it grows lighter, the landscape regains its colour, and the new day, July 28, begins its triumphal progress over the earth. Only an inspired pencil and magic colours could depict the scene that met my eyes when the whole country lay in shadow, and only the highest peaks of Gurla Mandatta caught the first gleam of the rising sun. In the growing light of dawn the mountain, with its snow-fields and glaciers, had shown silvery white and cold; but now! In a moment the extreme points of the summit began to glow with purple like liquid gold. And the brilliant illumination crept slowly like a mantle down the flanks of the mountain, and the thin white morning clouds, which hovered over the lower slopes and formed a girdle round a well-defined zone, floating freely like Saturn's ring, and like it throwing a shadow on the fields of eternal snow, these too assumed a tinge of gold and purple, such as no mortal can describe. The colours, at first as light and fleeting as those of a young maiden in her ball-dress, became more pronounced, light concentrated itself on the eastern mountains, and over their sharp outlines a sheaf of bright rays fell from the upper limb of the sun upon the lake. And now day has won the victory, and I try dreamily to decide which spectacle has made the greater impression on me, the quiet moonlight, or the sunrise with its warm, rosy gleam on the eternal snow.

Phenomena like these are fleeting guests on the earth; they come and go in the early morning hours, they are only seen once in a lifetime, they are like a greeting from a better world, a flash from the island of the phœnix. Thousands and thousands of pilgrims have wandered round the lake in the course of centuries, and have seen the dawn and sunset, but have never witnessed the display which we gazed upon from the middle of the holy lake on this memorable night. But soon the magical effects of light and colour, which have quickly followed one another and held me entranced, fade away. The country assumes its usual aspect, and is overshadowed by dense clouds. Kailas and Gurla Mandatta vanish entirely, and only a snowy crest far away to the north-west is still dyed a deep carmine, only yonder a sheaf of sunbeams penetrates through an opening in the clouds. In that direction the mirror of the lake is tinged blue, but to the south green. The wild-geese have waked up, and they are heard cackling on their joyous flights, and now and then a gull or tern screams. Bundles of seaweed float about. The sky is threatening, but the air is calm, and only gentle swells, smooth as polished metal, disturb the water, which looks like the clearest curaçāo. The boat moves with weary slowness to its destination, for now, at six o'clock in the morning, my oarsmen are tired and sleepy and quite at an end of their strength. They sleep and row alternately. "Hem-mala-hém" calls out Shukkur Ali, accenting the last syllable, when he energetically grasps his oar, but he goes to sleep between, and the oar hovers in the air; his own voice wakes him up, he dips the oar in and goes to sleep again.

The hours pass by, but there is no sign that we are nearing our destination. We cannot decide which bank is nearest, and we seem to be in the centre of this boundless lake. In the midst of Gurla Mandatta is seen a huge deeply eroded ravine, its entrance standing out picturesquely below the dense mantle of clouds. For a moment, when all around lay buried in shadow, the interior was lighted up by the sun, and it presented a fantastic appearance, resembling a portal into a hall of the gigantic dome lighted up by innumerable candles. The valleys and erosion channels between the different spurs of the massive are sharply defined, and wind down to the lake among flat cones of detritus, the outer margins of which cause the variations in the depth of the bottom. This now increases again to 200, 203, 213, and 240 feet. At fourteen points, these included, the bottom temperature is observed. The sounding occupies a considerable time. The line must first be paid out to the 230 feet, and then be held still till the thermometer has assumed the bottom temperature, and then it must be drawn up again, the depth must be noted, the thermometer read, the

248. Robert in the Boat.

temperature of the surface water and the air must be ascertained, and the log-reading taken.

Five furlongs to the north the smooth swell shows a curious fiery yellow colour, and I cannot make out the origin of this singular reflexion. The clouds gather in the south-west, and a breeze sweeps over the lake, producing waves which retard still more the progress of the boat. Rehim Ali cannot keep himself awake any longer, and Shukkur Ali is very comical in his overpowering sleepiness. The old man looks like a weather-beaten sea-dog in a south-wester—his Ladaki cap with its spreading flaps. He snoozes innocently with his oars up, and rows again and again in the air, still calling out his constant "Shu-ba-la-la." He talks in his sleep. Rehim Ali wakes up and asks him what is the matter, and no one knows what it is all about. Towards seven o'clock the dustman pays me a visit, but is not admitted. Only for a moment I see red wild asses running over the water, hear harps playing sweetly in the air, and behold the great black head of a sea-serpent rise above the waves and then sink down again; green dolphins and small whales arch their backs among the waves—but no, I must keep awake, for a storm may come down upon us any moment. I give my boatmen a good douche with the hollow of my hand, wash my own hands and face, and order breakfast—a hard-boiled goose egg, a piece of bread, and a bowl of milk, and then I light my pipe and am as lively again as a lark. At the twentieth sounding-place, 259 feet deep, the other two follow my example.

At nine o'clock, when we have been exactly twelve hours on the water, we sound a depth of 268.4 feet, but the south-western shore seems to our eyes as far off as ever. Rehim Ali thinks it is awful to have so much water under the keel. The clouds on Gurla lift a little, and we see deeper into the recesses of the great valley the more we come opposite its mouth. The lower points of the snowfields come into sight below the clouds. West of them is seen a broad erosion channel, grey with detritus and dotted with dark brushwood. The water reflects the forms of the mountains like a mirror; it turns blue when the sky is clear, but green again as soon as the clouds gather. A shoal of fishes plays in the water and splashes on the surface.

And again the hours of the day pass by. We glide slowly forwards, now over calm rising swell, whispering gently as spirit voices, now over small pyramidal waves produced by the meeting of two systems of undulations from different directions. Four small squalls from different quarters threaten us, but we catch only a flip of their tails, which cannot stir up the waves to a dangerous height. The last, from the south-east, is the strongest, and then the sail is hoisted. But still the shore seems far distant; perhaps Tsering was right with his Lamaistic wisdom.

All details, however, become sharper and clearer. Gurla turns three mighty gables towards the lake, and between them huge fans of detritus and erosion channels come to view. The fans become flatter towards the shore, and extend under the water down to the greatest depths of the lake; on the north shore, where a wide plain lies, the lake bottom might be expected to sink more slowly. Gurla is a splendid background to the holy lake—no artist in the world could conceive anything more magnificent and interesting.

Then we sounded 253, 243, 253, 223, 190, 177, and 82 feet, and perceived at length that the shore was near, for yaks and sheep were visible on the hills. The sea was now fairly high, and we had to bale the boat twice, and my fur coat on the bottom was wet. The two tired and sleepy men laboured painfully at the oars. We talked of how pleasant it would be to land, kindle a fire, and take our tea and food, but the shore still retired before us, and the hours of the afternoon slipped past. Gurla seemed to rise in the south directly from the water, its level skirts and low slopes being much foreshortened. The monks of the monastery here do not depend for water on the brooks, but drink the holy water of the lake, which has in reality the taste of the purest, most wholesome, spring water. Its crystal purity and dark greenish-blue colour are as beautiful as the flavour, and to pilgrims from a distance the water of Manasarowar is preferable to sparkling champagne.

At last we were released from imprisonment in the boat. We saw the bottom through the clear water, and a few strokes of the oar brought the boat to a wall of clay and decaying weeds, which the winter ice had pushed up on the bank. Inside the wall lies a longish lagoon, with mud in which one sinks to the knee. The time was half-past one, so we had been 16½ hours on the lake. But when we had reached the shore we found it impossible to get on land. After I had thought over the matter, while the men looked about them, we rowed northwards, and after an hour and a half discovered a place where the boat could be drawn ashore. Then we had been eighteen hours on the water.

A herdsman was seen, but he made off quickly. Fuel was collected and a fire lighted. Tea was infused and mutton fried, and when the three of us had eaten our dinner a temporary tent was constructed of the oars, mast, and sail, in which I lay down to sleep towards seven o'clock, wrapped in my fur, and with the life-buoys for a pillow. I had toiled for thirty-one hours continuously, so I went to sleep at once, and knew nothing of the storm which raged all night, or of the twenty-five pilgrims who passed by at dawn on their circuit of the holy lake.

CHAPTER XLV

MORE LAKE VOYAGES

I WAS awakened at six o'clock, having felt no cold in the night, for the minimum temperature was 40°. The morning was fine, only too warm; the pilgrims had gone away; we ate our breakfast, pushed the boat into the water, and rowed about 90 yards from the shore towards the north-north-east and north-north-west, describing a slight bend to camp No. 214. On our left hand was a row of pebble mounds, gradually rising to the top of the promontory which separates Manasarowar from Rakas-tal.

Soon the monastery Gossul-gompa was seen on its pebble terrace, nearly 130 feet high, like a swallow's nest hanging over the lake. A group of lamas stood silently watching the boat; they had never in their lives seen such a contrivance on the holy lake. When we drew near they vanished like rats into their holes, and only an old man remained sitting by a balustrade. I asked him the name of the monastery, and he said Gossul-gompa. The next point shut out the convent. The shore lagoons continue, though the margin below the hills is only 30 to 60 feet broad. The clay in which the lagoons are embedded is impermeable to water, but the lake has only to rise a couple of feet to find an outlet over the sandbank behind into the Rakas-tal, or Langak-tso, on the west. And when the channel at the north-west corner is silted up, as it is now, the Manasarowar has a subterranean outlet to the neighbouring lake, and its water consequently remains perfectly fresh.

I now intended to camp a little to the north at some

suitable spot, and thence row the following day over the lake to our headquarters near Serolung-gompa. We took bearings of a cinnabar-red hill lying on the north side of a slightly indented bay of the western shore. A fresh southerly breeze was blowing, we hoisted the sail, and flew whizzing over the lake. The pilgrims watched our voyage with the greatest astonishment, and the monks of Gossul cautiously followed us on the hills, no doubt wondering how such sacrilege would end. The wild-geese swam with their young ones out into the lake, while other swimming birds took themselves off some 100 yards inland, perhaps taking the boat for a curious water-bird of unusual size.

We went ashore at the red promontory, and while fuel was being collected and the camp arranged, I reconnoitred the neighbourhood from the heights above the landing-place. On the inner side of the shallow bay I found a hollow with its bottom lower than the surface of the lake, and filled with salt water, and on the west side of this swamp lies the lowest dip in the isthmus separating the twin lakes. Up there runs the pilgrim road, worn down by hundreds of thousands of weary feet. Three armed horsemen rode along the way. They came up without dismounting, and evidently did not know what to make of me. They could easily have taken me prisoner now that I was separated from my men, but they did not think of it, and rode on. A furious storm swept over the lake, its surface was wildly agitated, and covered with white horses. The farther, eastern part was of a deep green colour, while on our western shore it was lighter. The water of the shore lagoons was dark purple from the reflexion of the dense clouds. Towards four o'clock the air became oppressively still, then the wind sprang up, and an equally violent north-west storm came down raging and roaring. The wild south-easterly waves were suppressed by it, and the undulations remained uncertain till the new wave system was established. There was rain in many places round the lake, but we felt only a few drops. About six o'clock the sky looked threatening, with pitch-dark clouds all around, and not a trace could be seen of the eastern shore; we seemed to stand on the coast of the ocean. Soon after the wind veered round to the east-south-east, and then the surf beat all the evening against our beach. How fortunate that the weather had not been like this the evening before!

We sat two hours by the fire and talked. Its flames flickered and darted in all directions, so that they singed Shukkur Ali's goat's beard. The weather was still so threatening that we made a shelter of the boat, in which I lay down early to sleep. Before dozing off I listened to the roar of the waves, and thought I heard all kinds of mysterious sounds in the night, but it was only the cry of water-birds and the howling of the wind among the hills.

The men had orders to call me before sunrise, for we must hasten if we wished to reach camp No. 212 before darkness set in. It was scarcely light when I came out of my shelter. The last provisions were consumed by the morning fire, and then we put off about half-past four in dull, disagreeable weather. The strong west wind carried us rapidly away from the shore—indeed, it was really too strong for our sail and mast, but it took us on and doubled our pace. We had been sheltered under the hills, but when we were a few minutes from the beach the lake became uncomfortably rough. But it was of little consequence, for we sailed with the waves and took in no water.

The men, too, were more alive than on the first nocturnal voyage. They had evidently made up their minds to reach their destination before night, and they rowed like galley-slaves with the whip hanging over them; they seemed to run a race with the west wind, and try to get away before the waves rose too madly. The water hissed and foamed round the boat, and bubbled in the wake as when butter is browned in a pan, and beneath us the lake boiled up. It was a fine voyage as we rocked, spinning rapidly over the holy waves.

Shukkur Ali's refrain to the strokes of the oars is now "Ya paté, parvardigar Rabel, alehmin" or "Illallah," while Rehim Ali responds to the cry of his comrade with "Haap"

249. Sheep-shearing at Tugu-gompa on Manasarowar.

—the *p* jerked out quickly and loudly like an explosion —and with the refrain "Illallah," or "Svalallah." The Arabic words are, as usual in Ladak, much corrupted, but they lighten the work, and after Shukkur Ali had yelled them out thirty-five times in a minute for nine hours as loudly as his vocal cords would let him, he was dreadfully hoarse in the evening.

Then the soundings were 131, 171, 171, 177, 177, 185, 187, and 177. Out beyond the abrasion terrace and its rather steep escarpment, the lake bottom is practically level. Hanging cloud fringes show that rain is pouring down in torrents on most sides, but we escape it. My excellent boatmen row twice as fast as on the first night, but it is impossible to induce them to row in time. If I loose the rudder a moment, my boat falls off to the north or south instead of making east, where camp No. 212 lies. If it is dark before we reach the shore, our men are to light a pile of wood to guide us.

The day draws to an end, the wind sweeps away the clouds, and they seem to gather round the mountains, which form a grand wreath around this pearl of lakes. The wind dies quite away, the sun scorches my weather-beaten face, and it is trying to the eyes when the sparkling gold of the sunbeams falls straight upon them. Their blinding light makes it difficult to distinguish our goal, but I hold the compass in my hand. The waves sink and become more languid, and the sea is again smooth as glass. Now we move more slowly, for the wind no longer pushes behind, but the men are unwearied; their boat-song dies away over the water, awaking no echo. The hills of the eastern shore show no perceptible difference in size between one sounding-point and the next. I sit dreaming, the rhythmical song and the splashing of the oars exercising a soporific effect. I seem to hear the tramp of a horse which bears a rider in silver harness over the granite mountains of the Trans-Himalaya through an unknown land, and in the dream I perceive that the features of the rider are my own. Then I am sad, for the dream is false. I have certainly crossed the Trans-Himalaya by three passes, but the most important part of the exploration has not been accomplished. That I have done my utmost in dealing both with the Tibetans and the Chinese to gain access to the country north of the Tsangpo is no consolation to me. If one can storm the opposing bulwark of Nature, one should be able to overcome the obstinacy of man. Up yonder in the north, behind Kailas, the Trans-Himalaya extends its granite ramparts, and I must go there though it cost me my life. I must go there, if I clothe myself in the rags of a mendicant lama and beg my way from one black tent to another.

But we are still on the holy lake; it is a day of rest and a summer's day. I feel the skin of my face cracked by the burning of the sun. The hours crawl so slowly over the lake; patience, patience. The clouds display wonderful tone-effects; white and grey, sharply defined, they lie in different stages before the mountains, and behind them dark blue and purple curtains seem to hang down. We might be gliding over the bright floor of a temple hall, its walls richly decorated with flags and standards, which hang down from golden hooks on the ceiling of the sky, and touch the dust of earth with their fringes. The genii of Siva's paradise seem to hover round us. Now Shukkur Ali has taken to a new cry: "Ya aferin adétt," to which he adds "Ya, Allah," as he lifts his oar, and Rehim Ali chimes in with "Shupp." The depth still remains about 180 feet. To the south-east curious clouds are reflected in the lake, and a mist seems to be creeping over the water. All the tones are so light, airy, and grey that the landscape, which surrounds us like a ring where the water ends, seems hardly real. The twin summits of Pundi on the north-east are dark and solemn, and equally dark and solemn is the mirror of the lake. Silver beads drop from the oars and glitter like diamonds in the sun. I could live and die on this heavenly lake without ever growing weary of the wonderful spectacle always presenting fresh surprises.

Meanwhile a light south-easterly breeze disturbs again all the reflexions. The valleys Pachen and Pachung open their doors wider and wider, and allow us to see deeper into the recesses of the mountain. We recognize the hills above camp No. 212, but the tents are not visible. But we see a white spot on the northern shore which we take for a gompa. The depth is somewhat over 197 feet; "Ya bismillah hum!" is Shukkur Ali's exclamation. At the sixteenth point the depth has again decreased, the south-easterly breeze has ceased, and the lake is again a sheet of glass. Now the tents can be seen as tiny specks, and we hope to complete this line also without a storm. A long, low, smooth swell of closely following waves, like the wake of a distant steamer, comes to meet us. How has it been produced, since the lake is quite peaceful? Perhaps by a slight convulsion of the earth's crust, which has disturbed the shore. The undulations on this round lake are very peculiar. At point No. 20 the depth is only 128 feet, and now we have not far to go.

Crack! Shukkur Ali's oar broke off in the middle with a bang, and the boat drew rapidly away from the blade end, which had to be picked up. The good man was so dumbfoundered and bewildered that he stammered, "That does not matter," and went on rowing with the shaft in the air. Now, when the tents were so near, he had developed too much strength. "It is well that the old man does not burst himself," I thought. We tied the parts together with a piece of string. There was a stir on the shore when we landed. The waiting men showed by word and gesture how glad they were to have us back again after giving way to all kinds of dismal forebodings about our sad fate. Just as they caught sight of the boat out on the lake, Robert was about to send out patrols up and down the shore. All was well in the camp, except that the Tibetans were troubled because their provisions were at an end. I gave them money to buy *tsamba* at the monastery. In the evening I discussed with Robert a plan of rowing southwards to investigate the lake bit by bit. We bought a plank and two staves in Serolung, and on the first leisure day Shukkur Ali cut out with an axe two excellent oars, after a pattern I had cut for him from the lid of a cigarette box.

On the next day, the anniversary of my arrival in Leh, a new month began. Every time I write in my diary "the first," I wonder what the new month holds in its lap—new discoveries or new disappointments? But I hope always, and believe that all will come right at last. Rabsang and Tundup Sonam rowed, and Robert steered along the three-feet line about 55 yards from the land, while I sat in the bow, compass in hand, and drew a map of the shore-line, the hills and valleys, and all the details that are characteristic of a lake. Charles A. Sherring states in his book on western Tibet that Mr. Drummond, Commissioner of Bareilly, sailed in 1855 in a boat on Manasarowar, but no result has come to my knowledge; on the contrary, I find that the very latest map of the lake needs a thorough correction. Soundings had never been taken before, and the object of my boating expeditions was to collect material for a detailed isobathic map. When we left behind us the basin of the Brahmaputra at the pass Tamlung, I had already suspected that Manasarowar was a member of the hydrographic system of the Sutlej, and I wished to try if I could not make a contribution towards the solution of this problem. I knew that my investigations could only be inadequate, but they yielded a number of facts hitherto unknown. Among these are the systematic sounding of the bed, by means of which conclusions may be drawn as to the origin and formation of the lake. I soon convinced myself that the lake depression had been excavated by old glaciers from the southern mountains, as I at first conjectured, and was not dammed up by moraine walls across the broad valley. But want of space forbids me to enter fully into a discussion of this interesting question.

We glide in a flat curve to the south-west, and have to increase our distance from the shore that we may not run aground on the sandy bottom. The water at this season of the year has a fairly constant temperature of about 50°. Then we approach the mouth of the Tage-tsangpo. For about two-thirds of a mile the river flows parallel to the shore of the lake, being separated from it by an embankment 13 feet high, which has been cast up by the waves and the pressure of the ice. Here we encamped among drift-sand and bushes, and measured the Tage-tsangpo.

Its breadth was 56.8 feet, its maximum depth 3.4 feet, and its discharge 397.6 cubic feet a second, or 106 cubic feet more than where we last gauged it above the Na-marden affluent. I have already related how we first came in contact with this river at the pass Tam-lung-la; its source stream, the Gang-lung-chu or "water of the ice valley," comes from the Gang-lung mountain in the south, and so there is a glacier or "ice valley" in this mountain which is the origin of the Tage-tsangpo. It is seen from the Tam-lung-la, and is the glacier which I venture to call the Sutlej's genetic source or the real original source. We shall return to this attractive problem.

From every camp on the lake Robert rowed out with two men at right angles to the beach, sounding the depth every five minutes. By means of these radiating lines we discovered the saucer-shaped form of the lake, for, as I have already remarked, the lake bottom is on the whole very even. Now, from camp No. 215, Robert rowed out to a depth of 121 feet.

On August 2 we continued our boating excursion, while the caravan marched along the shore. All went excellently well, we heard not a word of any officials in pursuit of us, and the Tibetans placed yaks and mules at our disposal with the greatest willingness. A couple of showers fell, loud thunder rolled in Gurla Mandatta, and a violent south-westerly breeze forced us to come to a halt and wait at a place on the shore where the brook from the Nima-pendi valley debouches, forming a delta within a broken mole. Fish are plentiful in the brook, but here also the Tibetans asked us not to catch them, and we respected their wishes—only stupid and uncouth men wound the religious feelings of others. By this brook the lake receives a tribute of 49.4 cubic feet per second, while the Richung-chu entering farther to the west-south-west contributes 63.6 cubic feet.

We passed Yanggo-gompa under sail at a rather short distance, and steered straight for Tugu-gompa, picturesquely situated on a strand terrace. Here begin the long lagoons and mud embankment we had seen from the western beach, and we were carried comfortably ashore and greeted politely by a band of Hindus consisting of pilgrims and traders. A number of Tibetan shepherds from the north were staying here, where a not unimportant wool market is held every summer. A group of monks stood on the roof. Our camp was pitched close to the foot of the monastery, on the shore road, and had a fine view over the lake and Kailas behind it. At the southern wall of the convent is a yard enclosed by a stone wall, where 500 sheep were packed like herrings in a barrel, to be shorn in turn by Hindus and Botias who come from Almora and the border country in the south. The nomads receive eight annas (8d.) for every sheep, good interest on their live capital. The wool from 500 sheep is said to amount to 16 yak-loads (Illust. 249).

We paid at once a visit to the monastery, where the thirteen monks and their abbot, Tabga Rinchen, received us with the greatest kindness and politeness, showed us everything, and explained to us the various temple halls. They had heard of my voyages on the lake, and had now seen with their own eyes my boat sailing before a favourable wind, and they expressed their sincere conviction that I must possess occult powers to defy with impunity the god of the holy lake. But they understood that this was owing to my friendship with the Tashi Lama, who had given me his holy blessing. The monastery Tugu-gompa is a dependency of Shibeling-gompa in Purang, and most of the monks come from there to spend three years on the lake. They own herds in Chang-tang, trade, and seem to be in good circumstances; at any rate, they help the poor pilgrims who have nothing to eat on their wanderings round Tso-mavang. They receive gifts from well-to-do pilgrims. The temple halls are picturesque, handsome and in very good order. You enter from an upper balcony into an outer hall with wall paintings, among which is a picture of Tso-mavang with the fish-god, Madö Gemo, rising from the waves (Illust. 250). He has seven water-snakes in his hair, and the lower part of his body is like a green dolphin. The lake is as deep as it is broad, and concentric rings encircle the rising god. The abbot said that the fish-

250. The God of the Lake rising from Tso-mavang.

Sketch by the Author.

god comes up to greet the god of Tso-mavang, Hlabsen Dorche Barva, who gallops in a cloud of grey fiery tongues and smoke on a pink horse, and is armed with spear, bow and quiver. In the background stands Kang-rinpoche, the holy mountain. The whole picture is wanting in perspective and proportion, but it is curious and interesting, and the Lamaist artist has done his best to idealize the holy lake by his drawing and colouring. I made a copy of this work of art, which has some relationship with our old country paintings.

From the entrance hall a small door gives access to the holiest shrine in all Tugu-gompa, namely, the hall of the lake god. He is represented only as a mask, surrounded by *kadakhs*, and seems to peep out from between curtains. A couple of flames burn before him and the usual bowls are placed on a stool table. No man but the monks themselves may enter this little alcove, but I obtained permission to sit on the threshold and draw a sketch of it (Illust. 251). I regarded this unknown Hlabsen Dorche Barva almost with reverence, for he ruled over my beloved lake and had been so gracious to me.

But the finest sight of all was the view from the monastery roof. The highest parts of Gurla Mandatta, here called Mama-nani or Mamo-nani, were concealed by the lower flanks, for we were too near to it, but the surface of the lake stretched out northwards to an immense distance. A lama, who had served at several different times in the convent, asserted that the lake rose 24 to 28 inches in rainy summers, and declared that eighteen years before the water had reached to the foot of the red façade of the monastery. This seemed improbable, for the distance between the lake and the monastery was 323 feet, and the foot of the convent façade (the right corner looking from the strand) lay 20.67 feet above the level of the lake. I quote these figures to enable a future explorer to determine whether the lake has risen or fallen since August 2, 1907.

I passed the next days in the monastery, sketched the lamas at their various temple services, and fell in love with this pleasant, handsome Tugu-gompa. Punso Lama, a young monk, was my particular friend, and showed me everything with the inexhaustible knowledge of a trained museum attendant. Three officials of the Devashung had established themselves in the entrance hall in the company of the four ghostly kings, and mattresses, bundles, tables, swords and guns lay or stood in profane disorder at the entrance to the dwelling of the high gods (Illusts. 252, 253, 257).

Meanwhile Robert rowed out from the southern shore, and sounded the depths down to the contour of 207 feet. On August 5, we paid a visit to Yanggo-gompa, which contains ten monks and a nun. They told me that they came from the Hor country in the north of central Tibet, and therefore call themselves Horpa, but also Dokpa; the Changpa are the nomads of Chang-tang. The abbot is from Sekiya-gompa. In the monastery's *gunkang*, a dark subterranean crypt, hang masks, *kadakhs*, drums, spears and guns. I asked for what purpose the monks wanted the firearms, as one of their fundamental dogmas forbids them to extinguish the light of life, and they answered that with these guns many wild yaks had been killed, whose flesh had been used for human food, and that therefore the guns had been installed in a place of honour in the monastery. Yamba Tsering, a monk twenty-two years old, sat with his head against a wooden pillar, and gazed in silence at the dim light which fell into the crypt through an impluvium; he looked like a dreamer, a searcher after hidden truth (Illust. 256). Beside him sat the wrinkled nun. Both found their way into my sketch-book (Illusts. 258, 259). The foot of the monastery façade lies exactly $14\frac{3}{4}$ feet above the level of the lake, and the river Richen-chu, entering the lake behind the convent, discharges 62.15 cubic feet of water.

Yanggo-gompa was the third of the eight monasteries of the holy lake which I had visited, and I wished to see them all without exception. And I also wished to gauge all the streams falling into the lake. It fluctuates from day to day, according as there is rain or sunshine, but only by exact measurements could I arrive at the volume which is poured into the clear basin of Tso-mavang during a day of summer.

CHAPTER XLVI

A STORMY VOYAGE OVER THE HOLY LAKE

On August 6 we stayed at Tugu-gompa, one of the most interesting monasteries I have seen in Tibet. I was engaged all day long, with Robert and Rabsang to assist me, in measuring with a tape the dimensions of the three storeys, and drawing plans of them. The third, however, is little more than a roof balcony. I have no space to give the results here. As we were on the roof, eight monks were sitting in the inner court counting their receipts, which were duly entered in a cash-book. Their rupees and *tengas* lay in heaps on a short-legged table. I gave a handful of rupees, throwing them among the piles, and disturbing the calculations of the monks. However, they were very thankful for this unexpected contribution, which seemed to fall from heaven.

About thirty Hindu pilgrims set up their shabby tents near us. In the evening they lighted a fire on a flat metal dish, which was pushed out on to the water, and shone like a beacon fire by the bank. This floating pyre was meant as a homage to the lake.

On August 7 I was awakened early when the sun was pouring fresh gold over the blue lake, and a lama on the convent roof was blowing long-drawn heavy notes from his shell horn over the surface. I hastened to the shore where the boat lay, ready with its usual equipment, Shukkur Ali and Tundup Sonam put the sounding-line in order and stowed our baggage. The Hindus lined the bank like the wild-geese, left their clothing on land, and waded, with only a cloth round their loins, to bathe in the holy beatifying water of the lake. It must be very refreshing to people from the close jungles of India to wash in such a cool morning in water at only a few degrees above freezing-point. Most of them, however, go in no farther than up to their knees. There they squat down, or scoop up the water in their joined hands, and throw it over them. They make symbolical signs, fill their mouth with water and send it out in a stream, hold their hands flat against their faces and look at the rising sun, and perform all kinds of absurd, complicated manipulations, which I remember seeing at the ghâts of Benares. They are sunburnt, thin and miserable, and they are too thinly clad—I did not see a single sheepskin—and they complain of the severity of the climate, catch chills, and come to my tent for medicine. Some stood about an hour in the water before they returned to the beach to put on their clothing, and then they sat in groups talking. But they return to the valleys of India convinced that they have performed an action well-pleasing to the gods, and they take with them small metal bottles filled with holy water from Manasarowar to give to their relations. They believe that one of the ways of salvation runs past Manasarowar. They are always hopeful, and that is a fine thing for poor pilgrims on the face of the earth.

They stared with astonishment at our boat, which was driven out from the shore by powerful strokes, perhaps with envious eyes, for many asked me afterwards to let them go with me, that they might for the rest of their lives look back to the time when they floated on the sacred waves. The lake lay smooth and still, but at the first sounding-station (115 feet), the lake god shook himself, a north-westerly breeze sprang up, and the waves splashed and danced briskly against our bow, for our third line of soundings was carried north, 27° W., towards camp No. 214. We sounded 174, 207, 226, 236, 236, 246, and 253 feet, while the waves increased, and the boat rode well but with diminished speed. Gurla Mandatta was almost clear, but Kailas was buried in clouds. The wind fell and the sun glowed, and everything foretold a fine

251. TEMPLE HALL OF THE LAKE-GOD OF TSO-MAVANG.

252. CHENRESI'S IMAGE IN TUGU-GOMPA.

Sketches by the Author.

day. At the ninth point the depth was less, 246 feet; we had passed the line of soundings made in the night and its great depths. Afterwards the depths were 223, 197, 187, 194, and 200 feet.

The north-westerly breeze began to blow again, and at mid-day clouds gathered in the north. A heavy bluish-grey layer of clouds sank down slowly on the mountain flanks, and from its under side rain fringes hung down, greyish-purple on a compact dark background. All the mountains and the whole strand disappeared, and the masses of cloud seemed as though they would fall on the lake. We passed the fifteenth station, which showed a depth of 200 feet, and kept a steady course towards the red promontory. The rowers put forth all their strength when I had pointed out to them that we were drawing near to the shelter of the bank, and that the waves were becoming smaller the farther we advanced. We had left Gossul-gompa a good distance to the left; I could not see the monastery myself, but the men saw it as a small white speck in the distance.

Just before one o'clock yellow swirls of dust and sand appeared near the landspit which we were making for. They became denser and larger, and looked yellow and dismal on the dark purple background of gathering clouds. It was not the first time I had seen such storm warnings.

"We are in for a storm," I said quietly.

"God is with us," replied Shukkur Ali quite as calmly.

"Row on and we shall get in before the waves are high."

"If we turn straight to the shore, it will be nearer," suggested Shukkur Ali.

"No, we will not alter the course, we will make straight for our goal, and we shall soon be in the shelter of the hills on the shore; there are only three soundings to be taken, and they can be left for another time."

The wind fell again, and it began to rain in a few large drops, which on reaching the surface of the water remained an instant as separate round beads, as though they were covered with a film of oil. Then followed an extremely heavy shower of hail which lashed the water as it streamed down, enveloped us in semi-darkness, caused the lake to leap up in millions of tiny fountains, and in two minutes made the inside of the boat white. Nothing was visible but ourselves and the boat, only water and hail, which scourged the lake like rods and produced a hissing gurgle. Now and then the clouds were lighted up by quivering lightning, and the thunder growled heavily and threateningly in the north. Then the men turned round, but could see nothing in the mist; they were uneasy and we all felt that there was danger ahead.

The hail was followed by pelting rain, a downpour of such furious impetuosity that I could not imagine any more tremendous. It fell in such quantities and with such force that we were bowed down by it. I had on three shirts and a leather vest, but after a short time I felt that the water was streaming down my bare skin, which had this advantage that all the future douches that awaited us could make no further impression. I had my fur coat on my knees with the skin side up, and in all its hollows the water collected in small pools. A quantity of water fell into the boat and washed about with the stroke of the oars. The shore was not visible, and I steered by the compass.

"Row on, we have not much farther to go."

At length the rain became finer, but at four minutes after one o'clock, we heard a deafening roar in the north-east, a sound such as only a storm of the greatest violence can produce. Hail and rain were nothing to it; now that the heavy sheets of water were withdrawn the storm had a free course and swept suddenly and furiously over the lake. Why had we not started an hour earlier, instead of watching the religious ablutions of the Hindus? No, the god of Tso-mavang was angry and would teach us once for all not to treat so lightly the lake which splashes his dolphin's tail with its green water. How we envied the monks in Gossul-gompa, and our men down in the south under the peaceful walls of the Tugu monastery! What would they say, what would they do, if we were drowned like cats in this raging lake?

For a minute we struggled frantically to keep our

course in spite of the waves which swept upon us from the right. They swelled up with astonishing rapidity, and every wave which dashed against the taut canvas of the boat and dissolved into spray, made a cracking sound as though the little vessel were about to burst. The next was still larger; I warded it off with my Indian helmet, and Tundup Sonam received a cold buffet which disconcerted him for a moment. After the third, which threw its foaming crest over the gunwale, the water stood 4 inches deep in the boat, the little nutshell with the weight of three men lay far too deep in the water, and the water we had shipped gurgled, lapped, and splashed hither and thither with the roll of the boat.

Now I perceived that the attempt to hold our course was hopeless. We must fall off with the wind and waves. We had Gossul-gompa to the south, 50° W., and the storm was from the north-east; we could find refuge in the monastery, if we could get so far. The difficulty was to turn at right angles without capsizing. Twice I failed, and we shipped more water, but the third time I succeeded, and now, if we had any care for our lives we must prevent the boat from veering up into the wind; the storm came a little from the right. Tundup Sonam, who rowed the starboard oar in the bow, had all the work, while Shukkur Ali had only to dip in his oar occasionally at my command, but though outwardly calm he was too excited and eager, and when my voice could not be heard amid the howling of the storm, I put my hand on his knuckles to make him leave the oar alone.

Now began a voyage such as I had never experienced in all my journeys in Tibet. The storm increased to a hurricane, and under its pressure the waves became as high as the billows of the Baltic in stormy weather; a steamer would have rolled in such a sea, and we in the little canvas boat had to negotiate the unexpected cross rolls following one another. Lashed, hunted, and persecuted by the raging force of the wind, we swept over the lake. Every new wave that lifted us up seemed bigger than the last. Some had sharp smooth crests, as though moulded out of mountain crystal, and reflected the dark clouds in the north. It seemed as though a bottomless, watery grave yawned in front of us which might at any moment swallow up our boat. Others came rolling up foam-capped, hissing and thundering behind us, and we shuddered at the thought that they might fill the boat in an instant and send it to the bottom, but it rose bravely over the crests. The view was open on all sides, the sun was visible in the south, Gurla Mandatta was clear and sharp, to the south, 50° W., even the terrace on which Gossul-gompa stands could be seen, and it was black and threatening only in the north. During the second when the boat was balanced quivering on the crest of the wave, we might fancy ourselves transplanted to a lofty pass in Chang-tang with a world of mountain ranges all round us, while the foam of the waves had an illusive resemblance to the fields of eternal snow.

But this wave also passes on and the boat sinks into a hollow, we fall into a water grotto, the nearest waves conceal the view, the walls of the grotto are of the purest malachite behind us and like emerald in front. Now we are lifted up again—"At it, Tundup Sonam, or the huge foaming crest will thrust us down!"—he puts forth all his strength and the wave passes us. It is irregular and reminds us of the pyramidal summit of Kubi-gangri; two such crests tower up in front of us, and their edges are shattered into spray by the wind. They are as transparent as glass, and through one of them the image of Gurla Mandatta's bright white snowfields is refracted as in a magnifying glass. We have a watery portal in front of us and the tips of the waves are gilded with the faint reflexion of the sun in the south.

We struggle bravely and I sit on the bottom of the boat pushing the rudder with all my strength to keep the boat in the right direction, while the spray, lashed by the wind, spurts over us as from a fire-hose. Frequently a broken crest slips over the gunwale, but we have not a hand free to bale out the water. We see the boat filling slowly—shall we reach the bank before it sinks? The mast and sail lie with two reserve oars tied fast across the middle of the boat. If we could set a sail the

253. THE LHAKANG HALL IN TUGU-GOMPA.

Sketch by the Author.

boat would be easier to handle, but it is not to be thought of now, when we can hardly keep our balance sitting down and stiffening ourselves with our feet, with the heavy blows and the unexpected positions the boat assumes according to the form of the waves, their slopes, curves and curls. And, besides, in such a storm the mast would break like glass.

We had turned at right angles to our line of soundings for now we thought only of saving our lives, if that were possible—to reach the land before the boat sank. Then, in the most critical moment, when an irregular wave threatened the boat, I called on Tundup Sonam to put forth all his strength, and he did it too well, so that the oar broke with a crack. Now all hung by a hair, we could not manage the boat and it must inevitably capsize and be swamped under this foaming crest. But Tundup Sonam realized the danger, and with a quick grasp tore loose a reserve oar, while Shukkur Ali backed with the leeward oar; after another douche we trimmed the boat again.

The longer the storm lasts and the larger the expanse of lake left behind us in the north-east, the higher rise the waves; we are swept forwards, we rock up and down on the lumpy lake, and fresh cold douches are constantly poured over us from the crests as they split into spray like plumes of feathers. How small and helpless we feel in the presence of these roused infuriated forces of Nature, how imposing and awful, and yet how grand and splendid is this spectacle! The two men had never in their lives seen anything to equal it. I sit with my back to the pursuing billows, but the men have them before their faces, and I know when large waves are approaching by their muttered "Ya Allah!" Tundup is as pale as he can be with a sun-tanned skin; Shukkur Ali seems composed, but he does not sing to-day as he dips in his oar. Tundup afterwards confided to me that he was quite convinced that we should perish.

It is impossible to keep my eyeglasses dry and clear, and I have not for a long time had a dry thread on me. Shukkur Ali turns round and says that the monastery is in sight, but it is too far for my eyes. "Look at the wave yonder," I call out. "Is it not beautiful?" He smiles and murmurs his "Ya Allah." Its crest breaks close to us like a waterfall, and, air being forced into the water, it rises again in bubbling foam and the lake seems to boil and seethe. Hitherto there has been drizzling rain, but now the air is clear. The lake assumes a different hue, the waves are dark and bright, close to us black as ink, but lighter towards their tips, and the horizon of the lake is often seen through the next wave as through a sheet of ice.

Thus we are driven on, and the time seems endless. For five quarters of an hour we have striven with the freaks of the lake god, and every minute has seemed to us an hour. At last the monastery Gossul appears and grows larger, the details becoming distinguishable, and I see the white façade with its upper border of red, its windows and roof streamers, and some monks behind a balustrade with their eyes fixed on the boat. And below the cloister terrace there is wild foaming surf. How we are to land I cannot imagine; I have experienced such adventures before, but never anything as furious as to-day. We envy the monks up above with firm ground under their feet, and should like to be beside them. The log has been out all the time, and now I draw it in with a quick pull and call out to the men to be ready to jump overboard when I give the sign. I place the note-book and the map I have sketched to-day, all dripping with water, into the front of my leather vest, that at any rate I may not lose the figures I have obtained.

We have only a few minutes more. With the help of Shukkur Ali I manage to get out of my heavy soaked boots, and have scarcely done so when the boat is pitched violently into the breakers on the shore. Here the water is as brown as oatmeal, and the undertow sucks out the boat again. Now Tundup Sonam wishes to jump out of the boat but I advise him to try first with the oar if he can reach the bottom; he feels no ground and has to wait patiently. The boat receives a blow from behind and threatens to capsize; the oarsmen work as if they were

254. LAMA WITH PRAYER-DRUM.

255. LAMA BEFORE THE TEMPLE DOOR IN TUGU-GOMPA.

Sketches by the Author.

possessed to fight against the undertow, and before I am aware Tundup has jumped out, and, up to his breast in water, draws the boat shorewards with all his might. Now we two follow his example, and with our united strength succeed at last in drawing the boat up the beach before the raging surf can dash it to pieces. One more hard pull and we have drawn it up over the mud embankment into the lagoon, which the waves cannot reach.

Now we had had enough, and we threw ourselves down on the sand, quite tired out. The fearful excitement and tension of body and mind during an hour and a half was followed by stupor and weariness; we had nothing to say to one another, and I gave no orders for the night. We were shipwrecked men, and had every reason to be pleased and thankful that we had firm ground under our feet again, and had escaped safely from the green graves which had yawned below us, threatening to engulf us if we had not been on the alert in critical moments.

We had only dozed a few minutes when two monks and three young novices came gently over the sand and approached us cautiously, as if they were not quite certain whether we were alive or dead. When we got up they greeted us kindly, and inquired how we were and whether we needed help. They were deeply interested, and told us how they had seen from their balcony the boat tossing on the waves, and had been convinced that it must founder in the unusually violent storm that had swept over the lake. They had been frightened to death, and said that it was fearful to see the boat sink in the trough of the waves, and every moment they expected that it would not appear again. On landing we were immediately below them, and the sight was too terrible. Were we hurt at all, and would we come up into the monastery and spend the night in their warm rooms? But I thanked them for their kind offers and preferred to sleep as usual in the open air. If they could get us fuel and food we should be much obliged.

They bowed and disappeared in their maze of staircases, and presently came back with sacks full of dung, brushwood, and billets, and soon a grand fire was burning on the terrace. They kindled it themselves, for our matches and tinder were quite useless. Then they went off to fetch some eatables, for the contents of our packet of provisions were turned into paste by the water.

Meanwhile we made ourselves comfortable on the narrow strip of ground below the monastery. Two large caves opened into the terrace, their vaults black with smoke, for pilgrims and herdsmen spend the night in them. They would have sheltered us from the wind, but they were so dirty that we preferred to pitch our camp at the edge of the bank. It was wet with rain, but we scraped out dry sand with our hands. The boat was taken to pieces and emptied—it was half full of water—and then it was set up by the fire as a screen.

When the fire had burned up and was glowing hot, we stripped ourselves stark naked, wrung out one garment after another, and crouched by the fire to dry our underclothing and ourselves. Each had to look after himself, for we were all in the same plight. I spread out my things as near as possible to the fire and hung them over the oars and life-buoys to expose them to the wind and heat. Meanwhile I dried my woollen vest bit by bit, turned it inside out, held it to the fire on this side and that, out and inside, and when it was quite dry put it on again. Then came the turn of my unmentionables, then of my stockings, and so on. Nothing could be done with the leather waistcoat and the fur coat; they would not be dry by night, but what did it matter? It was at any rate better here than in the crystal halls of the lake king.

It is still broad daylight, but the storm rages, Gurla Mandatta and all the country to the south has disappeared, for the gale is passing off in that direction. There is fine close rain again. Falcons scream in the holes of the pebbly slopes—dangerous neighbours for the bluish-grey pigeons cooing on the rocks.

The monks came down again with sweet and sour milk and *tsamba*, tea we had ourselves, and the simple dinner tasted delicious. Then we sat a couple of hours by the fire while the storm continued. I dried my diary and entered the notes which form the contents of this chapter. Between whiles Shukkur Ali entertained me with stories of his adventures during his travels in the service of Younghusband and Wellby. Now that he had escaped death by the skin of his teeth, the past returned more vividly to his memory, and when once he was started on his reminiscences he could not be stopped, good old Shukkur Ali. I listened with one ear and wrote with the other — I had almost said — not to appear uninterested; and, after all, the chief thing to Shukkur Ali was that he could prattle.

At last the northern sky becomes clear, and all the mountains are white with snow; before only Kailas and its next neighbours were distinguished by white caps, but now all is white. We are certainly past the early days of August, but is it possible that autumn is already beginning? The summer has been so short that we have hardly had time to get accustomed to it.

Another night falls on the earth. Impenetrable darkness surrounds us, and only in the zenith a few stars sparkle. The swell still roars against the strand, but Tso-mavang is gently falling asleep. Above us towers the monastery on its steep wall like a fortress, and the monks have retired to rest. The falcons are heard no more, and the pigeons have sought their nests.

CHAPTER XLVII

ON THE ROOF OF THE GOSSUL MONASTERY

IN the middle of the night I was awaked by a terrible row; a dog from the monastery had crept under my men's half of the boat to see what it could find, but chanced to fall into the hands of Shukkur Ali, and got a good thrashing. The temperature fell to 37.4°. Rabsang came riding up at sunrise. The men had feared that we must have perished in the waves. He brought provisions and a packet of letters from Thakur Jai Chand, the British commercial agent in Gartok, who was at the time in Gyanima, where the fair was being held. He wrote that Colonel Dunlop Smith had directed him on June 27 to try to obtain news of me. Guffaru had performed his task satisfactorily, and all my baggage was safely deposited in Gartok, and my voluminous correspondence had been forwarded to Simla. From Mr. Sherring, who had made a journey to Manasarowar some years previously, I received a very kind letter; he had also had the kindness to send me his interesting book on western Tibet, while his wife had added a whole packet of English and French newspapers, literature the more acceptable that the extensive library presented to me by O'Connor had long been read through and dispersed to the four winds of heaven. It was a singular coincidence that where I had suffered shipwreck I was so unexpectedly brought again into contact with the outer world.

I was deeply moved by Rabsang's information that the monks in Tugu-gompa, when they saw the storm burst over our frail boat, had burnt incense before the images of the lake-god and implored him to deliver us from the waves. They had done it of their own accord, and not at the request of any one. They said it would be deplorable if we were lost; they had a heart, and were not so unfeeling as might be supposed. Few proofs of sympathy have touched me like this.

Accompanied by Rabsang, I ascended in the early morning the winding path up to the monastery. At the turns and projections stand cubical *chhortens* and votive cairns, and here and there a streamer flutters on a mast. A *samkang*, a hermit's dwelling, hangs over a cavern produced by the fall of a huge mass from the slope of the pebble terrace eleven years ago. I told the monks that they should not put too much confidence in the ground on which their monastery stands. They reckon millions of years for the soul's wanderings, but their earthly dwellings are not built for eternity. They answered calmly that the monastery had already stood for one hundred years, and that it would certainly stand as long as they were living there; for in general the monks are changed every three years, and they come here from the monastery Shibeling in Purang, by which they are maintained. There are only three of them, but I saw also four novices, seven, nine, ten, and eleven years old respectively, running about as actively as mice, and waiting on the monks. Their mother, a nun from Purang, also lives in the monastery. She had been married before she "took the veil," and when her husband died she dedicated herself and all her children to the Church. I afterwards learned that one of the "boys" was a girl; they were so like one another that I could not distinguish between them. At first they were shy and timid, but after I had given them a few silver coins they were soon at ease with me. They appeared small and stunted for their age, but the abbot told me that they had mourned so much at the death of their father that their growth was checked. Almost all the day they were bringing water from the lake in clay jugs, which they carried in a basket suspended by a strap round their forehead; they carry therefore with the muscles of the head and neck, which are consequently so much developed that they seem too large for the body. But they also receive instruction and take their first uncertain steps in the domain of wisdom; the eldest is said to have already acquired considerable knowledge.

I went into the temple and studied it thoroughly. I remained there twelve hours, drew, took measurements, made all kinds of inquiries, and took notes. Every part is handsome, interesting, and well-kept. The *lhakang* is like an old armoury, a museum of fine, rare articles, which show great artistic skill, and have been designed, carved, modelled, and painted with unwearied patience and real taste. The hall, supported by eight pillars, has two red divans; a statue of Buddha in gilded bronze, and a number of other idols; drums hanging in stands, lacquered tables with the usual religious objects, and a large quantity of votive bowls in the brightest brass and of uncommon, tasteful forms. On both sides of the pillars hang *tankas* in four rows, which are as long as standards and triumphal banners, and are so arranged that they do not prevent the light from playing on the faces of the gods. In a corner surely waves a Swedish flag? Ah, it is only a blue and yellow *tanka*, but it reminds me of the golden period of our fame and victories.

The *lhakang* of Gossul is not built on the usual plan; the skylight is wanting, and instead there are three windows in the façade facing the lake. But the gods do not see the lake, for the windows are pasted over with paper on a trellis-work of laths. Why is the beautiful view concealed and the daylight excluded? To enhance the mystical gloom within and excite the greater wonder and reverence in the minds of the pilgrims who come in half-blinded from the daylight, and that they may not see that the gold is only gilded brass, and that the marks of the brush and the chisel may not be too profanely evident. The poorer a monastery, the darker are its temple halls; the darkness hides their poverty and helps the monks to impose on the faithful.

Somchung is the name of a small compartment no larger than a cabin. On its divan are cushions and

256. Yanggo-gompa.

257. Interior of the Temple, Tugu.

Sketches by the Author.

pieces of cloth arranged in circles to form two nests, in which two monks sit during the night service. On the altar table before Sakya-muni's image stand forty bowls filled with water, and on another table some peacock's feathers in a silver vase, with which the gods are sprinkled with holy water to the cry "Om a hum."

In former times robbers and footpads harboured here, and had their hiding-places in the caves below the monastery. From these they fell upon the pilgrims and killed many of them. Then the god of Tso-mavang appeared to Jimpa Ngurbu, a noble lama, and ordered him to build the monastery, that it might be a sure stronghold for the protection of pilgrims, and for the honour of the gods. Even now the country is not safe. Last year two scoundrels, who had plundered the nomads, were taken and executed; and we ourselves saw ten Gurkhas, armed with guns, who rode past us in search of a robber band which had stolen their horses and sheep.

The monks said that the lake usually freezes in January; in stormy weather the ice breaks up, but when the weather is calm and the frost is sharp, the whole lake freezes over in a single day, and breaks up again in a single day when it is stormy. Unfortunately the statements made about the level of the water and the discharge are contradictory and untrustworthy. A lama, thirty-five years of age, now staying here, had lived on Tso-mavang as a child. He said that he well remembered the time when the water flowed out of the lake to Rakas-tal in such quantities that a horseman could not cross the channel, which is called Ganga, without danger. But now this channel had ceased to carry water for nine years. I was shown where the shore line ran last autumn, five fathoms farther inland, so that the lake must then have been 22½ inches higher. I was also shown a yellow block of stone, to which the water was said to have reached twelve years ago, and this point lay 10⅓ feet above the present level of the lake. Such a rate of fall is improbable, though this statement accorded fairly well with the information I had received at Tugu-gompa. The threshold of the one cave lay now 22.57 feet, and that of the other 120.4 feet from the shore, 18.86 feet above the water. I was told that when the monastery was built, one hundred years ago, the lake had reached both these caves, and that only a small path was left along the strand by which the caves could be approached. However, the dates of the Tibetans are exceedingly uncertain, and to arrive at safe conclusions we must resort to the statements of European travellers. I will make a few remarks on them later. When I asked one of the monks what became of all the water poured into Tso-mavang by all the rivers and brooks, he replied:

"However much it rains, and though all the tributaries are full to overflowing, no change is noticeable in the lake, for as much water is evaporated as flows in. In our holy books it is written that if all the tributaries failed, the lake would not sink and disappear, for it is eternal and is the abode of high gods. But now we see with our own eyes that it is always falling, and we do not know what this means."

The following records may be useful to future explorers: the lower edge of the massive threshold of the main gateway in the façade of Gossul-gompa lay on August 8, 1907, exactly 122.7 feet above the surface of the lake, as I ascertained by the help of a reflecting level.

We ascended to the roof of Gossul-gompa. It is flat, as usual, with a chimney, parapet, and streamers. No language on earth contains words forcible enough to describe the view from it over the lake. It was, indeed, much the same as we had seen from various points on the shore, but the light and shade was so enchanting and the colouring so wonderful that I was amazed, and felt my heart beat more strongly than usual as I stepped out of the dark temple halls on to the open platform. Tundup Sonam said in his simple way that the lake with its encircling mountains seemed like the sky with its light clouds. I, too, was the victim of an illusion which almost made me catch at the parapet for support. I wondered whether it was a fit of giddiness. I took, to wit, the border of mountains on the eastern shore for a belt of light clouds, and the surface of the sea for part of the sky. The day was perfectly calm and the lake like a mirror, in which the

258. A Dreamer. Lama in Yanggo-gompa on Manasarowar.
Drawn by T. Macfarlane from a Sketch by the Author.

sky was reflected; both looked exactly the same, and were of the same colour, and the mountains, which in consequence of the distance were all blended into a dark shadow, were like a girdle of clouds. The air was not clear, everything was of a dull subdued tone, there was no colour to speak of, but all was grey—sky, land, and water, with a tinge of blue, a fairy scene of glass, with decorations of white gauze seen through a thin blue veil of incense rising from the altar of the mighty god of the lake.

What has become of the earth, if all is sky and clouds? We are not totally bewitched, for we are standing on the roof of the monastery leaning against the parapet. A dream-picture in the most ethereal transitory tones floats before us. We seem to stand on a promontory jutting out into endless space, which yawns around us and in front. And where is now the holy lake, which yesterday nearly robbed us of life, and on which the storm was so furious that I still seem to feel the ground quaking under my feet? Has the Gossul monastery been changed by some whim of the gods into an air-ship which is bearing us away to another planet? Its streamers hang motionless on their poles, and nothing can be seen of the mountains, country, and ground.

"Oh yes, if you lean a little over the parapet," says a monk, smiling. True! Then the illusion vanishes, to my great chagrin. I should have liked to remain a while under its enchantment. Just below us runs the narrow margin on the bank, with its black dam of clay and water-weeds, and its elongated lagoons. Through the crystal-clear water we see the yellowish-grey mud on the lake bottom, the dark fringe of weeds, and the dark depths beyond. It is like a huge aquarium covered with plate-glass. Two flocks of geese are swimming on the water, producing diverging ripples. All is so indescribably quiet; so ethereal, transparent, and transitory, so subtile and sensitive, that I scarcely dare breathe. Never has a church service, a wedding march, a hymn of victory, or a funeral made a more powerful impression on me.

Did fate compel me to pass my life in a monastery in

Tibet, I would without hesitation choose Gossul-gompa. There I would observe the fluctuations of the lake and the annual curves of the temperature. I would sit up there like a watchman, gaze over the lake, and watch how its aspect changed every hour during the twelve months of the year. I would listen to the howling of the autumn storms, and would notice on calm November days how the belt of ice along the shore broadened from day to day, if only to melt again in the course of a day. The ring of ice would creep on ever nearer to the middle of the lake, be destroyed again and again by new gales, and then begin again to enchain the waters. And at length, on a day in January, when the layers of water were cooled through and through and no wind disturbed the air, I should see the god of Tso-mavang stretch a ringing roof of glass over his green palace, and the winter storms bestrew it with white powder and drive the whirling snow in dense clouds over the ice, with its smooth, dark-green surface peeping out here and there. And on calm days the lake would lie a white plain, lifeless and lonely under its white shroud, and I should sit by the bier of my friend longing for the spring. In vain would the first storms of spring contend with the solidity of the ice and its brave resistance, but at last the sun would come to help the wind, and would make the ice brittle and rotten. Leads and fissures would start up in all directions, and the next storm that swept over the ice would overcome all resistance, flinging about the ice blocks and piling them up one on another, driving them to the shore, and sweeping breakers over them so that they would be crushed, splintered, pulverized, and melted in the rolling surf. Then I should rejoice at the victory of the storm, the release of Tso-mavang and its restoration to life, and would listen to the song of the waves and the screaming of the wild geese.

Perhaps an hour such as I spent at the parapet of Gossul comes only once a year. The effect is the result of a certain temperature, a certain percentage of humidity, calm air, preceded by rain and a north-easterly storm. How seldom are all these conditions fulfilled? At most once a year, and just at this hour, this hour of all hours, I

259. THE OLD NUN IN YANGGO-GOMPA.
Sketch by the Author.

stood on the roof and saw the blue lake at rest after its play.

Wonderful, attractive, enchanting lake! Theme of story and legend, playground of storms and changes of colour, apple of the eye of gods and men, goal of weary, yearning pilgrims, holiest of the holiest of all the lakes of the world, art thou, Tso-mavang, lake of all lakes. Navel of old Asia, where four of the most famous rivers of the world, the Brahmaputra, the Indus, the Sutlej, and the Ganges, rise among gigantic peaks, surrounded by a world of mountains, among which is Kailas, the most famous in the world; for it is sacred in the eyes of hundreds of millions of Hindus, and is the centre of a wreath of monasteries where every morning blasts of conches sound out from the roofs over the lake. Axle and hub of the wheel, which is an image of life, and round which the pilgrims wander along the way of salvation towards the land of perfection. That is Manasarowar, the pearl of all the lakes of the world. Hoary with age when the books of the Veda were written, its blue billows have in the course of centuries seen innumerable troops of faithful Hindus and Tibetans arrive at its banks, there to drink, bathe, and find rest for their souls. There are certainly more beautiful lakes in the world. Its western neighbour, for instance, Langak-tso, is more picturesque. But there is none which unites with natural beauty such an influence on the faith and souls of men. That is why the roar of its waves is so attractive, and a sojourn on its shore so fascinating. Standing up on the convent roof, while silence reigns around, one fancies one hears innumerable wanderers approaching, and the echo of their stumbling feet on the holy path around the lake. And one casts a glance into the night of past centuries, which have left no trace of their aspirations and vain search after an imaginary blessedness. But Tso-mavang remains the same as it was then, and its azure-blue eye sees new generations treading in the footsteps of the old.

After such an hour everything else seems commonplace. Not till the blush of evening flooded the lake with a purple tinge could I tear myself away and go down to my camp on the shore. Once more I turned to Tso-mavang and called out a loud prolonged "Om a hum." Rabsang said nothing, but I could see that he was wondering whether I had become the latest convert of the Lamaistic church, and with the more reason because I had insisted on travelling round the lake in the orthodox direction—southwards by the east bank and northwards by the west bank.

The tracks of 120 yaks were discernible in the sand, which had passed northwards in the morning laden with brick tea. An old Hindu, who was performing the circuit of the lake in the same direction as the Tibetans, begged to be allowed to camp beside us, because he was afraid of robbers; we regaled him with tea, bread, and tobacco, and he asked us to accept a handful of rice. It is singular that the Hindu pilgrims seem to hold the Lamaistic monasteries in veneration; at least I saw them bow before the Lamaistic gods in Tugu-gompa, and place a handful of rice in the bowl which a monk held out to them.

After a temperature of 43.9° in the night the morning air seemed quite warm. A fresh easterly breeze ruffled the surface of the lake, and the foam-tipped waves shone in the sun, but the day was beautiful and I was full of life, and eager to go out upon the lake. The old Hindu said that he had resolved to postpone his pilgrimage and go with us in the boat, but I assured him that we would take no unnecessary ballast. But he followed us on the bank as we rowed through the surf to Camp No. 213, easily recognizable by its old fire-place, and when we steered thence seawards straight towards Tugu-gompa, visible as a white speck in the south-east, he was so eager to go with us that he ran into the water and did not turn back till it reached to his middle. He was certainly a little silly; he had talked nonsense all the evening, though no one had listened to him.

The new line of soundings was marked No. 4 on my map of the lake. Its greatest depth was 249 feet. At the ninth sounding-station the red metal disc of the current-meter became entangled in the sounding-line. It was torn away from its screws and twisted like a boomerang in mad gyrations down through the crystal-clear water to

260. The Holy Lake Manasarowar from Tugu-gompa, with Kailas in the background.

Water-colour Sketch by the Author.

a depth of 207 feet, there to sleep in the mud of Tso-mavang till the day of judgment. Fortunately it could easily be replaced.

When we landed at the monastery, all our men, and the monks and the pilgrims on the shore, were there to receive us. The first we caught sight of was the old crazy Hindu. His fellow-countrymen had taken it for granted that we must have perished in the storm, and therefore were very astonished to see us come back alive. But as I was now here again, they thought that they might take advantage of it, and asked me to present them one and all with new trousers, a request that I considered very importunate.

On August 10 I sat in my tent door and painted Kailas in different lights (Illust. 260). Its white summit stood out cold and bare against a bright blue cloudless sky, and the lake was of a deep, dazzling ultra-marine. When a breeze swept over the surface it was in the distance like clear green malachite. After sunset the sky was orange-coloured, and the lake, of just the same colour, reflected the outlines of the mountains in quivering serpentine lines. The evening before, the whole western horizon had glowed with bright red flames.

CHAPTER XLVIII

OUR LAST DAYS ON TSO-MAVANG

AT this time Robert had perfected himself more than I in the Tibetan language, and he talked it almost fluently. Therefore, while my whole time was taken up with other work, he was able to obtain information about the country and people, and perform certain tasks I set him. On the left, shorter wall of the vestibule of Tugu-gompa was an inscription for the enlightenment of pilgrims, and this Robert now translated into Hindustani and English. Freely rendered it runs as follows:

Tso-mavang is the holiest place in the world. In its centre dwells a god in human form, who inhabits a tent composed of turquoise and all kinds of precious stones. In the midst of it grows a tree with a thousand branches, and every branch contains a thousand cells in which a thousand lamas live. The lake tree has a double crown, one rising like a sunshade and shading Kang-rinpoche, the other overshadowing the whole world. Each of the 1022 branches bears an image of a god, and all these images turn their faces towards Gossul-gompa, and in former times all the gods gathered together here. Once golden water was fetched from the lake, and with it the face of Hlobun Rinpoche in Chiu-gompa was gilded, and what was left was used to gild the temple roofs of Tashi-lunpo. In old times the water of the lake flowed over a pass named Pakchu-la to the Ganga-chimbo. Water flows into the lake from all sides, cold, warm, hot, and cool. Water passes from the lake to the Ganga-shei and comes back again. Vapour rises annually from the lake and hovers over it once in the year, and then sinks down into the centre, and the next year the process is repeated. If any one brings up clay from the middle of the lake, that clay is really gold. The lake is the property of the lake-god. The lake is the central point of the whole world. Sambu Tashi grew out of the lake tree. Sochim Pema Dabge is of very holy, clear, and pure water. The Gyagar Shilki *chhorten* stands in the lake. The palace of the lake-god is in the lake. All the lamas there recite their prayers with one voice. All the gods assemble together in the lake and sit there among *chhortens* of all kinds, embellished with gold and precious stones. The spirit king of the southern land resides here in a golden house, and is not angry when any one comes to wash and purify himself. If we pray to the spirit king of the southern land, we shall be very wealthy and fortunate. Four large rivers and four small flow out of the lake by underground channels. The four large ones are one warm, one cold, one hot, and one cool. (The Karnali, Brahmaputra, Indus, and Sutlej.) If any one washes in the lake he is cleansed from sin and all impurities. If any one washes once in the lake, the sins of his forefathers are forgiven, and their souls are relieved from purgatorial fires. Datping Ngacha came with 500 pilgrims from Kang-rinpoche to wash in the lake. Lo Mato Gyamo met him and begged him to come to Tso-mavang. Dachung Ngacha and the pilgrims came with heaps of flowers and strewed them in the lake. Dachung Ngacha went three times round the lake and then ascended into heaven.

Of particular interest is the suggestion made here that the four large rivers stream out of Tso-mavang by subterranean passages. As regards the Sutlej this belief is, in my opinion, quite correct. I was told that the fifth Tashi Lama, whose mausoleum we had seen in Tashi-lunpo, once made the pilgrimage to Tso-mavang and went down to the shore at Tugu-gompa to offer a *kadakh* to the lake-god. The *kadakh* remained suspended in the air, that is, it was actually hanging on one of the branches of the holy tree, but as the tree is only visible to Rinpoches and genuine incarnations, the *kadakh* seemed to ordinary mortals to hang alone in the air.

On August 11 we bade a long farewell to the amiable monks of Tugu-gompa, and gave them liberal presents. They accompanied us down to the shore, when we put off on our voyage westwards. Into a large lagoon of the shore, brown and dirty owing to the numerous gulls and wild geese which here wallow in the mud, a brook from Gurla Mandatta runs, and now discharges 37.8 cubic feet of water in a second. All the way along runs a rubbish heap, the continuation of the pebble terrace on which

Tugu-gompa stands. The lake bed consists sometimes of sand, sometimes of detritus—offshoots of the detritus cone of Gurla Mandatta. Large collections of weeds form dark patches. Up above, at the mouths of two valleys of Gurla, are seen foaming streams, and it is strange that they do not debouch into the lake. But the explanation is easy. Twenty to fifty yards from the bank numerous small holes in the sand of the lake bed open and close like the valves of an artery, and the surface of the lake above them bubbles. These are springs. The streams disappear in the detritus cone, and the water runs below over impermeable layers of glacial clay. At the edge of the cone the water comes up again under the surface of the lake. I perceived, then, that I must gauge the rivers at the points where they emerge from the mountain valleys, if I would ascertain the exact amount of the tribute Tso-mavang receives.

Near camp 218, quite close to the shore, a spring came to the surface, and where it welled up it had a temperature of 38.1°, and therefore brought down the cold of the glaciers to the lake. As the melted water of the Gurla glaciers retains its low temperature on its subterranean course, it probably assists in keeping the water of the lake cool during the summer. Whole shoals of fish sported at the surface of the water, and snapped at plumed gnats, which were gathered in thick clouds.

On August 12 I rode with Rabsang and a Tibetan up to the foot of Gurla Mandatta. We crossed the great highway between Tugu-gompa and Purang. A wolf took to flight; occasionally a hare leapt up out of the steppe grass, and locusts flew about noisily. We rode into the mouth of the Namreldi valley, a resort of robbers, and its crystal stream, between walls of solid rock, carried 101 cubic feet of water, as compared to the 37.8 cubic feet at the place where it enters the lake. The rest of the water, therefore, pours into the lake under the detritus. A few miles farther west we halted at the mouth of the Selung-urdu valley, which has a glacier in its upper part. At half-past nine o'clock the bed was dry, but at half-past one a river with rapids and waterfalls poured down a volume of 63.9 cubic feet of exceedingly muddy water, which reached the lake in the subterranean springs. The view from this elevated spot is magnificent. We have a bird's-eye view of Tso-mavang, and in the west gleams the bright blue Langak-tso. The survey we can here take of the country is very instructive. The denudation cones of Gurla Mandatta, consisting of sand, rubbish, and boulders, extend northwards like inverted spoons; their extremities dip under the surface of the lake, and cause the fluctuating depths sounded on lines 1 and 2. From camp 218 Robert executed a line of soundings at right angles to the bank down to a depth of 190 feet.

Every day with its observations brought me nearer to the solution of the problem I had proposed to myself. As we rode northwards on the 13th along the western shore we dug wells at some places 10 yards from the bank. The ground consisted of alternate layers of sand and clay: on the top, sand; then a layer of decaying vegetable remains; then a foot and a half of sand which rested on clay. A pit 2 feet deep slowly filled with water up to the same level as the surface of the lake. The water permeates the sand and rests on the clay. If this layer of clay stretches, as seems likely, across the narrow isthmus to the shore of Langak-tso, it is evident that the water of Tso-mavang filters through the beds of sand and pebbles to the western lake. I was already convinced that even now when the old canal has ceased to act, an underground connection must exist between the two lakes. But the fact that the water of Tso-mavang is quite sweet is no proof that the lake has an outlet, seeing that it is only a few years since the canal was silted up.

Again we encamped below the hospitable monastery Gossul. On August 15 I rode with Rabsang and a Tibetan across the hilly isthmus between the two lakes in order to get a look at the country on this side also. We ascended sharply to the highest point of the ridge, where there is a fine view over Langak-tso with its picturesque rocky shores and projecting points and capes, its bays and islands, and its frame of steep mountains. In form it is very different from its neighbour, which is round and has no islands. We stood at a height of 16,033 feet, and therefore were 935 feet above the surface of Manasarowar. Then we rode down a valley clothed with brushwood, which emerges on to the flat, irregularly curved shore belt. Here are old, very plainly marked, shore lines, the highest 67.9 feet above the level of the lake. When the Langak-tso stood so high it had an outlet to the Sutlej, and the old bed of this river may be seen leading off from the north-eastern corner of the lake.

A strong south wind blew, and rolled the waves to the shore, where I sat a good hour, drawing and making observations. Then we rode again over the isthmus, at its lowest (15,289 feet) and broadest place. A salt swamp, begirt by hills, lies on its eastern half, quite close to the shore of Tso-mavang, with its surface 7.7 feet above that of the lake. In the sand and rubbish between the two are abundant streams of water, passing from the lake to the swamp. The swamp lies in a flat hollow of clay, in which the water evaporates, and the trifling quantities of salt contained in the lake water accumulate. At this place, then, the water of the eastern lake is prevented from seeping through to the western.

The following day we sailed with a favourable wind to the north-western corner of Tso-mavang, where Chiu-gompa stands on a pyramid of rock. This spot, camp No. 219, was to be our headquarters for several days. The outline of Tso-mavang is like that of a skull seen from the front, and we had now to explore the very top. A day of rest was devoted to a preliminary investigation of the channel where several cold and hot springs rise up; two of the latter had temperatures of 117° and 122° respectively, while in testing the third a thermometer graduated up to 150° did not suffice, and the tube burst. A spring of 117° in a walled basin is said to be used as a medical bath, but one must be a Tibetan to stew in water so hot. A small stone cabin beside it serves as a dressing-room. A little farther down the channel is spanned by a bridge constructed of four beams resting on two stone piers; it is in extraordinarily good condition, and is another proof that the canal contained water not so very long ago. On the piers of the bridge water-marks are still conspicuous 18½ inches above the present stagnant pools, smelling of sulphur and full of slimy weeds, which are fed by springs. Young wild-geese were swimming in one of them, and had great difficulty in protecting themselves from the brown puppy.

Chiu-gompa, the fifth of the eight monasteries of the lake which I visited, is small, and contains fifteen lamas who enter it for life, while the abbot is changed every three years. It owns some yaks, 500 goats, and 100 sheep, which are employed in transporting salt to Purang, where the monks barter it for barley. One monk, a youth twenty years of age, named Tsering Tundup, is one of the Tibetans whom I think of with particularly kind and warm feeling. His mother also lived in the monastery, and looked after the sheep and goats when they were driven in the evening into the penfolds. He was unusually handsome, refined, amiable and obliging, and showed me everything with full explanations. From his small bare cell he could dream and gaze at the holy lake in the east, and could see on the west Langak-tso, despised by the gods; but yet he was melancholy, and on that account we were sympathetic. He acknowledged openly that he was weary of the monotonous life in Chiu-gompa; every day was like the last, and the monks had hard work to procure a scanty subsistence, and must always be prepared for the attacks of robbers. It must be pleasanter to live as we did, and roam about freely among the mountains. He asked me if he might come with us, and I replied that I would willingly take him to Ladak. Then his face brightened, but he begged to be allowed to think over the matter until I returned from my next trip on the lake.

It rained all night, and in the morning everything was wet—even the things in my wind-beaten and torn tent, where little puddles had been formed. But Tsering came with the linen, so I was not so badly off. We had a long voyage before us, to camp No. 212, the first place we had encamped at on the holy lake. The programme of the excursion also included visits to the three other monasteries, the gauging of the volumes of water in the streams from the north, and the drawing of a map of the northern shore. We therefore took provisions for four days, which Rabsang and Adul were to transport along the bank on horses' backs. We were to meet them at the entrance to the valley Serolung, at Serolung-gompa. This last voyage was to complete my investigation of the lake, but precisely because it was the last it was looked forward to with fear by my men. They thought that I had so long defied the god of the lake that now my time was come, and that he would avenge himself and keep me for ever.

But the morning was beautiful, and when at half-past five we rowed out over the smooth lake, the temperature was 48.6°. The cloud cap of Gurla extended down to the water, and nothing could be seen of the country to the south. The Pundi mountain was covered with snow and had a wintry appearance. At the first sounding-station (66 feet) the tents were seen as white specks hovering above the lake. Chiu-gompa stands proudly on its rocky point, and is a landmark visible from all parts of the lake shore except from the west. At the second station the sounding was more than 130 feet. Shukkur Ali and Tundup Sonam row like galley-slaves, for they hope to finish this line, and then the work will be at an end. Sometimes the boat passes through belts of foam and weed. At the fifth station (161 feet) the tents can still be seen with the glass, but after that they disappear. Gossul's memorable monastery can also be dimly descried on its rock.

"Now we have traversed a third of the way," I said.

"Thank God!" replied Shukkur Ali. "I hope the weather will hold up to-day."

A large fish floated on the water, belly up; fish washed ashore are used by the people as medicine. The depths remain the same; the lake bed is very even. But at the thirteenth point we found 108 feet, and at the fourteenth 180 feet, which indicated a ridge in the lake bed or a cone of detritus from the foot of the northern mountains. At about an hour's sail from the eastern shore we saw Rabsang and Adul coming up, and they waited for us at the rendezvous. They proposed we should pass the night in a stone cabin at the right side of the mouth of the Serolung valley, but I refused, for pilgrims and tramps are wont to harbour there. Six monks from the convent, old friends of ours, paid me a visit, and four happy, laughing women, black and dirty, came rushing like a whirlwind down the slopes with baskets of fuel on their backs. Puppy had followed Rabsang, and had found at a monastery on the way an elegant little cavalier with a red collar and bells. With a feeling of satisfaction at having completed this last line of soundings, I went to sleep on the sandy shore under the light of the everlasting stars.

Next day I rode with Rabsang 17 miles to the north, in order to measure the volumes of water in the Pachen and Pachung valleys. We arranged to meet the others on the northern shore, whither they were to row with the baggage. Were we long away they were to light a beacon fire on a hill for our guidance. We followed for a time the shore with its banks of mud, small projections, and lagoons, and then we rode through the Samo-tsangpo from the Tokchen valley, and passed on the left hand two small lakes in the midst of rich pasturage, where a number of kiangs grazed, glared at us, pricked up their ears, and ran away at a slow gallop; then we crossed the *tasam*, or the great trunk-road, and rode up the sharply sculptured Pachen valley, with a foaming river carrying 69.9 cubic feet of water. Then we rode westwards, up and down hills, and enjoyed a new view of the holy lake with Gurla Mandatta in the background. The Pachung river carried 83.3 cubic feet of water. When our work was done we rode south-westwards. Wild asses were on the meadows; they are nearly tame, for no one puts an end to life on the shores of the holy lake. Thirty mares stood on a mound guarded by a stallion; the sun was sinking, and perhaps this is how these animals prepare for the dangers of the night. Now and again a mare left the group and made a circuit about her sisters, but the stallion ran after her immediately and forced her to return to the others. This game was frequently repeated, and it seemed to me that the mares were making sport of the stallion.

We ride over swampy meadows and small sandhills; nothing can be seen of the lake; we should like to hear its waves roaring under the south-west breeze, but new hills always crop up in front of us. At last we catch sight of the smoke of the camp-fire. Adul had caught a kiang foal four months old, which was ill and kept always turning round. The mother came to look after it in the night, but gave it up for lost, and it died soon after.

August 20 was spent in surveying a map of a part of the northern shore which is very slightly curved, and in a sounding excursion on the lake out to a depth of 154 feet. While the surface water had a temperature 55.6° everywhere, with an air temperature about constant, the temperature at the bottom sank from 56.1° to 46° at the depth of 154 feet.

We gradually began to suffer want. The collops which Adul tried to pass off on me on the morning of the 21st were decidedly bad, and therefore landed in Puppy's stomach. As Rabsang and I rode northwards to Pundi-gompa, the temperature was 56° and really too warm, so that a shower of rain was not unpleasant. Pundi lies on a rocky ledge in a ravine; its abbot is eighty years old, and has eight monks under him. One was a Chinaman from Pekin, who had lived forty years in the convent and had become a thorough Tibetan, though he had not forgotten his mother tongue. From there, too, there is a splendid view over the lake. As we were about to ride down to camp No. 222 on the shore, a messenger came from Robert with the news that the authorities in Parka had refused to provide us with transport animals or assist us in any way, for they had never heard that we were permitted to spend a whole month on the lake. He also said that our Ladakis were much frightened by all kinds of stories of robbers which were current in the neighbourhood, so that every one was anxious for my presence.

The camp was quite close to the monastery Langbonan, at the mouth of the Gyuma-chu. After we had measured this river and ascertained that it discharged 73.8 cubic feet of water, we had tracked up all the waters

261. Boy on the Upper Tsangpo.

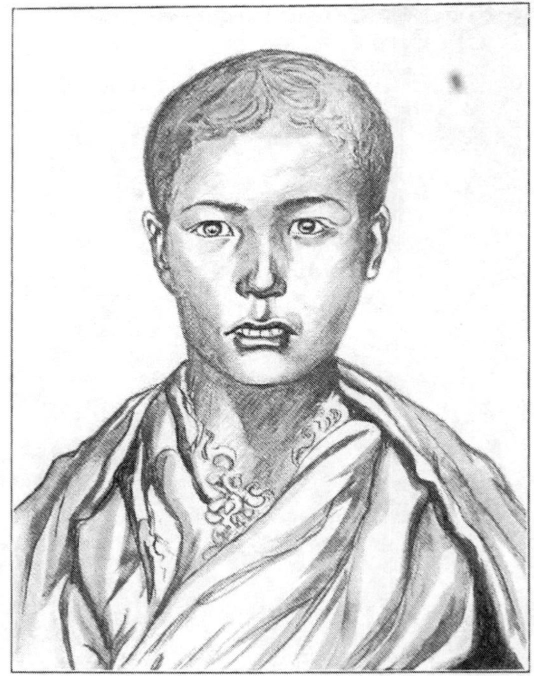

262. The Young Prior of Langbo-nan.

Sketches by the Author.

pouring into Manasarowar on the surface, and we found that the whole volume was 1094.8 cubic feet in a second, or 94,590,000 cubic feet in twenty-four hours, which would make a cube measuring nearly 456 feet each way. But how much water flows to the lake by underground passages which we could not measure? Probably a volume considerably in excess of the surface water; for Manasarowar lies in a trough between huge mountains which are constantly feeding the subterranean springs. At any rate the surplus water, so far as it is not lost by evaporation, filtrates through subterranean passages to the Langak-tso, which lies lower.

On the 22nd we again rowed straight out from the bank into the lake till we reached a place where the depth was 135 feet, and then sailed back with a favourable wind to the starting-point. It was the last time that I sank my lead in the holy water, and I was quite convinced that I should never do it again, for I had now 138 soundings, evenly distributed over the lake and affording ample material for the construction of an isobathic map. It was comical to hear Shukkur Ali when I remarked to him that this was our last voyage on Tso-mavang. He held his hands before his face as if he were about to pray, and said solemnly that in spite of all dangers "we had had the good fortune to bring our work to a successful conclusion by the favour of Allah, the favour of the Sahib, the favour of the papa and the mamma of the Sahib, and the favour of all his relations." I ventured to remark that he had forgotten the favour of the lake god, but he dismissed the suggestion with a wave of the hand, and said he had no more faith in the god.

Afterwards I rode with Rabsang up to the monastery Langbo-nan, while the others went on to Chiu-gompa. I shall omit here a description of this convent, where the most remarkable sight was the twelve-year-old abbot Tsering, an intelligent, frank, and lively boy, with sharp bright eyes, white teeth, a fresh, healthy complexion, and an attractive appearance (Illust. 262). He sat on a divan before a lacquered table in his library, called *tsemchung*, and showed a great interest in all my plans, glanced into my sketch-book, tried my field-glass, and asked me for a couple of pencils. During the hour I spent in his cell we became good friends, and when at length I bade him farewell we little thought that we should meet again only a year later.

As we made the round of the monastery we came in the gallery of the court upon a poor fellow who lay ill and seemed to be suffering. I asked him how he was, and he told me that on August 18, the day when Rabsang and Adul came to meet us, he was taking eleven mules and two horses laden with *tsamba* and barley to Parka, the Gova of which was the owner of the caravan. Where the Pachung river enters the eastern lagoon he was attacked at eleven o'clock in the morning by twelve robbers, who rushed down from the direction of the Pachung valley. They were all mounted, and armed with guns, swords, and spears, had two spare horses for provisions, and wore masks on their faces. They dismounted in a moment, threw a mantle over his head, tied his hands behind his back, and cleared him out, taking among other things 400 rupees, and then they rode off again to the Pachung valley, which Rabsang and I had hurriedly visited the next day. He then summoned help by shouting, and in a very pitiable condition found refuge in Langbo-nan. He showed us some deep stabs in his legs, his skin coat, and the saddle, which had suffered severely when he made a desperate attempt to defend himself. This was the incident which had so alarmed our Ladakis.

The way from here to Chiu-gompa is charming. Perpendicular, sometimes overhanging rocks of green and red schist fall to the shore, which here has a shingly beach only 20 yards broad. Two gigantic boulders stand like monuments on the shore, and on the rocky walls we see black caves and hermits' dwellings, and we often pass the usual three stones on which tea-kettles of pilgrims have boiled. Farther to the west the projections form a series of recesses in lighter tones; at one of these cliffs a new and fascinating view is displayed. A water mark lying $5\frac{1}{2}$ feet above the present level of the lake is very easily recognized. On the rocky pinnacles eagles sit motionless as statues, watching for prey.

Chergip-gompa is built on a terrace in the broad mouth of a valley. It is a small, poor monastery, but it has its *lhakang* and its vestibule with a large bronze bell, in which the six holy characters are cast. When the bell is rung at morning and evening the unfathomable truth is borne on the waves of sound over the lake, which, with its blue surface and its background of the snowfields of Gurla Mandatta, forms a charming landscape as seen from the court of the monastery. But its sound is heard by no one but Chergip's single monk. Poor man, what must be his feelings in winter evenings when storms sweep the drifting snow over the ice of Tso-mavang!

I remained with him fully two hours, for he had much to tell. He had travelled far, had been at Selipuk and the Nganglaring-tso, and offered to conduct me thence in twenty days to the Dangra-yum-tso; he had no suspicion that I was roaming about in the forbidden land under a political ban. But he revived my desire to visit the great unknown country to the north of the holy river. I was full of thoughts, full of plans, and full of an insatiable *desiderium incogniti* which never left me in peace, when at length I departed from the eighth and last monastery of Tso-mavang as the evening spread its dark veil over the lake I had conquered.

We had still a long way to go to the camp. At the last mountain spur stands a *chhorten*, from which our fire was visible. Soon we sat again among our companions. Late at night two horsemen rode past our camp; the watchmen called out "Who's there?" but they made no answer. Then Rabsang awoke and thoughtlessly sent a bullet after the unknown men, being convinced that they were robbers. My men had reached such a pitch of nervousness that they saw robbers everywhere.

This was our last night on the shore of the Tso-rinpoche, the "holy lake," and I listened sadly to the song of the surf dying away as the wind fell.

CHAPTER XLIX

ADVENTURES ON LANGAK-TSO

I HAVE not interrupted the description of my life on the revered lake with notices of our political troubles. Suffice it to say that we succeeded in staying there a whole month. Mounted and other messengers often came to make complaints, and then my men simply replied: "The Sahib is out on the lake, catch him if you can; he is a friend of the lake god, and can stay as long as he likes among the branches of the holy tree." And when I came back again they had gone off. In consequence of the boat trips they could not control my movements, but when we encamped by Chiu-gompa they became more energetic. During my absence came messenger after messenger with orders that I must at once betake myself to Parka and continue my journey thence to Ladak. On August 23 I sent Robert and Rabsang to Parka to make terms with the authorities, but they would not under any circumstances allow me to visit Langak-tso, my next stage. If I liked to stay a month or a year at Chiu-gompa it was nothing to them, for the monastery was not in their district, but the western lake was in their jurisdiction. They advised that I should come as soon as possible to Parka for my own sake, and would send in the morning fifteen yaks to carry my luggage.

But I wished to see Langak-tso at any cost. So when the fifteen yaks arrived next morning, I quickly made up my mind to send Tsering, Rabsang, and four men with the baggage to Parka, while Robert and the other six men would go with me to Langak-tso. Our own six

263. Temple Vessels in Chiu-gompa.

264. Two Children in Shigatse.

Sketches by the Author.

horses and the last mule from Poonch could easily carry the boat and our bit of luggage. The yaks were laden and my men disappeared behind the hills. My own small caravan had orders to camp on the shore of Langak-tso where the old channel enters. I went with Robert and two men on foot and executed a series of exact levellings over the isthmus separating the two lakes. At the same time I drew a map of the course of the channel. The measuring tape was nailed fast to an oar which Robert carried; the theodolite I carried myself. The distance between the pole and the instrument amounted to 55 yards, and was measured with tapes by our two assistants. The pole was placed on an iron dish that it might not sink into the soft ground.

The lakes were visited in 1812 by Moorcroft, who found no connecting channel. In October 1846 Henry Strachey found there an arm of the lake 100 feet broad and 3 feet deep. Landor declared that any connection was inconceivable, for, according to him, the isthmus was 300 feet high at its lowest part. Ryder found in the late autumn of 1904 no water running out of Manasarowar, but he heard from the natives that a little water passed through the channel during the rainy season. Sherring also saw no running water, but he thought it probable that the lake overflowed after rainy summers. As for me, I followed the bed of the channel from one lake to the other and found that in the year 1907 no water flowed from the eastern into the western lake, and in 1908 the condition was the same, though both my visits occurred in the rainy season. There must be very heavy falls of rain before Manasarowar can overflow, for the highest point of the channel bed lies more than 6½ feet above the level of the eastern lake.

The circumstance that different travellers in different years have given different accounts is, however, very easily explained. All depends on the precipitation: if it is abundant, the surface of Manasarowar rises; if it is very abundant its water drains off to the Langak-tso (Rakas-tal). If the summer is dry, as in the year 1907, the Langak-tso receives no water through the channel, but certainly by subterranean passages. On the whole, both these lakes are falling like the other lakes of Tibet, and the time is approaching when the subterranean outlet will be cut off and both lakes will be salt.

As we deliberately measured the channel and came to its highest point from which its bed dips towards the west, I threw a farewell glance at Tso-mavang, and experienced a feeling of bereavement at the thought that I must now leave its shores, and in all probability for ever. For I had known this gem of lakes in the light of the morning red and in the purple of sunset, in storms, in howling hurricanes when the waves rose mountain high, in fresh southerly breezes when the waves sparkled like emeralds, in full sunshine when the lake was smooth as a mirror, in the silver beams of the moon when the mountains stood out like white spectres after the dull yellow light of evening was extinguished, and in peaceful nights when the stars twinkled as clearly on the smooth surface of the lake as above in the vault of heaven. I had passed a memorable month of my life on this lake, and had made friends with the waves and become intimately acquainted with its depths. To this day I can hear the melodious splash of the raging surf, and still Tso-mavang lingers in my memory like a fairy tale, a legend, a song.

We went on westwards along narrow creeks and pools of stagnant water, but when the evening had become so dusky that I could no longer read the figures on the measuring pole, we gave up work, marked the last fixed point, and made for the camp, which we reached in complete darkness.

In the morning the work was continued. We had had a minimum of 22.6° in the night, and a violent south-west storm rendered it difficult to read the instruments. The hundred-and-fourth point was fixed at length at the edge of the water of Langak-tso. I have no space here to analyse the results. The channel runs west-north-west, and the line measured is 10,243 yards long, or twice as long as represented on the most recent maps. The surface of Langak-tso lay 44 feet below that of Tso-mavang, which agrees very well with the difference of height on Ryder's map, namely 50 feet. There is no water beyond the ninety-fourth fixed point in the bed, The Tibetans related a legend concerning the origin of the channel. Two large fishes in Tso-mavang were deadly enemies and chased each other. One was beaten, and in order to escape he darted right through the isthmus, and the windings of the channel bed show the course of the flying fish.

The morning of August 26 was dull, damp, and cold. Heavy clouds floated over the earth, heralds of the monsoon rains, and Langak-tso looked anything but inviting for a sail. But we had the whole day before us, and any moment horsemen might come from Parka, take us by the neck and lead us back, whether we liked it or not, to the path of duty. Langak-tso has a very irregular outline. Its chief basin in the south is begirt by rocks, in the north there is a smaller expansion, and between the two runs a contracted channel. All we could venture to do was to row over the small basin westwards and then to the south-east, to a place on the eastern shore whither our camp could be moved. It could be done in a few hours, so we took nothing but the mast and sail.

Tundup Sonam and Ishe were my boatmen, and we set out at half-past five o'clock. We were at first in the lee of a promontory, but when we had passed it the whole lake came down upon us with rolling, foaming billows, showers of spray, and threatening surge. The waves were crowded together in the narrows to leeward, and assumed curious irregular forms. Among them tossed masses of water-weed; the water was bright green and as clear and sweet as that of Tso-mavang. We are a little beyond the promontory; would it not be better to turn back? No; never turn back, never give in; still forwards! We were wet, but we kept our equilibrium and parried the cunning assaults of the rolling waves. "Row hard and we shall soon get into the shelter of the great point on the western shore." I even managed to take soundings, and found that the greatest depth was 54½ feet; the lake bottom was almost level. We had fought with the waves for four hours before we landed on the north side of the promontory, where we were sheltered from the wind.

Here we draw the boat to land and reconnoitre. The cape runs north-eastwards, and is covered with drift-sand which is in constant motion. On the shore plain to the south-west yellow sandspouts move about, whirling like corkscrews in the direction of the wind, and our promontory receives its share of this load of sand. On the north the dune is very steep; from time to time fresh sand falls down the slope and slips into the lake, where the waves sweep it away. From the sharp ridge of the dune the driftsand is blown like a dense plume to the lake, and the water is tinged with yellow for quite 200 yards in the direction of the wind by myriads of grains of sand, which fall to the bottom and build up a foundation under water on which the promontory can extend out into the lake. The wind has been strong, and now we have a storm. Patience! We cannot go back. The driftsand now floats so thickly over the lake that the eastern and northern shores are invisible; we might be sitting on a dune in the heart of the Takla-makan desert.

We slipped down to the sheltered side of the dune, but here, out of the wind, it was still worse. We were enveloped in clouds of sand which penetrated everywhere, into our eyes, ears, and noses, and irritated the skin where it came into contact with the body. The moaning howl of the storm was heard above and around us. My oarsmen slept or strolled about, but their footprints were at once obliterated by the wind. I played with the sand like a child—let it roll down the lee-side, built a small peninsula, which was immediately destroyed by the waves, and a harbour mole, which the sea beat over and broke up—and watched how new layers and clumps of dead seaweed appeared on the sand slope, and how the dry sand formed falls and cascades as it rolled down. But the storm did not abate.

We lay waiting there for four hours. On the eastern shore our men had moved the camp a little farther south. We saw the tents quite plainly. Should we venture to

265. Kailas behind Nyandi-gompa.

266. My Pack-Sheep.

creep along the shore southwards so as to reach a point opposite the camp? Out beyond the promontory the dark-green lake ran uncomfortably high, but we were a match for the waves—the men had only to put their weight on to the oars. So we crept along the shore, where we got some shelter, but we had to be careful that we were not carried out into the heavy seas. After rowing round two points we landed on the lee-side of a third, where the boat was drawn ashore again. Heavy seas with thundering, towering waves dashed against the southern side of the point, so that we could go no farther, for no pilot would encounter such billows in a canvas boat. I stood on the top of the promontory and enjoyed the fine spectacle. Robert's tent shone brightly in the setting sun. We saw the men, the horses grazing on the bank, and the smoke of the camp-fire beaten down by the storm. The crossing would barely take an hour, but between us and them yawned the dark-green abyss of tyrannical, all-conquering waves.

The sun sets and we still sit and wait, confused by the rush of the spirits of the air and water. This time they have played us a pretty trick, and we have been caught. To the north rises Kang-rinpoche, lofty and bright as a royal crown. Its summit is like a *chhorten* on the grave of a Grand Lama. Snow and ice with vertical and slightly inclined fissures and ledges form a network like the white web of a gigantic spider on the black cliffs.

And the day, a long day of waiting, neared its inevitable close. Shadows lengthened out over the foaming waves, the sun set, and the Pundi mountain, our old friend of Tso-mavang, glowed like fire in the sunset. Clouds of a deep blood-red colour, with edges of orange, and tinted above with reddest gold, hovered over its summit. It was as though the earth had opened and volcanic forces had burst forth. The hours passed by, the glow died out, the outlines of Pundi became indistinct and were at length swallowed up in the darkness. We were in the dark while the camp-fire blazed on the eastern shore. Our hopes were now centred on the night and the moon. The storm had raged thrice twenty-four hours, and it must end some time; but it was just as strong. And as it was useless to wait, and I could not appease my gnawing hunger with a piece of bread and a cup of tea, I wrapped myself in the sail, burrowed into the sand, and fell into a sound sleep.

The rain pelting down on the sail woke me twice, and about four o'clock in the morning the cold thoroughly roused me. A dreary, grey, rainy outlook. But Ishe proposed that we should try to get over, for the storm had slightly abated in consequence of the rain. We first made sure that the tackle was in good order, and then stepped into the boat and rowed out along the sheltered side of the promontory. But scarcely had the nose of the boat passed beyond the point when it received a shock that made all its joints crack. "Row, row as hard as you can," I yelled through the howling storm; "we shall get over before the boat is full. It is better to be wet than suck our thumbs for twenty-four hours more." To the south, 52° E., the tent canvas shone white in the morning grey. We strayed far out of our course, but cut the waves cleanly, and steered towards the surf. We just managed to get over. We were received on the other side by our men, who helped us to draw the boat ashore and had fire and breakfast ready for us.

Namgyal had returned from Parka and brought news that the Gova threatened to drive away my men in order to force me to leave Langak-tso. Bluff, however, has no effect on me. A more serious matter was that Puppy had not been seen for forty-eight hours, and that Shukkur Ali, who had gone the morning before to Chiu-gompa in search of her, had not been heard of since. Puppy at length found her way into camp herself, and then it was Shukkur Ali who was missing.

On the 28th the storm continued. We afterwards heard from Tibetans that stormy weather frequently prevails on Langak-tso, and the lake is agitated, when Tso-mavang is smooth and calm. Tundup Sonam concluded that Tso-mavang was a pet of the gods, while demons and devils ruled over Langak-tso. We had heard a tale in Gossul-gompa that the preceding winter five Tibetans, armed with swords and guns, had crossed the ice to reach Parka by a shorter way, but in the middle of the lake the ice had given way, and all five were dragged down by the weight of their weapons to the bottom.

I wished for fine weather that I might be able to cross over the lake to the islands. As, however, we were obliged to give up all thoughts of a voyage, I determined to pass round the lake and at any rate draw an outline map of it. We commenced, then, with the eastern shore, which makes a regular curve towards the east. The white mule from Poonch carried the boat. Some Ovis Ammons were seen on the rocks, which Tundup Sonam stalked unsuccessfully. Shukkur Ali turned up again as cool as a cucumber, having searched in vain for Puppy, which was snoring in my tent in most excellent condition.

August 29. We go to sleep amidst the roaring of the waves and the howling of the storm, and awake again to the same uproar. It is always in our ears as we ride along the shore. We might be at the foot of a waterfall. Now we follow the south shore westwards. Here the cliffs are almost everywhere precipitous, and the rocks are porphyry, granite, and schist; the shore strip is extremely narrow and steep, and is divided into sharply marked terraces. It descends right down to great depths, and shallow, gradually sloping places are not to be found. A human skull lay in a bay bobbing up and down in the waves, and not far off were other parts of a skeleton. Was it one of the men who had been drowned in the winter? At this discovery my men conceived a still greater aversion to Langak-tso, which even took human life. I perceived that they were wondering what further foolhardiness I might indulge in.

A sharp-pointed peninsula running north-westwards delayed us. On the bay beyond a caravan was camping, and we were glad to meet Tibetans again when all others had withdrawn from us; and they were glad to meet a European who had been at the Luma-ring-tso, their home. But they could not understand why we passed round all projections and went right round all the bays, instead of following the direct road running a little farther to the south. One of them held out his hands towards me with the fingers spread out, and said that the south shore of the lake had as many indentations. When I told him that I wished to draw a map of the lake, he said that it was of no consequence what the shore was like, as only egg-gatherers came there.

When we had passed two projecting points we encamped at the extremity of the cape which lies in a line with the southernmost island. It was stormy, but here we found shelter under a cliff with a streamer pole on the top. Stone walls, rags, and eggshells were evidence of the visits of men. On the east and west of the cape were open bays with heavy seas, and to the north, 19° E., we saw the southern point of the island—a dark precipitous rock, rising like a huge roll of bread from the waves. We had already heard of this island, Lache-to, on which the wild-geese lay their eggs in May, and are robbed of them by men from Parka who come over the ice. I could not therefore omit to visit it. The island lay quite near. We would return immediately, and Adul might begin to roast the wild-goose which Tundup had shot on the march. We wanted no provisions, but Robert advised Ishe to take a bag of *tsamba* with him, lest he should have to wait too long for his dinner.

These two men took the oars when we put off. The shelter of the cape was deceptive. Two minutes from the bank I tried to take a sounding, but the line made a great curve before it reached the bottom, for the storm drove the boat northwards. Then we fell upon another device: the boatmen had only to hold their oars in the air and let the wind carry the boat along. But a little farther out we could not sail so easily, for the wave system of the eastern open part of the lake came into collision with that from the west. Here the waves rose into hillocks and pyramids, and had to be negotiated with the oars. We rapidly drew near to the island, and its rocks became higher and looked threateningly dark and dangerous. When we were close to the southern point I perceived that it was impossible to land there. The bank of rubbish and blocks was very steep, and we and the

267. Part of Kailas.

Sketch by the Author.

boat would have been dashed in pieces in the foaming breakers. The situation was critical. Robert wished to land on the lee-side of the northern point, but that would have been risky, for the storm swept unchecked along the sides of the island, and if we did not get under the land at the right moment we should be driven out into the open lake at a distance of two days' voyage from the northern shore. We rocked up and down on soft green crystal. I steered close to the eastern bank, where the waves were just as high. Here we had no choice. I turned the bow towards the land, and the men rowed for all they were worth. A nasty billow threw us ashore. Robert jumped out, slipped, and got a ducking. Ishe hurried up to help him. Three billows broke over me before I got to land. We were all three drenched, but we were glad to have firm ground under our feet, and to have reached the island safely in spite of the treacherous storm which might have driven us past this open roadstead.

Then Robert and I went round the island while Ishe collected fuel. Though we could only walk slowly over the detritus, we took but twenty-five minutes to go round the island and ascertain its form by compass bearings. It is longish, runs from north to south, and consists of a single rock falling on all sides steeply to the water. During our walk the wind dried us. Then I drew a panorama of Gurla Mandatta, and after that the spot of earth to which fate had led us prisoners was subjected to a closer investigation. At the north-eastern foot of the elevation is a rather flat pebbly plateau. Here the wild-geese breed in spring, and here lay still several thousand eggs, in twos, threes, or fours, in a nest of stones and sand.

That was a discovery. Ishe had a bag of *tsamba*, but that was all. There was every probability that we should have to stay the night here, and now we had a quite unexpected store of provisions to last for months. And some time this persistent wind must cease. We played at Robinson Crusoe, and found our situation very advantageous. But the egg-collecting was the most interesting. The eggs were pretty and appetizing as they lay half embedded in the sand, and I pictured to myself the happy cackling that must go on in the spring when the goose mothers sit with expectant hearts on the hard nests, and the sun floods Gurla Mandatta with a sea of light.

We broke two. They were rotten. We tried others which lay in the shade and deeper in the sand. They gave out a horrible stench when the shell broke with a crack on a stone. But of about 200 eggs we broke, we found eight which were edible, and we did not want more. We helped Ishe to collect dry plants lying on the slopes, and at sunset we had a huge heap which we had piled within a small ring fence. In the middle the fire was lighted, and we sat leaning against the wall which sheltered us from the wind. We were warm and comfortable, and our satisfaction reached its height when Ishe's store of *tsamba* was divided into three equal portions, and was eaten out of a wooden bowl with the hand in place of a spoon. The greatest inconvenience was that we had no other vessel but Ishe's small wooden bowl, and therefore whenever one of us wanted a drink he had to tramp down to the shore.

The storm still howled over the rock and through the holes and crannies of the wall. Then the thought shot through my mind: "Is the boat moored securely? If it should be carried away! Then we are lost. Ah, but it may be cast ashore on the northern bank, and our men may fetch it and come across to the island. No, it will be filled with water, and be sunk by the weight of the zinc plates of the centre-boards. But then we can mount in the morning to the southern point and make our people understand by signs that we want provisions. We have drifted to the island in eighteen minutes. They can make a raft with the tent poles and stays, load it with provisions, and let it drift with the wind to the island. And we may find more fresh eggs."

Such were the thoughts that Robert and I exchanged while Ishe was feeling about in total darkness at the landing-place. "What if we have to stay here till the lake freezes over, four months hence?" I said. But at this moment we heard Ishe's steps in the sand, and he calmed us with the assurance that both the boat and the oars were safe.

Then we talked together again and kept up the fire. The storm had abated, but sudden gusts came down from all quarters. We inspected the water, and found that we could make for the mainland without danger. But first we took all the remaining fuel and piled it up into a blazing bonfire, which shone like a huge beacon over the lake. If any Tibetan saw it, he must have thought that an enchanted fire was burning on the desolate island.

The moon was high when we put off and the lake was still rough. But soon the black cape where our camp stood was seen on the southern shore against the dim background of mountains. In the middle of the sound the depth was 113 feet. We shouted with all our might, and were soon answered by a fire on the point, to which our people had come down. And the roasted wild-goose, which had waited so long for us, and a cup of hot tea tasted delicious in the early hours of morn. And still more delightful was it to creep into bed after our short visit to the goose island, which raised its dark, mysterious, dolphin-like ridge in the moonlight. Never again would my foot tread its peaceful strand.

CHAPTER L

THE SOURCE OF THE SUTLEJ

We had scarcely dressed in the morning before the storm raged again. Galsan and a gova from Parka overtook us here. The former brought provisions, the latter had strict orders from his chief, Parka Tasam, to tell me that if I did not at once betake myself to Parka, he would send off all my baggage to Langak-tso, and force me to move on to Purang. But the gova himself was a jovial old fellow, and he received my answer that if Parka Tasam ventured to meddle with my boxes, he should be immediately deposed. If he kept quiet a couple of days, I would come to Parka, and the rather that I found it impossible to navigate the lake at this season of the year.

Then we marched on westwards, in and out of the bays and round all the projections produced by a mountain elevation north of Gurla, which prolongs its ramifications to the lake. The constantly changing views, as we wind in and out and wander between land and water, are indescribably beautiful and charming. The two large islands lying far out in the lake we see wherever we may be. One is named Dopserma; other water-birds breed there, but no geese. In winter yaks and sheep are driven over the ice to the island, where there is good pasturage. When cattle disease rages in the country the animals on Dopserma do not suffer.

We passed round the sharp-pointed westernmost bay in a furious storm and blinding clouds of sand, and encamped on the shore again. The same agreeable weather continued also on the last day of August as we travelled north-eastwards and saw the Langak-tso in a new and beautiful aspect. The air was now clear, Kang-rinpoche and Gurla Mandatta were unclouded, and stood as sentinels above the lakes. We passed the point where Tundup Sonam, Ishe, and I had waited so long, and by the sand-dune where we had lain four hours.

At the north-western bay we cross the old bed of the Sutlej, consisting of treacherous, quaking bog or dry, hard clay; it is broad, has no terraces, and has been much degraded and smoothed down by deflation and driftsand in later times. Two springs rise up in the middle, and flow in the direction of the lake. Westwards the bed seems quite level, but actually it rises slowly and evenly to a flat culmination, on the other side of which it dips down towards the Indus.

Now it had become dark, and we rode hour after hour among low hills and dunes and over meadows and water channels. I thought we had lost our way, when the bells of grazing cattle were heard, a fire appeared, and Rabsang came to meet us with a lantern in order to lead us to the village Parka, where my tent was set up in a courtyard.

During the much-needed day of rest we allowed ourselves in Parka, I negotiated now and then with the govas of the neighbourhood. They asked me to set off definitely for the west next day, and I promised to do so, but on the condition that I might stay three days in Khaleb, half a day's journey to the west. They consented without inquiring into my further intentions. I wished, be it known, to pass round the holy mountain by the pilgrim road, but saw that the authorities would never grant their permission. It could be done only by stratagem.

Here I received a second very kind letter from Mr. Cassels, who happened to be in Gyanima on official business. Unfortunately the force of circumstances prevented us meeting. He gave me a pleasant surprise with three packets of tea, which were the more welcome as I had latterly had to put up with brick-tea.

Here also the truth of the report that had so long followed us, that six Chinese and Tibetan officials from Lhasa had been sent to bring me to reason, was at length made clear. The report was certainly true, but when the gentlemen on reaching Saka-dzong heard that I had marched on westwards some time before, they simply turned back again.

I obtained all kinds of information about the two lakes and their periodical outlets, from Tibetans who had long lived in the country. Four years before some water had flowed from Tso-mavang to Langak-tso, which confirms Ryder's statement. Twelve years ago the outflow had been so abundant that the channel could not be passed except by the bridge. The channel is sometimes called Ngangga, sometimes Ganga. The water of Langak-tso is said to drain off underground, and to appear again at a place in the old bed called Langchen-kamba, and this water is said to be the true source of the Sutlej, and to find its way to the large streams which form this river, called in Tibetan Langchen-kamba. Twelve years and forty-eight years ago the spring in the old bed is said to have emitted much more water than now. Sherring collected similar data in 1905.

Langak-tso is said to have been so poisonous in former times that any one who drank of its water died, but since the holy fish broke through the isthmus and passed into the lake, the water has been sweet. Langak-tso freezes in the beginning of December, half a month sooner than its eastern neighbour, and the freezing proceeds slowly and in patches, whereas Tso-mavang freezes over in an hour. Langak-tso also breaks up half a month before Tso-mavang. Both have ice 3 feet thick. In winter the surface of Tso-mavang falls 20 inches beneath the ice, which consequently is cracked and fissured, and dips from the shore; but Langak-tso sinks only one or two thirds of an inch. This shows that it receives water constantly from the eastern lake, but only parts with a trifling quantity in winter.

With regard to the goose island, I was told that three men are commissioned by the Devashung to settle on the island as soon as the wild-geese arrive, to protect them from wolves and foxes. They receive 8 rupees, a sheep, and a lump of butter as wages. At this time, in May, the ice is still two feet thick, but the egg-gatherers must take care that they are not cut off from the mainland by a storm. Some years ago it happened that two watchmen were isolated on the island in this way. They lived there eight months, subsisting on eggs and green food, and returned over the ice next winter as soon as the lake was frozen over. But one of them was so enfeebled that he died on reaching Parka.

After a lively feast held by the Ladakis in the evening, we rode on September 2 north-westwards, accompanied by an old grey-headed gova, who had become a particular friend of mine. The weather was fine, but we now felt biting cold in the morning, much as at home on the islets off the coast when the yellow leaves have fallen and a thin sheet of ice has spread over the inlets. All Parka was on foot to witness our departure. With us set out a high lama whom I had known in Leh. His retinue looked well in their yellow dresses against the grey and green ground. He had been in Shigatse, and had lately made the circuit of the holy mountain. During the march we waded through the rivers Dam-chu, Sung-chu, La-chu, and Khaleb, which together carried about 350 cubic feet of water per second to Langak-tso.

The nearer we came to the holy mountain, the less imposing it appeared; it was finest from Langak-tso. In form it resembles a tetrahedron set on a prism. From the middle of its white top a belt of ice falls precipitously down, and below it stands a stalagmite of ice, on to which a thick stream of water pours from above. The stream splits up into glittering drops of spray and thin sheets of water — a grand spectacle, which one could watch with pleasure for hours.

Our camp on the Khaleb moor had the advantage of being far from the haunts of men—a very necessary condition, for here I contrived to make three excursions without permission. The second of these took a whole day, September 6, and its aim was the old bed of the Sutlej. Where we reached it, the bed seemed to contain stagnant water both to the east and west, and the ground was quite level. At the place which seemed highest, we tested it with the boiling-point thermometer and found that it stood about 30 feet above the lake. Following the bed westwards we come first to a large pool of sweet water with large quantities of ducks and water-weeds, then to a series of freshwater swamps connected by channels, and at length to a brook, which flows slowly south-westwards. The brook pours into a large freshwater pool, No. 2, which has no visible outlet. But when we proceed farther west to the point where the bed is contracted between walls of solid rock, we come upon two springs forming a new brook, which flows through a clearly marked valley to the south-west. I am convinced that this water filtrates underground from Langak-tso. A year later I followed the old bed a day's march farther west, and found at Dölchu-gompa permanent springs of abundant water, which likewise well up on the bottom of the bed. From here and all along its course through the Himalayas the Tibetans call the Sutlej Langchen-kamba, the Elephant river; the hill on which the convent Dölchu-gompa is built is supposed to bear some resemblance to an elephant, and hence the name. The spring at Dölchu is called Langchen-kabab, or the mouth out of which the Elephant river comes, just as the Brahmaputra source is the Tamchok-kabab, or the mouth out of which the Horse river comes, and the Indus source is the Singi-kabab, or the mouth from which the Lion river comes. The fourth in the series is the Mapchu-kamba, the Peacock river or Karnali. The Tibetans assert that the source of the Sutlej is at the monastery Dölchu, not in the Himalayas or the Trans-Himalaya, from which, however, it receives very voluminous tributaries. They are also convinced that the source water of the Langchen-kamba originates from Langak-tso. And I would draw particular attention to the fact that the first of the two holy springs which pour their water into the Tage-tsangpo is also called Langchen-kamba (see p. 105), a proof that in old times the source was supposed to lie to the east of Tso-mavang.

Now I advise any one who takes no interest in the source of the Sutlej to skip the following quotation. During my stay in Kioto in December 1908, Mr. Ogawa,

268. Kailas from Diri-pu.

269. Confluence of the Two Arms of the Indus.

Sketches by the Author.

Professor of Geography in the University there, showed me a collection of Chinese books. One of them, *Shui-tao-ti-kang*, or *The Elements of Hydrography*, is a compilation of the author Chi Chao Nan in the 26th year of the Emperor Kien Lung, that is, the year 1762, and in this work, Book 22, is the following communication concerning the source of the Sutlej, which Professor Ogawa was kind enough to translate for me literally:[1]

The Kang-ka-kiang comes out from Kang-ti-ssu-shan, on the south-east of which there stands Lang-chuan-ka-pa-pu-shan (=Langchen-kabab), magnificent like an elephant. The relief is gradually accentuated more and more towards the south-western frontiers, and culminates at Kang-ti-ssu-shan (=Kailas). The mountain has a circumference of more than 140 li. On all sides the mountain forms precipitous walls more than 1000 feet high above the surrounding mountains, and accumulated snow seems as if hung on cliffs. Hundreds of springs pour down from the top, but flow under the ground on the foot of the mountain. It is situated in the extreme west of the Tsang region, 310 li north-east of Ta-ko-la-cheng in A-li, more than 5590 li south-west of Si-ning-fu in Shensi province. Its longitude is 36° 4′ W., and its latitude 30° 5′ N. In olden times the place was unknown, but can be doubtfully identified with A-nok-ta-shan in the annotation of Shui-ching. In the neighbourhood there are four high mountains, of which the southern is called Lang-chuan-ka-pa-pu-shan, lying 250 li south-by-east of Kang-ti-ssu-shan, and 270 li east of Ta-ko-la-cheng. The natives call it so, because the form of the mountain resembles an elephant. On the east of this mountain there stands Ta-mu-chu-ko-ka-pa-pu-shan (=Tamchok-kabab), which is the source of the Ya-lu-tsang-pu river (=Yere-tsangpo or Brahmaputra). Springs come out from the northern foot of the mountain, and accumulate into a lake (35° 5′ W., and 29° 1′ N.). The water flows north-westwards for 70 li, and receives a stream coming from the north-east. The stream lies in the mountains 80 li north-east of Lang-chuan-ka-pa-pu. Two streams flow westwards from the mountain and turn north-westwards after their junction. It now takes a sinuous course for 60 li, turns south-westwards, and joins the main river. This is a source.

The river flows further to the west-by-north for 40 li, then to the north-east, to be met by the water of lake Kung-sheng (=Gunchu-tso), which sinks under the ground of the lake basin, but which, after reappearing, and after receiving three northern affluents, runs south-westwards to the river.

[1] I have only omitted a couple of sentences, which have no immediate connection with the problem.

The lake of Kung-sheng-o-mo has two sources—one coming from the north-east, from Ta-ko-la-kung-ma-shan, and flowing 150–160 li; the other from the east, from the western foot of Ma-erh-yo-mu-ling (= Marium-la) in the western frontiers of Cho-shu-tê. This last-mentioned mountain forms the eastern boundary of A-li, and is the chief range going south-eastwards from Kang-ti-ssu. The water (of the lake Kung-sheng) flows westwards for more than 50 li, and forms another lake, 80 li wide, and without an outlet. However, more than 10 li farther to the west there is a third lake with a subterranean source and with a length of 30 li. A stream comes from the north to the lake. The river now flows south-westwards for 60 li, and receives a stream coming from the north-east. 40 li farther south-westwards it receives a stream coming from the northern mountains; farther south-westwards the river meets the water from Lang-chuan-ka-pa-pu-shan.

The water forms the lake Ma-piu-mu-ta-lai (= Tso-mavang). From south to north it is 150 li long, from east to west 80 or 100 li wide, and has a circumference of more than 200 li. On the northern side of the lake there are two streams coming from the north. The lake is situated 120 li to the south of Kang-ti-ssu. The water flows out from the west of the lake into the lake Lang-ka (= Langak-tso) at a distance of 60 li. The latter lake receives a stream coming from the north-east. Lake Lang-ka has a narrow rectangular shape, pointed and elongated, the length from south to north being 170 li, and the width from east to west 100 li. Its northern pointed corner has the stream coming from north-east. There are three sources on the southern foot at a distance of 70 li from a southern branch of Kang-ti-ssu; they flow southwards, unite into one stream, which takes a south-westerly course for 150–160 li before entering the lake. The lake is the same in circumference and area, but different in outline.

The water (of lake Lang-ka) flows out from the west, and after running westwards for more than 100 li it turns to the south-west, and is now called the Lang-chu-ho, and takes a sinuous course for more than 200 li. Then it receives the Chu-ka-la-ho coming from the north-east.

This description of the position of the source of the Sutlej is of such extraordinary interest that I do not like to reserve it for my scientific work, and the less so that it supports the theory I expressed when in India, that the Tage-tsangpo is nothing but the uppermost section of the course of the Sutlej, or, in other words, that the source of the Tage-tsangpo is also that of the Sutlej. Many quotations have been looked up during the discussion that has arisen on this problem, but they cannot compare in importance with the one just cited, which, moreover, is sixty years older than the oldest of the others, namely, Gerard's opinion that the Gunchu-tso is the source of the Sutlej.

The description in Chi Chao Nan's *Hydrography* is distinguished by the same careful conformity with the truth and conscientiousness as all other Chinese geographical descriptions. Compare the description of Kailas (Kangrinpoche) with what I have already said about it.

Lang-chuan-ka-pa-pu is the Chinese translation of the Tibetan Langchen kabab, which literally means the "Source of the Sutlej." When the Chinese author informs us that east of Langchen-kabab lies Tamchok-kabab, which is the source of the river Yere-tsangpo (Brahmaputra), we must admit that his description is quite in accordance with the truth, as I, the first European to visit this country, have myself discovered; for on the Tamlung-la I stood on the pass which parts the water between the Brahmaputra and Sutlej, and immediately to the south of the pass I saw Gang-lung-gangri and the glacier from which the Tage-tsangpo takes its rise, and in which the source of the Sutlej lies.

It is further said that the lake Gunchu-tso has two source streams—one from the north-east, from the mountain Ta-ko-la-kung-ma, which is evidently identical with D'Anville's Tacra-concla; the other from the west side of the pass Marium-la: an account which agrees with Ryder's map in all particulars. At present the Gunchu-tso is completely cut off and is salt; it therefore is no longer connected with the Sutlej system. But 147 years ago it had an outlet which ran partly underground, and then, rising up again, joined the Langchen-kamba or Tage-tsangpo. And that the Tage-tsangpo was at one time considered by the Tibetans to be the headwater of the Sutlej is apparent from the fact that its name, Langchen-kamba, is still applied to the upper of the two sacred source streams in the valley of the Tage-tsangpo.

And, again, it is said: This water, that is, the water of the Langchen-kabab, or the headwater of the Sutlej, forms the lake Ma-piu-mu-ta-lai, the Tso-mavang or Tso-mavam, as the name is also pronounced; on D'Anville's map (Map 2) it is written Ma-pama Talai, and D'Anville explains that Talai signifies lake. He might have added that it is the same word as in Dalai Lama, the priest, whose wisdom is as unfathomable as the ocean; for the Chinese word Talai or Dalai means ocean. By the use of this word the Chinese author wished to imply that Tso-mavang is much larger than the other lakes mentioned in his text.

The surplus water, as there is every reason to assume, flowed in the year 1762 from Tso-mavang through the channel to Langak-tso. The length of the channel was 60 li, which corresponds to my 5½ miles. All the northern tributaries which flow into the two lakes from the valleys of the Trans-Himalaya are correctly noted. The lake Langak is called Lang-ka. On D'Anville's map, the material for which was supplied by the Jesuits who lived in Pekin in the time of the Emperor Kang Hi (at the beginning of the eighteenth century), the lake is named Lanken. On the same map the river flowing thence westwards is called Lanc-tchou (Sutlej), but it is suggested, absurdly enough, that it is the upper course of the Ganges. D'Anville names the mountains south of Tso-mavang Lantchia-Kepou, which is Langchen-kabab, and the mountains lying to the south-east of them Tamtchou, that is, Tamchok, in which he quite correctly places the origin of the Yarou Tsanpou, the Brahmaputra. The material for the map of the whole Chinese Empire, which the Jesuits presented to the Emperor Kang Hi in the year 1718, was collected between the years 1708 and 1716, and the Emperor procured information about Tibet through natives, who were prepared for their work by the Jesuits, just as in later times English topographers have trained Indian pundits.

From D'Anville's map we learn that 200 years ago the Sutlej flowed out of Langak-tso through the bed I have already described. Professor Ogawa's translation of the Chinese text shows us that even in the year 1762, or perhaps some years before, the river still emerged from the Langak-tso. And it is expressly said that the river

Chu-ka-la-ho (Chu-kar, which, however, is said to descend from the north-east instead of the south-east) is only a tributary.

In the year 1846 Henry Strachey found no visible outlet, but he says that there is one underground, and considers it probable that the channel also may carry water when the lake has risen after heavy rains.

On July 30, 1908, I heard from the chief lama of the monastery Dölchu-gompa, who was born in the neighbourhood and was then fifty-five years old, that when he was quite young, water occasionally flowed out of the lake. But when he was ten years old, that would be in the year 1863, this water had failed, and since then no more had been seen. On the other hand, the springs in the bed are constant both in winter and in summer, and are independent of the precipitation. The monks believe that the water comes from Langak-tso, but nevertheless they call it the Langchen-kabab, the river which flows out of the mouth of the elephant.

My investigations on the spot, as well as the Chinese quotation, prove that Colonel S. G. Burrard is quite right in his masterly description of the rivers of the Himalayas and Tibet (Calcutta, 1907), when he includes Tso-mavang and Langak-tso and all their affluents in the drainage basin of the Sutlej, and therefore I will here cite two sentences of Colonel Burrard:

> The connection between the two lakes may be taken as established, but that between the western lake and the Sutlej basin is still open to question. If the water from Rakas-tal flows into the Sutlej once a century, and then only for such a short period as to be observed by no one, we shall still be justified in including the lakes in the catchment area of the river.

And in this connection I would point out that the water-level of Tibetan rivers and lakes is subject to periodical fluctuations, dependent on the precipitation, of the same kind as the Brückner periods. The level in the two lakes varies from year to year. At the present time they are very low, but there is nothing to prevent them rising gradually in a more or less distant future. Tso-mavang may rise so that its water may again flow through the channel to Langak-tso, and this lake at length may discharge its surplus water, as formerly, through the dry bed of the Sutlej. It is more probable, however, that Langak-tso is approaching a time when it will lose its subterranean outlet also, and be quite isolated, like Gunchu-tso and Panggong-tso, and consequently become salt in time. But after it has lost its outlet it may be a long time, as Professor Brückner informs me, before the lake becomes noticeably salt. The next step in the development will be that Tso-mavang will be cut off from Langak-tso and likewise become salt.

However, we need not plunge into speculations and prognostications of the future, which may have surprises in store about which we can form only more or less probable conjectures. It is our duty to rely solely on fact and observation.

And now that we are agreed that the two lakes belong to the drainage area of the Sutlej, the question is: Which of the rivers debouching into Tso-mavang is the head-water of the Sutlej? Naturally, the longest and the one which carries most water. The river which once flowed out of Gunchu-tso has no claim to this honour, and the Gunchu-tso must be rejected as the source of the Sutlej. The Tage-tsangpo discharged 388 cubic feet of water per second, while all the other streams entering Tso-mavang carried at most 100 cubic feet each. The source of the Tage-tsangpo in the front of the Ganglung glacier is therefore the source of the Sutlej.

270. Tibetan Female Pilgrims at Kailas.

CHAPTER LI

A PILGRIMAGE ROUND KANG-RINPOCHE

We are again on the Khaleb moor and the day is September 3, on which we are to begin the circuit of the holy mountain. The head Gova of Parka is with us to hold me in check, but I take very good care not to betray my plans. Tsering, Rabsang, Namgyal, and Ishe are to go with me; they are Lamaists, and are glad of the opportunity to come nearer the gates of salvation by wandering round the holy mountain. We take provisions for three days, the absolutely necessary instruments, sketch- and note-books. The stand of the large camera and one of the boat's tarpaulins are to serve as a tent. The whole baggage is only a light load for a horse. I ride my small grey Ladaki and the four men march on foot, for no one may ride round the holy mountain unless he is a heathen, like myself. The rest of the caravan is to wait for us in Khaleb, and my tent is to be left untouched that the Tibetans may think that I am expected back in the evening.

Tsering, Namgyal, and Ishe start early, and Rabsang and I a little later. The Gova and his men come to ask what it all means and whither I am going, but I answer only, "I shall soon be back again," and ride off to the north, 30° E., to the mouth of the Dunglung valley.

The others wait for us among the first moraines, and then we proceed in close column up and down among old moraines which have been thrust down by vanished glaciers. A party of pilgrims from Kham in the distant east are resting on the bank of the Dunglung river. They have pitched their tents, and their horses are grazing on the fresh grass. From the top of the moraine is seen the northern part of our stormy Langak-tso.

We ride up the valley and soon have on both sides solid rock of hard green and violet conglomerate, with huge cones of detritus at the foot of the slopes. Enormous boulders of conglomerate have fallen down here. On the left bank of the river, where the road comes up from Tarchen, stand a small cubical house and several *manis* and *chhortens* in long rows: it is a sacred road, the road of pilgrims round Kang-rinpoche.

The cliffs assume ever wilder forms, falling perpendicularly to terraces and pebble screes, forming steps and ledges, fortifications, battlements and towers, as though built by human hands. They consist of sandstone and conglomerate, and the strata dip 10° to the south, and to the eye appear horizontal. A small bridge spans the river. A party of pilgrims behind us is just crossing it. But we are on the right bank, and above us Nyandi-gompa is perched on its terrace. Above it rises the vertical wall of a huge mountain mass, a dangerous background for the monastery. Up on a ledge dwells a hermit, and quite at the top stands a streamer pole named Nyandi-kong. Five years ago a huge block fell down upon the monastery and laid half of it in ruins. The block still lies in the inner court. It was early in the morning after long-continuous rain; no one was hurt, but the monastery had to be rebuilt.

Two monks, two old women, and a boy received us kindly, and said it was the first time they had seen a European in Nyandi. The monastery, as well as the three others on Kailas, is under Tarchen-labrang, which is situated on the southern foot of the mountain, where the pilgrims begin and end their circuit. Curiously enough, these monasteries belong to Tongsa Penlop, the Raja of Bhotan. The preceding year, 1906, was a year of the fire horse, and the year 1918 will be a year of the earth horse; every twelfth year is a horse year, in which wood, fire, earth, iron or water is prefixed to the name horse; the Tibetan cycle (the period of time which is the base of the reckoning) extends over sixty years with the names of twelve different animals. Every horse year, and accordingly every twelfth year, crowds of pilgrims come to Kailas. The monks said that they cannot be counted, but they knew that in the year 1907 more than 5000 pilgrims had been at Nyandi, of whom the greater part came from Ladak.

The *lhakang*, or hall of the gods, is very original. Four pillars support the roof. The altar, like a Chinese kiosque of wood painted in colours, stands alone and in deep shadow, but so many votive lights are placed in front that they seem like a festival illumination. An especial lamp hangs before the image of Sakya-muni, which stands against a wall. In front of the altar is a huge copper vessel with a cover, which is called Tosungjön. It is said to have flown in old times from India through the air. In winter it is filled with butter, in summer with *chang*. A lama with a brass ladle poured the consecrated beverage into the bowls of my men, and out of the silver bowls with peacocks' feathers he poured holy water into the hollow of their hands; they drank of it and besmeared their faces with the rest. All, except Rabsang, paid due reverence to the statues and prayed, and Tsering had murmured his prayers all the way along and let the beads of his rosary slip through his fingers. Two fine elephant's tusks (*langchen-sala-rapten*) were set up before the altar.

In the Tsenkang hall is a figure of Hlabsen clothed in gold brocade and *kadakhs*, the god of Kang-rinpoche and Tso-mavang. In the ante-chamber is a whole arsenal of guns and swords and wooden and leathern shields, each with four iron bosses. On the outside of the monastery, which fronts the holy mountain, rows of artistically sculptured slabs are affixed. On six of them each of the holy characters is incised, and each of the gigantic characters is again filled in with the invariable alpha and omega of Lamaism, "Om mani padme hum." On other flagstones gods are carved with wonderful dexterity, and one feels a vain desire to buy one or two of them.

The view from the roof is indescribably beautiful.

The icy summit of Kang-rinpoche rises amid fantastic fissured precipitous rocks, and in the foreground are the picturesque superstructure of the monastery and its streamers (Illust. 265).

But time flies. After spending three hours in Nyandi, we say farewell to the monks, descend the steep path zigzagging among rubbish and boulders, and continue our journey to the north-north-east along the right bank of the river. At every turn I could stand still in astonishment, for this valley is one of the grandest and most beautiful in its wildness that I have ever seen. The precipice on the right side of the valley is divided into two stages with a terrace between them, and in the midst gapes a dark ravine. On the left side the rock forms a single vertical wall, and here the eyes fall on a succession of singular forms of relief, rocks like congealed cascades, citadels, church towers, and embattled fortifications, separated by cañon-like hollows. Water from melting snowfields pours down the steep slopes. One such jet of water is quite 800 feet high and white as milk; the wind turns it into spray, but it collects again, only to be split up against a projection. The rock around it is wet and dark with spurted drops. A natural rock bridge crosses a small cleft with vertical walls.

Immediately beyond the monastery the summit of Kailas is lost to view, but soon a bit of it is seen again through a gap. We passed twelve pilgrims, and soon after a second party resting on a slope. They put on solemn faces and do not talk with one another, but murmur prayers, walking with their bodies bent, and leaning on a staff—frequently, too, without a staff. How they have longed to come here! And now they are here and walk round the mountain, which is always on their right. They feel no weariness, for they know that every step improves their prospects in the world beyond the river of death. And when they have returned to their black tents in distant valleys, they tell their friends of all the wonders they have seen, and of the clouds, which sail like the dragon ships of old below the white summit of Gangri.

Small conical cairns are everywhere. Tsering never

omits to take up a stone from the margin of the road and lay it as his contribution on every such votive pile, and thereby he does a good deed, for he makes the way less rough for those who come after him. The sun looks out through a gap, and throws a bright yellow light into the valley, which otherwise is in shadow. The icy peak again appears much foreshortened. Several tributaries come in from the sides, and towards evening the river rises, containing quite 280 cubic feet of water.

A man from Gertse has been going round the mountain for twenty successive days, and now has just accomplished his tenth circuit. Dunglung-do is a very important valley junction, where three valleys converge—the Chamo-lung-chen from the north, 70° W., the Dunglung from the north, 5° W., and the third, called in its upper course Hle-lungpa, which we ascend. We now have granite on both sides. Kailas turns a sharp edge to the north, and from here the peak resembles a tetrahedron more than ever. Again the mountain is concealed by an elevation of the ring which girdles it as Monte Somma encircles Vesuvius. The main river swells up towards evening; the other two are spanned by bridges. Numbers of boulders lie all about. All is granite, and therefore the mountain forms are rounder and more lumpy (Illust. 267).

At length we see the monastery Diri-pu in front of us, standing on the slope on the right side of the valley. A huge block of granite beside the path up to it bears the usual sacred characters, and there also are long *manis*, streamers, and cairns. All the pilgrims we have overtaken in the course of the day turn into the monastery, where they can pass the night free of charge. The convent is crammed full after the arrival of a party of pilgrims belonging to the Pembo sect. These, of course, wander round the mountain in the reverse direction, and the orthodox cast contemptuous glances at them when they meet. I prefer to pitch my tent on the roof, where the luggage of the pilgrims is piled up. Here also there is a fine view of Kailas, raising its summit due south. With a temperature of 40° at nine o'clock it is cold and disagreeable, for a strong wind blows, and my tent, consisting only of the camera-stand covered with a linen cloth, is too small to allow of a fire being lighted (Illust. 268).

Since I had been successful in fixing the positions of the sources of the Brahmaputra and Sutlej, my old dream of discovering the source of the Indus was revived, and all my aspirations and ambition were now concentrated on this object. When I now learned from the monks that the point where the famous river issues forth from the "Mouth of the Lion" was only three days' journey to the north-east beyond a lofty pass, everything else seemed of trifling consequence compared to an advance into the unknown country in the north. We held a council of war; we had provisions only for two days more, and we had not brought enough money with us, and, moreover, the state of affairs in Khaleb was too uncertain to allow of greater hazards. I therefore decided to carry out my original plan in the meantime and complete the pilgrimage, and afterwards make the source of the Indus the object of a fresh excursion from Khaleb, or, if the worst came to the worst, from Gartok.

On September 4 we take leave of the monks of Diri-pu, cross by a bridge the river which comes down from the pass Tseti-lachen-la in the Trans-Himalaya, from the other side of which the water flows to the Indus, and mount in an easterly direction over rough steep slopes thickly bestrewn with granite boulders. On our right is the river which is fed by the glaciers of Kailas; it is quite short, but is very full of water. The path becomes still steeper, winding among immense blocks of granite, and leads up to the first hump, after which the ground is a little more even to the next break. Here we have a splendid view of the short truncated glacier which, fed from a sharply defined trough-shaped firn basin, lies on the north side of Kailas. Its terminal, lateral, and medial moraines are small but distinct. Eastwards from Kailas runs off an exceedingly sharp, pointed, and jagged ridge, covered on the north side with snow, and belts of pebbles in the snow give all this side a furrowed appearance. From all corners of the ice mantle and the snowfields foaming brooks hurry down to the river. On our left, northwards, the mountains consist

271. THE GOVA BY WHOSE HELP THE SOURCE OF THE INDUS WAS DISCOVERED (SEATED) AND TIBETANS AT KAILAS.

of vertical fissured granite in wild pyramidal forms. Kailas is protected on the north by immense masses of granite, but the mountain itself is in all probability of conglomerate, as shown by the nearly horizontal bedding plainly perceptible in the projecting ledges, sharply marked snow-lines, and belts of ice. The summit rises above this sea of wild mountains like a mighty crystal of hexagonal form.

A party of poor women and children climbed wearily up to the pass. An elderly man, who was now making his ninth circuit, made no objection to join our party; he knew the country and could give information about it. On another rise in the ground, called Tutu-dapso, we saw hundreds of votive cairns, 3 feet high—quite a forest of stone pyramids—like innumerable gravestones in a churchyard (Illust. 270).

Slowly and laboriously we climbed up this arduous pass, one of the most troublesome on the whole journey. Thicker and thicker lay the boulders, exclusively of granite in all possible varieties, some pink and some so light a grey as to be almost white. Between two boulders lay a suspicious-looking bundle of clothes. We examined it, and found that it contained the body of a man who had collapsed in making the tour of the mountain of the gods. His features were rigid, and he seemed poor and emaciated. No one knew who he was, and if he had any relations they would never learn that his pilgrimage had launched him into new adventures among the dark mazes of the soul's migrations.

Our old man stops at a flat granite block of colossal dimensions, and says that this is a *dikpa-karnak*, or a test-stone for sinners. A narrow tunnel runs under the block, and whoever is without sin, or at any rate has a clear conscience, can creep through the passage, but the man who sticks fast in the middle is a scoundrel. I asked the old man whether it might not happen that a thin rogue would wriggle through while a fat, honest fellow might stick fast; but he answered very seriously that stoutness had nothing to do with the result of the trial, which depended only on the state of the soul. Evidently our honest Ishe was not certain which way the balance of his conscience inclined, for, before we were aware, we saw him disappearing under the block, and heard him puffing, panting, and groaning, scratching with his hands and trying to get a foothold behind. But when he had floundered about inside long and vigorously, he was at last obliged to call for help in a half-strangled voice. We laughed till we could hardly keep on our feet, and let him stay a while in his hole because of his manifest sinfulness. Then the two other men dragged him out by the legs, and he looked extremely confused (and dusty) when he at length emerged again into the outer world, an unmasked villain. The old man told us that a woman had become so firmly fixed that she had actually to be dug out.

Some 200 paces farther in this maze of granite boulders, among which we wandered as in lanes between low houses and walls, stands a test-stone of another kind. It consists of three blocks leaning on one another, with two hollows between them. The task is to creep through the left passage and return by the right, that is, in the orthodox direction. Here Ishe made up for his previous discomfiture by crawling through both holes. I told him frankly that there was no skill required here, for the holes were so large that even small yaks could go through, However, the sinner had in this second stone an opportunity of preserving at least a show of righteousness.

Our wanderings round Kang-rinpoche, the "holy ice mountain" or the "ice jewel," is one of my most memorable recollections of Tibet, and I quite understand how the Tibetans can regard as a divine sanctuary this wonderful mountain which has so striking a resemblance to a *chhorten*, the monument which is erected in memory of a deceased saint within or without the temples. How often during our roamings had I heard of this mountain of salvation! And now I myself walked in pilgrim garb along the path between the monasteries, which are set, like precious stones in a bangle, in the track of pilgrims round Kang-rinpoche, the finger which points up to the mighty gods throned like stars in unfathomable space.

From the highlands of Kham in the remotest east, from Naktsang and Amdo, from the unknown Bongba, which we have heard of only in vague reports, from the black tents which stand like the spots of a leopard scattered among the dreary valleys of Tibet, from Ladak in the mountains of the far west, and from the Himalayan lands in the south, thousands of pilgrims come hither annually, to pace slowly and in deep meditation the 28 miles round the navel of the earth, the mountain of salvation. I saw the silent procession, the faithful bands, among which all ages and both sexes are represented, youths and maidens, strong men with wife and child, grey old men who would before their death follow in the footsteps of countless pilgrims to win a happier existence, ragged fellows who lived like parasites on the charity of the other pilgrims, scoundrels who had to do penance for a crime, robbers who had plundered peaceful travellers, chiefs, officials, herdsmen, and nomads, a varied train of shady humanity on the thorny road, which after interminable ages ends in the deep peace of Nirvana. August and serene Siva looks down from her paradise, and Hlabsen from his jewelled palace, on the innumerable human beings below who circle, like asteroids round the sun, in ever fresh troops, round the foot of the mountain, going up through the western valley, crossing the Dolma pass, and descending the eastern valley.

We soon discover that most of these simple pilgrims have no clear idea of the benefits their journey is supposed to confer on them. When they are questioned, they usually answer that after death they will be allowed to sit near the god of Gangri. But what they all believe most firmly and obstinately is that the pilgrimage will bring them a blessing in this world. It will ward off all evil from their tents and huts, will keep away sickness from their children and herds, protect them from robbers, thieves, and losses, will send them rain, good pasturage, and increase among their yaks and sheep, will act like a talisman, and guard themselves and their property as the four spirit kings protect the images of the temple halls from demons. They march with light elastic step, they feel neither the icy-cold cutting wind nor the scorching sun; every step is a link in a chain which cannot be broken by the powers of evil which persecute and torment the children of men. They start on their way from Tarchen-labrang, and every new turn in the road brings them a step nearer to the point where the ring closes. And during the whole peregrination they pray "Om mani padme hum," and every time this prayer is uttered they let a bead of the rosary pass through the fingers. The stranger also approaches Kang-rinpoche with a feeling of awe. It is incomparably the most famous mountain in the world. Mount Everest and Mont Blanc cannot vie with it. Yet there are millions of Europeans who have never heard of Kang-rinpoche, while the Hindus and Lamaists, all know Kailas, though they have no notion where Mont Blanc lifts up its head. Therefore one approaches the mountain with the same feeling of respect as one experiences in Lhasa, Tashi-lunpo, Buddh Gaya, Benares, Mecca, Jerusalem, and Rome—those holy places which have attracted to their altars countless bands of sin-burdened souls and seekers after truth.

Our volunteer guide said that he was on his ninth circuit of the mountain. He took two days to each, and intended to go round thirteen times. He called the track Kang-kora, the Gangri circle. Many years before, he had performed the meritorious feat called *gyangchag-tsallgen*, which consists in measuring the length of the way by the length of the pilgrim's body. One such pilgrimage is worth thirteen ordinary circuits on foot. My pilgrimage was of no value at all, because I was riding, the old man said; I must go on foot if I wished to derive any benefit from it.

When we came a second time to Diri-pu some days later, we saw two young lamas engaged in the prostration pilgrimage round the mountain. They were from Kham, and from that part of the country "where the last men dwell," and had been a year on the way to Kailas. They were poor and ragged, and had nothing to carry, for they lived on the alms of the faithful. They had come in nine days from Tarchen to Diri-pu, and reckoned that they had still eleven days to finish their round. I accompanied

272. GULAM RAZUL BESIDE BALES OF CHINESE BRICK-TEA.

them for half an hour on foot to observe their procedure. This consisted of six movements. Suppose the young lama standing on the path with his forehead held slightly down and his arms hanging loosely at his sides. (1) He places the palms of his hands together and raises them to the top of his head, at the same time bending his head a little down; (2) he lays his hands under his chin, lifting up his head again; (3) he kneels upon the ground, bends forwards and lays himself full length on the ground with outstretched arms; (4) he passes his hands laid together over his head; (5) he stretches his right hand forwards as far as it will reach, and scratches a mark in the soil with a piece of bone, which shows the line which must be touched by his toes at the next advance; and (6) he raises himself up with his hands, makes two or three strides up to the mark, and repeats the same actions. And thus he goes round the whole mountain.

It is slow work and they do not hurry; they perform the whole business with composure, but they lose their breath, especially on the way up to the pass. And on the way down from the Dolma-la there are places so steep that it must be a gymnastic feat to lie down head foremost. One of the young monks had already accomplished one round, and was now on the second. When he had finished, in twelve days, he intended to betake himself to a monastery on the Tsangpo and be there immured for the rest of his life. And he was only twenty years old! We, who in our superior wisdom smile at these exhibitions of fanaticism and self-mortification, ought to compare our own faith and convictions with theirs. The life beyond the grave is hidden from all peoples, but religious conceptions have clothed it in different forms among different peoples. "If thou lookest closely, thou wilt see that hope, the child of heaven, points every mortal with trembling hand to the obscure heights." Whatever may be our own convictions, we must admire those who, however erroneous their views may be in our opinion, yet possess faith enough to remove mountains.

OM MANI PADME HUM

CHAPTER LII

OM MANI PADME HUM

Now begins the last very steep zigzag in the troublesome path among sharp or round grey boulders of every form and size, a cone of blocks with steps in it. Dung-chapje is the name of a round wall of stone, in the midst of which is a smaller boulder, containing in a hollow depression a round stone like the cleft hoof of a wild yak. When the faithful pilgrim passes this spot, he takes this stone, strikes it against the bottom of the hollow and turns it once round like a pestle. Consequently the hollow is being constantly deepened, and one day it will be lowered right through the block.

We mount up a ridge with brooks flowing on both sides. On every rock, which has a top at all level, small stones are piled up, and many of these pyramidal heaps are packed so closely that there is no room for another stone. Thanks to these cairns the pilgrim can find his way in snowstorm and fog, though without them he could not easily find it in sunshine.

At length we see before us a gigantic boulder, its cubical contents amounting perhaps to 7000 or 10,000 cubic feet; it stands like an enormous milestone on the saddle of Dolma-la, which attains the tremendous height of 18,599 feet. On the top of the block smaller stones are piled up into a pyramid supporting a pole, and from its end cords decorated with rags and streamers are stretched to other poles fixed in the ground. Horns and bones, chiefly shoulder-blades of sheep, are here deposited in large quantities—gifts of homage to the pass, which is supposed to mark the halfway point of the pilgrimage. When the pilgrim arrives here, he smears a bit of butter on the side of the stone, plucks out a lock of his own hair and plasters it into the butter. Thus he has offered up some of himself and some of his belongings. Consequently the stone resembles a huge wig-block, from which black locks of hair flutter in the wind. In time it would be completely covered with Tibetan hair, were it not that the locks occasionally fall off and are blown away by the wind. Teeth are stuck in all the chinks of the Dolma block, forming whole rosaries of human teeth. If you have a loose tooth, dedicate it to the spirits of the pass. Tsering unfortunately was toothless, or he would gladly have conformed to this regulation.

Heaps of rags lie all around, for the pilgrim has always a spare shred to hang on a string or lay at the foot of the block. But he not only gives, but also takes. Our old man took a rag from the heap and had a large quantity of such relics round his neck, for he had taken one from every cairn.

The view is grand, though Kailas itself is not visible. But one can see the sharp black ridge lying quite close on the south side with a mantle of snow and a hanging glacier, its blue margin cut off perpendicularly at the small moraine lake on the eastern side of the pass.

While I sat at the foot of the block, making observations and drawing the panorama, a lama came strolling up leaning on his stick. He carried a book, a drum, a *dorche*, and a bell, and likewise a sickly-looking child in a basket on his back. The parents, nomads in the valley below, had given him *tsamba* for two days to carry the child round the mountain, whereby it would recover its health. Many pilgrims gain their livelihood by such services, and some make the pilgrimage only for the benefit of others. The lama with the child complained that he had only made the circuit of the mountain three times, and did not possess money enough to go round thirteen times. I gave him alms.

Then he sat down on the pass, turned his face in the

direction where the summit of Kang-rinpoche was hidden, placed his hands together, and chanted an interminable succession of prayers. After this he went up to the block and laid his forehead on the ground—how many times I do not know, but he was still at it when we descended among boulders to the tiny round lake Tso-kavála. We followed its northern shore, and our old friend told me that the ice never breaks up.

But time slips away and we must hasten on. We walk, slide, and scramble down steep slopes where it would be easy to tumble down head over heels. The old man is sure-footed, and these slopes are old acquaintances. But woe betide him if he turned round and went in the reverse direction. At length we reach the main valley, called in its upper part Tselung, and in its lower Lam-chyker. Through the large valley, which enters the main valley on the right side, and is called Kando-sanglam, we now look eastwards upon the highest pinnacle of the summit of Kailas, which has a sharp edge towards the north-east, and still looks like a crystal. At two *manis* erected side by side we pass the border of the granite and the conglomerate, which now appears again. The further we proceed the more numerous are the boulders of this kind of rock, while those of granite at length occur no more. We march south-west and bivouac on the roof of the monastery Tsumtul-pu. All day long, at all the cairns and all the resting-places, I have heard nothing but an endless murmur of the words "Om mani padme hum," and now, as long as I am awake, "Om mani padme hum" sounds in my ears from all nooks and corners.

The temple had no other curiosity but a statue of Duk Ngavang Gyamtso, 5 feet high, sitting as at a writing-desk, two not very large elephant's tusks, and a five-branched chandelier from Lhasa. Our visit, therefore, did not last long, and we rode down the valley in which the river gradually increased in size. Here, too, *manis* and *chhortens* are erected, and at the end of the valley, where again numbers of granite boulders are accumulated, we see once more Langak-tso and the grand Gurla group.

At Tarchen-labrang we reached the termination of the

273. Tibetan Tent.

274. Monastery of Gar-gunsa.

275. Images at Chushut.

pilgrimage. Here twenty-three tents were pitched, and we received the greatest attention, were refreshed with milk and *chang*, and rested two hours. Then we left the pilgrim road to the right, and came into sight of the fourth monastery, perched high up on a terrace in the valley below the holy peak. A curious local wind at the north-west corner of Langak-tso raised up clouds of dust like the smoke of a burning town. A short while after, we lay peacefully among our men in the camp on the Khaleb moor.

By this pilgrimage round the holy mountain, which I had been able to accomplish by an unexpected lucky chance, I had gained an insight into the religious life of the Tibetans. It had also been, as it were, a revisal of all the experiences I had already collected in this connection.

Our knowledge of Tibet is still defective, and some future traveller will find sufficient material to show on a map of the whole Lamaistic world all the great pilgrim routes to innumerable sanctuaries. On such a map numerous roads would converge, like the spokes of a wheel, to Da Kuren, the temple of Maidari in Urga. Still closer would the rays from every inhabited spot of the immense territory of Lamaism run together to their chief focus, Lhasa. Somewhat less thickly they would unite at Tashi-lunpo. Innumerable winding roads and paths would start from the farthest border countries of Tibet, all tending towards the holy Kailas. We know that they exist, and no great imagination is required to conceive how they would look on a map. But it is with the routes of pilgrims just as with the flight of the wild-geese: we know nothing of their precise course. Besides, among the principal foci are scattered a number of smaller centres whence radii diverge to a sanctuary, a lake, or a spring, and from the heart of all these wind-roses peals out a cry to the faithful, similar to the exhortation of Isaiah: "Look upon Zion, the city of our solemnities: thine eyes shall see Jerusalem" (Isa. xxxiii. 20).

In the ears of the Tibetan another saying rings, the mystical formula "Om mani padme hum," not only on his wanderings to the goal of his pilgrimage, but throughout his life. Concerning this Waddell makes, among others, the following remarks: "Om-ma-ṇi pad-me Hūṃ, which literally means '*Om!* The Jewel in the lotus!' *Hūṃ!*—is addressed to the Bodhisat Padmapāṇi, who is represented like Buddha as seated or standing within a lotus-flower. He is the patron-god of Tibet and the controller of metempsychosis. And no wonder this formula is so popular and constantly repeated by both Lāmas and laity, for its mere utterance is believed to stop the cycle of re-births and to convey the reciter directly to paradise. Thus it is stated in the Māṇi-kah-bum with extravagant rhapsody that this formula 'is the essence of all happiness, prosperity, and knowledge, and the great means of deliverance,' for the *Om* closes re-birth amongst the gods, *ma* among the Titans, *ṇi* as a man, *pad* as a beast, *me* as a Tantalus, and *Hūṃ* as an inhabitant of hell. And in keeping with this view each of these six syllables is given the distinctive colour of these six states of re-birth, namely: *Om*, the godly *white*; *ma*, the Titanic *blue*; *ṇi*, the human *yellow*; *pad*, the animal *green*; *me*, the 'Tantalic' *red*; and *Hūṃ*, the hellish *black*" (*The Buddhism of Tibet*, 148-9).

Köppen and Grünwedel translate the four words: "O, Jewel in the lotus-flower, Amen."

Wherever one turns in Tibet, he sees the six sacred characters engraved or chiselled out, and hears them repeated everywhere. They are found in every temple in hundreds of thousands of copies, nay, in millions, for in the great prayer mills they are stamped in fine letters on thin paper. On the monastery roofs, on the roofs of private houses, and on the black tents, they are inscribed on the fluttering streamers. On all the roads we ride daily past wall-like stone cists covered with slabs, on which the formula "Om mani padme hum" is carved. Seldom does the most lonely path lead up to a pass where no cairn is erected to remind the wanderer of his dependence all his life long on the influence of good and bad spirits. And on the top of every such *lhato* or *lhadse* is fixed a pole or a stick with streamers, every one proclaiming in black letters the eternal truth. At projecting rocks cubical *chhortens* or *lhatos* stand beside the road in red and white. On the sides of granite rocks polished smooth by wind and weather figures of Buddha are frequently cut, and below them, as well as on fallen boulders, can be read in gigantic characters "Om mani padme hum." On the piers between which chain bridges are stretched over the Tsangpo or other rivers, heaps of stones are piled up, and on all these innumerable votive cairns lie yak skulls and crania of wild sheep and antelopes. Into the horns and the bleached frontal bones of the yak the sacred formula is cut, and the incised characters are filled in with red or some other holy colour. We find them again in innumerable copies and in many forms, especially on the high-roads which lead to temples and pilgrims' resorts, as well as at all places where there is danger, as on mountain passes and river fords. And even the ferry boats of hide are decorated with blessed streamers.

In every caravan one man at least, and usually several, has a prayer-mill in his hand. This is rotated by means of a weight round the axle of the handle, and is stuffed full of paper strips bearing the holy formula in many thousands of impressions. All day long, whatever the duration of the journey, the believer turns his prayer-mill and babbles in chanting tones "Om mani padme hum." The militia who are called out to catch a robber band have on their ride more confidence in their prayer-mills than in their guns and sabres, and, sad to say, there are some even among the robbers who rattle off their Om and Hum in order to make their escape. Among the escorts which accompanied me on various occasions there were always one or two horsemen armed with a *mani* machine. One always sees this convenient praying instrument in the hands of the people one meets. The herdsman murmurs the six syllables beside his herd, his wife when milking the sheep, the merchant as he goes to market, the hunter as he stalks the wild yak on untrodden paths, the nomad when he sets out to move his tent to another pasture, the artisan as he bends over his work. With these words the Tibetan begins his day, and with them on his tongue he lies down to rest. The Om and Hum are not only the Alpha and Omega of the day, but of his whole life.

The mystic words rang constantly in my ears. I heard them when the sun rose and when I blew out my light, and I did not escape them even in the wilderness, for my own men murmured "Om mani padme hum." They belong to Tibet, these words; they are inseparable from it: I cannot imagine the snow-capped mountains and the blue lakes without them. They are as closely connected with this country as buzzing with the bee-hive, as the flutter of streamers with the pass, as the ceaseless west wind with its howling.

The life of the Tibetan from the cradle to the grave is interwoven with a multitude of religious precepts and customs. It is his duty to contribute his mite to the maintenance of the monasteries and to the Peter's pence of the temples. When he passes a votive cairn he adds a stone to the pile as an offering; when he rides by a *mani*, he never forgets to guide his steed to the left of it; when he sees a holy mountain, he never omits to lay his forehead on the ground in homage; in all important undertakings he must, for the sake of his eternal salvation, seek the advice of monks learned in the law; when a mendicant lama comes to his door he never refuses to give him a handful of *tsamba* or a lump of butter; when he makes the round of the temple halls, he adds his contribution to the collection in the votive bowls; and when he saddles his horse or loads a yak, he again hums the everlasting "Om mani padme hum."

More frequently than an Ave Maria or a Paternoster in the Catholic world, "Om mani padme hum" forms an accompaniment to the life and wanderings of humanity over half Asia. The boundless vista opened out by the six holy syllables is thus expressed by Edwin Arnold in the concluding lines of his poem, *The Light of Asia*:

> The dew is on the lotus. Rise, Great Sun!
> And lift my leaf and mix me with the wave.
> Om mani padme hum, the sunrise comes.
> The dewdrop slips into the shining sea.

276. THE POLICEMEN FROM SIMLA.

277. MY BOAT ON THE INDUS.

278. LADAKI WOMEN.

CHAPTER LIII

THE DISCOVERY OF THE SOURCE OF THE INDUS

IMMEDIATELY on my arrival in Khaleb I told the old gova, who had the hopeless and thankless task of watching my proceedings, that I now intended to take the road past Singi-kabab, or the source of the Indus.

"If you go thither, Bombo," he answered, "I shall at once send a courier to the Garpuns, the two chiefs in Gartok."

"I do not think that the Garpuns will have any objection to my taking a more northerly route."

"Oh yes, the Garpuns received orders from Lhasa five days ago to watch carefully that you followed no other way but the great high-road to Gartok. The Garpuns straightway sent couriers to twelve different places—Parka, Misser, Purang, Singtod, and others—to make it known that you were not permitted to travel on byroads. If this letter had not reached me, I would willingly have let you march northwards, but now I dare not for my own sake."

"What would you do if I quietly disappeared one night? I can buy yaks in Tarchen, and then I shall not be dependent on those I have from you."

"Yes, of course. A man lives in Tarchen who has sixty yaks, and will sell them as soon as he sees silver money. But I shall at once send word to the Garpuns, and they will send men after you and force you to come back. To buy yaks would therefore be useless waste of money. However, if you like to let the main part of your caravan follow the high-road, and make yourself an excursion of a couple of days northwards to the Singi-kabab, and then join your caravan again, I will put no obstacles in your way. But you do it at your own risk, and you will most certainly be caught before you reach the source of the Indus."

I was as much astonished as delighted by this sudden change in the attitude of the gova, and arranged with Robert that he should lead the main caravan in very short day's marches to Gartok, while I made as rapidly as possible for the source of the Indus. I took only as many things as a small leathern trunk would contain, and as companions only five men, among them Rabsang as interpreter and Adul as cook, with our own six animals and three dogs, one of which, a new purchase, ran away on the first day. I had Robert's small tent, and our arsenal consisted of two guns and a revolver, for robbers were said to make the country very unsafe. I could not find a guide, but on the way to Diri-pu, where I encamped once more, I came across an old man from Tok-jalung, who wished to make the round of Kailas thirteen times, and gave me much valuable information. But no money could induce him to accompany us farther.

On the 8th we continued our way through the valley that runs north-north-eastwards from Diri-pu to the Tseti-la. The stream, divided into many arms, was covered in the night by a thin coating of ice, smooth as glass, where the water had run off, but it disappeared when day came. The valley is broad, and the road showed traces of considerable traffic, though we did not meet a soul. The marmots whistled in front of their holes; the summer would soon be over for them. Kang-rinpoche can be seen from many places, and here pilgrims from the north have piled up cairns. Granite predominates everywhere, but crystalline schists occur here and there. We followed the fresh tracks of three horsemen. The gradient became steeper and the scenery assumed more of an alpine character. We mounted up among huge cones of detritus with babbling brooks of melted snow to the pass, which lay at a height of 18,465 feet. Its plateau is singularly flat. On its northern side camp No. 234 was pitched.

In the evening Rabsang reported that our fuel-gatherers had heard whistles, and that these signals had been answered from the other side. The men believed that there were robbers here, and did not dare to sit outside by the fire lest they should be good marks for shots out of an ambush. I quieted them with the assurance that no robber would venture to attack a European, but gave orders to the watchmen to keep an eye on our animals.

The night passed quietly and the minimum temperature went down to 16.2°; autumn was come again into dreary Tibet. I had supposed that the Tseti-la was the pass on the main divide, but we had not gone far when we saw its brook, which flowed northwards, make a bend to the west, and descend through a well-defined valley to the Dunglung. It therefore belongs to the catchment basin of the Sutlej and not to the Indus, and the Tseti-la is a pass of secondary order. But we soon reached the actual pass, an extremely flat threshold. Here lies a small muddy lake drained by a brook issuing from its eastern side, which we followed all day. This pass is the Tseti-lachen-la, and it is a water-parting between the Sutlej and the Indus. Its height is less than that of the Tseti-la, for it is only 17,933 feet; it lies on the main chain of the Trans-Himalaya. Kailas, therefore, lies a good day's journey south of the watershed of the two rivers, and belongs entirely to the basin of the Sutlej.

From the lake we follow the little affluent of the Indus northwards. The ground is marshy and rough. Here and there are seen three hearthstones. A dead horse lies among the luxuriant grass. It is singular that no nomads are encamped here. At length we see at a far distance quite down in the valley men going downstream with large flocks of sheep. Tundup Sonam and Ishe are sent after them, and by degrees the rest of us come up with the party. They are nomads from Gertse, who have taken salt to Gyanima and are now transporting barley on their 500 sheep. All the valley is dotted over with white sheep, which trip along actively, plucking the grass as they go. In front of us rises a steep purple mountain chain, and along the flank turned towards us the Indus is said to flow. We joined the men of the sheep caravan and camped together with them. There were five of them, all armed with guns, and they said that the district was frequently haunted by robbers, who at times seemed to vanish altogether, and then suddenly came down like a whirlwind, and no one knew whence they came.

Our camping-ground on the bank of the Indus (16,663 feet) is called Singi-buk. Eastwards the valley is broad and open, but the Indus itself is here an insignificant stream. I was therefore not astonished when I heard that it was only a short day's journey to the source, which, I was told, does not proceed from snow or a glacier, but springs up out of the ground. The men called the river the Singi-tsangpo, or Singi-kamba, and the source itself Singi-kabab, though we afterwards heard the word pronounced Senge more frequently than Singi.

It turned out that one of the five men knew all about us. He was a brother of the Lobsang Tsering on the Dungtse-tso who had sold us three yaks the winter before (see Chapter XV.). It was a singular chance that we should fall in with him. He said he had heard how well we had treated his brother, and offered us his services—for a good reward, of course. As he had travelled several times through this region, quite unknown to Europeans, and was acquainted with all the passes, roads, and valleys, I thought he would be very valuable to me, and I proposed to give him 7 rupees a day, that is about half a month's pay of one of my Ladakis. Of course he accepted the terms at once and soon became our intimate friend.

But these business matters were not yet settled. The man had a quantity of sheep and barley. He consented to let us eight sheep on hire, and sell us their loads, which would last our horses for a week. He was to receive a rupee for the hire of each sheep, which was high, for a sheep is worth only 2 to 3 rupees. The old man would therefore receive 18 rupees every evening as long as he was with us; but it was cheap after all, for the discovery of the source of the Indus was involved.

The large sheep-caravan had already started on Sep-

279, 280, 281. At the Monastery Door in Tashi-gang between Gartok and Ladak.

tember 10, when we, with our new guide, whose own *tsamba* was carried on a ninth sheep, followed in its track. After an hour's march we crossed a tributary, the Lungdep-chu, which comes from a valley in the south-east, with flattish mountains in the background.

A little farther up the Singi-kamba expands into a basin containing an abundance of medium-sized fish. As we passed, the fish were darting upstream in compact shoals, and passed a very shallow place with slight swirls. Here Rabsang attacked them, but all his catch was only one small miserable fish. Then we threw up a dam by the bank, with an opening on one side, and the men went into the water and drove in the fish with shouts and splashing. Then the entrance was built up. After we had repeated this diversion three times, we had procured thirty-seven fine fish, and I was eager for my dinner, which I usually looked forward to with some loathing, for the hard dried mutton had become thoroughly distasteful to me. Our old man, who sat and watched us, thought that we had taken leave of our senses. Farther up, the fish were so crowded in a quiet pool that they made the water seem almost black with their dark backs.

We rode up the valley, leaving on our right a red, loaf-shaped mountain called Lungdep-ningri. Opposite, on the northern side of the valley, were seen two fine Ovis Ammon sheep feeding on a conical elevation. They bore splendid horns, and carried their heads royally. They soon perceived us, and made slowly up the slope. But they paid too much attention to our movements, and did not notice that Tundup Sonam, with his gun on his back, was making a detour to stalk them from the other side of the hill. After a while we heard a shot, and a good hour later, when the camp was pitched, Tundup came back laden with as much of the flesh of his victim as he could carry. Thus we obtained a fresh addition to our somewhat scanty rations, and Tundup's exploit enhanced the glory of this memorable day. In the evening he went off again to fetch more meat, and he brought me the head of the wild sheep, which I wished to preserve as a memento of the day at the source of the Indus.

The ground rises exceedingly slowly. Singi-yüra is a rugged cliff to the north, with a large hole through its summit. Singi-chava is the name of a commanding eminence to the south. Then we wade through the outflow of the Munjam valley running in from the south-east. Above this the Indus is only a tiny brook, and part of its water comes from a valley in the south-east, the Bokar. A little later we camp at the aperture of the spring, which is so well concealed that it might easily be overlooked without a guide.

From the mountains on the northern side a flattish cone of detritus, or, more correctly, a slope bestrewn with rubbish, descends to the level, open valley. At its foot projects a slab of white rock with an almost horizontal bedding, underneath which several small springs well up out of the ground, forming weedy ponds and the source stream, which we had traced upwards, and which is the first and uppermost of the headwaters of the mighty Indus. The four largest springs, where they issued from the ground, had temperatures of 48.6°, 49.1°, 49.6°, and 50.4° respectively. They are said to emit the same quantity of water in winter and summer, but a little more after rainy seasons. Up on the slab of rock stand three tall cairns and a small cubical *lhato* containing votive pyramids of clay. And below the *lhato* is a quadrangular *mani*, with hundreds of red flagstones, some covered with fine close inscriptions, some bearing a single character 20 inches high. On two the wheel of life was incised, and on another a divine image, which I carried off as a souvenir of the source of the Indus.

Our guide said that the source Singi-kabab was reverenced because of its divine origin. When travellers reached this place or any other part of the upper Indus, they scooped up water with their hands, drank of it, and sprinkled their faces and heads with it.

Through the investigations made by Montgomerie's pundits in the year 1867 it was known that the eastern arm of the Indus is the actual headwater, and I had afterwards an opportunity of proving by measurement that the western, Gartok, stream is considerably smaller. But no

282. Dancing Women in Chushut, a Village on my Way back to Ladak.

pundit had succeeded in penetrating to the source, and the one who had advanced nearest to it, namely, to a point 30 miles from it, had been attacked by robbers and forced to turn back. Consequently, until our time the erroneous opinion prevailed that the Indus had its source on the north flank of Kailas, and, thanks to those admirable robbers, the discovery of the Indus source was reserved for me and my five Ladakis.

We passed a memorable evening and a memorable night at this important geographical spot, situated 16,946 feet above sea-level. Here I stood and saw the Indus emerge from the lap of the earth. Here I stood and saw this unpretentious brook wind down the valley, and I thought of all the changes it must undergo before it passes between rocky cliffs, singing its roaring song in ever more powerful crescendo, down to the sea at Karachi, where steamers load and unload their cargoes. I thought of its restless course through western Tibet, through Ladak and Baltistan, past Skardu, where the apricot trees nod on its banks, through Dardistan and Kohistan, past Peshawar, and across the plains of the western Panjab, until at last it is swallowed up by the salt waves of the ocean, the Nirvana and the refuge of all weary rivers. Here I stood and wondered whether the Macedonian Alexander, when he crossed the Indus 2200 years ago, had any notion where its source lay, and I revelled in the consciousness that, except the Tibetans themselves, no other human being but myself had penetrated to this spot. Great obstacles had been placed in my way, but Providence had secured for me the triumph of reaching the actual sources of the Brahmaputra and Indus, and ascertaining the origin of these two historical rivers, which, like the claws of a crab, grip the highest of all the mountain systems of the world—the Himalayas. Their waters are born in the reservoirs of the firmament, and they roll down their floods to the lowlands to yield life and sustenance to fifty millions of human beings. Up here white monasteries stand peacefully on their banks, while in India pagodas and mosques are reflected in their waters; up here wolves, wild yaks, and wild sheep, roam about their valleys, while down below in India the eyes of tigers and leopards shine like glowing coals of fire from the jungles that skirt their banks, and poisonous snakes wriggle through the dense brushwood. Here in dreary Tibet icy storms and cold snowfalls lash their waves, while down in the flat country mild breezes whisper in the crowns of the palms and mango trees. I seemed to listen here to the beating of the pulses of these two renowned rivers, to watch the industry and rivalry which, through untold generations, have occupied unnumbered human lives, short and transitory as the life of the midge and the grass; all those wanderers on the earth and guests in the abodes of time, who have been born beside the fleeting current of these rivers, have drunk of their waters, have drawn from them life and strength for their fields, have lived and died on their banks, and have risen from the sheltered freedom of their valleys up to the realms of eternal hope. Not without pride, but still with a feeling of humble thankfulness, I stood there, conscious that I was the first white man who had ever penetrated to the sources of the Indus and Brahmaputra.

CHAPTER LIV

A RESOLUTION

FROM the source of the Indus we travelled on north-eastwards with our friendly guide to a locality called Yumbamatsen, which lies in lat. 32° N. And thence I betook myself to Gartok, the chief town of western Tibet and the residence of the two Garpuns, where I arrived after many adventures on September 26, having crossed the Trans-Himalaya for the fifth time by the Jukti-la (19,111 feet high). I must, alas! omit a description of this journey for the present, though it passed for the most part through unknown country. Mr. Calvert crossed over the Jukti-la two years before.

In Gartok (14,656 feet) a new period began. This town is a turning-point in the chronicles of my journey. In the first place, I again came into contact with the outer world. Thakur Jai Chand, the British commercial agent, handed me immediately on my arrival a thick packet of letters, including a quantity from my dear home, and others from Lord and Lady Minto and their daughters, from Colonel Dunlop Smith, Younghusband, O'Connor, Rawling, and many other friends in Europe and Asia. Nothing, however, was heard of the heavy consignment I expected from Simla. But soon afterwards I heard from Dunlop Smith that all I had ordered was on the way and would arrive in due course, and meantime I had to wait in patience.

The Garpuns at once sent me presents as a token of welcome, with the usual polite phrases. They were of too great importance to visit me first, so next day I went to them. The elder was ill; the younger, a gentleman from

Lhasa, thirty-five years of age and of distinguished appearance, received me most cordially in his simple Government buildings, and was so little angry at the liberties I had recently taken that he did not even ask me where I had been. It was an irony of fate that a letter in most friendly terms and most liberal in its concessions, which I now received from Lien Darin by the hand of the Garpun, had not reached me until it was too late. When Lien Darin received my letter from Raga-tasam, he immediately sent off two Chinamen fully authorized to come to an agreement with me about the route I was to take. "For I shall be glad to know," said the Amban of Lhasa, "that you are travelling by the road that suits you." He was quite convinced that my movements, whichever way I took, would give no cause for political complications. And he concluded with the words: "Now, I hope that you will have a successful and peaceful journey, and I will pray for your health and prosperity."

How I regretted now that I had not stayed in Saka, and so much the more when the Garpun told me that the two Chinamen had arrived with an escort of four Tibetans only two weeks after we had left! But the Garpun was friendly disposed towards me; he was the most powerful man in western Tibet, and could still throw open all doors for me, if he dared and was willing to do so.

I was, indeed, pleased and thankful for the results which I had already been able to secure. Besides many other problems that had been solved, I had crossed the Trans-Himalaya by five passes, namely, the Sela-la, Chang-la-Pod-la, Angden-la, Tseti-lachen-la, and Jukti-la, of which the first four had been entirely unknown. But between the Angden-la and the Tseti-lachen-la I had been obliged to leave a gap of quite 330 miles in the exploration of the Trans-Himalaya. Of this region nothing was known but the summits Ryder had seen from his route, and which he and Wood had measured by observation. We also possessed some uncertain statements of Nain Sing's journey in 1873, but his route lay to the north of the blank patch, and this blank represented an area of 5300 square miles. I could not return home without having done all that was

283. OLD WOMAN.

284. LAMA IN CHUSHUT.

Sketches by the Author.

humanly possible to traverse the unknown country by at least one route. Precisely there was the line forming the watershed between the Indian Ocean and the inland drainage of the salt lakes on the Tibetan plateau. There many lakes and rivers might be expected to exist, and there lay the large province of Bongba, of which so many hazy reports had reached our ears from its northern, eastern, and southern boundaries. But the greatest and most important question of all was: Does the Nien-chen-tang-la run right through Tibet in a westerly and north-westerly direction to the north of the Tsangpo and the upper Indus? No European and no pundit had hitherto ventured on this problem; but Hodgson, Saunders, and Atkinson had many years before laid down a hypothetical range on their maps of Tibet. Did it actually exist? Or was a labyrinth of ranges hidden under the white space, or a comparatively flat plateau, on which foundation isolated snowy peaks and chains were based? Hypotheses are absolutely worthless compared to proved facts. Such facts I would procure. I knew that if I did not succeed now in penetrating into the country which on the latest English map of Tibet (1906, Map 1) bears only the word "Unexplored," one fine day another explorer would come and rob me of this triumph. And this thought I could not endure.

In Gartok my old friend from Leh, the rich merchant Gulam Razul, was staying (Illust. 272). I consulted him, and he was to be my delivering angel. He took a very sanguine view of our position, for the Garpun owed him 7000 rupees for goods delivered, and feared his influence; he could therefore put pressure on the Viceroy of western Tibet. He first tried stratagem, which, however, completely failed, for the Garpun replied he was too fond of his head to expose it to risk by assisting a European who had no permission to travel about the country. Then we tried gold, but the Garpun answered most theatrically: "If this house were of gold and you offered it to me, I would not take it. If you travel on forbidden roads, I will send armed men after you who will force you to return hither."

He was incorruptible, and he was too strong for us.

How sorry I was now that I had not proceeded eastwards when I was in enjoyment of complete freedom at the source of the Indus and in Yumba-matsen! But no, that was impossible, for my cash-box was then not full enough, I had only five men with me, and I could not have left the rest of my caravan to their own devices.

What if I went down into Nepal and came back again into Tibet by unguarded roads? No, that would not do, for snow would soon close the Himalayan passes. And if we tried to slink through to Rudok and thence make eastwards? No, Rudok swarmed with spies. And soon Gulum Razul learned also that the Garpun had sent orders throughout his territory to stop me in case I attempted to travel even to Ladak by any other than the main high-road.

Thus we planned this and that, and mused day and night, sometimes in my tent, sometimes in Gulam Razul's, and waited for the consignment from Simla, heard bells jingle when couriers came from the east, saw one merchant after another return from the fair in Lhasa, met the *serpun* or gold commissioner who came from Tok-jalung, and felt the cold of autumn cut our skins more sharply as the thermometer fell to $-11°$.

Then in lonely hours I came to the resolution to return to Ladak and thence, as in the year before, penetrate into Tibet from the north, traverse the whole country once more, and cross the blank space. I knew very well that by this roundabout way it would take half a year to reach districts situated only a month's journey from Gartok. A new caravan would be necessary, new dangers and adventures awaited us, and winter was before us with its Arctic cold. But it must be done in spite of everything. I would not turn back until the obstacles in my way became quite insuperable. To enter Ladak, a country under British protection, was a risk, and therefore I must make all haste to cross the frontier again. I could not avoid Rawling's and Deasy's country, but what did it matter? My aim was the unknown region, which I would try to explore by some route or other.

Gulam Razul and Robert were the only ones who were initiated into my new plans, for in them I could place the blindest confidence. During our conferences we spoke in Persian, and Robert kept a watch that no eavesdropper came near my tent. Gulam Razul undertook to get together the new caravan from Leh, and it was to reach at a certain time Drugub, where I meant to dismiss my last thirteen men; they were worn-out and longed to get home. Gulam Razul undertook the responsibility of finding me fresh men.

On October 20 we left Gartok to await in Gar-gunsa the arrival of the consignment from India. Gulam Razul, Thakur Jai Chand, the postmaster Deni Das, and the doctor Mohanlal, also moved thither. Robert had heard in Gartok the sad news that his elder brother had died in Further India, and now he received a fresh blow, for his little brother, ten years old, had been drowned in Srinagar. He was inconsolable, and begged me to let him go home to his mother, who had now only one son left. So I was to lose him also.

Gulam Razul had three large tents within his fence of boughs (Illust. 254). There he sat like a pasha on his divan, smoked a large silver narghilé, and received his guests with Oriental dignity. He was jovial and agreeable, undertook to do everything, and thought nothing of difficulties. There we made our plans and long lists of things to be bought, and as my arrival in Ladak could not be kept secret for long, we spread the report that I wanted a new caravan for a journey to Khotan, and that I intended to travel to Pekin in the spring. For the success of the plan it was essential that no one should have any suspicion of my real intentions; for in that case, especial orders would be sent to Rudok and to the nomads. My own servants and all Hajji Nazer Shah's household believed therefore that it was my settled purpose to go to Khotan, and that I had given up all thoughts of Tibet. I even went so far as to send a telegram from Drugub to Reuter's correspondent in India, my friend Mr. Buck, with the information that I was about to make a short journey to Khotan. The object was to mislead the mandarins. If no one else would help me, I must help myself, and, if necessary, with cunning and trickery. None of my Indian friends must have any suspicion of my real plans, not even Colonel Dunlop Smith; it would, of course, be silly to put them in a position where they must either betray me or be disloyal to their own superiors. Except Gulam Razul and Robert, only my parents and sisters were let into the secret. But, unfortunately, I had given them a far too optimistic estimate of the length of my enterprise, and therefore when they heard no news they became day by day more uneasy, and at last came to the conclusion that I had come to grief (Illust. 234).

On October 29, 1907, Gulam Razul's mules arrived, and were subjected to a thorough inspection. They were in splendid condition—small, sturdy, and sleek animals from Lhasa, accustomed to rarefied air, and, according to the owner, capable of enduring hardships of every kind. Gulam Razul even offered to buy them back at the price I paid, if they returned alive. I paid for all the twenty 1780 rupees. I still possessed five of my own animals, after a small white mule had been torn to pieces by wolves in Gartok. A whole pack had attacked our last six animals, the camp watchman had been unable to drive the wolves away, and the mule had been horribly wounded. He had been seen running before the wolves with his entrails trailing on the ground. The last mule from Poonch still survived, as well as my little Ladaki grey and one of his fellows, the veterans of Leh.

Gulam Razul also undertook to procure for me fifteen excellent horses from Ladak at a price of 1500 rupees. The other purchases consisted of: barley for the animals, 60 rupees; rice, 70 rupees; *tsamba*, 125 rupees; provender sacks, 60 rupees; clothes for the new men, 152 rupees; butter, 80 rupees; tea, 50 rupees; stearin candles and sugar, 104 rupees; a Lhasa skin coat for myself, 40 rupees; and a sleeping-bag of soft goatskin, also for myself, 25 rupees; in addition there was the hire of the pack animals which conveyed my baggage to Leh, 40 rupees, and the cost of transporting the newly purchased goods from Leh to Drugub, 20 rupees. Eleven men were to be enlisted in Leh, all having served in Hajji Nazer Shah's commercial house and known as honest respectable people. They

285. On the Way to Tankse.

286. In the Indus Valley on the Way to Ladak.

287. The New Horses and Mules at Drugub.

were to receive 15 rupees a month each, though their usual wages had not been more than 12, and three months' pay in advance. The caravan bashi was to receive 50 rupees a month and be selected with very great care. My whole debt to Gulam Razul amounted to nearly 5000 rupees, for those who had had the trouble of making all these purchases were to receive a douceur over and above. I sent a note of hand to Colonel Dunlop Smith, with directions that this sum should be paid to Gulam Razul, in order that he might have security if I did not return from this journey.

On October 30 Gulam Razul sent his son to Leh to equip the new caravan, which was to reach Drugub, ready in all particulars, on November 30. For the valuable services rendered me on this occasion Gulam Razul afterwards received from H.M. King Gustaf of Sweden the gold medal "for distinguished service," and I recommended him to the Indian Government for the title of honour, Khan Bahadur; of course I based my appeal in this case on the great commercial services he had rendered to the Indian Empire.

In Gar-gunsa I heard news of a new treaty between Great Britain and Russia, which had been concluded in October of this year. "Great Britain and Russia bind themselves not to allow any scientific expedition of any kind whatsoever to enter Tibet for the next three years without previous agreement, and call upon China to act similarly" (Illust. 274).

It seemed as though this clause were especially designed to meet my case. I said not a word to Gulam Razul about it. But I saw that I could no longer travel in Tibet as a European. Last year I had been successful when the political situation was still unsettled, but I had taught both the Chinese and Tibetans a lesson, and shown them that it was possible for a European to travel right across the country. I had also placed a weapon in their hands against me. I should not be able to manage it a second time. Now they would keep their eyes open along the periphery of the inhabited country. I must travel in disguise to attract as little attention as possible.

Another courier was therefore sent to Leh to procure me a complete Ladaki costume in Mohammedan fashion. Gulam Razul also was of opinion that, considering all circumstances, it would be wisest to travel as a merchant. The new caravan leader was to be our master, while I myself should figure as "the least of his servants," and keep myself out of sight in all negotiations.

The whole affair was a desperate game, a political and diplomatic game of chess, the stakes being my own life or great geographical discoveries. I, who had hitherto stood on the most friendly and confidential terms with the Tibetans, must now avoid them as enemies. I should not be able to see any Tibetan face to face, and should have to conceal my own eyes in order not to be caught. Therefore a large pair of round goggles with dark glasses was bought; inside them I fastened polished glasses of the strength suited to my sight. My European outfit was restricted as much as was at all possible; the large camera and the boat were sent to Leh with my other baggage, and I took with me only a small Richard's camera.

The main point was that in inhabited districts I should conduct myself with Oriental self-control and be entirely passive. The outcome of this mad plan was to me enshrouded in impenetrable darkness. I only knew that I must go northwards from Drugub in the direction of the Karakorum pass, then turn to the east and south-east, and endeavour to cross from Lemchung-tso the blank space lying to the south of Bower's route in 1891, and thence continue my journey through the great blank patch on the north of the upper Tsangpo. If I were successful, I would go south to India either through Nepal or through Gyangtse, where perhaps I might have an opportunity of meeting Major O'Connor, as I had always wished to do. Gulam Razul advised me to be very cautious, for the Rudok-dzong had a paid spy in Drugub, who had to report on the movements of Europeans on the English side of the frontier. This spy was one of the most dangerous reefs in my fairway; the suspicion of the Tibetans was at once roused when they found that I had bought twenty mules from Gulam Razul. The Garpun sent a messenger to find out what I wanted them for. He was told that they were for a journey to Khotan.

Thakur Jai Chand had an excellent *jamadar* whom he sent to meet the baggage coming from India. At length, in the beginning of November, we received news that the consignment was coming. Then Robert proposed to go to meet our wished-for guests with some of our new mules. Late on the evening of the 6th they all turned up when I was already in bed. They were five policemen from Rampur, one of them suffering from inflammation of the lungs and more dead than alive. When Robert met them they were so starved and exhausted that he had first to massage the whole party to put new life into them (Illust. 276).

I at once gave orders to light a roaring fire and serve tea. They came up with their laden mules, two Mohammedans, three Hindus—all in dark blue uniforms with tall blue-and-white turbans, rifles, and bayonets. I bade them welcome, thanked them for the excellent way in which they had performed their task, and made their corporal give me an account of their difficult and trying journey over the Ayi-la. Then they were shown to sleeping-places in a tent, and next day I looked through the nine chests sent to me by Colonel Dunlop Smith. Three of them contained 6000 rupees in silver, all of the Queen's reign, none of the King's, for the Tibetans will not take rupees on which King Edward's face is stamped. The other boxes contained tinned meat of all kinds, preserves, chocolate, cheese, cakes and biscuits; cigars, cigarettes and tobacco; gold and silver watches, and revolvers with ammunition, for presents; cartridges for two of our guns; note-books and map paper; a whole library of new novels, including Jack London's *The Call of the Wild*—a present from O'Connor and suitable reading for the adventurous time before us; an anemometer and a hydrometer, presents from the chief of the Central Meteorological Institute in Simla, Dr. Gilbert Walker; and a host of other necessary and acceptable articles. The amiable Colonel, his equally amiable sister, and his daughter, had had no end of trouble in selecting and purchasing the things, packing them up and transmitting them to Tibet. It was owing to their kindness that I was able for a long time to live like a prince, and I cannot be sufficiently grateful to them.

Now I had nothing more to wait for. The policemen were well paid, and I also bore the expense of their return journey and gave them winter clothing; took a hearty farewell of my sincere friend Gulam Razul, without whose help the new journey would have been impossible; thanked Thakur Jai Chand and the other Hindus for their kindness, and started off on November 9, 1907, north-westwards along the course of the upper Indus.

On the 26th we reached Tankse, where the dignitaries of the district and even the *tesildar* of Leh came to meet us. They had already heard that I intended to travel to Khotan in midwinter. The following day was to be a day of rest, for here I was to discharge all my old servants except Robert and the Gurkha, Rub Das. When I had breakfasted, Tsering carried out the plates and dishes, which now had many chips out of their enamel. "This is the last time, Tsering, that you will wait on me." Then the old man began to weep, and hurried out quickly.

Then I summoned all the men to my tent and made them a speech, telling them that they had served me faithfully and obediently, and had well earned the comfort and repose that awaited them by their domestic hearths in the bosom of their families. I wished them good fortune and prosperity in the future, and reminded them of the loss we had all sustained by the death of Muhamed Isa—good old Muhamed Isa, who, when we were last at Tankse, had made all arrangements so cleverly and conscientiously. And to show them that we were not the only ones who mourned for him, I read them what Younghusband, O'Connor, and Rawling had written to me about the deceased.

While their five horses and five yaks were being loaded with all their belongings, they came to me in my tent, one after another, to receive their pay and an extra present. Tsering, Rehim Ali, Shukkur Ali, and Tundup Sonam received especial gifts of money, the latter three

288. Robert in Winter Dress.

having exposed themselves to danger on my account. Old Tsering asked to be allowed to keep the lame dog from the Ngangtse-tso; its bark before his hut in Leh would remind him of the time when the dog kept watch at our camp-fires. Shukkur Ali kept another dog from the same country. Now I had only the brown puppy, which, with Robert and the mule from Poonch, were among the oldest veterans of the caravan, all three having accompanied me from Srinagar.

And then came the bitter moment of parting. So much grief, such loud weeping! They could hardly tear themselves away. The *tesildar* was quite overcome at witnessing the deep attachment of my simple followers. The bonds were strong that were now torn asunder, for there is nothing which knits men together so firmly as common sufferings and dangers. I myself felt a catch in my throat, and, as the men reluctantly followed their yaks down the road to Drugub, I stood and watched them until they were out of sight. Then I dried my eyes before going into my tent, where Robert and the *tesildar* were waiting for me with tea and cakes served up by Rub Das. I could not help thinking of a funeral repast after an interment, at which a wreath of violets had been laid on the grave of a departed friend.

Next morning I awoke to new surroundings. All my old companions were scattered to the four winds, and now they were gone all seemed empty and deserted. Robert read off the meteorological instruments as usual, and Rub Das laid my breakfast as noiselessly as an elf. I was glad that in spite of everything I felt not the slightest irresolution. The same angel who had protected me on my former journey would again attend my steps. I seemed to hear once more in the distance the rustle of his wings in the cold winter nights on the Chang-tang.

CHAPTER LV

A NEW CHAPTER

As soon as we were ready we mounted our horses and rode down to Drugub. Soon the old village came in sight with the house in which I had dwelt six years before, and the garden in which we had halted in the year 1906. On a terrace below the village stood our three tents and a fourth. The *jamadar* Ishe, old Hiraman, who never omitted to greet me, and young Anmar Ju, another of my old friends, salaamed and presented to me my new men. These three had orders from the *tesildar* to accompany me to Shyok.

"Who is the caravan bashi?" I asked.

"I am," answered a little wrinkled old man called Abdul Kerim, and wearing a large yellow skin-coat (Illust. 289).

"What are the names of the others?"

"Kutus, Gulam, Suen, Abdul Rasak, Sedik, Lobsang, Kunchuk, Gaffar, Abdullah, and Sonam Kunchuk."

"You are then eleven men altogether—three Lamaists and eight Mohammedans?"

"Yes, Sahib."

"I shall at some future time take down your names, ages, places of abode, the journeys you have made, the services you have been in, etc."

It turned out that very few of them had ever been in the service of a European, but all had been employed by Nazer Shah, and his son Gulam Razul answered for them. Four had been in Lhasa, and almost all the Mohammedans in Yarkand, and all seemed pleasant and cheerful, and were in the prime of life.

289. Abdul Kerim, the New Caravan Leader.

"Which of you is my cook?"

"I am," answered Gulam, a comical little fellow, who immediately received a lecture from Rub Das how I was to be attended on (Illust. 291).

"Are you all Ladakis?"

"Yes, Sahib, all except Lobsang, who is a Tibetan from Gar-gunsa, but has married in Leh and has served with the Hajji Nazer Shah."

I was somewhat loath to take a Tibetan with me on a journey where it was essential to keep the Tibetans as long as possible in the dark. If danger threatened, how easily he could betray me to his countrymen! I considered whether I would not exchange him for another man, or simply leave him behind. But how often had I reason subsequently to rejoice that I had not given effect to the suggestion! With the exception of the four Russian cossacks and Robert, Lobsang was the best servant who ever accompanied me on my journeys through the wilds of Asia. He was a splendid man, and I cherish a warm recollection of him (Illust. 290).

All were now welcomed into my service, and I expressed the hope that they would perform their duty as faithfully as their predecessors, promised them an extra donation of 50 rupees each if I were contented with them, and told them that I would pay the expenses of their return home from the point where our journey ended, just as I had done before. When it was known in Leh that I wanted fresh servants for the journey to Khotan, Guffaru and all the men I had sent home from Tokchen presented themselves and begged earnestly to be restored to my service. But the old Hajji had received strict directions from his son. Not one of my old servants might accompany me this time, for it would increase the danger if we met Tibetans with whom we were already acquainted.

The new horses seemed fine and strong, and stood, eating hay and barley, in a long row along a wall, beside the mules and the veterans from Leh. They were to be well fed, for the days of feasting would soon be over, and it would be well if they put on flesh, on which they could fall back in evil days. All the goods ordered were of the best quality, and packed in new strong boxes covered with leather (Illust. 287).

On the morning of November 29, 1907, three Tibetans came from Rudok-dzong and set up their tents on our left wing. There, I thought, now espionage is beginning. An hour later we heard the sound of bells up in the valley. The noise became louder and louder between the cliffs, and a great din was raised as thirty-four fine little mules with loads of salt passed by my tent. All had a chain of small bells round their necks, most of them were adorned with red and blue ribands, and some had large red tassels hanging at their chests, which almost touched the ground and swung about at every step. It was a bright and lively scene, and the jingle of bells allured me out to fresh adventures in distant regions. In the twinkling of an eye the animals were relieved of their loads and driven up the valley like a herd of wild asses, to graze on the scanty grass among the granite. The owners must then be traders. They afterwards came into my tent, took tea and cigarettes, and asked Abdul Kerim whither we were travelling. He answered without lying, "To Khotan." It was I who lied. But had I told the truth, I should have been stopped in fourteen days, and might as well have gone home at once.

We had three new tents. The two larger accommodated my eleven servants; the smallest, which was so small that one could only stand upright under the ridge-pole, and could only hold a bed and two boxes, was mine. I wished to have one as small as possible that it might more easily be kept warm. All my baggage was re-packed. I gave some superfluous articles to Robert and to the Rev. Mr. Peter in Leh. There was a very thorough sorting out, and only what was absolutely indispensable was packed, filling two boxes, one of which chiefly contained Swedish and English books, sent by my sister Alma and Colonel Dunlop Smith. As soon as they were read, they would be offered to the winds. When I moved at night into my new tent and laid myself to rest in the large sleeping-bag lined with sheep's wool, and covered myself, I was as warm and comfortable as in a bed at home.

290

291

292

290. Lobsang; 291. Gulam; 292. Kutus—my Last Trusty Followers.

Gulam Razul's son, Abdul Hai, visited me, and our business matters were transacted with him. Robert remained responsible for my heavy baggage until he had deposited it in the house of the Hajji Nazer Shah. It consisted of ten regulation horse-loads. In my leisure hours I wrote a heap of letters, which Robert was to hand in at the post-office in Leh.

We had now 21 mules and 19 horses, the brown puppy, and a large yellow dog from Gartok. All the mules and horses, except mine and Abdul Kerim's saddle-horses, carried loads (Illusts. 296, 297, 298). I rode my little white Ladaki, which had grown marvellously strong again, and was as spirited as one of the new horses. He and two others were the survivors of the large caravan which had, on the former occasion, set out from Leh. In order to make sure that Abdul Kerim took sufficient provender, I told him he must not think that I would follow the direct road like ordinary caravans. I might make excursions right and left, and often remain stationary for a week at a time. He must, therefore, provide barley for the animals for two-and-a-half months, and he must take care that the provender we took with us lasted out. But it is stupid to trust to others. All the heavy baggage from Simla, the silver money, and the tinned provisions made four loads; Gulam's chests of kitchen utensils, two; the tent, the bedding, and the belongings of the men made several loads; all the other animals were to be laden with rice, barley, and *tsamba*. We also took 25 sheep from Tankse.

In the night of December 3 the thermometer fell to −10.1°. Next morning all the baggage was packed up and carried down the valley to Shyok by coolies. Two fellows, as strong as bears, carried my two tent-boxes. The animals carried only their new saddles. One group after another marched off, and at last I remained alone. Then I shook hands with my faithful companion, Robert, thanked him for his invaluable services, his honesty, his courage, and his patience; asked him to greet for me the missionaries, Dr. Neve, and warm India; took leave also of honest Rub Das and all the others; mounted into my new Ladak saddle on my trusty white, and rode down to the Shyok valley with Anmar Ju. I was the last remaining of the original caravan, and was surrounded by men who were complete strangers to me. But I was also strange to them, and they had no suspicion of the foolhardy adventures I intended to lead them into. The wind, however, was the same, and the same stars would twinkle in the sky during the cold silent nights in Tibet. So I should not be quite alone.

It is little more than 6 miles to Shyok, and yet this short distance took almost eight hours. We had to cross the river six times, which just below the village of Drugub has cut a deep narrow passage between rocks of granite and gneiss. The first crossing was easy, for there the river had been frozen over in the night, and though the ice cracked, we passed over by a path strewn with sand. At the second passage the river was open, but broad and shallow, and the ice belts on both sides had been strewn with sand. The third, where we had to cross over again to the right bank, was very awkward, because ice belts suddenly ending in the middle were flooded in consequence of a damming up of the ice lower down. They could not therefore be strewn with sand, and we had to be careful lest we should fall out of the saddle when the horses set their feet down in the water 3 feet deep. It is little more agreeable when he jumps up on the opposite edge, and his hoofs slide about before he can get a firm foothold on the smooth ice.

Below this place was the fourth crossing—the worst of all—and here the whole train had come to a halt. On the right bank, where we stood, the river was broad and deep, with icy cold, dark-blue, transparent water winding down, but at the left bank lay a broad belt of ice. Suen, a tall, black-bearded man with very Jewish features, bared his body and examined the ford on horseback. In so doing he got into water so deep that his horse began to swim. Then he jumped in himself and swam to the edge of the ice, where it cost him great effort to climb up. Poor man! I shivered as I looked at him; he had been quite under water.

293. BEGGARS.

294. ABDUL KERIM'S NEW TENT.

Four of the others made an attempt a little higher up, and got over, but they were up to their necks in water. Then the whole troop of mules and horses were driven into the river; the horses managed best. One mule, I felt sure, would be lost. He made no attempt to hoist himself on to the ice until he had been pelted with stones from our bank. And when at length he was up and was following the track of the others, the ice cracked and gave way under him, and there he lay enclosed. All five men had to pull him out and drag him over the ice to solid ground.

Barely 100 yards farther down is the fifth ford. Between the two stands a steep, smooth, projecting rock, its foot washed by the river. It is, however, possible to climb over the rock up small fissures and over slight projections and thus avoid the two detestable fords. Here all the baggage was carried over by the coolies, and I myself climbed over the rocks barefooted; a short way beyond this crag a strong man carried me over smooth flooded ice. Here we had plenty of time for meditation, while the animals were again driven through such deep water that they almost had to swim. All were wet up to the root of the tail and many had water over their backs. The poor creatures stood together closely in a group, with pieces of ice hanging from their flanks and knocking together like castanets. We kindled a fire that the five men who had been in the water might undress, dry themselves, and change every stitch of clothing.

Then we went some distance downstream to a place where the heavy provisions were piled up on the bank, and the poor animals had to enter the icy water before they had got warm again. Here the baggage had to be carried over the river by stark-naked men, who tried with staves in their hands to keep their equilibrium among the treacherous rounded stones in the river bed. An elderly man was seized with cramp when he was half-way across, and could not move a step. Two bold youths jumped into the water and dragged him to land. Two mules, which could not be induced by coaxing or scolding to enter the water, were tugged over with a rope. I had a guide before my horse, which was wet half-way up the saddle, so that I had to tuck up my legs as high as possible, and in this position it was very difficult to keep my balance, as the horse made unexpected jumps among the blocks. The men raised such a loud hurrah that the mountains rang again when I was over the last ford with a whole skin; a blazing fire prevented any ill effects from my foot-bath. Every man, who came across shivering, dripping, and blue with cold, had to sit down immediately by the fire. I could not understand why they were not frozen to death.

Then we rode in the twilight up and down hill, and it was pitch dark before a welcome blazing fire showed us that we were near the village of Shyok. We gathered round it as we came up, and delighted in its radiating heat. I could not help consoling myself with the thought that, if any pursuers followed me up from the English side, they would at any rate get a cold bath before they found me.

In the night the temperature fell to only 15.4°, but here we were at a height of only 12,365 feet. We stayed on December 5 in Shyok, to dry the pack-saddles and give the animals a day's rest after their trying work. In the evening the men held a farewell festival, for Shyok was the last village in Ladak. As soon as the drums and flutes were heard, all the women and girls of the country flocked to the dance.

On December 6 we took leave of our last friends, and marched down the slopes to the floor of the Shyok valley, where the altitude is 12,300 feet; it was the lowest spot we were in for a long time (Illust. 300.) For from here we mounted northwards up the valley excavated by the great affluent of the Indus. There is no road or path to speak of, only rubbish and rounded boulders, but the scenery is wonderfully fine, and gigantic granite crags tower up on all sides. We crossed the river five times, which here carries about 420 cubic feet of water and has belts of ice of varying breadth. A solitary starved wanderer from Yarkand met us, and was given a meal of *tsamba*. We pitched our camp among the bushes in a bed of sand at Chong-yangal, where I had stayed in the year 1902.

We were now alone. Only one man not belonging to the caravan was still with us, Tubges of Shyok, who had charge of our sheep during the early days of our journey, especially at the fords. In the evening I had a conversation with Abdul Kerim, Kutus, and Gulam. I now told them that I would not travel to Khotan by the ordinary road, because I knew it already. We would strike more to the east, and the sooner we came up on to the plateau the better. They replied that Tubges knew the country well. He was called in to the consultation. What if we went through the Chang-chenmo valley to Pamzal and the Lanak-la? "No," he answered, "that is impossible; one can go as far as Oro-rotse, but there the valley becomes as narrow as a corridor, and ice cascades and boulders cover the bottom of the valley. Animals cannot get through even without loads." It was then evident that we must continue up the Shyok valley and watch for an opportunity of diverging eastwards.

So on the 7th we went on between grand mountain gables, silent and solemn, like Egyptian pyramids, like cathedrals and fortress towers. Between them detritus cones descend to the valley floor, where their bases are eroded by the high water of the summer flood and cut off in perpendicular walls. It must be a magnificent spectacle when the turbid thundering water rolls down from the melting snow of the Karakorum and fills all the valley, making its way with tremendous force to the Indus. An enormous block of perhaps 70,000 cubic feet has fallen down; it has cracked in falling, as though a giant had split it with his axe; one fancies one can see the gap it has left on the heights above. Four times the path crosses the stream, and the rather narrow opening of the Chang-chenmo valley is left on the right. We encamped among the dunes of Kaptar-khane. In the night the temperature fell to 2.5°.

The way is terribly trying, nothing but detritus and blocks of grey granite, against which the horses wear out their shoes. Again we crossed the river twice and set up our tents in the oasis Dung-yeilak, where a worn-out caravan from Khotan had already settled, and had sent a messenger to Nubra for help, as several of their horses had foundered.

As long as there was pasturage we could take matters quietly and make short marches. Only too soon the grass would come to an end, and then we must make more haste. So we rested a day when the merchant Muhamed Rehim from Khotan arrived at the oasis with his caravan. But he only remained an hour, for he wanted to reach warmer regions, and was glad to have the Karakorum pass behind him. He earnestly advised me to wait till spring, for the snow lay deeper than usual on the pass. One of his caravan men also came to me and gave me a handful of dried peaches. "Does the Sahib remember me?" he asked. "Certainly, you are Mollah Shah." The good fellow, now fifty-seven years old, and with his beard greyer, had never visited his home in Cherchen again since he had left my service in the spring of 1902. What a singular wandering life, full of toil and adventure, these Asiatics lead! He implored me to engage him again, but I told him he ought to be glad to go down into Ladak instead of returning to the frightful pass in the middle of the icy winter. It would certainly have been pleasant to have with me an old tried companion. But no, he would have been out of place in my Ladaki company. Mollah Shah told us for our encouragement that a large caravan had lost fifty-two horses on the pass, and had been obliged to leave behind the greater part of their goods.

None of my people knew yet my actual plans. As long as we were on the great winter route to Eastern Turkestan they must all believe that Khotan was my destination. We had also the advantage that all who met us would report in Ladak that they had seen us on the great highway, and thus no suspicion would be aroused.

December 10. It was colder, the minimum temperature being -2.4°. My Curzon hat was burned in the fire. In its place I put on a large skin-cap which Muhamed Isa had sewed together, and wound round it a pugree as a protection against the sun. Arms of the river with a gentle current were covered with glittering ice, but the main stream, now much smaller, was nearly free. At the camp at Charvak a spring brook dashed down the rocks in a tinkling cascade, though the cold did all it could to silence

 298

 296

 297

295. My Brown Puppy with my Cook, Tsering.
296, 297, 298. My White Ladaki Horse.

it. The animals were driven up the slopes where the grass was better. A huge fire was lighted when the day declined, and a narrow sickle of a moon stood in the sky. Where the animals were driven up, there was a thundering fall of stones in the night, and some blocks rolled down and lay among our tents. It was a dangerous place.

We had a cold march on the way to Yulgunluk. When thick snow-clouds cover the sky, the wind blows in the traveller's face, and the temperature at one o'clock is 14.9°, one feels the cold dreadfully, and has to tie a thick neck-cloth over the face. The valley is lifeless and deserted. Hitherto we had only seen a hare, an eagle, and a raven; the last followed us from camp to camp. Six times we crossed the stream; the brown puppy was carried over, but the yellow dog found his way across—he howled piteously whenever he had to go into the cold water.

In Yulgunluk also, at a height of 13,455 feet, we encamped a day. Now the thermometer fell in the night to −6.2°. This was the last really pleasant and agreeable oasis we came across. During the day of rest we heard the horses neighing with satisfaction on the pastures and the sheep bleating. The loads of provender were already smaller, so we could load four horses with good knotty firewood. On the right side of the valley rose a snowy mountain. As early as two o'clock the sun disappeared, but it lighted up the snow long after the valley lay in deep shadow; the sky was blue and cloudless. In the evening the men sang at the fire just the same melodies as their predecessors. The winter days are short, but they seem endlessly long to one tortured by the uncertainty of his cherished hopes. By eight o'clock the camp is quiet, and at nine Gulam brings in the last brazier after I have read the meteorological instruments. How I long to get out of this confined valley on to the plateau country! Here we are marching north-north-west, and I ought to be going east and south-east. If we could find a way up to the Chang-tang by one of the valleys to the east, we should be saved much time and many a weary step.

On December 13 we looked in vain for such a way. We crossed the river twice more on its ice-sheet. At the second ford the whole caravan passed over dry-shod, and only my small white horse broke through and I wet my feet. After a third crossing we camped in a desolate spot just opposite the Shialung valley. It looked promising. Tubges and Kutus were sent up the valley to spy out the land. In the evening they returned with the tidings that we could go a fairly long distance up the valley, but beyond it became impassable owing to deep basins, abundant ice, and large boulders, just as in the Drugub river. We must therefore keep on the route to the Karakorum pass. This increased the risks for the caravan, for it lengthened the distance; but, on the other hand, it lessened the danger of discovery, for when once we had got into Tibet we could avoid the most northern nomads.

Now Tubges begged permission to accompany me to the end, and his petition was eagerly supported by all the other men. I was the more willing to take him that he was a skilled hunter. I had now twelve men, and I made the thirteenth in the caravan. But we were not superstitious.

CHAPTER LVI

UP TO THE HEIGHTS OF DAPSANG

HEAVY clouds and piercingly cold wind increased the difficulty of our march on December 14 up the valley. We saw two bales of goods, sewed up in linen and with the stamp of a Turkestan firm, lying on the ground, as though they had fallen from a dying horse, the carcase of which we had passed. Higher up two more. They contained silken materials from Khotan. So far the caravans come with failing strength after excessive exertions on the pass. They are like ships which must throw their cargo overboard when they begin to sink. At Köteklik also we found passable grass and firewood. Gulam is a capital cook; he prepares me the most delicate cutlets and rissoles, and for a change gives me chickens and eggs.

On the 15th there is little water in the valley; it runs under rubbish, but farther up the river is again fresh and clear. We frequently pass the remains of unfortunate caravans—dead horses, bales of goods, and pack-saddles from which the hay has been removed to save the life of a dying horse. We travel west-north-westwards, and therefore ever farther from our goal. But at length we come to a valley which will lead us in the right direction. We leave the Sasser valley to the left and enter a valley portal full of treacherous ice, often as thin as skin. We wait till our scouts have tried the ice, which they declare to be impassable. Tubges, however, finds another, longer way, over steep hills, and at their foot we pitch our camp.

Next morning we went over a steep spur of porphyry

to reach a better place on the frozen river which was to afford us an easterly passage up to Murgu. We crossed again and again the strip of ice, which was first strewn with sand that the horses might not break their legs. As usual, two scouts went in advance. One of them came back and called to us from a distance that a fallen rock closed up the valley. On reaching the spot I found that a landslip had lately taken place. The blocks of porphyry barring the channel were as big as houses, and between them the river formed deep basins covered with a thin coat of ice. We had therefore to turn back and retrace our steps all the way down to camp No. 279, over the terrible rock, which on this side was so steep that each animal had to be shoved up separately, and the men had to look out for themselves when a pack got loose and rolled down the acclivity. Then we went some distance up the Sasser valley. A strong icy wind blew in our faces. Beside a wall of rock the dogs put up a hare which took refuge in a hole, but Kunchuk pulled him out again and he was condemned to be eaten. Our camp this time was in an almost barren place, and after all the fording of the river during the day icicles clinked on the flanks of our wearied animals.

It is evening again. The mountain spurs project, dark and rugged, into the valley like huge sarcophagi, and on them rest moon-lighted snowfields like shrouds. The Ladakis sing no more; their ditties are frozen on their lips. It is awfully quiet. The kitchen fire flickers with yellowish-red tongues in the white moonshine. One can almost hear the sound of the frost outside.

After Gulam has brought in the last brazier I undress myself, put on my large woollen dressing-gown, set myself a while right over the fire to get a little heat into my body before I creep into my lair of fur, and smile to hear the yellow dog, who is lying outside, and barks and snarls at the increasing cold in the angriest and most comical tones. No wonder he is enraged, for the thermometer falls in the night to $-12.8°$. Then I hear a singular squeaking in Gulam's tent. We had already anticipated a happy event, and now I inquired whether there was an addition to the

299. PANORAMA FROM CAMP 422, BONGBA.

300. PANORAMA FROM CAMP 277, SHYOK VALLEY.

Sketches by the Author.

Puppy family. Four small puppies had again come into the world. They had waited for the very coldest night we had yet experienced. Gulam had contrived a cage of frieze rugs in which Puppy lay, licking her young ones. Two of the tiny animals were of the female, two of the male sex; the former were drowned, for we thought that the others would grow stronger if they monopolized all the milk and heat that would otherwise have been divided among four. I sat by the hutch and studied the interesting group till I was so stiff with cold that I could hardly walk back to my tent. Next morning the tiny curs were going on splendidly; one of them whined in quite the orthodox fashion, and no doubt thought what a grim cold country fate had launched him into. We determined to take good care of them, for they would be pleasant companions for me. Up here they would at any rate be immune from the sickness which had carried off their elder sisters. Kunchuk had to carry them against his bare skin to keep them warm. Half-way Mamma Puppy was allowed to occupy herself for a while with her little ones, though these did not seem quite to understand the milk business.

We had a bad march on December 17. No shouts of encouragement were heard, but the caravan moved on slowly and apathetically. Within half an hour our feet were benumbed and lost all feeling. I wound the ends of my *bashlik* like a visor several times round my face up to the eyes, but the breath turned it into a thick crust of ice which froze to my moustache and beard, which I had allowed to grow since leaving Gartok to suit my intended Mohammedan disguise. All the men put on their furs. Dust and soil flew about, and our faces had a singular appearance.

At a place where a Yarkand caravan was encamped, we turned to the right up a very narrow valley, in which the floor, covered with bright milky-white ice, looked like a marble pavement between the rocky walls. Fortunately the Yarkand men had strewn sand over the ice, but still it did not prevent several of our animals from falling, so that they had to be loaded again.

When we at length camped in Long the temperature

was at zero even at three o'clock. A second large Yarkand caravan, on the homeward journey, was halting here. The leaders asked us to travel with them over the Karakorum, but I refused, with the excuse that we could make only short day's marches. Observation by any who might tell the Chinese in Yarkand that I had again passed over into Tibet was exactly what I must avoid above everything.

Here lay a poor man, both of whose feet had been frost-bitten on the Karakorum, so that the flesh and toes actually fell off. He crawled up to our camp and wept over his disastrous fate. He had been engaged with the Yarkand caravan we had met first, but as he had become incapable of work owing to his wounds, the barbarous merchant had dismissed him in the midst of the wilds and left him behind. In such a case it is hard to know what to do. We could not cure him, and to take him with us or give up a part of the caravan for him was out of the question. He said himself that he would crawl to Shyok, but how was he to get across the river? I let him warm himself at our fire, drink tea and eat, and on the 18th, when we went on after 56½° of frost in the night, I gave him *tsamba* for several days, matches, and a sum of money which would enable him to hire a horse from a caravan travelling to Shyok.

This day's march took us eastwards to a place called Bulak (the spring); it should properly have been called Guristan (the graveyard), for here lay at least twenty dead horses. During a ride of two hours I had counted sixty-three carcases of horses; it is wonderful that trade on this caravan route, the highest in the world, can be profitable.

From there the route ran up the narrow fissured Murgu valley, at first up and down over hills, where numbers of dead horses, which had once been strong and fat, showed us the way. Then we descended a break-neck path into the deep valley, where spring water at the bottom formed cracked domes of ice. Then on the slopes of the left flank we climbed again up a zigzag path; the snow became deeper and was piled up, especially on the path, so smooth that if the horses had made a false step we should have been lost beyond recovery. The landscape was magnificent, but it could not be properly enjoyed when the temperature about one o'clock was only 0.3°. And then again we went down headlong to the valley bottom, where we passed over a natural bridge of rock improved by the hand of man. Our direction had been east, but now we diverged more and more to the north and north-west.

The snow becomes deeper, the sun sinks, the shadows creep up the reddish-yellow hills, the wind is stronger, and one thinks: If this lasts much longer I shall freeze. At last we halt at the foot of a terrace on the right side of the valley, where the sheep are driven into a cave to keep them warm in the night. I slip down from the saddle with all my limbs numbed, and long for a fire. Not a trace of organic life was to be seen at camp No. 283. The horses and mules were tethered so that they stood in a close pack.

At this unlucky camp I made the first discovery on this new journey through Tibet. Abdul Kerim came to me at the fire and said:

"Sahib, we have barley for eight to ten days more; but in that time we shall reach Shahidulla, where we can get everything."

"Eight to ten days! Are you mad? Did you not obey my orders? Did I not tell you expressly to take barley for 2½ months?"

"I brought a supply with me which was enough for the journey to Khotan."

"Did I not tell you that I was not going to Khotan by the ordinary route, but by roundabout ways which would demand at least two months?"

"Yes, Sahib, I have acted wrongly," answered the old man, and began to sob. Abdul Kerim was an honest man, but he was stupid, and he had not the great experience of Muhamed Isa.

"You are caravan bashi, and the duty of a caravan leader is to see that there is sufficient provender for the journey. When the ten days are over, our animals will starve. What do you mean to do then?"

"Sahib, send me with some animals to Shahidulla. I can be back again in a fortnight."

"You know that everything that happens in Shahidulla is reported to the Amban of Khotan. The Chinese must know nothing of our intentions."

My first notion was to dismiss Abdul Kerim at once and to write to the Hajji Nazer Shah for more provender, which might be brought up on hired animals. But what would they think in western Tibet and Ladak if I sent for more provender from Leh when I was barely eight days' journey from Shahidulla, which lies on the direct road to Khotan? My whole plan would be betrayed and must fail. I should be stopped by the first nomads, perhaps by the English whom I had so happily escaped hitherto. It was only necessary to forbid the natives to supply me with provisions and baggage animals. And if I procured all we wanted in Shahidulla, the Amban of Khotan would send word to Kashgar, whence a telegraph line runs through Asia to Pekin, where His Excellency Na Tang proved so absolutely immovable when the Swedish Minister Wallenberg had given himself so much trouble to obtain for me permission for a new journey through Tibet. Up here in this desolate valley my position was strong. We had sneaked quietly and cautiously through British territory without exciting suspicion. But as soon as we came into contact with the outer world we should be caught.

I sat in my tent all the evening, considering the matter from all sides, and measured the distances on my map with compasses. We were about 100 miles from my camp No. 8 of the preceding year, where the grass was so good. So far we could travel without the least difficulty. But beyond we had 430 miles more, to the district on the Tong-tso. However, before we came there we must meet with nomads and grazing land. The horses, indeed, would be lost, but the Tibetan mules were, so Gulam Razul said, accustomed to shift for themselves, and they were not given barley. The first step was to reach the free open Chang-tang and get out of this frightful mousetrap, the Shyok valley, which was always taking us further north-north-west. Even if we had to sacrifice everything and creep on all fours to the nearest tent, I would not give in: I would not depart a hair's breadth from the original plan.

Night came with a clear sky, twinkling stars and sharp frost; by nine o'clock the temperature was down to −20.4°. The animals stood quietly crowded together to keep themselves warm. When I awoke occasionally I did not hear them, and they might have vanished. The minimum was reached at −31.2°. When I was awakened, Kutus had been out on the prowl into a broad valley, coming in from the east, and had found a road which, as far as he could see, was excellent. We had still two days' journey from camp No. 283 to the dreaded Karakorum pass, which I wished to avoid. If we ascended the side valley eastwards, we should soon arrive at the main crest of the Karakorum range and be spared two days' journey. I resolved to try it.

So we travelled on December 20 to the east-north-east over crunching snow. The valley looked very promising, especially as old horse tracks could be seen in some places. In the middle of the valley was the bed of a brook covered over with smooth, treacherous ice, but elsewhere there was nothing but detritus. After we had passed a hill thickly overgrown with *burtse* tufts, all vegetation ceased. At one o'clock the temperature was −5.8°. My beard was white with rime, my face-cloth turned into a mass of ice, and all the animals were white. For hours we slowly mounted upwards. In some places the valley was so contracted that it was only 2 yards broad. The best of the day was over when the caravan suddenly came to a halt. All was quiet in the front, and I waited with Kutus for whatever was to happen.

After a time came Abdul Kerim, much cast down, with the news that the valley was impassable at two places. I went to look. The first barrier of rocks might be forced, but the second was worse. We could certainly have dragged the baggage over the ice between and under the blocks, but there was no passage for the animals. Should we try to make a road along which the animals could be helped over the blocks by the united strength of the men? Yes; but first men must be sent up to find out whether there were more of such barriers to cross. When they came back with the news that the way was still worse above, I gave orders to pitch the camp, as the shades of evening were falling.

Good heavens, what a camp! Not a blade of grass, not a drop of water! Again we sat in a mousetrap between steep mountain walls, where, at any moment, devastating blocks might be detached from the sides by the frost. The horses scraped about in the snow looking for grass. During the night they roamed about, and stumbled over the tent ropes. The thermometer fell to – 30.6°. One puppy lost his way, got outside, and came of his own accord into my tent; fortunately for him I was awakened by his whining, and gave him shelter in my bed, where he was warm and comfortable.

A frosty morning! we must take care not to touch metal, for it burns like fire. A mule made his way into my tent and looked for something edible in my washing-basin. To his great astonishment it stuck to his nose, and he took it a few steps with him. The hungry animals had consumed two empty sacks and six ropes during the night, and played the mischief with one another's tails. In winter, life up here is a desperate struggle with the frost.

The orders for the day were to encamp in a place where there were stalks of *yapchan* and *burtse*, and remain there all the next day. I set out at a temperature of – 23.8° and found the camp all ready on the right side of the valley. The animals were immediately sent up the slopes, and there grazed with a good appetite on the dry frozen stalks. During the day of rest, pieces of ice were hewn out of the brook and melted in the two large kettles of the men. Horses and mules were then able to drink their fill.

In the night a most welcome change took place in the weather, the whole sky was overcast, and the thermometer fell only to 1°; it felt quite warm in the morning. Some mules had stampeded, but Lobsang found them after a diligent search. I set out with Kutus soon after the caravan. We had not gone far when we saw Muhamed Isa's white Shigatse horse lying frozen stiff in the snow.

He had been in a wretched state for some days, and the last hardships had been too much for him. Worn-out and emaciated he really needed a long, long rest.

After a while we passed the valley junction and the unlucky camp No. 283, and were again on the great caravan route, the road of dead horses. Four lay in a ravine quite close together, as though they did not wish to part even in death. A large dapple-grey showed no change, but another horse looked as if it were stuffed, and a third, with its outstretched legs, resembled an overturned gymnasium horse. Some were nearly covered with snow, and others had fallen in a curious cramped position, but most of them lay as though death had surprised them when they were composing themselves to rest after violent exertion. Nearly all were hollow: the hide was stretched over the backbone and ribs, and they looked intact from the back, but on the other side it could be seen that they were only empty, dry skeletons, hard as iron, which rattled when the yellow dog, who had nothing else to eat on the way, pulled them about. The dogs barked at the first carcases, but soon they became familiar with the sight of them. What sufferings and what desperate struggles for life these dreary mountains must have witnessed in the course of time! Lying awake at night one fancies one hears the sighs of worn-out pack animals and their laboured breathing as they patiently go towards their end, and sees an endless parade of veterans condemned to die who can endure no more in the service of cruel man. When the dogs bark outside in the silent night they seem to bark at ghosts and apparitions who try with hesitating steps to make their way out of the snowfields that hold them fast, and intervene between them and the juicy meadows of Ladak. If any road in the world deserves the name "Via dolorosa," it is the caravan road over the Karakorum pass connecting Eastern Turkestan with India. Like an enormous bridge of sighs it spans with its airy arches the highest mountain-land of Asia and of the world.

Higher and higher our slow train ascends the fissured valley where here and there small glacier tongues peep out between the steep crags. Frequently old camping-places are seen with ripped-up pack-saddles. Hurricanes from the south prevail here; fine red dust from weathered sandstone flies like clouds of blood through the valley and colours the snowfields red. The valley shrinks to a hollow way where a somewhat more sheltered spot bears the name "Daulet Bek ulldi" (where Daulet Bek died). Who was he? No one knows; but the name has remained. Probably an ordinary trader from Khotan or Yarkand, or a pilgrim who died on his wanderings, and therefore found the doors of paradise wide open. For over the Karakorum pass runs the main pilgrim route from Eastern Turkestan to Mecca.

The valley becomes ever smaller—a mere corridor between walls of red conglomerate. This is the Kizil-unkur, or the Red Hole, an appropriate name. Here the caravan has pitched its camp. Not a sign of organic life. The animals stand in a group, and the mules gnaw at the frozen dung of former visitors. From this hole the way rises up to the Dapsang plateau, where a snowstorm is now raging, and even in the valley flakes of snow dance and whirl in the air. In the twilight Tundup Sonam comes up with only twelve sheep; the others have been frozen to death on the way. Night falls threatening and awful on the everlasting snow. Everything up here is so dreary and cold (16,824 feet); there is nothing living far and wide, and yet the yellow dog fills the ravine with his barking.

The men set up the tents near together, and a very scanty fire burned among them, for we had to be economical with the firewood from Köteklik. The Mohammedans started a low charming song in rising and falling tones, and now and then a strong voice intoned a hollow "Allahu ekber." When Gulam came with the brazier I asked him what it meant, and he said that it was a *namas* or hymn of prayer to Allah, that the Most High might protect us in the morning from the snowstorm. For if a caravan is caught in a snowstorm on the heights of Dapsang it is lost.

I often heard this melodious hymn again in days of hardship, and it always affected me painfully. Not as the reproachful warning clang of church bells ringing for service, when I pass a church door without going in, but because the men sang the hymn only when they were out of spirits and considered our position desperate. It seemed as though they would remind me that defeat awaited me, and that this time I had aimed too high.

CHAPTER LVII

ON THE ROOF OF THE WORLD

ON Christmas Eve 1905 I had dined with Mr. and Mrs. Grant Duff in the hospitable English Embassy, and on another day supped with Count d'Apchier in the French Legation, and was invited to a reception by Count Rex in the German Embassy,—all in Teheran, now in such a disturbed state. The same day twelve months later I had still Muhamed Isa and Robert with me, and we were in inhabited country. Little I dreamt now that old Asia would demand still another Christmas Eve in my life, and that on December 24, 1908, I should sit at table amid a circle of pleasant and intelligent Japanese in distant Mukden, where a few years before the thunders of war had rolled above the graves of the Manchurian emperors. But this year, 1907, I was quite alone, and with twelve satellites on the way to my—Ukraine.

In the morning with a bright sun and calm weather the caravan marched slowly up towards the heights of Dapsang, while Kutus and I followed in the crunching snow. I had given Abdul Kerim orders to wait at the top. After I had read the instruments and found a height of 17,808 feet, I scoured the horizon with my field-glass—a confusion of snowy mountains. Only to the north-east a broad erosion furrow sloped gently down, and I chose that direction.

"Now we leave the Karakorum route and ride eastwards," I said; "follow my track; I will ride in front." The men stared in astonishment; they had looked forward to the gardens and vineyards of Khotan, and I offered them the granite and snowstorms of Chang-tang. They said nothing, however, but silently and patiently followed in my footsteps. It was not easy to lead the way, for the country was covered with deep snow. I directed Kutus, and he went before my horse to test the depth. The ground was quite level, but contained hollows where the snow lay 3 to 6 feet deep; and the crust was exceedingly treacherous, for sometimes it broke, and I was thrown out of the saddle, while the horse plunged and floundered like a dolphin, and was almost suffocated in the fine dry snow. We therefore turned back to try another direction.

Lobsang, who was always on the alert when we were in a critical situation, was already looking for a better way. But we must in any case cross the valley, and the men tramped out a furrow in the snow, through which the animals were led one at a time. The horses managed best, while the mules often fell and caused long delays. How far would this snow extend? It checked our progress and concealed any wretched pasture that might exist in some ravine. We crawled on like snails. I went on foot, and my skin coat felt as heavy as lead. But after several hours of hard toil we reached the terrace skirting the right side of the valley, where the snow was thinner and we made more progress.

Camp No. 287 was in the most desolate spot I can remember in all my travels, except the sandy sea of the Takla-makan desert. Behind us our trail wound through the white snow and in front all was snow. The animals were tethered close together, and they had a feed of corn in the evening.

After the day's work was over I lighted two candles —usually I had but one—and set up the portraits of my family on a box, as I had often done before on Christmas Eves in Asia. At half-past eight o'clock the moon rose gloriously over the mountains to the east-north-east, and at nine the thermometer had sunk to $-16.8°$. I could not get the temperature above $-4°$ in my tent, and my hands were so benumbed that I could not hold a book, but had to crawl into bed, which was the best thing to do—there one forgets Christmas with all its precious memories and its melancholy solitude.

The thermometer sank to $-37.5°$. A horse lay frozen hard in his place in the line; the others stood stupefied, with drooping heads, and great icicles on their noses. Christmas Eve brought us good weather. I almost longed for a snowstorm. We had no fear of pursuit, but if a Turkestan caravan now went down to Kizil-unkur, the men would see our trail in the snow and report that we were off to Tibet. A snowstorm would obliterate all traces.

Meanwhile we stumbled on eastwards through the snow. A spring supplied water where all the animals got a drink. We halted in a ravine with tufts of *yapchan* (17,087 feet). The animals made greedily for the dry hard stalks, which also provided us with a grand fire, and this evening it was warm and comfortable in my tent. I rejoiced to think that the days would again become longer, and subtracted the length of each day's march from the distance between us and the Tong-tso. Ah, would we were there! And there we should be only on the northern margin of the blank space. What an immensely long way we had to travel!

Next day we followed the same flat valley eastwards between mountains of moderate height, making use of a path worn down by Pantholops antelopes. The snow became less deep and was only occasionally troublesome, usually covered with a crust as dry as parchment. When we had encamped in a perfectly barren spot, I consulted with Abdul Kerim. Only two sacks of barley were left. I saw that he had been weeping, and therefore I restrained my wrath. The others, too, were astonished and doleful. I had not yet said anything to them, but they understood that there was no question of Khotan. The men had *tsamba* for nearly three months and rice for two. I therefore ordered that some should be given to the horses when the barley was finished, but enough should be left for the men to last two months. The others gathered outside the tent during the consultation. Lobsang was calm and unconcerned, and could be heard singing and whistling as he watched the animals. I took to him most, perhaps because he was a Tibetan; but I liked them all, for they were capital fellows. In the evening they sang hymns to Allah, knowing that our situation was exceedingly critical.

Next day we started early, and I rode at the head of the caravan. We all had severe headaches, but the height was enormous (17,644 feet). We had marched little more than a mile when we found sparse grass in a slight hollow on the northern slopes. That was a Christmas box. Here we pitched our camp. The animals ran up to the pasture with their loads on. How they ate! It was a pleasure to see them. Suen cut ridiculous capers between the tents. The men were in high spirits. I heard no more hymns to Allah, but the caravan bashi, who seemed to think he was in some degree responsible for the spiritual welfare of all the Mohammedans, usually read every evening at sunset one of the five daily prayers. Our supply of fuel was at an end, but Lobsang found a hard moss which burned for a long time and gave out plenty of heat. Now I perceived that when we should some time part, I should miss Lobsang most.

On December 28, leaden clouds lay over the earth, and therefore the cold was less severe. We continued our course eastwards, and marched slowly till we came to a spring, which at the orifice had a temperature of 33.6°. The water felt quite warm; it formed large cakes of ice in the flat valley, which looked from a distance like a lake. While the men set up the tents here, Puppy, as usual, took charge of her young ones in a folded piece of felt. One of them had a white spot on the forehead and was my especial favourite, for he never whined unnecessarily. To-day he had opened his eyes and given a short glance at the cold inhospitable world around him. However, before my tent was ready, he died quite suddenly, and was buried under some stones that the yellow dog might not eat him up. Mamma Puppy looked for him, but soon contented herself with the last of the four. We would do all we could to keep this little creature.

On the way to the next camping-place, No. 292, we still followed the same blessed valley which had afforded us such an excellent route since Christmas Eve. The minimum temperature had fallen to −21.8°, as though a cold wave were passing over the country. At one place some wild yaks had left their visiting cards, and the men collected a sack of dung. Evidently these animals come hither only in summer; the winter is too cold even for them. A mule died before we reached a spring surrounded by fair grazing. So far we had got on well, but had made little progress; on the past six days we had covered only 47 miles.

December 30. With a minimum of zero and a temperature at one o'clock of 3.2° the range between day and night is not great. But now the sky was covered with dense clouds; it snowed and became half dark; the men could not tell in which direction they were marching, and asked where the sun rose. We had the help of the longitudinal valley for another day's journey, and we followed it down to a junction of valleys where there was a huge sheet of ice. On the way I saw a flock of twenty-two wild sheep, which fled with great agility up a slope of detritus, bringing the stones rattling down.

In the evening I informed Abdul Kerim, Gulam, and Kutus that we were to advance into Tibet and steer our course past the Arport-tso to the upper Brahmaputra. And I told them that I should travel in disguise in order to escape notice. They were amazed, and asked if I should not expose my life to danger daily; but I calmed them, saying that all would go well if they only obeyed my orders implicitly. Our chief concern was to preserve our animals, for if the caravan were lost we should never get on. "Yes," answered the caravan bashi, "if we only find good pasture, so that the animals can rest and eat their fill, we can certainly hold out for two months, but they will not bear long marches."

Here we stood at a parting of the roads. Our valley opened into another, which came down from high mountains in the south, part of the Karakorum range. The united streams continued their course northwards, and could not be any other river but the upper course of the Karakash Darya; in its lower valley on the Khotan Darya I had many years before almost lost my life. Now the question was whether we should go up or down, and we decided to devote the last day of the year to finding out which was the better road, sending out Abdullah to reconnoitre south-eastwards, Tubges north-eastwards. As in any case we should have to cross the ice sheet, a path was sanded.

We packed the 6000 rupees Colonel Dunlop Smith had sent from India in two sacks, which were lighter than the wooden boxes, and these were to be used as firewood some time when all else failed. At every camp our baggage became lighter, as our provisions diminished, and I threw away one book after another after I had read them. I had received from home the numbers of a Swedish journal for half a year, and these were very useful in lighting our camp-fires. We had still nine sheep left, but the time was fast approaching when our meat supply would come to an end, for we could hardly reckon on finding game so soon.

New Year's Day 1908 was bright and sunny—a good omen as regarded the dark riddles this year concealed. The two scouts returned with the same report: that there were no obstacles in the way; and I let them discuss the question themselves, and decide which way was the best. They chose Abdullah's route, which led up the valley south-eastwards. The road here was excellent. At the mouth of the valley we found a couple of small round stone walls, which, however, might very well have been a hundred years old. The sight of a dead yak had an enlivening effect on us, contradictory as it may sound. Higher we mounted to where a lofty snow mountain with glaciers could be seen at the end of the valley. Then we stopped, and scouts were sent forwards. They declared that the way was impassable, and voted that Abdullah should be thrashed. But as such measures would have been of no use to us in our difficulty he got off with a good scolding. He admitted that he had not been so far up as we were now, yet on his return he had asked for, and been given, a bit of tobacco for his reconnoitring work. I told him that he had done a mean trick, and that he should never see the smoke of my tobacco again.

There was nothing to do but pitch our camp. A strong south-west wind blew, and fine snow was driven down from all the crests and summits. When the men went out to gather fuel they looked like Polar explorers. After all, New Year's Day had brought us no good luck, but, on the contrary, a retreat.

This was commenced early on the morning of January 2, and we passed again camp 293, and marched onwards over slopes of detritus on the eastern side of the ice sheet. At one spot spring water formed a little bubbling fountain in the midst of the ice. After the valley had turned to the east-north-east we encamped in a corner where driftsand was piled up into hillocks.

I wanted to get out of this labyrinth of mountains and valleys which pour their waters into Eastern Turkestan. We were still in the basin of the Karakash river, and must sooner or later cross a pass separating it from the salt lakes of the Chang-tang. On the 3rd we again mounted up one of the head valleys and camped in its upper part, while the country was enveloped in a furious snowstorm. It continued till late in the evening, and what was most remarkable was that the stars shone all the time though the snow was falling thickly. Before, there had been blue-black clouds above us without a snowflake. Extraordinary land!

Next day we rested. The animals had been without drink for a long time, fuel was abundant, ice was taken from the river bed and melted in pots.

In this region the mountains are less continuous, and form sharp peaks and pyramids of small relative height. It snowed all night, but the morning of January 5 was fine as we travelled eastwards along the route Kutus had investigated. It led up over snow-covered ground to a small pass (17,995 feet), on the other side of which another branch of the Karakash crossed our course. We must get out of this entanglement, which delayed our march and told on our strength. As long as the animals kept up we had nothing to complain of. I was glad of every day that brought us a little nearer to spring and out of the winter's cold. It penetrated through everything. My feet had no feeling in them. Gulam rubbed them and massaged me in the evening over the fire, but could not bring them to life. The ink was turned into a lump of ice and had to be thawed before the fire; when I wrote I had to bend over the brazier, and still the ink congealed in the pen and froze on the paper. Singularly enough I have still an unquenchable desire for ice-cold water and prefer it to warm tea, but the water we usually get is far from pleasant. It is generally Tubges who takes a spade and fills an empty sack with snow, and then melts it in a kettle. Gulam tries to persuade me to drink tea, and cannot understand how it is that I am not sick of water. It is no use being thirsty in the night: a cup of water standing near the brazier is frozen to the bottom in a quarter of an hour.

After a temperature of −28° and a stormy night, which drove the animals to seek shelter in the men's tent, we crossed the broad valley up to the next pass. We left a lofty snow-covered mountain to the south. At the foot of a hill a wild yak was musing. When he saw our dark train against the white snow he made straight towards us, but before long he took his way through the valley and dashed in wild flight to the north, followed by our two dogs. It was very encouraging to find something living in this God-forgotten wilderness; for now we had lost even the raven.

It was a steep and slow ascent up to the pass, which had a height of 18,005 feet. We were surprised to find that it was a snow limit, for east of the pass there was no snow at all. As we descended the other side along a broad, open, sandy valley we had to be careful that we did not find ourselves without water in the evening. Far to the south appeared an ice sheet, but it lay too far out of our course. We therefore filled two sacks with snow from the last drift, encamped where thin tufts afforded fuel, and sent five men with all the animals southwards to the ice in search of water and fodder.

The water question now became pressing, for apparently we could not count on snow much farther. And we could not dig for water, as before, for the ground was frozen into stone. We must therefore proceed cautiously. We had a great open wilderness in front of us; we must make our way from one point of support to another, and explore the routes in advance, lest we might come to a catastrophe. I therefore gave orders that, now that the loads were considerably smaller, a couple of our animals should carry snow or ice. At every camp we left an empty meat-tin. I think less of the time soon approaching when the excellent goods from Simla will come to an end than of the fact that the burdens of our animals are daily becoming lighter. The rock specimens I collect do not weigh much. Of course the provender has long given out, but where the pasturage is scanty or altogether absent, loaves of parched meal are kneaded together for the animals.

The men are to come back on the 7th, and we wait for them till mid-day. There, too, they come: the black group is plainly visible; they march and march, but come no nearer. Ah, it is only some black stones dancing in the mirage. A little later Suen reports that some of the animals have run away, and consequently we have to remain the whole day at this dismal camp.

How slowly the hours pass on a day like this! I am a prisoner in my own tent, for cold and wind keep me from work out of doors. As long as the sun is above the horizon I pass the time very comfortably, for I can see the mountains, these silent, dreary, lonely mountains, where men never wander, and I see the sandspouts whirling along before the wind. But when the sun sets, the long winter evening begins, and I hear only the howl of the storm without. Patience! Spring will come some time. Every day that passes we are a step farther from this horrible winter. Brown Puppy and her whelp keep me company, and I look upon them as comrades in misfortune. She has her mat in a corner of the tent, and takes her meals when I do. The whelp we call Black Puppy amuses me immensely. He has begun to take notice of the world and the life around him. When the big dogs bark outside the tent, he turns his head and gives a feeble growl. When his mother leaves him on the mat in the cold, he makes an attempt at a bark and seems to think it strange. He wanders about the tent, though he is still so unsteady on his legs that he constantly topples over. He has already conceived a highly salutary respect for the brazier, and sniffs and shakes his head when he chances to come too near it. Sometimes it happens that he misses his mother in the night, when there may be as many as 54 degrees of frost in the tent; but his complaining squeal awakens me, and I take him under the furs—an attention he is very fond of. One morning he wakened me by crawling of his own accord on to my pillow and trying to get into my bed. After that I felt no concern about his future; he must learn how to make his way in life, and that he was doing.

On the 8th we went over a small pass 17,569 feet high. A horse and a mule perished on the way. Camp 299 was pitched where the first pasture was found, in a valley on the other side (16,946 feet). There was no water, but we had four sacks of ice. Seven sheep were left, and the raven had also come again.

The aim of our next day's journey was to find water for the animals. My trusty white Ladaki horse, which I always rode, used to get my washing water every morning, and I used no soap that I might not spoil it for him. From a small rise in the ground we were able to enjoy the view I had so longed for—the great open plain we had crossed in the autumn of 1906. To the east-south-east I easily recognized the spur we passed then, and we could not be more than two days' march from the Aksai-chin lake. I had now followed for several days much the same route as Crosby, and at the lake I should cross my own route of 1906, after which we should go down towards the Arport-tso, and, as last year, intersect the paths of Bower, Deasy, Rawling, and Zugmeyer.

The whole country lay under a vault of dense clouds. After a march of only 3 miles we found a flowing spring of beautiful water (33°), where camp No. 300 (16,329 feet) was pitched. In the evening my servants sang bright and happy melodies again, and Suen performed his most ridiculous dances. We were again up on the roof of the world, and all dreary Tibet lay in front of us. Should we be able to cross it with our little caravan?

CHAPTER LVIII

FORTY DEGREES BELOW ZERO

WITH fresh blocks of ice in our sacks we set out on January 10 straight towards the projection at the foot of which camp 8 had been pitched, and where I knew that the grass was good. The great level barren plain stretched between us and the spot, and we had 15 miles to cover. The wind was boisterous, and we were frozen through in a minute. In the lee of the caravan, which went in advance, lay a cloud of dust like smoke. The yellow hue of the grass could be seen from a distance, and the sight so refreshed my men that they began to sing on the march. The animals understood that they were coming to good pasturage, and quickened their pace without any shouts from the men. The tents were set up in the same place as last year, and here I closed my long circuitous route through Tibet. It was with a melancholy feeling I saw this place again, where Muhamed Isa had raised his tall cairn. Now we had avoided all dangers from Rudok, and we minded little that England and Russia had promised each other not to let a European into Tibet for three years. The height here was 16,198 feet.

For several days I had spoken of this place with its good pasturage, and when we broke up our camp on the 11th I was able to promise my men a still better camp for the next night. They were astonished that I was so much at home in these dreary regions. The track of the great caravan of 1906 was blown away by the passage of many storms, but the Aksai-chin lake soon came into sight, its surface looking grey and dismal in the chilly

301. View from Camp 307.

302. The small salt Lake south of Camp 309. (Smudge in sky caused by the freezing of the colour.)

303. Horses going to drink at the lake near Camp 310. Abdul Kerim on the left.

304. Mountain north-east of Camp 310; the freshwater Lake in the foreground.

305. Storm Clouds over the snowy mountains south of Camp 312.

Water-colour Sketches by the Author.

weather. Six kiang spoors converged to the fine spring of fresh water near the shore, where we kindled our fires among the same stones as last time. Pasturage and fuel are abundant in the neighbourhood; it is a veritable oasis —the best camp we had had since Köteklik. But the storm still raged, and the salt waves rose high over the lake, cooled down to 20.7°, though there was no sign of ice. In the night it snowed hard again, and on the 12th, which was made a day of rest, the lake lay blue amidst a landscape of shining white.

When all goes well the Mohammedans read no prayers. Probably they think that when we can help ourselves it is unnecessary to disturb Allah.

We had to pay a horse as toll for the good pasturage. He lay frozen hard in the camp on the morning of the 13th, after a night temperature of −18.4°. The yellow dog remained beside him, and when he came late at night into the next camp, he was so fat and puffed up that it was evident he had stored up food for several days. Two ravens followed us with their hoarse croaking. Snow fell thickly and hid the view. A herd of antelopes disappeared like shadows in the mist. A sheep died on the way, and two more had to be killed, for they were worn-out; we had now only three left. The cold penetrated everywhere in the night, and the thermometer sank to −33°.

On January 14 we made south-eastwards over a plain of soft, tiring ground, which caused us the loss of a mule. The caravan moved very slowly forward and in close order; the animals marched more comfortably when they were together; those which would linger behind, overcome with fatigue, were driven forward by the Ladakis. At camp 304 the grass was poor, and two mules seemed to be near their end. The cold was fearfully sharp in the night. The thermometer fell to −39.6°, or to nearly 40 degrees below zero, and almost to the freezing-point of mercury. That was the lowest temperature I ever recorded in all my journeys in Asia.

But January 15 brought a fine morning and an Italian blue sky. Abdul Kerim and all the other Mohammedans waited on me, in a tragi-comical procession, with dried apricots and almonds, and a simultaneous cry of "Aid mubarek," or "A blessed Festival." One of the festivals of Islam fell on this day. Exceedingly comical was the procession of the four Lamaists, who came up as the others retired; and Lobsang, who led them, took off his cap and scratched his head in Tibetan fashion, but did not put out his tongue—he had no doubt learned in Leh that this performance was not pleasing to a European. I gave them 10 rupees each and handed the caravan bashi a watch, which he was to wind up well every evening to be sure of the time.

On we marched again, moving slowly, for the ground rose. We proceeded like a funeral procession, and Suen was the parson. There was no longer reason to fear thirst, for half the country was covered with snow. But every mile caused us a struggle, and it was long before we came to the cliff we were making for. We left a huge snowy massive on the right hand.

Next day's march took us over a flat saddle to a small side valley where there was some grass. The temperature had been down to $-29.9°$, and I could not by any means get life into my feet. Sometimes they ached, sometimes there was an uncomfortable pricking in my toes, and then again they lost all feeling. During the day's rest we allowed ourselves in camp 306 Tubges shot an antelope and an Ovis Ammon, a feat which prolonged the lives of our last two sheep. In the evening the men were cheerful and hopeful as they sat around the flesh-pot.

Gulam Razul had presented me with six bottles of whisky, which, sewed up in thick felt, had been brought all the way; for Ladakis maintain that when a mule shows signs of exhaustion and weakness it can be cured by giving it whisky or other spirits. But the bottles were heavy, so three of them were emptied and set up as a memorial on some stones. Perhaps some time or other they may be found by another traveller. The other three were kept.

On the 18th we continued to follow the same longitudinal valley. All the ranges in this country run east and west, the usual direction in Tibet. To the right was a lofty range we must cross if we would travel south-eastwards. Through a gap in the northern mountains was visible to the north-east the mighty snowy dome we had passed to the right of in 1906. Eastwards there seemed to be no obstacle in the way, but we diverged south-eastwards up a valley. Before we encamped (Illust. 301) another mule had fallen, and then we had lost a fourth of the caravan.

Next day we proceeded further up the valley. Sometimes it was only 10 yards broad between solid horizontal terraces. Below a steep crag lay five pot-stones, and therefore Tibetan hunters must have come thus far. The Ladakis were delighted to meet with signs of human beings again. The valley opened out into an extensive plain, and a gap was seen to the south-east, but as the ground was lower towards the east we turned our steps in that direction. From the low threshold the view was anything but encouraging—a world of mountains. We resolved to encamp where we were (17,405 feet high) and to try the other, southern, passage next day.

A miserable camp! The storm raged so violently that the tents could hardly be set up, and the iron tent-pegs beat together and rattled until they were fixed. We had first to make a fire before we could use our numbed hands, and a small stone wall had to be raised to prevent the fire from being carried away. Now Nature and the elements were against us, whereas we might in the future expect opposition from man. The pasture was wretched, and a grey horse and the last mule from Poonch lay dead in the morning. It was the senior of the veterans, for it had come with me all the way from Srinagar and had done good service, and I was grieved at losing it. Now there was only one creature left which had seen the first beginning of the caravan, namely, our brown Puppy. She and the little puppy kept me company in this oppressive, weary solitude.

From camp 309, where we stayed a day, there was an uninterrupted view over another longitudinal valley, to the south of the former. There lay a contracted salt lake. At almost every camp, as on the former journey, I drew a panorama of the surroundings, and tried sometimes to paint small water-colour drawings (Illust. 302). Then I had to sit in the opening of the tent and hold the block over the fire to prevent the brush freezing into a lump of ice. But the sky, which should have been of an even blue or grey tone, usually turned into a film of ice with strange stars and crystals.

In camp 310 we also remained a day, for the pasture was better than we had found for a long time. The grass grew in sand on the shore of a small freshwater lake with a free opening, where at length the animals got a good drink after having had to quench their thirst with snow. We had travelled 188 miles since Christmas Eve, or about 6½ miles a day on an average—a terribly slow pace. Now we had had a furious storm for three days, and here yellow whirls of sand flew over the ice and the wind moaned and rustled through the grass. Abdul Kerim sewed together a long Mohammedan coat for me, which I was to wear under my fur when I assumed my disguise.

On January 24 the whole country was covered with dazzling snow and the sun shone, but a stormy blast drove the fine snow particles in streaks over the land, and a roaring sound was heard. Antelopes careered lightly over the ground, dark against the white snow. A mule died on the way; not even Tibetan mules can bear this climate. I was benumbed and half-dead with cold before I reached the camp.

After a temperature of $-21.3°$ the neighbourhood was enveloped in semi-darkness by heavy clouds. The jagged mountains to the south reminded me of a squadron of armoured vessels at gunnery practice in rainy weather. Their grey outlines peeped out from the low clouds. The valley was about 6 miles broad. Towards the east the snow lay less thickly, and finally only the footprints of wild animals were filled with snow, like a string of pearls in the dark ground.

As I turn over the leaves of my diary of this terrible journey how often I come across the remark that this was the hardest day we had hitherto experienced. And yet days were always coming when we suffered still more. So it was on January 26. The sky was covered with such

306. Camp 307.

307. Camp 333. The Beginning of a Storm.

308. Camp 335. Lemchung-tso, looking East.

309. Camp 401. Kanchung-gangri from the North.
In the foreground Lapchung-tso, the source of Chaktak- or Charta-tsangpo.

compact clouds that we might fancy we were riding under a prison vault. The storm raged with undiminished violence, and a quarter of an hour after I had mounted my horse I was benumbed and powerless. My hands ached, and I tried to thaw my right hand by breathing on it whenever I had to take a note, but after reading the compass for two seconds my hands lost all feeling. My feet troubled me less, for I had no feeling at all in them. I only hoped I should reach the camp before the blood froze in my veins (Illust. 305).

Then we come at length to the Arport-tso and leave the northern basin of the lake on our left, while a large basin swells out like a fjord towards the south. A mountain spur sends out a cape into the lake, which has a very irregular outline. It stands in our way. Shall we leave it on the right or left? We come up to the middle of the lake shore and wait while Lobsang goes to see if the caravan can travel over the ice. He hurries forward and makes us a sign to follow. We go down to the beach and along a spit which narrows down to a fine point.

Here the ice on our left hand has been piled up into hummocks, 6 feet high, of grand transparent green flat slabs, but on the right, as far as we can see over the southern basin, the ice spreads its level smooth sheet of a beautiful dark green colour like leaves of laurel and lilac. We feel the usual fascination of the ice, and stand and stare down into the dark cold depths. Drifting snow sweeps like comets' tails over the smooth course. We stand on the very point of the promontory, with the narrowest part of the Arport-tso in front of us, for the lake is contracted like a wasp's waist. Here there are fences, walls, and barriers raised by ice pressure, and between them snow is drifted up, hard and dry on the surface. It would have been quite impossible to march over the bare ice; the caravan would have been carried away like chaff before the wind. But the snow affords us an excellent path. Lobsang leads the way, guiding us in many a wind, but we get across and come to the farther shore at the foot of a cliff.

Worse followed, for the rocky point fell straight down to the lake on its eastern side, and here we had slippery ice swept clear of snow which we sanded. One horse or mule after another slipped and fell. Some of them made no attempt to get up again, but were dragged over the ice to firm ground, where their loads were put on again. Some fell with a heavy thud on the hard treacherous ice. We had to double a whole series of points in this way till we came to one where further progress was impossible, for at its foot issued forth springs which produced large openings in the ice. There icy cold waves beat with a sharp sound against the edges of the ice under the lash of the wind, which drove continually clouds of snow dancing like elves over the dark green field of ice. We had to struggle up over steep slopes till at last we reached, thoroughly tired out, an inlet where a few leaves of grass grew. We had left a mule on the ice, and two men went back and gave it a drop of whisky so that it could come on to the camp. But my brown horse from Shigatse, which had so often carried me up to the east gate of Tashi-lunpo, remained behind for good. It is sad and depressing when a veteran dies.

Arport-tso lies at a height of 17,382 feet. The water, which was drawn from an opening in the ice, was quite potable. There was a high pass in front of us to the south-east, but we could not reach it in one day, and we camped on the plain at the south-east of the lake where Rawling had once stayed. It was little more than a mile thither, but the grass was good and the animals needed nourishment. It snowed thickly all day. It was warm and comfortable under cover, and we pitied the poor animals which were out grazing in the cold. The small puppy had grown so much that he could wander alone between the tents watching for an opportunity to steal meat. A sheep was slaughtered.

At night the cold was more severe again, and the thermometer sank to -30.3°. The sick mule sought shelter behind the men's tent, lay down at once, and gave vent to a piteous sound. I went out to look at it, and caused it to be put out of its misery.

On the morning of the 28th we found two horses dead on the grass. One was one of the veterans of Leh which Robert had ridden, and which also bore me to the springs

310. MY DYING PONY.
Sketched by the Author.

in the Sutlej bed. We had now only twenty-three animals left, and my small white Ladaki was the last of the veterans. Little I thought, as he carried me over the Chang-lung-yogma, that he would survive a hundred and fifty comrades. Every morning two long icicles hung down from his nostrils. He was taken great care of, and I always saved a piece of bread from my breakfast for him. I had a particular affection for him and for Brown Puppy. They had been with me so long, and had passed through so many adventures.

A loss of three animals in one day was serious for such a caravan as ours. How would it all end? We had still an immense distance before us. We struggled for three hours with halting steps up this terrible pass which had a height of 18,281 feet. We encamped in the shelter of a rock and killed the last worn-out sheep, and then had no live store of meat.

The temperature fell to $-24.5°$, and the first sound I heard in the morning of the 29th was the everlasting howl of the storm. We marched south-eastwards through snow a foot deep. "One of our worst days," it is styled in my diary. We cared about nothing except to get to our camp alive. I had a scarf wound several times over my face, but it was quickly turned into a sheet of ice, which cracked when I turned my head. I tried to smoke a cigarette, but it froze on to my lips. Two horses died on the way, and Abdul Kerim's horse took over the load of one of them, while the man himself went on foot like the others. I followed the track of the caravan with Kutus. Then we found Kunchuk Sonam and Suen unable to go further; they suffered from pains at the heart. I tried to cheer them up, and promised to give them medicine if they would follow slowly in the track of the caravan. Was it now the turn of the men after half the caravan had been lost? Quite overcome with fatigue they hobbled at twilight into camp.

Abdul Kerim came into my tent very cast down and asked if we should fall in with nomads within ten days, for otherwise he considered our condition desperate. In truth, I could give him no consolation, but could only tell him that we must go on as long as there was a single mule left, and then try to drag ourselves along to the nomads with as much food as we could carry. Now we thought no longer of pursuers behind, or of dangers before us, but only wished to preserve our lives and come to country where we could find means of subsistence. Behind us the snow obliterated our tracks, and the future awaited us with its impenetrable secrets.

CHAPTER LIX

IN THE SNOW

THE storm howled round us all night long, and our thin tent canvas fluttered in the blast. Gulam awaked me with the information, "It is nasty weather to-day; we can see nothing." Even the nearest mountains were hidden by the snow, and if I had not already taken a bearing along the valley in the direction south, 35° E., we could not have set out. This day, January 30, we had to keep together, for the driving snow obliterated the tracks immediately. We had two leaders, and I rode last along the trail, which at first was marked as a black winding line, but farther on, where the snow lay 2 feet deep, no ground or rubbish could be seen. A brown horse which carried no burden lay down and died in the snow. We could see the snow making ready its grave before it was cold. It vanished behind us in the dreadful solitude.

We move forwards at a very slow pace through the snowdrifts. The fury of the storm carries away the warning shouts from the lips of the guides and they do not reach our ears; we simply follow the trail. Lobsang goes first, and he often disappears in the dry loose snow and has to seek another direction. In the hollows the snow lies 3 feet deep, and we can take only one step at a time after the spades have cut us a ditch through the snow. One or other of the animals is always falling, and the removal of his load and readjusting it causes a block, for all must follow in the same furrow. All, men and animals, are half-dead with fatigue and labour for breath. The snow sweeps round us in suffocating wreaths; we turn our backs to the wind and lean forwards. Only the nearest mules are plainly visible, the fifth is indistinct, and those at the front are seen only as slight shadows amidst the universal whiteness. I cannot catch a glimpse of the guides. Thus the troop passes on a few steps till it comes to the next block, and when the mule immediately in front of me moves on again it is only to plunge into a hollow filled with snow, where two men wait to keep up its load. The direction is now east and the ground rises. A few such days and the caravan will be lost (Illust. 312).

At length we come to a low pass (18,268 feet high). Even at sea-level such a journey would be hard enough, but how much worse it is in a country which lies some hundreds of feet higher than Mont Blanc, and where there is nothing but granite. On the eastern side of the saddle the snow lay 3 feet deep in some places, and it seemed as though we should be stuck fast in the snowdrifts; and what had we to expect then? For the provender was coming to an end, and we must go on if we would find pasture. Now we went gently down, the snow became a little less deep, and we came to an expansion of the valley where there were stretches of ground swept bare by the blast. On the right appeared a slope where Abdul Karim thought he saw blades of grass sticking up out of the snow, and he asked permission to camp. It was difficult to set up the tents that evening. At dusk the two sick men came up, their faces blue and swollen.

A miserable camp! The storm increased to a hurricane, and nothing could be heard but its howling. When I looked out of my tent I could see nothing that was not white, and there was no difference between the ground, the mountains, and the sky—all being alike white. Not even the men's tent could be distinguished in the driving snow. The fine particles penetrated into the tent and covered everything with a white powder. It was impossible to look for fuel, and at three o'clock the temperature in the tent was 1.4°. I could see nothing living outside, and I might have been quite alone in this wilderness.

My trusty Gulam comes, however, at length with fire,

311. Lost beyond Recovery.

for Lobsang and Sedik have found some brushwood. Gulam says that Sonam Kunchuk is ready to lay himself down on the snow and die, but I advise him to take a good dose of quinine instead. Late at night the tones of the hymn to Allah reach my ears, sounding softer and sadder than usual amid the raging of the storm. We are moving towards a dark destiny, I have attempted too much, and any moment the catastrophe may come. We are snowed up here, the animals must die of starvation and I myself—well, it is but a question of time.

A little below the camp the valley made a turn to the right. Thither the animals had gone at night, but came back as there was no grazing. A grey mule had stayed behind to die. It lay in a curious position, as though it had died in the act of getting up—on its knees with its nose pressed against the ground, and was frozen hard in this position. Yet the temperature fell only to $-16.4°$.

The storm continued with undiminished violence on January 31. We loaded the nineteen mules and horses and marched down the valley at random in the same dense snow. The snow came down in incredible quantities; such a snowstorm I had never witnessed even on the Pamir. We could not travel more than $2\frac{3}{4}$ miles, and then we halted and pitched the tents, which looked dirty against the pure snow. Four big wild yaks were moving over the slopes, tramping like snow-ploughs. The dogs made after them, but soon gave up the chase, for they could not go far in the drifts. The animals received their allowance of rice, and then trailed off to a hill where they poked about for the scanty grass.

I examined all the baggage with the help of Abdul Kerim and Gulam, and discarded all that could be spared. Unnecessary clothing and worn-out boots were burned, and reserve garments were brought out. My articles, note-books, and instruments were stuffed into two small sacks. Writing materials and other things for daily use were packed in a small handbag from Stockholm. The other chests were used as firewood, when the men had stripped off the leather coverings to make new shoe-soles. Even the box for the cooking utensils and the provision boxes were burned, and all the baggage was henceforth carried in sacks. By this means the loads were made lighter and more convenient, though there was more trouble in turning everything out of a sack when anything was wanted from the bottom.

In the afternoon there was a short break in the snowstorm. Beyond the white limits of the valley was seen to the south-east the large lake Shemen-tso, with a dark purple sky above it, presaging more snow. I took bearings of the next day's route, and it was well I did so, for soon the snow began to fall again unusually thickly. It snowed all day and all night, and a swishing sound was heard as the snowflakes were driven by the wind against the canvas of the tent and from time to time slipped down. In the morning of February 1 piles of snow lay round the tents. The minimum temperature was only $-0.8°$, and it felt quite pleasant. We loaded our weary hungry pack animals and marched slowly south-eastwards. The gale blew from the south, and the snow pelted on to our faces.

Silently and heavily the fainting troop moved on towards the lake. All the men's beards and moustaches were white with rime, and we seemed all to have turned grey in a night. Abdul Kerim walked in front with his staff, but he took a wrong direction, and I chose another leader. In some places we were nearly suffocated in the snow, and the crestfallen men stood in the drifts, at a loss what to do. But we plunged and floundered on a bit, and then stood still; then a little bit further. The pass over which we had made our way the previous day was no doubt blocked by snow. Had we reached it two days later we should never have forced a way over it. Now our retreat was cut off, and we must seek safety southwards. It was some consolation to know that we had burned our ships.

Fortunately the ground sloped down, and as we toiled on hour after hour the snow diminished and travelling became easier. But the storm, which had now raged for a fortnight, showed no signs of abatement. Down on the western flat by the lake the snow mantle was thin, and we

312. "If this continues a few days longer, we are lost."

encamped in a spot where the grass was not bad. I gave the men some cigarettes every evening—at other times they smoked yak-dung and filled their narghilés with tea-leaves.

The night was unusually mild, with the minimum temperature only 5.2°, but the clouds were as dense as ever and the snow fell unceasingly. It was dark all day, as though a curtain hung over the forbidden land. We stayed at camp 319. The storm blew from the south-west more wildly than usual. The animals grazed with their heads to leeward, and had to be driven windwards again every time they came to the edge of the restricted area of grass. On February 3, also, we remained where we were. All night long the hurricane had raged, tearing, raving, ploughing up the ground like a gigantic plough, and endeavouring to pull down our tents. In the evening I secured everything that could fly away if the tent were overthrown. In the morning all the animals had disappeared as though they had been carried away by the blast; at any rate, they had gone with the wind to the northern shore of the lake.

Immediately beyond our camp was a spring of fresh water and a round fold for sheep. I had ceased to look forward to spring, it seemed so hopelessly distant, and to be farther off every day that passed. Brown Puppy and Little Puppy kept me company as usual, and we played together to pass the hours of our imprisonment. Gulam continued to rub my feet, but with little result, for they remained numb and cold as ice. Then he brought two pairs of *paipaks* of thick felt and a pair of *charuks* or Yarkand boots of soft leather outside. They were really warmer than my Kashmir boots, which were ruthlessly burned.

CHAPTER LX

DEATH OF THE LAST VETERAN

STUDDED with twinkling stars the winter sky stretched its dark-blue canopy over our lonesome camp, and 50 degrees of frost foretold a clear day. On February 4 not a cloud hovered over the mountains, and this plateau, abandoned by gods and men, which had lately been buried under the white shroud of winter, was again illumined by bright sunlight. Sad news was brought me in the morning: a horse and a mule lay dead beside the tents. With the seventeen remaining animals we continued our journey along the irregular northern shore of the Shemen-tso (16,266 feet). The quantity of snow became less, and at camp 320 the gravelly ground was almost bare. The view over the lake was grand. Captain Rawling's map of this district is executed with great accuracy.

On February 5, also, we encamped on the shore of the great lake, having followed the curves of its bays and capes. A mule died on the way. Though we had burned all we could dispense with, yet the loads were much too heavy for the surviving animals. A big strong mule always led the van, at the heels of Gulam; it carried at least two ordinary loads, and yet was fat and fresh. There was no sign of human beings. A flock of jackdaws were perched on a crag. At the camp the provisions were inspected, and we decided to relinquish three heavy sacks of rice. The rice was to be given on the following days, mixed with parched meal and water, to the animals. Of my provisions, only two boxes of tinned meat, some jam and biscuits, were left. We had not tasted meat for some time. The storm raged all day and the sun had vanished again.

On February 6 we passed a very abundant spring of water at a temperature of 46.2°, which poured into the lake. There flocks of sheep had recently drunk, and rows of cairns ran from the shore to guide antelopes into the traps in the ground. Now no game was seen except a single kiang. A mule died, and Abdul Kerim's yellow horse fell by the way. Only fourteen animals reached the camp this day, and of these my small white Ladaki was in the worst plight; he stumbled and fell, and I made a somersault over his head.

The day after, we made a short journey, left the lake and its barren shore behind us, and set up our tents amid good grass. The weather was fine; at one o'clock the temperature was 14°, and it felt as though spring had come. All the animals lay down to rest and warm themselves in the sun. Only my small Ladaki began to graze immediately; he would not die, but would follow me to the end. Wild asses and antelopes grazed on the steppe, and hares were plentiful. I was alarmed by a message that three men could be seen at some distance to the north, and the caravan bashi wished me to come and examine them through my field-glass. Apparently they were on the way to our camp. But I had plenty of time to put on my disguise. I watched them a long time, till at last they turned into three wild yaks which had been lengthened out by mirage. We had no need yet to trouble ourselves about men, but perhaps these yaks were forerunners.

Now I had ridden my small white horse for the last time. On February 8, when we continued our march east-south-east after a minimum temperature of – 18.9° he followed the caravan loose and unladen, and fell even without a rider. I rode instead a grey horse from Tikze. We made barely 5 miles, but yet the journey was full of events. On the other side on a low hill stood a Pantholops antelope, which did not run away though we were quite close. We soon noticed that it was held fast and was struggling to get free. The dogs rushed at it, but a couple of men hurried on to keep them off. The animal was fast in a snare laid in an antelope track, where also we noticed fresh footprints of two men. We were evidently not far from winter hunters, who perhaps had already caught sight of us. Perhaps they had seen me, the only one riding in European dress. Perhaps it was too late to disguise myself. All my plans would then be spoiled, and all the labours of the winter lost.

But at any rate we had now fresh meat. Let us examine the ingenious trap in which the game is caught. Plates of rib bones of antelopes are firmly fixed in a ring of hard twisted vegetable fibres, which form a funnel with the points in a ditch. The antelope is enticed into the trap by a row of small cairns, and tramps about in the funnel, the plates giving way, but forming immovable impediments when he attempts to draw his hoofs out. But the snare must be held secure if it is to have the desired effect. A rope as thick as a finger is made fast in the bottom of the ditch, which is filled with water, and after freezing becomes as hard as stone. The free end of the rope forms a noose above the ring of fibres, which tightens when the animal first attempts to lift his leg and holds down the funnel of ribs. The more the poor animal jumps about, the faster is the hold of the twisted snare.

The victim was slain; the dogs ate their fill of the entrails, and the meat made ordinary loads for four men. Then we went on. At the mouth of a valley to the south were seen a sheepfold and two black specks we took for stones. Beyond a grass-grown mound we found a pool of fresh water, and we pitched the camp near it. It was not long before the Ladakis were sitting round a fire and roasting pieces of delicate, much-appreciated meat.

Now, when we were evidently in the neighbourhood of human beings, it was time for me to give directions to my people. All were summoned to my tent. I told them that we should succeed in crossing the forbidden land only by craftiness and cautiousness, and that I had made the great sacrifices which they had witnessed only to see regions where no Sahib had ever been. If our scheme were to be successful, every man must do his duty and play his part well. Whenever Tibetans put the usual questions, whence we came and whither we were going, they should answer that we were all, without exception, Ladakis, in the service of a merchant named Gulam Razul, who had sent us to Chang-tang to find out how much wool could be bought from the nomads next summer. Abdul Kerim was our leader and chief, and had to manage our affairs. He was therefore given 100 rupees for expenses, and every evening when no one could spy upon us he was to render an account to me. I myself was one of his servants, a Mohammedan named—Abdurrahman, the caravan bashi suggested—but no; Hajji Baba sounded better to me. Accordingly, when we came among Tibetans, they should never forget and call me Sahib, but only Hajji Baba. All understood the matter and promised to do their best.

A little later, Lobsang came running up and declared that the two black stones were tents. We went out and examined them through the field-glass. Quite true; smoke rose from one of them, but neither men nor animals were visible. I at once ordered Abdul Kerim, Abdul Rasak, and Kutus to go and pay for the antelope, buy anything they could, and obtain information. They soon came back again and asked if it would not be wiser to avoid the tents and march on eastwards, the more so that the inmates might be robbers. No; these men had seen us and might send a report to Rudok, and then we should be stopped. It was best, then, to enter into friendly relations with the men and lull them into security. "Bismillah," cried the three and took themselves off, while the others sat by the fire in lively conversation about the incidents of the day and the prospects of the future. It was now sixty-four days since we had left the last village in Ladak, while on the former journey we had been in solitude for eighty-one days.

After three hours my men returned. The two tents contained nine inmates—two grown-up men, two women, three girls, and two boys. The older man was named Purung Kungga, and he owned 150 sheep and 4 dogs, but no other animals. During their journey from Yildan their tents and goods were carried by sheep. They had arrived two months before, and intended to stay half a month more. The day before they had just been to look at their antelope trap, when they were alarmed at the sight of the caravan. They took it for granted that only robbers could be travelling in this district, which lay outside the haunts of honest and honourable men. The antelope had, then, been not more than an hour in the trap. Abdul Kerim paid 3 rupees for it, 3 for a sheep, and 1 for milk and butter. We could get more milk early in the morning, but we should have to send for it, for the nomads dared not come to our tents. We might have kept the antelope without compensation, for we were wayfarers and had a right to take what we found. In answer to their inquiry who we were, Abdul Kerim repeated the yarn he had just learned. The country about camp 324 is called Riochung. In one of the tents lay the hides and meat of nine antelopes. The people lived almost exclusively on the game they caught in their snares.

So far we had been fortunate. With provisions for twenty-one days instead of for seventy-five, we had struggled up to the Karakorum instead of finding a passage to the east; we had been persecuted by raging storms, biting cold, and deep snow all the way, and yet we had lighted on the first men. They were like a rock in the ocean, and now again we were to venture over the raging waves. This day found us only a few miles up a gently sloping valley filled with ice. Little Puppy was let loose and had to look after himself a bit. But he was soon tired, and lay down till Kunchuk fetched him.

February 10. The valley bottom is full of ice sheets, which we often cross after they have been strewn with sand. We wander through a labyrinth of clay hills. In an expansion to the left are seen three stone cabins and some *mani* heaps; here is the gold placer which Rawling calls Rungma-tok, and the hunters we saw yesterday Getsa-rung. The gold-diggers come hither only in summer. The camp to-day, No. 326, is in an excellent spot, with a sandy soil, plenty of fuel, and an unfrozen brook. It is pleasant to listen to the purling water, a sign of approaching spring. East and south-east rises a wreath of lofty mountains, which we have to surmount. As long as the ground is flat and there is grass the animals do very well, but they cannot endure a high pass. My white Ladaki has picked up again, and the men are ordered to tend him carefully.

February 11. We ascend the valley, and the snow becomes deeper again. In one place are seen fresh tracks of three men. We camp behind a cliff to get shelter from the wind, but first we have to cross the ice belt in the valley bottom, where a path has been recently sanded. It is evident that we shall soon fall in with men—perhaps on the march between the two camps. Therefore I put on my new Ladaki costume with a girdle round the waist. The white turban is kept ready at hand in case we meet Tibetans. The *chapkan* looks suspiciously clean, but Gulam undertakes to soil it with fat and soot. My soft leather vest is sacrificed and cut up for soles. After this camp Lobsang and Kutus were required to give me every evening lessons in Tibetan, and I arranged all the new words in a vocabulary, which afterwards grew to a considerable size. Thus we spent a couple of hours each day when all my literature was at an end. I especially practised the answers I was to give in case I, Hajji Baba, were subjected to cross-examination.

On the 12th we marched up through the snowdrifts in the valley, where small, graceful, elegant Goa antelopes were seen on two occasions. The camping-ground was so wretched that all the animals wandered back in the night to the former camp, and therefore the next day was lost, and we waited wearily. In my grey *chapkan* I am too conspicuous among the other ragamuffins, and whenever I have an opportunity I smear soot and butter on it and cut holes in it here and there. A continuation of such treatment will at length make it as disreputable as the others. I also try to leave off washing my face and hands, but do not succeed in looking as dirty as my men. With them the dirt seems to be engrained and never to be removed, and they could grow potatoes under their nails. My desire was to become like them as soon as possible, that I might escape the notice of the Tibetans.

February 14. Temperature -22.9°. Again we are a

few miles nearer our destination and a day nearer spring. Our progress is slow, but we must be glad that we can get along at all. Camp 329 is in the valley leading to the pass, which we have taken several days to reach. A mule is fatigued and is relieved of his load. Some grass is again found, and all the animals go out to graze, except my small Ladaki, which stands beside my tent with drooping head and icicles under his eyes. He has been weeping, knowing well that he will never be able to cross over the pass and that we shall leave him. I sit beside him for several hours, patting and stroking him, and trying to induce him to eat lumps of meal mixed with rice. He revives again and goes slowly after his comrades.

February 15. Temperature -22.5°. A hard, toilsome day. Through ice and snow among sharp detritus we march up the valley. My white horse leads the way of his own accord and I ride in the rear. We keep together for some time, and ascend step by step towards the troublesome pass. But first one and then another lags behind. Among them is my white horse. I stop and whisper in pure Swedish into his ear: "Do not lose courage; put out all your strength and climb the pass, and then you will go down in a few days to fine rich pasture." He raises his head, pricks up his ears, and gazes at me as I go on up to the pass with Kutus and Gulam. Only a couple of lively mules follow my horse and halt where he halts, at every twentieth step.

At last we came up to the flat pass, which attains to the considerable height of 18,553 feet. Here we waited a long time. The large black mule passed first over the snowy threshold of the pass and then the others, till nine baggage animals had gone by and my grey Tikze horse last. Abdul Kerim reported that four animals were thoroughly tired out. I ordered that they should be led step by step even till night if necessary, and he went down to them again. A little later appeared Tubges and Abdullah carrying two loads. One of the four animals had already departed this life.

To the west-north-west, the direction from which we had come, the view was magnificent—a sea of wild, red, gigantic undulations, with snow crowning the summits and streaming down their sides. During the last days we had noticed schists, porphyry, red and grey granite. The country was absolutely barren, and we must try to reach the nearest grass in the descending valley, but it was full of snow, and the train moved slowly and wearily through the drifts. I went on foot like the rest; every man carried a load to help the animals. All were silent, and tramped and balanced themselves in the track marked by the leader. The valley contracted to a ditch, and where the first yak-moss grew we threw down our burdens. A sorry camp in the close dismal valley. The last animals stood tied together, and were fed with pulverized yak-dung and moss mixed with meal and rice.

At dusk the other men came up leading a mule. Three animals were gone, and one of them was my small white Ladaki horse. He had struggled up to the very top of the pass, where I had sat watching for him in vain, and then had laid himself down to die. He had served me and carried me faithfully and patiently for a year and a half, and had never from the first been missing from the camping-ground, and now that the last of the veterans was gone I felt very lonely. During the whole journey he had never reached a higher spot than that whereon he died; on the very saddle of the pass his bones would be bleached by the winter storms and the summer sun. The caravan this evening was empty and forlorn, for I had lost a trusty friend. Now Brown Puppy was my consoler, for she had been with me from Srinagar, and her little whelp was the youngest and least anxious member of our struggling troop.

Two mules had crossed the pass but died in the valley. If another such pass lay in our way the caravan would perish. The loads were much too heavy for the surviving animals. A thorough weeding-out was necessary. My ulster and most of my European clothes were burned. Felt mats, tools, kitchen utensils, and spare shoes for the horses were thrown away. My small Swedish bag was burned, and all the medicines except the quinine jar were sacrificed; my European toilet necessaries, including my razors, went the same way, and only a piece of soap was kept. All European articles that were not absolutely indispensable were cast into the fire. I tore out of Fröding's poems the leaves I did not know by heart, and left the rest at the camp. The remaining matches were distributed among the men; I kept myself twenty-four boxes, which must suffice until the time when we must use only flint and steel to preserve our incognito.

Cold and sad the night spread its wings over the silent valley where our lonely camp, a picture of desolation, was buried among black cliffs and white snowdrifts, while the stars came out above like lights burning round a bier.

While the lightened loads were being placed on the animals I started on foot followed by two men. One of them, Kutus, walked beside me, and I steadied myself by his shoulder as we floundered through the drifts. The wind blew furiously, and the snow danced in spirals and appeared as white clouds on all the crags and ridges. After a march of about 3 miles we encamped when we came to grass. Snow had to be melted in pots, for the animals had been long without drink. This process did not take so long now that only eleven animals were left.

With tottering steps we continued to the east-south-east on the 17th and 18th, sometimes along valleys, sometimes over open country, and always through deep tiring snow. Camp 333 (Illust. 307) was barely made ready when a terrible storm burst over us. The sky had been clear, and then all of a sudden the pure blue colour was wiped out by orange clouds of dust which swept up from the south-west. I was sitting in the lee of my tent when in an instant the contents of the brazier were carried away. A heap of wild asses' dung which the men had collected also flew away, and we saw the small round balls dancing up the slopes as though they were racing. A herd of antelopes cantered past our camp, and their smooth coats shimmered like satin and velvet according as the hair was exposed to the wind and the light. Again our ears are filled with the din of the storm. I hurry inside, and hear from time to time a shout when some part of the men's tent threatens to give way or the sound of iron against iron when the tent-pegs have to be driven in again, or a singing dying-away sound when my towel is seized by the blast and borne away towards the foot of the mountains. We might be on an unsound vessel with the sails flapping and beating in cracking strips, and the mountain spurs, which still peep obscurely from the mist, might be dangerous and threatening reefs, against which we are to be dashed in a moment. Grand and majestic is such a storm when it sweeps over the earth in unbridled fury.

CHAPTER LXI

THIRTY DAYS OF STORM

On February 19 we had good country for travelling, declining gently to the shore of the Lemchung-tso, which appeared in the distance. I travelled mostly on foot, as I could easily do, for the storm had abated, but, as usual, we were chilled through by the wind, though the temperature rose to 28° at one o'clock. At the foot of some hills in the south we perceived numbers of black spots, which we took for tame yaks. They soon resolved themselves, however, into whole troops of antelopes, which sped in light springs over the plain northwards. Now were often seen signs of the summer visits of the Gertse nomads. We had left Deasy's and Rawling's routes a couple of days behind us, and now found ourselves on the western margin of one of the largest blank spaces in the map of Tibet.

After a grey horse had perished in the night we had only ten animals left, or a fourth of the original caravan. They were fed in the morning with meal and spent tea-leaves in water, which they swallowed with avidity. Our store of provisions would last out barely a month.

We were 6 or 7 miles from the shore of the lake, and on arriving there we encamped close to a cave in which a millstone and a couple of yak hides had been left in the summer. Along the shore ran a path worn by the feet of men. We stayed here a day and sorted out the baggage again. All spare instruments, such as thermometers, measuring tape, eye-glasses, etc., as well as some European garments, a couple of caps, bandages, portfolios, were sewed up, together with some stones, in a sack, and sunk in a hole in the ice, which covered the lake to a depth of nearly 3 feet. Now I had only three changes of underclothing left, one of which might be sacrificed at the next sorting out—we were like a balloon from which ballast is thrown out to keep it in the air till it has crossed a sea and has firm ground below it.

In the evening we hear a whole orchestra of roaring winds. The air hurls itself down like cascades from the mountains on to the camp, and cannot rush fast enough over the clear ice of the lake, where the moon produces bright silvery streaks on the surface, while the mountains show a dark outline to the north. Grazing and fuel are plentiful to-day, and therefore we are in high spirits. The men sing, sometimes softly like a swinging lullaby or rounded billows in a bay, sometimes in the wild and passionate style of Asiatics, and dance around the fire. But when the most violent gusts rush down, they pause, prepared to prevent the tent from falling over the fire. They seem to sing responses to the storm, and I am pleased with the performance, for it chases away thoughts of the long hours of solitude, and calls forth pleasant dreams and hopes of spring, warm winds, discoveries and adventures in Tibet. I wonder daily how this journey will end, but every day I am a step nearer to the answer.

On February 22 we left the little fresh-water lake on our left hand, while the Lemchung-tso proper extended its partly frozen surface to the right. In the middle the water was quite open and of a dark-green colour, and was lashed into vapour by the storm. To the east-south-east the country seemed favourable—an open plain, where no obstacle came in our way. In front of us were two grazing animals—perhaps yaks or wild asses. Gulam, who went in front, held up a field-glass and reported that they were horses. So we were near nomads again. We searched about in every direction but could perceive no tent. Had, perchance, the horses strayed away? However, they were not shy, but became very sprightly when they caught sight of us, galloped straight to the caravan, and greeted every horse and mule individually. After this civility they followed us all the way, prancing and neighing.

They were three-year-old colts which had never carried a saddle or a load—fat, fresh, and nimble-footed, very different from our last three horses. When we encamped they went off to the south and were lost to sight. The storm increased in violence, and our last iron spade and a kettle were carried away by the wind, but were afterwards recovered.

February 23. The thermometer sank to − 19.8°. Our last ten animals made a short day's march along the same easy valley. I could perceive no trace of the "Snowy Range" of English maps in the prolongation of this valley. We observed a couple of tents in the mouth of a valley to the north, but we were now in no distress. I lived exclusively on tea, bread, and jam, of which there were still two pots left.

The storm continued next day also. We seldom covered more than 6 or 7 miles. In the past month we had travelled 220 miles, 30 more than in the previous month. During the evening and night the snow pelted on to our tents. I still had my warm comfortable bed, but at a pinch it would also go piecemeal into the fire. Everything that was discarded was burned or buried, lest, if it were left, it might arouse suspicions.

For another day's march we had the advantage of this fine longitudinal valley, which imperceptibly rises to a flat threshold, beyond which we passed a gold placer. The holes from which the auriferous sand is extracted are 3 to 16 feet in diameter, and little more than 3 feet deep. It is evident that some of them have been dug out last summer. A little farther down gold had been searched for some time ago. Folds, stone shelters for marksmen, and stone cairns were to be seen in several places.

Still lower down we came, on the following day, to a third placer, situated where the valley contracts to a trough. Here large sheepfolds and abundant tracks of men were found. The gold is washed out on flat stones in a flume 100 yards long. The valley afterwards contracts to a breadth of 5 yards, and the bottom is mostly filled with ice, here and there forming ledges. These had to be levelled with axes and strewn with sand, and each animal was led and held up by men. We could not afford to let any one of them

313, 314, 315, 316, 317. PANORAMAS FROM THE CAMPS 318, 333, 335, 359, 360; IN THE LAST TWO, SHA-KANGSHAM.

After Water-colour Sketches by the Author.

break his leg and be lost to us. Then the ice came to an end, the valley opened out, and we pitched our tents in an extensive flat. Towards the east the land was all favourable, and no "Snowy Range" stood in our way. We could see 25 miles ahead. Tubges shot five hares and we had a feast that evening. A pack of wolves howled round the camp at night.

February 27. A thousand wild asses were seen on the plain which sloped down gently to the east-south-east. They formed dark lines, sometimes large, sometimes small, sometimes spots like a rosary. Some herds galloped off to a point about two hundred yards in front of the caravan, where they stood and gazed and then dispersed, springing away in graceful movements. Perhaps they were here for a great spring congress, to decide questions relating to their territory and pastures. It is certain that, like the nomads, they migrate at fixed seasons, for they also are dependent on the occurrence of grass and its varying abundance at different heights and different times of the year.

Farther down the plain, beyond a small cliff, were five herds of kiangs, the nearest of which numbered 133 head. They came galloping almost up to us. Lobsang ran towards them. Then they set off in wild flight one after another, their hoofs thundering over the ground, made a wide curve behind us, and vanished in a dense cloud of dust, the hard beat of their hoofs being still audible. A strong puff of wind dispersed the cloud, and they came into sight again; they stood quaking with fear, and looked at us, pricked up their ears, dilated their nostrils, and sniffed the wind.

To the south of our route we perceived two tents among small scattered heights. Abdul Kerim and two men went off to them while we pitched camp 341. On their return they reported that the tents were the property of a certain Tsering Ngorpel from Gertse, who had come hither with his family for two months and was going back in a month. They were poor people, and owned only 70 sheep and goats, 6 yaks, and 1 dog. The neighbourhood of camp 341 the man called Senes-yung-ringmo, and he said that if we marched south-eastwards we should almost daily meet with nomads from Gertse and Senkor, districts in the south which I had passed through in 1901. They were afraid of our men and would not let them enter the tents. Two fine sheep and a lump of butter were bought, and rescued us from starvation for a time. The hare meat was discarded and given to the dogs.

We made the two sheep carry themselves our newly-acquired store of meat to camp 342; we had no room for extra loads. We mounted slowly to a flat pass. Three tents stood in a side valley and some men came out to look at us, but we passed on without exchanging questions and answers. On February 29 the wind raged furiously all day long. Clouds swept ceaselessly over the country, and at one o'clock the temperature was 22.1°, quite low enough to chill a rider down to the bones and marrow.

In front of us lay a large flat hollow, in the midst of which two small lakes shone white with ice. We slowly approached the isthmus between them. A herd of antelopes took to flight and nearly fell over a lonely wild ass, which looked at them uneasily, but at the last moment they turned off in another direction as though they were afraid of him. On the left, in a deep trough running towards the lake, a flock of sheep was driven along by two shepherds. Wait one moment. Hand me the turban. Gulam wound it round my head, and then I went on foot like the rest. Along the shore a young man was driving six yaks. Abdul Kerim and Gulam went up to him while we set up the tents on the shore (15,200 feet)

After a while they returned with the yak-driver, a boy of fourteen in a large white skin hood. He was terribly frightened, and could with difficulty be persuaded to come to our tents; our intention was that he should guide two of our men to his dwelling. He called the lake Lumbur-ringmo. As my disguise was now complete, I went to look at the boy, who did not seem at all suspicious.

Lobsang and Tubges followed the boy to his tent, and after a long time returned with unwelcome news. Two Tibetans had rushed out of the tent, stopped them, and asked roughly what they wanted. They replied very quietly that they wished to buy food; but there was nothing of the kind for sale.

"But who are you?" an elderly man asked.

"We are Ladakis in the service of a merchant, and we are on the way to Saka-dzong," they answered.

"No," the Tibetan exclaimed; "you lie. No merchant travels this way, least of all in winter; there is no trade in Chang-tang."

"We are not trading," Lobsang replied; "we are commissioned to inquire how much sheep's wool can be bought up next summer."

"Sheep's wool—in uninhabited districts! No; you are servants of a European, who keeps himself out of sight in one of your tents. Out with the truth, or it will be bad for you."

"Ask the boy here," returned Lobsang in his most innocent tone, "if he saw any European in our tent. We abhor Europeans as heartily as you. If you doubt us, you can come to our tents and see for yourself."

"No, thank you; we will not come to your tent," the old man answered, and disappeared with his people behind the black hangings.

Lobsang was very serious when he came back, and proposed that, if we had not already come to a standstill, we should in future set up our camp as far as possible from the nomads. I was alarmed, and I had a feeling that we should not advance much farther into the forbidden land. It was also disappointing to be so openly suspected to be a European.

Now good advice was precious, for evidently the nomads would betray us to the nearest authorities. At the evening's lesson in Tibetan, which occupied some hours, I discussed the situation with Lobsang and Kutus. It was resolved that Abdul Kerim should go early in the morning to the tent, and if the nomads were still hostile we would try to lengthen our day's march so as to get out of the way of a probable summons to stop.

This time Lobsang met with a better reception, as he could present our chief and leader, whom the nomads correctly addressed as *bombo*. The old man introduced himself under the name of Sogbarong Tsering Tundup—Sogbarong is his home in the west, and this name is placed before his own much as Anders Persson i Storgården. The old man invited his guests into his tent, took a couple of sheep's trotters, cut them in pieces with an axe, threw them into the caldron, and offered some broth to Abdul Kerim, saying it was the only tea he had. In the tent were five antelopes cut up, a gun, a knife, and other articles. The old man did not this time express any suspicions of us, but related that a European with a large caravan had crossed the country to the east more than a year ago. He did not suspect, of course, that that same European was hiding in one of our tents. When the messengers came back they had a fine fat sheep and a can of milk with them.

This day, March 1, the wind was so strong that it was impossible to travel. My tent fell over and was held fast by the load of sand and stones on its folds. Not a trace of the surroundings was visible, and I should have obtained no notion of country on the route. At two o'clock Tsering Tundup and another Tibetan came to return the visit. They emerged from the mist only when they were close at hand, and a couple of men hastened to protect them from the dogs. The visit was a complete surprise, but there was nothing which could excite the least suspicion. My things were crammed into a sack, and I was disguised as usual; indeed, I had now no other clothing to put on. Even if they had come and looked into my tent there would have been no danger.

Our guests had capacious sheepskin coats drawn up above the belt so as to form the usual protruding bag where a large part of their property is stored. They wore hoods of sheepskin and looked like Samoyeds or Chukchis. They stood a while and chatted with our men in the wind, but I did not hear a word, though they were standing only 3 yards from the loop-hole in my tent through which I was watching them. After some hesitation, they went into Abdul Kerim's tent, and then the yak question was discussed. They had only six yaks, which they required for their own journeys; but if we would buy sheep, they would let us have as many as twelve, and each sheep could easily carry a fifth part of a mule's load. The offer was accepted with pleasure, and the price was fixed at 38 rupees. Then they went off through the storm and I felt safe again.

The purchase was concluded on March 2, and the twelve sheep stood with their heads together in the shelter of the men's tent. To start on our travels was impossible, for we could not have kept our legs in such a storm. We therefore remained here another day, and the men had full occupation in sewing sacks for the sheep, arranging and weighing the loads. I was worse off, for I had nothing to do and nothing to read, but I sat and wrote Tibetan notes and entered new words in my lexicon. Then I heard a hasty step coming towards my tent; it was Kunchuk bringing fire. A rustle, an oath, all the contents are swept out of the shovel, and the man has to crawl back to the camp-fire for more embers. So the day passes and the storm roars, and every one is weary and listless.

During these stormy days our animals lay for the most part quietly in a hollow where they were sheltered from the wind. The storm kept them from grazing, and they were much enfeebled by fasting. A white mule, therefore, remained behind at Lumbur-ringmo-tso when we moved off south-eastwards on March 3 with 3 horses, 6 mules, and 12 sheep, delighted that we had passed this critical point with a whole skin. Freshwater springs formed a number of picturesque ice volcanoes on the shore of the small lake. Before we encamped behind a projecting cliff, we met three large flocks of sheep with their shepherds. On such occasions I always went on foot. The new sheep all carried burdens, and gave invaluable help to our tired animals. They were tied up every night between the tents that they might be safe from wolves, and the yellow dog from Gartok proved an excellent guard. They bleated piteously the first evening, probably distressed at leaving their native country. I was sorry for them, for they had been treated as cruelly as Uncle Tom, but in time they became quite accustomed to their new way of life.

Violent storms prevailed all day and all the following day, on which we passed two black tents. At every camp we had to take the greatest care that no pieces of paper, match-boxes, candle ends, or cigarette stumps were left lying about, for we might be sure that the Tibetans dwelling near would come and search about after we had left the spot. Our route took us over a low pass (16,030 feet). The rocks comprised weathered schists, quartzite, and granite—the last only in detached blocks. On the other side we followed a deeply excavated valley opening out on to a plain, and we were just setting up our tent by a projecting rock when two large black dogs came running towards us barking. Nomads, therefore, were encamping in the neighbourhood, and we must be on our guard. Abdul Kerim, who always showed himself prudent and tactful in delicate negotiations, went off to a tent which stood on the other side of the rock and was inhabited by four Senkor nomads who owned 400 sheep. The chief of them was named Shgoge, and sold us three sheep at 3 rupees a head, some butter and milk. He said that the country here, around camp 345, was called Pankur, and that we were three days' journey from the encampment of the Gertse Pun, or the chief of Gertse. With him, however, we had nothing to do. It was to our interest to avoid as much as possible officials of all kinds, not to approach Gertse or Senkor in the west too closely, and not too near my route of 1906 to the east. We must steer our way through many pitfalls. Just in this district we crossed the meridian of 84° E., and my plan was to travel due south from the Tong-tso right across the large blank space. The continual storms which had done us so much harm, were so far advantageous to us that they enabled us to cross the great wastes without being much noticed. This day all was hazy from the dust, and our neighbours' sheep, which passed my tent in long columns with shepherds and dogs, made a very curious spectacle in the dense mist.

March 5. Abdul Kerim obtained two more sheep, and now we had seventeen to help the mules and horses. Our intention was to increase our sheep caravan by degrees, and make ourselves independent of the other animals.

We must also have a spare horse for Abdul Kerim, for he was our master, and it was incongruous that he should go on foot while I, a simple caravan man, rode. This day we had the storm at our back, and we travelled $8\frac{1}{2}$ miles over the same even, excellent ground which had made progress easier since we left Lemchung-tso. We encamped at a sheepfold and enjoyed the feeling that there were no neighbours to spy on us. A sheep was slaughtered; only the worst were sacrificed for food, and were to be replaced by new ones when an opportunity presented itself.

CHAPTER LXII

ADVENTURES OF OURSELVES AND PUPPY IN NAGRONG

On March 6 we made another hop towards our destination. It is difficult to travel over the high plateaus of Tibet in winter, and we could not march more than four hours a day. The morning was clear, but we had not gone far beyond a small lake, with its mantle of ice covered with driftsand and dust, before the storm increased in violence and made me reel in the saddle. The clouds of dust became thicker, the sandspouts were dark reddish-brown at the base, and the gusts tore up furrows in the ground like ploughshares, while frequently spiral forms were seen which could only be produced by cyclonic whirlwinds. On the left hand shimmered a lake, its surface partly white with gypsum and salt, partly streaked brown with drift-sand, and with open water only in two places; it was the ghost of a lake which was doomed to disappear.

Two built-up fireplaces served us capitally for a camping-ground on the shore where the grazing was good. On the eastern side of the lake was a brick-red ridge of medium height, which I wished to paint in order to record the effective tones in the dust mist. I waited for the others with Kutus and Gulam, and we had scarcely induced a fire to burn before the storm rose at noon to a hurricane. Now everything vanished—lake, ridge, all except the nearest tufts of grass. The fire was fenced in with stones and clods lest it should be blown away, sand and minute pebbles beat against my dry skin coat, and I had to cover all my face, for the skin smarted as though lashed by whip-cord if it were exposed for a second to the wind. Fortunately the others made their way to us. Every man had to lend a hand to raise my tent. At length Gulam came crawling backwards and yelled into my ear that the tent was ready. With straddling legs and all my muscles on the stretch I fought my way to it, and was glad to catch hold of a tent rope before I was blown down. At last I was under cover and could recover my breath. The tent cloth was puffed out like a balloon, and threatened every moment to burst with a report. The sand and rubbish beat upon it, producing a deafening noise. It was as dark as at twilight, and the wind roared and whined through the grass. The men tried to set up their own tent, but when the wind had overturned it twice they let it lie, weighting it with the baggage that it might not fly away. Five Ladakis lay in the lee of my tent rolled up like hedgehogs, and I let them come in, where they sat silent and motionless for a couple of hours. The others had crept under the ruins of their unfortunate tent. Puppy and Little Puppy lay in a corner and kept each other warm. However, the temperature was 35.8°, and we had not had such warmth for three months. A long and dismal evening! It was with difficulty I got a piece of bread, a cup of tea, and a piece of dried meat. We were deaf and dizzy when at length we sought repose under our rugs, while the storm continued to rage outside.

I awoke to hear the same old music, and to go out to my horse was like plunging into icy-cold water. Neither the sky nor the horizon was visible, and the mountains were dim shadows. With Kutus and Gulam I led the way, following a path trodden by men. Dark, chill, and doleful was the land of eternal twilight, frost, and the wicked demons of the air. After a march of 8 miles we halted at the edge of a belt of ice, a frozen stream in several branches, which ran to the south-west. The gale flew over the clear sheet of ice, and the red dust was swept over it like flames. With the assistance of Kutus I slid over to the other side, and in the shelter of the opening of a small valley we made the usual fire.

The caravan came to the edge of the ice. It was impossible to sand a path, for the grains would have been swept away. The animals were led across singly, each helped over by several men. For all that a mule fell and gave a fearful wrench to one of its hind legs, and with great difficulty it was helped up to the camp. All of us had grey distorted faces, our eyes ran, full of sand and dust. My lips bled and my teeth were black. March is the worst month, but we had never experienced such bad weather before. What is the use of looking forward to spring when the days are darker as time goes on?

The injured mule had evidently dislocated its leg. It was thrown down and a rope was fastened round its hoof and the end was pulled by the men. When it was at full stretch Lobsang hit the rope hard with a tent-pole in order to set the dislocated joint in place again, but I could not perceive that the operation had any effect. No; the mule was lost to us just when we could ill afford to lose one of our best animals.

And it was lost indeed, for on the morning of March 8 it could not take a step. It was sad to pass the death sentence, and a pitiful sight when the fresh warm blood spurted out in powerful jets and moistened the barren soil. It lay quiet and patiently, and after a few convulsions expired, and was left in solitude when we moved on over the dreary waste.

But before starting I had ascended a hill and looked around. Which was more expedient—to travel north-east or south-west? Both directions lay out of our course. I decided for the south-west, and hastened down to my tent, where Gulam served up breakfast. Brown Puppy and Little Puppy gave me their company to get their share. Little Puppy had grown so much that he could do what he liked with his mother. When I gave her a piece of meat the young one flew upon her and took it away. I had to hold Little Puppy that his mother might eat in peace. When we set out, Puppy and the yellow dog remained behind with the slaughtered mule, finding a convenient point of departure in an open wound in the soft muscles of the neck. There they stood gorging when we started along the ice-belt of the stream towards the south-west.

With my usual followers I rode in advance. The

suffocating, blinding, deafening storm was right in our faces. Gulam walked in front, stopped, looked through the field-glass, and gave me the sign to dismount. The stream swept round the foot of a cliff in front of us.

"What is it?" I asked Gulam when we came up to him.

"A large stone house with a wall and a couple of smaller huts. They are not visible at this moment because of the mist, but they lie close to the foot of the mountain."

"Yes; now they can be seen. It is strange that no dogs rush at us."

"What is to be done? Shall we turn back? Surely a chieftain lives here, and he will come and search us down to the skin."

"No; it is too late, for we must have been seen already."

How I regretted that we had not travelled to the north-east! But we must put on a good face in our unlucky situation. We passed the village at a distance of 100 yards, and halted in the shelter of the dark porphyry crag crowned by two *chhortens* and a *mani*. At least it was pleasant to get shelter for a moment. It was like taking refuge in a gateway when it pours. All around was dead and dreary; no one was seen; only a couple of jackdaws croaked, and a hare sped out of its form so near us that we could have caught it with the hand if we had been alert. Kutus and Gulam went out to gather fuel. I searched the suspicious neighbourhood with the field-glass, where treachery seemed to lurk behind every projection. It cleared a little towards the south-east, enough for me to detect a black tent of unusual size about 200 yards off. Four strings with prayer-streamers were stretched out from a high pole. I had been in hopes that we should get past the first dwellings, as no dogs had shown themselves, but I had never heard of an uninhabited tent. And the outward appearance of this tent indicated the presence of an important chief. Thanks to the mist, we had stumbled right on to his camp, and he would not be caught napping by poor strolling Ladakis.

Gulam had been to the large house, the yard door of which stood open, and had found in a shed a large quantity of fuel of a kind of shrub the Tibetans call *ombo.* So we waited and waited, expecting to see the caravan emerge from the mist, but when nothing was heard of it Kutus went out to search. It had wandered quite out of its course, and had made a long circuit round the house and tent, for the leaders were convinced that I wished to slip by unnoticed. A horse had fallen, and now we had only two left, and 5 mules out of 40 animals.

The three tents were set up in a line close together, and Abdul Kerim went with Kunchuk to the large tent. We saw through the mist that a man came out to meet them, and that all three went into the tent, and then we waited with our hearts in our mouths. The men returned at dusk with good news. The tent was inhabited by a lonely old Amchi-lama, *i.e.* a monk-doctor, who at the same time looked after the souls of the Nagrong nomads, determined from astrological books the lucky and unlucky days for baptisms and other affairs, and assisted people with the same remedies when they were sick, died, and finally were buried. He was from Sera in Lhasa, and had lived three years in Nagrong. The tent was a movable temple, furnished inside with altars, burning butter lamps, and votive bowls, where the hermit performed service—we heard him beating a temple drum at midnight. It belonged, as well as the large house, to the Gertse Pun Bombo, or the chief of the Gertse district, who a few days before had gone off a day's journey to the east, with his flocks, children, and all, but was soon expected back in consequence of a dispute between two of his subjects. Perhaps, after all, it was well we travelled south-west instead of north-east, for we might have fallen into the jaws of the Gertse Pun himself. This potentate comes to Nagrong in late summer and takes up his abode in the stone house, while a hundred nomad tents are set up around and a fair is held.

The old lama had no servants, but every third day a man came to bring him wood. He must find it dull in the long winter evenings, when he hears the storm roaring outside, and silence reigns within around the gods who answer his prayers and the rolls of his drum with a smile of reconciliation. But probably he is a philosopher and has no fear of the dangers of the night. In his tent lay several sacks full of *tsamba*, barley, rice, and butter, but he had no authority to sell anything without the permission of the Gertse Pun. Instead, he pointed out where the tent of the Pun's brother-in-law stood, where all kinds of prime goods could be bought.

We therefore decided to remain where we were over March 9, and Abdul Kerim with three attendants sought out the brother-in-law, met with a friendly reception, and bought five sheep and two goats, besides two sheep-loads of rice and as much barley, and also a bag of tobacco, which the men had long wanted. All day long I was a prisoner in my tent; my period of freedom was over. And when the evening came and enveloped the dreary Nagrong valley in its shadows, I could think of nothing else but my old trusty comrade, the oldest of all that had been with me in Tibet, Brown Puppy. In the company of the yellow dog she had remained in the morning with the mule which had dislocated its leg, and I had seen nothing of her since. We had hoped, however, that she would find us again, as she had so often done before, but now we were convinced that she had lost our trail, and, desperate and crazy with anxiety, was seeking for us over hill and dale, only to wander farther and farther from the right direction. It was useless to send men after her, and it was not advisable to divide our small party at such a critical time. The dogs had remained a long time tearing at the mule's neck, and when at last they were satiated they had started to follow us and had lost our track in the terrible wind and sand clouds. If they once crossed over ice they would never find our track again. Now thoughts of my old tent companion worried me more than anything else. Only that very morning she had lain on her felt rug in the usual corner, and we had breakfasted together. Where was she? what was she doing at this moment? Day and night she would run barking and whining over desolate Chang-tang with her nose to the ground, searching for our track till her paws were torn and painful. What would she do when night came down with its dreadful darkness and its prowling wolves? Were the dogs keeping together, or were they seeking us along different paths, having lost each other? Would Puppy some time find a home with friendly nomads and lead a comfortable life again, or would she come to want and be tied outside a poor tent, and, pining in hopeless sorrow, remember her past life, which, from when she lapped milk in my room at Srinagar, had been spent in my caravan? I was never to receive an answer to these questions, for the parts she and the yellow dog played in our romance were ended. For the future her life would shape itself differently, but I was never to gain any knowledge of the remaining chapters of her existence. I lay awake at night thinking of her misfortune, and looked every morning to see if perchance she had come back in the night and was lying in her usual corner, and I fancied I heard her trotting outside my tent in the dusk, or thought I could distinguish the profile of a lonely half-starved dog on a mound or crag with its nose up and howling at the storm. For some time I suffered from a delusion, imagining that a shade, the restless soul, the invisible ghost of a dog followed me wherever I went. I felt the presence of an invisible dog which followed me into my tent, and among the Tibetans, and always whined and pleaded for help, and I was worried that I could give no help or consolation to my lost, wandering friend. But soon we had other things to think of, other dogs became my friends, and we were daily entangled in a skein of troubles which must lead to a crisis, and the cares of the past paled before the gravity of the moment.

March 10. Such a day as this is interesting to look back on, but it was hard and cruel as long as it lasted. Before six o'clock I was awakened with the disquieting information that two Tibetans were approaching our tents. I made haste to dress myself and paint my face and hands black with a thin coating. Meanwhile the strangers arrived and were invited into Abdul Kerim's tent, where I heard them talking pleasantly about sheep and money—so they

318. The Author as a Shepherd.

were not spies; our time had not yet come. One of the guests was the brother-in-law, the other a neighbour of his, who, when he heard what a good price we paid for sheep, said he was ready to sell us four he had brought with him, as well as a lively goat. Abdul Kerim had received a general order to buy all the sheep he could procure, so he took them. The goat was, as has been said, a lively beast, and he ran off at once and could not be caught again.

The two Tibetans went off to the lama's tent to drink tea, but the critical time was not yet over, for probably they would return to see us start. Therefore, while the tents were still standing, I set out with Tubges, Little Kunchuk, and "Snoring Kunchuk," as we called Sonam Kunchuk on account of his terrible timber-sawing propensities, when they drove our thirty-one sheep down the valley. As we went off the Tibetans came out and watched us, but did not suspect anything wrong. To escape detection I had hurriedly turned to sheep-driving (Illust. 318), but I soon found that I had no natural aptitude for this occupation, so invigorating, but so trying to the patience. I fancied I imitated my Ladakis as closely as possible, whistled and shouted in the same way, and threw out my arms when a sheep left the crowd, but the animals showed me not the least obedience, but went where they liked when I was near. After an hour's walk in the teeth of the wind I had had enough, and while the other shepherds went on with the sheep, Kunchuk and I stayed in a cranny out of sight of the lama's tent, while I could look over all the valley.

At length the other men came with Abdul Kerim riding at their head. Our coats and turbans were of the same colour, so that any Tibetans who happened to be watching could not tell if it were Abdul Kerim or I that was riding. I now took my horse and went on in front with my usual companions. At eleven o'clock the storm rose to a furious pitch and dashed in our faces. Driftsand swept over the ground in dense masses; we were nearly suffocated, and we seemed to stand still while the country moved past us at a giddy pace. We crossed the valley in order to follow its western flank. The clouds of dust obscured the sun; nothing could be seen beyond a distance of 20 yards; chaos surrounded us. We stopped to get our breath, and lest we should miss the others, but as soon as they appeared like phantoms in the mist we set off again. I have experienced many sandstorms in Takla-makan and the Lob-nor desert, but hardly any so bad as this was. In Turkestan one simply encamps when a storm comes on, but what is the use of encamping to await the end of a storm which lasts thirty days? We strayed among small dunes, and, though the valley fell in the direction we were travelling, we seemed as though we were mounting to a lofty pass in consequence of the pressure of the storm. The driftsand rattled against my dry, hard coat, which, from the constant friction, became heavily charged with electricity. About every other minute there was a discharge, and I felt uncomfortable and often painful prickings, especially in the soles of the feet, the hands, and knees. At every such discharge the horse also pulled up and became nervous. At last, when my grey Tikze horse refused to go further, and we had quite lost sight of the others, and could not see where we were going, we came to a halt and huddled together with our backs to the wind. The electrical discharges continued even now, but were weaker. If I placed the tip of a finger near Gulam's or Kutus' hand a small electric spark was felt and seen, and both of us felt the shock. The men were exceedingly astonished, and hoped it was not witchcraft.

We sat waiting for three hours, and were prepared for an uncomfortable night. But Kutus came upon the other men just when they were giving up all attempt to find us before night. We encamped among the dunes, and before long all articles which were set out in my tent vanished under a thick layer of sand.

On the morning of the 11th the storm had somewhat abated; and, wearied and stiff after our experiences of the previous night, we continued our journey southwards and encamped at a deserted sheepfold. By nine o'clock compact sandspouts twisted slowly over the plain like spectres, so the storm was again at its usual height. We had *tsamba* for only one day, but it did not count for much as long as we had such a good supply of meat. We were glad to get out of reach of the Gertse Pun; in this drifting sand it was impossible to find our trail—yes, even for our own dogs. Little Puppy did not miss his mother, but felt very important at being sole master on the ground, and barked at our sober sheep. It was, however, a serious matter for us that we were deprived of our night-watch in districts where we had most need of them. We must try to procure fresh dogs as soon as possible.

On March the 12th we marched the usual weary 6½ miles to the east-south-east through a fine, broad, longitudinal valley, and pitched our camp in a hollow full of rubbish. Our three tents were now always placed close together, so that, if any stranger came unexpectedly to my tent, I could crawl into Abdul Kerim's without being seen from outside. My Ladak *chapkan* began to assume a more satisfactory colour, but we still did all we could to defile it and make it sooty and greasy. Little Puppy lent me his assistance by biting and tearing the sleeves so that they hung in rags. It would not be long before I had the appearance of a regular ruffian.

It snowed heavily all night, and in the morning the snow lay so deep, and the country was so thickly covered, that we thought it best to remain stationary. We were still farther removed from Brown Puppy, and it was vain for her to seek our trail. Perhaps it was providential that both she and the white horse were lost before they could betray us. Tibetans have wonderfully sharp eyes for animals, and recognize them again when they have seen them only once. Now the danger was over, for all the veterans had gone. Perhaps Puppy sacrificed herself that I might be successful! All the same, I seemed to see her wandering disconsolate and distressed about the desolate wastes in the north.

CHAPTER LXIII

THROUGH THE HIGHLANDS OF BONGBA

WHEN I awake to another day of uncertain fortune and adventures life seems gloomy and solitary, and the longer the time the more I long for an end of my difficulties. When Gulam awoke me on the 14th, he complained that Abdul Kerim did not keep the watch I had given him in order; either the watch or the caravan leader was at fault, but he believed it was the latter, for the watch could not be blamed if it were wound up only every other day. Gulam affirmed that when Abdul Kerim was asked what o'clock it was, he always answered seven, whatever time it might be in the twenty-four hours.

The thermometer fell to $-11°$ in the night, but the day was fine. The wind blew as usual, but the sun came out and we thought of spring again. Three shepherds were taking some hundreds of sheep to the west, which had been driven off from their pasturage by the recent snow and were looking for uncovered land. We were only a day's journey from the Tong-tso (14,800 feet), they said, and the Tong-tso was the point from which we were to start southwards to traverse unknown country. If I succeeded in crossing it only by a single route, all the troubles of the past winter would not have been in vain. The shepherds' information was correct, for the next day we bivouacked on the western shore of the Tong-tso, which we found exactly at the place where the immortal pundit, Nain Sing, inserted it on his map. To the south-east towered the huge massive Sha-kangsham, along the northern foot of which I had ridden in 1901.

Now we had to find a convenient pass over the mountain which barred our way to the south. A gap was seen to the south-east, and we directed our steps towards it. On our right, two tents stood at the foot of a hill, and Abdul Kerim was sent to them while we encamped in a deep narrow ravine, at the bottom of which we found a large quantity of wind-driven kiang dung and dry tufts of grass. On his return, our good leader reported that he was rudely received by two men, named Nakchu Tundup and Nakchu Hlundup, who came from the district Nakchu, three days' journey distant to the south, and had a wife in common. They first asked how many we were and how many guns we had, just as though they wished to know whether they and their neighbours might venture to attack us. They then said that they had seen a man riding at the head of our party, while all the rest, Abdul Kerim included, went on foot, and that it was not hard to guess that the mounted man was a European. When Abdul Kerim replied that no Europeans travel in winter, for they are too much afraid of the cold, and that we were only wool-buyers from Ladak, the Tibetans shook their heads and answered that they had never heard of Ladakis travelling in this country in winter. But, nevertheless, Abdul succeeded in gaining their confidence, and when he had paid double the market price for two yaks and six sheep, the Tibetans forgot their suspicions, all for the sake of filthy lucre. The purchase was to be completed the following morning. Then the new animals were fetched, and their carrying power was a welcome assistance to our animals. Fortunately, the nomads had in general the greatest respect for our tents. It was important for us to make liberal bargains with men who at first had been hostile to us. On the other hand, they often abstained from betraying us, even if they had suspicions, for if it were known that they had been well paid, the nearest chief would confiscate their receipts and would also punish the unfortunate men who had dared to traffic with suspected individuals.

During the day's march I rode in front as usual, with my two companions on foot. A tent lay concealed behind a cliff, and we did not notice it until we were some way past it, and then it was too late to dismount. Two fellows were outside and looked after us, and if they compared notes with their neighbours they would have good cause for suspicion. At our camp that day we had a visit from an old man and two young people, who had their tent near and came to see what kind of men we were. They said that they were very poor, and begged for some coppers. We were on the border of the district Bongba-changma, which contains 300 tents, and, like the whole province of Bongba, is subject to the governor Karma Puntso, whose tent stood at a distance of six days' journey to the south. He was a man of twenty-five years of age, lived in a large tent, and had been in office only a year, since his father died. It was assuring to know that he could have no experience of Europeans and their crafty ways. After the strangers had received a couple of *tengas* from Abdul Kerim, they went home again in the rays of the evening sun, delighted to find that we were not robbers.

Then the temperature fell to $-16°$; the winter was remarkably trying, but the day, March 18, was still fine, and I travelled all the way on foot, driving the sheep while we were passing several tents. Among them was that of our old man of the day before, and he proved to be a man of property, who sold us various much-needed articles of food. On the way Tubges shot seven partridges, whereupon two Tibetans came forward and protested, saying that only Europeans shot partridges. Abdul Kerim assured them that he preferred partridges to mutton. Again there was talk of Karma Puntso. Perhaps it would be better to choose another way. No; then the governor would be still more suspicious. We encamped on the northern side of a small pass, where we had no troublesome neighbours.

March 19. Breakfast, a delicate partridge and a cup of tea, was just over when it was announced that three Tibetans were coming up to our tents. But they stopped at a respectful distance, and Abdul Kerim went up to them. My tent was opened in this direction, but was closed again just in time. The Tibetans' errand was to ask if we had any medicine suitable for a man who had a pain in the foot. In reality, their object was to spy upon us when we set out, for they stayed all the time and looked about. After my hands and face had been coloured black, I stole by the secret passage into Abdul Kerim's tent, while Kutus and Gulam crawled by the same way into mine to pack up. Then I went with Lobsang and Kutus, and drove the sheep up the track leading to the pass (16,135 feet). We had not gone far when Abdul Kerim came riding on my horse and made frantic gestures to us to stop. A Tibetan horseman, followed by a big dog, would meet us in a few moments on the path. We therefore took a roundabout way among hillocks, while the caravan encountered the Tibetan. In this way we escaped the danger. Soon came Kunchuk and Sedik, leading the dog with a rope on either side—a savage brute, which barked till he foamed at the mouth, and tried to bite those who were taking him away from his master. He was of the species called *takkar*, and Takkar was his name. He reminded me of a St. Bernard; he was coal black, with a white patch on the chest and neck, and was as savage as a wolf. They had bought him for 2 rupees.

Moreover, Abdul Kerim had also bought the rider's horse for 86 rupees, and he came jogging cheerfully after us as we rode down from the summit of the pass to a longitudinal valley abounding in tents and herds of sheep and yaks, and at two spots were seen mounted men, who looked uncomfortably like a levy. The new horse was eleven years old, the owner said, and if he passed well over his fifteenth year, he would live to thirty—but we did not want him so long. He was a new member of our troop and excited general interest, and Takkar became quieter when he saw an old friend and comrade in misfortune.

At the camp we had to be careful, for nomads dwelt near and shepherds wandered with their flocks on the slopes around. To prevent Takkar from running away he was tied by the neck to a tent pole, an operation by no means easy. He was tied fast with ropes, his legs were fettered, and a felt mat was thrown over him, on which four men sat while the others made him fast to the pole.

Immediately he was let loose he rushed at those nearest him, but was held back by the pole. It was a sin to drag him from home against his will; he was another Uncle Tom who suffered for our sake, but I hoped that we should soon understand each other. To console him in his captivity he was given the blood and entrails of the slaughtered sheep.

We crossed another small pass (19,537 feet) on the 20th, and the insignificant lake Shar-tso, where a fine spring bubbles up out of the ground by the shore. From a couple of tents to the west we bought tea, butter, and *tsamba* sufficient for several days, and heard again about Karma Puntso. This time it was said that he lived three days to the west, and we hoped to slip past without any disturbance. The country about camp 359 is called Luma-shar, and we stayed on the northern bank of the large river Kangsham-tsangpo, which comes from the northern flank of Sha-kangsham, the huge massive which I left to the south of my route in 1901, and which showed us a magnificent view of its western side. The mountain lay about a couple of days' journey to the south-east.

The next day we were to cross the river, an exceedingly unpleasant business; for though there had been 32 degrees of frost in the night the ice, except close to the bank, would not bear. Abdul made an attempt with his horse, but the animal came down on his nose in the middle of the river. Then Lobsang took off his boots and went across the river barefooted, and came back again to help in conducting our pack animals gently and firmly across. To get the sheep over was the worst difficulty; they had to be pushed and pulled by the horns, one at a time. Almost all the men of the caravan got a refreshing bath in the stream (Illust. 363).

On the other side we ascended to a small pass where there was a splendid view over the ridge, which seemed to run west-south-west from Sha-kangsham and which barred our way to the south. Abdul Kerim, Kunchuk, and Sedik went with an exhausted mule to a few tents standing to the right of our route, with the object of bartering the worn-out beast for a couple of sheep, but the nomads said they would not take it as a gift. Instead, our men bought rice, sour milk, butter, salt, and a sheep, so that we were provided for some days. From the camp also Abdul Kerim took a long walk to some tents in the neighbourhood. Now poor Abdul Kerim had to do penance for his sins, and if he had erred in taking too little barley from Ladak, he made up for it by his conduct on this adventurous journey.

From camp 360 the highest peak of Sha-kangsham lay south, 73° E. (Illust. 317).

Takkar is still irreconcilable, and heartily detests Kunchuk who bought him. But he also barks at us as soon as we show ourselves outside the tents. On the march he is resigned as long as he is near our new horse, but at other times he is savage. The only one that dares go near him is Little Puppy, who teases and sports with him and bites his ears. Takkar treats Little Puppy with supreme contempt, and only when the young one presumes to snatch his new uncle's food he growls angrily, but then Little Puppy pricks up his ears, puts his head on one side, and looks at him. He little thought that the new dog could have bitten off his head like a chicken's if he had wished. In reality, Takkar was glad to have a playfellow in his captivity, though at first he held himself aloof to maintain his dignity.

The next morning Lobsang and Tubges went back to the nomads' tent and returned with three more sheep, a lump of butter, and a bag of tobacco. Their appetites were wonderful to behold. The others had left for them half a pot of tea mixed with butter, thick and red. One cup disappeared after another, and they emptied the pot to the last drop. Then they took some meat out, which they ate up like wild beasts. What was left they stuffed into their waistbelts, to have it handy in case they were hungry before we reached the next camp.

We continued on our way to the south, passing on our left hand an open plain which extended up to the foot of the skirts of Sha-kangsham. We passed tents and flocks at one or two places, and encamped on a hill of loose material beside a spring. The nomads around had nothing to sell, but gave Abdul Kerim much valuable information. On such occasions Kunchuk used to sit and secretly note down all the geographical names. Among other details we now heard that if we held on our journey to the south for seven days we should fall in with a rich merchant from Lhasa, named Tsongpun Tashi, who was wont to take up his quarters in winter in the heart of the Bongba province to sell tea to the nomads. We might be certain that if we came into the neighbourhood of his camp we should again be in a critical situation.

Now Lobsang and two weather-beaten Ladakis complained that they slept badly, because it was too warm in the tent. The former wore a set of underclothes, and above only a garment of thin woollen material. In this costume he had travelled all the way from Drugub, and slept in 72 degrees of frost with only a couple of sacks over him, for he had sold his skin coat to one of his comrades at the commencement of the journey. Only a Tibetan can survive such an experience.

On March 23 we struggled up to the Chaklam-la, which we also heard called Amchen-la. The path up to it is steep, and we moved exceedingly slowly up the ascent. The sheep and the two yaks beat us hollow. From the last tent the path was visible all the way up to the pass, so I was obliged to travel on foot, and I might have collapsed from palpitation of the heart and loss of breath if Lobsang had not gone behind and pushed me. The lives of two mules had been ebbing away during the previous days, so the animals were left where nomads could take possession of them. A black horse was also giving in, and the newly bought one had to take over his load. My grey horse was no longer worth much. Chaklam-la, with its 17,339 feet, was a heavy trial to us, and I was not delighted with the view which unrolled itself to the south—a labyrinth of mountains, where it was plain to see that the ranges all stretched from east to west. From the pass there is a steep descent to the river Sangchen-chu, which flows westwards. We encamped on its bank. Now Takkar was becoming resigned to his fate. He was certainly annoyed at being tied to the pole, but he found that he got good and plentiful food and that we were kind to him. He barked only at Kunchuk, whom he could never forgive.

When we broke up our camp on March 24, we hesitated whether we should make for the south-west or south-east, for high mountains rose to the south. If we went south-westwards we should come too near to Karma Puntso, and so we chose the south-easterly route. We had first to cross the ice of the river, 130 yards broad, where a path was sanded. The sheep had to be dragged over one by one by the horns, and the yaks would not venture on the ice till they saw that it bore the horses and mules. Gulam went first on foot, and had the usual order to give a sign if he saw a tent or shepherds. We had not gone far when he stretched out his left hand, which meant that I must dismount and go on foot while Abdul Kerim rode my horse. It was only a shepherd with his flock. As soon as the danger was past I exchanged places with the caravan leader.

A little farther on I found that I had lost my cigarette case, which also contained some unmounted family portraits and one or two pieces of sticking-plaster. It would be terrible if a Tibetan found it. Only a European could own such a thing. Lobsang and Kutus went back and searched along the track while I lay and waited on a bank. They found the case, and each received a cigarette as a reward, and we sat and smoked while Abdul Kerim with Kunchuk and Tubges went down to a tent, where there were only women, and bought some provisions. At the camp in the evening snow fell, and at night the thermometer sank to zero. Now we had only 21 sheep left, and we must try to increase our flock, or, still better, buy a dozen horses. In this region, and in Bongba generally, it was difficult to buy sheep. Everywhere the nomads complained that their flocks had been decimated by the cold, wind, and snow, and the pasturage was unusually poor, because the rains had failed at the end of the preceding summer. Sheep-breeding is their means of subsistence, and if they lose their flocks they are impoverished and can do nothing but wander about begging from more fortunate people. They have therefore a decided objection to diminish their flocks by artificial means, as we may say; the flocks must fluctuate, increasing in good times and diminishing in bad, but they must not be reduced by sale. Therefore they often refuse to sell even at double the proper price. Still harder was it to buy horses in Bongba.

In the night our animals wandered back to the former camp. While Lobsang and Kutus went after them most of the day slipped by, and therefore we remained at camp 363. Kunchuk and Tubges spied a tent in a valley to the south, where they bought rice, barley, *tsamba*, milk, and *chura*—a kind of cheese, so that we had food for several days. Thus we got our livelihood in small portions, bit by bit and from tent to tent. Our own flock had now shrunk to 21 head, all carrying burdens.

A solitary wild-goose flew screaming over our camp. Had he got lost, or was he a scout sent out to see if the ice were broken up on the lakes to the north? Doubtless he would soon return to his tribe and make his report. It seemed to me that he had been despatched too soon.

From February 24 to March 24 we had traversed only 190 miles, owing to the cutting storm, loss of animals, and now at length the difficult country. We now seldom made a day's march of as much as 7 miles.

It is most irritating that a tent, like a sentinel-box or a spying eye, always stands at the northern foot of a pass, so that I have to walk all the way. This day also, when we crept up to the Sanchen-la, a small shelter stood on the saddle, 17,572 feet high. Southwards there were still more mountains. At a distance of 20 to 25 miles north, 60° E., rose the highest peak of Sha-kangsham, a fine sight in the beautiful weather, when not a cloud obstructed the view. Five Ovis Ammons careered in nimble and elastic springs over the heights, and small agile Goa antelopes leaped along the southern slope, where we scrambled down among detritus. The Pantholops antelope is not seen in this region.

Close to where we encamped at Nema-tok was a tent, and the inmates sold us a sheep's load of rice. An old man, whom my fellows called familiarly *ava* or father, came to look at our black horse which we wished to sell, as it could evidently not travel much farther. But the old man said he would not give a rap for the horse. He informed us that in nine days nomads from all quarters would repair to the place where Karma Puntso dwelt, to buy tea and pay their taxes to the Government. Tsongpun Tashi was a powerful and influential man, he said. We drew near to this potentate with a feeling of uneasiness and growing respect. He enjoys peculiar privileges from the Devashung. He sells tea to the nomads on credit. When they sell their sheep's wool in summer at the *tasam* they pay their debts to him in *tengas* or in goods. Tsongpun Tashi makes a good profit on these transactions, and therefore it is to his interest to stand well with the Devashung. If he, who must have the reputation of being more intelligent and sensible than the simple nomads, were to let us pass by with impunity, he would have to answer for it to the Devashung and would lose his privileges. We were therefore evidently coming to a most critical moment.

Nothing venture, nothing have! If I would explore the blank space in the heart of which I now found myself, I must expose myself to various annoyances and run great risks. For a moderately intelligent man it could be no particular pleasure to go on foot through desolate wastes like a vagabond, and drive a flock of refractory sheep. I was already thoroughly weary of this work, for I had no talent or training to perform it properly. I had to paint myself black every morning like a negro, and I sat with a brush before the looking-glass, smearing my face three times over to produce an evenly dark complexion. My eyes were concealed with a pair of large round Tibetan spectacles with my own polished glasses fixed inside. This time I was much more carefully disguised than in 1901, when I tried to get through to Lhasa as a Mongol, but was held fast in the strong claws of Kamba Bombo. My turban was too white, so it was dipped in a dye of boiled butter and ashes, and became at once quite shabby. My soft leather boots were in holes, so that the toes came out. It was well that I ran no risk of meeting acquaintances from Stockholm or London.

This journey was painful and trying to the nerves. Day and night I lived in the greatest anxiety lest I should be discovered and ignominiously unmasked. The farther we advanced southwards the more I was troubled by this apprehension. Should we succeed, or should we be forced back when we had traversed only half the distance across the blank space? Should I never cross the Trans-Himalaya again? At every stage our watchfulness and cautiousness increased, and also the tension of our nerves. I must always be on my guard and never hold a cigarette in my hand when we were on the march. My map sheets and compass I thrust into my bosom to be near at hand. When I collected a rock specimen, took a bearing with the compass, or made a drawing near a tent, Lobsang had to screen me, and he became astonishingly adept at this game. The sun I could observe only when we were quite sure that no Tibetan could see the instrument. Sometimes I sat and drew a panorama through a peephole in the tent cloth. The sheep were my refuge, and with them I set out first, and had not to take part in the packing and loading, and I was spared from watching the animals at night, as in 1901. In both cases I was practically a prisoner in my tent, where the evening hours seemed very long. Nothing is so trying and irritating to the mind as this anxiety in which I lived, travelling in disguise, and expecting any moment to come to a crisis in my fate.

CHAPTER LXIV

TSONGPUN TASHI

MARCH 27. Nearly $-4°$ in the night—still winter. But at one o'clock the temperature rose to $46\frac{1}{2}°$—spring was coming.

An old man sold us four sheep in the morning, and then prowled about our tents. He could not at all understand why we had come hither, especially at this season, but Abdul Kerim told him that when we left Tok-jalung the most severe cold was over. This was a new story we had invented, because it was more probable than the former, and would pass better in the southern parts of the country.

Here, also, stood the usual tent with a view up to the pass, and I was obliged to go on foot up to the summit of the Ladung-la with its 17,395 feet. But here the view was encouraging; we had level or declining ground before us for four days. The descent from the pass to the south was precipitous, and we stumbled and slid through the rubbish, which rattled down behind us, and I had the satisfaction of ruining my boots and clothes more than ever. The valley turned off to the right, south-west, and in the Janglung district, where we encamped, a young shepherd informed us that we should come to Tsongpun Tashi's tent next day.

Numerous springs bubbled up from the valley bottom and formed a little clear brook full of fish between grassy swards. Here some of us halted and used Kutus's girdle as a net. At the first haul we caught 18 fish, and we did not cease till we had 160—not large ones, but quite sufficient to feed all thirteen of us. It was amusing to see Little

Puppy as he stood watching attentively and regarding the sprawling fishes, barking and shaking his head. He had never in his life seen running water before, and must have supposed that he could walk upon it as safely as on clear ice. Quite unsuspiciously he jumped down from the grass, where the brook was 2 feet deep, and entirely disappeared under the water. When he had, with much difficulty, struggled up again, he was much amazed and disconcerted, and prowled about growling with displeasure at the cold bath. After that he kept far away from the deceitful brook.

March 28. Now we saw that we could trust Takkar, so we let him loose. He did not run away, but was in the best of tempers, and flew like an arrow over the slopes, enjoying his freedom, and played with Little Puppy, who became furious when the huge brute came racing down on him with playful leaps, so that he rolled over and over on the ground.

Abdul Kerim was to go on the new horse with the Ladaki saddle, accompanied by two men, to look out for Tsongpun Tashi. He had plenty of money to buy anything he might find, and in reply to searching questions he was to say that we had orders from Gulam Razul to meet one of his caravans in Raga-tasam, which in about ten days was to leave Lhasa, and then accompany it to Ladak.

I had to ride my grey horse barebacked, but I had not got far before we passed two tents, where four Tibetans came out to look at us. Two of our men went and talked to them while the rest of us followed the brook through the valley. A little further and we had to be careful again, for there were three more tents and two large flocks, the owner of which possessed 3000 sheep. Sheepfolds, old camping-places, and *manis* were all around, for we were on a great highway, and therefore I kept close to the sheep, and whistled and shouted at them. At the mouth of a side valley, on the left, stood a large white tent with blue borders, which was said to belong to the chief of the district, the Gova Chykying. A man came out of the tent, hurried after us, and asked whence we came and whither we were going. Two women came out of a tent inhabited by beggars, and put the same questions. A mile or so farther we were out of sight of tents, and I jumped on my grey horse, but I could not ride far, for more tents appeared farther down the valley. We encamped by the side of the brook in the Kung-sherya country, where the valley is very broad and open, and tents are seen in many directions. From one of these, which stood below ours, a man came and made inquiries. He said that one of the tents, which looked large and important, belonged to Takyung Lama, abbot of Mendong-gompa, a monastery three days' journey to the south-east. Now we were in a warm corner, with the district chief, a high lama, and Tsongpun Tashi as near neighbours, and the Governor of the great province of Bongba not far off. It would be a marvel if we succeeded in making our way out of this wasps' nest. One thing was certain, that we must make off next morning, before news of our arrival had spread about.

After we had waited several hours Abdul Kerim came. We could see at a long distance that he had bought a horse, which was laden with sacks and bags containing rice, barley, butter, and *tsamba*. Tsongpun Tashi proved to be an old man of a poverty-stricken and mean appearance, but his large tent was full of goods, sacks, and packets of tea, and his movable shop was very well stocked. Naturally he was much surprised at the visit, but he swallowed the story that Abdul Kerim dished up for him. He had even given him the names of all the places where we ought to camp on the way to Saka-dzong and Raga-tasam, and advised us to be well on our guard in a district he called Bupgo-lathit, where there were always robbers. He related that a band of robbers had, a few weeks before, attacked and plundered Targyaling-gompa, the monastery where we had met with such a hostile reception in June of the preceding year. Forty men with horses and guns had been levied to chase the band, but Tsongpun Tashi said that these forty men were little better than robbers themselves, and that we ought to inquire about them, so as to avoid them as they returned. Abdul Kerim promised Tsongpun Tashi to barter our sick black horse for some provisions, but Abdul

Kerim did not know that Abdullah had already exchanged the horse at the beggars' tent for two sheep and a goat. There the faithful horse would see happy days again when the grass grew up.

After Abdul Kerim had drunk tea he went on to visit the Gova Chykying, who came out of his tent and said that Takyung Lama had that very day imposed on him eight days' *yangguk*—that means that he must not transact any kind of business, but must devote himself entirely, on account of his sins, to contemplation in his own house. That was fine for us; the Gova was reduced to a negligible quantity.

March 29. Temperature 13° in the night, and 55° at seven o'clock—this is spring. Welcome mild salubrious breezes, come to thaw our frozen joints!

Early in the morning came a couple of our men tramping along with another dog, light yellow, dirty, and loathsome. He was inhospitably received by Takkar, who immediately gave him a sharp pinch in the neck, and seemed to think that the new member of the caravan was quite superfluous as long as he kept watch himself.

Far in the north a solitary Tibetan appeared, and approached our camp. I was sitting at breakfast, and was hoping that we should soon leave this dangerous place. I went out and looked through the field-glass; the stranger was making straight for our tents. Soon Abdul Kerim came and said that it was Tsongpun Tashi himself. He stopped at some distance and called to us to tie up our dogs, for Takkar had rushed at the old man, who defended himself with stones. The men were purposely slow in fastening up the dogs, in order to give me time to put the interior of my tent in order. On such occasions my note-books and instruments were crammed into a rice sack, which always stood ready. There was no other furniture, for we had burned all European articles and boxes long before.

Meanwhile, Abdul Kerim conducted Tsongpun Tashi into his tent, which stood close against mine, and I listened to their conversation at a distance of little more than a yard. By degrees the talk became, to say the least of it, lively. Tsongpun Tashi raised his voice more and more, and Abdul Kerim was evidently in a serious dilemma.

"Did you not promise to give me the black horse in exchange for butter? Bring the horse immediately. If you do not keep your word, I will detain the whole pack of you here. We do not let men that break their word escape in Bongba. I thought yesterday that you were honest men, but now I see what you are up to. Now I shall begin by searching your tents."

With that he got up as angry as a wasp and went out. But Gulam, who was always alert and never lost a word of a conversation, had let Takkar loose again. As soon as Tsongpun Tashi showed himself at the tent door the dog flew at him again. He backed, and Abdul seized the opportunity to call out in a gruff voice: "Kutus, take Hajji Baba with you and go and look for the lost horse."

"What horse is that?" asked Tsongpun.

"It is one of our horses which has run away up the mountain, and we cannot set out till we have found him."

"What colour is he?" asked Tsongpun with uncomfortable inquisitiveness.

"Grey," replied Abdul Kerim, who had difficulty in concealing his uneasiness, for it was he who had pledged the black steed without knowing whether it was still in our possession.

"Very well, I shall stay here till you have found the grey horse."

During the minute this conversation lasted Tsongpun Tashi had walked towards the opening of my tent, when Kutus came running up from the other side, seized me by the collar, and whispered "Come." We hurried off to a crag on the north-east, and so just escaped the clutches of Tsongpun.

"What man is that?" the old man asked, pointing at me, as I was making off with clumsy waddling steps.

"Hajji Baba, one of my servants," answered Abdul Kerim, without moving a muscle.

We did not look round as we went off to the point, and were glad when at length we were hidden by a projecting rock. Then we scrambled up a fissure whence we could see all around. Here we lay a weary time with our hearts in our mouths, while Tsongpun Tashi waited for the runaway horse, which had not run away at all, for all our animals stood ready laden before our tents. But he must have lost patience. After Gaffar had gone to the tent to try and get back the black horse, but met with a refusal, for the horse had been fed with barley and was getting on splendidly, Tsongpun Tashi seemed to make in that direction himself, accompanied by Gaffar. But he changed his mind, for he turned back half-way, and soon we saw him going to the fine tent of the soul-doctor, which stood about 300 yards farther down the valley. He was attended by one of our men, who helped him to carry the sacks in which the goods acquired the previous day were packed.

We remained quiet in our hiding-place of much-weathered green schist, full of quartz veins, from which we could peep out without being seen. We were supposed to be looking for the lost horse. But now the caravan was ready, and began to move down the valley past the abbot's tent. Tsongpun Tashi's errand had been to take farewell of the prelate, who was setting out this day for Mendong-gompa, absolutely unknown in all the maps in the world, and his yaks stood tethered and surrounded by a troop of servants. Abdul Kerim was shrewd enough to send no messenger after us, but leave us to take care of ourselves. And so we did when we had had enough of the green schist —we could not lie still till doomsday. But we had to pass the abbot's tent, and there sat Tsongpun Tashi, unless he were among the men outside. We sneaked on. Kutus walked next the tent to screen me. My disguise was perfect, and I had a black face. We passed with some trepidation quite close to the tent; two savage dogs rushed at us and we threw stones at them, thereby deranging our order of march and making a change of front. Confounded dogs! We had passed the tent, and, so far, had done well. But if Tsongpun Tashi noticed us—and he could scarcely fail to do so, for the dogs barked so furiously—he would certainly wonder in which direction the grey horse had made off. If he had no suspicion of us he must be, beyond comparison, the greatest ass that I had ever fallen in with.

We made haste and soon overtook the others, and were lost among them. The valley sloped down—a fortunate thing for me, as I had to travel on foot where so many pitfalls surrounded me on all sides. Abdul Kerim rode grandly on my horse at the head of the party. On the left were a white-and-blue and a black tent with twenty yaks. Two men hurried up to us, and Abdul Kerim met and spoke to them. We marched along the ice belt of the brook, and passed five more tents, and, at all, the men came out to look at us. I walked with the sheep farther from the tents than the caravan. We passed twenty tents that day; it was a dangerous stretch of country, and it was strange that we came through safely.

A woman, carrying a load of wool on her back, overtook us. She was so bold as to join herself to the caravan and ask to be allowed to put her wool on one of the yaks. Never have I so heartily wished a woman at the devil. Abdul Rasak took the woman in hand and offered to carry half her load to her tent, and so they jogged along the road far ahead, and freed us from her suspicious company.

We took it for granted that she was a spy. When we encamped below a sheepfold, there she was again, established herself inside the fold, lighted a fire and fetched water. She must drink tea before she went on homewards, she said; but fortunately she toddled off before dusk.

I sat in the setting sun and noted down the varied incidents of the day. I sat in the opening of my tent enjoying the soothing rustle of the spring, when what should I see but Takkar himself, who came up to me anxiously and humbly, made the most expressive gestures, put his head on one side and began to paw my arm. I looked at him and he looked at me, and at last we understood each other.

"I could not know," he said, "that you were nice men when you tied me by the neck to this horrible tent pole. I thought that you would tease and torment and starve me, and throw stones and dirt at me, as the Tibetans have done ever since I can remember. But I see that you are well disposed towards me, and give me two good meals of mutton every day. I know that you, in spite of your rags, are a bombo-chimbo, and that Abdul Kerim is only a servant. Be at ease, I will not let any one come near your tent; I will watch over you at night, I will never betray you, I will follow you everywhere; you may trust in me. But now come and play with me a little; take away this useless tent pole, and let us be no longer strangers."

His shrewd brown eyes showed plainly that this was what he meant to say, word for word. I took his shaggy head in my arms and squeezed it. Then he jumped up on me and began to dance and yelp with joy, and enticed me out of my tent. Then I took hold of him again, untied the knots, and released him from his pole, to the great astonishment of my men, who were sitting in the open around a fire. No one had ever ventured so near to Takkar, except Little Puppy, and without the slightest jealousy the little cub joined in the game, which henceforth whiled away daily a couple of hours of my weary captivity.

CHAPTER LXV

BUPTSANG-TSANGPO, ONE OF THE LARGEST RIVERS OF THE HEART OF TIBET

It was with a feeling of relief that we broke up our camp on March 30, after we had succeeded in extricating ourselves from the net which had so nearly held us fast in its meshes. Through here runs the so-called Serpun-lam, or gold-inspectors' road, which extends through the interior of Tibet from Lhasa to Tok-jalung, and is one of the greatest high-roads of the country. We did not yet feel quite safe, but we had heard some assuring news: Karma Puntso had taken a journey of several days northwards to a place in Chang-tang where he owned large flocks of sheep. Most of the nomads in Bongba had sent their sheep to the north, where the grazing was much better. This was of great advantage to us, for now only women, old men, and children remained in the tents of Bongba, while most of the men were following the sheep. It was part of the trial of my patience that I could not have the slightest dealings with Tibetans, for I should have betrayed myself at once by my defective utterance of the language. I never talked with them, but pulled the strings of my marionettes from my place of concealment.

The wild-geese had now commenced their migrations, and we constantly heard their cries above our tents. On March 30 we found an excellent path along the river in which we had caught fish just below Ladung-la. The country was very open and flat, and we passed at some distance from twelve tents. Near the last we pitched camp 368, and bought a black horse. We had now four horses, of which one was a veteran from Ladak; now I rode the first horse we had bought—a brown one. The last three mules and the two yaks from the Tsong-tso were in good condition. When we encamped near natives, Takkar was tied up outside the entrance to my tent to keep off inquisitive visitors. He had been bred and reared among Tibetans, and had never seen any other people in his life till lately, and yet now he became mad with rage if he saw a Tibetan only at a distance. I had often to pay various sums in rupees to those of his two-legged fellow-countrymen whose unprotected legs he had bitten, and he was never contented without a slight effusion of blood.

We followed the river south-south-westwards for another day's journey to camp 369, where some poor nomads were encamping by a sheet of snow. Sha-kangsham's summit came into sight again, this time to the north, 30° E., rising like a gigantic beacon above the mountains. Five days' journey to the west-north-west was pointed out the salt lake, Tabie-tsaka, the position of which I had sought in vain to ascertain from the *tasam*. In the afternoon when I sat outside to draw a panorama, nomads were strolling and peering about, so that I had to post watchmen. In the evening all around was pitch-dark: there was no moon, only dense clouds. Our animals had disappeared, and as there was good reason to fear wolves and horse-stealers, eight men were sent out to look for them. They had revolvers, and fired a few shots to let any possible disturbers of the peace know that we were armed. The animals would not freeze, for the temperature fell in the night only to 18°, and in the morning they had come back again all right. The only one missing was the greyish-yellow dog; thinking, perhaps, that he had fallen into bad company, he had gnawed through his rope and run home in the night to his miserable tent.

Now the path runs south-south-west up to the little easy pass Satsot-la (15,932 feet), in red porphyry and with a way-mark. In the wide valley in front of us lies the lake Chunit-tso, and on its farther side rises a red mountain of regular form. We pass several *manis*, and on the right hand a miniature lake called Chabuk-tso, where Tubges shot two wild-geese. The honorary huntsman often supplied me with game; he was called by his comrades simply Shyok, after his home, just as we call one of our acquaintances Jönköping or Falsterbo.

We crossed a great road running to the north-west; hundreds of yaks had recently passed—no doubt a salt caravan on the way to Tabie-tsaka. Then we passed a circular wall, where a solitary man came out and looked at us, but retired behind the wall when he found that we would have nothing to do with him. A fine *mani* decorated with horns stood on a terrace, and just below it we halted for the night by a sheet of ice produced by springs. We had scarcely set up the tents when a caravan of several hundred sheep, laden with salt, came along from the north-west. Only two armed guides were with it; they had been to Tabie-tsaka, and were now going home to Yangchut-tanga, twenty days' journey to the south-east. In the same direction 400 yaks were grazing, which were said to belong to the Gova of the district. In the evening we had a visit from a traveller who was going home to his tent farther south. He promised to sell us three sheep in the morning. Would he keep his word?

Yes, certainly; he met us with the sheep next day as we were passing along the western shore of the Chunit-tso (15,574 feet) southwards. At the northern extremity of the lake a warm sulphurous spring burst forth. We were told that if a man drinks of it he becomes ill, but if he mixes the water with some from an adjacent cold spring he is cured of any complaint he may suffer from. Sick sheep and goats are dipped in the warm water and become well again at once. The spring is holy, and a *mani* heap is set up near it. The lake is slightly salt and frozen. Two small brooks enter it from the mountains on the west; a third brook, Lungnak-bupchu, formed a large sheet of ice, and in the mouth of its valley stood a couple of tents, and their dogs came down on us like a whirlwind, but received such a thrashing from Takkar that they showed themselves no more that evening.

April 3. We left the southern end of the lake behind us and ascended a small valley leading up to the low pass Nima-lung-la, near which we encamped in a barren spot between granite crags. An eagle-owl sat in a cleft and at twilight uttered its shrill piercing cry. Lobsang said that this bird was thought much of in Tibet, because it warns honest men of thieves and robbers. When the eagle-owls sit and scream, robbers are certain to be in the neighbourhood.

On April 4 we had only half an hour's march to the threshold of the Nima-lung-la (16,017 feet), from which there is a magnificent view over the Trans-Himalaya—a series of dark rocks with black, snow-crowned peaks. Between us and the range extended a wide, perfectly level plain, full of pools, marshes, and rivulets. At one of them sat two Tibetans cutting up a yak which had died. They confirmed the information we had received before, that we were now in the district Bongba-kemar, a day's journey from Bongba-kebyang, and that we must follow the river Buptsang-tsangpo for several days upwards to reach Saka-dzong by the pass Samye-la. I had still a very dim and indistinct notion of the geographical configuration of this region. Was the range in front of us to the south a continuation of Nien-chen-tang-la, which I had crossed at the Sela-la, Chang-la-Pod-la, and Angden-la; or was it another range disconnected from the former? During the following days we should obtain an answer to this question. Should we be successful, and be able to complete this exceedingly important meridional traverse through an unknown part of Tibet? It would be more than provoking to be stopped just at the northern foot of the Trans-Himalaya.

Camp 374 was pitched below the opening of a valley where there were two tents. The nomads warned us against the water in the pools of the plain: our horses would lose their hair if they drank of it. "Snoring" Kunchuk complained of toothache, but was cured at once by two resolute comrades. The operation was performed with pincers properly intended for horse-shoe nails. To get at the tooth better, they put a stone in the patient's mouth. "Do not kill me," he shrieked when the tooth jumped out.

On April 5 we travelled altogether 10¼ miles to the south. The country was perfectly barren, and the ground was entirely covered with red porphyry detritus. A small spring surrounded by grass seemed to us quite an oasis, and there we encamped near a sheepfold and a *mani* heap.

Another day's march and we came to the Buptsang-tsangpo, "the deeply excavated river," and followed it to the south. The river is divided into several arms, and already contained a deal of water, though for the most part it was frozen. This valley is about 3 miles broad and has a very gentle slope. The locality where we encamped after passing fourteen tents was called Monlam-gongma (15,820 feet). Hence the river was said to flow five days' journey to the north-north-west and pour into a large lake, called the Tarok-tso. We might have attempted to make an excursion in that direction, but it was more important to complete the meridional line while the country was still open to us. Two huge snowy peaks which the nomads here, as on the *tasam*, called Lunpo-gangri, or "the great ice mountain," were said to lie to the right of the route we ought to follow to Saka-dzong. This information was exceedingly puzzling, and I saw that Lunpo-gangri with the summits triangulated by Ryder and Wood could not be a prolongation of the mighty range I had crossed by three passes, and which, farther east, bears the name Nien-chen-tang-la.

After a vain attempt to get rid of our enfeebled yaks, we continued up the great river along its right or eastern bank terrace. A south-westerly storm which commenced some days before still continued. In the Amchung country (camp 376) we had a neighbour called Kamba Dramdul, who could not give much information, but what he said was of deep interest. We had still some days' journey to the Samye-la—all up the Buptsang-tsangpo valley, with *gangris* or snowy heights on both the right and left sides. On the pass we should be quite close to the peaks of Lunpo-gangri. I already suspected that the great range we had on our left—that is, towards the east—was a continuation of Nien-chen-tang-la, while Lunpo-gangri was a quite independent chain without the least connection with the former.

The eastern range increased in magnitude on the following day's march, and among its dark ramifications rose some rather flat summits capped with eternal snow. We kept for the most part to the top of the terrace on the right bank, which was 50 to 65 feet above the river, and fell steeply to the even valley bottom where the stream meandered. Here the valley was about 2 miles broad. The ice mantle of the river became wider and thicker the higher we mounted, but the rise was very gradual. From camp 377 the culminating peak of Lunpo-gangri lay south, 23° E. Every day's journey we accomplished without adventures strengthened our position. The nomads must think: If these men travel right through the whole of Bongba without being stopped, they cannot be impostors.

On April 10 we travelled 8½ miles up the Buptsang-tsangpo, and we were astonished to find so voluminous a river up on the isolated plateau country. On its banks ducks and geese cackled in large numbers. Tubges shot several of them; it was a sin to disturb their dreams of spring and love. No human being was seen this day. I had a feeling of repose when we could see no black tents, and for the sake of peace I would readily abstain from sour milk. The view to the south-south-east was magnificent; the peaks of Lunpo-gangri stood out against the pure blue sky in dazzling white, with shades of light blue indicating ice. On the east also of our route appeared a whole world of mountains. Most unexpectedly the summits of Lunpo-gangri have a much grander and more imposing appearance from the northern side, towards the plateau country, than from the south side, the valley of the Brahmaputra, most probably because on the southern side they are too near. Up in the north we saw them at all distances, and for several days we had them right in front of us.

In the night of April 11 the temperature sank to −1.7°, and on the preceding nights to 3.7°, 13.5°, and 17.2°. The cold increased as we mounted higher. We came to an expansion in the valley where three glacier streams unite to form the Buptsang-tsangpo, just as in the case of the Brahmaputra, and also on the northern flank of one of

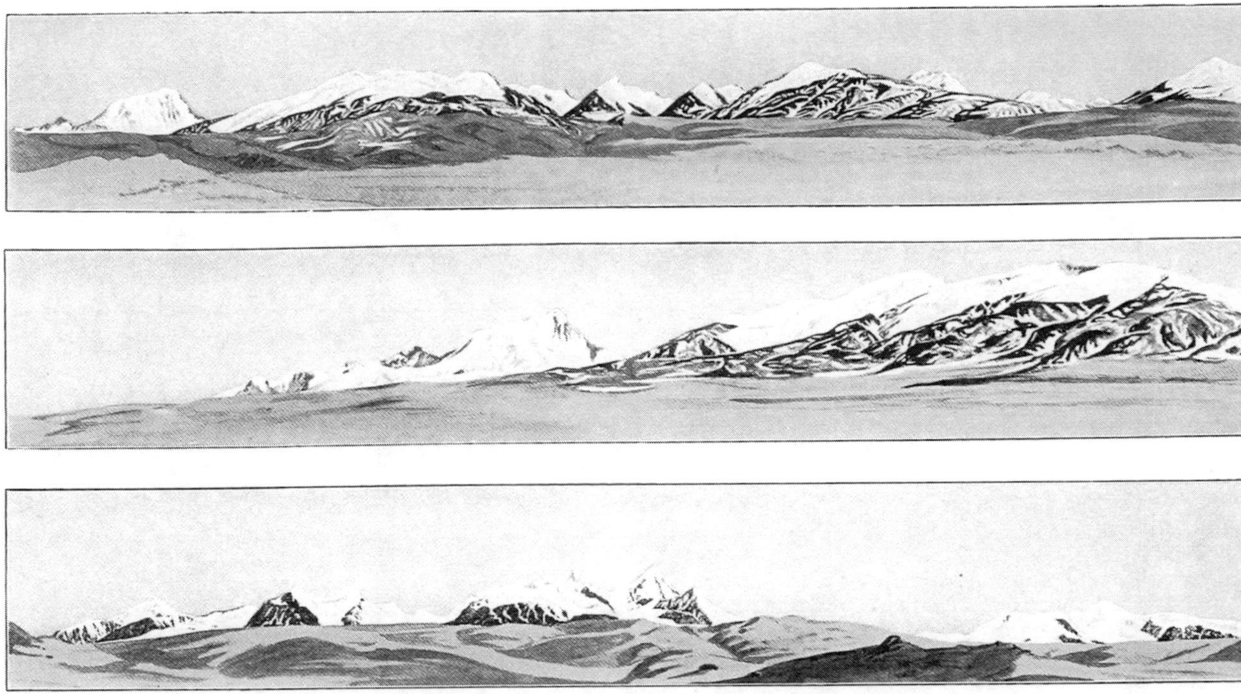

319

320

321

319, 320, 321. THE SUMMITS OF LUNPO-GANGRI FROM CAMPS 379, 381, AND 383.
From Water-Colours by the Author.

the world's mightiest mountain systems. Our camp 379 (16,112 feet) was pitched close to the river in Bupyung-ring. The eastern headwater comes partly from the Samye-la, partly from mountains adjoining on the south-west. The middle one descends from a massive called Yallak-mallak, and the western from Chomo-gangri; south-east of this mountain is Lunpo-gangri, which is drained to the sea, both from its northern and its southern flank (Illusts. 319, 320, 321).

Bupyung-ring is one of the finest and most beautiful regions I have seen in Tibet. The flat wide valley, surrounded by mountains with ice and snow, is clothed with abundant grass and traversed by numerous water-courses. Everywhere are seen traces of camping-places. At the time we passed through only a few tent villages remained, but the valley is full of life in summer when the nomads come down from the north. When the melting of the snows properly sets in during summer, and afterwards in the rainy season, the Buptsang-tsangpo swells up so tremendously that the river cannot be crossed for three months, and communication between the banks is interrupted. From its source to its outlet in the Tarok-tso the river is probably nearly 100 miles long, and is possibly the largest river in Tibet which does not flow to the sea. The only rivers that can vie with it are the Sachu-tsangpo, which flows into the Zilling-tso, and the Soma-tsangpo, which falls into the Teri-nam-tso. The Sachu-tsangpo was far larger than the Buptsang when I crossed it in the rainy season in 1901. But the Buptsang is also a large river in spring, and in the rainy season must swell as much as the Sachu. The Buptsang-tsangpo has hitherto been unknown to Europeans, but we find the Tarok-tso on D'Anville's map, and a river entering the lake from the south, which no doubt is identical with the Buptsang-tsangpo. The Jesuits who resided in Pekin two hundred years ago, and were ordered by the Emperor Kang Hi to compile a map of the whole Chinese Empire, procured information even about this remote region from Chinese and Tibetan sources.

During the past days our two yaks had become so

wearied and footsore that we had to get rid of them at any price. We therefore stayed a day in Bupyung and bartered them for nine sheep, which took over the loads of the yaks. Now we had again thirty-one sheep and some goats.

On the 13th we came to the foot of the mountain where commenced the actual steep ascent to the pass itself. Here were four tents inhabited exclusively by women and children. The men had gone a couple of days before to Gova Tsepten's tent. It is incumbent on this chief to collect a certain number of men and yaks, which for about three months are posted on the *tasam* ready to transport goods on behalf of the Devashung without compensation. This is a kind of *corvée* which is exacted not only all along the road between Lhasa and Ladak, but on all other great high-roads in Tibet. Naturally this injudicious system is a great annoyance to the nomads, who have to leave their flocks in the meantime to the care of women and children. If any one wishes to escape this compulsory service he must supply a substitute, pay him, and furnish him with yaks and provisions. The year before, when we travelled with hired horses from Shigatse, the poor nomads served us, but we always paid them honourably and gave them handsome gratuities as well.

After a night temperature of −0.8° we rode up to the pass on the 14th, over and between hills and across the brook which brings its tribute from the Samye-la to the Buptsang-tsangpo. Solid rock could not be found, but all the detritus and boulders were of grey granite; seldom was a piece of porphyry noticed. The usual observations were made on the pass, and the boiling-point thermometer was read off. The view of Lunpo-gangri was grander than ever, now that its peaks were quite near. The distinctly marked valley of the Buptsang-tsangpo disappeared in the distance to the north-north-west, while to the south-east nothing could be seen but a flat saddle, whence I concluded that we were not yet on the actual water-parting pass. We had not followed the track of the caravan far, before we saw a brook coming from the south-east, which also belonged to the Buptsang-tsangpo. On its bank, where we also halted, was encamped a caravan of 8 men and 350 yaks, which was carrying salt to Saka-dzong, six days' march farther. These men could not understand why we, merchants from Ladak, chose such a way, and asked how we found it out. They were treated to the usual story about the wool-trade in summer, and they regretted that they could not serve us with their yaks, as they were called out for Government transport on the great high-roads. Now we wondered whether they would let the Governor of Saka-dzong know that they had met with a party of Ladakis on byways, and if this news would injure us. Perhaps, after all, it would be best to avoid Saka-dzong altogether.

On April 15 it was our chief desire to get in advance of the yak caravan. Before they had begun to load up their animals I started off with the sheep, and came in good time to the summit of the Samye-la with its streamer-decked poles. Though we were all the way in sight of the yak-men's camp, I must, at any cost, determine the height of the pass, and the distance was so great that they could not see what we were doing. After boiling the thermometer, whence we obtained a height of 18,133 feet, I also drew a panorama. To the south and south-east was a world of mountains belonging to the Lunpo-gangri range, which lay to the south, and to Nien-chen-tang-la on the north. We were therefore standing on the actual watershed between two gigantic ranges, which are both members of the Trans-Himalayan family. And this pass, the Samye-la, occupies the highest and most important rank from a hydrographic and orographical point of view that any pass in Asia can lay claim to, for it is a divide between the isolated drainage area of the plateau on the north and the boundless ocean on the south. It ranks, then, with the Sela-la, Chang-la-Pod-la, and Angden-la, and is much more important than the Tseti-lachen-la, which is only a watershed between the Sutlej and the Indus, and than the Jukti-la, which parts the waters between the two arms of the Indus. At the Samye-la I attained my chief desire, to cross the Trans-Himalaya between the Tseti-lachen-la and the Angden-la, and gain another point on the immense boundary line on the north of the basins of the great Indian rivers, and I succeeded in proving the unbroken continuance of the Trans-Himalaya for 118 miles west of Angden-la. A most extraordinarily interesting discovery also was that the Angden-la and the Samye-la, though of exactly the same value as watersheds, do not lie on the same chain. The Angden-la is situated on the western prolongation of the chain which stands on the southern shore of Tengri-nor and is known by the name of Nien-chen-tang-la, but the Samye-la lies in a longitudinal valley between this chain and Lunpo-gangri. Accordingly, I could strike out once and for all the continuous mountain range which Hodgson and Saunders constructed at their writing-table, and represented as running north of the upper Brahmaputra. Here also I considered what name I should give to the colossal mountain system which runs in the north parallel to the Himalayas. The name Lunpo-gangri had at least as much claim as Nien-chen-tang-la, but both were unsuitable, as they only denoted certain ranges in a whole system, and therefore had only local significance. Then it came to me like a flash—Trans-Himalaya is the name which I will attach to this gigantic mountain system.

While I sat and pondered over the great idea which had come to me this day without any merit of my own, I was recalled to the business of the moment by Lobsang, who informed me that the yaks were moving in a black line up to the pass. Then we got up and went on foot down the slopes bestrewn with troublesome rubbish and granite boulders. Soon trickling rivulets collected into a small brook. I regarded with pleasure this little stream leaping among the stones, and listened to its purling song. It was the old melody, and we had recently heard it from the brooks of the Buptsang-tsangpo. And yet I seemed to hear an undertone of another kind, a sound in the water which suggested a new aim. The Buptsang-tsangpo is doomed to final annihilation in the Tarok-tso and Tabie-tsaka, where the water is evaporated and dispersed to the four winds of heaven. But the brook we now followed debouches into the Chaktak-tsangpo and Brahmaputra, and its destiny is the Indian Ocean, over which runs the way to my home.

We had just set up our tents before the yaks came tramping up in close order, followed by their whistling and singing drivers. They went round, not to come too near us. Were they afraid of us or were they suspicious? Were they a cloud, no larger than a man's hand, from which, in due time, a destructive tornado was to burst over our little band, which now for the second time crossed the forbidden land without leave?

CHAPTER LXVI

IN THE ROBBERS' PARADISE

In former times the glacier tongues of Lunpo-gangri ran down into the valley, and traces of them were very conspicuous as we descended to lower country on April 16. The valley is quite full of old moraines, consisting exclusively of granite, and some of them are superficially concealed under fine matter and moss. We passed the large yak caravan again, which was encamping after a very short march. Evidently the men intended to stay over the next day, for the loads were taken off the yaks and piled up. When they mean to set out again the next day they leave the loads on the yaks, for they think it too much trouble to load and unload 350 yaks for a single night. They might stay for us as long as they liked; we should get in advance and pass by Saka-dzong before we were denounced. But no, it would be wiser to avoid Saka-dzong altogether; not to escape the sight of Muhamed Isa's grave, but not to needlessly expose ourselves to suspicion. It was perfectly evident that the authorities would wonder why a small party of Ladakis went along byways instead of following the great *tasam*, and they would hold an inquiry over us.

After the moraines came to an end we traversed a more open expansion of the valley, with luxuriant grass and millions of detestable mouse-holes. We were right glad when Takkar pinched the necks of one or two of these obnoxious rodents. Tubges supplied me with partridges, and one of our goats yielded me a drop of milk. From camp 383 Lunpo-gangri's summits are seen foreshortened, and

323

324

325

322. Wrestling. 323. Two Guides. 324. Boy with Hat. 325. Shepherd Boy.
(Inhabitants of the Province of Bongba.)

Sketches by the Author.

one of them is as small as an umbrella. Several peaks are seen to the east-south-east, the continuation of the range, and it is not difficult to infer that Chomo-uchong, the isolated mountain beside the *tasam*, lies in the eastern prolongation of Lunpo-gangri. I took bearings of the higher summits in the neighbourhood from every camp, and shall hereafter make known the results.

The other men make the "Snorer's" life miserable. At eight o'clock he crawls into his lair beside the sheep, and immediately begins his wood-sawing. Some one yells at him, and he wakes up and makes some witty remark, which makes the men laugh, and he never loses his temper. In two minutes he is asleep again and sawing as hard as ever, and is roused by another shout. Only when the others have fallen asleep is he left in peace, and can saw as hard as he likes.

Little Puppy behaves splendidly, is lively, playful, and affectionate. At night he sleeps on the rugs at my feet and helps Takkar to keep watch. They are my companions, and it will be hard to part from them.

April 17. 0.7°. How long this winter has been! Now Lobsang has come to the conclusion that the yak drivers will not denounce us, for fear lest they should be called to account for not spying upon us better. We continue our way down the valley. How delightful only to go for some days to lower country. In some places we see summer camping-grounds; now the country is desolate and deserted.

The river carries down about 70 cubic feet of clear water per second; it has open water only in the middle, and elsewhere is covered with margins of ice 2 feet thick, and icicles hang from their edges. On the banks, field-mice dart about between their holes. The valley contracts and the river often skirts steep cliffs of schist. Most of the tributaries, and the largest of them, come from the chain which is the immediate continuation of Nien-chen-tang-la. The ice becomes thicker the more the valley contracts and the longer it is in shadow. We often cross it from one bank to the other, where it forms a bridge. Stags' horns are set up on a *mani* heap; where do they come from? This valley runs between the two ranges like the

Buptsang-tsangpo. On this day we never see a man or a tent.

In the evening a night owl again sat screeching above the camp, and the Ladakis were convinced that it meant to warn us against robbers. If these knew that a European with European weapons was in the caravan they would not attack it; but we were only Ladakis, and the Tibetans despise Ladakis and look upon them as cowards.

On the 18th we travelled southwards to the place (15,407 feet) where our valley enters the Rukyok valley, running down from the west-north-west, at the bottom of which some of the Lunpo-gangri summits were again visible. Still no men were to be seen, only numerous summer camping-places. Two horsemen rode past our camp on the other, right, side of the valley. What did they want? Were they spies? We had every reason to suspect a spy in every human being. No; they were kiang hunters from Gertse, who had left their home and were seeking new dwellings in another province, because of some unpleasantness with the Gertse Pun, the potentate whom we were carefully making away from. They informed us that we were a day's journey from Pasa-guk, where I had encamped the year before, and three short marches from Saka-dzong. It was hazardous to pass so near a governor's residence. Abdul Kerim bought one of the riders' horses for 100 rupees.

This day I put on for the first time a new Ladaki costume. The other was too warm, and, being red, was conspicuous among the others. The new coat was made of worn, tattered sackcloth, and was stained with ashes and soot. In this I looked just like the other men. Now I painted my face regularly every day, and he must be a very smart fellow who could find out that I was not a genuine Ladaki. We had hitherto got on remarkably well, and had only a day's journey to a place where I had been the year before. But the nervous tension increased more and more, and I wondered every morning what surprises the new day had in store for us.

April 19. As we were starting, two men passed on foot, driving before them 200 sheep laden with salt. Our

327

329

326. Sonam Ngurbu, Chief of the Chokchu Province. 327. Dorche Tsuen, Governor of the Saka Province. 328. Man with a Singular Cap, in Sonam Ngurbu's Escort. 329. Tagla Tsering, the Chief who refused to let me go to the Dangra-yum-tso.

Sketches by the Author.

way was the same as theirs and we had to pass them. While I drove our own sheep down the road, Abdul Kerim stopped and talked with the men, to draw off their attention; but we could see that they were interested in our strange party, and looked closely at us. I limped, thinking that the Tibetans had never seen a lame European, if they had seen any European at all. But the people had seen me in Pasa-guk and Saka-dzong the year before, and then I did not halt. I had come off well from our troublesome neighbours and also past the large yak caravan, which a couple of days ago had turned off another way but had now come into ours again. We met a large sheep caravan with a mounted party; a woman was said to be the wife of the Gova of Rukyok. The people we had just met were not so dangerous as those that followed.

We left the Rukyok river farther and farther to the right, and directly to the south appeared quite close the lofty summit which rises above Pasa-guk. We had left the salt-laden sheep and the yaks behind us, and we came at length to the bank of our old friend the Chaktak-tsangpo, which was considerably smaller than at the end of May and beginning of June the year before. Here we left the high-road to the south, and marched northwards along the Chaktak-tsangpo's right, or western bank, where we soon encamped on a meadow (15,203 feet).

When Abdul Kerim came back he was very solemn. He had had great difficulty in answering questions why we followed a byway along the Chaktak-tsangpo instead of taking the highway to Saka-dzong as all other travellers did. He had replied that we were sent to find out how much sheep's wool would be for sale in the country next summer. Then the men of the salt caravan had said: "You cannot be afraid of robbers; they frequent the mountains up here. Are you well armed?"

"Yes, we have two guns and some revolvers."

"You will want them. We see that you are peaceful people, so we warn you. Six days ago a robber band, eighteen men strong, each with his horse and gun, attacked a tent village here in the neighbourhood. They pillaged 3 tents, took 400 sheep and about 200 yaks, and made off by the road you intend to follow. Men were collected and sent after them, but two were killed and the others ran away. No one knows where the band is now. If you value your lives, keep a sharp watch at night. If they attack you, let them plunder you; you are only thirteen, and cannot defend yourselves."

This was why Abdul Kerim looked so anxious, and it was not to be wondered at. Now we also ran the risk of a night attack, as if it were not trying enough to travel in disguise by byways through the forbidden land. As long as there was daylight the animals were allowed to wander about and graze, but at dusk they were driven up near to the tents. In the evening the men could talk of nothing but robbers. Lobsang, who was a Tibetan himself, took the matter quietly. He said that there were organized bands of as many as a hundred men with a chief at their head, who ordered where raids should be made. But at this season of the year they sat round their fires and tried to look innocent. In his opinion the air must be warmer before they would move. If a robber was caught in the neighbourhood of Gartok, his head and one arm must be sent as a proof to Lhasa, he added. In the principal towns punishment is very severe. For theft an eye is taken out and a hand cut off. A Gova or other magistrate who catches a robber receives a reward or promotion, but one who neglects his duty is punished. We heard that the district near Geddo by the upper Raga-tsangpo is notorious as a regular nest of robbers, and is visited by professional freebooters from Nakchu.

In the twilight the Mohammedans among my Ladakis sang the same melodious hymn I had first heard at Kizil-unkur. "Allahu ekber" echoed among the rocky cliffs; "and it is very effective in protecting true believers against the wiles of the heathen." They had all at once become deeply religious again in the robbers' paradise. "Allahu ekber," God is great.

The night passed peacefully, and early the next morning it was reported that five horsemen were approaching our tents from the north. The field-glass reduced them to two men, a woman, and some yaks. They made a circuit as though they were afraid of us, but Abdul Kerim hailed them to get information about the road. Then we marched on directly eastwards along the northern bank of the Chaktak-tsangpo. The ascent was very gradual, the valley fairly broad and with abundant pasture. No tent was seen, but summer camps were numerous. A cairn marks the place where the Chaktak-tsangpo, coming from the north, 10° W., unites with its tributary the Gebuk-chu from the east. To the north-north-east rise two snowy peaks of medium height with small glaciers. It was evident that the Chaktak-tsangpo flows from the country to the north of them, for the deeply excavated transverse valley of the river could be clearly traced. The main river may carry down about 250 cubic feet in a second, and the affluent about 70. In this district the river is called Kamchung-chu; the name Chaktak-tsangpo (Charta-tsangpo, as it is incorrectly called by Nain Sing) is not applied to it above Pasa-guk. We encamped in the angle between the two rivers near a meadow where three horses were feeding. Their owners, who were bivouacking behind a projection near at hand, were from Rukyok and had lost many of their sheep in winter from disease, and had been to a warm spring to dip and save the remainder. We were here about due north of Saka-dzong and about two days' journey from it. But between us and the Governor's residence rose a ridge which is a link in the chain of Lunpo-gangri. In the evening and at night our watchmen fired, as usual, some revolver shots, to inform any chance robbers that we were on our guard.

April 21. As the tents were being taken down, our neighbours went by with 200 sheep. I turned my back to them and busied myself with loading a mule. Then I travelled with the sheep, for there were several more tents farther up, and I could not ride till we came to an uninhabited part of the valley. Several side valleys opened on the left, and at their ends could sometimes be seen a part of the main crest. We know absolutely nothing of the country to the north of it, but that it cannot be the watershed between the plateau and the sea is evident, and was shown by the Kamchung transverse valley.

After crossing the river twice over bridges of porous ice we encamped near a sheepfold where dry dung was plentiful. The last nomads had told us that next day we should come to a large tent, the property of an influential old man named Kamba Tsenam, who owned 1000 yaks and 5000 sheep. He would evidently be our next difficulty, and if we slipped past him the country would be open to us as far as Raga-tasam. We are satisfied when, as on this day, we have again gained nearly 9 miles without being interfered with; but how shall we fare to-morrow?—this is the standing question we ask ourselves every evening. It is certainly an advantage to travel along out-of-the-way paths where we escape notice, but if any sharp gova or governor hears us spoken of, he cannot help being suspicious of our strange proceedings, and institute a close inquiry. Now the salt caravan which we passed has already arrived at Saka-dzong; we are, indeed, to the east of that place, but we travel so slowly that we can never escape pursuit. Our excitement grows daily. I am tired and weary of this self-imposed confinement, and long for it to come to an end. What shall we do then? That I know not. We have penetrated so far that a crisis must come. I have managed to travel through Bongba, but my plans for the immediate future are very indefinite and depend on circumstances. We will get on as far as we can.

April 22 was a day when we knew that the definite crisis was coming very much nearer. Abdul Kerim, Kunchuk, and Gaffar set out first to pay a visit to Kamba Tsenam and keep his attention riveted on the sale of food and horses. We followed after, and crossed the river twice on cracking bridges of ice, kept along the northern bank, and passed a side valley, at the mouth of which stood three tents, where our men were in the midst of a group of Tibetans who were showing their horses. Gulam had warned me in time, so I dismounted and went and looked after our last mules. As soon as we were concealed by a bank terrace I could ride again. The pleasure did not last long, for at the next side valley on the north I had to dismount again before another tent, where a pack of savage dogs were encountered by Takkar and Little Puppy, who, save the mark, would help to defend us, but received a nip in the neck and had to be rescued. Here we lost Kutus and Tubges, who remained at the tent, while our diminished party continued on its way eastwards.

At a spur on the northern side of the valley a couple of elegant *mani* heaps were erected, and by one of them a streamer pole was set up. It had snowed thickly ever since eight o'clock, but the valley was so narrow that we could not pass all the tents unseen. Just at the projecting point a large valley ran in from the north: we only guessed at it, for everything was hidden in the snowstorm. Gulam went a little way ahead and gave me the sign to dismount. Immediately in front of the point stood four tents and a small stone cabin, where a man stood watching us, and also a chief's tent of such huge dimensions that I never saw its like; it was as large as a house. Here we left Lobsang and Abdul Rasak, and went on eastwards with a much diminished party. The chief volume of the Gebuk-chu comes from the northern valley; in our valley, which we knew led to the Gebuk-la, only a brook was left. We set up our tents on the terrace at the mouth of a northern side valley. All the country was white, and not a shadow could be seen of the surroundings.

Our three tents stood as usual close together, mine with its opening up the valley, that is, eastwards. After a while the men left behind came up and gave their reports in turn. They had bought provisions for two days, and had learned that the district was called Gebuk-yung. The next day we should go over the Gebuk-la and encamp at the foot of the Kinchen-la, from the top of which we should see Raga-tasam the following day. Of course it was risky for three parties of our men to visit three tents near together, for the Tibetans always asked about the routes we had followed and our plans, and our men might in their haste give discordant answers. In the large tent Lobsang had been cross-examined, and had answered that we came from the Gertse Pun, who had advised us to take this byroad because we should reach Raga-tasam two days sooner than if we went through Saka-dzong. "Quite true," the Tibetans answered, but also warned us against robbers, for thirteen Ladakis would be but a mouthful for an ordinary robber band, and the country was very unsafe. "It is well for you that you have good weapons," they said.

Lastly, Abdul Kerim turned up with his purchases. He had learned that all the tents we had seen in the day belonged to Kamba Tsenam, who lived himself in the largest, but he happened to be in Saka-dzong, where an assembly had been convened in anticipation of an impending visit from a high Chinese official, and the question what present should be made to him had to be decided. Kamba Tsenam owned thirty-five horses, which were grazing beyond Gebuk-la, and if the rich nomad returned in the evening we should certainly be able to buy some from him.

"You say," declared an elderly man in Kamba Tsenam's service, "that you are a *tsongpun* (merchant) from Ladak. Why then do you travel by this dangerous side route? Here you can drive no trade. How have you found the way? Why have you travelled in winter? Why do you ask the names of the valleys?"

"I have to write down all the names," he answered, "that we may find the way again in summer, for I am commissioned to make large purchases of wool."

"That is well, you shall have several hundred bales of sheep's wool from us. I will give you a guide in the morning; you will pay him a rupee for two days. Without him you cannot find your way over the Gebuk-la, especially when the ground is covered with snow."

Abdul Kerim had thanked him for his kindness and then had come to look for us. We were sitting and deliberating when two riders armed with guns came up to our tents. They were close upon us when they appeared out of the snowstorm. We just managed to close my tent and fasten up Takkar before the entrance. The elder man was Abdul Kerim's friend from the large tent, the other the youth who was offered to us as a guide. They tied up their horses and went nonchalantly into Abdul Kerim's tent. Here they sat and gossiped for an hour, and offered a large handsome white horse for sale at the price of

331

333

330. Travelling Ladaki Merchant in West Tibet. 331. Oang Gye, Son of the Governor of Saka. 332. Panchor, the Yak-slayer, my Guide on the Journey to the Teri-nam-tso. 333. Woman of Yumba-matsen.

Sketches by the Author.

127 rupees. Abdul Kerim bought it, whereupon they asked how much money he had with him, and whether he was not afraid of being attacked. Afterwards they went about the tents and looked around, and I drew a breath of relief when they at last vanished in the snow with the other horse.

Now we considered the situation. To refuse the guide would seem extremely suspicious, for the snow already lay a foot deep, and the path—all we had to depend on—was covered up. But to have a stranger, a spy, in the caravan for two days and a night was still more dangerous. When Kutus and Sedik went back a little later to the large tent to fetch a bowl of sour milk, they were told to say that our *tsongpun* did not want a guide, for we should remain quiet a day, either here or at the next camp. "Your *tsongpun* speaks with two tongues, he does not know what he wants," the men answered.

We left this dangerous place on April 23 before the sun was up, and I went first with the sheep in case our neighbours paid a morning visit. The weather cleared and the sun came out, and then the snow quickly evaporated. Farther up all the valley floor was covered with a continuous sheet of ice. In front of us was seen the pass Gebuk-la. Here a little old man was following ten mares. He pretended not to see us, but he was soon overtaken by Abdul Kerim and Kunchuk, who kept him company most of the day. With Lobsang I rested half an hour on the pass, at a height of 16,978 feet. To the east and south-east of us lay an entanglement of mountains and valleys, and without the horse-tender we had so fortunately found it would have been quite impossible to find our way over the succession of small saddles which followed. To the south-south-east the snowy massive of Chomo-uchong rose in radiant sunshine; to the north was a huge crest, which I, like Ryder, took for the main range of the Trans-Himalaya and the watershed, but this turned out afterwards to be a mistake.

The horse-driver took us up a secondary saddle, at the eastern foot of which runs a deeply eroded valley, which, coming from the north, 10° E., is the upper section of the valley we followed last year, and which runs down to Basang, where I saw Muhamed Isa for the last time among the number of the living. Here was the driver's tent, and to escape his company during the night we continued our march after the stranger had given us instructions about the way. Our camp 390 was situated in the mouth of a small valley on the ascent to the Kinchen-la, where we were overwhelmed in a terribly dense and violent snowstorm.

The guide, who had so fortunately appeared at the right moment, had said in the presence of our men that he was Kamba Tsenam's brother and a great yak-slayer. The year before he had seen in Saka-dzong a European whose caravan leader, a big strong fellow, had inspired respect wherever he showed himself. But he had died suddenly in Saka, and his comrades had digged a long hole in the ground where they had laid him. He thought it strange that Ladakis, who were of the same faith as the Tibetans, would travel with and serve the hated Europeans.

For the future we determined to observe yet greater caution. Two or three Ladakis should always wear dark eye-glasses, so that mine might not seem so peculiar. As soon as we could buy woollen material all the men should have new clothes, so that I in my rags would seem the poorest and meanest of the party.

CHAPTER LXVII

APRIL 24

IN these days our life was dismal and lonesome, and our future uncertain. We went as in the dark, feeling with our hands lest we should fall. Every day which passed without any untoward event came upon me as a complete surprise. We had now only two days' journey to Raga-tasam on the great highway, where caravans and travellers fare to and fro, and Government officials are responsible that no unauthorized person slips past. I was thoroughly sick of my disguise and the constant uncertainty, and longed for a crisis to free me from my embarrassment. But to deliver ourselves, of our own free will, into the hands of the Tibetans was out of the question. They must detect us themselves, and till then the strain on our nerves must continue.

April 24—the anniversary of the *Vega's* return to Stockholm in 1880! At sunrise the whole country lay under a bright wintry shroud of white snow. The thermometer had fallen to 2½°, but when the sun mounted up the horses steamed, and light clouds of vapour rose up from the snow, so that we might have been riding through a land of solfataras and fumaroles. Our caravan animals struggled bravely up the tough ascent. Of sheep we had only twenty left, and two of them were veterans from Lumbur-ringmo-tso. Twice we thought that the pass, Kinchen-la, was just before us, but new heights rose farther back, and we worked our way up hills, among which brooks run down towards Basang and Saka-dzong, where Muhamed Isa sleeps in his mound. To the south-west Chomo-uchong's summits presented a grand sight. At length we made the last ascent up to the top of the pass, where the height is 17,851 feet above sea-level. At the other side a river runs north-east, one of the headwaters of the Raga-tsangpo. To the west there is a brilliant spectacle, the summits of Lunpo-gangri rising in sharp and savage beauty from a maze of mountains and ridges, which shine in lighter bluer shades the more remote they are. To the north-east we catch a glimpse of an outlying ridge covered from foot to crest with new-fallen snow. The broad flat valley of the Raga-tsangpo stretches eastwards as far as the eye can see. In the far distance to the east-south-east a grand snowy crest shines forth, the northernmost of the Himalayan system (Illust. 199).

We stayed a long time at the top, and I sketched a panorama. Then we followed the track of the caravan over the lower shoulders of two mountains, and found our camp pitched in a valley with good grass and a brook partially frozen. My tent looked towards its bank, and all three stood as usual in a line. This day also had passed satisfactorily, but all would be different next day, for then we should come to Raga-tasam, where we encamped last year and stayed a week. Camp 391 was, then, the last where we could still feel at ease, for we had seen no living being all day long, and had no neighbours. Here, then, we must arrange some fresh safeguards.

We must sort out from our already scanty baggage all articles that might excite suspicion, as, for example, the small padded leather box in which the theodolite was packed; for the future it would be rolled with its inner wooden case in my bed. Further, the hypsometer's leather case and the actinometer, which probably would never be used again. Whatever was combustible was to be thrown into the fire and the rest buried. A couple of rugs of camel's wool were also to be discarded.

To begin with, we must make a change in our housing arrangements. I was to sleep for the last time in my old weather-beaten tent, where our chief, Abdul Kerim, was henceforth to set up his quarters and receive guests. For me a compartment of about 2 square yards, not larger

334. Tibetans with Yaks.

335. Dorche Tsuen on the March.

than my bed, was partitioned off in Abdul Kerim's tent. This crib, which, when the camp was set up, was enclosed on all sides, was henceforth to be my prison cell. It was like a secret drawer in a bureau, and when it was ready I inspected it and found it somewhat narrow but comfortable.

Suen was my hairdresser, and he had just completed his business when Abdul Kerim looked in at the tent opening and whispered that four men with yaks were coming up the valley on the road we had to go down from the Kinchen-la. I hurriedly set my disguise in order and wound the turban round my head, while the flap was fastened, and Takkar was tied up before my tent. Then I looked through the peephole in the tent canvas on the side towards the upper end of the valley, and saw eight men on foot in dark-blue and red dresses, with red scarves round their heads, all armed with guns and swords, and leading nine horses; one man led two laden horses. What in the world did this mean? They were not robbers, for they come suddenly and at night. They seemed rather men in Government service; the two in front were certainly officials. My men occupied themselves at their fire; I could see that they were a prey to the greatest uneasiness.

The strangers came straight to our camp-fire as if it were the end of their journey. They formed a circle round Abdul Kerim, Lobsang, Kutus, and Gulam, and began an animated but subdued conversation. Three of them, evidently servants, led the horses to a spot barely thirty paces from my tent and right in front of it. There they took off all the saddles and loads, sent off the horses to graze, brought out pots and cans, arranged three stones in order, collected fuel, made a fire, fetched water in a large pot and cooked tea. It was plain that they intended to camp here for the night, and that they had intruded on us for the purpose of watching us.

The other five entered Abdul Kerim's tent, threw themselves down, and continued the conversation in the same low quiet voice and in thoroughly polite and measured tones. I could not catch what they said, but that the affair was serious I could only too plainly perceive, for I heard my name mentioned—Hedin Sahib. After a good hour's conversation they went out again and made a tour round my tent, but the furious Takkar would not let them approach the door. But they discovered the peephole in the side of the tent, and a man put his finger in and looked through the hole, but I was lying against the folds of the tent on the same side, so he could not see me. Then they went and threw themselves down in a circle round the fire, brought out their wooden cups and drank tea. They sat right in front of the entrance to my tent, and I could not get out without being seen.

Then Abdul Kerim whispered from the back of my tent and inside his own, and told me what the men had said. The leader, a stoutish young man of good appearance, had put the usual questions and received the usual answers. Then he had uttered the following words in a serious and decided tone:

"News of your arrival has come to the Governor of Saka-dzong through two salt caravans which passed your party above Pasa-guk. As it has never occurred that a merchant from Ladak has come from the north and has travelled on the byway through Gebuk, the Governor and the other authorities in Saka suspected that Hedin Sahib might be concealed among you, and the more so because he himself expressed his wish last year to come back again and travel through the mountainous regions in the north. Therefore my comrades and I received orders to follow your trail, overtake you, and subject you to the most searching examination. We are in no hurry, and in the morning we shall get several yak-loads of provisions. You protest that Hedin Sahib is not among you disguised as a Ladaki. Well, it may be that you are telling the truth. But remember, *tsongpun*, that we shall carry out our orders to the letter. You are thirteen men from Ladak, you say, and I can see only ten. Where are the others?"

"They are out collecting fuel."

"Good. When you are all assembled here we intend to search you down to the skin. Then we shall turn out all your baggage and empty every sack we find in your tents. And if in this examination we find nothing belonging to a European, it will remain for you to give a written declaration that no European is among your party concealed or disguised, and under this declaration you must set your name-stamp. Then you can travel early in the morning where you like, and we shall return to Saka."

When I heard this report the situation became quite clear to me, and I at once decided what I would do. But first I crept by the secret way into the caravan leader's tent, where I found myself surrounded by my retainers, except three, who were to warn us if the Tibetans came back again.

"What is to be done?" I asked Abdul Kerim.

"The Sahib knows best himself. As far as I can see, our condition is hopeless," answered the honest man, who had got us out of many a scrape before.

"What does Lobsang think?"

"It would not be wise to give them such a declaration," he answered with a very troubled face.

"Sahib," suggested Kutus, "if they give us breathing-time till night, the Sahib and I can hide among the mountains as at the time when we were close to Tsongpun Tashi. When the search is over we can rejoin the caravan farther down. I can carry the Sahib's papers, and other European articles can be buried in the ground under the tent."

"They know that we are thirteen," remarked Gulam.

Under the force of circumstances we had made our way right across Tibet with a trumped-up story, but to let Abdul Kerim confirm a false document with his name-stamp on my account was a little too strong even for my geographical conscience. I could not consent to that. Whatever might happen, our position was still a strong one. We were in the heart of Tibet. The next move would be that we should be sent out of the country, and by whatever way we were obliged to go, I should certainly gain something more. I would absolutely refuse to go to Ladak, but I would be content to go to India through Nepal, or, better still, through Gyangtse.

"No," I said to my men as I rose up, "I shall give myself up to the Tibetans."

Then they were all amazed, and began to cry and sob like children.

"Why do you weep?" I asked.

"We shall part here for good, and the Sahib will be killed," they answered.

"Oh no, it is not so bad as that," I said, for it was not the first time I had been caught by Tibetans.

When I walked out of the tent I heard behind me the murmur of Mohammedan prayers: "Allahu ekber—Bismillah rahman errahim."

In my usual disguise from top to toe, and with my face painted black, I walked with slow, deliberate steps straight to the circle of Tibetans. When I was close to them they all rose up, as if they knew that I was no ordinary Ladaki.

"Sit down," I said, with a dignified gesture of invitation, and sat down myself between the two principal men. In the one on my right hand I recognized at once the Pemba Tsering of the year before. I clapped him on the shoulder, saying, "Do you know me again, Pemba Tsering?" He answered not a word, but looked with wide-opened eyes at his comrades, and nodded towards me, as much as to say "It is he." They were mightily dumbfoundered and disconcerted: no one spoke, some looked at one another, others gazed into the fire, one threw a couple of sticks among the stones, and another took small sips of tea.

Then I spoke again: "Yes, truly, Pemba Tsering, you are quite right; I am Hedin Sahib, who visited Saka-dzong last year. Here you have me again; what do you mean to do with me?"

Abdul Kerim, Lobsang, and Kutus stood behind, trembling like aspen leaves, and expecting that preparations for an execution would be the next move.

Still they made no answer, but began to whisper together in groups. The younger official, who was evidently the cock of the walk, for the others looked at him and waited for him to speak, began to look through his papers, and picked out one which he read in silence. As they were so long in recovering from their consternation —for they had not expected to get hold of me so easily—

336. Farewell Entertainment for the Tibetans on May 5, 1908.

I sent Kutus for a box of Egyptian cigarettes, and offered them all round. Each took one with thanks, and lighted it after I had set an example and showed them that the cigarettes were not filled with gunpowder. Then the ice was broken, and the leader began to speak very softly and without looking at me.

"Yesterday strict orders came from the Devashung that the Governor of Saka would be held responsible for Europeans who might sneak into the country from the west, and if any European showed himself he must be immediately forced to return by the way he came. When the report reached Saka of a caravan two days' journey off, the Governor suspected that it might be you, Hedin Sahib, and we have now accomplished our task. In the Governor's name we forbid you to take another step eastwards. We beg you to conform in all things to our directions; our heads and your personal safety are at stake. To-morrow you will follow us over the Kinchen-la to Saka-dzong."

"I said last year that I must and would see the mountain region north of Saka. Now I have seen it, and you have not been able to prevent me. You see then that I can do more in your country than yourselves. Now I intend to travel back to India, but by which way only Lien Darin, Amban of Lhasa, shall decide. It is therefore my intention to write to him, and I shall not go anywhere before his answer comes."

"We do not wish you to travel by any other way than the one you choose, but we have no authority to forward a letter to Lhasa; the Governor will decide the question himself. It is with him you must treat; you must meet him personally. Therefore we will accompany you to-morrow to Saka-dzong."

"No, sir, anywhere else you please, but not to Saka-dzong. You know that my caravan leader died and lies buried there. It is against my principles to visit a place where I have buried a faithful servant. You shall never get me to Saka-dzong even if you raise all Tibet."

"If it would trouble you to see Saka-dzong again, we will certainly not urge you to go thither. Will you instead have the kindness to follow us to Semoku by the Tsango, on the *tasam*, which is only two days' journey to the south-west? I will then write to the Governor and ask him to meet you there."

"Good; I will follow you to Semoku to-morrow."

"Thanks; I will at once send an express messenger to inform the Governor, so that you may not have to wait at Semoku. But tell me why you have come back again? You travel and travel in Tibet and you are always sent away, but always come back again. Had you not enough last year, when you were obliged to leave the country by the road to Ladak? And now you turn up again among us. How is that possible, and why are you come?"

"Because I love your country and your friendly people to such a degree that I cannot live without them."

"H'm! It is very kind of you to say so, but would it not be better if you were to love your own country a little more? As long as we do not travel in your country, you should not travel in ours; we remain at home, and the best thing you can do is to remain in your country."

"As long as I can sit in a saddle I shall come back. You can inform the Devashung at your leisure that their Excellencies may look for more visits."

They laughed pleasantly and looked at one another, as much as to say: "If he likes to come back, he is welcome as far as we are concerned." And my Ladakis laughed and were extremely astonished that our last day of freedom had come to so peaceful and merry an ending. The Tibetans were exceedingly agreeable, polite, and gentle, and never uttered a hard or peevish word about the trouble that I had again brought upon them. And when the old wool story, which Abdul Kerim a little while before had tried to cram down their throats, was referred to, they laughed heartily and thought that it was a grand device. They are so accustomed to lie themselves that they have a great admiration for any one else who succeeds in deceiving them. They thought it very wonderful that we had been able to cross the whole country without detection, and believed that I must possess some mysterious powers of

337

338

339

340

337, 338, 339, 340. THE DANCERS AT THE CAMP-FIRE: TURGES, KUNCHUK, SUEN.

which they knew nothing, and that they must be very cautious in dealing with me.

The young official, who was named Rinche Dorche, but was called Rindor, a contraction of the two names, wrote a long letter to the Governor of Saka, saying that I was the same Hedin Sahib who had been here the year before, that we had come to a friendly agreement to proceed to Semoku, that I did not wish to travel to Ladak but straight to India, and that Lien Darin alone was to decide on the route. The letter was sealed, and despatched by a mounted courier over the Kinchen-la.

Then we talked and jested again, and before sunset we were as intimate as though we had been friends from childhood. We might have made an appointment to meet in this barren valley and been glad to have found one another. It was easy to understand that the Tibetans were pleased. They little thought when the sun rose that they would make such a good catch before evening. The successful issue of their mission would be of great advantage; they would be commended by the Governor and gain promotion. For my part I had a feeling of unmixed satisfaction. Our freedom was at an end, but for me it had been nothing but an exceedingly enervating captivity. Now, for the first time, I felt perfectly free, and was no longer a prisoner in my own tent; I should have no need of that wretched hiding-hole in Abdul Kerim's tent. The Tibetans laughed loudly at my ragged, smutty, greasy dress of coarse grey sackcloth, in which I looked like a convict, or, at best, like a begging monk of the Grey Friars' confraternity. Then they understood how I had succeeded in crossing Bongba unseen and unknown. How delightful it would be to throw my rags into the fire and clothe myself in a clean neat Tibetan costume, to be no longer obliged to hide my papers and instruments in rice sacks, and not to have to paint my face black as a Moor's instead of washing myself. As soon as we had parted from our new friends in the evening, Gulam took a hand-basin of warm water into my tent, and then I had a good scrubbing from top to toe, and the water showed that I wanted it. He had to change the water four times before I was tolerably clean. Then I clipped my Mohammedan beard to the skin, and sadly missed the razors I had thrown away. But I was glad that we had not burned the things we had condemned some hours earlier.

Rindor begged the loan of one of our tents, as their own transport train was not expected till the morning. Besides Pemba Tsering, there were two other men I had known the year before. They were all very friendly, and said that we had tipped them very generously. There was also a wrinkled old man in the party, who was always smoking a Chinese pipe. His name was Kamba Tsenam, and it was his tent near which we had so nearly been detained two days before.

Thus ended April 24, 1908. Strange, melancholy thoughts took possession of me when I went to bed. The Tibetans had again thwarted my plans—I know not how many times they had done so. Our future was dark as ever, but it had arrived at a new stage, and on the 25th we should wake up to begin a new chapter. The deep silence in the valley was only disturbed occasionally by Takkar, when the faithful dog barked at the Tibetans. His bark was re-echoed from both flanks as though three dogs kept guard over us. And the everlasting stars glittered as before over our lonely tents.

CHAPTER LXVIII

HIS EXCELLENCY THE GOVERNOR OF SAKA

On April 25 we rode in a compact body to the mouth of a valley east of Chomo-uchong, called Radak. Six Tibetans guarded me on both sides, and our journey had some resemblance to a convict train. Now I was not obliged to dismount before we passed a tent. On the left hand was a large open plain where Raga-tasam is situated. A shot was heard in the deserted country, and Rindor sent two men to see what it was. An antelope hunter! He was arrested and beaten; for the Government, at ecclesiastical instigation, had forbidden the extinction of life for three years, except in the case of sheep and yaks. I was reminded of the agreement to forbid Europeans to travel in Tibet for three years.

Now I drew my map of the route, took compass bearings, and sketched a panorama quite at my ease. The Tibetans wondered at me and questioned me, but did not trouble themselves much about my work. And I had plenty of time to think of the line of policy I should adopt during the following negotiations. I knew that they would urge me to return by the way I had come, through Bongba, or by the road I had taken to Ladak the year before. For my part, I had now had enough of Tibet and I longed to get home, and wished to avoid routes that involved loss of time and that I knew already. Now I only wished to travel to India *viâ* Shigatse and Gyangtse, and I would try to obtain permission to travel to these towns by roads where no one had been before. After the excitement in which we had lived so long came a reaction. I was worn-out, weary, and indifferent to everything except the nearest way home. Therefore I sat down and wrote a letter of fifteen pages to Lien Darin, referred to his friendly letter sent to Gartok, gave an account of our last journey, pointed out to him that no Great Power could take it amiss if I travelled out of the country through Gyangtse, promised that in return I would give him information about the occurrences of gold and salt I had seen, and about the measures which should be taken for the promotion of sheep-breeding,—all natural resources, which would contribute to the advancement of China's newest province, Tibet. And I concluded my letter with wishes for the happiness and prosperity of Lien Darin himself and peace to his forefathers' graves.

I did not doubt a moment that he would give his consent to such a modest request, and I saw in my mind's eye the dramatic scene when I should make my first call on Major O'Connor in Tibetan dress, and have a little fun with him before I made myself known. But I may as well say at once that this long epistle to Lien Darin was never sent. My opponent's tactics lured me to a contest in which he was checkmated in two moves. My merit was as little now as formerly; I was always a marionette, and the hands which held the strings hung over the paths where the clouds and stars move.

In the evening I had a visit from Pemba Tsering and Kamba Tsenam. The former was much more gentle and friendly than the year before; the latter was a great humorist, who did not seem at all annoyed that he had omitted to close the bag when he had us in it, and had let a valuable booty fall into the hands of another. They had heard of my adventurous voyages on Tso-mavang, and were astonished that I had escaped with my life.

Two short days' marches took us over the pass Kule-la and down to the valley where Semoku stands on the great high-road. Here stood some scattered tents, and the Governor and his colleagues had established themselves in the small stone house of the station. All the more important posts in Tibet are entrusted to two gentlemen: thus, for example, there are always two garpuns or viceroys

341. Inner Court of Selipuk.

342. Dorche Tsuen and Ngavang on Horseback.

in Gartok, a system adopted with the intention that one shall control the other or shall inform of the other if he is guilty of any roguery. In Saka-dzong, however, the one governor seemed to be of higher rank than the other; at any rate, he conducted all the negotiations as though he possessed greater authority.

As soon as we were ready Rindor and two other men came into my tent and brought a message from the Governor that he awaited me in the station-house. I answered, that if he wanted anything of me he might come to my tent. It was not long before a party of men crossed the hundred yards between our dwellings. I went out to meet them, invited them to come in and sit down as far as the space allowed, took up my position on my bed, and had before me three gentlemen, namely, Dorche Tsuen, *pun* or Governor of Saka-dzong (Illust. 327), Ngavang, his colleague, and Oang Gye, his eighteen-year-old son (Illust. 331). A crowd of servants, nomads, and soldiers massed together at the tent door.

Pun Dorche Tsuen is an unusually tall Tibetan, forty-three years old, of sympathetic and refined appearance, dressed in a Chinese costume of silk, with a small silk cap on his head, a pigtail behind, and velvet boots. He is a man of wealth, owning large flocks in the province over which he rules and a stone house in Lhasa, his home, for he is an *upa* or domiciled inhabitant of the province U, the capital of which is Lhasa. There dwell three of his four sons, and one of them is a young lama. His wife has been dead some years.

Ngavang, his coadjutor, is a little, fat, kindly man in Tibetan costume, but with a Chinese cap and pigtail. Oang Gye wears his hair in Tibetan fashion, wears no head-covering, and, like his father, is exceedingly sympathetic and good-natured.

"I hope that you have had a successful journey and have not suffered much from cold," said Dorche Tsuen.

"Oh, it was cold, and we have lost our caravan, our clothes are in rags, and our provisions are at an end, but, as you see, that is of no consequence to us."

"At the time of your visit to Saka-dzong last year I was in Tsonka, but I received an account of your movements. You were sent away. Why have you come back again?"

"To visit the districts I was then prevented from seeing. I am ashamed to have given you the trouble of coming here from Saka-dzong. I hope that we shall soon come to an agreement about the route I am to take in order to leave the country."

Now I should have to play my cards well. I had changed my mind during the last few days. I had rested, the reaction after the excitement of travelling in disguise had passed away, and I was exceedingly eager to attempt some new discoveries before I gave up the game. I had, it is true, succeeded in making a very valuable traverse across Bongba. I had travelled straight across the word "Unexplored" on the latest English map of Tibet—yea, I had passed between the *p* and *l*, so that "unexp" lay on the west side of my route and "lored" on the east (see Map 1, Vol. I.). But I had left quite untouched two extensive stretches of the large blank patch, and I dreamed of nothing else than to cross Bongba again by two fresh routes. It would certainly take four or five months to return to India after a northerly zigzag course, instead of a couple of weeks if I made for British territory through Gyangtse, as I intended at first. But if I succeeded in making the northerly detour I should carry home material of perhaps greater value than the discoveries already made. Dorche Tsuen answered with firm decision:

"As to your way back, I will tell you at once: not a step further east; my head depends on it. Here you see the order I received a couple of days ago from the Devashung. I will read it to you. Last year you travelled without leave to Nepal, to Kubi-gangri, across the holy lake, round Kang-rinpoche, and to Yumba-matsen. I know exactly where you went. You cannot do the same this year. It is probably in consequence of your journey in all sorts of forbidden directions that the Devashung has distributed through the country instructions regarding Europeans. Two officials have recently been sent from

Lhasa to Shansa-dzong to see that no European approaches the holy city from Naktsang. Some time ago a Chinese officer with 200 soldiers was moved to Tingri to guard the country from intrusion from the south. Not even a Gurkha or a Hindu can now travel in Tibet without especial permission. The other day I received a letter from the Chinese frontier official in Tingri which I will read to you. As you see, he orders me to force any European who may come to Saka from the north to return in his own footsteps. If he refuses, I have to send off a messenger to Tingri, and shall receive assistance in a few days from the soldiers stationed there. Times are changed in Tibet. If you will not listen to me and travel back by the way you came, I will send a messenger to Tingri. But, like you, I hope that we shall come to an agreement without unpleasantness and outside interference."

My next move was a feint, namely, to try for the Gyangtse route; I would in the end conform to his wishes and give up the Gyangtse route under the condition that I should not be compelled to travel along roads I knew already. I pointed out how near we were to Gyangtse, and how easily he would get rid of me if I went thither, but nothing made any impression on him. He only answered, "All that is true, but the road is closed to you."

"Well, I will give it up for your sake, but only on condition that you forward a letter from me to the British Trade Agent in Gyangtse. You can understand that my family are disturbed at my long absence and are looking for news of me."

"Yes, I can understand that, but I regret to say that I cannot forward your correspondence. All the authorities in Tibet are strictly forbidden to assist a European in any way, as he has no right to travel in the country."

"You will perhaps allow two of my own servants to carry a letter from me to Gyangtse?"

"No, never!"

"Well, at least, you can inform the Devashung of my arrival, and ask the Government to send notice of it to Gyangtse."

"I sent a messenger to the Devashung as soon as I

received the letter from Rindor. They will know in Lhasa in a few days that you are come here again."

I had never induced any Tibetan magistrate to forward my letters. That Dorche Tsuen refused to do me such a trifling service had the deplorable consequence that my family did not receive any reliable report of me till September, and therefore supposed that some misfortune had befallen me. Instead of reaching the frontier in a couple of weeks, I was sent back again into the silence of Tibet, and the waves washed again over our track. But I took it for granted that news of our arrival on the *tasam* would penetrate to Gyangtse both officially and through reports, and would then be made known everywhere. Such, however, was not the case, and after we left the *tasam* our fate was buried in the same complete silence as before.

"No, Hedin Sahib," Dorche Tsuen cried out, "the only way open to you is the one by which you came from the north."

"I will never travel by that road. It is no use talking about it."

"You must."

"You cannot force me to do so. To begin with, I will not let you know which way I came, and I travelled in disguise."

"It does not matter. It is very well known that you came from the Samye-la and the Kinchen-la. Beyond that the escort I shall send with you will ask the way from tent to tent."

"The nomads will answer that they have seen no Ladakis, for fear of being punished."

"I shall find means of making them confess more than you think."

"You can kill me if you like, but you shall never force me to travel over the Samye-la. Remember that I am a European and a friend of the Tashi Lama. You may lose your button."

Much disturbed, Dorche Tsuen conferred in whispers with Ngavang.

"I will give way so far for your sake that I will allow you to return to Ladak by the same road you followed

343. THE AUTHOR IN TIBETAN DRESS.
From a photograph by the Rev. Mr. Marx, in Poo.

last year, through Tradum, Tuksum, Shamsang, Parka, and Gartok."

That was the very solution I most feared. If there were any road in all Tibet that I wished to avoid at any cost it was the road to Ladak. I answered:

"Never! Not a step on the great highroad to Ladak!"

"But why? You ought to be thankful for so great a concession."

"It is forbidden by the laws of my country for a man to return in his own footsteps. You can cut my throat, but you will not force me to do anything of the sort."

"You must have strange laws in your country. May I hear which way you really wish to take?"

"I have already said through Gyangtse. You refused and I understand your motive. You have urged me to go back to the north. Even in this respect I will conform to your wishes, but only on the condition that I am not obliged to retrace my steps. I will go over another pass east of the Samye-la and northwards to the Teri-nam-tso and then westwards by the shortest way out of Tibet."

"That is not to be thought of. But let us take the matter quietly. Will you agree to accompany me to Kamba Tsenam's tent, four days' journey from here? You have been there already, and before we reach it we shall have come to some understanding."

"Yes, willingly."

Opposition spurred me on. It now became a point of honour to win a new game of chess. My position was very strong. The *tasam* was eliminated. If I could only cross the Trans-Himalaya by a more easterly pass, I should by some ruse or other gain the Teri-nam-tso, Mendong-gompa, the lower Buptsang-tsangpo, the Tarok-tso, Selipuk, and an eighth Trans-Himalayan pass. Yes, now I must, if ever, play my cards well. I still felt young and strong. The political entanglement which encompassed me on all sides in Tibet rendered it difficult for me to make geographical discoveries, but it stimulated my ambition. Therefore I remember with particular warmth and sympathy all those who, in virtue of their temporary power in the world, sought to raise obstacles in my way.

We then talked on various subjects. He wished to see our weapons, and asked if he could buy a revolver. "No; you shall have it as a present, cartridges and all, if you will let me go the way I have proposed."

"H'm!"

"You must procure us all the provisions we need for two months, besides new shoes, clothing, tobacco, horses, mules, yaks."

"With pleasure; make out a list of all you want."

It was done at once. Meal, *tsamba*, tea, sugar, Japanese cigarettes, which were said to be procurable—all was to be brought from Tsongka, whither mounted men were sent the same day across the Tsangpo and over the Nevu-la. Everything was to be in our tents in a week. The rest could be obtained from Saka-dzong. In the evening I paid an equally long return visit to my valiant friend Pun Dorche Tsuen, and at night I consigned my letter to Lien Darin to the flames. Ah no! no Chinese interference in Tibeto-Swedish affairs.

On the 28th we remained quiet and visited one another by the hour together. The two governors sat on benches fastened to the wall, Rindor and Oang Gye on mats on the floor, and all four played at dice. The two dice were shaken in a wooden bowl, and turned out on to a round piece of skin. The markers were small Indian snailshells. Then they played with Chinese dominoes. Meanwhile they drank tea, smoked pipes, sang, joked, laughed, and moved the bricks with wonderful and graceful dexterity. Ngavang won ten *tengas* and was greatly elated. In this way they pass the time when the day's work is done. Rindor is the Governor's private secretary, and on a bench and a table lay piles of documents and letters, written on coarse Chinese paper, and folded up one on another. The Governor's correspondence now comes to Semoku, and his daily work must run its course. His province, Saka, is very extensive, and he states with some pride that his power stretches to Sangsang in the east, to the Nevu-la in the south, to the Marium-la in the west, and northwards some days' journey beyond Kamba Tsenam's tent.

The illustrious gentlemen were much amused with my

44

345

346

347

344, 345. Soldiers of the Garrison of Saka-dzong, belonging to our Escort. 346. Armed Tibetan from the Country between the Teri-nam-tso and the Dangra-yum-tso. 347. Boy with Small Gun on the Southern Shore of the Teri-nam-tso.

costume. "You are a Sahib," they said; "you were for six weeks the guest of the Tashi Lama; you employ one caravan after another, and leave a quantity of money behind you, and yet are dressed more shabbily than any of your servants."

At night their horses and mules were driven to the station-house by soldiers, and we ought to have taken the same precaution, for our horses were attacked by wolves. The brown horse we had bought two weeks before for 100 rupees had his two right feet tied together lest he should run away, and the wolves directed their attack on him, as he could not escape, ate him up, and took the head off with them. At any rate it was missing in the morning from the skeleton, which was pretty closely stripped.

On April 29 we rode together on the road down the Semoku valley, which runs to the upper Brahmaputra (Illust. 335). This we left on the left hand, as well as the *tasam*, and ascended a valley where the little village of Ushy with its stone huts and barley fields is situated. The 150 inhabitants are at home only at seedtime and harvest; the rest of the year they are away, tending their sheep. Thence we proceeded the following day to the pass Ushy-la. The way is marked by a succession of *mani* heaps and *chhortens*, and the pass by rods so thin as to be invisible at a distance, and the streamers they carry look like a flock of tied birds. A little farther to the north-west we crossed the pass Gye-la, where Chomo-uchong makes a fine display, and soon after we were on the main pass of the same name (16,135 feet). From a hill near, the eye can sweep over all the horizon, the peaks and glaciers of the Himalayas, Chomo-uchong, and close at hand to the south-south-east the Brahmaputra valley with the river meandering in several arms. We encamped on the bank of the Sachu-tsangpo, which flows into the Chaktak-tsangpo west of Saka-dzong. Here also lies a votive block of a hard green rock, covered with offerings, bits of butter, and streamers.

The 1st of May was celebrated by a march over the Lamlung-la, a difficult pass, on the saddle of which,

16,791 feet high, the traveller is again rewarded by a magnificent view over this complicated sea of mountains. From here Chomo-uchong's seven summits appear in a compact group; the central one is of a regular conical shape and is pure white all over; the others consist chiefly of black cliffs and projections, from among which issue small blue-tinged glaciers. The length of the massive corresponds to that of Lunpo-gangri, of which it is a continuation.

In the Namchen valley our united camp formed quite a little village, for all the chiefs of the country were convened to a consultation. And here it was that Rindor and Pemba Tsering joined us with all the goods we had ordered from Saka-dzong. We stayed here two days. The weather was raw and chilly, and the temperature constantly fell to 8.2°. There was no spring as yet. But the wild-geese were on their migration, and when Tubges once shot a gander at a neighbouring brook, Oang Gye came to complain to me. He was quite overcome at this brutal murder, and could not conceive how my servant could be so heartless and cruel.

"You are right," I answered; "I am myself sorry for the wild-geese. But you must remember that we are travellers, and dependent for our livelihood on what the country yields. Often the chase and fishing are our only resources."

"In this district you have plenty of sheep."

"Is it not just as wrong to kill sheep and eat their flesh?"

"No!" he exclaimed, with passionate decision; "that is quite another matter. You surely will not compare sheep to wild-geese. There is as much difference between them as between sheep and human beings. For, like human beings, the wild-geese marry and have families. And if you sever such a union by a thoughtless shot, you cause sorrow and misery. The goose which has just been bereaved of her mate will seek him fruitlessly by day and night, and will never leave the place where he has been murdered. Her life will be empty and forlorn, and she will never enter upon a new union, but will remain a widow, and will soon die of grief. A woman cannot mourn more deeply than she will, and the man who has caused such sorrow draws down a punishment on himself."

The excellent Oang Gye was quite inconsolable. We might shoot antelopes, wild sheep, and partridges as much as ever, if only we left the wild-geese in peace. I had heard in the Lob country similar tales of the sorrow of the swans when their union was dissolved by death. It was moving to witness Oang Gye's tenderness and great sympathy for the wild-geese, and I felt the deepest respect for him. Many a noble and sensitive heart beats in the cold and desolate valleys of Tibet.

CHAPTER LXIX

KAMBA TSENAM, FATHER OF THE ROBBERS

At the Namchen camp we bought a large supply of rice, meal, barley and *tsamba*, sugar, stearin candles, soap, and five hundred cigarettes,—all procured from Tsongka. A rich merchant, Ngutu, who owned fifty horses and mules and two hundred yaks, sold us two mules and a horse, besides cloth for new garments, boots, and caps. Abdul Kerim hastened to make me a Tibetan costume of fine Lhasa cloth; on my head I wore a Chinese silk cap swathed with a red turban; I stalked about in silk Chinese boots, and had an elegant sword in my girdle. In my Ladaki saddle with its variegated fittings, and riding a milk-white stallion, I looked in this makeshift outfit quite like a Tibetan of rank (Illust. 343).

Here a large meeting was held in Dorche Tsuen's tent, where the question of my return route was discussed. Dorche Tsuen insisted on the necessity of my crossing the Samye-la again, and I answered, as before, that I intended to take no other way than over a pass east of the Samye-la. Then he appealed to the nomads at hand, who no doubt had received their instructions beforehand, and they all affirmed that the Chang-tang could be reached by no other pass than the Samye-la. However, we had heard from the horse-driver on the Gebuk-la that a way led over the mountains directly north of Kamba Tsenam's tent. But then the nomads, who would have to let us yaks on hire, replied that the road was so bad that we could not reach the Tarok-tso in three months, and that, for their part, they would not let their yaks go, and come to

348

350

348. Trooper of the Escort. 349. Tibetan of Teri-nam-tso.
350. Young Shepherd of Bongba.

Sketches by the Author.

grief on the detritus of the pass. Then we offered to buy yaks, but found no one who would sell his animals. After Dorche Tsuen had informed me that those who travelled from Saka into Bongba with hired yaks had to change both men and pack animals at Buptö on the upper Buptsang-tsangpo, I proposed to divide my caravan into two sections, one of which, under Abdul Kerim, would cross the Samye-la, while I with the other half marched over the eastern pass; we would meet on the lower course of the Buptsang-tsangpo. Ngutu, a genial old man of Mongolian origin, supported me, giving it as his opinion that it was of no consequence which pass I crossed myself, provided that the main part of the caravan went over the Samye-la; but Dorche Tsuen was still obstinate, and tried to frighten me with a tale of ten well-armed robbers whose haunts were in the country north of the mountain I wished to pass over.

"If the country is unsafe," I returned, "it is your duty to provide me with an escort of ten soldiers."

"The soldiers belong to the garrison of Saka-dzong, and cannot be employed elsewhere."

"Listen to me, Dorche Tsuen, and do not be so short-sighted. If you give me ten soldiers, you will be able to control my movements. I will pay them 2 rupees a man per day for their services, that is, 20 rupees a day altogether. You can well believe that I cannot afford such a great expense for a long time, and therefore you will have a guarantee that I shall not take a long round-about way. When I have rejoined Abdul Kerim's party I shall be beyond the limits of your province, and the escort can return."

"That is true," exclaimed two voices in the crowd; "if he pays 20 rupees a day, he cannot go far."

Dorche Tsuen rose and called some of the other men to a consultation outside the tent, and when he came back again he said that I might have my wish, if I would sign a written declaration that I took upon myself all responsibility for the consequences, for he wished to be free from blame if any misfortune befell me. Of course I promised to sign such a document with pleasure.

Thus the matter was arranged. Nima Tashi (Illust. 353), a powerful man of pleasant aspect, and dressed in a loose sheepskin, was to be chief of the bodyguard, and as he said he did not know the road to the north, Panchor (Illust. 332), a man fifty-five years of age, was ordered to act as guide. He was called into the tent. I had not seen him before, but Abdul Kerim said that he was the same man who on April 23 had shown us the way to the foot of the Kinchen-la, and that he had seen me and Muhamed Isa last year in Saka-dzong. He was a little, thin, wiry man who had killed eighty yaks with the gun he always carried. To everything that was said to him he agreed submissively with "La lasso, la lasso." We could see that he was sly and knavish—just the stuff we wanted.

With him and all the other company we rode on May 4 over the pass Gara-la, and from its rather flat threshold saw Kamba Tsenam's tent still in the same place. Here we crossed, then, our route of April 22, and had made a loop round the snowy massive Chomo-uchong.

Panchor was the elder brother of Kamba Tsenam, and it struck me as curious that when the Governor of Saka pitched his tent beside that of the wealthy nomad, the latter did not come out to welcome him. Now a collection of tents had sprung up in the valley larger than at any of the foregoing camps. Couriers and messengers came and went, small yak caravans came up to the tents with provisions for the officials, and nomads had come in from the neighbourhood to have a look at the eccentric European who had come down like a bomb into the country and had been caught at last.

Late in the evening Kamba Tsenam came sneaking into my tent. He was very mysterious, and said that the Governor and his people had no notion that he was paying me a visit in the darkness. He wished only to say that Panchor could very well contrive that I should go almost anywhere I liked. The escort had strict orders from the authorities, but only Panchor knew the way, and could easily throw dust into the eyes of the other men. I had only to make my wishes known to Panchor and he would

351. GUESTS AT THE OPENING OF MY TENT ON THE BANK OF THE TERI-NAM-TSO.
(Over the opening a plaid is stretched as a protection against the sun.)

352. THE YAKS FORDING THE RIVER SOMA-TSANGPO.

manage the rest. If also a band of fifty robbers swept down on us like a whirlwind, they would disperse like sheep as soon as they knew that Panchor with his never-failing gun was with us. Kamba Tsenam thus revealed himself as a cunning rogue, who had not the slightest respect for the authorities of Saka. The old fool promised that I should travel by the roads I wished if, in return, I would contrive that he should be governor of Saka. What he said was only idle talk, and he himself was a fellow to be on our guard against. There was not a man in Bongba who had ever heard of him, and his great power existed only in his own imagination. In his own village he was known and flattered on account of his great wealth, and he boasted that no robber dared to touch his flocks, for he was their trusted friend. "I am the father of all the robbers," he said modestly.

I willingly accepted his invitation to visit his tent next morning. When I had passed it the first time it was in a snowstorm, and I had looked upon it as a serious menace to my plans and my freedom. Almost like a thief in the night, expecting to be discovered every moment, I had stolen past the black nomad dwelling. Now I approached it as an honoured guest, only barked at by dogs.

The huge tent, made of a number of pieces of material, is supported by three veritable masts, firmly fixed in the ground. A stone wall runs along the inner side, and in front of it are heaps of *tsamba*, rice, and corn sacks. Baskets and boxes stand full of clothing. The altar, a wooden shelf and a table are laden with *gaos*, images, votive bowls, praying mills, and holy books. In one corner stand perhaps a dozen guns with streamers on their rests, and in another as many swords. On the hearth, built on the left of the entrance, always stands a large tea-kettle boiling, ready for any guests that may come in. A battery of wooden cups stands on a stone slab ready for use. The bluish grey smoke rises up towards the chimney opening. Far away from the entrance, at the right corner, the master of the house has his seat of honour, a small divan with a stool table before it, and before this again a fireplace, like a hollow cracked cannon-ball, filled with reeking dung embers. Some of Kamba Tsenam's shepherds are sitting in a group drinking tea, in another part some small black children are playing, and in a third the women of the tent are tittering. With pure white short hair, wrinkled like crushed parchment, stone-blind, and dressed like Monna Vanna only in a cloak, Kamba Tsenam's eighty-three-year-old mother sits on her bed and swings her prayer-mill with the right hand, while her left hand keeps the beads of her rosary in constant motion. She prattles and murmurs prayers, sometimes drops her rosary to catch a troublesome insect, and sometimes lets the prayer-mill stop when she is plunged in vague dreamy thought. Twice she asked if the European were still there and if he had been offered tea and food.

May 5, the last day we enjoyed Dorche Tsuen's society, had to be celebrated in some way. I invited the whole party to a festival in the camp. The two Governors and Oang Gye took their places in my tent, in the middle of which our tea-cups were filled on an improvised table. The day had been cold and muggy and snow fell, but we warmed our hands over the fire, and sat wrapped in skin coats like four Tibetans of rank, while the populace formed a circle outside. A fire was lighted in the middle and was maintained by dung from four sacks. It was pitch dark outside, but yellow flames threw a bright gleam over the dark Tibetans, servants, herdsmen, nomads and soldiers, women and children, youths and old men. They stood in wondering groups in their skin coats blackened by the smoke of fires, bare-headed, with long black tresses hanging over their shoulders. The light from the fire made a vain attempt to gild them. They stood out in sharp effective relief against the deep shadows (Illust. 336).

I charged Abdul Kerim to do his very best, and he informed me that the programme would contain fifteen items, song and dance following alternately without a pause. The first item was a dance with sticks to represent swords; the second, a hunting episode: a wild animal, composed of two crouching men with a piece of felt over them and two sticks for horns, went prancing round the fire; a hunter with his gun crept about, took aim at the

353. Nima Tashi,
Commandor of the Government-Escort
on the way to the Teri-nam-tso.

354. Nuns of Mendong.

355. A high Lama of Chokchu.

366. The Prior of Selipuk.

Water-colour Sketches by the Author.

monster, killed him with a single shot, and performed with his friends a triumphal dance around the carcase. Then followed a Ladaki dance, little Gulam leading the troop, and after that Suen executed his remarkable dance before a lady, represented by a stick he held before him. All the others kept time by clapping their hands, and invited the Tibetans to join in, and my guests in the tent were convulsed with laughter.

The Mohammedans executed a Yarkand dance with Kutus as leader. They danced round the fire, swinging their arms and skirts, and between the fire and the tent they appeared only as black profiles, while on the other side they were lighted up by the reddish-yellow flames, and their perspiring faces shone like bronze. A song followed, waking a sonorous echo in the mountains, and the Tibetans recognizing the air joined in, and all the while the men clapped their hands. The smoke from the fire took part in the dances and sometimes flew right in the faces of the spectators, the singing became louder, the merriment more uncontrolled, and the nomads laughed till they had to support themselves with their hands on their knees, as Suen revolved in grotesque pirouettes over the arena and the nomads tried to imitate him. The clumsy Abdullah performed an indescribable dance with his back bent back, and when he bent himself so much that he fell backwards to the edge of the fire, the delight of the spectators was unbounded: they laughed till they were breathless, hopped about and uttered wild yells, while the performer shook the sparks from his coat and retired to his corner (Illusts. 337, 338, 339, 340). The Tibetans evidently enjoyed themselves; perhaps they had never had such an amusing evening in their lives. Dorche Tsuen said something of the sort. Ngavang gave way to his kindly laugh, and Oang Gye enjoyed the unwonted spectacle like a child. For my part, I dreamed awhile and thought of the unexpected and singular manner in which fate had allowed me to choose my course. Through the clouds of smoke I seemed to see all old Asia before me, and the adventures of past years behind me. A carnival of old camp-scenes danced before my mind's eye, expiring like shooting-stars in the night—merry songs which came to an end among other mountains and the dying sound of strings and flutes. And I was surprised that I had not had enough of these things and that I was not tired of the light of camp-fires.

The wind rises, the snow falls thickly and hisses in the fire, and the flakes are lighted up from below. With white hair and shoulders the Tibetans look like mist figures, and behind them hang the dark curtains of night, from which is heard from time to time a pony's neigh or a dog's bark. The last sack of fuel is emptied over the leaping flames, burns up and sinks, and only embers are left, glowing in the ceaselessly falling snow. Then my grateful guests rise at midnight, distribute gifts to the performers, say farewell, and vanish like ghosts in the darkness to seek their own tents. Now night reigns alone over the valley, the surroundings lie silent and still, and only the pelting snow makes a swishing sound against the tent.

On the morning of May 6 the country was again white as in the depth of winter. Quietly and lightly as cotton-wool the flakes fell, and all, the Tibetans included, were more wrapped up than usual. The Governors and their retinue came to pay a farewell visit, and then I went out with them to their horses, took a last farewell, and thanked them for all the kindness they had shown me in spite of the trouble I had given them. Dorche Tsuen expressed a hope that we should meet again. It is much easier to get on with men and lead them where you wish if you treat them kindly and gently; you gain nothing by violence, harshness, and threats. The Governor was a fine upright figure on his horse; his face was entirely covered with dark spectacles and a red hood to protect it from the blast (Illust. 342). His troop of mounted men was considerably diminished after his escort had been told off to follow me. They struck their heels into their horses and soon disappeared up the hill on the way to the Gara-la.

My caravan was now to be divided into two parties. Only five men were to follow me, namely, Gulam, Lobsang, Kutus, Tubges, and Kunchuk. We had eight goats

357. Two Lamas of Mendong.

358. My Sheep crossing the River Soma-tsangpo.

to supply milk; our old sheep had been sold for a mere trifle. A hundred rupees for the first five days were paid in advance to the escort under Nima Tashi. No agreement was made with Panchor, but he was to be paid well if he took me where I wished. The other seven Ladakis were ordered to proceed under the command of Abdul Kerim over the Samye-la to the Buptsang-tsangpo, follow the stream slowly downwards, and wait for us near its mouth in the Tarok-tso. Whatever they did, they were not to leave the Buptsang-tsangpo, or we might lose one another. Rindor and Pemba Tsering were deputed to follow them over the Samye-la to Buptö, to bring the Kebyang people to reason if they refused transport animals. My baggage was reduced to a minimum, and I took with me only a thousand rupees. Abdul Kerim was responsible for the remainder of the cash. He was an honest man, but a noodle. Some nomads accompanied us with six yaks for the baggage (Illusts. 344, 345, 348).

Though, according to our plans, we were to be separated only a few weeks, the parting was touching, and many childish tears trickled down weather-beaten cheeks. We had bought more horses, and all my five Ladakis could ride. We rode up the valley in close order; the bottom was full of loose rotten ice, lumpy tufts of grass with mice-holes among them, frozen springs, and detritus of hard green schist. We marched north-eastwards, and then due west, over the small double pass Shalung-la, and down to the Gyegong valley, where we encamped at Kamba Tsenam's sheepfolds to buy some sheep for food. The escort had got there first, and sat in their black tent drinking tea.

We sat talking with Kamba Tsenam and Panchor when a tall and strongly built young fellow came and sat down at the opening of my tent.

"I have seen the Bombo before," he said, "in the neighbourhood of Nakchu. You had a Buryat and a lama with you. That is seven years ago."

"Quite right. Have you brought me a message?"

"No; I only wish to ask if you are disposed to buy two

good yaks from me. You can have them for half their value."

"Thanks; we do not want any yaks now. What is your occupation?"

"Robber!" he answered, without blinking.

After he had gone, Kamba Tsenam informed me that some time ago the man had killed a nomad in Rukyok, and now was come to treat about the compensation for the murder. The authorities were looking eagerly for the band to which he belonged, and Kamba Tsenam and Panchor knew exactly where they were hiding, but would not betray them lest they should be robbed of their property in revenge. Kamba Tsenam and his brother were evidently on very confidential terms with the robbers of the country, and I very much suspected that they were in league with some of them. In Panchor we had certainly an actual robber chief as guide. He himself told us that the Devashung had tried to engage him in their service as a spy and guide, when they wished to track up an evaded robber band, but he would not consent. He knew that we had a large quantity of money with us, and we were not too safe in his company. He could very well arrange a night attack and in the end play the innocent. He pretended not to know the country beyond a couple of days' journey to the north, but when he inspected our six horses he said: "This one you bought from an old nomad to the west of Sha-kangsham, and this one from Tsongpun Tashi." If he knew every horse in the country, he must also know the country very well. I asked him to go over the names of our camping-places to the north, but he gave only the first two, and added: "The rest you will know as you go on, and if I cannot find them myself, there will always be some robbers I can ask."

On May 7 we took leave of the old robber chief Kamba Tsenam, and rode in close order up to the pass Gyegong-la, which has a height of 18,012 feet. The pass stands on a distinctly marked chain, which is called Kanchung-gangri, and it was very interesting to find that all the water on the northern side of the pass flowed to the upper Chaktak-tsangpo. Kanchung-gangri is therefore not part of the main range of the Trans-Himalaya, and the Gyegong-la is only a secondary pass. The great watershed lay some days' journey farther to the north.

On the northern side we passed a warm spring, Memo-chutsen, which at the orifice had a temperature of 93.6°, while in another the water boiled and steamed. The springs are surrounded by sinter, terraces, and basins in which sick people bathe.

Panchor had an old field-glass and diligently looked out for robbers and wild yaks. He said that we ought always to keep together in case we were attacked by robbers he did not know, and he bade us help with our weapons in the defence.

The camp this day was No. 400.

CHAPTER LXX

THE SEVENTH CROSSING OF THE TRANS-HIMALAYA—TO THE HEAVENLY LAKE OF THE THRONE MOUNTAIN

TWENTY-NINE degrees of frost on the night of May 8. Winter instead of spring might be coming. A month ago it was much warmer in Bongba. But now we are mounting up to the heights of the Trans-Himalaya, the weather is cold, raw, and windy, the temperature seldom above freezing-point, and to-day the whole country is again buried in snow.

We ride northwards and descend from a small saddle to the Chaktak-tsangpo, near which we have to halt a while to warm ourselves at a fire. The river bends to the west-south-west to break through Kanchung-gangri. On its bank is seen a tent, eight horses, and a hundred sheep. Panchor went off to-day to stalk a herd of ninety wild yaks, and Nima Tashi, the captain of the bodyguard, was sure that a robber band was in the tent, for no nomads are seen in this cold country. The escort, particularly Nima Tashi, were dreadfully afraid of robbers; and Panchor had told us that we could make them go anywhere by frightening the soldiers with robbers. When Panchor appeared again, he said that the suspected tent was really inhabited by the band which had the murder in Rukyok on its conscience, and he added that if the people in Rukyok would not let the matter rest, the band threatened to commit new crimes in the country. I asked why the authorities did not seize the chief now when he was so near, but Panchor shook his head and said that if he was taken and killed, thirty others would be down on the country, and that

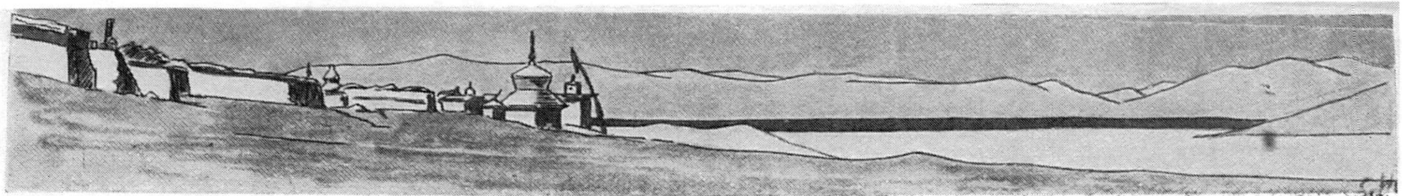

359. Village below Lunkar-gompa on the Tarok-tso.

360 Mendong Monastery west of the Teri-nam-tso.

361. Selipuk Monastery south-west of the Nganglaring-tso.

Water-colour Sketches by the Author.

362. Holiday Costumes and Ornaments of Tibetan Women of Kyangrang in the Trans-Himalaya.

Water-colour Sketches by the Author.

would be worse. A bandit's life in Tibet is on the whole a very pleasant one.

Following the stream upwards we came to the small lake Lapchung-tso, entirely covered with ice, and set up camp 401 (17,037 feet) on its eastern shore. It is enclosed among hills and surrounded on all sides by lofty mountains. To the south Kanchung-gangri appears in all its splendour. The snow is much more abundant on its northern than on its southern side, and in the hollows between its summits three large and several small glaciers, short and steep, are seen. From all the valleys on the north, north-west, and north-east brooks descend to the Lapchung-tso, and from the southern extremity of the lake the Chaktak-tsangpo issues, and a little distance farther south-west breaks through Kanchung-gangri.

May 9. −0.9° at this time of year! We move north-eastwards along the eastern shore of Lapchung-tso, and follow a well-beaten road consisting of quite fifty parallel paths. It is very interesting to draw another line on the map of Tibet through a part unknown before. Here travel the merchants whose destination is east Bongba and Chokchu, and here passes a large part of the salt traffic from Tabie-tsaka, as well as pilgrims on their way home from Kang-rinpoche. The last usually follow the *tasam* on their outward journey, but return by the northern route—this is, that the whole pilgrimage may make a *kore* or a loop of salvation.

Our direction becomes now more northerly and we go up the Sangmo-bertik valley, where the bottom is filled with ice clear as glass, but there is good pasturage on the flanks. The country is quite flat between Kanchung-gangri and the main crest of the Trans-Himalaya. In the longitudinal valley between the two we see to the north, 60° W., the comparatively low saddle Dicha-la, which is, however, a watershed of the first rank, for it parts the water flowing to the ocean from the isolated drainage of the plateau. Over the Dicha-la runs the lately mentioned road to the Buptsang-tsangpo and Tabie-tsaka. North, north-west, and north-east are several *gangris* with firn-fields and snow, all belonging to the main range of the

Trans-Himalaya. To the east lies a pass, the Nakbo-kongdo-la, with the Nakbo-gongrong-gangri; over this pass, which also seems to lie on the main watershed, a road runs to Targo-gangri and Dangra-yum-tso. Between Raga-tasam and Ombo a road crosses the Tsalam-nakta-la, mostly frequented by salt caravans. From camp 402 we could still see Chomo-uchong to the south, 13° E.

A member of the robber band we saw the day before paid us a visit and was evidently an old friend of Panchor. He gave us many interesting details of the Teri-nam-tso and Mendong-gompa, which were afterwards found to be perfectly correct. I never could make out Panchor. Either he was in league with the devil himself, or he was a fully fledged knave at his own risk and reckoning. He now assured me that it would be the easiest thing in the world to take me to the Teri-nam-tso and perhaps also to the Dangra-yum-tso. O gods of Naktsang, slumber in this cold spring and do not warn your earthly vassals until it is too late! Yes, if I could only contrive to cross the Trans-Himalaya twice more, I would then willingly leave this mighty range to rest a thousand years under a veil of clouds and glittering snowfields. It is strange that this wide country, so near to the Indian frontier, should have remained absolutely unknown till our late times. I am proud and delighted to know that I am the first white man to penetrate to this wilderness.

Panchor advised us to stay a day in the valley, for we should not find pasture as good as here for a long time. I wondered how he could know that, seeing that he had said recently that he had never been north of the Sangmo-bertik-la.

On the night of May 11 the thermometer fell to 3°. We found ourselves in a great enlargement of the Trans-Himalaya called Lap, and this region is noted for its severe climate. Even in the middle of summer, when it is warm everywhere else, it is cold in Lap. The ice breaks up on Lapchung-tso only in the beginning of June after all the other ice is melted. From the map it is seen that many considerable rivers, flowing north and south, take their rise in this lofty swell.

363. Crossing the Kangsham River.

The day's march took us up to higher ground, and the way was dreadful—not a road at all, but a track winding among granite boulders and yak-moss. And next day it was still worse. In raw wintry weather, with a temperature of 1.2°, we wound up the ascent extremely slowly, where all small and loose material had been removed, so that the animals might at any moment break their legs among the stones. Here no other vegetation was seen but a moss, yellow as the yolk of an egg, and another shading into red. On the left we passed three small glaciers with a blue tinge on their fronts. By one of them some wild yaks walked meditatively. The weather was so cold that we had to stop frequently to warm our hands at a small dung fire. Panchor insisted strongly on these halts "in order that the Bombo may not be tired"; but I suspect it was chiefly because he wanted a puff from his Chinese *gansa*.

Though it was a great struggle for our horses, we came at last to the Sangmo-bertik-la, at the giddy height of 19,094 feet, and now I stood for the seventh time on the main crest of the Trans-Himalaya and the watershed of the great Indian rivers. The view was closed in on all sides and limited by adjacent heights. On a sharp ridge to the north-west seven yaks were tramping in the snow. Panchor and one of the soldiers went on foot in pursuit of them—to mount these steep hills on foot and carry heavy, clumsy guns is tough work. We rode on among the granite boulders; lower down green porphyry begins. The gradient became more gentle, and where we encamped we could scarcely perceive in which direction the valley sloped.

The day had been stormy, and the blast continued on May 13. Little Puppy went out to look at the morning, but crept back again and lay on his mat. Takkar was still irreconcilable towards his countrymen, the Tibetans, and inspired the greatest respect in all the escort and Panchor. We rode on through the valley northwards, past numerous summer camping-grounds, and recognized the characteristic low relief of Chang-tang in contrast to the more deeply excavated valleys on the southern side of the Trans-

Himalaya. At the mouth of a side-valley running in from the west the escort came to a halt, and Nima Tashi explained that our road to Buptö, where we had agreed to meet Abdul Kerim's party, ran up this valley, and that they did not intend to go farther north. They now showed their teeth for the first time, and were not so pliant as we thought. They excused themselves on the ground that their yaks were tired, that their provisions were at an end, and that they had no orders to accompany us more than fourteen days. Panchor, the scoundrel, took their part, and frightened us with the chief of Bongba-chushar, who took tribute from all the robbers of the country, and would certainly plunder us if we passed through his domain. After long consideration we decided to camp where we were, to thoroughly discuss the situation. Before the sun had set I had won them over, though it was chiefly the chink of silver rupees which made them forget all their scruples. It was agreed that they should receive their 20 rupees every evening, and I gave them a goat in addition, as their supply of meat was at an end.

So on May 14 we rode farther north in blinding snow, and passed numerous *manis*, nine standing in one row. The valley became more open, and was more than a mile broad. We found no water at the camp, but two of our yaks were laden with blocks of ice. Every evening we sat an hour conversing with Panchor, and it was easy to check his statements. I told him once for all, that if he did not speak the truth he would receive no extra gratuity. In the evening he declared that there were dreadful apparitions at Muhamed Isa's grave, and that at night fearful shrieks and groans could be heard from beneath. He was quite convinced that spirits and demons haunted the grave, and said that no Tibetan ventured to go near the place ; this was well, for consequently the grave would not be desecrated.

He gave me also much valuable information about the country round Nam-tso or Tengri-nor, where he was born. He had gone twice round Nam-tso, thrice round Tso-mavang, and twelve times round Kang-rinpoche, which he intended to visit again soon, to complete the thirteenth

364. THE VILLAGE OF LUNKAR.

365. GROUP OF TIBETANS AT THE TERI-NAM-TSO.

circuit of salvation. He considered it superfluous to make the circuit of Dangra-yum-tso and Targo-gangri, for he had already tramped so far that all his sins must be forgiven, and he was sure of promotion in the next incarnation. Panchor had not the slightest doubt that a man or horse which had drunk of the water of Tso-mavang or Nam-tso was for ever immune from illness, robbers, and wolves. "It is just as though a fire blazed out of that part of the body where the wolf intends to seize him," he affirmed. But he considerably modified his statements after I had told him that we had a mule which had drunk for a whole month of the water of Tso-mavang and yet had been torn in pieces by wolves at Gartok. "Yes," he replied, "the protection is only for Tibetans and their animals, not for Europeans and their animals. And if the wolf itself drank of the holy water it would avail nothing; he would still seize his prey."

On the 15th of May we set out again in a snowstorm, whereas I had been looking forward ever since January to spring. It caused great merriment, both among the Tibetans and the Ladakis, when one of the escort who did not know Kunchuk's name, spoke of him as "that there calf." We had travelled a good long way before they ceased to laugh at the newly invented title, which stuck to Kunchuk ever after.

The valley opens out on to a plain where kiangs, Goa and Pantholops antelopes are plentiful. From the ridge of a hill we see to the east another still larger plain, beyond which Targo-gangri would be visible if the mountain were not shrouded in clouds and falling snow. Buchu-tso is a small pool which dries up in summer. There lay three black tents, and beyond another hill in the locality Kangmar, seven. When we encamped, sixty men, women, and children came out and watched us. They had gathered together here to pay their taxes to a collector from Saka. The district is called Bongba-chushar, and the elderly Gova came to visit us. He was a discreet man and put no awkward questions. Panchor, who was accustomed to run with the hare and hunt with the hounds, had probably given him an account of us beforehand. It seems he was terribly frightened, for he had never in his life seen a European. However, he gave us much valuable information about the country, among other things, that the little twin lakes Mun-tso lay to the north of the Barong-la and east of the Teri-nam-tso, not south of the Dangra-yum-tso as on Nain Sing's map, which I had myself found to be incorrect. On the way to the Teri-nam-tso we should be able in two places to steal goose eggs; it was forbidden to the Tibetans for three years to take them, but a European could permit himself anything without having to answer for it to the gods of heaven and earth.

After a day's rest we marched north-north-east to the broad longitudinal valley of Soma-tsangpo. The river descends from the east-south-east, and probably has its source in the great mountain system we saw from the Shuru-tso. Here it runs west-north-west, but afterwards turns north and north-eastwards, and therefore makes a sharp curve before it enters the Teri-nam-tso. Its bed is flat and shallow, and at the time carried down about 280 cubic feet of water per second, but it is so full in summer that sometimes it cannot be forded. We camped at a spring in a valley at the farther side, and on May 18 ascended the adjacent pass, Dongchen-la, and on its south slopes twenty-four Ovis Ammon sheep were a fine sight.

On the night of the 19th, the minimum temperature was 29.5°, and now it felt as if spring were really come, or even summer. The way ran north-west up a steep valley, where granite and dark schists were twice observed *in situ*, to the small pass Teta-la (16,266 feet), where we had at length a free view over the longed-for lake Teri-nam-tso, Nain Sing's Tede-nam-tso, which he never visited nor saw, but only heard of, and inserted with a broken line quite correctly on his map. The only mistake he made was to draw the lake longer from north to south instead of from east to west.

To obtain an uninterrupted view we climbed up a height on the north side of the pass (16,972 feet). The scene here displayed in all directions was one of the grandest and most memorable tableaus I have seen in Tibet. The "heavenly lake" lay like a great flat-cut turquoise framed in mountains and hills shaded in pink, red, yellow, and purple, which, towards the horizon, gradually passed into a light blue veil. Only to the south-east quadrant is the view obstructed by adjacent heights belonging to the chain on the crest of which we stand, and which runs along the southern shore of the lake, but elsewhere the view is open, dizzy, boundless, and the eyes scan both Sha-kangsham's majestic peak and Targo-gangri's many-headed ridge, and the seven-times-mounted main range of the Trans-Himalaya, with its snow-crowned heights rising in a row of bright white domes to the south. Many other peaks and domes with eternal snow rise over this sea of tumbled waves, but, after all, the finest sight is the lake itself, which charms and fascinates the spectator by its intense ultramarine hue, a couple of shades deeper and stronger than turquoise. When one first comes to the saddle of the pass and this wealth of colouring strikes the retina, one can scarcely restrain an exclamation of astonishment and admiration. We look down straight on the lake, and its southern shore is just below us. To the west it extends for two days' journey, and widens out enormously, while to the east it contracts and seems to stretch a good day's journey. Due north-east the blue surface is broken by a steep rocky islet, with a level shore only in the east, and further east one fancies one can detect the hollow where the basin of the Dangra-yum-tso skirts the northern foot of the divine Targo-gangri mountain.

Beautiful weather, not a cloud on the blue vault of heaven, calm and quiet, only the gentlest whisper over the hills sounding in the ears like the tinkle of small bells and the vibration of strings. One feels overwhelmed by this grand beauty, which speaks more powerfully to the senses than the high mass of any archbishop. I stood several hours up here and made a hopeless attempt to sketch the landscape, but succeeded in producing only a feeble imitation of the reality. From the Teta-la one commands a very considerable area of the heart of Tibet. How extensive is the line of Sha-kangsham! How many are the points from which I have viewed this wonderful mountain on different journeys! Like a gigantic beacon, a marvellous landmark, it raises its snow-covered dome above desolate Tibet. And we were far from its dripping glaciers when for the last time it sank below the horizon like a dream of snow and roses.

At last we had to drag ourselves away and follow the track of the other men to a little dreary valley where they had encamped near a couple of tents. Even here the view was remarkable. How I now missed my old tried boat, and how gladly I would have glided with sail and oar over the heavenly lake!

We remained four whole days at this miserable camp with its fine view (15,646 feet). The fact was that Dangra-yum-tso now for the fourth time began to haunt my dreams, and as the holy lake was only four days' journey to the east, I would try to reach its shore. But Nima Tashi and Panchor put all kinds of difficulties in the way: their yaks would perish where there was no grazing, and it was impossible to hire yaks, for all had lately gone to Tabie-tsaka for salt. I proposed to go on my own horses and meet them at Mendong-gompa after the excursion, and to this they made no objection at first. If I had not been by this time heartily sick of Tibet, I would have played them a pretty trick, and gone not only to Dangra-yum-tso, but further eastwards until I was stopped. But I was weary of geography, discoveries, and adventures, and wanted to get home. And besides, on comparing the lands east and west of the Teri-nam-tso, I considered the latter far better worth visiting. The former I had traversed by three routes, and two other travellers had been there, but no one had been in the west, and we knew nothing about it except the uncertain data which the Jesuits had gathered from the natives two hundred years ago. In fact this land was the least known part of Tibet, and the road to the Nganglaring-tso crosses the blank patch in its longer direction. If the authorities had asked me which way I would choose, I should have answered, the way to the Nganglaring-tso. It would have been wisest to close at once with Nima Tashi's suggestion to go straight to Mendong-gompa. But their opposition

366. THE VILLAGE OF LUNKAR FROM THE TEMPLE HILL.

367. THE SOUTHERN SHORE OF MANASAROWAR WITH GRAZING YAKS.

egged me on to break another lance for Dangra-yum-tso. I ought to have remembered that he who grasps at all loses all, for I was within an ace of losing Mendong-gompa into the bargain.

For when Nima Tashi saw that he could not make me give way, he secretly sent a message to Tagla Tsering, the chief of Sangge-ngamo-buk, the district we were in and which is subject to Naktsang. And Tagla Tsering came. Last year he had been in Lundup's train when the latter had stopped us at the foot of Targo-gangri and prevented us from going to the shore of the holy lake. Now he looked very grand and important. Over a mantle of panther skin he wore a belt of six bright silver *gaos*, and in the belt was stuck a sword with a silver scabbard inlaid with turquoise and coral, and at his side rattled knives and other pendent articles. Over all, he wore a long reddish-violet mantle, and on his head a Chinese silk cap. He was accompanied by six horsemen, and, the day after, twenty more arrived, all armed to the teeth with guns, swords, and lances; all in picturesque bright-coloured costumes, some with tall brimmed hats on their heads, others with bandages round their foreheads, Tagla Tsering evidently took the matter seriously, and tried to get over me by talking of raising the militia (Illust. 329).

The powerful chief meanwhile entered my tent, friendly and pleased, and, like an old friend, bade me heartily welcome, and expressed his great astonishment that I had come back again, though I had been forced the year before to turn back. Had I not already brought about Hlaje Tsering's fall, and would I cause the new Governor of Naktsang to meet the same fate? Or what did I mean?

"No, Hedin Sahib, you cannot travel to Naktsang. Turn to the west. Nima Tashi had no authority to lead you even to the Teri-nam-tso; it was on the Buptsang-tsangpo you were to meet the caravan. You talk of Mendong-gompa. You have no right to travel thither. There is a nearer way to the rendezvous. Mendong-gompa does not lie in my district, but all the same I have sent written notices to all the govas in the country to stop you if you travel to the monastery."

Poor Nima Tashi was half dead with fright. He had thought to frighten me, but now he saw that the chief and I sat together like old friends, drinking tea and smoking cigarettes, while he was reprimanded for bringing me too far. I told him afterwards that he was a noodle, and if he now got into trouble in Saka it was his own fault. Tagla Tsering's good humour was much enhanced when I promised to turn back and conform to the arrangements of the chiefs on the way to Mendong, if by any chance I was prevented from approaching the convent.

We said farewell on May 24, and continued our journey westwards along the southern shore of the lake. The water is salt and has an extremely unpleasant taste, and cannot be drunk in any circumstances. Lamlung-la (16,880 feet) is a commanding pass, which must be crossed to cut off a peninsula. The rocks are granite and green schist. Hares and wild-geese are very plentiful. Here and there are freshwater lagoons on the shore, which forms a very narrow belt at the foot of the mountains. The northern shore belt seems to be much broader. We followed the southern shore another day to the spring Tertsi at the western extremity of the lake, which forms a large regular expansion.

I heard the name of this lovely lake variously pronounced by different nomads. Nain Sing's Tede-nam-tso is incorrect. The Gova of Kangmar insisted that Tsari-nam-tso was the correct pronunciation, and said that the name was bestowed because *ri di tsa-la tso yore*, that is, "The lake situated at the foot of the mountain." The nomads on the shore, however, said Tiri- or Teri-nam-tso. At our camp 411 were two small mountains on the shore, called Techen and Techung, or the Great and Little Te, or more correctly Ti. *Ti* is a lama's throne in a temple, *ri* signifies mountain, *nam* heaven, and *tso* lake. The whole name therefore has the poetical meaning of the Throne-mountain's Heavenly Lake. Its height above sea-level is 15,367 feet, or 413 feet lower than Mont Blanc, which, if it lifted up its head from the turquoise billows of the lake, would look like the small rocky islet in its eastern half.

CHAPTER LXXI

ANOTHER JOURNEY ACROSS THE WHITE PATCH

We left on May 26 the heavenly lake, the shore of which had never before been trodden by European or pundit, and saw its blue surface diminish to a sabre blade between the mountains, and finally disappear in the east, while we rode westwards over a wide plain, which was formerly under water. Kutus, Lobsang, and Panchor accompanied me. We must hasten to descend on the monastery before the monks got wind of us, and the caravan and escort could come after and encamp near Mendong-gompa. Panchor disappeared at the first tent we passed, and was not seen again all day. He was a coward, and did not wish to be suspected of showing us the way to the sanctuary. We had therefore to shift for ourselves and find our way thither.

Two men and a woman came out of a nomad encampment to the track we followed, and asked if we had seen the European who was said to be travelling about Bongba. In order to preserve my incognito till I came to Mendong, I answered that he was coming behind with his caravan, and if they kept on the look-out they would see an amusing figure. Probably they had long given up all hope of seeing the stranger. My involuntary disguise therefore did me good service, for the nomads took me to be, like the other two men, servants of the expected European.

Hour after hour we rode on westwards and looked in vain for a monastery. But at last it cropped up all of a sudden. We were on the top of a bank terrace 30 feet high, skirting on the east the channel of the Soma-tsangpo, and saw at the foot of the opposite terrace the quadrangular stone house of the monastery with its white walls and red frieze, *chhortens*, *mani* heaps, and streamers, and on the east and west of it two tent villages, the upper inhabited by sixty monks, the lower by forty nuns (Illust. 360). The Soma-tsangpo, also called Nyagga, or Soma-Nyagga-tsangpo, now carried down 350 to 420 cubic feet of water, which, divided into four channels, glided over a treacherously deepening bottom. We managed, however, to ford it, and rode up to the gate of the monastery, where ten monks, good-natured but reserved, met us. I have no space to describe the religious organization of Mendong-gompa. It is enough to say that hitherto it was quite unknown even by name, like so many of the convents we visited the year before. The peculiarity of this monastery is that the brothers and sisters live in black tents, and every tent is a cell. The tents had a very comfortable and attractive appearance, but the sisters, of whom I took some portraits, were hideous to behold—old unwashed harpies, barbarous and demoralized. That there is anything idyllic and fascinating in life in a nunnery in the wilds is a pure illusion, which vanishes at once at the sight of these old apes. They have also a puzzling resemblance to their male colleagues, and it is often difficult to decide whether one of them is a man or a woman (Illust. 354).

When we left the solitary monastery on May 28 we decided to make for the rendezvous on the Buptsang-tsangpo, where Abdul Kerim would no doubt be uneasy at our prolonged absence. It had been arranged that we should be separated only two weeks, but before we reached the river a whole month would have passed away.

So we set out early, followed the right bank of the Soma-tsangpo southwards, and crossed the range, from the top of which, at the Teta-la, we had first seen the Teri-nam-tso. The valley is quite 2½ miles broad, the strand terraces are well developed, the fall is slight, and the rush of water is seldom heard; here and there stands a tent with grazing flocks. One more sunrise and we ride through the river (Illust. 358), which, with the Sachu-tsangpo, Buptsang-tsangpo, and Bogtsang-tsangpo, shares the honour of

368. Lunkar-gompa.

369. Selipuk-gompa.

being one of the largest in the interior of Tibet. Through the valley Goa-lung we rode up on May 30 to the pass Goa-la (17,382 feet), flat and easy, lying amidst pink and grey granite, and affording an instructive view over the Trans-Himalaya to the south. To the south-west we see, close below the pass, the small lake Karong-tso—a new discovery, like everything else in this country. Our route ran to the west, when we, on June 1, rode, with the Karong-tso on our left hand, and a crest of medium height on our right, through the district Bongba-kemar, following the great route of the salt caravans between Raga-tasam and Tabie-tsaka, which crosses the already mentioned pass Tsalam-nakta-la. A high-road from Naktsang joins this. At camp 417 we had the Chunit-tso near us on the north-west.

Although we were at the beginning of June, the minimum sank below freezing-point; in the night of the 1st the thermometer fell to 16.3°. But the day was warm, nay hot, when the sun shone and the air was still. The dreary barren valleys lay waiting for the rainy season. The grass was more than scanty, for last summer the rains failed. Our direction turned more to the south-west. From camp 418 we saw, to the south, 60° E., the opening of a valley through which a highway runs through Bongba-kyangrang over the Dicha-la to Lapchung.

Our Tibetans know excellently well how to look after themselves on the journey. On the march they twist string, talk, sing and whistle, and shout at their yaks. In pitching their camp they set up their black tent in a moment, first stretching out the ropes and fastening them into the ground with wooden pegs, and then throwing the cloth over the poles. The animals are unloaded and sent off to feed, and the men gather fuel and make a fire in the tent, where all assemble to drink tea and sleep. After a couple of hours they come out again, wrestle, play and laugh. In the dusk one may be heard singing a monotonous ballad, which must, however, be amusing, for the others laugh heartily at every verse. Morning and evening they gabble their prayers, all together, murmuring like bees in a hive. An old man, whom I knew the year before, has a riding yak of his own, and brandishes the escort's prayer-mill. He is never seen without this ingenious instrument. The men are always good-natured and polite, help us to collect fuel, set up the tents and load the animals, and frequently pay us a visit. We know them all by name and are the best of friends.

The temperature sank in the night only a few degrees below freezing-point, and yet a snowstorm raged almost all day long on June 3. We rode past a large marsh in the valley and up to the flat saddle Merke-sang, with a view over the plain we crossed exactly two months before on the way to the Buptsang-tsangpo. Camp 419 lay therefore in the Bongba-kebyang district again. To the south-east is the pass Chiptu-la, with the pilgrim route from Nakchu to Kang-rinpoche. To the south, 27° W., rises a snowy summit, at the foot of which a road leads over the Dsalung-la to Tradum. As a watershed this pass is of the first rank, and it sends off a voluminous tributary to the Buptsang-tsangpo. The escort sent off a messenger in advance to this river to look out for Abdul Kerim's party.

June 4. It had snowed all night long, and we set out in the wildest snowstorm. It was half dark, with heavy leaden clouds; not a glimpse could be seen of the surrounding mountains; all was wet, muddy, and evil-smelling; pools of melting snow lay on the ground, and seven pilgrims from Kang-rinpoche were close upon us before they emerged from the mist. We splashed through the soaked soil, but when we encamped on the shore of the Buptsang-tsangpo the weather was much clearer.

Before I proceed further I will mention that the great province of Bongba is divided into twelve *tso* or districts, namely: Parryang, Laktsang, Buptö, Tsaruk, Yeke, Tarok, Kebyang, Kemar, Parma, Changma, Kyangrang, and Chushar. To each of these district names is usually prefixed the name of the province, as, for instance, Bongba-parryang, Bongba-laktsang, etc. We were now in Bongba-kebyang.

Some tents stood on the river bank. The nomads reported that Abdul Kerim had gone a week before by a cross-cut over the mountain on the right, down towards the

370. The Trans-Himalaya from Abuk-la. (The three parts in the illustration form a continuous panorama from East to S.S.W.)

371. Storm over the Trans-Himalaya. (To the left the way up to Samye-la; valley of Buptsang-tsangpo.)

Sketches by the Author.

Tarok-tso. There was no Gova here, but two natives were ready to let us on hire the five yaks we required. They were shy and timorous, but Panchor, the rogue, spoke well of us, and it was agreed that they should accompany us to the boundary of Tarok-tso. On the morning of June 5 we took farewell of Nima Tashi and his soldiers and of Panchor, and rode between the hills on the left side of the valley down the course of the Buptsang-tsangpo. Soon the valley contracted to a ditch, but before long expanded again. On our left hand we had the main range of the Trans-Himalaya, which, however, did not present an imposing appearance, for we were always close to its foot. At times we were enveloped in a snowstorm, and at Mabie-tangsam-angmo, where we camped, we made haste to get a cover over our heads. When Little Puppy heard the thunder rumble for the first time in his life, he was very disturbed and barked with all his might, but he could not make out whence the noise came, and he found it safest to fly into the tent and hide himself behind my bed-head.

June 6. Hail and snow! The whole country is hidden under newly-fallen snow, as far as we can see. Is June to be reckoned among the winter months? We have already had nine of them. It seems as though summer were missed out this year and we were approaching another winter. But the precipitation is welcome to the nomads, for it promotes the growth of fresh grass. We march sometimes on the top, sometimes at the foot of a lofty erosion terrace 80 to 100 feet high, which is a characteristic feature in this large valley. Geese, wild asses, Goa antelopes, and foxes are everywhere. A sharp bend in the river forces us to the north-north-east for a time, and the valley is again narrow and picturesque. At Tuta, which belongs to Bongba-tsaruk, we encamp close by the Buptsang-tsangpo, where the wild-geese swim with their yellow chicks in the clear water.

Eighteen degrees of frost on the night of June 7. Yet the day was fine, and flies, gnats, and other insects were more numerous than before. As on the two preceding days we crossed several small affluents from the Trans-Himalaya. The Buptsang valley expanded more and more, and at length became 13 miles broad. We encamped in sight of the Tarok-tso, on a level plain about 16 feet above the surface of the lake, and with two nomad tents as our nearest neighbours. The height here was 15,197 feet.

Our guides were the pleasantest and most complacent we had ever had, our movements were not controlled by chiefs and soldiers, and Karma Puntso's camp was far away—we might have travelled wherever we liked. But the Buptsang-tsangpo and the Tarok-tso were the most interesting geographical features in Bongba, and now we saw the lake close in front of us.

Our plan was to make on June 8 for Lunkar-gompa, which was seen perched on its hill with a view over the lake. But it was not to be, for at six o'clock Gova Pensa arrived on horseback accompanied by two servants. He was dressed in a handsome blue cloak, looked about fifty-five years old, and greeted us in a kind and friendly manner. After a while came half a dozen more horsemen—evidently we were held up again. Gova Pensa asked us to remain where we were for the day, for Gova Parvang, the district chief of Tarok-shung, would come in the afternoon. He said it was impossible to see Lunkar-gompa, for both the head lamas, with most of the other twenty monks, were gone two days before to Kang-rinpoche, and had left the temple gates locked. Only four nuns and two monks had been left behind. Of Abdul Kerim's party he only knew that they had met Gova Parvang, but did not know where they were now.

Gova Parvang did not put in an appearance, but sent instead his lieutenant, old Yamba, and seventeen other unarmed men to my tent. Yamba had orders not to let us go to Tabie-tsaka if he valued his head. But he added that if we went there of our own accord and with our own horses he could not stop us, but yaks and provisions would not be supplied, and the nomads had orders to avoid us like the plague. Would we, on the other hand, go up a valley which opened out to the south-south-west by which we could reach Tuksum in seven days over the Lungnak-la, he would let us hire yaks, would sell us provisions, and provide us with guides. Or if we would go over the

Lunkar-la north-westwards to Selipuk, he would also do his best to serve us. He advised us to take the latter route, for he had been present when Gova Parvang forced Abdul Kerim to take the direct road to Selipuk between the Tarok-tso and Tabie-tsaka. We had, then, three different routes to choose from, which led over the blank space on the map of Tibet, where there are no other black lines but the meridians and parallels and the word "Unexplored." I did not take a minute to choose; the middle road over the Lunkar-la was naturally the most desirable, for I knew that it would yield me most details to complete my knowledge of the intricate orography of the Trans-Himalaya. On the morning of June 9 we hastily concluded our business, obtained yaks and guides, bought barley, rice, and *tsamba*, took farewell of the chiefs of Bongba-tarok, and steered our course direct to the temple. We passed several tent villages, for the country is densely peopled. At the foot of the mountain, on the left, a warm spring rises out of the ground. Below the monastery hill stand twenty small white stone cabins, each with a red frieze under the eaves and a small quadrangular yard. In front of the village are two *chhortens* (Illusts. 359, 366). behind which two women with their children were hiding, While the caravan continued up the Lunkar valley, I, with Lobsang and Kutus, ascended the porphyry hill to the temple, which is surrounded by a quadrangular wall. Some savage dogs rushed upon us and snapped at Little Puppy, but there was no other sign of life. We went into the court and found the temple door closed, and fastened with a great iron lock. As I was sketching a panorama of the great beautiful lake and its wreath of mountains, six men came up and told us in an angry voice to go away. I rose up, went straight to the nearest of them, and, pointing to the path down to the village, told them that if they did not immediately make off they must put up with the consequences. They turned round meekly without saying a word.

The lake stretches from north, 26° W., to north, 57° E., but extends further eastwards hidden behind a mountain. To the north-north-east two rocky islets are seen near the northern shore. To the north-east the Buptsang-tsangpo enters a bay, and in the far distance in the same direction our old Sha-kangsham appears. The water of the Tarok-tso is said to be sweet, but I had no opportunity of confirming this statement. If it is correct, the lake must have a subterranean outlet to the Tabie-tsaka lying to the north, though a small mountain offshoot lies between the two lakes.

We left the small inhospitable monastery and a couple of small white and red houses, where the nuns have their cells, and soon rejoined our men in the Lunkar valley.

In the night the temperature was above freezing-point for the first time. Our path ascended steeply to the south-west and south, and in three hours we were at the streamer-decked cairn on the Lunkar-la, where the height was 18,274 feet. From a height to the north-east of the pass the Tarok-tso lies below the spectator as on a map, and in the north from 20° to 26° E. is seen the white and yellow saline depression of Tabie-tsaka, renowned throughout Tibet. At Goang-shung we got three new guides with four yaks, who took us to the bank of the Gyenor- or Goang-tsangpo—a small river which, coming from the mountain Kapta in the south-east, falls into the Poru-tso. To the west rises a chain of mighty snowy peaks. On the morning of June 12, after 8.8 degrees of frost, the stream was covered with a third of an inch of ice, and I missed the pleasant rippling sound of the evening. But the ice broke up in the sunshine and rattled down in large flakes. We were conducted still to the south-west; on the next day when we encamped on the lake shore the direction was nearer west. From camp 428 (17,067 feet) we had a fine view over the small lake Poru-tso, also called Yeke-tso because it is situated in the district Bongba-yeke, the westernmost in the large province of Bongba, which is under the control of Karma Puntso. To the west of it follows Rigi-hloma or Rigi-changmo, which is subject to Ngari-karpun, as the Garpun of Gartok is called here. Puru-tso is drying up; the highest shore-line lies 354 feet above the present level of the lake. The water is not fit for drinking, but, curiously enough, it still contains fish.

372. SONAM NGURBU AND HIS FOLLOWERS ON HORSEBACK.

373. SOME OF OUR HORSES ON THE WAY TO KAMBA TSENAM'S TENT.

An extremely disagreeable odour rises from the beach. The lake stretches from north-east to south-west.

On June 14 we rode westwards and crossed the broad valley watered by the Nyapchu-tsangpo, which, descending from the Men-la due south, falls into the Poru-tso. The Men-la, a day's journey off, is a pass in a longitudinal valley between two of the ranges of the Trans-Himalaya. Over its threshold a road runs to Shamsang on the upper Tsangpo. A day was spent on the bank of the Surle-tsangpo, which also flows to the Poru-tso, and in the evening carried quite 210 cubic feet of water per second.

Here I was waited on by Gova Pundar of Rigi-hloma, an elderly man, who gave me a *kadakh*, butter, meal, and milk, and sold us all the provisions we required for several days, and his goodwill knew no bounds. The people in this part of Tibet were always very friendly disposed. In the Lob country the natives called me Padishahim or "Your Majesty," a title that more than satisfied my ambition; but in Bongba and Rigi I was often called Rinpoche or "Your Holiness," which I thought a little too strong. But they meant well, and I accepted their civilities as the most natural thing in the world. Gova Pundar knew every inch of his country, and I pumped him thoroughly. Among other interesting details, he informed me that thirteen days' journey to the north, near the Lakkor-tso, was a monastery Marmik-gompa, a dependency of Sera, with twenty-five monks and four nuns. In the year 1901 I had been at the Lakkor-tso, and had heard the blast of the shell-horn at the other side of a ridge, but I did not enjoy the same freedom as now, and could not visit the monastery.

We rode on the 16th in a snowstorm, with fresh men and yaks, through the picturesque Surle valley, and on the 17th over stony moss-grown slopes to the pass Sur-la or Sur-la-Kemi-la, 19,134 feet high, which, like the Lunkar-la, is of the second order, for it is a divide between the Poru-tso and the Shovo-tso. Before reaching the actual pass we had a striking view west-south-west over a world of firn-fields, peaks clothed with eternal snow, and glaciers, one of which, of large dimensions and bluish green in front, with numerous moraines and rivulets, descends to the Surle river. Here grey granite predominates; wild yaks are everywhere; the country is barren and of a high alpine character. On the other side of the Sur-la the ground descends rapidly among quantities of medium-sized granite boulders.

At camp 431 we were, then, in the district Rigi-changma. When we went on farther down the valley from the pass on June 18, we suddenly heard wild yells from a whole choir of four large and six small wolves, which were strolling along a slope immediately to the left of the path. They were greyish yellow, and seemed hungry and in a very vicious humour. Takkar rushed heedlessly at them, but they faced him, and he thought it better to turn back. They showed no signs of fear, but held their ground even when we threw stones at them. At that moment two horsemen with weapons and red hats came down from the Sur-la. They were pursuivants sent out in advance to Selipuk to make preparations for the arrival of the *serpuns*, or gold commissioners. These gentlemen are sent annually from Lhasa to Tok-jalung, and their journey is burdensome to the nomads, for they exact pack animals and food without payment. They take the road north of the Teri-nam-tso and Tabie-tsaka, which is one of Tibet's great arteries. It is called the Ser-lam, or the "gold road."

Over a small saddle we came to the Pedang-tsangpo's valley, 6½ miles broad, which starts from the Trans-Himalayan pass Pedang-la, and runs almost due north. Camp 432 was pitched on the river bank in a place quite devoid of life. Our guides wished to turn back with their yaks, but were persuaded to accompany us to the nearest tent village. What could the Tibetans be thinking of? They left us without the slightest supervision, and we enjoyed more freedom than ever before. We could now have travelled anywhere we liked, eastwards to Tabie-tsaka or southwards over the Trans-Himalaya; but the lakes in the north had most attraction for me, and we should have to cross the lofty mountains in the south at some time.

CHAPTER LXXII

THE LAST DAYS IN UNKNOWN COUNTRY

On June 19 we proceeded north-north-east down the Pedang-tsangpo's gently declining valley, sometimes near, sometimes at a distance from, the fairly large river. On the right was the ridge of the Sur-la with its snowy summits and small glacier tongues, and far in the north was seen a huge crest called Ganglung-gangri, a prolongation of the Sur-la. We found that this colossal range, like its eastern and western neighbours, runs from north-north-west to south-south-east, and that the orographical configuration is totally unlike the scheme set forth by Hodgson, Atkinson, Saunders, and Burrard, for these gentlemen, quite hypothetically, inserted a single chain parallel to the upper Brahmaputra. In reality one wanders here in a labyrinth of mountain ranges, one and all only parts of the gigantic system of the Trans-Himalaya.

The road was excellent, and after a long ride we set up our two tents on the bank of a glacier stream while snow squalls and showers of pelting rain came down alternately. Here we had to stay a day, that the genial nomads of the neighbourhood might send for the district chief; for we had nothing to eat, but had to buy whatever we could get. He came, and we bought provisions for 50 rupees, and gave him 20 for his kindness. Our treasury was almost empty, and I looked forward with trembling to the time when we should be obliged, like wandering Jews, to sell watches, revolvers, and horses to gain a livelihood. For here, in Rigi-changma, no one had heard of Abdul Kerim and his men. We could not tell what had happened. Had he gone quite off his head? He had 2500 rupees with him; had he decamped, or had he been robbed? A letter was despatched to Gova Parvang saying that if he did not get news of them in a week he would have all the Devashung and the Mandarins about his ears. At any rate we had made a splendid journey through unknown country, and now we must make our way to the Shovo-tso we had long heard spoken of. Properly we ought to have gone over the Pedang range on the west direct to Selipuk, but it was not difficult to talk over the Gova, and on June 21 he had fresh yaks and guides ready. The latter were a young man and a boy ten years old in a blue sheepskin. With these we could have gone off anywhere, but I was tired and longed to get home. The valley of the Pedang-tsangpo took us further to the north. It is unusual to find in Tibet such a great longitudinal valley running north and south, for they lie almost always east and west, and produce the peculiar parallelism so characteristic of the country. We passed sixteen tents, and near the last we crossed the Pedang-tsangpo, which runs to the Shovo-tso by a more easterly course. Lobsang caused great amusement when he was attacked by a furious dog, and, having no stones, threw his bright sheath-knife at him; he missed, but the dog took the knife in his teeth and ran off to his master's tent.

Then we rode up to the Abuk-la pass, with a view both magnificent and instructive. The bluish-green Shovo-tso is, like Poru-tso, longest from north-east to south-west, and is surrounded by huge mountains, some of them with eternal snow. To the north, 30° E., we see the pass Ka-la, over which the "gold road" runs. The name Ka-la occurs on a map of one of Montgomerie's pundits by a single isolated mountain summit. In reality the Ka-la is the very opposite of a mountain summit, namely, a depression or saddle in a mountain range. We encamped on the southern shore of the Shovo-tso, which lies at an absolute height of 15,696 feet. The water is salt, and round the shore are seen old shore-lines of about the same height as at Poru-tso.

June 22. When we left the western extremity of the

374. LAMA OF CHOKCHU TAKING LEAVE OF THE PRIOR OF SELIPUK.

375. LAMA OF CHOKCHU ON HORSEBACK.

Shovo-tso we saw a large caravan of yaks and sheep which seemed to have the same destination as ourselves. Lobsang found out that the people were *nekoras* or pilgrims on the way to Kang-rinpoche, and that the owner of the caravan was the Governor of Chokchu, Sonam Ngurbu (Illust. 372). We left them behind and rode up to the pass Tela-mata-la. A horseman approached us at a gallop, and made signs to us to halt. We waited for him, all on the tiptoe of expectation, for we made sure that he brought us a message from Abdul Kerim. Bah! it was only one of Sonam Ngurbu's soldiers who wanted to ask our guides if a spring on the way to Selipuk had any water in it this year. Sonam Ngurbu's caravan had come from Tabie-tsaka and had not heard a word of our men. It seemed as though the earth had swallowed them up. My orders had been that, whatever else they did, they should wait for us on the Buptsang-tsangpo. Doubtless they had been plundered by robbers; and we had only 80 rupees left. I blessed the hour when I decided to keep myself all the maps, notes, sketches, and rock specimens when we parted at Kamba Tsenam's tent. We could obtain money by selling some valuables, and from Selipuk I could send a courier to Thakur Jai Chand in Gartok.

From Tela-mata-la we have again a striking view over almost all the Sur-la range and over the mountainous region of Lavar-gangri to the south of Selipuk. With every day's march the orographical configuration becomes clearer, and soon the leading features of the blank space will be nearly all ascertained.

The temperature again sank at the midsummer season below freezing-point, the reading on June 23 being 25.9°. We rode through a small steep valley up to the Tayep-parva-la (17,887 feet). The ground was so honeycombed with mouse-holes that the horses trod on two or three at once. Little Puppy caught a couple of field-mice by the neck, and we did not pity them. A marmot which had ventured too far from its hole almost fell into Takkar's clutches, but just saved himself in time. At the pass we made the usual halt for observations, and I drew a panorama of the surroundings. Between north and north-west the horizon is far distant and the country level; only to the north, 5° W., appears a small snow-capped dome, but not another *gangri*. The view over Nganglaring-tso, just below, is grand, all the mountains in shades of pink, and the water of a deep ultramarine. A large part of its eastern half is occupied by a large island, a mountain mass rising out of the water with a contour as irregular as that of the lake itself, all promontories, bays, and capes. To the north-west lie three small islands. No European had ever seen Nganglaring-tso before, nor any pundit. But the pundit sent by Montgomerie in 1867 to Tok-jalung obtained some hazy information about the district "Shellifuk" and the great lake "Ghalaring-tso," which was afterwards inserted in maps of Tibet. The form given by the pundit to the lake, namely, an egg-shape with the longer axis from north to south, does not at all correspond to the reality; for the lake stretches east and west, and its contour could not be more irregular than it is. The pundit places a small island in the northern half, and adds the legend "Monastery on Island." In reality Nganglaring-tso has at least four islands, but not a single monastery.

On Midsummer Day we encamped by the roaring surf (15,577 feet), and on the 25th we crossed the last hilly mountain spur which still separated us from the extensive plain of Selipuk. From its height we again saw the great chain of Sur-la, and to the south the Trans-Himalaya with sixty-three snowy peaks, regular as the teeth of a saw. On the 26th we rode over level country to the west-north-west. On the plain two mounted Tibetans were pursuing a wild ass, which was wounded in the near foreleg and had four dogs at his heels. The dogs did not bite him, but tried to chase the animal in a certain direction. Time after time the men were close on the game and dismounted; they did not shoot, but threw up dust with their hands to frighten the wild ass and drive him as near as possible to their tent, that they might not have to carry the meat far (Illust. 356).

Camp 439 was pitched on the bank of the river Sumdang-tsangpo, which flows into the Nganglaring-tso

377

379

376, 377. Boys sitting. 378. Young Lama. 379. Old Woman.

Sketches by the Author.

without joining the rivers Lavar-tsangpo and Aong-tsangpo, farther west, which unite and enter the lake's most western bounds. Here Lobsang caught a wolf cub, a small wild rogue, which much interested Takkar. But Takkar had a great respect for his hereditary enemy and ventured to bite only his tail. Afterwards he became bolder, and when the little creature found himself in a desperate situation, he threw himself into the river to swim over to the other side. Then Takkar gave a yell, jumped in and caught the cub, thrust him down with his paws, seized him with his teeth and brought him to land, where he ate every bit of him.

We followed the river upwards on June 27 and encamped again on its bank opposite the monastery Selipuk-gompa (15,696 feet), the abbot of which, a Kanpo-lama, Jamtse Singe, was also chief of the district in secular affairs (Illusts. 356, 374, 369, 341). Neither he nor any one else had heard anything of Abdul Kerim, but he was so good as to search in his holy books to find out where our men were, and he came to the conclusion that they were somewhere to the south, and that in twenty days we should either meet them or hear some reliable news of them.

On June 28, at half-past nine in the evening, the country was shaken by an earthquake—the only one I ever experienced in Tibet. However, it had no effect on the good relations between me and the monks and Sonam Ngurbu, the Governor (Illusts. 326, 375), who was also a guest in the monastery, and had a high lama from Chokchu (Illust. 355) in his party. The Governor gave us as much *tsamba*, rice, and sugar as would at a pinch last us till we came to Tokchen, and he received a watch in exchange. Of money we had only a few rupees left. I had never been in such straits before. If I ever meet Abdul Kerim again, I thought, he shall get what he deserves and a little more.

When we set up our tents on the last day of June on the Rartse plain, south of Selipuk, Lobsang announced at dusk that four men and four mules were coming to the camp. They were Abdul Kerim, Sedik, Gaffar, and a Tibetan. Our caravan bashi came frightened and confused to my tent, and I thought it better that he should give an account of his stewardship before I passed sentence on him. He reported that they had come to the appointed rendezvous at the proper time, but there he had been hard pressed by six Govas—Gova Parvang among them, who took the lead, and ordered them to leave the place at once and go on to the Tarok-tso. As they had no passport from Lhasa, they could expect no mercy, he said. So they betook themselves to the northern shore of the Tarok-tso, where they waited fourteen days, as the grazing was good and no one interfered with them. They heard contradictory reports about us. At length a nomad died on the lake shore, and a monk from Lunkar-gompa was summoned to his tent to read the prayers for the dead. They met this man, and he said that we had passed the monastery nine days previously. Then they packed up all their belongings, intending to hurry after us next morning. But horse-stealers had come in the night and stolen my grey Tikze horse and a mule from Saka-dzong. This event cost them three days, but they never recovered the stolen animals. While Suen, Abdullah, Abdul Rasak, and Sonam Kunchuk followed slowly, the three others made forced marches westwards, and now at last they were here and had all our cash with them. Abdul Kerim escaped with a slight reprimand, but I afterwards heard the other men badgering him. We found the others in Kyangrang, and so the whole strength of the company, thirteen men, was complete when, on July 8, we crossed the pass Ding-la (Illust. 213), 19,308 feet high, the loftiest pass we had crossed in all this journey in Tibet, and on past the small lake Argok-tso, which lies in the basin of the Aong-tsangpo; and on July 12 we crossed the Surnge-la (17,310 feet). Two days later we came to Tokchen, where another political entanglement detained us nine days. But I cannot stay to give an account of it, for I reached the limit of the space allowed me at Chapter LXIV., and my publisher is impatient.

CHAPTER LXXIII

THE TRANS-HIMALAYA

On the map of the Jesuits, now two hundred years old (D'Anville, 1733) (Map 2), a series of mountains runs on the north side of the upper Brahmaputra, bearing from east to west the following names: Youc, Larkin, Tchimouran Coïran, Tchompa, Lop, Tchour, Takra concla, Kentaisse (Kailas) Latatsi, etc. These mountains and ranges have never been transferred to modern maps of Tibet, probably because geographers regarded the material collected by trained Tibetans as too unreliable and indefinite. Yet these chains of mountains are nothing else but the Trans-Himalaya, though the representation is confused and inexact.

When Brian Hodgson in his map of southern Tibet (*Selections from the Records of the Government of Bengal*, No. xxvii.), here reproduced in facsimile (Map 3), drew a huge unbroken chain north of, and parallel to, the Tsangpo, he took a step which could only be based on the Jesuits' map and the data he received in the year 1843 from the Maharaja of Nepal. No doubt lofty mountains existed to the north of the Tsangpo—that was known to the Jesuits even in the time of Kang Hi. But Hodgson's hypothetical Nyenchhen-thangla (Trans-Himalaya), which he looks upon as a prolongation of the Karakorum, and the natural boundary between northern and southern Tibet, is by no means an original conception, and is no advance on previous knowledge, or, more correctly, theory. For already, in the year 1840, Dufour had inserted a similar huge uninterrupted chain north of, and parallel to, the Tsangpo, on the map which illustrates the famous description of the travels of the Lazarist missionary, Father Huc (Illust. 381)—*Souvenirs d'un Voyage dans la Tartarie, le Thibet et la Chine, 1844-46*. Dufour's map is even better than Hodgson's, for he has adopted from the Jesuits' map a northern affluent to the Tsangpo, passing through the great range, which, like the Jesuits, he calls Mts. Koïran.

Huc and Gabet were probably the first Europeans to cross the Trans-Himalaya, and one wonders where they made the passage. Probably by the Shang-shung-la along the Mongolian pilgrim road from Kuku-nor and Tsaidam to Lhasa. It is vain to seek any information on the subject in Huc's famous book. During the two years Huc stayed in Macao he worked up the scanty notes he had made on his journey. He mentions Burkhan Bota, Shuga, and Tang-la, and also the large village Nakchu, where the caravans exchange their camels for yaks, but he says not a word about the pass by which he crossed one of the mightiest mountain systems of the world. He says, indeed, that he went over a colossal mountain range, and as its position agreed with that of the Mts. Koïran of Dufour and the Jesuits, he adopts this name, which he certainly had never heard on his journey, and which probably was changed on its way from Tibet to the Jesuits' note-books in Pekin. All he has to say of his journey over the Trans-Himalaya is contained in the following sentences: "La route qui conduit de Na-Ptchu à Lha-Ssa est, en général, rocailleuse et très-fatigante. Quand on arrive à la chaîne des monts Koïran, elle est d'une difficulté extrême" (ii. p. 241).

Another attempt to represent the course of the Trans-Himalaya was made by Trelawney Saunders in his map of Tibet (Map 6), which is found in Markham's *Narratives of the Mission of George Bogle to Tibet, and of the Journey of Thomas Manning to Lhasa* (London, 1879), and in Edwin T. Atkinson's *The Himalayan Districts of the North-Western Provinces of India* (Allahabad, 1882). Like Dufour and Hodgson, Saunders draws a huge continuous chain all through Tibet. For the western parts, north of Manasarowar, and for the eastern, south of Tengri-nor, he has relied on the cartography of the pundits; the rest, between 82° and 89½° E. long., is partly a reproduction of the Jesuits' map, partly pure fancy, and has not the remotest resemblance to the reality, as will be apparent from a comparison of Saunders' map with mine. I will only point out that the Trans-Himalaya consists not of one chain but of many, and that the source of the Chaktak-tsangpo lies to the south, not to the north of the principal one. All the central and largest part of the system, which I explored, is therefore quite incorrect on Saunders' map.

In the year 1867 Colonel Montgomerie (Illust. 380) sent out three pundits for the purpose of compiling a map of the country north of Manasarowar. One of them was the incomparable and wonderful Nain Sing, another was the man who was at Yiachan prevented from discovering the source of the Indus. On their way to Tok-jalung they crossed the Trans-Himalaya at the Jukti-la, which they called Gugti-la, assigning to it a height of 19,500 feet: I found its height was 19,070 feet. Mr. Calvert crossed the same pass a year before me. On their return they crossed the Trans-Himalaya by following the eastern branch of the Indus down to where it breaks through the range and unites with the Gartok branch.

A pundit also went between Manasarowar and Tok-jalung, past the Ruldap-tso—a name and lake I sought for east and west in vain, but I will not therefore deny its existence. Moreover, of this pundit's route I have no precise details. It seems likely that he crossed the Trans-Himalaya by a pass called Sar-lung.

On January 8, 1872, one of Montgomerie's explorers, a young trained Tibetan, travelled over the Trans-Himalaya by the Khalamba-la, 17,200 feet high. In Markham's account of this journey it is said that he returned across the mountains by the Dhok-la, though the actual water-parting pass he came to was much more probably the Dam-largen-la. This pass was crossed the following year (1873) by Nain Sing on his famous journey from Leh to Lhasa, which is described so conscientiously by Colonel

Sir Henry Trotter. Nain Sing assigns to Dam-langren-la a height of 16,900 feet.

The great pundit A. K., or Krishna, who contends with Nain Sing for the foremost place, crossed the most easterly parts of the Trans-Himalaya on his journey in 1881, and more probably by the pass Shiar-gang-la than the Nub-kong-la, as I have already suggested; but from his map it is difficult to decide whether the Shiar-gang-la is a dividing pass of the first rank or not. In any case, it is situated on the chain which forms the watershed between the Salwin and the Brahmaputra, and is undoubtedly an immediate continuation of the Nien-chen-tang-la, or Trans-Himalaya. A similar assumption is also made by Colonel S. G. Burrard in his and Hayden's admirable work, *A Sketch of the Geography and Geology of the Himalaya Mountains and Tibet* (Calcutta, 1907). On map xvii. in this work Burrard has, quite rightly in my opinion, inserted the prolongation of the range, though we have no sure data about its course.

Thus we find that after Father Huc several of Montgomerie's and Trotter's pundits, as well as Mr. Calvert in the year 1906, crossed the Trans-Himalaya in Tibet. So far as I know, there are only two more names to be added to these—namely, Littledale, who on his bold journey in 1894-95 passed over the system by the pass Guring-la (19,587 feet), and Count de Lesdain, who crossed it by the Khalamba-la in 1905. Both describe the magnificent spectacle Nien-chen-tang-la presents from Tengri-nor, but the latter added nothing to our knowledge of the Trans-Himalaya, for he made use of the same pass, the Khalamba-la, as Montgomerie's pundit. In his narrative, *Voyage au Thibet, par la Mongolie de Pékin aux Indes*, he mentions not a single pass, much less its name. But he followed the western shore of Tengri-nor, and he says (p. 340): "Des massifs de montagnes très durs et absolument enchevêtrés formaient un obstacle insurmontable. En conséquence, je résolus de suivre le premier cours d'eau, dont la direction ferait présumer qu'il se dirigeait vers le Brahmapoutra. C'est ainsi que nous cheminâmes plusieurs jours en suivant les bords d'une rivière sans

380. COLONEL T. G. MONTGOMERIE.

381. ABBÉ HUC.

For the portrait of T. G. Montgomerie my thanks are due to the Colonel's widow, and for that of Père Huc, probably not published before, to Mr. E. Schwartz, Paris.

cesse grossissante, appelée Chang-chu. . . ." This river is the Shang-chu, which comes from the Khalamba-la.

Two Frenchmen and two Englishmen have, then, crossed the Trans-Himalaya before me, besides half a dozen pundits. Farther west in English territory innumerable Europeans have passed over the system, especially by the Chang-la, where I surmounted it three times. Between the Indus and the Panggong-tso I travelled over the system on November 22, 1907, by the easy pass Tsake-la.

An extraordinarily valuable contribution to the knowledge of the Trans-Himalaya was afforded us by Ryder and Wood on their remarkable journey up the Brahmaputra in the year 1904. They had no opportunity of crossing the system, or even of penetrating a day's journey into the southern transverse valleys, but they took bearings of all the summits visible from their route. And some of these, particularly Lunpo-gangri, are among the very highest which, under a mantle of eternal snow, rise up from the Trans-Himalaya. The absolutely highest is, according to Ryder, 23,255 feet, and is therefore little inferior to Nien-chen-tang-la with its 23,900 feet. Ryder and Burrard took it for granted that these summits stood on a single continuous range, which they represent on their map as the northern watershed of the Brahmaputra. In his text (p. 95), however, Burrard rightly points out that this chain, which he calls "the Kailas Range," is not the watershed, for in some places it is broken through by affluents from the north. Burrard commits the same mistake as Dufour, Hodgson, Saunders, and Atkinson, in assuming the existence of a single continuous range to the north of the Tsangpo. I pondered much myself over this problem, and on a general map of the ranges of Tibet (1905) I inserted two ranges north of the Tsangpo, a conception in accordance with F. Grenard's in his *Carte de l'Asie Centrale* of the year 1899.

A history of geographical exploration in a region so little known as the Trans-Himalaya must naturally be exceeding short and meagre. With all my researches I have not been able to discover any other predecessors than those already mentioned—that is, in those parts of the system which lie within the bounds of Tibet—and not a single one in the central regions of the Trans-Himalaya. That such an extensive region as southern Tibet has been quite unknown till now, though it lies close to the Indian frontier, has given rise to much reasonable astonishment, and in many circles arguments and proofs, based on more or less apocryphal records and vague hypotheses, have been laboriously sought out to prove that my discoveries have not the priority claimed for them. The maps I have reproduced in facsimile, when carefully compared with my own maps, render any discussion on my part quite superfluous.

I cannot, however, pass over in silence an insinuation that the discoveries I have made are to be found indicated on the famous wall-maps in the Doge's Palace at Venice. The Chief Librarian of the Royal Library in Stockholm, Dr. E. W. Dahlgren, writes in a letter to me: "Only the grossest ignorance and silliness can find on these maps traces of any discoveries previous to yours." Before my return home Professor Mittag-Leffler, Director of the mathematical school in the University of Stockholm, had sent for photographs of these maps with a very detailed description, and he has kindly placed this material at my disposal. This book is not the place in which to publish it, and, besides, the following statement which Dr. Dahlgren has obligingly drawn up at my request makes all further comment unnecessary:

The Wall-Maps in the Sala dello Scudo, in the Doge's Palace at Venice

These maps, four in number, were constructed by the noted cartographer Giacomo Gastaldi in the middle of the sixteenth century, to take the place of older maps which were destroyed by fire in the year 1483; at least, it may be safely assumed that two of them, those of East Asia and Africa, are the work of Gastaldi.

The maps represent:

1. Asia from the mouth of the Indus eastwards to China and Japan, as well as the Pacific Ocean and part of America.

382. Altar Table with Images of Gods in Mangnang-gompa.

Water-colour Sketch by the Author.

2. Asia from Asia Minor to India (Kashmir).
3. Africa.
4. Italy.

Only maps Nos. 1 and 2 have any interest for Sven Hedin. They correspond completely with the photographs procured by Professor Mittag-Leffler.

All the maps were restored by Francisco Grisellini about the middle of the eighteenth century. In map No. 2 great alterations seem to have been made in geographical details as well as in the text and in the decoration. As the map extends no farther east than Kashmir it has, of course, no connection with Sven Hedin's discoveries.

Map No. 1, on the other hand, has in many essential respects preserved its original character. We can undoubtedly form a good notion of its original appearance by comparing it with the maps in Ramusio's work *Delle Navigazioni e Viaggi* (2nd Edition, Venice, 1554) and with Gastaldi's *Tercia Parte dell' Asia* (Venice, 1561). The resemblance to the former is very striking. In these maps, as in the wall-maps, the south is to the top.

On all these maps there is very great confusion in the representation of the river systems of the Ganges and the Brahmaputra. The mountains are drawn in at random, and even the Himalayas cannot be identified with complete certainty, much less the ranges of Central Asia. As the map was chiefly designed to illustrate the travels of Marco Polo, it naturally gives no information about countries he did not visit.

E. W. Dahlgren.

Father Huc concludes the account of his journey with the following remarkable words: "Mais il ne suffit pas toujours du zèle de l'écrivain pour faire connaître des contrées où il n'a jamais mis le pied. Écrire un Voyage en Chine après quelques promenades aux factories de Canton et aux environs de Macao, c'est peut-être s'exposer beaucoup à parler de chose qu'on ne connaît pas suffisamment . . . il est en général assez difficile de faire des découvertes dans un pays sans y avoir pénétré."

It was with such truths in my mind that I began the journey described in this book, the object of which was that set forth by Sir Clements Markham, when in connection with Littledale's last journey he made the following statement (*Geographical Journal*, vol. vii. p. 482): "In the whole length from Tengri-nor to the Mariam-la pass no one has crossed them (the Trans-Himalaya), so far as we know . . . and I believe nothing in Asia is of greater geographical importance than the exploration of this range of mountains."

It is not for me to decide how far I have achieved my aim, but when I passed over the Trans-Himalaya for the eighth time at the Surnge-la, I had at least the satisfaction of seeing all the old hypotheses fall down like a house of cards, and a new ground-plan laid down on the map of Asia, where before the blank patch yawned with its alluring "Unexplored."

I have no space here for a complete monograph of the Trans-Himalaya, or, indeed, the material for it, until the bearings and heights of the peaks have been worked out, the rock specimens identified, and a detailed map constructed from the sheets I drew. It will take a couple of years to work up the material. I will here only communicate some general facts, and will begin by citing the passes of first rank as watersheds, appending the names of the travellers who have crossed some of them:

Shiar-gang-la	Krishna, 1881	
Shang-shung-la	Huc, 1845	
Dam-largen-la	Nain Sing, 1873	16,903 feet.
Guring-la	Littledale, 1895	19,587 "
Tsebo-la		
Shugu-la		
Khalamba-la	Pundit, 1872	17,200 "
Do.	de Lesdain, 1905	
Sela-la	Hedin, 1907	18,064 "
Chang-la-Pod-la	Hedin, 1907	18,284 "
Sha-la		
Angden-la	Hedin, 1907	18,514 "
Tsalam-nakta-la		
Dombe-la		
Nakbo-kongdo-la		
Sangmo-bertik-la	Hedin, 1908	19,095 "
Saggo-la		
Dicha-la		
Samye-la	Hedin, 1908	18,133 "
Dsalung-la		
Lungmar-la		
Pechen-la		

383. The Author in Tibetan Costume at the Mission Station in Poo.
Photograph by the Rev. Mr. Marx.

Lungnak-la		
Yor-la		
Ganglung-la		
Men-la		
Pedang-la		
Gebbyi-la		
Yilung-la		
Tarkyang-la		
Surnge-la	Pundit? Hedin, 1908	17,310 feet
Tseti-lachen-la	Hedin, 1907	17,933 „
Jukti-la	Nain Sing, 1867	
Do.	Calvert, 1906	
Do.	Hedin, 1907	19,070 „

It has, then, been my lot to cross eight Trans-Himalayan passes, while seven have been crossed by other travellers. Seven of my passes were unknown before. Of the others I have seen the Dicha-la and Men-la, while of the remainder I have only gathered oral information. The Jukti-la is the watershed between the two headwaters of the Indus, the Tseti-lachen-la between the Sutlej and the Indus, the Surnge-la between the Sutlej and the Nganglaring-tso. Shiar-gang-la and Shang-shung-la lie on the watershed between the Salwin and the Brahmaputra. All the others lie on the great continental watershed between the ocean and the isolated drainage of the plateau. It appears from the list that all the passes crossed before by Europeans and pundits belong to the eastern and western parts of the system. Between the Khalamba-la and the Surnge-la the Trans-Himalaya had not been crossed in a single line, and it was exactly between these two passes that the great white space was situated. All that was known of it was the peaks fixed by Ryder and Wood, and some summits seen by Nain Sing from the north. If the Pundit's journey between Manasarowar and Ruldap-tso be disregarded, of which I have no information, the interval between the Khalamba-la and the Jukti-la measures 590 miles, or about as far as from Linköping to Haparanda, or from London to Dornoch Firth. And between these limits lie all the passes by crossing which I was able to trace the course of the Trans-Himalaya, and prove that its known eastern and western sections are connected and belong to the same mountain system, and that this system is one of the loftiest and mightiest in the world, only to be compared with the Himalayas, the Karakorum, Arka-tag, and Kuen-lun. Between the Shiar-gang-la and Yasin, not far from the sharp bend of the Indus, its length amounts to 1400 miles, but if it can be shown that the Trans-Himalaya merges into the Hindu-Kush and continues along the Salwin, its length extends to 2500 miles. On the north and south its boundaries are sharp and clearly defined; the northern is formed by the central lakes discovered by Nain Sing and myself, and the southern by the unheard-of Indus-tsangpo valley. In breadth it is inferior to the Himalayas, and its peaks are lower, but the heights of the Trans-Himalayan passes are considerably greater than those of the Himalayas. The average height of the five following Himalayan passes—Shar-khalep-la, Man-da-la, She-ru-la, No-la and Kore- or Photu-la—is 16,736 feet, while the average height of my first five Trans-Himalayan passes is 18,400 feet. It may be said generally that the dividing passes in the Trans-Himalaya of the first rank are 1600 feet higher than in the Himalayas. But the highest peak of the Himalayas, Mount Everest, with its 29,000, is 5100 feet higher than the Nien-chen-tang-la, the culminating point, as far as we know. Herewith are connected the different forms of relief predominating in the two systems; the crests of the Trans-Himalaya are flatter, its valleys shallower and broader, while the crests of the Himalayas are sharp and pointed, its valleys deep and much eroded. The former system is more compact and massive than the latter, as we may expect if we remember that the Himalayas are deluged by the precipitation of the south-west monsoon, and that its waters have for untold thousands of years degraded its valleys, while the Trans-Himalaya on the dry plateau country receives a comparatively insignificant share of the monsoon rain. Were it possible to compare the volumes of the two systems, we should no doubt find that the northern is much more massive than the southern, for such a comparison must proceed from sea-level, and though the Trans-Himalaya is the narrower of the two, its ascent begins from heights of 10,000 to 16,000 feet, from the

Tsangpo valley, while the Himalayas rise from sea-level or a few hundred feet above it. As a watershed the Trans-Himalaya occupies a higher and more important place than the Himalayas. In the west the Himalayas parts the waters between the Indus and some of its tributaries, and in the east the system is a divide between the Brahmaputra and the Ganges. But every drop of water which falls on the Himalayas goes down to the Indian Ocean. On the other hand, all the central Trans-Himalaya is a watershed between the Indian Ocean on the south and the enclosed drainage area of the plateau depression on the north. Only in its western section is the Trans-Himalaya also a watershed between the Indus and some of its right-hand tributaries, and in its eastern between the Salwin and Brahmaputra. Within the boundaries of Tibet there is only one river which takes its rise from the northern flank of the Trans-Himalaya and breaks through the system by a transverse valley; but this river is a lion, and is called by the Tibetans the Lion river, the Singi-kamba or Indus. The Salwin also springs from the northern flank of the system, but finds its way to the ocean without passing through the mountains. All the other rivers rising on the northern slopes, of which the Buptsang-tsangpo and the Soma-tsangpo are the largest, flow into the undrained salt lakes on the north. Only in the central parts of the Trans-Himalaya, stretching, however, over a distance of nearly 600 miles, does the continental watershed coincide with the main axis of the system, for to the west the watershed runs northwards from the source of the Indus, and then westwards, so as to leave the Panggong-tso within the isolated drainage basin of Tibet, and in the east runs northwards from the region between the source streams of the Salwin and Tengri-nor.

I have called this book Trans-Himalaya, because the incidents and adventures described in these two volumes occurred in this huge mountain system lying to the north of the Tsangpo and in the country to the north and south of it. When I first crossed the dividing range at the Sela-la I thought of retaining the name Hodgson had assigned to it, that is, Nien-chen-tang-la, and I did not change my mind after crossing the Chang-la-Pod-la and Angden-la, for these three passes lie on one and the same range, which on the southern shore of Tengri-nor is called Nien-chen-tang-la. After crossing the Tseti-lachen-la and the Jukti-la I supposed that these passes lay on the western prolongation of the Nien-chen-tang-la, and that the conception of Hodgson, Saunders, Atkinson, Burrard, and Ryder was correct. But after the second journey right through Tibet, and after I had crossed Bongba in several directions and found that there was no question of a single continuous range, but that a whole collection of ranges quite independent of one another existed, I perceived that the name Nien-chen-tang-la, which only denotes one of all these ranges, could not be given to the whole system. Equally inappropriate would be the names Lunpo-gangri, Kamchung-gangri, Targo-gangri, or any other local name. Saunders' "Gangri Mountains" I consider still more unsuitable, for every mountain in Tibet clothed with eternal snow is called a *gangri*, and the name in this connection would have a meaningless sound. Neither could I accept Burrard's "The Kailas Range." A name must be found suited to the whole of this intimately connected association of mountain ranges, a geographical conception which would leave no room for misunderstanding, and I decided to call the whole system, the connection and continuity of which I had succeeded in proving, the Trans-Himalaya.

Among English geographers many have approved of this name and an equal number have disapproved. To the latter category belongs Colonel Burrard, who points out that for some years back all the regions lying beyond the Himalayas have been called Trans-Himalayan. And in a letter he has lately written to me he says:

> Pupils of Montgomerie naturally ask why an old word should be given a new meaning when it is possible to invent any number of new names for newly discovered mountains. I do not see that it is necessary to give an important name to newly discovered mountains. A new name will become important because of the mountains to which it is attached, and your mountains would have rendered any new name important.

I cannot share Colonel Burrard's view, for I answer that

384. THE LAST MEMBERS OF THE LAST EXPEDITION IN POO.

just because of the circumstance that Montgomerie's pupils, officials of the Survey of India and pundits, have for fifty years and more called the country north of the Himalayas "The Trans-Himalayan regions," it was incumbent on me not to reject this name for the mountain system which can be nothing else but the Trans-Himalaya *par excellence*.

To give a quotation from the other side, I will here reproduce an expression of opinion from Lord Curzon, formerly Viceroy of India, whose knowledge of Asia is unsurpassed. In the *Geographical Journal*, April 1909, he says:

> Alongside of this great discovery (Bongba and Chokchu) I would place the tracing for hundreds of miles and the assurance of a definite orographical existence to the mighty mountain palisade or series of palisades to which he has, in my opinion very appropriately, given the title of the Trans-Himalaya. This range has been surmised to exist in its entire length for many years; it has been crossed at its extremities by Littledale and by native surveyors. But it was reserved for Dr. Hedin to trace it on the spot and to place it upon the map in its long, unbroken, and massive significance. . . . It is no mean addition to human knowledge that we should realize the assured existence of one of the greatest mountain masses in the world. As regards the name which Dr. Hedin has given to it, I will only say that the desiderata for the title of a new and momentous geographical discovery appear to be these: (1) that the name should if possible be given by the principal discoverer; (2) that it should not be unpronounceable, unwriteable, over-recondite, or obscure; (3) that it should if possible possess some descriptive value; and (4) should not violate any acknowledged canons of geographical nomenclature. The name Trans-Himalaya combines all these advantages, and it has a direct Central Asian analogy in the Trans-Alai, which is a range of mountains standing in the same relation to the Alai that Trans-Himalaya will do to Himalaya. I am not in the least impressed by the fact that the name was once given to another range, where its unsuitability secured its early extinction. Any attempts to substitute another title on the present occasion will, in my opinion, be foredoomed to failure.

My long journey backwards and forwards over the Trans-Himalaya cannot be regarded as more than a cursory and defective reconnaissance of a country hitherto unknown. It is easier to go to Lhasa with a force armed to the teeth, and shoot down the Tibetans like pheasants if they stand in the way, than to cross Tibet in all directions for two long years with four Governments and all the authorities of the land as opponents, twelve poor Ladakis as companions, and not a single man as escort. It is no merit of mine that I was long able to maintain a position which from the first seemed untenable. The same lucky star looked down, as often before, on my lonely course through vast Asia, and it is twenty-four years since I first took up my pilgrim staff. I have been able to follow and lay down only the chief geographical lines; between my routes many blank spaces are still left, and there is sufficient detailed work for generations of explorers and travellers more thoroughly prepared and better equipped than myself.

Go, then, out into the world, thou ringing and sonorous name for one of the world's mightiest mountain systems, and find thy way into geographical text-books, and remind children in the schools of the snow-crowned summits on the Roof of the World, among which the monsoon storms have sung their deafening chorus since the beginning. As long as I live, my proudest memories, like royal eagles, will soar round the cold desolate crags of the Trans-Himalaya.

CHAPTER LXXIV

SIMLA

Like a troop of beggars and knights of the road my twelve servants and I left Tokchen on July 24. We had stayed there nine days with nothing to do but watch the monsoon rain, which I had incautiously promised the natives, pelting down on the hills. The authorities of the place insisted this time that, as we were not furnished with a passport from Lhasa, we had no right to make use of the great high-road to Ladak, but must turn back to the interior of Tibet whence we had come. If I had not already had enough of the great blank, I would have agreed to their demand with pleasure, but I was now weary and longed for home, and as they refused the assistance and the transport facilities we required, we set out on foot with the baggage on our last ten horses and mules. I had still the white horse from Kamba Tsenam's tent at my disposal. We had no escort, for the authorities wished to be quite clear of blame in case they were called to account. By the holy lake, where we followed the northern shore by known ways, we at length found a tramp who offered to show us the way to the Totling monastery.

In Langbo-nan I visited hastily the young abbot, as sympathetic and good-natured as the year before, and at Chiu-gompa we met our old friend Tundup Lama, fretful, melancholy, and weary of his lonely cloister life. Large streams now emptied their water into both lakes, and with a feeling of regret I left again the scene of so many precious memories.

Before we came to the monastery of Tirtapuri we had

to cross several of the rivers which bring their tribute from the Trans-Himalaya to the Sutlej. Three of them were enormously swollen after the continuous rains, and rolled their volumes of greyish-brown foaming water over treacherous blocks. It boiled and seethed between the cliffs, and it carried along and overturned the slippery boulders. How I trembled in mortal anxiety lest the harvest so laboriously gathered in the last long winter should all be lost by a single false step.

We came to the temple of Tirtapuri in pouring rain. Lobsang, Gulam, Kutus, Tubges, Suen, and Kunchuk were to accompany me hence to Simla, but Abdul Kerim and the other five received their pay and gratuities, and took their way home to Leh through Gartok. I did not know the road to Simla, but on the map it seemed to be nearer than to Ladak, and therefore I expected that my party would arrive first at its destination. But this road is very wild and romantic, and the land is deeply excavated by the affluents of the Sutlej, and one might imagine that one had suddenly been transported to the cañons of the Colorado. One day we marched rapidly up an ascent of 3000 feet, and the next we went down as far, so that the distance was at least double as great as it appeared on the map, and Abdul Kerim reached Leh long before I was near Simla. Therefore the first news of us came from him, and not from myself, and in some quarters the worst fears were entertained for my safety. It seemed strange that my servants reached their home safe and sound while I myself was still missing.

We parted with floods of tears on August 1, and my party travelled past the three monasteries, Dongbo, Dava, and Mangnang (Illust. 382), and came to Totling-gompa on the 13th, near which Father Andrade, three hundred years ago, lodged in the now decayed town of Tsaparang. Here I met the Hindu doctor Mohanlal, who gave me the first news of the outer world. Through him I heard, with deep regret, of the death of King Oscar, which had occurred more than eight months before. Mohanlal also informed me of the growing unrest in India and of the anxiety my friends felt on my account. Thakur Jai Chand had been

385. My Puppy.

386. Takkar in his New Home with the Missionaries in Poo.

instructed by the Indian Government to spare no efforts to find out whether I was still living or not. He had sent out some Tibetan freebooters in various directions, and promised 50 rupees to any one who could furnish any certain information of my fate—this is the price he valued me at. Abdul Kerim had reached Gartok in the best of health, and was summoned to the Garpun, who exclaimed: "Your Sahib is a dreadful man; he will not be satisfied until I lose my head!" Old Hajji Nazer Shah, who had so conscientiously equipped my last caravan, had died the preceding winter.

When we left Tokchen on July 24 we were delighted at the thought that we should at every step be nearer to lower country and a denser and warmer atmosphere. A month later we were at a greater height than at Tokchen, and saw the country covered with snow, and heard the hail patter on our dilapidated tents. But at Shipki we again set them up in a garden dressed in the rich beauty of summer, and heard the wind murmur in the spreading crowns of the apricot trees. Shipki is the last village in Tibet. From this garden oasis begins the steep ascent to the Shipki-la, which is reached after attaining a height of six Eiffel Towers one upon another. Here we stood on the frontier between Tibet and India. I turned and let my eyes roam once more over these awfully desolate and barren mountains where my dreams had been realized, and my lucky star had shed a clearer and more friendly light than ever before. Farewell, home of wild asses and antelopes, holy land of the Tashi Lama, of Tso-mavang and the Tsangpo, into whose mysterious valleys the stranger has found his way only by enduring two Arctic winters and by driving a flock of refractory sheep! I seemed to take farewell of the best of my youth and the finest chapter in the story of my life.

On August 28 we encamped in the village of Poo (Illusts. 383, 384), and I spent two memorable days in the hospitable house of the Moravian missionaries. Messrs. Marx and Schnabel and their amiable families overwhelmed me with kindness, and now I was deluged with news from the outer world—it was like listening to the breakers on the coast of the ocean. I had not seen a European for more than two years, and I looked myself like a Tibetan footpad. But the missionaries rigged me out at once in European summer clothes and set an Indian helmet on my head.

A few days later we came to Kanam-gompa, where Alexander Csoma Körösi eighty years ago studied Lamaist learning as a monk, and more than any one else communicated to the scholars of the West the occult mysteries of this religion. How silent and quiet our life had been up on the expanse of Chang-tang! Now the dizzy depths of the valley are filled with the roar of the falling stream, and the thunder of the water is re-echoed from the precipitous cliffs. How bare and scanty was the soil of Tibet, and now we listen daily to the whisper of mild breezes in the deep dark coniferous forests that clothe the slopes of the Himalayas.

Still lower runs the road, still warmer is the air. My trusty friend, big shaggy Takkar, looks at me with questioning eyes. He loves not the summer's perfumed garlands nor the variegated zone of meadows. He remembers the free life on the open plains, he misses the fights with the wolves of the wilderness, and he dreams of the land of everlasting snowstorms. One day we saw him drink of a spring which poured its water across the path, and then lie down in the cool shade of the forest. He had done so many times before, but we should never see him repeat it. He turned and galloped up towards lonely Tibet. He parted with sorrow in his heart from his old master, I knew; but he thought he would ask the missionaries in Poo to send me a greeting. One morning he was found lying outside the gate to the court of the Mission-house, and, true to his old habit, he would let no one go in or out. He was hospitably received, and started a new life with a chain round his neck. I still receive from time to time, through Mr. Marx, greetings from old Takkar, who so faithfully defended my tent when I travelled in disguise through his own country (Illust. 386).

In the Club des Asiatiques in Paris I once dined with

387. SIMLA.

Madame Massieu, who has accomplished so many wonderful journeys in Asia. Roland Bonaparte and Henry of Orléans were present, as I vividly remembered when on September 7 I met the far-travelled Parisian lady in the station-house of Taranda. We had much to talk about when we contributed to the cost of a common dinner. Untouched by years, youthful and enthusiastic, Madame Massieu afterwards undertook a bold journey to Khatmandu.

With growing uneasiness I approached the hour when, after nearly a year's complete silence, I was again to receive letters from home, and I wondered whether I should break them open and read them without any cause for sorrow. The post met me at Gaura on September 9. I read all the evening, all night, and all the following day, and I was able to take the last days' journey to Simla in comfort, for I was spared any untoward news and knew that all was well at home. Now the wind whispered more gently than ever in the Himalayan cedars, and the roar of the Sutlej sounded like the roll of drums in a triumphal march.

In Kotgar I was present at evensong in the missionaries' church. How strange to hear again the soft soothing tones of the organ, and as an unworthy Christian pilgrim in a Christian temple remember the solitude of the past years.

The following day I marched along the road in the company of my men for the last time, for near Narkanda a rickshaw met me, sent by Colonel Dunlop Smith. I left them, to hurry on without delay, while they were to follow in the usual order of march. How pleasant to lean against the back of the little two-wheeled vehicle and roll away at a rapid pace under the shady canopy of the deodars!

September 15 was a great day for me. I stayed at the bungalow of Fagu, and this camp, where I was quite alone, was No. 499. Simla, therefore, would be 500. It felt very strange to stand on the boundary between the wilderness and the most refined civilization. At the breastwork of the excellent carriage-road sat a gentleman in his rickshaw; it was my friend Mr. Edward Buck, Reuter's correspondent. This is the beginning, I thought; and on I went on this last day's journey. The fine imposing town appears in the distance on the slopes of its hills and the white houses peep out from among the trees (Illust. 387). A young maiden takes a snap of us with her camera, but it is early in the morning, and without further adventures we take refuge at a gentleman's outfitters, for in spite of the clothes from Poo I must undergo a complete renovation before I can present myself before the doors of the Viceregal Lodge.

What a total contrast to the lonely life I had led for two long years! On September 16 a State ball took place, and I heard again the crunching sound on the sand of the court as innumerable rickshaws bore guests to the ball. Rustling silk, glittering jewels, brilliant uniforms—in an unbroken line the *élite* of Simla pass between satellites with their tall turbans and shining lances. God save the King! Followed by their staff Their Excellencies enter, and open the dance to the notes of a waltz of Strauss. It was just as in May 1906, and the twenty-eight months that had intervened seemed to me like a strange fantastic dream.

The first days I stayed in the house of my noble old friend Colonel Dunlop Smith, and had now an opportunity of thanking him and his amiable ladies for the trouble they had taken in connection with the consignment to Gartok the year before. Then I moved over to the Viceregal Lodge, and again enjoyed the same boundless hospitality of Lord and Lady Minto. From my window I saw again, sharp and clear, the crests of the Himalayas, and beyond the mountains and valleys of Tibet stretched out in a boundless sea. What wealth and luxury! I lived like a prince, walked on soft rugs and meditated, lay and read Swedish journals in a deep soft bed, by electric light, and bathed in a porcelain bath, attended by Hindus in the viceregal livery—I who had lately gone in rags and tended sheep.

On September 24 a hundred and fifty ladies and gentlemen in full dress were assembled in the State room

388. The Last Members of the Expedition at the Entrance of the Viceregal Lodge in Simla.

in the Viceregal Lodge. The occasion was a lecture, and on the dais hung with gold-embroidered brocade, where the thrones usually stand, was set up a large map of Tibet. The front seats were occupied by the Commander-in-Chief of the Indian Army, Lord Kitchener of Khartum, the Governor of the Panjab, the Maharajas of Alwar and Gwalior; and among the guests might be seen generals and superior officers, State secretaries, men of science, and members of the diplomatic corps then present in Simla. The Military Secretary, Colonel Victor Brooke, came forward and announced the arrival of the Viceroy and Lady Minto. I was trembling with stage fright, but before I knew anything about it, my opening words, "Your Excellencies, Ladies and Gentlemen," sounded through the brilliant saloon, and then followed an account of my last journey. It was one o'clock in the morning before I concluded, and after a most flattering speech from Lord Minto the guests withdrew to the late supper.

My six Ladakis and our seven remaining animals stayed in a *serai* below the palace. I often went and talked to them, and played a while with my old travelling companion Little Puppy. But the time passed quickly, and soon the last day came. I embraced and squeezed Little Puppy, stroked his head, and found it hard to tear myself away. He was put out by his master's elegant costume, and had a melancholy questioning expression, as though he suspected that the bond between us was loosed, and that we should never see each other again. We had shared everything in common from the time he was born below the snowy Karakorum pass, and to part from dogs is the hardest trial of all; to bid men farewell is not so distressing.

At our arrival in Simla I had given them 60 rupees each for new clothing, and in the bazaar they had found some old cast-off uniforms with bright metal buttons, which they thought grand and becoming. On the neck lappets were the words "Guard, London S.W. Railway," and how they found their way to India I do not know. But in these uniforms and in red fezzes my men assembled in the palace court on the last day of September (Illust. 388). They were allowed to keep our seven horses and mules, saddles, tents, skin coats, bed furniture, and everything. My white horse they were to sell in Leh and divide the price. Gulam took charge of Little Puppy, and undertook to see that he did not suffer want in the future—it was like breaking up an old home. Besides his pay, every man received a present of 100 rupees, and their expenses to Leh four times over. Lord and Lady Minto were present at the last farewell, and the Viceroy made them a short, cheery speech. It was a sad parting, and even the calm Lobsang, who was amazed at the wealth and splendour of Simla, wept like a child as with heavy step he followed his comrades down to their waiting animals. "What faithfulness! what devotion!" exclaimed Lady Minto with feeling; "their tears are more expressive than words."

At the beginning of October the Viceroy and Lady Minto set out on an excursion into the mountains, and after a hearty farewell and warm thanks for all the kindness they had showered on me, I remained lonely and forlorn in the great palace. My steamer would not leave Bombay for a week, and I was delighted to be the guest of Lord Kitchener in his residence, Snowdon, during the five days I was yet to stay in Simla. I shall never forget these days. My room was decorated with flowers, and on a table stood fourteen books on Tibet, chosen from the General's library to supply me with entertaining reading. With the aides-de-camp Captains Wyllie and Basset, merry fellows and good comrades, we lived like four bachelors, took breakfast, lunch, and dinner together, and spent the evening in the billiard-room, on the mantelpiece of which was the appropriate motto, "Strike, and fear not."

In the afternoon the General took me out along the road leading to Tibet. We then talked of the future of Europe in Asia and Africa, and I gained a greater insight than I had ever done before into Lord Kitchener's life and work in Egypt.

But the days at Snowdon also came to an end, and on October 11, when the people were flocking to church, I was driven by the victor of Africa to the station, where I took a last farewell of the man for whose exploits I have always felt a boundless admiration. At Summerhill station, below the Viceregal Lodge, I exchanged a last shake of the hand with my dear friend Dunlop Smith, and then the white houses of Simla vanished in the distance, and the train rolled down to the heat of India and the great lonely sea.

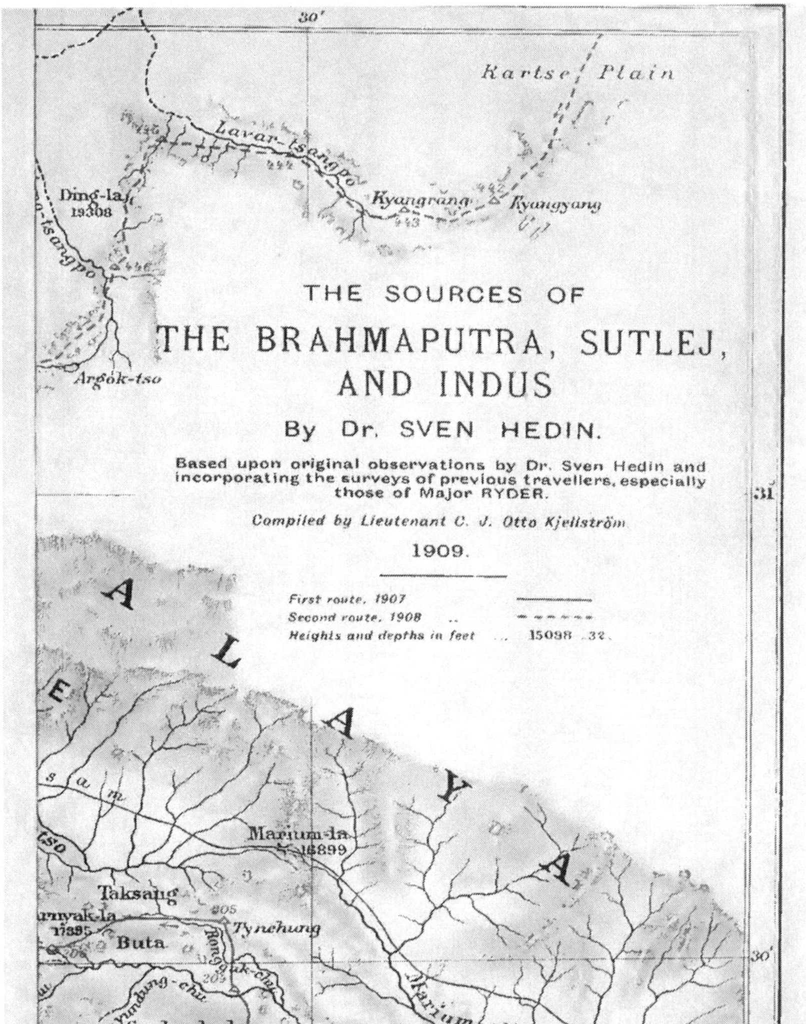

THE SOURCES OF
THE BRAHMAPUTRA, SUTLEJ, AND INDUS
By Dr. SVEN HEDIN.
Based upon original observations by Dr. Sven Hedin and incorporating the surveys of previous travellers, especially those of Major RYDER.
Compiled by Lieutenant C. J. Otto Kjellström
1909.
First route, 1907
Second route, 1908
Heights and depths in feet .. 15098 .32.
Kartse Plain
Lavar-tsangpo
Kyangrang
Kyangyang
Ding-la
19308
Argok-tso
A
L
A
Y
A
Marium-la
Taksang
Tynchung
Buta
Sen-kamba-la
Tugri-la
Dara-sumka
Sheryak
15991
Kargan-la
Tso-niti-kargang
Kubi-tsangpo
Dongdong-chu
Tse-chung-tso
Source of the Brahmaputra
Mikchung-simo
Absi
Ngomo-dinding
KUBI-GANGRI
Marium-chu
Tok-jonsung
Chema-yundung
Umbo
Laktsang
15410
Chema-yundung-chu
30'
31°
Stanford's Geog. Estab. London

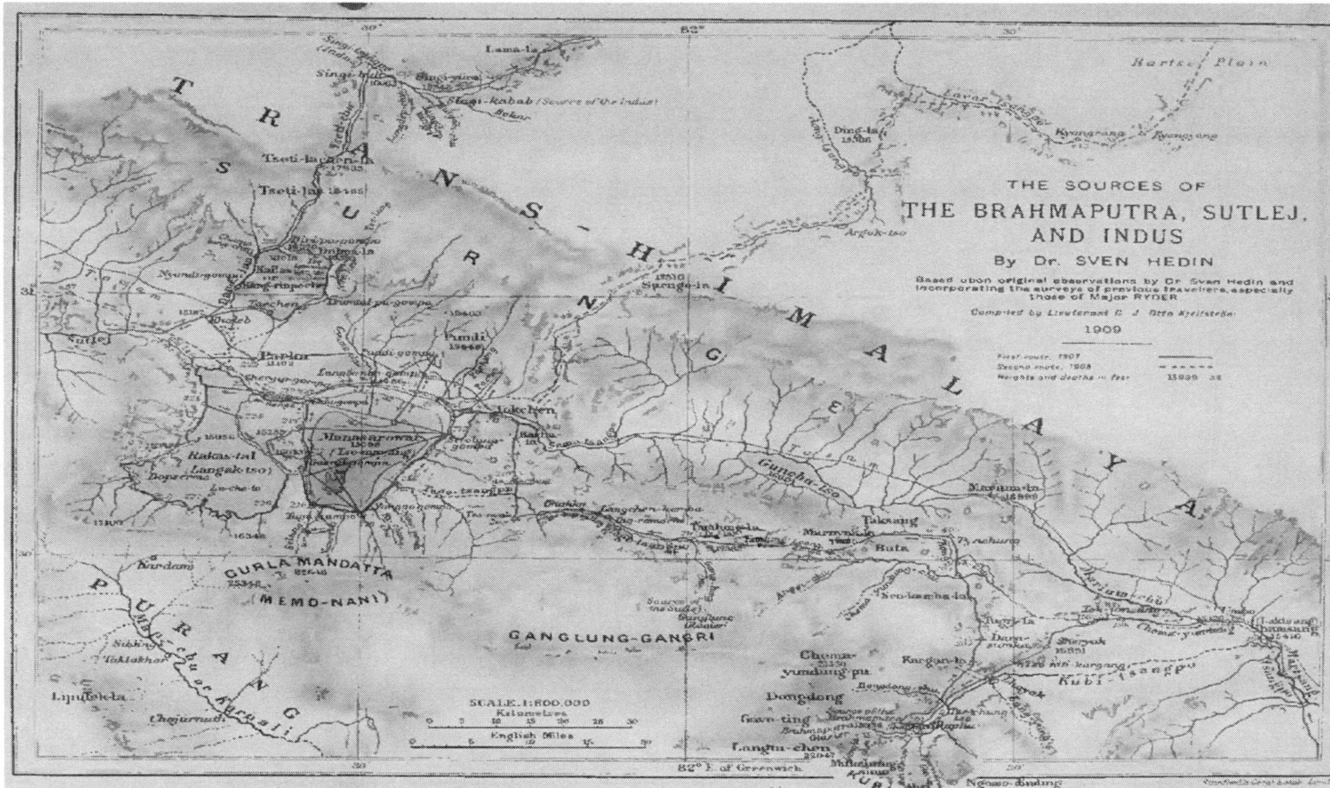
THE SOURCES OF
THE BRAHMAPUTRA, SUTLEJ, AND INDUS
By Dr. SVEN HEDIN
Based upon original observations by Dr Sven Hedin and incorporating the surveys of previous travellers, especially those of Major RYDER
1909
TRANS-HIMALAYA
GURLA MANDATTA
(MEMO-NANI)
GANGLUNG-GANGRI
PURANG
KUBI-GANGRI
Hartse Plain
Singi-kabab (Source of the Indus)
Tseti-la
Parka
Pundi
Sutlej
Rakas-tal
Langak-tso
Manasarowar
Gunchu-tso
Kubi-tsangpo
Dongdong
Langtu-chen
Ngomo-dingding
SCALE 1:800,000
Kilometres
English Miles
82° E. of Greenwich
London Macmillan & Co Ltd

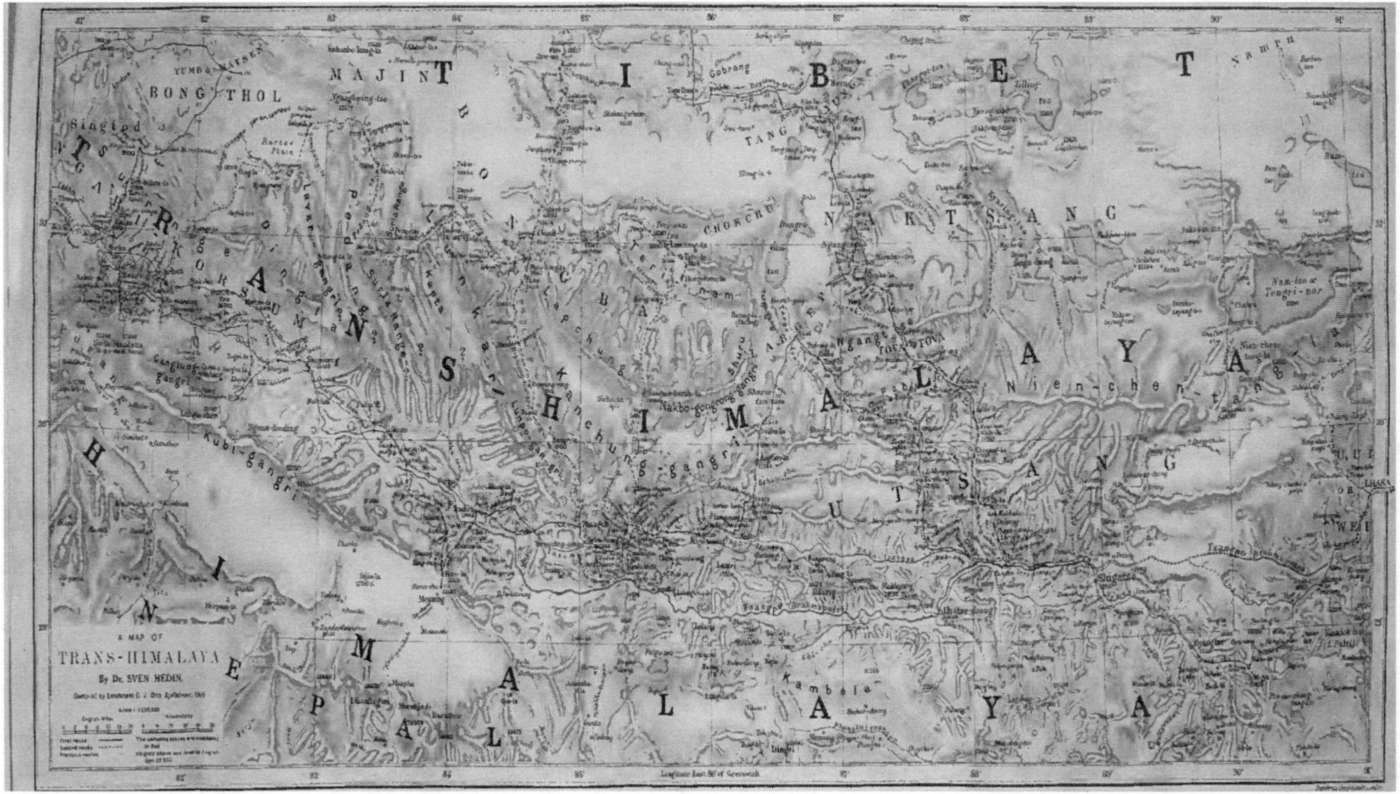

A MAP OF
TRANS-HIMALAYA
By Dr. SVEN HEDIN
TIBET
NEPAL
TRANS-HIMALAYA
HIMALAYA
BONG-THOL
YUMBA-MATSEN
MAJIN
NAKTSANG
CHORCHU
TANG
Gobrang
Singtod
UTSANG
Nien-chen-tang-la
Kubi-gangri
Kanchung-gangri
Lapchung
Lunpo-gangri
Surla Range
Lavar-gangri
Kanchung
Kambela
Ngangtse
Nam-tso or Tengri-nor
LHASA
Shigatse
Tsangpo (Brahmaputra)
Longitude East 86° of Greenwich

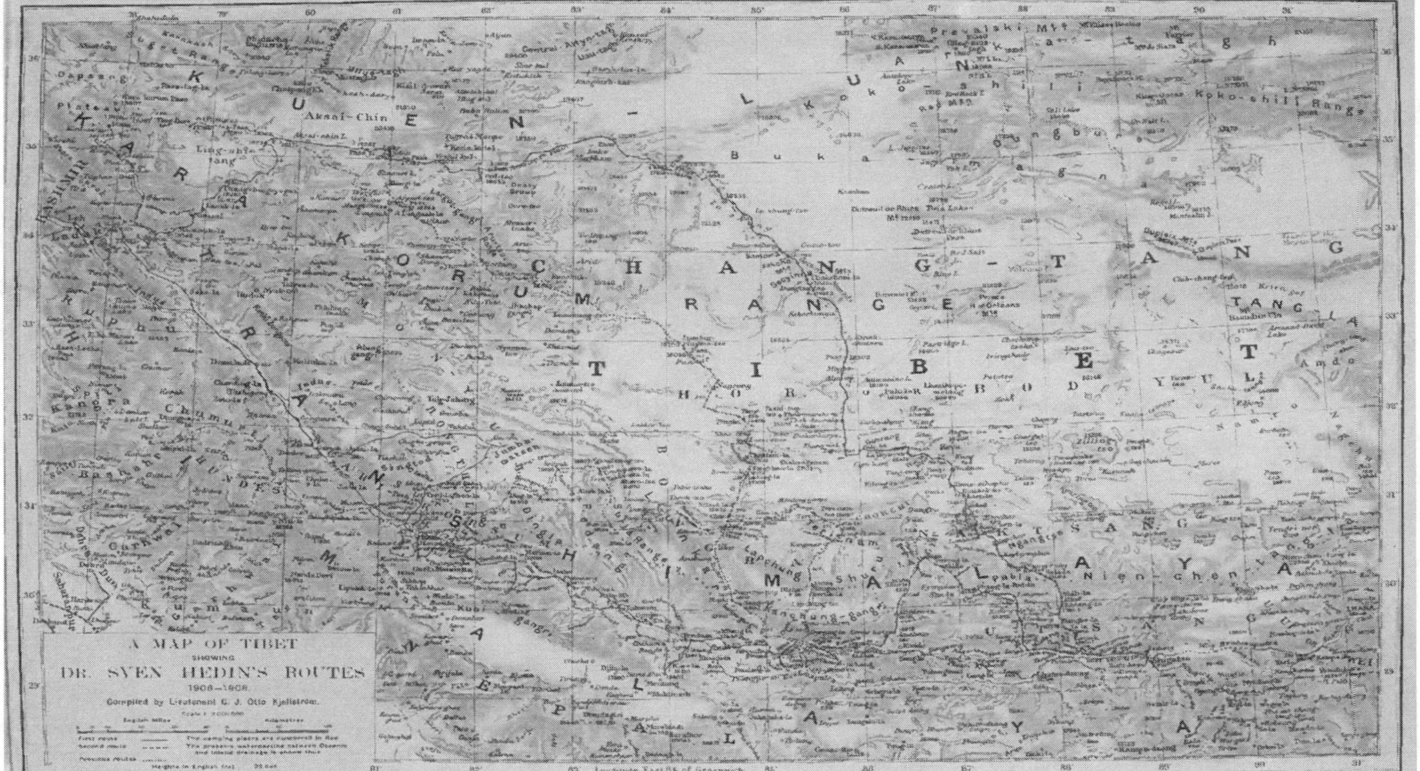
A MAP OF TIBET
SHOWING
DR. SVEN HEDIN'S ROUTES
1906–1908.
Compiled by Lieutenant C. J. Otto Kjellström.
Longitude East 84 of Greenwich
KUEN-LUN
KARAKORUM
CHANG-TANG
TRANS-HIMALAYA
TIBET
HIMALAYA
Aksai-Chin
Koko-shili Range
Nien-chen-tang-la
NEPAL

INDEX

THE END

TRANS-HIMALAYA

TEMPLE VESTIBULE IN TASHI-LUNPO. TWO OF THE SPIRIT-KINGS WHICH GUARD THE ENTRANCE.

Frontispiece.

TRANS-HIMALAYA

DISCOVERIES AND ADVENTURES IN TIBET

BY

SVEN HEDIN

WITH 156 ILLUSTRATIONS FROM PHOTOGRAPHS, WATER-COLOUR SKETCHES, AND DRAWINGS BY THE AUTHOR AND 4 MAPS

VOLUME III

MACMILLAN AND CO., LIMITED
ST. MARTIN'S STREET, LONDON
1913

ISBN : 978-81-212-0343-2

Published, 2018

Published by

Gyan Publishing House
5, Ansari Road
Daryaganj, New Delhi-110002
Phone: 011-47034999, 9811692060
www.gyanbooks.com
E-mail: books@gyanbooks.com

Printed at: G. Print Process, Delhi.

PREFACE

THE publication of this third volume of *Trans-Himalaya* fulfils a promise I made three years ago in the preface to the first volume.

Then I proposed to describe also my recollections of Japan, Korea, and Manchuria, and I intended to conclude with an account of my journey home through Siberia. But as soon as I began to look through my diaries and see what I had written about the source of the Indus, the highlands of western Tibet, and the Sutlej valley, I perceived that the third volume would be as bulky as the other two, and that no space could be spared for the extreme East if the material were to be dealt with as fully as it deserved. So now Japan, Korea, and Manchuria are omitted. For why should I encroach on space already scanty enough with accounts of countries visited annually by innumerable tourists, when I could present to my readers impressions of regions never before trodden by the foot of a white man, or where, at any rate, I had not a single rival? Besides, I have depicted several scenes in the great Orient in my book for young people, *From Pole to Pole.*

In three chapters of the present volume I have given a succinct historical review of all the journeys of exploration which have touched the margin of the central chains of the Trans-Himalaya, and have shown how immense was the area of this mountain system completely unknown before my journey.

Three other chapters contain *résumés* of those journeys which had the sacred lake of Manasarowar and the source regions of the great Indian rivers for their goal. Herein I demonstrate that before me no European, nor even an Asiatic of note, had penetrated to the true sources of the Indus and the Sutlej, and that the position of the source of the Brahmaputra had never been determined, though it might be guessed whereabouts the head-stream gushed forth from the foot of the glaciers. A polemical tone was unnecessary, for no allegations worthy of credit have ever been made to the contrary. I let the facts speak for themselves; they are, as always, very eloquent.

I have avoided all wearisome citations in the popular scientific chapters. I am treating the same questions fully in the scientific work which will shortly be issued, and in which all sources will be carefully indicated.

My thanks are due to Dr. Nils Ekholm for the calculation of absolute heights, to Professor Anders Hennig of Lund for the identification of rock specimens, and to Lieutenant C. J. Otto Kjellström for the general map.

The illustrations should be leniently criticized; with one or two exceptions they are from my own photographs and sketches. Perhaps they will give the reader some notion of the lonely country, the dizzy heights of the Trans-Himalaya, and of my old friends, the amiable, unassuming nomads.

SVEN HEDIN.

STOCKHOLM, *October* 1912.

CONTENTS

CHAPTER XXVII

CHAPTER XXVIII

CHAPTER XXIX

CHAPTER XXX

CHAPTER XXXI

CHAPTER XXXII

CHAPTER XXXIII

CHAPTER XXXIV

ILLUSTRATIONS

MAPS

CHAPTER I

FROM THE SOURCE OF THE INDUS THROUGH UNKNOWN COUNTRY

At camp 236 my horses and mules crop the tender grass that grows round the source of the Indus. The new-born stream babbles noisily among the stones in its bed, and I hear it in front of my tent like the roll of an organ in a classical mass. Its song will swell out to crashing thunder on the way through the Himalayas, but the melody is always the same, and to the music of the Indus ripples the Macedonians once defeated the peoples of the East (see Vol. II. p. 213).

My tent is anchored by its iron pegs in ground on which no European has set his foot. I am proud of being the first to visit the source of the Indus, and yet meekly thankful. From this point, where the river springs from the bosom of the earth, the increasing volumes of water hurry down towards the sea. The height is stupendous. I am resting at 16,946 feet above the level of the ocean. An Eiffel Tower on the summit of Mont Blanc! Not the eternal river alone, but the whole earth lies at my feet. I have crossed the Trans-Himalaya a fourth time and have at last reached the goal I aimed at.

Of the source of the Indus the geographers of old—Greek, Roman, and Arabian—knew nothing. Since the day when the claws of the British lion closed round the land of the Hindus, the cradle of the Indus has been repeatedly moved and located now here now there. At length English officers sent out native scouts to search for it, and these men found the head-stream, but not the source itself. And now I listened to its monotonous murmur.

I had five of my best men from Ladak with me. They had accompanied me on my adventurous march right through Tibet; they had endured a bitterly cold winter, and surmounted the Trans-Himalaya by unknown passes; with deep devotional feeling they had heard the chants resounding through the cloister courts of Tashi-lunpo, had visited the shores of the holy lake, and on the summit of Kailas had raised their eyes towards the paradise of Siva.

I spoke Jagatai Turkish with my men, and Rabsang translated for me into Tibetan. Tundup Sonam took care of our guns and Adul stirred the pots as they simmered over the cooking-fire.

A lucky chance had thrown a Tibetan nomad named Pema Tense in my way. Allured by the liberal remuneration in bright rupees which chinked in my hand, he had let his comrades go their way and offered me his service on the route north-eastwards through unknown country. From him we hired eight sheep and bought their loads of barley. Thus my own baggage animals were not overladen, and could now and then get a good feed in a country as bare and naked as immediately after the deluge.

We set out on the morning of September 11, 1907, and the hoofs tapped again on the hard frozen soil. The temperature had fallen in the night to 11.3°. In Tibet winter is a guest which comes early and stays late. The sky was light blue and clear, and the rainy season, which we had scarcely felt, was over. But the winds of the south-west monsoon howled and moaned over the highlands, and where the soil was loose dust flew up from the hoofs of the horses.

The land lies flat and open before us. It is the "Northern Plain," the Chang-tang of the Tibetans, the high plateau with its flattened surface forms. Behind us rises the Trans-Himalaya with its wild precipitous rocks. The valley we follow is broad and enclosed between high irregular mountains. The Bokar-tsangpo, one of the head-streams of the Indus, glides noiselessly between its

1. Source of the Indus.

2. A Mani Wall.

Sketches by the Author.

ice-lined banks. Its water is cold and crystal clear, and it is evident that it comes from snow-fields and springs and not from glaciers.

In an expansion between the heights to the left of our route white rings of salt glitter round the small vanishing lake Jekung-tso. The same name is given to the pass to which we ascend along a ravine between bare weathered cliffs. The Bokar-tsangpo is left behind us, but in the south-east we see the bluish heights with the thin snow-fields whence the brook draws some of its water.

On the other side of the pass also we are still in the basin of the Indus, for the rivulet which meanders among small clumps of faded grass down the Lamo-latse valley joins the Bokar-tsangpo.

Pema Tense waddles whistling and singing behind his eight sheep and is always ready to give me any information I ask for.

"What is the name of this place?" I ask him at a spot where a row of cairns covered with *mani* stones crosses the path.

"Shantse-gong," he answers. "Here the pilgrims greet the gods of Kang-rinpoche, for from here the actual summit of the holy mountain first comes into sight." Pema must have been imposed on with this tale, for not a glimpse of the mountain can be obtained from the cairns.

Some tiny rivulets still trickle down through the yellow moss, the only vegetation visible, to the Lamo-latse brook. I mention them because the easternmost rivulet should perhaps be regarded as the true source of the Indus.

Another obstacle appears in our way, and then the path leads to the pass of Lamo-latse sunk in a steep crest of quartz porphyry. Here is the watershed of the Indus. To the east stretches an elevated country which has no drainage to the sea. We are at a height of 17,802 feet. Two cairns mark the top of the pass, decked with yaks' horns and rags, the offerings of pious superstitious pilgrims. The six holy syllables "Om mani padme hum" are inscribed in black on coloured streamers, and when the rushing wind makes the streamers flap and crack, one can fancy that "Om mani padme hum," uttered by many voices, is borne by the wind over the desolate plateau to bring blessing and happiness to the troops of pilgrims.

Yes, up here the stormy wind rages furiously. I have to place myself with my back sheltered from the wind when I read the instruments, so as not to be carried away. And what a prospect towards the east-north-east! Do you imagine it is beautiful? It is terribly desolate, almost awful. I feel as lonely and forlorn as in the midst of a sea, a petrified sea with bell-shaped billows that are black and red near at hand and pass into yellow, green, and violet in the distance. I seem to stand on the crest of a wave looking down on all the others. Space without end! I should have to wander about for days and years to reproduce all these details on my map sheets. Here I take in at a single glance an enormous block of the earth's crust. Waste, cold and lonely. No men, no animals, no plants! But the sun lights up the ground and the wind howls among the rocks. There is no other sign of life.

It is pleasant to encamp (camp 237) after such a day. We pitch the tents as quickly as possible to get shelter from the storm which sweeps the ground like a stout besom. But the air is clear, for there is nothing loose to sweep away from this ground polished by the wind during millions of years. We look in vain for a yellowish-green patch which might be pasture land, and so one of the sheep is relieved of its load of barley.

When the camp is pitched at three o'clock, the afternoon seems long and the hours of solitude seem never to come to an end. I write down in my diary a description of the bit of earth I have seen since sunrise. The rock specimens I have picked out of the hills with my geological hammer are numbered and wrapped up in paper. And then Pema Tense must give me his company for a while.

"What is the name of this valley?" I ask him.

"It is called Lamo-latse-lungpe-do, and it opens after three days' journey into a large plain."

"Where is your home, Pema?"

"My tent stands in Gertse, sir."

"How far off is it?"

"Oh, quite fifteen days' march. We reckon eleven days' journey from Yumba-matsen to Gertse."

"Are there many nomads in Gertse?"

"My tribesmen live in two to three hundred black tents, and we own large flocks of sheep which are our only wealth."

"Tell me something about the profits you derive from your sheep."

"Well, you see, some nomads shear their sheep themselves in Gertse, and carry the wool on yaks thirteen days' journey to Tok-jalung, whither merchants from Ladak and Hindustan come to market. Others let the sheep carry their wool to market, and the purchasers do the shearing. But those nomads do best who break salt out of the beds of dried-up lakes, pack the lumps of salt on their sheep, and tramp in midsummer all the way to market at Gyanima and to the shore of Tso-mavang, where the sheep are shorn, for they make a profit on the salt as well as on the wool. And when they travel home again their sheep are laden with barley, which they have obtained by barter. Such a journey, outwards and homewards, occupies the greater part of the summer. The sheep graze by the way, no permission being asked, and so we nomads spare our own grass for the winter."

The Tok-jalung gold-field, at a height of 16,340 feet, is one of the highest permanently inhabited places in the world. Pema Tense had often been there, and told me that in summer 300 tents sprang up out of the earth, for at that time gold-diggers came thither from Lhasa and other places. During the winter only some thirty tents stood there. It is bitterly cold, and often a storm of powdery snow sweeps over the broad expanse.

Pema Tense looked out through the tent opening, and when he saw that the twilight was falling over the earth he rose and went out to look for his sheep and tie them up by the tents for the night. Then, after chatting a while at the camp fire of the Ladakis, he rolled himself up in his skin coat like a hedgehog and fell into a sound sleep. He had given us due notice that he intended to make off altogether as soon as we met travellers or caught sight of a tent, for if he were caught travelling about with strangers and guiding them into the forbidden land he would be beheaded as surely as twice two make four. Therefore, he wanted his rupees paid to him every evening; and he always got them in full.

The storm keeps us company all night long. There is something depressing in this constant wind, which, according to Pema, will last quite eight months. It makes the tent cloth flap and beat like a sail and it whistles and groans among the ropes, and a cold draught sweeps over the ground where I lie wrapped up in furs and felt rugs. The temperature sinks to 18° in the night; but at seven o'clock it is already up to 40.3°.

I slip quickly into my clothes and am hardly dressed when Adul comes in with my breakfast consisting of two vertebræ of the last-killed wild sheep, fresh bread and tea. Outside the Ladakis are shoeing my white steed, the faithful animal which has carried me many hundred miles through dreary Tibet. On this troublesome ground of thick accumulations of detritus the horses become footsore and must be carefully attended to.

We long to get out of this country which has nothing to offer but water and wind. The path is easily recognizable, and winds along like a light-coloured riband. Innumerable men and animals have trodden it down and sunk it in the ground. Pilgrims have swarmed from Gertse, Senkor, Yumba-matsen, and other regions of Tibet to the holy mountain and the wonder-working lake. Here and there are seen signs of their camps, a slab of stone blackened by fire, and three stones between which blue flames have flickered above yak dung and brought the water in a kettle to the boil.

Hour after hour our little company marches onwards. There is seldom anything unusual to attract our attention. Here lies the bleached skull of a wild sheep, *Ovis ammon*, with its heavy beautifully curved horns. The valley opens on to a plain and we turn aside from the brook which disappears northwards. Its water murmurs melodiously under a thin sheet of ice. A small herd of wild asses or kiangs is disporting itself on the plain, but makes off when

3. Pema Tense, my Guide to the Source of the Indus and to Yumba-matsen.

Sketch by the Author.

we set up our tents at camp 238 beside a wall of dry yak dung. The nomads, who have collected this fuel and are now feeding their flocks in some other spot, will certainly be surprised to find that most of their store of fuel is gone. If we could get no other luxury we would at any rate enjoy a large roaring fire at even.

The next day's journey brings us to a small pass through cliffs of porphyry; on the farther side Pema Tense leads us through a valley deeply sunk between wild weathered walls of rock, and with its bottom covered with a deep layer of sharp pebbles. At times a small patch of yellow grass appears with stems as hard and sharp as needles. In two sheltered gullies hairy ragged nettles struggle for life. Otherwise the country is everywhere dismally barren, dried-up and desolate.

Beyond a second saddle consisting of limestone we at last meet a solitary traveller.

"Where do you come from?" Rabsang asks him.

"From Yumba-matsen," he answers shortly, quickening his pace.

"Where are you going?"

"To a tent not far from here?"

"What have you to do there?"

"I have left a boot behind," he replies, making off as quickly as possible. Certainly an absent-minded gentleman! Pema Tense thinks that the man belongs to a band of robbers.

A gradually ascending path brings us to the Tsalam-ngopta-la pass, 16,660 feet high, adorned with two cairns and the usual prayer streamers. All round the horizon the view reveals nothing new. Still on all sides stretches the same dismal country. No black tents, no flocks. We have marched north-eastwards for six days and only met a single traveller.

Here at any rate we run no risk of being stopped by dictatorial governors and militia levies. We feel ourselves to be the lords of the land. If I had a larger caravan, more men and more provisions, I could travel unhindered a very long way eastwards. There is a peculiar charm in the adventures and excitement of a forbidden route. But the object of the present excursion—the source of the Indus—has been attained, and the main caravan is waiting for us at Gartok. Well, it may wait. As all is going well, we will try to advance two days' journey farther to the north-east. We leisurely descend the slope from the pass and prepare for the night in the Gyamboche district at camp 239.

On setting out on September 14, we decided that our next business was to look out for the tent of the headman of Yumba-matsen, who, Pema Tense believed, was staying in the neighbourhood. Every hill which seemed to promise a wide prospect was climbed by one of our party. Several times we thought we saw black tents to the north-east, but in the telescope they resolved themselves into heaps of rubbish or ring fences, which the nomads use as sheep-folds. The only thing we discovered was the small lake Nyanda-nakbo-tso.

Singular country! The mountains do not form continuous chains but rise in rolls of weathering products or steep humps of solid rock, apparently without any order. They are yellow and red, violet, grey and black. The surface is coloured, but the tones are subdued and solemn.

The people of the country seem to have fled before us, but to-day signs of man appear. The way passes twelve *mani* walls with stones bearing the everlasting "Om mani padme hum." Round an open pond four such votive cairns are erected. The animal life also announces a more favourable country. A covey of partridges chirps on the pebbles of a slope, and five of them are a welcome addition to our store of provisions. They are plucked at once and their feathers whirl in the air like wind-driven smoke. They are cleaned on the march, and are tied together and secured on the back of the white mule, where the head of a wild sheep, killed at the source of the Indus, is already enthroned and nods at every step of the mule. Wild asses are also seen more frequently than before.

The view in front is again barred by a small ridge at the foot of which grass more luxuriant than we have hitherto seen grows round a spring. A long well-kept *mani* wall runs up the slope, and not far from it stand perhaps a dozen cairns in a row. There must be men here. We hurry up to the crest, keenly expectant, and hope to catch sight of black tents on the other side, but not even the field-glass can detect a single Tibetan. Only wild asses wander over the plain, two hares race along a slope, and some bluish-black ravens circle leisurely above our heads. For the rest the desert stretches silent and dreary before us, and in the background shimmers the little lake.

Disappointed we move onwards. We approach the lake basin and the air becomes milder. Were it not for the horrible wind we could enjoy here a last touch of departing summer.

After a time the desert scene is enlivened by 500 sheep which trot before us in the same direction. Ah! there are our friends from Singi-buk, Pema Tense's comrades, with their caravan. They took another route and now we are following in their track. Gertse is their destination. The sheep carry small loads of barley, for which the herdsmen have bartered the easily won salt they have taken from the ground.

Now we are on the steppe round the lake where grasshoppers fill the air with their rattle, and lizards dart noiselessly over the sand. We notice on a slope by the farther shore fifteen *mani* walls. Astonished at finding them piled up so far from the track, I ask Pema Tense about them, and he asserts that they are tombstones of dead Tibetans.

A second lake now appeared behind a small isolated hill of limestone, and thither we directed our steps. The water may be drunk by any one who is not too particular. But we did not put our stomachs to the proof as Ishe, one of our Ladakis, discovered a spring of fresh water near the eastern shore. There we made ourselves comfortable enough to spend a night in the desert. The arrangements had been partially provided by the nomads, who now and then pitch their tents on the lake shore and feed their yaks and sheep on the good pasturage. There is a steep wall of phyllitic schist which can easily be split into slabs, and several small *mani* walls are built of them. On the top of one sits a yak skull with huge horns; the six holy syllables are carved in its white forehead and filled in with ochre so that they are red as blood. An old skin coat and a vest had been left among the stones.

Out on the lake a flock of ducks were quacking, and at dusk twenty wild geese alighted on the shallow water. Then a shot cracked and put an end to their repose. Three of the far-travelled visitors found their way into our kitchen. When the darkness of night fell over the earth we heard again an eager conversation among some sixty wild geese as they splashed in the water or whizzing down folded their wings above the surface. They came from the south-west and were off again next morning before us. Soon cold weather would cover the mud with a crust of ice and force the wild geese to return to lower, warmer regions.

After sunset deep violet shadows rose up in the east, turquoise-blue tints lingered a while in the zenith, while sulphur-yellow flames hovered over the western horizon. They soon paled and went out, and the camp fires burnt all the brighter. Out in the lake, which has a very slowly falling bottom, were heard splashing footsteps. It was Tundup Sonam returning with his game. At the foot of cliffs of schist the dogs barked at the echo of their own voices. Their bark pierced sharp and shrill through the otherwise silent night.

4. Snapshots in Camp.

Sketches by the Author.

CHAPTER II

THE NOMADS OF YUMBA-MATSEN

THE thermometer fell at night only to 20.8°, and yet a clear sheet of ice was formed over the old lake. We were not the only visitors resting on the shore. A caravan from Gyanima had come up early in the morning in three detachments, and one of the party cautiously approached our camp to find out what sort of men we were. Rabsang entered into conversation with the man, and asked him if he had any eatables to sell. Oh yes, he could spare a little butter and rice, and he would go at once to fetch them. However, he had hardly had time to exchange a few words with his friends, when they hastily loaded their yaks and sheep and disappeared northwards up the valley leading to Gertse. Did they take us for highwaymen?

We take down our tents and load our animals, I swing myself into the saddle, and off we go through the hopelessly dreary country. Wild asses scamper in herds over the plain by the shore. They are shy. At Tso-mavang one can go near them whenever one likes. No one sends a bullet after a kiang within sight of the mountain of the gods, and the animals know that the holy lake and its shores are a sanctuary. But here, where there are no holy places, the wild asses are quite aware that the wolf is not their only enemy.

The plain rises imperceptibly to the eye towards the valley opening Gyekung-sherma. Where are the nomads in this God-forsaken land? A mountain flank to the south is spotted black. Can it be grazing yaks?

No, the field-glass shows us that it is only heaps of fuel and small cairns. The country cannot be uninhabited everywhere, for we have seen so many traces of old camps.

To-day there is no wind. In the valley where the sun has heated the limestone rocks it is actually hot. The valley is short, and is bounded in the background by a low pass. At last! There comes a troop of black yaks trotting down the slope. Are they roving tribesmen from Yumba-matsen or another caravan from Gertse, which crosses our course like a ship on the sea without sending us a greeting across the waves? At all events we will not let these free rovers escape us. We must procure provisions and means of transport at any price, and if the men grumble we will treat them in Asiatic fashion, just as if the days of Timur had returned.

My men longed to see men of any kind; only Pema Tense was in despair.

"It must be the chief of Yumba," he said. "If he catches me he will beat me to a jelly, and then take from me the ninety-six rupees I have received from you."

"Then perhaps it will be best for you to pack up your things and be off, Pema."

"Yes, but let me stay here a while until Rabsang has been up the valley to reconnoitre."

Rabsang went and returned after an hour. It was really nomads from Yumba-matsen who were just moving their quarters. Two tents were already set up. The yaks would graze a while, and then be driven back over the pass again to fetch another part of the movable property of their masters. A large heap of various articles and packages containing meat, barley, and *tsamba*, was already piled up on the new camping-ground.

Now all was plain. The barley still left was put on one of our horses, we said good-bye to Pema Tense, and wished him every good fortune on his long journey to Gertse, and went on up the valley. We saw him sit down on the detritus and quietly light his pipe. There he remained for a time looking after us, and then he gathered his sheep together and walked down towards the lake.

He would soon overtake his comrades, and would return home in their company.

We were going to make new acquaintances. Two Tibetans came to meet us, saluting us in an embarrassed manner when we came near their tents. We immediately drew from them by questions all they knew about the geography of the country; they told us that Yumba-matsen is the name of a district lying east-north-east of the pass. There, there are forty-five tents under the command of the Gova or headman. Their flock graze in summer in a region lying still farther to the north-east. At the end of October they come down to the shores of the Mugu lake, and remain there during the coldest winter months. As soon as the early spring has succeeded to the sharpness of winter, they return slowly to Yumba-matsen.

In this way the nomads describe an orbit through one region after another as the seasons change. In summer they are to be found in one valley, in autumn in another. When the frost of winter covers the Mugu lake with a sheet of ice the wild asses know that it is time to depart. Thus it has been from father to son since the most remote antiquity. The experience possessed by the nomads of to-day is a heritage from innumerable preceding generations. They have discovered that the pastures in Yumba-matsen are best suited for summer grazing, and that the meadows round the lake suffice for their winter needs. When the winter herbage is consumed they return gradually to their summer dwelling-places. A people whose existence depends entirely on sheep-rearing, develops those powers of observation which are useful in the improvement of their flocks. They know every spring, every cave in their home country, and know what poisonous plants make the pastures dangerous. They wean the lambs from the ewes at the right time, and carefully accustom the sheep to carry small burdens. Against the wolves of the wilds the nomad is always on his guard, and in all the vicissitudes of life goes to work carefully with his inherited knowledge.

The chieftain of Yumba-matsen owns 500 sheep, and all his tent community 8000. Two hundred yaks and fifteen horses also belong to his subjects. The sheep are sheared in the middle of August, and the wool is sold to dealers who come from Ladak and the Indian frontier. A large sheep yields half a rupee. At Tso-mavang the wool is dearer, but there the purchaser is saved a large part of the cost of transport.

Our Tibetans were in the service of the Yumba chieftain, and could not help us without permission from their master. Therefore I sent one of them back over the pass to request the Yumba-matsen-chigep, as he is styled, to come to us. By that time it was evening, and we could not expect him before the next morning.

The evening was cold and calm. We had 3½° of frost at nine o'clock, and 23½° in the night. The bluish-grey smoke whirled from the fire like dancing elves down the valley, driven by a slight breeze from the pass. The vault of heaven, dark blue and clear, spanned the earth, the stars shone like sparkling jewels, the wreath of mountains formed a straggling coal-black frame round the camp, and above a ridge the moon displayed its silvery disc.

I lie awake for a while listening to the mysterious silence. The moonlight casts a subdued light through the tent covering, and here and there a bright shaft finds its way through a hole. We are all soon fast asleep in this singular, mysterious Tibet.

When I went out of my tent in the morning, two well-to-do nomads were sitting talking to my men. They wore loose black skin coats, soft felt boots with red ties, and red turban-like bandages on their long shaggy hair.

They rose, scratched their heads, and put out their tongues according to the custom of the country. It was no wonder that they were a little embarrassed, for they had never seen a European before. But the negotiations had hardly commenced when their shyness disappeared.

"Which of you is the Yumba-matsen-chigep?" I inquired.

"Neither. The chief could not come himself, but he has sent us with his greeting. Where do you come from, sir, and whither are you travelling?"

"I come from Kang-rinpoche and am on my way to Gartok."

"But why are you travelling north-eastwards when Gartok lies to the south-west?"

"I have come hither to buy provisions and hire baggage animals. To-morrow, five horses and as many yaks must stand before my tent ready for travelling."

"On that matter only the chief can give you an answer. When the Serpun, the gold commissioner, travels through our country he is empowered to use the baggage animals of the nomads without remuneration. But you have no *lamik* (passport). We have not been informed of your coming even by a *jaik* (message stick). Therefore the chief cannot grant your request."

"Very good, then I will send two of my men to Gartok and will remain here in the meantime. But if you will yourselves bring up the animals I require, I will pay two rupees a day for each horse and one rupee for each yak, and besides give a liberal recompense to the drivers I want. Do you agree?"

"The horses and yaks shall stand ready before your tent to-morrow," they answered, after I had paid them the money for the first day. Now they became agreeable and accommodating, and paid not the slightest heed to all the prohibitions issued from Lhasa. They could rely upon the silence of their fellow-tribesmen, and the wild geese tell no tales.

"Tell me what you know of the country to the east," I begged them. And they told me all sorts of things, but their range was limited. They knew the Lakkor-tso which I visited in 1901, had heard of the Dangra-yum-tso which I had lately seen in the distance, and had often ridden to Selipuk and the Nganglaring-tso, sometimes by the northern road across a gold-field, sometimes by the southern, which passes the source of the Aong-tsangpo, a river entering the Nganglaring-tso. By either way the journey takes four days; nomads of the Rundor tribe have tents round the lake.

We started on September 17, after a cold night. Forty fully-laden yaks tramped slowly and heavily down the valley. It was a new association formed of four tent groups which was migrating from Yumba-matsen to the mouth of a side valley situated farther down. Each tent community has its own camp, and there are no disputes about pasturage where the old customs are rigorously adhered to.

The baggage animals ordered were punctually provided. The horses were small and shaggy but remarkably plump and well-fed considering that they had been reared in such a wilderness. When the chase has been productive they are fed on dried meat; and this perhaps helps to make them look so round and sleek. The Tibetans shoe their horses only for long journeys, and then usually only on the forefeet.

Now my horses were to travel unburdened, for the yaks took the loads. My men, who had worn out their soles during a journey of 110 miles, were to ride. Our new guides went on foot, shouting and whistling as usual. Their right arms and bare right shoulders shone in the sunshine like polished bronze.

We bade farewell to the friendly nomads of the Gyekung valley and marched off by the way we had come, down the valley again. At the lakes, however, we diverged to the west, leaving our old road to the left behind us. Continuing the line of the small lakes a salt plain, the Mugu-telep, stretches out. Here the Tibetans halted beside a pond of fresh water and advised us to camp here for the night, because the next spring was a long distance off. Some kiangs, Pantholops antelopes, and wild geese vacated the ground as we came up. A westerly storm arose at mid-day, and the fine white powdery salt from the Mugu-telep plain whirled like clouds of steam over the lakes.

The camp was larger and more animated than usual. We were eight men with fifteen baggage animals and three dogs. The Tibetans did their best, collecting yak dung for the fires, carrying water, leading the animals to good pasturage, and then entertaining us with all kinds of stories. But the day seemed long. It is trying to the patience to lie at anchor when one would like to be getting over the ground and hurrying on to new fortunes.

5. NATIVES WATCHING MY DEPARTURE.

6. NATIVES WATCHING MY DEPARTURE.

In the evening some fifteen wild geese came and circled screaming above the pool. But when they found the place occupied the leading geese drew off their party to the lakes. The sun had just sunk below the horizon, and all the plain lay in shadow. But the pilgrims of the air and their pinions were lighted below by the sun, and stood out bright and white against the blue expanse of heaven. Had they come a minute later they would have been hidden by the shadow of the earth.

At dusk some riders were seen on a distant height. Our Tibetans thought that they had come out to look for a flock of sheep which a few days ago had disappeared in broad daylight when the shepherd was asleep. Probably some bandits had seized the opportunity to gain possession of the sheep. The old Ladak songs sounded round the blaze of the camp fire, soft and melodious as in the days of old. I had heard them times without number in the long winter evenings on Chang-tang, but I was never tired of the plaintive tones.

The temperature down to zero on the night of September 18! That is severe so early in autumn. If one has not put oneself in a state of defence on getting into bed, one is soon reminded by the creeping cold that furs are necessary. The pond was covered with a bright sheet of ice. The air was clear and calm, and the sun rose in splendour. By seven o'clock the temperature rose to 38° and at one o'clock to 64.8°. A range of temperature of more that 64° between night and day!

Our road runs north-westwards past two long salt lakes, called Tso-longcho, swarming with wild geese. The sun is burning and there is no wind. Now and then only a rushing sound is heard, and, turning in the saddle, I see a dust-spout coming; it whirls the sucked-up sand in helices and whizzes like a ghost over the plain. It rushes past us, revolving as it goes, thins out and vanishes in the distance; soon another follows.

Sigu-ragling-la is a small flat pass on our way over a ridge of quartzitic limestone that rises above the plain. This country is a desert that reminds me of certain parts of Eastern Persia. At a considerable distance are seen small hilly ridges of pink, light brown, or reddish colours; between them lies the plain so slightly undulating that I should not notice the inequalities did not the caravan far in front of us disappear now and then in a hollow, and after a time appear again on a rise in the ground. The road is excellent, with fine gravel thinly spread on firm yellow loam, but a blade of grass is nowhere visible. This track leads us north-westwards and, therefore, not in the direction of Gartok. I ask one of our guides the reason, and he replies that a detour is necessary because the springs are so few on the direct course.

Two small lakes are seen to the north, the Tso-kar or white lake and the Pul-tso or salt lake. The circular walls on their banks are signs of winter visitors.

The hours pass by and the landscape still remains monotonous. We pass a dark hill of schist with a spring at its foot, and then the light pink quivering tints of the desert plain come back again. A country like this is uncommon in western Tibet, where the mountain ranges are usually pressed together into innumerable folds.

About 150 wild asses disport themselves at some distance to the south side of our route, where, no doubt, there is grass. They lie down in herds or feed singly or in pairs. But they are always charming to look at as they skim like ships over the sea of the desert. When the dust-spouts pass over the herd they look like the smoke of burning vessels.

At length tents appear. They are pitched at a height of 15,138 feet among the fresh-water ponds of Luma-ringmo. It is like anchoring in a water channel in the midst of an archipelago. The mountain ridges stand up on all sides like holms, seeming to hover a little above the ground owing to the mirage.

7. A Nomad of Yumba-matsen.

Sketch by the Author.

CHAPTER III

OVER THE INDUS AGAIN

On September 19 our march ran due west.

"What is that curious erection?" I ask the guide who always walks beside me, as we pass twelve upright stones a yard high near a deserted camping-ground. One need not be an archæologist to perceive that they have been set up by human hands.

The Tibetan turns his head and replies: "There is no one in our country who knows what they mean."

Probably they have stood there for ages and are memorials of the time when Buddhism was introduced into Tibet. Some powerful chief had perhaps placed his tent there, or human sacrifices were offered between the stones to the dreaded spirits which inhabit the mountains and lakes.

An interruption occurred in our monotonous journey as we rode by two projecting black cliffs of porphyrite and volcanic tuff. I held in my left hand a folding cardboard case to protect the loose leaves on which I drew the daily course and the adjoining topography. With the right I was marking on the map the last bearing I had taken. Consequently the horse was left to his own devices. A violent gust swept over the plain and the map sheets began to flutter and flap. The small shaggy black animal from the Gyekung valley which I rode was frightened out of his senses, bolted, and sped like an arrow over the gravelly soil. I was about to thrust the map case into my leathern vest for safety when a crack in the ground caused the horse to swerve suddenly to one side, whereupon the saddle turned and I shot head downwards to the ground, where for the fraction of a second I saw brilliant fireworks. The Indian cork helmet I wore was crushed flat but it saved my head. My left temple bled and my goggles were bent up. When I had recovered a little from my consternation I got up cautiously and stretched out my arms and legs to make sure that nothing was broken. I might easily have been killed or have broken a leg, and then, patched up temporarily, I should have had to spend a full month in a waterless desert.

The horse came back at last to his comrades, breathless and trembling, with froth on his bridle and sweating flanks. The saddle hung loosely under his belly, and the dangling geological wallet had no doubt helped to alarm the animal. He had certainly done all he could to get rid of me, but nevertheless we rode on together as if nothing had happened. A slight headache, a swollen eyelid, and a purplish ring round the left eye were the only results of my somersault.

The boundless plain is before us, bestrewn with fragments of lava, tuff, and porphyrite polished by the wind. From a spoon-shaped swell in the ground I let my eyes roam over the hopelessly dismal country we have crossed. There are seen the small lakes, narrow and bright like a sabre blade, in the midst of extensive plains bounded far to the east by the dull pink mountains of Yumba-matsen. The spring by which we pitched camp 244 at a late hour is called Sariyol.

Next morning a thick veil of mist lay over the land, making all the colours faint and the outlines indistinct. We rode over slopes of detritus and again approached the watershed of the Indus, which we soon crossed by the Bokar-la pass, 16,989 feet high. Here, then, we left the enclosed basin and came on to ground which is drained to the sea. The view from the pass embraces an enormous extent of country. We still looked in vain for tents and flocks. Nothing could be seen but stone, sometimes as rock *in situ*, sometimes in pebble slopes, in heaps of weathering products, or accumulated in valley bottoms. No verdure adorns the flanks, no streams glisten in the sun. Here all is empty, dead, and dry, and one can understand why the source-stream of the Indus which drains this country has so little water.

From the Bokar-la a path runs down at first steeply and then with an imperceptible fall to a valley where the water of a few springs collects into a winding brook. The valley gradually contracts between its walls of quartz porphyry, and beside it rise terraces of erosion, more or less continuous, which are often twenty feet high, and testify to abundant precipitation in earlier geological periods. We encamped at a spring near the point where this side valley opens out to the Indus valley, and the usual fuel, furnished by the herds of the nomads, was not wanting.

We had neighbours also. One of our guides took Ishe to a hidden tent camp, and he soon returned with two natives and a grand supply of sweet and sour milk. Here we were again in known country. In the year 1867 two of Colonel Montgomerie's pundits explored this country, and in 1906 Mr. Calvert, employed by the Indian Government, crossed the region on his journey from Gartok to Tok-jalung. The district round the uppermost Indus is named Singtod, and lower down lies another, Singmet, that is, the upper Indus district and the lower, for Singi-Tsangpo is the Tibetan name for the Indus, and Singi-kabab is the source of the Lion river. A day's journey down-stream is a small temple inhabited in winter only by a solitary lama. He must be a philosopher, poor man! How dreary and comfortless his life must be when the frost crackles in the rocks and a snowstorm howls round the corners of his dwelling! But spring will come at last and then he can go out again. It is a consolation to know that he is not walled up in darkness like the monks in the grottoes of Linga.

During the night our caravan animals stampeded down the valley pursued by wolves. The alarm was given, the men followed the track, and came up just in time to save the horses and mules. Two hours later they were laden again, and the train descended the Indus valley which is enclosed by rather high mountains. The rocks on the left side are steep, and the river, invisible at present from our road, skirts their foot. Here and there we cross a rivulet trickling down to the Indus. A tent stands close to the river, a little farther off seven close together, and then again three. Here there are men at least.

A herd of yaks is grazing on a slope. What can the animals find to eat there? I cannot perceive the slightest tinge of green. The velvety yak grass hides itself among the stones, as also the mosses and lichens which the yaks lick up with their tongues rough as graters.

The place where our loads were again removed from the animals' backs, and where we set up our camp 246, is called Hlagar. Here the Indus takes a sharp bend, turning northwards through wild picturesque rocks of porphyry. My airy dwelling was set up on the brink of the right bank, and from my tent I could enjoy the sight of the proud river rolling its crystal clear water noiselessly among the mountains.

A stone's throw away stood two tents, and the inmates could not do enough for us. So we lived as princes in this wild lovely country, which seemed to us the more charming because we had of late seen nothing but desert. The dogs, which had long been on short rations, were not forgotten. Tundup Sonam brought partridges in abundance to the kitchen, and I preferred them to the perpetual mutton. Sour milk was to be had in gallons, and bread was baked in yak-dung ashes. Could a man fare better in such a country?

The day was glorious, the air in the deep valley warm and quiet, the temperature 55.6° at one o'clock, and 54.3° in the river. Now and then a puff of wind came down from the nearest ridge.

Two chiefs bearing the title of Gova appeared before my tent with tongues protruded and polite bows.

"I am glad to see you; be seated," I say to them.

"We are come to serve you to the best of our power, sir; you have only to command and we will obey."

"That's well. The men who have brought us here with horses and yaks from Yumba-matsen return in the morning to their tents. I shall therefore need horses and

8. ONE OF THE CHIEFS AT HLAGAR.

Sketch by the Author.

yaks and fresh guides who are thoroughly acquainted with the country on the way to the Jukti-la."

"Sir, we are sorry to say that yesterday the Serpun came here from the gold-diggings at Tok-jalung and was in great haste to reach Gartok, so we had to give him all the horses at hand. But if you will put up with yaks for riding and transport, you shall have as many as you wish."

I thankfully accepted the offer of yaks, and in two minutes we were as confidential as friends from childhood. They were ready to talk and had no secrets. I fear, however, that the information would not be so interesting to the reader as to myself, when the Tibetans of Hlagar spoke of their habits and their migrations. From time to time they go off to the salt lake Tsak-tsaka, five days' journey to the north-east. There they break up the salt, pack it in sacks which they fasten on their sheep's backs, and return to Hlagar to rest a while, and then continue their journey for nine days to Gyanima.

The road between Tok-jalung and Gartok is a *tasam* or post-road for riders, as the nomads informed me. Therefore they live all the year in Hlagar, to furnish horses to travellers of importance. Another road runs down the Indus valley past the tent village Pekiya and the mouth of the Langchu river as far as the confluence of the Gartong, the southern branch of the Indus. The Indus has only a slight fall all the way; no cascades and rapids disturb its peaceful course.

At Hlagar, situated at an absolute height of 15,328 feet, the Indus freezes over at the beginning of winter, but the water of permanent springs gurgles under the ice. About midwinter snow sometimes falls so thickly as to form a layer four inches deep. The cold is sharp but not so intense as in Tok-jalung. The summer rains are seldom so heavy that the river overflows its banks and cannot be forded. At the time of our visit the Singi-kamba, as the Indus is called here, flowed in two separate channels, which together discharged 212 cubic feet of water per second. The largest arm was at most 16 inches deep, and the average velocity of the water 26 inches a second.

On the morning of September 22 seven strong yaks grunted in camp 246. Some bore loads, others were to be ridden, and I received a well-rested horse. Rupees chinked in the black paws of the weather-beaten mountaineers, and the nomads of Gyekung set off to return to their home. We bade a friendly farewell to all, and with two young guides splashed through the famous river, so insignificant here near its source, and yonder, where its huge volumes of water roll over the plain at the foot of the Himalayas, so gigantic.

Throwing a glance north-north-west we see the Indus valley disappear among its mountain ranges. Our road to Gartok runs up the side valley Terruk. The sharp-edged porphyritic detritus that covers the ground thickly makes our march very trying. We are therefore glad to find that the valley is short and that the path has imperceptibly mounted to the pass Terruki-la (15,990 feet), where granite is found on the saddle. The wind has free play on the summit, and the pennants of the pass cairn crack like whips.

Here the country is extraordinarily dissected. The next valley, excavated in porphyrite and higher up in granite, leads to another pass, the Sertsoki-la, and beyond a valley trough there is a third, the Dotsa-la (16,552 feet). Camp 247 is pitched not far from its ridge at the Dotsa spring.

A splendid panorama to the south-west and south-south-west attracts the eye irresistibly. Dark and gloomy, but softened by the distance, a mighty range with pyramidal snow-crowned domes rises under the setting sun like the back scene of a theatre. It is the Trans-Himalaya. The sun declines, and the snow-fields, just now glistening like metal, vanish beneath the sharply defined outline of the crest.

The evening glow has paled. Another night creeps on from the east. The moon in splendid majesty pours its cold silvery light over the silent land. The background of the Trans-Himalaya appears only as a faint haze, but the firn-fields illuminated by the moon seem to hover like white clouds on the margin of the horizon.

The wind has fallen and we seem to miss something.

9. A Mendicant Lama.

10 and 11. Friendly Neighbours.

Sketches by the Author.

Deep silence lies over the mountains. My tent looks out on interstellar space, boundless emptiness. My men are still talking in low tones. The yaks tethered to a rope scrape from time to time their horny callosities with their teeth. Sometimes a dog barks and the dung crackles as the fire blazes up again.

But soon all is still. The men are tired and lie down to sleep. The yaks slumber and dream. The dogs curl themselves up, poking their noses under their tails, and the fire goes out from lack of fuel. The silence is oppressive and uncanny. There is something grand in such a night. We sleep as in a temple hall ready to awake on the threshold of eternity.

On September 23 we directed our steps still towards the west-south-west through a rugged weathered country where quartz-porphyrite, porphyry, and basalt form a labyrinth of small ridges, crests, and saddles. Here and there nothing is left of a disintegrated hill of rock but white coarse-grained sand. To the north, however, lies a wide plain covered with detritus which makes it look as dark as the Kevir desert in Persia. Far to the north this plain is bounded by the chains which enclose the valley of the Singi-kamba.

Hleri-kunglung is a dark cone, Lumbo-seju a larger mountain of a reddish colour, both to the south. They raise their heads like signposts or lighthouses above the irregular country, and it is many hours before we have got past them. The Trans-Himalaya rises up in the south-west like a huge wall, looking down with contempt on this weathered and dried-up battlefield where former mountains have struggled in vain against the forces of the atmosphere, and where now only isolated hills of harder rock withstand the process of disintegration that levels all before it.

We make a long march to get across this new desert zone as quickly as possible. The ground is firm enough and is covered with fine gravel and coarse sand; a better riding track could not be wished. We look in vain for water, and animal and vegetable life is also absent; only a contented lizard occasionally darts over the sand. The temperature is 59°. Not a cloud floats in the sky. No wind-driven dust obscures the view. As far as sight can reach, the mountains stand out sharp and clear.

Now the country in the direction we are travelling is as level as a sheet of water. One guide marches in front of the caravan, a ragged, good-natured old man. He has just delighted us with the information that this desert plain will never come to an end, however vigorously we may march. Well, then, we may as well rest for a quarter of an hour and refresh ourselves with the cold milk we have brought with us in a can. I search the horizon with my field-glass. Nothing living can be seen. Wild asses have left no tracks and antelopes no longer show themselves. We are the only living creatures in this desert; even ravens shun it.

We do not follow a path. Where our train moves along no one has yet travelled. The old man at its head says that it is all the same where we walk provided that we do not lose sight of the conical and pyramidal mountains to the south. The scattered footsteps of travellers are soon swept away by the wind. The name of the desert is Chaldi-chüldi.

A dark hill rises in the distance, the end of the day's journey. It seems to be out of reach; as the hours pass by it grows very slowly larger. But patience overcomes all resistance; we ride past the hill and perceive on the other side an oasis, Nyanda-nakbo, where luxuriant grass grows round a small swampy lake. Smoke rises alluringly from the smoke vents of half-a-dozen black tents, and two Indian wool caravans are resting at the spot.

As soon as my tent is ready I send for the Hindus to question them. They come from Rampur and have bought wool in Gertse, which they will carry to Gartok and India on five hundred sheep which they have also obtained in Gertse. They have paid two rupees for each sheep. About sixteen Indian caravans in the year are said to fetch wool from Gertse, and no doubt their profits are large.

The Gova of Nyanda told us of an attack made by robbers two weeks before on a nomad community living in seven tents. Eight scoundrels, armed with knives, sabres

12. My Tent.

and guns, fell upon the village under cover of darkness. The inhabitants did not even attempt to make a defence, but fled into the mountains as hard as they could run. When the band retired they carried off with them everything that was not immovably fixed, all the eatables, all the clothing, thirty pots, cans and dishes, besides 740 sheep and 69 yaks. They left scarcely anything but the bare tents and the dogs. The plundered nomads were living in the direst poverty, wandering through the country and begging from tent to tent. But vengeance was not asleep. Sixteen horsemen were on the track of the robber band. Large herds of yaks and sheep could not possibly disappear among the mountains without leaving a trace. The disturbers of the peace would soon be caught. In such a case there is no talk of pardon. The heads and hands of the felons are sent to Lhasa.

Next morning four women from the pillaged tent village came to me, and were thankful for the presents I was able to give them.

A short day's march through pathless country brought us to the bank of the brook Jukti-loen-chu. This descends from the great pass on the Trans-Himalaya which still separated us from Gartok. There is a choice of three passes, our guide informed us—the Jukti-hloma and Jukti-changma, or the southern and northern Jukti passes, and the Lazar-la lying a little to the north of them. The roads over them soon unite, however, on the southern side of the crest. In the middle of December all three are closed by snow, and then it is impossible for four months to cross the Trans-Himalaya in this neighbourhood.

There are, however, other routes for those travellers who wish to go from Nyanda to the lower Gartong. They follow the foot of the mountains north-westwards and make use of the low sand-covered pass, Pele-rakpa-la, which is never rendered inaccessible by snow. The Lapta-la is a fifth pass lying still farther to the north-west. And lastly the breaching valley of the Indus can always be traversed, and thus all elevations are avoided.

It is plainly evident that the main chain of the Trans-Himalaya, which here rises between the two branches of the Indus, collects almost all the moisture brought by the south-west monsoon which has not been intercepted by the Himalayan region. We have seen ourselves that the land to the north-east of the Trans-Himalaya is a real desert, and we are no longer astonished that the Singi-tsangpo, the head-stream of the Indus, is unable shortly after the end of the rainy season to collect more than 212 cubic feet of water per second.

13. Visitors in my Tent.

14. My Tent being packed.

CHAPTER IV

OVER THE TRANS-HIMALAYA TO GARTOK

THE morning of September 25 broke clear, cold and calm, and the 28 degrees of frost in the night had covered the quiet stretches of the brook with bridges of ice which rested against the stones lying in the bed. But as we moved slowly up the valley between walls and buttresses of granite and porphyry, we soon met more water which the morning sun had released from its fetters on the heights and which made the blocks of ice a night old ring out.

Here and there we see a spring opening with water frozen by the cold. Deserted camping-grounds indicate visits of nomads and pilgrims. Often the pebbles cease for a short distance, and moss and fine alpine grass form a carpet under the hoofs of the animals, over which the caravan moves noiselessly. There marmots have their holes.

The wild yak shuns the desolate region we have left behind us, but here, on the heights of the Trans-Himalaya, he finds a refuge and the pasturage and cold which suit him. A noted hunter from Nyanda had lately wounded a yak bull on the slopes of the Jukti pass and had nearly paid for it with his life. Foaming with rage, the animal had attacked the man with his horns, and the hunter only just succeeded in saving himself by running between two blocks of stone so close together that the yak could not squeeze through.

The valley expands into a steeply rising trough. At Changsang-karpo, where the rock is light-coloured porphyry, the path is charming. A giant seems to have thrown down a cartful of huge blocks to close the way, and the path winds up in zigzags between the blocks to the pass. Often the animals can hardly squeeze through the narrow openings. Some ascents are so steep that it is preferable to walk. Vainly we look upwards, hoping that the cone will soon come to an end, but it continues to rise in front of us, and our train ascends over more piles of blocks, and with repeated interruptions, to the Jukti-la.

Our hired yaks march lightly and nimbly, and I constantly wonder that the horses do not break their legs in the dark, treacherous holes that frequently yawn between the stones. Sometimes we find under a boulder a frozen green-shining pool of fair size. To the south two steeply hanging glacier tongues push their way between dark rocky shoulders on the crest of the range. The ice of the glacier-fall shines like polished steel.

The ascent becomes gentler, but we have still a long way to go north-westwards before we reach two small cairns with fluttering streamers and strings. They are at the top of the Jukti-la. Here the west wind blows half a gale, raw and freezing. The caravan must continue its march at once and move down into the sheltered valley on the other side. I remain behind with three of my men on the pass to determine its height above sea-level. It is my fifth crossing of the Trans-Himalaya. The Jukti-la has indeed been crossed by Mr. Calvert and the pundits, but I wish to obtain an accurate reading of the height with a boiling-point thermometer. All I have to do is to bring the water to the boil with the last drop of spirit that the lamp contains.

Tundup Sonam and Rabsang formed a screen with their skin coats, I put a light to the wick, the water in the vessel began to hum and sing, and soon the mercury rose in the tube of the thermometer. Then the lamp went out. But if I had to wait there all day I would ascertain the height. Never again would fate bring me to the Jukti-la, and if I missed this opportunity I should bitterly regret it afterwards.

Rabsang had good lungs. He had to hurry after the caravan and fetch me some stumps of stearin candle. It is impossible to run at a height where one is subject to

15. NOMADS ON THE MARCH.

16. HALT ON A PASS.

giddiness and among nasty boulders of porphyry, so we had to wait patiently. I had only a waterproof to protect me from the cutting wind. I crouched down with my back to the wind and my body leaning forward, hummed an air, and was nearly frozen. Tundup Sonam and the Tibetan guide squatted close together, and my riding horse stood half asleep with hanging head, his tail and mane flapping in the wind.

An hour passed and the second also came to an end. These hours are terribly long, when you feel the blood slowly congealing in your veins until at length you can hardly move a limb. At last shuffling footsteps were heard, and after a time the boiling-point of water was properly determined. The Jukti-hloma-la is 19,110 feet high, more than 3000 feet higher than Mont Blanc, and it is the second highest pass I crossed on this journey. The highest of all was the Ding-la, 19,308 feet.

After such a contest with the wind we packed up our belongings with satisfaction. I was too stiff to ride and went on foot to loosen my limbs. It is impossible to walk quickly at such a height, for the air is rare and the heart beats as if it would burst. I soon took to the saddle again. The wind was straight in our faces, shooting down as if from a spring-board.

A small side valley opens on our right.

"What is the name of this valley?" I ask the guide, as usual.

"It is the way from the Jukti-changma-la," he replies. Just then there appears one of the men from Rampur, leading the van of the sheep caravan.

"Why did we not take the same road as those men?" I ask.

"The Jukti-changma is partially frozen over and horses cannot cross it, while it is nearly impossible to drive sheep through the boulders of the Jukti-hloma."

The Dunglung-chenmo valley opens on the left, displaying snow-fields and insignificant glaciers in the background. We pass along the right side of the main valley. All the ground is covered with boulders and débris of granite and porphyry which seldom leave room for small patches of grass. The valley leading down from the two Jukti passes is deeply sculptured and is hemmed in by wild rugged walls of rock. It is lifeless as a desert; neither wild nor tame animals are to be seen. The guide tells us, however, that there are many wolves and lynxes in the neighbourhood.

After the awful heights with their cold and wind it was delightful to dismount at Dunglung-sumbo (16,966 feet), where the camp was ready for us and the brazier spread a welcome warmth through my tent. We had descended 2144 feet, and here the valley Lazar opened out, which comes down from the third pass, the Lazar-la.

September 26 was our last day on this excursion. We were to go down to Gartok, where letters from India awaited me and I should at last receive news from Sweden and my home. Therefore we started earlier than usual, and rode at a smart pace down the rather narrow valley. The rocks on the right side fall steeply, and the brook from the three passes murmurs at their foot. After a while the last ridges move aside, and through the portal of the valley mouth is disclosed a view over the great valley through which the southern branch of the Indus, the Gar-chu or Gartong, flows in a north-westerly direction. In the background, beyond the river-bed, rise mighty mountain masses belonging to the Himalayas.

At Hlande-tsogsa four conical stone heaps are piled up beside the road, but they do not breathe a single "Om mani padme hum." The guide says that the place has a bad name as a haunt of evil spirits.

We find ourselves in the valley mouth, where the porphyrite stands in vertical dikes. Now Gartok (14,656 feet) comes in sight, the capital of western Tibet and the residence of the two Garpuns or viceroys. It is a village of the simplest kind, some white and black tents besides several modest huts. But to us, coming from the desolate regions about the source of the Indus, Gartok seems like a capital. Temperature 57°! Delightful after all the cold we have endured during the past days. Tents and huts grow slowly larger, the Jukchi brook vanishes to the left, and we are down on the level valley bottom. Shaggy dogs

17. MY BAGGAGE YAKS.

18. TIBETAN GUIDES.

bark us a greeting, and I am soon sitting in my large comfortable tent, and reading my eagerly expected letters.

But the new equipment and the chests of silver coin I had ordered from India had not arrived. A wearisome time of waiting was in prospect for us. Autumn was come, and winter would soon set in in Tibet, and day after day passed by, but the consignment from India could not be heard of. I read my letters over again and studied the year-old newspaper, not even skipping the advertisements and time-tables. I drew and photographed, sat over my maps and forged new plans. The authorities would prevent me from tracing fully the main lines of the Trans-Himalaya. Well, I would do it. I was forbidden to return into unknown country. I would go there all the same. Winter, too, would place obstacles in my way. Then the new caravan must march through piles of snow to reach its destination, and enable me to fill up the blank space still covering the middle part of the Trans-Himalaya.

In my spare time I visited new and old friends. Chief among the latter was the great merchant, Gulam Razul, for whom I afterwards procured from the Viceroy of India the honorary title of Khan Bahadur. It was he who arranged my new caravan, providing me with men as well as animals and provisions. He had several roomy tents in Gartok, furnished with carpets and divans and heated with iron stoves. They were full of bales of cloth, and their walls were lined with large iron-bound chests containing Chinese silver coins, Indian rupees, gold-dust, and turquoises. A smaller tent was his mosque wherein he spent his hours of prayer. Round the tents ran a wall of brick-tea sewed up in bales. Every bale was worth 70 rupees and he had hundreds of them.

Gulam Razul told me various interesting details of his trade. His caravans bring beads, coral, and turquoise, English cotton goods and other wares to the markets in Gartok and Gyanima and to Lhasa. Carpets, felt rugs, Russian woollen materials, silk fabrics, and nephrite are purchased in Eastern Turkestan, and are transported over the Karakorum to Leh and Tibet. From Lhasa he imports brick-tea, Tibetan wool manufactures, Lamaist drugs, and other goods into Ladak. In Tok-jalung he buys gold-dust, which is subsequently sold again in Leh and Lhasa. During the fairs in Gartok and Gyanima, which are held in the three summer months, Gulam Razul sells goods to the value of 25,000 rupees. His exports to Lhasa amount to 40,000 rupees, and his imports from there to 35,000. Gulam Razul's family holds the Lopchak monopoly, a privilege of trade between Kashmir and Lhasa, in which is included free transport on Tibetan territory. The Tibetans enjoy a similar monopoly in the opposite direction. The distance from Leh to Gartok is reckoned at twenty-two caravan days' marches, from Gartok to Shigatse forty-five, and thence to Lhasa eleven.

Smaller traders from Ladak resort to Gartok with dried apricots and raisins, which they transport on asses, and barter for sheep's wool.

Dava Shah was a prominent merchant from Leh who was about to travel on to Lhasa. He visited me in my tent and asked if he might lend me 3000 rupees in cash, which made his chests heavy. But I had already sent for money to India and had therefore no need to avail myself of his kindness. He would have been glad to avoid the risk and trouble of transport, and he knew that the loan would be repaid to the last anna.

One day I betook myself to the small temple of Gartok, the Gar-yarsa-gompa, a cloister with eight monks under the control of Tashi-gang. The temple hall is a small dark closet. A red-painted *tanka* hangs before the altar and the statue of the Palden Hlamo is hidden among bunches of ribands and rags. The water in the metal cups on the altar table was frozen to the bottom; no other offerings are presented to the gods in this cold sanctuary.

It was much more comfortable in Gulam Razul's dwelling. He sat on a divan in the middle of his large tent, smoking his silver-studded narghileh, and receiving his guests with amiable dignity. We spoke Persian, joked and laughed heartily. Tea was handed round in Chinese porcelain cups, and the raisins, apricots, and slices of bread which accompanied it on pewter plates from Leh. One faggot after another was thrust into the stove, which

19. Camp in the Trans-Himalaya.

20. A Riding Yak.

became glowing red and crackled, spreading an invigorating heat through the tent. Some fat, greasy, good-tempered traders from Lhasa squatted in a corner arranging their silver *tengas* in piles for counting. The next day they were returning to the holy city, and now they were preparing to pay their debts before leaving. Two Hindus were likewise waiting on the great pasha of Gartok. They were extreme revolutionists, and poured forth the vials of their wrath on the English in India. I let them chatter for a time and then gave it them hot and strong, and they begged me earnestly not, for heaven's sake, to betray their rash speech. Political babblers, who call themselves heralds of freedom, are the same in all lands.

In these days of expectant waiting we found relief even in folklore and legends. In ancient times a lama of the Pembo sect and an orthodox lama met one day at the foot of Kang-rinpoche, the holy mountain. There they made a bet together. The one who should reach the summit of the mountain when the sun gilded the peak on the following morning should for ever retain possession of Kang-rinpoche. The heretical lama started at once up the southern flank, while the other lay down to sleep. When day dawned his servant perceived his master's rival close to the summit and waked the sleeping monk. He answered with a smile, "Keep calm, let the sun rise first." And when the sun appeared above the horizon the orthodox lama ascended on a sunbeam to the summit, while the Pembo lama was floundering painfully through the firn snow.

A dark vertical line of bare rock is still visible in the snow on the southern flank of the mountain. It shows the track of the heretic and does not reach quite to the top. For as the climber was approaching his goal he threw a glance up to the apex of the mountain and saw the other lama standing on it. He was so astounded that he fell down the slope, losing his prayer-drum, which his rival seized to play an accompaniment to his song of triumph. The defeated monk humbled himself, and begged his successful rival to give him at least a souvenir of the holy mountain. The victor took a handful of snow from Kang-rinpoche and threw it to the summit of the Pundi mountain, which stands to the north of Tso-mavang. The Pembo lama went thither, and since that time there has always been a small patch of snow on the Pundi. When this snow disappears at the end of time, then will the snow mantle of Kang-rinpoche also melt away and the earth will be destroyed.

In Gar-yarsa, where we were staying, the two Garpuns dwell only in summer. In winter they live at Gar-gunsa, a few short days' journey down-stream. Though the difference of height is only 591 feet, Gar-gunsa (14,065) has a much milder climate and, as a rule, little snow.

I determined for the sake of a change to remove my camp to Gar-gunsa. I paid no farewell visits to the viceroys. One of them was ill and the other had not deigned to return my visit on arrival. He had, however, to provide me with yaks of burden, and two of his men were to accompany me all the way to the frontier of Ladak, to see that I did not run off along forbidden roads.

It is pleasant to pack up my things, shake the dust off my feet, mount my horse and ride away from the small, miserable windy Gartok, where soon only two families will be left to pass the winter in their huts.

Not far from the town of Gartok we ride through the numerous channels of the Gartong. Two of its arms are quite small, one of them is frozen to the bottom and the horses slither over the ice, while the others still fight against the cold of night, and have only strips of ice along their banks. The bed is broad, though at this late season it contains little water. But we perceive that it can hold a considerable stream when abundant rain falls in late summer. Along the left bank runs an erosion terrace 13 feet high. The road passes along the top and the river vanishes for a time from our sight.

The valley is broad and grand. On the right we have the Trans-Himalaya, on the left the Tibetan slopes of the Himalayas. Small, boldly excavated side valleys display their portals on both sides. Flat cones of rubbish spread out like fans from their openings, and shallow runnels, now dry, wind downwards to the river.

21. BAGGAGE YAKS.

The valley contracts. The Himalayas and the Trans-Himalaya stretch out hands to each other. A narrow passage appears in front of us which the river has carved out. This passage is called Nima-lung, and here we pitch our tents. Here all the arms of the river are collected into a single channel, and the water glides between terraces 60 and 100 feet high, as it is slowly sucked into the narrows. Where the river again divides below these narrows I might drift with the current down to Gar-gunsa. The young Eurasian, Alexander Robert, who had waited for me at Gartok, had become a skilful boatman on the holy lake. He could steer the boat while I marked down the course of the stream on my map. A map survey of the valley had been made by Englishmen, but the river with all its windings was not drawn on it.

We would first make a short trial trip. The boat was put together and manned, and the current carried us slowly and easily towards the narrow gorge. But at the entrance there was a change. Here we darted like an arrow past the banks and entered the rapids; now it was too late to change our minds, and we had to go on as the water was sucked in as into a funnel. We warded off the boat with oars from the threatening blocks covered with smooth or foaming bells of clear water. In one sharp bend the boat could not turn quickly enough with the current and rushed at full speed on to a humpy block of stone where we were within an ace of capsizing. But before we were aware of our danger the stream had released the stern of the boat and we were again afloat rushing madly through the wild gorge.

Now we heard the roar of a rapid. We tried with all our might to hold back the boat with the oars, but the current was too strong, and we neared the danger at a giddy speed. One glance sufficed to convince us that it was impossible to thread our way safely through the blocks which formed a barrier all across the bed. This waterway was not made for canvas boats. The boat would either be overturned or torn to pieces. Just above the rapids the current was less rapid and gave us time to force the boat with firm thrusts behind a block at the bank, whereupon Robert jumped into the water and drew our small craft ashore. This much our trial trip had taught us, that it was wisest to keep on dry land for the present.

During the night we posted a strong watch, for wolves swarmed in this country, and at Gartok one of our mules had fallen a victim to a pack of Isegrims.

22. CROSSING A RIVER.

23. ON THE WAY TO CHUSHUL.

CHAPTER V

TO THE CONFLUENCE OF THE INDUS ARMS

THE road from Nima-lung winds through dry clefts between rocky hills up to the Chagring-la, a small swell on which a streamer pole is set up on a heap of stones. The view from it is hardly more extensive than from any other point in the valley. Far to the south-east are still seen the mighty mountains standing beyond Gartok, and to the north-west we perceive a succession of spurs which we shall pass one after another. The valley is now broad and open, and the Gar-chu, beside which we are travelling, does not glide so noiselessly as farther up, but murmurs gently and forms rapids which indicate a greater fall.

The valley lies before us in solemn stillness as on a Sunday ; men and herds are absent, and all is deadly quiet and as deserted as though a hostile army had marched plundering through the country. A *mani* wall and the road to Ladak are the only signs left by human hands and feet. At Namru alone meagre bushes grow among rank grass, and a field on which barley is sown in favourable years is the first specimen of agriculture we have seen in western Tibet.

In the background of the Shinkar side valley rises a dark mountain mass with snow-covered summits—a passing glimpse of the huge crest which we shall follow to Ladak and which has been named the Ladak range by English topographers. It forms the watershed between the Indus and the Sutlej. In former times its slopes and steep walls have been washed by tremendous floods of rain, as is proved by river terraces 160 feet high which we notice at the mouth of the Shinkar valley.

Chusan, the "warm water," is a name we frequently meet with in Tibet. Here also a group of hot springs bubble out of the ground close to the left bank of the Gar-chu and 6 feet above the surface of the river. One of them forms a small open basin, the clear water bubbling up at its bottom; it has a temperature of 141°. At the orifice of another spring the water is boiling, and therefore must be heated to more than 212°. A third shoots up like a tiny geyser, and its eruptions follow one another at intervals of a minute. The water is collected from all sides by small runnels into a large basin, in which invalids bathe to restore their health. A stone wall affords protection against the wind, and another serves as a dressing-room. We encamp just beyond the springs on the depastured meadow of Luma-ngoma (camp 253).

The valley bottom stretches before us as level as a floor as we move on next day towards the north-west. The ruins of two huts are the old Gar-gunsa, the guide says. At one time the river of a side valley flooded the place, and Gar-gunsa was therefore removed farther down the stream. We see its tents and fences of brushwood in the distance, but it is a long way to it over an extensive plain covered here with sand, there with grass, with bushes or swampy patches. Here are grazing a number of yaks and horses, and we perceive that the winter migration from Gartok has commenced.

In Gar-gunsa my long period of waiting came at last to an end. The post came from India with provisions, money, arms, and ammunition, and on November 9 we were able to start for Ladak.

Now the caravan is again large and imposing and winds like a dark snake over the grey ground. In Gar-gunsa I bought mules from Gulam Razul. They are allowed to travel without loads that they may save up their strength for the hard winter campaign which awaits them in the north. Hired yaks carry all our baggage, and the Tibetan escort, two horsemen of the Garpuns' guard at Gartok, arrange everything at the camping places. They really

24. THE LADAK RANGE SOUTH OF THE INDUS.

25. VIEW NORTH-WESTWARDS FROM THE INDUS VALLEY.

accompany us to watch our movements, but I do not mind that, so long as we remain on the great high-road, and I have no intention of giving them any trouble—at least not for the present.

I ride my little Ladaki horse, which after the long rest is fresh and plump. Our four-legged escort consists of a whole pack of dogs of all kinds, our own caravan dogs and other freebooters and tramps which have made friends with them in Gartok.

The valley slopes down imperceptibly to the eye; no obstacles come in our way, and the ground consists of the finest dust, on which grow tall yellow hard grass and *ombo* bushes peeled by the early winter. We therefore make quicker progress than usual. Two mules carry bells and sleigh-bells, which tinkle merrily to their tripping steps; from time to time are heard the shouts of the drivers, horses neigh, yaks grunt, the dogs dart like rockets after startled hares, and I draw the monotonous road to Ladak on the map sheet in front of me.

Here stands a solitary tent, there two *mani* walls remind the passer-by of the wanderings beyond the valley of the shadow of death, and here again come shaggy yaks carrying fuel to Gar-gunsa, where the two Garpuns are expected to arrive this evening.

The train comes to a halt. Ah! here are two branches of the river in front of us, frozen hard as stone. A path on the ice is strewn with sand and then we move on again. The road crosses the valley to the foot of the mountain on the left side, where some lively wild asses look down on us with curiosity from the top of a flat cone of detritus at the mouth of a transverse valley. The level bottom of the main valley has a yellowish tinge from the strips of meadow between the arms of the river, and here and there is a dark patch of bushes. The weather is splendid, clouds and winds have taken a holiday, summer still lingers in the sun, but my right foot, which is always in the shadow of the horse, is as cold as an icicle.

Tibetans have set up their tents at the spring Chiu, and we let our horses loose to graze, but at sunset they will be again tethered in camp. The neighbourhood is noted for wolves which attack cattle in packs. In the night gun-shots and loud cries are heard near at hand; some of our men are out driving off a pack of Isegrims. The night before a wild ass dashed into our camp mad with fright and tried to hide himself among our animals. His upper lip was torn off and red froth lay round his mouth; evidently he had only just escaped with his life. There are said to be two kinds of wolf in this country, one with a light grey, almost white, coat, the other dark grey.

From the Chiu spring we catch sight to the north-east of the gradually ascending flat pass Pele-rakpa-la, of which we have heard before. On the farther side lies the valley of the Lang-chu river.

At night my men were in high spirits. Grand fires flamed and crackled among the copses of *ombo* bushes, and the men, wrapped in their sheepskins, sat in groups as close as possible to the flickering fire. The brown weather-beaten faces beamed with pleasure at the thought that Ladak was near. In the bright yellow and red light the half-wild figures stood out sharply against the black night behind them. We felt that winter had laid its hand in earnest on the earth. By nine o'clock the temperature had fallen to 2.1°; terrible cold after the warm day. The air was perfectly still, the flame of my lamp showed not the slightest flicker, the tent flap hung limp and motionless, and the smoke of the camp-fires rose straight as a candle up towards the stars. The sickle of the moon hovered above the mountains in a cold blue winter sky; we should have light nights all the way to Ladak.

When I came out into the bright morning light after 41.8° of frost in the night, all the bushes and grass stalks, tents, saddles, and chests, nay, even the yaks and horses, were covered with the whitest rime. I felt as though everything had turned into marble and would crack like glass if it were too roughly handled. But the sun soon destroyed the illusion, and when we continued our journey over the hard frozen ground, the landscape had assumed its usual appearance. The belt of vegetation remained on the right while the path ran over barren land bestrewn all over with granite débris. Here stood a *mani* wall, the

26. Thakur Jai Chand (sitting), the English Agent in Gartok, with some of his Servants.

27. Camp at Gar-gunsa.

28. The Indus covered with Ice.

letters cut out in its granite slabs silently proclaiming the holy words.

Farther on the ground becomes sandy and lumpy owing to the numerous tufts of grass, and the road skirts the foot of the screes of the Ladak chain. These cones spread out from the mouths of side valleys and succeed one another on either side of the main valley alternately as far as the sight can reach. Between their lowest margins the breadth of the level valley bottom is about 6 to 9 miles. The dark rocky gables which the Ladak chain sends out to the main valley form an endless perspective fading away in ever lighter and more airy tints in the far distance. Between them yawn the short narrow and gloomy ravines of the transverse valleys. Up on the left bank terrace we are at a higher level than the river and therefore have a good view of its winding course. On the other side rise the more hilly heights of the Trans-Himalaya, which are far lower than those of the Ladak chain. Therefore the rubbish cones also of the Trans-Himalayan side valleys are smaller. Such is the scene day after day. But these chains are both important main features of the physical geography of Tibet; the Ladak chain on account of the part it plays as a watershed, and the Trans-Himalaya as the true boundary range of the elevated country.

The main valley is singularly straight. Therefore, from a high detritus cone the sight can sweep far to the north-west, far beyond Demchok and the western boundary of Tibet to the pink and brownish-red mountains which stand in Ladak. Beyond these mountains appear other summits in light steel-blue tones which we can only just perceive. In the foreground, and yet a good day's journey off, the monastery Tashi-gang is enthroned on a small rock in the midst of the valley. The air is so clear that distances appear insignificant. Lastly, we descry to the right the valley through which the Singi-kamba, the Indus proper, emerges from the mountains to join the Gar-chu. There the main valley expands into quite a plain tinged yellow by grass and spotted brown by bushes.

We soon reach the small village Langmar, where six or

seven families dwell in black tents, protected from wind and cold by brushwood fences. To guard against the evil spirits which live in the air their dwellings are adorned with poles, strings, and streamers.

Scarcely has the sun gone down in the west when the night frost comes creeping on and penetrates everywhere. Then the ink freezes in my pen as I sit cross-legged on my bed entering my observations in my diary. Then the fires burn more briskly and a freshly filled brazier is more frequently brought into the tent. The thermometer sank in the night before November 11 to $-12.6°$.

On this day we made only a short march. Its goal was the point where the two head-waters of the Indus flow together. The Gartong or Gar-chu streams along slowly and quietly, but the Singi-kamba rushes furiously and gleefully out of its gate in the Trans-Himalaya. We pitched camp 256 on the grassy bank on the left side of the Gartong. I had a beautiful and uncommon view over large ice-covered expanses of water.

Now my task was to measure the two rivers. Perhaps the reader may think such work superfluous and uninteresting. But there he is mistaken. A hundred years ago only the Gartong arm was known and was supposed to be the true source-stream of the Indus. Afterwards a more northern river, the Singi-kamba, was heard of, but some fifty years ago opinions were much divided as to which of the two rivers should be considered the main stream and which the tributary. In 1867 it was proved by Montgomerie's pundits that the Singi-kamba was considerably longer than the Gartong. But the mere length of the course is not decisive. The volume of water is at least as important. However, the example of the Tibetans was followed at that time, and the Singi-kamba was allowed to be the source-stream of the Indus. No exact measurement was undertaken. Therefore, I pitched my tents on November 11, 1907, at the confluence of the two Indus arms.

I could see that no easy task was before me, for the Gartong was fast frozen over save for a narrow channel in the middle. An opening was hacked out in the ice on

29. Little Puppy keeps Guard.

30. The Village of Langmar.

31. Demchok.

our bank and then from the boat we attacked the ice sheet with spades and axes. We wanted an open passage across the river that we might measure the depth and velocity without difficulty. Scarcely was our channel finished before huge ice-blocks came down from above, stopping up the passage worse than before. The boat also was nearly torn to rags.

A change of scene occurred at noon. The ice-drift diminished, the blocks in the choked passage began to press and rub together, and the whole mass set itself in motion with a grinding roar and floated off down-stream. Where the bed was narrowest and the current swiftest the surface was almost free of ice. In a moment a rope was stretched across the river, and I measured the depth at eight points at equal distances apart, and the velocity at the surface, at the bottom, and half way down. The results showed that the Gartong was 190 feet broad, had a mean depth of 15.9 inches and a maximum of 30.7, flowed at an average rate of 11 inches a second, and discharged 231 cubic feet of water per second. A small branch behind a mud-bank brought the volume of water up to 235.5 cubic feet.

The Singi-kamba was divided into two arms near the confluence, and it seemed as if this river must form an extensive delta after heavy rainfall, whereas the Gartong is always confined to a narrow trench. The upper branch of the Singi-kamba had the following dimensions: breadth 30 yards; average depth 12 inches; maximum depth 20 inches; average velocity 26.7 inches, and the volume of water 200 cubic feet, per second. The dimensions of the lower arm were: breadth 107¼ feet; mean depth 11⅛ inches; maximum depth 19 inches; average velocity 17¼ inches, and discharge 145 cubic feet, a second. The whole river therefore discharges 345 cubic feet of water, or 110 more than the Gartong.

Accordingly the Singi-kamba, the Lion river, is not only the longer but also the more voluminous of the two head-streams, and the problem is solved. Certainly it may be suggested that the dimensions given above only apply to late autumn and winter, for in summer and especially during the rainy season very different conditions may prevail. No doubt this is the case. The rainfall diminishes north-eastwards, and therefore more rain falls in the basin of the Gartong than in that of the Singi-kamba, which may be robbed of moisture by the Trans-Himalaya. The spring flood consequent on the melting of the snows is also greater in the Gartong. How often irregularities must occur in consequence of the direction of the wind and the capricious variations of temperature! In the meantime we may consider it probable that the Gartong carries during the whole year more water than the Singi-kamba, but we have at least discovered that the Singi-kamba is the larger stream when no disturbing influences are at work, when there is no precipitation, and when the temperatures in the two river basins may be considered identical.

The Singi-kamba traverses the Trans-Himalaya in a breached valley, while the Gartong flows in a tectonic valley between huge folded mountains. Therefore it is the latter which determines the direction of the united Indus. From Gar-gunsa the Gartong skirts the foot of the mountains on the right side of the valley, but just at the confluence the Singi-kamba forces it over to the left side. The mud delta of the Singi-kamba fixes the position of the confluence.

After 25 degrees of frost in the night the river was covered next morning with a thin sheet of ice. Only a few small channels remained open, through which the current carried quantities of porous ice-blocks, which rang clearly as they struck the ice attached to the banks. Over the top of the flat tongue of land between the two rivers we saw the ice of the Singi-kamba hurrying down to the Gartong. Here the name Gartong is lost in the waves of its comrade, for the Tibetans name the Indus, as far as they know its course north-westwards, the Singi-kamba or Singi-tsangpo, the river of the Lion.

We rested here a day. In the afternoon all the shore ice and all the ground ice vanished, but quite by seven o'clock more blocks came down, and at night the ice made a noise like a sugar saw. The landscape presented a curious spectacle in the moonshine. The mountains under

32. ROBERT'S TRIAL TRIP ON THE INDUS.

33. AT THE CONFLUENCE OF THE TWO INDUS ARMS.

34. THE INDUS VALLEY AT TASHI-GANG.

the moon were inky black profiles, the illuminated cliffs just opposite only faintly perceptible. The whole valley bottom between the two seemed to be full of water, and the drift-ice glided along like a moving pavement of glass sherds and glazed porcelain.

CHAPTER VI

IN DARK, DANK CLOISTER WALLS

On November 13 our train proceeds farther down the Indus valley, which has such a slight fall that the eye cannot perceive it. The river therefore flows slowly and peacefully, and its considerable breadth makes it look larger than it really is. Beyond the town of Leh it contracts in its narrow valley, and then becomes deep and impetuous.

Numerous springs well up along the road. Their rivulets are frozen up, and the ice sheets spread over the lumpy withered meadows. Occasionally a field appears surrounded by a stone wall and destined for barley cultivation, and there is no lack of *mani* rows with their prayers in stone. What is wanting in this terribly sparsely peopled and poor country, next neighbour to the fertile India, is human beings.

Right in front of us the monastery Tashi-gang gradually grows larger. Its walls are erected on the top of an isolated rock of solid porphyrite, which crops up from the bottom of the Indus valley like an island drawn out from north to south. As a whole it vividly reminds me of the village Yezdikast in Persia, and the fortified rock villages in Transcaucasia. The best view of the monastery buildings is from the east, and here, at the foot of the hill, lies the small wretched village of Tashi-gang, with its twenty low stone huts roofed with brushwood.

While the tents were being set up on the left bank of the Indus, I took a walk round the singular lama fortress. Its dirty greyish-yellow and red walls slope slightly inwards; up under the eaves runs a border of the colour of hawthorn blossoms. The windows, too, have frames coloured red. The *lhakang*, or hall of the gods, is a little higher than the other buildings, and on its roof flutter the usual bunches of streamers and all the decorations that pacify the spirits of the air, fend off evil powers, and bring peace to the abode of the gods.

Before the eastern façade of the temple a long fine *mani* wall is erected; on the short side stand two round free-standing towers, and here and there are seen red and grey *chhortens*. The whole is surrounded by a moat 10 feet deep, interrupted only on the east where communication with the village is kept open. On the same side stands the main portal. It gives access to a court full of rubbish, offal, and savage, dirty dogs. A second open space is like the court of a Turkish caravanserai with two storeys of verandahs resting on wooden pillars. The *lhakang* has a small court of its own, also surrounded with verandahs and with small panels adorned with paintings.

All the monks that were at home, perhaps about twenty, followed at my heels, a silent troop, in the usual garments like Roman togas. Several faces were still rosy red, but many had lost their original complexion and were turning black under the influence of tea and butter, dirt, grease, and poverty.

As I mounted the steps to the temple hall the monks woke up, calling out to me that the hall was not open to strangers, and could not be shown without permission from the lords of Gartok. If I forced my way in, I should arouse the anger of the gods, and misfortune would befall Tashi-gang. Neither could I inspect the *manekang*, the room with the large prayer-mill, or the storeroom where the religious masquerade dresses and the drums, trombones, and cymbals are kept, for the prior had the keys and he was then staying at Gartok.

It was vain to tell them that I had already been admitted without difficulty into about thirty convents in Tibet.

"Well, then," they retorted, "as Tashi-gang is much the same as all the others you can very well do without seeing it." They were quite right—I should lose nothing by not seeing Tashi-gang.

"If you come again to-morrow, the fifty monks of the monastery will drive you off," declared a tall lama.

"You said just now that there were only twenty-five monks in Tashi-gang," I replied, and I rode down to my camp, which now stood ready on the river bank 200 yards from the monastery.

In the twilight my Ladakis started a tremendous fight with the villagers and the priests. Two of my men had asked to be allowed to buy straw for our mules, but the headman of the village had refused without any reasonable excuse. Then the Ladakis held a council of war, armed themselves with bludgeons and tent-poles, and moved out in close order against the inhabitants of Tashi-gang. I was just writing in my tent when I heard loud shouts and war-whoops from the village. I went out with my field-glass to find out what was the matter. The fight was in full swing, and it looked really serious. Stones rained down, clubs whistled through the air, and the sons of Ladak and Tibet beat one another heartily in a closely packed crowd, which now and then disappeared in a cloud of dust. It would have been a pity to disturb them while they were so hard at work. Sometimes a man was shot head foremost out of the struggling throng, but he soon got up and plunged again into the mêlée. After they had pounded one another at close quarters for three-quarters of an hour they seemed to grow tired of the game, for they separated into smaller groups, which had an inexhaustible store of abusive terms at their command. At length peace was restored and the whole party marched to our camp.

The heroes, breathless, dripping with perspiration and with clothes torn, took up a position in front of my tent, each side shouting out its complaints and trying to drown the voices of the other. My men from Ladak maintained that the Tibetans had begun the quarrel, but the latter swore by all the gods of Tashi-gang that the strangers had attacked them with blows and buffets. I proposed to them that they should drink tea and rest an hour, and then settle

36. Gar-gunsa Monastery.

37. Chhorten near Tashi-gang.

38. Tashi-gang Monastery.

the dispute by another combat in the moonlight. The side that was then victorious should be held to be in the right, and should receive its reward. But they had no stomach for this. They stood confounded and went away. A Tibetan with a bloody head was given a plaster for his wound, and a rupee was slipped into his hand. The feud had the excellent result that all the mules got straw.

There is a slight touch of psychology in this incident so trifling in itself. Rabsang had been most violent, for he was the strongest and wildest, and had no proper feeling. Therefore he got what he deserved when I scolded my men.

"As long as we were in the heart of Tibet," I said to them, "you were always peaceable and well-behaved and did no harm to the Tibetans. But now, when we are on the frontier, at the last village but one and the very last monastery, you do not control yourselves at all, but behave like robbers."

"Sahib," answered Rabsang for himself and his comrades, "we have so often been annoyed when the Tibetans have stopped you, that we have watched for an opportunity of giving them a thorough hiding for once."

"Why should the poor people of Tashi-gang suffer for the sins of others? Here no road has been closed to us, and no harm has been done to us. Oh no, I know you. Right in Tibet you dared not make a commotion, but here on the frontier of Ladak, and in a small miserable village, you have plucked up courage."

"Sahib," stammered Rabsang, "it was our last opportunity, and the main thing was that the people were Tibetans."

"You are cowardly fellows, nothing else. Off with you!"

So the heroes retired to their camp-fires where they sat together till late in the night boasting of their exploits. None omitted to tell the others how many Tibetans he had struck and where.

Whether the scrimmage had made a deep impression on the monks, or whether other influences had soothed their tempers, at any rate I was informed next morning that

I should be welcomed in the monastery—without Ladakis, but I must make haste that I might look into the temple hall while the sun was still shining on the façade, for only from the threshold might I encounter the gaze of the gods.

I entered the small court. On the stone steps and in the anteroom with black draperies stood all the monks like a guard. I asked them to move aside a little that I might see the spirit kings, and the different pictures of other temple towns which decorated the outside walls.

Grey curtains hung before the doors. Seriously and hesitatingly an elderly monk came forward to draw them aside. The massive doors, with their quaint brass mounts and iron rings, were fastened, but the monk had brought the key and he opened the ponderous lock. After he had pointed out the place on the threshold where I was to crouch down, he made the doors turn on their creaking hinges, and the darkness of the holy of holies yawned before me.

I shook my head. The monk smiled and said, "Patience." Then some beams of light appeared, and when I had become accustomed to the scanty illumination I was able to distinguish the details. It was a small temple hall well kept with all its simplicity. A forest of painted *tanka* cloths with images of the gods hung down from the roof, reminding me of regimental colours in an arsenal, or of the trophies in an armoury. The *tankas* deepened the gloom of the interior.

As usual, an aisle passes through the hall up to the altar, bordered on either side by four red pillars draped with ribands and coloured hangings. There, too, are placed red divans on which the monks sit when they perform the Lamaistic service, and murmur the daily-repeated prayers. At the end of the aisle a pyramidal stand faces the altar full of offering-bowls of brass and small lamps fed with lumps of butter, their flickering flames struggling vainly with the darkness.

Yigde is the name of the principal god whose praises are sung in this sanctuary. He surmounts the altar, painted on a *tanka*, and his countenance is buried in a thicket of votive scarves called *kadakhs*. Beside him, to the left of the spectator, stands a cast statue of the reformer, Tsong Kapa, with mild, dreamy features. On the right the unfathomable scriptures are stored on firm bookshelves. The *lhakang* of Tashi-gang, here called *tsokang*, is only scantily furnished with idols, but the atmosphere is dark and mystical, such as is generally characteristic of lama worship.

When the monks murmur their prayers in the *lhakang* in a half-singing tone and at a bewildering rate, a lama sits in the *manekang* turning the great prayer-mill, which sends forth from its interior innumerable "Om mani padme hums" to plead for the mercy of the eternal powers.

The tea-kettle boils in the kitchen on the hearth of masonry, and the ecclesiastical cooks appear like mist forms through the thick clouds of steam. In the court before the kitchen-door stands a *hla-tamchen* or faggot, in which every twig is hung with coloured strips and every fragment bears the holy syllables. The bundle is housed in a cubical niche, its walls decorated with gaudy and inferior paintings.

The lama superior of Tashi-gang bears the title of *Umsed*, which properly signifies leader of the choir. He had come here three years before from the large monastery Sera near Lhasa, and he had still to complete a year's service in far western Tibet. The rest of the brotherhood are recruited in Totling, Chumurti, and other districts in the neighbourhood. I was told that Tashi-gang formerly belonged to Ladak, but that not long previously an exchange had been effected, in consequence of which Tashi-gang is now under the authority of Sera while the Maharaja of Kashmir has acquired some kind of right of possession over Misser lying between Gartok and the Rakas-tal.

"How do your monks get their living?" I asked.

"We hire out a hundred yaks and as many sheep for transport, and, besides, the Garpuns are bound to provide us with all the parched barley (*tsamba*) we require."

"Then you live peacefully and free from care?"

"No; Tashi-gang has seen better days, and has had larger property. Then we had the means necessary for keeping up our buildings. Now we receive barley sufficient to maintain ourselves, and we have to let the monastery fall into decay. The holy Yigde is a cruel, hard-hearted god, and his service must never be neglected ; he must be constantly appeased. The viceroys fear his power and visit him annually with offerings. Nor do they neglect their duty towards us, the servants of the god."

The outward decay gives Tashi-gang the appearance of a mediæval castle which is proudly enthroned on its rock, something between a strong fortress and a ruin, a memorial of a departed age. With every year that passes over the stronghold of the god Yigde, decay leaves new seams and gaps in the walls. From the broad frieze up above under the eaves blood-red streaks run down to the ground below. They are the work of the summer rains, which have so disfigured the walls that here they are brick red and there are tinged with pink. Here and there the plaster has been removed, and chips of stone have fallen ; in this case it is weathering, the change from burning sunshine to cold cutting frost, which has brought the cloister walls a step farther on the way to destruction. The streamers on the roof flutter in tatters that can hardly hold together ; there it is the wind that lords it over the home of the gods.

A small number of windows and a few loopholes pierce the wall facing west. On the southern end the windows are arranged unsymmetrically, and a small balcony hangs high above the ground, a quiet peaceful resort in this otherwise dismal, gloomy cloister. Here is the *labrang*, where the abbot dwells.

The whole monastery is formed of a long, irregular collection of buildings and walls enclosing courts also of a long shape. They are separated from one another by small internal walls, and are also connected by doors usually approached by steps, for the surface of the rock is uneven. In the peripheral buildings are the cells of the monks, and the whole edifice is dominated by the *lhakang*, the hall of the gods, on a polygonal ground-plan.

The mountains to the north-east and south-west rise out of the valley in majestic imposing masses, in steps,

39. CAMP IN THE INDUS VALLEY.

40. IN GAR-GUNSA. MY SERVANT RABSANG IN THE FOREGROUND.

41. CAMP ON THE INDUS.

42. CAMP IN DEMCHOK.

ridges, and summits. Tinted violet and yellowish-brown, their outlines are sharply and vividly defined at all hours of the day. At sunset the monastery glows bright yellow. Then the shadows creep up the flanks until the highest pinnacles shine in purple gleams. The Indus valley, upwards in the direction of Gartok and downwards towards Ladak, presents a boundless perspective. The appalling distances make one take deeper breaths, and one experiences an oppressive feeling of being shut in between two immense folds of the earth's crust—the Himalayas and the Trans-Himalaya.

Owing to its breadth and its slow fall the river has a grand appearance. We descend from the heights behind on our way north-westwards, and therefore there is little drift-ice, only a small border here and there along the bank. At some places wild ducks are heard quacking, but the wild geese have at this season no taste for Tibet, and they will not change their abode again this year.

The bright scene in clear colours and sharp contours became blurred in the afternoon owing to a violent storm from the west, which rushed down on the valley, stirring up great clouds of dust. The monastery looked as shadowy as a ghostly castle through the mist, the surface of the river rose in white foaming billows, and the ripples beat solemnly against the bank.

So ended our second day at Tashi-gang. A liberal present of silver rupees was distributed among the monks, silver rupees with the crowned head of the queen—they would not take the rupees with the uncrowned king's head. I had to make amends in this way for the misbehaviour of my Ladakis on the previous evening, and, moreover, I pitied the dreadful solitude of the priests in their greyish-red prison walls. Did an unlucky fate compel me to take monkish vows and spend my days in Tashi-gang, I should die of weariness and disgust at the unutterable dogmas opposed to freedom of thought of any kind. In the cavernous darkness of the temple hall the wicks of the butter lamps smoke while the sun shines outside. I should even grow tired of the view from the sunlighted balcony. The freedom of the Himalayas and the wild Sutlej valley to the south would irresistibly arouse my longing. In summer it would be all very well, when the liberated water of the Indus flows down the valley on its way to the sea. But what of winter, when the river is frozen over and silent, when snowstorms howl mournfully round the corners of the cloister buildings, and when the wind screams and whistles in the window openings as though ghosts and hobgoblins were at play?

1

2

3

4

43. THE MONASTERY TASHI-GANG.

1. From the West.
2. From the South.
3. From the East-South-East.
4. From the North.

Sketches by the Author.

CHAPTER VII

THE LAST DAYS ON THE INDUS

WHITE wreaths and atolls of ice covered half the river on the morning of November 15. The air was clear and calm, not a breath ruffled the water of the Indus, on which sluggish eddies formed pleasing designs as they revolved down to an unknown destination. Everything tempted me to a boat voyage, and I would let the proud stream carry me all the way to the next camping-ground. I myself took my seat in the front half of the boat, and drew every bend we passed on my map. In the stern half Robert was responsible for the oars and the management of the boat. Rabsang and Tundup Sonam accompanied us on the bank with the horses.

Where the river is broadest the ice drifts down noiselessly and slowly. In the narrower windings the floating blocks bump against the bank, and then a scraping noise is heard again. Above us rise the crests of the lofty mountains, and the land is still and peaceful. The temple fort of Tashi-gang on its hill is visible for a time, and is then concealed by the bank terraces and the inequalities of the ground.

The water is not quite clear; the depth varies generally from 23½ to 27½ inches, and the bottom can be seen only through 20 inches. The bed is regularly formed. Sometimes we float over water a foot deep, and then the bottom seems to move up, and the boat stops. The drift-ice warns us of shallow places. Where the porous ice blocks are piled up in hummocks in the middle of the channel we steer past the shoals where the current is broadest.

The river is remarkably straight and the bends that occur are far from sharp. We sail along the cliffs of the right side of the valley from which boulders and pebbles have fallen into the bed. Here a series of beautiful scenes are displayed, and we glide along a pathway full of crystals glittering in the sunshine. A light south-easterly breeze drives us forwards. I enjoy to the full the rest, the beauty of the country, and the consciousness that I am borne along by one of the most regal rivers of the world.

The bank on our side is silent and desolate. Occasionally only are seen *mani* walls or a small ring fence of stone, within which some hunter is wont to lie in wait for antelopes. Farther down a herd of yaks is grazing, and two of the animals get wind of us and sniff with an air of surprise. Yonder at the bend a fox prowls about, his mouth watering at the sight of a flock of chattering ducks that are swimming by the opposite bank.

Terraces 10 and 14 feet high confine the river bed, and bear witness to a more abundant precipitation in earlier times. The fall is slight, and seldom do we hear the water murmur gently at a bend. At a projecting point of rock rapids are formed and we are drawn in at a swift pace among treacherous blocks.

The day is cool, and it is a chilly pastime to sit hour after hour in a canvas boat among the drift-ice. Now we skim with great velocity along the foot of a precipitous cliff, and excitement makes us hot. Bushes grow in sheltered fissures, but otherwise the banks are bare. We often pass deserted camping places which are visited by nomads in summer. On a steep acclivity near us some wild sheep are feeding.

A row of small cairns was erected on a promontory. Between some of them strings were stretched, and a solitary Tibetan with his gun on his shoulders moved about setting his nooses. When antelopes see their path crossed by such a contrivance they cannot make up their minds to spring over it, whereby they would escape, but they run along the row of cairns to the end, just where the hunter has laid a snare on the ground, if he is not lying in wait himself.

Wind ahead, our course is checked! Tundup Sonam must come aboard and help to row. The drift-ice is carried by the wind to the right bank, and makes more noise than before. The thermometer at one o'clock falls to freezing-point in the water. The drift-ice maintains its hold. It gains ground from day to day as the winter draws on, and at last comes a day when a translucent bridge spans the river with its vault from bank to bank.

We glide at a rapid pace over shallow water, the keel grazing the gravel at the bottom, and lo! now we are fast aground. The drift-ice sweeps past us and bumps against the fragile boat. We row with all our strength, float off at last, and drift again down the Indus.

On the right opens the portal of the Potaö-sang valley, with a brick-red mountain peeping out from its background. Through this valley runs a way three days' journey long to Rudok on the Panggong-tso.

The current becomes swifter among a succession of small rapids. The river narrows with the valley, and we shoot at a dizzy speed to the new camp where strong hands hold up the boat. Then we make ourselves once more at home on a foreign shore.

Two fine specimens of the Ammon sheep were grazing on a slope, and Tundup, the hunter, wished to try his luck again. He made a détour through furrows and dells up to the ridge to catch the animals from the rear. I saw him through the field-glass sneaking along like a panther, and seeking cover behind the inequalities of the ground. But the senses of the animals are extraordinarily sharp. Suddenly I saw both raise their heads and gaze in the direction of the hunter. The wild sheep turned as at a given signal and dashed furiously down the steep rocky declivity. It was a grand sight to watch them come down in a cloud of dust to the level ground, and in two seconds ascend with unchecked rapidity the flank of another projection and disappear behind its top.

A raging storm from the south-west howled through the cordage and tore at the tent cloth when we woke next morning. Dust and withered grass whirled into the tents, the sky was covered with dense clouds, and the weather was raw and chilly when we rode away.

The valley contracts, its bottom becomes hillocky, and is covered with pebbles. The river keeps obstinately to the right side, but on the left, 80 feet above the valley bottom, stands a very old terrace, rounded by time and often broken through by side valleys. Beyond the side valley Tavuk, the mountains on the right side of the Indus valley become steeper than before, and here also are seen fine terraces in which a horizontal bedding of the detritus is plainly perceptible.

Beyond the hill Tsenmo, with its now empty summer camp, lies a row of *mani* walls, now more and more resembling in form those found in Ladak—long walls of boulder stones covered with flat slabs.

Rolled stones play an important part in the country which we have now reached. The whole of Demchok, the last village on the Tibetan side, is built of them. It consists, however, of only four or five huts with brushwood roofs. Walls of boulder stones also surround the miserable fields of barley, the sheep-folds, and the level floors of hard stamped earth where the grain will presently be threshed. A tattered old man and a famished youth were the only inhabitants that showed themselves. Our mules strayed about the stones nibbling at the refuse and sheep's dung, and the scanty grass growing between the springs and ice-flakes on the river strand was little better.

Our Tibetan guides looked upon Demchok as the frontier of the states of the Maharaja, for the power of the Devashung and the Dalai Lama, they said, extends no farther. Really, however, the frontier is a short day's journey farther down. My Ladakis were delighted, but I was grieved at leaving Tibet behind me with so many problems unsolved. But I was determined that I would be in the unknown land again a few months later.

On November 17 we bid farewell to the last village in Tibet, and ride down the detritus fan of Demchok to the bank of the Indus. Fishes lie in close shoals under the belt of ice attached to the margin, and when they are frightened away by stones they return at once, probably because the water is warmer under the cover of the ice-flakes. The valley assumes a peculiar form; while the road continues straight along the left side, the river makes a curve to the north and north-east to pass round an isolated ridge through a wild bed it has excavated along its foot.

The ground falls sensibly. Barrenness and desolation everywhere! Now comes a herd of yaks on the march from Ladak. It was good to see at last some life on this road, which, indeed, shows signs of no little traffic between the two countries, but on which we had hitherto been alone.

A cairn marks the highest point of a small swell in the ground, and the usual streamers hang on strings stretched between sticks. Our Tibetans march round the cairn to show reverence to the spirits of the earth. In the distance a huge light-blue and white mountain mass appears, not far from the village Chushul, which is five days' journey off. Numbed by the stormy wind which has blown right in our faces during the last hours, we are glad to see at last our tents pitched at the spring Na-gangkal (camp 261), and to hurry under their sheltering roofs. The place was bare enough. There was water in abundance but no pasture at all, and not a scrap of fuel. We therefore sacrificed two boxes which were worn out.

Two dogs deserve honourable mention. We had nine four-legged sentinels, a guard of Asiatic tramps, pariahs, which had come and offered their services without waiting for an invitation. In the case of most of them we could not find out where their homes were and where the tents stood which they had deserted to follow us. The Brown Puppy was the only one which had shared in all our adventures. She was a veteran from Srinagar, but her days in our service were numbered, for she was lost in a storm the next winter. She had her corner and felt rug in my tent where she slept at night. She used to tease in perfect friendship a yellow dog from Gartok, and he was her unfortunate companion in the storm.

Among our old friends was also the aged limping camp watcher from the country north of the Ngangtse-tso, who had been with us about a year. His coat hung down to the ground and he looked like an old yak, and he could not run like the others but crawled along step by step. He started in the morning with the laden yaks, but was soon tired and lay down beside the road to wait for me. Then he kept me company as long as his strength allowed, and laid himself down until Tsering came up in the rear with my tent and kitchen utensils. Finally he dropped behind Tsering also, and turned up a solitary wanderer at a late hour in the camp, breathless and panting. In spite of his unattractive appearance and his infirmities, or perhaps because of them, he enjoyed greater popularity than any other member of our foreign legion. Puppy played with him, jumping over him as with drooping head and shuffling steps he struggled to get over the long journey. When all our dogs barked together at night it was not easy to get any rest.

We set out on another day's march. The cold in the night has sunk only to 10.2°, but the river is frozen over here and there in quiet places. Beyond a yellow quartzite promontory the Indus returns to the part of the valley we travel along, and the beauty of the landscape is enhanced by the crystal-clear bluish reaches of water vainly contending against the cold of winter. At Puktse, where a bush grows here and there amongst the withered grass, a small ice bridge spans the river and cracks when my men test its carrying power.

Rich in colour and enchanting in spite of its terrible desolation, the landscape lies under the bluest of skies in which not a cloudlet or rising mist is to be seen. Therefore distance and perspective are unaffected by disturbing influences in the atmosphere. A countless number of spurs of the mighty ranges that enclose the valley appear in succession in front of us to the north-west. Between them flows the famous river by whose bank we tramp along the endless road to Ladak.

At Puktse our Tibetan escort had fulfilled its task and was to return to Gar-gunsa. They had accompanied us to prevent digressions along forbidden roads. Nevertheless, I was pleased to reward them liberally, for their conduct had been beyond all praise, and they had obeyed the orders given them and performed their duty.

The Gova and the whole population of the neighbouring village of Kuyul came to wait on us. They were all polite and agreeable but poor and wretched, since a robber band from the Tibetan side of the frontier had shortly before thoroughly pillaged their small community, the extreme outpost of the states of the Maharaja. The people had, indeed, addressed complaints to the authorities of Ladak, and these had promised to do their best, but the best that a district judge in Leh does is—nothing at all. The good folks of Kuyul are subjects of the famous monastery of Hemis. In outward appearance they resemble the last Tibetans except in clothing. Their skin coats hang down and are not drawn up and puffed out above the girdle as in Tibet. Their headgear is the characteristic Ladaki cap of sheep-skin, which can be turned down to protect the ears and the nape of the neck.

The men of Kuyul stayed over night in our camp, finding free quarters under the open sky. These sons of the wilderness are, indeed, accustomed to cold, but they must feel it through their ragged skin coats when the thermometer falls to 5 degrees below zero. They looked like ruffled horned owls when we left them to their fate in the morning, accompanied by the Gova and two of his men.

The Indus, which hitherto has stuck faithfully to the foot of the Trans-Himalaya, now flows down the middle of the valley and winds more frequently between its bushy banks. The ground is covered with the coarse sand produced by weathering, which remains after the wind has finished its sorting work and has carried away the finer drift-sand. We often ride over barren stretches as level as the finest parquetry flooring. Such is the ground where silt in microscopic particles has been deposited by rain-water in shallow hollows.

An excellently built stone wall with slabs bearing large letters in red and white is named Mani-tumtum. Not far from it the caravan crosses the river at a point where the flakes of drift-ice have been thrust over one another and frozen together into a firm mass.

Accordingly the camp (263) Dungkang is on the right bank. Here the river was 259 feet broad; its mean depth was 18.1 inches, while its maximum was 31, and its velocity 14.2 inches. The Indus here carried about 460 cubic feet of water, and had therefore lost quite 120 feet since we last measured its volume. At this season the cold increases day by day, the springs cease to flow, and the tributaries freeze up. Farther west, however, in Ladak, the river increases gradually, and at Nurla its volume in January is greater than at Dungkang in November.

Another day's journey on November 20 without any noticeable change. The eye falls on the same mountain masses to the south-east which we remember at Demchok; to the north-west the snowy group we have seen so long grows larger. Left and right tower the huge chains we have been familiar with since our halt at Gartok, and in the middle of the valley meanders the river which has supplied us with water for the past two months. Now a sheet of ice covers most of the Indus. But snow is still absent even from the flat hilly crests of the Trans-Himalaya, and on the Ladak range small remnants of snow remain throughout the year only in shady ravines. Grass now grows everywhere, and here and there bushes also stand fairly close. But no tents, no huts, neither herdsmen nor herds! Where the river crosses over to the left side of the valley we pitch our camp on its bank for the last time.

At this camp, which is numbered 264, the Indus is almost free except where small strips of ice skirt the brink. The dark blue water glides along lazily in noiseless eddies and spiral dimples, and forces its way south-westwards in a transverse valley through the Ladak chain. To the north-west we catch sight of the Tsake-la pass on the watershed between the Indus and the Panggong-tso. It is not a pass on a crest but a flat neck between two mountain ranges, the Trans-Himalaya and the Ladak chain.

The old west wind with cutting frost and icy cold howled over the banks of the Indus, and would have swept our tents into the river if we had not secured them extra firmly with ropes. The constant west winds of the

Chang-tang had again commenced their lively dance over the highest elevated region of the world. I recognized their mode of attack, and understood that the storm challenged me to share his dominion with him. And I smiled over the camp-fire at the thought that I had already accepted the invitation, and that the new caravan which was to lead me up there would listen in a few days to the first reveille. "Choose between the winter of Tibet and the perpetual summer of India," whispered the wind in the grass by the Indus bank. I had already made my choice without hesitation, and yet I experienced a certain feeling of self-pity as I thought of the terrible cold that awaited us.

In violent gusts the wind rushes over us and rolls in wild cascades down from the heights. We close our tents and creep into our lairs, while a roaring tumult rages outside all night long.

CHAPTER VIII

IN LADAK FOR THE LAST TIME

AFTER nearly 18° of frost in the night the west wind waked us with its roar on November 21, and our path led us into higher regions again from the bank of the Indus, where we lay in camp 264, at a height of 13,711 feet above the level of the sea. The grass of the steppe, now turned yellow, stands thickly on the clayey soil in which drift-sand is also abundantly mixed, which at times forms dunes with ridges turning along the mountain flanks northwards. Many dunes, however, are compelled by the grass roots to give up their wanderings.

The valley by which the Indus breaks through the mountains remains behind us to the left, and the path winds up to the pass Tsake-la. Grey and purple débris of granite, porphyry, and quartzite covers the ascent, which is not very steep. Here nothing grows. There is only a small oasis, Tama-yaghgang, where grass and bushes surround a spring.

The northern mountains are built up of green and violet porphyrite, but higher up grey granite prevails. To the south smoke rises from the stone huts of the village Salma, in the midst of barley-fields. We approach the Tsake-la, but ere we have reached it we halt for the night at the springs of Dunglung, which form flat ice-flakes among the thriving grass. The height is 14,597 feet, and therefore we have mounted 886 feet from our last camp on the Indus. From here we can perceive in the distance the mountains round Demchok. The Indus valley stretches in endless perspective to the south-east, its bottom tinted

44. A Girl of Chushul.

Sketch by the Author.

yellow with the colour of the steppe, but the river itself we cannot see for the distance is too great.

Next morning we are up in good time at the pass Tsake-la and its cairns adorned with horns and streamers. Here the height is 14,840 feet, and the wind is cutting at a temperature of 23°. We hurry down on foot to bring our blood into circulation again. Valleys, rocky promontories, and *mani* walls succeed one another, and the scanty vegetation struggling for existence forms yellow patches round the springs. The lofty snow-covered mountain we have seen so long is now near to us, but its firn-fields are hidden by intervening heights. The Panggong-tso is not visible, though the crests rising from its northern shore are in sight.

We descried from the pass the projecting mountain behind which our camping-ground for the day lay at the village Chushul. But hours passed and the day declined before we reached it. The path follows the left side of the valley. A succession of projecting heights appeared in front of us. The sun sank and the shadows grew longer. Again we rode past a jutting rock. Was not this the last? No, still appeared ever fresh promontories on the road, and the wind was so icily cold that we had to walk to keep warm. Twilight deepened, the road became less distinct, the wind rose still more. Should we reach our destination by this road? Four long *mani* walls and a small *chhorten* indicated the proximity of a monastery, but we could scarcely see them for it was dark.

At length the last mountain spur was passed, and the fires of the camp at Chushul flashed before us. The brook of the little village was half frozen over. The horses slipped and slithered over rounded ice-humps, plumped into the water, balanced themselves on the uneven bottom, and at last with a jump reached the grassy slope of the farther bank. We were tired and frozen as we turned our steps to the fire and lighted our pipes.

We had deserved a day's rest, and the headman of Chushul did all he could to pay honour to his far-travelled guests. The entertainment, which a European can hardly escape when he is a guest in a Ladak village, began before noon. In July 1906 dancing and music festivals had been held in my honour in every village on the way to Leh, and now on my return the rural performances began again. The twelve beauties of Chushul danced in slow rhythmical time in front of our tents. They were dressed in green and red sheep-skins, finery of all kinds bedecked their tresses, and ribbons adorned with turquoises fell from their crowns down their backs. Their eyes were turned to the ground and their expression showed no passion, no joyousness; sometimes they raised their right hands, sometimes their left, and they turned themselves round as they slowly advanced in Indian file. They were certainly not lovely, these ladies of the mountains, but they made up for it by dirtiness, shyness, and modesty. There was no hurry with the ballet in Chushul. They danced for hours, and the dance presented no surprising or alternating modifications. An old man accompanied it on a string instrument; and as the only drum in the village was cracked, our kitchen staff brought their most sonorous saucepans to enhance the brilliance of the festival.

The sights of Chushul are soon enumerated. The village consists of some twenty huts and two temples, the one at the foot of the hill, old and in ruins, while the other, Lundup-Chüding-gompa, has been built on a rise at the expense of a wealthy man, whose son, the lama Kunchuk Tingsin, now provides for the upkeep of the monastery. I was told that thirty monks served in the temple, but that they now lived scattered about, each in his own home, and that only the superior was then in the cloister; his portrait is in Vol. II. p. 216, Illust. 284.

In the other temple courtyard a streamer pole and a *chhorten* stand between dilapidated huts containing monks' cells. The façade is whitewashed, and the antechamber, with the indispensable spirit kings, is closed by a red-painted wooden grille. The temple hall is well provided with images, some life size, others rather smaller. The sunlight penetrates in above their heads more freely than elsewhere through a quadrangular opening. A passage runs round the group of gods, along which the pious make their rounds. In the middle of the group sits Guru Rinpoche,

45. Singing Beauties of Chushul.

46. Dancing Girls of Chushul.

Sketches by the Author

with a grey mask in his hand, and round him stand in inextricable confusion Tsepakmet, Chenrezi, Tsong Kapa, in red mantle and pointed yellow cap, and several statues of lamas with dreamy meditative countenances.

The superior told me that a short time before thieves had broken into the cells of the lamas and carried off articles to the value of 200 rupees. The robbed priests knew how to take care of themselves. To make up for their loss they extracted some precious stones from the statues of the gods and sold them to dealers in the neighbourhood. This theft, however, was detected, and a thorough investigation had been commenced into the conduct of these pious desecrators of the temple.

At evening the ballet was repeated. But this time my men were the hosts at their own fires. There was dancing, singing, and cither-playing, tea-kettles boiled, and the *chang* jugs filled with the light beer of the country made their rounds. The brave men were lively and excited; they were home again in Ladak, to them the finest country in the world, the country where their mothers had carried them in their arms, where their fathers had hunted the ibex and wild sheep among the rocks. Home-sickness was over and all the trials they had endured were forgotten. But the songs were the same that they had sung in Chang-tang, when the storm howled round the tents and the flames of the camp-fires fluttered and flickered like bunches of streamers on temple roofs.

The next day, on November 24, we rode away from the houses of Chushul and the frozen canals, which during the warmer seasons irrigate the barley-fields of the village. On this road also stand numerous *mani* walls looking like petrified railway trains. The road runs uphill north-westwards, and on the right rises the mighty snowy mountain. Down below at its foot trips along a sheep caravan, 500 animals laden with barley on their way to Rudok. Some of them are painted red and look like bleeding sacrificial lambs. In front marches a wether with his eyes constantly fixed on the path, while the whole herd follows him listlessly, half asleep, but dexterously balancing their loads. The shepherds that bring up the rear can quite depend on the toiling animals keeping on the path to Rudok.

We ourselves work our way laboriously up to the pass Kongta-la, a pebble-covered saddle 16,605 feet above sea-level. My men burst out with a loud yell of delight before its conical cairn and its votive pile of horns, stakes, streamers, and rags.

The valley Ar finds its way hither from the south-west through a cutting in dark porphyrite rocks, here filled with boulders and there leaving room for a path beside the brook which is frozen to the bottom. In the mountains on the north-east side of the pass grey granite predominates. The fall from the Kongta-la north-westwards is imperceptible. We pass six tents and two flocks of grazing sheep before we pitch our camp at the rocky promontory of the Lung-kongma valley.

The day was dull, grey, and cold, but at sunset the sky cleared in the west and the mighty masses of the granite mountain glittered like the reddest gold.

Another day breaks over the earth, the tents are folded up, the horses are saddled, and we continue our long wanderings. The valley falls more steeply and its bottom is full of granite blocks troublesome to pass, among which a brooklet murmurs under its crystal roof of ice. It grows gradually, receiving tribute from all the springs in the valley, until at length it unites with the Shyok, the great affluent of the Indus. At one place where we cross the brook the ice mantle is thin and transparent as glass, but nevertheless bears the horses as they are led carefully one by one over a sand-strewn path.

The day comes to an end, and the valley is again shrouded in shadows while the sunbeams are still gilding the lofty summits around us. A huge sheep caravan is encamped, and its owners have piled up the sacks of barley into walls; in their shelter the evening fires blaze cheerfully and pleasantly. A second caravan has not taken the trouble to remove the loads from the sheep, and the animals have to pass the night with the sacks on their backs. We, too, camp near them, in a place called Sara. Here the warrior chief Soravar Sing defeated the Tibetans,

47. On the Kongta-la.

48. The Village of Drugub.

49. Chhortens in Drugub.

as he some seventy years ago took Ladak from the Maharaja of Kashmir.

We noticed daily that we were approaching civilization. At every camp we met horsemen with news of my new caravan which was to assemble at Drugub. They brought also welcome additions to our provisions—fowls, eggs, and apples, and one of them handed me a kind letter from my old friend, Colonel Sir Francis Younghusband, who was then Resident in Kashmir.

November 26 was the last day I was in the company of my old servants. We follow the brook in the usual order of march. The path, however, climbs gradually up a small rise and remains at a considerable height above the valley floor. The landscape is wild and imposing. At our feet the brook creeps under its ice mantle. The narrow path covered with blocks and rubbish runs along the precipitous edge like the eaves of a roof. During a short halt we roll some loose boulders over the edge of the road. They thunder in mighty leaps, twisting as they fall down the steep walls, and with a tremendous noise smash to pieces the ice of the brook.

Now there is a rapid descent. We recognize more and more clearly the wild-fissured vertical sculpture that characterizes all the side valleys of the Indus. A cluster of huts surrounded by their fields, thin poplars, and the usual symbols of Lamaism in stone, bears the famous name of Herat. Chilam is a village a little farther down, where our yaks can only be induced by coaxing and threats to trust themselves on a swinging bridge of stone slabs supported by two tree trunks.

The valley becomes wilder and more enchanting the farther we descend. The uniform monotony of the plateau country is no more, but we find ourselves in a country where the rivers succeed in breaking their way through the stupendous mountain masses which stand in their way. More frequently we perceive traces of the struggle of man with uncontrolled Nature. The path is more clearly trodden out as it twists in thousands of bends among the trouble-some boulders, the fields increase in number and extent, and the ever-present *mani* walls cry to heaven from the depths of the valley. Here and there landslips have occurred on the precipitous walls, and on our left open three side valleys together, all contributing their shares to the water of the main stream. The erosion terraces are well developed, their lowest steps lying about 60 feet above the brook. We can hear and see how these rivulets work continually to cut their channels into the solid crust of the earth and deepen the valleys.

We have reached an important point. The Ladak chain, which we have so long had on our right, drops behind us, and the brook turns sharply to the north-east to break through a transverse valley in the chain which separates us from the country of the Panggong-tso. This breached valley is picturesquely hemmed in between high steep granite rocks, and its fall is so rapid that ice has not been able to form on the foaming rapids. Only occasionally is there room for a hut and patch of cultivated land.

In such a spot Tundup Sonam had his home. He hurried forward to greet his old mother and his brothers, and the whole family beamed with joy at the return of the bold hunter. They all stood by the road as I rode past, and were rewarded with Indian silver money for their gift of welcome, which consisted of dried apricots and bowls of milk.

A party of horsemen appears among the huge granite boulders. There they come, my old friends Anmar Ju and Hiraman, to witness my fourth entry into Ladak and offer their services.

The valley becomes still narrower. It is as narrow as a cutting. The path winds up and down over the detritus cones. Two *chhortens* are erected on the top of a block of rock. At a very narrow spot two huge boulders have fallen and made a bridge across the stream, and below them a deep basin of dark blue water has been formed.

Now we are near the end. There lies Tankse in its cauldron, and there stand the poplars under which Muhamed Isa in August 1906 sewed together the black tent and mended the mules' pack-saddles. The whole village turns out to meet us. Everything is the same only

50. MUSICIANS AT DRUGUB.

that all is cold, frozen, and leafless, and the grand caravan leader sleeps in his grave at Saka-dzong.

Here the circuit which we had for fifteen months described through the interior of Tibet was closed, here all ties were loosed, my old servants were dismissed to their huts, and a new and serious chapter was commenced.

A few days later I was in the neighbouring village of Drugub among new men. With them I began the hardest journey I have ever accomplished in Asia. On December 4 we started for the Karakorum Mountains, crossed in mid-winter with a temperature of $-40°$ the loftiest heights of Chang-tang, and on April 24, 1908, were held up by Dorche Tsuen, the Governor of Saka-dzong, and his men. After much palaver I obtained permission to go my own way, which of course took me up and down over the blank space where the central chains of the Trans-Himalaya raise their heads. Tibetan soldiers escorted me to the Tarok-tso, where I had arranged a rendezvous with the caravan leader Abdul Kerim and six of my men from Ladak. Five Ladakis accompanied me, namely, Gulam, Lobsang, Kutus, Tubges, and Kunchuk. This arrangement, unpractical in itself, was forced upon me by the Tibetans that they might keep a tighter hold of me.

I travelled westwards past the Teri-nam-tso, over the Lunkar-la pass, 18,274 feet high, and came at last at the Nganglaring-tso into country of which the pundits had collected a few extremely meagre and indefinite reports. The Selipuk monastery is the chief place in this part of Tibet.

There I had to leave the reader in the second volume of this book. The space at my disposal was filled up and I could not describe my journey through the Sutlej valley to Simla. And yet this route deserves description, for it is one of the most beautiful, wildest, and grandest in the world. The mighty river has excavated its valley right through the chains of the Himalayas. Certainly the well-known road from Rawal-pindi to Leh, which traverses the same ranges, abounds in enchanting scenes, but it has been constructed and improved by human hands, and solid bridges cross the rivers. The route through the Sutlej valley, on the contrary, has been for the most part left untouched, and its beauty increases with every day's journey from the holy lake.

The following chapters are devoted to the road between Selipuk and Simla (see Vol. II. p. 399).

51. MERCHANTS OF KASHMIR IN DRUGUB.

52. THE TESILDAR.

53. MERCHANTS OF RUDOK IN DRUGUB.

CHAPTER IX

THE SELIPUK MONASTERY

HALF a year has passed over dreary Tibet since we started from Ladak. Now our camp is pitched on the bank of the river Sumdang-tsangpo, a river which derives its origin from sources in the Trans-Himalaya, and mingles its fresh water with the briny waves of Nganglaring-tso. During the latter days we have ridden along among the rocks on the southern shore of this lake, which the pundits had heard mentioned. But the blue sheet of water, the pink irregular shores, and the rocky islands which rise out of the salt lake, had never been beheld by a white man.

It is midsummer. I write June 26, 1908, in my diary. A year of adventures lies behind me, and only the retreat remains to be accomplished. I have with me four Ladakis and a Tibetan, the excellent Lobsang, besides two guides and owners of yaks, who have accompanied me through Rundor-changma to Selipuk. Abdul Kerim and his companions have not yet joined us, and we have quite made up our minds that we shall never see them again.

In the course of the day a violent wind has swept over the country, and a little rain has fallen. The season of the south-west monsoon has not yet reached this lofty remote region, and the Sumdang-tsangpo carries only 88 cubic feet of water, but in consequence of its breadth and depth has the appearance of a fairly large river. At the left bank the water flows clear and pure, but on the right it is turbid and white as though milk had been poured into it. Probably wild geese or gulls have stirred up the bottom somewhere above the camp. At sunset the gulls sit in hundreds meditating on a mudbank, and shine in the distance like chains of white pearls.

The interior of Tibet is a dry, barren, mountainous wilderness, far away from all the seas of the world, and higher above the ocean than any other country. The traveller longs for water, and likes to camp on the shores of bluish lakes or murmuring streams. Such a camp we occupied now. The sea-blue surface of the great lake stretched away northwards, and the river flowed a pace from my tent. The Sumdang-tsangpo, however, does not murmur, and could tell no experiences from its home in the Trans-Himalaya to the sharply defined grass-grown banks which scarcely rose above its surface.

A felt rug is stretched between two stakes firmly rammed into the ground in front of my tent-opening, so that I can sit cross-legged out of doors, as in a shady verandah, and let the pencil or pen glide over the paper. When it is too dark to work, and too early to light a candle, I still sit there, smoking my pipe, and watching the heralds of night chasing the fleeing day over the western mountains. I am longing to go home. For two long years I have not seen a European. Solitude is pleasant, but one gets tired of it at last, and longs to see men of one's own race. When the last bright gleam pales, and dusk is all around, it is still three hours before night comes and puts an end to my yearning.

I look back with singular melancholy on those endlessly long evenings, when the ticking of my watch was the only sign that time was passing. If I had only had books to read! But our baggage animals had broken down, and my collection of books had long before been scattered to the winds, one volume after another. Only a Bible, a Swedish hymn-book, and Fröding's poems were left. The Old Testament helped me through many lonely hours. At last our situation was so critical that Fröding too was added to the ballast we discarded. The leaves which I knew by heart were torn out, but I could not retain in my memory the contents of some of them.

Lobsang and Kutus, my teachers in the Tibetan

Gulam. Tubges.

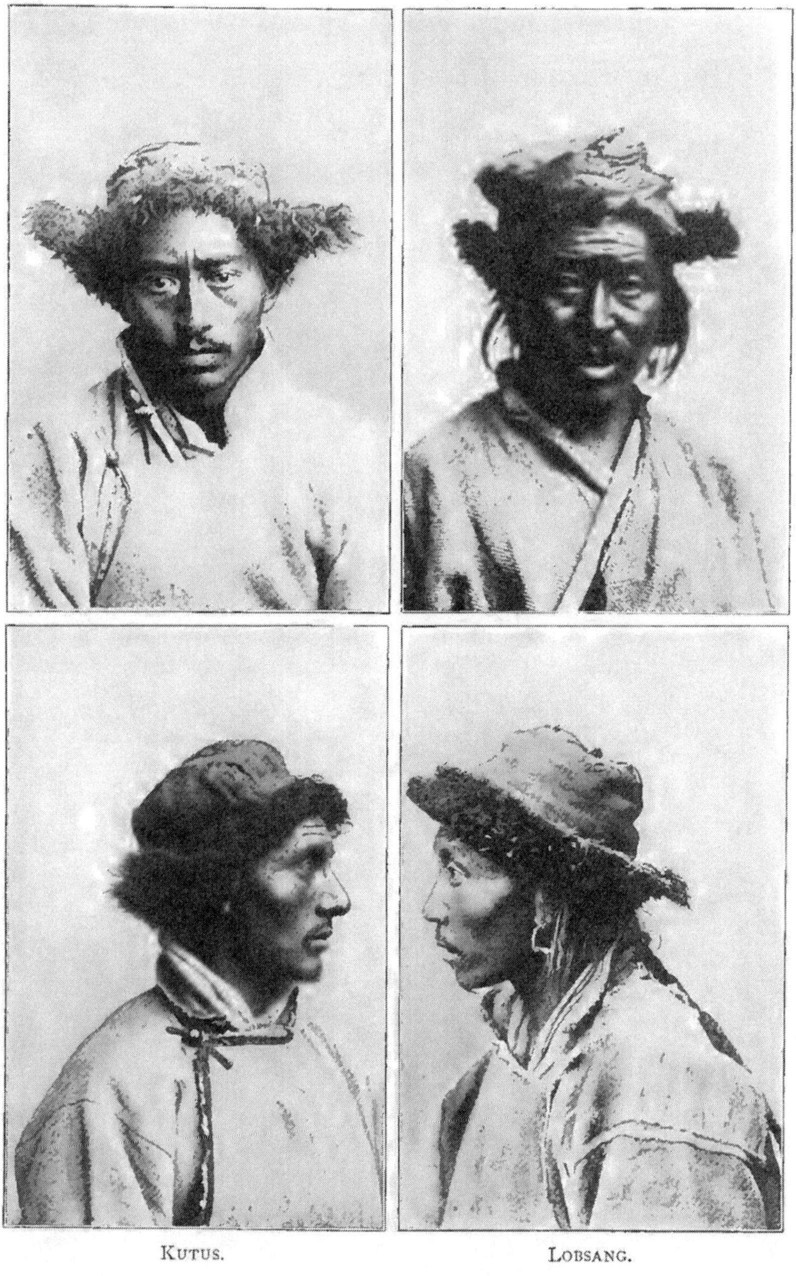

Kutus. Lobsang.

54. My Faithful Servants.

language, gave me their company every evening, and after they had withdrawn I wrote down the words I had learned in a vocabulary. Then Little Puppy came into the tent to play a while with me—the black pup born in the Shyok valley, which had had the giants of the Karakorum for sponsors, and received its name at the font when there were fifty degrees of frost. Gulam brought in a very simple supper of mutton—always mutton. I had a thorough dislike to this dish, and contented myself with bread. At nine o'clock I read off the meteorological instruments, and a little later Gulam tucked me up in my furs and closed up the tent. Then came blessed night with rest and forgetfulness.

This particular night was cold for the season—25°. So it is in the height of summer at Nganglaring-tso at a height of 15,570 feet. In the daytime the temperature may rise in the shade to 59°. Then, with a calm air and a clear sky, it is burning hot. But scarcely has the sun sunk when the cold breath of night steals over the brow of the earth.

Early in the morning a pack of wolves made a fearful commotion round the camp. They accused us of murder, and wished to recover a cub which Lobsang had caught and given for supper to our big watch-dog Takkar. Four fully grown and as many young wolves prowled about the farther bank where two mounted Tibetans tried to kill the young ones. We had seen wolves in the country before. They are very common here, and owing to their voracity are a scourge to the flocks. Every one who kills a wolf receives from the nomads who have suffered from the beast a *shanglung* or wolf-fee. In one camp he receives a bowl of *tsamba*, in another a silver coin, perhaps even a goat or sheep. At any rate he reaps a good harvest.

I sit on horseback, my men go on foot, driving our remaining baggage animals over the steppe, scantily covered with grass, which separates us from the monastery Selipuk. We see it before us in the distance. One is almost tempted to take it for a curious vessel with masts, rigging, ropes, and pennants, or even for a Viking ship adorned with flags for a festival.

A whole village of black tents has sprung up on the plain. The white tents indicate the presence of some chief. We soon learn that the owner of the whole village is the chief of the district Chokchu, which lies to the west of the Dangra-yum-tso. At the Shovo-tso we had seen his caravan on the march westward, and we knew that he and his family and retainers were on a pilgrimage to Kang-rinpoche. The Sumdang-tsangpo flowed between his camp and the cloister hill, and we camped on the left bank at the foot of the cloister hill.

Our situation was extremely uncomfortable. We came, six ragged fellows, from no one knew where. I was dressed as a Tibetan, though I had no longer the slightest cause to preserve my incognito. I wore the Tibetan costume for the simple reason that I had no other. How would the monastery, or rather its monks, who had in all probability never seen a European, treat us? All had heard of Younghusband's expedition to Lhasa, and knew that the white intruders had shot down the Tibetans like partridges. And now one of the white demons had come hither. What would the chief of Chokchu say, who was here in his camp surrounded by a retinue armed to the teeth? We might have avoided Selipuk if we had been frightened, but we were not. We pitched our camp on the bank of the Sumdang-tsangpo just between the chief of Chokchu and the prior of the monastery.

We had scarcely made our tent ready when the Gova of the village appeared attended by ten men. They took their seats uninvited under my felt roof, and made a great noise in their desperate endeavours to find out what country I came from, India, Turkestan, or Ladak. A white man in Tibetan dress? They could make nothing of me.

"Question me, you fellows, and you shall get information," I called out to them.

"What country are you from?" was asked on all sides at once.

"Peling" (European).

"Where do you come from?"

"From India and Ladak, but I have been at Shigatse; from the Dangra-yum-tso, but I have roamed round the holy lake; from the east, but I have been in the west; from the north, but I have travelled all through southern

55. A Nomad's Tent.

56. Transport of Sheep's Wool.

57. My Tent with the Awning.

Tibet. My main caravan has gone astray. Get it me back."

They hardly attempted to understand such a complicated answer. However, they understood so much, that we had now come from the east, and had two young guides who at the same time were the owners of our yaks. These were to return to the Shovo-tso, and then we should have no means of transport.

"We are on the way to Tokchen," I told them. "The Tibetan chiefs have provided us with baggage yaks and guides from Saka-dzong. Now it is your turn to perform your duty towards foreign visitors."

"We know of no such duty," answered the Gova. "Selipuk is not one of the places which supply yaks to travellers. Those who are marching to Rudok or the gold-diggings in Tok-jalung change their yaks in Yumba-matsen."

"Yumba-matsen does not lie on the way to Tokchen. We must hire fresh animals here in Selipuk."

"We will gladly oblige you if we receive orders from Lhasa. But you have not even a passport; and we do not know whether you have any right to wander about our country."

"I can assure you that we have no right whatever. But here we are and wish to go away. Give us yaks and you will get rid of us."

"Let your guides from the Shovo-tso take you wherever you wish to travel."

We talked and talked but came to no agreement. Our fellows from the Shovo-tso would not accompany us farther; their Gova had ordered them to bring us only to Selipuk. I had already been in the Yumba-matsen country. Now I must cross the Trans-Himalaya for the eighth time. Straight to Tokchen and then along the Sutlej to India. I would not consider any other programme. We could stay a couple of days at Selipuk, and, meanwhile, something might turn up to our advantage. Abdul Kerim, the scoundrel, who had our money-chest, might appear again. No one had heard of him and his caravan. I could not account for their disappearance. When we had paid for the hire of the yaks we should have only 10 rupees in hand. Then necessity would oblige us to barter a horse for two sheep, a baggage yak for a sack of *tsamba*. I still possessed two gold watches intended as presents for chiefs who rendered us conspicuous services. Who lived here in Tibet in such circumstances that he could buy a gold watch? I had paid ten pounds each for them. Now we might have to sell them for bread and butter. Never had I been in such straits in Tibet, poor as a pilgrim.

But wait! here is a rich man, the Governor of Chokchu. The gods of Tibet seem to have thrown a means of escape in my way. I must try what I can do with him. Lobsang and Kutus went off as an embassy extraordinary to his tent, chiefly to see what he looked like at close quarters, but also to inquire politely if he had any eatables to sell. The chief made a deep impression on my men. He was rich and a man of importance, that was evident. He would not trade in eatables, he told them, but we might have a loaf of sugar, and he would come next day to visit us and see how we lived.

At the same time Kunchuk spied about in the monastery where he looked up the Kanpo Lama, who is the prior of Selipuk and, besides, the *Pun* or administrator of the surrounding country. This man had spoken with great caution, but he might perhaps sell us some *tsamba* if we paid him well.

The day drew to a close and our situation was not improved. Tibetans passed to and fro among the tents of the chief of Chokchu, and his yaks, sheep, and horses fed in herds on the steppe. Compared to myself he was a Crœsus. I could not give anything to the beggars who sat before my tent.

In every camp and on every pass I used to draw a panorama embracing the whole horizon. And so I did here, in Selipuk, on the morning of June 28. Immediately the sketch was finished a Tibetan who knew the country was asked to provide material for the text. "There," he said, pointing N. 30° W., "runs the road over the Sigge-la to Yumba-matsen, which is two days' journey from here. The mountains you see to the south-west are the Lavar-

58. On the Way to Selipuk Monastery.

59. On the Way to Selipuk Monastery.

gangri group (a part of the Trans-Himalaya); among those mountains are the sources of the Lavar-tsangpo, which flows into the western part of the Nganglaring-tso. And the Sumdang-tsangpo rises close to the Sumdang-la, which lies southwards from here." And he showed me also the passes Oyar-la and Gebye-la, which are both on the Trans-Himalaya.

While we were engaged in orientation I could see that the chief of Chokchu was preparing for his promised visit. Handsome white mules and small plump horses were led to his tent and there saddled. The distance was only 200 yards, but the river was between us, and also he wished to impress us with his pomp and state and a numerous following. The wild troop presented a fine sight as it rode at a smart trot to the bank and plunged and splashed through the river. The chief and his brothers had panther-skins for saddle-cloths, and the wooden frames of their saddles were decorated with bright yellow metal studs and plates. They themselves wore cerise mantles with long turned-up sleeves, low leathern boots of Mongolian style, girdles round the waist, and at the left side valuable châtelaines with dagger and fire-steel on gold and silver chains. The sabre was stuck across through the girdle, and its silver-mounted scabbard was richly decorated with turquoises and imitation coral.

My tent, which had suffered severely from many a storm, was far too poor a reception-room for such illustrious guests. The sun, wind, and rain in succession looked in through innumerable rents, and the Pun of Chokchu and his two younger brothers smiled at one another as they took their seats on a ragged felt rug which had been spread out for them. I sat myself on my bed which also was laid on the ground. The furniture was of the same style as all the other things. Our boxes and our European things had been smashed, and my belongings lay there stowed in sacks. The eyes of the guests examined this curious interior; they had never seen the tent of a sahib so simply furnished. They also gazed at my costume but would not at first ask about it. Dishevelled Tibetan heads and sunburnt weather-beaten roguish faces crowded the tent door.

Sonam Ngurbu, the chief of Chokchu, was a man of forty, short, but strongly built, energetic and yet simple, bold and inquisitive, and yet reserved and polite. He is one of the personalities in the land of snow which I cannot forget. I see him still before me as he sat cross-legged in my tent, bareheaded, and with a regular lion's mane of black, thick, and no doubt very populous hair.

Sonam Ngurbu did not talk much. His questions were short and clear, and after receiving an answer he sat silent as though he were trying to grasp its meaning. After a short time came the usual question, "Have you anything to sell?" Yes, certainly we had, and the Huskvarna gun was brought out. We could well do without it as only two cartridges were left. Unfortunately Sonam Ngurbu had no use for a gun without ammunition. It might be worth 10 rupees, he thought. Many thanks, but it cost 300. So the gun was put aside.

Now we tried to catch him with the gold watch. The chief thought it bright and pretty, and could not conceive how men could make such small fine things. The whole escort now took it in turns to hold the watch to their ears and listen to its tick. But at last Sonam Ngurbu declared roundly that it seemed to him unnecessary and superfluous to keep a little machine of the kind to measure time. It was all the same to him whether it was eleven or twelve o'clock. He divided his day according to the sun and the weather, his occupations and journeys by the pasturage and the seasons. And, moreover, how could he know that the thin yellow metal was really gold?

The only thing that pleased Sonam Ngurbu was my Swedish revolver. "Will you sell it me for 60 rupees?" he asked. But my pride was aroused.

"What do you take me for? Do you think that I am a pedlar trapesing about to sell revolvers? In your country where one is never safe from attacks I want a revolver myself. And 60 rupees more or less are of no consequence to me."

Thus our honour was saved for the time, though we were aware that we could not live long on honour, water, and air.

60. The Chief Sonam Ngurbu (on the left), and one of his Brothers. Wives and Servants behind.

The chief took farewell of the revolver and soon after of its owner, rose, swung himself on to his panther-skin and splashed again through the river accompanied by all his motley crew.

The custom of the country and my own interests demanded a return visit. Lobsang and Kutus were to accompany me and interpret for me when my own stock of words did not suffice. I wound my red turban round my black cap, had the worst of the dust brushed out of my red mantle, thrust a short sabre into my girdle, and mounted my worn-out steed. To give my satellites a civilized appearance was a hopeless undertaking; they were and remained landloupers. I, however, endeavoured in the days of poverty and humiliation to retain a reflexion of vanished greatness by outward composure and dignity.

Sonam Ngurbu came to meet me at the entrance of his splendid tent, ornamented with festoons of blue ribands. The ground within was covered with carpets—what luxury! and square cushions were laid round a low table. Here we took our seats, and an interminable palaver began.

"Where does your tent stand, Sonam Ngurbu, when you are at home in Chokchu?"

"In the country Kasang-tota, two days' journey to the east of the Teri-nam-tso and one west of the Dangra-yum-tso."

"How far is it from Kasang-tota to Selipuk?"

"I have been fifty days on the way," he said.

From his description it appeared that he had travelled along the north side of the Trans-Himalaya, and had to cross only one pass of importance, the Ka-la, which lies not far east of Nganglaring-tso.

"Whither are you now travelling, Sonam Ngurbu?"

"To Tokchen, Parka, and Tarchen."

"How many days do you reckon it to Tokchen?"

"Twenty."

"Then you must travel extremely slowly?"

"Yes. We are not in a hurry. We remain several days where the pasture is good for the sake of the animals."

"How large is your retinue?"

"More than a hundred men, including an armed escort. I have sixty horses, four hundred yaks of burden, and as many sheep, of which many, however, are slaughtered during the journey."

Our host told me further that he was a powerful and respected man, not only in his own home between the lakes, but also in the interior of Tibet, especially in the province of Bongba. His reputation there was founded chiefly on his ability to track out robbers and bandits with the help of his horsemen. The Devashung, the government in Lhasa, was on that account particularly well disposed towards him, and applied to him when there was any trouble with bandits. He had more armed horsemen under his command even than the Governor of Saka-dzong. Whenever people had been attacked and robbed, he let loose his men like bloodhounds, and they seldom missed their mark.

On his journey to Selipuk also he had occasion to exercise his office of chief constable of police. Cattle thieves had played their pranks between the monastery Chiu-gompa and Tirtapuri, and retreated with six hundred stolen sheep to the mountainous regions of Bongba. He, Sonam Ngurbu, had been informed, and had organized a drive to catch the villains. As usual, he had succeeded in laying his hands on the scoundrels, and he had now arranged a meeting with one of the Garpuns of Gartok in a district called Tashi-tse-buk, and lying west of Selipuk. There the two potentates would discuss the robber question. As Sonam Ngurbu was always at feud with freebooters and knaves, he probably thought it safest to take all his possessions with him when he was going on a journey.

"What is really the motive of your present journey?" I asked.

"I am on a pilgrimage to Kang-rinpoche; there I shall make three circuits of the holy mountain and one of the holy lake. I make a pilgrimage thither every third year."

"What do you gain by it?"

"Good fortune and prosperity for myself, my family, and my flocks."

"And if you omitted the pilgrimage?"

61. Sonam Ngurbu.

62. Sonam Ngurbu's Brother.

"Then robbers would pillage my tents, rain would not fall, and my sheep would starve."

Sonam Ngurbu sat silent awhile, observing me closely. Then he said:

"Our paths have crossed before. You, Sahib, may not know it, but I have seen you often. I had been a month in Shigatse when you came thither last year. In the press of pilgrims during the feast days I could not have drawn your attention. But I saw you going up daily to the temples of Tashi-lunpo, and I heard that you were a friend of His Holiness the Tashi Lama. I perceived, then, that you are a man of consequence, though your caravan is so small and unpretentious."

The good Tashi Lama thus came unexpectedly to our help in a difficult situation. Sonam Ngurbu told every one who would listen that he had seen me at the temple festivals, and this increased my importance. It was understood that I was not a man to be treated like any ordinary knight of the road. No doubt, though poor and ragged, I was a high lama from Western lands.

Now all I had to do was to procure money. I wrote to Thakur Jai Chand, the agent of the Indian Government in Gartok, begging him to send the necessary sum to Tokchen where I should soon arrive. The only difficulty was to send the letter without money. I told Sonam Ngurbu the state of affairs fully, and asked him to send a man of his numerous retinue to Gartok with the letter.

"If you were with me at home," he replied, "I would willingly forward your letter, but here I am myself a stranger, and it would cost me my head were I to meddle with the affairs of another province."

While we were discussing the matter a servant came in to announce that Jamtse Singe, the prior of the monastery, was coming. We hurried out to see the show. It was an exceedingly comical sight. His reverence walked with slow solemn steps and bowed head, letting the beads of a rosary slip through his fingers. He was not alone, but walked in a procession. Beside him strode another lama, two younger monks followed, and two novices came last. In consequence of the mixture of affected simplicity and pompous solemnity the procession was indescribably ridiculous. The servants of the church, however, caused a great stir among these children of the world, and inquisitive Tibetans stood gaping at all the tent doors.

The prior did not vouchsafe us a single glance. He stalked slowly past us, making for the tent tenanted by a lama of Chokchu who was one of Sonam Ngurbu's followers, Namgyal Dorche. First the church then the temporal rulers!

But it was not long before another messenger announced that the prior, this time alone, was on his way to Sonam Ngurbu's tent. Then we went out again, and the chief's brothers as well as some other gentlemen joined us. All saluted Jamtse Singe with the greatest respect, bowing low and throwing themselves on the ground. He passed his hand in blessing from one head to another, and held out both his hands to me.

Now there was much affectation, and many ceremonious speeches were made on the question of who should occupy the seat of honour opposite the entrance. Every one knew that the seat was by right the prelate's, but the host had much trouble to induce him to take possession of it. At last he succeeded, and Sonam Ngurbu and I placed ourselves beside him with the low table between us. I recognized herein the Chinese ceremonial which does not at all suit the natural rude character of the Tibetans.

On hearing the self-conscious bandit-catcher and the right reverend monk pay court to each other in a flood of flattering speeches, one could not help thinking that they must be close friends and entertain unbounded respect for each other. One would never imagine that they were really like cat and dog. Sonam Ngurbu was superstitious, and had a bad conscience like all pilgrims in Tibet. He feared that the monk by cunning incantations might spoil all the fruits of his pilgrimage and turn them to evil. This was also why he had taken his own confessor with him. Jamtse Singe, on the other hand, as he afterwards told me himself, regarded the temporal chief as a spy, who might at any time calumniate him to the Devashung in Lhasa. Therefore, he was very reserved towards me as long as

63. Soldiers of Sonam Ngurbu.

Sketches by the Author.

Sonam Ngurbu was in Selipuk, or the latter might have reported him for showing hospitality to a European.

Sonam Ngurbu did not change his bearing towards me on account of his guest. On the contrary he dwelt on my friendship with the Tashi Lama, and the prelate became decidedly more affable. He smiled and listened with interest as I enumerated all the monasteries I had visited in southern Tibet and related some adventures. There were several among the men present who could confirm my statements. For instance, the steward of Selipuk had been the year before in Raga-tasam, and a lama, twenty years old, had been in Lehlung-gompa when I drew the pillars of the temple hall. A man in the service of Sonam Ngurbu had been present when Lundup Tsering and his horsemen had protected the Dangra-yum-tso from my intrusion. Here, then, were four men who had seen me before at different places, and perhaps this was partly the reason why no alarm had been raised at my arrival in Selipuk. What could be done with such a bird of passage? And, besides, a caravan of only six men with six horses and mules could not be dangerous.

"Well, now, let me see at least the temple hall of Selipuk," I proposed.

"Never! A European has never been here. If a Peling were admitted into the hall of the gods all the monks would die."

"Nonsense! You have heard that I was repeatedly in Tashi-lunpo, and that the Tashi Lama has not died in consequence."

"Yes, he is great and powerful and can exorcise every danger. But I possess no such power, and have no authority to show the monastery to strangers."

Our conversation was interrupted by the cook, who looked into the tent to announce that dinner was ready. I never ate except in the morning and evening, but now out of regard for my host I had to greet with a friendly smile the china bowl in which the soup, the *pièce de résistance* of the meal, was served. Such a bowl was placed before each guest, but the host had one of costly nephrite. The soup was very strong. It contained solid pieces of yak meat, rice, and Chinese macaroni, all flavoured with onions, pepper, and salt. It was eaten with pewter and wooden spoons, and the Tibetans, both laymen and ecclesiastics, exhibited an enormous appetite. They held their soup-plates close under their mouths, supped and smacked their lips and fished the scraps of meat up with the spoons, never removing their eyes from their food. They ate like gourmets, silent and serious ; they might have been engaged in a religious function which might not be disturbed by everyday talk. For the credit of the cook, and as an excuse for the gentlemen's appetites, I must say that the soup was really excellent. Boiling hot and nourishing, it spread an agreeable glow all through the body ; the macaroni and rice were done to death ; the rest might be left by one who was not armed with Tibetan fangs which can chew to pieces tough yak meat and gutta-percha. The Tibetans began with the meat, then scooped out the rice and macaroni, lastly drank up the liquid, and put the empty plates on the table again with a sigh and other Asiatic noises betokening satisfaction. They did not remain long there. The cook, who was watching at the tent door, fetched them out, refilled them and placed them before the guests to be cleared again.

After dinner the massive black teapot of burnt clay was passed round. Dinner, indeed, is only an interruption of the tea-drinking which goes on all day. The Tibetans have a remarkable capacity for drinking one cup after another of thick muddy brick-tea. I should have burst if I had attempted to emulate their achievements in this respect. The tea is of the poorest kind, the refuse and small twigs from Chinese tea plantations. It is compressed into brick-like blocks which are wrapped in paper, sewed up in bales, and despatched to Tibet. The porcelain cups also come from China. They are always tasteful and delicate, and have generally saucers and shield-shaped covers of silvered metal. The beverage is mixed with butter, which floats in small yellow blobs on the top of the tea. All who drink it have a shining ring of butter round their mouths. When you have taken a drink the waiter comes at once with the black pot to fill up the cup again.

64. A Nepalese in Tokchen.

65. An Old Man (Tibetan).

66. A Nomad.

Sketches by the Author.

Sonam Ngurbu, puffed out and satiated, stark naked down to the hips, and with waving hair hanging down over his copper-brown shoulders in tangled locks, at last took his long thin Chinese pipe, filled and lighted it, smoked and puffed and filled the whole tent with the acrid fumes of bad tobacco from Bhotan. The metal bowl of the pipe is small and contains only enough tobacco for a couple of puffs. When the fine yellow powder is burnt out, the pipe is emptied by tapping it on a wooden disc attached to the châtelaine, and when refilled is lighted from the embers thus preserved. In this way the tedious business with glowing coals and flint and steel is avoided in a country where matches are still unknown.

Jamtse Singe had only the right arm bare. He wore a violet vest with yellow borders and over it the usual blood-red lama toga. His head was uncovered and his grey-besprinkled hair was cut short. His portrait is on the coloured plate facing p. 368 in Vol. II.

When Jamtse had enjoyed enough of the good things of this world he said good-bye to Sonam Ngurbu, laid his hand on his head to bless him, and returned to the tent of the lama of Chokchu, whither I followed him. This prelate was named Namgyal Dorche, and he was a small agreeable and humorous man. He was also exceedingly picturesque in appearance. He wore a yellow mantle with wide sleeves over his red toga, a rosary wound twice round his neck, and a silver case containing a small image hanging by a string. A shield-shaped hat of gilded wood covered his head and was fastened by a string under his chin. He had on his nose Chinese spectacles with large round glasses of rock crystal which gave him the air of a learned theologian. With this colleague Jamtse Singe was frank and unembarrassed, and he even promised to do his best to get my letter sent to Gartok.

Sonam Ngurbu had two brothers. The three had two wives among them, which works out at two-thirds of a wife per man. These ladies left much to be desired in feminine grace, cleanliness, and youthfulness, and it is no wonder that his share was enough for each brother. Their faces were painted dark brown, they wore in their ears silver plates and pendants of beads and turquoises, ribands hung from their pigtails down their backs, whole sashes, with shells, rupees, and silver ornaments sewed thickly on them. How matrimonial squabbles are settled in such a singularly composed family is hard to understand. Probably they do not occur. In Tibet jealousy is unknown, and conjugal fidelity is an unknown and superfluous virtue.

Not till dusk did Kutus go for my riding horse. Meanwhile I took leave of Sonam Ngurbu, who was sitting in the women's tent with only ladies about him. Some of the beauties who were not painted looked quite pretty, but they are always substantially built and masculine.

Then I returned to my own home on the river bank. There the Gova of Selipuk and his staff were waiting for me. He had considered the matter and now promised to send my letter to Yumba-matsen in two days, and thence in nine days more to Gartok. It would be carried from tent to tent and reach its destination over the Jukti-la.

The day abounded in varied incidents, and it ended in an unusual manner. It was half-past six o'clock, I had gone to bed, and the light was out. A violent gust of wind swept over the country and was followed by a strong earthquake. The first shock passed immediately into a circular movement of the earth's crust. Then came a vibration twice repeated, and finally a short tremble was felt which became weaker and then ceased altogether. Ten minutes later came a second shock, succeeded after five minutes by a third. The first shock gave us a feeling of uneasiness and insecurity. Kutus called out, "Ya Allah!" and the other men awoke and talked excitedly. Only the dogs took no notice. This was the second time I had experienced an earthquake during the twelve years I had spent in Asia. The first was in the year 1895 at Tash-kurgan on the Pamir.

No frost on the night of June 28; the minimum was only 33°. Two monks visited me, sent by the prior of Selipuk, to inquire if I had felt the earthquake and what it meant. Earthquakes had been felt before in this country, but not often. They also wished to know if I could control at pleasure the weather, winds, and rain, and, if so,

67. Two of Sonam Ngurbu's Horsemen.

would I summon the rain-clouds to water the dried-up meadows of Selipuk. But I assured them that I had nothing to do with the precipitation, and could not alter the paths of the winds and clouds. But one can always prophesy, so I foretold heavy rains in the near future. Fortunately I was right. The reader will soon be convinced of this when we are beyond the holy lake. There I often rejoiced as I heard fresh showers patter on the slopes, and thought of my dear nomads and of the grass that would spring up, sucking moisture out of the earth to feed the flocks and bring general prosperity to the black tents during the coming winter.

As early as about six o'clock the Tibetans of Chokchu began to drive their yaks, sheep, and horses into camp from the pastures. The great Sonam Ngurbu would continue his pilgrimage to expiate his sins by walking round the holy mountain. But he would not leave without bidding me good-bye, and honoured me with an early visit to my tent, bringing me as a token of friendship a present of sugar, rice, *tsamba*, and delicious white Chinese wheaten flour, which postponed the terrible moment of starvation for a few days more. In return I gave him a silver watch and chain, and we parted the best of friends.

It was an age before the immense caravan was ready to march. The tethered yaks stood in long dark rows waiting hours for their loads. The horses became impatient and made their way off to the pastures again. However, the tents were taken down one by one and packed up, and by eleven o'clock the van of the yak detachment was ready to set off westwards. Half an hour later the next column followed in the track of its comrades, and still another after an hour more. The yaks grunted and marched lazily under light loads in a closely packed mass; the drivers and leaders followed at their heels, some of them armed with guns, others with a cudgel horizontally across their backs and tightly held under their arms. All marched bareheaded with light quick steps and whistled merrily, shouted, and sang.

Then came the turn of the sheep which, nodding and tripping like a lively brook, waltzed through the Sumdang-tsangpo. Sitting under my felt awning I observed with attentive eyes this cheerful departure, this wandering of men and animals to the mountain of the eternal gods. The horses were again collected, and most of them were saddled while the rest carried loads; we counted sixty of them.

At last the white and blue tent of the chief stood on the plain alone, surrounded by a dozen horses and mules. At the moment he stepped out we saw the tent lowered to the ground, quickly rolled up with its poles and ropes, packed on horses and carried away. When the pilgrims were in the saddle I went off to the place where their path crossed the river. The troop reached the bank in a short gallop and plunged through the water to the spot where I was waiting. Here all the riders dismounted except the women. We once more said good-bye, expressed our pleasure that fate had brought us together, wished one another a good journey, and hoped to meet again at Tokchen.

Then Sonam Ngurbu leapt on to his white horse, which bore a coloured cloth under its saddle, and handsome trappings, and was decked with tassels and other ornaments. He had confined his unkempt hair under a red turban, and round his neck he wore a rusty arrow-head, which brought him good fortune in war and success in thief-hunting. At his left side hung a large silver case, a portable temple, and his sabre stuck out horizontally from his girdle. The wives sat man-fashion on their little spirited horses, with their felt boots thrust into the stirrups, and their hoods over their heads. The rest of the troop were equipped as for a campaign. They carried sabres and long lances with flat steel heads, and polished strips of steel wound like snakes round the shafts hung by straps from their shoulders. They were also encumbered with clumsy muskets and their long sharp-pointed forks, which would prick the eyes and ears of their next neighbour if he did not look out. Now the wild horsemen thrust their lances against the ground and swung themselves into their saddles with the dexterity of acrobats, and the troop dashed away in a cloud of dust, and soon disappeared behind the monastery hill.

68. Soldiers of Sonam Ngurbu.

Sketches by the Author.

After Sonam Ngurbu had gone the steppe looked empty and desolate. Only two poor nomad huts stood there, and two dogs rummaged about for offal.

Feeling lonely I went up to the monastery, the doors of which had hitherto been as firmly closed to us as the Mendong and Lunkar monasteries before. But now they were opened to me without hesitation. The *nerpa*, the steward of Selipuk, came to meet me, and led me through a great gate into a forecourt, where bales of provisions were piled up against the walls, and were sewed up in yak hides with the hair outside. The bales contained tea and barley, *tsamba* and salt. The wooden saddles of the transport yaks were heaped together in a corner. Various guns and sabres hung on a wall in picturesque confusion. Evidently Selipuk was prepared to defend itself in case of attack.

The *nerpa* told me that the cloister owned 61 yaks and 1012 sheep, which were partly hired out to caravan, partly employed by the monks on their own account. For the rest the monks lived on the voluntary offerings of the nomads. Three monks had attained the rank of a *Kanpo*, six were *Gelong*, and three *Getsul* or novices; besides these there was the *nerpa*, who attended to their worldly business.

A staircase leads into a cave-like room called *simkang*, which is dim even in the middle of the day. On a bench against the wall sat the prior entertaining Namgyal Dorche, his brother in Buddha. They were feasting and drinking tea. The guest from Chokchu held in his hand a leg of mutton, and cut pieces off it, which were quickly crunched by his strong teeth. The meat was raw, old, and dried, and consequently as hard as wood. Dried peaches, raisins, and sugar were placed before me. We talked and jested together, but they would not let me into Buddha's temple.

Then the visitor rose. He belonged to Sonam Ngurbu's household, and must not be late in overtaking the others. We accompanied him down into the court, where two novices were waiting with three red-bridled horses. In his red cowl with his gilded shovel hat above it, this bundle of clothes was a splendid incarnation of the Lamaist cult.

He said farewell politely to the prior and myself, and off he went over the hill.

As long as a glimpse was to be seen of the departing guest and his two companions, Jamtse Singe stood in silence, but as soon as they disappeared his manner changed as though by magic. He suddenly became another man. With a sly smile he invited me to go up into the *simkang* again, and there he was excessively lively. I understood him. He felt now free from all supervision and espionage. He was now sole master in the house, and could do as he liked. The other monks also came in, and were equally delighted.

Then appeared my friend the village headman, accompanied by some other Tibetans. They handed me a lump of barley-sugar and a copper bowl of milk, and then they threw themselves down full length in front of me, touching the ground with their foreheads, and behaved just as if I were an image of Buddha. I asked in astonishment what this conduct meant, and learned only too soon the answer to the riddle. It was a long tale.

The sheep of the monastery had just returned from a district in the north where a fine and much-prized china clay occurs. They were laden with it, and were now to go on to the fair at Gyanima, where the china clay was expected to fetch two rupees a sheep's load. All the men of the monastery were, then, required as drivers, and they must withdraw their promise to forward my letter to Gartok.

I pretended to be enraged.

"Did you not tell me yourselves that there were 60 tents under the rule of the monastery? Did you not say lately that the nomads brought the wood and water that the monks required, and watched their flocks on the pastures? And now you are supposed not to have a man free to ride to Yumba-matsen."

"Forgive us, Sahib, all are now engaged. Permit us to oblige you in some other way."

"Very well, I will forgive you if you show me the hall of Buddha."

"With the greatest pleasure," cried Jamtse Singe rising and drawing us all in procession to the *lhakang*. The doors were opened wide, and the mysteries were exposed to my

69. SONAM NGURBU LEAVING SELIPUK.

70. SONAM NGURBU'S DEPARTURE FROM SELIPUK.

gaze. But there was really nothing worth looking at. The hall was small and dark. An assemblage of gods stood on the altar table, among them Sakya-toba (Buddha) and Tsong Kapa. All the usual strips and pictures hung from the roof, and spears, sabres, and guns were fastened to the pillars. The whole show was like a marine store, a scene of religious still life faded and corroded by time and covered with the dust of centuries. The shelves were almost breaking under the weight of the holy books, hideous masks grinned out of the corners, and two temple drums stood between the pillars, waiting to rouse the attention of the gods when the monks mumbled their prayers in the day or night.

My stock question: "How old is this monastery?" was answered as usual with the words: "It has been here from the beginning." This has the same significance as the first words of the Bible and one thinks of an astounding age. But when the prior subsequently admitted that a *Rinpoche* or incarnation named Gerung Lama had founded Selipuk, its age was considerably reduced. To judge by its exterior the monastery can scarcely be more than two hundred years old.

The portal of the *lhakang* faces east as always. Numerous *mani* walls surround the cloister compound, and a wall which forms a forecourt and a fold for the sheep of burden. There, too, lies the holy monastery dog chained up, which barks whenever any one approaches.

At dusk I bade farewell to the friendly monks.

When night came on the sound of noisy music reached my tent. Drums rolled, flutes were blown, and bells and rattles rang. Service was being held in the hall of Buddha.

The noise died away, and Jamtse Singe came alone to us in the darkness. He called out to us from a distance to keep hold of our dogs that he might gain my tent without being bitten.

"Do not be cross, Sahib," he said, "because I have not returned your visit before. I durst not as long as Sonam Ngurbu was here."

"It is of no consequence. You are always welcome. Sit down and take tea with me."

"When are you coming to us again, Sahib?"

"Perhaps in two years," I answered, as if it were quite a settled matter.

"Will you be so good then as to bring me two presents, first a revolver and then some kind of salve which will make hair grow. I intend to grow a moustache."

"What in the world do you, being a monk, want with a moustache?"

"Well, I was in Lhasa four years ago when the English broke into the Potala, and one of the strangers assured me that a man who wore a moustache could never fall ill."

"That is all a lie, I can assure you. But now, tell me, have you kept your promise of yesterday and consulted your holy books about the fate of my lost caravan?"

"Yes, certainly. The books say that your servants are alive and that all is well with them. They are now somewhere to the south of this, and in twenty days you will meet them, or at any rate receive reliable news of the caravan."

Truly the answer of an oracle! Within four-and-twenty hours I was to have good reason for abandoning faith in the utterances of Lamaist books.

Jamtse Singe was given a few trifles I was able to spare. In return he gave me a *tenga*, barely 6d., adding that the sum was certainly small but that the coin would have the effect of a talisman; as long as I retained it in my possession I should never come to want. Then he rose, rubbed his forehead against mine as a sign of friendship, and styled me "Lama Sahib," or, freely translated, Doctor of Divinity.

After he had returned to his small close cell with a hearth in the middle of the clay floor and chests and the bed against the walls, we held a short consultation, and decided to travel on next morning to Tokchen, though we had no money and no provisions.

71. THE INNER COURT OF SELIPUK.

72. ENTRANCE TO THE SELIPUK MONASTERY.

CHAPTER X

THE MODELS OF KYANGYANG

THE journey I commenced on June 30 was a reckless undertaking. We could hold out a few days more with the presents we received in Selipuk, and the two youths who had accompanied us with yaks from the Pedang-tsangpo fortunately allowed themselves to be persuaded to travel a little farther with us. But first they wanted their arrears of pay. After they had been paid out to them there remained in our money-chest two small silver coins, a *tenga* and a six-anna piece, amounting together to about a shilling. The beggars who crowded round us at our departure thought us stingy because we did not give them even a copper farthing.

I do not know exactly what my thoughts were. I seemed to be venturing ever farther on thin ice which would break at last. The main thing was to keep the men from Pedang as far as Tokchen, if possible, whence I might be able to send a messenger to Gartok. But what would happen if they struck in the middle of the Trans-Himalaya? Well, time would show. One can bear a great deal before one dies, and we must make our way by some means or other.

So we marched past the monastery walls. There Jamtse Singe came out, took hold of my horse by the bridle, and led it for a time with his own holy hand. Then he bowed his adieu, and soon the monastery disappeared behind the hills and was included in the treasure of kind friendly memories I retain of Tibet.

The path traversed an immense plain, the largest I have seen north of the Trans-Himalaya. Three tents and some grazing yaks, otherwise quite lifeless. Hard grass grows in clumps and tufts on hillocks or domes of roots, and the horses are often in danger of tumbling over head first on the uneven ground. We twice cross the winding Sumdang-tsangpo. Its bottom is treacherous, and the horse which Kutus rode almost sank into the mud.

The part of the steppe on which shepherds feed their flocks is called Rartse. There we pitched camp 441. According to my custom I drew a panorama of the mountains around us. Here especially a picture was important for orientation, for the compact walls of the Trans-Himalaya rose in the south. I had just finished the drawing and was inserting the compass bearings of the high summits and deep valleys, when Lobsang came to inform me that four men and as many laden mules were approaching our camp. Astonished and doubtful I examined the little party through my field-glass. They came nearer and grew larger. Mirage made them appear to float a hair's-breadth above the ground.

"The man in the yellow mantle is Abdul Kerim," cried Kutus.

"Sedik and Gaffar are also with him," said Gulam.

"The fourth is a Tibetan," declared Lobsang.

A short time later all our perplexities were cleared up and our anxiety was over (see Vol. II. p. 400). The future shone again in a rosy light. Abdul Kerim brought our remaining 2684 rupees sewed up in small bags, and my financial circumstances were now brilliant. We need deny ourselves nothing on the way to Simla, and the men from Pedang, who had adhered to us in evil times, should be royally rewarded.

Four of our men were still absent; they had baggage yaks and therefore they marched more slowly, but they were now on the right track. The caravan was, at any rate, considerably strengthened when we moved farther over the steppe on July 1, after nine degrees of frost in the night. The belt of grass came to an end after a time, and in its place an extraordinarily flat fan of rubbish and sand stretched up to the foot of the mountain. On its slope there could be distinguished a whole series of old shore embankments. We could see distinctly how closely they followed the contours of the hills and projecting rocks, how the intervals between them increased over gently sloping ground, and how they closed up together on steep declivities. The highest beach wall stood perhaps 23 feet above the neighbouring ground, and at the uppermost plainly recognizable beach line (15,990 feet) we were 413 feet above the surface of the Nganglaring-tso.

So far the lake had formerly extended, during a period when the precipitation was more abundant than at present. The whole plain near Selipuk then lay under water, and the Tengri-nor in the east had a worthy counterpart in the west, on the northern flank of the Trans-Himalaya. In the course of time the quantity of precipitation diminished, the great lake contracted, and in our day only the salt lake is left, which fills the basin round the rocky islets of Nganglaring-tso. But the old shore lines and beaches still remain, and in them slumbers a fossilized echo of the murmur of the surge of ancient times.

The way led south-west over a small pass and up a grass-grown valley, where we passed the night at the spring Kyangyang (camp 442). Five nomad tents were set up there. Two men hurried out of one of them to advise us not to encamp there for our own sakes, because an old man was dying of an infectious disease in one of the tents. It was the old story. We might be vagabonds, and so they were anxious to get rid of us, and tried to scare us away with smallpox and plague.

Light showers had been falling since noon, and I was glad for the sake of Jamtse Singe and the shepherds. Towards evening arose a south-westerly storm which howled fearfully through the valley. The brazier was more necessary than ever; we wrapped ourselves in our furs and could almost believe that another winter was coming on.

We spent three whole days in the Kyangyang valley or, as the whole district is called, in Kyangyang-lobchang, in which two valleys to the west are included. We had to wait here for the four men still missing, Suen, Abdullah, Abdul Rasak, and Sonam Kunchuk. On the evening of July 3 we saw them making with all speed for our camp, and it was touching to witness their joy at seeing us again. They threw themselves down on the ground before me, and embraced their comrades with tears. Abdul Rasak wept so that he could not stand still for excitement. He lifted one foot and then the other, stamping as in a wine-press. I was hard-hearted enough nearly to kill myself with laughing at the sight of this uncontrolled delight.

Before the three days were over the people at the spring of Kyangyang had recovered from their fright: they perceived that our intentions towards them were good. An elderly man who had once been the Gova of the place promised us the thirteen yaks we wanted if we would have patience for a couple of days more, and so we could dismiss the men from the Pedang-tsangpo. They received double pay. They had rendered us excellent service, had helped us to discover the Shovo-tso, and to reach the Nganglaring-tso. They set out well satisfied on the same evening to return to their home.

The heralds of the south-west monsoon skimmed like dark shadows over the valley, and on July 2 it rained and snowed alternately almost all day long. The snow did not fall in flakes, but in small round grains which soon melted. In the Trans-Himalaya it snows even in summer; but then our camp stood 16,330 feet above the sea.

On July 3 also the rain pattered down monotonously until evening. The nomads were delighted. We had brought with us the first rainy days of the year, and perhaps on that account they were so friendly to us. It was impossible to work out of doors. And I could not endure to sit idle all day and listen to the rain beating down on my dilapidated tent. So our neighbours were informed that every female who presented herself in Abdul Kerim's large white tent to have her portrait drawn should receive a rupee, and every male a *tenga*. The women were to put on their best clothes, and all the ornaments they could get together out of their hiding-places.

An hour passed, and then another, but no models appeared. There was ample excuse for them; they were bashful, and wondered what this invitation meant. Filthy lucre at last overcame their scruples. I heard chains and châtelaines clinking, and saw them coming slowly across the meadows like a wedding procession, with bridesmaids, witnesses, and guests. The Tibetans stood loitering awkwardly between the tents. Then the rain began to pour down more violently, and our guests were glad when Lobsang drove them into Abdul Kerim's tent. It had a long smoke vent in the top through which light entered, but, unfortunately, rain also, and therefore an improvised umbrella had to be rigged up over my drawing-board.

They were really stylish, these ladies of the Kyangyang valley. Some of them are depicted on the coloured plate facing p. 374 in Vol. II., where the name is incorrectly spelt Kyangrang. At first they sat silent looking about the tent or blowing their noses loudly with their fingers. But they soon laid aside their shyness. The Ladakis joked with them, and before long the country beauties were heard chattering and laughing with them as freely as if they too had been born in Ladak. When I told the models that I had finished, and that they might go home, they still remained sitting with us in the tent.

They answered fearlessly my questions about their ages and names, and a young maiden told me with evident pride that the long back cloth was called *pale* in Tibetan, the metal plates *raktig*, and the shells sewed on it *dundok*.

A worthy matron, the thirty-eight-years-old Norsum, wore on her brow a row of silver rupees strung on threads of coral. On the top of her head she had a red cloth closely studded with cheap coral and inferior turquoise. Her hair was divided into a number of thin tails, into which chains of white and blue glass beads were woven. Her neck was hidden by many rows of coloured glass beads. The two cloths which hang like veils from the top of the head down over the back are patchwork of green and red stuff in geometrical figures. They are decorated above with rupees, anna-pieces, and Indian copper coins, and little four-cornered silver plates are sewed on in the midst of this collection. Farther down follow scallop shells in double rows, and at the bottom are fixed a number of Indian uniform buttons, some of brass, others silvered, all with the arms of Great Britain, or the initials of a regiment.

The Tommy Atkins who wore these buttons could hardly have foreseen that they would one day be the pride of a woman in the eternal snow mountains of Tibet.

I value such a costume at 250 rupees, or about £17. There were 100 rupees on it in cash. The older the ladies the finer they are decked out; the young ones had at most a chain of beads round the neck, and the ornaments of their back cloths were of copper. It must certainly require a long time to complete the collection. All depends on the rain. After copious rain the grass is juicy, the sheep are healthy and grow fat. Then the well-being of the nomads increases, and their wives can afford to buy a necklace from some travelling trader, or sew a rupee on their mantillas. Or a new uniform button reaches Tibet in some mysterious way, and they buy it. Now each of the models could add another rupee to her finery.

Two old women had no ornament at all, but still they waited patiently till their turn came. Apparently they had reached the age when the mother resigns her trinkets to a daughter who has found a bridegroom, or to a young girl who will become her daughter-in-law, at least in part. Thus it may happen that an outfit may take two generations to complete it. Hardly more than two, for life in Tibet is uncertain; if the rain fails the grass dries up, the flocks are decimated, and the nomads find themselves compelled by want to sell their trinkets.

The following day I was almost flooded with models. They came from other tents in the neighbouring valleys, where the rumour of an easily-to-be-earned rupee had spread. But now the occupation had ceased to amuse me, and I could spare no more paper. But they received their rupees all the same for their goodwill, and as friendly souvenirs.

The feast of reunion was held on a pitch-dark night, when the rain hissed in the flames of the camp-fire. Suen was master of ceremonies in the caravan. He danced round the fire and led the gleeful songs of Ladak.

The night of July 4 brought us 11.3 degrees of frost. Thirteen yaks stood ready in the morning to take over our baggage. Our own animals were to be spared as much as

73. Abdul Kerim's large Tent

74. Inquisitive Visitors.

possible; we might want them in districts where the people were less friendly disposed than the inhabitants here in the interior, who had never seen a European. The ex-Gova of Kyangyang provided us with a sheep and goat, and procured barley for the horses and butter for the men. He had felt so much at ease in our company that he asked to accompany us for a day's journey, and he was very welcome to me for the sake of the information he could give me about the route.

We ride slowly up between the porphyry rocks of the valley to the pass Kyangyang-la (16,920 feet). Sheep and yaks feed in large numbers on the thriving grass on ground honeycombed with mouse-holes. From the saddle of the pass we perceive near to us the somewhat flat snowy summit of the Lavar-gangri, which we first made acquaintance with at Selipuk. On the farther side of the pass the valley of the Lavar-tsangpo and the river itself come into view, and eleven black tents are set up on its banks. Here we pitched our camp 443.

In the night the temperature sank to 12.4°, on July 6 in 31½° N. lat.! The absolute height explains it. In such a country no mercy is to be expected from winter. For two whole days we followed the left bank downwards, and saw the river gradually increased by water flowing out of the side valleys. At the point where we leave the Lavar-tsangpo we see the river winding off northwards to its confluence with the larger Aong-tsangpo. But before it reaches it the river almost touches the Damrap-tso, a small long lake with banks white with salt. Every step we take is over unknown country never pressed by any but Tibetan soles. The land is still very sparsely peopled, but game occurs in larger quantities than before; I saw kiangs, Pantholops and Goa antelopes, and swarms of hares.

On July 8 we awoke in camp 445 (17,048 feet) in cold windy weather to an interesting day's march. I could perceive myself that we should have to surmount a mountain chain of the first rank, for during the past two days I had seen the snow-crowned crest of a mighty range through the portals of several side valleys. But I did not know whether this range formed the watershed of the Nganglaring-tso.

We had camped in the mouth of the Ding-la valley, where a narrow strip of grass grows by the bank of a babbling brook. The valley is so narrow that there is no room for a path. We therefore clambered over the steep flank of the left side of the valley bestrewn with sharp pebbles of grey granite. Not a square foot of the slope is bare; the ascent is sharp and the horses got sore feet. The yaks did not mind, for no way is impassable for them. Over this detritus the pilgrims tramp to Kang-rinpoche.

The path runs rather high above the bottom of the Ding-la valley, sometimes southwards, sometimes south-westwards. We had therefore a splendid view over the massive, lofty, and wildly fissured mountain barrier along the opposite right side of the valley, which culminates in three similar humps with caps of eternal snow; the lappets of these caps, turned into ice, descend to the valley in the form of hanging glaciers.

A last curve in the road brings us in a southerly direction through more accumulations of granite rubbish up to the hilly saddle which is known as the Ding-la. The streamers of the pass flutter on their stakes in the highly rarefied air, and the cairn, a brother of the clouds, is perhaps the highest on earth that marks a caravan route. It is erected at a height of 19,308 feet above sea-level. In Europe the ascent of Mont Blanc is a height record, and there one has the continent of the white men at his feet. But on the Ding-la one is 3526 feet higher.

And yet the view is less extensive than one would expect. The near-lying crests hide the distant horizon to the north. Only the quadrant between south-east and south-west presents an uninterrupted prospect. There rises a continuous range with a row of small snowy peaks. It appears much less imposing than the Ding-la range. But as a watershed it takes a much higher rank, for from its flanks the water drains to two seas, the Gulfs of Arabia and Bengal, and its brooks flow northwards to the Ngang-laring-tso. The Ding-la range must accordingly be broken through by these streams, and is of the second order.

With one of the Tibetans acquainted with the country by my side I scan the southern horizon. Near by to the south-east towers a snowy massive, which sends out from its firn basins short glacier tongues into rocky abysses. S. 22° E. another snowy giant exhibits its royal crown among the clouds, and at its western foot opens the valley Da-teri, its floor still covered with winter ice. Due south we descry the small lake Argok-tso barely a day's journey distant.

After we had listened long enough to the "Om mani padme hum" of the streamers of the Ding-la pass, we worked our way painfully down through the granite pebbles of the other side and encamped at the spring-fed rivulet Lumanakbo, at a height of 16,857 feet (camp 446), where the frozen snow was lashed by the wind against our tents.

CHAPTER XI

OVER THE TRANS-HIMALAYA FOR THE LAST TIME

On July 9 we directed our march southwards through the labyrinth of the Trans-Himalaya, and then my hydrographical conceptions were gradually made clear. To the east is seen the Ding-la range with its gables and firn-fields and its glacier tongues, from which the melted ice collects into a brook carrying 88 cubic feet of water per second. To the right stands a smaller crest without snow. Large pasture lands lie among the mountains and remains of old nomad camps are numerous.

After a time we are on the bank of another brook which comes from the south, meandering through a broad open valley. Its water, 175 cubic feet per second, is rather turbid and of a dirty green colour; farther down it receives the above-mentioned brook. The united stream then breaks through the Ding-la range in a narrow valley. When I inquired why the road did not rather run along the river instead of mounting the laborious ascents to the Ding-la pass, our Tibetans replied that the narrow passage was quite impracticable.

We lingered a while on the bank of this watercourse, the largest we had met with for a long time. Gulam had always fishing tackle with him, and he caught a good number of fish.

"What is this river called?" I asked one of the Tibetans.

"Nya-mangbo-tsangpo," he replied, without moving a muscle of his face. *Nya* signifies fish, *mangbo* much, and *tsangpo* river; the whole means, then, the river abounding in fish, a name which my informant had apparently coined for this occasion.

"The river is called Argok-tsangpo, sir," affirmed another guide; "it comes from the Argok-tso."

"Which way does it take?"

"It unites in the district Aong-dunker with the Aong-tsangpo. The water collects from all the mountains and valleys you see to the south to the Argok-tso, and therefore the Argok-tsangpo is the largest brook in this country." We were also able afterwards to ascertain that the Argok-tsangpo is the main stream and the Lavar-tsangpo only a tributary. The united river is the largest watercourse that pours its water into the Nganglaring-tso.

One is surprised to find the watershed between the Sutlej and the Nganglaring-tso so far to the south. Somewhere or other in the north-west there must be a triple watershed which sends out brooks to the Indus as well as to the Sutlej and the salt lake. But the country there is unknown, and future explorers will find plenty to occupy them in that region. My journey was only a reconnaissance.

Over undulating ground, between densely overgrown swamps fed by springs, our road passes south-westwards. The view is frequently quite obscured, for heavy leaden clouds sweep over the ground and often a shower of hail beats in our faces. The Argok-tso is near to us, and, as far as we can see, it has a fairly round form. At the foot of our hills flows a third brook, the Surnge-chu, which discharges into the Argok-tso. We pitched camp 447 beside it.

Dark heavy rain-clouds again moved over the mountain crests and thunder growled dully. The camp was hardly ready when the storm broke in earnest. Hail beat on the tops of the tents and now and then a rain shower pattered down. A large sheet had to be laid over my tent which leaked on all sides. So it had to be! Now the flocks of the nomads were safe for the coming winter, and their owners could live without anxiety for the next twelve months.

Towards evening the rain changed into snow, which fell for hours without intermission, this time in large light flakes, which grazed the tents noiselessly, and spread their white carpet all over the country. At night the clouds parted for a time and the moon stood in the gap, sad and blurred, and threw its pale light over the wintry scene around us. The temperature fell to several degrees below freezing-point and the snow crunched under the feet. And, moreover, this was the hottest time of the year. We might fancy ourselves back in the winter of Chang-tang. Our camp stood 16,913 feet above the sea.

Wolves howl near us during the night. We are accustomed to them and take no notice of their ghastly barking. But we have always to think of our horses and mules, which are grazing out in the snow watched by two men. The wolves are certainly bold, for two revolver shots resound through the valley, then all is quiet.

The new day dawned gloomy and threatening, and our march was continued west-south-westwards, over wintry white hills and through crunching snow. The god of storms drove his rumbling chariot through the world of mountains that surrounded us on all sides. The snow lay half a foot deep and covered the treacherous mouse-holes in which the horses stumbled. It caked also, and hemispherical soles clung to the hoofs of the animals. Later in the day, however, the sun got the upper hand, the snow mantle disappeared, and the ground was quite bare when we reached our camp for the night.

The day's march had led us along the Surnge-chu, and we had waded through a large number of its tributary brooks. How different from the dried-up region in which the Indus has its sources! The camping place is called Takche, and six-and-twenty black tents in two villages were our neighbours. The Gova of the place had gone to Purang, but his deputy, a little plump big-boned Tibetan, promised to obey all my commands. I could have as many yaks for the journey to Tokchen as I wanted. The man told me that Sonam Ngurbu had left Takche the same day; he had prepared the nomads for our visit, and told them they had nothing to fear from us. So the nomads of Takche were friendly towards us from the first.

The men from Kyangyang had done their work and could go. They were well paid and also took with them two dogs which we had no use for. The one was dirty yellow and a disagreeable animal; Little Puppy and Takkar could not bear him. The other was a little brown tyke called Kamduk. Both had joined us of their own free will, and barked all night long without the slightest provocation. Now they were led on the leash back to Kyangyang. But at the very next camp Kamduk was back again, wagging his tail vigorously and barking for joy. After this proof of faithfulness he was spoiled by every one, and he accompanied us all the way to India until he stopped behind of his own accord in one of the first villages. He feared the heat and wished himself back again in the summer snow of the Kyangyang valley.

We stayed a day more in Takche. We wanted to buy sheep, *tsamba*, and milk, and barley for the horses. The weather, too, was not inviting for riding. There was a continual downpour of rain, and the ground was converted into one great swamp of mud. The grass here was more juicy than it had been for several years. I beguiled the time with the pencil and I had not to wait for sitters. They came in shoals, of both sexes and all ages, filling Abdul Kerim's roomy tent, where the atmosphere, laden with the evaporation from dirty nomads and their soaked clothing, soon exhaled a sweet Tibetan aroma. There was sunshine in the tent, while outside the rain ceaselessly swilled the tightly-stretched tent cloth. It was really a great pleasure to sit all day among the sons and daughters of the wilderness, to see them close at hand in garments that had grown on their sheep and yaks, and listen to their unrestrained gossip and their hearty laughter. In a corner sat a young mother with her baby. She was wretchedly clothed in rags, but well developed, and with an energetic expression. Every time the model's seat was free she came forward and declared that it was her turn, and at last she got her wish.

Quite a popular assembly crowded before the tents when we set out on July 12. They could not possibly be all from the black tents of Takche, and it turned out that many had come from the neighbouring valleys. They had heard that the portrait-drawing would be continued, and they hoped to earn a rupee or *tenga* themselves. But their hopes were crushed, for a new drove of fine yaks was already waiting with their drivers, and the neighbours of Takche could only witness our departure.

The whole country was veiled in a curious mist. The ground seemed to steam, near objects were only faintly visible and the distant heights were quite hidden. The phenomenon was evidently due to the heavy rain of the day before followed by the cold of the night. In the forenoon a smart hail shower fell, and the guide, who had always to walk beside me, said that the hail was of no use, for only the rain could refresh the grass roots. Farther westwards, he said, the pasturage was better, and in a week the community of Takche would remove thither, for so long there would still be grazing on the Surnge-chu.

The ground rises exceedingly gently. We are close to the Surnge-la, a water-parting pass of the first order in the Trans-Himalaya, and yet the land before us is practically level. Mountains stand on both sides but we march along an open valley between them.

"Here is the Surnge-la," remarks my attendant.

"Impossible! The ground is quite level; this is not a pass."

"Yet this is what we call the Surnge-la," he replies.

A singular pass! Not the smallest gutter of water betrayed a fall in any direction. The ground was perfectly level. After a few minutes, however, we came to a tiny bed running southwards. Now the question was settled; the boiling-point thermometer was brought into action and gave a height of 17,310 feet. The numerous cairns on the pass are misleading, for they are set up a good way to the west of the highest point.

The structure soon becomes more apparent; we ride down a slowly falling valley, the Surnge-lungpa, drained by a brook belonging to the drainage basin of the Sutlej. We had, therefore, crossed the Trans-Himalaya for the eighth time. The Surnge-la pass was much easier than any of the others. It can scarcely be called a pass; it is only a slight flattened rise in a very low part of the system.

From camp 449 (16,132 feet) in the mouth of the

75. On a Pass of the Trans-Himalaya.

Panglung valley we saw to the west-south-west an old acquaintance, the Pundi mountain, which stands at the northern shore of the holy lake. The Surnge-lungpa continues on in the same direction, and now proved to be the upper part of the Pachen valley, to the mouth of which I had made a short visit the year before. During the following day's march we left this valley on the right, and crossed instead over the small pass Yübgo-la and a succession of low hills, and finally through a narrow winding valley.

We had just pitched camp 450 when the sky darkened as at eventide. A little later the hail burst its bonds and clattered down with indescribable violence. The whole country became dead white again, but the white covering was soon washed away by closely falling rain. Only the higher parts of the mountains, where precipitation always takes the form of hail or snow, remained white. There is a splashing and squelching in the wet outside. Little Puppy comes running in, and of course contrives to shake the water out of his coat on to my note-books and maps just under my nose. Then he rolls himself up on his mat in the corner to dry. But he cannot rest. When he hears steps outside he must go out to inspect the passer-by and growl at him, and then he comes in again to give me another douche.

Towards evening the rain passed into snow. Such is always the order of the weather in high Tibet. First a violent hailstorm, which then passes into rain, and ends in a fall of snow. But how different were the two rainy seasons of 1907 and 1908! During the former there were only some sprinkles of rain a couple of times, while now violent and continuous downpours were always falling.

The next day's journey brought us down the Gelle-lungpa valley, wedged in between cliffs of hälleflinta and grauwacke. At a place where the valley widens out twelve horsemen overtook us, driving in great haste a herd of yaks and a number of sheep before them. They were from Nepal, and I asked them as they passed, why they were in such a terrible hurry. "Thieves from Tibet stole our cattle," they replied, "so we at once pursued the band. We overtook them two days ago, and we thrashed the scoundrels so soundly that they could hardly walk. But we recovered our animals, and now we are riding hard to get quickly over the frontier and home."

"Where do we cross the frontier?"

"At the pass Chakpalung-la." A name of ill-omen, for it means "Pass of the Robbers' Valley."

"Do not the authorities help you, if you make a complaint to the Devashung?"

"No. The Tibetan Government will not lift a finger to assist foreigners who have been plundered. When we are robbed by Tibetans all we can do is to rush off with all speed into the enemies' country and recover our property by force, or it vanishes like smoke. As you see, we are well armed. Good-bye!"

The spokesman of the Nepalese hurled another curse at the Tibetan scum, and then the singular troop disappeared round a bend of the valley.

We are now in the domain of Tokchen. The district that we have passed through last is named Hor-paryang. We have still a small pass to cross, the Rigong-la; from its top a small corner of the holy lake is seen in S. 69° W. Otherwise the view is not worth much. Heavy leaden blue-black clouds hang over the whole country, hiding everything. The road passes at last over gently swelling hills down into the valley of the Samo-tsangpo. We pitch our camp on the left bank of the river close to the place where the Gova of Tokchen has set up his summer tents.

As usual the camp was ready and the smoke rose from the fire when I rode up. I dismounted, handed Lobsang my riding-whip, let Gulam draw off my leather boots and untie my sash, threw back my Tibetan mantle, went into the tent, and thanked God that He had permitted my strenuous work to come to a successful end.

Then I lay down on my bed and pondered. Seven months had passed since we left Ladak. I had traversed in many directions the great blank space north of the Tsangpo, the upper Brahmaputra. I had gained my end, done my duty, and could now take the road to India with an easy conscience.

But before we commence our journey back through the

Sutlej valley let us pause a moment here after the eighth crossing of the Trans-Himalaya and recall to mind what was known in past times of this mountain system. And let us pay homage to the memory of those men who have contributed, each his share, to the knowledge of the Trans-Himalaya. They touched principally the eastern and western wings. The centre, the "white patch," remained for me. Therefore I had the good fortune to be able to set aside theories which had been formulated on various occasions, to connect together the two wings, and prove that the Trans-Himalaya is a single, connected system consisting of a host of different ranges, a folded system of the earth's crust, which, indeed, is surpassed in loftiness by the Himalayas, but is their equal in massiveness and importance.

CHAPTER XII

THE TRANS-HIMALAYA IN ANCIENT TIMES AND THE MIDDLE AGES—THE CATHOLIC MISSIONARIES

It seems to us wonderful that huge areas of southern Tibet, a country so near to the frontier of India, and only two hundred miles distant from English railway stations, have preserved their secrets until the present day, and that no European eyes have beheld their scenery. Five years ago I succeeded in forcing my way through their once inexorably closed portals of rock, in sketching the main lines of hitherto unknown mountain ranges, in tracing watercourses of which no rumour of their existence had penetrated into the world of white men, and in pitching my tent by the shores of lakes where till then no European had listened to the song of the waves.

The goal of aspiration for centuries, the poles of the earth have in the course of those five years been reached. They were considered inaccessible. Nothing could be harder of accomplishment than to travel to one of the poles with dog teams. And yet both poles have been conquered in the exciting chase, for which national vanity and the palms of victory waving at the end have supplied the impulse. Bold men were pressing on towards the poles at a time when so many mysteries lay unsolved in the deep valleys where the Indo-European rivers have excavated their channels. Flags were planted at the poles before the storming of the heights of Gaurisankar, Kanchanjanga, or Mount Everest had even commenced. The future will show that the loftiest peaks of the world are less easy of access than the two points through which the axis of the earth passes. The fact that the country to the north of the upper Brahmaputra was only attained a few years before the poles, shows that the roads leading over the boundaries of Tibet into the interior are not strewn with roses.

From the jungles of Bengal, from the luxuriant vegetation of the Ganges valley, and from the plains of the Punjab, wooded heights rise up to bare steep cliffs and precipitous ramparts, to wildly-fissured jagged mountain massives, and finally to the domain of the petrified kings, crowned with eternal snow, that look down over suffocating steamy India. Out of reverence to this mysterious icily cold and inaccessible world the old Hindus, the people of the plain, located the habitation of their gods and their holiest places in those high regions which were beyond the reach of mortals.

But the religious faith of the Hindus has not peopled all the Himalayas with gods, and not everywhere in the high mountains are there pilgrimage resorts. The central Himalayas play no part in their imaginings. The land of Nepal also is mentioned in their classical literature only in obscure and indefinite terms, and the Hindus have travelled so far only in recent times. On the other hand, they have made pilgrimages from remote ages to the source of the Ganges, and they placed their principal gods in that part of the Himalayas where the large rivers rise and collect all the volumes of water which make corn grow on the plains of India and ripen into golden harvests.

The Indian Aryans came from the north-west and passed over the mountains into Kashmir, to the Punjab, and down to the countries of the Indus and Ganges. An original knowledge of the regions where their deified forefathers lived and roamed, remained in their consciousness as a misty remembrance from the hoary past, and therefore the country round the holy lakes and the river sources were also the dwelling-places of their gods. (See Anton, Freiherr von Ow, *Hom, der falsche Prophet aus der noachitischen Zeit*, p. 152; and "Religionsgeschichtliches aus Sven Hedins Transhimalaya," in *Anthropos*, v.

(1910), Nos. 5 and 6; also Lassen's *Indische Altertums-kunde*, etc.)

According to the ancient Vedic books Asia lay floating as a lotus blossom (*padma*) on the surface of the ocean. The blossom had four petals, and the one pointing south was India. Amidst the mighty mountain summits which fructified the earth with their rivers stood Meru, the mountain of the gods, the loftiest elevation in the world, like a fruit germ in the middle of the flower. Meru included the whole high region which extends northwards from India. All Tibet belonged to it. Not only the Aryan Hindus raised their hands to the mountains from which, according to their belief, their help came, but other people also living in the surrounding lands lifted their eyes to the mysterious heights. To the Burmans the snowy land is the dwelling of the departed after death, and even the Chinese have chosen the Kwen-lun, a part of Meru, as the abode of their oldest saints.

From this Meru flow five enormous rivers, the Ganges, the Indus, and the Oxus to the south and west, the other two to Siberia and China. Threefold ranges of mountains border Meru on the south and north. The three on the south are: Himavan or Himalaya, close to India; Hemakuta, or the mountains with the gold-glittering summits; the third, "The Best among the Mountains," serves as the throne of Indra, the god of rain and storms, who launches the glistening bridge of the rainbow across the vault of heaven after he has made his thunder rumble over the earth. This third range is Kailas, the paradise of Siva, the home of the gods. Beyond the holy lakes, and beyond the holy sources of the Indus, Sutlej, Brahmaputra, Ganges, and Jumna, it lifts its sunlighted head above a country unmatched on earth for lofty majesty and grand solitude.

Mythical poesy has peopled Kailas with a host of wonderful figures. Above it rises the heaven of Siva, and to attain to it after death is the object of the most deeply felt desire—a feeling shared also by the Tibetans. In the *Cloud Messenger* Kalidasa sings of the aerial flight of the holy alpine swans to Kailas and its neighbours, which shine like white lotus blossoms high above all the lands of the world, a reflexion of the smile of Siva and the light of Mahadeva. Kailas, the crystal, is the origin of the divine rivers, and there is worshipped the imprint of Rama's foot.

Thus the old Aryans, forefathers of the Hindus, enveloped this world of impenetrable mountains in a tissue of legends and lyrics, and made them the scene of heroic deeds and of the wonderful incidents of epical and mystical fancy. Out of the darkness of Indian legends a scarcely audible whisper from the Himalayas at last reached the west, by means of accounts based on rumours and attributable to Phœnician and Persian merchants. Herodotus tells of the gold-digging ants to the north in cloudland, a tale which originated among the old Hindus. He says that the singular ants are smaller than dogs, but bigger than foxes. Nearchus states that he had himself seen a skin of the gold-digging animal in Alexander's camp, and found that it resembled the fur of a panther. In our days the legendary ants have been turned into marmots, which dig holes in the ground, and throw up heaps of earth and sand before the entrances of their retreats, in which perhaps some gold-dust may occasionally be found.

The geographical writers and historians after the time of Alexander mention only the lofty chain which skirts India on the north. Megasthenes calls the Himalayas Emodos, a name which Pliny also employs. Arrian gives the name of Caucasus to the western part of those mountains. Pomponius Mela makes the Taurus the northern boundary of India, which extends its mighty ridge, in his opinion, which had also been that of Eratosthenes, from Asia Minor to the farthest east. Strabo states that as a traveller proceeds eastwards from the Hyrcanian or Caspian sea the mountains lie to his right, which the Greeks name Taurus and which extend to the Indian sea. Of the lofty mountain masses which lie beyond Bactria and Sogdiana and the land of the wandering Scythian herdsmen, he says: "All other mountains, from the land of the Aryans onwards, the Macedonians named Caucasus, but among the barbarians the various parts bear the names Paropamisus, Emodus,

Imaus, and others of similar sound." In another place he repeats the same idea in the following words: "India is bounded on the north, from Ariana to the eastern sea, by the last parts of the Taurus, which the natives call by the names Paropamisus, Emodus, Imaus, and others, while the Macedonians name them Caucasus."

In the second century A.D. Ptolemy, the greatest geographer of antiquity, wrote his famous work, laying the foundation on which in later times Arabians and Europeans built.

The name Imaus in Ptolemy's system embraces not only the eastern part of the Hindu-kush and the western part of the Himalayas, but also the eastern marginal chains of the Pamir. Accordingly the Imaus, which runs north and south, divides the western Scythia from the eastern, while the part that runs east and west, corresponding to the Himalayas, forms a boundary wall between India intra Gangem fluvium and Scythia extra Imaum montem, the country in the southern part of which are piled up the mighty chains of the Trans-Himalaya.

The whole of the Middle Ages lived, so to say, on the wisdom of Ptolemy, and his world system acquired dogmatic sharpness in the minds of the learned. For eleven hundred years the high-born rivers flowed down from their holy sources, and the dark cloud-masses of the monsoon struggled with the sunshine for lordship over the Trans-Himalaya and its neighbours. Europeans had no suspicion of the existence of the highest elevation on earth. Like a fortress protected by massive ramparts and full moats, unknown Tibet dreamed in undisturbed peace. How long would it be before the outer walls fell? Seventeen hundred and fifty years were the winter storms to sing their ancient hymns over the lofty mountain land of Bongba before its last defences fell before the assault of European exploration.

When the earth had made its eleven hundredth revolution round the sun, the first meagre report of Tibet reached Europe. The Mongols had fallen upon the world of the white men, devastating all the country. To obtain information about the home and conditions of life of that warlike people, the Pope in the year 1245 sent Piano Carpini to the Great Khan. This ambassador heard of Tibet during his long journey. "The inhabitants of that land are pagans," he says; and then adds: "They have a most astonishing or rather horrible custom, for when any one's father is about to give up the ghost, all the relatives meet together, and they eat him, as was told to me for certain."

On his celebrated journey, during the years 1253–1255, the object of which also was the court of the Great Khan, the excellent Franciscan monk William de Rubruquis learned that beyond the Tanguts dwell the Tibetans, "a people in the habit of eating their dead parents so that for piety's sake they should not give their parents any other sepulchre than their bowels. They have given this practice up, however, as they were held an abomination among all nations. They still, however, make handsome cups out of the heads of their parents, so that when drinking out of them they may have them in mind in the midst of their merry-making. These people have much gold in their country, so that when one lacks gold he digs till he finds it, and he only takes so much as he requires and puts the rest back in the ground; for if he puts it in a treasury or a coffer, he believes that God would take away from him that which is in the ground. I saw many misshapen individuals of this people."

Rockhill, who has edited and annotated the best edition of Rubruquis' narrative, doubts whether the Tibetans were cannibals in the Middle Ages. On the other hand, there is still at the present day scarcely a temple in Tibet where human skulls are not used, both as drinking vessels and as religious drums. (Such a drum is depicted on p. 1174 of the second volume of my book *Through Asia.*)

During the twenty years (1275–95) of his sojourn at the court of the Emperor Kublai Khan, Marco Polo, the most illustrious traveller of the Middle Ages, heard various reports of Tibet and describes it as follows:

This province, called Tebet, is of very great extent. The people, as I have told you, have a language of their own, and they are idolaters, and they border on Manzi and sundry other regions.

Moreover, they are very great thieves. The country is, in fact, so great that it embraces eight kingdoms and a vast number of cities and villages. It contains in several quarters rivers and lakes, in which gold-dust is found in great abundance. Cinnamon also grows there in great plenty. Coral is in great demand in this country and fetches a high price, for they delight to hang it round the necks of their women and of their idols. They have also in this country plenty of fine woollens and other stuffs, and many kinds of spices are produced there which are never seen in our country. Among this people, too, you find the best enchanters and astrologers that exist in all that quarter of the world; they perform such extraordinary marvels and sorceries by diabolic art, that it astounds one to see or even hear of them. So I will relate none of them in this book of ours; people would be amazed if they heard them, but it would serve no good purpose. These people of Tebet are an ill-conditioned race. They have mastiff dogs as big as donkeys, which are capital at seizing wild beasts (and in particular the wild oxen which are called *Bayamini*, very great and fierce animals). They have also sundry other kinds of sporting dogs, and excellent lanner falcons (and sakers), swift in flight and well trained, which are got in the mountains of the country.

In conclusion Marco Polo states that Tibet is subject to the Great Khan.

In the year 1328 the Franciscan monk Odorico de Pordenone travelled from Shan-si through Shen-si, Se-chuan and Tibet. Henri Cordier, who has prepared the best edition of the monk's narrative, supposes that in the second section of his journey, of which no report is extant, the monk passed through Badakshan, Khorasan, Tabriz, and Armenia, back to Europe, where he arrived in the year 1330. His name deserves to be kept in memory, not only because he achieved one of the most remarkable journeys through the midst of Asia, but also because he was the first European to pass through Tibet and to visit Lhasa, that maiden city which for five hundred years longer excited the curiosity of European travellers, and in their imagination displayed façades towering to the skies under golden temple roofs. Odorico mentions Lhasa Gota, which, according to Cordier, is a corruption of the name Potala borne by the monastery palace of the Dalai Lama. The country he calls Riboth; he knows that it borders on India, and says:

76. MOUNTAIN LANDSCAPE, SOUTH-WESTERN TIBET.

> This kingdom is subject to the Great Khan, and there are found bread and wine in much greater abundance than in any other part of the world. The people of this country live in tents of black felt. Their chief city is very fine, all of white stone, and the streets well paved. It is called Gota. In this city none dare shed human blood, nor of any beast, out of reverence to an idol they worship there. In this city dwells the *obassy*, that is to say their pope in their language. He is the chief of all the idolaters, and bestows the benefices of the country at his pleasure.

Odorico also knows how the Tibetans deal with their dead, that the priests cut off the head from the body and give it to the son, who makes of it a drinking-cup, from which he drinks to the memory of his father; while the body is cut up and thrown to eagles and vultures, who, like the angels of God, conduct the departed to the joys of paradise.

Again three hundred years passed away without any new information reaching Europe about the Land of Snow, as the Tibetans often call their home among the mountains and valleys. Three hundred years the fortress held out, and strangers never crossed its fosses. Storms swept the snow down the flanks as before, and caused it to flutter down like white kerchiefs from crest and peak. The wind groaned and piped round the rocky spurs, and the waves beat sadly against the lonely shores of the lake of Brahma and the Tengri-nor. Safe and undisturbed as in a sanctuary, the nomads migrated with their black tents from one pasture to another just as in the days when Odorico was in their country.

In the year 1625 Father Antonio de Andrade travelled to Tsaparang. We shall speak of him later when we come to that country. Now we will cite only those travellers who have touched on the Trans-Himalaya during their wanderings. We have seen that the Hindus of ancient times knew no other part of this system than Kailas. Whether Odorico crossed the eastern ranges of this system is unknown. But now modern times have instituted a more thorough knowledge of the earth by their more rigid demands. During this period the wings of the Trans-Himalaya will be made known by degrees.

In the exploration of the earth there is hardly a grander and more enchanting problem conceivable than the connection of these two wings and of the delineation of the whole system. At any rate I have never faced a more splendid task. Therefore I dwell with pleasure on the remembrance of those travellers who in earlier and more recent times have contributed stones to the tremendous structure which is now completed in its main features. Perhaps it is also worth while to inquire how one of the most gigantic folds of the earth's crust, which stands as firmly in its rigidity now as in the days when the Vedas were written, gradually emerged from the night of folklore and legend, how it was unveiled little by little, grew more and more towards completion on the maps of Europeans, like a game of patience, and at last stood fully revealed to geographers as one of the loftiest, longest, and greatest mountain systems in the world.

The last section, which was yet wanting to form a complete representation of the whole, had an area of about 42,000 square miles, and was therefore larger than Bavaria, Württemberg, and Baden together. On the map were to be read there the words "terra incognita," and they had to be wiped out. When this was done the game was won.

The first traveller who brought back to Europe fuller and more valuable information about Tibet, and who is known with certainty to have crossed the eastern Trans-Himalaya, was the Jesuit father Johannes Grueber, who left Pekin in the year 1661, accompanied by Albert Dorville, a member of the same order, with the intention of travelling through all eastern Tibet by the Kuku-nor, Lhasa, Shigatse, and Khatmandu, and, after his journey was successfully accomplished, came to Agra in 1662. The description of this journey does not do justice to its importance. Athanasius Kircher and Thévenot have published a small number of letters and notes from Grueber's hand, the latter in his noted work *China Illustrata*, which appeared at Amsterdam in 1760.

From this we learn that the two priests crossed the Hwang-ho twice, and that, after passing Sining-fu, they travelled for three months through the desert of the Tatar Kalmukhs before reaching the kingdom of Lhasa, which was called by the Tatars Barantola. Their route ran over plains and mountains, and through rivers with grassy banks, where the herds of the nomads found pasture in sufficient quantity. "There are many who believe that this desert stretches from India to the Arctic Sea." There no other animals occur but "wild bulls." The inhabitants dwell in "portable houses," as Grueber calls what Odorico three hundred years earlier had correctly styled "black felt tents."

In the southern part of the land thus described, between Nakchu on the Salwin and the Reting monastery, south-east of the Tengri-nor, Grueber and Dorville passed over the heights of the Trans-Himalaya without suspecting that they had thereby added another discovery to the many they had already made during their long journey. That this mountain system does not stand out in Grueber's notes in the sharp relief that is really due to it, and that Kircher does not even mention it, is not to be wondered at, for the ranges on the south of Tsaidam, the huge Tang-la, which, two hundred years later, excited the astonishment and awe of Father Huc, seem to have left no impression on Grueber's memory.

What he seems to have retained better and has described in vivid colours, are the Langur mountains south of the Tsangpo, which correspond to the northern water-parting chain of the Himalayas between Shigatse and Khatmandu. There he was attacked by mountain sickness, and he has ventured to make some very hazardous conjectures to explain the unbearable headaches that throbbed in his temples, all which have been accepted with blind faith by his Catholic successors on the elevated roads of Tibet.

He says that the Langur mountains are so high that men cannot breathe there because the air is much too "subtle," and he adds: "In summer certain poisonous weeds grow there which exhale such a bad-smelling dangerous odour that one cannot stay up there without risk of losing one's life, nay, not even cross the mountains without danger to life." For a whole month one must cross immense mountains and march along awful abysses before reaching the first town in Nepal.

In Kircher's work we read also of the audience the Grand Duke of Tuscany granted to the good Grueber on his return home. Among other questions the Grand Duke inquired whether Father Johannes had travelled from Tatary or the land of the Usbeks into the empire of the Great Mogul, or whether he had come from the east, and whether he had become acquainted with the countries of Tibet which Antonio de Andrade had described. To this Grueber replied that he had marched westwards from Pekin to Sining-fu, and that he had been forced by the Great Wall to take a south-westerly course. To reach the territories of the Great Mogul he had wandered through the desert of Tatary and the kingdoms of Barantola, Nepal, and Maranga, and had at last come to the Ganges. "As to the kingdom of Tibet, my knowledge of this country is fairly exact, for both our Jesuit fathers and the Christians who have been there have given me thorough information."

When the Grand Duke inquired whether Father Johannes thought of describing the provinces and states lying outside China, and whether he intended to publish geographical maps of them, he received the regrettable answer that since Father Athanasius Kircher had already made known in his work *China Illustrata*, everything of importance about Grueber's journey, it would be a waste of trouble "to add anything to what had already been said by so great a man and to write a separate book." It seems as if Grueber considered it impertinence or even insubordination towards Kircher to pretend that he could write himself anything better and more complete than was contained in *China Illustrata*.

We recognize on one of Kircher's maps the Himalayas in the "Montes Tibetici," though Kailas, which belongs to the Trans-Himalaya, is included among them. To the north of this mountain we read the words "Tibet Regnum."

Fully fifty years vanished down the stream of time without an echo reaching Europe from the land where the mountains of the Trans-Himalaya bathe their summits in storm and sunshine. Then occurred in Rome an incident which paved the way to the mysterious country. The Capuchin fathers of the province of Ancona applied for an exclusive right to establish missions in Tibet, and they acquired it by a special order of the Congregatio de Propoganda Fide. Accordingly Father Felice da Montecchio, Father Domenico da Fano, and other members of the Capuchin order set off from Rome in the year 1704 to travel to India and Tibet. Fano arrived at Lhasa in 1707. In his efforts to establish a mission station in the capital of the Dalai Lama he encountered great difficulties, and he returned to the eternal city to obtain more vigorous support from home. In the year 1715 he was again in India, equipped for another attack on Tibet.

Meanwhile the Jesuit father, Ippolito Desideri, had received permission from the general of his order to convert the Tibetans, and after receiving a blessing from the Pope he too started on his way. From India he took with him Father Manuel Freyre. The two travelled through Kashmir to Leh, where they spent the summer of 1715 in learning the language, in the hope of sometime "seeing fruits well pleasing to God's majesty sprout up among the mountains of Tibet."

Desideri left Leh in August 1715 and travelled in the train of a Tatar princess with a large caravan and many attendants through Gartok and past Manasarowar to Lhasa, where he arrived in March 1716. He had accomplished a journey which ought to make his name for ever famous. It was not till quite 188 years later that the next European expedition—under Captain Rawling and Major Ryder—passed through the valley of the upper Brahmaputra. Father Desideri was the first European who travelled along the whole of the Trans-Himalaya along its southern flank.

For nearly two hundred years nothing was known of that journey except what Desideri imparted to Father Ildebrand Grassi in a letter written in Lhasa on April 10, 1716, which was afterwards printed in the *Lettres Edifiantes*. In some ten others he does not touch on any geographical questions. At last a full and detailed manuscript in his handwriting was found in his native town, and this precious document was published at Rome in 1904. Desideri is the most prominent among the Catholic missionaries who visited Tibet early in the eighteenth century.

He rode for months together past the holy lake and along the Tsangpo valley, always having on the north side rocky buttresses and spurs of the Trans-Himalaya, which looked down into the valley like house gables into an old alley. Nevertheless, Desideri has hardly anything to say about these mountains, but, like Grueber, speaks only of the Langur mountains. When one follows the same route as Desideri it is not hard to understand him. The Langur mountains, which he crossed with much toil, made a deeper impression on him than the Trans-Himalaya, of which he obtained only partial views from the Tsangpo valley. Seen from the comparatively deep trough of this river, the system makes a grand effect only at two places; elsewhere the near-lying mountains which hide the main crest are not very high.

But Desideri is the first European who saw Kailas and has told about it. He relates that he left Gartok in the middle of October, and on November 9 reached the greatest heights he had to surmount on the way to Lhasa. Here, in the province of Ngari, he says, is an extraordinarily high mountain of considerable compass, covered with eternal snow and enveloped in the most terrible cold. Perhaps he wandered round Kailas, for he speaks of the trains of pilgrims and of the religious significance of the mountain.

He knows the various roads from Lhasa to Sining-fu, and he knows that Tibet borders in the east and north-east on China and Tatary, and in the north on wild desolate countries and the kingdom of Yarkand. He tells those who were not to know of his writings till two hundred years later, that Shigatse is the capital of the kingdom of Tsang; that Lhasa, the heart of the central province of Tibet, which is called U, lies among high mountains; and that lofty crests also rise to the north of the Sera monastery.

Desideri's description, however, has never to our minds

conveyed the idea of a continuous mountain system along the way from Ladak to Lhasa. Such an idea existed even in the year 1904 only in theory. In the same year appeared Desideri's description, but it did not enlarge our views or clear up our notions of the mysterious mountains.

But the Langur mountains did make an impression on the father. "They have the peculiarity that every one who crosses them experiences acute discomfort, especially severe headache, nausea and want of breath, accompanied by fever." Desideri has a much more sensible and correct explanation of mountain sickness than Father Huc, who attributes it to poisonous exhalations of carbonic acid rising from the ground. The former says:

> Many people believe that the discomfort one experiences arises from the reek from certain minerals that occur in the interior of the Langur mountains; but, as no unmistakable traces of such minerals have been found hitherto, I rather believe that the unpleasant symptoms are due to the thin sharp air. I am the more inclined to this view, because my pains became still more unendurable when the wind rose, and I suffered from excruciating headache just on the tops of the Langur mountains.

One would have thought that during the long period of nearly four decades, when the Capuchin mission, certainly with some interruptions, was at work in Tibet, quite a literature of the remarkable country would have grown up, for at that time many priests travelled backwards and forwards over the Himalayas. And yet the geographical results are meagre. The most important work of the time is Georgi's *Alphabetum Tibetanum*, for which Orazio della Penna and Cassiano Beligatti supplied almost all the material. Then there is Beligatti's own narrative, which was recently discovered at Macerata in the communal library Mozzi-Borgetti, and was published at Florence in 1902.

Beligatti, born at Macerata in 1708, consecrated his life at seventeen years of age to the service of religion, and went out in 1738 as a missionary to Tibet, where he remained two years. He returned in 1756 through Nepal and Bengal to Italy, and died in 1785 in his native town.

He made his journey to Tibet in the company of

Father della Penna. The Capuchin mission had meanwhile passed the height of its prosperity, and not even the last reinforcement it received from Rome could enable it to maintain the holy fire in opposition to the Dalai Lama and the divine images in the Potala. In April 1745 the flame expired entirely when the last missionaries left Lhasa. Their houses were destroyed, and a hundred years were to elapse before missionaries from Europe—the Lazarists, Huc and Gabet—again penetrated into the holy city. Yet still in the year 1904 the English under Younghusband found a bronze bell in the Potala which had once rung for service in the Capuchin church. "Te Deum laudamus" could be read in the bronze, and the Ambrosian hymn of praise seems to linger in the waves of sound when the bell is set swinging by pagan hands, and the melancholy and victorious echo rebounds from the rocks of Tibet.

Beligatti tells of his long tramp from his native place all the way to Paris, of his taking ship at Lorient for the port of Chandernagore, which he reached half a year later, and whence he and his comrades travelled on in December 1739 to Patna. From here eight brethren and sixteen native servants set out on Shanks's pony to follow the rough paths through Nepal.

As soon as Beligatti in his narrative has passed the Tibetan frontier we read on with redoubled interest, wondering whether he will vouchsafe us a glance at the Trans-Himalaya. But we wait in vain for the rise of the curtain, and freely pardon Fra Cassiano for this omission when we remember that the distant view was perhaps limited by the enveloping draperies of the monsoon clouds.

On the heights of the Langur mountains he cannot refrain, any more than his predecessors, from alluding to the "singular influence which the mountains exercise over both men and animals, whether this arises from the rarefaction of the atmosphere or from deleterious exhalations." With three saddle-horses, on which the most exhausted of the party rode, the ecclesiastics painfully toiled up the steep mountain flanks. In a shed on the road they, their men and steeds, and some travellers from Lhasa, spent a

77. A Tibetan Woman.

78. The Governor of Saka-dzong.

Sketches by the Author

night which reminded them of "purgatorial fires and hell." Some whimpered, others cried out aloud, while those lying beside them gave themselves up for lost or raved. They could not eat, and their four-legged companions did not contribute to raise their spirits. Next day they crossed the pass, and when they reached Tingri on the other side, all their troubles were over.

He depicts in the same masterly style as Desideri the daily work during his journey, and describes how the camp was pitched and the animals let loose to graze, the camp-fire lighted and food cooked, while some of the brethren read the breviary; how they set out again to make new efforts, scolded refractory mule-drivers, and watched the reddish-yellow swift-footed kiangs which circled round the caravan; how they were troubled by the violent wind which often interfered with their cooking; and how they came to one village after another, and constantly to a new monastery. Beligatti's route may be easily traced on a modern map.

The priests stayed two days in Gyangtse to keep Christmas. Then they went on over the Karo-la to the singular lake Yamdok-tso, with its peninsula and nuns' convents. Next they marched up to the pass Kamba-la, which lies in the range dividing the Yamdok-tso from the Tsangpo. Here, too, nothing is said of the view on the northern horizon, which must have enchanted them. But he, or perhaps Della Penna, who accompanied him on this journey, told Father Georgi what they saw, for the *Alphabetum Tibetanum* draws aside a corner of the curtain, and in the following words: "E vertice Kambalà prospicitur nova quaedam series elatiorum nivosorumque montium ad Boream. Hinc eos adorant Indi ac Tibetani viatores," or "From the summit of the Kamba-la one perceives a new series of lofty snow-covered mountains to the north. From here Tibetan and Indian travellers worship them (the mountains)."

The snow-covered crests far to the north are the part of the Trans-Himalaya which the Tibetans call Nien-chen-tang-la, and which are holy in their eyes. If the sky were clear, Odorico de Pordenone, Grueber and Dorville, Desideri and Freyre, and all the Capuchins who crossed the Kamba-la, must have beheld the same sight, and yet they have not disclosed anything of the imposing scene displayed before the eyes of the traveller as he looks northwards.

At length they crossed the Tsangpo in the boats of yak hides, which are used at the present day, and on the morning of January 5, 1741, "il Padre Prefetto" (Della Penna) and Father Floriano hurried on to Lhasa to put in order the dwelling in which all were to meet on the following day. Beligatti followed at the head of the rest of the party; he passed the large Brebung monastery on the left, skirted the outer wall of the Potala, and entered the holy city on January 6.

At the end of his narrative Beligatti tells of the handsome monasteries, Sera and Galdan, of the manner in which the missionaries were received by the "King," of their visit to the Chinese Resident, of a Tibetan banquet, of the temple festivals at the New Year, and of the entry of the Grand Lama into Lhasa.

A large part of the original manuscript has been lost, but the portion which has been unearthed from the dusty twilight of the library archives, and has been published 160 years after it was written, throws new light on the life of the Capuchins in Lhasa, and their toilsome journeys over the Langur mountains and the Kamba-la. Thus, then, Fra Cassiano also has at last emerged from the realm of shadows, and has in the narrative of his journey raised a worthy memorial of his life's work.

From Della Penna's hand there is a description, as excellent as it is short, of Chang-tang, the "Northern Plain," as the Tibetans call the plateau land. It is entitled "Breve Notizia del regno del Tibet." He speaks also of the "Duchy of Dam," lying eight days' journey from Lhasa and two from Nak-chu. There is now no such duchy, but there is a village Dam, and a pass of the same name leads over the Trans-Himalaya south-east of the Tengri-nor.

In a short essay Della Penna devotes a few words to the memory of the famous Dutch traveller Samuel van de Putte, who journeyed between 1723 and 1738 from India through Lhasa to Pekin, and returned to India by the same route. Grueber and Dorville followed nearly the same road as Huc and Gabet were afterwards to try. Van de Putte stayed a long time in Lhasa, and then continued his journey, disguised as a Chinaman, in the train of a Lama embassy to the Son of Heaven. He died at Batavia in 1745. In his will he expressed a wish that all his manuscripts should be burned, for he feared that his short notes written on loose leaves might be wrongly interpreted; they might convey erroneous notions of all the wonders he had seen and experienced, and thus cast a slur on his name.

CHAPTER XIII

THE JESUITS—D'ANVILLE—THE FIRST ENGLISHMEN—RITTER, HUMBOLDT, AND HUC

When the great Emperor Kang Hi (1662–1722) had rounded off the frontiers of his realm by the conquest of Mongolia, Formosa, and Tibet, he decided in the year 1708 to have a map compiled of his immense territories. He entrusted the execution of this work to the learned Jesuits, who sojourned in Pekin and enjoyed his especial favour. At first he confined himself to the countries about the Great Wall, but when the Jesuits, after the lapse of a year, spread out a map 15 feet long before the eyes of the Emperor, he was so delighted that he wanted his whole empire to be surveyed in this manner. The Jesuits began with Manchuria and the province Chi-li, a work which occupied two years. After that not a year passed without one or more provinces being added to the great cartographical work. It reflects great credit on the Chinese that the Jesuits found in every province home-made maps that had been compiled long before. Only Tibet had never been surveyed.

The most prominent of the Jesuits was Father Régis, who lived 36 years in China, and wrote in Du Halde's great work on this country articles on Korea and Tibet. The Emperor Kang Hi sent an embassy to Lhasa to win over the Tibetan princes to the policy of China, and the envoy was also charged with the hopeless task of seeing that a map of all the lands under the rule of the Dalai Lama was compiled.

In the year 1711 this map was delivered to Father

Régis, who found it useless. The Emperor, however, did not give up the scheme. Two Lamaist monks, who had been educated in Pekin, were instructed to survey the mountainous country from Sining to Lhasa and the sources of the Ganges, and to bring to the Son of Heaven revivifying water from that holy stream. In the year 1717 the map was completed and the Emperor sent it to his friends the Jesuits.

After a few slight improvements which were made in consideration of the school from which the two Lamaist topographers came, the sheets of their survey were incorporated in the whole cartographical representation of China, which was laid entire before the Emperor in the year 1718. A copy of this work was sent to the King of France, and from it D'Anville drew his famous map, but he also introduced improvements which were not always successful.

Just at the time when the Lamaist monks were busy at their work war broke out in Tibet, the Dzungarian Khan, Tsagan Araptan, having despatched his commander-in-chief, Seren Donduk, from Khotan to Lhasa with an army. It is a unique record in the annals of warfare that an invading army should march 900 miles through a hostile country for the most part uninhabited and almost everywhere as high as Mont Blanc, and yet be successful. On this campaign the Dzungarians crossed the Kwen-lun, the Karakorum, and the Trans-Himalaya, but of their fortunes we know little or nothing. We know, however, that the country round Lhasa was plundered and devastated, the temples robbed of their immense treasures, and that the enemy put all the lamas that were caught in sacks and carried them off to Tatary. The two lama topographers very nearly fell into their hands. When they heard of the approaching danger they hurried on their work and were solely concerned for their own safety.

The result of their travels was D'Anville's map of the year 1733, which was published in his atlas of China, 1737 (see *Trans-Himalaya*, end of Vol. I.). We find on it lakes and rivers that are difficult to identify; we find mountain ranges which run in all directions, but mostly from north-east to south-west, whereas the actual direction is from north-west to south-east. As European geographers had no other map than D'Anville's, they had to be content with his representation. It seemed, however, at least clear that the country north of the Tsangpo was a mountain land, and that from the crests and peaks of those mountains rivers rushed down and discharged into lakes without outlets. For long the influence of D'Anville's map was perceptible in every European atlas. Such is the case with the Tibet sheet in *Stieler's Handatlas* of the year 1875. Later, however, the whole area in which the central part of the Trans-Himalaya lies, having a length of 560 miles and a breadth of 75, was wiped out. Even the Tarok-tso and Tabie-tsaka were sacrificed, two lakes which D'Anville has reproduced very well. But how was one to know what was good and what bad? Everything was doubted. No European had been there. What was old and unreliable was rejected. Even in 1889 Dutreuil de Rhins refrained from inserting any Tibetan ranges on his great map of Central Asia, "car la plupart n'ont pas été même entrevues par les explorateurs modernes." Here there was work enough for the travellers of the new age. A hundred and ninety years after the first Chinese exploration a little order was to be introduced into this labyrinth of mountains.

The deeply indented valleys of the Indo-Chinese rivers have been considered to present the most intricate problems in Asia. And with these must be reckoned the country north of the Tsangpo. Through the efforts of Kang Hi and his friends the Jesuits, an inextricable chaos of peaks and crests began to peep out of the mist in the north. Even to the end of the eighteenth century the geographers of Europe seemed to have placed greater faith in the classical representation than in the Chinese. Afterwards the two changed places, and D'Anville was preferred to Ptolemy. Other sources were wanting, and when Major Rennell says in the text accompanying his map of Hindustan, published in 1785, that from the top of the Kamba-la "may be seen towards the north a range of still higher mountains covered with snow," we recognize Georgi's statement almost word for word.

When George Bogle left Calcutta in May 1774 as ambassador of the great Governor - General Warren Hastings to the Tashi Lama, he was also enjoined to question the natives about the countries lying between Lhasa and Siberia. In his memorandum to the ambassador Warren Hastings says:

> Tibet is a cold, high, mountainous country. . . . I have been told that a large river forms a boundary between China and Tibet, which was carefully guarded by the troops of both countries; and that Tibet received European commodities by the valley of Kashmir. But I have learned nothing satisfactory on these subjects. . . . The great rivers of the south and east of Asia appear to issue from its mountains. It is probably, therefore, the highest land in the old continent, and this circumstance, together with the difficulty of access to it, give it a striking analogy to the valley of Quito, in South America.

Warren Hastings had a clearer head than Bogle. The latter travelled to Tibet, crossed the Tsangpo and entered the Shang valley, and repaired to the monastery Namling, where he carried out his mission. But he made no inquiries about the farther course of this road, by which a pundit made his way just a hundred years later up to the Khalamba-la pass in the Trans-Himalaya, and which on the northern side runs down to the Tengri-nor. Though he ascended for a considerable distance the Shang valley, one of the southern valleys of the Trans-Himalaya, he has no suspicion of the existence of this gigantic system. And when he describes the character of Tibet in general terms he says only that—

> It is full of hills; they might be called mountains . . . however, one has few of them to climb, the road leading through the valleys. . . . The country is bare, stony and unsheltered; hardly a tree is to be seen, except in the neighbourhood of villages, and even there in no great numbers.

Bogle is the first Englishman and one of the few Europeans who have at any time come into contact with the Trans-Himalaya. Yet he took no notice of it. He cannot be compared with Desideri, Beligatti, and Della Penna.

In 1783–84 Samuel Turner travelled to the ecclesiastical court on a similar errand—to open up commercial relations between Tibet and India—and brought back a fine map of his route, the first existing 120 years later when Younghusband marched to Lhasa. Turner went only to Tashi-lunpo, and from his windows in the monastery was able to see the roads leading to Bhotan and Bengal, to Ladak and Kashmir, to Nepal, Lhasa, and China. He mentions the road to Sining in a few words which are not at all to be compared with Desideri's clear description of this route. On the Trans-Himalaya he is silent; indeed he could see nothing of its rocky ramparts from his windows in Tashi-lunpo. But if he had questioned the monks he would at least have learned something of the "nivosi montes" visible "ad Boream," about which Georgi drew information from Capuchin sources.

Equally blind to the mountainous region in the north was the bold but very ignorant Thomas Manning, who tried to reach Lhasa in 1812 on his own account, and succeeded. His report of the journey is marvellous for its emptiness and stupidity. He does not even know the name of Kamba-la. In Lhasa he hears nothing and learns nothing. His path to the mysterious city is like the track of a sailing ship on the sea, where the waves close up again behind the vessel. Younghusband, who followed in the steps of Manning a hundred years later, characterizes it as a meagre description of an important journey.

In the same year William Moorcroft betook himself to Manasarowar, and acquired there valuable information about the holy lake. On his map a range of mountains runs north of the lake, the Cailas mountains, but they are drawn as if they were the escarpment of a plateau country falling steeply to the basin of the lake. This, then, is the part of the Trans-Himalaya of which Desideri speaks. Desideri was there a hundred years earlier, but his description was not known until a hundred years after Moorcroft's.

During the first decade of the nineteenth century several Englishmen visited Nepal. It would be cruel to expect from them any new information about the mountains to the north. In his excellent work, *An Account of the Kingdom of Nepal* (1811), Kirkpatrick has practically nothing to say about Tibet. But Francis Hamilton allows us to catch at least a glimpse of the Trans-Himalaya, when he says that three ranges start from the Manasarowar, of which the southern two belong to the Himalayas, while the most northern approaches India only near the holy lake, bearing in its central part the peak of Kailas. This was told him by natives of Nepal, who also knew that the most northern range lay to the north of the Indus and Brahmaputra. He has not, however, ventured to extend the chain eastward on his map. He has left it to others to construct at the writing-table a continuous line of mountains up to the Nien-chen-tang-la of the Chinese maps. Of the salt lake, Tabie-tsaka, which had long been known to the Chinese, Hamilton cites a doubtful report:

> Borax and salt are said to be brought from a lake, which is situated nearly north from Kathmandu, about fifteen days' journey beyond the Brahmaputra. They are conveyed to Nepal on the backs of a large kind of sheep, of which many have four horns, and which seem to be the common beasts of burden in all the countries towards the sources of the Indus, Ganges, and Brahmaputra.

Another hundred years passed away. The reign of Ptolemy was over. The Chinese sources were discredited. Europeans tried to draw aside the curtain from the forbidden land themselves. But still the words "terra incognita" stretched across the map to the north of India and the Himalayas, a country which had remained a closed book during the century.

In the year 1895 Professor Vasilief published in St. Petersburg a description of Tibet, which had been composed by a Mongol named Minkhul Khutukhtu, who died in 1839, after having been employed in the lama temples in Pekin. This author also is indefinite, and states only that to the north of the Himalayas "there is a snow-covered mountain chain, which, as many believe, is identical with the Gandise (Kailas); but to me it seems more correct to apply this name as nomen appellativum not only to the Gandise but also to many thousands of other mountains between Kabul and Kam" (eastern Tibet). He mentions also "one of the four stormy snow-covered mountains, the gNyanchen-tan-lkhai-gans-ri," the Nien-chen-tang-la of the Tibetans and Chinese. Minkhul Khutukhtu knew, then, the two end columns in the east and west, between which the mighty wrinkles of the Trans-Himalaya are imprinted on the face of the earth.

A new period in the knowledge and geography of central Asia opens with Karl Ritter. He distinguishes two chains in the interior of Tibet; the Khor mountains which run from the Kwen-lun across to the Tengri-nor, and the Dsang mountains which skirt the Tsangpo valley on the north, are connected with the "extraordinarily lofty glaciated group Nien-chen-tang-la," and stretch west of the town Tsindo far towards the north-east.

In Ritter's time (1833) no other journeys had been accomplished into the heart of Tibet than those I have just described. His chief sources were therefore Klaproth's translation of Chinese works. Ritter is the first who has in a geographical handbook recognized Chinese learning so far that, relying on it, he has spoken of a continuous chain to the north of the Tsangpo. But he also accepts as trustworthy information certain false statements which may be traced back to mistakes of the lama topographers. According to Ritter the Dsang range is the eastern continuation of the Gangdisri (Kailas), and the whole system divides Tibet into two halves, the southern being the inhabited Tibet proper, and the northern the land of the Mongolian nomads.

The indistinct notions of the Chinese geographers have accordingly been remodelled and systematized by Ritter. He has made the oriental conception comprehensible and acceptable also to the peoples of the West. But he readily concedes that the knowledge of our Trans-Himalaya, which he calls "the entirely unknown northern range," must at the time be defective.

From the year 1833 we can then start with the fact that the greatest geographer then living was convinced of the existence of a continuous chain to the north of the Tsangpo, though he held it to be quite unknown with the exception of the mountain groups Kailas and Nien-chen-tang-la.

The next man of importance is the great Alexander

79. The Summit of Kang-rinpoche.

Sketch by the Author.

von Humboldt. He makes four huge mountain waves extend east and west through all the interior of Asia: the Altai, Tian-shan, Kwen-lun, and the Himalayas. Like Ritter, he places the two ranges Khor and Dsang in the high country between the Kwen-lun and the Himalayas, and says of the Dsang that it skirts the long valley of the Tsangpo, and runs from west to east in the direction of the Nien-chen-tang-la, a very high summit between Lhasa and the Tengri-nor.

In all this we recognize Ritter. The two German geographers have made use of the same sources, the statements of the lama topographers and other Chinese works. Many of them were translated by Klaproth, and Ritter and Humboldt drew their information from his work. Humboldt showed (1844) that the Chinese sources were more reliable than the Greek, Roman, Arabian, and Indian. Many circumstances contributed to this result, such as China's wars with peoples on the western boundary of the empire, the great pilgrimages in Buddhistic Asia, the religious reverence with which all lofty mountains were regarded, and lastly the compass. And yet the conspicuous parallelism which is characteristic of all the ranges of Tibet never struck the Chinese, and consequently Humboldt also was beguiled into assuming a meridional ridge east of Manasarowar, a watershed between the Indus and Sutlej on the north-west and the Tsangpo on the east.

Humboldt considers the mountain skeleton of Asia very simple and regular, and on his map the various systems were drawn with the greatest geometrical preciseness. Instead of the complicated ganglion of the Pamir he has a meridional chain, the Bolor, which long figured on maps of Asia. The Karakorum and the Trans-Himalaya are absent from his review of the great mountain systems, but they are to be found at least in fragments on his map. He has no great faith in D'Anville's representation, and is of opinion that it originated in a time when the most confused notions prevailed about the lofty mountains of Tatary, and it was assumed that they ran off in every direction without any defined order. And yet D'Anville was, on the whole, nearer to the truth than Humboldt.

In order not to lose the red thread in the knowledge of the Trans-Himalaya, we must remember that both Ritter and Humboldt represented the Dzang mountains north of the Tsangpo as one continuous chain. This quite erroneous conception has later been obstinately adhered to, though it is a step backwards compared to D'Anville's idea of southern Tibet.

On my return in the year 1909 I was astonished to find a statement in the *Geographical Journal* that my Trans-Himalaya had been known "for more than half a century." It was affirmed that Brian Hodgson showed it on his map as the Nyenchhen Thangla chain, and added in his text, "separating southern from northern Tibet." The other authorities supposed to have taken part in this discovery are Nain Sing, Ryder, Wood, Rawling, Markham, Saunders, Atkinson, and Burrard.

What, then, I had considered to be one of the most important discoveries any one could make in Asia had, forsooth, been known in England for more than fifty years.

As far back as the year in which I was born (1865) the great pundit, Nain Sing, travelled up the Tsangpo, and he shows on his map an uninterrupted mountain system up in the north. But of a continuous mountain system on the north side of the river he says not a word, and he has not marked it on his map. Ryder, Rawling, Wood, and Bailey made in 1904, after the march to Lhasa, a brilliant expedition, especially as regards topographical and trigonometrical work. They followed in the footsteps of Nain Sing, and had no opportunity of leaving the Tsangpo valley and making an excursion into the unknown country north of it. As to the other authorities none of them was in Tibet.

The last edition of the sheet Tibet in *Stieler's Hand-atlas*, issued before my last incursion into the forbidden land, shows nothing but a white patch to the north of the Tsangpo, and at the same time only the word "Unexplored" covered this region on the Royal Geographical Society's map of Tibet. And yet the country had been known for more than fifty years! Is it conceivable that the writer of the short notice referred to had sources of knowledge unknown to the Royal Geographical Society, and that the Geographical Institute of Justus Perthes in Gotha, the first in the world, had made the blunder of forgetting the records from which the blanks on the map might have been filled up?

The short notice made a great sensation, and went the round of the world's periodicals, and not least in Sweden, where it appeared in the papers on the day in January on which I reached home. What was the public to believe? Had I gone blindly to work, and had I claimed a priority rightly due to others?

We have followed step by step the explorations on the outer edge of the Trans-Himalaya down to the time of Humboldt, and have thus far found no fixed and certain points but Kailas and the Nien-chen-tang-la. Now we are on the threshold of the period for which Hodgson has been chosen as the standard-bearer. It will be worth our while to examine closely the sources and the data which have been brought forward as possessing a claim to accuracy. To me this is an affair of honour. I have waited three years, but it takes time to search in the recesses of libraries.

Brian Hodgson was born in the year 1800; he went in 1818 to India, and two years later betook himself to Nepal, where he acted as Vice-Resident from 1825 to 1833 and as Resident from 1833 to 1843. After he had stayed a long time in Darjiling, and had been altogether forty years in India, he returned home and died there in 1894, after a life of constant pioneer work, both as an investigator in humanistic and natural science and as a diplomat and politician.

Two years after Hodgson's death Sir William Hunter published his biography in a volume of nearly four hundred pages. I have read the book through from the first page to the last. It contains lists of innumerable articles and essays on every imaginable subject, which Hodgson scattered in profusion among periodicals in various languages. Yet in this memoir, which gathers together the most minute particulars of a brilliant career, not a word is said of the Nien-chen-tang-la, and not a line is devoted to the mountains north of the Tsangpo.

Well, then, it may be that the biographer has omitted the most important link in an otherwise complete chain. We have therefore no choice but to turn to Hodgson's own writings.

In an article (*Journal of the Asiatic Society of Bengal*, 1853, note on p. 122), the contents of which are chiefly on a linguistic subject, Hodgson says of the Nien-chen-tang-la:

> This important feature of the geography of Tibet is indicated by the Nian-tsin-tangla of Ritter's "Hoch Asien" and by the Tanla of Huc. I have, following native authority, used in a wide sense a name which those writers use in a contracted sense; and reasonably because the extension, continuity and height of the chain are indubitable.

That is all! Not a word on what Ritter twenty years before had stated in a fuller and more systematic manner. For the rest Hodgson speaks only of the property of the chain as a boundary wall between northern and southern Tibet and of the Turkish and Mongolian tribes that are said to dwell on its northern side. Hodgson's entire originality consists in having clothed Ritter's description in other words. His error of bringing into connection Ritter's Nien-chen-tang-la and Huc's Tanla, and combining into one chain two systems running parallel to each other, with an interval of two degrees of lattitude, was an exceedingly unfortunate misconception, of which Ritter had already been guilty several years before Huc's journey.

In the year 1856 Hodgson made the conjecture that the Karakorum and the Nien-chen-tang-la belonged to one and the same system. But Humboldt, with whom Hodgson was in correspondence, had expressed the same opinion in 1831. In 1853 Hodgson sees in the Nien-chen-tang-la a worthy rival of the Kwen-lun and the Himalayas, but three years later he adopts Humboldt's four systems, the Altai, Tian-shan, Kwen-lun, and Himalayas, without even mentioning the Nien-chen-tang-la. The statement that this chain divides northern from southern Tibet is borrowed entirely from Ritter.

Hodgson published in 1857 the map which is reproduced at the end of the first volume of this book. It is from first to last a fanciful representation in everything connected with the mountains north of the Tsangpo. D'Anville had given us 124 years before from Chinese sources a cartographical picture in which, as far as was possible, he endeavoured to follow the actual contours, and in which some details were strikingly accurate, especially the country round the Manasarowar. But Hodgson spoiled everything, both what was correct and what was defective.

Here we have to do with a retrograde step in our knowledge of those mysterious mountains. The little that was known in the 'fifties of the nineteenth century of the Trans-Himalaya, and which for the most part bore the label "made in Germany," Hodgson distorted, explained incorrectly, and imported into England. If he had only taken the trouble to cast a glance at Stülpnagel's map of India and Tibet in *Stieler's Handatlas* of the year 1849, he would there have found a representation of Tibet which contrasts as advantageously with his own as D'Anville's map with that of Ptolemy.

The process was as follows: Klaproth translated the Chinese authors, and his writings were quoted by Ritter and Humboldt. Both these German authors were consulted by Hodgson, but he filled in the space at his writing-table out of his own head. It is easy to set down a range of mountains on the blank space of a map theoretically and without a shadow of proof, if one is convinced of its existence. But no one has the right to appeal to the result of such a process as to a gospel and a dogma, and least of all at a time when it has at last been proved that such a mountain chain does not exist, and when the central Trans-Himalaya has been resolved into a labyrinth of different ranges.

This is how the matter stands with regard to the statement that Hodgson knew these mountains more than fifty years before my journey.

On their famous journey in 1845–46 from Manchuria to Lhasa, the two Lazarists, Huc and Gabet, crossed the whole of eastern Tibet, and in so doing passed over the eastern part of the Trans-Himalaya. Near Kuku-nor they with several Mongolian caravans joined themselves to a Tibetan embassy which was on its way home. The whole company numbered 2000 Tibetans and Tatars; all the horsemen were armed and 500 Chinese soldiers escorted the embassy to the Tibetan frontier; 15,000 yaks and 1200 camels carried the baggage, and 1200 horses bore riders. In his admirable description of the journey Huc exclaims: "How astonished these endless silent deserts must be when they are so suddenly surprised by such a great tumultuous party!"

Kuku-nor was left behind and the travellers came up to the highlands of Tibet where difficulties soon accumulated in their way.

> The deserts of Tibet are certainly the most dreadful country conceivable. The ground seems to rise continuously, the vegetation grows poorer the farther we advance, and the temperature falls alarmingly. Now death, too, began to lie in wait for our poor caravan. Want of water and fodder soon exhausted the strength of the animals. Beasts of burden had to be left behind daily, for they could drag themselves along no farther. Afterwards came the men's turn.

On the stupendous heights to the south of the Murui-ussou or upper Yang-tse-kiang, horses, mules, and camels died in shoals, and forty men had to be left behind. Father Gabet was then attacked by an illness which put an end to his life before he could return to France.

> Then we began to ascend the huge chain of the Tanla mountains. After six days' climbing over the slopes of mountains lying as in an amphitheatre behind and above one another, we reached at last that famous plateau which is perhaps the highest country in the world. From the margin of the grand plateau we perceived at our feet peaks and summits which surmounted various gigantic mountain groups, their farthest offshoots extending to the horizon.

Nakchu on the Salwin was the first Tibetan village. There were black Tibetan tents as well as Mongolian kibitkas. We are now approaching the eastern wing of the Trans-Himalaya, and wait with eagerness to learn what an educated European, who travelled right across the system, has to relate about it; he must surely have something to say. Yet Huc hardly mentions those mountains, and we have only an inkling of their presence in the following sentence: "The road leading from Nakchu to Lhasa is in general stony and very troublesome, and when the range of the Koïran mountains is reached, it is very trying." These Koïran mountains are the eastern continuation of the Nien-chen-tang-la, and therefore a part of the Trans-Himalaya; apparently they made no very deep impression on Father Huc.

Soon the road becomes better, villages and fields occur more frequently, and after a last tiring pass the two Lazarists enter the city of the Dalai Lama on January 29, 1846. Huc is one of the most brilliant and sympathetic personalities that have ever written their name on the brow of Asia.

CHAPTER XIV

THE TRANS-HIMALAYA FROM THE MIDDLE OF THE NINETEENTH CENTURY UP TO THE PRESENT

In the middle of last century three famous English doctors—Hooker, Thomson, and Campbell—contributed in a meritorious manner to extend in Europe the knowledge of the Himalayas, their geology and natural characteristics. They did not extend their theories beyond their own range of vision, and carefully abstained from building up mountain ranges which would perhaps in a few years have fallen to pieces.

Sir Joseph Hooker (1848–50) saw from the pass Donkia-la, which forms the boundary between Sikkim and Tibet, on the farthest horizon to the north-west and north of Nepal, "some immense snowy mountains, reduced to mere specks on the horizon," and adds that snow-topped range rose over range in the clear purple distance. He was convinced that they lay beyond the Tsangpo in the country of the salt lakes, where the most conspicuous characteristic features were the immense heights and the colours which contrasted sharply with the dark, snow-clad rocks of the Himalayas. The distance to these mountains seemed to him enormous. Previously he had looked upon Tibet as a flat country falling in sloping steppes gently to the Tsangpo valley. It is difficult to make out from Hooker's description which mountains he meant, but in his remarks about the view from the Donkia-la we seem to catch a glimpse of the Trans-Himalaya, and to find a suggestion of a world of unknown mountains—"nova quaędam series elatiorum nivosorumque montium ad Boream."

80. THE ROBBER CHIEF, KAMBA TSENAM.

Sketch by the Author.

Hooker looks upon the highlands round the Manasarowar as an important centre from which four mountain ranges diverge—the eastern Himalayas, the north-western Himalayas, the Kwen-lun, and "the chain north of the Yaru (Tsangpo) of which nothing is known."

Hooker published his *Himalayan Journals* in the year 1854. The year before appeared the article in which Hodgson mentioned the Nien-chen-tang-la. If Hodgson had really known these mountains, Hooker would not have described the country north of the river as a terra incognita, and he would have been less likely to do so, because the two explorers were personal friends and were in the forefront of the progress of their time, especially in their knowledge of the Himalayas.

Sir. Alexander Cunningham introduced the name Trans-Himalaya in the year 1854, giving it to the range which separates the upper Sutlej from the Indus. But as this range is part of the Himalayas proper the name soon disappeared from geographical literature. For the mountains north of the Manasarowar he proposed the name Kailas or Gangri range, which was retained for a long time after. But about the direction of the range, or even of its prolongation beyond the Kailas mountain, Cunningham does not say a word, or even make a guess about it.

In the year 1865 occurred Nain Sing's famous journey. He belonged to Captain Montgomerie's school of topographers, which was composed of experienced pundits or educated Hindus and natives from the upper valleys of the Himalayas. Montgomerie drew up the plan for Nain Sing's journey of discovery, and provided his protégé with a sextant, a compass, a chronometer, thermometers, and other instruments. The pundit travelled on foot and took with him a prayer-mill and a rosary. In the former he kept thin strips of paper on which he noted down his observations, and he let a bead of the latter pass through his fingers every hundred paces, reckoning in this way the distance he had traversed.

Nain Sing started from Khatmandu. We cannot follow him step by step. He visited Lhasa, passed up the Tsangpo valley to the Manasarowar, and returned to British India after a six months' journey. Montgomerie worked out Nain Sing's results and expressed his disappointment that it was so difficult to gather an idea of the country from the pundit's description.

Between Manasarowar and Tradum, Nain Sing saw no important heights. A little farther east the mountains were even fairly low. Still farther east, however, appeared to the north a very high snowy range which ran parallel to the Tsangpo for 20 miles. From the Kamba-la, where the Capuchins caught sight of lofty snow mountains, the pundit saw only comparatively low elevations.

Any one who has passed through the Tsangpo valley will understand the pundit's impressions. Except Desideri, only five Europeans have seen this country, and of these four belonged to the same party, namely, those under the leadership of Captain Rawling. I followed in their track three years later. Crests and ramifications lying close at hand shut out the view towards the north. Where Nain Sing could see no heights of importance to the north, I crossed a range by the Ding-la, a pass not less than 19,308 feet high. Such secrets are not to be discovered from the Tsangpo valley, for the southernmost offshoots are as little transparent as other mountains. It is not enough to look at the margin of an unknown country; if we would know what is hidden in the interior, we must cross it along several lines. There, a little farther to the east, where the height of the mountains seemed to Nain Sing to diminish still more, are hidden to the north the mighty central ranges of the Trans-Himalaya, the Lunpo-gangri, the Lunkar, the Lapchung, and the Kanchung-gangri. Of the lofty snowy range the pundit mentions I have seen only the western part which belongs to the Kanchung-gangri. Nain Sing travelled a distance of 400 miles between Shigatse and the Marium-la, of which only 90 were immediately along the north bank of the river. The journey of the pundit revealed nothing of a continuous mountain system, nay, nothing of an unbroken range, and could not reveal anything of it. Montgomerie has no suspicion of its existence, at any rate he does not mention it. He does not refer to Hodgson's hypothetical range, and makes no allusion to the

Nien-chen-tang-la. Only on the map to Nain Sing's narrative one notices mountains skirting the river which might, however, very well be the outer edge of a plateau. In this respect D'Anville gives us more. We are not content with the peripheral parts of this terra incognita so difficult to conquer; we must force the outer works and penetrate into the interior.

Pundits effected such an incursion to the north in the year 1867 on their journey to Tok-jalung. As usual the plan was made by the indefatigable Montgomerie. The Aling-gangri was discovered, a snow-clad mountain group, the relation of which to the Trans-Himalaya has not yet been ascertained. On this journey one of the pundits approached the source of the Indus within five days' journey, but was driven back by robbers. Thus the discovery of the Singi-kabab, the source of the Indus, was postponed for forty years, and fell to my lot.

In 1868 those regions were again visited by pundits. They heard of Selipuk and the Nganglaring-tso, and I subsequently confirmed their existence by visiting those places.

In connection with the discoveries of the pundits in western Tibet, Sir Henry Rawlinson expressed the view that if a traveller were once over the Indus and the inner northern range, he would find himself up on the plateau of Tatary, and could drive with horse and carriage to the great desert without crossing a single pass. In a carriage over the Karakorum, the Arka-Tag, and the Kwen-lun, where one may thank God if one gets over safely on horseback! So little was known forty years ago of the highest mountain land in the world. It is amusing to read how the great geographers of that time argued for or against the existence of those mountains. As a rule they only "believed" that the configuration was so or so, but why, no one knew. Rawlinson only believed that a man could drive to Eastern Turkestan. And yet it became evident to Strahlenberg during his long sojourn in Siberia after the wars of Charles XII., that Eastern Turkestan must be bounded on the south by mighty mountains.

One of Montgomerie's natives accomplished an important journey in 1871–72, passing up the Shang valley to Namling, as Bogle had done a hundred years before. He was not content, like Bogle, with the Namling monastery, but continued his journey northwards, and crossed the Kalamba-la pass to the "great heavenly lake," the Tengri-nor. This route was to serve for thirty-five years as the eastern boundary of the land which still remained unknown when I started on my last journey.

The traveller could see from a monastery by the lake a number of fine grand snow peaks which are called the Ninjinthangla. The lamas said that the highest peak was a god, and that three hundred and sixty smaller snow peaks surround it which serve as his suite. From the lake shore all these peaks presented an imposing appearance. This was the first time that a trustworthy traveller confirmed the existence of the famous Nien-chen-tang-la, which the Capuchins had seen raising its sun-bathed bonnets of snow above a petrified sea of bare many-coloured rocks.

On his return the traveller crossed the Trans-Himalaya a second time by the pass Dam-largen-la, and in the village of Dam recalled to memory Della Penna's duchy of the same name.

Montgomerie was justly proud of the harvest thus gathered in, and wrote in 1875 that he had tried from time to time to obtain enlightenment about the unknown country to the north of the river by means of the men he sent out. But even then he did not speak of a continuous chain. Only the Nien-chen-tang-la was known through the crossing of the Kalamba-la and the Dam-largen-la. Westwards the land was still terra incognita. Montgomerie did not suspect that this alluring inscription would stand for thirty-one years more on English maps.

The great Nain Sing set out again in 1873, this time from Leh to Lhasa, and at the instance of Captain Trotter. This journey is one of the most brilliant ever achieved in Tibet. He found the Targot Lha, my Targo-gangri, which had already appeared on D'Anville's map, discovered a range which runs thence for 180 miles eastwards, and fixed a number of its summits. He saw the Targo-gangri only from a distance of 100 miles and the range from 60 miles.

Much that he says is therefore incorrect, and, what is worse, he inserted farther south, from mere rumours, large rivers which figured for thirty years on all maps of Tibet, until I was able to remove these imaginary streams from the earth for ever.

After Nain Sing had discovered a series of large lakes he proceeded lastly over the Dam-largen-la to Lhasa, and when he returned to Calcutta he had executed a survey of 1200 miles of unknown country.

During their journeys from 1865 to 1875 the pundits crossed four passes of the Trans-Himalaya, two in the west and two in the east. They defined by their routes the limits of the unknown mountain country, which, as late as 1906, was marked on all maps by blank spaces with the inscription "Unexplored."

The story of the Himalayas goes farther back; it begins in the mythical obscurity of the Indian hymns, and the outlines of these mountains stand out clearly in classical literature. The Chinese knew the Kwen-lun from remote times, and it is on European maps of the beginning of the eighteenth century, though in rough outlines and only partially. But the Trans-Himalaya! How hopeless has the contest been against its giants! Heated controversies have often been carried on by learned men on the structure of the Himalayas, on the architecture of the Kwen-lun and the Karakorum. But no sound has disturbed the crests of the Trans-Himalaya, the silence of ignorance has reigned on its heights, an eloquent, unbroken, and solemn silence. The country was unknown. While waiting for exact information first hand, men took the side of D'Anville or Klaproth. Students at home could draw mighty ranges across the blank spaces of the map at their own will and pleasure without criticism having a word to say against them. Not till the years 1906–8, when the central ranges had been discovered, did a slight dispute arise. This is always the way of the world. Imagination is tolerated, but the truth is rejected.

For a long period of years Henry Strachey was the chief authority on the geography of Tibet. On his important journey in 1846 to the Manasarowar he saw from the Himalayan pass Lankpya Dhura, "through the opening northwards, a glimpse of distant blue mountains, part of the Gangri range, perhaps, on the north side of the Sutlej." On his way to the lake he made the following observation :

> The north-west horizon is bounded by the Gangri range of mountains moderately tipped with snow, and remarkable for the deep purple-blue colour of their inferior rocky parts; and about the middle of this range rises the snow-capped Peak of Kailas, somewhat higher than the rest of the line. I do not believe these mountains are nearly so lofty as the main ranges of the Indian Himalaya.

He takes the Marium-la for the eastern boundary pillar of the Gangri range, and does not believe in the existence of any ranges north of the Tsangpo; for beyond the Marium-la "eastward, extends table-land with smaller, more irregular and detached hills, all the way to Lhassa, and as far as my informant knows to the northward." At that time, then, some believed in the existence of a huge range, others in a flat plateau studded with scattered hills.

The brothers Schlagintweit, the first Europeans who crossed the whole great upheaval of Tibet between India and Eastern Turkestan, knew of three systems, the Himalayas, Karakorum, and Kwen-lun. They regarded the Karakorum as the backbone of inner Asia, which was prolonged westwards by the Hindu-kush and branched out in the east—how could they know this, as no one had been there? Tibet is a valley bordered by the Karakorum and the Himalayas. This view Hermann von Schlagintweit did not alter even after Nain Sing's first journey, which shows that he did not at all receive the impression from the pundit's description that there was another range bordering the Tsangpo valley on the north. But the existence of the Nien-chen-tang-la could not be overlooked, so this range was simply connected with the southern branch of the Karakorum, and thus came into existence a monstrous bastard between two different ranges.

In his book *Indische Altertumskunde*, which appeared in 1867, Christian Lassen has attempted to draw the main lines of the mountain skeleton of Asia according to the

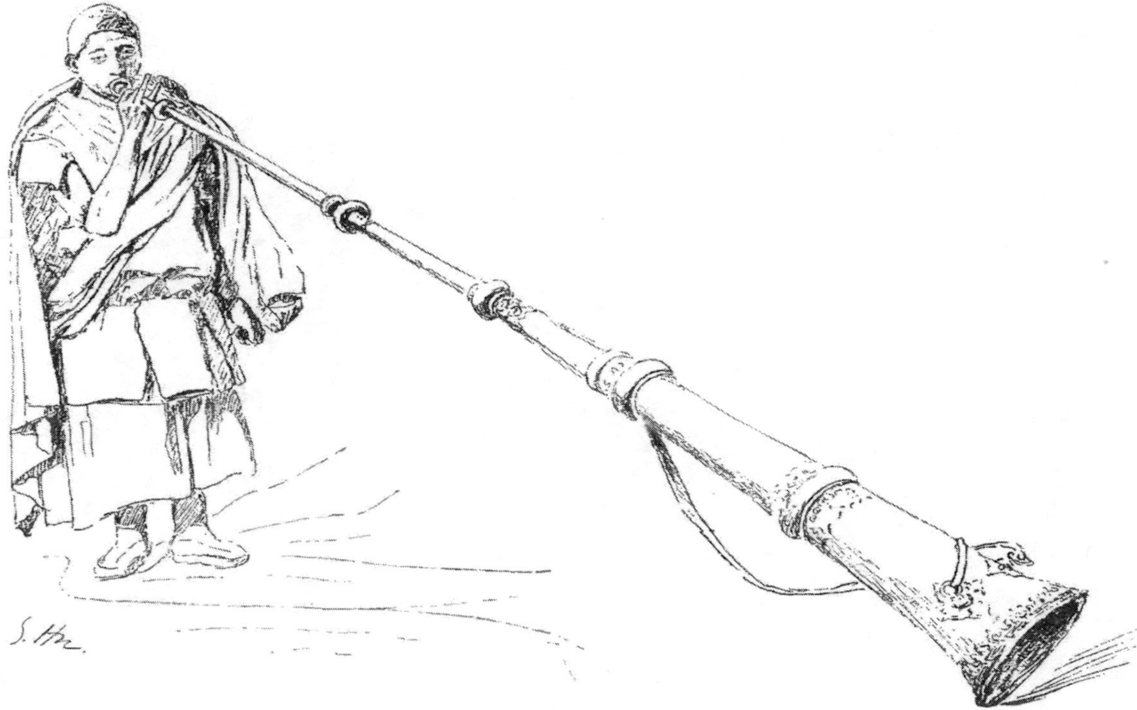

81. Lama with a Copper Trumpet ten feet long.

Sketch by the Author.

knowledge of his time. He conceives the Kailâsa or the Gangdisri range, the western wing of the Trans-Himalaya, to be a ramification of the Karakorum, which is itself an offshoot from the Kwen-lun. In the Kailas peak the Gangdisri range comes into contact with the Himalayas, without, however, belonging to them. Lassen therefore builds a bridge of mountains from the Pamir to the Himalayas, and with all his diligence cannot ascertain that the various ranges belong to different systems and are parallel folds of the earth's crust.

The noted geographers Sir Clements Markham and Trelawney Saunders discussed in the middle of the 'seventies of the nineteenth century the structure of the Himalayas, and at the same time alluded to its connection with the mountains in the north. Markham distinguishes three ranges—the southern, which bears the great peaks of the Himalayas; the middle, which is the watershed between the Ganges and Brahmaputra; and the northern, which is a prolongation of the Karakorum. He therefore includes the Trans-Himalaya, so far as it was known, in the system of the Himalayas and calls it the "northern range." He places on its southern flanks the sources of the Indus, Brahmaputra, and Sutlej. I have succeeded in proving that the Sutlej and Brahmaputra rise on the northern flank of the Himalayas, and that the source of the Indus lies to the north of the western Trans-Himalaya, though all three rivers receive large affluents from other directions.

Saunders considers the Kwen-lun to be the northern boundary of the Tibetan highlands and says:

> But all detailed knowledge of the interior of this extraordinary country is wanting, and it must continue a sealed book to Europeans until friendly pressure is put upon the Government of Peking to allow European intercourse between India and the Chinese dominions.

Several leaves of this sealed book belong to the chapter Trans-Himalaya.

Saunders' text is not quite clear. At one time he says: "The mountains on the north of the Sanpu are the contreforts, buttresses, slopes or escarpments of the table-land which they support," and at another time declares that "the Gangri Range is only known at its extremities." The last affirmation was correct and remained so for thirty years. In September I telegraphed to the reporter of the *Times* at Simla: "The eastern and western parts of the Trans-Himalaya were already known, but its middle and highest part lies in Bongba and was unexplored." Saunders maintains that a mountain system must be crossed before it can be said to be known, and he points out that these mountains had never been crossed along a single line between the Manasarowar and the Tengri-nor. He repeats Ritter's mistake of making the Nien-chen-tang-la continue northwards and merge into the Tanla of Father Huc.

On the other hand Saunders does not hesitate a moment to insert Hodgson's hypothetical range on his map (a copy is given at the end of Vol. I.), which he endeavours to fit in as well as he can with some of D'Anville's lakes and rivers. The result has a certain appearance of probability but no resemblance to the truth. How little was known of these mountains is proved by the fact that Saunders, in the year 1877, drew a single continuous range to the north of the river, while Richthofen in the same year—in his famous work *China*—set down four parallel ranges in the west, two and three in the middle, and one in the east. Both were equally wrong; it could not be otherwise. Neither had been there, and each could design his map in the manner which seemed to him most probable.

In his work *The Himalayan Districts of the North-Western Provinces of India* (1882), E. T. Atkinson mentions cursorily a range of high peaks north of the river, but he adds that it is impossible to give a general description of the Tibetan highlands based on actual observation. But from the little that is known, he thinks it may be assumed that Tibet is crossed by lofty mountains, and it seems to him certain that the Kwen-lun and the Himalayas are the northern and southern margins of the country. The map which Atkinson published in his book is a copy of Saunders' map, but yet Atkinson is referred to as an authority on the Trans-Himalaya. He could, of course, have read in books what had been achieved in the western and eastern parts, but of the main mass, the central regions, he had not, and could not have, the slightest smattering of knowledge.

In the same year, 1882, Elisée Réclus issued the seventh volume of his admirable *Nouvelle Géographie Universelle*, wherein he suggests the name Trans-Himalaya for the northernmost range of the Himalayas which runs immediately beside the Tsangpo on the south. Cunningham had confined this name to a range in the west. Of our more northern mountains Réclus says: "On the north of the depression, in which the Tsangpo flows, is the Tibetan plateau, carved by running water into innumerable valleys." He assumes, however, like the Englishmen, the existence of a great range, the Gang-dis-ri north of the Tsangpo, and makes it join the Nien-chen-tang-la in the east.

About the year 1896 Richthofen wrote the Tibetan chapter of the third volume of his work *China*, which was only published a short time ago by Dr. Ernst Tiessen, seven years after the death of the Professor. Richthofen there collected all the notices that exist on the mountains of Tibet, and came to the conclusion that a very lofty range, already indicated by D'Anville, rises to the south of the Tengri-nor, which abounds in glaciers and rocky pinnacles, and extends from west-south-west to east-north-east, and forms the watershed between the Tengri-nor and the Ki-chu, the river of Lhasa. Westwards this range takes a more westerly direction, and from its southern flank the water flows down to the Tsangpo. He seeks in vain to obtain an idea of the geographical configuration of the country from the maps of Nain Sing, Bower, and Littledale—from them such a "scheme is not to be drawn." But here he refers to the country north of the Trans-Himalaya. If countries which had been traversed by three travellers still remained obscure, what could be expected of those in which no one had been? There the imaginary continuous chain, called sometimes Nien-chen-tang-la, sometimes Gangri, Gang-dis-ri, or Kailas, had been so firmly fixed in the minds of many that even Richthofen believed in its existence.

But if we search through writings and examine records with the microscope of criticism, we look in vain for information about the proper central Trans-Himalaya. In past years we find not a line, not a single word about it. We come always upon Kailas and the Gangri mountains in the west and the Nien-chen-tang-la in the east. There Europeans and Asiatics have been. But if one inquires about the range supposed to stretch like a bridge from the one terminal pillar to the other, it turns out on close examination that it has been constructed in Europe or India, but has never been explored on the spot. It was a creation of the imagination; its days were numbered, and when the time came it was found to have no claim to existence.

When we now turn to the three European expeditions which have come into contact with the Trans-Himalaya in our own days, we find that they have all travelled to the range and summits which have for ages been known by the name Nien-chen-tang-la. They have confirmed the existence of those mountains, but have thrown no new light on our system.

Gabriel Bonvalot, accompanied by Prince Henry of Orleans, accomplished in 1889 that remarkable journey on which he traversed the whole of eastern Tibet and reached the northern foot of the eastern Trans-Himalaya. Coming from the north, Bonvalot approached Tengri-nor full of expectation. At last the path led up the last elevation which intercepted the view towards the south.

> As we come to the top of the pass we catch sight of the Ninling Tanla and the eastern edge of the lake. Hastening our steps, we climb the neighbouring heights to enlarge our horizon. . . . The Ningling Tanla holds our eyes the longest. This range stretches just in front of us its snow-besprinkled crest and quite closes in our view. The height and regularity of this line of grand summits is astonishing; they rise above spurs which descend to the lake, drawn up in rank like the tents of a military camp. And the whole is dominated by four lofty and majestic peaks of ice, which the Tibetans worship, for behind them lies Lhasa, the spiritual city. Turning our eyes to the northern shore of the lake we perceive no snow on the small ridge which skirts it, while the flanks of the Ningling Tanla are white, and the truth of the Tibetan saying is

82. Tibetan Hunter.

83. Monks with Clarinet and Conch.

Sketches by the Author.

evident: "The water of the Namtso is formed from the snow of the Ningling Tanla."

It was not written in the stars that the noted French expedition should cross the Trans-Himalaya and penetrate into the forbidden land behind the high snow mountains. But Bonvalot did ascend the Dam pass, where Nain Sing had tried his luck.

Immediately to the south of the Ningling Tanla appears on Bonvalot's map a second and higher range with the text: "Sommets très élevés (dominant la chaîne)," a feature in the sculpture not to be found in any other map. Even here in the part of the system best known at that time the data are extremely contradictory.

Four years later another French expedition beheld the heavenly lake, that of Dutreuil de Rhins and Grenard, who writes:

> On November 30 we discovered, from the top of the last ridge, the lake of heaven, which is honoured as sacred and divine, its dark calm blue contrasting strongly with the blinding white of the mountains with their thousand peaks, which rise from the southern shore and resemble the waves of a stormy sea.

The expedition was stopped by the Tibetans, and fifty days were wasted in useless negotiations. After a short visit to the foot of the Dam pass, the Frenchmen had to draw off north-westwards, where a sad fate was to befall Dutreuil de Rhins, who fell a victim to Tibetan bullets.

The explorer St. George Littledale was more fortunate when he came to the lake of spirits from the north in 1895. Like his predecessors, he was struck by the magnificent view.

> On the south it (the lake) was fringed by the magnificent range of the Ninchen-Tangla—a succession of snow-clad peaks and glaciers, partially hidden in clouds and vapour, which added to their size and grandeur, while above all towered with cliffs of appalling steepness the great peak of Charemaru, 24,153 feet.

In this name we recognize D'Anville's "Tchimonran." Littledale's route passed over the pass Goring-la. Since the time of Father Huc no European had succeeded in crossing the eastern Trans-Himalaya.

A new point of departure was marked in the year 1904 by the journey of the four officers, Ryder, Rawling, Wood, and Bailey, after the English expedition to Lhasa, when they travelled on the track of Nain Sing up the Tsangpo. The chief result of this journey is the exact survey of the valley and the triangulation which connected all visible summits. Ryder described this journey to the Royal Geographical Society in London. He certainly mentions a snowy range with summits attaining to a height of 23,200 feet which was visible from the hills lying north of Tradum. But neither he nor Rawling in his book on the journey says a word about any continuous mountain system; rather he discountenances the view that such exists, and we find none shown on his map. There it seems as though there were the margin of a plateau country bearing scattered summits. It was not until I had in India an opportunity of imparting my results to Major Ryder that he readily admitted that "a lofty complicated mountain system" runs north of the Tsangpo parallel to the Himalayas.

Now the last visitor to the Trans-Himalaya before my journey remains to be mentioned. In the year 1905 Count de Lesdain came down from the north, and at the sight of the heavenly lake and the peaks rising to the sky, exclaimed:

> Towards evening on September 13 we discovered the Tengri-nor, which stretched out majestically in front of us. It is impossible to conceive a more beautiful and grander spectacle. Beyond its broad deep-blue mirror appeared the huge chain Nien-chen-tang-la, covered with eternal ice. The highest points were reflected in the calm transparent water of the lake. These stupendous heights form a more glorious frame than any of the Swiss lakes can boast of.

That is all! We can only conclude from his small sketch-map that he crossed the Trans-Himalaya by the Kalamba-la, and therefore by the route already known since 1872 from the journeys of the pundits. He says nothing of a connected system.

It seems as though a magic charm hovered round the summits of the Nien-chen-tang-la. They rise like the points of a kingly crown high above the earth, higher than any other part of the Trans-Himalaya. Thus they looked for endless ages on the nomads before northern Buddhism had penetrated into Tibet; thus they looked down on the Chinese who collected the first notices of the holy land; they excited the admiration of the Capuchins as a line "nivosorum montium ad Boream"; they cast a pale reflexion of the abode of eternal snow into the study where the learned Klaproth dived into the annals of the Chinese; and they illumined the now faded leaves stored in German archives, to which the old masters Ritter and Humboldt confided their thoughts. They excited the astonishment of the intrepid pundits, who brought the first certain information to Europe, shone like beacons before the three French expeditions, which approached them from the north, and even roused the quiet, imperturbable Littledale to a burst of enthusiasm.

But the threads that have been spun round those giants are few, and these few are weak. We know hardly anything of those mountains. Rhapsodies, full of poetic expressions, that is really all. There are glaciers and firn-fields, which are reflected in the azure-blue lake, giddy heights, and restricted horizons. But what else? Photographs and maps there are none, and not a single rock specimen has been taken from the lap of the mountains. And the passes to the east and west, the Dam-largen-la, the Kalamba-la, and the Goring-la! We must be thankful that we at least have learned their names and heights.

The Nien-chen-tang-la is like a Catholic cathedral in which a funeral mass is always being celebrated. One approaches it in reverent silence. One is overwhelmed by what one sees and is struck dumb. No one has succeeded in breaking through the charm. Round the Nien-chen-tang-la it is always peaceful. And before one is aware the hymns have died away and one is again led out to the black tents of the Tibetans.

And yet the Nien-chen-tang-la is a part of the Trans-Himalaya. Six expeditions had visited it, four of which had crossed the system. To the west of it no one had been.

We owe the last theoretical representation of the Trans-

Himalaya to the map of Colonel S. G. Burrard in the first part of his book *A Sketch of the Geography and Geology of the Himalaya Mountains and Tibet*, which appeared in the year 1907, that is, about the time when I had made three of my eight crossings of the mountains. On this map, too, a range runs on the north of the upper Indus and the Tsangpo. In its western part it is called the Kailas range, in its eastern the Nien-chen-tang-la range. It forks, however, on the 85th meridian of east longitude; the eastern arm lies between the Raga-tsangpo and the Tsangpo. Farther to the east the northern arm splits up again twice. Such conclusions might be drawn from the material then available, but as regards the central Trans-Himalaya they had nothing to do with the reality.

After Littledale's lecture to the London Geographical Society in 1896, the President of the Society, Sir Clements Markham, rose and said:

> I will say a few words respecting the chain of mountains which Mr. Littledale actually crossed and which he mentions as throwing up peaks 20,000 feet high. . . . These mountains are of the greatest possible importance and interest; they have only been crossed by native explorers and by Mr. Littledale opposite the Tengri-nor, and in the whole length from Tengri-nor to the Marium-la no one has crossed them, so far as we know. One of the last suggestions by General Walker was that a rough survey should be undertaken of these northern parts of the Himalayan system, and I believe nothing in Asia is of greater geographical importance than the exploration of this range of mountains.

In the same year Sir Clements Markham remarked in a presidential address to the Society:

> It is to the desirability of completing the exploration of this mighty range that I am anxious to turn the attention of geographers. . . . But I think that it is to the mountains which form its southern buttressing wall, and which rise from the valley of the Tsanpu or Brahmaputra, that the efforts of explorers should now be directed. . . . It appears to be a magnificent range of mountains.

He goes on to speak of the work of the pundits and of Littledale, and resumes:

> This I believe to be the whole of the knowledge we now possess of this most interesting range of mountains. . . . The portion of

84. Mendicant Lama.

Sketch by the Author.

this northern Himalayan chain from Kailas to the Goring-la of Littledale, a distance of 600 miles, requires to be explored. . . . A more accurate knowledge of its configuration is a great geographical desideratum. . . . Here, then, is a piece of work which is well calculated to arouse the ambition of future explorers.

In another presidential address in 1899 Markham repeats:

One of the most interesting pieces of geographical work that remains to be achieved in Central Asia is the detailed examination of the great chain of mountains bounding the Tsanpu valley on the north.

Again in the year 1904 Markham complains:

In my address of 1896 I drew attention to the importance of exploring the great northern range of the Himalaya from Kailas to the Goring-la of Littledale, and I got together all available information on the subject. But this is a work which still remains to be done.

In the autumn of 1905 I wrote the last chapters of my book, *Scientific Results of a Journey in Central Asia, 1899–1902*, concluding with the following words:

The extreme south of Tibet, the Tsangpo valley, has recently been investigated by members of the English expedition (Ryder and Rawling); but all the wide region between this part and my route to Ladak (1901) is an absolute terra incognita. The explorer who tries to give an account of the general features of the Tibetan highlands will in this gap never fail to lose himself in guesses and theories without an atom of foundation. Rather than expose myself to such a risk I have determined to explore the unknown country myself, and see it with my own eyes. Then only, when the gap has been filled up and the blank spaces on our maps have given place to new lakes, rivers and ranges, will it be possible to give a correct picture of the morphology of the Tibetan highlands. . . . Therefore I prefer to postpone a general description of the country until my return from the journey on which I am about to start. The work which I hope then to write must be considered an immediate continuation and completion of this which I have now brought to an end.

I therefore started with a definite object. The aim of my journey was to fill up the huge area of the middle Trans-Himalaya. How far I succeeded in carrying out my plans is related in this book. The Trans-Himalaya was crossed along seven independent lines, the outlines of its configuration were laid down on a map, and I proved that the whole was a connected system, the greatest, indeed, in the world. Instead of the single stereotyped range which had been conceived in European studies, I found a labyrinth of lofty ranges, and by this discovery wiped out for ever the "Unexplored" which appeared on English maps in the region north of the Tsangpo.

After my lecture in London on February 23, 1909, a communication from Sir Clements Markham was read in which he said:

> The so-called Nien-chen-tang-la mountains were unknown from the Tengri-nor to the Maryum-la pass, and I always looked upon their discovery, on those meridians, as the most important desideratum in Asiatic geography for many reasons.

And he expressed his pleasure that the wished-for discovery had been at last achieved.

What was known of the geology of the Trans-Himalaya before 1906? The extreme tip of its western wing was known where it touches British territory, and Stoliczka was the first who tried some forty years ago to introduce order into the confused chaos. In the east a line had been determined, the road from Sikkim through Gyangtse to Lhasa. The Director of the Geological Survey of India, Dr. H. H. Hayden, who took part in Younghusband's expedition, has given us geological maps and detailed descriptions of the structure of that region.

But of the central part nothing was known. The side of the moon turned towards the earth was better known as regards its orography than the inner parts of the middle Trans Himalaya, so what could be expected of its geological structure? A single continuous chain had been drawn theoretically on the north of the Tsangpo. As the river received large tributaries from the north it was safe to assume the existence of high mountains in their source regions. But there was no foundation for geological hypotheses. There was only one resource for any one who wished enlightenment on the subject—let the mountains speak for themselves.

At all the places where my route came in contact with rocks *in situ* I took rock specimens, and there also I always determined the strike and dip of the strata. On the other hand, where rock *in situ* did not crop out, or could not be reached, rock specimens were collected from the weathered ruins of former mountains. It often happened that to spare my horse and my own heart, I rode past a cliff rising too high. Therefore in my series of 1170 specimens many gaps occur, which might easily have been filled up in a country in which one has not constantly to fight against the deadly rarefaction of the air. To put it plainly, there is often the painful choice of killing one's horse or completing the collection of specimens. And as a journey in Tibet depends almost entirely on the endurance of the caravan, the collection must often suffer.

But every rock specimen from a hitherto unknown country is a gain, and an undoubtedly extensive selection of such specimens from one of the mightiest mountain systems of the world must throw a clear light on the fundamental outlines of its architecture. I am therefore convinced that the stones which I knocked out of the rocks of the Trans-Himalaya during my toilsome wanderings will give us at least a provisional insight into the geological structure of the system, when they have been examined under the microscope of an expert, compared together, and exhibited on a map in cross sections with different colours. They will give us some notion of the forces which were active in the earth's crust when the brow of Asia was first wrinkled by the folded ranges of the Trans-Himalaya, when its crests were thrust upwards, and its towering peaks lifted their icy battlements towards the sun.

After my return the geological material was entrusted to Professor Anders Hennig of Lund. With unremitting care and constantly growing interest he has plunged into my collections, let the stones speak in their silent language, and drawn out the secrets concealed in the form of crystals. They have been like Tibetan bells, the metal of which has been first made sonorous in Sweden. Every stone is to me a souvenir of a pass, a camp, or a windy day—a microscopical fragment of my own Trans-Himalaya. And Professor

Hennig has received them with the same reverence with which I entrusted them to him.

I perceive the defectiveness of my own share of the work. My fellow-worker cannot wring more from the insufficient material than it is able to supply. But I believe, nevertheless, that his conclusions will be held to mark a new departure, for they give a geological purview of a hitherto unknown land, extremely difficult of access, and, besides, deal with one of the mightiest mountain systems of the world. Professor Hennig's work will appear shortly as a volume of the scientific results of my last journey. The following lines, written by Professor Hennig at my request, will certainly awaken interest among geologists:

The older deposits consist of white, grey, or dark grey quartzites and phyllitic schists, as well as subordinate beds of slaty crystalline limestone; the series is so strongly metamorphosed that if it contained originally fossil remains, these are quite destroyed. The series is penetrated by an intrusive formation mentioned below, and in connection with the eruption has suffered a plainly perceptible metamorphosis by pressure; it is therefore older than the other. Most certainly it forms a direct prolongation running east and west of the Jurassic schists and quartzite with limestone which Hayden has described from Lhasa and the country north-west of the town of Gyangtse. The formation has its chief extension in the Brahmaputra valley, but still it occurs, though very seldom, on the northern flank of the Trans-Himalaya and in western Tibet.

Younger than this series are the dark grey and reddish limestones which constitute the main mass of the base of the west Tibetan highlands. The limestones contain species of Orbitolina and radiolites, and correspond to the Aptian and Albian Cenomanian. Still younger sedimentary rocks, containing fossils, have not been found in the region traversed by Dr. Sven Hedin.

The above-mentioned Jurassic and Cretaceous deposits are, as stated, intersected by an eruptive formation, which, in the Brahmaputra valley, consists of ultrabasic peridotites, varieties of gabbro and granites, the first of which are often converted into serpentine. This formation forms a part of the eruptive formations known both in the eastern and western parts of the Himalayas which are in general ascribed to the Eocene age. Within the Trans-Himalaya itself it consists of intrusive granites (white granite associated with alkali and lime, and grey hornblende granite or quartz biotitic diorite of the Kyi-Chu type), pegmatites, granitic porphyries, diorite por-

85. LAMA WITH A TEMPLE DRUM.

Sketch by the Author.

phyrites, diabase, etc., of real vitrified surface lavas, as liparites, trachytes, dacites, andesites and basalts, as well as sub-aerial volcanic tuffs.

More recent than these formations, and lying unconformably upon them, is a formation of greyish-green, violet or reddish-brown conglomerates, sandstones, and schists, of which it has in many cases been shown that it has been produced at the expense of the porphyry-like intrusive rocks in the granites and peridotites, and therefore is of later than Eocene age. The formation, which is often developed as a very insignificant product of weathering, has no fossils at all.

It is overlaid unconformably in the Brahmaputra valley by a grey horizontal deposit of sandstone conglomerate which belongs to what is described by the geologists of the Geological Institute of India as Pleistocene.

It is worthy of remark that the foundation of the Brahmaputra valley, except for the younger tertiary deposits which occur throughout the area examined, is built up of older Jurassic deposits and low down of parts of the Eocene eruptive formation, while the base of the heights of the Trans-Himalaya and of the western Tibetan plateau consists of Cenomanian limestones and also—in the Trans-Himalaya—of a plainly recognizable system of dikes and intrusive sheets of the above-mentioned eruptive formation. These circumstances show that the Brahmaputra valley, which separates the Himalayas and the Trans-Himalaya, must be considered in its present condition as a deeply excavated erosion valley, and that faults do not play the leading part here which Oswald has assigned to them in his article based on Dr. Sven Hedin's preliminary communications.

CHAPTER XV

A CRITICAL SITUATION

However warmly one loves cold Tibet, yet after two years on the storm-lashed heights of this country, one longs to return to the perpetual summer of India. I had already exceeded the space of time for which one can endure without injury a continued sojourn in highly rarefied air, and at Tokchen I revelled in the thought that only one more high pass lay on the route which would lead me down to the shade of Himalayan cedars and the palms and mango trees of India.

So I thought in my innocence. I knew the road through the Sutlej valley only from maps on a small scale which I had with me, and from the succinct descriptions published by Ryder and Rawling. Their expedition had started from Gartok, and had therefore to cross the Ladak range by an awkward pass before it reached the Shipki. I, on the other hand, intended to follow the course of the Sutlej straight from the holy lake and the Langak-tso. The Englishmen had made their march in midwinter and yet had not encountered any serious difficulties, while I had midsummer before me and therefore ought to perform the task more easily.

Yes, summer is a glorious season in Tibet. But in the higher regions of the Sutlej's course winter is much more preferable. The rainy season did not neglect its duties this year, and we had been thoroughly soaked several times already. The rivers might be swollen so that they overflowed their banks, and we might get into great difficulties in crossing the tributaries. I did not think of

86. A Young Tibetan.

Sketch by the Author.

these things beforehand. But the day was to come when I should envy those who could avail themselves of the bridges of ice over the Sutlej in winter. My great aim now was to be on the road as soon as possible. I felt that I should soon be at home. But the way to India was much longer than I expected when I measured the distances on my map with compasses in Tokchen.

Even in Tokchen a formidable obstacle presented itself. I had thought of travelling on the next day, and I had to wait here nine days before setting out. The long wait had not the slightest results. Yes, one! Our animals had a thorough rest to prepare them for the hardships to come. And I was compelled to take a much-needed rest which otherwise I should never have allowed myself. I was deadly tired and quite exhausted after the wearing marches in the Trans-Himalaya, and after the past winter with its terrible cold. I lay all day long like an invalid, had lost all energy, was indifferent to everything, and tired of everything.

On the very first evening the bother began. My friend of the year before, the Gova of Tokchen, came into my tent with a friendly smile, handed me a *kadakh*, a thin white strip of stuff, as a sign of welcome and respect, and gave me a lump of *korum*-sugar from Purang, wrapped up in leaves. He was invited to take his seat on the usual felt rug, and his first question was:

"How is it possible that you are again in Tibet, Sahib? You left the country a year ago. Whence do you come now?"

"I have come over the northern mountains in order to see the innermost parts of Tibet which were closed to my caravan last year. I told you then that I should come back, and here I am."

"I cannot understand you, Sahib. Last year I was duly informed of your approach. This time I have only heard it said that you had turned up at Saka-dzong, and that it had been proclaimed all along the *tasam* that you were staying in the country without permission, and were not authorized to travel anywhere but towards the north.

I have received no orders, however, and I really do not know what to do with you."

"Oh, I can tell you that. You must get for me to-morrow morning early the yaks I need, and see that I travel safely on the road to Tirtapuri. You know that the authorities in Lhasa are, as usual, anxious to get rid of me. Well then, help me on. I promise that from Tirtapuri I will follow the course of the Sutlej down to India."

"Tirtapuri! yes, that is all very fine. But I have not yet received any orders, either from Lhasa or Gartok. I know only too well what happened last year. Then you asked me for means of transport to the Tso-mavang. I helped you to reach the lake and then you remained there a whole month. Afterwards I had to bear the blame."

"I hope you were not punished?"

"No, but I was warned not to meddle with Europeans in future without orders. And I was reprimanded for not having prevented you from sailing in your boat on the holy lake."

"The boat did not do any harm to the holy lake?"

"The gods may be angry. The lake is their property. The pilgrims finish their pilgrimage round its shores. The Tso-mavang is too good to be navigated by boats."

"This year you need not be alarmed. The boat is not with me; you may convince yourself of that. I will not stop a day at Tso-mavang, but will travel straight to Tirtapuri. No one has refused us yaks hitherto. The Governor of Saka-dzong supplied the first; the last are from Takche. We must have fresh ones the day after to-morrow at latest."

After long consideration the Gova answered:

"I will consult with my people and then give you my answer."

And so he went. I knew him for an honest man. Now he stood between two fires. He would gladly have obliged me, but he could not be unfaithful to his duty. Experience had made him wary. He had a grudge against me because I had been before in Tokchen and thereby got him into trouble. And it is always more difficult to wriggle out the second time. Dorche Tsuen had given notice all along the *tasam*, the great high road to Ladak, that I must not travel in any direction but to the north, the way I had come. I was now apparently stuck fast, and my fortune was about to take a very peculiar turn.

After an hour our three yak-drivers from Takche came to the tent door. The oldest, in great excitement, and his voice interrupted by sobs, said:

"Sir, the Gova of Tokchen and five other men have threatened us with a hundred stripes each, because we have brought you here without permission."

"Impossible! Do not be alarmed; whoever promises you a beating will have to deal with me."

"Yes, sir, there is one way of saving us from it, that is, if you will go back with us over the Surnge-la to Takche."

"No, listen to me. I have at last reached here, and I must hurry off to India as quickly as possible."

"Yes, but the Gova says that he will let us off the beating if we take you home with us."

"What have I to do at Takche? I cannot stay there for ever."

"You are to go on from there to Kyangyang and the Pedang-tsangpo. We are told that you must return by the very same way you came."

And thereupon the yak-drivers with their lachrymose faces threw themselves down before me, begging me in the most beseeching terms to accompany them back to their tents.

Now I perceived that it was only by pure good luck that I succeeded in passing through the forbidden land. If the nomad chiefs on the Pedang-tsangpo, at Selipuk, in the Kyangyang valley, and at Takche had known what the Gova of Tokchen knew, they would not have given us a yak on hire nor sold us a handful of *tsamba* unless we had consented to turn back and travel eastwards. How often had we met with the same experience as now! Each magistrate wished to relieve himself of all responsibility, and therefore tried to persuade me to return to the place I had come from. One would have thought that the Gova of Tokchen would have been satisfied if he saw me disappear in the direction of India. But he thought only of his own safety. No one should reprimand him for helping me to pass through his territory. As I had now come from the north, there was nothing for it but to drive me back to the north. The situation was critical. I must watch the course of events.

Darkness had come when another guest visited us, this time a welcome one—rain. It fell closely and heavily and pelted monotonously over all the country. The valley was turned into a swamp, and the mud squelched under the feet. Two tired horses, which had had a feed of barley by the tents, stood half asleep under their soaked rugs, with dripping manes and trickling tails. We could not help wondering whether this deluge would ever thoroughly dry up again. My tent was strengthened by extra covers and a ditch was digged round it, or I should have been in danger of being drowned as I lay in my bed on the ground. All night long the rain fell in torrents, but when the morning sun poured its gold down on the valley of the Samo-tsangpo out of a clear blue sky, all the mountains of the country glistened with blinding white new-fallen snow, as if winter had spread its pall over the bier of the too-soon-departed summer.

The Gova presented himself at my tent with his suite. He looked depressed and it was some time before he could find words. At last he began:

"I have consulted with my people. We are all agreed that I cannot and dare not have anything to do with you. I was warned the last time, and if I help you again I shall be punished. It is best for us all that you should return to Takche."

"You can quite understand," I returned, "that I have no thought of marching farther northwards when I must hasten into India as quickly as possible. But I do not wish to involve you in any unpleasantness, so, if you will send an express to Lhasa to ask for instructions, I am ready to wait until the answer arrives."

"You cannot wait so long, Sahib. I will hold counsel with my people once more."

Then the party trooped off, but only to be succeeded by

a new figure, a *yango* or inspector of transport animals and caravan traffic on the section of the *tasam* lying between the stations Parka and Shamsang. In this capacity he is generally on the road, and it was only by chance that he was in Tokchen. He came most humbly, almost crawling, into the tent, and the bale of red woollen material from Lhasa, which he begged me to accept as an offering of friendship, showed that he had a particular favour to ask.

"You say that you wish to travel to Tirtapuri, Sahib. Why did you not go through Yumba-matsen when you were at Selipuk? If you will promise to go straight to Parka, I will provide you with baggage animals, but you certainly may not travel by the holy lake to Tirtapuri. Oh, Sahib, for the sake of the Lama Kunchuk, for the gods' sake, turn back to Takche! The men and the yaks from there will be detained here for you. They had no right to bring you here, and you have no passport from Lhasa. The instructions the government has issued are much stricter than before. Oh, Sahib, go back to the north!"

I smiled, patted the *yango* on the shoulder, and answered slowly, accentuating every word:

"My way runs along the Tso-mavang to Tirtapuri. There is no other way for me."

He rose angrily, received his bale of material back again, and tramped off to the black tents.

A year, almost to the day, had passed away since I had for the first time pitched my tent in Tokchen. When I then asked permission to explore the forbidden roads over the mountains to the north, I received a peremptory no in reply. Now I was begged and implored in the most moving terms to go thither, and prayers and threats were employed to induce me. Yaks and guides were kept ready. I might have laid down the condition: "Procure me ten good horses and provisions for two months; let me choose my own route over the mountains, and I will promise you to go to Takche." This would certainly have been agreed to, only to see me disappear in the direction I had come. A curious fate, a singular country! When I try to steal into Tibet I find the frontier closed. And when I have succeeded and wish to slip out again the frontier is also closed with locks and bars. Never had such a good opportunity presented itself, and I had plenty of money. I might have gained two more Trans-Himalayan passes and established my headquarters beside some lake or other. Why did I not do it? Yes, it was stupid of me. But I had left my relations far too long already without news of me, and I knew that their anxiety would increase with every day that passed. And last but not least—I was tired of Tibet! I had now had enough of it; another autumn and a winter among the everlasting heights would have been too much for me.

One day followed another without anything remarkable happening. One day the *yongsun*, or head of the privileged commercial mission from Tibet to Ladak, came to Tokchen. He had brought red Tibetan woollen materials for sale, and I made a large purchase, for all my twelve men wanted new suits. The transaction had also the good result that the men were fully employed for some days. Abdul Kerim's tent was turned into a tailor's shop and clothes were cut out, sewed and fitted on all day long.

Our friend Sonam Ngurbu made another interruption in the monotony in which we lived. He had been delayed on the way through the nomads in the Paryang valley refusing to supply him with provisions. Unfortunately they had bravely resisted the strange chief and his unfair demands, and therefore Sonam Ngurbu was in exceedingly bad temper when he reached Tokchen. His love for the Swedish army revolver had not cooled down, and he tried to wheedle me into an exchange of the revolver for an old rotten wooden saddle. As this failed, he said that the Garpun would soon come down upon me and drive me up to the Chang-tang.

The Gova of Tokchen remained friendly and sent secret messengers to my tent at dusk to ask me to keep quiet and wait. Two officials were hostile to me, but they would soon leave, and then we should have our hands free. Indeed! those officials seemed not to go away. On the contrary, more were fetched by messengers, the Govas of Pangri and Hor, through whose districts I had passed last.

87. INHABITANTS OF TOKCHEN.

It was like a little political congress in which no one was willing to take any responsibility. The Tibetans held councils all day long, and we saw them going from tent to tent or sitting in small warmly-disputing groups out in the sunshine. If I would only return to Takche they would willingly defray all the expenses. But I would not.

One day came our friend the ex-Gova of Kyangyang, and he was soundly rated by his colleague of Hor for letting us travel to Hor without permission. Now Kyangyang would abuse Pedang, and so on along the whole line. Saka-dzong, where we had received the first yaks, would be the last in the sequence. A terrible tumult might be anticipated in the labyrinths of the Trans-Himalaya, and it was a real stroke of luck that it had not broken out before, or it would have been all up with the last discoveries.

Some fine summer days followed, and I delighted in the warmth of the sun on the thin tent. The Samo-tsangpo, which had lately been much swollen, fell again. On July 22 autumn returned and rain washed the valley. The brook increased into a dirty grey, rumbling volume of water measuring 173 cubic feet per second.

On July 23 I hoped that the days of imprisonment had come to an end. The chiefs, accompanied by their servants, came to visit me, and, as far as room permitted, they were all accommodated in Abdul Kerim's tent. The Gova of Pangri took the lead and spoke in the name of the others. He capitulated all the reasons which made a retreat northwards necessary. As he showed no signs of coming to an end, I interrupted him and reminded the assembly that the Gova of Pangri had no authority in Tokchen. Another speaker interfered and told me that all the chiefs would be shortened by a head if I did not return to Takche. In order to bribe me, every one of them laid a parcel of woollen material before me.

I perceived that I should never prevail with them, so to put an end to the discussion I asked:

"Then you will give me no yaks for Tirtapuri?"

"No!" they replied with one voice.

I got up quickly and went across to my tent, while the Tibetans looked silently and doubtfully at one another.

Then the Gova of Pangri came and begged for another word with me.

"Sahib," he began, "as I shall at any rate be beheaded because I have let you through my district, I may as well give you yaks for a journey to Parka."

"Good! Parka is at least a little nearer to Tirtapuri. Have the yaks ready to-morrow."

"But I have no yaks myself. You must hire them in Tokchen."

The Gova of Tokchen was asked, but he had no mind to agree to the proposal. So we had to give up this plan also.

I relate all these consultations to show how things go in Tibet. They are extremely characteristic, and most travellers have had some such experiences. The authorities are stubborn, but always polite and friendly.

It was evident that I must help myself. The caravan consisted of ten horses and mules. Nine should be laden and I would ride the white horse I had bought from Kamba Tsenam in the far east. We could not expect the honest Tibetans to get themselves into difficulties on our account.

"We start to-morrow morning," was the order I gave my men.

So our last evening in Tokchen came on. Rain poured down from heaven, and thunder rolled so heavily in the mountains that the earth trembled, and the turbid stream rose more rapidly than before.

Early in the morning of July 24 the tents were taken down, and the loading had already commenced when a messenger announced that I should have yaks if I would wait a little. Of course I was so obliging as to wait till the Gova of Tokchen came with a new proposal.

"We have decided that all the chiefs now assembled in Tokchen shall escort you to Parka in order to explain there the state of affairs and to see that all goes well. We need, however, a day to get ready. To-morrow you shall have the yaks."

"I have waited long enough. I have no more faith in you."

"I will give you an undertaking in writing that everything shall be ready to-morrow."

"Very well, then, I will wait until the document is ready."

Lobsang went with the Gova to his tent, but soon came back with the information that the Gova had repented of the matter.

Thereupon the signal for starting was given. The horses and mules were quickly laden, and we moved off down the valley in the sight of all the Tibetans of Tokchen. The animals had rested and were in fairly good condition. Their loads were heavier than usual as there were no yaks to help in transport. Our party marched on over meadows and screes on the left bank of the Samo-tsangpo, passing the bend of the river where we had pitched camp 211 the year before. Now the valley expanded and we saw the great holy lake again. Yonder appeared also the summit of Kailas, the holy Kang-rinpoche. Lobsang and Kutus threw themselves full length on the ground and touched it with their foreheads to salute the gods of the mountain.

The camp was pitched just below the mouth of the valley on the right bank. The day was bright and clear, the sunshine glittered on the blue mirror of the Manasarowar, and, unconscious of its own beauty, spread around me one of the grandest and most famous landscapes on earth. I felt that I was free and on my way home. Yet why did no dark troop of horsemen appear in the mouth of the valley? Why did they not come after us, all those chiefs of Tokchen, Pangri, Hor, and Purang, who had recently told us we must not on any account pass along the shore of the holy lake? We were only thirteen men and badly armed. The Tibetans despise the men of Ladak. I was the only European, but I was in Tibetan costume. They might have compelled us to do anything. They might have driven away our horses under cover of night, and thus have fettered us. And if nothing else would do, they might have called out the nomads of the country and armed them with guns and sabres. But not a hand moved when we tore off the bonds of our imprisonment before their eyes. Was it my lucky star or a reflexion from the holiness of the Tashi Lama which accompanied me? Perhaps the Tibetans simply looked upon me as an *enfant terrible* whom it was vain to watch. I had always been turned out everywhere, and yet I had crossed the country in all directions, and had turned up in places where I was least expected. I was like the wind, no one knew whence I came or whither I went.

However it might be, no horsemen showed themselves at the mouth of the Samo valley. We were left alone and slept peacefully on the sacred shore.

CHAPTER XVI

TO THE CONVENT OF "ST. SOW"

WHEN in the previous year I spent a memorable summer month at Tso-mavang, the Manasarowar of the Hindus, and lived on its waters, I felt like a master in my own country and a seafarer over my own water. Now we were only a flight of birds of passage which longed to leave the holy districts.

We marched over the steppe by the shore where grass grew thick and freely after the abundant downpours of rain. There were grazing 4000 sheep, with loads of salt on their backs. Their drivers had set up their tents close together, and they said that they came from Chang-tang and were on their way to the fair at Gyanima.

On the left lay the surface of the holy lake with its changing shades, while to the right we had the large lagoon into which flow the brooks from the valleys Pachen and Pachung. The water which streams from the lagoon into the lake had the year before formed a small brook, but now, after the heavy rains, we found ourselves suddenly on the bank of a considerable river almost a hundred yards wide. It looked, however, worse than it really was. The current was extremely slow, and the depth was only three-quarters of an inch. The whole discharge amounted only to about 185 cubic feet a second. The fording of the river was troublesome only on account of the mud, in which the toiling animals sank up to the knee.

We encamped on the compact sand and gravel of the beach. To the north we could see Pundi-gompa on its cliff on the flank of the Pundi mountain, and a small white spot which had been visible in front of us all the day proved to be the monastery Langbo-nan. Two of my men thought they could see Tugu-gompa also; they had eagle's eyes; to me this monastery was invisible even through the field-glass. Kang-rinpoche and Gurla Mandatta were veiled in clouds, and only late in the day did the mountain of the gods look out distinctly from between white clouds. Camp 453 was pitched on the bank of the Gyuma-chu, which carried 140 cubic feet of water.

All night the country lay under a dark awning of clouds, and the temperature did not fall below 45°, quite a summer night once more. While the caravan was following the shore to the Chiu-gompa, I, with Lobsang and Kutus, visited the young prior Tsering in Langbo-nan. Everything was the same in his roomy cell; he sat on the same divan behind the same red lacquered table, and the sacred books lay, as before, on their dusty shelves. His portrait is in Vol. II., Illust. 262, facing p. 162. The only difference was that Lama Tsering was a year older; he was now thirteen. The older monks of the monastery kept him company. There he had sat all the year day after day, had heard the paper in the window frames rustle and crackle, and had listened to the winter storms as they swept howling over the heights. He drank his morning tea out of a small child's cup and counted the beads of his rosary. In the presence of the monks he must put on the dignity of a prior. But the rogue's eyes flashed, and he laughed childishly when I related some of my adventures.

"Why are you dressed this year like a Tibetan?" he asked. "Last year you wore a European suit."

"I should never have got through to Bongba and Saka-dzong in European costume," I replied.

"True, true! Are you coming here again?"

"Yes, I hope to see you again, Lama Tsering."

We had no time to sit long. A bag of flour and a lump of sugar were handed me as a present, and were requited with a handful of silver rupees. In the court, where a cloister servant held my horse, we said good-bye to the monks, and as I rode away the young prior, sitting at the window, nodded farewell with a friendly smile.

The monastery Chergip-gompa lies lonely and forlorn in its valley mouth. We do not stop there, but hurry past the well-known boulders, caves, and *chhorten* of its mountain spur, and make ourselves comfortable below Chiu-gompa on the same spot as last time. The position of the shore line seems unchanged, the heavy rains not having raised the level of the lake appreciably. But the rainy season has only just begun this year, and no doubt long continuous rains would cause Tso-mavang to rise.

In Chiu-gompa also we found old friends. Chief among them was the young monk Tundup Lama, who, with a lump of butter as a gift of welcome and with protruded tongue, found his way into my tent. He had become thinner and bent, dragged his feet as he walked, and had a bad cough. But he was still the same kindly, cheerful cloister brother as at our last meeting, and I was grieved that he should pass a purposeless life between the dark mouldy walls of his cell, while I enjoyed unbounded freedom among the fresh glorious mountains. All the inmates of the monastery visited us, monks, herdsmen, fuel-gatherers, and water-carriers, nay, even Tundup Lama's old mother, and every one received a small present for old friendship's sake.

A party of Hindu pilgrims were camping on the shore under the open sky. One of them was a very comical freak, about fifty years old, copper-brown, with black whiskers, red turban, a tattered mantle, which a merchant of Ladak had given him, and a pilgrim staff in his hand shod with an iron ferule. He wanted to return to India through Taklakot, and begged for a rupee that he might eat his fill for once.

Chiu-gompa was a critical point, as I knew very well from the year before. But the night passed quietly and without disturbance, and no dark horsemen appeared in the morning. We left the monastery people in their fearful isolation, and heard the murmur of the holy waves die away behind us as we marched down the Ganga bed between the two lakes. The path to the next camping-ground ran over flat hills and swampy meadows on the north shore of the Langak-tso. Here the inhabitants of the district Parka are wont to feed their flocks in winter. Now we saw only a solitary herdsman and some yaks.

On the way we came upon a tramp hideous to behold, dirty, hungry, and clothed in nothing but rags. He defended himself stoutly with a thick stick when the dogs attacked him.

"Give me a copper, sir," he begged in a whining tone.

"Do you know any by-way to Tirtapuri south of the *tasam*?" I asked.

"Yes, I know one."

"If you will show us the way you shall be paid a rupee a day besides free rations."

"Gladly! But if suspicious horsemen appear I must make myself scarce, or I shall be beaten to death."

The new pilot of the caravan, which the wilderness had given us, was called by my men simply the "Beggar," and this name he retained as long as he was with us.

At sunset a violent south-west wind arose and the waves beat against the shore. The clouds round the crown of Kang-rinpoche parted, and a faint purple gleam lighted up the royal mountain. I had fixed it on my photographic plates the year before and drawn it from all sides. Now I saw it for the last time. I asked no more from it, for I had looked enough at it and now saw it only as in a dream.

From a small hill near the camp we could perceive the tents and huts of Parka. Of course our white tents and our camp-fires must be as plainly visible from there. Why, then, did no one come to force us to take the great high road to Ladak again? I do not know, but no one came, and this night also passed quietly.

Close to the west side of the camp the river flows through the plain from the valley which runs due east of Kang-rinpoche, where the monastery Tsumtul-pu-gompa lies at the mouth. This river, too, had received its share of rain; it carried 530 cubic feet of water and was 140 yards broad. Its bottom was extraordinarily dangerous, so that the men had to carry the loads over. My horse nearly stuck fast in the viscous mud and almost threw me into the water.

The old dried-up Sutlej bed lies to the left as we march

88. A Lama in Chiu-gompa.

Sketch by the Author.

over the level ground, where the horses and mules become restive at the sight and smell of the juicy pasturage, and walk with their noses to the ground all the way. Then we cross the Sutlej bed, in which the rain-water has collected into large pools. At the place where we crossed the river bed next day, July 29, its bank terraces were as perfect as though they had been exposed to erosion at the present time. Here also were the ponds we had seen in the year 1907; they were no larger, for they are constantly fed by springs and are independent of rain.

We leave behind us on the left the narrow valley in which the Sutlej, after apparently losing itself in Tso-mavang and the Langak-tso, is born again of spring rivulets, gradually to grow into a great river along which we shall travel through the Himalayas. For a short distance therefore we lose sight of the river, which is here an insignificant brook, and pitch camp 457 on the hills to the north of it. Here grow large quantities of wild leeks, and Gulam gathers a good supply to season the inevitable mutton cutlets which daily grace my table.

It was all we could do to set up the tents before the rain came. The clouds lay actually on the ground, and there was not a glimpse to be seen of the mountains. Twenty ditches had to be digged to guard against flooding. The rain poured down in bucketsful and produced a combination of singular notes. Sometimes it sounded like military music, sometimes like a vibrating roll on tightly stretched drum parchment. But amidst it all we seemed to hear the bleating of fat sheep and the grunting of sleek yaks. Lambs and calves rained down from heaven, milk and butter for the poor nomads.

I listen and to my ears comes the sound of boiling pots filled with fat meat and of singing kettles in which the tea mixed with butter is prepared. Prosperity and happy days descend with the heavy drops. I hear the ornaments of the women tinkle and the noise and laughter of little naked well-fed children who are playing round the black tents. The nomad lays his gun under the border of the tent cloth; he is not, as in lean years, dependent on the chase, but can afford to kill a sheep now and then.

The rain continues heavily and monotonously. Beyond the mist I seem to see it fall like the whitest cotton-wool on the high alpine firn-basins, the cradle of the rivers. Outside there is a swelling roar; it is the Sutlej, which rolls its volumes of water beyond Tirtapuri. The river is as yet a child playing in the valley, but it soon grows larger and stronger, and every drop of rain falling in the mountains adds to the immense force with which the river saws its valley through the Himalayas. The rain still falls and pelts and patters on the grass. I seem to hear the streamers on the passes flutter and the prayer-mills hum; a thousand voices seem to cry from heaven over the blessed land, "Om mani padme hum."

The rain pours down all night and we march on in the morning in heavy rain. The air is raw, damp, and chilly, and I wrap my Tibetan skin coat about me and draw the hood over my head. The men tie round them empty sacks. Dripping and uncomfortable we splash along to the west-north-west over a small rise, and then direct our steps down to the right bank of the Sutlej, where the small monastery Dölchu-gompa is built on a hill, while steep mountain walls flank the left bank.

There is not much to be said about Dölchu-gompa. In its present form it was erected about the time when Soravar Sing conquered Tibet. A Kanpo Lama, four Getsul or novices, a superintendent, and a steward were now the ecclesiastical inmates of the monastery. The golden Sera near Lhasa is said to be the mother cloister of Dölchu, and to give the monks 600 *tenga* yearly for their maintenance. With this allowance they have to manage as well as they can, and in return they must undertake the care of souls in their district. The *lhakang* or hall of the gods is poor. In the middle of the altar table stands a small *chhorten* with the ashes of the lama Lobsang Dentsing who founded the Dölchu monastery two hundred years ago. So at least declared the lama who showed us the sanctuary.

Fourteen tents were pitched at the foot of the cloister hill. Their inmates were not nomads but wool-dealers from Nepal and Ladak. They told me that it paid them to buy up wool in this country and that salt was the only other article of trade on which a profit could be made. Five sheep's loads of salt were equivalent to four sheep's loads of barley, and the value of every sixth load of salt was the duty demanded by the Government.

Dölchu is particularly interesting because here the springs well up in the Sutlej bed which are now the apparent sources of the river, if we neglect the real genetic and historical source lying to the south-east of the Tso-mavang. The name Langchen-kabab, or source of the Sutlej, is used of both places. The hill on which Dölchu-gompa stands is supposed to have the form of a *langchen* or elephant.

In the evening a strolling lama, a mendicant monk from Kham in the extreme east of Tibet, came into our camp. He was equipped with a spear, a drum, and a flute made out of a human shank bone. I promised him a rupee if he would stand still for half an hour, but I had not sketched much of his portrait when the wanderer decamped hastily.

"You must keep to your bargain," growled Lobsang after him.

"I will have none of the bargain or rupee. The fellow bewitches me with his eyes."

Another promise was not fulfilled, but for sufficient reasons. A Ladaki had promised to let me have nine asses on hire for the journey to Tirtapuri. But when he learned that the tributaries to be crossed on the way were so swollen that no ass would be stupid enough to venture through them and endanger his life, he sent me word that he could not let me have them.

We had therefore to look after ourselves. We waded just below the monastery through the crystal-clear brook fed by the springs. It was the young Sutlej, which was to keep us company from here all the way to Simla. If we had always camped on the river bank, every new camp would have stood at a slightly less elevation above the sea than the preceding. At Dölchu we were already a little lower than the Langak-tso; the lake has a height of 15,056 feet, while the monastery stands at a height of 14,820 feet. As we proceeded farther it turned out that no rule held good with regard to the relative heights.

The days of childhood soon pass away. It was not long before the Sutlej had left its infancy behind. In an expansion of the valley we hear the roar of great volumes of water rolling down. The affluent Chukta falls through a gap in the erosion terrace and divides into five delta arms with thick greyish-brown foaming water above the gravelly ground. The fifth arm of this river, which rises in the Trans-Himalaya, was 58 yards broad and discharged 530 cubic feet per second. It was, indeed, about fifty times as large as the source-stream of the Sutlej, but the latter flows all the year round, whereas the Chukta swells up after rain but fails altogether in the cold of winter.

After we have passed over without a wetting we follow the right bank of the united river, and then march along the river bed itself at the foot of an erosion terrace 25 to 30 feet high. On both sides old terraces rise about 130 feet above the valley floor, evidence of a time when larger volumes of water than now poured down the valley and when the lakes had a constant outflow.

After a time we come to another break in the right terrace, and another tributary, the Goyak, empties itself into the Sutlej. The Goyak discharged probably 100 cubic feet of yellowish-brown water thick as pea-soup. We are always crossing feeders, each contributing its mite, and the river gradually increases.

The Sutlej valley has here a westerly direction ; it may be about 1¼ miles broad, but if only the level valley floor be estimated, the breadth is one to two hundred yards. Some stretches are clothed with excellent grass, and we wonder that no nomads make use of it. There is no life except some hares scuttling through the grass. The camp this day, 459, is pitched on the bank of the Sutlej at a height of 14,574 feet. Here the outflow of a spring debouches, and its bluish-green water is at once swallowed up in the yellowish-brown tumbling flood of the river. In the middle of the day the spring water had a temperature of 52.8°, while the river was warmed up to 61.3°.

We had become tired of the peaceful repose of the highlands, and now we were to hear noise enough. It was not only the loud heavy roar of the river, no—rain, too, pelted down on the slopes, and thunder rolled over the valley. When we broke up camp on August 1 the rain still poured down from heaven. Now the rainy season was in full swing, and we, moreover, had travelled from the central parts of Tibet to the peripheral Himalayan regions which catch the greater part of the precipitation of the south-west monsoon.

About a hundred yards below the camp the Sutlej enters a corridor-like trench between precipitous cliffs, which it is impossible to pass through. The path therefore mounts to the ridge on the right side of the valley. We have not proceeded far up there when we are stopped by another valley excavated deep as a grave below our feet. As far as we can see through the rain it comes from the north-east. Grass lends a greenish tinge to the valley bottom, and in the middle shines a winding river like a bright yellow riband. We halt at the edge from which the path winds in steep zigzags to the bottom of this side river; the difference of height is only 165 feet. The river looks small in the distance. But we soon hear its rushing roar, and when we reach the bank we are quite dazed when we look at the heavy reddish-brown stream of water. The river is called Tokbo-shar. A short distance below the ford the valley narrows and the Tokbo-shar forces its way through a rocky portal to join the Sutlej.

We deliberated a little on the feat before us. The rain fell in bucketsful, and it was almost a consolation that we were already wet, for it would be a miracle if we got across this river, which seemed red with blood, without a good bath. All the loads carried by the horses and mules were piled up as high as possible and roped very securely. Some of the men searched for a convenient ford. Where the water rises in high boiling domes, smooth treacherous stones may be expected on which the animals may slip and fall, while at places where the water forms small regular waves, a level bottom is probable. The fording-place finally chosen looked anything but inviting, but there was none better and we must get over.

The river consisted of three narrow arms with breadths of 23.7 and 36 feet; in the middle one the depth was 40 inches. This is not much, but it is more than enough when the water forms rapids and threatens to sweep down man and beast. The aggregate volume was 953 cubic feet, so that the Sutlej received a considerable addition to its water.

First the ford had to be tested. Rasak and the Beggar undressed, took hold of each other, and rolled and staggered like drunken men in the water. They really needed a bath. But it was rash of the Beggar to expose his back, for it was striped like a zebra by the strokes of a whipping which had been administered to him somewhere or other. He therefore stood confessed a notorious rogue. But what did that matter to us? Now he belonged to our travelling company and he played his part excellently. Both crossed all three arms without falling and came back to act as pilots.

Now all my men undressed. The baggage animals were led over one by one; two men walked on either side of a wading animal to lay hold at once if he fell. I was in great anxiety about my maps, notes, and sketches. But all went well, and I rode last through the river preceded by a pilot.

When the men had dried and clothed themselves again, we rode on along the terrace platform. We had not gone far when the same scene was repeated. A new tributary boiled and foamed below our feet, the Tokbo-nub, which had carved out a channel just as sharply marked as its neighbour's, and also flowed to the Sutlej through a rocky portal. We had no choice.

Again the ropes were tightened round the loads, the men undressed, horses and mules plunged into the water, stumbled over the boulders and planted their feet firmly so that they should not be washed away. We did not hear the pelting rain as the Tokbo-nub rolled 850 cubic feet of water past the waders.

The path along the gravelly terrace is marked by cairns and *mani* walls, indicating the proximity of a temple. The Trans-Himalaya, where the two tributaries collect rain-water in the southern valleys, is not visible in this weather, and to the left we only dimly perceive the deep corridor of the Sutlej, cut through solid rock and now completely filled with floods of water.

The wet, tiring day's journey nears an end. A *mani* wall, a hundred yards long and unusually well kept, points to the monastery Tirtapuri, which stands on a terraced slope and is surrounded by a guard of *chhortens*.

I rode up to the sanctuary. The prior, a Kanpo Lama, did not deign to show himself, but sixteen out of the twenty-one monks of the cloister were present and had no objection to take me round. They pronounced the name of the place Tretapuri, but the word Tirtapuri is of Indian origin and signifies "pilgrimage resort." Sakya-toba, softly smiling and plunged in thought, is enthroned on the altar in the *lhakang*, which otherwise contains nothing out of the common. But yes, I was shown some flat dark stones cut round, which might be diabase or porphyry. They bore distinct and rather deep impressions of the hands and feet of holy men long fallen asleep in Buddha. In one also was the imprint of a horse's hoof. *Pia fraus!* The great thing is that the crowd believes in them and continues to humbly make offerings to the monastery.

In the anteroom of the *lhakang* two *nekora*, or pilgrims from Lhasa, had taken up their quarters, and a Hindu was in their company. The object of his journey was Manasarowar and Kailas. He had holy water from the Ganga lake in a brass can, and this miraculous fluid he wished to exchange for my horse. But I had no inclination for this stroke of business; there might be only ordinary water from a village pond in the can, and I wanted my horse myself.

Through an alley of *chhortens* the path runs down to another shrine, the Dorche Pagmo *lhakang*, where the saint of this name sits in the company of Buddha and other potentates of the Lamaist theocracy. Dorche Pagmo is an abbess, who, like the Dalai Lama and the Tashi Lama, never dies but only renews her earthly shell. She lives in the handsome nunnery on the peninsula in the Yamboktso. The curious name signifies the "holy sow" or the "diamond sow," and the proof of her reincarnation is a birth-mark on the nape of the neck resembling a pig's snout. Her hall at Tirtapuri is damp, dark, and dismal, and only after one has become accustomed to the gloom can one distinguish the stereotyped smiles of the gods.

Outside the rain poured down and trickled over the rocks. The caravan had pitched camp 460 beside a shelf of limestone sinter where warm springs bubbled up. The rain shut us in like a glass house. We waited therefore a while in the doorway of the dark pigsty of "St. Sow." Behind us yawned a mystical "Gotterdämmerung," outside freedom sang in the roar of tumbling cascades. How could the monks hesitate in their choice between the two? Well, in the cloister they obtained *tsamba*, tea, and bread without working. Their days slipped by peacefully and without anxiety in the service of the eternal gods. To hold services, clean lamps, perform incantation dances in costumes and masks during the great festivals of the temple, and have the care of souls among the nomads of the neighbourhood, all this was far more comfortable than to wander about with caravans, tend sheep and yaks, or break up salt in Chang-tang.

The rain did not cease. But now we had enough of the holy sow and her monks, so we wrapped ourselves in our mantles and hurried down to our tents.

CHAPTER XVII

MANASAROWAR IN ANCIENT AND MODERN TIMES

THERE is no finer ring on earth than that which bears the names of Manasarowar, Kailas, and Gurla Mandatta; it is a turquoise set between two diamonds. The grand impressive silence which reigns around the inaccessible mountains, and the inexhaustible wealth of crystal-clear water which makes the lake the mother of the holy rivers, the toilsome rocky paths that lead thence over the heights of the Himalayas, everything has aided in rendering from ancient times this wonderful country one of the most holy pilgrimage resorts or *tirta* of the Hindus. Whoever is of a pure and enlightened mind and bathes in the waves of Manasarowar attains thereby to a knowledge of the truth concealed from other mortals. Still at the present day the stranger stands on the lake shore, meditating deeply as he watches the troops of pilgrims wading into water sacred to the gods, and seeking truth there and a solution of the problem of life.

Mânasa Sarôwara means "Mânasa, the most beautiful of lakes." Mânasa means "created by the soul," for the lake was created by the soul of Buddha.

In the Skanda Purana there is a tale of Manasarowar, which is called Manasa-Khanda. The holy lake and its creation are there described in the form of a dialogue. Prince Janamejaya asks Suta, a pupil of Viasa, how the world was created. Suta relates that Dattatreya Rishi, one of the seven human incarnations of Vishnu, after he had visited the Himalayas betook himself to Benares, and loudly praised to the Raja Danvantari the beauty of the

Himalayas. He extolled that part of the mountains where Siva dwells, and where the Ganges like a lotus blossom on its stalk emerges from the foot of Vishnu.

> I saw Manasarowar where Siva dwells in the form of a Rajahansa or a royal swan. This lake was formed by Brahma's soul and therefore received the name of Manasa-sarowara. There dwell also Mahadeva and the gods, thence flows the Sarju (the Karnali, called by the Tibetans Map-chu, or the Peacock river), besides other female streams and the Satadru (Sutlej) and other male streams. Whoever touches his body with earth from Manasarowar and bathes in its waters will attain to the paradise of Brahma, and whoever drinks the water will ascend to the heaven of Siva and be washed pure from the sins of a hundred incarnations, and even the animals which bear the name Manasarowar will enter into Brahma's paradise. The water of the lake is like pearls. There are no mountains that can compare with the Himalayas, for in them are Kailas and Manasarowar. As the dew is dried up by the morning sun, so are the sins of men blotted out at the sight of the Himalayas.

On the creation of Manasarowar it is said:

> The sons of Brahma betook themselves to the countries lying north of the Himalayas and fasted on Kailas. They beheld Siva and Parvati, and there they remained twelve years, praying and fasting. At this time little rain fell, water was scarce, and in their necessity they went to Brahma and worshipped him. Then Brahma asked what they wanted. They answered: "We are engaged in meditation on Kailas and have to go down thence to Mandakini to bathe; make us a place where we can bathe." Then Brahma created Manasarowar by an effort of his will. They went home rejoicing at the success of their journey, and again gave themselves up on Kailas to prayer and fasting, worshipping the golden symbol of fecundation which rose in the middle of the lake above the surface.

When the Prince asks "Which road leads to the holy lake?" Dattatreya enumerates the chief places on the way and speaks of the duties of a pilgrim, of which the following must be performed at the lake shore:

> He should bathe there and pour a libation of water to the shades of his forefathers and worship Mahadeva (Siva) in the form of a royal swan. He should there make the *parikrama*, or the circuit of the holy Manasa lake, gaze at Kailas, and bathe in all the neighbouring rivers.

Kailas is the Olympus of the old Hindu world, the

scene of action of the heroic figures of mystic poetry. At its foot dreams the holy lake, now quiet and smooth as a mirror, showing images of the sun and stars, now beating a melody against the shore in time with the rapid dance of the monsoon clouds on their course through the heavens from the sultry plains of India to the heart of the cool and lofty Tibet.

The clouds come trooping over the Himalayas from the south-west. The stranger who rows in his boat over the lake or wanders round the shore from one monastery to another, knows the ways of the clouds and what they mean. They are the heralds of the south-west monsoon, which does not reach Tibet till late summer. They collect their moisture from the sea, caress the coasts between Ceylon and the mouth of the Indus, bring new life to the palms and jungles, draw up the crops from the earth, and bless men with cool weather. They rush up the flanks of the Himalayas and dissolve in abundant rains. Only a small part of the rain-clouds crosses the barrier and bedews the slopes of the Trans-Himalaya, benefiting also the pastures of the nomads. Scorched and squeezed dry like a bath-sponge the rest of the clouds pass on over the high country and are lost in the air before they can reach the desert regions of Central Asia.

According to the mythology of the Hindus the Yakshas are a kind of divine beings of lower rank in the service of Kuvera, the god of wealth, who guards hidden treasures in the Kailas mountain. There dwells the powerful Kuvera with his divine court. He had committed the care of the golden lotus lilies in the Manasa lake to a Yaksha. Absorbed in his love for his beautiful wife the attendant neglected his duty, and one night the lilies were trodden down by the world elephants which keep watch at the eight corners of the earth. Then Kuvera was wroth and sentenced the Yaksha as a punishment to live apart from his beloved wife for a whole year.

Consumed by sorrow and desire the exile spent the weary lonely days in the south, in the holy forests of the Rama mountain.

The legend is two thousand years old. Kalidasa, one

of the greatest masters of Hindu literature, the author of the *Sakuntala*, has ennobled the theme and has composed a lyrical poem with the holy mountains round Manasarowar as background. The poem is called *Meghaduta*, or the *Cloud-Messenger*, and it abounds in the gorgeousness of the East and in spirited songs, glows with love and longing, and contains a host of the finest, grandest descriptions of nature.

One day one of the rain-clouds of the monsoon was floating over the summit of the Rama mountain, and the banished Yaksha called out to the rain-giver that he wished him to take a greeting to his wife in the Kailas mountain. For the clouds are Indra's envoys, and Indra is the god of the sky. First the Yaksha presents flowers to the Cloud-Messenger, and then he describes the course of the cloud before the monsoon wind from the Rama mountain to Kailas, where the deserted one dwells. He speaks in lofty verse to the messenger, which sends his proud thunder rolling among the hills and is accompanied by the royal swans, the Rajahansas, who migrate to the Manasa lake when the rainy season begins in India. In the language of poetry the wild geese which make their nests every spring on the islands of Rakas-tal are styled swans.

Kalidasa unfolds before our eyes an extremely enchanting panorama of plains and meadows, forests and groves, towns and rivers, which the Cloud-Messenger beholds on his aerial journey. Often these descriptions are involved in a cloud of mythological allusions and relieved by scenes of pomp and love, but just as frequently we come upon passages over which the cloud casts its shadow.

This is especially true of the end of the Cloud-Messenger's journey; the following lines are from the translation of Professor H. H. Wilson (Calcutta, 1813):

Ascended thence a transient period rest,
Renowned Cailása's venerated guest;
That mount whose sides with brightest lustre shine,
A polished mirror worthy charms divine;
Whose base a Rávan from its centre wrung,
Shaken not sundered, stable though unstrung,
Whose lofty peaks to distant realms in sight
Present a Siva's smile, a lotus white.

Now on the mountain's side like some dear friend
Behold the city of the Gods impend;
Thy goal behold, where Ganga's winding rill
Skirts like a costly train the sacred hill;
Where brilliant pearls descend in lucid showers
And clouds like tresses clothe her lofty towers.

To those loved scenes repaired, that awful size,
Like a young elephant, in haste disguise,
Lest terror seize my fair one, as thy form
Hangs o'er the hillock, and portends the storm.
Thence to the inner mansion bend thy sight,
Diffusing round a mild and quivering light,
As when through evening shades soft flashes play,
Where the bright fire-fly wings his glittering way.

The tresses are the clouds, the costly train is the Ganges, which girdles Alakâ,[1] and which, therefore, in Kalidasa's poem is supposed to have its source on Kailas. It is little more than a hundred years since this erroneous view was definitely confuted.

The Yaksha exhorts the Cloud-Messenger, after his task is accomplished, to end his long journey on the summit of Kailas in the form of an elephant. Among the Tibetans, too, whose wisdom is borrowed from India, the elephant plays a certain part in this country. In the Nyandi monastery at the western foot of Kailas two elephant's tusks, *langchen-sala-rapten*, are set up before the altar; all that the monks could say about them was that they had been there as long as the monastery itself. A monastery on the northern shore bears the name of the elephant, Langbo-nan, and, finally, the Sutlej, which periodically flows out of the lake, is called Langchen-kamba, the Elephant river.

But now let us leave the region of legend and poetry, where we vainly grope for firm ground, and search historical chronicles to see what they have to report about the holy lake.

Manasarowar does not figure in the campaign of the great Macedonian. Ptolemy did not know of the lake. Marco Polo and other travellers in the Middle Ages did not hear its name. The migrations of nations took other

[1] The town of Kuvera and the Yaksha.

routes and left Manasarowar undisturbed, a wild rose among inaccessible mountains. For hundreds of years the wild geese continued to fly over the Himalayas, and pilgrims bent their steps towards the lake of truth and enlightenment, and its name was never borne on the wings of fame to Western lands.

When at length, in comparatively recent times, we seem to catch a glimpse of the lake, we still find ourselves left in uncertainty and know not what to believe. In the year 1553 the Khan of Yarkand sent his general, Mirza Haidar, with an army to raze to the ground the idol temple in Lhasa. The army made havoc in the country like a plague, but was itself decimated and did not attain its proper object. In the description of his campaign, Mirza Haidar says: "After a journey of a month a country was reached where there is a lake: it has a circumference of forty farsakh, and on the shore stands a fortress called Luk-u-Labuk. There we halted for the night." This lake can be no other than Manasarowar, for Mirza Haidar travelled along the same road as Desideri two hundred years later.

In old writings on the Himalayan regions a Jesuit, Father Antonio de Monserrate, is mentioned, who in the year 1581 accompanied the Emperor Akbar on his progress to Kabul, and is said to have heard of a lake Manasarowar. I have obtained information about him only at second and third hand; I have not succeeded in finding any report from his own hand.

François Bernier, who accompanied the Great Mogul, Aurangzeb, on his journey to Kashmir, and described his experiences in 1699, could not compare with Ptolemy in his knowledge of the courses of the great Indian rivers, though he lived fifteen hundred years after the time of the great master. But in his scheme of the mountains in the north of India he is on a par with Ptolemy. He gives us a single mountain range named Caucasus, and Tibet shrinks up to nothing. On a map in Bernier's work, however, we find to the east of Kashmir a "Petit Thibet Royaume." The chief branch of the Indus comes from Mont Caucase, and the river receives no water from lands beyond the boundary of Kashmir. Though the French traveller inquired of merchants about the roads to the north and east, he heard nothing of the holy lake.

D'Anville's "Carte Générale du Thibet" (1733), which is reproduced at the end of Vol. I. of this book, supplies for the first time a clear trustworthy representation of Manasarowar and the Rakas-tal. This ground was investigated by Kang Hi's lama topographers. They must have stayed a long time at the lakes, for this region far in the west of great Tibet is better and more exactly surveyed than any other part of the country. The wreath of mountains round the basin gives us a correct picture of the reality. To the north rises Kentaisse or Kailas, in the south-east a brook emerges from the Lantchia Kepou mountains and corresponds to my Langchen-kabab, the headwater of the Sutlej. In the year 1907 I obtained the same results as Kang Hi's topographers. The rivulet represented as flowing to the lake from the south-east is the Tage-tsangpo, which I have called the origin of the Sutlej. Here we come to a problem which in connection with the holy lake will claim our attention more than once in the following description.

D'Anville, following his Lamaist authority, gives the lakes Tibetan names, the eastern lake Mapama and the western Lankan, instead of the names Tso-mavang and Langak-tso, which are more correct. Of the former a better map was compiled than we find one hundred and fifty years later. Between the two runs a connecting river course. This, too, is a link in the chain of the Sutlej. In the years 1907 and 1908 the bed of this channel was dry, as it had often been before. Here we come to a second problem, the question of the periodical variations of precipitation, which are the cause why water flows out of Manasarowar only in rainy years. During certain periods the rain is so abundant that the Langak-tso or Rakas-tal also discharges water, and then only has the river an uninterrupted course. This was the case when Kang Hi's topographers reconnoitred the country and correctly named the river running out of the lakes Lan-chou or Lang-chu, that is Langchen-kamba, Elephant river, Sutlej.

But who is to blame for the fatal error which the

Seigneur D'Anville, Géographe du Roi, has perpetrated? He makes the Lan-tchou identical with the Ganges, and the upper Indus a tributary entering that river. In his great work, *Description de la Chine*, Father du Halde states that the two lamas sent out by Kang Hi obtained their information about the source of the Ganges from "lamas living in the neighbouring pagodas and from documents found in the palace of the Grand Lama in Lhasa." This statement cannot be right, for the monks round Manasarowar knew very well that the river issuing from the lake was the Sutlej and not the Ganges.

The first traveller who described Manasarowar in words was the incomparable Father Desideri. He relates that he and Freyre reached the highest elevations on the road from Leh to Lhasa on November 9, 1715, and says that "the water which streams thence westwards is the origin of the Indus, while that which runs eastwards forms the Ganges."

In the following lines he is the first to allude to the problem, since then become so difficult, of the relations of the great rivers to Manasarowar.

We travel on over a plain called Retoa, where there is a large lake, which it takes several days to go round, and from which, it is supposed, the Ganges originates. But from all that I was able to observe on my journey and the confirmatory statements of men who were acquainted with this country as well as with the empire of the Great Mogul, I am forced to conclude that the mountain Ngari Giongar (Kailas) is not only the source of the Ganges, but also of the Indus. As this mountain is the highest point from which the land falls in both directions, the water flowing down from the western side—whether it be rain-water or melted snow—runs to the second Tibet (Ladak), which is evident from the actual conditions, and after traversing it (Ladak) passes through Little Tibet (Baltistan). Then it rolls down through all the mountains of Kashmir, and at length reaches Little Guzaratta to form the mighty navigable Indus. In the same way the water descending from the east side of Ngari Giongar (Kailas) runs first into the already-mentioned lake Retoa (Manasarowar), and then continuing its course downwards forms the Ganges. A proof of this is furnished by the following circumstance. In the writings of our forefathers there is much talk of the golden sand of the Ganges. If, then, we were to assume that the origin and source of that river lay anywhere else we should give our forefathers the lie, for at no other part of the river's course (except at Kailas and Manasarowar) can a trace of such sand be detected. If, however, my theory is approved, namely, that the source of the Ganges lies on that summit and in the lake Retoa, the statements of old authors are quite in harmony with my views. For, as is known—and, I venture to say, known throughout the world—there is much gold dust on the shores and in the sand round this lake, which the rivers descending from Kailas and other adjacent mountains wash down from the surface of these mountains. Tibetans and a number of traders resort from time to time to the lake to search for and collect the gold, and derive a large profit from it. The lake is, moreover, the object of great reverence among this superstitious people; therefore they make pilgrimages from time to time to this district and wander round the lake with deep devotion, for they believe that thereby they will secure forgiveness of sins and obtain many special indulgences.

These words were written by a Jesuit priest two hundred years ago. Desideri, who travelled with a Tatar princess and her immense retinue, had probably no opportunity of making the circuit of the lake himself and ascertaining what rivers flowed out of it. But he believes from his observations and the reports of Indian pilgrims that the farthest roots of the Indus as well as of the Ganges are to be found in Kailas. The Singi-kabab, the source of the Indus, lies not far off in the north of the Trans-Himalaya. But the Ganges! Desideri has confused the Sutlej with the sacred river of Benares, and was loath to disturb the harmony between the assertions of "our forefathers" and the occurrence, "known throughout the world," of auriferous sand on the banks of Manasarowar. We may be pretty certain that on that winter day when Desideri rode beside Manasarowar no European except himself and Freyre had any suspicion of the existence of this lake.

In winter most of the streams fail or are frozen up. If, furthermore, a snowstorm sweeps over the country, all is levelled down, and the most concentrated attention is required to unravel the hydrography. The Hindus have known of old the high alpine valley where the spring gushes forth which gives birth to the river of Benares. The Tibetans are equally aware that the watercourse which at times issues from Manasarowar is the Elephant river, the Sutlej. But if the monks living in the Chiu monastery are asked the name of the channel, they answer to this day Ganga or Nganga. Possibly this name misled Desideri. At all events it was not his fault that English topographers in much later times confused the Sutlej with the Ganges. He was the pioneer. Who could demand of him that he should grasp in two days the scheme of these singular waterways, about which explorers and travellers have disputed and squabbled for two hundred years after his time. To me, who have explored all round the lakes for a longer time than any of my predecessors, it is consoling and refreshing to find again "il lago di Retoa" in the old diary of Father Desideri.

In the report of Father Souciet (*Observations mathématiques, etc., faites à la Chine*, Paris, 1729) Father Gaubil publishes a memoir on the sources of the Ganges "according to Chinese and Tatar maps." That we may not have to dip into Gaubil's text, I refer to his map; it is valuable and interesting. When compared with my map it is easy to understand. The Mont Cantés is Kailas. On its north-western flank we have the source of the Indus. Why of the Indus? Well, along its course we find Tashi-gang and Ladak, though the names are a little distorted. It is the southern branch, the Gartong, which is meant; the main branch from the Singi-kabab was not known.

South-east of the holy mountain the three head-streams of the Ganges flow into the lake Lapama or Manasarowar. Thence a stream pours out to the Lanka lake or Rakas-tal and leaves it again to run on westwards. This river is the Sutlej. Why should it be the Sutlej? Because we recognize along its course the names Guge, Tsaparang, and Chumurti, also corrupted.

Again we come across the serious misconception of uniting the Indus and Sutlej to form the Ganges. D'Anville committed the same mistake. Therefore it is clearly evident that D'Anville and Gaubil drew their information from the same origin—the exploration of Kang Hi's lamas. These did not travel far enough westwards to ascertain the ultimate fate of the two rivers. The drawing of the ground is in the main correct, and the hydrography accords with the reality; the only error is that the name Ganges is inserted instead of Sutlej.

When we hear next of Manasarowar the Jesuit father Joseph Tieffenthaler is our informant. He was born at Bozen in 1715, went at twenty-eight years of age to Goa, and then for a long series of years wandered through different parts of India, noting down anything remarkable that he saw and experienced. Then in 1765 he betook himself to Bengal and applied for assistance "to the famous English nation which is well known for its generosity and its pity for the poor and wretched."

It is not always possible to gather from Tieffenthaler's reports whether they are the result of his own observations or whether he relied on hearsay. One is often tempted to apply his remarks on the classical authors, who named the Himalayas of Kumaon Imaus, to himself: "They did not see these countries and are usually wrong in their descriptions of distant regions." But we are ready to forgive him because he says quite correctly that the source of the Indus must be sought for in the mountains of Tibet.

Of Tibet he has heard that it lies for five months under a covering of snow. Thence come the softest wool, musk, and white oxtails. The land is governed by a spiritual ruler, the Lama Goru, whom he calls "magnus magister"; he belongs to an order of hermits and is worshipped as a god. He lives in Patala. Information of this kind had reached Siberia fifty years earlier, and the Swede Strahlenberg, who was living there as a Russian prisoner of war, collected invaluable geographical material.

But now we are concerned only with the miraculous lake and the sacred rivers.

Tieffenthaler entered into correspondence with the famous Anquetil du Perron, who looked through his material and published it in his *Description historique et géographique de l'Inde.*

As regards the source of the Ganges Tieffenthaler affirms that it will never be discovered because the way beyond the gorge of the "cow's mouth" is impassable. His commentator observes that there are no impassable roads for those who have legs to walk—"invia tenaci nulla est via." As an excuse for the father, Anquetil mentions that the sources are considered inaccessible both in Bengal and Tibet, because the holy river comes from heaven. He has no faith in the expedition which the great Emperor Akbar sent out at the end of the sixteenth century to search for the source of the Ganges. The envoys saw the water of the river gush out in great abundance in a ravine under a mountain which resembled a cow's head. Anquetil does not believe that the cow's head can rise above the real source, which must rather be looked for in the great Tatary. English explorers, however, were soon to establish the fact that the information which Akbar's envoys brought to their master was correct.

There is every reason to suppose that the maps which Tieffenthaler sent to Anquetil du Perron had been originally drawn by natives for the Emperor Akbar. For the father acknowledges that he had never been himself in the high regions but had heard news about them.

In Anquetil's description it is said of the two lakes:

> The eastern, called Mansaroar or Mansara, is very famous in the country and has, according to Father Tieffenthaler's notes, a circumference of 60 *coss* (Indian miles). The western is named Lanka and has a circumference of more than 11 *coss*. According to the statement of the learned missionary, the Brahmaputra river, which flows to Assam and Rangamati, comes out of the lake Mansaroar. From the upper part of Mansaroar, that is the north-western, a river issues, beside which is written in Persian: "the great river Sutlej which goes in the direction of the Punjab—consequently westwards."

To this sensible and correct Persian statement, which probably dates from the end of the sixteenth century, Anquetil adds the unfortunate remark: "It is asserted that the Sutlej, which flows to Bilaspur and Ludiana, comes down from that lake; but this affirmation is unworthy of credit, for it is more probable that the river flowing out of the lake unites with the Alaknanda which waters Badrinat and Srinagar."

The Alaknanda is one of the eastern headwaters of the Ganges. Here, then, there is another example of the confusion of the Sutlej and Ganges, or at any rate a tributary of the latter.

On Rakas-tal we read: "Beside the large lake Mansaroar and on its west side is the Lanka lake, which the German missionary writes Lanka Dhé. This lake, out of which on the west the Sarju river flows, is much smaller than Mansaroar." It was already stated in the Skanda Purana that the Sarju or Gogra, the Map-chu or Peacock river of the Tibetans, comes from the lakes, not, however, from Rakas-tal but from Manasarowar. Tieffenthaler is here not sure of his facts. He says himself: "Certiora alias exploranda."

Anquetil is all the more positive. He inquires how far D'Anville is right in naming the river issuing from Lanka or Rakas-tal the Ganges. We hope in vain that he will after all decide that the river flowing out of the lake is the Sutlej. But no, he points out that it is an affluent of the Ganges, the Gogra or Peacock river. He says that D'Anville's map of the lamas is incorrect, yet this map was very much better than Tieffenthaler's.

He is more fortunate in his conjecture that the Tsangpo is the upper course of the Brahmaputra; but while Father Régis is satisfied with placing the source of the Tsangpo in the neighbourhood of Manasarowar, Anquetil takes Tieffenthaler's bait and makes the river flow out of that lake.

In conclusion he summarizes the data about the two lakes supplied by Tieffenthaler's map, namely, "the hitherto unknown sources of the three greatest rivers of that country: the Sarju, which flows out of the Lanka lake, and the course of which is marked on no European map; the Sutlej, which runs north-westwards from Manasaroar and flows towards the Punjab; and the Brahmaputra or Tsangpo, which springs from the outflow of this lake on the eastern shore, and which traverses a large part of Tibet before it makes a bend to the south-west to pour into the Ganges below Daka."

It must have been a delight to the learned Anquetil thus to revel in the wealth of knowledge placed at his disposal by Tieffenthaler. Like Gaubil and D'Anville, he exercised all the acuteness of his intellect in determining the source of the Ganges from Chinese, Tatar, and Indian chronicles and records. Ritter placed no confidence in the oriental statements. He calls them ostensibly official, and yet in every respect, if not entirely false, at any rate only half true. Among these he reckons also the maps which Father Tieffenthaler sent to Europe from Hindustan. Therein Ritter is too severe. It is not difficult with the light of our present knowledge to interpret and understand the attempts made by the peoples of the East.

When the curious map sent by Tieffenthaler to Anquetil is compared with the map in the second volume of *Trans-Himalaya*, it must be admitted that the resemblance is very slight. The most singular feature is the hydrography. We see the Brahmaputra flowing out of Manasarowar on the east. How is that possible? Shah Akbar's envoys no doubt went round the lake. The Persian note on the map runs: "The great river which goes in the direction of the Punjab." If a Hindu had given the information the error would have been easier to understand, for he would have been influenced by religious prejudices and have been blinded by them. The Manasarowar was created from the soul of Brahma and the Brahmaputra is Brahma's son. But a Mohammedan wrote the Persian inscription. Possibly Hindus may have drawn the map and the writing was added by Mohammedans in India.

There is actually a river, which interrupts the regularity of the eastern shore line, but this river flows into the lake, not out of it. It is our old Tage-tsangpo, the source stream of the Sutlej, which debouches there. Perhaps the natives who are responsible for the map had simply forgotten in which direction the water ran, and did not perpetrate the mistake until after their return to India.

The map gives no information about the river in the south-west. We may, therefore, consider it certain that it represents one of the rivers that descend from Gurla Mandatta to the lake. We may be the more certain of this because the map shows in the same neighbourhood a temple with hermits' cells, which is evidently the great monastery Tugu-gompa.

The river flowing out of the lake north-westwards especially attracts our attention. Here we have only to keep to the original genuine statement in Persian which says: "The great river Sutlej which goes in the direction of the Punjab." Whenever the map was drawn, the Sutlej then streamed out of the lake. But how is it that the draughtsman did not know that the river entered Rakas-tal? Probably because he had crossed it only at the shore of Manasarowar and had not troubled himself further about it. Owing to this neglect he has made two rivers run out of the lakes westward instead of one. For he saw that a river issued from the Rakas-tal, his Lanka Dhé, and thought that this river was the Sarju, Map-chu. He will have nothing to do with any water connection between the two lakes. Manasarowar belongs to the system of the Sutlej, Rakas-tal to that of the Ganges. If he had examined the isthmus between the two lakes, he would have found that his Sutlej flowed out of Manasarowar into Rakas-tal, and that the river draining the western lake was still "the great river Sutlej which goes in the direction of the Punjab."

Tieffenthaler's map conjures out of the mirror of Manasarowar a monstrous bifurcation, which, as unique on the earth's surface, really ought to have roused the suspicion of Anquetil du Perron—two gigantic rivers running out of the same lake, the Brahmaputra flowing eastwards, the Sutlej westwards.

At first sight the map of Eastern Asia seems more than fanciful. After closer examination we detect its meaning. It shows that at the end of the sixteenth century, and perhaps before the time when Tieffenthaler sojourned in India, the two lakes were closely connected with the river system of the Sutlej, the upper course of the stream passing through both, and then continuing on its headlong path through the Himalayas, past Tirtapuri, Totling, and Kanam. In a recently published book, *Les Royaumes des Neiges*, Charles Eudes Bonin has instituted an excellent comparison of Tieffenthaler's map with my results.

In Chapter L. of the second volume of *Trans-Himalaya*, "The Source of the Sutlej," I have already given the notable contents of a Chinese work, *Shui-tao-ti-kang*, or *The Elements of Hydrography*, which was published in the year 1762. Therein the earliest wanderings of the river are depicted in a manner which agrees in details with the reality, and shows that the Chinese then also, as in the time of Kang Hi, were much better informed about those waterways than modern Europeans who had not been there, but thought that they could solve the problem out of their own heads. The Chinese text states in short decided sentences that the water of Lang-chuan-ka-pa-pu-shan, or the mountain Langchen-kabab, forms the lake Ma-piu-mu-ta-lai, or Manasarowar, and then adds: "The water (that is, the Sutlej) flows out from the west of the lake into the lake Lang-ka (Rakas-tal) at a distance of 60 li. The water (of lake Lang-ka) flows out from the west, and after running westwards for more than 100 li it turns to the south-west, and is now called the Lang-chu-ho." *Lang* signifies bull or elephant, and *chu* means water in Tibetan, while *ho* is the Chinese word for river.

When Major J. Rennell published in the year 1782 his fine map of Hindustan, in which southern Tibet appears in part, he had for this country no other material to guide him but D'Anville's map which had appeared fifty years earlier. He makes the Indus rise in the mountainous regions west of Kashgar, and the Sutlej descend from the southern flank of the Himalayas. But he lets the true upper Indus, which flows through Ladak, and the upper Sutlej, which runs past Totling, be captured by the basin of the Ganges. Rennell, however, confesses that he has made use of D'Anville's map only from want of better material, and he expresses a doubt whether the headwaters of the Ganges can extend so far north-westwards as they are shown on D'Anville's map. He considers it certain, however, that the Ganges and Brahmaputra rise on either side of the same ridge east of Manasarowar, and that after enormous detours—one to the west, the other to the east—they debouch into the sea at the same place.

Rennell was subjected to pretty sharp criticism, by

Anquetil du Perron, for instance, who pointed out that he had shown the defectiveness of D'Anville's map in 1776, for the Gogra, and not the Ganges, rose in the same ridge in Tibet as the Brahmaputra. It was not discovered, however, until some fifty years later that both Rennell and Anquetil were wrong in their explanations of the maps of D'Anville and Tieffenthaler.

When, then, Rennell's map shows a watercourse between the two lakes and a river issuing from Rakas-tal on the west, which is called the Ganges, we recognize on the one hand the correct interpretation discovered by the lama topographers, and on the other the usual confusion of the Ganges with the Sutlej.

In the Anglo-Indian periodical *Asiatick Researches* for the year 1798, there is an article with the title, "An Account of Two Fakirs," published by a Mr. Duncan. In this also Manasarowar passes rapidly before our eyes.

One fakir, Purana Poori of Benares, held his folded hands above his head until his arms grew stiff in this unnatural position. He was an intelligent and trustworthy man, and narrated his adventures in 1792. On his wanderings through the world he had visited Balkh, Bukhara, Samarcand, Badakshan, and Kashmir. He had been at the Gangotri, the source of the Ganges, and had found that the river at its origin was so narrow that a man might jump over it. From Khatmandu he had travelled into the interior of Tibet, to Lhasa and Shigatse. Thence he marched in eighty days to the lake "Maun Surwur."

Of this lake the fakir gave the following account:

> Its circumference is of six days' journey, and around it are twenty or five-and-twenty *goumaris* (or religious stations or temples), and the habitations of the people called Dowki, whose dress is like that of the Thibetians. The Maun Surwur is one lake, but in the middle of it there arises, as it were, a partition wall, and the northern part is called Maun Surwur, and the southern Lunkadh or Lunkadeh. From the Maun Surwur part issues one river, and from the Lunkadh part two rivers. The first is called Bráhma, where Puresram making Tupieya, the Brahmaputra issued out, and took its course eastward; and of the two streams that issue from the Lunkadh, one is called the Surju, being the same which flows

by Ayóddjà or Oude; and the other is called Sutrooda (or in the Puranas Shutudru, and vulgarly the Sutluje), which flows into the Punjaub country; and two days' journey west from the Maun Surwur is the large town of Teree Ladác. . . . Proceeding from Ladác seven days' journey to the southward there is a mountain called Caílasa Cungri (Cungur meaning a peak), which is exceedingly lofty, and on its summit there is a Bhowjputr or Bhoojputr tree, from the root of which spouts or gushes a small stream, which the people say is the source of the Ganges, and that it comes from Vaicont'ha or heaven, as is also related in the Puranas.

It is not said when the fakir travelled to the lake; perhaps ten years before he recounted his observations, perhaps even twenty. At any rate his memory played him false. He has confused Kailas with a mountain of the same name lying more to the south. Like Tieffenthaler's informants, he makes the Brahmaputra begin at Manasarowar. The only accurate detail he has given is the outflow of the Sutlej from the Langak-tso. Though he made the circuit of Manasarowar, which is prescribed to pilgrims, it never occurred to him that the Sutlej runs out of this lake. The origin of the Sarju river is a reminder of Tieffenthaler's map, and the spelling of the names is also similar.

The other fakir had nothing to tell of the complicated waterways. He only noticed that four countries met at Maun Talai (Manasarowar), namely, China, the "Lama Land," Beshahr, and Kulu.

Year after year pilgrims have wandered round the lake for the purification of their souls and in hopes of attaining to the paradise of Brahma and the heaven of Siva. But they have taken their experiences with them when they entered on the dark road beyond the pyre on the quay at Benares, and their knowledge has vanished in the ocean of oblivion just as thoroughly as their ashes have been borne down by the eddies of the Ganges to the Bay of Bengal, and been there lost in the briny deep. Oh, if we possessed a chronicle of all that they have seen every year for many centuries! They have trodden out paths on the margin of the shore with their pious feet. For thousands of years Siva's guests have performed the round dance

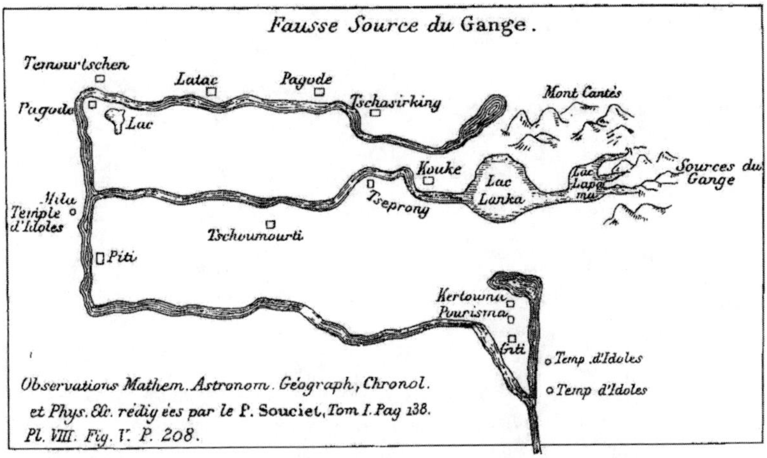

GAUBIL'S MAP OF THE TWO LAKES AND THE SOURCE OF THE GANGES.

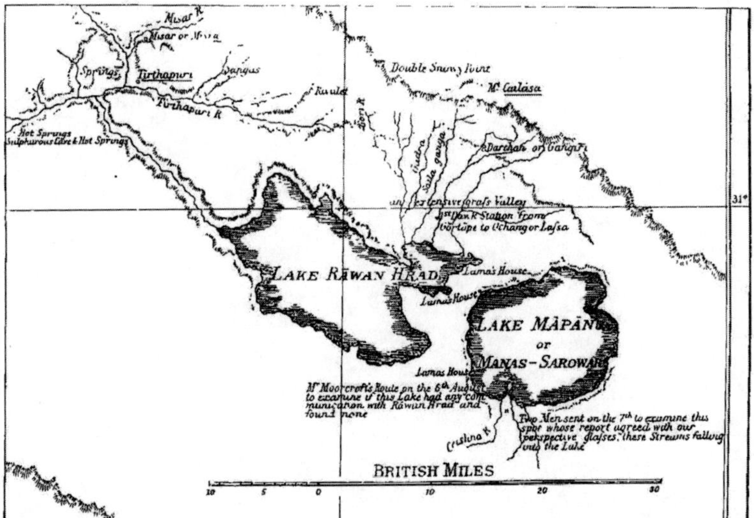

MOORCROFT'S MAP OF MANASAROWAR AND RAKAS-TAL.

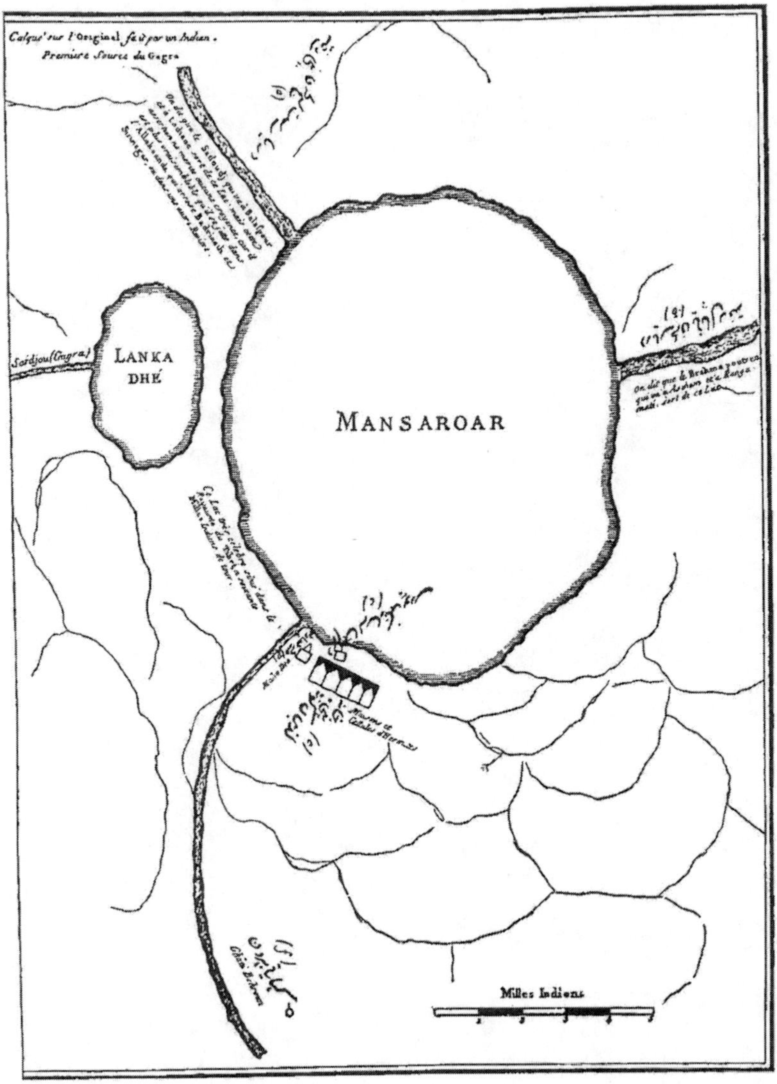

ANQUETIL DU PERRON'S MAP OF MANASAROWAR AND RAKAS-TAL.

which was to lead them to an imaginary heaven. If only one devotee each year had recorded what he saw on a stone tablet in a pagoda!

Some of them have seen the Sutlej come forth from Manasarowar, and to get over the river have crossed the bridge which stood just below the Chiu monastery and was restored from time to time. It still stands there, and old water-marks may be seen on the conglomerate blocks of the bridge-heads. Others have seen a miserable thread of water trickling down the bed, while others again have found not a drop in the channel and have crossed dry-shod.

If we knew now what was known to those wanderers of the age when the first pilgrim made his round of the lake, we could draw a curve of the periodic rise and fall of the lake level. We should see how the lake rose after rainy summers, and how it fell in years of drought. The effect of the monsoon on the highlands would be apparent, and we should perceive that the lake created from the soul of Brahma is living, and that its pulse beats in rhythmical periodic time in obedience to the unknown laws of heaven. But the pilgrims have not revealed their secrets, and nothing remains for us but to search out and collect the notes made by a small number of travellers.

CHAPTER XVIII

THE FIRST ENGLISHMEN AT THE HOLY LAKE

CAPTAIN F. WILFORD, in his "Essay on the Sacred Isles in the West," which appeared in 1808, has communicated what he heard from the famous Purangir, a man who was repeatedly employed by Warren Hastings as interpreter and spy in Bhutan and Tibet, accompanied Bogle and Turner on their journey, and in the year 1779 the Tashi Lama on his march to Pekin. Purangir was a Brahmin, and had made the pilgrimage to Manasarowar, probably shortly before 1773. During his visit there he heard that the lake was wont to overflow during the rainy season, and that the channel then carried water, but failed during the dry season. It should be noted that the surface of the lake rises and falls every year, but that the bed remains dry in some years even during the rainy season.

Purangir believed that the Ganges had its source on Kailas, and flowed thence to Manasarowar. He describes the circle of mountains; he says correctly that the lake has the form of an irregular oval approaching to a circle; he took five whole days to walk round it, and on the south bank he visited the principal temple, the present Tugu-gompa. "The Ganges issues from it (the lake), and during the dry season its stream is hardly five or six inches deep. It does not go through the lake called Lanken in the maps; it flows to the south-east of it at the distance of two or three *coss.*"

Here we have, then, a notice that the water about the year 1770 issued from Manasarowar even during the dry season, and, as usual, we have the name Ganges put in the place of Sutlej. Purangir denies that the river runs through Rakas-tal. But of this he knows no more than other pilgrims. They never turned their steps towards the other lake. It is not holy, and is not touched by the pilgrim route. Purangir, therefore, did not see for himself in which direction the false Ganges flowed, and he did not know that the river by which he stood certainly does not take the way to Benares, but cuts its bed through the Himalayas to make for the Indus.

Wilford makes some bold statements, and perhaps these caused Klaproth to write such a biting criticism of the work. For Wilford says that Pliny and Ctesias mentioned the lake, and Marco Polo described it, whereas their writings contain not a word about Manasarowar.

How dangerous it is to attempt to draw geographical conclusions from religious errors and articles of faith may be seen from the statement of Wilford, that "the four sacred rivers, springing from the Mánsarovara, according to the divines of Tibet, are the Brahmá-putra, the Ganges, the Indus and the Sitá. The Ganges is the only one that really issues from that lake, and if the three others do, it must be through subterranean channels; and such communications, whether real or imaginary, are very common in the Puránas." The four rivers which the Tibetans connect with the holy lake are those which gush forth from the mouths of the lion, the elephant, the horse, and the peacock. But the Ganges, from the head of the sacred cow, is not among them. The fourth is the Gogra or Map-chu, the Peacock river. The nomads, who are less imbued with Lamaistic ideas, say quite plainly that only the Sutlej flows out of the lake, and this only at times.

D'Anville's map shines like a lighthouse over Tibet. Some parts of it have been proved incorrect by later English explorations, and therefore its authority has been undermined. Other regions were for nearly a hundred years accepted as represented. The rest was, as we have seen, rejected only in the second half of the nineteenth century. The most remarkable feature in D'Anville's map is the indication that the Ganges issues from Manasarowar; this was a burning question a hundred years ago. In the year 1812 H. T. Colebrooke published an article "On the Sources of the Ganges in the Himádri or Emodus." As we have had so many false data on this subject, it may not be amiss to consider the discovery of the Ganges source.

Colebrooke had great doubts as to the accuracy of the statement made by Kang Hi's lamas. Hindu pilgrims were wont to follow the Ganges up to the foot of the snowy mountains, while Kang Hi's lamas advanced to the lakes and Kailas in the west. Between these terminal points rise the mighty Himalayas, and it is impossible to determine from their southern side the courses of rivers in the north.

If geographers had been asked in the year 1906 to point out on a large-scale map of western Tibet the source of the Brahmaputra, they would have been considerably perplexed, and each would have laid his finger on a different place. Even those who knew Ryder's results would have given undecided answers. No one, not even Ryder himself, could have placed the point of the compasses on a particular point and said "Here." The position of the Sutlej source would have been fixed with still greater uncertainty, and only those who knew the records would have answered that the question had not yet been decided. The source of the Indus might have been located within a narrower circle, though its radius would have measured twenty miles; but no European had tried to reach it, and Montgomerie's pundits had been obliged to turn back when they were still several days' journey from the source.

At last in the year 1907 I succeeded in finding my way to the sources of all three rivers. I succeeded because I was determined to find them, and because I did not give myself up to chance like chaff driven before the wind. In the case of the Brahmaputra and Indus I followed the streams upwards, which is the surest method. In the case of the Sutlej I followed the river down from its source, and not until I had collected all my data could I prove that the end of the Ganglung glacier, from which the Tage-tsangpo flows, is the source of the Sutlej.

A hundred years earlier the question of the Ganges source was much more vague. It is, of course, owing to the difficulties always placed in the way of Europeans by the Tibetans, and the aversion of the Indian Government to any complications on the frontier, that Englishmen have not long ago penetrated into the country and discovered the sources of the Brahmaputra, Indus, and Sutlej. My success was due to the respect towards Europeans with which Younghusband's expedition inspired the Tibetans, and also to the fact that I received no instructions from the Indian Government. The source of the Ganges was discovered in 1808, those of the other three rivers in 1907. On the former event Colebrooke says:

> Perhaps the national credit was concerned not to leave in uncertainty and doubt a question which the English only have the best opportunity of solving, and one at the same time interesting, as that of exploring the springs of one of the greatest rivers of the old continent, and whose waters fertilize and enrich the British territories which it traverses in its whole navigable extent.

The expedition was accomplished by Lieutenant Webb and the Captains Raper and Hearsey. It followed the track of Antonio de Andrade. Two hundred years earlier this traveller on his way over the Mana pass to Tsaparang had, without knowing it, passed by the source of the Ganges. The sources of the Indus, Sutlej, and Brahmaputra neither Catholic missionaries nor any one else had passed before the year 1907.

The instructions given to Lieutenant Webb by the Supreme Government of Bengal contain the following paragraph:

> To ascertain whether this (*i.e.* the cascade or subterraneous passage at Gangotri) be the ultimate source of the Ganges; and in case it should prove otherwise, to trace the river, by survey, as far towards its genuine source as possible. To learn, in particular, whether, as stated by Major Rennell, it arise from the lake Manasarobar; and, should evidence be obtained confirming his account, to get, as nearly as practicable, the bearing and distance of that lake.

Webb accomplished his task, and reported that the Ganges rose on the southern slope of the Himalayas and that, as trustworthy natives had informed him, "no river, except one, exists westwards of the Manasarowar lake; that this river is called the Saturaj (Satalaj) river."

Captain Raper has given an excellent description of that important journey. Gangotri was the source of the Ganges. The problem of a connection between the Ganges and Manasarowar was finally settled. But which river was that which had figured so long between the lakes and to the west of Rakas-tal? This question had yet to be answered.

On a later occasion, in the year 1816, Webb learned from a Tibetan border chief that more than a hundred streams poured into Manasarowar, but that the lake had only one outlet to the Rakas-tal, a channel which, however, was often dry.

William Moorcroft was a veterinary surgeon who in 1808 went to Calcutta at the invitation of the directors of the East India Company. His name is famous in connection with Manasarowar, and his narrative of the journey he undertook with Captain Hearsey in 1812 to the north-western shore of that lake, is some of the best literature we have on the holy lake. But his hydrographical results were negative. Thus Colebrooke says in his introduction to Moorcroft's narrative: "He ascertained the existence and approximately determined the situation of Mánasaróvara, verifying at the same time the fact that it gives origin neither to the Ganges nor to any other of the rivers reported to flow from it." Colebrooke, however, adds the suggestion that the lake when it rises sufficiently may discharge its surplus water to Rakas-tal, from which the Sutlej originates.

Moorcroft travelled over the heights of the Himalayas. At the sight of the huge snow-clad mountains he could not understand why people had not been content to ascribe the Ganges to them, but insisted on bringing the river out of a lake, which also must be constantly fed by rivulets. This truth has been forgotten by some learned men of our days. It is not enough to say that Manasarowar is the source of the Sutlej. The largest of the streams that feed the lake is the uppermost course of the Sutlej. And as the Tage-tsangpo is very much larger than all the rest, there can be no doubt where the real source lies.

They gained Tibet over the Niti pass (17,568 feet).

The pass was so high that a handful of resolute men could have held it against a whole army by rolling down large blocks of stone. The two Englishmen travelled in disguise and gave themselves out for merchants. They got safely past Daba and came to Gartok. The Garpun had no objection to their extending their journey to Manasarowar. But when Moorcroft asked to be allowed to make the journey back over some other pass than the Niti, the answer was "No," for the Garpun would lose his head if the strangers did not go back by the same way they had come—just as at the present day.

Moorcroft proceeded south-eastwards and found at the foot of the rock on which the Tirtapuri cloister is built "a very rapid stream, which is said to proceed from a lake at the foot of the Himálaya, called Ráwanhrád (Rakas-tal), and to constitute the principal branch of the Satúdrá." We will not do more than mention that the words in the text do not agree with Moorcroft's map. Worthy of notice is the circumstance that, according to the statement of the lamas of Tirtapuri, the Sutlej came from Rakas-tal, though the channel between the two lakes was dry, and therefore no water could flow out of the western lake unless through subterranean passages. Hence it seems that the monks trace back the Sutlej to Rakas-tal, in spite of climatic variations which cause the water to fail periodically.

After two more days' journey Moorcroft descried to the south "a large sheet of remarkably blue water at the foot of the mountains to the right, called Ráwanhrád, said to give rise to the principal branch of the Satúdra, and to communicate by a river with the lake Mansarowar, named by the natives Mapang." Moorcroft therefore approached the holy lake with the conviction that the water ran through both lakes. That the Ganges does not receive a drop of water from this direction had already been proved by Webb's expedition. Now Moorcroft had to find out how matters stood with regard to the Sutlej.

On August 6, 1812, Moorcroft walked along the shore of Manasarowar to Chiu-gompa, and mounted a hill on its southern side. He looked in vain for an outlet. As far as the eye could perceive through the field-glass there was no depression between the two lakes, no interruptions in the hills. He sent scouts to the southern shore, and they returned with the news that no drainage stream issued from the lake.

He returned to his camp convinced that no rivers flowed out of Manasarowar. And yet on his walk near Chiu-gompa he had twice crossed the dry bed without remarking that it might at times at any rate serve as an outlet. The next day he again sent men off along the western shore to confirm his observations. When they returned they assured him that they had not even found a sign of any old dried-up bed.

An old pundit named Harballabh, who was Moorcroft's companion on this journey, assured him before they reached the lake that a watercourse issued from Manasarowar, entered the Rakas-tal, and left it again on the western shore as the Sutlej. Harballabh was vexed at the result of the investigation, for it seemed to cast an aspersion on his credibility. He affirmed with great positiveness that sixteen years before, that is in 1796, he could not have crossed the channel between the eastern and western lakes if there had not been a bridge below Chiu-gompa. Also a man from Ladak told how, eight years before, or in 1804, he had seen the stream flowing out of the lake, which had subsequently ceased to run, and that then the bed had dried up and been filled with sand.

Again Moorcroft sent out scouts who returned with the same negative result. After all he could only explain the phenomenon by supposing that an earthquake had produced alterations in the ground. And yet the explanation was not far to seek! That stream had only a periodical existence, depending on variations in the rainfall which, sometimes abundant, sometimes slight, was carried up by clouds of the south-west monsoon into the mountains.

Moorcroft thought he saw in the distance a stream issuing from the western shore of Rakas-tal; but, unfortunately, an attack of fever prevented him from examining it more closely. As regards this he must have relied on the statements of the natives, for it is beyond doubt that the channel from the Rakas-tal was dried up in the year 1812.

After Moorcroft had solved the problem of the lakes and the mysterious river, as he supposed, he took his way back through Daba and over the Niti pass; and rejoiced when he saw the first trees on the south side of the Himalayas. In Kumaon the strangers awakened suspicion by clothing themselves again in European costume, and in consequence of orders from Khatmandu, the capital of Nepal, they were imprisoned with great brutality. Moorcroft, however, by his courage and energetic conduct succeeded after a time in regaining his freedom, and in November 1812 the whole expedition reached British territory in safety.

A singular fate seems to have pursued this, the first Englishman to reach the holy lake. After his famous and meritorious journey thither, he directed his eyes from the shore yet farther into the heart of Asia, on to that world of unknown mountains, which, since the time of Marco Polo and Benedict Goes unknown and unvisited, form a partition between the countries of India and the focus of the immense empire once ruled by the iron hand of the victorious Timur. In the year 1820 we find Moorcroft in Leh, but having waited there for two years without finding an opportunity of travelling northwards he returned to Kashmir and the Punjab in order to make for Bukhara through Cabul and by unknown roads. On his return thence he died of fever at Andkhoi, on the 4th or 5th of August 1825, it was said, but as his countryman Trebeck and his Asiatic fellow-travellers all perished, there is every reason to suppose that they were the victims of a hostile attack. It is the more probable that such was the case because the expedition was received with hostility by the people and princes in Timur's country. Moorcroft was the first to die; there is a letter in Trebeck's handwriting still extant which confirms his death.

It therefore excited no little astonishment when Father Huc related in his noted work, *Souvenirs d'un voyage dans la Tartarie, le Thibet et la Chine*, which appeared in 1853, that during his stay in Lhasa he was one day visited by the chief of the Kashmirian merchants, who introduced to him one of his subordinates named Risan, and told him that the man had served Moorcroft for many years during his sojourn in Lhasa.

Huc had never heard anything of Moorcroft, and now he was assured on all sides that the English traveller had arrived at the capital of the Dalai Lama in 1826. He had come from Ladak, was dressed as a Mohammedan, and spoke Persian only. He had hired a house and lived in it twelve years with his servant Risan. Herds of yaks and goats which he bought were tended by Tibetan herdsmen on the mountains, and under the pretence of keeping an eye on them he had been able to wander about unmolested in the mountainous regions, making notes and drawing maps. After the twelve years had passed the stranger had given Risan a letter, and told him that he would make his fortune if he showed it in Calcutta. Then he left Lhasa by the road to Ladak which passes by Manasarowar, so excellently described by him. Near the lake he was attacked by robbers and murdered.

By order of the Tibetan Government the robbers were pursued and overpowered. The property of the dead man was brought to Lhasa, and there the geographical maps, the notes, and the instruments revealed that the supposed Kashmiri was an Englishman.

Huc tried in vain to clear up the mystery, for after his return to France he learned that in Ritter's *Asien* Moorcroft's death in Bukhara in 1825 was announced. The same statement was made in Professor Wilson's book on Moorcroft published in 1841. Lieutenant Burnes on his journey to Bukhara in 1832 had visited his grave.

Perceval Landon, correspondent of the *Times* with the expedition of Younghusband to Lhasa, suggests that Moorcroft's papers were carried after his death in Bukhara by Kashmiris to Lhasa, and that their owner was afterwards murdered or plundered at the holy lake on his journey home. The supposed Moorcroft was, then, a man from Kashmir. This is perhaps the true explanation. But Huc spoke himself with the man who had served the stranger for twelve years, and he justly asks what reason the inhabitants of Lhasa, Tibetans and Kashmiris, could have for imposing on him with such anecdotes. At any rate

Moorcroft's fate is involved in darkness. According to the former version he died alone in Bukhara in 1825, according to the other he was killed in 1838 near Manasarowar.

Among the names connected with Manasarowar, Moorcroft occupies the first place. He, indeed, visited only the western shore, but I have realized on the spot how accurate and reliable his observations were. His countrymen have not always estimated him highly enough. Various attempts have been made to explain on more or less probable grounds why he did not see the river bed near Chiu-gompa. It is, however, by no means extraordinary if this bed is so sanded up as to be unrecognizable after the water in the lake has stood for several years at a low level. Moorcroft's omission was that, owing to fever, he did not go a few hundred yards beyond the monastery Chiu-gompa; then the circumstances would have been clear at once. If Harballabh and the Ladaki, whose words he could not make up his mind to trust, had only led him to the bridge, he would have admitted that abundant floods must at times pass under its beams.

Three years after Moorcroft's journey to Manasarowar, his countryman, James B. Fraser, reached the Jumnotri, the source of the Jumna, and availed himself of the opportunity to gather information about the country in which the Sutlej collects its first drops of water. The natives could only inform him that the river came from a great distance and had its source behind the Himalayan chain. They knew nothing more definite. He himself believed that the river was fed chiefly by melted snow from the mountains, which lifted their white summits on all sides. The narrative of this journey appeared two years after Moorcroft's. But the author does not know the work of his countryman, and seems hardly to have heard of the first Englishman who crossed the western Himalayas. Or he would have said a word or two about the map printed two years before, which shows Rakas-tal as the source of the Sutlej.

In the years 1817 and 1818 the brothers, Captain Gerard and Doctor Gerard, travelled through the western

Himalayas and made valuable contributions to our knowledge of those mountains. They did not, indeed, advance as far as our lake, but they obtained information about it from natives. Captain Gerard states:

> I have seen more than one hundred people who have travelled up the Sutluj, not exactly to its source, but to within ten or twelve miles of it, to the place whence the road turns off to Mansurowur. All the accounts agree that the largest stream issues from the western corner of Rawun Rudd (Rakas-tal), or Langa, and, even close to that lake, it is stated to be thirty feet broad and one-and-a-quarter deep, in the dry season, and very rapid.

From this report we may conclude that the precipitation increased from 1812 to 1817, and then reached a maximum which allowed both lakes to overflow. This conclusion, however, is afterwards contradicted in Captain Gerard's report, wherein it is said that the natives affirmed most positively that the Manasarowar had about twenty years before sent out a stream westwards, which had to be crossed by a bridge, but that it had subsequently failed. But the monks living on the shore believed that the outflow still continued, though by subterranean passages.

Especially interesting is Gerard's remark, that a river flowing into Manasarowar on the east is known to the natives as the Sutlej, and that it comes from the Gunchu-tso. But here he misunderstood his informant, for the river which comes from the direction of the Gunchu-tso is the Samo-tsangpo, while that which must be regarded as the uppermost course of the Sutlej is the Tage-tsangpo. The Gunchu-tso has no outlet; the lake is salt and it is scarcely credible that it had an outlet to Manasarowar a hundred years ago.

Another of the great pioneers in the western Himalayas was Captain J. D. Herbert, who travelled along the Sutlej in 1819 and drew up a map of the part of the river which lies in British territory. He was unable to advance beyond the frontier village Shipki. Like the Gerard brothers he was forced to turn back at the Tibetan boundary. The suspicion of the authorities seems to have been aroused after Moorcroft's visit; even natives were often refused permission to cross the frontier, for it was feared that they might be disguised Europeans. Therefore Herbert could do nothing towards solving the problem, but like the Gerard brothers had to content himself with questioning natives; they informed him that a connection existed between the two lakes during the rainy season.

We often wonder at the absence of Moorcroft's name in descriptions of Himalayan journeys of this period, though he was the first authority on the country round the lakes. We wonder why natives of more or less credibility were subjected to a cross-examination when an Englishman had shortly before given such an exact and detailed account of the origin of the Sutlej and its upper course. It is the same with Francis Hamilton, who set out in 1814 and gave to the world his excellent book *An Account of the Kingdom of Nepal in 1819*. He has included a quantity of contradictory statements he received from a certain Hariballabh, in whom we have every reason for recognizing Moorcroft's old pundit Harballabh. The pundit affirmed that a river flowed out of each of the lakes, and Hamilton considers that this statement agrees on the whole with D'Anville's map. Why did he not consult Moorcroft's map, which was much newer and was the work of an Englishman?

During the thirty-four years which intervened between Moorcroft's first journey and Henry Strachey's visit to Manasarowar hardly any information on western Tibet reached Europe. Students certainly spoke now and then of the holy lake, and slight allusions were made to it in geographical literature. Minkhul Khutuktu wrote his description of Tibet, which, however, was not translated into Russian until much later, and in which the courses of the four famous rivers are fancifully drawn.

Meanwhile the discovery of the source of the Sutlej gave rise to a dispute as to priority in the *Journal Asiatique*. The great geographers Saint-Martin and Klaproth believed that they could prove that Tieffenthaler and Anquetil du Perron had solved the problem in 1784, or twenty-eight years before Moorcroft's journey, and that therefore the honour of the discovery was due to the Germans and French and not to the English. It was clearly shown on Tieffenthaler's map, they maintained, that Manasarowar was the source of the Sutlej. "From this lake flows the river Langtchou or Sutledj, which runs westwards to cross the Langa lake, which the Hindus call Ravanhrad. Accordingly, there exists a connection between the two lakes, which Moorcroft has disputed without reasons and proofs; the farthest source of the Sutledj is in the lake Manasarowar, and not in Ravanhrad." Therefore, the two learned men think that it is time that the credit of the discovery should be assigned to the Germans and French, to whom it is justly due.

It is the old story, but remains ever new. Ritter had already said that a single observation on the spot was worth all the cheap hypotheses that can be manufactured at home. Here we have on the one side sound unpretentious personal observations, and on the other, theoretical speculations of doubtful value. First of all, Kang Hi's lama topographers long ago had surveyed the lakes, and proved their close hydrographical connection with a river which was the Sutlej, though they mistook it for the Ganges. To them, then, belongs the honour of the first discovery, though it was reserved for Moorcroft to prove that the river was the Sutlej. It was reprehensible that two men like Saint-Martin and Klaproth should put the authority of their famous names in the scale against Moorcroft, and throw a cloud over a discovery which was worth a hundred times as much as all that Tieffenthaler and Anquetil du Perron had written on Manasarowar. Ritter alone defended Moorcroft as the "only eye-witness," and he expressed briefly the sharp-sighted suspicion that the outflow of the lake might be periodical. He could appreciate all the troubles and dangers to which the native topographers were exposed and the risk Moorcroft ran in travelling in disguise when he made his discoveries. How easy and safe it was, on the other hand, for a man to sit at his writing-table and in categorical statements hurl his thunderbolts at the real discoverers who had seen lands, rivers, and lakes, and cite against them authorities who had never crossed the bounds of Tibet!

Lieutenant J. D. Cunningham, who wrote in 1844,

collected the most recent data concerning the lakes, and supplemented them by reports he received himself from natives. He arrived at the conclusion that, if a water channel had ever connected the two lakes, it no longer existed, and that no stream still flowed out of Rakas-tal.

Shortly after, in the autumn of 1846, Henry Strachey accomplished his well-known journey to the frequently discussed lake district, turning his steps first to Rakas-tal, which was less known, and which seemed to him more interesting, because the Sutlej ran out of its north-western corner. His examination convinced him that no visible watercourse left the lake, and that the only outlet he could find was through the permeable ground. But he did not deny that abundant precipitation might raise the surface of the lakes to such a degree that the surplus water might flow away through the bed still visible in the north-west. He also puts the question whether the Darma-yankti, a tributary coming from the south and joining the Sutlej of Tirtapuri, may not be the true source of the Sutlej. The decision, however, he left for exact measurements. Undoubtedly the Darma-yankti carries at certain times more water than the branch of Tirtapuri. But if we are to move the source from one point to another according to the volume of either stream, we may as well give up the problem as insolvable. Reckoned from the source of the Tage-tsangpo the Tirtapuri branch is the longest. But the decisive point of view is that of the Tibetans and Chinese, that the two lakes lie on the Sutlej source-stream like pearls on a string. When Rakas-tal is finally cut off from the Sutlej, and its water begins to turn salt, then must the two lakes be regarded as an isolated hydrographic system.

Then follows the surprising discovery which Strachey made on October 5 when he had left the north-eastern bight of Rakas-tal behind him and was marching eastward. Only a mile from the lake shore he came across "a large stream 100 feet wide and 3 deep, running rapidly from east to west through a well-defined channel; this was the outlet of Manasarowar."

Thereby Henry Strachey proved that the account given by Kang Hi's lamas was correct. Only Moorcroft could have seen the channel, and again a shadow of doubt was cast upon his efforts. Strachey endeavours to explain the matter by supposing that the discharged water broke through a shore bank of sand and gravel and was hidden by it, and that it did not collect into a stream until it emerged on the other side of this bank. For otherwise Moorcroft must have noticed it.

Yet never did the essence of the problem stand out so clearly as now. Some years the channel contained water, in others it was dry. Its water was therefore a periodical appearance, and Moorcroft had made his observations as surely as the envoys of Kang Hi, or as Henry Strachey, though he visited these regions at a time when the monsoon rains were scanty and caused a low level of water in the lakes.

Two years later, in the autumn of 1848, Henry Strachey's brother Richard succeeded in making his way to the forbidden lakes. He passed along the southern shore of Rakas-tal and marched northwards on the isthmus between this lake and Manasarowar until he reached a rise near Chiu-gompa, from which he looked down on the stream which connected Manasarowar with Rakas-tal. Then also the eastern lake had an outlet to its western neighbour.

CHAPTER XIX

THE LATEST REPORTS

DURING the twenty years which passed between the journeys of the Strachey brothers and the departure of Montgomerie's pundits, we search in vain for any valuable information about the disputed country which the inaccessible walls of the Himalayas so effectually protected. I find only that a Mr. Drummond, Commissioner of Bareilly, sailed in a boat on the holy lake in the year 1855, or according to other accounts in 1860, but I have obtained no information as to what his aim was on this journey, or what he accomplished.

In his classic account of Ladak Sir Alexander Cunningham relies on the experiences of the brothers Strachey, and rightly says that the true sources of the Sutlej must be sought among the streams which flow into Manasarowar from the east. It is remarkable that then no European had visited the eastern shore and that nothing was known of the waters that debouched there. The source of the Indus, on the other hand, he misplaced into a quite absurd spot, believing that Moorcroft had discovered it and had seen the water of the Indus flow north-westwards past Gartok to Ladak. He knows nothing of the north-eastern arm which descends from the true source.

The legend of the four beasts' mouths, from which the famous rivers rise, is, according to Cunningham, of Indian origin. The Tibetans could not know of the elephant and peacock except from there. And the Tsangpo, the river of the horse's mouth, is so named in honour of Buddha's steed. The name Singi-kamba, the Indus, refers rather to the tiger than the lion.

On their long and meritorious journeys through the western Himalayas during the years 1855 to 1857, the Schlagintweit brothers did not succeed in advancing to our lakes. They had, like Cunningham, to content themselves with quoting Strachey, and spoke therefore of a river which connected the two lakes throughout the year.

There is also no lack of apochryphal accounts. In June 1865 Captain H. R. Smith and A. S. Harrison reached the village Darchen at the southern foot of Kailas, and also marched along the northern shores of both lakes. They traversed the mountains for sport, and not much can be expected from their powers of observation. It would have been wiser, therefore, if Captain Smith had forborne to criticize the Strachey brothers, the most thorough and reliable explorers who had then travelled in Tibet. Smith actually asserts that it is a physical impossibility that water should flow to the Sutlej from one or both of the lakes, for in that case it would have to flow up a steep hill. He also disputes the existence of any trace of an old river bed. Every native he questioned confirmed his own observations, and, besides, he had found the circumstances so easily comprehensible that all inquiries were superfluous. At the meeting of the London Geographical Society, when the Captain gave an account of his astonishing discoveries in the Himalayas, the Himalayan explorer Dr. Thomson was present, and he effectively defended the honour of the brothers Strachey.

Captain A. Bennett advanced the same year to Daba, and added his contribution to the solution of the problem in the naïve and superficial opinion on the sources of the Sutlej and Indus that both rivers rise here, the former in some lakes, the latter in the hills behind them.

At the same time as the last-mentioned, Thomas W. Webber and three other Englishmen travelled to the country south-east of the holy lake to hunt there. Webber describes the journey in a book which appeared in 1902, nearly forty years after the journey. Therein he reports the curious discoveries made by himself and his companions, discoveries which quite overthrew all that Moorcroft, the brothers Strachey, and the pundits had achieved. The pundits certainly travelled two years after Webber, whose book takes no notice of their experiences.

Webber believed himself to be in the higher regions of the Brahmaputra when a very surprising change of scene occurred:

> On another occasion we crossed another very lofty divide, and found ourselves suddenly out on the northern slopes of another watershed, none other than that of the mighty Indus. Far beneath us, some miles away, lay the most brilliantly beautiful blue sea, the celebrated Manasarowar lake, as it proved, which we had promised not to approach.

It is hopeless to try to reduce this confusion to order. They stand on a watershed between the Brahmaputra and Indus and see Manasarowar a mile in front of them! On a map, which I have reproduced at the end of Vol. I., Webber has placed the source of the Indus south of Manasarowar and the source of the Ganges on the southern flank of Gurla Mandatta. On the east side of the same mountain rises the Brahmaputra. It is inconceivable how such a map could have been printed in England and in the year 1902. Kang Hi's lamas confused the Sutlej with the Ganges, and that was pardonable. And so it was in Desideri's case. But the source of the Ganges had been known for nearly a hundred years in 1902, and for as long a time it was known that the stream flowing out of the lakes was the Sutlej, and not the Indus. When Webber's book appeared all these facts were known, but he has erased them with one stroke of the pen. Of Gurla Mandatta he says: "This conspicuous mountain might appropriately be called the Peak of Asia, as from its glaciers the three great rivers, Indus, Ganges, and Brahmaputra, take their rise." The Ganges and the Brahmaputra have nothing whatever to do with Gurla. The source of the Indus lies to the north, beyond the Trans-Himalaya. The Sutlej is certainly an affluent of the Indus, but its sources do not lie on the slopes of Gurla. The whole account is a romance—a phantom picture from the time of the Jesuits and Capuchins.

On his noted journey in the years 1885 and 1886 along the Tsangpo, the upper Brahmaputra, Nain Sing passed both lakes on the northern side. Montgomerie, who sent him out, led astray by Nain Sing's route, thought that the position of the Brahmaputra's source might be fixed in the mountains to the east of the lakes. It is, then, astonishing to hear two such famous presidents of the London Geographical Society as Murchison and Rawlinson say that the pundits returned along the bank of the Brahmaputra to the source of this river in Manasarowar. This was really to return to Father Tieffenthaler's view, and to ignore one of the most important watersheds in all Asia.

We have a reliable statement from the year 1868 by one of Montgomerie's pundits, who walked round Manasarowar without finding any outlet. But it is added that "at one point on the west the ground near the Ju monastery was low and looked as if water had perhaps at one time flowed through towards the Rakas-tal lake, though it is now too much above the lake to admit of it." Twenty years earlier, when the brothers Strachey visited the lake, water was still flowing out. Now the channel was dry. There is, then, a periodical depression, a fall in the curve.

Spirits dwell in the sacred mountains of Tibet, and it almost seems as if the Europeans who wandered along the foot of the steep rocky cliffs were blinded and stupefied by the magic power of the spirits and forgot to solve the problems for the sake of which they made such great efforts. Such was the case with the Nien-chen-tang-la, which several Europeans saw, and yet always remained a gigantic mark of inquiry on the shore of its holy lake.

A similar enchantment has bewitched Manasarowar and Rakas-tal. Now there are four great rivers, which, each on its side, draw water from this inexhaustible reservoir, now it is the Ganges which rises there, then again the Indus, the Sutlej, the Map-chu, and the Brahmaputra, which are accused of exacting toll from the beneficent waves of the lake. And then dim rumours crop up that it is a physical impossibility that a single drop of water can escape from the margin of the lake basin.

Yet in the year 1891 Colonel Tanner, who knew the

Himalayas thoroughly, wrote: "I here remark that the moot question as to whether the Satlaj actually comes from the Mansorawar lake or not, does not appear to have been definitely settled."

The extraordinary Münchhausen romance which an English newspaper writer named Landor narrated, and which quite set aside all the conscientious reliable descriptions of Moorcroft, Strachey, and the pundits, had no effect whatever. Among the uncritical, sensation-loving public Landor had a certain temporary success; but among geographers, especially in London, he was received with justifiable suspicion.

The Japanese priest, Ekai Kawaguchi, who travelled through India and Tibet in the years 1897 to 1903, caused less sensation. He makes some very valuable observations, but also commits some dreadful mistakes. He has no high opinion of the sharp-sightedness of Europeans. He himself is honest and ingenuous, and does his best to find out the truth. His mission was not geographical; he wished only to study religious literature and compare the Chinese translation of the Buddhist books with the Tibetan.

From Khatmandu and Muktinath Kawaguchi proceeded to Tibet, crossed the streams which form the Tsangpo, and travelled in a north-westerly direction to Manasarowar. He drew no maps, and his compass bearings are often absurd. Consequently, one is frequently uncertain which rivers and mountains he really refers to. But when he follows a river for four miles and then sees it debouch into the south-eastern part of Manasarowar, this can only be the Tage-tsangpo. He calls the source of this river the "Chumik Ganga, or the source of the Ganges," and he adds: "I took a deep drink of the holy water." Of this and another spring he says: "Hindus and Tibetans consider these two sources to be the origin of the sacred Ganges, and regard them with religious awe."

Here, then, the Ganges again crops up among our lakes. Nevertheless, Kawaguchi's narrative possesses a certain interest. His two springs are probably identical with those I passed on the course of the Tage-tsangpo, as

I have mentioned in Vol. II. p. 105. He calls the first Chumik Ganga; Chumik is Tibetan, and signifies spring, while Ganga is the Indian name of the Ganges. When I asked the name of the spring I was told that the brook is the Langchen-kamba or the Sutlej river; the Langchen-kabab, the source of the Sutlej, lies a little farther south-east. But the channel between Manasarowar and Rakas-tal was named to me the Ganga. This appears to imply that the connecting channel is regarded as a continuation of the Tage-tsangpo, a view which is quite correct, and agrees both with D'Anville's map and the Chinese description in the work *The Elements of Hydrography*. Kawaguchi is a Buddhist priest, and perhaps religious dogmas obscured his judgment. It is not easy to sound the soul of a Buddhist priest. It is credible that his informant saw in the Sutlej a tributary of the Ganges, and that consequently, in his opinion, the source of the Sutlej might be described as that of the Ganges. But such speculations are unnecessary, for a little later in his narrative Kawaguchi himself declares that the Gogra, Sutlej, Indus, and Brahmaputra are all said to flow out of the lake, leaving out the Ganges, though it was the only river of which he had drunk water at the holy source. He adds, quite correctly, that the origins of these four rivers must be sought for in the neighbouring mountains and not in the lake. And he says that only "the source of the Brahmaputra has hitherto defied exploration." In reality he had no notion where the sources of these rivers are. Who could expect a Buddhist pilgrim to be acquainted with the geographical literature of Europe?

Kawaguchi, with the greatest assurance, gives the circumference of Manasarowar as 200 miles, though actually it is only 45. He also boldly finds fault with the form given by Europeans to the lake on maps, and ascertained himself that its outline was that of a lotus. *Ad maiorem Dei gloriam!*

In connection with the water communication he made a still more remarkable discovery. He walked out from Tugu-gompa on to the isthmus, and from its hills he could overlook Rakas-tal.

A mountain of about two and a half miles in circumference rises like a partition between the two lakes, and where this mountain dips down to a trough it seems as though there was there a connecting channel between the two lakes. I found, however, that no such channel really exists, but instead I discovered that Rakas-tal lies higher than Manasarowar. I was afterwards told that the waters of the two lakes really mingle every ten to fifteen years, after extraordinarily violent deluges of rain, and that on those occasions Rakas-tal discharges its water into Manasarowar. Hence arises the Tibetan saying that the bridegroom Rakas-tal visits the bride Manasarowar every fifteen years.

Here we have in addition to all the former absurdities the statement that the water flows backwards. For the surface of Rakas-tal lies about 40 feet lower than Manasarowar. Such a mistake Kawaguchi ought not to have committed, for when he afterwards crossed the Sutlej, which he calls the Langchen Khanbab, he says: "My companion told me unasked that this river comes from Manasarowar." Poor as the narrative of the Japanese priest is in geographical matters, it is still interesting reading. He recounts the smallest details of his adventures, and all the little dangers to which he was exposed. As the noble Sakya-muni triumphed over the tempter at Buddh Gaya, so Kawaguchi turned a deaf ear to the fervid declarations of love with which Dava, a child of Manasarowar, nineteen years old, assailed him; a maid of the wilderness who tried to allure him with the hundred yaks and four hundred sheep of her father. "I could not help pitying this innocent little creature," he says chivalrously; "pretty she was not, but not ugly; she was a smart little figure. . . . Dava of course could not compare with the daughters of the archfiend in attractiveness; but she could weep and implore just as well as they." Kawaguchi, however, was adamant, and did not forget the vow which binds the priests of Buddha. So Dava's dream came to nothing; she was never to exchange the snow-clad summit of Siva's mountain for a sight of the peak of Fuji-yama, the sacred mountain of the Japanese.

Kawaguchi performed the circuit of Kailas, prescribed to pilgrims. Among the troop of pilgrims he made the acquaintance of a robber from Kham, who accompanied his steps with the following lamentations:

> O holy Kang-rinpoche! O great Sakya-muni! O all Buddhas and Bodhisattvas at the ten corners of the world and in all ages that were and are and are to come! I have been a wicked man. I have murdered several people. I have stolen all sorts of things that did not belong to me. I have carried off wives from their husbands. I have again and again stirred up strife and have beaten people cruelly. All these great sins I now repent of and now do solemn penance for them on this mountain. By this act of confession and repentance I believe that I shall escape the penalty of those sins. I also perform this penance for my future sins, for it may be that I shall again commit sin, and that I shall rob men of their goods, carry off their wives, beat them to death or thrash them.

But we cannot accompany Kawaguchi on his farther wanderings through Tibet. From every page of his book a puff comes to us of the pure, unadulterated Asia, where everything—even the huge mountains and the turquoise-blue lakes—is involved in a network of religious preconceptions and legends, and where the image of the noble Sakya-muni, serene and dreamy, seems ever to hover before the eyes of the wanderer and conceal from him the world of reality.

What does the lately deceased English missionary, Graham Sandberg, say of the regions which have now so long occupied our thoughts? He was never in Tibet himself, but he made this country the object of a thorough study, and in 1904 published a valuable work upon it. He gives an account of the history of exploration since 1623, and arrives at the conclusion: "The sources of the shortest great river rising in and flowing out of Tibet, the Sutlej, are not to this day absolutely known." He continues: "It is still a subject of mystery and speculation where so familiar a river as the Indus takes actually rise." Three years later these questions were no longer a riddle; but by that time the missionary had gone where we must all go some time.

In his *Handbook of Tibet*, which also appeared in the year 1904, the well-known Asiatic explorer, Sir Thomas Holdich, remarks: "The Indus rises on the slopes of

89 MAJOR RYDER.

Kailas, the sacred mountain, the Elysium or Siva's paradise of ancient Sanskrit literature." This was also the opinion of Desideri two hundred years earlier. Holdich places the source of the Sutlej on the southern flank of Kailas. Now we know that the Indus starts from the country on the northern side of the Trans-Himalaya, and that the Sutlej springs from the northern flank of the Himalayas.

Major Ryder and Captain Rawling marched along both lakes in the end of November 1904, that is, precisely at the same season as Father Desideri in 1715. The ice-blocks which choked up the channel between the two lakes came, it was discovered, from springs in the bed, and the surface of Manasarowar lay 2 feet below the highest point of the bed. But the monks of the Chiu-gompa declared that some water flowed out of the holy lake every year in late summer. Such an outflow had not occurred from Rakas-tal for fifty or sixty years.

Rawling is near the true solution when he says that the question is still open, whether one of the brooks entering Manasarowar from the east should not be held to be the source of the Sutlej. But he does not follow up this theory, and, like Ryder, he excludes the lakes entirely from the river system of the Sutlej, leaving the determination of the actual site of the source to future explorers.

The decisive words were spoken in the year 1907, just at the time when I was in southern Tibet, by Colonel Burrard, who proved quite conclusively that both lakes then belonged to the Sutlej system, even if they sent out an insignificant brook to the bed of the river only once in a hundred years (see Vol. II. p. 187).

We have now only to refer to the last visitor to the lakes before my journey, Mr. Charles Sherring, who made the circuit of them in 1905. He makes the Indus rise in the Kailas range, which in itself is an indefinite statement. The Brahmaputra he brings down from the Marium-la, or the country lying in the immediate neighbourhood of this pass, which is not according to the facts. On the source of the Sutlej he can only say that Moorcroft saw it, and that it *now* lies near Dölchu-gompa. He gives an excellent photographic panorama of the channel between the two lakes, and says that from this picture any one can decide whether there is a connection and how it is formed. He is quite right. Even in 1904 and 1905 photographic views were necessary to convince certain doubters of the existence of a channel which the Chinese knew of two hundred years ago.

In 1905 no water passed through the channel, but Sherring heard that there was an outflow after heavy rains.

We are now at the last pulsation in these much-discussed waterways. I have already given an account of my own observations in the second volume of this book. There I have told that the lakes were in 1907 cut off from each other, and also from a connection with the Sutlej, unless there were a subterranean outlet to this river. This year was unusually dry even in the rainy season—August and September—and only twice did light showers fall on the highlands. The nomads generally complained of the drought; the pastures were yellow, the grass was poor, and it was expected that the famished flocks of sheep, which had suffered from scanty fodder during the warm season, would not have enough stamina to get through the following winter.

Many beds and ditches were quite dried up. The twelve beds carrying water which debouched into Manasarowar, and which I measured, discharged 1010 cubic feet of water per second, or 88 million cubic feet in the day. And yet it was not nearly sufficient to compensate for the loss by evaporation. The surface of Manasarowar stood 7.4 feet below the top of the sill of the bed near Chiu-gompa. Three years before Ryder had found there a difference of level of only 2 feet. It was plainly evident that only heavy deluges of rain could raise the surface of the lake to such a height that water could pour into the channel past the monastery.

In the summer of 1908, when I visited Manasarowar the second time, no change had occurred. Yet during the rainy season of this year the south-west monsoon did its duty thoroughly. Often the rain poured down in torrents during my march along the Sutlej valley. It may be safely assumed that the twelve larger streams and the innumerable small rivulets, which collect into Manasarowar, then brought to the lake ten times as much water as in 1907. Just as certain is it that the lake level was rising slowly but steadily.

I suspected that the period of drought was over, and that another, characterized by more abundant precipitation, would follow. But how was I to learn whether I was right or not?

Then I remembered my friend Gulam Razul, the rich merchant in Leh, who sends caravans annually from that town to Lhasa. He was a clever, educated man, and had helped me before. I wrote to him asking him to inquire what the rainy seasons had been like in the last years, and whether water had flowed out of the eastern lake into the western, and out of the western into the Sutlej.

In a letter dated Leh, June 12, 1911, he informed me that a very large quantity of rain fell in the autumn of 1909, and that the rainy season of 1910 lasted nearly three months, with far more plentiful precipitation than in the previous year. All the watercourses were filled, and a roaring stream was in the bed near Chiu-gompa. The water poured into Rakas-tal. Thus one link in the broken chain had been inserted. The other link, the outflow from Rakas-tal to the Sutlej, had not, however, been renewed. Thakur Jai Chand, the agent of the Indian Government at Gartok, confirmed, I should like to add, Gulam Razul's statements.

It is clear that only after several successive seasons of heavy rainfall does the lower lake rise high enough to overflow into the river bed.

It would take us too far afield were I to enter here into all the interesting questions connected with this hydrographical problem, such as the advance and retreat of glaciers, the rainfall at the meteorological stations of the western Himalayas, the famine years in India, etc. I only wish to show that the apparently contradictory statements of different travellers may be explained by the periodical variations which cause the lakes to overflow at times, and then again to be cut off from the Sutlej.

All reports from the years before 1904 speak of an

outflow from Manasarowar. In 1812 and 1816 the lake was isolated; in 1817 to 1819 it discharged water; in 1843 it appears to have been cut off; from 1865 to 1900 there are only three reports of any value, and these all speak of the isolation of the lake, but notwithstanding it is quite possible that the lake may have overflowed occasionally, though no one happened to be there to confirm the fact. In the year 1904 the bed may have carried water, but from 1905 to 1908 it lay dry. In the year 1909 began a new period of discharge.

The lower lake had certainly an outflow in the years 1715 and 1762 to the Sutlej. We have no reliable data for later years. It seems probable that the lake has been isolated for nearly a century, and the statements of Tibetans to the contrary are too contradictory. This much is certain, that the periods relating to Rakas-tal are of greater length than those of the oscillations of Manasarowar. The former extend to a century, perhaps two, but the latter last only a few years. Thus we find that in the interval during which Rakas-tal has been cut off from the Sutlej, Manasarowar has had five periods of discharge and as many without.

The two lakes therefore act as the most delicate and sensitive instruments under the influence of wind and weather. No apparatus designed by man could indicate more exactly the sway of the south-west monsoon over the country between the lofty mountains, and no rain-gauges, however closely they might be installed, could give a clearer and more homogeneous notion of its relation to the surface water flowing off through the bed of the Sutlej. It is a pity that it is so seldom that any one has taken the trouble of going up there to read off this excellent record of the rainfall.

As the periodical variations of the discharge of Manasarowar are still in progress, there is nothing to prevent the same phenomenon occurring in the case of Rakas-tal in the future. At present this lake is at a downward section of the curve, or the absolute height of the surface is, perhaps, at a stationary minimum. But this curve may bend up again, and, finally, the surplus water may pour once more into the Sutlej as in the days when Kang Hi's topographers drew up a map of southern Tibet.

The water of Manasarowar is sweet like river water, as is to be expected seeing that the lake has an outlet, though only periodically. The flavour of the water should not be tasted at the shore, for there decayed fucus and algæ are packed together into brown or black clumps. One of the European visitors to the holy lake thought he perceived a disagreeable after-taste in the water, but if he had had an opportunity of rowing out far enough from the shore in a boat, he would readily have admitted that no better drinking-water can be drawn from any glacier lake.

Rakas-tal, which lost its superficial outlet perhaps a hundred years ago, is, nevertheless, as sweet as its neighbour, whence it may be inferred that its water is renewed constantly by a subterranean inflow. Until the water of the lake acquires a decided briny taste, we cannot affirm that it is cut off from the Sutlej system.

The extraordinarily dry summer of the year 1907 was very favourable for river measurements. No local torrents of rain caused particular streams to swell. All were quietly and regularly fed under similar conditions. Of the 1010 cubic feet of water which flowed per second into Manasarowar 397 were discharged by the Tage-tsangpo. The next largest brook, which descends from Gurla Mandatta, carried only 100 feet, or a quarter of the volume of the Tage-tsangpo. It is, therefore, easy to decide which of the two should be called the headwater of the Sutlej. Chinese and Tibetans say that it is the Tage-tsangpo, and they are quite right.

In his delightful article on the far too meagre and superficial notes on religious history contained in the first two volumes of this book, Baron Anton von Ow exclaims on the Manasarowar of the Hindus and the Tso-mavang of the Tibetans:

> Here on the most remarkable heights of the globe we have actually before us the lake which was celebrated thousands of years ago as the mythical lake of Haoma and Siva; here we have the mythical Pushkara, the lotus pool from which Brahma rose—here the Chin lake of the Chinese myth, in the midst of which the divine Buddha child reposes on a bed of lotus blossoms!

Celebrated in grand hymns by the poets of remote antiquity, a dwelling-place of mighty gods, a mirror beneath the paradise of Brahma and the heaven of Siva, the goal of innumerable yearning pilgrims, a refuge of the royal swans of romance, the wild geese of reality, the most wondrous lake on earth lies dreaming among the snow-clad summits of lofty mountains. Manasarowar is not dead like the thousand salt lakes of Tibet. It sleeps only on calm nights, when the silence of death hovers over its bright mirror and the silvery wake of the moon quivers behind the boat of the stranger. But it lives and breathes when the storm sweeps with raging fury over its liquid expanse and raises emerald-green crystal billows on its bosom, and when the surf beats heavily and monotonously against the shore. It opens wide its arms to receive the foaming brook which dashes down from Gurla, glistening like gold in the sun as soon as its water emerges from the shadow of the mantle of clouds and from the granite ravine. One seems to hear the pulse of the lake-god beat when the water escapes at times through the veins of the Ganga channel. One seems to hear the morning prayer of the lake when the copper trombones sound on the temple roofs, and the pilgrims of Buddha murmur their never-ending "Om mani padme hum."

In lights and shadows, in colour and illumination, in moods that change from hour to hour and season to season, in charming views and fascinating perspectives, Manasarowar is the most beautiful of the lakes of Tibet. Once when I had pitched my camp on the western shore, I perceived the threatening calm after a windy day which is the forerunner of a storm. To the north the sky was dark, heavy bluish-purple clouds passed over the heights. The knobs of the Pundi mountain stood out black against the first bluish-grey fringes, the heralds of the storm-clouds. The foot of the mountains had a brick-red hue which contrasted strongly with the malachite-green water. Shortly after the hurricane broke, the lake boiled up into white foaming waves. Far away to the east its tumultuous surface was as green as laurel and syringa, but towards the western shore the tones grew lighter, and near this margin the water glittered in the green colour of the birch's spring foliage. The calm lagoons, sheltered by banks of mud from the onset of the waves, were tinted bluish-violet by the reflexion of the storm-clouds in the colourless waves. (See the coloured picture facing p. 152, Vol. II.)

Bewitching and romantically beautiful is the scene displayed westwards in the evening hour. The sun has just set, but its streaks of yellow gold still linger, a dazzling sheaf of rays, on the edge of the horizon. The whole sky is vividly yellow and the lake looks like liquid amber. After a time the western sky flares up in ruddy hues, a sharp background to the pitchy black mountains. The steel-grey summit of Kailas rises in its eternal majesty to the north, and soon the new night spreads its shadows over its firn-fields.

But the scene is finest in the morning, when the sun begins his triumphal course over the earth, first clothing the summits in purple flames and then pouring his gold over the eternal lake and its holy mountains.

The sight of the lake makes the stranger involuntarily meditative. His thoughts are not disturbed by the nomads who inhabit the country with their black tents and white flocks, nor by the monks who are for ever turning their prayer-mills. This lake is itself a huge prayer-mill, as it were, a ring of pious pilgrims revolving round its axis. As far back as traditions and legends carry us, Manasarowar has attracted the aspirations of men and their prayers. On its banks we tread on ground which was already classic when Rome was founded. Here legends and fairy tales whisper round the cliffs and precipices, and here Siva swims in the form of a swan by the foot of the mountain of the gods.

Therefore is the Sutlej also so important among the rivers of the land of lamas. Now and then he reposes in the arms of the holy lake, as though he would there forget the furious combats that await him on his long way to the coast. But when the hours of rest are over, which in their brevity and transitoriness are like geological seconds, then the newborn river gathers up its strength and breaks through the isthmus. If his strength is great enough he also bursts the fetters in which Rakas-tal confines him. Unlike the Indus and Brahmaputra his youth is short, being marked by the parallel ranges of the Himalayas and the æolian basin in Hundes. Already at Shipki begins his ripe age, the time of roaring stormy labour, when the river with irresistible energy cuts his way through the Himalayas. Wearied and silent, majestically calm and dignified, he emerges from the mountains to traverse the Punjab; this is the time of old age. At last he joins his fortunes with the Indus. Turbid and weighted with the soil of India, the dying streams glide gently and quietly into the desolate ocean which encircles the globe with its waters.

90. YAKS CROSSING THE RIVER.

CHAPTER XX

A DIZZY PASSAGE OF THE SUTLEJ

THE gates of Indra's heaven stood open and the monsoon rains poured down. How the Sutlej would swell up when the ground was soaked and the rain-water could find a way straight down to the rivers! At Tirtapuri, however, it was still possible to cross the river. A yak caravan from Gyanima had encamped on the left bank. The drivers began to unload the animals; evidently they meant to defy the river, lest they should be compelled by continuous rain to make a long detour past Dölchu-gompa.

Immediately above the monastery the river bed is rather broad. Two drivers mounted their most powerful yaks and plunged into the rushing waves. The baggage yaks were driven in a compact black mass into the river and guided by whistling, shouting drivers. Only the heads of the yaks, the riders and the loads were visible above the water. The animals did their work capitally. They were strong, sure-footed, and never lost their hold, however much the current endeavoured to carry them away. Dripping like sponges the yaks clambered up on to our bank and then stalked on.

I decided to dismiss half my men at Tirtapuri. The men who had been the nucleus of the caravan during the severe winter—Lobsang, Gulam, Kutus, Tubges, Suen, and Kunchuk—should accompany me to Simla; Abdul Kerim and the other five should return to Ladak through Misser and Gartok. As usual they submitted to their fate without a murmur. They received their pay, and I gave them in addition a liberal gratuity; an extra sum for new clothes, and their travelling expenses were also counted out to them. After this severe bleeding I had only 650 rupees left, and therefore had to be careful afterwards.

Before the sun rose on August 2 I thanked my returning men for the last time for their faithful service and bade them farewell. They had only two hours' journey to Misser, so Kutus and Suen were allowed to accompany them and transport their belongings on our own mules. In Misser the authorities were unfriendly at first, but when they knew for certain that I was not with the men they allowed them to hire the yaks they needed.

In the course of the afternoon our much-diminished caravan was made ready. As though to make up for the loss of our men, a young lama came down from the convent and offered to act as guide on the way to Kyunglung. He was received as a rescuing angel, and our tramp with the wealed back received his dismissal and also ten rupees; he thought himself rich. With bundles on their backs and staves in their hands five poor pilgrims came up and reminded us of our duty to pay toll to all those who are on a pilgrimage.

Curious creatures! They wander about by the year together, living entirely on alms. They pass their nights in monastery courtyards in the company of the half-wild sacred dogs, or in the antechambers of the temples under the protection of the spirit kings. Where there are neither tents nor sanctuaries, they seek a lodging in caves and clefts, and light their evening fires with flint, steel, and tinder. They are a terrible burden to the nomads living on the highroads, for who can have the heart to cruelly turn away a man on his way to or from a holy place?

Below Tirtapuri the valley expands considerably. Our path runs north-west along the foot of the lowest erosion terrace, over fresh juicy meadows here and there interrupted by spots which have been flooded, and where the clayey mud is still shiny with moisture. The river prefers the left side of the valley; on its slopes are seen four sharply marked terraces like the seats in a circus. Another tributary rushes down from the north-east; its name is

Misser-chu, its sources lie among the recesses of the southern flank of the Trans-Himalaya, and its volume is now 565 cubic feet a second. In the rain-mist one can only imagine the lofty regions among the snow-clad crests whence this watercourse descends.

We passed the night on the pasture-land Gerik-yung, where the height was 13,830 feet. The rain pelted drearily on to my tent and all the streams swelled up still more. Next morning a small yak caravan passed by.

"Where are you travelling to?" we asked.

"To Totling-gompa with tea."

"Have you *tsamba* or any other edibles to sell?" we inquired, for we were living from hand to mouth and had no stores left.

"No," the yak men replied, "only tea, and that is not for sale, for it is intended for the use of the monastery."

"Well, be off, then."

A shrill whistle, and the yaks trip down to the gloomy portal of the narrow ravine to which the Sutlej valley now contracts.

Samtang Rangdol, the young lama of Tirtapuri, rides on a yak beside me that he may be always at hand to give me information.

"What is this place called?" I ask at the first promontory round which the path winds.

"Palgye-pugu," he answers; "up above on the top are the remains of old ramparts; once a royal mansion stood there, named Kardong."

"Now tell me the name of this side valley."

"We call it Chornak; it comes down from the Jarko-la pass over which the *tasam* runs."

The Jarko-la is an important pass, for it is on the watershed between the Indus and the Sutlej. Ryder and Rawling crossed it in December 1904. Now the brook in the valley carried 388 cubic feet of water as black as if it had flowed through vegetable soil or coal. Exactly opposite, on the left side, the Sutlej receives a large affluent, the Haltshor-chu, which descends from the hills round the high plateau of Gyanima. Samtang Rangdol affirmed that this river had as large a volume of water as the Sutlej itself, and therefore was held by some to be the present headwater of the Sutlej. But in a previous chapter I have shown that the Haltshor must be relegated to the position of a tributary. The volume of the Sutlej below its confluence with the Haltshor may be estimated at 6350 cubic feet per second, or twice that of the Brahmaputra at Tuksum at the beginning of July the year before. But in the year 1907 there was hardly any rain, and hence the great difference.

We waded through the broad but shallow Chornak-chu, and saw at the foot of the next projection ten ruined *chhortens* which had been erected, Samtang Rangdol told me, by Pembos, the schismatics who used to come hither in former times to worship an image somewhere in the surrounding mountains, but as their rites caused annoyance at the orthodox Tirtapuri, this pilgrimage was forbidden.

Here, too, the Sutlej rushes furiously along the left side of the valley. But the expansions have now come to an end and the river cuts its bed with irresistible force through a narrow winding chasm where only the rock pigeons can follow its course. Therefore the road deserts the river and runs up the mountain on the right side of the valley in innumerable zigzags. We first cross the mouth of a small transverse valley, called Tsaldöt, which comes not from the Trans-Himalaya, like the former, but from the Ladak range, the mighty partition between the Indus and Sutlej. And then we work our way up to the small saddle Tsaldöt-la, where the height is 14,748 feet.

The mist hides the distant view, but as far as we can see the landscape is uncommon and grand. Deep down below us yawns the gigantic abyss which the grinding waters have carved out through countless ages. The sides fall down sheer and the river cannot be seen, but its heavy hollow roar resounds among the mountains like growling thunder. Soon the heights of the Ladak range will screen the Trans-Himalaya, but we should still see some of its ridges did not the opaque rain-clouds envelop them. Behind us gleam the green meadows of Tirtapuri, but all on our way in front is of the greyest grey.

From the ridge of the pass the wildly fissured mountain looks fairly uniform, but much foreshortened. We are astonished at the view of the Sutlej valley and its great tributaries which are all very steeply or even vertically cut down into the earth's crust, forming a maze of ditches and corridors, which are nearly allied to the cañons of the Colorado. We seem to be on the limit of two different forms of landscape. We have left the horizontal lines, the gentle undulations of the earth's surface. Now vertical lines begin to come into prominence, the grand rugged sculpture that is eaten down with unsparing energy. The mountain ranges stand like weathered ruins on the pedestal of the plateau country, and the disintegrated material contributes to fill up the hollows in the ground, and smooth down the surface. But here in the wonderful land we are now entering the products of weathering are washed away by the ever-flowing rivers.

Slowly and cautiously the caravan advances along the steep precipices. Sometimes we are three hundred feet above the level of the river, sometimes nearly six hundred; we ascend, descend, turn to the left, then to the right, and struggle painfully and slowly over small ditches among pebbles and small boulders. Often we ride along the edge of a precipice, where a single false step would hurl us into the depths.

Before me rides the lama, Samtang Rangdol, on his black yak, wrapped in his red monk's toga and with a cloth wound round his head. My curiosity amuses him, and he gives me scraps of information even when I do not question him. Now he leads us up to another saddle and again we stop dumb with admiration and astonishment at the bold peculiar sculpture of the Himalayas. The cloud masses of the south-west monsoon hang like a gloomy canopy over the brow of the Himalayas, and send down lighter rain fringes over the valley, at the bottom of which the Sutlej plays its funeral march in ever rumbling organ tones.

A green spot glimmers among the grey indistinct rain-washed mountains—the meadows near the Kyung-lung monastery. We are a day's journey from that place which yet looks so near. The time of straight lines and long days' marches is over; here the path winds along as often precipitous as horizontal. A point may seem quite near, while the distance to it is hopelessly long by the path which twists in all directions.

At length the path runs down over a chaos of ridges and rocky spurs of micaceous quartzite, separated by deeply excavated valleys and troughs. Now we ride on the left side and then on the right side of a ridge, and in either case have a deep ravine on our other side. Over the last declivity we come down to an expansion of the valley and pitch camp 462 a yard from the bank of the Sutlej and a yard above the water. We are 14,003 feet above the sea, and have descended only 253 feet from Tirtapuri and 1053 from the Langak-tso.

Immediately above this fine camping-ground the narrow corridor which forced us to climb the heights comes to an end. Proud and mighty, like a king among rivers, the Sutlej comes forth from its rocky portal and spreads out in an expansion of its valley. Its thick turbid and brownish-grey water rushes in a compact mass of foaming and heavily thundering billows out of the chasm. The depth might then be 6½ feet, perhaps 10 or even 13 in the deepest channel of the bed. Our lama told us that there is a ford here which may be used in the dry season. It is then better to pass over to the left bank instead of climbing up again over the mountains on the right.

The way we take over the Himalayas may certainly be called a *high* road, an imperial route if one likes to call it so, but it is not a grand trunk road, a main artery where Indian and Tibetan traders meet to barter the coral and pearls of the warm seas for the sheep's wool and yak hides of the land of snow. All day we meet not a single soul, no travellers, no animals, wild or tame. Seldom do we see a smoked slab of stone, the ashes of a dung fire, or the stones of a fireplace where a black tent has stood over the flames.

Here peace rules. The mighty river reigns in majestic solitude. I could not take my eyes away from its brown bubbles as they hurried on their headlong descent to India. We should soon follow it. I loved this stream, for no

91. IN THE UPPER SUTLEJ VALLEY.

92. THE SUTLEJ IN A WILD RAVINE.

white man had ever seen its source before me. I was to follow its course to the sea with increasing interest and ever greater eagerness. It was grand to fall asleep by its dull roar and hear it again when I awoke.

During the night the river rose $1\frac{1}{2}$ inches. The temperature did not fall below 43.5°; it must gradually rise as we come down to lower levels. But at present the land of warm nights is far away.

From the camp the path runs uphill over the terraces and hills of the right bank, and after a short time we find ourselves at an unpleasant place which Samtang Rangdol had prepared us for beforehand. Here I preferred my own feet to those of the horse.

The path clings like a cornice to the precipitous flank. We creep into every gully and cleft of the precipice, wind round every outstanding rock, mount and descend and avail ourselves of every capricious curve of the solid rock. Irregular staircases run up and down in the bare calcareous sandstone and quartzite, where man's hand has never been raised to remove an obstacle from the path or level an inequality. It takes us quite two hours to get over a length of little more than a hundred yards. The loads are unstrapped and carried by the men. Only two energetic mules contrive to get over the ground safely with the sacks and tents with which they are laden. The worst spot is a steeply sloping flat, the surface of a stratum without fissures or inequalities to give a sure foothold. The animals have to slide down this toboggan with stiffened legs, while one man leads each by the halter and two others hold it by the tail to put the brake on.

Then the animals were loaded again and we crossed two deep troughs down to the river. The path ran between the bank and the foot of the lowest erosion terrace. Old terrace shelves skirt the steep walls of the left bank, often projecting in cornices and overhanging slabs, and rising 230 to 260 feet above the valley floor. Various bands of gravel, sand, and clay crop out in its exposures. Not much room is left for the path during the rainy season, and there is seldom space enough for a strip of fair grass. At the entrance of a large side valley on the left there is an open flat where a vividly green field of barley is ripening for harvest. But there is not a man to be seen. Perhaps the owner of the field lives in Kyung-lung, whither a road runs along the left bank, passing two large *mani* walls.

Among light-coloured rocky slabs, knobs, and ridges of very fantastic forms, the valley again contracts to a wild narrow chasm. We were just at its commencement, when a man came running after us shouting loudly. At last a human being in this lifeless country! Or perhaps it was the outrider of a troop which would force us to return to the path of duty. No, not at all! When the man came nearer we recognized our striped friend, the tramp of Chiu-gompa, who trotted up breathlessly swinging his cudgel to keep off the dogs, which had always held him in suspicion.

"What do you want, 'Beggar'? Did you not receive your pay, and were you not dismissed for good?"

"Yes, sir; but just as you rode away a Gova and his men came to Tirtapuri, and the monks complained to him that I had shown you the way to the monastery. Then the Gova threatened to take me bound to Gartok, there to be brought before the Garpun and be beaten."

"How did you contrive to escape?"

"I managed to steal away from Tirtapuri in the dark, and now I have almost run myself to death in trying to overtake you."

"And now you wish to travel with us again?"

"Yes, sir, let me go with you to India. If I return to Tibet I shall be beaten to death without ceremony."

"Well, come along in the meantime."

But now we have something else to think of. Before us yawns the chasm which the river in its fury has cut through the living rock, which, as expert evidence informs us, consists of micaceous quartzite and concretions of carbonate of lime. What a difference between this river and those we have known up in Tibet! They glided smoothly and noiselessly along their beds. Here, on the contrary, we see a river which collects all its energy to eat down like a saw blade into the rocks and free itself from its gaol of

93 AND 94. AWKWARD PLACES ON THE MARCH.

solid stone. It no longer babbles clearly with a rippling lapping murmur, but roars with a dull heavy din which fills the narrow valley, that valley where all loose products of weathering are swept away from the sides, and where we feel as if the rocky foundation trembled beneath the weight of the 6350 cubic feet of water per second.

But what is become of the majestic river that we have just seen? The Sutlej has shrivelled up to nothing; it is smaller than the Tokbo-shar. Ah, it is only an illusion; the velocity is tremendous, the depth must be enormous. Look at this wild tumultuous sheet of water which is thrown up into permanent waves, their form and position prescribed by the inequalities, windings, and coves of the river-bed. See these rounded domes which resemble in form a propeller blade and are always boiling at the same spot. And there a comb foams with hissing flakes which remind us of the clods torn up by the ploughshare. And here is a row of undulations which curve their backs gracefully and like dolphins and porpoises shoot along in merry, careless play.

All this water is thick as pea-soup owing to the solid matter washed down by rain and torn up by erosive action, which enables the river to deepen its bed more effectually. Here, at Kyung-lung, the river has to contend with the first formidable obstacle, a bar across its course. We shall find many such obstacles on the march before us. They increase in size on the way down, as the river does in breadth. One of the finest, most imposing breached valleys in the world is that which the Sutlej has cut through the Himalayas. Our suspense increases day by day. We look on the map and wonder if the river will carry out its intention successfully.

We are down at the bridge of Kyung-lung, where for the first time we pass, not through the Sutlej, but over it. Here beside the bridge-head on the right bank is a red and white *chhorten*. It has no more to do with the structure of the bridge than the small kiosk-like chapels which stand at the right bridge-head of the Nicolas bridge at St. Petersburg, and in which peasants and citizens kneel and cross themselves before the pictures of saints. The difference is only that the *chhorten* of Kyung-lung, perhaps from time to time restored and improved, stood as a protecting bastion of the bridge many centuries before St. Petersburg was founded.

What does this *chhorten* mean? Just what the decorated cairn does on a pass or a *mani* wall on a road: an offering, a homage, an appeal to the powerful spirits of the river not to make use of their physical superiority against helpless man. It stands there as an eloquent witness that the bridge is under the protection of the gods, and that the traveller may confidently entrust his life to its bending planks. Were the *chhorten* removed from Kyung-lung the spirits of the Langchen-kamba would be angry and demand a human sacrifice; the bridge would give way under the weight of the traveller, and the victim would perish in the seething whirlpool.

Not far from the bank stands a row of red-painted *mani* walls and pyramidal *chhorten*. About three hundred feet above the river the monastery of Kyung-lung is poised like a swallow's nest on the top of a singularly modelled pebble terrace. The rain-water has washed out cones and shafts, walls and towers in its steep front. Quite at the top of this apparently frail substructure is throned Kyung-lung, turning a brick-red façade towards the river, and it reminds us of Lamayuru in Ladak, though it is much smaller. A building on a lower shelf is said to contain monks' cells and storerooms. Dark holes and embrasures in the vertical wall of the terrace indicate cave-dwellings. A splendid position, a wonderfully beautiful prospect! The Tibetan lamas have a sharp eye for architectural beauty, lines of solid simplicity, and show a highly educated taste. The brotherhood of Kyung-lung consists of eight persons, and, like most others in the neighbourhood, they belong to the Gelugpa or orthodox sect.

Lama Samtang Rangdol has taken leave of me and is gone up to the monastery. While my Ladakis unload the animals, I examine the bridge, which is in the usual Asiatic style.

The bridge spans the Sutlej where the river is narrowest, two projecting rocks approaching each other with an interval

95. Kyung-lung-gompa and the Sutlej.

Sketch by the Author.

of 43 feet. Four layers of short beams are walled into the precipitous faces opposite each other, the uppermost, which rests on and receives support from the three others, being longer and slanting outwards. On their extremities rest the two round and swinging tree trunks of the suspended bridge, which in their turn bear the planks. The unevenness in the footway left by the axe has been removed by wear, rain, and sunshine. The woodwork is greyish-white, peeled and fragile, and the whole structure shakes under the feet. It is putting one's life in peril to cross, not knowing when the limit of elasticity will be reached.

The bridge is only 45 inches broad, and there is no handrail to give protection. The depth of the river here must be considerable; the breadth was not more than 45 feet, but the velocity of the current was tremendous. Even if we had possessed poles long enough to measure the depth, we could not have used them, for the pressure of the compressed volume of water would have broken them like reeds. Immediately above the bridge some bosses of solid rock and white pinnacles of stone rise above the surface, while between them the raging stream boils and whirls before forcing its way into the narrow trough below the bridge with deafening roar, hissing crests of foam and showers of spray.

A Tibetan came running up on the farther bank. He made gestures with his arms as though to keep us back, and we could see that he was shouting something, but it was impossible to hear anything but the roar of the river. We made signs to him to come over to us and he came.

"What is the matter?" we asked him.

"The bridge will not bear the weight of a horse, but the mules may perhaps cross without the beams breaking."

"Do you suppose that we are going to leave our horses here?"

"They can swim across the river farther down. You see that the Langchen-kamba widens out there and is quiet."

"If the bridge will bear the mules it will the horses also. We shall see. I only hope that it will not collapse when half the caravan is over and split it in two."

"I advise you to be careful. The bridge is rotten and bad."

"How old is it then?"

"It is ten years since it was last renewed. The bridge-heads were built thirty years ago."

The Ladakis are accustomed to dangerous bridges at home. They walked over carrying the loads on their backs with firm straddling steps. Only one man on the bridge at a time! I saw the last load laid down on the farther bank with a feeling of relief, then crossed and stationed myself beside the left bridge-head.

Now come the animals. We had bought ten goats which supplied me with milk. Let them try the bridge first. Goats are not endowed with much sense. The whole pack remains standing, as though rooted to the ground, where the planks join the firm bridge-head. They want to turn back, scenting something disagreeable. The river seethes below them. Here there must be some pitfall which some villains have placed in the way to destroy them.

"On with you, you beasts!" shouts Tubges, the herdsman.

If only they had sense enough to cross over singly! But no, they must, of course, crowd up together, with the danger of pushing one another off the bridge. They do all get over, but with a close shave.

"One of the mules to the front!"

A little animal from Lhasa is driven up. He has surely seen a bridge before, for he is quite calm, and manages the feat very cleverly. He steps on to the planks without hesitation, and counteracts the swing of the bridge by loose elastic movements of the knee. He bends his head down and smells the bridge as he goes, keeping exactly in the middle. His comrades cross with the same composure.

Horses are more stupid than mules, at least in crossing bridges. Ours were from Chang-tang, and had never seen a bridge in their lives. The first that was driven up shied, turned round and ran away. Number two followed his example. So they had to be led across. But, in order not to load the beams with too heavy a weight, the rope was made as long as the bridge, and two men laid hold of it and pulled with all their might, while two others lashed the horse from behind until the refractory animal ventured out on to the planks, and, trembling as much as they, tramped across heavily and stupidly.

Now remained the two white horses I had bought of the robber chief Kamba Tsenam. The one, a large powerful animal, reared and preferred blows and stripes to the awful bridge. Perhaps the goats would encourage him. So they had to take the walk again. Then the horse plucked up courage and galloped across so fast to reach firm ground again that he was within a hair's-breadth of trampling a goat to death. At last came the turn of my riding horse, which had carried me 500 miles from Kamba Tsenam's tent, and had twice crossed the Trans-Himalaya through the labyrinth of the Bongba mountains, passing lakes and fording rivers. I looked upon him as a friend and helper who had shared in my discoveries. He was snow-white and in capital condition, much too good to be drowned in the Sutlej.

Now the horse must submit to his fate. What could he do when the men with united strength tugged at the rope and two others drove him on from behind? He looked very unhappy and anxious, and trembled in all his limbs as he ventured on to the treacherous planks. All would have passed off well if he had only gone straight on. He had seen that the bridge had borne all the other animals, and he must, as usual, have wished for their company. But when he was in the middle of the bridge he was overcome by fear. Regardless of the rope attached to his halter he stopped and turned to the left, so that he stood across the bridge and looked upstream. He gazed into the rushing whirling torrent below. His eyes glared, his nostrils expanded, he snorted loudly, and then he leapt to meet his death in the raging boiling flood below.

His hind hoofs struck against the edge of the bridge, so that the horse made a somersault and struck the water with his back. Of course he is dashed to pieces, I thought. It was fortunate that I had not ridden over this superb bridge. We rescued the saddle, and the only thing lost was the rope, which the men let go when they saw what the end would be.

At the moment when the horse struck the surface of the water he was seized by the furious current, and disappeared at once. We rushed down from the bridge-head to see if the mangled carcase would be brought up again to the top of the rolling swirling waters.

"There he is!" cried Lobsang.

"Impossible! Yes, by Jove!"

Yonder some seventy yards down his white head rose out of the waves. The Sutlej was much broader at that place, as though it would rest after its exertions.

"He is alive, he is swimming!" cries Kutus. No one troubles himself about the other animals.

"Bravo, he is swimming towards the left bank!"

"Yes, or he would have to make another jump."

"Fancy his taking such a roundabout way when he had only half the bridge to cross, hardly ten paces!"

"He must have lost his senses."

However, the white horse had by no means lost his energy. A few powerful strokes brought him to the bank, and with two lively jumps he was on dry ground, where he began to graze at once as if nothing had happened. He snorted once or twice, and shook the water off, but all his limbs were sound, and he had not broken any of his legs. The bath seemed, indeed, to have refreshed him.

I hastened to my four-footed friend, wiped the water out of his eyes, and patted him. He was now doubly dear to me. The Sutlej had been unable to separate us, and now we should enjoy each other's society on the road to India. I admired his reckless courage, but had no mind to rival him in boldness. No doubt the horse had been caught up in the volume of water, had become part of it, and had been carried down without striking against a projecting rock. The spirits of the Langchen-kamba had favoured him. That is the advantage of having a *chhorten* erected at a bridge-head!

From the ravine it was not many hundred yards to the next meadowland. The animals were laden again and we set out. Then we missed the dogs. They were on the

96. THE SUTLEJ BRIDGE NEAR KYUNG-LUNG.

97. CAIRN ON STEEP EDGE OF THE SUTLEJ VALLEY.

right bank, and we could see that they were barking. They sniffed at the river, but it was too furious, and neither of them would cross the bridge to save his life. Then Kunchuk went over with Little Puppy on his arm. When he was in the middle he set the dog down, thinking that he would run over the other half by himself. Not if he knew it! He did not, indeed, act like the white horse, but laid himself down on his belly, crouched down close to the planks, and howled piteously, not daring to move a paw, and quite paralysed by terror. There he waited until he was carried over the other half. But he was so frightened that he sobbed badly all the rest of the day. Takkar was dragged unmercifully over the bridge by strong hands.

CHAPTER XXI

THE RAVINES OF THE SUTLEJ

A CLEAR spring gushed up on the meadow of Kyung-lung. We bought provisions, butter and *tsamba* from our neighbours inhabiting five black tents. Two elderly genial monks visited us and presented me with a *kadakh.*

"Can we do anything for you, sir?" one of them asked.

"Why, yes; I want a guide to Daba."

"All right; I will guide you thither if you will give me the same pay as Samtang Rangdol."

"Agreed; and if you serve me well you shall get something over."

But when it grew dusk the lama sent an excuse. An important monk from Totling-gompa was expected every moment, and he would be very angry if one of the brothers of Kyung-lung were absent. Samtang Rangdol, too, could not be persuaded to accompany us farther, but he begged me to keep the beggar from Chiu in my service, or he would murder him to get possession of his money. The beggar was allowed to remain with us; we should be able to make use of him: there is always plenty to do in a caravan.

However, as we started on August 5, we obtained a guide quite unexpectedly. A tea caravan of five men and fifteen yaks which had rested at Kyung-lung, and was travelling to Totling, set off at the same time. The leader was named Samye Karmo, and he was promised a recompense if he answered honestly all the questions put to him. In the end he went off without his gratuity, so his answers were not much to be relied on.

The yaks, laden with large bales of tea sewed up in

hides, and escorted by their drivers, two of whom carried guns, tramped over rubbish and grass, over rivulets and slopes. They had come into the world as tiny calves in Chang-tang, and found the climate of the confined valley much too hot for their thick coats. So they seized every opportunity of taking a footbath in the margin of the river. One of them went out too far into the water, sinking deeper and deeper. Samye Karmo and his party shouted and threw stones over the yak into the water. But the animal liked the cool water which soaked through his hair up to his back, he snorted and shook his head at the stone-throwing, and went on until he began to swim, the bales of tea acting like a cork jacket. He did not suspect that with his shagginess his life hung by a hair. If the sucking stream had caught him, then——! But he escaped it, and dripping like a sponge he climbed up to the bank again. Both concerned in this freak, Samye and the yak, suffered from the consequences, the tea being no better for the wetting and the load twice as heavy.

We had a long distance to the next place where we could ride a whole hour by the Sutlej bank. Meanwhile we said good-bye to the stream. It rushes into another chasm where the volumes of water splash up along the foot of the mountains on the left. Here the precipice is not vertical but hangs over, being undermined by the eroding force of the river. There is, then, no other choice but to climb the limestone cliffs in short steep zigzags and get up to the top. The river disappears below; its roar becomes fainter and at last is heard no more.

Our road mounts higher and higher. The eyes can roam over greater distances and the horizon retires backwards. The gradient becomes less steep and at last we are on a dome-shaped summit named Munto-mangbo—if Samye Karmo told us the truth. A row of cairns stands at the edge of a vertical wall. The sides of the trench which the river has here cut into the earth's crust are precipitous cliffs. The Sutlej works incessantly down below. Blocks loosened by the winter frosts are always falling, and are used by the river as tools to chisel out and deepen its bed.

We follow the Chinese tea slowly and gently over the hills and down the steep cliffs, and cross two deeply excavated side valleys without water. We have to cross all those troublesome side valleys which make the journey to India so terribly long. And then we pass over gently undulating heights. The eyes roam over immense distances. One forgets the vertically sunk cañons, and one might suppose that between the low crests and peaks to the north the country is quite level.

Place two rectangular plates slightly inclined to one another and leave a small interval at the bottom; that is the Sutlej valley. But imagine further that the plates are indented with innumerable grooves all running down to the trench in the middle. Such is the country traversed by the road to India, a road which has a superb contempt for the horizontal curves of the map. For half an hour it may run on an even dome between two side valleys and then plunge headlong into an abyss which takes a whole hour to cross. We stand at the edge and see that the opposite edge is only a gunshot off. We should like to jump or fly over, and we see in imagination the viaduct which will never span the valley with its spidery web. But it is no use. We must clamber down the hundred steep zigzags and then climb up again on the other side to reach at last the opposite edge.

Now we remain for a good while up above, for the road runs south-westwards nearly parallel to two cañons. The path is well trodden down, for numbers of men and animals have tramped along it in the course of time. Now it is empty and desolate. If there are tents and huts here, they are hidden down below where brooks irrigate the meadows and barley thrives. Up here the ground is covered with fine gravel, hard and dry. Only tufts of hardy grass are kept alive by occasional showers. A flock of twelve Ammon sheep flies before us with graceful leaps. Now and then we come across the skull of a wild sheep bleached and worn by sunshine and rain.

Ah! now the level road ends. The bottomless abyss of the cañon Shib or Shibe-chu, mightier than its predecessors, yawns at our feet. As we stand at the extreme

98. THE EYES ROAM OVER IMMENSE DISTANCES.

99. ON A VALLEY BOTTOM.

edge and look down we can see the grand river winding along the bottom. At this height the water below seems motionless, but the river twists like a riband from S. 12° W.

Traveller, dismount here, I advise you, or you will be shot over the head of your horse. There are other ways of reaching the valley bottom quicker than you would like, for the ground is often hard and covered with detritus, in which both men and horses slide down if they cannot put on the brake in time. I had put on excellent foot-gear, a cross between a boot and a stocking, made of white felt and ending in a sock of wild ass's hide, but without solid soles. A practical but not an elegant foot-covering. It was warm and soft for riding, but was awkward to walk in over pebbles. But one can endure much without dying, and when the socks are worn through they can be replaced by new ones in a moment.

At any rate we get down, and camp 464 is pitched on the meadows of the Shibe-chu. Next morning the river carried 406 cubic feet of water, and its tributary, the Lunak, which comes from the south-west, 81 feet. The united stream flows through a wild narrow chasm to the Sutlej.

A perplexing country! If I did not draw on my map every bend of the road, every rise and every dip in the ground, I should never be able to disentangle this complicated labyrinth. Where we ride on terrace platforms of earlier or later origin and up hill and down dale in trenches and side valleys, no guide is necessary. But frequently the road runs for a time in a valley bottom and is lost to sight, being swept away by the swollen water. There we should be lost if we had not Samye Karmo. He is really pleasant company. So the little pug-nosed Chinese lap-dog with the collar of bells seemed to think, which Samye had carried day after day in his arms all the way from Lhasa. The caravan had been four months on the journey, but it had made long halts wherever the pasturage was good. Samye Karmo entertained us with the gossip of the capital. The Dalai Lama was on his way to Pekin, he declared.

"How do you know that?"

"It was the common talk in the streets of Lhasa four months ago."

"When is he coming back to the Potala?"

"I do not know."

"Do they miss him?"

"Not exactly! As for myself, I do not care a rap about him."

No doubt the good Samye was more civil-tongued when the Pope of Lamaism again entered his capital at the beginning of the year 1910. Perhaps also he prayed "Om mani padme hum" with greater fervency than on the road to Daba when the Dalai Lama prepared to make his entry into the Potala, this time from India. At any rate, that pontiff is an important historical personage. He has fought with India and China, and never has Chenrezi been incarnated in an earthly shell which has travelled so far.

So we march on, Samye Karmo beguiling the length of the way with his conversation. He leads us up barren heights and down a steep path into the narrow valley Sang-serpo, where a spring feeds a clear rivulet rippling brightly through luxuriant grass.

"Here we stop," says Samye.

"Why not go on to Dongbo-gompa—it cannot be much farther?"

"No, it is not far; but there is no good grazing there. And, besides, it is dangerous to turn the animals loose at Dongbo-gompa, for there are barley-fields there and the damage the animals do has to be paid for."

"How much is exacted for trampling down the corn in the fields of the Dongbo monastery?"

"As a rule, one has to pay a rupee for every hoof-mark on the field."

"That may be an expensive business if there are many horses."

"Of course; and I advise you to remain here to-day and pass by Dongbo-gompa to-morrow."

We therefore set up our tents, lighted our dung fires, and were glad to be under cover when the rain began. But it was a ruse of the rogue Samye Karmo. He wanted to shake us off, because it might be dangerous to march up to a monastery in the company of a European. After the yaks had grazed awhile on the grassy margin of the brook, they were assembled in marching order by their drivers, and the men from Lhasa went down the valley with their far-travelled tea, singing and whistling. We might have followed their example, but we had already made ourselves comfortable for the night, and did not care to move in the rain.

Good heavens, how it rained that night! The pattering and trickling made it almost impossible to sleep. But though it still rained, we followed next morning the trail of the yaks from Lhasa down the narrow valley and up over hills where the mist shut out the view. Then we lost the track, and the beggar from Chiu who led the van had certainly no notion where the monastery lay. It was by pure good luck that we found it.

A curious scene presents itself in the mist when we come suddenly to the edge of another side valley. The edge seems to end in space, and below us yawns bottomless emptiness. We let ourselves slide down the steep soaked slopes, and thus reach the valley floor, where a flock of sheep tells us that men are near. A tethered horse is grazing on the meadow. A streamered cairn and a pyramidal waymark show us that we have struck the right road. It runs over a confusion of hillocks and trenches to the north. On the left is another abyss, a side valley of the first rank. Its lower slopes are vividly green with fields of barley which promise a good harvest.

This valley is called Dongbo, and soon we see Dongbo-gompa peep out through the mist from the commanding hill on which it is proudly enthroned. The road ascends steeply, sometimes winding among humps of living stone, sometimes running like a cornice along the foot of vertical pebble terraces, into which caves open, blackened by the smoke of camp-fires.

Like so many other monasteries in Tibet, Dongbo-gompa seems to have seen better days. The first impression is one of neglect and decay—ruins of houses and walls, heaps of sweepings and offal, offensive to the nose, savage measly dogs which rush at us and get a warm reception from Takkar, dirty ragged villagers and monks. If the people had only been civil! But Samye Karmo had warned us against them. They had nothing to sell and would have nothing to do with us. What they had they wanted themselves, and it was no use to chink our rupees in their ears.

While the caravan marched down the bottom of the valley, I stayed awhile above with Kutus and Lobsang to inspect at any rate the outside of the monastery. A dark covered cloister where pilgrims made the *kore* or beatifying circuit of the sanctuary was the only thing out of the common. The gate of the *lhakang* was locked.

I draw a hasty sketch of the monastery and the Dongbo valley which winds down to the Sutlej. But the rain begins again and I cannot draw on wet paper. The weather is too wet both for monks and laymen, and they vanish one after another into their musty holes. The water trickles and drops from the roofs and from our caps, little muddy rivulets ripple down the slopes, for to-day the south-west monsoon gives the Himalayas a thorough drenching, and it would be no harm if Dongbo-gompa and its refuse heaps were one day washed away. The monastery, dismal, lonely, and desolate on such a day, must be a charming and romantic object when bathed in sunlight or lighted up by the full moon on clear nights. But in this weather it hangs like a ghostly castle above the abyss.

As the rain did not abate we made up our minds to hurry down the steep declivity. We were wet through when we reached the camp, which stood at a height of 13,390 feet. We had never been so low since we left the Langak-tso. The barley-fields were better than any we had seen before, and our animals had to be closely watched lest they should be tempted to run into the fields. They had to be content with a small meadow by the Dongbo-chu, which carries down to the Sutlej 140 cubic feet of water per second. The tents were pitched close to the stream, which filled the valley with a roar magnified a thousand times by the echo. Again I listened to the monotonous rattle on my tent and the drippings which formed little puddles inside.

100. View from Dongbo-gompa over the Sutlej Valley towards the North-East.

Sketch by the Author.

We were badly off for provisions. The men had only half a brick of tea left, and there was nothing more for me but a small bag of wheaten flour, tea and sugar. Not to go to bed hungry, we resolved with bleeding hearts to sacrifice one of the goats. It was cruel, but it had to be. The goat was thin and miserable, but it performed its last act of friendship as well as it could. In the evening my men sang the old songs, but they sounded more subdued than usual, for both the river and the clouds chimed in with powerful lungs.

The temperature at night falls to 40.3° and we have not yet received a greeting from the summer of India. But we are travelling, as on the upper Indus, parallel to the Himalayas, for the actual breach does not begin before Shipki.

Close to the camp begins the steep ascent that leads up to the open heights and distant views. Again we see the general dip of the surface towards the Sutlej valley and the dark straight lines which mark the cañons. And we have to cross them all. The first two are not so bad, but the third is a valley of the first rank. At its margin I turn my eyes in all directions. N. 25° E. is seen a flat summit covered with snow; it rises up from the Ladak range, which we remember as the watershed between the Sutlej and Indus. The range we have seen for several days to the south is named Zaskar, and on its mighty crest lies the Shipki-la, at the foot of which the Sutlej breaks through the main wall of its prison.

We slip and slide down the sloping flanks and platforms to the bottom of the large valley which the Yungu-tsangpo has carved out. We see this tributary emerge from a rocky ravine a little above the road and then spread itself out on the expanded valley floor which crosses our route. The river carries 350 cubic feet now, but we perceive by the empty beds, some still damp and others containing longish pools, that it has lately been much more swollen. We have now waded through 7400 cubic feet of water, but as we have not seen the tributaries on the other side of the valley we must estimate the volume of the Sutlej as at least 10,600 cubic feet.

A young Tibetan on horseback overtook us at the river. Was he a traitor or the outrider of a party which would force us to turn back? No; he was only taking a message to Daba, and as he warned us that we should not find water again until we were there, we set up our camp here.

The barley-fields on the lowest terraces of the western side of the valley promised an abundant harvest. Only two poor families lived in ruined huts; the men were not at home, but the women showed that they could very well take care of themselves. They appeared at sunset before my tent where they behaved like suffragists.

"Your cursed goats have trampled down a field of crops. Will you pay for the damage, you villains, or must we complain of you to the monastery?"

"What is the value of the corn destroyed?"

"At least ten rupees."

"Then they must have eaten up all there was."

"No haggling, but down with the cash."

Two of my men looked at the place and found that the goats had indeed been feasting there—and very welcome they were—but that they could not have destroyed barley of more than the value of a rupee. The women received three rupees and went back smiling and satisfied. They had themselves driven the goats into the corn and thus made a little profit even before the grain was ripe. But as I could not afford at the time to pay extra corn duties, I gave my men notice that in future they would be responsible for all forbidden grazing on our neighbours' fields.

On August 9 we ride up out of the valley of the Yungu-tsangpo; up on the *tanga*, the tableland, we find ourselves 1150 feet higher than in our camp down on the valley bottom. How long will this amusement continue? Eight small side valleys are crossed, a perpetual up and down. The air line may be short, but our road is long and tiring.

After a time the direction is north-westerly, and a new ravine of the first rank gradually opens on the left. To the right begins a small side valley which gradually deepens as it runs down to join the larger. The even elevation on which we ride gradually narrows into a wedge with a point projecting like a springboard into space between the two valleys. It is as though the earth ended at this point and space began. It is too magnificent. I must remain here a long time until I have looked enough.

The caravan may continue its march to the camping-ground of the day. I take my seat at the end of the point, and there I am surrounded by dizzy abysses on all sides except the one from which I came. The view commands all the region between the ranges on the north and south. To the north-west it is unlimited, the yellowish-brown land vanishing into the horizon. I can perceive the position of the Sutlej valley to which the innumerable profound valleys make their way.

The air is clear and not a cloud is in the sky. North and south the view is limited, in the former direction by the Ladak range, in the other by the Zaskar range, both looking rather unimportant and showing small patches of firn on their flat summits. The interval between them may amount to 40 or 45 miles. The cross sectional profile is the curve of a tightly stretched rope, the fall therefore decreasing towards the middle where the Sutlej flows. This, however, applies only to the original valley with its loose deposits and its filled-up basins as seen from any point up on the *tanga*. Seen from a point, such I was on now, vertical and steeply inclined lines predominate. Cut up and hollowed out by rain-water and by rivers which during a damper climatic period were more voluminous than at present, the country with the wonderfully carved ravines at my feet is like a gigantic cathedral turned upside down. The point on which I sit surrounded by ravines has perpendicular sides. Below follows a steep declivity, and then again the fall is very sudden if not vertical. The lowest descent to the valley bottom is less steep, owing to fallen débris which has here accumulated into a fan. Exactly opposite, on the farther side of the main valley, is seen much better and more distinctly a similar formation, a succession of perpendicular and steep declivities from the top down to the valley bottom. In all the corners between the valleys accumulations are collected of closely packed loose material consisting of the finest dust, sand, and gravel. Fractures and landslides frequently occur, but on the whole the formation is characterized by a regularity which extends over the whole country and lends it a striped, checked appearance. The vertical lines are fissures and drainage channels into which the rain-water penetrates, causing landslips. As far as the eye can reach, the same regular design prevails. Over the flat surface of the opposite side of the valley still more valleys can be descried in tones growing fainter and in ever greater foreshortening. Only the uppermost slope is seen in all cases. After the masterly delineations of American geologists I can recognize with the greatest ease the same eroded sculpture, the same picturesque formation, which have made the cañons of the Colorado river so famous.

On one of the lowest shelves on the western side of the great valley below us the Daba-gompa stands perhaps somewhat more than 300 feet above the valley floor. Below the monastery stands the village of Daba enclosed as in a niche by pyramids, cones, and shafts of detritus. This village is the most important trade-centre on all the road to the frontier.

We have now seen enough, and we go down into the valley which we had shortly before on our right. From small beginnings it eats its way deeper down, and through its shelving labyrinth of small trenches, projections, and hills we descend to the bottom of the Daba valley. The river of the same name is divided into several arms, and carries only 159 cubic feet per second. Camp 468 stood on its left bank below the monastery village.

101. Laden Yaks on the March.

102. Carrying Loads over the Sutlej Bridge near Daba.

CHAPTER XXII

A PICTURESQUE MONASTERY

I DECIDED to remain two nights in the camp at Daba. The animals had had no day of rest since we had left Tokchen, and we had to procure provisions at any price. There were no pasture grounds but the juicy barley-fields, so our horses and mules had to be tied up.

First of all I drew a panorama of all the castles, towers, and crenellated walls which turned their fantastic fronts to the lane of the Daba valley, and had been modelled by rain and rivulets in the lowest declivity of the left flank. I had not yet finished when Kutus and Lobsang returned from a first reconnoitring expedition in the village; they had bundles full of rice and *tsamba*, as well as barley for the animals. We were, then, safe from famine in the meantime. They had also found some bad tobacco and filled their pipes at once; at any rate it had a sweeter aroma than the yak-dung they had puffed of late. Several Indian merchants were staying in Daba, and inquiries for provisions should be made at their camps next morning.

Before I was dressed my good fellows had again added to our supplies. Gulam, the cook, beaming with satisfaction, came to show me his booty—half a sack of potatoes, a bag of the small sweet raisins called *kishmish* in Turkestan, a whole apronful of dried plums, two packets of stearin candles, and three plump sheep. We had scarcely ever been so well off since we left Drugub the year before. The potatoes were the best of all. Roasted potatoes and milk in Daba tasted to me better than oysters and champagne in the Grand Hotel at Stockholm.

Accompanied by my usual satellites, Lobsang and Kutus, I betake myself at seven o'clock to the village, where I spend the whole day till darkness drives me back home. I should like to stay there for a week, for I have never seen subjects so alluring for the brush and so charming for the pencil since I left behind me the temple courts of Tashi-lunpo. The village lies like a bird's nest at the mouth of an extremely short semicircular valley, a niche, or whatever this pocket-like recess may be called. It lies in the pebble terrace amid a forest of stone pyramids and cones separated from one another by vertical clefts often so narrow that a man could not squeeze himself into them. A fissured wall; a background scene of the wildest, grandest sculpture; a row of pillars in several storeys attached to a wall behind; an immense organ with closely crowded pipes. Between the different stages the original horizontal bedding crops out here and there, and it is not hard to perceive that one here is in an æolian district of löss, which owes its fantastic forms to running water.

A wall protects the valley niche on the river-side. Through its gate, with a threshold of roughly hewn beams, we enter a market-place, or perhaps it might be called a broad bazaar street, between two rows of inhabited houses and rural caravanserais. Two *chhortens* stand like enigmatical milestones in the centre of the market, and Daba is beflagged with innumerable streamers which are fixed on a rope stretching over the whole village, so that they flutter blessings and good wishes over traders and cloister brothers in a silent chorus.

Here and there a merchant has set up his tent, while the nomads have piled up in blocks and walls their sacks containing salt from the *tsakas*, the dried-up lakes of western Tibet. Brick tea, sent from Lhasa, seems to be in great demand, and also rice, barley, meal, brown sugar, dried fruits, and other goods from India.

Daba is an emporium of the barter trade in this part of the province of Ngari-korsum or Hundes. Some fifty Hindus, most of them from Niti-rong, a valley lying on the south side of the Niti-la pass, and from Garhwal, had now come to the fair at Daba.

103. Through a Ravine to the Sutlej Valley.

104. The Valley Floor near Daba.

It seemed to me like a whiff of home to hear these copper-brown men from the frontier of India talking together in their language, and I was glad to meet these cheerful heralds of a fairy land, whose palms I longed to see. But what a difference there was between them and my old Tibetans, to whom to my sorrow I must soon bid a long farewell! As regards their build and the form of the head, the features and the dress, as well as regards their language and religion, we are confronted by representatives of a new type, another race. The face is more finely cut, more harmonically drawn, and in better proportion than that of the Tibetans—that is, according to Aryan ideas—and we recognize therein a transition to the pure Indo-Germanic type. The body is more slender and graceful, perhaps an inch or so taller than among the sons of Tibet, who are distinguished by their powerful muscular development, their squat roundish build, their measured, steady, and never hasty movements, the broad Mongolian form of head and massive skull.

These strangers from warmer valleys, with their raven-black hair hanging down in smooth locks, wear a small round skull-cap often ornamented with simple embroidery. Most of them wear long, light-grey kaftans gathered in by a girdle at the waist, narrow trousers fitting closely at the ankles, and low shoes ending in turned-up points. The whole appearance of the Hindu is more delicate and effeminate than that of the Tibetans. The sons of the Land of Snow are men hardened by their struggle against the dread forces of nature and a bitterly cold climate.

Some of the houses in the great market of Daba are more neatly and solidly built than any we have seen since our departure from the town of Shigatse. A broad red or blue band runs along the top under the roof, and light-blue bands are painted round the windows. The architecture reminds one of Italy. The Daba-dzong, the town hall, or perhaps more correctly the "government house," like that of an Indian town, first attracts our attention. It is a group of buildings painted all over hawthorn red, and its flat roof is decorated with many exorcising streamers and poles with ribands. A *chhorten* before the front indicates that the Daba-dzong is not only the headquarters of the town authorities but is also under the control of the state church. *Dzong* is a secular term. But the red house is also a *labrang*, or the seat of the lama superior of the monastery, who is named Tugden Nima. In Daba we find the same organization as in Selipuk, where the abbot of the monastery also holds in his hands the reins of secular power.

From the market we come into a quadrangular court, where the never-absent dog is chained up and rouses the echo of the rain-carved colonnade of the valley with his furious bark. Another gate, a stone staircase, an antechamber. Lay and ecclesiastical servants greet me politely as I enter. A lama invites me to enter the abbot's study, which is also the justice room. I stalk in with my two satellites, and next moment find myself in a larger room with a pillar in the middle, which is fitted up and furnished in the solid Lamaist style we remember so well in the red chamber and other principal monks' cells and priests' dwellings in Tashi-lunpo.

Exactly opposite the entrance sits Tugden Nima, with his back to a large window filled with panes of thin paper through which a subdued light penetrates. Against the light Tugden Nima is seen only as a dark profile, and his features are imperceptible. I can only make out that he wears the toga of a monk and has short hair, and also that letters and documents are piled up among writing materials on a low, lacquered table.

When I had come up to the table I made a slight bow which the temporal and spiritual judge of Daba returned with an inclination of exactly the same angle. But he did not rise from his divan, which was covered with a mat. He looked with a smile at my weather-beaten features. My face had frequently changed its skin in the rarefied air, and the last integument was tough as parchment and was darkened by the scorching sun of Tibet. He also examined my dress. A Sahib in Tibetan costume! My green velvet cap had once been thought worthy to adorn the head of a Tatar khan; now, from constant changes of rain and sunshine, it had assumed a hue for which language

105. Lama Dwellings in Daba-gompa.

106. Part of the Village of Daba.
Sketches by the Author.

has no name and the colour scale no shade. A brick-red turban scarf was wound round its border. The blood-red kaftan, confined at the waist by a grey girdle, had seen better days. In honour of Tugden Nima I had put on Mongolian leather boots with strong thick soles. The satellites were in every respect worthy of their master. Ragged from top to toe, Kutus could not expect to be taken for anything but a genuine vagabond from Ladak. Lobsang wore a kaftan of the same kind as mine, but fresher in colour, for it had been made in Tokchen.

"Sit down, Sahib," said Tugden Nima after he had surveyed long enough the far-travelled wanderer who had come so unexpectedly into his room. Some lamas, silent and motionless as pillars, Hindus and Tibetan laymen, lined the walls watching attentively to see what would happen. Tugden Nima had a pleasant face and good manners, and he was friendly towards us from the first, not coarse and repellent like the monks of Dongbo.

"I have heard of you, Sahib, and I know that you sailed over Tso-mavang in a boat. Singular that you came off with your life from such an exploit. You might have aroused the wrath of the gods, and I suspect that you were exposed to danger more than once, were you not?"

"Certainly, storm often overtook us, and the boat was cast ashore by the waves. But if I had displeased the gods I should not now be sitting on a divan and talking to you, Tugden Nima."

"You are a friend of the Panchen Rinpoche in Tashi-lunpo—that explains everything. And I have also heard that you have visited many monasteries, and have consorted with the monks on a friendly and confidential footing. Which monasteries have you seen?"

I took a good drink from my tea-cup, and then gave him the whole list, from Tashi-lunpo to Tirtapuri.

"You have seen more of them than I," he exclaimed.

"Now, tell me something about yourself," I asked, when the string of his tongue was loosed, and he had shown himself to be a good-tempered and sympathetic, as well as a well-informed and interesting man.

"Where stood the tent of your mother when you were

born, how old are you, where did you spend your youth, and what are you doing here?"

"I was born in Lhasa, and at a very early age entered the Sera monastery as a novice. I am now 40 years old, and I have been chosen by the Devashung to put in order and manage the affairs of Daba-dzong. I have, then, as you must have seen from the papers on the table, quite enough to do, and you must excuse me if I cannot give you as much of my time as I should like. You wish to see the monastery. A lama has already been ordered to show you everything. Let me know if I can do anything else for you."

When I had thanked him for his kindness, he said, suddenly:

"This is a lucky year. You have seen how it has rained. The harvest will turn out well, the grass is shooting up in the valleys and the nomads will have a good winter. You know, of course, the great water festival in Lhasa, from hearsay at least? Well, when the rains fail this festival is held with great state to mollify the heavens. This year the water festival will be a simpler ceremony, for the rain is coming of itself."

I understood his meaning; we too know that

> When the Devil was sick, the Devil a monk would be;
> When the Devil was well, the devil a monk was he!

Our conversation was interrupted by some Hindu merchants and their Tibetan customers, who had fallen into a dispute about a commercial bargain. Tugden Nima, the judge, not the abbot, waited in silence until the contending parties had exhausted the whole stock of ugly words the Tibetan language contains.

Meanwhile I could look a little round the room, which, after the desolate regions where I had lived for so many months, seemed palatial. The walls were covered with Chinese paintings on paper, and bookshelves almost breaking under the weight of the holy scriptures. On the altar table small statues of the gods smiled in silver and copper cases, and the light of flickering flames burning in bowls fell on their faces. The usual Lamaist furnishings, the bells, *dorches* or thunderbolts of brass, the prayer-mill and other religious objects, were also present. Over the door hung a portrait of the Emperor William, a coloured print, which had somehow found its way to Daba-dzong.

But both Tugden Nima and myself had other things to think of, so I rose, took my leave and went out to the market, where I was again most unexpectedly reminded of Germany. A Hindu came to me, bowed and said:

"Salaam, Sahib. Will you take me into your service? I have been employed by Europeans before."

"No, thank you; I have just sent off six servants, and I do not want any more."

"Do take me! I will show you a testimonial given me by a European whom I served a long time."

And with that he brought out a folded yellow paper. I read it quickly through, and then asked him, "How old are you?"

"Forty years."

"Well, this testimonial was written fifty-three years ago, according to its date."

"Yes, you see, it was my brother who actually received it, and he is much older than I."

"If you will sell me the testimonial, you can make a few rupees by it."

"No, Sahib, I will not sell it; it is a very valuable document."

He was right. I would have kept it as an autograph. It contained a few lines of thanks in English to a certain Mance, who had provided a European expedition with excellent sturdy coolies. And the classical names subscribed below were "Adolph and Robert Schlagintweit, Badinath, September 5, 1855." The testimonial had therefore been drawn up two years before the murder of Adolph Schlagintweit in Kashgar.

Now we toil up a narrow steep gully in the freakish slope of the pebble bed to reach the level terrace in front of Daba-gompa. An old lama comes to meet us; he is charged to show us the monastery and the temple halls. First he conducts us into a forecourt, partly roofed over. Here we see the usual arrangement, the portal of the *lhakang*, with its red door panels decorated with iron and brass mounts, the blue pillars attached to the wall on the sides, and yellow and pink draperies above.

The lama is about to unlock the door and take us in, but I restrain him and take out my sketch-book and small paint-box. The portal and its surroundings are too interesting. The four spirit kings are at their posts. The figures are coarsely painted, with little art, and, judged by the faded colouring and the gaps caused by the fall of the distemper, fairly old. In the corner to the left lie heaps of discarded streamers, temple draperies, *kadakhs* and strips of coloured cloth all dusty and time-worn, torn by the winds of the highlands or bleached by burning sun. A cracked drum stands silent in its stand; a rotten table can no longer bear the weight of heavy images; two stools which have lost a leg are left to perish, and some temple vessels of copper and brass can no longer resist verdigris and corruption.

Now the red doors are opened and the mouldy close darkness of the *lhakang* or *chamkang*, as this, the principal hall of the gods is called, stands before us. *Chhortens* are erected on either side of a Chamba statue, the one on the left called Pöchöge-kudung, the other on the right covered with gold. Other images are faultlessly arranged in regular ranks on tables and shelves between vessels for offerings and lamp-bowls. The truths of Lamaism lie on dark sheets of paper between their old wooden covers, wrapped in green and blue cloths. The holy legends are to be read in coloured pictures amid a forest of *tankas*, and the usual strips of cloth are wound round the pillars.

A smaller hall is called *Lama-lhakang*, after Yabyan Shin Tibi, a priest who is supposed to have founded the monastery at the time when the walls of Tashi-lunpo were reared. However that may be, his ashes are said to be contained in the large *chhorten*, Lami-kudung, which stands in the middle of the hall. Sitting statues of Tsong Kapa, three feet high, protect the dust of the deceased saint, and the reformer can enjoy the sight of coloured artificial flowers in vases. Here, too, stand cast idols in close rows, and

107. THE VILLAGE OF DABA.

108. TERRACE IN DABA-GOMPA.

among the temple vessels four silver beakers with one foot are conspicuous.

I have very great doubts whether my honest Lobsang is strong in the faith. But he might be seen humbly making his rounds in the terrestrial Valhalla of Lamaism, and throwing himself down before every one of these golden idols, so that his forehead touched the floor of hard-stamped clay. He even begged our lama to be allowed to keep a *kadakh* that he might have a good journey to India in its blessed atmosphere. My dear Lobsang was much too sound in mind to believe in this hocus-pocus. But he did not wish to hurt the feelings of the old lama, so he observed the outward forms and practices of the religion he had inherited from his parents.

A third temple, the *dukang*, was closed, and the lama who had the key happened to be in one of the adjacent valleys, looking after the salvation of a dying nomad to the best of his ability.

Daba-gompa belongs to the Gelugpa sect, and its brotherhood consists of fifteen monks. They are of the Gelong and Getsul orders, and only Tugden Nima has attained the rank of Kanpo Lama.

Though it is small, the monastery vividly reminds me of Tashi-lunpo. Here also we find a collection of stone houses, which produce a pleasing effect. The walls are painted red, here and there relieved by white panels. The *chamkang* is covered with a roof jutting out into curved angles after the Chinese style. The greater part of its original gilding has been washed away by the monsoon rains. Streamers flutter on the roofs, and bells hang at all the projecting corners with feathers tied to their clappers. The slightest breeze that breathes over Daba-gompa calls forth from this carillon a melodious symphony that speaks of peace.

How willingly we linger by the hour in this remarkable picturesque monastery! From whichever side we behold it new surprises meet our eyes. Like eagles' eyries, a row of white houses with red and blue friezes and window frames hangs above the village down in the valley; in them are the cells of the yellow confraternity. The greyish yellow pebble terrace with its countless shafts and pyramids makes an effective background to the particoloured houses. The parts illumined by the sun stand out sharp and strong, while the shadows are faint owing to the reflexion from all sides; only the deeply-eroded vertical furrows between the pillars are black.

Now summer reigns in the Daba valley. Summer is the time of life and movement. Then the Hindus of Niti-rong bring their goods over the mountains and trade in the fair of the Tibetans. During late autumn life gradually declines. Then follows winter when the Himalayan passes are closed, and, cut off from communications, Daba is left in solitude. The cloister brothers spend their lonely days in the white houses and hold services in the dim temple halls. They see the snow fall in thick flakes, and listen to the mystical dialogue between the wind and the bells. But the noisy chatter of the rocky bed and the Sutlej, their Langchen-kamba or Elephant river, does not reach their ears.

Evening draws on and we begin the descent, but we must linger once more at the steep wall where half a dozen *chhortens* of fine and stately form stand, having an air of antiquity owing to the commencement of decay. A cubical foundation with plinth and ornamentation bears a contracted cupola with an onion-shaped turret ending in a gilded crescent encircling a disc. They are painted red, white, and greyish-blue, and on the sides two horses are portrayed.

The shades of evening fall early on the village of Daba; a pale light illumines the façades and groups of houses, while the eastern side of the valley is lighted up a little longer by the rays of the setting sun.

The Hindus have their regular abode just opposite Daba-dzong, in a small house with an open platform in the court in front of the building. There the men from Niti were assembled, and their expressive songs charmed our ears as we went home in the twilight.

"Come up to us for a time, Sahib, listen to our songs, and watch the dances," one of our new friends asked us. Very gladly. A carpet was laid down for me, and as a

109. CHHORTENS IN DABA-GOMPA SEEN FROM ABOVE.

110. THE VILLAGE OF DABA WITH THE MONASTERY.

gift of welcome two dishes were handed to me piled up with grains of rice and sugar, which I more than paid for in cash. Two men sang some unintelligible words, accompanying themselves on drums which looked like hour-glasses, and which they beat with their fingers. In front of them a pretty brown young maiden, with smoothly combed black hair, black dreamy eyes, and silver rings in her nostrils, danced a whirling circling dance. She had thrown a pink transparent veil carelessly over her hair, and wore a black jacket, a white skirt which stood out from her hips like an open parasol, and closely fitting trousers tied round the ankles. Her prettily formed bare feet turned round swiftly and gracefully in the dance.

The darkness came down on us. The camp-fire spread a bright light down by the bank. All the poor of Daba waited patiently for my return, and received small presents. Lastly, Suen danced round the fire, and the songs of the Ladakis sounded cheerfully in the cold valley.

CHAPTER XXIII

IN THE SANCTUARY OF THE MANGNANG MONASTERY

THOUGH Simla lies almost due west of Daba, the road runs for several days' march to the north and north-west, and passes along tributaries between regions which are quite impassable for man and beast. There is no possibility of advancing along the shortest way marked out by the Sutlej. We remember the appearance of the river bed below the monastery Kyung-lung. The irresistible mass of water dashed with a deafening roar between vertical and overhanging cliffs of solid rock. We must cross the Sutlej four times more before we come to Simla, and at every crossing we shall gain a fresh insight into the secrets of the remarkable valley. Where the rocks reach out towards each other, and where the river, narrow and squeezed together, tumbles between them, there only has it been possible to construct a bridge, and only there do we see the Elephant river. Its rule, however, extends over the whole Himalayan region which we traverse.

A short distance between the cliffs on either side is not the only condition demanded for bridging over the river. Such places are numerous. We may be sure that the Sutlej flows all the way in a deep trough. Wet shining ramparts of rock descend from colossal heights to its banks. Long reaches of the river have never been seen by human eye. The wild sheep can find no way to them, and the chamois has nothing to attract him thither. Only rock pigeons, falcons, and eagles know the deep, shady, and cold vault-like corridors where the river tosses without rest or pause. No, the Tibetan road and river engineer-

111. In the Temple of Daba-gompa. To the left a Case with the Holy Books.

Sketch by the Author.

ing corps demands also for bridge-building that the shore supports of the bridge-head shall lie only a few feet above the water, for usually the road follows the valleys of tributaries and avoids all ridges and crests that are difficult of access.

On the road to Daba we are during two days' journey at a distance of six to ten miles from the Sutlej, and not till the third day do we approach the river at a sharp angle. But even the smallest side valley is imbued with its spirit. The rain of the south-west monsoon, which washes these rocks and terraces, is tributary to the Sutlej and is bound to trace back the course of this river from its own home, the Indian Ocean. During our journey I always longed to see the main river, but had to patiently wind along the terrible detours between the bridges.

The mountain land south of the Sutlej is Hundes proper; Chumurti lies north of the river. Both are characterized by their cañons, their fearfully wild vertical sculpture. The Ladak and the Zaskar ranges gradually diverge, and therefore the affluents become longer, and probably on the whole more voluminous. After a single traverse, however, no law can be laid down as regards this. The rain is unequally distributed. A small tributary may rise until it overflows after sharp local downpours, and a larger one may fall considerably after a couple of bright days.

From Daba we have to mount again up to the heights which separate us from the next side valley. The road crawls up the gully cut out in the terraces just above the village. Consequently the friendly monastery vanishes out of sight at once, as we turn northwards into such a steep trench that the loads are always slipping off as the animals struggle up. The men push behind, shouting and whistling. Yonder one of our horses has stopped with his load hanging under his belly, and a long halt follows. Two minutes more and another load is almost off. The soil of this torrent bed, only six feet wide, is yellow clay, so that we are nearly choked with the dust the animals kick up. On either side pillars and blocks of rolled stone,

60-100 feet high, rise perpendicularly or hang over in a threatening manner. Now we do fairly well, but this road must be delightful after continuous rain. Then there is danger of being struck down by falling stones and boulders, then the viscous plastic clay is smooth as soap, then neither man nor beast can keep his feet, and if any one falls he slides with alarming rapidity down to the bottom of a grand toboggan.

Scarcely have we reached the top when the path, perhaps the most capricious in the world, takes us down again into a gully which opens into a medium-sized valley. A small brook trickles down its bed. There is no wind here. A touch of the sun of India lies over this desolate disintegrated country. Horses and mules make for the brook to drink. The men scoop up water with their hands and pour it over their heads and faces.

After thus refreshing ourselves, we ascend another rolling mountain, but only to plunge down again into the next valley. This, too, is watered by a rivulet which has produced a narrow strip of grass. Ruins of old houses, a row of *chhortens*, two small barley-fields and a brook are the sights of the next valley. Then follows a labyrinth of small valleys and furrows, an inextricable confusion of all kinds of troughs, some of which we cross right over, and others come in contact with only at their heads where they are not cut deeply into the ground. A larger dale winds off north-eastwards, and the descent into it is so steep that two loads slip over the heads of the animals, which have to stand with their noses to the ground until help comes.

A last rise separated us from the valley Manlung, where we had had enough for one day. Here also stood a hut to protect the barley on the fields which are watered by a rivulet from a spring. I would have travelled further but I yielded to my men's desire for rest. The good living in Daba had made them heavy and lazy; of course they had eaten as much *tsamba* and mutton as they could force down and a little more.

Just at mid-day the sun was burning hot, but half an hour later the sky grew dark in the south and the monsoon again drove heavy masses of cloud over the Himalayas. A

112. WALL OF DABA-GOMPA.

113. CHHORTENS AT DABA.

Sketches by the Author.

distant murmur is heard; it becomes louder; a hailstorm comes; it rushes down upon us, and the air is immediately cool and fresh. As soon as the hail is over steady rain commences. We had been warned at Daba of the Mangnang-tsangpo. This river swells up after heavy rain so that it cannot be forded. It would be pleasant if, on reaching its bank, we had to stop waiting for days, when we were so anxious to reach India.

August 12 broke clear after a minimum of 45° in the night. The rain had cooled the air and the Mangnang-tsangpo would not prove an obstacle to our march. As usual we had to climb a steep slope; we always camp at the bottom of a valley and travel straight across innumerable valleys. Another chaos of troughs and then a rapid descent between yellow colonnades carved out fantastically in the detritus down into the narrow Anggong valley, where a brook is ensconced between grassy banks.

A horseman flies past us without answering when we inquire his destination. A second follows at a quick trot, his saddle-bags bulged out with their contents. He, too, has no intention of detaining us. The destination of both is evidently Totling. Perhaps this large convent is the stone in our way which will trip us up. At Tokchen the authorities wished to drive us back into the interior of the country. We must wait and see if the men of Totling have the assurance to do the same, so near the frontier.

The small Anggong brook soon enters the large Mangnang valley, and even from the junction of the two valleys we can hear in the distance the roar of a great river. We make a circuit to the left and south-west and cross many waterless but still wet beds, with their banks sparsely begrown with bushes. The river with its rapid raging current and its breadth of 72 yards was formidable, but it was easy to ford at a place where its 700 cubic feet of water was distributed among four arms. We had now passed 8500 cubic feet of water in the tributaries of the Sutlej. With the addition of the water running in on the opposite side the Sutlej must here carry 16,000 or even 17,500 cubic feet.

Glad to have the obstacle we had been warned of safely

behind us, we pitched camp 470 on a meadow by the left bank close to the monastery Mangnang-gompa, which, curiously enough, is built on the level valley floor and not on the heights above, as is the case with most convents. It is eleven o'clock, and we have the day before us. Little we care though thunder rolls among the Himalayas and heavy clouds congregate in dark blue cumuli over the southern mountains. We shall be caught by the first drops, but it is only a couple of strides to the forecourt of the monastery. Just as we have got under cover the rain begins and pelts all day on to the ground.

The village of Mangnang contains three or four simple huts surrounded by walls, and stands in the midst of larger and more thriving barley-fields than we have hitherto seen. In five weeks the scythe will sever the corn, and the crop is sure for this year, even if the rain stops altogether. Ten days ago the river was much swollen and could not be forded without danger. The distance to its source on the slopes of the snow-clad mountains of the Gangman-gangri is reckoned to be three short days' marches.

We are at a height of 13,176 feet, and are 1880 feet lower than the Rakas-tal lake. Here we come to the upper limit of arboreal vegetation, and we greet the first heralds of the Himalayan forests in the form of a green grove of a dozen leafy poplars beside the village. If the whole country as far as sight can reach were not overshadowed by rain-clouds, I would have my tent set up under the crowns of the trees; I should delight in the pale green subdued light that filters through the foliage, and would listen to the rustle of twigs and leaves that seems to speak of home. The traveller from India here takes leave of the last grove, and never sees a tree again till he comes to Ladse-dzong and Ye-shung in the far east, or to Chushul and Tankse, if he marches westwards. But if he directs his steps northwards, through Chang-tang, he finds the shadow of a tree only when he reaches the oases of Eastern Turkestan.

Mangnang-changchugling-gompa, what a charming, appropriate name for a hermitage where the days are long and there is time enough to spare! The monastery turns its rose-coloured walls to the outer world, and the stranger is agreeably surprised to find a large, richly-decorated *lhakang* within. Eight pillars of sound timber support the roof, and in the nave between them we see for the fiftieth time the red divans on which the monks sit cross-legged as they murmur their prayers during the services. The prior has a special seat at the upper end of the row. Hangings, painted banners and pennants hang from the ceiling and pillars like trophies of a holy war. The theological library consists of the *Kanjur* scriptures, while the 208 folios of the *Tanjur* are only found in monasteries of the rank of Totling-gompa. Fresco paintings in fresh sober colours cover the walls, and the pictures exhibit an artistic sense that is not without merit.

A host of 330 divine images is placed on the altar table; the reader will find them depicted on a coloured plate in Vol. II. p. 406. There we see Tsong Kapa in three copies, all adorned with cloth caps. They are made of brass, but the dust of years and the smoke of guttering butter wicks have covered them with a black film. The monks of the monastery asserted that these images had been made on the spot by a lama skilled in metal work, but this statement is doubtful. Perhaps he only repaired some broken images.

Above all the rest and behind them a huge rosy red statue of Buddha stands in the shaft of light from the impluvium. His eyes stare into the hall, his lips are swollen, his cheeks stand out, and his long ears are partly covered with a veil. His hands he holds laid palm to palm as if in prayer, but they are entirely hidden in a *kadakh*, the offering of pious pilgrims. A subdued light, contrasting with the gloom which prevails in the hall, falls on his face, a gleam of the Nirvana in which the unapproachable princely son of the Sakya tribe dreams in solemn silent repose.

"Let me buy some of your gods," I begged one of the monks who showed the deities.

"You would be welcome to do so if every article in the Mangnang *lhakang* were not ticketed with a number, which is entered in the inventory of the monastery. A strict check is kept; and when a new prior comes he at once inspects all the movable property of the monastery and looks if anything is wanting. If anything has been taken away his predecessor must replace it. Therefore we cannot sell you the smallest cloth."

Red, yellow, and brown cloths covered the front of the altar table. Only the boldly carved feet on which the table rests were visible; two brazen cymbals, an important instrument in church music, leaned against them. Lamps burned not before the altar table but on a table at one side. New wicks were placed in the butter, all the bowls were filled with grains of rice and water, and the brazen vessels shone like gold. A cloister brother was sweeping the earthen floor, but was kind enough to stop when I asked him to let the dust settle a while. On the outer court also besoms were flying about.

"You are surely preparing for a festival?" I asked.

"No, we are expecting a Kanpo Lama from Lhasa. He is to relieve the prior of Totling, whose four years of service are at an end. On his journey thither the new prior inspects all the monasteries on the road through Ngari-khorsum, so we sweep and clean inside and out to give a good impression."

"But you keep the yearly church festivals in Mangnang?"

"No; for the great festivals we go, like the lamas of Daba and Dongbo, to Totling."

"To which mother cloister is Mangnang affiliated?"

"The Brebung monastery near Lhasa."

"But you belong to Tsong Kapa's yellow sect, the Gelugpa?"

"Yes, certainly."

To the red carved door-posts in the antechamber, the *Dukang-gumchor*, some small bronze gods, were irreverently hung by strings, an arrangement I have never seen elsewhere. The four spirit kings, called collectively Galchen Dirgi, are represented on the walls with force and elegance.

I sat for hours, painting in water-colours, in the *lhakang* of Mangnang, where silence hovered with motionless wings over the assemblage of deities. Subdued colours, dreamy eyes, gently smiling lips; trombones and drums which

114 Ravine on the way to Totling.

115. Daba.

could make a noise but were now dumb; a spider lazily climbing up its thread which hung down from the ceiling —all had a soporific effect on my senses. Outside was heard the swish of the steadily falling rain. Lobsang, who had held a long conversation with a lama, at last fell asleep, and slumbered like an innocent child, leaning against a pillar and sitting with wide-spread legs on a divan, properly intended for use in divine service. He dreamed of the fearful winter in Chang-tang, which lay behind us, or of the summer of India, to which we drew nearer every day. His deep breathing made the silence still more striking. I seemed as though shut up in a burial vault waiting until the breathing was over that I too might fall asleep. Why did not ghostly forms come forth from the dark corners of the temple hall? Why did not the divinities in the mural paintings step down and execute incantation dances before the altar? Eternal Buddha, unfathomable deity on thy throne in the cup of the lotus flower, why didst thou not utter words of wisdom in this sanctuary erected in thine honour?

My eyes turn from the haloes of the gods to the brush and paper. I look round. Lobsang's head is nearly slipping off its resting-place, and he sleeps with open mouth as soundly as a dormouse. The lama, with whom he had been talking, sits upright, and in silence lets the beads of his rosary slip through his fingers. I begin unconsciously to whistle, as though to give a rhythmical swing to my sketching. But then the lama rises, comes gently up, and begs me not to disturb the peace of the sanctuary.

The light that falls on Buddha's face grows fainter, for the evening advances with rapid strides.

"Good morning, Lobsang!" I call out so loudly that the lama, but just now motionless as Buddha, starts and drops his rosary. Lobsang yawns and rubs his eyes. We go out into the rain.

"Who rest here?" I ask our lama as we pass by some large *chhortens*.

"Monks of high rank who have died and been cremated in Mangnang."

He tells me that after the bodies have been consumed

on the pyres the ashes are mixed with moist clay and kneaded into small figures called *tsatsa*, which are of the form of a cylinder and a cone in one. On every *tsatsa*, while it is still moist, some sacred word or sentence is printed with a stamp. The ashes of a dead man suffice to make a couple of thousand *tsatsa*, which are deposited in a hollow of the solid base of the *chhorten*. This *chhorten* is therefore the grave of the dead man as well as his monument.

Darkness descends on Mangnang, and soon the shadows of night draw their veil over the countenance of Buddha. Some poor small children, only half-clothed in rags, accompany me down to the camp to get a piece of bread and a copper. And then night opens its arms to receive cenobites and pilgrims, and we for some hours wander through the fairyland of dreams and oblivion.

CHAPTER XXIV

HIS EXCELLENCY THE CHURL

IMMEDIATELY below the cloister village the road winds up three sharply marked terraces which all indicate former levels of the valley of the tributary. Up on the top the road takes a bend to north and north-east; it is tiresome, when Simla lies to the west. But the road must accommodate itself to the configuration of the country and creep through where the land presents no insurmountable obstacles.

Suddenly our small party comes to a halt on the edge of a fearfully deep valley, a cañon which is one of the right-hand branches of a whole system of gigantic erosion troughs. From the edge we look down perpendicularly into a dizzy depth of several hundred yards. The whole precipice is seen foreshortened, and we get an excellent notion of its different beds of varying thickness, vertical where the material is hard, and with a very slanting dip where it is looser; down at the bottom the last detritus fan passes into the floor of the narrow channel. The uppermost layer on which we stand consists of a bed of reddish-brown detritus 16 feet thick. The wind blows over its level surface and its sides are vertical. From one convenient spot we can catch a glimpse of its lower limit, for the underlying bed of yellow clay is softer and more easily attacked by denudation. The detritus bed, therefore, projects forward like a cornice from which loosened blocks threaten to fall at any moment.

On the top from which the descent commences we are at an absolute height of 13,176 feet. The scene before our eyes is truly wonderful, and no pen can describe its extraordinary forms. A yellow map is unrolled beneath our feet; a labyrinth of deep, precipitous erosion valleys, corridors, and trenches, separated by wedge-shaped blocks of pebble and clay. Thanks to the expansion round Totling, the Sutlej is visible to the north, but at this distance its line of foaming rapids looks only like a fine thread. We think we can perceive that below Totling and Tsaparang, which cannot be distinguished at so great a distance, the Sutlej valley again contracts to a narrow ravine. But where does the path run? Is it possible to get down through this maze and along these declivities without breaking a limb?

From the point on the edge where the cairn stands we plunge down headlong. The scene changes at every bend of this sharply winding zigzag path. We slide down slopes, creep almost all round hillocks and boulders, nay, must often toil up again to find a less steep descent, and then go down once more. On the whole the path runs north-west, though at times we are walking south-east—indeed, towards all points of the compass.

The spacious landscape we have seen from the top vanishes at once when we are buried in the deep cañon excavated with fantastic irregularity in a typical deposit of löss. We are, therefore, enclosed between yellow precipitous walls of clay, and regard with astonishment a confusion of yellow towers, walls, and castles standing, as it were, in the narrow lane of an enchanted town.

Now the path lies like a narrow shelf on a precipitous slope and below us yawns a dry ravine. The fine powdery dust rises in yellow clouds behind the hoofs of our animals. This road is impassable after rain. We were afterwards told so at Totling, but we could see ourselves that it must be so. On all sides there are perfect tobogganing slides. How slippery they must be when all this clay is wet!

The free outlook we enjoyed on the shelf was lost again when the road crept down into a very deep trough between walls of löss 100 feet high. Loose dust lay on the bottom, on which we seemed to walk as on eiderdown cushions. Above our heads only a narrow strip of sky was visible.

Then it grows lighter again. On the left the wall of clay is still perpendicular, but it is interrupted on the right, or is replaced, by a row of yellow pillars and cubical blocks forming a loggia, a gallery, which affords through its loopholes a view over the Sutlej valley. How often I should like to stop and sketch on the way! But it is better to hurry on. The sky is dull, rain may come, and then we should be stuck fast.

Now we bend round an isolated conical hill and crawl along a ridge between two trenches. The next moment we cross some trenches. We walk up and down hill, to right and left, through dust and vapour. The animals manage splendidly. The loads slip off only twice, causing stoppages.

Step by step we work our way down through the löss bed, coming to older and older horizons of the immense filled-up basin. In two hours we have moved down deposits which must have taken at least ten thousand years to accumulate. We have gained a grand insight into the work of the forces of denudation and accumulation during earlier periods.

The bed of detritus above, which covers the whole as with a mantle, must certainly increase in thickness towards the foot of the mountains and thin out towards the Sutlej. Under this bed we see a series of different deposits, and at the bottom of all occurs rock *in situ*, which, however, crops out only on the banks of the Sutlej.

If we could clear away all this loose alluvium, we should see a flat open strath between the Ayi-la in the northern, and the Gangman-gangri in the southern, mountains with a breadth of 60 miles. Such was this country in a remote period when an alteration took place in the climate, transforming everything. The climate became dry, precipitation almost ceased, the highlands were converted into steppe, but the wind continued its dance over the wilderness. On its wings it bore along the fine dust weathered from the mountains, which by degrees fell to the earth and formed æolian deposits. It was long before the trough valley was filled up with a thickness of many hundred feet. But when this filling up was complete, Hundes had a form of surface exactly of the same kind as the basins of China and Mongolia, which are filled up with dust borne by the wind and which Richthofen calls "*lössmulden.*"

Such a hollow may be closed in on all sides and have no drainage. Then all the solid matter carried by wind and water to its centre remains within its bounds. But if it has an outlet to the sea, like the Sutlej valley, erosion and running water exercise their force when the time is ripe.

And in the Sutlej valley the water has again acquired its rights. A new change of climate occurred, this time from drought to abundant precipitation. The transition must have extended through thousands of years. The precipitation increased slowly and steadily, perhaps with periodical interruptions. At last the south-west monsoon flooded the Himalayas with extraordinarily heavy deluges of rain. The water collected into mighty rivers which cut their channels vertically through the löss deposits of the steppe period. The result is the wild dissected cañon country we have around us on all sides.

The thorough change of climatic conditions which in Hundes and in many other parts of Asia exhibited itself as a pluvial period with abundant precipitation, produced in more northern regions the Great Ice Age, when Scandinavia and extensive areas of northern Europe lay under a mantle of ice. The pluvial period has left conspicuous traces, and not in Hundes only; the huge terraces on the banks of the Indus and the concentric beach lines round all the salt lakes of Tibet are memorials of this period. Then Manasarowar and Rakas-tal were filled to overflowing, and the upper Sutlej streamed through them constantly. But the inland ice retreated northwards and disappeared at the time when the rainfall diminished on the Himalayas. It seems as though the climate in the present period were tending towards greater dryness. We have seen that the Sutlej was cut off from Rakas-tal barely a century ago, though this event may very well be only a moment in a period.

Step by step and turn after turn we have worked our way down the steep walls; at length only a succession of round flat hills remain before we can ride on over level or slightly undulating ground. A streamer cairn on one of the last hills announces the proximity of Totling-gompa. Now the sharply limited quadrangular cloister town appears on the left bank of the Sutlej. Is it possible? A town in this unproductive country all of yellow clay! Yes, truly; yonder we see the crowded temple buildings surmounted by Chinese roofs and the tall *chhortens*, the emblems of transitoriness and recollection. These ancient weather-worn memorial stones of Lamaism speak of neglect and decay. Tottering houses still defy time among the ruins of others which have long fallen in. The red-painted monastery buildings bear the marks of rain, frost, and sun, and poverty peers out from the holes and chinks of the dilapidated walls, to announce to the stranger that Totling's period of grandeur is now only a tradition.

The monastery town is built on a terrace perhaps 60 feet above the level of the Sutlej. At the foot of this terrace the dirty grey eddies of the great broad river roll along with a much slower speed than at the last place we heard their roar. A mile and a quarter higher we can just descry the narrow, sharply cut, rocky portal from which the river emerges, foaming and turbulent, into the expansion at Totling. This is one of the places where the Sutlej rests on its journey. But the royal river longs for more deeds of heroism. Immediately below Tsaparang it renews its furious combat with the rocks.

As the most noted and perhaps also the largest of the ecclesiastical strongholds of Tibet, Totling should have shown itself off on our arrival by a grand procession of its monks, clothed in red togas, and marching along as solemn and dignified as Roman senators. But not a priest was to be seen; no children of the poorer classes played among the ruins; no horse stood tied up before a cloister cell. Were the monks afraid of us? Very well, we would look them up. Not that I had anything to say to them, but when fate had brought me to Totling, why should I neglect the opportunity of obtaining a general impression and a remembrance of its temple halls to take back with me home?

But look, there are three monks standing in a corner. Cool and unembarrassed as usual, and with both hands clasped behind his back, Lobsang walks up to them and asks:

"Have you heard whether a messenger is come from Gartok? Our Sahib expects one from Thakur Jai Chand."

"We do not keep a look-out for your messenger," a lama answered drily and coldly.

"Whose is the white tent that stands yonder outside the village?"

"Go and find out for yourself."

With imperturbable composure Lobsang turns his back on the priests. Our friend, Samye Karmo, who is now staying in Totling, but keeps out of our way, has evidently announced that we were on the way and were travelling without a passport. The monastery authorities are therefore prepared, and have put themselves in a state of defence.

Two roads meet at Totling, the one along which we have travelled from Tirtapuri, and the highroad from Gartok to Simla. The latter is open for trade between India and Tibet, and Totling is consequently an important place, and its authorities are wont to exercise control over travellers. I had a premonition that this place might be a stone of stumbling to us, and the conduct of the only three monks we had seen promised nothing good. It seemed as though the lay and clerical inhabitants of the village had received orders not to show themselves to us. The authorities would wait to see what we on our part meditated doing. The three monks were only spies who wished to find out what we looked like at a little distance.

The caravan pitched camp 471 at the foot of the terrace on the river-bank. I remained above with my satellites and my sketch-book. After looking about in vain for a suitable guide, we passed through two gates into an open irregular court faced by several temple buildings and dwelling-houses. It was no use to be nice about our seats on this ground bestrewn with dirt and sweepings. I had to sit somewhere in order to draw a portal with a projecting balcony supported by pillars and adorned with painted figures in many colours. Monks, novices, and lay attendants peeped through windows and loopholes and crawled one after another from their dens to observe more closely this impudent proceeding.

What a priesthood! So dirty, so uncivilized, and so unapproachable! Water they never thought of, though the proud Sutlej flowed just under their noses. Their bodies were covered with rags ripe for the dust-heap. The togas, once red, hung round them in dark greasy tatters, harbouring dirt and vermin. The inhabitants of Totling are as wretched and debased as those of the monastery. It was no more than I had expected of this frontier fortress of religion on the highroad in western Tibet.

They stand in a compact group, silent and motionless, and their eyes follow my pencil attentively. If I address a question to them, they do not answer; if I press them, they say they do not know; if I ask them to sell us a sheep or some *tsamba*, they shake their heads in refusal; if I ask to speak with the prior, they only laugh scornfully; and if I order them to open the doors of the temple hall, they shrug their shoulders and go away. I had never met with such unfriendly monks before except in Targyaling, Lunkar, and Dongbo. And I should like to add that such passive stand-offishness is the extreme form of unfriendliness lamas ever display. They never give way to abusive words and insults. At any rate I have never met with blackguardly treatment in Tibet.

I get up and walk to the *labrang*, a large house of several storeys. Its windows and balconies are like those of Tashi-lunpo and, like them, are partially hidden under black curtains with horizontal white stripes. An Indian trader, the owner of the white tent, salutes me politely.

"Have you heard whether a messenger from Gartok is waiting for me here?"

"No, Sahib; if one had come, I should certainly have heard."

"Have you any edibles to sell?"

"No, Sahib; but if you like to buy a hundred cigarettes, the last I have, you are welcome to them."

I was glad to do so, for my tobacco was at an end.

I had just finished the outlines of the façade, sketched in two balconies and was engaged at a third, when a servant came out of the door, walked straight up to me, and said:

"Come with me up into the *labrang*."

"Certainly. Does the Kanpo Lama wish to speak to me?"

"No, the prior is not at home; he has been living for some days in a tent outside the monastery."

"Who is it, then, who wishes to see me?"

"The Changtsö."

We now learn that this potentate is a kind of superintendent of the secular and business affairs of the monastery, and has his office up a staircase in the *labrang*.

I left off drawing, and with my men followed the messenger up the stairs and through a dark passage to a small long room with a paper window looking out into the monastery court.

Here sits His Excellency, the Changtsö, on a divan behind a red lacquered table and a brass-bound box. He sits like a stern inflexible judge, and seems to be waiting until the criminal is brought before him. I think I see him now; his portrait is indelibly impressed on my memory. I feel that I am smiling at this ridiculous figure, this fat, sleek, and wrathful spirit-king in human form, who sits before me so arrogant and so puffed up like a bull-frog, ready to keep off any demons or Europeans from the sacred halls of Totling by his grim and awful countenance.

The substratum of the Changtsö was concealed by the table and chest, and the rest of his sleek body shone with fat and grease. He had a violet vest drawn over his shoulders, which left a pair of fat arms exposed; a Chinese skull-cap surmounted his bullet-shaped head. His brows were knitted in deep wrinkles, and beneath his forelock his eyes flashed with ire. His nose was as round as a potato, and his lips were fleshy—what juicy curses could pour out of them! His cheeks were as full as those of a trumpeting angel, and beautified by thin grey whiskers, which had an indescribably comical effect in a country of beardless men. Yes, there he sat, the Changtsö, and I stood before him in Tibetan costume, but with folders on my nose, and felt at the moment farther from India than on the day I set out from Tokchen.

"Aha, you old scoundrel!" I thought to myself; "you may make a show of your power and authority for a time, but you will have to knuckle down in the end. You do not bend your head, you give me no word of greeting, you do not invite me to take a seat on the ragged cushion in the window. All right; I will sit down for all that, for I, too, can be bumptious when necessary, and it is no use your trying to cow me with your greyish-brown, red-rimmed, rolling eyes."

Lobsang and Kutus, who at my orders sat themselves down at the door, felt very small in the presence of this churl. But I felt inclined for sport and had no intention of suppressing my feelings. Look out, Changtsö! Tibet is all behind me, and I have only a few days' journey more to the Indian frontier. Try to scare me back to Gartok, if you can. By the earrings of Sakya-toba, you shall not succeed.

The spirit-king began his interrogation. I had expected a voice which would roll like thunder through the small chamber, but he spoke in a low tone without expression, which made him still more forbidding.

"Where do you come from?"

"From Chang-tang, from Tashi-lunpo, from the *labrang* of the Tashi Lama, from Tashi-gompa, from Tso-mavang"; and I came out with a whole string of names which I gabbled like a lesson learned by heart.

"I know it. You have been with the Tashi Lama, you have sailed your boat on Tso-mavang, and you have been turned out by an order from Lhasa, and have to leave Tibet by the great highroad to Ladak. I know everything."

"Then questions are unnecessary."

"I wish also to know why you have returned to Tibet,

which is closed to Europeans, and I want to know what you are doing here, in Totling."

"You wish to know this and to know that, and I intend to travel all about Tibet. No one has been able to stop me yet from wandering where I would. You may try it, but you will suffer for it."

"Have you a passport from Lhasa?"

"No."

"Then you have no right to show yourself in Totling."

"No, none. And for that very reason it is incumbent on me to leave the country by the shortest way to India."

"We will see about that. First of all I will take down some notes. What is your name?"

"Sven Hedin."

"That I know."

"Then why do you ask me?"

"To check my information. It is my duty to know what kind of people pass through Totling, especially when they are travelling without passports. What is the name of your country?"

"Svidingvé."

"Right! How many men and baggage animals have you?"

"Six men and ten baggage animals."

"That agrees. I shall send this very day a report about you to Lhasa. Why have you just drawn the temple gate and the *labrang*?"

"To take the drawings with me as a remembrance of Totling, and to show my countrymen what things are like here."

"No one is privileged to draw anything here. I have no mind to lose my head on your account. You have sketched Dongbo, Daba, and Mangnang also. The monks who permitted such things will be punished."

"You will perhaps leave Tugden Nima alone?"

"Show me your drawings."

"With pleasure!" I answered, handing him the case in which I had only two loose sheets, that a shower of rain might not spoil all. He took out a sheet and asked:

"What does this represent?"

"The temple portal out there."

"This is not a temple portal."

"No, certainly not, when it is held upside down."

"I shall keep your drawings."

"Then you are a thief."

"It is you who act as a thief when you go about drawing without permission. However, you may have the temple portal, but I shall keep the *labrang*."

"Listen to me, Changtsö; you had better be civil. Beware of the Tashi Lama; he is my friend, and I may complain of you to him. You are a Gelugpa, so take care!"

"It is true that I am a Gelugpa, but in secular affairs I obey no one but the Dalai Lama and the Devashung. I have nothing to do with the Tashi Lama."

"I have come here to inspect the temple halls of Totling. Be so good as to order all the doors to be opened."

"Ha, ha, ha! A European in the temple halls of Totling! No, never!"

He lent back on his divan and laughed and snarled and laughed in his cold room like an old tom-cat. But he had thawed a little, and the thunder-cloud on his brow had passed off.

"Can you sell us provisions, Changtsö? I pay well."

"So I have heard from Daba. I will inquire; you shall have an answer to-morrow. Your caravan is no doubt well armed?"

"We have a gun and two revolvers."

"Can I see your weapons?"

Kutus was sent off at once to fetch our arsenal. The Changtsö became still more friendly; he balanced the small revolver in his hand, and said in a questioning tone:

"I should like to buy this."

"It is not for sale."

"Oh, surely; tell me how much you want for it; I can pay you."

"But I do not want money. Let me see the temple and you shall have the revolver as a present."

"No, that will not do," and he gave me back the revolver.

"Very well, if you can do without the revolver, I can dispense with the temple. If the inside is not better kept up than the outside the loss is not great."

Now I had had enough of the Changtsö. I rose and departed after a polite leave-taking on both sides. A heavy shower of rain pattered down on us as we walked down to the tents. The sprouting barley-fields got a good drenching; yellow rivulets streamed down from the terraces and emptied their muddy water into the Sutlej. The road we had just traversed became impassable in a moment, and it was lucky that we were just descending the slope.

When the day was declining I sat in my tent, looked over the great river, and listened to the patter of the rain on the gravel of the bank. Suddenly the neigh of a horse was heard. A stranger appeared at the tent door. Aha! Mohanlal, the Hindu doctor, whose acquaintance I had made the year before in Gartok. Abdul Kerim had, then, duly delivered my letter to Thakur Jai Chand, and he had kindly sent Mohanlal with all the necessaries I had asked for, and two books as well. It was August 13. Since October 1907 I had heard no echo of the outer world. The good Mohanlal was certainly not well posted up in the events of the great world beyond the mountains and seas, but it was a great pleasure to hear all he knew. He gave me a very acceptable account of the remaining thirty days' marches to Simla, with distances in English miles. Twenty days earlier we had left Tokchen with the feeling that we should soon be home. And now we had a whole month more.

We smoked cigarettes, drank tea, ate supper, and talked till midnight. Mohanlal was really entertaining. Among other items he told me a tragi-comical incident which had taken place in Gartok.

One of Thakur Jai Chand's friends on the south side of the Himalayas had sent by a mounted messenger a request for a loan of a thousand rupees. The money was counted out and sewed up in a double bag, which the messenger tied with his knapsack and clothes behind his saddle. He set out on August 2, escorted by two servants of Thakur Jai Chand, who were to show him the ford through the

116. The Bridge of Totling.

much-swollen Gartong. The river was divided into three arms, two of which were easily forded. Therefore the messenger, apparently a thoughtless youth, sent the men back and proceeded to cross the third arm, wading through the water alone. The left bank was high, and when the horse made ready to jump up out of the water, which was 3 feet deep, the saddle got loose and slipped down into the stream with everything on it. The poor man began at once to fish, and fished the whole day and all the next, and for four days grubbed about in the mud in spite of the rapid current. On the fifth day he found the saddle, the garments, and the knapsack, but not the money-bag. When Mohanlal rode past the spot the incautious and unfortunate wight was quite in despair, and was still waiting on the bank until the river should fall after the rainy season and give up its booty.

The once noted Tsaparang, which stands on the left bank of the Sutlej, just below Totling, is now even more decayed than the monastery village. A *dzong* is said to administer justice in Tsaparang, but only during two winter months, and for the rest of the year it is removed to another village. Only sixteen men live in the place, and grow barley. The background consists of the high yellow löss terraces with their fantastically modelled forms. Below the village the Sutlej sings a ballad of a king who three hundred years ago brandished his sceptre over the valley and defended his kingdom with horsemen and lances.

CHAPTER XXV

THE FIRST JESUIT IN TIBET

AN unpretentious little book lies open in front of me during the hours I devote to my own recollections of Totling and Tsaparang, and I can hardly keep my eyes away from it. The book has only thirty-one pages, and yet I had to pay eighty gulden for it in a Dutch old-book shop. The pompous title, *Novo Descobrimento do Gram Cathayo, ou Reinos de Tibet, pello Padre Antonio de Andrade da Companhia de Iesu, Portuguez, no anno de 1624. Com todas as licenças necessarias. Em Lisboa, por Mattheus Pinheiro, Anno de 1626*, is out of proportion to its contents and size.

Do not suppose that I bought it to read. Its contents are translated into other tongues, which are more easily understood by readers of Germanic race. But I wished to have the original report in my fairly complete collection of Tibetan literature; I wished to turn over the leaves and to gaze on these faded reddish leaves; I would inhale the atmosphere around these remarkable lines, and piously stroke my fingers over the fine dust which adheres to the paper after a lapse of nearly three hundred years.

There is something peculiar about old books. For my part I regard them with the deepest reverence. They are like voices speaking from past centuries. Searching eyes, which have scanned the printed lines, have long been closed for ever, but the books still live. This *Novo Descobrimento* still utters the same words and speaks in the same language as in the days when King Gustavus Adolphus reigned over Sweden. I regard this book with the feeling expressed in the classical words of Tegnér: "What do I care for living duffers when I have the heroes of humanity in my bookcase?" I love it because Antonio de Andrade is the author, and because it was printed when the famous Jesuit still lived and sojourned in Tibet; yes, it passed through the press in Lisbon in the year when he laid the foundation stone of a Christian church in Tsaparang, where we have hastily examined the miserable huts down by the Sutlej river. What does it profit that Odorico de Pordenone was the first European to visit Tibet? His recollections are far too scanty and indistinct. Padre Antonio is the first who brought to the world reliable information from that country. He is the first European who crossed the Himalayas and penetrated into Tibet from the south, and also the first who followed the Ganges of Vishnu to its source. He stands like a milestone on the highroad of the centuries, a boundary cliff in the stream of time, and he marks the point from which the history of Tibetan exploration really begins. I myself am for the present, perhaps, the last in the sequence. At any rate I have heard of no successor in the regions which I have revealed. Only in Tsaparang, that old town so closely associated with Antonio's name, do our routes touch, though there was an interval of three centuries between us. It is no wonder that I regard the faded book with peculiar tenderness and devoutly repeat its last words, "Laus Deo!"

Antonio de Andrade was born in the year 1580 at Oleiros in Portugal. At sixteen he entered the Order of Jesuits, and was sent in 1600 to Goa on the west coast of India. There for some years he took an active part in the work of the Order, and there one day a vague report reached his ears that there were Christians among the peoples of Tibet. C. Wessels says of these reports that they had their origin "in a superficial resemblance of some of the ceremonies of the Buddhist church to those of the Catholic." Andrade declared himself that he undertook his journey only for the glory of God, and that the Portuguese had long wished for an opportunity of *discovering* Tibet.

Antonio had sojourned a quarter of a century in Goa

when he found an opportunity, in 1624, of travelling to the snowy mountains in the north. Accompanied by Father Manuel Marques and two Christian servants, he left Agra on March 30, and at Delhi joined a caravan of Hindu pilgrims, who intended to make a pilgrimage to the holy places on the upper Ganges. The route probably ran past Hardwar, "the Gate of Vishnu," through countries subject to the Raja of Srinagar, and never before seen by a white man. The party marched over slippery rocks and under the dense leafy vaults of forests. In the depths below roared the Ganges. The bold Portuguese shrank from no danger, and when he was suspected of espionage in Srinagar and imprisoned, he succeeded by his calmness and prudence in regaining his liberty.

His journey took him to still higher regions along the banks of the Vishnu-Ganga, along the same route which Webb and Raper followed 180 years later, quite ignorant that the Portuguese had been there before them. In his excellent account of his journey Raper does not say a word about Andrade, but he confirms the accurate observations Andrade had made. C. Wessels has compared the two travellers in a meritorious study lately published in *De Studien, Tijdschrift voor godsdienstwetenschap en letteren*, vol. 77 (1912), No. 4, under the title, "Antonio de Andrade, S.J. Een ontdekkingsreziger in de Himalaya en in Tibet (1624-1630)." His essay is the best we have on the old Jesuits. Wessels has eradicated many errors which have made the round of descriptions of Tibet. The absurd notion that Andrade travelled through Kashmir and on his way discovered Manasarowar, the Tso-mavang of the Tibetans, was not the least of such mistakes. Andrade's Srinagar is not the capital of Kashmir, but the town of the same name on the Alaknanda. As to the lake which he discovered, and has been mistaken for Manasarowar, we shall return to that presently.

The missionaries continued their journey and reached Badrinath, where one of the holiest shrines of the Hindus in this part of the Himalayas attracted crowds of pilgrims. At a later time Webb and Raper advanced as far as the village Mana on the Saraswati, the upper course of the

Vishnu-Ganga. But Andrade went on further, undismayed, up to the eternal snows and to quite unknown Tibet. On this road he approached the highest crest of the Himalayas. The sufferings and privations of the little party became here intense. Marques had remained behind, and Andrade had with him only the two Christians and a guide from Mana. He is very reticent in his little book. The geography of the country no longer attracts his attention; he is exclusively occupied with his struggle for victory, and tells of the scanty food, the parched barley-meal steeped in water, which the travellers subsisted on, and how they were inconvenienced by the poisonous gases which rose from the ground.

On the third day they were overtaken by three men from Mana who depicted in startling colours all the dangers, including death, they would have to encounter if they continued on the way to the pass. Andrade and his two servants were not deterred by fears, but the guide returned with the messengers. The way up to the pass became worse and worse. They floundered up to the knee in snow, and sometimes they sank to the chest or the armpits; they often hitched themselves along over the crust with the movements of a swimmer, so that they might not be suffocated in the loose snow. At night a mantle was laid over the snow and the three men lay upon it, covering themselves with the other two mantles. Sometimes snow fell in such quantities that they had to get up and shake it off the mantles lest they should be buried alive. The snow blinded their eyes, their hands and feet were numbed with cold, and yet Andrade went on. And at last we read in his little book, *Novo Descobrimento*, the following pregnant words which for three hundred years have been misunderstood and falsely interpreted: "Nesta forma fomos caminhando atê o alto de todas as serras, onde nasce o Rio Ganga de hum grande tanque, & do mesmo nasce tamben outra, que rega as terras do Tibet." That is, he continued his march "as far as the highest point of the rocks where the Ganges rises in a large pool, in which pool also another river has its source, which irrigates the lands of Tibet."

Note that he speaks of a "tanque," not of a "lago." He means, as C. Wessels has clearly shown, the glacier pool Deb-tal, 400 yards long, which lies at the top of the Mana pass, and from which springs the Saraswati, the stream that flows to the Ganges. The other river which runs northwards and irrigates the lands of Tibet is, of course, a brook, which rises on the pass or in its immediate neighbourhood and enters the Sutlej near Totling. The discoverer Andrade was, then, quite right, and it is not his fault that Markham and others have misunderstood him, and ascribed to him the discovery of Manasarowar. Holdich seeks to detract from his fame, saying that he is only a doubtful authority. It is singular how easily the geographers of our time can make negative discoveries in countries where they have never set a foot. Without contributing a single positive item to our real knowledge, they content themselves with pulling down what others have built up. Wessels has done a good deed in breaking a lance for the honour of Andrade, and he now, after three centuries, secures full justice for the heroic exploits of the Portuguese, when the voice of the Jesuit has long been silent, while his little book still preserves the truth between its cracked boards.

But Andrade was misunderstood centuries ago. In his noted work *China Illustrata* (Amsterdam, 1670) the learned Jesuit father, Athanasius Kircher, collected some remarkable tales about Andrade's journey. Andrade was, Kircher remarks, fortunate in making several striking discoveries in Tibet, among others the sources of the Ganges and the Indus. This was communicated to Kircher by a baptized Hindu, named Joseph, who had accompanied Father Andrade on all his travels and at the age of eighty-six was staying in Rome. Father Henrik Roth, also, told Kircher in Rome all he knew about the Portuguese missionary.

Let us hear what Kircher has to say:

> On the highest mountains of Tibet, covered with eternal snow, there is a large lake in which rise the greatest rivers of India; for from this sheet of water issue the Indus, the Ganges, the Ravi, and the Atenh. The Ganges flows to a chasm where its cascade makes

a terrific roar, and then after irrigating a lovely valley it rolls on to the sea into which it pours. As to the Indus and the other rivers, they stream slowly along the mountains as we see on the map.

At another place in his book Kircher says of Father Antonio that from Tsaparang he crossed "a high mountain on the top of which is a large lake, which, from what he says about it and from what he could see, is the source of the Indus, the Ganges, and the other large rivers of India."

It would take us too far if we were to enter here upon a discussion of this interesting problem. Suffice it to say that I cannot share Wessels' opinion, but believe that Kircher really meant Manasarowar, of which Joseph and Roth had gleaned reports. Kircher afterwards mixed together in his own storeroom the communications of these two and Andrade's own narrative, which, indeed, contains not a single word indicating that he had the slightest knowledge of that lake. It is inconceivable that he could have lived for years on the banks of the Sutlej and yet not know whence the river came. It is enough that he says nothing about it.

But Kircher goes much further. He makes Father Andrade continue his journey from the enigmatical lake through Rudok and the lands of the Tanguts and Tatars to China. He makes him travel in two months all through Asia! The title of the little book lying on the table before me is doubtless to blame for Father Kircher's mistake, *Novo Descobrimento do Gram Cathayo* . . . for "Gram Cathayo" is the "Great China." Curiously enough the learned orientalist, J. Klaproth, has calmly accepted this statement, for he writes quite confidently:

> In the year 1624 the Portuguese Jesuit Antonio de Andrade undertook a journey from Tibet to China. He set out from the realm of the Great Mogul, took the road through Garhwal, crossed Tibet and came safely to China.

But I am forgetting! We have left the good Father and his two Christians on the Mana pass. From the top he looked forth, as he expresses himself, over the kingdom of Tibet. All was white there, covered with deep snow. Their snow-blinded eyes could detect no road.

The two servants were tired to death and were obliged to turn back. Andrade took pity on them and accompanied them lest they should perish in the snow. After three days they fortunately met scouts of Bothia, who had been sent out from Mana, and after three more days' march they pitched their camp in a cave, where Marques, who brought provisions, joined the party again. Then they rested a month while the summer sun melted the snow. Then the missionaries marched up again with better success, crossed the pass, and were soon after received by envoys from the king of Tsaparang. In the early days of August 1624 they reached the "Cidade Real," the royal city, below Totling, where now only sixteen inhabitants dwell in dilapidated huts.

The king and the queen overwhelmed Father Antonio with tokens of hospitality, and he enjoyed greater freedom than any of the travellers who, during nearly three centuries, have followed in his footsteps and have set out for adventures in Tibet. He remained, nevertheless, only a month in Tsaparang, about which town he has nothing to say but that it lies on a river. At the beginning of November we find him again in Agra, and there he wrote the little book which I have told about, and which is dated November 8, 1624.

In the following year he set out on his second journey to Tsaparang, and during the next twenty-five years about eighteen missionaries followed his example. In 1642 Marques stayed at Tsaparang, and Cacella died in 1630 in Shigatse; six years later Alano dos Anjos died in Tibet. C. Wessels has promised us an essay on his fortunes, of which only a faint echo has come down to our times.

How long Andrade stayed on his second visit to Tsaparang is not known. He reached the town on August 28, 1625. On April 11, 1626, he laid the foundation stone of the first Christian church in Tibet. The narrative of his second journey is dated August 15 in Tsaparang. He was still there in September 1627, as appears from his letters. But in the year 1630 he was staying in Goa, and the year after he despatched four missionaries to Tsaparang. At the beginning of the year

1634 he made ready for a third journey, with six companions, to the snowy country in the north, but on March 19 he was removed by death and was buried at Goa. It is believed that he died of poison.

Two hundred years passed by before a European came again to Tsaparang. Kircher and D'Anville had inserted the town on their maps and in later times English travellers had heard it spoken of. In the year 1855 Tsaparang was visited by Adolph Schlagintweit who found at this famous place fifteen houses.

Now I take from my bookshelf another small volume as old and discoloured as the first. It contains the description of Andrade's experiences on his journeys and is, as mentioned, dated August 15, 1626. It was printed in Paris in 1629, and its title is *Histoire de ce qui est passé au Royaume du Tibet*. At that time Lhasa had not attained its present renown, Hundes stood for Tibet, and Tsaparang was the largest town in the country.

My affection for this book is not less than that I cherish for Andrade's first book. Perhaps even greater, for I can read it easily. Here Andrade mentions that he, very different from myself, received a passport from the Great Mogul to the "little kings in the mountains," and his journey was easier than the former. In Tsaparang a house was placed at his disposal close to the palace in which the king's son resided.

The little book is full of amusing descriptions of the lama monks of Tibet, their manners and customs, their religious views, and their useless exchange of opinions and disputes with the steadfast Father.

> When they prepare for worship (he relates) they blow trumpets of metal; but trumpets are also made of leg and arm bones of dead men, and they also make use of rosaries with beads made from dead men's skulls; and when I asked the reason of this, the lama, who is the king's brother, answered that they used such trumpets in order that the people might remember the dead when they heard the blare, and that they often drank out of skulls that they might retain a lively remembrance of death.

One day when attending a festival, Andrade expressed to the brother of the king his astonishment that the lamas danced and said that "our priests were so earnest and dignified that they would not for all the world be seen in such an indecent act and one so unworthy of the profession to which they were consecrated." "Do not be surprised," returned the lama, "for in this performance the young lamas represent angels"; and he added that just as we (Europeans) depict our angels singing and playing on musical instruments, so they (Lamaists) represented angels—that they danced was only a minor detail—and he said that he had seen a small picture of the birth of Christ in which several angels were depicted, who in their joy at the birth of the Redeemer sang and played on musical instruments.

Father Antonio had a sharp eye for all that related to religion, and forgot to tell future generations about the mysterious country which lifted its lofty snowy peaks around him, and about the great river which he saw rolling its waters down the valley with a thundering roar. Only the following lines contain some slight reference to a temple festival in Totling-gompa:

> Not long ago I went off to a town which lies about half a day's journey from Tsaparang. I accompanied the King who wished to visit his mother, the Queen, who had undertaken a pilgrimage to this place, where there are several temples and five hundred lamas. As crowds of people flocked on this day from all sides to the place, their number amounted to two thousand. When we arrived, we found those on whom the King would wait drawn up in perfect order, two and two like our priests in a procession; and they extended over a considerable length of road, singing after their fashion, and the more important persons carrying various banners in their hands. When the King caught sight of them, he at once dismounted from his horse, and standing on a long silken carpet, laid down for him by the lamas, made three genuflexions to the whole assembly, lowering his head and hands to the ground. Then the whole company made six similar obeisances to the King. This shows what great respect this prince shows to the lamas when they appear before him as a body corporate, whereas when he meets them singly he does not salute them at all, except, of course, their superior, who now happens to be the King's brother.

He speaks of the great friendship of the good King to the Jesuits, and of his reverence for the only true church, which he regarded with much greater affection than the religion of his own country. On one excursion the King showed much greater honour to Father Andrade than to his guest, the king of Ladak, "ruler of a neighbouring kingdom." When they came near the town and the people streamed out to see the spectacle, the King again dismounted and took his seat on a carpet, placing his son on his left side and Father Andrade on his right. When the missionary modestly declined to sit down while the Queen and all the others were standing, the King said: "You are a priest and our father, are you not?" All this, besides the supposed desire of the King for baptism and Christianity, makes us suspect a pious fraud on the part of the missionary who wanted money from home to enable him to continue his work. And the two superior lamas may be excused for reproaching the King because he had been induced in six months to turn his back on the faith of his fathers and adopt another. But Andrade characterized their conduct as "tricks of the devil," prayed and fasted in order to gain the soul of the King, and arranged a disputation with the Buddhist priests in the illustrious presence of His Majesty. On this occasion he decoyed them into slippery places. They had no answers to give, tried to shirk the question, and scoffed at the Jesuits.

Another time (relates Andrade) I asked a lama in the presence of the King what means of salvation a sinner could use to be restored to the grace of God, and he replied that it was sufficient to utter the words *Om ma'ny patmeonry* (*Om mani padme hum*), which is equivalent to saying: however much I have sinned, I shall still get to heaven. If that is true, I retorted, take a dagger and stab a man to the heart, rob the King of the pearls he wears, insult us with the most extravagant abuse, and then say simply *Om ma'ny patmeonry*, and you are at once absolved and purified from all sins. Do you think that is reasonable?

The Father assured the lama that in spite of all his fine talk he would, without good works, be condemned to the fires of hell. Then the King turned to those present and mocked the lama so severely that Andrade had to beg him not to let it be known that he, the Jesuit, had imparted to him the knowledge he possessed. Then Andrade asked the Tibetan monks what the formula, which they had always on their lips in season and out of season, precisely meant; and none of them could answer. Then said Andrade, "As you patter these words like parrots which do not understand what they say, know that *Om ma'ny patmeonry* signifies Lord, forgive me my sins." And from that hour all the monks assigned this meaning to the mysterious words.

The good Jesuit continues:

> They show the greatest reverence to our sacred images, and our church is quite full of such. Thither the people of rank resort, worship and throw themselves on the ground, for they are accustomed to adore holy images in this fashion. They are always asking us to hold the holy book (so they call the missal) over their heads, for thereby we shall receive strength to unfold to them the mysteries of the Gospel. When the King was in our church not long ago with a large retinue, I had to explain to him what the Christ crucified, the figure in front of us, meant, and it was a strange sight to see him turn to those present and say: "Here you see that it is true that the Son of God is a living book, very different from that which the lamas read, which is not God and cannot be God." . . . Some natives from the town of Utsang (Lhasa), where there are many churches, have told me that they have seen in them many sacred images similar to our own. Who can doubt that it is the will of Heaven that they shall soon be drawn to the worship of the true God?

Once the lama, the brother of the King, came to Andrade's church and gave him seven copper bowls, saying that water should be offered in them daily to the God of the Christians. "So they do themselves, and they believe that it is also the custom with us." The chalice especially excited his interest, and he begged to be allowed to witness the ceremonies at Andrade's service.

> After the lama had seen everything, he told me that the Grand Lama in Utsang (the Dalai Lama) offers small quantities of bread and wine, that he eats and drinks of them himself and distributes the remainder to the other lamas, and that he blows and breathes with his mouth over the wine he presents to God, which he alone and no one else may do. And he added that this Grand Lama wears on his head a tiara like mine but much larger.

Father Antonio de Andrade entertains greater hopes

of being able to convert the Tibetans than Father Gerbillon, who says of the Mongolian Lamaists:

> I believe that they would become ardent Christians, if they accepted the true religion; but, as it is, they are, to tell the truth, so obstinately rooted by the lamas in their false doctrines that there is little hope of converting them to the faith.

With regard to Father Andrade's vain search for traces of an old Christianity in south-western Tibet, Ritter, in *Asien* (vol. ii. p. 447), expresses the opinion that the reports which the Catholic missionaries heard in India, as has so often been the case, mixed up the ceremonies of the Lama cultus with those of the Catholic church.

In taking leave of Andrade and his naïve but interesting communications, we are naturally confronted with the question to which Ritter alludes in the words above.

CHAPTER XXVI

LAMAISM AND CATHOLICISM

How little I thought during the memorable days I spent in Tashi-lunpo that the observations I made at the New Year's festival and noted down would two years later call forth protests and disapproval from many sides in Central Europe! I ventured in the first volume of this book to dwell on the many points of similarity between the external forms of Lamaism and Catholicism. I did not allow myself to be influenced by any preconceived opinions, but relied simply and solely on my own judgment. My own impression was strong and clear, but I only touched on it lightly in describing my days in the cloister court of the Tashi Lama. I called the *labrang* the Vatican, and the Tashi Lama, Pope, and said that, like the Pope in Rome, he was a prisoner in the Tibetan Vatican. I remarked on the monastic and cloister life, on the processions and the funeral rites, and saw in the gifts of hard cash, which the pilgrims have to present to the clergy, a counterpart to the Peter's pence of Rome.

It would have been vulgar and reprehensible if I had intended thereby to irritate the Catholics from sheer wantonness. It would have been stupid and unseemly, for I have so many sincere friends among the Catholics and so many ineffaceable memories of their domestic hearths. Had I not been the guest of Catholic missionaries under the palms of Baghdad, the city of the *Thousand-and-One Nights*, and in the imperial city of Calcutta? Had I not sat at the table of their brethren in Lian-chu-fu and Pekin, and had I not returned home with an extraordinary admiration for all I had seen among the amiable learned Jesuits in Hongkong and Sikawei? I was received as a welcome guest by them all, and all gave me valuable information about the districts to which they were voluntarily banished, and in which they worked. Why should I have any intention of wounding them in their most sacred feelings, and offending the immense hosts that stood behind them?

The gigantic work that Catholic missions have accomplished for centuries in purely geographical investigations throughout Asia is worthy of the greatest admiration. They have opened roads into the heart of the largest continent of the world. As far back as the Middle Ages the Franciscan monks Piano Carpini and Wilhelm Rubruquis brought to the West the first news of the boundless empire of Mangu Can. No words of praise are extravagant for the Jesuits who executed a topographical survey of the whole Chinese Empire in the time of the immortal Kang Hi. The oldest explorers after the monk Odorico were Jesuits, namely, Andrade, Grueber, Dorville, and Desideri. Capuchins dwelt for several decades in Lhasa, and were instrumental in opening a connection between the Land of Snow and the world of white men. Huc and Gabet were Lazarists; one cannot think of Tibet without calling to mind Huc, the incomparable Abbé Huc, overflowing with kindness of heart, cheerfulness, and wit.

My quite innocent utterances have aroused among several Catholic organs of the press a displeasure which is unmistakably betrayed in strong language. It was said that I was guilty of gross shamelessness, and had committed an indecency "in comparing Catholicism with the darkest heathenism and idolatry." Two ultramontane newspapers declared in indignant terms that my comparison of the two religions was an exhibition of stupidity, ignorance, and bad manners. But their passion was quite misplaced and unnecessary, for I never made the slightest attempt to gainsay their characteristics. Some Catholic priests in southern Germany and Poland honoured me with letters in which they complained that I had sadly shocked their religious feelings. Should a new edition of *Trans-Himalaya* be published the unfortunate passages must be struck out, for they gave a thoroughly false impression of Catholicism.

And yet it had never been my intention to support in the slightest degree the movement called "away from Rome." A small storm raged over my quiet study and made a vain attempt to disturb me in my tranquil work. I seemed to see grim cloister brothers and reverend prelates pointing the finger at me and denouncing me as an arch-heretic. Catholic bells sounded in my ears, I perceived an aroma of incense, heard the mass being sung, and saw monks and nuns walking in procession to the church festivals. And all this grand attractive church pomp I had compared to Lamaism! I had committed a misdemeanour, and it almost seemed as if I were making a pilgrimage to do penance, to confess and promise amendment, when I travelled to Rome, sauntered under the dome of St. Peter's, and waited upon the good old venerable Pius X.

Then I had neither time nor inclination nor means of answering these attacks. Since then two years have elapsed, and during this time I have studied old and new sources for a history of journeys of discovery in Tibet. Without looking for them I have come across several accounts of Lamaism, and I am armed to the teeth now that I take the field, not to cause annoyance to Catholics, but to prove that I was quite right when I spoke of the similarity of the outward forms of Lamaism and Catholicism.

The subject is not a new one. It is as old as the Bohemian forest. The monks of the Middle Ages noticed the striking similarity, and were astonished at it. Many Catholic missionaries have remarked on it in plain words without being attacked on that account by their brethren in the faith. Often the statements are unreliable and amplified with a wealth of detail that raises suspicion. Some authors have drawn on the experiences of others without referring to their sources. Often also mistakes have been made by great authorities. Thus, for example,

Professor Kuchner, in his brilliant work on Tibet, *Opisanie Tibeta* (Vladivostok, 1907), asserts that Rubruquis, who travelled in 1253, "gives in many places information about Lamaism, and points out many curious points of resemblance between the rites of this religion and the Catholic divine service." In W. W. Rockhill's excellent translation of *The Journey of William of Rubruck to the Eastern Parts of the World, 1253–55* (London, 1900), not a single word on this subject is to be found on pp. 199 and 232, and the word Lamaism does not occur. Rubruquis speaks on one occasion of a "priest from China," and on another of a reincarnation, and Rockhill supposes that he meant thereby priests from Tibet. On the other hand, the Franciscan frequently mentions Nestorian Christians whom he met on the way, and who had had numerous congregations in the countries north and east of Tibet for 600 years before his time.

Recently an interesting inquiry by Richard Garbe with the title, "Has the Development of Buddhism been influenced by Christianity?" has appeared in *Deutsche Rundschau* (No. 14, April 15, 1912, p. 89 *et seq.*), edited by Julius Rodenberg. Before we proceed further it may be instructive to give a hasty glance at its contents.

In the middle of the third century B.C. Buddhism spread over north-western India, and there was developed and flourished till the eighth century the school which differentiated the northern Buddhism from the southern, and is known by the name of Mahayana or the "Great Ship." In this modification of the original dogmas some investigators see the effect of Christian influence. One of them, the Jesuit father Joseph Dahlmann, against whom Garbe's criticism is chiefly directed, has lately gone so far as to ascribe the victorious progress of Buddhism over half Asia and a third part of the human race, not to its own strength, but to the Christian thoughts and ideas which it had adopted in north-western India. Dahlmann therefore maintains that this disguised form of Christianity explains the immense extension of the new religion.

In the Catholic press Dahlmann's supposed discovery

was hailed with delight, nay, often with enthusiasm. At last a sagacious investigator "had made an end of the humbug of Buddhism."

Relying on the best authorities to be had, on Grünwedel, M. A. Stein, etc., Garbe examines the demonstration of Dahlmann in the smallest details, and blows it bit by bit into the air. It would carry us too far were we to enter deeply into this matter. Suffice it to say that chronological impossibilities confront the Father. Garbe proves with irreproachable perspicuity that the Mahayana Buddhism has made its triumphant progress through the east Asiatic world owing to its own vigour. On the other hand, he is disposed to answer in the affirmative the question whether Christianity has left in later times traces in northern Buddhism.

Padma Sambhava in the middle of the eighth century instituted Tibetan Lamaism, which thrust out the indigenous Shamanism. The founder of Lamaism was, however, shrewd enough to incorporate various dogmas and customs of the Shamans in his form of Buddhism, which was already mixed with Sivaist elements.

Christian influence first becomes possible in the year 635, when the Nestorians began to send missionaries into those regions. And it was after this time that the belief in an almighty, omniscient, primordial Buddha arose in Tibet and Nepal—a monotheistic deviation from the original atheistic Buddhism. Garbe thinks it not unlikely that this almighty god may have been borrowed from the Nestorians. With much greater confidence he insists on the influence of Christianity on the later development of the Lamaist cult, "which has been even styled a caricature of the Catholic cult."

Among other striking similarities Garbe cites the fact from Waddell that high lamas cross themselves before the commencement of a religious rite. They also hold a ceremony which has a remarkable resemblance to the Eucharist. Bread and wine are distributed to the worshippers. The bread consists perhaps of small butter puffs, and the wine is perhaps a kind of beer called "chang." But whoever partakes of it is long-lived. Garbe says:

Strictly Catholic, too, seems to us a fundamental idea of Lamaism that the priests have in their possession the keys of heaven and hell, for they have invented the universally received maxim: "Without a lama before one, one cannot approach God."

Garbe asks in conclusion whether the similarities between the Catholic and Lamaist cults may be explained by the assumption that the minds of men, when they move along the same lines of feeling and thought, also tend towards the same outward forms. "But," he answers, "the concordances are so numerous and close that we cannot escape from the assumption that borrowing has taken place." It is of course certain that Catholicism has stamped its image on Lamaism, and not *vice versa.* And just as evident is it that the two religions have in essential matters developed quite independently of each other.

After this introduction I will proceed to cite some older expressions of opinion. In a German collection of various narratives of travel with the title *Allgemeine Historie der Reisen zu Wasser und zu Lande; oder Sammlung aller Reisebeschreibungen*, etc. (Leipzig, 1750), there is in vol. vii. p. 212 a whole section with the promising superscription, "The Religion of Tibet and its astonishing Agreement with the Romish." Herein it is said somewhat scoffingly that the missionaries who visited Tibet—that is, Grueber, Desideri, Della Penna, and others—"did little more than notice the similarity between the religion of Tibet and their own." Some missionaries explain this agreement by the supposition that Christianity was perhaps preached in Tibet in the time of the Apostles. If other missionaries are to be believed, this agreement is very close, "and involves almost all the doctrines and ceremonies of the Romish church." Gerbillon mentions the following ceremonies:

(1) Holy water; (2) singing in divine service; (3) prayers for the dead; (4) the clothing of the priests, which is such as the Apostles are represented as wearing, and the caps and capes such as bishops wear; (5) their Grand Lama is much the same to them as the Pope is to those of the Romish confession. They made the offering of the Mass with bread and wine, gave extreme unction, blessed those who wished to marry, prayed over the sick, honoured

the relics of demigods, had monks and nuns, sang in the choir like monks, observed certain annual festivals, submitted to severe penances, including flagellation, consecrated bishops and sent out missionaries, who lived in extreme poverty, and travelled barefooted through the desert to China.

According to this collection of travels the Prefect of the Capuchin mission, Orazio della Penna, is the author of the following lines:

> The religion of Tibet is in the main a copy of the Roman. They believe in a God and a trinity, but full of errors, paradise, hell, and purgatory, also full of errors. They have prayers, alms, vows, and offerings for the dead, have a large number of monasteries with monks numbering thirty thousand, who take the three vows of poverty, chastity, and obedience, and others besides. They have their confessors, who are selected by their superiors, and receive a licence from the Lama—as from a bishop—without which they cannot hear confessions. The church organisation is ordered as in the Romish church.

Régis and certain other Catholic missionaries report that they did all that was possible to prevent this similarity being known, for it would be injurious to Catholicism if it were compared with a religion which practised the grossest idolatry, and such a revelation would bring water to the Protestant mill.

When the Pope and the congregations in the 'forties of the eighteenth century refused to grant more money to the Capuchin mission in Lhasa, an appeal was made to public charity by a circular printed in Rome in the year 1742. The document represented Tibet as for the most part converted; only a few more missionaries were required to bring the work to an end. A criticism of the time dealt severely with this appeal. It was asked what doctrines were preached that the people of Tibet had so readily accepted Christianity. The Holy Scriptures or the confession of Pius VII., or the rules of the order of the Capuchins? Jesus Christ was never mentioned. On the other hand, the outward resemblance of the order of the church was insisted on. But this very similarity must be an obstacle, the critic remarks, for if the real difference was only that the lamas of Tibet had to learn the Latin

Mass in order to be Christian lamas, they would dispense with conversion. It was also cited as an advantage that the Tibetans might have only one wife. Why was nothing said of the custom of a woman having husbands by the half-dozen? The women would fight against the new teaching, and defend their rights with teeth and nails.

It was the Prefect Della Penna who worked on behalf of the Capuchin mission in Tibet. He related that he had had many a hard battle with the Lamaist monks, and had once written a long letter to the king in Lhasa in defence of Catholicism. In his reply the king extolled the advantages of his own religion and called Christianity a lower form of belief, though there was good in both.

Honour to the Capuchins in any case! They behaved themselves like men in Tibet. We have no reason to be angry with them because they or their speaking trumpet, Father Georgi, in his noted but ill-written book *Alphabetum Tibetanum* (Rome, 1762), lays the blame for the similarity of the two religions on the old Manichaeism. The heresiarch Manes is said to be responsible for all the devil's work in Tibet, but we do not hear in what wonderful way his doctrines reached that country. In one place (p. 543) Georgi expresses the following apprehension: "Antiquum hoc et portentosum connubium Manichaiae hydrae cum Paganismi monstro in Tibeto commixtae, terret me plurimum, ac nescio quid mali in posterum futurum portendere videtur Ecclesiae." (Compare also *Relazione inedita di un viaggio al Tibet del Padre Cassiano Beligatti da Macerata* [Florence, 1902, pp. 7 and 11].) It is not right, as Dr. Gutzlaff does in the *Journal of the Royal Geographical Society*, 1851, p. 226, to look for similarities between the rituals of the Capuchins and of Shamanism, and to assert that on that account the missionaries were regarded as lamas from western lands. For what has Shamanism to do with Catholicism?

We can go back further than the time of the Capuchins. It is very significant that the first European to enter Tibet, as far as we know, the Franciscan monk Odorico de Pordenone, calls the Grand Lama in Lhasa, Pope. He means the abbot of the principal temple, for the office of

Dalai Lama did not exist then. His own words run: "In this city dwells the Obassy, that is to say their pope in their language. He is the chief of all the idolaters. . . ." In a Latin translation (by Hakluyt) it is given: "Papa eorum qui est caput & princeps omnium Idolatrorum . . . sicut noster Papa Romanus est caput omnium Christianorum." (Henri Cordier, *Les Voyages en Asie au XIVe siècle du bienheureux Frère Odoric de Pordenone* [Paris, 1891, p. 450]; compare also Henry Yule, *Cathay and the Way Thither*, p. 149.)

Our friend Andrade says of the monks of Tsaparang that they live together "just as our cloister people." They do not marry, and the young ones sing chants clear, loud, and expressive "after our style." Their temples are like our churches but finer and cleaner, are painted and adorned with golden statues. He had seen an image supposed to represent the Mother of God, and had found there confession, holy water, and a sprinkling which might be compared to baptism.

Athanasius Kircher in *La Chine Illustrée*, etc. (Amsterdam, 1670, p. 97), says of the Dalai Lama that he sits on a cushion in a room lighted by many lamps. Thither come the pilgrims, who cast themselves down before him, touching the ground with the forehead as a sign of homage. They are not allowed to kiss his feet as is customary with the "pontifical sovereign in Rome." Here are plainly evident the wiles of the Devil. To make a mock of holy things and rob God of the honour due unto Him the Evil One has by a trick of his usual cunning caused these barbarians to imitate us, and induced them to pay to a human being the reverence due to God and Jesus Christ alone. He profanes the most holy mysteries of the Catholic Church by forcing these poor wretched creatures to celebrate these mysteries at the place where they keep their hideous idols. Because he has observed that Christians call the Pope Father of Fathers, he makes these idolatrous barbarians call that false god Grand Lama or high priest.

This Kircher was himself a Jesuit. He explains the resemblance between the two religions as a device of the

Devil. Grueber fell back on the same expedient in 1661. "Nothing," writes Richthofen in the first volume of his *China* (p. 672), "struck him more than the resemblance of the worship to that of Catholics, which he regarded as a device of the Devil."

Apparently they are the views of Father Régis which we find in the following words of the author Du Halde in his *Description de l'Empire de la Chine*, etc. (vol. iv. p. 469). He says that able missionaries have come to the conviction that traces are to be found in the old books of Tibet of "our holy religion" which was preached there in the times of the Apostles, but in the course of centuries has through lack of knowledge been mixed with errors which have finally gained the upper hand.

The indications on which they base their assumption is the dress of the lamas, which is very similar to that in which the Apostles are represented in old pictures; the subordination which is found among them and has some resemblance to the Roman hierarchy; several of their ceremonies which are not far removed from our own; their idea of an incarnation, and lastly the doctrines which their most eminent doctors promulgate. All this, indeed, makes it necessary to subject their books which are found in Lhasa and the monuments existing there to a thorough examination.

This Du Halde was likewise a Jesuit.

Now let us hear what missionaries of later times have to say. The immortal Huc, Prêtre missionnaire de la congrégation de Saint-Lazare, records in his *Souvenirs d'un voyage dans la Tartarie, le Thibet et la Chine* (Paris, 1853, vol. ii. p. 110 *et seq.*):

If we examine, even most superficially, the reforms and innovations introduced into the Lamaist cult by Tsong Kapa, we are quite unavoidably struck by their resemblance to Catholicism. The crozier, the mitre, the chasuble, the cardinal's robe, or the choir robe which the higher lamas wear on journeys or in performing certain ceremonies, the double choir at divine service, the chants, the exorcism, the censer with five chains which can be opened and closed at pleasure, the blessing which the lamas impart by extending the right hand over the heads of the faithful, the rosary, the celibacy of the clergy, their separation from the world, the worship of saints, the fasts, processions, litanies, holy water; these are the points of contact the Buddhists have with us. Can we say that these points of contact have a Christian origin? We believe so, and though we have no positive proof of such a derivation in tradition or in the antiquities of the country, it is nevertheless permissible to express conjectures which in every respect are highly probable.

We know that in the fourteenth century, during the supremacy of the Mongol emperors, Europeans were often in communication with the peoples of Central Asia. We have already in the first part of our narrative of travel spoken of the famous embassies which the Tartar conquerors sent to Rome, France, and England. Undoubtedly these barbarians must have been so struck by the pomp and grandeur of the ceremonies of Catholic worship that they took back with them to their deserts an ineffaceable remembrance of them. We know also that about the same time priests of various orders undertook long journeys to introduce Christianity into Tartary; they must at the same time have penetrated into Thibet and reached the Si-fan people and the Mongols on Koko-nor. Jean de Montcorvin, Archbishop of Peking, had established a choir in which numbers of Mongolian monks practised daily the recitation of Psalms and Catholic rites. When we remember that Tsong Kapa lived at the time when Christianity gained an entrance into Central Asia, we shall not be astonished that there are such striking resemblances to Christianity in reformed Buddhism.

And can we not say something still more positive? May not those legends of Tsong Kapa which we collected ourselves at his birthplace, hearing them direct from the lamas, serve to support our view? After eliminating all the extraordinary details which the imagination of the lamas has added to the narrative, we can affirm that Tsong Kapa was a man pre-eminent by his genius and perhaps by his virtues; that he was instructed by a stranger who came from the West; that the pupil after the death of the master moved westwards, and that he remained in Thibet where he promulgated the doctrines he had been taught. Was not the stranger with the large nose a European, one of the Catholic missionaries who at that time penetrated in large numbers into Central Asia? It is no wonder that Lamaist traditions have preserved the memory of that European face, of a type so different from the Asiatic. During our stay in Kum-bum we heard lamas remark more than once on the strangeness of our appearance, and they said without hesitation that we must be from the country of Tsong Kapa's teacher. We may assume that an early death prevented the Catholic missionary from completing the religious education of his pupil, and that the latter, when he wished afterwards to become an apostle, thought only of introducing a new liturgy, whether because he possessed only a defective knowledge of Christian dogmas or because he had fallen from the faith. The slight resistance his reforms encountered appears to indicate that the progress of Christian ideas in those countries had severely shaken the foundations of the Buddhist cult. There remains only to be investigated the question whether the numerous points of contact between Buddhists and Catholics are helpful or unfavourable to the spread of the faith in Tartary and Thibet.

These similarities apply of course only to forms of worship. Referring to doctrine Huc says in *Le Christianisme en Chine* (Paris, 1857, vol. iv. p. 11):

Father Desideri, in our opinion, has very extravagant notions on the points of contact he thinks he has discovered in dogma between Christianity and the Lamaist teaching. It is true that in Thibet are found astonishing reminders of the great primitive traditions and unmistakable traces of the Catholic missionaries of the Middle Ages; but it is not true that the Buddhists have any clear and definite idea of the Holy Trinity, the salvation of men, the incarnation of the Son of God, and the holy eucharist. The germs of all these dogmas may possibly underlie their creed, but they are certainly not firmly established.

In another passage of the same work Huc exclaims:

La coïncidence des lieux, celle des époques, les témoignages de l'histoire et de la tradition, tout démontra donc jusqu'à l'évidence que la hiérarchie et le culte lamaïques ont fait des empruntes considérables au christianisme.

The amiable Abbé C. H. Desgodins, who lived in the extreme east of Tibet for a generation, endeavoured to explain away the resemblance between the two religions. In his work, *Le Thibet d'après la correspondance des missionnaires*, is a special rubric on the subject, "Hiérarchie lamaïque comparée à celle de l'église catholique," in which he says:

Certain writers have gone even so far as to compare the Lamaist hierarchy to the Catholic church, its Pope, its cardinals, its primates, its archbishops, and its bishops. The comparison is more than clumsy, for in Catholicism the hierarchy is among the secular clergy, from the Pope down to the lowest pastor; the fundamental hierarchy of the church and its religious societies are nothing but useful though not indispensable auxiliaries. In Tibet, on the other hand, the whole hierarchy is entirely monastic, and there is not the slightest trace of a secular clergy.

In fact the organization of religious bodies in Tibet is fundamentally far more similar to Protestantism than to Catholicism (!). On both sides we find a striking parallelism in the independent rival sects, very little cohesion among the clergy of each sect, and the association and interference of the civil power in the sphere of religion and in religious affairs. The only similarity common to Lamaism and Catholicism we find in the form of monasticism, which in the Catholic church is a secondary matter, but in Tibetan Buddhism is fundamental. If we go back to the 13th century we find that history throws a light on the previous development of this form, and we hope that it will finish its work and yield us infallible proofs that the form of monasticism as well as many other ceremonies in the outward rites of worship are simply borrowed from Christianity.

An anonymous writer in the *Calcutta Review* (1877, vol. lxiv. p. 115) says of George Bogle's description of the ceremonies in Tashi-lunpo in the year 1774, that some of them "irresistibly lead us to comparisons between the Buddhism of Tibet and the Roman Catholic religion. The mind reverts to the scene at St. Peter's on Easter-day, as we read of the Teshu Lama seated under a canopy in the court of the palace and a vast crowd around awaiting his blessing." After enumerating a host of points of contact, in the spirit of Huc, he instances the analogy between the Buddhistic system of incarnations and the dogma of the apostolic succession. He gives the preference to the Buddhist invention. The idea of letting the spirit of a deceased lama pass without human intervention into the body of a child, he considers much more elevated and purer, as well as more in harmony with the feelings, than to let this transference be decided by the votes of a college of cardinals.

About the same time as the ambassador Bogle, John Stewart expresses in the *Annual Register* (1778, "Characters," p. 36) his astonishment that the Dalai Lama "often distributes little balls of consecrated flour, like the *pain bénit* of the Roman Catholics." And he reckons up a number of resemblances, and thinks that it is no wonder that the Capuchins thought they could detect among the lamas of Tibet every trait of their own worship.

In the notes to the French edition of Carl Peter Thunberg's narrative of travel (*Voyages de C. P. Thunberg au Japon* [Paris, 1796], iii. p. 248) L. Langlès makes some profound reflexions on Buddhism and Christianity. In Buddhism he finds counterparts of the saints and the canonized Popes of the Catholic church. He quotes also the passage in the *Histoire du Japon* of the Jesuit Charlevoix where it is said: "The remarkable circumstance is that in the midst of this formless chaos of religion we find traces of Christianity, that we have scarcely a mystery, a dogma, or even a precept of charity, that apparently are not known already to the Japanese." The illustrations in the work of Father Georgi show, as Langlès remarks, a striking similarity between the dress of the lamas and the clothing of Catholic priests. All this, according to him, is quite comprehensible if we take "Tibet or the plateau of Tartary" to have been the cradle of all knowledge.

Perhaps I have already wearied my readers with all these quotations. Well, there are only a couple more. The subject is very absorbing, and it has drawn under its yoke even men like Napoleon and Voltaire, for a few minutes at least. The latter does not, indeed, mention our analogies, but he makes a droll remark about the Dalai Lama, wherein he has certainly not hit the mark any more than in his reflexions on Charles XII. Thus he says in his *Essai sur les mœurs et l'esprit* (Paris, 1775, ii. p. 143): "It is certain that the part of Tibet where the Grand Lama rules belonged to the empire of Jinghis Khan, and that the high priest was in nowise molested by the monarch, who had in his army many worshippers of this god in human form." Abel Rémusat replies to this (*Mélanges Asiatiques* [Paris, 1825] vol. i. p. 129 *et seq.*) that Jinghis Khan never had an opportunity of manifesting such respect for the high priest, "for in the time of Jinghis Khan there was no Dalai Lama in Tibet."

Napoleon's grand personality passes only by pure chance before our eyes. Captain Basil Hall landed at Jamestown in August 11, 1817, and two days later had an audience with Napoleon. Hall quotes from the conversation that he "appeared well aware of the striking resemblance between the appearance of the Catholic priests and the Chinese Bonzes; a resemblance which, as he remarked, extends to many parts of the religious ceremonies of both. Here, however, as he also observed, the comparison stops, since the Bonzes of China exert no influence whatsoever over the minds of the people, and never interfere in their temporal or external concerns." (Compare Frémeaux, *Les derniers jours de l'Empéreur.*)

The great Sanskrit scholar H. H. Wilson says, with regard to the men of the Capuchin mission in the *Journal* of the Royal Asiatic Society of Great Britain and Ireland (1843, vol. xi. p. 293): "They all agree in the resemblance between the religion of the Lamas and Christianity." This remark occurs in a note to the account of Mir Izzet Ullah of a journey from Ladak to Yarkand, in which the Mohammedan dares to make the following impertinent statement: "There is likewise an obvious affinity between the Lamas of Tibet and the monks of Christian countries." Mir Izzet Ullah made this journey by order of the Manasarowar explorer, Moorcroft, who, at his visit to Daba in 1812, observed that on the death of a rich Tibetan a considerable part of his fortune escheated to the church, and an idol had to be presented to those priests who prayed for the repose of the soul of the deceased, just as in the Roman Catholic church. (Compare *Asiatick Researches*, 1818, xii. p. 437.)

The bishop Dr. Nicholas Wiseman (afterwards cardinal) delivered in Rome in the year 1835 twelve lectures, which were published with the title *Twelve Lectures on the Connection between Science and revealed Religion.* In the eleventh lecture Wiseman discusses the religious conditions of Tibet, saying:

> When Europe first became acquainted with this worship, it was impossible not to be struck with the analogies it presented to the religious rites of Christians. The hierarchy of the Lamas, their monastic institutions, their churches and ceremonies, resembled ours with such minuteness, that some connection between the two seemed necessarily to have existed.

Relying on the authority of Abel Rémusat and two other scholars, Wiseman comes to the following conclusion:

> At the time when the Buddhist patriarchs first established themselves in Thibet, that country was in immediate contact with

Christianity. Not only had the Nestorians ecclesiastical settlements in Tartary, but Italian and French religious men visited the court of the Khans, charged with important missions from the Pope and St. Lewis of France. They carried with them church ornaments and altars, to make, if possible, a favourable impression on the minds of the natives. For this end they celebrated their worship in the presence of the Tartar princes, by whom they were permitted to erect chapels within the precincts of the royal palaces. An Italian Archbishop, sent by Pope Clement V., established his see in the capital, and erected a church, to which the faithful were summoned by the sound of three bells, and where they beheld many sacred pictures painted on the walls.

Nothing was easier than to induce many of the various sects which crowded the Mongol court to admire and adopt the rites of this religion. Some members of the imperial house secretly embraced Christianity, many mingled its practices with the profession of their own creeds, and Europe was alternately delighted and disappointed by reports of imperial conversions and by discoveries of their falsehood. . . . Surrounded by the celebration of such ceremonies, hearing from the ambassadors and missionaries of the west accounts of the worship and hierarchy of their countries, it is no wonder that the religion of the Lamas, just beginning to assume splendour and pomp, should have adopted institutions and practices already familiar to them, and already admired by those whom they wished to gain. The coincidence of time and place, the previous non-existence of that sacred monarchy, amply demonstrate that the religion of Thibet is but an attempted imitation of ours.

Wiseman, then, defends the view that the Lamaist cult was imported into Tibet from Europe. Most, however, of what he has to say on the subject is borrowed from the works of Abel Rémusat. The latter says in his "Discours sur l'origine de la hiérarchie lamaïque" (*Mélanges Asiatiques*, Paris, 1825, vol. i. p. 129):

The first missionaries who came into contact with Lamaism were not a little astonished to find in the heart of Asia numerous monasteries, as well as solemn processions, pilgrimages, religious festivals, the court of a high priest and colleges of lama superiors, who elect their chief, the prince of the church and spiritual father of the Tibetans and Tatars. But as faith in their creed was in no small degree a virtue, they did not think of concealing these points of contact but, in order to explain them, regarded Lamaism as a degenerate kind of Christianity, and in the details which seemed to them so surprising they saw traces of a former intrusion of the Syrian sects into this country.

Abel Rémusat shows that just at this time when ambassadors and Catholic monks travelled from Europe to the East, the new residences of the Buddhist patriarchs were established in Tibet. "Is it to be wondered at if they, in the desire to increase the number of their adherents and to lend their religion greater lustre, adopted certain liturgical practices and something of the foreign pomp which imposed on the masses?"

Abel Rémusat seeks, then, to prove that the purely outward resemblances that exist have arisen owing to Lamaism having in later times adopted part of the splendid ritual of the Catholic Church. Accordingly he is opposed to the view that Lamaism is a degenerated Christianity. Among those who have maintained this opinion he mentions Thévenot, the Abbé Renaudot, Andrade, Della Penna, Georgi, Deguiques, Lacroze, "and many others." However the resemblance between the two churches may be explained, it is evident from Abel Rémusat's exposition that such a resemblance has really been observed by a large number of Catholics.

Henry T. Prinsep, in his little book *Tibet, Tartary, and Mongolia* (London, 1851, pp. 5, 12, 136, 141, 165, etc.), says of Lamaist Asia:

> The extraordinary similitude in many parts of the doctrine, and of the books, and ritual, and forms, and institutions of this religion with those of Romish Christianity, which was remarked by the Jesuits who visited Tibet in the seventeenth century, and even by Father Rubruquis in the thirteenth, might lead to the belief that they had been borrowed entirely from this latter. . . . The discipline, the habits, and even the ritual of these monasteries of Tibet and Tartary, have also a remarkable resemblance to those of the churches of Rome and Constantinople in the middle ages.

Prinsep refers also to Turner's astonishment at the Tibetan antiphonal singing between the priests and people, and its similarity to the grand ceremonies of the Romish Church. Csoma de Körös has translated some of the Tibetan church canticles, and Prinsep says of them that he is himself astonished at their resemblance in spirit and tone to parts of the litany and the psalms which are sung or recited in the same manner in the Catholic Church.

In the *Géographie Universelle* of Malte-Brun, published in Paris in 1860, I find (vol. iii. p. 255) the following sentence:

> Rome and Lhasa, the Pope and the Dalai Lama, present to us very interesting points of contact. The Tibetan Government, which is entirely Lamaist, seems to be to a certain extent a copy of the ecclesiastical administration of the States of the Church.

In conclusion one more quotation from Koeppen's noted book *Die lamaische Hierarchie und Kirche* (Berlin, 1859), p. 116 *et seq.*:

> Older and later travellers who have penetrated into the Land of Snow, or into one of the countries converted by it, have often expressed their astonishment at the numerous relations between the forms of the Catholic and Lamaist cults, the similarity, nay, identity of the ceremonies, priest's dress, sacred utensils, etc. In the times of gross superstition this circumstance was ascribed to the author of all evil, Satan. The Devil—it was said—the "Ape of God," had imitated even the Christianity of the Lord God, and founded a church which outwardly mimicked the Catholic, but was essentially and truly nothing but a heathen creation of the Devil. The Capuchin missionaries of last century put in the place of the Devil the heresiarch Manes, whom they identified with Buddha, and made the founder of Lamaism. The latest emissaries of the Propaganda who visited Lhasa arrived at the conviction that all the analogies of Lamaism and Catholicism, even the pontificate, the celibacy of the clergy, the adoration of saints, confession, fasts, processions, etc., as well as the use of exorcism, holy water, and lastly, bells, rosaries, mitres, and croziers, etc., were all borrowed from Christianity, and were first introduced into the Lamaist ritual in the train of the innovations of the doctor bTsong kha pa. . . . It is hardly possible to discuss more closely the question exactly what Lamaism has borrowed from Christianity, and what on the other side Catholicism has borrowed from Lamaism or Buddhism; we will only remark that it is a mistake to ascribe to bTsong kha pa such far-reaching reforms that he first created the whole Lamaist cult as it now is, and that it is, on the other hand, quite uncritical and unhistorical to consider primitive Buddhist institutions and usages, such as celibacy, confession and fasting, which are all demonstrably older than Christianity, as innovations and, moreover, imitations of Catholicism.

The rosary, too, is older in India and even Tibet than in Europe. Koeppen (on p. 319) says:

The home of the rosary appears to be India, whence Muslim, and through them probably Christians, have received it, for we cannot well credit the human brain with having twice invented this peculiar implement.

On baptism he says (on p. 320):

Baptism, that is, the custom of sprinkling children with water immediately or soon after birth, or dipping them in it, and at the same time giving them a name, is not exclusively a Christian sacrament, but is to be found in many so-called heathen religions, even among quite rude Shamanist peoples, and expressly as an act of religious consecration and expiation, as a spiritual purification. That the Lamaist Church observed the rite is a matter of course with its hierarchical tendency.

As regards marriage Koeppen points out a difference between the two churches (as on p. 321):

According to the decisions of Catholic councils a man is cursed who maintains that the status conjugalis is as pure and holy as the status virginitatis. It is, therefore, a glaring inconsistency that the celebration of marriage, that is, the act whereby two persons pass from a more holy to a less holy state, should be held to be a sacrament in the Catholic Church.

Koeppen also has his opponents. Thus W. L. Heeley in *The Calcutta Review* (1874, lix. p. 139) says of him that he is evidently a freethinker, has a bad opinion of the priests and their ways, and "hates the lamas because they remind him of the Catholic Church as much as some of the Catholic missionaries hate them because they parody the church."

In the first volume of Adrien Launay's *Histoire de la Mission du Thibet* (p. 23) I find the following:

In the seventeenth century Indian caravans reported that there were Christians in Thibet; they had no doubt been misled, like some historians, by the similarities between the Catholic and Lamaist ceremonies.

One of the men of the time most renowned for his knowledge of Buddhism, Dr. T. W. Rhys Davids, concludes his excellent little handbook, which has run through many editions, *Buddhism: being a Sketch of the Life and Teach-*

ings of Gautama, the Buddha (London, 1903, p. 250), with the following words:

> Lamaism, indeed, with its shaven priests, its bells and rosaries, its images and holy water and gorgeous dresses; its service with double choirs, and processions and creeds and mystic rites and incense, in which the laity are spectators only; its worship of the double Virgin, and of saints and angels; its images, its idols and its pictures; its huge monasteries and its gorgeous cathedrals, its powerful hierarchy, its cardinals, its Pope, bears outwardly at least a strong resemblance to Romanism, in spite of the essential difference of its teachings and its mode of thought.

In the first volume of my book I have only slightly touched on some similarities between the two churches. Now I have shown by all sorts of quotations that not only Protestant students of religion, but also a large number of Catholic missionaries, who have lived for years in Tibet, have gone much further in their comparisons than I. Let the reader decide for himself whether I am the one who has committed a sin against religion, or whether the Catholics who have poured forth the vials of their wrath over my head should not be reproached for having permitted themselves serious deviations from the paths of truth.

We have been lured aside into long bypaths from the majestic valley of the Sutlej by Father Antonio de Andrade's successful missionary journeys to the old kingdom of Tsaparang. It is now time to take up again the thread of the narrative. We leave the dying village to its dreams of vanished greatness beside the roar of the royal river, and prepare to depart from a country where once the first Christian bells in Tibet rang in clear tones over the desolate heights.

CHAPTER XXVII

IN THE LABYRINTH OF TRIBUTARIES

THE height in the camp at the foot of the monastery terrace of Totling was only 12,140 feet. We were decidedly going down. A pleasant feeling, after years of sojourn at immense elevations, to descend again into denser layers of air! Two years in the highly rarefied air 16,000 to 19,000 feet above sea-level is about as much as a European can endure. His heart and lungs are not adapted to the scarcity of oxygen which is found up on the borders of interstellar space. When the Dalai Lama travels to Calcutta, he is perhaps troubled by the heat, but he must feel the increase of the oxygen in the air agreeable. It is otherwise with the European. When he leaves half the atmosphere below him, the muscles and the beating of his heart are excessively strained; he is afflicted day and night with the languid feeling of a convalescent after a serious illness, which is not driven off by ten hours' rest in the night.

I noticed the following symptoms in my own case: the temperature of the body fell a couple of degrees below the normal, the respiration and the pulse were quicker than usual, and the slightest movement produced shortness of breath; I became at last indifferent to everything, except the road to India; the two meals of the day I regarded as a punishment for my sins; hot tea and ice-cold water I always liked, and tobacco was an indispensable companion during the terribly long hours of solitude. A limitless impregnable ocean extended ever around me, and its petrified billows, which towered above me month after month, seemed as though they would never come to an end. I had made my voyage long enough in calm waters, and now I came to the strand of the sea of mountains, where the surf stormed and tossed, and with every day it became more apparent that the conquest of the Himalayas was no child's play.

Now we were going down towards happy India. After the grey unfruitful country of high Tibet, the barley-fields on the affluents of the Sutlej seemed delightfully green, and presently we heard tepid summer winds rustle through the thick foliage of poplars. Even the pattering rain was warm and pleasant; I could throw off the felt rug at night, for the temperature did not fall below 48°. We seemed to be going to meet the spring. I began to enjoy life again; my hours of rest had more effect, and my appetite came back. Therefore it was so inexpressibly delightful to have descended from high elevations.

Even the Changtsö, who was at first so high and mighty, ended in becoming quite agreeable. He procured the provisions we wanted, and bartered a saddle for a revolver. We had no other need for his gracious assistance, for Thakur Jai Chand had sent with Mohanlal a young Tibetan named Ngurup Dorche, who was to act as guide. He knew the roads to Poo, and I might take him with me to Simla if I wished.

Ngurup Dorche headed the party when we left Totling on August 15. We were not long to enjoy a comparatively low altitude. From Mangnang we had descended rapidly to the monastery which stands on the bottom of the Sutlej trough, and now we had to mount again into higher regions, where the road traverses the land of Chumurti in a wide curve to the north of the river.

Our little party marches along the terrace of the left bank before the cloister town, where temple buildings and *chhorten* pyramids rise among the ruins, and here and there a lama gives us a parting look from a dark lancet window. The path follows up the stream north-eastwards, then turns northwards and makes straight for the bridge over the Sutlej. Between sheer cliffs of sandstone, running 18° N. 85 E., the great river contracts to a breadth of about 80 feet; its depth must be considerable. The huge volumes of dirty grey water roar and toss along the narrow chasm, and present, as one looks up-stream, a grand, fascinating spectacle of irresistible strength. Immediately below the bridge the river expands again and becomes quieter; the mountains recede, leaving space for level strips along the bank, where the erosion terraces are, however, sharply marked or are broken through by small tributaries. But the expansion of the valley is short, for at Tsaparang the river again bores its way through a narrow corridor.

The bridge of Totling is a solid structure, and horses may be trusted on its planks without the slightest anxiety. The bridge-heads are perhaps 40 feet above the water, and are built in the form of stone tunnels on shelves of rock. Between the upper surfaces of the tunnel walls two powerful iron chains are stretched from bank to bank, and from them hangs the wooden pavement of the bridge. The whole is so firmly jointed together that the bridge does not perceptibly tremble under the weight of a horse. The chains serve also as a handrail, and my white horse had no opportunity of trying his luck in another leap.

On the right bank our direction is again westerly, and the road runs over watercourses between hillocks of löss and gravel. The largest of all is the valley through which the road comes down from Gartok and the Ayi-la to Totling. Now about 175 cubic feet of muddy water streamed down its bed, hindering, as usual, the progress of foot-passengers. Our path follows the river bank just opposite Totling, and we have an excellent view of the decayed monastic town. It finally vanishes out of sight as we turn up a side valley, where a brook flows among fresh meadows. Steep walls of clay, sand, and pebbles rise beside it—the cañon country has not yet come to an end. Such is the scenery until we come to a place where Ngurup Dorche proposes to encamp. The height is 12,290 feet. From the north-east descends a valley named Natang, in which barley is cultivated.

Hardly had the tents been set up, when the south-west monsoon laid a blue-black wing over the country, the day grew dark, and the heralds of Indra blew a rumbling blast.

117 AND 118. THE BRIDGE OF TOTLING.

The echo answered in the mountains and valleys, lightning flashed like sword-blades crossing in the fight, the clouds were rent and the rain pelted down heavily on the Natang valley. Later in the afternoon a dull growl was heard from up the valley. Was a violent thunder-squall coming or a cloudburst? No, it was the rain-water which had collected from all sides into a torrent, and was rolling its heavy volumes down to the Sutlej. The noise became slowly but steadily louder, and at last was deafening. Every man to his feet! The ground was quickly examined. The tents stood in the middle of the valley. Is it possible that the whole camp may be washed away? If the whole valley bottom is filled with this raging water, we shall be as in a mouse-trap under a stream of water, for the slopes are so steep that we cannot escape by flight.

It is too late to pack up and look about for a safer place. Look yonder at the nearest corner above the camp! A dark greyish-brown wall is rolling down upon the tents. Yes, it actually rolls over the ground, foaming and roaring, and takes with it all the loose dust, sand, and gravel, and all the dry grass stalks. It is impossible to make ourselves heard. Now the air groans and the ground shakes. At the last moment I seize my papers, resolved that, as far as lies in my power, my notes and maps shall not be lost.

Wonderfully fine and grand is such a spectacle, and at the sight one almost forgets that danger threatens. I cannot take my eyes away from the billow of rolling water. Our excitement increases. But the torrent does not advance as rapidly as might be expected. It fills one yard of the bed after another, and approaches with crushing force the place where I am standing. Now it is here. Will it seize the tents and carry us off with it in its triumphal course? Must I run off quickly to find a safer spot? The water rises and will soon reach me. No, this time it does not touch us. The tents stand on a slight rise which bears no signs of former flooding. We are on an island which the water cannot reach. But it was a near shave, and had this deluge caught us in one of the narrow passages farther down we should have been in a desperate situation.

For fully two hours this flood of 1000 cubic feet of water continued to rush down the valley. Towards evening the volume diminished, and by the next morning was reduced to a small brook. The water was so full of clay that if you put a hand in it and then let it dry in the air it was covered with a glove of the finest mud. Immense quantities of solid matter are thus washed down into the Sutlej, and do not come to rest until the river can build up banks of mud and sand in some expansion of the valley. How much more powerfully and energetically this diluvial action must have been during the pluvial period! It is easy to see that erosion working through a thousand years can have produced no other result than that here presented to the eye—a labyrinth of deeply cut cañons.

The Sutlej is the main artery for all the rain water draining off Hundes. The river is composed of the united volumes of innumerable tributaries which swell up and fall according to the unequal rainfall in their basins. One day the Natang valley may contain a small brook and the next a great river. But in the main trench of the Sutlej the variations are smoothed out. At Bilaspur, where the river leaves the Himalayas and emerges into the plains of the Punjab, we shall certainly find that when the rainy season commences, and days with rain become more and more numerous, the volume of the Sutlej increases steadily to a maximum, and then diminishes as regularly when rain becomes scarcer in autumn.

In the night of August 15 rain fell steadily and heavily, and we made haste next day to leave the Natang valley before the next flood came down upon us. The small side valley which we followed northwards is excavated in yellow löss loam which the water had made as smooth as soap. The animals were unsafe on their feet; they slided forwards or paddled in the worst mud soup. There was generally a porridge on the bottom of the drainage bed of the valley which looked like freshly-stirred mortar, and when we had to wade through it the animals were in danger

119. VALLEY OF THE NGARI-TSANGPO.

120. GULLY NEAR NATANG.

of drowning. The cañon type still prevailed. We marched between vertical or very steep walls of yellow æolian dust; huge free-standing blocks, towers, and pillars reminded us, as so often before, of the streets and lanes of a town lying in an enchanted sleep. Innumerable ravines of all sizes opened at the sides, and their channels spread out like the spokes of a quadrant of a wheel. Some of these unpleasant ditches were a yard deep and a foot broad. Had the loam been dry it would easily have borne the weight of the animals, but it was softened by the rain; it gave way, and one horse or mule after another tumbled on to his nose in the treacherous pitfalls. When the leader of the train had performed his tumble, the animals behind tried another place.

This valley is sterile, dreary, and silent. The gradient is slight. But when we come to higher regions the landscape changes its appearance. A bush or two, a hardy plant, and a little grass have here and there found a refuge at the foot of a steep wall. The loose deposits which once filled all the Sutlej basin gradually increase in thickness, and at the corners and projections rock *in situ*, phyllitic schist, often crops out. At the last bend in the road hills and domed summits appear in the background like holms and peninsulas in the desert of the clay formations. Before reaching this ground which the æolian deposits have left untouched, we make a short halt at a small spring where the grass is not sufficient to satisfy our ten animals.

Another day's march and the façades of the sleeping town become lower. Occasionally an undermined block of clay has fallen and strewed the valley floor with cubical sharp-edged fragments. Now we have reached the cairn which is erected on the boundary between the æolian accumulations and the heights of Kaling-tang, covered with pebbles and thinly clothed with tall grass. Marked by smaller cairns and *mani* stones the path winds up to the top of a commanding elevation, a stone pyramid visible from all sides. Here it will repay us to rest a while and slowly scan the edge of the horizon. We have just been shut up in the narrow valley where we saw nothing but the nearest cliffs of clay and the next bend of the valley. Now we can breathe freely, now we can see our position, and gain a general view of this singular country, where atmospheric agents and the forces which transform the earth's surface have worked more capriciously and left more distinct traces than in any other part of Tibet.

North-westwards the country retains the same character as heretofore; an inextricable confusion of valleys, ravines, and furrows carved into the æolian clay, a maze of ramifications and drainage channels of every kind and dimension down to the most insignificant and minute runnel of water. A snowy crest towers above the yellow earth to the north-east, belonging to the Ladak range. Westwards the horizon is shut in by stunted domes with small shining snow-caps, which lie not far from Shipki.

The pyramid of rock, conspicuous from a long distance, stands on an upheaval between two valley systems. When we leave its stones, lashed by the wind and doomed to destruction by weathering, we follow first one of the smallest runnels, then larger and larger gullies and ravines, cut ever deeper into the loose crust, until the last corridor passes into the large Shangdse valley, which runs south-westwards down to the Sutlej. Juicy barley-fields and marshy meadows line its brook, and amidst them stand about fifty square grey-washed houses decorated with streamers, which together constitute the village of Shangdse. A solitary more pretentious house with a *chhorten* before it is the dwelling of the headman. Shangdse-gompa is built on a hill on the right side of the valley, and consists of two red houses and a white building surrounded by the usual memorial pyramids. Seven lamas of the Gelugpa sect are said to live and labour in this monastery.

The Shangdse brook carried 280 cubic feet of water, but the following morning, after a fine night, had fallen to 180. The day had been burning hot, and with 70° at one o'clock it was suffocatingly hot, and so much the more as the air was still. The height was 13,760 feet.

As soon as camp 474 was pitched, lamas, villagers, and women came up to the tents, where they sat down quite at their ease and began to talk to us. There was not a sign of the mistrust which we met with in Totling. How

121. THE SHANGDSE VALLEY.

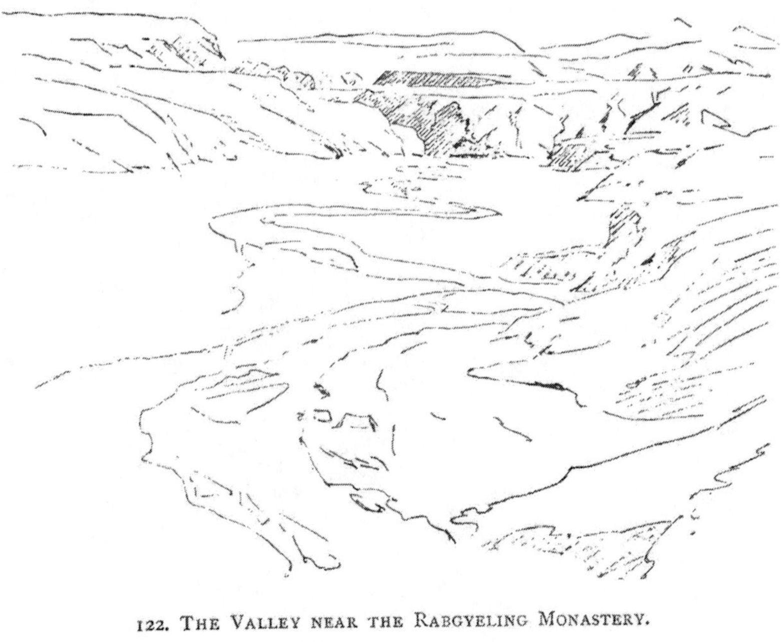

122. THE VALLEY NEAR THE RABGYELING MONASTERY.

Sketches by the Author.

could they suspect a caravan which came from Totling and had a Tibetan guide? Now that we had got past Totling we should no doubt find a free passage everywhere.

The next day's march was like the preceding. We travelled north-westwards up a narrow gradually rising valley to another hilly elevation, and saw from its cairn a view now well known to us; then we descended the next valley, Choktse, which is just like the Shangdse valley. The inhabitants of the Choktse valley dwell like ants on the löss walls of the right flank, where they have a small number of exceedingly primitive huts. They were at the time out in their barley-fields attending to the irrigation which is effected by two spring-fed brooks. The fields are in tiers of terraces, and the water runs through open pipes from the higher to the lower in a fixed order. The industry and watchful care of the good men and their wives showed that they entertained good hopes of the year's harvest.

Oxen and cows were grazing on the meadows near the village, the first we had seen for a long time, another hint of warmer regions. We had, indeed, seen in the course of the day two wild asses, and on the slopes cheerful marmots piped shrilly from their holes. But what of that? We were, nevertheless, about to leave the high, cold, and bare Tibet; we were—heavenly thought—on the way to India, the land of legends and jungles. Barley-fields we had seen for many days past, but now we had reached the first agricultural village, a settled population instead of wandering nomads, cattle took the place of yaks, and sheep-rearing, which was everything up on the heights, was of only secondary importance to the peasants whose villages we now visited.

We have nothing to do in Choktse, so we ride past the village, up more valleys, over more heights, and perceive the monastery Rabgyeling-gompa on its hill in front of us. It is melancholy and affecting to see all these religious houses in so desolate a country. The cloister cells claim far too large a percentage of the male population; the men could employ their time and strength much better than in cleaning lamps and prostrations before golden idols.

And yet I say, "Long live monasticism." Only bright memories linger in my mind from its misty light.

Juicy meadows on the left bank of the Rabgyeling river tempt us to encamp. I have just ordered a halt when Ngurup Dorche cries out, "No, we cannot camp here, sir."

"Why not? The grass is good, the water clear, and the weather settled."

"Quite true, but if rain comes in the night, we shall be cut off, for this river has a bad reputation, and is very difficult to ford on account of its depth."

"Very well; then we will stay on the right bank."

We waded through the pure fresh water, and then let the animals go back to the meadows on the left bank. If rain came we could fetch them in time.

Picturesque, rich in colouring, and mysterious as a fairy castle, Rabgyeling-gompa lifts its streamer-adorned battlements above the valley. On the highest point of the summit of the hill a red-painted *lhakang* defies the destructive forces of the atmosphere, the water, and the earth, resembling the capital of a pillar or an eagle's eyrie hanging over the abyss. The insecure substratum of pebbles looked as though it must yield to the weight of the next rain. It seems like braving God to sleep a single night in the building. A second shrine stands at the foot of the hill among the huts and yards of the village and a whole tangle of *chhortens*. The dwellings of the monks form a small village compound, begirt by a wall of its own.

Conducted by two monks I paid a short visit to the lower temple and saw there some artistically executed mural paintings, which, however, had suffered much from damp and the water that trickled from the roof. Otherwise the interior was the same as usual. The two divans were there, as well as the eight pillars with their banners and ribands. Piles of loose sheets replaced the bound treasures of the shelves. In the middle of the back wall sat Buddha, six feet high and clothed in a yellow mantle. Before him on the altar table the *dii minores* were set up in rows, with lamps in brazen bowls burning in front. The

123. Rabgyeling-gompa.

124. Chhortens in Rabgyeling.

Sketches by the Author.

whole was blended into a harmonic, subdued, and sufficiently dirty tinge of colour.

A *kore*, or open passage, with balustrade and a free view on all sides, runs all round the outside of the temple and lay-village, passing by some *chhorten* pyramids. In niches at their sides are rows of prayer cylinders. When the pilgrim or monk, in making the circuit of the *kore*, comes to them, he never omits to set with his hand all these machines revolving round their upright iron axles, and their humming and grating accompany his steps. This action has the same effect as if the wanderer gabbled off all the prayers written on long strips of paper in every one of the prayer-mills. But woe to him who turns the mills the wrong way! Both the rotation and the circuit of the *kore* must be performed in the direction of the hands of a watch.

Through a loophole in the inner side of the passage I could look down into a partially underground crypt, into which the monks would not let me enter. I could see, however, that medallions in bas-relief, representing Buddha, painted in colours and partly gilded, adorned the longer wall. Some freshly cut *mani* stones lay on the earthen floor and a finely chiselled stone image; I would have purchased it with silver coin but my offer was refused.

Eleven serving monks lived in Rabgyeling. The outer walls of their houses were painted greyish-blue, red and white, in vertical stripes, a pattern intended to proclaim the connection of the monastery with Sekiya. The monks were as friendly disposed as the laity and their wives, who came to our tents to sell us small pats of more or less rancid butter.

In the light of the evening sun the higher *lhakang* shone red as blood on a sacrificial stone. The shadows grew longer, filling the valley, where the stillness was broken only by the murmur of the river. The stars, friends of all pilgrims and wayfarers, twinkled brighter than usual in the clear evening. The temperature sank in the night to 34.2°. We were at a height of 13,668 feet, and therefore 1528 feet higher than at Totling.

CHAPTER XXVIII

THE DEVIL'S CAULDRON OF THE NGARI-TSANGPO

ASTONISHED that the upper *lhakang* had not fallen down in the night, but still stood red and massive on its mountain spur, I set out next day with my people from Rabgyeling. We climb in zigzags up the heights along a narrow path, which hangs over deep ravines and precipitous cliffs. Before we are aware we are again descending into a deep valley, the upper part of which is called Rildigyok, and the lower Changtang. We stay a while on the bank of its brook and refresh ourselves with a drink of clear cold water, which ripples down with a murmur to bring its appointed tribute to its master, the Sutlej.

The huts, fields, and *chhorten* of Rildigyok are not such as to excite any curiosity. We pass on up to more heights and over ridges between deep ravines. As usual, we pass up and down over a succession of valleys before we halt at Karu-sing, which affords spring water and pasture but contains no human dwellings. A *dakpa*, a Tibetan post-runner, passed our tents at a gentle trot, carrying Thakur Jai Chand's English post in a small satchel; he had been, he told us, three days on the way. The satchel, which, between Simla and Gartok, passes through several hands, would soon be forwarded by a fresh Marathon runner.

This night also the minimum temperature is very close to freezing-point, but the height is considerable, 14,108 feet. We have derived no advantage from the regular fall of the Sutlej, for here we are 1968 feet higher than at Totling. This road to India is drearily long. We seem to have travelled six miles and yet we have only covered three, or even less. And the distance to the frontier and the forests on the south side of the Himalayas seems as long as ever.

On August 20 we had still the same country, a succession of troublesome valleys separated by heights and elevations. Rock *in situ* crops out more frequently, and it is a strongly folded, much weathered, phyllitic schist. In one of these valleys lies Sumur-gompa, quite a small cloister, with two monks and two huts. A side valley opening on the right is called Ldat; its springs and meadows exhort us to set up camp 477 at a height of 12,556 feet. In a terrace wall close by the camp there was a cave with a barred door and closed window openings. A devout monk had passed the whole of the preceding year in its darkness, and was soon to return to his voluntary confinement.

Whistles and the tramp of horses sounded in the valley. A lama in a skull-cap came with two natives from Beshahr, driving before them some horses and a mule.

"Where are you going?" we asked.

"To Bongba in Tibet."

"What is your business there?"

"We own three hundred sheep, which are guarded and tended up there by Tibetans. Now we mean to fetch the wool and carry it to the Indian side."

"Do you go up every summer?"

"Yes, but this year we have something else to see after as well. We have heard that a fellow from Ladak has stolen some of our sheep and has gone off to Nubra with his booty. We are going to pursue the scoundrel."

"Good luck, and farewell!"

The road had been terrible enough before, but I had never found anything so topsy-turvy as on August 21. As usual we began the day with a troublesome climb up steep slopes, reaching at last the pass Dato-la sunk in a sharp rocky ridge. I walk up to the cairn, and am astonished and dumbfoundered at the sight before me. How in the world are we ever to get down into this abyss? The largest, deepest erosion valley I have hitherto seen yawns between us and a point as high on the other side. Here a huge piece of the earth's crust is wanting. Has it subsided and left a trough in its place? No, running water has ploughed out this trench in the course of enormous periods of time; the Ngari-tsangpo has eaten its way downwards, carrying away one grain of dust after another, one boulder after another, and is still continuing its work, though at a slower rate than in the pluvial period.

I remain a while standing at the cairn. The height is 16,165 feet. Only a short step separates me from the rocky ledge opposite, and the journey thither takes four hours! No words can do justice to the bird's-eye view over this grand, richly and fantastically sculptured valley. It will be difficult to tear myself away and travel on again. It is better to be cautious, and not allow myself to be bewitched by the imposing scene. There rise rocky pinnacles and spurs, and behind them lies the abyss and the opposite flanks. But where is the path? To my eyes it seems as though it vanished under overhanging cliffs. Hallo, here it is, dizzily steep! Do not lose your footing, keep hold of the side of the cliff, take care that your legs do not slide from under you, or you will come a terrible cropper down a blood-dripping channel.

Now it is better. The road makes a turn to the right, is less precipitous, and has a stone parapet on the outer side. But our delight is short-lived. Again we go down headlong until we reach the top of a ramification, which helps us for a time. Once we go up again, and then follow steep slopes between jutting rocks and sheer precipices, with an awful deeply excavated trough on the outer side, which opens into the valley of the Ngari-tsangpo.

We slide, glide, and plant our feet firmly again, and feel the strain at the back of the knee. We take care not to walk in front of the caravan, lest we should be struck on the head by pebbles and small stones loosened by the horses' feet, which roll down flying and twisting through the air.

The first hour is over, but there are plenty more. Now the path creeps into a very steep trough, so narrow that the outstretched arms can touch both sides. Take care that the animals keep in Indian file! If they enter

125. THE LITTLE BRIDGE OVER THE NGARI-TSANGPO.

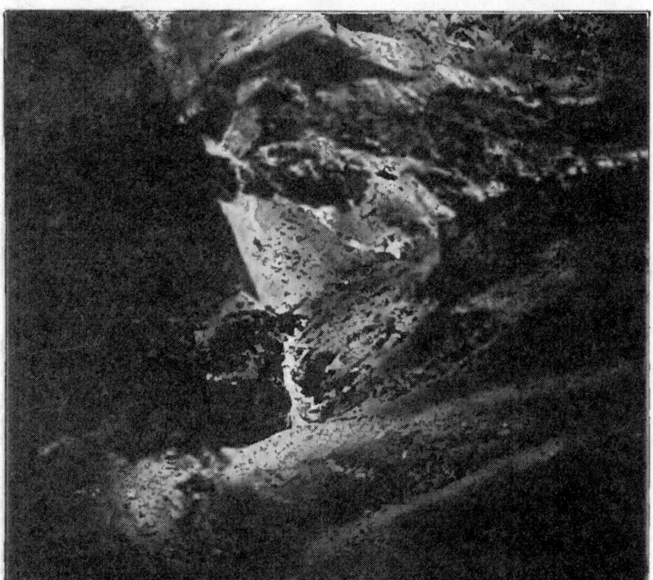

126. RAVINE NEAR OPTIL.

this hole in couples they will stick fast in it, and cannot be drawn out. There a load has fallen off and is rolling down on its own hook to tickle a lively mule on the hind legs. He kicks out behind, with the result that his own load slips off. It is best to put him right again first, or the trench will be closed up like a corked bottle.

It would be good sport to toboggan down the pebble-covered slopes, if the slide were not so long and did not lead straight into the jaws of death. Look, there to the right, at the stupendous cliffs falling sheer to the valley floor. The Ngari-tsangpo has cut its way straight through the mass. We perceive gaps or niches left in the rough wild ramparts of schist and quartzite by colossal blocks which have at some time fallen out and dashed with terrific noise down into the valley to form the natural bridge over the Ngari-tsangpo.

Ah, here we are nearly at the bottom. Yes, but the last bit is the worst. A series of very steep staircases in the solid rock. If one slips down one step, it will not be the last. It is best to put on the brake in time; it would be a pity if we broke our necks just at this moment when the bottcm is so near.

At last we are down and all the bones in the caravan are whole. The sight of the cliffs as we look back is much less awful than the view down into the yawning gulf, for projecting points and knobs of rock hide the declivities and so the slope cannot be seen as a whole.

On the margin by the cairn not a sound of the whirling grinding water was audible. Half-way down a low murmur reached our ears which increased in strength as we descended. And now when we have reached the valley floor, we hear the water tossing madly among rocks and boulders. We see only two stretches of the river as we climb down. All the rest is hidden by cliffs and projections. The erosion downwards has progressed so powerfully and rapidly that the weathering of the valley slopes has not been able to keep pace with it. In places the river has worked so far in advance that whole cliffs are undermined and lean like arches over the water.

Here, too, in the depth of the valley the wild, bold

sculpture makes a grand effect, and we shall be glad to pause a while on the small, very original bridge. But where is the bridge and where is the river? The green foaming water seems to dive into the earth and disappear. Wait, here is the bridge. It is just six and a half feet long. Did we not see it with our own eyes, we should by no means credit the statement that the largest of the northern tributaries of the Sutlej, which drains vast areas of the highlands of Chumurti, can find room under a bridge six and a half feet long. Even if the bridge were to fall in, foot passengers at any rate could still cross the river. But the leap would be dangerous and a false step would infallibly lead to death.

Two huge blocks of stone several thousand cubic feet in dimensions have fallen into the narrowest part of the river channel and have taken up a most favourable position. The tops are on the same level and similarly flattened above and form a vault under which the river forces its way. But the vault has a gap, for the blocks do not touch each other. A gap six and a half feet broad separates the two. At first sight one would bet ten to one that they were part of a sill of solid rock, for their lower edges are covered with smaller boulders, pebbles, and sand. But a moment's thought convinces us that so great a river could not have cut its way into so narrow a trench without widening its bed sideways by means of loose blocks, sharp-edged detritus, and other polishing material. Ngurup Dorche also knew that, according to local tradition, the blocks had actually fallen down and built excellent bridge-heads. The two were originally one block and were broken in two by the fall.

After nature had accomplished the hardest part of the work, all that men needed to do was to lay two short tree trunks over the gap between the blocks. Boughs and joists were laid crosswise on the trunks and the whole was covered with hard stones. The bridge, five feet broad and without a parapet, hangs some 65 feet above the water. It is heard boiling and fuming down below, but the river is not visible, for the trench-like abyss is pitch dark. The fissure widens out just below the bridge, and there the foaming arched billows are seen fighting with boulders and rocky points. The unfortunate man who fell into this whirlpool would be torn into small pieces. A huge spout of water, as powerful as the flywheel of a machine, shoots down at one spot and then wells up in another in flat hissing bubbles, and next moment forces its way into a narrow gorge. And if the lost one survived the first billow, and did not lose consciousness, he would grope in vain for a point of rock to which to cling. These walls are vertical, polished, and smooth, and no power on earth could resist the pressure of the water from above and withstand the wild rush of the waterspouts.

The bridge is called, like the country, Optil. The Ngari-tsangpo rushes on foaming to the north-west, and, as far as can be seen in either direction, the valley is equally deep and wild, though the channel is more contracted just at the bridge than elsewhere. Ngurup Dorche was quite right in saying that the whole wide detour which the road makes on the north side of the Sutlej is rendered necessary solely by the Ngari-tsangpo, which cannot be crossed at a single place below the bridge of Optil. The stretch of the river which we see immediately above the bridge at the foot of vertical undermined cliffs, gives an idea of its general appearance. The water here forms rapids in a small foaming bed between great masses of rounded boulders, and it strives to eat its way into the base of the cliffs. Possibly the river is as deep as it is broad, and therefore it is difficult to estimate its volume. Such a river cannot be forded; the bed is too narrow and too deep, its fall is too great, and its water possesses irresistible force. Therefore there is no choice but to travel by a roundabout way and over the tiny bridge which spans the huge channel like a match.

We test the bridge. Wind and weather have half-consumed its beams, and it is much too heavily weighted with stones, which only serve to prevent the feet of the animals sinking in between the planks in passing over. Yet nasty holes yawn between the slabs; they have to be covered up with more stones. Two men try their luck on the wretched thing and walk rolling and stamping across the chasm. A mule is led over. The bridge holds. A second crosses with his load on. The shy horses from Chang-tang stop, cock their ears, and start at the heavy awful thunder that rises from the bosom of the earth. A stroke of the whip loosens their legs; the bridge is only six and a half feet long, and in two strides they are safely over.

Huge volumes of water groan, splash, and tumble against the slabs and blocks of stone, and yet we cannot draw a drop of water if we have no mind to fall into the bed above the bridge. We all prefer to wait till the next spring, but we wish we were there. For in the Devil's Cauldron of the Ngari-tsangpo a different climate reigns than on the free open heights above, where the winds of heaven whistle freely round the cairn. The thermometer marks 71.2° in the shade; not a breath of air stirs in the confined valley and the suffocating heat is very oppressive. I have discarded my Tibetan mantle and appear in a dress which is light indeed, but comical rather than becoming.

At the cairn of the pass we had been at a height of 15,279 feet; the height at the bridge of Optil was 12,556 feet, a difference of 2723 feet, three Eiffel towers on the top of one another in an hour and a half! The cairn stood 223 feet above the surface of the Langak-tso, and now we were 2500 feet below the lake. Such figures give a notion of this road. On the Tibetan side of the Himalayas one cannot dance light-footed and gleefully as on roses. But it is grand, bewitching, and enchanting, and inspiriting to travel over the tributaries of the Sutlej, where the rivers strike their chords in accompaniment to the wanderer's steps, and their ringing metallic music calls forth a thousand echoes from the steep rocky cliffs.

How different from the valley of the Tsangpo! There a difference of level amounting to three thousand feet took as many months to descend as here it takes hours. That is the difference between the plateau country, where horizontal lines predominate, and the peripheral Himalayan region, the country of vertical lines. In the enclosed basin of Chang-tang all the products of weathering are carried towards the centre and have contributed for countless ages

127. THE DEVIL'S CAULDRON OF THE NGARI-TSANGPO.

to level down the country. Here, on the other hand, they are all washed away and the earth's crust is cut down deeply. One is awestruck at this transition from the flat landscape to the sculptured. I know nothing which can compare in overpowering beauty with the scenes which are displayed at every turn before the eyes of the traveller as he witnesses the combat of the Sutlej with the Himalayas. Nature affords no grander parallel to the fight of St. George with the Dragon. The Himalayas lie pierced through at our feet, while the river sings its pæan of victory, tossing to the end of time.

The ascent begins again. We must climb up just as high as we have slid down on the steep slopes of the left side. We strive and struggle, and yet cover no appreciable distance. If we could place all the ascents together and all the descents, the result would be a length of road amounting to several times the distance of an air line over the Himalayas.

On the flank of the left side we notice the marks of a stupendous landslip. A mass equal in volume to all the pyramids of Egypt together has broken loose and fallen to the bottom of the valley. The path runs up between its fragments and the remaining precipitous cliff, past boulders, through detritus, and over hillocks, ravines, and furrows. A small clear and icy cold rivulet takes pity on our thirst, and we all drink deep draughts of it. Then we go on again. The gradient is steep, and we zigzag up at a terribly slow pace. The animals labour, sweat, and pant in quick and hasty gasps; one would think they must burst from want of breath. The valley we follow leads up to a small saddle, and beyond this we cross another valley hollow, where the water collects into a bed which also pays tribute to the Ngari-tsangpo. At the top a view again opens out over the wild valley, and now we can see the Dato-la and its stone pyramid, beside which we stood not long ago. But of the roar of the river not a whisper reaches us.

Grass, herbs, and thorny bushes form here and there ragged clumps. Otherwise the path winds through bare boulders and weathered débris, and schist stands *in situ.*

The strike and dip of the rock, about 30° to the north-west, is the same on both sides. The valley is isoclinal, and the river has a tendency to follow the top of the fold; therefore the flanks on the left side are the steeper, and the Ngari-tsangpo is undermining them.

The camp this day was pitched at the spring Koldoktse, at a height of 14,275 feet. No rain was heard in the night, though the sky threatened rain. But after a minimum of 45.3° in the night the storm broke loose at daybreak, and as we packed up our things the rain pelted down on the flanks of the mountains.

The spring Koldoktse was only a stage on the way to the pass Dambak-la. After this saddle is reached we go down rapidly to the valley Sasser, watered by a small brook. Then we climb again up the Tsanglangma-kesa side valley and come to Sanak among jagged rocks and over flat or steep hills into higher regions, marching in a west-north-westerly direction. At last we are up at the cairn on the flattened pass Pooche-la, where the instruments give a height of 16,165 feet above sea-level, or 3609 feet above the bridge of Optil.

A brook rises just at the top, and we follow it down to an expansion of the valley called Manchu-chen, where a circular stone sheep-fold stands on a flourishing meadow. Sumbu-tar and Bichutse are other valleys on our way; in the latter we encamp at a spring.

During the day we had the wind in our faces, with rain and hail, and I was glad to have the Tibetan mantle. Thunder rolled and the weather was raw and cool. At one o'clock the thermometer marked 43.5°, or nearly two degrees lower than the minimum of the preceding night. This was somewhat different from the summer heat in the gorge of Optil, where we had had nearly 72°. The night of August 22 was starlight and calm, and the air was cooled down to 29.5°. Such cold we had never felt since we had left Tokchen a month before. The morning sun shed its gold brilliantly and clearly over the earth, but its shafts were crossed by the monsoon which began early to drive its blue-grey cloud chariot over the mountains.

We travelled in a subdued light and comfortably warm

air to the pass, and thence down into the Chuwang-chung valley, the brook of which unites with the Gyesowang river. The landscape now assumes a different character. Beyond the pass Piang-la the ground falls to the north and north-east, and where the path makes a bend to the south-west the ascent is continuous. To the right of our road rises a very considerable range with snowy peaks, and contours which vividly remind us of the Surla range in the Trans-Himalaya. It seems to run west-north-west.

From a valley in this range runs the voluminous Tokchen-chu river, receiving additions from several transverse valleys. We do not allow ourselves to be tempted to encamp by the attractive meadows of these valleys, but try to get down to the mouth of the Lungun valley, where four black nomad tents beside the brook present an unusual sight. We encamp near them (camp 480) at a height of 15,594 feet. We were quite in the highlands of Tibet again. Shepherds driving at even their gently bleating lambs and ewes into the folds, grunting yaks, columns of greyish-blue smoke rising from black tents, no fixed settlements, no tilled fields, and no poplars. A heavy snowfall, now and then interrupted by rain, darkness spread by thick clouds over the earth—all seemed to indicate that we had again returned from the depth of the warm valleys into lofty Tibet, to say a last farewell to the friendly amiable nomads.

27° in the night of August 23! This degree of cold also was a parting greeting from the home of eternal winter. It seemed as though summer were passing us by, followed by early autumn. But wait! The next night we were to have it 21° warmer, and two days later the minima would be higher than the maxima here. And in a few weeks we should be almost melted by the heat, and think with regret of the fresh mountain air and the cool summer snow.

But when I awoke in the Lungun valley, felt the icy cold air, and saw the threatening sky, the bare hills of detritus and the snow-clad mountains, I thought that we had not gained much by our month's journey from Tokchen. It was still cold and raw, and we were still at the same enormous height above sea-level. What good had the two crossings of the Sutlej at Kyung-lung and Totling done us, and why had we worn out ourselves and our animals among the innumerable side valleys? Warmth, life and Simla were just as far off, and we had not yet even commenced the actual crossing of the Himalayas. The Sutlej still streamed north-westwards. At Shipki the river first makes a decided turn to the south-west to begin its stormy course through the Himalayas, overcoming all the obstacles it encounters. The Indus takes a step farther, and in the neighbourhood of Gilgit bends at right angles to break through the mountains by the shortest way. And farther than all travels the Brahmaputra, which flows through two-thirds of Tibet parallel to the Himalayas before it puts forth its strength on the noted breach of the Dihong valley.

The country round Lungun was a boundary stone on our way. Now we had done with the deep trying side valleys, and we had passed successfully through the cañon country. Another country awaited us, other forms of surface, which were not less grand than the former, nay, even more stupendous and astonishing. But now the breach through the mightiest mountain system of the world was before us.

CHAPTER XXIX

DOWN TO THE SUTLEJ

Now came days of excitement.

A quickly passing hail shower rattled down on the mountain flanks as we took down the tents on August 24, and saw for the last time Tibetan herdsmen go to pasture with their sheep, and drive up their yaks to be milked. We ascended to the pass over a gently rising flat of gravel. To the right of the road ripples the brook Neribke, and beyond Kongkong-la rises the lofty range with its snow belts. At length the road comes up to the Dungmar-la pass, which is adorned at the top by an elegant cairn, resembling, with its red-painted poles, streamers and horns, a bloody sacrificial stone dedicated to heathen gods.

To the south the eyes rove freely over the mighty Himalayan range, which we shall soon cross by the Shipki pass, and on this side of its steep flanks we can perceive the deep wild valley of the Sutlej. At a short distance to the west stands a crest with fields of firn and grey pinnacles. Now and then we hear stones and rocks sliding down the nearest declivities; they are the voices of weathering which announce the law of transitoriness to mountain masses of the hardest granite.

At the stone pyramid of the Dungmar pass we are at a height of 15,919 feet above the sea. Now comes something different. Our road runs south-west, and we go headlong over endless declivities. What a wonderful view! We feel so helpless, small, and lost in this grand, wildly dissected country. Tagha and Shing-chig-ma are names the guide whispers into my ear. The Chang-tang with its nomad life lies far behind us. We are coming to agricultural villages and men who are alike in all respects to their congeners on the heights except in the words of greeting, borrowed from Mohammedans of India, "Salaam, Sahib." But they are just as good Lamaists as any citizen of Lhasa, as is proved by the well-kept *mani* walls and streamered cairns which line the road.

Gradually we come down from great elevations into lower regions. I lean with my right hand on the left shoulder of Lobsang, and thus walk more surely and quickly over hillocks of nasty granite blocks, through sand and rubbish which gives way under the feet, and over slopes of soil scantily clothed with grass and halms. I feel the air growing denser and warmer. Down in the valley below us I perceive the Tomlang-tsangpo as a motionless, noiseless thread of bluish-green, interwoven with white foaming rapids.

Still we go on. We pass down the last slopes, and find at the bottom an irrigation channel which conducts water from the river to the barley-fields of the village of Tangmet, which lie on a sloping ledge high above the valley bottom. Splashing among round polished blocks of light-coloured granite the Tomlang-tsangpo forces its 350 cubic feet of water in a single shoot between the stone walls abutting on the banks, which support a small awkward bridge. It consists of two slender tree-trunks a foot apart, and is simply covered with a row of stone slabs. This small wicked-looking frame may be safe, but it is prudent to keep in the middle of the stone pavement, for otherwise, as one trunk bends more than the other, one may fall head first into the greenish-white spray. My men carried the baggage over, supporting one another, and the animals were driven through the river farther down, where the water was quiet.

Here is active life, here the spirits of earth toil and do not sleep, as on the heights of Chang-tang. Here the water dashes through steep valleys eager to reach the sea. See that brook, which has washed itself out a ravine in the high mountains away to the west, and now rushes merrily through a rocky portal into the Tomlang-tsangpo. The

128. Bridge over the Tomlang-tsangpo.

129. Mountain Range on the Frontier of Tibet and India.

village of Pera lies on a cornice above the valley in the middle of its fields, *mani* walls and *chhortens*. The road passes the village. It is rough and dangerous, and takes us up to the small Puge-la saddle, and then goes down again in sharp zigzags very rapidly nearly to the bottom of the valley, where the village of Puge stands, on the top of a terrace like those on which Tangmet and Pera have found sites. The barley fields stretch to the very edge of the terrace, and the heavy swelling ears ripening for harvest undulate over the valley.

We do not stop, but pass by Puge's stone houses, their projecting windows and balconies raised on piles, which give us a foretaste of the architecture in vogue in the Himalayas. Two willows with dense foliage enhance the charm of the little village. The men from Ladak are here reminded of their home and raise a cheerful song as we troop by. Shy villagers come out to gaze at us; the dogs bark till they are almost hoarse, and come to loggerheads with Takkar and Little Puppy, while the river roars in the valley below. It is really a joyous life, a foretaste of the days awaiting us on the way to Simla.

Beyond the village the path is disagreeable, for now it runs as a small ledge along a slope bestrewn with sharp-edged phyllitic schist and light-coloured gneiss, but soon it goes down to the village Yer, a closely packed cluster of stone huts on the left bank of a side valley which opens on the right. The Buddhist religion is highly honoured by the people of Yer, as may be seen from the silent monuments and speaking stones. Three *chhortens* raise their pyramids in the middle of a field, and from the ashes within blessings pour forth over the thriving corn in its bright dress of juicy green.

A sorry bridge crosses the brook of the side valley. Takkar, who had crossed the bridge of Pera with the greatest caution, found the bridge of Yer below all criticism, and preferred the 280 cubic feet of water which separated him from the farther bank. When all the caravan had crossed, heroically but howling piteously he plunged into the swirling waves, and was in a moment swept away to a block of stone, on to which he crawled up with an effort, quite dizzy already. There he sat very mournfully, a prey to bad luck; he coughed and cleared his throat after all the cold water he had had to swallow, and then howled at the sight of the billows that boiled and foamed on both sides of the block. We pitched our camp on the right bank and amused ourselves vastly, though perhaps heartlessly, at the pitiful situation into which the big dog had fallen. After Takkar had made himself ridiculous long enough, and had done penance enough for his fear of the bridge, he slipped yelping into the water, fought bravely with the waves, and came again safely but dripping wet on to dry land.

It was long since so charming a landscape had surrounded our tents. They stood on a narrow strip of ground between a vertical cliff and the murmuring brook. Mild breezes rustled through the crowns of the willows and set the bright green barley fields in motion against the background of grey sheets of rock. The prayer streamers fluttered lazily on their poles; half-naked, dear, dainty little children played on the flat roofs of the huts, and their bright laughter echoed among the hills. Now and then was heard the bark of the village tykes, and the river ceaselessly sang its plaintive ballad of the endlessly long journey to the sea.

Between Dungmar-la and Yer we had descended 3524 feet in two hours. How delightful it was to breathe this dense warm air! The thermometer marked about one o'clock P.M. 70.7°, against 44.1° on the preceding day, and the minimum at night was only 48°. Well may white men be eager to escape from the suffocating heat of India to the cool air of Simla, or of some other hill station on the southern flank of the Himalayas. But it is still more glorious to come down from the cold rarefied air of Tibet into the warmth of deep valleys. It is a feeling like that of convalescence after an illness, like rest after hard work, and like pleasant dreaming on flowery meads on mild days beside the sea. Even the nights are delightful; there is no need to load the body with warm skins and rugs, and I lie long awake just to enjoy breathing freely, for respiration is a pleasure and no longer a bodily exertion. Sleep is heavenly and waking is pleasant. And if I do not sleep so many hours as up yonder, I derive greater benefit from the night's rest.

Our elation increases as the heights diminish. The boundless level expanses of Tibet and the extensive views are gone, and we find ourselves in a country where the horizon hangs above our heads in a jagged line. When I get into the saddle in the morning I know that a series of surprises await me. Such was the case also when we left Yer. At the first bend in the valley we ride for a long time along the fields of the village of Tsar and between the willows on a small hill. Another bend and Shinggun-gompa, the village of Pude and its grove of dense foliage are left behind. A tributary intercepting our road is crossed without a bridge. Near the village of Niru we again leave the valley bottom to mount the heights.

We have to cut across a tip of the great range which rises between our valley and that of the Sutlej. There is said to be another path down below, but only foot-passengers can make use of it. Uphill, then, and over steep slopes, over ledges of solid rock in natural staircases, among boulders and detritus. The path is often exceptionally steep and is always troublesome. We rise ever higher above the valley floor, and the murmur of the stream dies away. At length we are up on the Rongtotke-la pass, with its cairn standing at an elevation of 13,690 feet.

Dumb with astonishment at the magnificent view which here meets my eyes, I remain for a time by the cairn to admire it. In the depths below the Sutlej lies as in a trough, and the famous river flows down from the south-east. Confined between its precipitous cliffs, which form corridors and huge stone columns, it winds along like a greenish white belt, apparently motionless and silent as the grave. The horizontal distances are insignificant, the vertical appalling. One would think a shout could be heard at the village of Shipki to the south-west, so plainly visible are its huts, terraced fields, and orchards. Above the village rears itself the mighty crest which has had to wait for our coming; but now we shall soon be there. The Shipki-la is sunk in its ridge, and just to the right of it we perceive the huge deeply excavated breached valley of the Sutlej. Unfortunately the magnificent view is a little blurred by fine rainy drizzle, and wisps of white cloud which sail like warships about and beneath the crests. But the Shipki-la is not as near as we think. We must first clamber down as low as we can, down to the level of the Sutlej, and then mount to dizzy heights on the other side. The thought that the Shipki-la is the last pass along the whole road to Simla consoles us, however, and after an unusually long rest we leave the Rongtotke-la to the mercy of the winds and begin the endless descent.

Now come numerous zigzags running down steep declivities and banks, deeply cut wedge-shaped ravines, and bending round shoulders of mica-schist, the road runs rapidly down slopes bestrewn with sharp rubbish, destructive to my Tibetan boots. A little brook has worn out a cleft in the rock, and the road again hangs like a cornice over the depths. If the loads are packed too broad the animals may be pushed over the edge. Then come more steep slopes full of boulders and pebbles. We are still far off, but the roar of the river reaches our ears as a slight murmur. Down below we see the bridge of Lopchak. It looks fearful in the distance, weak and fragile as a match.

One steep slope after another is left behind, and we go down lower and lower. The river looks larger, the roar sounds louder through the denser air and in the contracted valley. We stumble down another length and reduce the height by a hundred yards, and then by another, and thus gradually approach the great river. The view contracts as the mountains rise ever higher. Now the roar of the river fills all the valley. The bridge is the central feature in the scene; over its swinging hammock runs the road to Shipki.

We traverse a few more hundred yards and hurry down the last slopes of detritus. The gradient becomes less, and at last we are down on the flat meadow on the right bank of the Sutlej, in a locality called, like the bridge, Lopchak. The tents are set up near the well-situated village of Korang. Fancy always having the enjoyment of such a view! To see the river rise during the rainy season and slowly fall in autumn and winter until it reaches

130. Goats on the Lopchak Bridge.

131. On the Shipki-la.

its lowest level; to follow the struggles of water against the cold, and to watch the belt of ice on the banks growing broader, while snow accumulates on the flanks of the valley which are not too steep to retain it. At last the river is spanned by a bridge of ice, and the white covering holds it in its clutches. Then comes spring, the snow and ice melt, and the river rises; the passes that have been closed by snow so long are open again for traffic. The Sutlej comes to life and the people of Korang can hear the pulsations of its movement month after month.

From Rongtotke-la to the bridge of Lopchak we descended 3906 feet in two hours, for the Sutlej here lies at a height of 9784 feet.

While the men were putting the tents in order I made a closer examination of the bridge. As at Kyung-lung and Totling nature has done most of the work. A huge boulder lies on the right bank of the river, and there is solid rock on the left. Between the two the river is squeezed up to a breadth of 74 feet. A broad flight of stone steps leads to the upper slab of the right bridgehead, where a passage or portal of stone bears a small white *chhorten.* The vaulted roof of the portal is richly ornamented with fresh paintings and prayer formulæ for the edification of those who trust their lives to the wretched planks that swing over the stream. The usual trunks which support the bridge itself are firmly fixed in the Cyclopean wall of the bridgehead. The upright stone pier of the left bridgehead is built on a slanting ledge of rock, and looks as if it might at any moment slip down into the river. In this wall also tree trunks are inserted, and thus the span of the bridge is shortened by several yards. In other respects the construction is of the usual design, two beams with joists of wood, planks, and boughs irregularly placed. These are held in position by posts attached to the beams below the wooden joists. The beams are fastened at the bridgehead by blocks of stone, which unnecessarily add considerably to the weight.

I take up my position where the suspended part of the bridge commences, and there can see that the whole structure dips under its own weight in an uncomfortable curve.

Below me the great river tosses as it is sucked in furiously between the bridgeheads. Any one who is not quite sure on his feet had better keep off this bridge, for it is narrow and has no balustrade, and through the chinks between the planks the boiling water is seen, and one feels as though the bridge were rushing upstream. An involuntary start may pitch a man over. A skilled swimmer, however, would probably work his way out again. In the middle of the bridge the woodwork is 24½ feet above the water.

The bridge was doubtless not so bad when it was new and the two beams were fairly straight. But now it is old and badly worn, and hangs askew in an alarming manner. Its woodwork has been drenched by heavy rains, heated and scorched by the sun, covered with snow in winter and eaten into by frost, and under a load a trifle too heavy the two beams would snap like glass. The worst is that the beam on the upstream side makes a much greater curve than its neighbour, so that the whole bridge as seen from the right bank tilts to the right. There is, therefore, a danger of slipping and falling, and all the more because several cross planks have been worn smooth.

The inhabitants of the village of Korang, who are responsible for it, said that they had intended to restore the bridge during the last low water, but after mature consideration they came to the conclusion to rely another year on the protection of the *chhorten* tower. I expect that the bridge will one day strike work, when it can no longer bear the traffic. "If I can only get over safely, it may do what it likes afterwards," is, no doubt, the thought of every traveller. So I, too, thought as I sat up there looking at the rotten planks which hung over the formidable Sutlej, and shook and swayed back and fro even in the gentle breeze blowing in the valley.

I drew for perhaps an hour. But no one came. Was the critical moment so near that no one would venture over any more? No! Tripping steps are heard on the steps. Two Tibetans drive fifty goats laden with salt up to the small open platform of the bridgehead. The men shout and whistle shrilly, but the goats will not move from the spot. And when goats get any notion into their heads,

132. The Caravan after safely crossing the Lopchak Bridge.

there is nothing to be done with them. One man seizes two goats by the horns and drags the refractory, jumping and rearing animals out on to the bridge, while his comrade drives some others after him. Encouraged by this sight, the whole troop dashes suddenly over the chasm. It is a wonder that none of the four-footed lunatics is pushed over the edge. The bridge sways up and down; surely one more goat would cause it to give way. I drew a breath of relief when the whole troop was over and disappeared in a cloud of dust among the hills on the other side.

CHAPTER XXX

FAREWELL TO TIBET

SUCH heat as in the night of August 25 the minimum thermometer had not marked for two whole years; we had 54.1°. Accompanied by Tubges I went off to the bridge. As a herdsman from the Shyok valley, accustomed to the wildly fissured dales and the foaming summer floods and the shaking bridges of Ladak, he was considered by us all as the most surefooted, and therefore my maps and notes were to be committed to his care. The valuable results of nine months' work lay packed in three small boxes from Tokchen, and Tubges was to carry them over one at a time, so that should he stumble all would not be lost. He crossed over safely with one box, balancing himself on straddling legs, before I thought of suggesting that he should crawl over and push the boxes before him. When the other two were safely deposited on the other bank I felt relieved, and sat down on them to watch what would happen next.

With a bale on his back Suen came up to the bridge-head. But when he saw the swinging stage and looked down on the whirling water he stopped, shook his head, and turned round. The bursts of laughter of his comrades goaded him on, and holding his breath and carefully balancing himself, he walked on, and when he had come safely over began to dance and sing, and he took a solemn oath that he would never set foot again on this bridge. Gulam, Kutus, and Lobsang went backwards and forwards to carry tents, bags, and saddles over to the left bank, and soon all the baggage was transported.

Now came the mules and horses. A smart old man of

Korang, who knew all about the bridge, came of his own accord to offer his assistance. The first mule crossed, feeling his footing at each step, and his comrades followed with the same cool composure and intelligence. Then the old man from Korang led a black horse safely over the bridge, and was just as successful with another. A third horse did not like the look of things, but soon consented to follow his leader.

The two white horses were the worst, as usual. The large one jibbed at the sight of the bridge, backed so far over the top of the stone wall that his hind legs slipped over the edge, and he would certainly have fallen and broken his neck if two Ladakis had not rushed forwards and held him till help came. While he was recovering from his fright the old man took my riding horse by the halter and stepped on to the bridge. I expected to see him plunge over again, but the horse kept quite quiet, and followed the man, only quickening his pace a little as he neared firm ground.

The old man of Korang seemed to possess an especial gift of overcoming the fear of refractory steeds for the bridge. He induced the other white horse also to follow him, but the animal wished to make short work of the job and began to gallop so fast that the bridge shook more than ever. It was a grand feat to gallop over the wretched thing without slipping or putting his feet between the joists. He came over trembling in all his limbs, and then there was general jubilation.

The caravan was laden and the day's march was commenced along the left bank, where a fine long *mani* wall was erected, and the river roared beneath us. Rokti-chu is a small side valley with a turbulent brook, spanned by a bridge of the usual kind. Then the slopes become less steep, and we recede from the Sutlej.

A bend in the road and then the roar of rapids again reaches our ears. Beyond it lies the village of Chok, the most idyllic spot I have seen in Tibet. The road traverses quite a park of poplars and willows, and half-ripe yellow fruit hangs on the apricot trees. Small runnels ripple among the trees, and pleasant cool shade is afforded by the dense vaults of foliage. Here and there a hut peeps through the leaves, and a streamer pole stands beside the smallest temple I have ever seen. Above the park stands the village itself in the form of an amphitheatre, with a grand view of mountains and valleys, and the road runs on a level with the roofs of the uppermost row of houses, on which apricots are spread out to dry.

For a time we follow the foot of a cliff, and then mount rapidly over solid rock, gneiss, and mica-schist, where the road is improved with stone walls and hurdlework. Then over more rapids we come to Largyep, where the villagers are engaged in mowing their fine crop of barley. Up and down we go into valleys and out again, past long *mani* walls and through a solitary *chhorten* gateway with portraits of Buddha as ceiling paintings, to whom the gods of the mountains pay silent homage. At last the path shoots headlong to the bottom of a valley, where the brook Salve-chu tumbles down with a deafening noise.

The bright frothy water rushes in reckless rapids over round, smoothly-polished boulders, hisses, whirls, and seethes as if it could not get down quickly enough to the Sutlej. A firm bridge affords us a passage over the Salve-chu to the left bank, and over steep rocky slopes we come to the end of our day's march, Shipki, our last camp on the sacred soil of Tibet.

Shipki was also my finest camping ground in Tibet. The tents were pitched on a grassy slope, where there was a sweet fresh odour of soil and juicy grass, and the apricot trees afforded cool shade. The wind blew in strong gusts, and produced a pleasant rustle in the trees, while the Salve-chu murmured at the bottom of the scarp. On a higher slope of the bank stood an agricultural village, and gigantic peaks kept guard in the background, veiled in dense clouds. As though to render our halt near the village more agreeable, men and women presented themselves, calling out politely, "Salaam, Sahib," and bringing small presents of butter, milk, and fruit. No one showed any disposition to stop us on the threshold of India.

The night was calm and mild, with a temperature of

133. The Lopchak Bridge.

134. The Sutlej Valley below Lopchak.

56.3°; the stars twinkled through the foliage of the apricot trees, and blustering wind and rushing water lulled us to sleep. We were in marching order early in the morning, and prepared to mount to greater heights, accompanied by crowds of beggars and flies. The former placed themselves in our way at every turn, holding out small bouquets of flowers. They were the last Tibetans I saw, and how could I refuse them a trifle? They gradually disappeared, and the winged pests also became fewer as we mounted. The flies which swarmed round us on the other side of the pass were British subjects.

We had, fortunately, picked up five yaks in Shipki. We could, therefore, spare our own animals in crossing the pass. The climb begins as soon as we leave the yards, fields, and conduits behind us. The path winds steeply up between boulders and pebbles, over marshy furrows with rank grass, over purling brooks, and along troublesome slopes and dome-shaped hills. In the narrow hollow of a flat ravine lies the last tilled field belonging to Shipki. At Yayur begins the hardest ascent, and here we must go slowly. The animals take two steps, and then have to stop to recover their breath. Even the yaks breathe heavily. They stare with their bloodshot eyes, and their purplish tongues hang dripping from their mouths.

High up on the other side of the Sutlej monks of the monastery Puri-gompa enjoy a splendid view from their loopholes. Yonder rises the wildly fissured, wonderfully beautiful summit of the Rio Porgyul above this world ot majestic mountains, but clouds often spread their veil over the brow of this giant. It stands there like an outpost of the series of royal peaks which stretch their arc along the north of India, and contain among them the highest in the world.

Behind us, in the direction of the bridge of Lopchak, we see the Sutlej meandering down below and struggling with the mountains, an overpowering view, a scene of sublime grandeur such as only the Himalayas can display. The whole valley lies like a bottomless abyss below us, and around us tower the crests, their battlements piercing the clouds. We have ourselves climbed so high that wisps of cloud, pure white like steam, conceal the valley from us at times. Now and then a little drizzle falls, and the air is cool. Not far to the right we descry the point of the rocky ridge up which we are painfully toiling to the Shipki-la. From its edge there is a sheer fall to the dizzy abyss in which the Sutlej has carved out its wild breach. Never has human eye beheld the cliffs of that dim foaming cutting. Will a way ever be blasted through it, a road which will save caravans the crossing of the Shipki-la?

After a last very trying ascent we are up at the cairn. The yakdrivers called the pass Pimig-la, but said that it was frequently named Shipki-la, after the village. The height is 15,404 feet, and we have mounted 5620 feet again from the Lopchak bridge, so deep has the Sutlej cut into the Himalayas at this point. Unluckily, the view over the mountains on the Indian side was intercepted by thick clouds, beneath which only the huge valley was visible, but not the river, as it lies in too deep a trough.

It is the last time we shall be so high above sea-level. Now we are going definitely downwards. But not at once. First, we must cross a bowl-shaped hollow, with a pool called Tsokam and a small glacier brook. Here, at Pashagang, is the boundary between India and Tibet. I stop a couple of minutes on the farther margin of the hollow to bid farewell to Tibet. My sight did not range far into the realm of the Trans-Himalaya, but a motley procession passed before my eyes of wonderful memories and strange adventures among the mountains that shut in the prospect. Here ended not a chapter, nay, a whole book was closed at the Shipki-la.

On Indian ground we speed down quite passable slopes, but soon the gradient becomes steeper, and we return ever more rapidly to the denser layers of air above which we have been raised for a few hours in crossing the pass. Stones and rubbish rattle round our feet, a flock of sheep slips past us in a hollow, a crystal clear rivulet shoots down a granite ledge in the entrance of the valley Kamlung, and finally we slide down a steep gully between bushes and boulders to a point where a view opens on the village of

135. A Typical Village on the Tibetan Frontier.

Photographed by Mr. Marx of Poo.

Namgya-rijing, its waving fields, its leafy groves, and its jungles of luxuriant vegetation.

A field just mown offered a suitable site for camp 484. The height was less, but we were still far above the Sutlej. Down below are seen more villages on their flat platforms. On the right side wild precipitous rocks rise to dizzy heights above the river. This view is unspeakably fine and fascinating. Violent gusts of wind sweep the steep flanks and whistle through the hedge of wild roses which barricades our tents.

The villagers are Lamaists, speak Tibetan, and wear round their necks cords with sacred talismans. The loose bulging skin coats are seen no more, the fashions being modified from the Indian side, and the men wear thin close-fitting coats. Our host had a short cut grey beard and a little cap on the crown of his head. He was named Hira, and was the Numberdar, or headman, of Namgya-rijing. He had seen many Sahibs, and when he came to us to give me an armful of sugar beet, he asked if he could oblige me in any way. Yes, he could request his colleague in Poo by letter to have everything ready for our passage of the Sutlej on the following day. He told us that lower down in the village of Tovaling ten persons had lately died of smallpox. An Indian doctor had come up and vaccinated all the inhabitants. When the yak drivers from Shipki heard this they begged me to let them go back at once. They were well paid, and they made their way up to the pass again. With them the last band was severed which had connected me with Tibet.

I write August 28 in my diary. The road runs down shelving declivities full of rubbish, and is lined on both sides with thorny thickets. Near it lies Namgya proper, and is succeeded still lower down by the village of Kapp on a hilly terrace. Here the Sutlej emerges from its corridor, the descent becomes more gradual, and beyond a *chhorten* portal we march along the bank some 150 feet above the water. But still we go up and down according to the form of the steep slopes. Here it is not pleasant to ride on a horse which comes from the more level parts of the Trans-Himalaya. Often the road runs like a narrow stripe over an extremely steep declivity, falling immediately down to the heavily thundering water. The cliffs on the right bank seem perpendicular, and dirty grey waves wash their feet. Granite alternates with dark mica-schist. The bottom of the grand valley, which we saw so far below us from the Shipki pass, is a fine sight. Now we are, as it were, in a mouse-trap, and feel uncomfortable at being below colossal cliffs and peaks. A landslip, and all thought of escape would be absurd.

Ah! I cannot suppress an exclamation of astonishment as I look into the Tidang valley, where a mountain stream forms a white foaming fall with a tremendous roar, and carries perhaps 530 cubic feet of water. It is pleasant to linger a few minutes at the fine bridge below the fall. A little farther down the Sutlej makes a bend to the right, and in a valley to the left lies the village of Tovaling which has been attacked by smallpox.

Here the messenger Ngurup Dorche, who had to carry the message to Poo, dashed past us. It was when we had only a short length of road to traverse to the passage of the Sutlej. The message stick was handed to him, and he vanished swiftly along the road with it.

We follow in his track. A landslip which has carried away the road detains us a good hour. We have to dig a new path with our own spades in the steep slope, after which the men lead the animals carefully past the place lest they should fall into the river, and then carry over the baggage. Again the road runs upwards and skirts the outer edge of a cliff which falls vertically, or even overhangs. Grass and shrubs have taken root at the very margin. Whoever stumbles here falls head first into the river. The right bank is similarly formed, and the river passes through a gigantic trench deeper than it is broad, and both in front and behind its cross section is that of a dark rocky portal.

Down here it is warm. The confined air lies dense and heavy over the river. We halt and drink from springs and rivulets which bubble up from the bosom of the earth. Here no breeze can reach us.

At last a precipitous cliff forces us to descend to the

136. GOAT CARAVAN AT THE TOP OF THE SHIPKI-LA.

137. ROAD IN THE SUTLEJ VALLEY.

edge of the water, where we see the billows of the river rolling swiftly beside us. Then we go up a slight rise again to the platform of a projecting rock that hangs fearfully over the deep trough of the river, and where not the ghost of a bridge is to be seen. But Poo lies on the other side, and we must get over.

CHAPTER XXXI

BETWEEN SKY AND WATER

We had now arrived at the head of the bridge which is described in Captain Rawling's narrative *The Grand Plateau* (p. 303). Accompanied by Major Ryder and the other members of the expedition to Gartok, he crossed the Sutlej here just at the end of the year 1904. He says:

> Ten miles below Khub (Kapp) a great cantilever bridge, regarded as an engineering triumph, spanned the Sutlej, carrying the road from the left to the right bank. It had only been completed and opened for traffic in the autumn, and was looked upon by the natives with awe and admiration. But for us it was to be of no use. The timber, obtained from the neighbourhood, proved to be exceptionally brittle, for, three weeks before our arrival, the lower beams gave way close to the piers, and the whole structure was precipitated with a crash into the torrent below.

For the Englishmen a temporary bridge was built between the ice-lined banks. But for us there was no other resource but to trust ourselves and our belongings to a cable of wire strands stretched between the stone piers.

We collected our animals on the stone ledge above the left bridge-head, and looked around in vain for the help without which the caravan could not make use of the cable. Not a living creature could be seen, not even a wretched hut was erected as a watch-house beside this dangerous passage. Imagine a pitch-dark night, dense fog, and a traveller who, trusting in the existence of a bridge, climbs to the bridge-head, and thence, stepping

138. Bridge over the Sutlej near Shipki.

139. Cable over the Sutlej near Poo.

Sketches by the Author.

into empty space, falls into the Sutlej. Poo stands high up, and is hidden by the mountain flanks. Neither by shouts nor signs can we attract the attention of the inhabitants, and a gun-shot would hardly be heard over there.

I step out on to the balks of the bridge-head. They project like a spring-board into empty space. Eighty feet below me seethes the compressed river. It seems as though our progress were stopped here and Simla hopelessly far away. I learned afterwards that the passage was purposely closed on account of the smallpox, and no travellers were allowed to come from the other side.

It was therefore no wonder that the messenger had shown such carelessness in delivering his message. Ngurup Dorche was sitting brooding at the bridge-head when we came to the unlucky spot. A man must be an acrobat to wind himself over on the cable without assistance. There are many such acrobats among the natives. They simply sling their cammerbands over the cable and hitch themselves along backwards. Ngurup adopted another method. He took the wooden frame of a mule's pack-saddle, placed it astride on the cable, wound a rope a couple of times round the wood, and put his legs into the loops thus made. When he was satisfied that all was secure, he grasped the cable with both hands and drew himself along backwards. I must admit that it was an awful sight when he had passed the outer edge of the spring-board and was dangling above the chasm. As long as the cable dipped down to the lowest point of its curve it was easy to move along, but hard on the ascending section. I breathed more freely when I saw him hanging over the right pier of the bridge. There he sprang out of the loops and vanished like an ibex over the hill on the way to Poo.

While we waited a fire was lighted, and Gulam put on water for tea. I examined the nasty place more closely. Mica-schist crops out on both banks, and the tall piers between which the bridge once spanned the river rest on a firm foundation of rock. The right bridge-head consists of an upright buttress in which balks of timber are built in horizontally, and the cable is carried at a height of six feet above the level stone platform to a perpendicular post, and thence to its anchorage in the ground beyond. On our side the wooden beams of the bridge are still in the stone dam and carry a platform with a parapet. The cable passes above the boarded footway, here also at a height of six feet, to the top of a firm post, beyond which it is wound round a capstan, and therefore it can be tightened when it has stretched too much. Usually travellers and goods are transported over the river by means of a pulley, which slides along the cable and is fixed in a block which keeps it in place. Men and animals are secured to a hook underneath the block and are drawn over easily and quickly. But now the pulley was broken, and we had to resort to some other contrivance.

I lay myself down on the bridge platform and carefully hitch myself forward to the edge. Just below me tumbles the mighty river, one of the giants of the Himalayas. Immediately below the stone pier two colossal boulders have fallen into the bed, and between them and the right rocky wall the river is compressed into a space of perhaps twenty-five feet. The whole Sutlej seems here changed into a squirting jet which bores through the mountains with marvellous energy. The white foaming volumes seem to dive under the boulders and disappear, only to shoot up again in boiling bells and vaulted hillocks of water. The whole is like a gigantic boiling cauldron. The noise is like growling thunder: it reverberates among the cliffs, it is deafening to the ear, and one feels dizzy and under the influence of some magic power that playfully attracts one down to the flakes of foam under which the Sutlej dances along its Berserker course raging furiously and white with wrath. I can hardly help feeling frightened. What if the beams now gave way while I am lying here gazing into the depths? What if the cable parted with a loud report as I hang over the river? Well, all would soon be over. Before I could really feel my heart coming up into my throat with horror I should come out of the whirlpool between the blocks as a chopped-up, well-soaked beef-steak.

140. THE SHIPKI-LA.

141. WIRE-ROPE BRIDGE NEAR POO.

But the cable will hold, I am told, though it is as thin as a cord. It is said to be 115 feet long.

It must be a good way to Poo, for Ngurup does not come back. Patience! Out with the sketch-book; I shall never forget this place. The stone platform of the dam on the right bank is only a stone's throw off, but the way to it lies through the valley of the shadow of death. All Tibet lies behind us, and yet we have never stood in front of such an awful fissure.

At last our waiting comes to an end. Yonder a party of men are hurrying down the slope. They are natives of Poo, but there are also two Europeans with walking-sticks and sun-helmets. They mount the dam quickly, and greet us politely. I have forgotten how to take off my hat, though fortunately I do not put out my tongue, but flourish my sketch-book frantically. We can see how eager they are to get me across as soon as possible. Ngurup has given them my letter. They know, then, who it is that now wishes to return to civilization after a sojourn of two years in Tibet—contrary to the wishes of four governments, of England and India, Tibet and China, not to mention the treaty concluded in 1907 between Great Britain and Russia, one of the objects of which was to prevent anything in the way of exploration for three years. They know that during that time I was my own master, and are curious to know how I have got on.

A native named Deva Ram, village magistrate of Poo, comes dangling under the mule saddle over to our side. We can see that he is accustomed to this little game, and would do for an aviator. After he has landed safely and saluted us politely, he ties some sacks and a tent under the saddle, to which a strong thin cord is attached and held by the men on the other side. Deva gives the signal, and soon the whole load is in their hands.

Now the Europeans begin to gesticulate, make signs, and point towards Poo. I do not understand them. One of them writes a few lines on a piece of paper which comes over with the saddle. The message is: "Please wait a little longer; we have sent to the village for a pulley-block." All right. The saddle, then, is not safe, and I am glad to wait.

The block came, and was drawn over to us. Kunchuk tried his luck. It was a joke to see the faces of Suen and Lobsang when their comrade was suspended over the chasm. They were almost sick with horror, and had to turn away. Suen rolled himself up like a hedgehog behind the capstan, and wept bitterly.

"What is the matter with you?" I asked.

"It is terrible that we must all die here after we have come so far and have only a little farther to go."

"Oh, do not be stupid, Suen; there is really no danger."

At the bottom of my heart I envy Kunchuk, who has already made the deadly passage. But in the meantime I have to see that my valuable notes are securely fastened and go over safely. And then I want to know what is to be done with the animals. One of the sensible mules is led up, and stands just under the block. Four strong bands of rope are put round him, one under the root of the tail, one supporting the neck, the third slung round the body in front of the hind-legs, and the fourth behind the fore-legs. The eyes of the victim are covered. The mule stands patiently quiet, but the trembling of his legs shows that he suspects some dirty trick. Ready! The men on the other pier begin at a given signal to pull with all their might. The block slides slowly along the cable. The mule is forced to move, and he walks with unsteady steps towards the river, after a vain attempt to resist with outstretched hoofs. He feels his feet leave the ground, and stretches his legs out, but cannot touch anything. Next moment he is sailing through the air above the tossing river. He has submitted to his fate, and his legs hang limp. What else could the poor creature do? But the agony is short; his forefeet strike the edge of the stone pier, he feels firm ground under his feet, and stands as patiently as before until he is freed from all his fetters and is sent off to graze on a bank.

Now it is my turn. "The earth vanishes; the Gyallar horn sounds the summons to the feast of the gods."

142. Deva Ram on his Way to us.

Deva Ram must think I am very heavy for he ties me up as fast as a dangerous criminal. I slip my legs into the loops of rope, and grasp the front cheek of the block firmly.

"Off!" I call out.

"No, Sahib, not yet," answers Deva Ram.

"What more is wanting?"

"The tackle will hold all right, there is no fear of it; but any one who is not accustomed to see the river below him may become giddy, lose his senses, relax his hands, throw himself backwards, slip out of the loops, and fall head first into the Langchen-kamba."

"I shall not be giddy."

"Still, for safety's sake, we will take a turn of rope, or better two, round your body and the other ropes. There, now all is right. Now you may loose your hands, Sahib, without falling."

"Off," I cry more loudly than before.

Deva Ram gives the signal, the block begins to glide, and I am suspended beyond the brink, and see the greyish billows of the river rolling beneath me. It seems an age. Why am I not already across? It is only 115 feet. Above on the heights is my old Tibet; down in the plains is India. My caravan is torn asunder. I myself am dangling between heaven and the murderous Sutlej. I have explored this river and discovered its ultimate source. Surely the discovery demands a victim! I never entertained such great respect for this grand majestic river as at this moment, and suddenly I realized the meaning of the *chhorten* pyramids and cairns of the Tibetans on banks and bridges, those cries for help against the uncontrollable powers of nature, and those prayers in stone to inexorable gods. My eyes fall on the gigantic white cauldron boiling in the abyss below. How magnificent, how ravishingly beautiful! Language has no words to describe it; no artist can depict this scene, the dizzy bird's-eye view cannot be reproduced on canvas. Only a model could give some notion of it. Only the droning of the thundering water is heard, repeated every moment. It fills the narrow chasm, and I hover among a chaos of sound waves crossing one another from all sides.

I swing about at every jerk caused by the pull on the rope. Halloh! Only two yards to the edge of the stone pier. Beautiful land! As the cable has held so long surely it will not now split with an ominous crack. Pull away! Only a yard more. With a comfortable feeling of security I glide over the pier, and in a moment am freed from all bands and fetters.

The two Europeans give me a hearty welcome in German, and congratulate me on having performed the short aerial journey without mishap. They are Moravian missionaries, and are named Marx and Schnabel. In a minute we are as well acquainted as friends of youth. We stay a short time on the platform to see Lobsang swung over with blindfolded eyes, for he could not trust his head, and he was very agitated when he landed. I also receive my white steed, and stroke his eyes and nose to quieten him. The others might look after themselves, and they were all over before eight o'clock, so that the whole crossing lasted quite five hours. The missionaries told me that an Englishman had turned back on seeing the cable.

Now we go up the steep ascent to Poo. Just as twilight comes we enter the narrow, lifeless streets of the village. Only a group or two of inquisitive women and some lonely strollers are out when we pass over the little market-place, where the villagers assemble on winter evenings to amuse themselves with dance, song, and string music. At last we come to the missionaries' compound, and find that it forms a pretty little neatly-kept village. A brand-new house in a garden is my abode during the days of rest.

I had not seen an European since August 14, 1906, and now I wrote August 28, 1908. For two long years I had associated with Asiatics, and I was glad to see men and women of German race again; and worthier specimens of the white race than these Christian apostles and their wives I could not have met with. They shamed me with their hospitality and spoiled me like a child. They served me with the best the house afforded, clothed me anew, gave me books and newspapers to read, and were never impatient at my cross-fire of questions: Was the world at peace or did

143. "I DANGLE BETWEEN HEAVEN AND THE MURDEROUS SUTLEJ."

Photographed by Mr. Marx of Poo.

the torch of war blaze in any country; how is it with the unrest in India; have you heard any news from Sweden? It is certainly pleasant to be spared for two years newspapers, telephone calls, stupid letters, idiotic receptions, and the inane chatter of the world. In so-called civilization we lead an artificial life, lose our individuality, and are picked to pieces by the gossip and base scandal in which society revels. It is pleasant to seek great solitudes where no commotion penetrates. But still, when the time of isolation is over, it is also delightful to find oneself in the swim again. One soon becomes accustomed to it, though one looks back not without sadness to the grand time when only a thin tent cloth separated one from the nights of the wilderness and the eternal stars.

I slept in a proper bed, and had a view of the garden where my men pitched their tents, and our tethered horses and mules could console themselves with better grass than they had ever seen before. Takkar and Little Puppy did not feel at home in these strange surroundings, and their Tibetan coats were not suited to this warm, oppressive air. They lay with their mouths open, gasped for breath, and snapped at the troublesome flies which left them no peace.

The village is divided into two sections. The poor live above, the well-to-do and rich below, the mission station. There are here 600 to 700 inhabitants, all Lamaists, who speak a dialect of Tibetan more akin to the language of Darjiling than to the patois of neighbouring districts. The caste system has spread hither from India. The blood also is not free from a Hindu admixture, and on the way to Simla it may be observed that Tibetan blood thins out, while Hindu blood becomes more conspicuous.

Wheat is cultivated here, barley and millet, besides buckwheat, which yields two crops a year. Only the missionaries try rye, and it thrives well. Poo lies too high for grape culture, but there are juicy bunches down by the river. Potatoes are planted in some fields, while beet, turnips, and radishes are grown generally. The mountain breezes rustle through the crowns of the walnut trees, and apricots and apple trees adorn the outskirts of the village. Of course poplars and willows are not absent, and the cedar or *shukpa* is the object of religious reverence. Spruce and birch occur above the village, but the deodar or Himalayan cedar thrives only on the west side of the Sutlej. Among bushes the wild rose and the whitethorn are the commonest.

Two monasteries belong to Poo. The upper is named Chila-gompa, the lower Poo-gompa. Thirty lamas of the red sect live there; these monks are allowed to marry. Most of the nuns live in the village, and occupy themselves in secular affairs.

Poo lies, indeed, high above the Sutlej, but yet in a hollow depression between lofty snowy mountains. In the height of summer a close stagnant heat, especially deleterious to European children, prevails in this hollow. All the white children that have died in Poo have been carried off in July or August. If a small child lives through August its parents may hope to keep it for another year. In September the nights become pleasant and people revive. Frost comes with the new year, and at the end of January the river freezes for five weeks. Only its quieter reaches have a proper covering of ice. One such place is above the cable; here the river may be crossed on planks which are laid on two boulders which stand at the edge of the ice fringe.

August 30 was a Sunday, and a service was held in the small chapel of the mission. The congregation consisted of perhaps fifty people, including a few children. The men sat on the right, the women on the left of the pulpit. My men also attended and listened with great astonishment to the singing and the words of the preacher. The tones of the organ sounded gentle and peaceful, and in the tongue of their country the Christians sang a psalm to the tune of "Glory to God in the Highest." It was wonderfully beautiful. I wept from emotion in the little lonely church among the majestic mountain masses of the Himalayas. The two years flew like a dream before my mind. Through the window is seen the bright sunny landscape, the threshold of my beloved Tibet, the royal

144. Aerial Passage of the Sutlej.

Photographed by Mr. Marx of Poo.

demesne of unfettered freedom, and now I am about to bid it a long farewell.

Festoons of ripening apples hung down among the leaves, and cackling hens stalked leisurely about the yard. Quiet and devout the congregation listened to the words of the preacher which sounded through the small building with gentle conviction.

Amen! Our Father. . . . Another hymn was sung, and with solemn faces the Christians dispersed to their homes.

The missionaries take me round the premises of the station. They tell me that the Himalayas are in the Moravian mission district No. 13, and that work was commenced in 1853. The Poo station was founded in 1865, and the first couple of missionaries were Mr. and Mrs. Pagell, who both died at their post in 1883, and were buried in the little graveyard above the chapel. A stranger stands thoughtfully and bareheaded before such a grave. They went into exile of their own free will, and sacrificed their lives for their faith. At home only a few friends inquired about them, and here perhaps they met with little gratitude and encouragement, but these preachers of the gospel fought for the highest of all earthly aims.

How sad and affecting to see these children's graves with their fresh or already faded wreaths! There one can read the names of many children who only came into the world to be baptized and to die, and of many who during their brief existence saw no other white faces than those of their parents, and no other scene than the Himalayas round Poo. Unknown to the world, pure and innocent, the little people slumber under the perishable inscriptions of their tombstones. Mr. and Mrs. Schnabel had three children in this churchyard, and one had died in the Red Sea on the voyage home. Mr. and Mrs. Marx had consigned their only child to the soil of the Himalayas fourteen days before, and fresh wreaths adorned the little mound. Some gravestones had inscriptions in Tibetan characters, not the everlasting, inane "Om mani padme hum," but Christian words, for beneath them rested villagers of Poo who had received baptism.

Solemn and profound is the atmosphere which reigns round these abodes of peace and forgetfulness. The eyes roam over wild grand valleys, and on all sides sharp pinnacles of rock form a guard of honour. The troop of monsoon clouds floats under the vault of heaven towards Tibet, and the stars of the winter night sparkle gently over the graves of Poo.

CHAPTER XXXII

A LEARNED LAMA FROM HUNGARY

When I set out from Poo on August 31, I had 200 miles to travel to Simla. A few hearty words of thanks to the missionaries' wives, a vigorous shake of the hand with the missionaries who escorted us to a bend in the road, and then we go off along the winding path through the state of Beshahr.

Here I travelled over a country which had been well known for a hundred years, and which had been thoroughly mapped by the topographical survey. I could therefore pack up my map-board and ride on free and unhampered without having to think of minutes and bearings. For two years I durst not omit to notice the smallest crook in the road, but now I had a holiday after a long period of work. Now I looked as long as I pleased at this wonderful country, noticed the villages and men who now become ever more common appearances, and gazed at the lofty mountains, the foaming river, and above all the vegetation which became more and more luxuriant, and passed gradually from high alpine forms to sub-tropical, and, finally, at the foot of the Himalayas, into tropical. As before, I could remark the increase of heat with the decrease of height, and the life and activity of man which beat with a stronger pulse every day we drew nearer to our destination.

After Poo our animals have no work to do. We employ coolies, in the English fashion, to carry our baggage. Fifteen coolies, men and women, carry our loads on their strong shoulders, while our animals tramp unladen, and even without burdens have to exert themselves enough to get over some awkward places. Beyond a sharp ridge of rock we have the Sutlej far below us on our left. Then follows a series of small projections and spurs, where the road is so dangerous that we must often help ourselves with our hands, if we would not lose our balance and fall into the water that rolls hundreds of feet below us. The road clings like a cornice to the cliff which often overhangs. Imagine this road where nature has done everything and man has not assisted with a single blasting charge! Branches, boughs, and slabs have, indeed, been thrust into all the crevices to provide steps and some little protection on the outer side, and at two places there is some attempt at a balustrade, but otherwise this road, with its abrupt sections and dangerous slides, has been formed by weathering.

Accustomed to the fresh air of elevated Tibet we are always perspiring; 77.7° in the shade is too much for us, and yet this is only the beginning of the heat which awaits us, and from which I shall not escape until I come to Shanghai and Japan. My men will have done with it when they get home to Ladak.

The rocks on the left side are just as abrupt, and there also a path has been levelled which connects Tovaling with Nesang and Morang. In the distance it looks like a fine thread on the cliff, a suitable contrivance for rope-dancers and suicides.

Beyond a difficult passage through strongly folded dark mica-schist, we march up a rise with a cairn, and then go down headlong by many hundred zigzags to the bottom of the side valley Sha-lungpo. There flows a river with water of the purest bluish-green, and the foam flakes of its falls and rapids float like white soap-suds on its surface. A small level spot on the left bank affords room for our two tents and the camp-fires.

Ngurup Dorche had left us and gone off to his home in a village close to Poo. The beggar from Chiu-gompa was still with us, and like the others had nothing to do. Beside me walked a young guide who was smart and active as a cat. We had passed our coolies half-way along the road and had to wait a long time down by the river bank before the undulating file appeared as small dots on the slopes. We saw sometimes their fronts, sometimes their backs or sides, according to their position on the zigzags; gradually they grew larger, and at last laid down their loads among the tents. There were some young girls among them and two of these were really handsome. I felt ashamed that these princesses of the wild mountains had to burden their shoulders with my baggage, while I was so comfortable myself. But my chivalry was out of place in the Himalayas, and the young ladies were quite pleased to work for their four annas a stage. I gladly doubled their pay, not only because it is absurdly small for such toil, but also because the black-eyed portresses were so indescribably charming.

On this road every fresh camping-ground surpasses the last in wild romantic beauty. In the Sha valley one seems to be shut up in a maze, and wonders how in the world one is to get out. On all sides nothing can be seen but narrow dells among abrupt wildly-fissured slopes. The Shalungpo leads like a corridor down to the colonnades of the Sutlej valley. It is no use to try and make oneself heard here. The Sha river, with its 700 or 800 cubic feet of water per second, forces its furious way through all obstacles to reach the Sutlej, and tumbling volumes of water drum against blocks and ledges a loud sonorous march of victory over the mica-schist. The heat confined in the valley lies heavy and oppressive over the water. But I have only to stretch my hand out of the tent door to fill a cup with wonderfully refreshing water at a temperature of only 50°. During the night the temperature did not fall below 62.1°.

The shades of evening fall sooner in the narrow valley, and it is dark earlier than on the open flats above. The fires flame up high and cast a yellowish red light on the faces of the cliffs. The men move about like ghosts; they can only be seen, for their steps cannot be heard nor their voices, only the overpowering roar of the river. The tent stands open to let in the light draught produced by the stream.

The sun rises on another brilliant day. We have now to cross the river. After rain this river rises tremendously and floods the small spot where our camp is pitched. It is much too broad to be bridged over. It was now impossible to wade through with laden animals, for probably a horseman would have been swept down to the Sutlej. Therefore, a cable, as at Poo, has been stretched across the bed which in the middle of the valley is only 11½ feet above the water. Now only a third of the cable need be used, for the river runs in a single channel along the right bank, where the cable is anchored in a very steep slope above a level stone wall which serves as a landing-place. The loads are carried to the bank, and at the top of a stone heap lying in the bed are fastened to the block of the running pulley. Then the whole pack is drawn over to the stone dam on the right bank, where fresh coolies are waiting to take charge of them.

The men are conveyed across in the same way. The horses have to look after themselves, and can scarcely keep their feet on the bottom of the bed, and resist the rush of the water. Two small mules are pulled across with a rope. Takkar swims over, but Little Puppy is sent by cable.

The Sha river is said to be the boundary of the Kanam district. The ascent from the right bank is very perceptible, and the road makes sharp short windings through abrupt fissures, where high shafts of masonry have been built up to support the path, past shady nooks and under dark-green canopies of pine-trees, higher and higher, until at length we reach a saddle called Tungnang-la.

Just below us we see the Sutlej and the place where the metallic green water of the Sha river is swallowed up by the dirty muddy flood of the main river and disappears instantly. A small commencement of a pebbly delta has been mercilessly cut off as with a knife. The Sutlej suffers no useless hindrances on its way. Just opposite on the left bank debouches the Tomba-chu valley with its stream, and therefore the place is called Sumna, or the meeting of three valleys.

The Tungnang-la does not suffice us; we mount still higher and pass a cairn which stands like a landmark high above the wildly tossing river. But now the corridor is so steep and deep that we only now and then catch sight of a small stretch of the Sutlej. It would be dangerous to ride here, so I go on foot. Tubges, Kunchuk, and Suen drive our unladen animals past us: the effect of the refreshing bath has not lasted long; they are sweating and their heads droop; but they keep up well.

Takkar is in a worse case; he must suffer terribly, for he takes short quick breaths and lets his dripping tongue hang out of his mouth. Whenever he sees a cleft with cool shadow he stops to rest there. Then he runs past us to crawl into some other hole. He drinks from every rivulet, laying himself down on his stomach in the water. He is afraid of the heat, smells danger, and broods over secret plans. What is he thinking of? He perhaps recalls to mind his youth on the bare breezy heights of the province of Bongba, and thinks of the March day when he was forced to leave his master and his home for ever. He had offered desperate resistance and none of us durst go near him. Afterwards he had quietly submitted to fate and had been as true to us as gold. How often had he saved me from spies, keeping jealous guard before my tent? Now he is thinking it all over and believes that he has been betrayed by us. Totling was all very well, and the Shipki-la was a glorious place which reminded him of Bongba. There he saw yaks for the last time. But the heat of Poo was detestable, and now we were still following the great river down towards the sea. Takkar told himself that it must become hotter the farther we descended, and the scenes of Bongba returned more clearly and sharply to his memory. Thus he thought as he ran from one shady place to another. He felt that all ties were loosened and that really he was a stranger among us. He felt like a hen when she sees the duckling she has hatched swimming in the water and cannot follow it. Now he rushes past us to look for another shady spot.

We march on and neither see nor hear anything of him. Perhaps he will wait and follow our track in the evening. No, there he comes again. I call to him, but he does not obey as usual, he does not see or hear, he throws himself helplessly under an arching rock. He is in despair, and knows that we are leaving him for good.

Parango is the name of a place where the path runs across a huge detritus fan. The guide informs us that it is dangerous in winter when avalanches roll down and landslips fall. After heavy rains also it is wise to make all speed in passing Parango.

Tsarak-tatang is a side valley with a murmuring brook; high up on a hill at its flank stands a hut among tilled fields. Here and there conifers make a rather thin wood, and a rest is agreeable in a ravine near Kamurti. Immediately opposite we have a bird's-eye view of the large Nesang river, throwing up white froth against the boulders that fill its rapids, but flowing calmly with a dark-green colour at its mouth.

From a commanding promontory where the cairn Kanam-laptse stands we enjoy for a moment a magnificent prospect. Deep down in a side valley lies the village of Kanam, and farther off Pill and other villages. But the finest sight is the background formed by the nearest snow-clad summits of a huge Himalayan massive which is known by the famous name of Kailas. In the peculiar illumination, and in an atmosphere apparently saturated with warm vapour, its firn-covered peaks make a deep and imposing effect. Steely-blue clouds and round white fleeces form white beds round the higher parts of the mountains, and the blinding white summits rise above this sea of aerial surge.

We descend to the village of Kanam. Without a guide we should surely go astray in this confusion of narrow lanes, passages, and small squares between houses, walls, terraces, fields, and gardens, among which canals here and there cool the air with tiny waterfalls, or which are interrupted by actual jungles of extremely luxuriant vegetation. The houses remind me of Kashmir; frequently the beams project on all sides beyond the walls to form verandahs and a shelter from the rain.

Our tents were erected in an open yard in front of the lower sanctuary which is called the *Kanjur-lhakang* because the holy scriptures are kept there. Naturally the first thing we do is to inspect the theological library. The hall is plain and not to be compared with those we have lately seen in Tibet. In the centre of the altar chancel towers a large *chhorten* called *Kudung*.

"Whose ashes does this *chhorten* contain?" I ask a monk.

"The ashes of a Grand Lama, Lotsava Rinpoche, who lived two or three centuries ago," he answers.

Locked cupboards stand on both sides and are opened at my request. They contain a number of small clay images. The Kanjur and Tanjur scriptures are kept in two clumsy heavy bookcases. Some volumes of the former are absent, for the monks are reading them in their cells.

The *Kache-lhakang*, standing higher up the village, is more important. The name signifies the "Mohammedan hall of the gods."

"Why is it so called?" I ask one of our priestly ciceroni.

"Because a converted Mohammedan served the temple." But one of his colleagues said, "No, simply because the architect was a Mohammedan."

The latter explanation was the more probable, for the whole architecture of the cloister court was exactly like the caravanserais in Yarkand. As there, the two-storeyed galleries were turned to the court, in the middle of which a thick-stemmed apple tree lifted up its crown. Such courts are, indeed, not uncommon in Tibet, but here the Mohammedan style is more pronounced than usual.

Stone steps lead up to the temple hall, where we meet again our old friends Sakya-toba, Chenresi, and Tsong Kapa. Some new *tankas* hang down from the roof and through its large impluvium daylight falls, gilding the pillars of the shrine.

"Where is the monk's cell which the European lama

inhabited when he lived here?" I asked Gachen Lobsang Tarva, a monk about fifty-five years old, who was very amiable and friendly.

"Come with me, sir," he said, and led me on to the flat roof. From here we mounted an outside staircase ending in a verandah before a small room.

"Who lives here?" I asked.

"Lotsa Rinpoche, a Kanpo Lama, who is now on a visit to the Tashi Lama. But this is also the room in which a lama from Europe once lived."

A lama from Europe! It sounds very improbable and yet it is quite true. A wonderfully entrancing human story is indissolubly connected with the monastery of Kanam. A true story, in which the wildest adventures of Hajji Baba are combined with superhuman patience and the finest example of the suppression of self in the interests of science. We stand on the threshold of the cell in which the Hungarian philologist, Alexander Csoma of Körös in Transylvania, spent three years of his life.

His greatness and his reputation survive in the works he published. But his personality and his life are little known, and hence the mystical charm surrounding his name. A few letters from him and about him afford an insight into his thoughts and schemes. In the narrative of one or another Himalayan journey his image flashes only rapidly before our eyes. It would take too long to dwell on all these narratives of travel. We will give here only a specimen. Captain C. Johnson on his journey from April to October 1827, visited the village of Kanam, and says in the *Journal of the Royal Geographical Society*, 1834, p. 56:

> There is in this city a Lama temple, and an excellent library. . . . Here they met with Tchoma de Coxas, an Hungarian traveller, who was there for the purpose of ascertaining the origin of the Huns. . . . He had been in Luddak, and had acquired a knowledge of the language, but having become an object of suspicion, he had come south, and buried himself in the library at Kanum. . . . He was not very communicative, and lived the life of a hermit, upon an allowance granted him by the Company.

In the book already quoted, *Die lamaische Hierarchie und Kirche* (vol. ii. p 286), Koeppen writes of Csoma

145. Gachen Lobsang Tarva.

146. Yangpur, the Oldest Man in Kanam.

Sketches by the Author.

. . . who had made it the task of his life to track down the Uigur, the supposed ancestors or at least fellow-tribesmen of his people, the Hungarians, and he hoped, after searching fruitlessly for several years in Persia, Afghanistan, and Turkestan amidst hardships and privations, to finally discover them in some corner of the closed land of snow. But before trying to penetrate into that country he resolved to learn the Tibetan language, and studied it first in Ladag, then in Yangla, and lastly from 1827 in the monastery of Kanam on the Sutlej under the guidance of a literate lama, in spite of cold and want, with such heroic energy that at last he mastered it, the first European to do so, and at the same time acquired an exhaustive knowledge of Tibetan literature.

We can obtain a notion of the importance of Csoma's work from the following words of the present American Ambassador in Constantinople, the profound and learned Asiatic investigator W. W. Rockhill, in *The Life of the Buddha*:

Any one who has glanced at the analysis of the Tibetan Bkah-hgyur by Alexander Csoma de Körös, published in the 20th volume of the *Asiatick Researches*, must have been struck with the wonderful patience and perseverance of this extraordinary scholar. Some idea of the extent of the researches which are embodied in his analysis of the Dulva, about the tenth part of the whole Bkah-hgyur, may be had when it is known that it occupies more than 4000 leaves of seven lines to the page, each line averaging twenty-two syllables.

Let us take a glance at the career of this extraordinary man. I follow here the account given by Dr. Th. Duka in his book *Life and Works of Alexander Csoma de Körös. A Biography compiled chiefly from hitherto unpublished data* (London, 1885). Körösi Csoma Sandor, or Alexander Csoma of Körös, was born in the year 1784, and in his youth devoted himself enthusiastically to the study of oriental languages, theology, history of the world, and geography. When he was thirty-six years old he left his country for ever, and commenced the long journey which was to make his name known and renowned in the scientific world. He traversed the Balkan countries, sailed to Alexandria, and then made his way through Aleppo, Mosul, Baghdad, Kermanshah, and Hamadan to Teheran. At that time no Europeans lived in the Persian capital, except those attached to the embassies. Here Csoma enjoyed English hospitality until in the spring of 1821 he left Teheran in Persian dress to follow the ancient caravan road to Meshed, Bukhara, Balk, Kulm, Bamian, and Kabul. He almost always travelled on foot. From Constantinople to Bukhara he followed pretty nearly the same route as his famous countryman, Professor Arminius Vambéry, forty-two years later. It was a heroic deed he accomplished. At that time it was more difficult than now to traverse these regions unscathed. Csoma has left no account of his adventures, but from Vambéry's graphic description we may gain some conception of the troubles and dangers which Csoma must have encountered. In the year 1890 I travelled along the same road as Csoma, and can very well imagine the privations he must have endured seventy years earlier.

Csoma passed through Lahore and Kashmir to Leh. On his journey back from Leh he met Moorcroft in July 1822, who had accomplished his memorable journey to Manasarowar ten years before. In Moorcroft Csoma found a sincere friend, stayed with him half a year, and received from his benefactor money as well as books and letters of introduction. Thus Csoma, through Moorcroft's intervention, was enabled to spend sixteen months in the monastery of Yangla in Sanskar, where with a learned lama and a servant he occupied a cell thirty square feet in area, and there plunged into the study of the sacred writings. He found that the 320 volumes which are the foundation of all Tibetan learning and religion are a translation of an Indian Sanskrit original. In grinding poverty and amid great privations he worked his way into this new world of knowledge. Winter was a hard time, the little room could not be warmed, and Csoma had no money for lights. Wrapped in a sheep-skin he sat all day over the Tibetan folios while snowstorms howled outside in the mountains.

In the year 1825 the Indian Government accepted his offer to continue his investigations at their expense. English rule had begun to extend itself over India, and it was important to learn something of the languages and religions of neighbouring peoples. The Government offered him a remuneration of 50 rupees a month. It was a gigantic work Csoma had undertaken. He found that the Kanjur consisted of 98 volumes, each two feet long and eight inches broad, and containing more than 300 leaves. The Tanjur had 224 volumes with 76,409 leaves in the aggregate, and had been translated and arranged by 3000 persons.

These years Csoma spent partly at Sabathu in Kulu, partly at Pukdal in Sanskar. On one of his journeys he came to Kanam, and there heard that the holy scriptures were kept in the monastery of the village, whither they had been brought from Tashi-lunpo fifty years before. Therefore he determined to continue his studies in Kanam and received the sanction of the Government to a sojourn of three years.

About this time Dr. Gerard, who did such good service in connexion with the geography of the Himalayas, travelled through these regions and came to Kanam. In an interesting letter, dated at Sabathu on January 21, 1829, Gerard relates that he had seen the learned Hungarian in the little romantic village where he was dwelling amongst his books in the dress of the natives, and living like them on buttered tea. Under circumstances which would have driven most men to despair, he had collected 40,000 Tibetan words. His teacher and assistant was a highly educated and amiable lama named Bande Sangs-Rgyas PHun-Tsogs. The Hungarian reminded the English doctor of the philosophers of antiquity, for like them he was completely absorbed in his researches, and was blind and deaf to everything that was going on about him. But he was delighted with the unsuspected treasures he had brought to light from the gold mines of Tibetan wisdom, which would one day excite the astonishment of the learned world. He expressed, however, a fear that the Government might not appreciate his work; but on the day when he could hand over his grammar and his lexicon he would be the happiest man on earth, for then he would have carried out his engagement and could die contented.

He lived in poverty, for the 50 rupees a month were

his only income. Half he paid to his teacher, his servant received 4 rupees, and his dwelling cost a rupee a month. Twenty rupees were, then, left to provide him with food, clothing, writing materials, and all other necessaries.

Gerard says:

> Mr. Csoma's hamlet is at the extreme upper limit of the village of Kanum, at an absolute elevation of 9500 feet. Around him are the romantic abodes of monks, whose religious ceremonies, their pious incantations, etc., have a singular affinity to Romish customs. Below is the monastery containing the Encyclopædia. . . . Mr. Csoma showed me some improvements he had made to his cottage; one was a fireplace, which had cost him twelve rupees. . . . Two rustic benches and a couple of ruder chairs are all the furniture in his small abode.

In spite of all his poverty he retained an indomitable pride, and could not be induced to accept the smallest present from Gerard. Even the English newspapers Gerard sent him were refused. Rice, sugar, clothes, all were returned. The only things he kept at Gerard's earnest entreaty were an English Bible, which he read through in eight days, a Latin and a Greek dictionary.

Poverty had no power over him. He seemed to be raised above all worldly things. He had travelled for years through western and southern Asia on a mere pittance, and had laid the foundations of a new branch of science for the pay of a lacquey. He never went out except to fetch more volumes from the library. In summer he wore the coarse garments that could be procured in Kanam, and in winter he wrapped himself in his sheep-skin. The work itself was his life. He would earnestly and faithfully fathom the depths of Tibetan knowledge, hand over the results to the Government in Calcutta, and then continue his researches in Lhasa and pass at last into Mongolia. Finally he would search out the original home of the Magyars in Asia. But man proposes, God disposes.

News reached Calcutta that Moorcroft had died at Andkhoi in Bukhara. It was proposed to send Csoma thither to recover the papers of the deceased explorer, but the plan was never carried out. The Asiatic Society

147. Ravine in the Sutlej Valley.

148. View of the Sutlej Valley near Kanam.

in Calcutta assigned 50 rupees monthly for Csoma's maintenance, but he was offended by the wording of the generous offer and refused it.

At the end of 1830 he left Kanam, where he had sojourned over three years, and took leave of his teacher, the good Bande Sangs-Rgyas PHun-Tsogs, and went to Calcutta, where he was for several years librarian of the Asiatic Society, and superintended the printing of his large quartos, the grammar and the dictionary. Here he also wrote a number of learned essays and translated parts of the Bible into Tibetan for the missionaries.

He did not alter his Spartan mode of life in the capital. He took no part in society functions. He was not seen in the street. Silent as a Brahmin, he arranged the Tibetan manuscripts in the library and shut himself up among his own papers in his room, where he lived like a hermit and a misanthrope. Yet he had some intimates, a couple of friends who visited him frequently. The great Himalayan explorers, Moorcroft, Gerard, Wilson, Prinsep, Hodgson, Campbell, and others, came in contact with Csoma. The singular taciturn student could be lively and talkative when any one spoke of Hungary with kindly interest.

When he was fifty-eight years old Csoma resolved to travel to Lhasa and Central Asia. In Lhasa he would find the perfection of Tibetan learning, and in Central Asia would find the original home of the Magyars. He would devote ten years more to the East before he returned home. Probably he started from the Hugli by boat and then, travelling on foot through the fever districts south of the Himalayas, arrived on March 24, 1842, at Darjiling, among the cool mountains which separated him from his desired bourne.

Here he met Dr. Campbell who afterwards expressed his admiration of Csoma's learning, and his astonishment at the curious mixture of pride and humility which formed the groundwork of his character. He knew a number of languages, says Campbell, and was conversant with still more—Hebrew, Arabic, Sanskrit, Pushtu, Greek, Latin, Slavonic, German, English, Turkish, Persian, French,

Russian, Tibetan, Hindustani, Mahratta, and Bengali, and he had a dictionary of every language with him. He had spent twenty-two years in travel, or a longer time than any European since Marco Polo. An official in the service of the Raja of Sikkim was astounded at his Tibetan and Lamaist knowledge; a European who knew the languages and literature more thoroughly than any Kanpo Lama or Rinpoche!

Dr. Campbell recognized Csoma's worth, liked his society, and visited him frequently. He found him in a miserable hole sitting on a mat among four boxes of books. In this room, which was nothing better than a closet, Csoma worked, took his simple meals of tea and rice, and slept in a coarsely woven blue wrapper. And in this closet Campbell found him on April 6, ill of fever, and tried in vain to make him swallow a febrifuge. On the 7th Csoma was better, and he spoke cheerfully and with lively interest. "What would not Hodgson, Turner, and some philosophers of Europe give to be in my place when I come to Lhasa?" he several times exclaimed. He told with pride of his long journeys and his years of solitude on the frontier of Tibet, and was delighted with the sensation his literary researches had aroused among the learned men of Europe.

Campbell listened with almost religious reverence to his conversation, and thought that Csoma wished that not a single word should escape the attentiveness of the Englishman and not a syllable be forgotten. For now he spoke of the original home of the Hungarian race in Asia, of the Huns and the Uigurs, and of the key to the dark riddle which lay hidden in Lhasa and Kham in the extreme east of Tibet.

On April 9, the indefatigable pilgrim again lay in high fever. His complexion was yellow, his cheeks had fallen in, and his thoughts wandered along misty paths vainly groping after the original home of the Magyars. Now the doctor succeeded in inducing him to take medicine. But it was too late. On the evening of the 10th Csoma fell into a comatose slumber, and early the following morning he had ceased for ever his search for the open tablelands where the forefathers of the Magyar had once ridden about on wild horses.

On April 12 the dead hero and martyr was borne to the grave. Campbell read the prayers as the coffin was lowered; all the Englishmen present in Darjiling attended the funeral. The Asiatic Society erected a monument over the grave, and the inscription on the tablet contains the following words:

. . . and after years passed under privations, such as have been seldom endured, and patient labour in the cause of Science, compiled a Dictionary and Grammar of the Tibetan language, his best and real monument.

On his road to Lassa, to resume his labours, he died in this place, on the 11th April 1842.

Requiescat in pace.

Csoma had devoted the years of his manhood to Tibetan studies and also sacrificed his life for them. His was a tragic fate, to be snatched away just as he was about to cross for the first time the frontier of the promised land, the forbidden land of the sacred books. On my way from Tibet, where I had spent more than two years, I had now arrived at Csoma's farthest point from the opposite direction. I trod with the feelings of a pilgrim the lanes and banks over which Csoma had wandered in solitude to and fro between the library and his monk's cell high up in the village. I cherished a slight hope of finding some memorial of his sojourn in this place, though seventy-eight years had passed since his time.

Therefore I turned to Gachen Lobsang Tarva, the representative of the superior of Kanam. I have already mentioned that he had led me to the small room in the upper monastery enclosure.

"Do you know nothing of that Lama-Sahib?" I asked him.

"No, nothing at all. But Yangpur, an old man of eighty-two, is the oldest inhabitant of Kanam; he may be able to tell you something."

"Let him come at once."

A messenger was despatched, and after a time we had old Yangpur with us.

"Do you remember the Lama-Sahib who lived here?" I asked him.

"No, sir; I was a child when he left Kanam. But I remember very well that my father used to speak of him, and said that he lived some years in the monastery dressed just like our own lamas and regarded by them as a colleague."

"Do you remember his name, Yangpur?"

"Yes, he was named Ganderbek," the old man answered without a moment of hesitation. In the evening I wrote in my diary: "This name Ganderbek can be nothing else but Iskander Bek, the name by which Alexander the Great is known in western Asia, especially as Csoma's Christian name was Alexander." Now I find that Moorcroft begins a letter of introduction, written in Kashmir in the year 1823, with the following words: "The object of this address is to bespeak your good offices for Mr. Alexander Csoma, or Sekunder Beg, of Transsylvania, whom I now take the liberty to introduce." Alexander, Sekunder, Iskender, Iskander Gander, Iskender Bek was certainly Csoma's *nom de guerre* in Asia.

"How did this Ganderbek occupy himself?"

"That I do not know, but I remember from my childhood that every one spoke well of him, and that he was highly respected."

"Is it certain that he lived in this little house?"

"Yes, that is quite certain; it was always said so from the time of my childhood. Ten years ago the house was shaky and the beams were jointed more firmly together, but just in the same form as before."

A low door and a small window open on to the verandah, both with red-painted frames while the other parts of the wall are white. The inner walls are of stone recently white-washed, and therefore it is useless to look for any remarks written or scratched on the walls. On the long side opposite the door and window stand a wooden bench and a small cupboard, both roughly made in European, not Asiatic, form. Yangpur asserted that they had belonged to Ganderbek. In addition there was a simple wooden couch. Narrow beams supported the

149. Csoma's Cell.

150. Csoma's House in Kanam.

Sketches by the Author.

roof and the floor was constructed of thicker boards. The whole accords exactly with Gerard's description: "Two rustic benches and a couple of ruder chairs are all the furniture in his small abode." Now the chairs were gone, that was all. The position of the house in the village and with relation to the *Kanjur-lhakang* is just as described by Gerard.

One of the finest landscapes on earth was displayed to the eyes of the student when he stepped out on to the verandah. Deep down at the bottom of the valley the narrow wild Sutlej winds through abrupt corridors, and in the background rise the sharply cut pyramids of the Kailas group. Dark-green patches are seen on some slopes—coniferous woods. How often must Csoma have looked at these mountains and valleys during his years of solitude! I could not gaze at them long enough, monuments erected to his memory as they seemed to me.

But the hours had slipped away and it was time to go down to the tents. Half-way down we looked for a moment into a third small temple, the *Tarbaling-lhakang*, which had been redecorated five years before and was bright with gaudy colours. The old gods keep their places. Chamba sits there, ten feet high, with dangling legs and a crown-shaped diadem on his head. The monks differ from their brethren in Tibet in wearing small yellow caps and beards. Young bareheaded nuns carried water up to the monastery. Twenty monks and twenty-three nuns, belonging to the yellow sect, are said to serve in the sanctuaries of Kanam.

We had seen enough and, indeed, could see no more, for the darkness was deepening, and just as we prepared to go on again the conch summoned the monks to evening service, and a lama on the roof of the *Tarbaling* intoned in a loud clear voice "Om mani padme hum." The six holy syllables sounded as melodiously as the call to prayer of the muezzin from the platform of a minaret at sunset. The dogs barked in the yards and the grasshoppers kept up a shrill concert in the thickets. But above every sound was heard the roar of the mighty river down in the valley.

When I reached the tents Little Puppy came to meet

me barking a welcome. But why did not Takkar come? He was not lying at his usual post among the tents. Two of my men went out to look for him, scoured the roads and bridges in the neighbourhood, shouted his name, and called him with piercing whistles. But he did not hear, and never showed himself again. He had turned round and run back to Poo.

CHAPTER XXXIII

MY AMAZONIAN ESCORT

THE morning of September 2 was pleasant and cool after 55.9° in the night. The gnats did their best to disturb me in my sleep, and it would have been well if I had had a mosquito net; but what did it matter, for I had run the gauntlet and was now immune?

Noisy music of drums, cymbals, and trombones from the roof of the upper monastery of Kanam awoke me early in the morning, and when I looked out of my tent a new relay of coolies was waiting for our baggage. They wished to set out early that they might not have to march during the hottest hours of the day. Only two were men, and all the rest women, in frocks of coarse material and black, brown, or grey vests, which left the arms and shoulders bare. Silver pendants dangled from the lobes of their ears, bangles of brass adorned their wrists, and their naked feet surprised me, for they might have to walk over sharp rubbish and unmade paths where even horses get sore feet. But their soles are hardened by constant wear, and are as little sensitive as the callosities of a camel's foot. Our noble portresses had never touched the water of the brook of Kanam, but they were jolly, fresh, and dainty. Mothers and young girls slung our baggage by cords and straps on to their backs in a moment, and vanished with it into the shady lanes of Kanam.

A little later we followed in their footsteps along the bank of a canal shaded by leafy walnut trees. Blessed summer, lovely vegetation, how long it is since I saw such wealth! We are soon out of the maze of Kanam; the memorable village and its picturesque houses like swallows' nests disappear among the hills, and we go down to a bridge over the brook and up on the other side to the village of Kyap. Pill, too, and other villages, we pass on the road, which is still bad. I prefer my own legs to those of my horse, especially as a huge overhanging rock obliges me occasionally to bend my head sideways over the yawning abyss. We are now no longer so high above the rushing whirlpools of the Sutlej. The current is no longer so swift, and one feels much inclined to try a raft on this restless water.

We are at a sharp corner where the great side valley Kirang comes down to the Sutlej. The bridge over the tributary stands rather far up the valley, so the road runs up to a sharp point. From the corner we descend at first. The landscape is magnificent and fascinating. Old fir-trees spread over us their refreshing sweet-scented crowns, while below us the cliffs fall suddenly to the Kirang river, hiding it from us in the meantime. In only two bends of its bed can we see the stream tossing in white foaming falls and rapids over boulders and bars, and we perceive that the pure cold water of the Kirang is able, on account of its greater velocity and huge volume, to thrust out a light-green semicircle into the grey dirty Sutlej. Up the valley are seen fields and villages, one of them being Kirang. Just by the solid bridge the river forms thundering falls, dashing over gigantic rounded boulders. Wherever one turns the eyes fall on a charmingly beautiful scene. Let us linger a moment in the shadow of a rock to drink a cup of the cold water of the Kirang, which brings fresh greetings from glaciers and firns to the heat prevailing here. Life is worth living!

Here one might forget all his duties to stay for years as Csoma of Körös did. But we must go on, up the right bank where the road runs through fine woods of firs. Here I can ride again. From the Kirang bridge the road is excellent, for so far the trade highway, planned by the Indian Government to the Tibetan frontier, is finished. Above Kirang also we had seen preliminary work at many places. Will the Tibetan Government follow this example on the other half of the route, from the frontier to Gartok? Yes, if they are compelled by a treaty, not otherwise. On the Tibetan side, moreover, there are greater difficulties to contend with. But, as it is, the stranger from Tibet gives a sigh of relief when he is past the Kirang valley. He enters on a splendidly made road, which avoids all dangerous precipitous cliffs or abrupt slopes, and has everywhere a regular gradual ascent.

And here! Another reminder of the power of England and the proximity of civilization. A small black tablet on a milestone bears in white oil-colour the inscription, "Simla 165," and for greater assurance a light-coloured board with black figures proclaims once more "165." So many English miles still separate us from our destination. We regard this milestone with a certain respect; it knows more than we do. It has 164 comrades, and we must pass them all. With growing elation the pilgrims watch the numbers fall and the distance shorten. 165 miles more to Simla—a mere trifle when I think of the distance I have travelled!

I sit dreaming on my white horse as though spellbound. The whole air sings, there is a buzz and murmur in the forest and in the depth of the valley. What is it, then? Ah, our guard of Amazons is climbing the heights. Look there, how they stride along between the trees in a row, with heavy firm steps and swinging gait. How charming sounds the song from young, almost childish, throats, and how happy! Before we overtake them they have halted to take a rest. Gulam and Kunchuk, who accompany them, have never enjoyed themselves so well in their lives; they dance for pleasure and are quite beside themselves.

I wish to hear them sing again and wait therefore until they troop off under the dark pines. The rhythmical sonorous singing peals out through the forest and is not overpowered even by the roar of the Sutlej. We might be in a theatre. And what a theatre! Look at the background formed by the mountains on the left side of the Sutlej! Look at those gloomy recesses of dark-green conifers! The setting is the best after all. And round about whisper gentle zephyrs with the odour of the forest, and the roar of the victorious river resounds among the mountains. We travel as to a festival in these heavenly Himalayas. How different from dreary Tibet, where no forests overshadowed our road, no rivers made for the sea, and no women sang!

I ride in front. The singing becomes fainter and dies away in the distance. Only occasionally when we, the choir of singers and myself, find ourselves at the same time on a projecting spur of rock, can a few low notes be heard. But beyond the next corner of mica-schist I hear the song no more.

When I reached the village of Gyengring our horses and mules were already grazing on a meadow, and I rode off to our first bungalow, the last shelter on the Tibetan road. The keeper stood squarely in front of the door and told me that I could not pass the night there without a permit from Simla. A permit from Simla, when I came from Tibet! In Totling the doors were shut in our faces, but here we were on English ground. "Out of the way, old man." The lock must have been out of order for the door opened when I grasped the knob, and in a minute I had made myself comfortable in a pleasant room with a bedstead, table, and chairs. The yard where the men set up their tents stands like a platform above the valley, and the view over the Sutlej is charming.

Our female coolies laid down their loads in front of the bungalow and sat down to wait for their pay. And they had to wait for a while until I had drawn the portraits of some of them. Then they received an extra douceur for their pretty cheerful singing.

Little Puppy made me laugh by the extraordinarily cautious way in which he crossed the threshold of the bungalow. Apparently he thought it was some kind of bridge. "It is surely some new devilry," as Sancho Panza says at a historical moment in the edition of *Don Quixote*, which wiled away many a long evening in Tibet. When Little Puppy had convinced himself that the deals of the floor did not shake like the bridges of the Sutlej, he picked up courage and laid himself down in the shade.

151. View from Camp 478.

152. Cable over the Sha River.

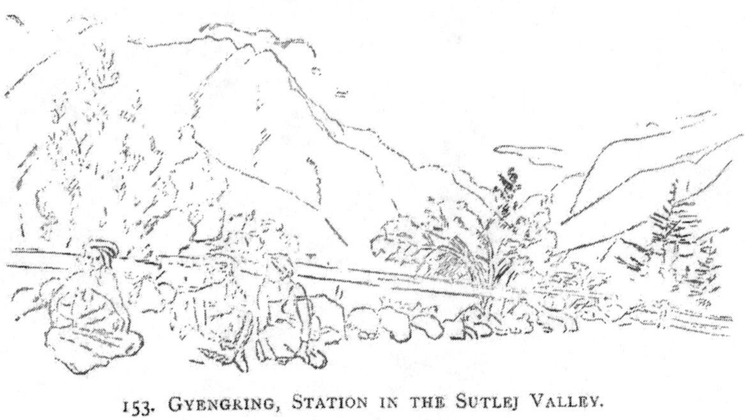

153. Gyengring, Station in the Sutlej Valley.

Sketches by the Author.

On September 3 our loads were transported, not by Amazons, but on mules, a striking contrast. But the Sutlej remained with us, and the road was always beautiful. On the farther bank opens the great side valley Rangri, and snow mountains shimmer in the background. Above the villages Morang and Risba, Kailas, or Keila as the name is pronounced here, towers among the clouds, a huge dome of snow and ice, with a circle of sharp pinnacles like a royal crown.

We have come somewhat lower, and the roar of the river is louder. The village of Apek lies behind us, and Aren below us; we pass by Riberang on the left bank and by Rarang. I scorn the bungalow of the latter, but turn my attention to its *chhorten* portal and its *mani* walls; they convince me that here Lamaism still holds its own. A man passing by gives me a fine bunch of grapes; the berries are very sour but refreshing, and the main thing is that they are actually grapes. The heat is not great; there is a wind, and the forest is dense; the dark-brown or grey stems of the conifers often stand among large boulders of granite and mica-schist. Where the road has been damaged by landslips and the decay of the timber, navvies are at work with spades and picks, and they always beg for a trifle to recompense them for their labour on behalf of travellers. We are now close to the Sutlej, and the noise is quite deafening. The river is larger than we have yet seen it, and is encumbered with foaming rapids. It would be death to attempt a voyage on a raft.

Two men on foot in Indian uniform came up and saluted us. One bore on his shoulder-strap a metal plate with the inscription, "His Highness the Raja of Beshahr."

"What do you want?" I asked.

"The Tesildar of Chini has sent us to attend on you and look after the transport."

"How did he know that I was coming?"

"Deva Ram of Poo has sent a runner."

And now we go uphill again, but not for long. Where we come down to the river again the road describes a double loop in the form of the figure 8. Chutar-kar is a large side valley with a fine river, crossed by a bridge of two arches. The valley is sunk between vertical cliffs; its fall is rapid, its channel full of blocks. The river fights its way down with frantic fury and forms a succession of white foaming falls. Here we halt for a while to watch the struggle of the water with the stones. The noise of the Sutlej is lost in this thundering tumult.

Beyond the bridge comes another stretch of fine coniferous forest, so dense that it is twilight under the crowns. A sunbeam breaks through here and there, and makes a granite boulder glow like fire. But the country is most beautiful where we see nothing on all sides but perpendicular cliffs. Here the road is blasted out of the rock, and the schist, gneiss, or granite forms an arched roof over our heads. Owing to the blasting the rock presents a fresh surface of fracture. On the outer side the road is protected by a low stone wall with small drainage holes.

In a valley trough on the left bank we perceive the village of Pundam with its huts, fields, and groves. On our side the fresh dark-green forest increases in extent, and we enjoy the strong odour of pines. The road forks; its right branch leads up to the comfortable bungalow of the village Pangi, where I can lie and stretch myself in a deck chair on the balcony, and where white Vandals have perpetuated their unknown names on the table top. Illustrated papers and ragged novels are also signs of tourists' visits.

Early next morning the whole Sutlej valley lay buried in white mist, through which only the nearest trees were faintly visible—otherwise the verandah of the bungalow might have been an airship floating among the clouds. Soon the mist parted and the peaks of Kailas appeared again brightly lighted by the morning sun, with the turquoise-blue sky as background.

A short way beyond the bungalow we pass the village of Pangi and then through the well-watered Kojang valley, in which stand clapping mills and neat compounds. Farther down we come to Chini. While the caravan is proceeding to Rogi I go up to visit the missionaries, Mr. and Mrs. Bruske, and talk with them a while about the Land of Snow, for they have long watched for an opportunity of travelling to Tibet to preach the Gospel to the followers of Buddha. I could not encourage their hopes of better times and an open road over the frontier. They proposed to give up their fixed dwelling and travel about among the villages to address the people. In Chini "Om mani padme hum" has not all its own way with the souls of men. We are now in a district where Lamaism is losing its hold and Hinduism has the upper hand. Only a quarter of the population is Lamaist, and there is one Lama monastery for two Hindu temples. Several new *chhortens* and *mani* walls seem to indicate a chance revival of the Tibetan religion. The village is said to contain 500 inhabitants, who all belong to one tribe called Kanauri and are divided into three clans, each with its own language, or at least a dialect widely different from the other two, in which many Tibetan words are incorporated.

Time flies quickly in pleasant company, and all too soon I am obliged to leave the kindly missionary couple, and ride on along the road which, for the most part, is blasted out of vertical cliffs and has a crenellated breastwork. It is not much farther to Rogi, where we make ourselves at home in the bungalow. The camping place is numbered 490, and we have only ten days' journey to Simla. It would be bad luck if the mad dog were to bite us, which is rendering the roads of the neighbourhood unsafe according to the warning "Cave canem" displayed on posters.

Here we are at a height of 9350 feet. The minimum at night is 57.7°, and the air is fresher than it was higher up. We still see the peaks of Kailas, partially veiled in a dense mantle of cloud. Granite surrounds us and black mica-schist dipping to the north.

I write September 5. Again milky-white impenetrable mist fills the valley, but it is almost gone by nine o'clock, leaving only thin wisps of light gauzy cloud. The forest becomes thinner, the road runs through tracts of bare rock, the Sutlej is out of sight but its roar fills the mountains and valleys. I have forcibly to suppress an exclamation at a corner of the road where the indescribably magnificent valley of the Sutlej again comes into view. Look on the other side at that wild side valley, Bosba-garang, with its great river rushing for better or worse to the Sutlej. The main river grows with every fresh tribute of water which it mingles with its own. Just hear it roar. Look how it works to cut ever deeper into the heart of the Himalayas. Think of the pressure of this volume of water, and remember that it is in constant movement and rolls boulders and pebbles down its bed. No wonder that the valley is so deep, and that the landscape which fascinates our eyes assumes such grand contours and wildly-fissured forms.

In a small, deep side valley with a brightly-rippling brook we meet a mule caravan with loads which can only belong to a white man. There he comes, the owner, on foot, in a light summer scouting suit with a white Indian helmet on his head. Of course I dismount, and we salute each other. It is Lieut.-Colonel W. W. Norman, of the 22nd Regiment of the Frontier Force, with whom I have the honour to converse. We talk perhaps an hour in the shade before we go on, each in his own direction.

We have now descended, and the noise of the river increases in force. Ah, there is another side valley, the deep channel of the Yula-garang, which has cut down into the solid rock with furious violence. Beyond its bridge the road mounts again up to the bungalow of the village Urni. I wonder if anywhere in the whole world there can be a camping-ground in a finer situation than this, hanging over the valley of the Sutlej and commanding a charming view of the gigantic chasm up-stream. The station buildings have been purposely erected at the grandest point of view, in order to attract tourists from Simla.

Atmospheric effects presented a singular spectacle at Urni. The valley became suddenly filled with white vapour, which completely veiled all the environs and was not dispersed even by the heavy rain which poured down for an hour and a half. But when the rain ceased, a light breeze swept away the mist little by little, and white cloudlets came sailing along like dragons, while others in the form of balls and bells rose slowly upwards like balloons. The bottom of the valley was still filled with clouds of fog. The whole scene was extremely curious and perplexing. A sea of milk from which rose islands and holms. Air, water, earth, everything is alive in the Himalayas. In the heart of Tibet there is life only in the air, and the water is only occasionally roused from its torpid sleep when the storm wind lashes the lakes, and the surf strums its melancholy hymns on the beach.

The next milestone announces that we have only 126 miles to travel. 7874 feet above sea-level say the hypsometrical instruments. And the minimum thermometer declares that we had $61\frac{1}{2}°$ in the night of September 5.

Now we go down again, and after two hours are barely 65 feet above the river, and its din is overwhelming.

"What is the name of this river?" I ask the guide.

"Ganga," he replies.

"Not Langchen-kamba?"

"No, I have never heard that name." The Tibetan appellation stops at the frontier. The answer of the guide might seem to imply another confusion of the Sutlej with the Ganges, but *ganga* means simply "The River."

Our road skirts the bank. At one place three huge boulders have fallen into the river and the water flows between as through a gateway. A dangerous-looking path also runs along the left bank where a small deeply excavated valley opens—the Ramni-kar.

The gneiss stands in abrupt cliffs facing the valley, and huge blocks lie more frequently in the bed, like signs of warning to travellers and caravans of the danger that is ever present there. The water has eaten into them until they have been worn round, and a patient stream of water has hollowed out holes and indentations in their sides, flat surfaces and curved ridges—gutta cavat lapidem. It is their fate to be annihilated in time and be replaced by new blocks. Round them the water dances in foaming waves, showers of spray shoot up from hissing cascades between narrow apertures, and small falls pour down in bright domes of water which passes below into foaming whirlpools and witches' cauldrons. A raft would be of no use here; it would be dashed to pieces before one had time to look round, however stoutly it might be built.

A new surprise awaits us at a place where the rocks

fall perpendicularly to the river, or slightly overhang. To blast out a gallery in the rocks would have been too expensive, for the distance is a hundred yards. Therefore all that has been done is to fix stanchions into borings in the rock and lay over them an open bridge with a rail on the outside. The height of this bridge above the river is perhaps a hundred and thirty feet, and when one leans over the railing the Sutlej is immediately below. Here the view is splendid, almost awful.

Beyond this bridge clinging to the precipice the valley contracts, though all dimensions are still colossal. Caves and gigantic potholes, once worn out by the water of the river, yawn empty and dry on both sides of the valley, showing how deep the river has cut its way down since they were formed. Again a noise of thunder is heard in front of us. The side valley, Pabe-kar, sends its great stream down to the Sutlej. A white imposing waterfall leaps down above the bridge over the Pabe. This bridge does not spoil the landscape. It rests on natural piers and dams, on boulders that have fallen into the bed. Overcome with astonishment and admiration I remain standing and sacrifice two of my last copper coins.

The next surprise in our way is the fine Wang-tu bridge, which, borne by ten wire cables anchored in the rocks, throws its solid roadway across the Sutlej. We have never been so low (5361 feet) and we are only six feet above the river. But we do not enjoy the satisfaction long, for on the left bank the path winds up again to the rest-house of the village of Nachar.

One of our horses from Bongba was resting with his leader at a bend in the road. He stood on trembling legs and whinnied with pleasure as he saw his white companion and his countryman pass by. But he saw us for the last time and his whinny was a parting greeting. Why did he stand in the broiling sun, when there was only a mile to dense forest with its cool shade? He could go no farther, he was worn out. His sight would soon be dimmed by other shades, darker than those of the forest.

154. Himalayan Scenery.

155. The Road in the Sutlej Ravine.

CHAPTER XXXIV

THE LAST

I MIGHT have come to a conclusion at the turn of the road where the Bongba horse died. The remaining nine days' journey is only the last section of my retreat from the Tibetan frontier, which passed through well-known country. Many Englishmen travel annually along this road, and I have nothing to relate which has not already been seen and described by others. But we will let the line run out.

From the bridge of Wang-tu over the Sutlej we ascend 1770 feet to the bungalow of Nachar. During the next day's journey we descend the height of an Eiffel tower to Paunda, passing over open slopes or through fine groves of Himalayan cedars and copses of alder. The traffic increases and we meet travellers, small herds of black and white cattle, handsome and well fed, and sometimes with loads, sometimes without.

Next morning nine coolies stand before the house in Paunda, waiting for our dilapidated packs, and with them we descend to the valleys of Soldam which run together just below the road. Here stands a last Lamaist road-portal with the usual painting under its arch and a *mani* wall beside it. The religion of Tibet burns in these valleys with an expiring flame. Here waterfalls and cascades shoot down, here rivers murmur among stones and boulders, here the environment is quite different from that in the quiet, majestic repose of Tibetan monasteries with their peaceful solemn gloom. We are again so low down that forest cannot flourish, but we see its dark masses on the heights to the left of our road.

When we leave the Soldam valley we again mount to the forest zone and soon enter its dark shady canopy. Our coolies march up leaning forwards and with slow steady steps, often resting and propping their loads against blocks and ledges without taking them off. At the bungalow of the village Taranda we are again 7020 feet above sea-level.

It rained heavily in the evening and night, and when we set out next morning the road was slippery with mud, and drops fell from the drenched foliage. But the air was beautifully cool, and there was a pleasant odour from the forest. Sometimes we went down gradually, sometimes remained for a good way at the same height. We crossed three side valleys and a small pass before we reached the rest-house of the village Sarahan.

Here I was surprised by a letter written in English from the Raja of Beshahr, Shumshir Sing by name, who in polite terms asked if he might pay me a visit. I should think so! A Raja asking for an audience! "Your Highness will be heartily welcome," I wrote back. And His Highness came, but not a highland prince with light elastic gait. He was a very shrivelled old man, who, from age and infirmities, could no longer stand on his feet, much less walk, but was carried on a litter by turbaned servants. They helped him to an easy-chair in my room and then a very singular conversation began. The noble prince was almost stone deaf and I had to yell into his ear to make myself audible. His English was not easily comprehensible to any one who can hear as well as I can. But for all that we chatted away, both at the same time, and before I had thought of giving directions to Gulam my guest gave his own orders.

"Bring me some tea and cake, and put tobacco before me, for I will smoke a pipe."

Meanwhile he looked round at all the trifles lying about, and, without a change of countenance, and without speaking a word, put two of my last pencils into his pocket. No doubt it had become a habit of his to plunder the visitors to the bungalow in this harmless fashion, and I would willingly have given him a whole cart-load of pencils if I had been able.

"How old is Your Highness?" I asked.

"Forty-nine years," he answered boldly, and without a moment's hesitation, though he must certainly have seen eighty springs pass over the lovely country of Sarahan.

"How old is Your Honour?" he asked me.

"Forty-three," I replied.

"Then I am three years older than you."

"Just so," I answered, for I would not make a fuss about a paltry difference of three years, when he himself had so coolly taken off some thirty years. Thereupon this remarkable visit came to an end. My offer to return his visit was decidedly refused. Early next morning the old Raja was announced again, but I sent word that I unfortunately could not see him, and made off quickly with my pencils.

The next day's journey took me over the side valley Manglard-kard to the bungalow of Gaora, which was, indeed, smaller and more unpretentious than the foregoing, but to me dearer and richer in memories. For here a messenger sent from Simla by my gallant friend, J. R. Dunlop Smith, brought me a large bag of letters from Stockholm. Now I forgot everything about me; the proud heights of the Himalayas towering above me vanished; it was a whole year since I had heard a word from home.

At Gaora the height above the sea is 6024 feet, and the temperature fell in the night of September 10 to 40.8°, so that it was quite cold in the morning. But it was to be very different during the day. The road runs down all the way, and I went on foot through this incomparable country. In the large village of Rampur on the Sutlej I was only 3870 feet above the sea, so that I had descended 2150 feet during the day. The air was damp, warm, and close as in a conservatory. The breath of the hot Indian summer fanned our faces. The Sutlej foams some thirty yards below the village, and its well-known roar again salutes the ear. The river is imposing here. Its droning murmur seems to announce that it is proud of its work.

It has overcome the loftiest wildest ranges of the Himalayas, and has only small crests to cut through. But it is tired of its exertions, and longs to get out of the mountains to the open plains of the Punjab and the boundless sea—Thalassa, Thalassa!

Raj Sahib Mangat Ram, one of the officials of the little state, had come half-way to meet me, and while I sat writing at the large table in the verandah of the bungalow, he had twelve dishes laid on a carpet on the floor, containing piled-up rice, spices, sweet biscuits, and fruit. Also a servant dragged in a struggling sheep. I made my acknowledgments for the attention, fully determined to make good the value of the presents in full. For Beshahr is a poor state, and its officials certainly cannot afford to present fruit and refreshments to all the white visitors who choose to put in an appearance at Rampur. The state revenue is said to amount to thirty thousand rupees. When it was proposed to build a new bridge near Poo, where we dangled under the fearful cable over the river, not more than eighteen hundred rupees could be spared for its construction. The new bridge would have gone the same way as the old. The budget has also other expenses to provide for; thus the state minister receives for the invaluable services he renders to the principality two hundred rupees a month, and there can be very little left for the little Raja who is so fond of pencils.

Yet the Raja could afford to live in Rampur in a palace called Shishe Mahal, or the Glass Palace, a commonplace building in debased oriental style, with coloured glass windows, badly-painted portraits of the owner and other princes, and cheap, showy knick-knacks on the walls and in the verandahs. The court bears the pretentious name of Top-khaneh, or Artillery Court, and two old rusty muzzle-loaders actually stand in it. All bears the imprint of decline, decay, and bad taste. Give me the monasteries of Tibet, their solid architecture and pure unadulterated style.

There is little else to see in Rampur. But yes! A bridge over the Sutlej, a bazaar street with shops and workshops just as in India, a post-house, a school, and two

Hindu temples, which contend successfully with a Lamaist monastery for the souls of the inhabitants. In the last a solitary lama showed us the great prayer-cylinder with its 187,000 *manis*, which was just then being turned by a believer. He told me also that this is the last monastery on the road from Tibet. Then farewell ye monks with your everlasting "Om mani padme hum!"

Next morning all the office-bearers presented themselves for a farewell visit, now reinforced by the postmaster, the schoolmaster, and a fat pundit named Narayan Dutt. After all who had been attentive to us had received liberal gratuities, I wished to pay for the entertainment of the previous day and for the sheep. The rupees were counted out on the table, but the noble gentlemen declared magnanimously that the edibles were a state affair, a gift of welcome in the name of His Highness the Raja of Beshahr, and that compensation was out of the question. So I thanked them for their liberal hospitality, bade them send my acknowledgments to the Raja, and mounted the tall black horse which I hired here, and which was to carry me to Simla instead of my faithful white friend from Kamba Tsenam's tent.

The good men and women escorted me in procession when I left Rampur. The schoolboys were drawn up in two ranks on the road, and giggled and salaamed as we rode past. "Good luck to you, boys," I called out, and then I begged the procession to wear out no more shoe-leather on my account. Glad to be released from the constraints of politeness, they bowed low and returned to the village.

I ride on along the Sutlej river. The majestic stream is quieter and smoother. The valley widens a little, the slopes become less abrupt, the road runs thirty to sixty feet above the water, and on the bridge over the tributary Nogri we can again admire foaming emerald green volumes of water which disappear in the lap of the Sutlej. Beyond the village of Date-nagar the river makes a sharp bend, and at the narrowest point a rope bridge hangs between the banks. This long hammock does not look exactly trustworthy, but it is grand compared to the cable near Poo.

In Nirit we are at a height of 3658 feet, and at one o'clock read off 87.8°. This seems oppressively hot to those who have spent two years in Tibet. Even night does not bring coolness here, for the minimum is 70.5°.

I must relate an amusing little incident in Nirit. As I sat writing, Gulam came into the verandah, quite excited and boiling over with rage, to tell me that when he, who always remained behind us to pack up the last articles, was about to leave Rampur, a bill was quite unexpectedly presented to him. The good hosts demanded compensation for the sheep and the other delicacies I wanted to pay for. As Gulam had no money with him, the man wanted to take his revolver. At last it was agreed that one of the men should accompany him to Nirit and lay his claim before me. And now he presented himself, and when Gulam saw him his anger burst forth again. He gave him a couple of such sound buffets that the man tumbled over into the bushes, and then quickly took to flight. When Gulam had retired to the kitchen, the unexpected creditor came back and received compensation not only for the entertainment but also for the thrashing given him. He was allowed to keep the sheep, which, curiously enough, had lived through all the squabble. One has always to be cautious about presents in the East.

September 13 was a Sunday, and I had a delightful ride to Kotgar. We had to ascend from 3658 feet at Nirit to 5610 at Kotgar, or the height of two Eiffel towers, towards cooler regions. For a time, however, the road skirts the bank of the famous river. It is still quieter. There are, indeed, rapids here and there, but the grey turbid water no longer tosses and foams as violently as farther up. The Sutlej is tired after its work; the huge volumes of water need no longer toil, and they glide lazily down to the plains, no longer singing loudly and triumphantly, but still humming the old song. At times the river is quite silent, and then it lifts its voice in new rapids. I hear it once more and see it disappear for the last time behind the hills as I ride away from its bank to the heights round Tanadar.

How pleasant it is to leave behind the suffocating

valley and its close humidity. The air becomes cooler and fresher the higher we mount, and small white clouds cast shadows on the ground. In the distance appears Kailas again, the abode of eternal snow.

Several Europeans were staying just then in Kotgar, and I was entertained with extraordinary hospitality. Among them was the missionary Bentel, who had worked thirty-eight years as a preacher. I attended the English Church in the evening and heard again a Christian service. The caravan reached the yard of the bungalow at Kotgar later than usual. One of the horses from Chang-tang had been unable to climb the ascent from Tanadar; it had fallen down a precipice and been killed on the spot. Of ten animals, three had fallen victims to the road from Tokchen to Simla.

September 14, fifty miles more. At a bend in the road I met six runners with an empty rickshaw. It was a pleasant change to take my seat in a light two-wheeled carriage and be borne over high dome-shaped crests and ridges. I smoked cigarettes, wrote down my notes, and let my eyes rove freely over deep valleys and far-stretching distances. I had no need to be anxious lest my runners should tire. A new team awaited me at every bungalow, and I could travel on as long as I liked. At Narkanda we were higher than we had ever been since leaving Rogi, 8790 feet above the sea. In Theog I stopped for dinner, and then travelled in the dark with lamps on the shafts. The wheels creaked, the bare soles of my runners tapped on the hard smooth road, and the light danced merrily in front of our party. But it was a pity to lose the beautiful view, and I did not wish to arrive at Simla in the middle of the night, so I camped for the last time on this long journey in the bungalow of Fagu, at a height of 8200 feet.

The last day breaks! The morning is fresh and bright, and I set out early for the beautiful place which bears the camp number 500. My runners skim along as if they were oiled, and the rickshaw rolls down the gently-falling ridge towards Simla. The cheerful white summer houses on the cedar-clothed hills grow larger, and soon we are speeding through the luxuriant pine forests which hang over deep valleys.

I frequently gaze with pleasure out of my windows in the hospitable Viceregal Lodge. Now flooded with sunshine, now overshadowed by heavy rain-clouds, the Himalayas display their wonders around me. I am stranded on a reef in a boisterous sea. Beyond the ridges to the east, I know, the holy mountain lies where Brahma is enthroned in his heaven and Siva dwells in his paradise. And beyond the darkness of legends my royal Trans-Himalaya lifts its snow-clad ranges to the sun.

Westwards the crests of the Himalayas sink down to low hills, which finally pass into the boundless plains of the Punjab. On the edge of the horizon these waves fade away like petrified surf on the coast of a desert sea. Amid the yellow haze at the foot of the mountains a dark riband is seen in the distance meandering past Firazpur to the Indus. It is the Sutlej. The roar of its water still lingers in my ears, and I still seem to hear the proud river sing of its yearning for the sea.

Trans-Himalaya Vol. III.

WESTERN TIBI

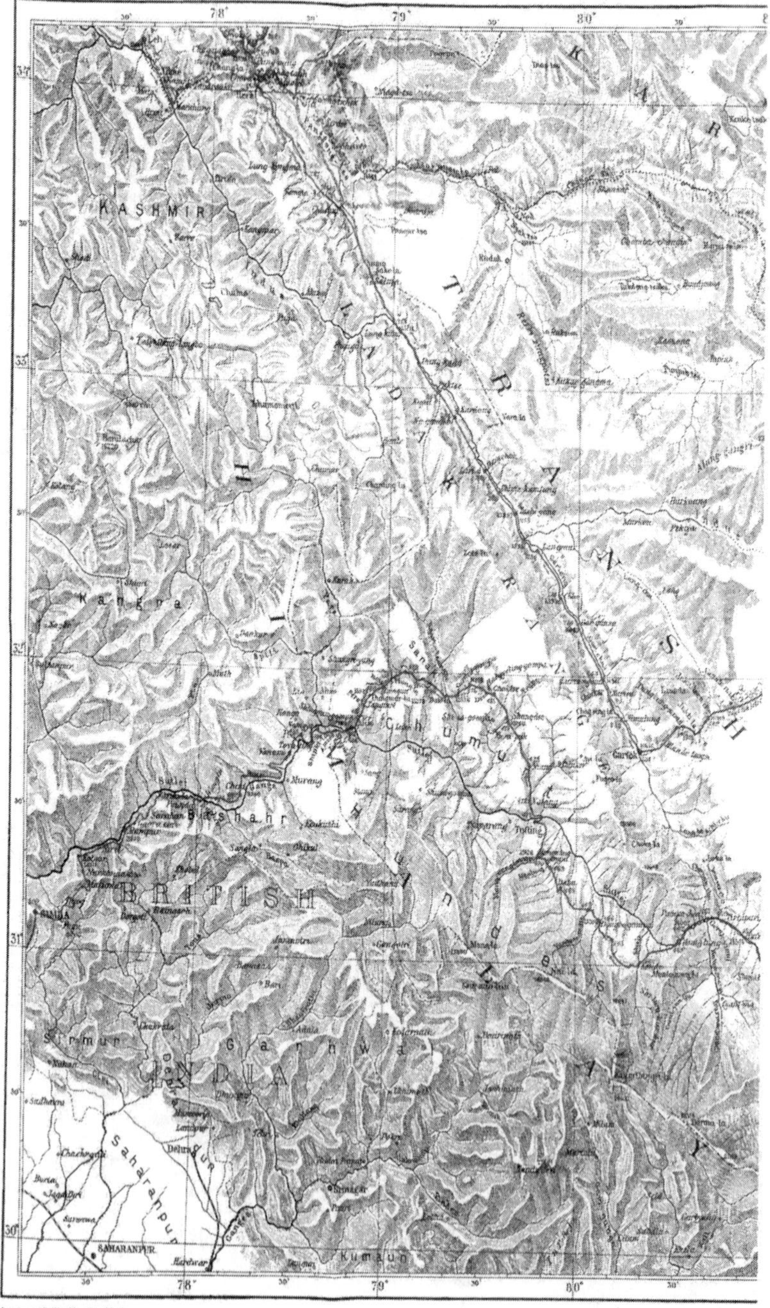

Reproduced at Stanford's Geog.l Estab.t London

Scale 1:1,500,000

Dr. Sven Hedins routes in 1906

" " " " 1907

London Macmillan & Co. Ltd.

IBET

Drawn by Lieutenant C. J. Otto Kjellström

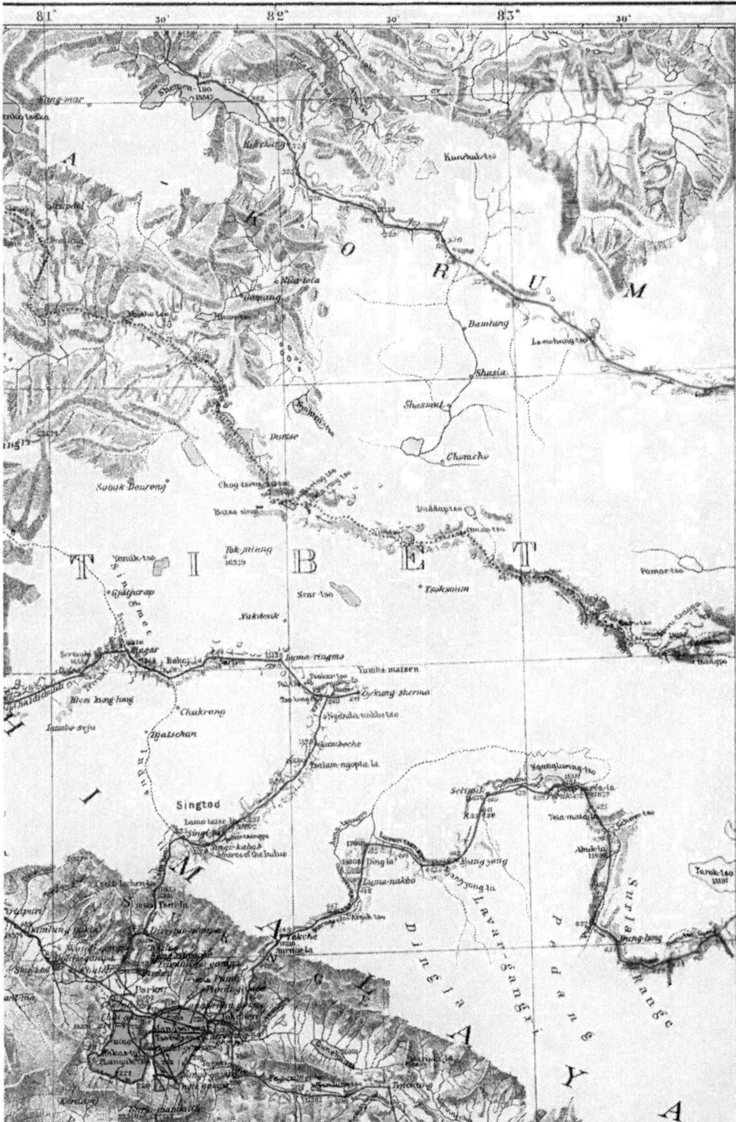

100 kilometres

Heights in English Feet

Generalstabens Litogr. Anst. Stockholm

1906 - 1908.

1901 - 1902.

INDEX

THE END